ESSENTIALS OF ECONOMICS

THIRD EDITION

Green type indicates global example

ESSENTIALS OF ECONOMICS

THIRD EDITION

Paul Krugman • Robin Wells
PRINCETON UNIVERSITY

Kathryn Graddy
BRANDEIS UNIVERSITY

WORTH PUBLISHERS
A MACMILLAN HIGHER EDUCATION COMPANY

Senior Vice President, Editorial and Production: Catherine Woods
Publisher: Charles Linsmeier
Marketing Manager: Tom Digiano
Marketing Assistant: Tess Sanders
Executive Development Editor: Sharon Balbos
Associate Development Editor: Mary Melis
Senior Consultant: Andreas Bentz
Senior Media Editor: Marie McHale
Associate Media Editor: Lukia Kliossis
Director of Market Research and Development: Steven Rigolosi
Director of Digital and Print Development: Tracey Kuehn
Associate Managing Editor: Lisa Kinne
Senior Project Editor: Liz Geller
Art Director: Babs Reingold
Cover Designer: Kevin Kall
Interior Designers: Charles Yuen, Kevin Kall, Lissi Sigillo
Layout Designer and Illustrations: TSI Graphics and Lyndall Culbertson
Photo Editor: Cecilia Varas
Photo Researcher: Elyse Rieder
Production Manager: Barbara Anne Seixas
Supplements Production Manager: Stacey Alexander
Supplements Project Editor: Edgar Bonilla
Composition: TSI Graphics
Printing and Binding: Quad/Graphics, Inc.

See page xxxi for credits information. Page xxxi is an extension of this copyright page.

ISBN-13: 978-1-4292-7850-8
ISBN-10: 1-4292-7850-1

Library of Congress Control Number: 2013938794

Printed in the United States of America

First printing

Worth Publishers
41 Madison Avenue
New York, NY 10010
www.worthpublishers.com

To beginning students everywhere,
which we all were at one time.

ABOUT THE AUTHORS

Paul Krugman, recipient of the 2008 Nobel Memorial Prize in Economic Sciences, is Professor of Economics at Princeton University, where he regularly teaches the principles course. He received his BA from Yale and his PhD from MIT. Prior to his current position, he taught at Yale, Stanford, and MIT. He also spent a year on the staff of the Council of Economic Advisers in 1982–1983. His research is mainly in the area of international trade, where he is one of the founders of the "new trade theory," which focuses on increasing returns and imperfect competition. He also works in international finance, with a concentration in currency crises. In 1991, Krugman received the American Economic Association's John Bates Clark medal. In addition to his teaching and academic research, Krugman writes extensively for nontechnical audiences. He is a regular op-ed columnist and blogger for the *New York Times.* His latest trade book is *End this Depression Now!* Recent best-sellers include *The Return of Depression Economics and the Crisis of 2008,* a history of recent economic troubles and their implications for economic policy, and *The Conscience of a Liberal,* a study of the political economy of economic inequality and its relationship with political polarization from the Gilded Age to the present. His earlier books, *Peddling Prosperity* and *The Age of Diminished Expectations,* have become modern classics.

Robin Wells was a Lecturer and Researcher in Economics at Princeton University. She received her BA from the University of Chicago and her PhD from the University of California at Berkeley; she then did postdoctoral work at MIT. She has taught at the University of Michigan, the University of Southampton (United Kingdom), Stanford, and MIT. The subject of her teaching and research is the theory of organizations and incentives.

Kathryn Graddy is the Fred and Rita Richman Distinguished Professor in Economics and Chair of the Department of Economics at Brandeis University. She received her BA and BS from Tulane University, her MBA from Columbia University, and her PhD from Princeton University. She regularly teaches introduction to economics at Brandeis, and her research focuses on the economics of art and culture and industrial organization.

BRIEF CONTENTS

CONTENTS

PREFACE

"Stories are good for us, whether we hear them, read them, write them, or simply imagine them. But stories that we read are particularly good for us. In fact I believe they are essential."
Frank Smith, *Reading: FAQ*

FROM PAUL AND ROBIN

More than a decade ago, when we began writing the first edition of this textbook, we had many small ideas: particular aspects of economics that we believed weren't covered the right way in existing textbooks. But we also had one big idea: the belief that an economics textbook could and should be built around narratives, that it should never lose sight of the fact that economics is, in the end, a set of stories about what people do.

Many of the stories economists tell take the form of models—for whatever else they are, economic models are stories about how the world works. But we believed that students' understanding of and appreciation for models would be greatly enhanced if they were presented, as much as possible, in the context of stories about the real world, stories that both illustrate economic concepts and touch on the concerns we all face as individuals living in a world shaped by economic forces. Those stories have been integrated into every edition, including this one, which contains more stories than ever before. Once again, you'll find them in the openers, in boxed features like Economics in Action, For Inquiring Minds, and Global Comparisons, but now in our new Business Cases as well.

We have been gratified by the reception this storytelling approach has received, but we have also heard from users who urged us to expand the range of our stories to reach an even broader audience. In this edition of *Essentials of Economics* we have tried to expand the book's appeal with some carefully selected changes.

As in the previous edition, we've made extensive changes and updates in coverage to reflect current events—events that have come thick and fast in a turbulent, troubled world economy, which is affecting the lives and prospects of students everywhere. Currency is very important to us. We have also expanded our coverage of business issues, both because business experience is a key source of economic lessons and because most students will eventually find themselves working in the business world. We are especially pleased with how the new Business Cases have turned out and how they augment the overall number and richness of our stories.

We remain extremely fortunate in our reviewers, who have put in an immense amount of work helping us to make this book even better. And we are also deeply thankful to all the users who have given us feedback, telling us what works and, even more important, what doesn't.

Many things have changed since the second edition of this book. As you'll see, there's a great deal of new material, and there are some significant changes (and, we hope, improvements) in pedagogy. But we've tried to keep the spirit the same. This is a book about economics as the study of what people do and how they interact, a study very much informed by real-world experience.

FROM KATHRYN

I enjoyed working on this third edition of *Essentials of Economics*. Much of the book is based on the third edition of Paul and Robin's *Economics,* which is their excellent, entertaining, and up-to-date principles text for the two-semester course. Feedback from reviewers on the second edition of *Essentials,* along with my own experience teaching a one-semester survey course, has guided the revision of this third edition.

In a one-semester course it is always a challenge to balance the depth of coverage of specific topics with breadth of coverage of essential topics on economics. My hope is that this third edition achieves this balance and at the end of the course leaves the students interested in economics and eager to learn more. A focus on global examples is once again an important feature of the book, reflecting both Paul and Robin's international experiences and my twelve years of living and working in the United Kingdom.

The Third Edition: What's New

We have learned with each new edition that there is always room for improvement. So, for the third edition, we undertook a revision with three goals in mind: to expand the book's appeal to business students, to be current in terms of topics covered and examples included, and to make the book more accessible. We hope that the following revisions lead to a more successful teaching experience for you.

New Business Case Studies

Now, more than ever, students entering the business community need a strong understanding of economic principles and their applications to business decisions. To meet this demand, each part now concludes with a set of real-world Business Cases, showing how the economic issues discussed in the part's chapters play out in the world of entrepreneurs and bottom lines.

The cases range from the story of the trading firm Li & Fung, which is in the business of making money from comparative advantage, to a look at how apps like TheFind are making the retail market for electronics much more competitive, to an examination of how lean production techniques at Boeing and Toyota have impacted comparative advantage in the airline and auto industries. The cases provide insight into business decision making in both American and international companies and at recognizable firms like British Airways and Priceline.com. Lesser-known firms are also used to illustrate economic concepts behind the supply costs of labor during seasonal work (Kiva Systems and the debate on human versus robotic order fulfillment), and the positive externalities of economic geography during the digital boom (Silicon Valley in California and Route 128 outside Boston).

The chapters on the macroeconomy are treated in business cases as well, ranging from the 2009 bankruptcy of General Motors, once the symbol of American economic success, and its rebound in 2010, to a look at companies like Macroeconomic Advisers and the nonprofit Institute of Supply Management that forecast changes in GDP, to an examination of the productivity surge in retailing driven by improvements in global logistics at Walmart. The cases also place the individual consumer and firm in the macroeconomy with examples that illustrate the changing job market during a recession (Monster.com), the role of gift cards in secondary markets (PlasticJungle.com), and the value of "breakage" when individual consumers fail to pay down their gift cards completely.

Each case is followed by critical thinking questions that prompt students to apply the economics they learned in the chapter to real-life business situations (answers to these questions are found in the Instructor's Resource Manual).

New Chapter: "Crises and Consequences"

This new chapter provides an up-to-date look at the 2008 financial crisis and the aspects of the banking system that allowed it to take place. Starting with the story of the Lehman Brothers collapse, the chapter integrates coverage on the dangers of banking, the trade-off between liquidity and rate of return, the emergence of "shadow banks," and the early bank runs of the recession. Also covered: asset bubbles, financial contagion, financial panic, and a look at how the financial crisis fits into a long history of economic crises. The chapter concludes with a discussion of why banking crises are so bad for so many, and the role the government and regulation play in crises.

An Emphasis on Currency and Visual Exposition

The third edition is updated to remain the most current textbook on the market in its data, examples, and the opening stories—a currency that drives student interest in each chapter.

Economics in Action: A Richer Story to Be Told

Students and instructors alike have always championed *Essentials of Economics* for its applications of economic principles, especially our Economics in Action feature. In the third edition, we have revised or replaced a significant number of Economics in Action applications in every single chapter. We believe this provides the richness of content that drives student and instructor interest. A list of all Economics in Action boxes appears on the inside front cover.

Opening Stories We have always taken great care to ensure that each chapter's opening story illustrates the key concepts of that chapter in a compelling and accessible way. To continue to do so, almost every story in the third edition was updated and nearly a third were replaced in an effort to bridge the gap between economic concepts and student interest in the world around them. New openers include the story of Boeing's Dreamliner and its genesis in the wind tunnels that the Wright brothers built at Kitty Hawk, the story of how flooding in Pakistan led to higher prices for blue jeans here at home, and we tell the story of China's economic rise, surpassing Japan as the second largest economy, and the means economists use to measure such trends.

Worked Problems Virtually every chapter concludes with a worked problem that poses a realistic economic question and then uses the concepts presented in the chapter to help students solve it, step-by-step. Each worked problem has been carefully reviewed and revised in keeping with our emphasis on currency. New worked problems have been added on China's exports of rare earths and on Tesla Motors, the producer of electric cars. Other worked problems have been updated using current examples and data. A full list of the Worked Problems can be found on the inside front cover of this book.

A More Visual Exposition The research tells us that students read more online, in shorter bursts, and respond better to visual representations of information than ever before. In the third edition, we've worked hard to present information in the format that best teaches students.

We've shortened our paragraphs for easier reading and included numbered and bulleted lists whenever content would allow. You will find helpful new summary tables in this edition. And, most helpful, are the new visual displays in the book, including the dynamic representations of the factors that shift demand (p. 78) and the factors that shift supply (p. 85), among others.

Tools for Learning Every chapter is structured around a common set of features that help students learn while keeping them engaged.

CHAPTER 3

Supply and Demand

BLUE JEAN BLUES

Ciaran Griffin/Thinkstock

How did flood-ravaged cotton crops in Pakistan lead to higher-priced blue jeans and more polyester in T-shirts?

WHAT YOU WILL LEARN IN THIS CHAPTER

- What a **competitive market** is and how it is described by the **supply and demand model**
- What the **demand curve** and the **supply curve** are
- The difference between **movements along a curve** and **shifts of a curve**
- How the supply and demand curves determine a market's **equilibrium price** and **equilibrium quantity**
- In the case of a **shortage** or **surplus,** how price moves the market back to equilibrium

Chapter Overviews offer students a helpful preview of the key concepts they will learn about in the chapter.

IF YOU BOUGHT A PAIR OF BLUE jeans in 2011, you may have been shocked at the price. Or maybe not: fashions change, and maybe you thought you were paying the price for being fashionable. But you weren't—you were paying for cotton. Jeans are made of denim, which is a particular weave of cotton, and by late 2010, when jeans manufacturers were buying supplies for the coming year, cotton prices were more than triple their level just two years earlier. By December 2010, the price of a pound of cotton had hit a 140-year high, the highest cotton price since records began in 1870.

And why were cotton prices so high?

On one side, demand for clothing of all kinds was surging. In 2008–2009, as the world struggled with the effects of a financial crisis, nervous consumers cut back on clothing purchases. But by 201[illegible] with the worst apparently over, bu[illegible]

production. Most notably, Pakistan, the world's fourth-largest cotton producer, was hit by devastating floods that put one-fifth of the country underwater and virtually destroyed its cotton crop.

Fearing that consumers had limited tolerance for large increases in the price of cotton clothing, apparel makers began scrambling to find ways to reduce costs without offending consumers' fashion sense. They adopted changes like smaller buttons, cheaper linings, and—yes—polyester, doubting that consumers would be willing to pay more for cotton goods. In fact, some experts on the cotton market warned that the sky-high prices of cotton in 2010–2011 might lead to a permanent shift in tastes, with consumers becoming more willing to wear synthetics even when cotton prices came down.

At the same time, it was not all bad news for everyone connected with the

weather and were relishing the higher prices. American farmers responded to sky-high cotton prices by sharply increasing the acreage devoted to the crop. None of this was enough, however, to produce immediate price relief.

Wait a minute: how, exactly, does flooding in Pakistan translate into higher jeans prices and more polyester in your T-shirts? It's a matter of supply and demand—but what does that mean? Many people use "supply and demand" as a sort of catchphrase to mean "the laws of the marketplace at work." To economists, however, the concept of supply and demand has a precise meaning: it is a *model of how a market behaves* that is extremely useful for understanding many—but not all—markets.

In this chapter, we lay out the pieces that make up the *supply and demand model,* put them together, and show how this model can be used to understand how many—but not all—markets behave. ■

Opening Stories Each chapter begins with a compelling story that is often integrated throughout the rest of the chapter. More than a third of the stories in this edition are new, including the one shown here.

ECONOMICS ➤ IN ACTION

BEATING THE TRAFFIC

Global Stamps identify which boxes, cases, and applications are global in focus.

Economics in Action cases conclude every major text section. This much-lauded feature lets students immediately apply concepts they've read about to real phenomena.

traffic problems, and many local authorities try to discour- e crowded city center. If we think of an auto trip to the city people consume, we can use the economics of demand to ies.

is to reduce the demand for auto trips by lowering utes. Many metropolitan areas subsidize bus and rail ure commuters out of their cars. An alternative is to mplements: several major U.S. cities impose high taxes ing garages and impose short time limits on parking e revenue and to discourage people from driving into

s—including Singapore, London, Oslo, Stockholm, and villing to adopt a direct and politically controversial ongestion by raising the price of driving. Under "congestion pricing" (or "congestion charging" in the United Kingdom), a charge is imposed on cars entering the city center during business hours. Drivers buy passes, which are then debited electronically as they drive by monitoring stations. Compliance is monitored with automatic cameras that photograph license plates. Moscow is currently contemplating a congestion charge scheme to tackle the worst traffic jams of all major cities, with 40% of drivers reporting traffic jams exceeding three hours.

Cities can reduce traffic congestion by raising the price of driving.

The current daily cost of driving in London ranges from £9 to £12 (about $14 to $19). And drivers who don't pay and are caught pay a fine of £120 (about $190) for each transgression.

Not surprisingly, studies have shown that after the implementation of congestion pricing, traffic does indeed decrease. In the 1990s, London had some of the worst traffic in Europe. The introduction of its congestion charge in 2003 immediately reduced traffic in the London city center by about 15%, with overall traffic falling by 21% between 2002 and 2006. And there was increased use of substitutes, such as public transportation, bicycles, motorbikes, and ride-sharing.

In the United S s implement-ed pilot program Some trans-portation experts rices, raising prices during pea icing may be controversial, it a

Check Your Understanding questions allow students to immediately test their understanding of a section. Solutions appear at the back of the book.

▼ Quick Review

- The **supply and demand model** is a model of a **competitive market**—one in which there are many buyers and sellers of the same good or service.
- The **demand schedule** shows how the **quantity demanded** changes as the price changes. A **demand curve** illustrates this relationship.
- The **law of demand** asserts that a higher price reduces the quantity demanded. Thus, demand curves normally slope downward.
- An increase in demand leads to a rightward **shift of the demand curve:** the quantity demanded rises for any given price. A decrease in demand leads to a leftward shift: the quantity demanded falls for any given price. A change in price results in a change in the quantity demanded and a **movement along the demand curve.**
- The five main factors that can shift the demand curve are changes in (1) the price of a related good, such as a **substitute** or a **complement,** (2) income, (3) tastes, (4) expectations, and (5) the number of consumers.
- The marke demand curve is the horizontal s the **individual demand curves** sumers in the market.

CHECK YOUR UNDERSTANDING 3-1

1. Explain whether each of the following events represents (i) a *shift of* the demand curve or (ii) a *movement along* the demand curve.
   a. A store owner finds that customers are willing to pay more for umbrellas on rainy days.
   b. When XYZ Telecom, a long-distance telephone service provider, offered reduced rates on weekends, its volume of weekend calling increased sharply.
   c. People buy more long-stem roses the week of Valentine's Day, even though the prices are higher than at other times during the year.
   d. A sharp rise in the price of gasoline leads many commuters to join carpools in order to reduce their gasoline purchases.

Solutions ap

Quick Reviews offer students a short, bulleted summary of key concepts in the section to aid understanding.

PAY MORE, PUMP LESS

For a real-world illustration of the law of demand, consider how gasoline consumption varies according to the prices consumers pay at the pump. Because of high taxes, gasoline and diesel fuel are more than twice as expensive in most European countries as in the United States. According to the law of demand, this should lead Europeans to buy less gasoline than Americans—and they do. As you can see from the figure, per person, Europeans consume less than half as much fuel as Americans, mainly because they drive smaller cars with better mileage.

Prices aren't the only factor affecting fuel consumption, but they're probably the main cause of the difference between European and American fuel consumption per person.

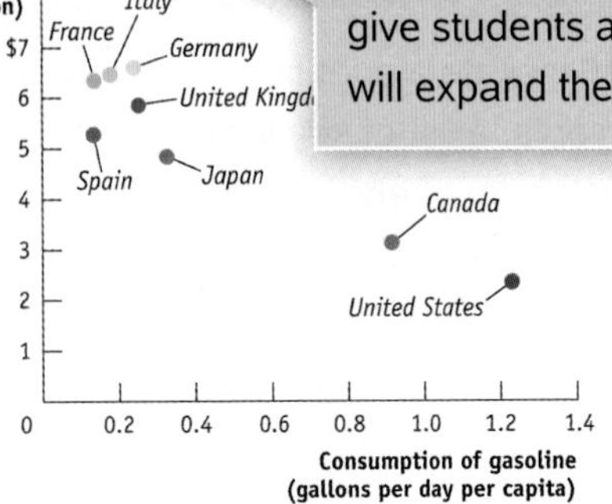

Source: U.S. Energy Information Administration, 2009.

Global Comparison boxes use real data from several countries as well as colorful graphs to illustrate how and why countries reach different economic outcomes. The boxes give students an international perspective that will expand their understanding of economics.

WORKED PROBLEM

Production Challenges for Tesla: The Model S

Tesla Motors, founded in 2003, exclusively produces electric cars and electric powertrains in a former Toyota factory in Fremont, California. The Tesla Roadster, a sports car, was the company's first design. Their newest design, available for 2012 delivery, is the Tesla Model S, a luxury sedan. The Model S uses no gasoline, has a range of up to 300 miles per charge, and has zero tailpipe emissions. Although demand for the car has been strong, production of the Model S at the Fremont plant is currently less than Tesla had anticipated.

Let's assume that Tesla engineers knew they needed to either build or buy a new factory in order to produce the new Model S. And, suppose that Tesla engineers and accountants estimated the following hypothetical cost structure per year based on full-year production at plants of different sizes.

	Total cost (hundreds of millions of U.S. dollars)		
Plant size	10,000 cars sold	20,000 cars sold	30,000 cars sold
A	$1.75	$3.25	$5.5
B	2.0	3.0	5.0
C	2.5	4.0	4.5

When Toyotas were built there, the Fremont plant produced about 80,000 vehicles per year. Suppose that Tesla equipped the plant with the hopes of producing 30,000 Tesla vehicles per year, yet in its first few years of production, Tesla predicted sales would be only 20,000 vehicles per year. But, by 2012, because of production delays, actual sales dropped to less than 10,000 cars per year. Using the table, find Tesla's average total cost of production per car at a size C plant if only 20,000 cars are built. At a size C plant, what is the average total cost of production if only 10,000 cars are built?

Worked Problems
Chapters conclude with a worked problem that presents a realistic economic question and then helps students answer it, one step at a time, by applying key concepts from the chapter.

PITFALLS

DEMAND VERSUS QUANTITY DEMANDED

When economists say "an increase in demand," they mean a rightward shift of the demand curve, and when they say "a decrease in demand," they mean a leftward shift of the demand curve—that is, when they're being careful. In ordinary speech most people, including professional economists, use the word *demand* casually. For example, an economist might say "the demand for air travel has doubled over the past 15 years, partly because of falling airfares" *quantit*

It's conver nomic distinct deman

Pitfalls boxes clarify concepts that can be easily misunderstood by students new to economics.

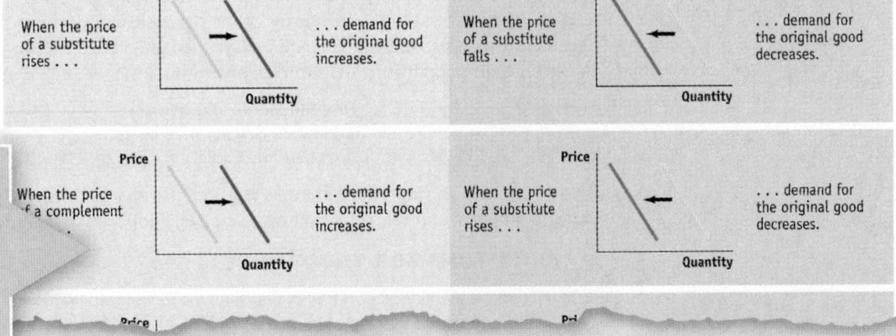
TABLE 3-1 Factors That Shift Demand

When this happens . . .	. . . demand increases		But when this happens . . .	. . . demand decreases	
When the price of a substitute rises . . .	[graph]	. . . demand for the original good increases.	When the price of a substitute falls . . .	[graph]	. . . demand for the original good decreases.
When the price of a complement	[graph]	. . . demand for the original good increases.	When the price of a substitute rises . . .	[graph]	. . . demand for the original good decreases.

New! Summary Tables serve as a helpful study aid for readers. Many incorporate visuals to help students grasp important economic concepts.

SUMMARY

1. The **supply and demand model** illustrates how a **competitive market,** one with many buyers and sel' 's, none of whom can influence the market price 's.
2. The 'schedule shows the quantity ... esented graphi- ... of demand says ...; that is, a higher ... ple to demand a

ing supply, they mean **shifts of the supply curve**—a change in the quantity supplied at any given price. An increase in supply causes a rightward shift of the supply curve. A decrease in supply causes a leftward shift.

8. There are five main factors that shift the supply curve:
   - A change in **input** prices
   - A change in the prices of related goods and services
   - A change in technology
   - A change in expectations
   - A change in the number of producers

End-of-Chapter Reviews include a brief but complete summary of key concepts, a list of key terms, and a comprehensive, high-quality set of end-of-chapter problems.

PROBLEMS

1. A survey indicated that chocolate is Americans' favorite ice-cream flavor. For each of the following, indicate the possible effects on demand, supply, or both as well as equilibrium price and quantity of chocolate ice cream.
   a. A severe drought in the Midwest causes dairy farmers to reduce the number of milk-producing cattle in their herds by a third. These dairy farmers supply cream that is used to manufacture chocolate ice cream.
   b. A new report by the American Medical Association reveals that chocolate does, in fact, have significant health benefits.

Case 2: There i... which is repor...

b. The market fo...
Case 1: The Ra...
Case 2: The pr...

c. The market fo...
Case 1: People...
Case 2: People... cooked breakf...

d. The market fo...

KEY TERMS

Competitive market, p. 66
Supply and demand model, p. 66
Demand schedule, p. 67
Quantity demanded, p. 67
Demand curve, p. 68
Law of demand, p. 68
Shift of the demand curve, p. 70
Movement along the demand curve, p. 70
Substitutes, p. 71
Complements, p. 71
Normal good, p. 72
Inferior good, p. 72
Individual demand curve, p. 73
Quantity supplied, p. 76
Supply schedule, p. 76
Supply curve, p. 77
Shift of the supply curve, p. 77

BUSINESS CASE • The Chicago Board of Trade

Jim West

To understand the concept of an equilibrium price, it's helpful to do what we did in the discussion of demand: imagine that buyers are wandering around comparing the prices offered by different sellers. Some markets really do wo... way. But cotton, wheat, and many other commodities are traded on "excha... which make prices much more transparent and make the movement to ... equilibrium almost instantaneous.

Modern exchanges began with wheat trading at the Chicago Board of ... founded in 1848. But in 1848, St. Louis, not Chicago, was the leading city ... American West, and it dominated the wheat trade. The wheat market in ... was freewheeling and a lot like the story we told in the text. There ... marketplace; sellers set up in various warehouses, or even stacked sa... on the levee, and buyers wandered around looking for the best deal.

In Chicago, however, sellers had a better idea. The Chicago Board of Tr... association of the city's leading grain dealers, created a system in which w... traders gathered in one place—the "pit"—where they called out or accepted ... to buy or sell. The Board guaranteed that these contracts would be fulfille... system meant that buyers could very quickly find sellers and vice versa, reducing the costs of doing business. It also ensured that everyone could see the latest price, so the price rose and fell very rapidly to clear the market. For example, news of bad weather in a wheat-growing area hundreds of miles away would send the price in Chicago soaring in a matter of minutes.

The Chicago Board of Trade went on to become the world's most important trading center for wheat and many other agricultural commodities, a status it retains to this day. And the Board's rise helped the rise of Chicago, too. The city, as Carl Sandburg put it in his famous poem, became

Hog Butcher for the World,
Tool Maker, Stacker of Wheat,
Player with Railroads and the Nation's Freight Handler

By 1890, Chicago had more than a million people, second only to New York. Making a better market, it turned out, was very good business indeed.

QUESTIONS FOR THOUGHT

1. In the text we mentioned how prices can vary in a tourist trap. Why was the wheat market in St. Louis a bit like a tourist trap, and why was Chicago different?
2. What was the advantage of h... buyers and sellers gathered in one place?

New! Business Cases close each section, applying key economic principles to real-life business situations in both American and international companies. Each case includes critical thinking questions.

Advantages of This Book

Our basic approach to textbook writing remains unchanged:

- **Chapters build intuition through realistic examples.** In every chapter, we use real-world examples, stories, applications, and case studies to teach the core concepts and motivate student learning. The best way to introduce concepts and reinforce them is through real-world examples; students simply relate more easily to them.
- **Pedagogical features reinforce learning.** We've crafted a genuinely helpful set of features that are described in the preceding section, "Tools for Learning" on pages xxi–xxiv.
- **Chapters are accessible and entertaining.** We use a fluid and friendly writing style to make concepts accessible and, whenever possible, we use examples that are familiar to students.
- **Although easy to understand, the book also prepares students for further coursework.** There's no need to choose between two unappealing alternatives: a textbook that is "easy to teach" but leaves major gaps in students' understanding, or a textbook that is "hard to teach" but adequately prepares students for future coursework. We offer the best of both worlds.

Supplements and Media

Worth Publishers is pleased to offer an enhanced and completely revised supplements and media package to accompany this textbook. The package has been crafted to help instructors teach their principles course and to give students the tools to develop their skills in economics.

For Instructors

Instructor's Resource Manual with Solutions Manual The Instructor's Resource Manual, revised by Nora Underwood, University of Central Florida, is a resource meant to provide materials and tips to enhance the classroom experience. The Instructor's Resource Manual provides the following:

- Chapter-by-chapter learning objectives
- Chapter outlines
- Teaching tips and ideas that include:
  - Hints on how to create student interest
  - Tips on presenting the material in class
  - Discussion of the examples used in the text, including points to emphasize with your students
- Activities that can be conducted in or out of the classroom
- Hints for dealing with common misunderstandings that are typical among students
- Web resources (includes tips for using EconPortal)
- Solutions manual with detailed solutions to all of the end-of-chapter problems from the textbook

Test Bank *Coordinator:* Carlos Aguilar, El Paso Community College. The Test Bank provides a wide range of questions appropriate for assessing your students' comprehension, interpretation, analysis, and synthesis skills. Totaling over 4,500 questions, the Test Bank offers multiple-choice, true/false, and short-answer questions designed for comprehensive coverage of the text concepts. Questions have been checked for continuity with the text content, overall usability, and accuracy.

The Test Bank features include the following:

- To aid instructors in building tests, each question has been categorized according to its general *degree of difficulty.* The three levels are*: easy, moderate,* and *difficult.*
  - *Easy* questions require students to recognize concepts and definitions. These are questions that can be answered by direct reference to the textbook.
  - *Moderate* questions require some analysis on the student's part.
  - *Difficult* questions usually require more detailed analysis by the student.
- Each question has also been categorized according to a *skill descriptor.* These include: *Fact-Based, Definitional, Concept-Based, Critical Thinking,* and *Analytical Thinking.*
  - *Fact-Based Questions* require students to identify facts presented in the text.
  - *Definitional Questions* require students to define an economic term or concept.
  - *Concept-Based Questions* require a straightforward knowledge of basic concepts.
  - *Critical Thinking Questions* require the student to apply a concept to a particular situation.
  - *Analytical Thinking Questions* require another level of analysis to answer the question. Students must be able to apply a concept and use this knowledge for further analysis of a situation or scenario.

- To further aid instructors in building tests, each question is conveniently cross-referenced to the appropriate topic heading in the textbook. Questions are presented in the order in which concepts are presented in the text.
- The Test Bank includes questions with tables that students must analyze to solve for numerical answers. It also contains questions based on the graphs that appear in the book. These questions ask students to use the graphical models developed in the textbook and to interpret the information presented in the graph. Selected questions are paired with scenarios to reinforce comprehension.
- Questions have been designed to correlate with the various questions in the text. *Study Guide Questions* are also available in each chapter. This is a unique set of 25–30 questions per chapter that are parallel to the *Chapter Review Questions* in the printed Study Guide. These questions focus on the key concepts from the text that students should grasp after reading the chapter. These questions reflect the types of questions that the students have likely already worked through in homework assignments or in self-testing. These questions can also be used for testing or for brief in-class quizzes.

The Test Bank is available in CD-ROM format for both Windows and Macintosh users. With this program, instructors can easily create and print tests and write and edit questions. Tests can be printed in a wide range of formats. The software's unique synthesis of flexible word-processing and database features creates a program that is extremely intuitive and capable.

Lecture PowerPoint Presentation Created by Amy Scott, DeSales University, the enhanced PowerPoint presentation slides are designed to assist you with lecture preparation and presentations. The slides are organized by topic and contain graphs, data tables, and bulleted lists of key concepts suitable for lecture presentation. Key figures from the text are replicated and animated to demonstrate how they build. *Notes to the Instructor* are also included to provide added tips, class exercises, examples, and explanations to enhance classroom presentations. The slides have been designed to allow for easy editing of graphs and text. These slides can be customized to suit your individual needs by adding your own data, questions, and lecture notes. These files may be accessed on the instructor's side of the website.

For Students

Study Guide Prepared by Elizabeth Sawyer Kelly, University of Wisconsin–Madison, the Study Guide reinforces the topics and key concepts covered in the text. For each chapter, the Study Guide is organized as follows:

Before You Read the Chapter

- Summary: an opening paragraph that provides a brief overview of the chapter.
- Objectives: a numbered list outlining and describing the material that the student should have learned in the chapter. These objectives can be easily used as a study tool for students.
- Key Terms: a list of boldface key terms with their definitions—including room for note-taking.

After You Read the Chapter

- Tips: numbered list of learning tips with graphical analysis.
- Problems and Exercises: a set of 10–15 comprehensive problems.

Before You Take the Test

- Chapter Review Questions: a set of 30 multiple-choice questions that focus on the key concepts from the text students should grasp after reading the chapter. These questions are designed for student exam preparation. A parallel set of these questions is also available to instructors in the Test Bank.

Answer Key

- Answers to Problems and Exercises: detailed solutions to the Problems and Exercises in the Study Guide.
- Answers to Chapter Review Questions: solutions to the multiple-choice questions in the Study Guide—along with thorough explanations.

Online Offerings

sapling learning

www.saplinglearning.com

Sapling Learning provides the most effective interactive homework and instruction that improves student-learning outcomes for the problem solving disciplines.

Sapling Learning offers an enjoyable teaching and effective learning experience that is distinctive in three important ways:

- **Ease of Use:** Sapling Learning's easy-to-use interface keeps students engaged in problem solving, not struggling with the software.
- **Targeted Instructional Content:** Sapling Learning increases student engagement and comprehension by delivering immediate feedback and targeted instructional content.
- **Unsurpassed Service and Support:** Sapling Learning makes teaching more enjoyable by providing a dedicated Masters- or PhD-level colleague to service instructors' unique needs throughout the course, including content customization.

Aplia

Worth/Aplia courses are all available with digital textbooks, interactive assignments, and detailed feedback. With Aplia, you retain complete control of and flexibility for your course. You choose the content you want students to cover, and you decide how to organize it. You decide whether online activities are practice (ungraded or graded). For a preview of Aplia materials and to learn more, visit http://www.aplia.com/worth.

The integrated online version of the Aplia media and the Krugman/Wells text includes:

- Extra problem sets (derived from in-chapter questions in the book) suitable for homework and keyed to specific topics from each chapter
- Regularly updated news analyses
- Real-time online simulations of market interactions
- Interactive tutorials to assist with math and graphing
- Instant online reports that allow instructors to target student trouble areas more efficiently

CoursePacks Plug our content into your course management system. Whatever you teach, or whether you use Blackboard, Canvas, Desire2Learn, Angel, Sakai, or Moodle to manage your course, we have free content and support available. Registered instructors can download cartridges with no hassle, no strings attached. Content includes our most popular free resources and book-specific content. For more information, go to http://worthpublishers.com/catalog/Other/Coursepack.

Further Resources Offered

CourseSmart eBooks

http://www.coursesmart.com/ourproducts

CourseSmart eBooks offer the complete book in PDF format. Students can save money, up to 60% off the price of print textbooks. With the CourseSmart eBook, students have the ability to take notes, highlight, print pages, and more. A great alternative to renting print textbooks!

Faculty Lounge Faculty Lounge is an online community of economics instructors. At this unique forum, economics instructors can connect, interact, and collaborate with fellow teachers and economics researchers, sharing thoughts and teaching resources. Instructors can upload their own resources and search for peer-reviewed content to use in class. Faculty Lounge is a great place to connect with colleagues nationwide who face the same challenges in the classroom as you do. To learn more, ask your Worth representative or visit www.worthpublishers.com/facultylounge.

Worth Noting Worth Noting keeps you connected to your textbook authors in real time. Whether they were just on CNBC or published in the *New York Times,* this is the place to find out about it. Visit Worth Noting at http://blogs.worthpublishers.com/econblog/.

i>clicker Developed by a team of University of Illinois physicists, i>clicker is the most flexible and reliable classroom response system available. It is the only solution created *for* educators, *by* educators—with continuous product improvements made through direct classroom testing and faculty feedback. You'll love i>clicker, no matter your level of technical expertise, because the focus is on *your* teaching, *not the technology.* To learn more about packaging i>clicker with this textbook, please contact your local sales rep or visit www.iclicker.com.

Dismal Scientist A high-powered business database and analysis service comes to the classroom! Dismal Scientist offers real-time monitoring of the global economy, produced locally by economists and professionals at Economy.com's London, Sydney, and West Chester offices. Dismal Scientist is *free* when packaged with the Krugman/Wells textbook. Please contact your local sales rep for more information or go to www.economy.com.

ECONPORTAL IS NOW LAUNCHPAD

Because Technology Should Never Get in the Way

LaunchPad

LaunchPad is an online homework, e-Book, and teaching and learning system that can be used as a stand-alone course management system or integrated into many campus course management systems such as Blackboard, Canvas, Desire2Learn, and others. And now, drawing on what we've learned from thousands of instructors and hundreds of thousands of students over the past several years, we are proud to introduce a new generation of Macmillan's Portals—***LaunchPad***.

LaunchPad features include:

- **LaunchPad Units** that provide the ability to build a course in minutes. LaunchPad offers selected resources compiled into ready-to-use teaching units, complete with problem sets, activities, e-Book sections, and state-of-the-art online homework and testing. Instructors can quickly set up their course using precreated LaunchPad units for each chapter. They can also enhance LaunchPad units or create their own original assignments, adding selections from our extensive resource library of questions and activities, and their own materials as well.
- **LearningCurve:** A popular student resource, LearningCurve is an adaptive quizzing engine that automatically adjusts questions to the student's mastery level. With LearningCurve activities, each student follows a unique path to understanding the material. The more questions a student answers correctly, the more difficult the questions become. Each question is written specifically for the text and is linked to the relevant e-Book section. LearningCurve also provides a personal study plan for students as well as complete metrics for instructors. Proven to raise student performance, LearningCurve serves as an ideal formative assessment and learning tool. For detailed information, visit http://learningcurveworks.com.

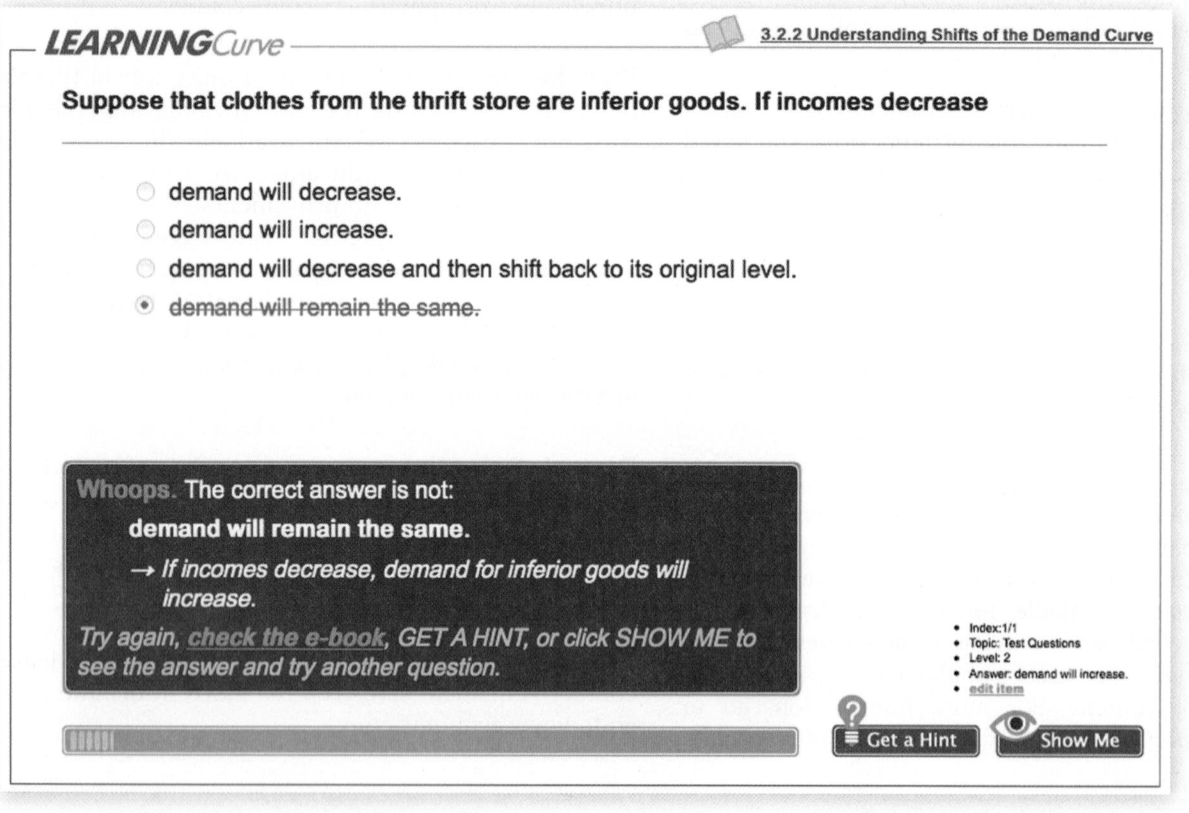

- **Clear, consistent interface:** LaunchPad integrates and unifies a consistent series of resources—LaunchPad units, the e-Book, media, assessment tools, instructor materials, and other content—to a degree unmatched by other online learning systems.
- **Robust, interactive e-Book:** The e-Book offers powerful study tools for students and easily customizable features for instructors. Our simple note-taking tool allows instructors to post notes, hyperlinks, content and more with a few simple clicks. Students can also take their own notes and can view all notes within each chapter to allow for easy study and review. Students can also highlight, access a glossary, and enlarge images within the text.
- **Powerful online quizzing and homework:** In addition to the LaunchPad units, instructors can create their own assignments using their own questions or drawing on quiz items within EconPortal, including:
  - **The complete test bank** for the textbook for use in creating exams, quizzes, or homework problems. Instructors can use built-in filters and settings to ensure the right questions are chosen and displayed to their preferences.
  - **The end-of-chapter problem sets** from the textbook which are carefully edited and available in a self-graded format—perfect for in-class quizzes and homework assignments.
  - **Electronically gradable graphing problems** using a robust graphing engine. Students will be asked to draw their response to a question, and the software will automatically grade that response. Graphing questions are tagged to appropriate textbook sections and range in difficulty level and skill.

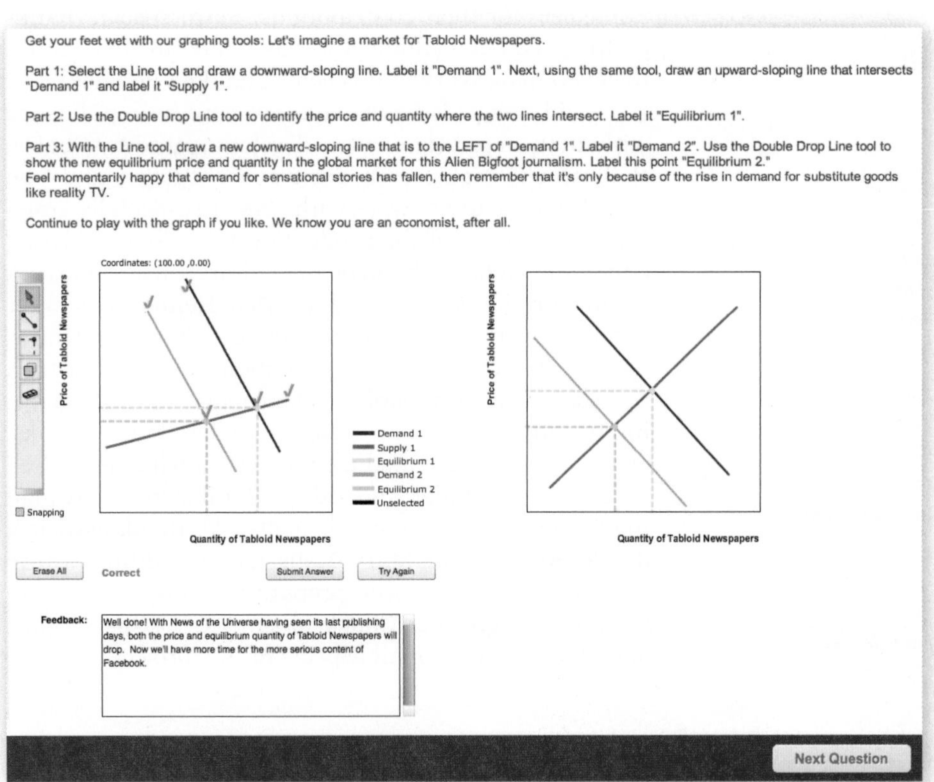

Acknowledgments

We are indebted to the following reviewers for their suggestions and advice on this third edition.

Semih Emre Cekin, *Texas Tech University*
Abel Embaye, *University of Arkansas*
Matthew Jaremski, *Colgate University*
Nicholas Karatjas, *Indiana University of Pennsylvania*
Susan Kask, *Warren Wilson College*
Katie Kontak, *Bowling Green State University*
Parul Mathur, *Simpson College*
Marshall Medoff, *California State University, Long Beach*
Amy Scott, *DeSales University*
Chace Stiehl, *Bellevue College*
Robert Teitelbaum, *State University of New York, Empire State College*
Theo Thedford, *Shorter University*
Matt Warning, *University of Puget Sound*

Once again, we would like to thank the following reviewers for their input on the second edition.

Jack Amariglio, *Merrimack College*
Rob Catlett, *Emporia State University*
Eric Chiang, *Florida Atlantic University*
Michael Coon, *University of Wisconsin–Milwaukee*
Tom Creahan, *Morehead State University*
Jose Esteban, *Palomar College*
Randall Filer, *Hunter College, CUNY*
Todd Gabe, *University of Maine*
Seth Gitter, *Towson University*
Devra Golbe, *Hunter College*
Patricia Graham, *University of Northern Colorado*
Thomas Hardin, *Mater Dei Catholic High School*
Terence Hunady, *Bowling Green State University*
Arthur Janssen, *Emporia State University*
Hisaya Kitaoka, *Franklin College*
Andrew F. Kozak, *St. Mary's College of Maryland*
Richard Langlois, *University of Connecticut*
Stephen Lile, *Western Kentucky University*
Dennis C. McCornac, *Anne Arundel Community College*
Mary Helen McSweeney-Feld, *Iona College*
Diego Mendez-Carbajo, *Illinois Wesleyan University*
Garrett Milam, *University of Puget Sound*
Ellen Mutari, *Richard Stockton College of New Jersey*
Kevin O'Brien, *Bradley University*
Inge O'Connor, *Syracuse University*
John Perry, *Centre College*
H. Mikael Sandberg, *University of Florida*
Elizabeth Sawyer-Kelly, *University of Wisconsin–Madison*
Amy Scott, *DeSales University*
Patrick Taylor, *Millsaps College*
Thomas Watkins, *Eastern Kentucky University*

We owe a special thanks to those people who provided guidance in creating the first edition of *Essentials of Economics*:

Carlos Aguilar, *El Paso Community College*
Irma T. Alonso, *Florida International University*
Clive Belfield, *Queens College, CUNY*
Norman R. Cloutier, *University of Wisconsin–Parkside*
Jose L. Esteban, *Palomar College*
Devra Golbe, *Hunter College, CUNY*
Frances F. Lea, *Germanna Community College*
Noreen E. Lephardt, *Marquette University*
Chris N. McGrew, *Purdue University*
Abdulhamid Sukar, *Cameron University*
Jose J. Vazquez-Cognet, *University of Illinois at Urbana-Champaign*

We must also thank the many people at Worth Publishers for their contributions. Extra-special thanks go to special consultant Andreas Bentz, for his careful review of new Worked Problems and data updates.

In addition, this book could not have been published without the input of executive development editor Sharon Balbos, who makes everything come together and who is truly a pleasure to work with. We are especially grateful for the input of the production team: senior project editor Liz Geller, who kept the editorial team on track during production; copyeditor Deb Heimann, for her excellent work; associate managing editor Lisa Kinne, for her project oversight; production manager Barbara Seixas, for her invaluable guidance; and Kevin Kall, for his beautiful cover and design updates. Many thanks, as well, to associate media editor Lukia Kliossis, as well as Stacey Alexander and Edgar Bonilla for coordinating the production of supplements. We thank associate development editor Mary Melis for her administrative assistance and turnover preparation. Finally, we are grateful to publisher Chuck Linsmeier, for his support and able oversight of all aspects of this project.

CREDITS

Cover Photo Credits

First Row: Bike rider: *Flat Earth Images;* Cornstalks: *Stockbyte;* Oil rig workers: *istockphoto.com;* Logs on truck: *Photodisc;* Oil refinery: *Photodisc;* Machine worker: *Digitalvision;* Farmer on tractor: *Photodisc.* **Second Row:** Collection of dyes: *Digital Vision/Getty Images;* Man driving forklift: *Clerkenwell/Getty Images;* Steam: *Photodisc;* Pineapples: *Photodisc;* Cows: *Stockbyte;* Couple buying car: *Photodisc;* Color buildings: *Photodisc.* **Third Row:** Woman smiling: *Photodisc;* Highways: *Fotosearch;* Powerlines: *Digitalvision;* Red Factory shot: *Digitalvision;* Glass facade: *Veer;* Flowers in a field: *Stockbyte;* Hay in snow: *Photodisc.* **Fourth Row:** Cars in traffic: *PhotoDisc;* High-speed train: *Flat Earth Images;* Hong Kong intersection: *Photodisc;* Boy: *Photodisc;* Big truck: *Phil Whitehouse/Flickr;* Surgeon: *Stockbyte;* Red factory shot: *Digitalvision.* **Fifth Row:** Lightbulbs: © fStop/Alamy; Flags: *Photodisc;* Steam: *PhotoDisc;* Tugboat: *Flat Earth Images;* Fisher: *Photodisc;* Boy with flowers: *Photodisc;* Vancouver skyline: *Photodisc.* **Sixth Row:** Hybrid car: *istockphoto;* Wind turbines: *Beverett/Dreamstime.com;* Man with sign during Great Depression: *Archive Holdings Inc./Getty Images;* Wall Street sign: *Nikada/ iStockphoto;* Ship: *Photodisc;* Skyline: *Photodisc;* Sewage treatment plant: *Digital Vision.* **Seventh Row:** Tax form: *D. Hurst/Alamy;* Man with iPad: *Veer;* Evening dining: *Photodisc;* Grocers: *Photodisc;* Woman with blue scarf: *Photodisc;* Wheat: *Stockbyte;* Oil refinery at night: *Digitalvision.* **Eighth Row:** NY Stock Exchange: *Image Source;* Chemical plant: *Brand X Pictures;* Gas prices: *Courtesy Patricia Marx;* Wiretubes: *Digitalvision;* Currency: *Photodisc;* Golden Gate Bridge: *Photodisc;* Pipes in oil field: *Photodisc.* **Ninth Row:** Girl smiling: *Photodisc;* Can tops: *Brand X Pictures;* Tokyo Stock Exchange: *Media Bakery;* Oil worker: *Corbis;* Smiling woman: *Photodisc;* Trees: *Photodisc;* Double-decker bus: *Flat Earth Images.*

Text Credits

Chapter 5, Source information for Table 5-1 on page 147: ***Eggs, beef:*** K. S. Huang and Biing-Hwan Lin, *Estimation of Food Demand and Nutrient Elasticities from Household Survey Data,* United States Department of Agriculture Economic Research Service Technical Bulletin, No. 1887 (Washington, DC: U.S. Department of Agriculture, 2000); ***stationery, gasoline, airline travel, foreign travel:*** H. S. Houthakker and Lester D. Taylor, *Consumer Demand in the United States, 1929–1970: Analyses and Projections* (Cambridge, MA: Harvard University Press, 1966); ***housing, restaurant meals:*** H. S. Houthakker and Lester D. Taylor, *Consumer Demand in the United States: Analyses and Projections,* 2nd ed. (Cambridge, MA: Harvard University Press, 1970).

First Principles

WHAT YOU WILL LEARN IN THIS CHAPTER

- A set of definitions relating to economics and the economy
- A set of principles for understanding the economics of how individuals make choices
- A set of principles for understanding how economies work through the interaction of individual choices
- A set of principles for understanding economy-wide interactions

COMMON GROUND

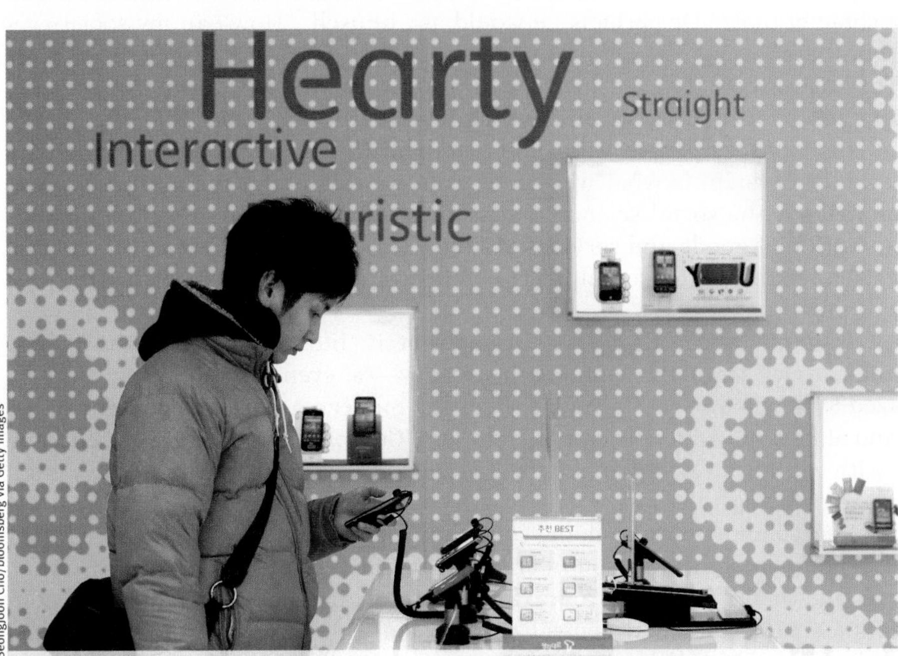

Seongjoon Cho/bloomsberg via Getty Images

One must choose.

THE ANNUAL MEETING OF THE American Economic Association draws thousands of economists, young and old, famous and obscure. There are booksellers, business meetings, and quite a few job interviews. But mainly the economists gather to talk and listen. During the busiest times, 60 or more presentations may be taking place simultaneously, on questions that range from financial market crises to who does the cooking in two-earner families.

What do these people have in common? An expert on financial markets probably knows very little about the economics of housework, and vice versa. Yet an economist who wanders into the wrong seminar and ends up listening to presentations on some unfamiliar topic is nonetheless likely to hear much that is familiar. The reason is that all economic analysis is based on a set of common principles that apply to many different issues.

Some of these principles involve *individual choice*—for economics is, first of all, about the choices that individuals make. Do you save your money and take the bus or do you buy a car? Do you keep your old smart-phone or upgrade to a new one? These decisions involve *making a choice* from among a limited number of alternatives—limited because no one can have everything that he or she wants. Every question in economics at its most basic level involves individuals making choices.

But to understand how an *economy* works, you need to understand more than how individuals make choices. None of us are Robinson Crusoe, alone on an island. We must make decisions in an environment that is shaped by the decisions of others. Indeed, in a modern economy even the simplest decisions you make—say, what to have for breakfast—are shaped by the decisions of thousands of other people, from the banana grower in Costa Rica who decided to grow the fruit you eat to the farmer in Iowa who provided the corn in your cornflakes.

Because each of us in a *market economy* depends on so many others—and they, in turn, depend on us—our choices interact. So although all economics at a basic level is about individual choice, in order to understand how market economies behave we must also understand *economic interaction*—how my choices affect your choices, and vice versa.

Many important economic interactions can be understood by looking at the markets for individual goods, like the market for corn. But an economy as a whole has ups and downs, and we therefore need to understand economy-wide interactions as well as the more limited interactions that occur in individual markets.

Through the study of economics, we will discover common principles about individual choice and interaction. In this first section, we define key terms in economics. We then look in detail at twelve basic principles of economics—four principles involving individual choice, five involving the way individual choices interact, and three more involving economy-wide interactions. ■

An **economy** is a system for coordinating society's productive activities.

Economics is the social science that studies the production, distribution, and consumption of goods and services.

A **market economy** is an economy in which decisions about production and consumption are made by individual producers and consumers.

The **invisible hand** refers to the way in which the individual pursuit of self-interest can lead to good results for society as a whole.

The Ordinary Business of Life

Imagine that you could transport an American from the colonial period forward in time to our own era. (Isn't that the plot of a movie? Several, actually.) What would this time-traveler find amazing?

Surely the most amazing thing would be the sheer prosperity of modern America—the range of goods and services that ordinary families can afford. Looking at all that wealth, our transplanted colonial would wonder, "How can I get some of that?" Or perhaps he would ask himself, "How can my society get some of that?"

The answer is that to get this kind of prosperity, you need a well-functioning system for coordinating productive activities—the activities that create the goods and services people want and get them to the people who want them. That kind of system is what we mean when we talk about the **economy.** And **economics** is the social science that studies the production, distribution, and consumption of goods and services. As the great nineteenth-century economist Alfred Marshall put it, economics is "a study of mankind in the ordinary business of life."

An economy succeeds to the extent that it, literally, delivers the goods. A time-traveler from the eighteenth century—or even from 1950—would be amazed at how many goods and services the modern American economy delivers and at how many people can afford them. Compared with any past economy and with all but a few other countries today, America has an incredibly high standard of living.

So our economy must be doing something right, and the time-traveler might want to compliment the person in charge. But guess what? There isn't anyone in charge. The United States has a **market economy,** in which production and consumption are the result of decentralized decisions by many firms and individuals. There is no central authority telling people what to produce or where to ship it. Each individual producer makes what he or she thinks will be most profitable; each consumer buys what he or she chooses.

The alternative to a market economy is a *command economy,* in which there *is* a central authority making decisions about production and consumption. Command economies have been tried, most notably in the Soviet Union between 1917 and 1991. But they didn't work very well. Producers in the Soviet Union routinely found themselves unable to produce because they did not have crucial raw materials, or they succeeded in producing but then found that nobody wanted their products. Consumers were often unable to find necessary items—command economies are famous for long lines at shops.

Market economies, however, are able to coordinate even highly complex activities and to reliably provide consumers with the goods and services they want. Indeed, people quite casually trust their lives to the market system: residents of any major city would starve in days if the unplanned yet somehow orderly actions of thousands of businesses did not deliver a steady supply of food. Surprisingly, the unplanned "chaos" of a market economy turns out to be far more orderly than the "planning" of a command economy.

In 1776, in a famous passage in his book *The Wealth of Nations,* the pioneering Scottish economist Adam Smith wrote about how individuals, in pursuing their own interests, often end up serving the interests of society as a whole. Of a businessman whose pursuit of profit makes the nation wealthier, Smith wrote: "[H]e intends only his own gain, and he is in this, as in many other cases, led by an invisible hand to promote an end which was no part of his intention." Ever since, economists have used the term **invisible hand** to refer to the way a market economy manages to harness the power of self-interest for the good of society.

The study of how individuals make decisions and how these decisions interact is called **microeconomics.** One of the key themes in microeconomics is the validity of Adam Smith's insight: individuals pursuing their own interests often do promote the interests of society as a whole.

So part of the answer to our time-traveler's question—"How can my society achieve the kind of prosperity you take for granted?"—is that his society should learn to appreciate the virtues of a market economy and the power of the invisible hand.

But the invisible hand isn't always our friend. It's also important to understand when and why the individual pursuit of self-interest can lead to counterproductive behavior.

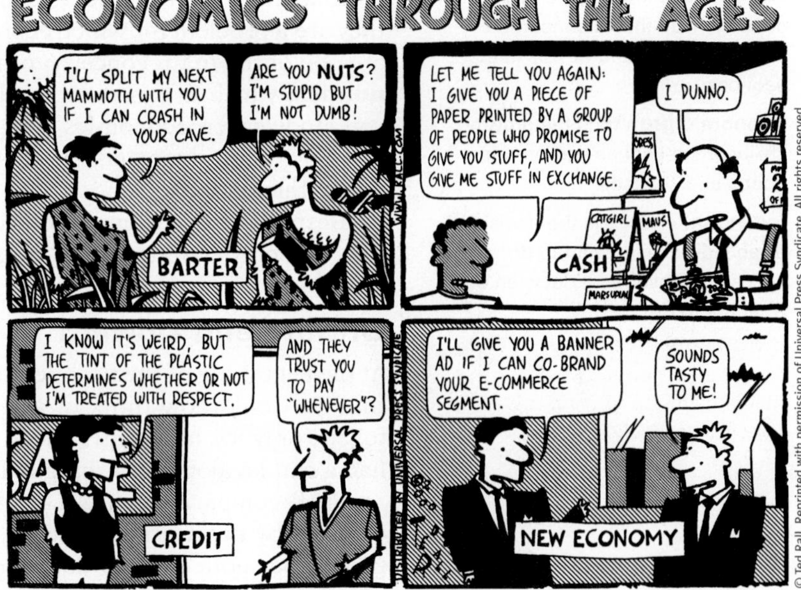

My Benefit, Your Cost

One thing that our time-traveler would not admire about modern life is the traffic. In fact, although most things have gotten better in America over time, traffic congestion has gotten a lot worse.

When traffic is congested, each driver is imposing a cost on all the other drivers on the road—he is literally getting in their way (and they are getting in his way). This cost can be substantial: in major metropolitan areas, each time someone drives to work, instead of taking public transportation or working at home, he can easily impose $15 or more in hidden costs on other drivers. Yet when deciding whether or not to drive, commuters have no incentive to take the costs they impose on others into account.

Traffic congestion is a familiar example of a much broader problem: sometimes the individual pursuit of one's own interest, instead of promoting the interests of society as a whole, can actually make society worse off. When this happens, it is known as **market failure.** Other important examples of market failure involve air and water pollution as well as the overexploitation of natural resources such as fish and forests.

The good news, as you will learn as you use this book to study microeconomics, is that economic analysis can be used to diagnose cases of market failure. And often, economic analysis can also be used to devise solutions for the problem.

Good Times, Bad Times

Normally our time-traveler would find shopping malls crowded with happy customers. But during the fall of 2008, stores across America became unusually quiet. The U.S. economy was depressed, and businesses were laying off workers in large numbers.

Such troubled periods are a regular feature of modern economies. The fact is that the economy does not always run smoothly: it experiences fluctuations, a series of ups and downs. By middle age, a typical American will have experienced three or four downs, known as **recessions.** (The U.S. economy experienced serious recessions beginning in 1973, 1981, 1990, 2001, and 2007.) During a severe recession, millions of workers may be laid off.

Microeconomics is the branch of economics that studies how people make decisions and how these decisions interact.

When the individual pursuit of self-interest leads to bad results for society as a whole, there is **market failure.**

A **recession** is a downturn in the economy.

Macroeconomics is the branch of economics that is concerned with overall ups and downs in the economy.

Economic growth is the growing ability of the economy to produce goods and services.

Individual choice is the decision by an individual of what to do, which necessarily involves a decision of what not to do.

Like market failure, recessions are a fact of life; but also like market failure, they are a problem for which economic analysis offers some solutions. Recessions are one of the main concerns of the branch of economics known as **macroeconomics,** which is concerned with the overall ups and downs of the economy. If you study macroeconomics, you will learn how economists explain recessions and how government policies can be used to minimize the damage from economic fluctuations.

Despite the occasional recession, however, over the long run the story of the U.S. economy contains many more ups than downs.

Onward and Upward

At the beginning of the twentieth century, most Americans lived under conditions that we would now think of as extreme poverty. Only 10% of homes had flush toilets, only 8% had central heating, only 2% had electricity, and almost nobody had a car, let alone a washing machine or air conditioning.

Such comparisons are a stark reminder of how much our lives have been changed by **economic growth,** the growing ability of the economy to produce goods and services. Why does the economy grow over time? And why does economic growth occur faster in some times and places than in others? These are key questions for economics because economic growth is a good thing, and most of us want more of it.

The "ordinary business of life" is really quite extraordinary, if you stop to think about it, and it can lead us to ask some very interesting and important questions.

In this book, we will describe the answers economists have given to these questions. But this book, like economics as a whole, isn't a list of answers: it's an introduction to a discipline, a way to address questions like those we have just asked. Or as Alfred Marshall put it: "Economics . . . is not a body of concrete truth, but an engine for the discovery of concrete truth."

So let's turn the key and start the ignition.

Quick Review

- **Economics** is the study of the production, distribution, and consumption of goods and services and how the **economy** coordinates these activities. In a **market economy,** the **invisible hand** works through individuals pursuing their own self-interest.
- **Microeconomics** is the study of how individuals make decisions and how these decisions interact, which sometimes leads to **market failure. Macroeconomics** is concerned with economic fluctuations, such as **recessions,** that can temporarily slow **economic growth.**

CHECK YOUR UNDERSTANDING 1-1

1. Which of the following statements describe features of a market economy?
   a. The invisible hand harnesses the power of self-interest for the good of society.
   b. A central authority makes decisions about production and consumption.
   c. The pursuit of one's own self-interest sometimes results in market failure.
   d. Growth in a market economy is steady and without fluctuations.

Solutions appear at back of book.

Principles That Underlie Individual Choice: The Core of Economics

Every economic issue involves, at its most basic level, **individual choice—** decisions by an individual about what to do and what not to do. In fact, you might say that it isn't economics if it isn't about choice.

Step into a big store like a Walmart or Target. There are thousands of different products available, and it is extremely unlikely that you—or anyone else—could afford to buy everything you might want to have. And anyway, there's only so much space in your dorm room or apartment. So will you buy another bookcase or a mini-refrigerator? Given limitations on your budget and your living space, you must choose which products to buy and which to leave on the shelf.

The fact that those products are on the shelf in the first place involves choice—the store manager chose to put them there, and the manufacturers of the products chose to produce them. All economic activities involve individual choice.

Four economic principles underlie the economics of individual choice, as shown in Table 1-1. We'll now examine each of these principles in more detail.

TABLE 1-1 The Principles of Individual Choice

1. People must make choices because resources are scarce.
2. The opportunity cost of an item—what you must give up in order to get it—is its true cost.
3. "How much" decisions require making trade-offs at the margin: comparing the costs and benefits of doing a little bit more of an activity versus doing a little bit less.
4. People usually respond to incentives, exploiting opportunities to make themselves better off.

Principle #1: Choices Are Necessary Because Resources Are Scarce

You can't always get what you want. Everyone would like to have a beautiful house in a great location (and have help with the housecleaning), a new car or two, and a nice vacation in a fancy hotel. But even in a rich country like the United States, not many families can afford all that. So they must make choices—whether to go to Disney World this year or buy a better car, whether to make do with a small backyard or accept a longer commute in order to live where land is cheaper.

Limited income isn't the only thing that keeps people from having everything they want. Time is also in limited supply: there are only 24 hours in a day. And because the time we have is limited, choosing to spend time on one activity also means choosing not to spend time on a different activity—spending time studying for an exam means forgoing a night spent watching a movie. Indeed, many people are so limited by the number of hours in the day that they are willing to trade money for time. For example, convenience stores normally charge higher prices than a regular supermarket. But they fulfill a valuable role by catering to time-pressured customers who would rather pay more than travel farther to the supermarket.

This leads us to our first principle of individual choice:

People must make choices because resources are scarce.

A **resource** is anything that can be used to produce something else. Lists of the economy's resources usually begin with land, labor (the time of workers), capital (machinery, buildings, and other man-made productive assets), and human capital (the educational achievements and skills of workers). A resource is **scarce** when there's not enough of the resource available to satisfy all the ways a society wants to use it. There are many scarce resources. These include natural resources—resources that come from the physical environment, such as minerals, lumber, and petroleum. There is also a limited quantity of human resources—labor, skill, and intelligence. And in a growing world economy with a rapidly increasing human population, even clean air and water have become scarce resources.

Just as individuals must make choices, the scarcity of resources means that society as a whole must make choices. One way a society makes choices is by allowing them to emerge as the result of many individual choices, which is what usually happens in a market economy. For example, Americans as a group have only so many hours in a week: how many of those hours will they spend going to supermarkets to get lower prices, rather than saving time by shopping at convenience stores? The answer is the sum of individual decisions: each of the millions of individuals in the economy makes his or her own choice about where to shop, and the overall choice is simply the sum of those individual decisions.

A **resource** is anything that can be used to produce something else.

Resources are **scarce**—not enough of the resources are available to satisfy all the various ways a society wants to use them.

The real cost of an item is its **opportunity cost**: what you must give up in order to get it.

But for various reasons, there are some decisions that a society decides are best not left to individual choice. For example, the authors live in an area that until recently was mainly farmland but is now being rapidly built up. Most local residents feel that the community would be a more pleasant place to live if some of the land was left undeveloped. But no individual has an incentive to keep his or her land as open space, rather than sell it to a developer. So a trend has emerged in many communities across the United States of local governments purchasing undeveloped land and preserving it as open space. We'll see in later chapters why decisions about how to use scarce resources are often best left to individuals but sometimes should be made at a higher, community-wide, level.

Principle #2: The True Cost of Something Is Its Opportunity Cost

It is the last term before you graduate, and your class schedule allows you to take only one elective. There are two, however, that you would really like to take: Intro to Computer Graphics and History of Jazz.

Suppose you decide to take the History of Jazz course. What's the cost of that decision? It is the fact that you can't take the computer graphics class, your next best alternative choice. Economists call that kind of cost—what you must give up in order to get an item you want—the **opportunity cost** of that item. This leads us to our second principle of individual choice:

> ***The opportunity cost of an item—what you must give up in order to get it—is its true cost.***

So the opportunity cost of taking the History of Jazz class is the benefit you would have derived from the Intro to Computer Graphics class.

The concept of opportunity cost is crucial to understanding individual choice because, in the end, all costs are opportunity costs. That's because every choice you make means forgoing some other alternative. Sometimes critics claim that economists are concerned only with costs and benefits that can be measured in dollars and cents. But that is not true. Much economic analysis involves cases like our elective course example, where it costs no extra tuition to take one elective course—that is, there is no direct monetary cost. Nonetheless, the elective you choose has an opportunity cost—the other desirable elective course that you must forgo because your limited time permits taking only one. More specifically, the opportunity cost of a choice is what you forgo by not choosing your next best alternative.

You might think that opportunity cost is an add-on—that is, something *additional* to the monetary cost of an item. Suppose that an elective class costs additional tuition of $750; now there is a monetary cost to taking History of Jazz. Is the opportunity cost of taking that course something separate from that monetary cost?

Well, consider two cases. First, suppose that taking Intro to Computer Graphics also costs $750. In this case, you would have to spend that $750 no matter which class you take. So what you give up to take the History of Jazz class is still the computer graphics class, period—you would have to spend that $750 either way. But suppose there isn't any fee for the computer graphics class. In that case, what you give up to take the jazz class is the benefit from the computer graphics class *plus* the benefit you could have gained from spending the $750 on other things.

Either way, the real cost of taking your preferred class is what you must give up to get it. As you expand the set of decisions that underlie each choice—whether to take an elective or not, whether to finish this term or not, whether to drop out or not—you'll realize that all costs are ultimately opportunity costs.

Sometimes the money you have to pay for something is a good indication of its opportunity cost. But many times it is not. One very important example of how poorly monetary cost can indicate opportunity cost is the cost of attending college. Tuition and housing are major monetary expenses for most students; but even if these things were free, attending college would still be an expensive proposition because most college students, if they were not in college, would have a job. That is, by going to college, students *forgo* the income they could have earned if they had worked instead. This means that the opportunity cost of attending college is what you pay for tuition and housing plus the forgone income you would have earned in a job.

It's easy to see that the opportunity cost of going to college is especially high for people who could be earning a lot during what would otherwise have been their college years. That is why star athletes like LeBron James and entrepreneurs like Mark Zuckerberg, founder of Facebook, often skip or drop out of college.

You make a **trade-off** when you compare the costs with the benefits of doing something.

AP Photo/Jeff Chiu

Mark Zuckerberg understood the concept of opportunity cost.

Principle #3: "How Much" Is a Decision at the Margin

Some important decisions involve an "either–or" choice—for example, you decide either to go to college or to begin working; you decide either to take economics or to take something else. But other important decisions involve "how much" choices—for example, if you are taking both economics and chemistry this semester, you must decide how much time to spend studying for each. When it comes to understanding "how much" decisions, economics has an important insight to offer: "how much" is a decision made at the margin.

Suppose you are taking both economics and chemistry. And suppose you are a pre-med student, so your grade in chemistry matters more to you than your grade in economics. Does that therefore imply that you should spend *all* your study time on chemistry and wing it on the economics exam? Probably not; even if you think your chemistry grade is more important, you should put some effort into studying economics.

Spending more time studying chemistry involves a benefit (a higher expected grade in that course) and a cost (you could have spent that time doing something else, such as studying to get a higher grade in economics). That is, your decision involves a **trade-off**—a comparison of costs and benefits.

How do you decide this kind of "how much" question? The typical answer is that you make the decision a bit at a time, by asking how you should spend the next hour. Say both exams are on the same day, and the night before you spend time reviewing your notes for both courses. At 6:00 P.M., you decide that it's a good idea to spend at least an hour on each course. At 8:00 P.M., you decide you'd better spend another hour on each course. At 10:00 P.M., you are getting tired and figure you have one more hour to study before bed—chemistry or economics? If you are pre-med, it's likely to be chemistry; if you are pre-MBA, it's likely to be economics.

Note how you've made the decision to allocate your time: at each point the question is whether or not to spend *one more hour* on either course. And in deciding whether to spend another hour studying for chemistry, you weigh the costs (an hour forgone of studying for economics or an hour forgone of sleeping) versus the benefits (a likely increase in your chemistry grade). As long as the benefit of studying chemistry for one more hour outweighs the cost, you should choose to study for that additional hour.

Decisions about whether to do a bit more or a bit less of an activity are **marginal decisions**. The study of such decisions is known as **marginal analysis**.

An **incentive** is anything that offers rewards to people who change their behavior.

Decisions of this type—whether to do a bit more or a bit less of an activity, like what to do with your next hour, your next dollar, and so on—are **marginal decisions.** This brings us to our third principle of individual choice:

> ***"How much" decisions require making trade-offs at the margin: comparing the costs and benefits of doing a little bit more of an activity versus doing a little bit less.***

The study of such decisions is known as **marginal analysis.** Many of the questions that we face in economics—as well as in real life—involve marginal analysis: How many workers should I hire in my shop? At what mileage should I change the oil in my car? What is an acceptable rate of negative side effects from a new medicine? Marginal analysis plays a central role in economics because it is the key to deciding "how much" of an activity to do.

Principle #4: People Usually Respond to Incentives, Exploiting Opportunities to Make Themselves Better Off

One day, while listening to the morning financial news, the authors heard a great tip about how to park cheaply in Manhattan. Garages in the Wall Street area charge as much as $30 per day. But according to the newscaster, some people had found a better way: instead of parking in a garage, they had their oil changed at the Manhattan Jiffy Lube, where it costs $19.95 to change your oil—and they keep your car all day!

It's a great story, but unfortunately it turned out not to be true—in fact, there is no Jiffy Lube in Manhattan. But if there were, you can be sure there would be a lot of oil changes there. Why? Because when people are offered opportunities to make themselves better off, they normally take them—and if they could find a way to park their car all day for $19.95 rather than $30, they would.

In this example economists say that people are responding to an **incentive**—an opportunity to make themselves better off. We can now state our fourth principle of individual choice:

> ***People usually respond to incentives, exploiting opportunities to make themselves better off.***

When you try to predict how individuals will behave in an economic situation, it is a very good bet that they will respond to incentives—that is, exploit opportunities to make themselves better off. Furthermore, individuals will *continue* to exploit these opportunities until they have been fully exhausted. If there really were a Manhattan Jiffy Lube and an oil change really were a cheap way to park your car, we can safely predict that before long the waiting list for oil changes would be weeks, if not months.

In fact, the principle that people will exploit opportunities to make themselves better off is the basis of *all* predictions by economists about individual behavior. If the earnings of those who get MBAs soar while the earnings of those who get law degrees decline, we can expect more students to go to business school and fewer to go to law school. If the price of gasoline rises and stays high for an extended period of time, we can expect people to buy smaller cars with higher gas mileage—making themselves better off in the presence of higher gas prices by driving more fuel-efficient cars.

One last point: economists tend to be skeptical of any attempt to change people's behavior that *doesn't* change their incentives. For example, a plan that calls on manufacturers to reduce pollution voluntarily probably won't be effective because it hasn't changed manufacturers' incentives. In contrast, a plan that gives them a financial reward to reduce pollution is a lot more likely to work because it has changed their incentives.

FOR INQUIRING MINDS

CASHING IN AT SCHOOL

The true reward for learning is, of course, the learning itself. Many students, however, struggle with their motivation to study and work hard. Teachers and policy makers have been particularly challenged to help students from disadvantaged backgrounds, who often have poor school attendance, high dropout rates, and low standardized test scores. In a 2007–2008 study, Harvard economist Roland Fryer Jr. found that monetary incentives—cash rewards—could improve students' academic performance in schools in economically disadvantaged areas. How cash incentives work, however, is both surprising and predictable.

Fryer conducted his research in four different school districts, employing a different set of incentives and a different measure of performance in each. In New York, students were paid according to their scores on standardized tests; in Chicago, they were paid according to their grades; in Washington, D.C., they were paid according to attendance and good behavior as well as their grades; in Dallas, second-graders were paid each time they read a book. Fryer evaluated the results by comparing the performance of students who were in the program to other students in the same school who were not.

In New York, the program had no perceptible effect on test scores. In Chicago, students in the program got better grades and attended class more. In Washington, the program boosted the outcomes of the kids who are normally the hardest to reach, those with serious behavioral problems, raising their test scores by an amount equivalent to attending five extra months of school. The most dramatic results occurred in Dallas, where students significantly boosted their reading-comprehension test scores; results continued into the next year, after the cash rewards had ended.

So what explains the various results? To motivate students with cash rewards, Fryer found that students had to believe that they could have a significant effect on the performance measure. So in Chicago, Washington, and Dallas—where students had a significant amount of control over outcomes such as grades, attendance, behavior, and the number of books read—the program produced significant results. But because New York students had little idea how to affect their score on a standardized test, the prospect of a reward had little influence on their behavior. Also, the timing of the reward matters: a $1 reward has more effect on behavior if performance is measured at shorter intervals and the reward is delivered soon after.

Kris Timken/Getty Images

Cash incentives have been shown to improve student performance.

Fryer's experiment revealed some critical insights about how to motivate behavior with incentives. How incentives are designed is very important: the relationship between effort and outcome, as well as the speed of reward, matters a lot. Moreover, the design of incentives may depend quite a lot on the characteristics of the people you are trying to motivate: what motivates a student from an economically privileged background may not motivate a student from an economically disadvantaged one. Fryer's insights give teachers and policy makers an important new tool for helping disadvantaged students succeed in school.

So are we ready to do economics? Not yet—because most of the interesting things that happen in the economy are the result not merely of individual choices but of the way in which individual choices interact.

ECONOMICS ➤ IN ACTION

BOY OR GIRL? IT DEPENDS ON THE COST

One fact about China is indisputable: it's a big country with lots of people. As of 2011, the population of China was 1,344,130,000. That's right: over *one billion three hundred million*.

In 1978, the government of China introduced the "one-child policy" to address the economic and demographic challenges presented by China's large population. China was very, very poor in 1978, and its leaders worried that the country could not afford to adequately educate and care for its growing population. The average Chinese woman in the 1970s was giving birth to more than five children during her lifetime. So the government restricted most couples, particularly those in urban areas, to one child, imposing penalties on those who defied the mandate. As a result, by 2011 the average number of births for a woman in China was only 1.5.

But the one-child policy had an unfortunate unintended consequence. Because China is an overwhelmingly rural country and sons can perform the manual

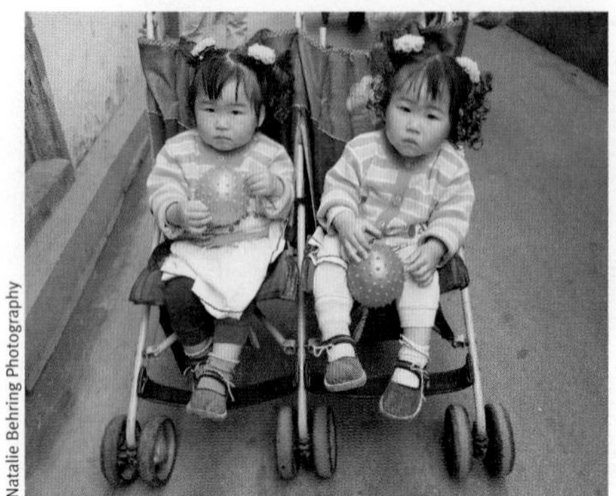
Natalie Behring Photography

The cost of China's "one-child policy" was a generation of "disappeared" daughters—a phenomenon that has itself begun to disappear as economic conditions have changed.

labor of farming, families had a strong preference for sons over daughters. In addition, tradition dictates that brides become part of their husbands' families and that sons take care of their elderly parents. As a result of the one-child policy, China soon had too many "unwanted girls." Some were given up for adoption abroad, but all too many simply "disappeared" during the first year of life, the victims of neglect and mistreatment.

India, another highly rural poor country with high demographic pressures, also has a significant problem with "disappearing girls." In 1990, Amartya Sen, an Indian-born British economist who would go on to win the Nobel Prize in 1998, estimated that there were up to 100 million "missing women" in Asia. (The exact figure is in dispute, but it is clear that Sen identified a real and pervasive problem.)

Demographers have recently noted a distinct turn of events in China, which is quickly urbanizing. In all but one of the provinces with urban centers, the gender imbalance between boys and girls peaked in 1995 and has steadily fallen toward the biologically natural ratio since then. Many believe that the source of the change is China's strong economic growth and increasing urbanization. As people move to cities to take advantage of job growth there, they don't need sons to work the fields. Moreover, land prices in Chinese cities are skyrocketing, making the custom of parents buying an apartment for a son before he can marry unaffordable for many. To be sure, sons are still preferred in the rural areas. But as a sure mark of how times have changed, Internet websites have recently popped up that advise couples on how to have a girl rather than a boy.

Quick Review

- All economic activities involve **individual choice.**
- People must make choices because **resources** are **scarce.**
- The real cost of something is its **opportunity cost**—what you must give up to get it. All costs are opportunity costs. Monetary costs are sometimes a good indicator of opportunity costs, but not always.
- Many choices involve not *whether* to do something but *how much* of it to do. "How much" choices call for making a **trade-off** at the margin. The study of **marginal decisions** is known as **marginal analysis.**
- Because people usually exploit opportunities to make themselves better off, **incentives** can change people's behavior.

CHECK YOUR UNDERSTANDING 1-2

1. Explain how each of the following situations illustrates one of the four principles of individual choice.
   a. You are on your third trip to a restaurant's all-you-can-eat dessert buffet and are feeling very full. Although it would cost you no additional money, you forgo a slice of coconut cream pie but have a slice of chocolate cake.
   b. Even if there were more resources in the world, there would still be scarcity.
   c. Different teaching assistants teach several Economics 101 tutorials. Those taught by the teaching assistants with the best reputations fill up quickly, with spaces left unfilled in the ones taught by assistants with poor reputations.
   d. To decide how many hours per week to exercise, you compare the health benefits of one more hour of exercise to the effect on your grades of one less hour spent studying.
2. You make $45,000 per year at your current job with Whiz Kids Consultants. You are considering a job offer from Brainiacs, Inc., that will pay you $50,000 per year. Which of the following are elements of the opportunity cost of accepting the new job at Brainiacs, Inc.?
   a. The increased time spent commuting to your new job
   b. The $45,000 salary from your old job
   c. The more spacious office at your new job

Solutions appear at back of book.

Interaction: How Economies Work

The **interaction** of choices—my choices affect your choices, and vice versa—is a feature of most economic situations. The results of this interaction are often quite different from what the individuals intend.

An economy is a system for coordinating the productive activities of many people. In a market economy like we live in, coordination takes place without any coordinator: each individual makes his or her own choices. Yet those choices are by no means independent of one another: each individual's opportunities, and hence choices, depend to a large extent on the choices made by other people. So to understand how a market economy behaves, we have to examine this **interaction** in which my choices affect your choices, and vice versa.

When studying economic interaction, we quickly learn that the end result of individual choices may be quite different from what any one individual intends. For example, over the past century farmers in the United States have eagerly adopted new farming techniques and crop strains that have reduced their costs and increased their yields. Clearly, it's in the interest of each farmer to keep up with the latest farming techniques.

But the end result of each farmer trying to increase his or her own income has actually been to drive many farmers out of business. Because American farmers have been so successful at producing larger yields, agricultural prices have steadily fallen. These falling prices have reduced the incomes of many farmers, and as a result fewer and fewer people find farming worth doing. That is, an individual farmer who plants a better variety of corn is better off; but when many farmers plant a better variety of corn, the result may be to make farmers as a group worse off.

A farmer who plants a new, more productive corn variety doesn't just grow more corn. Such a farmer also affects the market for corn through the increased yields attained, with consequences that will be felt by other farmers, consumers, and beyond.

Just as there are four economic principles that underlie individual choice, there are five principles that underlie the economics of interaction. These five principles are summarized in Table 1-2. We will now examine each of these principles more closely.

TABLE 1-2 The Principles of the Interaction of Individual Choices

5. There are gains from trade.
6. Because people respond to incentives, markets move toward equilibrium.
7. Resources should be used as efficiently as possible to achieve society's goals.
8. Because people usually exploit gains from trade, markets usually lead to efficiency.
9. When markets don't achieve efficiency, government intervention can improve society's welfare.

Principle #5: There Are Gains from Trade

Why do the choices I make interact with the choices you make? A family could try to take care of all its own needs—growing its own food, sewing its own clothing, providing itself with entertainment, writing its own economics textbooks. But trying to live that way would be very hard. The key to a much better standard of living for everyone is **trade,** in which people divide tasks among themselves and each person provides a good or service that other people want in return for different goods and services that he or she wants.

The reason we have an economy, not many self-sufficient individuals, is that there are **gains from trade:** by dividing tasks and trading, two people (or 6 billion people) can each get more of what they want than they could get by being self-sufficient. This leads us to our fifth principle:

There are gains from trade.

Gains from trade arise from this division of tasks, which economists call **specialization**—a situation in which different people each engage in a different task, specializing in those tasks that they are good at performing. The advantages of specialization, and the resulting gains from trade, were the starting point for Adam Smith's 1776 book *The Wealth of Nations*, which many regard as the beginning of economics as a discipline. Smith's book begins with a description of an eighteenth-century pin factory where, rather than each of the 10 workers making a pin from start to finish, each worker specialized in one of the many steps in pin-making:

> One man draws out the wire, another straights it, a third cuts it, a fourth points it, a fifth grinds it at the top for receiving the head; to make the head requires two or three distinct operations; to put it on, is a particular business, to whiten the pins is another; it is even a trade by itself to put them into the paper; and the important business of making a pin is, in this manner, divided into about eighteen distinct operations. . . . Those ten persons, therefore, could make among them upwards of forty-eight thousand pins in a day. But if they had all wrought separately and independently, and without any of them having been educated to this particular business, they certainly could not each of them have made twenty, perhaps not one pin a day. . . .

In a market economy, individuals engage in **trade**: they provide goods and services to others and receive goods and services in return.

There are **gains from trade**: people can get more of what they want through trade than they could if they tried to be self-sufficient. This increase in output is due to **specialization**: each person specializes in the task that he or she is good at performing.

"I hunt and she gathers—otherwise we couldn't make ends meet."

The same principle applies when we look at how people divide tasks among themselves and trade in an economy. *The economy, as a whole, can produce more when each person specializes in a task and trades with others.*

The benefits of specialization are the reason a person typically chooses only one career. It takes many years of study and experience to become a doctor; it also takes many years of study and experience to become a commercial airline pilot. Many doctors might well have had the potential to become excellent pilots, and vice versa; but it is very unlikely that anyone who decided to pursue both careers would be as good a pilot or as good a doctor as someone who decided at the beginning to specialize in that field. So it is to everyone's advantage that individuals specialize in their career choices.

Markets are what allow a doctor and a pilot to specialize in their own fields. Because markets for commercial flights and for doctors' services exist, a doctor is assured that she can find a flight and a pilot is assured that he can find a doctor. As long as individuals know that they can find the goods and services they want in the market, they are willing to forgo self-sufficiency and to specialize. But what assures people that markets will deliver what they want? The answer to that question leads us to our second principle of how individual choices interact.

Principle #6: Markets Move Toward Equilibrium

It's a busy afternoon at the supermarket; there are long lines at the checkout counters. Then one of the previously closed cash registers opens. What happens? The first thing, of course, is a rush to that register. After a couple of minutes, however, things will have settled down; shoppers will have rearranged themselves so that the line at the newly opened register is about the same length as the lines at all the other registers.

How do we know that? We know from our fourth principle that people will exploit opportunities to make themselves better off. This means that people will rush to the newly opened register in order to save time standing in line. And things will settle down when shoppers can no longer improve their position by switching lines—that is, when the opportunities to make themselves better off have all been exploited.

A story about supermarket checkout lines may seem to have little to do with how individual choices interact, but in fact it illustrates an important principle. A situation in which individuals cannot make themselves better off by doing something different—the situation in which all the checkout lines are the same length—is what economists call an **equilibrium.** An economic situation is in equilibrium when no individual would be better off doing something different.

Recall the story about the mythical Jiffy Lube, where it was supposedly cheaper to leave your car for an oil change than to pay for parking. If the opportunity had really existed and people were still paying $30 to park in garages, the situation would *not* have been an equilibrium. And that should have been a giveaway that the story couldn't be true. In reality, people would have seized an opportunity to park cheaply, just as they seize opportunities to save time at the checkout line. And in so doing they would have eliminated the opportunity! Either it would have become very hard to get an appointment for an oil change or the price of a lube job would have increased to the point that it was no longer an attractive option (unless you really needed a lube job). This brings us to our sixth principle:

An economic situation is in **equilibrium** when no individual would be better off doing something different.

Because people respond to incentives, markets move toward equilibrium.

As we will see, markets usually reach equilibrium via changes in prices, which rise or fall until no opportunities for individuals to make themselves better off remain.

FOR INQUIRING MINDS

CHOOSING SIDES

Why do people in America drive on the right side of the road? Of course, it's the law. But long before it was the law, it was an equilibrium.

Before there were formal traffic laws, there were informal "rules of the road," practices that everyone expected everyone else to follow. These rules included an understanding that people would normally keep to one side of the road. In some places, such as England, the rule was to keep to the left; in others, such as France, it was to keep to the right.

Why would some places choose the right and others, the left? That's not completely clear, although it may have depended on the dominant form of traffic. Men riding horses and carrying swords on their left hip preferred to ride on the left (think about getting on or off the horse, and you'll see why). On the other hand, right-handed people walking but leading horses apparently preferred to walk on the right.

In any case, once a rule of the road was established, there were strong incentives for each individual to stay on the "usual" side of the road: those who didn't would keep colliding with oncoming traffic. So once established, the rule of the road would be self-enforcing—that is, it would be an equilibrium. Nowadays, of course, which side you drive on is determined by law; some countries have even changed sides (Sweden went from left to right in 1967).

But what about pedestrians? There are no laws—but there are informal rules. In the United States, urban pedestrians normally keep to the right. But if you should happen to visit a country where people drive on the left, watch out: people who drive on the left also typically walk on the left. So when in a foreign country, do as the locals do. You won't be arrested if you walk on the right, but you will be worse off than if you accept the equilibrium and walk on the left.

The concept of equilibrium is extremely helpful in understanding economic interactions because it provides a way of cutting through the sometimes complex details of those interactions. To understand what happens when a new line is opened at a supermarket, you don't need to worry about exactly how shoppers rearrange themselves, who moves ahead of whom, which register just opened, and so on. What you need to know is that any time there is a change, the situation will move to an equilibrium.

The fact that markets move toward equilibrium is why we can depend on them to work in a predictable way. In fact, we can trust markets to supply us with the essentials of life. For example, people who live in big cities can be sure that the supermarket shelves will always be fully stocked. Why? Because if some merchants who distribute food *didn't* make deliveries, a big profit opportunity would be created for any merchant who did—and there would be a rush to supply food, just like the rush to a newly opened cash register. So the market ensures that food will always be available for city dwellers. And, returning to our fifth principle, this allows city dwellers to be city dwellers—to specialize in doing city jobs rather than living on farms and growing their own food.

A market economy, as we have seen, allows people to achieve gains from trade. But how do we know how well such an economy is doing? The next principle gives us a standard to use in evaluating an economy's performance.

Principle #7: Resources Should Be Used Efficiently to Achieve Society's Goals

Suppose you are taking a course in which the classroom is too small for the number of students—many people are forced to stand or sit on the floor—despite the fact that large, empty classrooms are available nearby. You would say, correctly, that this is no way to run a college. Economists would call this an *inefficient* use of resources. But if an inefficient use of resources is undesirable, just what does it mean to use resources *efficiently*? You might imagine that the efficient use of resources has something to do with money, maybe that it is measured in dollars-and-cents terms. But in economics, as in life, money is only a means to other ends. The measure that economists really care about is not money but people's happiness or welfare. Economists say that *an economy's resources are used efficiently when they are used in a way that has fully exploited all opportunities to make everyone*

An economy is **efficient** if it takes all opportunities to make some people better off without making other people worse off.

Equity means that everyone gets his or her fair share. Since people can disagree about what's "fair," equity isn't as well defined a concept as efficiency.

better off. To put it another way, an economy is **efficient** if it takes all opportunities to make some people better off without making other people worse off.

In our classroom example, there clearly was a way to make everyone better off—moving the class to a larger room would make people in the class better off without hurting anyone else in the college. Assigning the course to the smaller classroom was an inefficient use of the college's resources, whereas assigning the course to the larger classroom would have been an efficient use of the college's resources.

When an economy is efficient, it is producing the maximum gains from trade possible given the resources available. Why? Because there is no way to rearrange how resources are used in a way that can make everyone better off. When an economy is efficient, one person can be made better off by rearranging how resources are used *only* by making someone else worse off. In our classroom example, if all larger classrooms were already occupied, the college would have been run in an efficient way: your class could be made better off by moving to a larger classroom only by making people in the larger classroom worse off by making them move to a smaller classroom.

We can now state our seventh principle:

> ***Resources should be used as efficiently as possible to achieve society's goals.***

Should economic policy makers always strive to achieve economic efficiency? Well, not quite, because efficiency is only a means to achieving society's goals. Sometimes efficiency may conflict with a goal that society has deemed worthwhile to achieve. For example, in most societies, people also care about issues of fairness, or **equity.** And there is typically a trade-off between equity and efficiency: policies that promote equity often come at a cost of decreased efficiency in the economy, and vice versa.

Construction Photography/Corbis

Sometimes equity trumps efficiency.

To see this, consider the case of disabled-designated parking spaces in public parking lots. Many people have difficulty walking due to age or disability, so it seems only fair to assign closer parking spaces specifically for their use. You may have noticed, however, that a certain amount of inefficiency is involved. To make sure that there is always a parking space available should a disabled person want one, there are typically more such spaces available than there are disabled people who want one. As a result, desirable parking spaces are unused. (And the temptation for nondisabled people to use them is so great that we must be dissuaded by fear of getting a ticket.) So, short of hiring parking valets to allocate spaces, there is a conflict between *equity*, making life "fairer" for disabled people, and *efficiency*, making sure that all opportunities to make people better off have been fully exploited by never letting close-in parking spaces go unused.

Exactly how far policy makers should go in promoting equity over efficiency is a difficult question that goes to the heart of the political process. As such, it is not a question that economists can answer. What is important for economists, however, is always to seek to use the economy's resources as efficiently as possible in the pursuit of society's goals, whatever those goals may be.

Principle #8: Markets Usually Lead to Efficiency

No branch of the U.S. government is entrusted with ensuring the general economic efficiency of our market economy—we don't have agents who go around making sure that brain surgeons aren't plowing fields or that Minnesota farmers aren't trying to grow oranges. The government doesn't need to enforce the efficient use of resources, because in most cases the invisible hand does the job.

The incentives built into a market economy ensure that resources are usually put to good use and that opportunities to make people better off are not wasted. If a college were known for its habit of crowding students into small classrooms while large classrooms went unused, it would soon find its enrollment dropping, putting the jobs of its administrators at risk. The "market" for college students would respond in a way that induced administrators to run the college efficiently.

A detailed explanation of why markets are usually very good at making sure that resources are used well will have to wait until we have studied how markets actually work. But the most basic reason is that in a market economy, in which individuals are free to choose what to consume and what to produce, people normally take opportunities for mutual gain—that is, gains from trade. If there is a way in which some people can be made better off, people will usually be able to take advantage of that opportunity. And that is exactly what defines efficiency: all the opportunities to make some people better off without making other people worse off have been exploited. This gives rise to our eighth principle:

> ***Because people usually exploit gains from trade, markets usually lead to efficiency.***

As we learned in the first section of this chapter, however, there are exceptions to this principle that markets are generally efficient. In cases of *market failure*, the individual pursuit of self-interest found in markets makes society worse off—that is, the market outcome is inefficient. And, as we will see in examining the next principle, when markets fail, government intervention can help. But short of instances of market failure, the general rule is that markets are a remarkably good way of organizing an economy.

Principle #9: When Markets Don't Achieve Efficiency, Government Intervention Can Improve Society's Welfare

Let's recall the nature of the market failure caused by traffic congestion—a commuter driving to work has no incentive to take into account the cost that his or her action inflicts on other drivers in the form of increased traffic congestion. There are several possible remedies to this situation; examples include charging road tolls, subsidizing the cost of public transportation, and taxing sales of gasoline to individual drivers. All these remedies work by changing the incentives of would-be drivers, motivating them to drive less and use alternative transportation. But they also share another feature: each relies on government intervention in the market. This brings us to our ninth principle:

> ***When markets don't achieve efficiency, government intervention can improve society's welfare.***

That is, when markets go wrong, an appropriately designed government policy can sometimes move society closer to an efficient outcome by changing how society's resources are used.

A very important branch of economics is devoted to studying why markets fail and what policies should be adopted to improve social welfare. We will study these problems and their remedies in depth in later chapters, but, briefly, there are three principal ways in which they fail:

- Individual actions have side effects that are not properly taken into account by the market. An example is an action that causes pollution.
- One party prevents mutually beneficial trades from occurring in an attempt to capture a greater share of resources for itself. An example is a drug company that prices a drug higher than the cost of producing it, making it unaffordable for some people who would benefit from it.
- Some goods, by their very nature, are unsuited for efficient management by markets. An example of such a good is air traffic control.

An important part of your education in economics is learning to identify not just when markets work but also when they don't work, and to judge what government policies are appropriate in each situation.

ECONOMICS ➤ IN ACTION

RESTORING EQUILIBRIUM ON THE FREEWAYS

Back in 1994 a powerful earthquake struck the Los Angeles area, causing several freeway bridges to collapse and thereby disrupting the normal commuting routes of hundreds of thousands of drivers. The events that followed offer a particularly clear example of interdependent decision making—in this case, the decisions of commuters about how to get to work.

Glowimages/Getty Images

Witness equilibrium in action on a Los Angeles freeway.

In the immediate aftermath of the earthquake, there was great concern about the impact on traffic, since motorists would now have to crowd onto alternative routes or detour around the blockages by using city streets. Public officials and news programs warned commuters to expect massive delays and urged them to avoid unnecessary travel, reschedule their work to commute before or after the rush, or use mass transit. These warnings were unexpectedly effective. In fact, so many people heeded them that in the first few days following the quake, those who maintained their regular commuting routine actually found the drive to and from work faster than before.

Of course, this situation could not last. As word spread that traffic was relatively light, people abandoned their less convenient new commuting methods and reverted to their cars—and traffic got steadily worse. Within a few weeks after the quake, serious traffic jams had appeared. After a few more weeks, however, the situation stabilized: the reality of worse-than-usual congestion discouraged enough drivers to prevent the nightmare of citywide gridlock from materializing. Los Angeles traffic, in short, had settled into a new equilibrium in which each commuter was making the best choice he or she could, given what everyone else was doing.

This was not, by the way, the end of the story: fears that the city would strangle on traffic led local authorities to repair the roads with record speed. Within only 18 months after the quake, all the freeways were back to normal, ready for the next one.

▼ Quick Review

- Most economic situations involve the **interaction** of choices, sometimes with unintended results. In a market economy, interaction occurs via **trade** between individuals.
- Individuals trade because there are **gains from trade,** which arise from **specialization.** Markets usually move toward **equilibrium** because people exploit gains from trade.
- To achieve society's goals, the use of resources should be **efficient.** But **equity,** as well as efficiency, may be desirable in an economy. There is often a trade-off between equity and efficiency.
- Except for certain well-defined exceptions, markets are normally efficient. When markets fail to achieve efficiency, government intervention can improve society's welfare.

CHECK YOUR UNDERSTANDING 1-3

1. Explain how each of the following situations illustrates one of the five principles of interaction.
   a. Using the college website, any student who wants to sell a used textbook for at least $30 is able to sell it to someone who is willing to pay $30.
   b. At a college tutoring co-op, students can arrange to provide tutoring in subjects they are good at (such as economics) in return for receiving tutoring in subjects they are struggling with (such as philosophy).
   c. The local municipality imposes a law that requires bars and nightclubs near residential areas to keep their noise levels below a certain threshold.
   d. To provide better care for low-income patients, the local municipality has decided to close some underutilized neighborhood clinics and shift funds to the main hospital.
   e. On the college website, books of a given title with approximately the same level of wear and tear sell for about the same price.

2. Which of the following describes an equilibrium situation? Which does not? Explain your answer.
   a. The restaurants across the street from the university dining hall serve better-tasting and cheaper meals than those served at the university dining hall. The vast majority of students continue to eat at the dining hall.
   b. You currently take the subway to work. Although taking the bus is cheaper, the ride takes longer. So you are willing to pay the higher subway fare in order to save time.

Solutions appear at back of book.

Economy-Wide Interactions

As we mentioned earlier, the economy as a whole has its ups and downs. For example, business in America's shopping malls was depressed in 2008, because the economy was in a recession. By 2012, the economy had somewhat recovered. To understand recessions and recoveries, we need to understand economy-wide interactions, and understanding the big picture of the economy requires understanding three more important economic principles. Those three economy-wide principles are summarized in Table 1-3.

TABLE 1-3 The Principles of Economy-Wide Interactions

10. One person's spending is another person's income.
11. Overall spending sometimes gets out of line with the economy's productive capacity.
12. Government policies can change spending.

Principle #10: One Person's Spending Is Another Person's Income

In 2006, home construction in America began a rapid decline because builders found it increasingly hard to make sales. At first the damage was mainly limited to the construction industry. But over time the slump spread into just about every part of the economy, with consumer spending falling across the board.

But why should a fall in home construction mean empty stores in the shopping malls? After all, malls are places where families, not builders, do their shopping. The answer is that lower spending on construction led to lower incomes throughout the economy; people who had been employed either directly in construction, producing goods and services builders need (like wallboard), or in producing goods and services new homeowners need (like new furniture), either lost their jobs or were forced to take pay cuts. And as incomes fell, so did spending by consumers. This example illustrates our tenth principle:

One person's spending is another person's income.

In a market economy, people make a living selling things—including their labor—to other people. If some group in the economy decides, for whatever reason, to spend more, the income of other groups will rise. If some group decides to spend less, the income of other groups will fall.

Because one person's spending is another person's income, a chain reaction of changes in spending behavior tends to have repercussions that spread through the economy. For example, a cut in business investment spending, like the one that happened in 2008, leads to reduced family incomes; families respond by reducing consumer spending; this leads to another round of income cuts; and so on. These repercussions play an important role in our understanding of recessions and recoveries.

Principle #11: Overall Spending Sometimes Gets Out of Line with the Economy's Productive Capacity

Macroeconomics emerged as a separate branch of economics in the 1930s, when a collapse of consumer and business spending, a crisis in the banking industry, and other factors led to a plunge in overall spending. This plunge in spending, in turn, led to a period of very high unemployment known as the Great Depression.

The lesson economists learned from the troubles of the 1930s is that overall spending—the amount of goods and services that consumers and businesses want to buy—sometimes doesn't match the amount of goods and services the economy is capable of producing. In the 1930s, spending fell far short of what was needed to keep American workers employed, and the result was a severe economic slump. In fact, shortfalls in spending are responsible for most, though not all, recessions.

It's also possible for overall spending to be too high. In that case, the economy experiences *inflation*, a rise in prices throughout the economy. This rise in prices occurs because when the amount that people want to buy outstrips the supply, producers can raise their prices and still find willing customers. Taking account of both shortfalls in spending and excesses in spending brings us to our eleventh principle:

> ***Overall spending sometimes gets out of line with the economy's productive capacity.***

Principle #12: Government Policies Can Change Spending

Overall spending sometimes gets out of line with the economy's productive capacity. But can anything be done about that? Yes—which leads to our twelfth and last principle:

> ***Government policies can change spending.***

In fact, government policies can dramatically affect spending.

For one thing, the government itself does a lot of spending on everything from military equipment to education—and it can choose to do more or less. The government can also vary how much it collects from the public in taxes, which in turn affects how much income consumers and businesses have left to spend. And the government's control of the quantity of money in circulation, it turns out, gives it another powerful tool with which to affect total spending. Government spending, taxes, and control of money are the tools of *macroeconomic policy*.

Modern governments deploy these macroeconomic policy tools in an effort to manage overall spending in the economy, trying to steer it between the perils of recession and inflation. These efforts aren't always successful—recessions still happen, and so do periods of inflation. But it's widely believed that aggressive efforts to sustain spending in 2008 and 2009 helped prevent the financial crisis of 2008 from turning into a full-blown depression.

ECONOMICS ➤ *IN ACTION*

ADVENTURES IN BABYSITTING

The website, myarmyonesource.com, which offers advice to army families, suggests that parents join a babysitting cooperative—an arrangement that is common in many walks of life. In a babysitting cooperative, a number of parents exchange babysitting services rather than hire someone to babysit. But how do these organizations make sure that all members do their fair share of the work? As myarmyonesource.com explained, "Instead of money, most co-ops exchange tickets or points. When you need a sitter, you call a friend on the list, and you pay them with tickets. You earn tickets by babysitting other children within the co-op."

In other words, a babysitting co-op is a miniature economy in which people buy and sell babysitting services. And it happens to be a type of economy that can have macroeconomic problems. A famous article titled "Monetary Theory and the Great Capitol Hill Babysitting Co-Op Crisis," published in 1977, described the troubles of a babysitting cooperative that issued too few tickets. Bear in mind that, on average, people in a babysitting co-op want to have a reserve of tickets stashed away in case they need to go out several times before they can replenish their stash by doing some more babysitting.

In this case, because there weren't that many tickets out there to begin with, most parents were anxious to add to their reserves by babysitting but reluctant to run them down by going out. But one parent's decision to go out was another's chance to babysit, so it became difficult to earn tickets. Knowing this, parents became even more reluctant to use their reserves except on special occasions.

In short, the co-op had fallen into a recession. Recessions in the larger, nonbabysitting economy are a bit more complicated than this, but the troubles of the Capitol Hill babysitting co-op demonstrate two of our three principles of economy-wide interactions. One person's spending is another person's income: opportunities to babysit arose only to the extent that other people went out. And an economy can suffer from too little spending: when not enough people were willing to go out, everyone was frustrated at the lack of babysitting opportunities.

And what about government policies to change spending? Actually, the Capitol Hill co-op did that, too. Eventually, it solved its problem by handing out more tickets, and with increased reserves, people were willing to go out more.

iStockphoto

As participants in a babysitting co-op soon discovered, fewer nights out made everyone worse off.

Quick Review

- In a market economy, one person's spending is another person's income. As a result, changes in spending behavior have repercussions that spread through the economy.
- Overall spending sometimes gets out of line with the economy's capacity to produce goods and services. When spending is too low, the result is a recession. When spending is too high, it causes inflation.
- Modern governments use macroeconomic policy tools to affect the overall level of spending in an effort to steer the economy between recession and inflation.

CHECK YOUR UNDERSTANDING 1-4

1. Explain how each of the following examples illustrates one of the three principles of economy-wide interactions.
   a. The White House urged Congress to pass a package of temporary spending increases and tax cuts in early 2009, a time when employment was plunging and unemployment soaring.
   b. Oil companies are investing heavily in projects that will extract oil from the "oil sands" of Canada. In Edmonton, Alberta, near the projects, restaurants and other consumer businesses are booming.
   c. In the mid-2000s, Spain, which was experiencing a big housing boom, also had the highest inflation rate in Europe.

Solutions appear at back of book.

SUMMARY

1. An **economy** is a system for coordinating society's productive activities, and **economics** is the social science that studies the production, distribution, and consumption of goods and services. The United States has a **market economy**—an economy in which decisions about production and consumption are made by individual producers and consumers pursuing their own self-interest. The **invisible hand** harnesses the power of self-interest for the good of society.
2. **Microeconomics** is the branch of economics that studies how people make decisions and how these decisions interact. **Market failure** occurs when the individual pursuit of self-interest leads to bad results for society as a whole.
3. **Macroeconomics** is the branch of economics that is concerned with overall ups and downs in the economy. Despite occasional **recessions,** the U.S. economy has achieved long-run **economic growth.**
4. All economic analysis is based on a set of basic principles that apply to three levels of economic activity. First, we study how individuals make choices; second, we study how these choices interact; and third, we study how the economy functions overall.
5. Everyone has to make choices about what to do and what *not* to do. **Individual choice** is the basis of economics—if it doesn't involve choice, it isn't economics.
6. The reason choices must be made is that **resources**—anything that can be used to produce something else—are **scarce.** Individuals are limited in their choices by money and time; economies are limited by their supplies of human and natural resources.
7. Because you must choose among limited alternatives, the true cost of anything is what you must give up to get it—all costs are **opportunity costs.**
8. Many economic decisions involve questions not of "whether" but of "how much"—how much to spend on some good, how much to produce, and so on. Such decisions must be made by performing a **trade-off** *at the margin*—by comparing the costs and benefits of doing a bit more or a bit less. Decisions of this type are called **marginal decisions,** and the study of them, **marginal analysis,** plays a central role in economics.
9. The study of how people *should* make decisions is also a good way to understand actual behavior. Individuals usually respond to **incentives**—exploiting opportunities to make themselves better off.
10. The next level of economic analysis is the study of **interaction**—how my choices depend on your choices, and vice versa. When individuals interact, the end result may be different from what anyone intends.
11. Individuals interact because there are **gains from trade:** by engaging in the **trade** of goods and services with one another, the members of an economy can all be made better off. **Specialization**—each person specializes in the task he or she is good at—is the source of gains from trade.
12. Because individuals usually respond to incentives, markets normally move toward **equilibrium**—a situation in which no individual can make himself or herself better off by taking a different action.
13. An economy is **efficient** if all opportunities to make some people better off without making other people worse off are taken. Resources should be used as efficiently as possible to achieve society's goals. But efficiency is not the sole way to evaluate an economy: **equity,** or fairness, is also desirable, and there is often a trade-off between equity and efficiency.
14. Markets usually lead to efficiency, with some well-defined exceptions.
15. When markets fail and do not achieve efficiency, government intervention can improve society's welfare.
16. Because people in a market economy earn income by selling things, including their own labor, one person's spending is another person's income. As a result, changes in spending behavior can spread throughout the economy.
17. Overall spending in the economy can get out of line with the economy's productive capacity. Spending below the economy's productive capacity leads to a recession; spending in excess of the economy's productive capacity leads to inflation.
18. Governments have the ability to strongly affect overall spending, an ability they use in an effort to steer the economy between recession and inflation.

KEY TERMS

Economy, p. 2
Economics, p. 2
Market economy, p. 2
Invisible hand, p. 2
Microeconomics, p. 3
Market failure, p. 3
Recession, p. 3
Macroeconomics, p. 4
Economic growth, p. 4
Individual choice, p. 4
Resource, p. 5
Scarce, p. 5
Opportunity cost, p. 6
Trade-off, p. 7
Marginal decisions, p. 8
Marginal analysis, p. 8
Incentive, p. 8
Interaction, p. 10
Trade, p. 11
Gains from trade, p. 11
Specialization, p. 11
Equilibrium, p. 12
Efficient, p. 14
Equity, p. 14

PROBLEMS

1. In each of the following situations, identify which of the twelve principles is at work.

a. You choose to shop at the local discount store rather than paying a higher price for the same merchandise at the local department store.

b. On your spring break trip, your budget is limited to $35 a day.

c. The student union provides a website on which departing students can sell items such as used books, appliances, and furniture rather than give them away to their roommates as they formerly did.

d. After a hurricane did extensive damage to homes on the island of St. Crispin, homeowners wanted to purchase many more building materials and hire many more workers than were available on the island. As a result, prices for goods and services rose dramatically across the board.

e. You buy a used textbook from your roommate. Your roommate uses the money to buy songs from iTunes.

f. You decide how many cups of coffee to have when studying the night before an exam by considering how much more work you can do by having another cup versus how jittery it will make you feel.

g. There is limited lab space available to do the project required in Chemistry 101. The lab supervisor assigns lab time to each student based on when that student is able to come.

h. You realize that you can graduate a semester early by forgoing a semester of study abroad.

i. At the student union, there is a bulletin board on which people advertise used items for sale, such as bicycles. Once you have adjusted for differences in quality, all the bikes sell for about the same price.

j. You are better at performing lab experiments, and your lab partner is better at writing lab reports. So the two of you agree that you will do all the experiments and she will write up all the reports.

k. State governments mandate that it is illegal to drive without passing a driving exam.

l. Your parents' after-tax income has increased because of a tax cut passed by Congress. They therefore increase your allowance, which you spend on a spring break vacation.

2. Describe some of the opportunity costs when you decide to do the following.

a. Attend college instead of taking a job

b. Watch a movie instead of studying for an exam

c. Ride the bus instead of driving your car

3. Liza needs to buy a textbook for the next economics class. The price at the college bookstore is $65. One online site offers it for $55 and another site, for $57. All prices include sales tax. The accompanying table indicates the typical shipping and handling charges for the textbook ordered online.

Shipping method	Delivery time	Charge
Standard shipping	3–7 days	$3.99
Second-day air	2 business days	8.98
Next-day air	1 business day	13.98

a. What is the opportunity cost of buying online instead of at the bookstore? Note that if you buy the book online, you must wait to get it.

b. Show the relevant choices for this student. What determines which of these options the student will choose?

4. Use the concept of opportunity cost to explain the following.

a. More people choose to get graduate degrees when the job market is poor.

b. More people choose to do their own home repairs when the economy is slow and hourly wages are down.

c. There are more parks in suburban than in urban areas.

d. Convenience stores, which have higher prices than supermarkets, cater to busy people.

e. Fewer students enroll in classes that meet before 10:00 A.M.

5. In the following examples, state how you would use the principle of marginal analysis to make a decision.

a. Deciding how many days to wait before doing your laundry

b. Deciding how much library research to do before writing your term paper

c. Deciding how many bags of chips to eat

d. Deciding how many lectures of a class to skip

6. This morning you made the following individual choices: you bought a bagel and coffee at the local café, you drove to school in your car during rush hour, and you typed your roommate's term paper because you are a fast typist—in return for which she will do your laundry for a month. For each of these actions, describe how your individual choices interacted with the individual choices made by others. Were other people left better off or worse off by your choices in each case?

7. The Hatfield family lives on the east side of the Hatatoochie River, and the McCoy family lives on the west side. Each family's diet consists of fried chicken and corn-on-the-cob, and each is self-sufficient, raising their own chickens and growing their own corn. Explain the conditions under which each of the following would be true.

a. The two families are made better off when the Hatfields specialize in raising chickens, the McCoys specialize in growing corn, and the two families trade.

b. The two families are made better off when the McCoys specialize in raising chickens, the Hatfields specialize in growing corn, and the two families trade.

8. Which of the following situations describes an equilibrium? Which does not? If the situation does not describe an equilibrium, what would an equilibrium look like?

a. Many people regularly commute from the suburbs to downtown Pleasantville. Due to traffic congestion, the trip takes 30 minutes when you travel by highway but only 15 minutes when you go by side streets.

b. At the intersection of Main and Broadway are two gas stations. One station charges $3.00 per gallon for regular gas and the other charges $2.85 per gallon. Customers can get service immediately at the first station but must wait in a long line at the second.

c. Every student enrolled in Economics 101 must also attend a weekly tutorial. This year there are two sections offered: section A and section B, which meet at the same time in adjoining classrooms and are taught by equally competent instructors. Section A is overcrowded, with people sitting on the floor and often unable to see the chalkboard. Section B has many empty seats.

9. In each of the following cases, explain whether you think the situation is efficient or not. If it is not efficient, why not? What actions would make the situation efficient?

a. Electricity is included in the rent at your dorm. Some residents in your dorm leave lights, computers, and appliances on when they are not in their rooms.

b. Although they cost the same amount to prepare, the cafeteria in your dorm consistently provides too many dishes that diners don't like, such as tofu casserole, and too few dishes that diners do like, such as roast turkey with dressing.

c. The enrollment for a particular course exceeds the spaces available. Some students who need to take this course to complete their major are unable to get a space even though others who are taking it as an elective do get a space.

10. Discuss the efficiency and equity implications of each of the following policies. How would you go about balancing the concerns of equity and efficiency in these areas?

a. The government pays the full tuition for every college student to study whatever subject he or she wishes.

b. When people lose their jobs, the government provides unemployment benefits until they find new ones.

11. Governments often adopt certain policies in order to promote desired behavior among their citizens. For each of the following policies, determine what the incentive is and what behavior the government wishes to promote. In each case, why do you think that the government might wish to change people's behavior, rather than allow their actions to be solely determined by individual choice?

a. A tax of $5 per pack is imposed on cigarettes.

b. The government pays parents $100 when their child is vaccinated for measles.

c. The government pays college students to tutor children from low-income families.

d. The government imposes a tax on the amount of air pollution that a company discharges.

12. In each of the following situations, explain how government intervention could improve society's welfare by changing people's incentives. In what sense is the market going wrong?

a. Pollution from auto emissions has reached unhealthy levels.

b. Everyone in Woodville would be better off if streetlights were installed in the town. But no individual resident is willing to pay for installation of a streetlight in front of his or her house because it is impossible to recoup the cost by charging other residents for the benefit they receive from it.

13. On August 2, 2010, Tim Geithner, the Treasury secretary, published an article defending the administration's policies. In it he said, "The recession that began in late 2007 was extraordinarily severe. But the actions we took at its height to stimulate the economy helped arrest the free fall, preventing an even deeper collapse and putting the economy on the road to recovery." Which two of the three principles of economy-wide interaction are at work in this statement?

14. In August 2007, a sharp downturn in the U.S. housing market reduced the income of many who worked in the home construction industry. A *Wall Street Journal* news article reported that Walmart's wire-transfer business was likely to suffer because many construction workers are Hispanics who regularly send part of their wages back to relatives in their home countries via Walmart. With this information, use one of the principles of economy-wide interaction to trace a chain of links that explains how reduced spending for U.S. home purchases is likely to affect the performance of the Mexican economy.

15. In 2005, Hurricane Katrina caused massive destruction to the U.S. Gulf Coast. Tens of thousands of people lost their homes and possessions. Even those who weren't directly affected by the destruction were hurt because businesses failed or contracted and jobs dried up. Using one of the principles of economy-wide interaction, explain how government intervention can help in this situation.

16. During the Great Depression, food was left to rot in the fields or fields that had once been actively cultivated were left fallow. Use one of the principles of economy-wide interaction to explain how this could have occurred.

Economic Models: Trade-offs and Trade

FROM KITTY HAWK TO DREAMLINER

Mark Ralston/AFP/Getty Images

AP Photo

The Wright Brothers' model made modern airplanes, including the Dreamliner, possible.

WHAT YOU WILL LEARN IN THIS CHAPTER

- Why **models**—simplified representations of reality—play a crucial role in economics
- Two simple but important models: the **production possibility frontier** and **comparative advantage**
- The **circular-flow diagram,** a schematic representation of the economy
- The difference between **positive economics,** which analyzes how the economy works, and **normative economics,** which prescribes economic policy
- When economists agree and why they sometimes disagree

ON DECEMBER 15, 2009, BOEING'S newest jet, the 787 Dreamliner, took its first three-hour test flight. It was a historic moment: the Dreamliner was the result of an aerodynamic revolution—a superefficient airplane designed to cut airline operating costs and the first to use superlight composite materials. To ensure that the Dreamliner was sufficiently lightweight and aerodynamic, it underwent over 15,000 hours of wind tunnel tests—tests that resulted in subtle design changes that improved its performance, making it 20% more fuel efficient and 20% less pollutant emitting than existing passenger jets.

The first flight of the Dreamliner was a spectacular advance from the 1903 maiden voyage of the Wright Flyer, the first successful powered airplane, in Kitty Hawk, North Carolina. Yet the Boeing engineers—and all aeronautic engineers—owe an enormous debt to the Wright Flyer's inventors, Wilbur and Orville Wright. What made the Wrights truly visionary was their invention of the wind tunnel, an apparatus that let them experiment with many different designs for wings and control surfaces. Doing experiments with a miniature airplane, inside a wind tunnel the size of a shipping crate, gave the Wright Brothers the knowledge that would make heavier-than-air flight possible.

Neither a miniature airplane inside a packing crate nor a miniature model of the Dreamliner inside Boeing's state-of-the-art Transonic Wind Tunnel is the same thing as an actual aircraft in flight. But it is a very useful *model* of a flying plane—a simplified representation of the real thing that can be used to answer crucial questions, such as how much lift a given wing shape will generate at a given airspeed.

Needless to say, testing an airplane design in a wind tunnel is cheaper and safer than building a full-scale version and hoping it will fly. More generally, models play a crucial role in almost all scientific research—economics very much included.

In fact, you could say that economic theory consists mainly of a collection of models, a series of simplified representations of economic reality that allow us to understand a variety of economic issues. In this chapter, we'll look at two economic models that are crucially important in their own right and also illustrate why such models are so useful. We'll conclude with a look at how economists actually use models in their work. ■

A **model** is a simplified representation of a real situation that is used to better understand real-life situations.

The **other things equal assumption** means that all other relevant factors remain unchanged.

Models in Economics: Some Important Examples

A **model** is any simplified representation of reality that is used to better understand real-life situations. But how do we create a simplified representation of an economic situation?

One possibility—an economist's equivalent of a wind tunnel—is to find or create a real but simplified economy. For example, economists interested in the economic role of money have studied the system of exchange that developed in World War II prison camps, in which cigarettes became a universally accepted form of payment even among prisoners who didn't smoke.

Another possibility is to simulate the workings of the economy on a computer. For example, when changes in tax law are proposed, government officials use *tax models*—large mathematical computer programs—to assess how the proposed changes would affect different types of people.

Models are important because their simplicity allows economists to focus on the effects of only one change at a time. That is, they allow us to hold everything else constant and study how one change affects the overall economic outcome. So an important assumption when building economic models is the **other things equal assumption,** which means that all other relevant factors remain unchanged.

But you can't always find or create a small-scale version of the whole economy, and a computer program is only as good as the data it uses. (Programmers have a saying: "garbage in, garbage out.") For many purposes, the most effective form of economic modeling is the construction of "thought experiments": simplified, hypothetical versions of real-life situations.

In Chapter 1 we illustrated the concept of equilibrium with the example of how customers at a supermarket would rearrange themselves when a new cash register opens. Though we didn't say it, this was an example of a simple model—an imaginary supermarket, in which many details were ignored. (What were customers buying? Never mind.) This simple model can be used to answer a "what if" question: what if another cash register were opened?

As the cash register story showed, it is often possible to describe and analyze a useful economic model in plain English. However, because much of economics involves changes in quantities—in the price of a product, the number of units produced, or the number of workers employed in its production—economists often find that using some mathematics helps clarify an issue. In particular, a numerical example, a simple equation, or—especially—a graph can be key to understanding an economic concept.

Whatever form it takes, a good economic model can be a tremendous aid to understanding. The best way to grasp this point is to consider some simple but important economic models and what they tell us. First, we will look at the *production possibility frontier,* a model that helps economists think about the trade-offs every economy faces. Then we will turn to *comparative advantage,* a model that clarifies the principle of gains from trade—trade both between individuals and between countries. In addition, we'll examine the *circular-flow diagram,* a schematic representation that helps us understand how flows of money, goods, and services are channeled through the economy.

In discussing these models, we make considerable use of graphs to represent mathematical relationships. Graphs play an important role throughout this book. If you are already familiar with the use of graphs, you may feel free to skip the appendix to this chapter, which provides a brief introduction to the use of graphs in economics. If not, this would be a good time to turn to it.

FOR INQUIRING MINDS

THE MODEL THAT ATE THE ECONOMY

A model is just a model, right? So how much damage can it do? Economists probably would have answered that question quite differently before the financial meltdown of 2008–2009 than after it. The financial crisis continues to reverberate today—a testament to why economic models are so important. For an economic model—a *bad* economic model, it turned out—played a significant role in the origins of the crisis.

"The model that ate the economy" originated in finance theory, the branch of economics that seeks to understand what assets like stocks and bonds are worth. Financial theorists often get hired (at very high salaries, mind you) to devise complex mathematical models to help investment companies decide what assets to buy and sell and at what price.

Finance theory has become increasingly important as Wall Street (a district in New York City where nearly all major investment companies have their headquarters) has shifted from trading simple assets like stocks and bonds to more complex assets—notably, mortgage-backed securities (or MBS's for short). An MBS is an asset that entitles its owner to a stream of earnings based on the payments made by thousands of people on their home loans. Investors wanted to know how risky these complex assets were. That is, how likely was it that an investor would lose money on an MBS?

Although we won't go into the details, estimating the likelihood of losing money on an MBS is a complicated problem. It involves calculating the probability that a significant number of the thousands of homeowners backing your security will stop paying their mortgages. Until that probability could be calculated, investors didn't want to buy MBS's. In order to generate sales, Wall Street firms needed to provide potential MBS buyers with some estimate of their risk.

In 2000, a Wall Street financial theorist announced that he had solved the problem by employing a huge statistical abstraction—assuming that current homeowners were no more likely to stop paying their mortgages than in previous decades. With this assumption, he devised a simple model for estimating the risk of buying an MBS. Financial traders loved the model as it opened up a huge and extraordinarily profitable market for them. Using this simple model, Wall Street was able to create and sell billions of MBS's, generating billions in profits for itself.

Or investors *thought* they had calculated the risk of losing money on an MBS. Some financial experts—particularly Darrell Duffie, a Stanford University finance professor—warned from the sidelines that the estimates of risk calculated by this simple model were just plain wrong. He, and other critics, said that in the search for simplicity, the model seriously underestimated the likelihood that many homeowners would stop paying their mortgages at the same time, leaving MBS investors in danger of incurring huge losses.

The warnings fell on deaf ears—no doubt because Wall Street was making so much money. Billions of dollars worth of MBS's were sold to investors both in the United States and abroad. In 2008–2009, the problems critics warned about exploded in catastrophic fashion. Over the previous decade, American home prices had risen too high, and mortgages had been extended to many who were unable to pay. As home prices fell to earth, millions of homeowners didn't pay their mortgages. With losses mounting for MBS investors, it became all too clear that the model had indeed underestimated the risks. When investors and financial institutions around the world realized the extent of their losses, the worldwide economy ground to an abrupt halt. To this day, it has not fully recovered.

Trade-offs: The Production Possibility Frontier

The first principle of economics we introduced in Chapter 1 was that resources are scarce and that, as a result, any economy—whether it's an isolated group of a few dozen hunter-gatherers or the 6 billion people making up the twenty-first-century global economy—faces trade-offs. No matter how lightweight the Boeing Dreamliner is, no matter how efficient Boeing's assembly line, producing Dreamliners means using resources that therefore can't be used to produce something else.

The **production possibility frontier** illustrates the trade-offs facing an economy that produces only two goods. It shows the maximum quantity of one good that can be produced for any given quantity produced of the other.

To think about the trade-offs that face any economy, economists often use the model known as the **production possibility frontier.** The idea behind this model is to improve our understanding of trade-offs by considering a simplified economy that produces only two goods. This simplification enables us to show the trade-off graphically.

Suppose, for a moment, that the United States was a one-company economy, with Boeing its sole employer and aircraft its only product. But there would still be a choice of what kinds of aircraft to produce—say, Dreamliners versus small commuter jets. Figure 2-1 shows a hypothetical production possibility frontier representing the trade-off this one-company economy would face. The frontier—the line in the diagram—shows the maximum quantity of small jets that Boeing can produce per year *given* the quantity of Dreamliners it produces per year, and vice versa. That is, it answers questions of the form, "What is the maximum quantity of small jets that Boeing can produce in a year if it also produces 9 (or 15, or 30) Dreamliners that year?"

There is a crucial distinction between points *inside* or *on* the production possibility frontier (the shaded area) and *outside* the frontier. If a production point lies inside or on the frontier—like point *C*, at which Boeing produces 20 small jets and 9 Dreamliners in a year—it is feasible. After all, the frontier tells us that if Boeing produces 20 small jets, it could also produce a maximum of 15 Dreamliners that year, so it could certainly make 9 Dreamliners. However, a production point that lies outside the frontier—such as the hypothetical production point *D*, where Boeing produces 40 small jets and 30 Dreamliners—isn't feasible. Boeing can produce 40 small jets and no Dreamliners, *or* it can produce 30 Dreamliners and no small jets, but it can't do both.

In Figure 2-1 the production possibility frontier intersects the horizontal axis at 40 small jets. This means that if Boeing dedicated all its production capacity to making small jets, it could produce 40 small jets per year but could produce no Dreamliners. The production possibility frontier intersects the vertical axis at 30 Dreamliners. This means that if Boeing dedicated all its production capacity to making Dreamliners, it could produce 30 Dreamliners per year but no small jets.

The figure also shows less extreme trade-offs. For example, if Boeing's managers decide to make 20 small jets this year, they can produce at most 15 Dreamliners; this production choice is illustrated by point *A*. And if Boeing's

FIGURE 2-1 The Production Possibility Frontier

The production possibility frontier illustrates the trade-offs Boeing faces in producing Dreamliners and small jets. It shows the maximum quantity of one good that can be produced given the quantity of the other good produced. Here, the maximum quantity of Dreamliners manufactured per year depends on the quantity of small jets manufactured that year, and vice versa. Boeing's feasible production is shown by the area *inside* or *on* the curve. Production at point *C* is feasible but not efficient. Points *A* and *B* are feasible and efficient in production, but point *D* is not feasible.

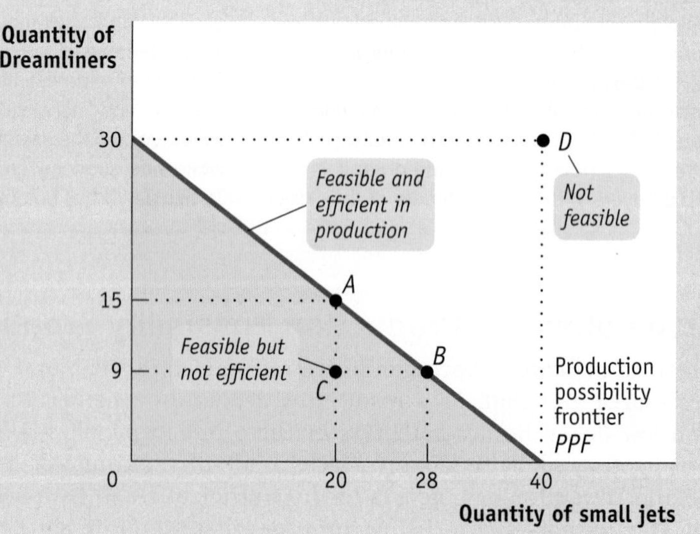

managers decide to produce 28 small jets, they can make at most 9 Dreamliners, as shown by point *B*.

Thinking in terms of a production possibility frontier simplifies the complexities of reality. The real-world U.S. economy produces millions of different goods. Even Boeing can produce more than two different types of planes. Yet it's important to realize that even in its simplicity, this stripped-down model gives us important insights about the real world.

By simplifying reality, the production possibility frontier helps us understand some aspects of the real economy better than we could without the model: efficiency, opportunity cost, and economic growth.

Efficiency First of all, the production possibility frontier is a good way to illustrate the general economic concept of *efficiency.* Recall from Chapter 1 that an economy is efficient if there are no missed opportunities—there is no way to make some people better off without making other people worse off.

One key element of efficiency is that there are no missed opportunities in production—there is no way to produce more of one good without producing less of other goods. As long as Boeing operates on its production possibility frontier, its production is efficient. At point *A*, 15 Dreamliners are the maximum quantity feasible given that Boeing has also committed to producing 20 small jets; at point *B*, 9 Dreamliners are the maximum number that can be made given the choice to produce 28 small jets; and so on. But suppose for some reason that Boeing was operating at point *C*, making 20 small jets and 9 Dreamliners. In this case, it would not be operating efficiently and would therefore be *inefficient:* it could be producing more of both planes.

Although we have used an example of the production choices of a one-firm, two-good economy to illustrate efficiency and inefficiency, these concepts also carry over to the real economy, which contains many firms and produces many goods. If the economy as a whole could not produce more of any one good without producing less of something else—that is, if it is on its production possibility frontier—then we say that the economy is *efficient in production*. If, however, the economy could produce more of some things without producing less of others—which typically means that it could produce more of everything—then it is inefficient in production. For example, an economy in which large numbers of workers are involuntarily unemployed is clearly inefficient in production. And that's a bad thing, because the economy could be producing more useful goods and services.

Although the production possibility frontier helps clarify what it means for an economy to be efficient in production, it's important to understand that efficiency in production is only *part* of what's required for the economy as a whole to be efficient. Efficiency also requires that the economy allocate its resources so that consumers are as well off as possible. If an economy does this, we say that it is *efficient in allocation*. To see why efficiency in allocation is as important as efficiency in production, notice that points *A* and *B* in Figure 2-1 both represent situations in which the economy is efficient in production, because in each case it can't produce more of one good without producing less of the other. But these two situations may not be equally desirable from society's point of view. Suppose that society prefers to have more small jets and fewer Dreamliners than at point *A*; say, it prefers to have 28 small jets and 9 Dreamliners, corresponding to point *B*. In this case, point *A* is inefficient in allocation from the point of view of the economy as a whole because it would rather have Boeing produce at point *B* rather than at point *A*.

This example shows that efficiency for the economy as a whole requires *both* efficiency in production and efficiency in allocation: to be efficient, an economy must produce as much of each good as it can given the production of other goods, and it must also produce the mix of goods that people want to consume. (And it must also deliver those goods to the right people: an economy that gives small jets to international airlines and Dreamliners to commuter airlines serving small rural airports is inefficient, too.)

In the real world, command economies, such as the former Soviet Union, are notorious for inefficiency in allocation. For example, it was common for consumers to find stores well stocked with items few people wanted but lacking such basics as soap and toilet paper.

Opportunity Cost The production possibility frontier is also useful as a reminder of the fundamental point that the true cost of any good isn't the money it costs to buy, but what must be given up in order to get that good—the *opportunity cost*. If, for example, Boeing decides to change its production from point *A* to point *B*, it will produce 8 more small jets but 6 fewer Dreamliners. So the opportunity cost of 8 small jets is 6 Dreamliners—the 6 Dreamliners that must be forgone in order to produce 8 more small jets. This means that each small jet has an opportunity cost of $6/8 = 3/4$ of a Dreamliner.

Is the opportunity cost of an extra small jet in terms of Dreamliners always the same, no matter how many small jets and Dreamliners are currently produced? In the example illustrated by Figure 2-1, the answer is yes. If Boeing increases its production of small jets from 28 to 40, the number of Dreamliners it produces falls from 9 to zero. So Boeing's opportunity cost per additional small jet is $9/12 = 3/4$ of a Dreamliner, the same as it was when Boeing went from 20 small jets produced to 28. However, the fact that in this example the opportunity cost of a small jet in terms of a Dreamliner is always the same is a result of an assumption we've made, an assumption that's reflected in how Figure 2-1 is drawn. Specifically, whenever we assume that the opportunity cost of an additional unit of a good doesn't change regardless of the output mix, the production possibility frontier is a straight line.

Moreover, as you might have already guessed, the slope of a straight-line production possibility frontier is equal to the opportunity cost—specifically, the opportunity cost for the good measured on the horizontal axis in terms of the good measured on the vertical axis. In Figure 2-1, the production possibility frontier has a *constant slope* of $-3/4$, implying that Boeing faces a *constant opportunity cost* for 1 small jet equal to $3/4$ of a Dreamliner. (A review of how to calculate the slope of a straight line is found in this chapter's appendix.) This is the simplest case, but the production possibility frontier model can also be used to examine situations in which opportunity costs change as the mix of output changes.

Figure 2-2 illustrates a different assumption, a case in which Boeing faces *increasing opportunity cost*. Here, the more small jets it produces, the more costly it is to produce yet another small jet in terms of forgone production of a

FIGURE 2-2 Increasing Opportunity Cost

The bowed-out shape of the production possibility frontier reflects increasing opportunity cost. In this example, to produce the first 20 small jets, Boeing must forgo producing 5 Dreamliners. But to produce an additional 20 small jets, Boeing must forgo manufacturing 25 more Dreamliners.

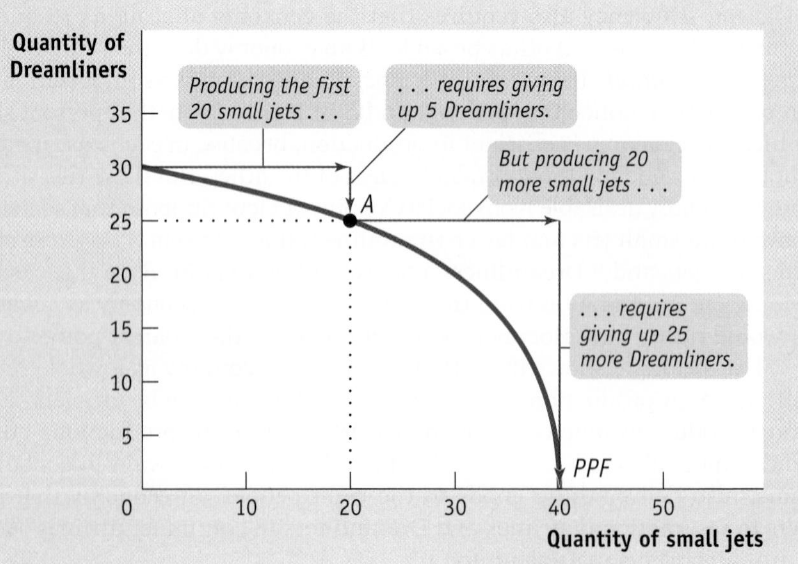

Dreamliner. And the same holds true in reverse: the more Dreamliners Boeing produces, the more costly it is to produce yet another Dreamliner in terms of forgone production of small jets. For example, to go from producing zero small jets to producing 20, Boeing has to forgo producing 5 Dreamliners. That is, the opportunity cost of those 20 small jets is 5 Dreamliners. But to increase its production of small jets to 40—that is, to produce an additional 20 small jets—it must forgo producing 25 more Dreamliners, a much higher opportunity cost. As you can see in Figure 2-2, when opportunity costs are increasing rather than constant, the production possibility frontier is a bowed-out curve rather than a straight line.

Although it's often useful to work with the simple assumption that the production possibility frontier is a straight line, economists believe that in reality opportunity costs are typically increasing. When only a small amount of a good is produced, the opportunity cost of producing that good is relatively low because the economy needs to use only those resources that are especially well suited for its production. For example, if an economy grows only a small amount of corn, that corn can be grown in places where the soil and climate are perfect for corn-growing but less suitable for growing anything else, like wheat. So growing that corn involves giving up only a small amount of potential wheat output. Once the economy grows a lot of corn, however, land that is well suited for wheat but isn't so great for corn must be used to produce corn anyway. As a result, the additional corn production involves sacrificing considerably more wheat production. In other words, as more of a good is produced, its opportunity cost typically rises because well-suited inputs are used up and less adaptable inputs must be used instead.

Economic Growth Finally, the production possibility frontier helps us understand what it means to talk about *economic growth*. We introduced the concept of economic growth in Chapter 1, defining it as *the growing ability of the economy to produce goods and services*. As we saw, economic growth is one of the fundamental features of the real economy. But are we really justified in saying that the economy has grown over time? After all, although the U.S. economy produces more of many things than it did a century ago, it produces less of other things—for example, horse-drawn carriages. Production of many goods, in other words, is actually down. So how can we say for sure that the economy as a whole has grown?

The answer is illustrated in Figure 2-3, where we have drawn two hypothetical production possibility frontiers for the economy. In them we have assumed once

FIGURE 2-3 Economic Growth

Economic growth results in an *outward shift* of the production possibility frontier because production possibilities are expanded. The economy can now produce more of everything. For example, if production is initially at point *A* (25 Dreamliners and 20 small jets), economic growth means that the economy could move to point *E* (30 Dreamliners and 25 small jets).

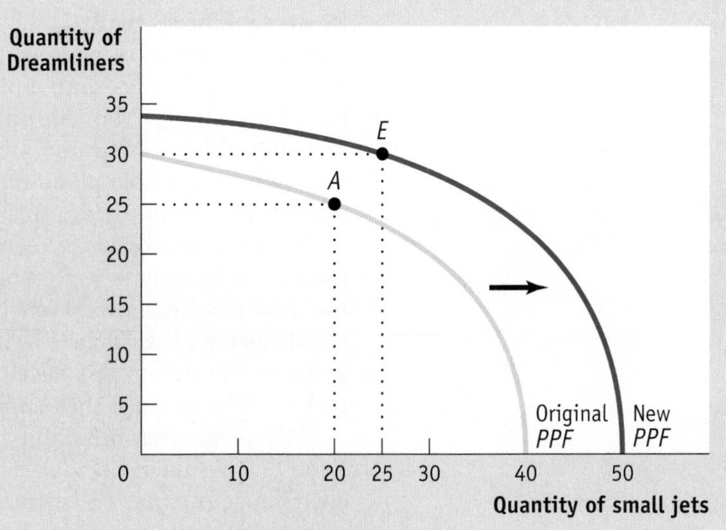

Factors of production are resources used to produce goods and services.

Technology is the technical means for producing goods and services.

again that everyone in the economy works for Boeing and, consequently, the economy produces only two goods, Dreamliners and small jets. Notice how the two curves are nested, with the one labeled "Original *PPF*" lying completely inside the one labeled "New *PPF*." Now we can see graphically what we mean by economic growth of the economy: economic growth means an *expansion of the economy's production possibilities;* that is, the economy *can* produce more of everything. For example, if the economy initially produces at point *A* (25 Dreamliners and 20 small jets), economic growth means that the economy could move to point *E* (30 Dreamliners and 25 small jets). *E* lies outside the original frontier; so in the production possibility frontier model, growth is shown as an outward shift of the frontier.

What can lead the production possibility frontier to shift outward? There are basically two sources of economic growth. One is an increase in the economy's **factors of production,** the resources used to produce goods and services. Economists usually use the term *factor of production* to refer to a resource that is not used up in production. For example, in traditional airplane manufacture workers used riveting machines to connect metal sheets when constructing a plane's fuselage; the workers and the riveters are factors of production, but the rivets and the sheet metal are not. Once a fuselage is made, a worker and riveter can be used to make another fuselage, but the sheet metal and rivets used to make one fuselage cannot be used to make another.

Broadly speaking, the main factors of production are the resources—land, labor, physical capital, and human capital. Land is a resource supplied by nature; labor is the economy's pool of workers; physical capital refers to created resources such as machines and buildings; and human capital refers to the educational achievements and skills of the labor force, which enhance its productivity. Of course, each of these is really a category rather than a single factor: land in North Dakota is quite different from land in Florida.

To see how adding to an economy's factors of production leads to economic growth, suppose that Boeing builds another construction hangar that allows it to increase the number of planes—small jets or Dreamliners or both—it can produce in a year. The new construction hangar is a factor of production, a resource Boeing can use to increase its yearly output. We can't say how many more planes of each type Boeing will produce; that's a management decision that will depend on, among other things, customer demand. But we can say that Boeing's production possibility frontier has shifted outward because it can now produce more small jets without reducing the number of Dreamliners it makes, or it can make more Dreamliners without reducing the number of small jets produced.

The other source of economic growth is progress in **technology,** the technical means for the production of goods and services. Composite materials had been used in some parts of aircraft before the Boeing Dreamliner was developed. But Boeing engineers realized that there were large additional advantages to building a whole plane out of composites. The plane would be lighter, stronger, and have better aerodynamics than a plane built in the traditional way. It would therefore have longer range, be able to carry more people, and use less fuel, in addition to being able to maintain higher cabin pressure. So in a real sense Boeing's innovation—a whole plane built out of composites—was a way to do more with any given amount of resources, pushing out the production possibility frontier.

Because improved jet technology has pushed out the production possibility frontier, it has made it possible for the economy to produce more of everything, not just jets and air travel. Over the past 30 years, the biggest technological advances have taken place in information technology, not in construction or food services. Yet Americans have chosen to buy bigger houses and eat out more than they used to because the economy's growth has made it possible to do so.

The production possibility frontier is a very simplified model of an economy. Yet it teaches us important lessons about real-life economies. It gives us our first clear sense of what constitutes economic efficiency, it illustrates the concept of opportunity cost, and it makes clear what economic growth is all about.

Comparative Advantage and Gains from Trade

Among the twelve principles of economics described in Chapter 1 was the principle of *gains from trade*—the mutual gains that individuals can achieve by specializing in doing different things and trading with one another. Our second illustration of an economic model is a particularly useful model of gains from trade—trade based on *comparative advantage*.

One of the most important insights in all of economics is that there are gains from trade—that it makes sense to produce the things you're especially good at producing and to buy from other people the things you aren't as good at producing. This would be true even if you could produce everything for yourself: even if a brilliant brain surgeon *could* repair her own dripping faucet, it's probably a better idea for her to call in a professional plumber.

How can we model the gains from trade? Let's stay with our aircraft example and once again imagine that the United States is a one-company economy where everyone works for Boeing, producing airplanes. Let's now assume, however, that the United States has the ability to trade with Brazil—another one-company economy where everyone works for the Brazilian aircraft company Embraer, which is, in the real world, a successful producer of small commuter jets. (If you fly from one major U.S. city to another, your plane is likely to be a Boeing, but if you fly into a small city, the odds are good that your plane will be an Embraer.)

In our example, the only two goods produced are large jets and small jets. Both countries could produce both kinds of jets. But as we'll see in a moment, they can gain by producing different things and trading with each other. For the purposes of this example, let's return to the simpler case of straight-line production possibility frontiers. America's production possibilities are represented by the production possibility frontier in panel (a) of Figure 2-4, which is similar to the production possibility frontier in Figure 2-1. According to this diagram, the United States can produce 40 small jets if it makes no large jets and can manufacture 30 large jets if it produces no small jets. Recall that this means that the slope of the U.S. production possibility frontier is −3/4: its opportunity cost of 1 small jet is 3/4 of a large jet.

FIGURE 2-4 Production Possibilities for Two Countries

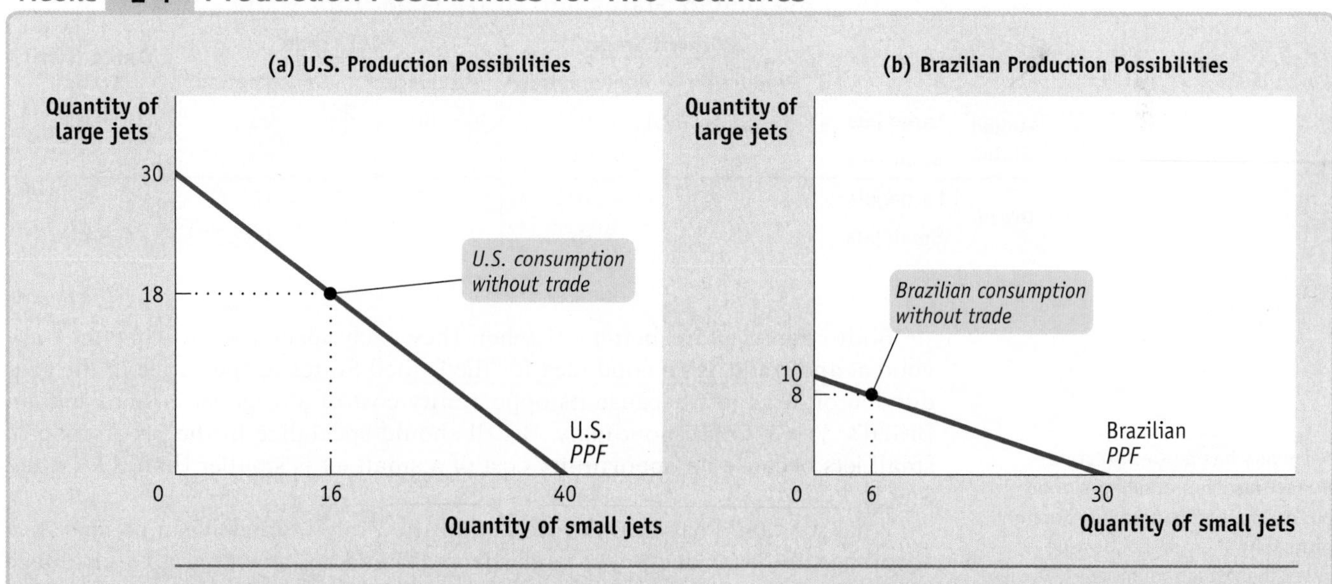

Here, both the United States and Brazil have a constant opportunity cost of small jets, illustrated by a straight-line production possibility frontier. For the United States, each small jet has an opportunity cost of 3/4 of a large jet. Brazil has an opportunity cost of a small jet equal to 1/3 of a large jet.

Panel (b) of Figure 2-4 shows Brazil's production possibilities. Like the United States, Brazil's production possibility frontier is a straight line, implying a constant opportunity cost of a small jet in terms of large jets. Brazil's production possibility frontier has a constant slope of –1/3. Brazil can't produce as much of anything as the United States can: at most it can produce 30 small jets or 10 large jets. But it is relatively better at manufacturing small jets than the United States; whereas the United States sacrifices 3/4 of a large jet per small jet produced, for Brazil the opportunity cost of a small jet is only 1/3 of a large jet. Table 2-1 summarizes the two countries' opportunity costs of small jets and large jets.

TABLE 2-1 U.S. and Brazilian Opportunity Costs of Small Jets and Large Jets

	U.S. Opportunity Cost		Brazilian Opportunity Cost
One small jet	3/4 large jet	>	1/3 large jet
One large jet	4/3 small jets	<	3 small jets

Now, the United States and Brazil could each choose to make their own large and small jets, not trading any airplanes and consuming only what each produced within its own country. (A country "consumes" an airplane when it is owned by a domestic resident.) Let's suppose that the two countries start out this way and make the consumption choices shown in Figure 2-4: in the absence of trade, the United States produces and consumes 16 small jets and 18 large jets per year, while Brazil produces and consumes 6 small jets and 8 large jets per year.

But is this the best the two countries can do? No, it isn't. Given that the two producers—and therefore the two countries—have different opportunity costs, the United States and Brazil can strike a deal that makes both of them better off.

Table 2-2 shows how such a deal works: the United States specializes in the production of large jets, manufacturing 30 per year, and sells 10 to Brazil. Meanwhile, Brazil specializes in the production of small jets, producing 30 per year, and sells 20 to the United States. The result is shown in Figure 2-5. The United States now consumes more of both small jets and large jets than before: instead of 16 small jets and 18 large jets, it now consumes 20 small jets and 20 large jets. Brazil also consumes more, going from 6 small jets and 8 large jets to 10 small jets and 10 large jets. As Table 2-2 also shows, both the United States and Brazil reap gains from trade, consuming more of both types of plane than they would have without trade.

TABLE 2-2 How the United States and Brazil Gain from Trade

		Without Trade		With Trade		Gains from Trade
		Production	Consumption	Production	Consumption	
United States	Large jets	18	18	30	20	+2
	Small jets	16	16	0	20	+4
Brazil	Large jets	8	8	0	10	+2
	Small jets	6	6	30	10	+4

Both countries are better off when they each specialize in what they are good at and trade. It's a good idea for the United States to specialize in the production of large jets because its opportunity cost of a large jet is smaller than Brazil's: 4/3 < 3. Correspondingly, Brazil should specialize in the production of small jets because its opportunity cost of a small jet is smaller than the United States: 1/3 < 3/4.

A country has a **comparative advantage** in producing a good or service if its opportunity cost of producing the good or service is lower than other countries'. Likewise, an individual has a comparative advantage in producing a good or service if his or her opportunity cost of producing the good or service is lower than for other people.

What we would say in this case is that the United States has a comparative advantage in the production of large jets and Brazil has a comparative advantage in the production of small jets. A country has a **comparative advantage** in producing something if the opportunity cost of that production is lower for that country than for other countries. The same concept applies to firms and people: a firm or an individual has a comparative advantage in producing something if its, his, or her opportunity cost of production is lower than for others.

FIGURE 2-5 Comparative Advantage and Gains from Trade

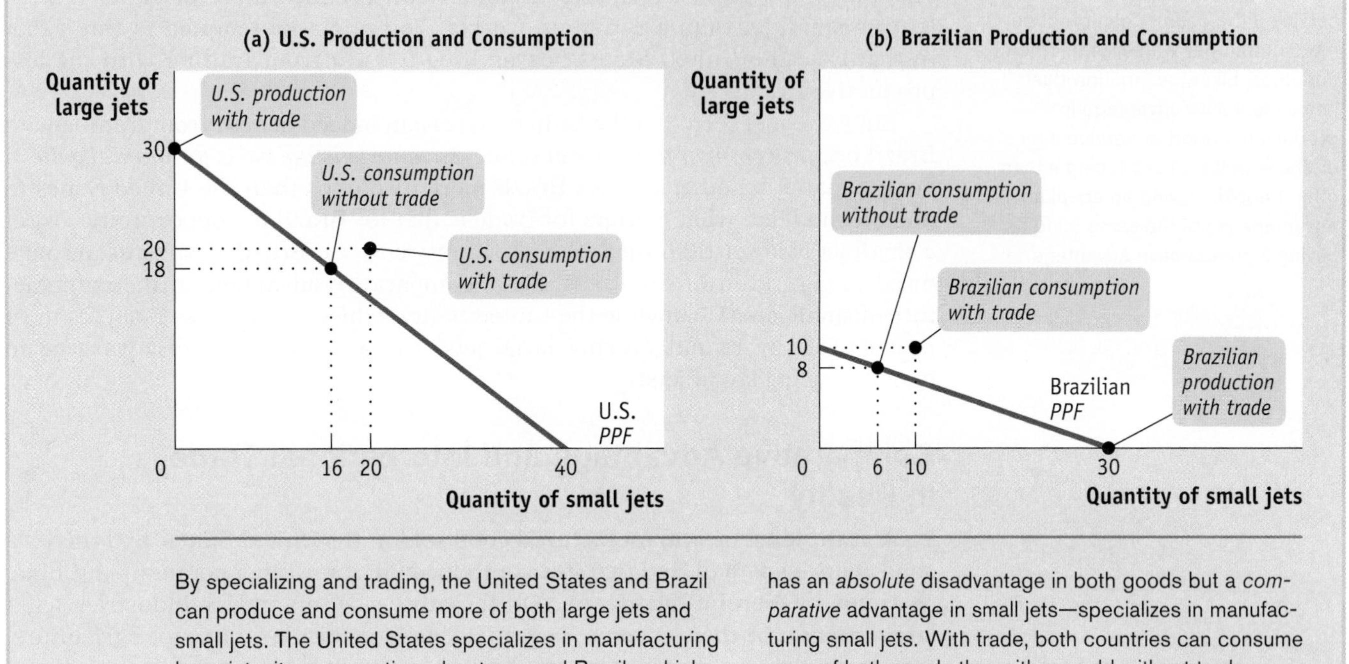

By specializing and trading, the United States and Brazil can produce and consume more of both large jets and small jets. The United States specializes in manufacturing large jets, its comparative advantage, and Brazil—which has an *absolute* disadvantage in both goods but a *comparative* advantage in small jets—specializes in manufacturing small jets. With trade, both countries can consume more of both goods than either could without trade.

One point of clarification before we proceed further. You may have wondered why the United States traded 10 large jets to Brazil in return for 20 small jets. Why not some other deal, like trading 10 large jets for 12 small jets? The answer to that question has two parts. First, there may indeed be other trades that the United States and Brazil might agree to. Second, there are some deals that we can safely rule out—one like 10 large jets for 10 small jets.

To understand why, reexamine Table 2-1 and consider the United States first. Without trading with Brazil, the U.S. opportunity cost of a small jet is 3/4 of a large jet. So it's clear that the United States will not accept any trade that requires it to give up more than 3/4 of a large jet for a small jet. Trading 10 jets in return for 12 small jets would require the United States to pay an opportunity cost of 10/12 = 5/6 of a large jet for a small jet. Because 5/6 > 3/4, this is a deal that the United States would reject. Similarly, Brazil won't accept a trade that gives it less than 1/3 of a large jet for a small jet.

The point to remember is that the United States and Brazil will be willing to trade only if the "price" of the good each country obtains in the trade is less than its own opportunity cost of producing the good domestically. Moreover, this is a general statement that is true whenever two parties—countries, firms, or individuals—trade voluntarily.

While our story clearly simplifies reality, it teaches us some very important lessons that apply to the real economy, too.

First, the model provides a clear illustration of the gains from trade: through specialization and trade, both countries produce more and consume more than if they were self-sufficient.

Second, the model demonstrates a very important point that is often overlooked in real-world arguments: each country has a comparative advantage in producing something. This applies to firms and people as well: *everyone has a comparative advantage in something, and everyone has a comparative disadvantage in something.*

Crucially, in our example it doesn't matter if, as is probably the case in real life, U.S. workers are just as good as or even better than Brazilian workers at producing small jets. Suppose that the United States is actually better than Brazil at all kinds of aircraft production. In that case, we would say that the

A country has an **absolute advantage** in producing a good or service if the country can produce more output per worker than other countries. Likewise, an individual has an absolute advantage in producing a good or service if he or she is better at producing it than other people. Having an absolute advantage is not the same thing as having a comparative advantage.

United States has an **absolute advantage** in both large-jet and small-jet production: in an hour, an American worker can produce more of either a large jet or a small jet than a Brazilian worker. You might be tempted to think that in that case the United States has nothing to gain from trading with the less productive Brazil.

But we've just seen that the United States can indeed benefit from trading with Brazil because *comparative, not absolute, advantage is the basis for mutual gain.* It doesn't matter whether it takes Brazil more resources than the United States to make a small jet; what matters for trade is that for Brazil the opportunity cost of a small jet is lower than the U.S. opportunity cost. So Brazil, despite its absolute disadvantage, even in small jets, has a comparative advantage in the manufacture of small jets. Meanwhile the United States, which can use its resources most productively by manufacturing large jets, has a comparative *dis*advantage in manufacturing small jets.

Comparative Advantage and International Trade, in Reality

Look at the label on a manufactured good sold in the United States, and there's a good chance you will find that it was produced in some other country—in China, or Japan, or even in Canada, eh? On the other side, many U.S. industries sell a large fraction of their output overseas. (This is particularly true of agriculture, high technology, and entertainment.)

Should all this international exchange of goods and services be celebrated, or is it cause for concern? Politicians and the public often question the desirability of international trade, arguing that the nation should produce goods for itself rather than buying them from foreigners. Industries around the world demand protection from foreign competition: Japanese farmers want to keep out American rice, American steelworkers want to keep out European steel. And these demands are often supported by public opinion.

Economists, however, have a very positive view of international trade. Why? Because they view it in terms of comparative advantage. As we learned from our example of U.S. large jets and Brazilian small jets, international trade benefits both countries. Each country can consume more than if it didn't trade and remained self-sufficient. Moreover, these mutual gains don't depend on each country being better than other countries at producing one kind of good. Even if one country has, say, higher output per worker in both industries—that is, even if one country has an absolute advantage in both industries—there are still gains from trade. The upcoming Global Comparison, which explains the pattern of clothing production throughout the global economy, illustrates just this point.

PITFALLS

MISUNDERSTANDING COMPARATIVE ADVANTAGE

Students do it, pundits do it, and politicians do it all the time: they confuse *comparative* advantage with *absolute* advantage. For example, back in the 1980s, when the U.S. economy seemed to be lagging behind that of Japan, one often heard commentators warn that if we didn't improve our productivity, we would soon have no comparative advantage in anything.

What those commentators meant was that we would have no *absolute* advantage in anything—that there might come a time when the Japanese were better at everything than we were. (It didn't turn out that way, but that's another story.) And they had the idea that in that case we would no longer be able to benefit from trade with Japan.

But just as Brazil, in our example, was able to benefit from trade with the United States (and vice versa) despite the fact that the United States was better at manufacturing both large and small jets, in real life nations can still gain from trade even if they are less productive in all industries than the countries they trade with.

PAJAMA REPUBLICS

Poor countries tend to have low productivity in clothing manufacture, but even lower productivity in other industries (see the upcoming Economics in Action), giving them a comparative advantage in clothing manufacture. As a result, the clothing industry tends to dominate their economies. An official from one such country once joked, "We are not a banana republic—we are a pajama republic."

The figure to the right plots per capita income (the total income of the country divided by the size of the population) against the share of manufacturing employment devoted to clothing production for several countries. The graph shows just how strongly negative the relationship is between a country's per capita income level and the size of its clothing industry: poor countries have relatively large clothing industries, while rich countries have relatively small ones.

According to the U.S. Department of Commerce, Bangladesh's clothing industry has "low productivity, largely low literacy levels, frequent labor unrest, and outdated technology." Yet Bangladesh devotes most of its manufacturing workforce to clothing, the sector in which it nonetheless has a comparative advantage because its productivity in non-clothing industries is even lower. In contrast, Costa Rica has "relatively high productivity" in clothing. Yet, a much smaller and declining fraction of Costa Rica's workforce is employed in clothing production. That's because productivity in non-clothing industries is somewhat higher in Costa Rica than in Bangladesh.

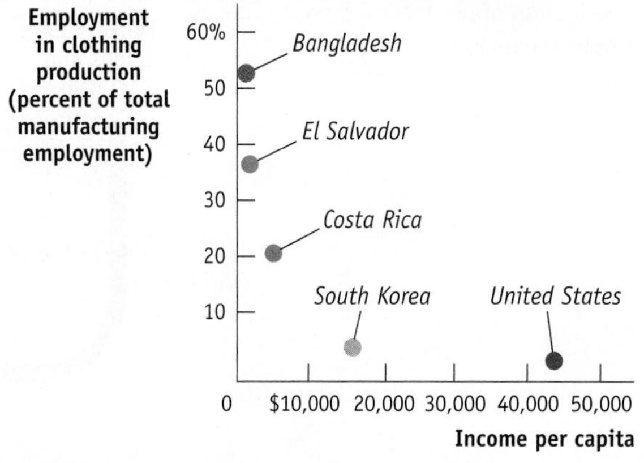

Source: World Bank, World Development Indicators; Nicita A. and M. Olarreaga, "Trade, Production and Protection 1976–2004," *World Bank Economic Review* 21, no. 1 (2007): 165–171.

Transactions: The Circular-Flow Diagram

The model economies that we've studied so far—each containing only one firm—are a huge simplification. We've also greatly simplified trade between the United States and Brazil, assuming that they engage only in the simplest of economic transactions, **barter,** in which one party directly trades a good or service for another good or service without using money. In a modern economy, simple barter is rare: usually people trade goods or services for money—pieces of colored paper with no inherent value—and then trade those pieces of colored paper for the goods or services they want. That is, they sell goods or services and buy other goods or services.

And they both sell and buy a lot of different things. The U.S. economy is a vastly complex entity, with more than a hundred million workers employed by millions of companies, producing millions of different goods and services. Yet you can learn some very important things about the economy by considering the simple graphic shown in Figure 2-6 on the next page, the **circular-flow diagram.** This diagram represents the transactions that take place in an economy by two kinds of flows around a circle: flows of physical things such as goods, services, labor, or raw materials in one direction, and flows of money that pay for these physical things in the opposite direction. In this case the physical flows are shown in yellow, the money flows in green.

The simplest circular-flow diagram illustrates an economy that contains only two kinds of inhabitants: **households** and **firms.** A household consists of either an individual or a group of people (usually, but not necessarily, a family) that share their income. A firm is an organization that produces goods and services for sale—and that employs members of households.

As you can see in Figure 2-6, there are two kinds of markets in this simple economy. On one side (here the left side) there are **markets for goods and services** in which households buy the goods and services they want from firms.

Trade takes the form of **barter** when people directly exchange goods or services that they have for goods or services that they want.

The **circular-flow diagram** represents the transactions in an economy by flows around a circle.

A **household** is a person or a group of people that share their income.

A **firm** is an organization that produces goods and services for sale.

Firms sell goods and services that they produce to households in **markets for goods and services.**

FIGURE 2-6 The Circular-Flow Diagram

This diagram represents the flows of money and of goods and services in the economy. In the markets for goods and services, households purchase goods and services from firms, generating a flow of money to the firms and a flow of goods and services to the households. The money flows back to households as firms purchase factors of production from the households in factor markets.

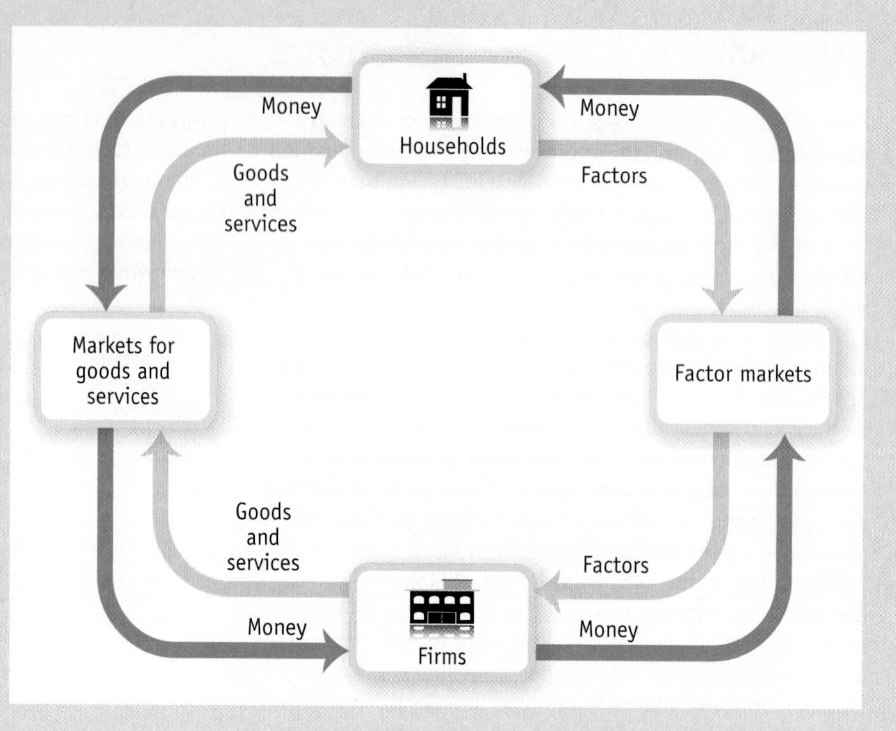

This produces a flow of goods and services to households and a return flow of money to firms.

On the other side, there are **factor markets** in which firms buy the resources they need to produce goods and services. Recall from earlier in the chapter that the main factors of production are land, labor, physical capital, and human capital.

The factor market most of us know best is the labor market, in which workers sell their services. In addition, we can think of households as owning and selling the other factors of production to firms. For example, when a firm buys physical capital in the form of machines, the payment ultimately goes to the households that own the machine-making firm. In this case, the transactions are occurring in the *capital market,* the market in which capital is bought and sold. Factor markets ultimately determine an economy's **income distribution,** how the total income created in an economy is allocated between less skilled workers, highly skilled workers, and the owners of capital and land.

The circular-flow diagram ignores a number of real-world complications in the interests of simplicity. A few examples:

- In the real world, the distinction between firms and households isn't always that clear-cut. Consider a small, family-run business—a farm, a shop, a small hotel. Is this a firm or a household? A more complete picture would include a separate box for family businesses.
- Many of the sales firms make are not to households but to other firms; for example, steel companies sell mainly to other companies such as auto manufacturers, not to households. A more complete picture would include these flows of goods, services, and money within the business sector.
- The figure doesn't show the government, which in the real world diverts quite a lot of money out of the circular flow in the form of taxes but also injects a lot of money back into the flow in the form of spending.

Firms buy the resources they need to produce goods and services in **factor markets.**

An economy's **income distribution** is the way in which total income is divided among the owners of the various factors of production.

Figure 2-6, in other words, is by no means a complete picture either of all the types of inhabitants of the real economy or of all the flows of money and physical items that take place among these inhabitants.

Despite its simplicity, the circular-flow diagram is a very useful aid to thinking about the economy.

ECONOMICS ➤ *IN ACTION*

RICH NATION, POOR NATION

Try taking off your clothes—at a suitable time and in a suitable place, of course—and taking a look at the labels inside that say where they were made. It's a very good bet that much, if not most, of your clothing was manufactured overseas, in a country that is much poorer than the United States—say, in El Salvador, Sri Lanka, or Bangladesh.

Robert Nickelsberg/Getty Images

Although less productive than American workers, Bangladeshi workers have a comparative advantage in clothing production.

Why are these countries so much poorer than we are? The immediate reason is that their economies are much less *productive*—firms in these countries are just not able to produce as much from a given quantity of resources as comparable firms in the United States or other wealthy countries. Why countries differ so much in productivity is a deep question—indeed, one of the main questions that preoccupy economists. But in any case, the difference in productivity is a fact.

But if the economies of these countries are so much less productive than ours, how is it that they make so much of our clothing? Why don't we do it for ourselves?

The answer is "comparative advantage." Just about every industry in Bangladesh is much less productive than the corresponding industry in the United States. But the productivity difference between rich and poor countries varies across goods; it is very large in the production of sophisticated goods like aircraft but not that large in the production of simpler goods like clothing. So Bangladesh's position with regard to clothing production is like Embraer's position with respect to producing small jets: it's not as good at it as Boeing, but it's the thing Embraer does comparatively well.

Bangladesh, though it is at an absolute disadvantage compared with the United States in almost everything, has a comparative advantage in clothing production. This means that both the United States and Bangladesh are able to consume more because they specialize in producing different things, with Bangladesh supplying our clothing and the United States supplying Bangladesh with more sophisticated goods.

1. True or false? Explain your answer.
   a. An increase in the amount of resources available to Boeing for use in producing Dreamliners and small jets does not change its production possibility frontier.
   b. A technological change that allows Boeing to build more small jets for any amount of Dreamliners built results in a change in its production possibility frontier.
   c. The production possibility frontier is useful because it illustrates how much of one good an economy must give up to get more of another good regardless of whether resources are being used efficiently.
2. In Italy, an automobile can be produced by 8 workers in one day and a washing machine by 3 workers in one day. In the United States, an automobile can be produced by 6 workers in one day and a washing machine by 2 workers in one day.
   a. Which country has an absolute advantage in the production of automobiles? In washing machines?

Quick Review

- Most economic **models** are "thought experiments" or simplified representations of reality that rely on the **other things equal assumption.**
- The **production possibility frontier** model illustrates the concepts of efficiency, opportunity cost, and economic growth.
- Every person and every country has a **comparative advantage** in something, giving rise to gains from trade. Comparative advantage is often confused with **absolute advantage.**
- In the simplest economies people **barter** rather than transact with money. The **circular-flow diagram** illustrates transactions within the economy as flows of goods and services, **factors of production,** and money between **households** and **firms.** These transactions occur in **markets for goods and services** and **factor markets.** Ultimately, factor markets determine the economy's **income distribution.**

Positive economics is the branch of economic analysis that describes the way the economy actually works.

Normative economics makes prescriptions about the way the economy should work.

A **forecast** is a simple prediction of the future.

b. Which country has a comparative advantage in the production of washing machines? In automobiles?

c. What pattern of specialization results in the greatest gains from trade between the two countries?

3. Using the numbers from Table 2-1, explain why the United States and Brazil are willing to engage in a trade of 10 large jets for 15 small jets.

4. Use the circular-flow diagram to explain how an increase in the amount of money spent by households results in an increase in the number of jobs in the economy. Describe in words what the circular-flow diagram predicts.

Solutions appear at back of book.

Using Models

Economics, we have now learned, is mainly a matter of creating models that draw on a set of basic principles but add some more specific assumptions that allow the modeler to apply those principles to a particular situation. But what do economists actually *do* with their models?

Positive versus Normative Economics

Imagine that you are an economic adviser to the governor of your state. What kinds of questions might the governor ask you to answer?

Well, here are three possible questions:

1. How much revenue will the tolls on the state turnpike yield next year?
2. How much would that revenue increase if the toll were raised from $1 to $1.50?
3. Should the toll be raised, bearing in mind that a toll increase will reduce traffic and air pollution near the road but will impose some financial hardship on frequent commuters?

There is a big difference between the first two questions and the third one. The first two are questions about facts. Your forecast of next year's toll collection will be proved right or wrong when the numbers actually come in. Your estimate of the impact of a change in the toll is a little harder to check—revenue depends on other factors besides the toll, and it may be hard to disentangle the causes of any change in revenue. Still, in principle there is only one right answer.

But the question of whether tolls should be raised may not have a "right" answer—two people who agree on the effects of a higher toll could still disagree about whether raising the toll is a good idea. For example, someone who lives near the turnpike but doesn't commute on it will care a lot about noise and air pollution but not so much about commuting costs. A regular commuter who doesn't live near the turnpike will have the opposite priorities.

This example highlights a key distinction between two roles of economic analysis. Analysis that tries to answer questions about the way the world works, which have definite right and wrong answers, is known as **positive economics.** In contrast, analysis that involves saying how the world *should* work is known as **normative economics.** To put it another way, positive economics is about description; normative economics is about prescription.

Positive economics occupies most of the time and effort of the economics profession. And models play a crucial role in almost all positive economics. As we mentioned earlier, the U.S. government uses a computer model to assess proposed changes in national tax policy, and many state governments have similar models to assess the effects of their own tax policy.

It's worth noting that there is a subtle but important difference between the first and second questions we imagined the governor asking. Question 1 asked for a simple prediction about next year's revenue—a **forecast.** Question 2 was a "what if" question, asking how revenue would change if the tax law were changed. Economists are often called upon to answer both types of questions, but models are especially useful for answering "what if" questions.

The answers to such questions often serve as a guide to policy, but they are still predictions, not prescriptions. That is, they tell you what will happen if a policy were changed; they don't tell you whether or not that result is good. Suppose your economic model tells you that the governor's proposed increase in highway tolls will raise property values in communities near the road but will hurt people who must use the turnpike to get to work. Does that make this proposed toll increase a good idea or a bad one? It depends on whom you ask. As we've just seen, someone who is very concerned with the communities near the road will support the increase, but someone who is very concerned with the welfare of drivers will feel differently. That's a value judgment—it's not a question of economic analysis.

Still, economists often do engage in normative economics and give policy advice. How can they do this when there may be no "right" answer?

One answer is that economists are also citizens, and we all have our opinions. But economic analysis can often be used to show that some policies are clearly better than others, regardless of anyone's opinions.

Suppose that policies A and B achieve the same goal, but policy A makes everyone better off than policy B—or at least makes some people better off without making other people worse off. Then A is clearly more efficient than B. That's not a value judgment: we're talking about how best to achieve a goal, not about the goal itself.

For example, two different policies have been used to help low-income families obtain housing: rent control, which limits the rents landlords are allowed to charge, and rent subsidies, which provide families with additional money to pay rent. Almost all economists agree that subsidies are the more efficient policy. And so the great majority of economists, whatever their personal politics, favor subsidies over rent control.

When policies can be clearly ranked in this way, then economists generally agree. But it is no secret that economists sometimes disagree.

When and Why Economists Disagree

Economists have a reputation for arguing with each other. Where does this reputation come from, and is it justified?

One important answer is that media coverage tends to exaggerate the real differences in views among economists. If nearly all economists agree on an issue—for example, the proposition that rent controls lead to housing shortages—reporters and editors are likely to conclude that it's not a story worth covering, leaving the professional consensus unreported. But an issue on which prominent economists take opposing sides—for example, whether cutting taxes right now would help the economy—makes a news story worth reporting. So you hear much more about the areas of disagreement within economics than you do about the large areas of agreement.

It is also worth remembering that economics is, unavoidably, often tied up in politics. On a number of issues powerful interest groups know what opinions they want to hear; they therefore have an incentive to find and promote economists who profess those opinions, giving these economists a prominence and visibility out of proportion to their support among their colleagues.

While the appearance of disagreement among economists exceeds the reality, it remains true that economists often *do* disagree about important things. For example, some well respected economists argue vehemently that the U.S. government should replace the income tax with a *value-added tax* (a national sales tax, which is the main source of government revenue in many European countries). Other equally respected economists disagree. Why this difference of opinion?

FOR INQUIRING MINDS

WHEN ECONOMISTS AGREE

"If all the economists in the world were laid end to end, they still couldn't reach a conclusion." So goes one popular economist joke. But do economists really disagree that much?

Not according to a classic survey of members of the American Economic Association, reported in the May 1992 issue of the *American Economic Review*. The authors asked respondents to agree or disagree with a number of statements about the economy; what they found was a high level of agreement among professional economists on many of the statements. At the top, with more than 90 percent of the economists agreeing, were "Tariffs and import quotas usually reduce general economic welfare" and "A ceiling on rents reduces the quantity and quality of housing available." What's striking about these two statements is that many noneconomists disagree: tariffs and import quotas to keep out foreign-produced goods are favored by many voters, and proposals to do away with rent control in cities like New York and San Francisco have met fierce political opposition.

So is the stereotype of quarreling economists a myth? Not entirely: economists do disagree quite a lot on some issues, especially in macroeconomics. But there is a large area of common ground.

One important source of differences lies in values: as in any diverse group of individuals, reasonable people can differ. In comparison to an income tax, a value-added tax typically falls more heavily on people of modest means. So an economist who values a society with more social and income equality for its own sake will tend to oppose a value-added tax. An economist with different values will be less likely to oppose it.

A second important source of differences arises from economic modeling. Because economists base their conclusions on models, which are simplified representations of reality, two economists can legitimately disagree about which simplifications are appropriate—and therefore arrive at different conclusions.

Suppose that the U.S. government were considering introducing a value-added tax. Economist A may rely on a model that focuses on the administrative costs of tax systems—that is, the costs of monitoring, processing papers, collecting the tax, and so on. This economist might then point to the well-known high costs of administering a value-added tax and argue against the change. But economist B may think that the right way to approach the question is to ignore the administrative costs and focus on how the proposed law would change savings behavior. This economist might point to studies suggesting that value-added taxes promote higher consumer saving, a desirable result.

Because the economists have used different models—that is, made different simplifying assumptions—they arrive at different conclusions. And so the two economists may find themselves on different sides of the issue.

In most cases such disputes are eventually resolved by the accumulation of evidence showing which of the various models proposed by economists does a better job of fitting the facts. However, in economics, as in any science, it can take a long time before research settles important disputes—decades, in some cases. And since the economy is always changing, in ways that make old models invalid or raise new policy questions, there are always new issues on which economists disagree. The policy maker must then decide which economist to believe.

The important point is that economic analysis is a method, not a set of conclusions.

ECONOMICS ➤ IN ACTION

ECONOMISTS, BEYOND THE IVORY TOWER

Many economists are mainly engaged in teaching and research. But quite a few economists have a more direct hand in events.

As described earlier in this chapter (For Inquiring Minds, "The Model That Ate the Economy"), one specific branch of economics, finance theory, plays an important role on Wall Street—not always to good effect. But pricing assets is by no means the only useful function economists serve in the business world. Businesses need forecasts of the future demand for their products, predictions of future raw-material prices, assessments of their future financing needs, and more; for all of these purposes, economic analysis is essential.

Some of the economists employed in the business world work directly for the institutions that need their input. Top financial firms like Goldman Sachs and Morgan Stanley, in particular, maintain high-quality economics groups, which produce analyses of forces and events likely to affect financial markets. Other economists are employed by consulting firms like Macro Advisers, which sells analysis and advice to a wide range of other businesses.

Last but not least, economists participate extensively in government. According to the Bureau of Labor Statistics, government agencies employ about half of the professional economists in the United States. This shouldn't be surprising: one of the most important functions of government is to make economic policy, and almost every government policy decision must take economic effects into consideration. So governments around the world employ economists in a variety of roles.

In the U.S. government, a key role is played by the Council of Economic Advisers, whose sole purpose is to advise the president on economic matters. Unlike most government employees, most economists at the Council aren't longtime civil servants; instead, they are mainly professors on leave for one or two years from their universities. Many of the nation's best-known economists have served at the Council of Economic Advisers at some point in their careers.

Economists also play an important role in many other parts of the government, from the Department of Commerce to the Labor Department. Economists dominate the staff of the Federal Reserve, a government agency that controls the economy's money supply as well as overseeing banks. And economists play an especially important role in two international organizations headquartered in Washington, D.C.: the International Monetary Fund, which provides advice and loans to countries experiencing economic difficulties, and the World Bank, which provides advice and loans to promote long-term economic development.

In the past, it wasn't that easy to track what all these economists working on practical affairs were up to. These days, however, there is a very lively online discussion of economic prospects and policy, on websites that range from the home page of the International Monetary Fund (www.imf.org), to business-oriented sites like economy.com, to the blogs of individual economists, like that of Mark Thoma (economistsview.typepad.com) or, yes, our own blog, which is among the Technorati top 100 blogs, at krugman.blogs.nytimes.com.

Quick Review

- **Positive economics**—the focus of most economic research—is the analysis of the way the world works, in which there are definite right and wrong answers. It often involves making **forecasts.** But in **normative economics,** which makes prescriptions about how things ought to be, there are often no right answers and only value judgments.
- Economists do disagree—though not as much as legend has it—for two main reasons. One, they may disagree about which simplifications to make in a model. Two, economists may disagree—like everyone else—about values.

CHECK YOUR UNDERSTANDING 2-2

1. Which of the following statements is a positive statement? Which is a normative statement?
   a. Society should take measures to prevent people from engaging in dangerous personal behavior.
   b. People who engage in dangerous personal behavior impose higher costs on society through higher medical costs.
2. True or false? Explain your answer.
   a. Policy choice A and policy choice B attempt to achieve the same social goal. Policy choice A, however, results in a much less efficient use of resources than policy choice B. Therefore, economists are more likely to agree on choosing policy choice B.
   b. When two economists disagree on the desirability of a policy, it's typically because one of them has made a mistake.
   c. Policy makers can always use economics to figure out which goals a society should try to achieve.

Solutions appear at back of book.

WORKED PROBLEM

It's Not Magic

In the third book of the bestselling *Inheritance Cycle* fantasy series by Christopher Paolini, the hero, Eragon, extracts gold from the earth using magic. Eragon learned from his mentor, Oromis, that the earth contains minute particles of nearly every element. While these elements are too expensive to mine, they can be extracted by magic.

In the real world, these elements, called rare earths, aren't extracted by magic but by Chinese companies. Rare earths are important for the operation of lasers, cell phones, computer hard drives, and many of the appliances we use daily. But they are also scattered about in small amounts, making them very difficult and expensive to mine. China currently controls about 95% of the world's production of rare earths.

Meanwhile, the United States is the largest producer of chicken in the world. Fortunately, the United States and China can trade with each other. But what if China refused to export rare earths, forcing the United States to find ways to extract these rare earths on its own? What if China stopped importing chicken and reverted to self-production?

Now suppose that China and the United States can produce either chicken or rare earths—a hypothetical example based on an actual trading pattern. Assume that the production possibilities for rare earths and chicken are as follows:

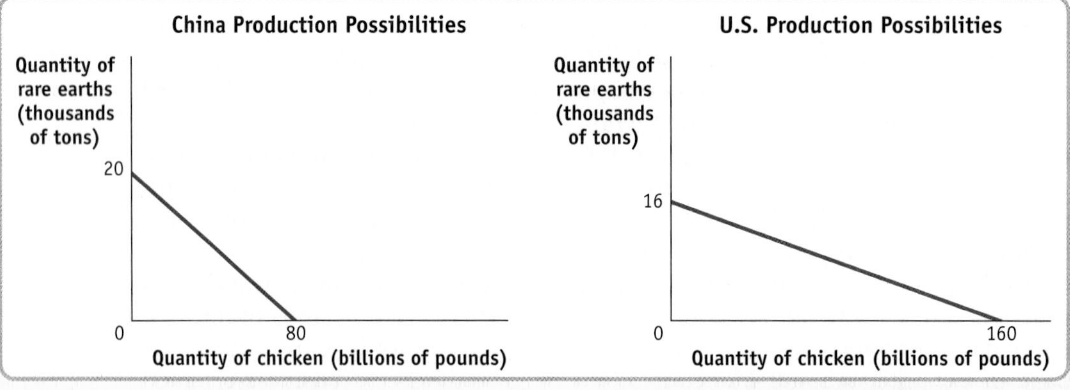

Calculate the opportunity cost of rare earths and chicken for both countries. Does the United States have a comparative advantage in producing rare earths? Suppose China wishes to consume 64 billion pounds of chicken and 12 thousand tons of rare earths. Show this point on a graph of the production possibilities. Is this possible without trade?

STEP 1: Calculate the opportunity cost of rare earths and chicken for both countries.

Review the section "Comparative Advantage and Gains from Trade" on pages 33–36.

The production possibility frontiers for both countries are straight lines, which implies a constant opportunity cost of chicken in terms of rare earths. The slope of China's production possibility frontier is $-\frac{1}{4}$ (the slope is defined as the change in the y-variable—rare earths—divided by the change in the x-variable—chicken—which in this case is $-\frac{20}{80} = -\frac{1}{4}$), and the slope of the production possibility frontier for the United States is $-\frac{1}{10}$. Thus, the opportunity cost for China of producing 1 thousand tons of rare earths is 4 billion pounds of chicken, and the opportunity cost for the United States of producing 1 thousand tons of rare earths is 10 billion pounds of chicken. Likewise, the opportunity cost for China of producing 1 billion pounds of chicken is ¼ of a thousand tons of rare earths (250 tons), and the opportunity cost for the United States of producing 1 billion pounds of chicken is 1⁄10 of a thousand tons (100 tons) of rare earths.

STEP 2: Does China have a comparative advantage at producing chicken?

Review the section "Comparative Advantage and Gains from Trade" on pages 33–36.

A country has a comparative advantage in the production of a good if the opportunity cost of production is lower for that country than for another country. In this case, the opportunity cost of producing 1 billion pounds of chicken is ¼ of a thousand tons of rare earths (250 tons) for China and 1⁄10 of a thousand tons (100 tons) of rare earths for the United States. Since 1⁄10 is less than ¼, the United States, not China, has a comparative advantage in the production of chicken.

STEP 3: Suppose China wishes to consume 64 billion pounds of chicken and 12 thousand tons of rare earths. Show this point on a graph of the production possibilities. Is this possible without trade?

Once again, review the section "Comparative Advantage and Gains from Trade" on pages 33–36, and especially Figure 2-5.

As shown on the following graph, China's consumption of 64 billion pounds of chicken and 12 thousand tons of rare earths, demonstrated at point B, is outside the production possibility frontier without trade. If China consumed 64 billion pounds of chicken, without trade, it could consume only 4 thousand tons of rare earths, shown at point A. Thus, without trade, this level of consumption of both goods would be impossible.

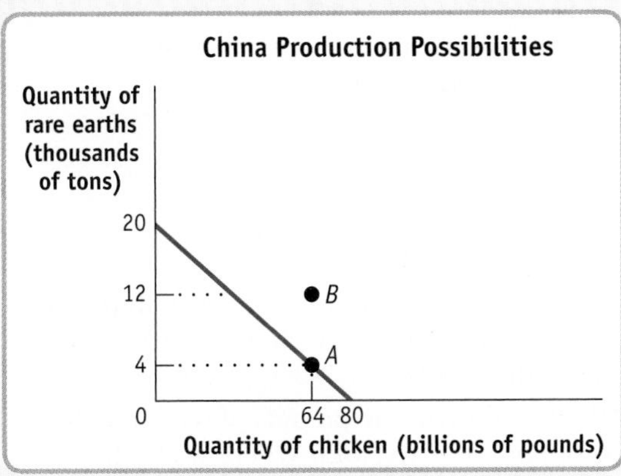

SUMMARY

1. Almost all economics is based on **models,** "thought experiments" or simplified versions of reality, many of which use mathematical tools such as graphs. An important assumption in economic models is the **other things equal assumption,** which allows analysis of the effect of a change in one factor by holding all other relevant factors unchanged.

2. One important economic model is the **production possibility frontier.** It illustrates *opportunity cost* (showing how much less of one good can be produced if more of the other good is produced); *efficiency* (an economy is efficient in production if it produces on the production possibility frontier and efficient in allocation if it produces the mix of goods and services that

people want to consume); and *economic growth* (an outward shift of the production possibility frontier). There are two basic sources of growth: an increase in **factors of production**—resources such as land, labor, capital, and human capital, inputs that are not used up in production—and improved **technology.**

3. Another important model is **comparative advantage,** which explains the source of gains from trade between individuals and countries. Everyone has a comparative advantage in something—some good or service in which that person has a lower opportunity cost than everyone else. But it is often confused with **absolute advantage,** an ability to produce a particular good or service better than anyone else. This confusion leads some to erroneously conclude that there are no gains from trade between people or countries.

4. In the simplest economies people **barter**—trade goods and services for one another—rather than trade them for money, as in a modern economy. The **circular-flow diagram** represents transactions within the economy as flows of goods, services, and money between **households** and **firms.** These transactions occur in **markets for goods and services** and **factor markets,** markets for **factors of production**—land, labor, physical capital, and human capital. It is useful in understanding how spending, production, employment, income, and growth are related in the economy. Ultimately, factor markets determine the economy's **income distribution,** how an economy's total income is allocated to the owners of the factors of production.

5. Economists use economic models for both **positive economics,** which describes how the economy works, and for **normative economics,** which prescribes how the economy *should* work. Positive economics often involves making **forecasts.** Economists can determine correct answers for positive questions but typically not for normative questions, which involve value judgments. The exceptions are when policies designed to achieve a certain objective can be clearly ranked in terms of efficiency.

6. There are two main reasons economists disagree. One, they may disagree about which simplifications to make in a model. Two, economists may disagree—like everyone else—about values.

KEY TERMS

PROBLEMS

1. Atlantis is a small, isolated island in the South Atlantic. The inhabitants grow potatoes and catch fish. The accompanying table shows the maximum annual output combinations of potatoes and fish that can be produced. Obviously, given their limited resources and available technology, as they use more of their resources for potato production, there are fewer resources available for catching fish.

Maximum annual output options	Quantity of potatoes (pounds)	Quantity of fish (pounds)
A	1,000	0
B	800	300
C	600	500
D	400	600
E	200	650
F	0	675

   a. Draw a production possibility frontier with potatoes on the horizontal axis and fish on the vertical axis illustrating these options, showing points *A–F.*
   b. Can Atlantis produce 500 pounds of fish and 800 pounds of potatoes? Explain. Where would this point lie relative to the production possibility frontier?
   c. What is the opportunity cost of increasing the annual output of potatoes from 600 to 800 pounds?
   d. What is the opportunity cost of increasing the annual output of potatoes from 200 to 400 pounds?
   e. Can you explain why the answers to parts c and d are not the same? What does this imply about the slope of the production possibility frontier?

2. In the ancient country of Roma, only two goods, spaghetti and meatballs, are produced. There are two tribes in Roma, the Tivoli and the Frivoli. By themselves, the Tivoli each month can produce either 30

pounds of spaghetti and no meatballs, or 50 pounds of meatballs and no spaghetti, or any combination in between. The Frivoli, by themselves, each month can produce 40 pounds of spaghetti and no meatballs, or 30 pounds of meatballs and no spaghetti, or any combination in between.

a. Assume that all production possibility frontiers are straight lines. Draw one diagram showing the monthly production possibility frontier for the Tivoli and another showing the monthly production possibility frontier for the Frivoli. Show how you calculated them.

b. Which tribe has the comparative advantage in spaghetti production? In meatball production?

In A.D. 100 the Frivoli discover a new technique for making meatballs that doubles the quantity of meatballs they can produce each month.

c. Draw the new monthly production possibility frontier for the Frivoli.

d. After the innovation, which tribe now has an absolute advantage in producing meatballs? In producing spaghetti? Which has the comparative advantage in meatball production? In spaghetti production?

3. According to the U.S. Census Bureau, in July 2006 the United States sold aircraft worth $1 billion to China and bought aircraft worth only $19,000 from China. During the same month, however, the United States bought $83 million worth of men's trousers, slacks, and jeans from China but sold only $8,000 worth of trousers, slacks, and jeans to China. Using what you have learned about how trade is determined by comparative advantage, answer the following questions.

a. Which country has the comparative advantage in aircraft production? In production of trousers, slacks, and jeans?

b. Can you determine which country has the absolute advantage in aircraft production? In production of trousers, slacks, and jeans?

4. Peter Pundit, an economics reporter, states that the European Union (EU) is increasing its productivity very rapidly in all industries. He claims that this productivity advance is so rapid that output from the EU in these industries will soon exceed that of the United States and, as a result, the United States will no longer benefit from trade with the EU.

a. Do you think Peter Pundit is correct or not? If not, what do you think is the source of his mistake?

b. If the EU and the United States continue to trade, what do you think will characterize the goods that the EU sells to the United States and the goods that the United States sells to the EU?

5. The inhabitants of the fictional economy of Atlantis use money in the form of cowry shells. Draw a circular-flow diagram showing households and firms. Firms produce potatoes and fish, and households buy potatoes and fish. Households also provide the land and labor to firms. Identify where in the flows of cowry shells or physical things (goods and services, or resources) each of the following impacts would occur. Describe how this impact spreads around the circle.

a. A devastating hurricane floods many of the potato fields.

b. A very productive fishing season yields a very large number of fish caught.

c. The inhabitants of Atlantis discover Shakira and spend several days a month at dancing festivals.

6. An economist might say that colleges and universities "produce" education, using faculty members and students as inputs. According to this line of reasoning, education is then "consumed" by households. Construct a circular-flow diagram to represent the sector of the economy devoted to college education: colleges and universities represent firms, and households both consume education and provide faculty and students to universities. What are the relevant markets in this diagram? What is being bought and sold in each direction? What would happen in the diagram if the government decided to subsidize 50% of all college students' tuition?

7. Your dormitory roommate plays loud music most of the time; you, however, would prefer more peace and quiet. You suggest that she buy some earphones. She responds that although she would be happy to use earphones, she has many other things that she would prefer to spend her money on right now. You discuss this situation with a friend who is an economics major. The following exchange takes place:

He: How much would it cost to buy earphones?

You: $15.

He: How much do you value having some peace and quiet for the rest of the semester?

You: $30.

He: It is efficient for you to buy the earphones and give them to your roommate. You gain more than you lose; the benefit exceeds the cost. You should do that.

You: It just isn't fair that I have to pay for the earphones when I'm not the one making the noise.

a. Which parts of this conversation contain positive statements and which parts contain normative statements?

b. Construct an argument supporting your viewpoint that your roommate should be the one to change her behavior. Similarly, construct an argument from the viewpoint of your roommate that you should be the one to buy the earphones. If your dormitory has a policy that gives residents the unlimited right to play music, whose argument is likely to win? If your dormitory has a rule that a person must stop playing music whenever a roommate complains, whose argument is likely to win?

8. A representative of the American clothing industry recently made the following statement: "Workers in Asia often work in sweatshop conditions earning only pennies an hour. American workers are more productive and as a result earn higher wages. In order to preserve the dignity of the American workplace, the government should enact legislation banning imports of low-wage Asian clothing."

a. Which parts of this quote are positive statements? Which parts are normative statements?

b. Is the policy that is being advocated consistent with the preceding statements about the wages and productivities of American and Asian workers?

c. Would such a policy make some Americans better off without making any other Americans worse off? That is, would this policy be efficient from the viewpoint of all Americans?

d. Would low-wage Asian workers benefit from or be hurt by such a policy?

9. Are the following statements true or false? Explain your answers.

a. "When people must pay higher taxes on their wage earnings, it reduces their incentive to work" is a positive statement.

b. "We should lower taxes to encourage more work" is a positive statement.

c. Economics cannot always be used to completely decide what society ought to do.

d. "The system of public education in this country generates greater benefits to society than the cost of running the system" is a normative statement.

e. All disagreements among economists are generated by the media.

10. Evaluate the following statement: "It is easier to build an economic model that accurately reflects events that have already occurred than to build an economic model to forecast future events." Do you think this is true or not? Why? What does this imply about the difficulties of building good economic models?

11. Economists who work for the government are often called on to make policy recommendations. Why do you think it is important for the public to be able to differentiate normative statements from positive statements in these recommendations?

12. The mayor of Gotham City, worried about a potential epidemic of deadly influenza this winter, asks an economic adviser the following series of questions. Determine whether a question requires the economic adviser to make a positive assessment or a normative assessment.

a. How much vaccine will be in stock in the city by the end of November?

b. If we offer to pay 10% more per dose to the pharmaceutical companies providing the vaccines, will they provide additional doses?

c. If there is a shortage of vaccine in the city, whom should we vaccinate first—the elderly or the very young? (Assume that a person from one group has an equal likelihood of dying from influenza as a person from the other group.)

d. If the city charges $25 per shot, how many people will pay?

e. If the city charges $25 per shot, it will make a profit of $10 per shot, money that can go to pay for inoculating poor people. Should the city engage in such a scheme?

13. Assess the following statement: "If economists just had enough data, they could solve all policy questions in a way that maximizes the social good. There would be no need for divisive political debates, such as whether the government should provide free medical care for all."

EXTEND YOUR UNDERSTANDING

14. You are in charge of allocating residents to your dormitory's baseball and basketball teams. You are down to the last four people, two of whom must be allocated to baseball and two to basketball. The accompanying table gives each person's batting average and free-throw average.

Name	Batting average	Free-throw average
Kelley	70%	60%
Jackie	50%	50%
Curt	10%	30%
Gerry	80%	70%

a. Explain how you would use the concept of comparative advantage to allocate the players. Begin by establishing each player's opportunity cost of free throws in terms of batting average.

b. Why is it likely that the other basketball players will be unhappy about this arrangement but the other baseball players will be satisfied? Nonetheless, why would an economist say that this is an efficient way to allocate players for your dormitory's sports teams?

15. Two important industries on the island of Bermuda are fishing and tourism. According to data from the Food and Agriculture Organization of the United Nations and the Bermuda Department of Statistics, in the year 2009 the 306 registered fishermen in Bermuda caught 387 metric tons of marine fish. And the 2,719 people employed by hotels produced 554,400 hotel stays (measured by the number of visitor arrivals). Suppose that this production point is efficient in production. Assume also that the opportunity cost of 1 additional metric ton of fish is 2,000 hotel stays and that this opportunity cost is constant (the opportunity cost does not change).

a. If all 306 registered fishermen were to be employed by hotels (in addition to the 2,719 people already working in hotels), how many hotel stays could Bermuda produce?

b. If all 2,719 hotel employees were to become fishermen (in addition to the 306 fishermen already working in the fishing industry), how many metric tons of fish could Bermuda produce?

c. Draw a production possibility frontier for Bermuda, with fish on the horizontal axis and hotel stays on the vertical axis, and label Bermuda's actual production point for the year 2009.

16. According to data from the U.S. Department of Agriculture's National Agricultural Statistics Service, 124 million acres of land in the United States were used for wheat or corn farming in 2004. Of those 124 million acres, farmers used 50 million acres to grow 2.158 billion bushels of wheat and 74 million acres of land to grow 11.807 billion bushels of corn. Suppose that U.S. wheat and corn farming is efficient in production. At that production point, the opportunity cost of producing 1 additional bushel of wheat is 1.7 fewer bushels of corn. However, because farmers have increasing opportunity costs, additional bushels of wheat have an opportunity cost greater than 1.7 bushels of corn. For each of the following production points, decide whether that production point is (i) feasible and efficient in production, (ii) feasible but not efficient in production, (iii) not feasible, or (iv) unclear as to whether or not it is feasible.

a. Farmers use 40 million acres of land to produce 1.8 billion bushels of wheat, and they use 60 million acres of land to produce 9 billion bushels of corn. The remaining 24 million acres are left unused.

b. From their original production point, farmers transfer 40 million acres of land from corn to wheat production. They now produce 3.158 billion bushels of wheat and 10.107 bushels of corn.

c. Farmers reduce their production of wheat to 2 billion bushels and increase their production of corn to 12.044 billion bushels. Along the production possibility frontier, the opportunity cost of going from 11.807 billion bushels of corn to 12.044 billion bushels of corn is 0.666 bushel of wheat per bushel of corn.

Graphs in Economics

A quantity that can take on more than one value is called a **variable**.

Getting the Picture

Whether you're reading about economics in the *Wall Street Journal* or in your economics textbook, you will see many graphs. Visual images can make it much easier to understand verbal descriptions, numerical information, or ideas. In economics, graphs are the type of visual image used to facilitate understanding. To fully understand the ideas and information being discussed, you need to be familiar with how to interpret these visual aids. This appendix explains how graphs are constructed and interpreted and how they are used in economics.

Graphs, Variables, and Economic Models

One reason to attend college is that a bachelor's degree provides access to higher-paying jobs. Additional degrees, such as MBAs or law degrees, increase earnings even more. If you were to read an article about the relationship between educational attainment and income, you would probably see a graph showing the income levels for workers with different amounts of education. And this graph would depict the idea that, in general, more education increases income. This graph, like most of those in economics, would depict the relationship between two economic variables. A **variable** is a quantity that can take on more than one value, such as the number of years of education a person has, the price of a can of soda, or a household's income.

As you learned in this chapter, economic analysis relies heavily on *models*, simplified descriptions of real situations. Most economic models describe the relationship between two variables, simplified by holding constant other variables that may affect the relationship. For example, an economic model might describe the relationship between the price of a can of soda and the number of cans of soda that consumers will buy, assuming that everything else that affects consumers' purchases of soda stays constant. This type of model can be described mathematically or verbally, but illustrating the relationship in a graph makes it easier to understand. Next we show how graphs that depict economic models are constructed and interpreted.

How Graphs Work

Most graphs in economics are based on a grid built around two perpendicular lines that show the values of two variables, helping you visualize the relationship between them. So a first step in understanding the use of such graphs is to see how this system works.

Two-Variable Graphs

Figure 2A-1 shows a typical two-variable graph. It illustrates the data in the accompanying table on outside temperature and the number of sodas a typical vendor can expect to sell at a baseball stadium during one game. The first column shows the values of outside temperature (the first variable) and the second column shows the values of the number of sodas sold (the second variable). Five combinations or pairs of the two variables are shown, each denoted by *A* through *E* in the third column.

Now let's turn to graphing the data in this table. In any two-variable graph, one variable is called the *x*-variable and the other is called the *y*-variable. Here

FIGURE 2A-1 Plotting Points on a Two-Variable Graph

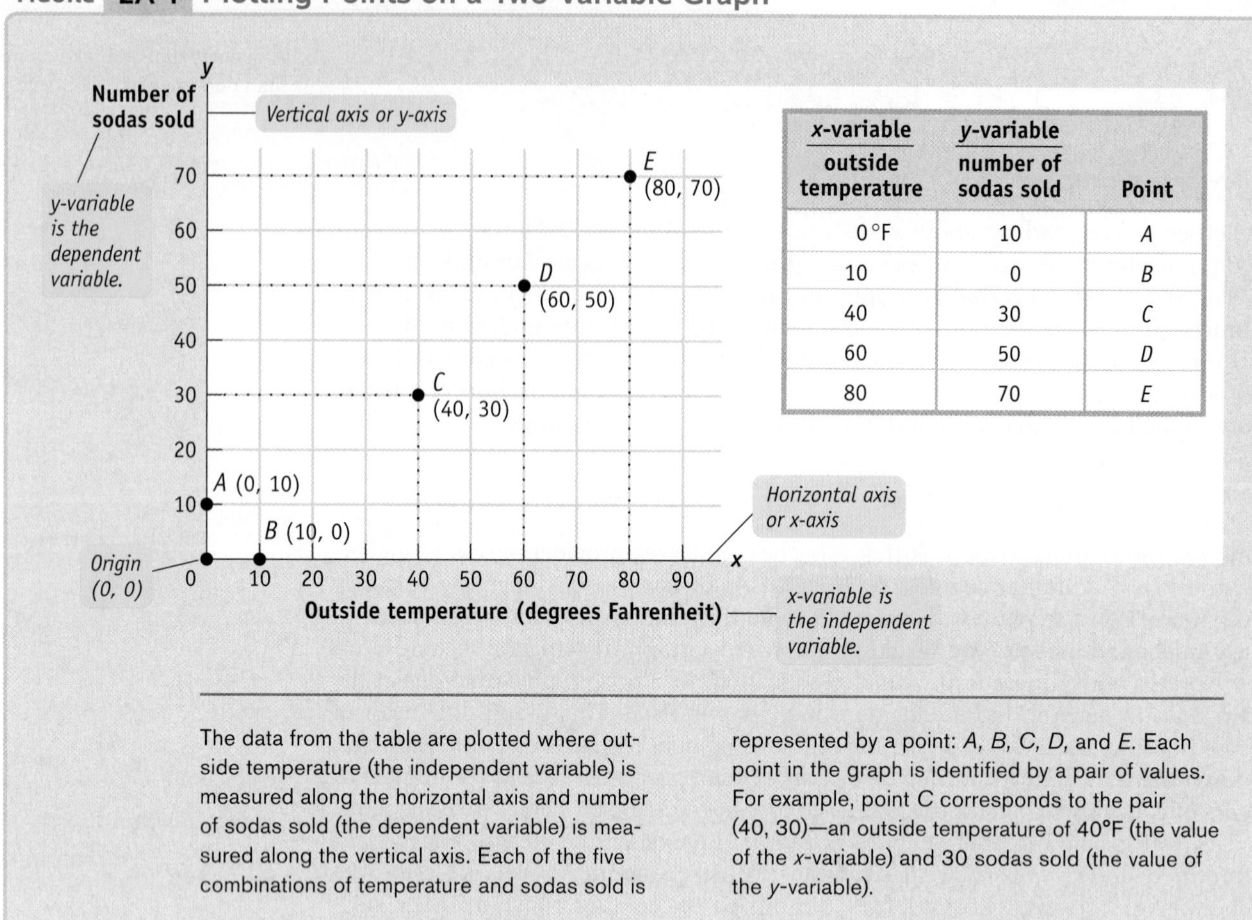

x-variable outside temperature	y-variable number of sodas sold	Point
0°F	10	*A*
10	0	*B*
40	30	*C*
60	50	*D*
80	70	*E*

The data from the table are plotted where outside temperature (the independent variable) is measured along the horizontal axis and number of sodas sold (the dependent variable) is measured along the vertical axis. Each of the five combinations of temperature and sodas sold is represented by a point: *A*, *B*, *C*, *D*, and *E*. Each point in the graph is identified by a pair of values. For example, point C corresponds to the pair (40, 30)—an outside temperature of 40°F (the value of the *x*-variable) and 30 sodas sold (the value of the *y*-variable).

we have made outside temperature the *x*-variable and number of sodas sold the *y*-variable. The solid horizontal line in the graph is called the **horizontal axis** or ***x*-axis,** and values of the *x*-variable—outside temperature—are measured along it. Similarly, the solid vertical line in the graph is called the **vertical axis** or ***y*-axis,** and values of the *y*-variable—number of sodas sold—are measured along it. At the **origin,** the point where the two axes meet, each variable is equal to zero. As you move rightward from the origin along the *x*-axis, values of the *x*-variable are positive and increasing. As you move up from the origin along the *y*-axis, values of the *y*-variable are positive and increasing.

You can plot each of the five points *A* through *E* on this graph by using a pair of numbers—the values that the *x*-variable and the *y*-variable take on for a given point. In Figure 2A-1, at point *C*, the *x*-variable takes on the value 40 and the *y*-variable takes on the value 30. You plot point *C* by drawing a line straight up from 40 on the *x*-axis and a horizontal line across from 30 on the *y*-axis. We write point *C* as (40, 30). We write the origin as (0, 0).

Looking at point *A* and point *B* in Figure 2A-1, you can see that when one of the variables for a point has a value of zero, it will lie on one of the axes. If the value of the *x*-variable is zero, the point will lie on the vertical axis, like point *A*. If the value of the *y*-variable is zero, the point will lie on the horizontal axis, like point *B*.

Most graphs that depict relationships between two economic variables represent a **causal relationship,** a relationship in which the value taken by one variable directly influences or determines the value taken by the other variable. In a causal relationship, the determining variable is called the **independent variable;** the variable it determines is called the **dependent variable.** In our example of soda

The line along which values of the *x*-variable are measured is called the **horizontal axis** or ***x*-axis.** The line along which values of the *y*-variable are measured is called the **vertical axis** or ***y*-axis.** The point where the axes of a two-variable graph meet is the **origin.**

A **causal relationship** exists between two variables when the value taken by one variable directly influences or determines the value taken by the other variable. In a causal relationship, the determining variable is called the **independent variable;** the variable it determines is called the **dependent variable.**

sales, the outside temperature is the independent variable. It directly influences the number of sodas that are sold, the dependent variable in this case.

By convention, we put the independent variable on the horizontal axis and the dependent variable on the vertical axis. Figure 2A-1 is constructed consistent with this convention; the independent variable (outside temperature) is on the horizontal axis and the dependent variable (number of sodas sold) is on the vertical axis. An important exception to this convention is in graphs showing the economic relationship between the price of a product and quantity of the product: although price is generally the independent variable that determines quantity, it is always measured on the vertical axis.

A **curve** is a line on a graph that depicts a relationship between two variables. It may be either a straight line or a curved line. If the curve is a straight line, the variables have a **linear relationship.** If the curve is not a straight line, the variables have a **nonlinear relationship.**

Curves on a Graph

Panel (a) of Figure 2A-2 contains some of the same information as Figure 2A-1, with a line drawn through the points *B, C, D,* and *E.* Such a line on a graph is called a **curve,** regardless of whether it is a straight line or a curved line. If the curve that shows the relationship between two variables is a straight line, or linear, the variables have a **linear relationship.** When the curve is not a straight line, or nonlinear, the variables have a **nonlinear relationship.**

A point on a curve indicates the value of the *y*-variable for a specific value of the *x*-variable. For example, point *D* indicates that at a temperature of 60°F, a vendor can expect to sell 50 sodas. The shape and orientation of a curve reveal

FIGURE 2A-2 Drawing Curves

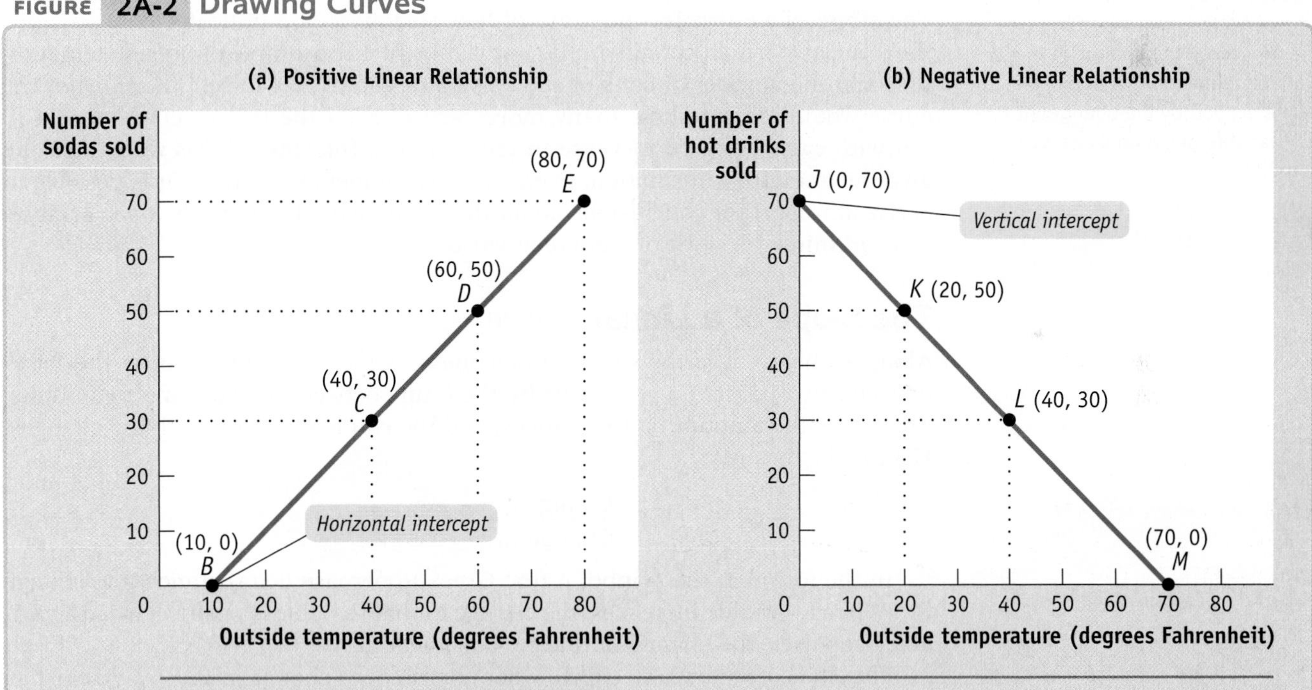

The curve in panel (a) illustrates the relationship between the two variables, outside temperature and number of sodas sold. The two variables have a positive linear relationship: positive because the curve has an upward tilt, and linear because it is a straight line. It implies that an increase in the *x*-variable (outside temperature) leads to an increase in the *y*-variable (number of sodas sold). The curve in panel (b) is also a straight line, but it tilts downward. The two variables here, outside temperature and number of hot drinks sold, have a negative linear relationship: an increase in the *x*-variable (outside temperature) leads to a decrease in the *y*-variable (number of hot drinks sold). The curve in panel (a) has a horizontal intercept at point *B*, where it hits the horizontal axis. The curve in panel (b) has a vertical intercept at point *J*, where it hits the vertical axis, and a horizontal intercept at point *M*, where it hits the horizontal axis.

Two variables have a **positive relationship** when an increase in the value of one variable is associated with an increase in the value of the other variable. It is illustrated by a curve that slopes upward from left to right.

Two variables have a **negative relationship** when an increase in the value of one variable is associated with a decrease in the value of the other variable. It is illustrated by a curve that slopes downward from left to right.

The **horizontal intercept** of a curve is the point at which it hits the horizontal axis; it indicates the value of the *x*-variable when the value of the *y*-variable is zero.

The **vertical intercept** of a curve is the point at which it hits the vertical axis; it shows the value of the *y*-variable when the value of the *x*-variable is zero.

The **slope** of a line or curve is a measure of how steep it is. The slope of a line is measured by "rise over run"—the change in the *y*-variable between two points on the line divided by the change in the *x*-variable between those same two points.

the general nature of the relationship between the two variables. The upward tilt of the curve in panel (a) of Figure 2A-2 means that vendors can expect to sell more sodas at higher outside temperatures.

When variables are related this way—that is, when an increase in one variable is associated with an increase in the other variable—the variables are said to have a **positive relationship.** It is illustrated by a curve that slopes upward from left to right. Because this curve is also linear, the relationship between outside temperature and number of sodas sold illustrated by the curve in panel (a) of Figure 2A-2 is a positive linear relationship.

When an increase in one variable is associated with a decrease in the other variable, the two variables are said to have a **negative relationship.** It is illustrated by a curve that slopes downward from left to right, like the curve in panel (b) of Figure 2A-2. Because this curve is also linear, the relationship it depicts is a negative linear relationship. Two variables that might have such a relationship are the outside temperature and the number of hot drinks a vendor can expect to sell at a baseball stadium.

Return for a moment to the curve in panel (a) of Figure 2A-2 and you can see that it hits the horizontal axis at point *B*. This point, known as the **horizontal intercept,** shows the value of the *x*-variable when the value of the *y*-variable is zero. In panel (b) of Figure 2A-2, the curve hits the vertical axis at point *J*. This point, called the **vertical intercept,** indicates the value of the *y*-variable when the value of the *x*-variable is zero.

A Key Concept: The Slope of a Curve

The **slope** of a curve is a measure of how steep it is and indicates how sensitive the *y*-variable is to a change in the *x*-variable. In our example of outside temperature and the number of cans of soda a vendor can expect to sell, the slope of the curve would indicate how many more cans of soda the vendor could expect to sell with each 1 degree increase in temperature. Interpreted this way, the slope gives meaningful information. Even without numbers for *x* and *y*, it is possible to arrive at important conclusions about the relationship between the two variables by examining the slope of a curve at various points.

The Slope of a Linear Curve

Along a linear curve the slope, or steepness, is measured by dividing the "rise" between two points on the curve by the "run" between those same two points. The rise is the amount that *y* changes, and the run is the amount that *x* changes. Here is the formula:

$$\frac{\text{Change in } y}{\text{Change in } x} = \frac{\Delta y}{\Delta x} = \text{Slope}$$

In the formula, the symbol Δ (the Greek uppercase delta) stands for "change in." When a variable increases, the change in that variable is positive; when a variable decreases, the change in that variable is negative.

The slope of a curve is positive when the rise (the change in the *y*-variable) has the same sign as the run (the change in the *x*-variable). That's because when two numbers have the same sign, the ratio of those two numbers is positive. The curve in panel (a) of Figure 2A-2 has a positive slope: along the curve, both the *y*-variable and the *x*-variable increase. The slope of a curve is negative when the rise and the run have different signs. That's because when two numbers have different signs, the ratio of those two numbers is negative. The curve in panel (b) of Figure 2A-2 has a negative slope: along the curve, an increase in the *x*-variable is associated with a decrease in the *y*-variable.

Figure 2A-3 illustrates how to calculate the slope of a linear curve. Let's focus first on panel (a). From point *A* to point *B* the value of the *y*-variable changes from

FIGURE 2A-3 Calculating the Slope

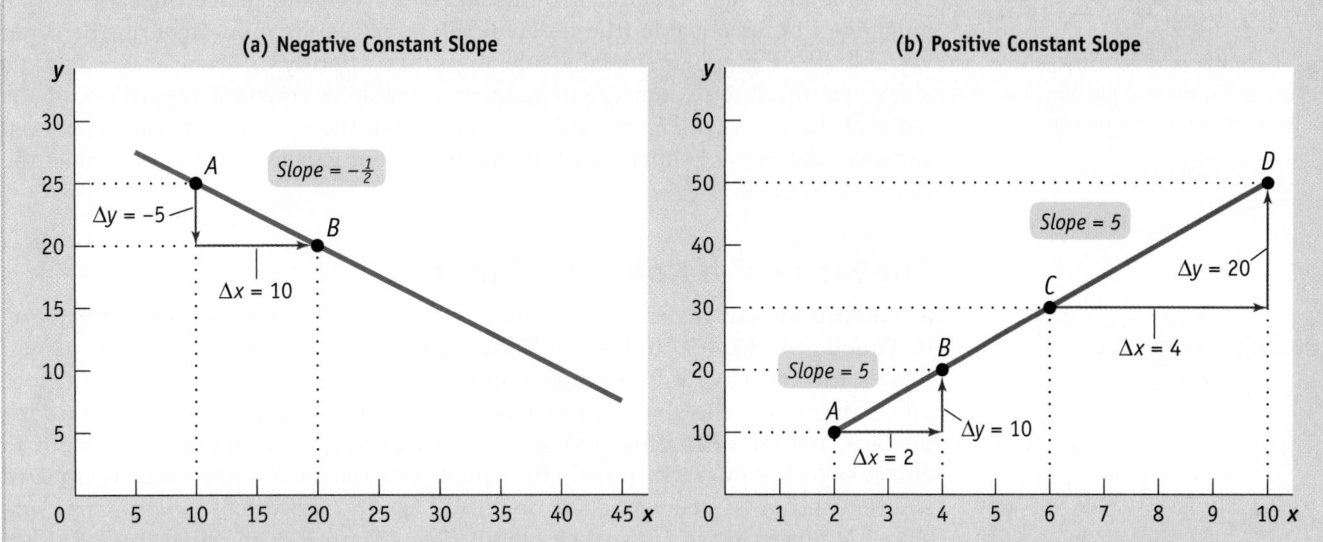

Panels (a) and (b) show two linear curves. Between points *A* and *B* on the curve in panel (a), the change in *y* (the rise) is −5 and the change in *x* (the run) is 10. So the slope from *A* to *B* is $\frac{\Delta y}{\Delta x} = \frac{-5}{10} = -\frac{1}{2} = -0.5$, where the negative sign indicates that the curve is downward sloping. In panel (b), the curve has a slope from *A* to *B* of $\frac{\Delta y}{\Delta x} = \frac{10}{2} = 5$. The slope from *C* to *D* is $\frac{\Delta y}{\Delta x} = \frac{20}{4} = 5$. The slope is positive, indicating that the curve is upward sloping. Furthermore, the slope between *A* and *B* is the same as the slope between *C* and *D*, making this a linear curve. The slope of a linear curve is constant: it is the same regardless of where it is measured along the curve.

25 to 20 and the value of the *x*-variable changes from 10 to 20. So the slope of the line between these two points is:

$$\frac{\text{Change in } y}{\text{Change in } x} = \frac{\Delta y}{\Delta x} = \frac{-5}{10} = -\frac{1}{2} = -0.5$$

Because a straight line is equally steep at all points, the slope of a straight line is the same at all points. In other words, a straight line has a constant slope. You can check this by calculating the slope of the linear curve between points *A* and *B* and between points *C* and *D* in panel (b) of Figure 2A-3.

Between *A* and *B*: $\frac{\Delta y}{\Delta x} = \frac{10}{2} = 5$

Between *C* and *D*: $\frac{\Delta y}{\Delta x} = \frac{20}{4} = 5$

Horizontal and Vertical Curves and Their Slopes

When a curve is horizontal, the value of the *y*-variable along that curve never changes—it is constant. Everywhere along the curve, the change in *y* is zero. Now, zero divided by any number is zero. So, regardless of the value of the change in *x*, the slope of a horizontal curve is always zero.

If a curve is vertical, the value of the *x*-variable along the curve never changes—it is constant. Everywhere along the curve, the change in *x* is zero. This means that the slope of a vertical curve is a ratio with zero in the denominator. A ratio with zero in the denominator is equal to infinity—that is, an infinitely large number. So the slope of a vertical curve is equal to infinity.

A **nonlinear curve** is one in which the slope is not the same between every pair of points.

The **absolute value** of a negative number is the value of the negative number without the minus sign.

A vertical or a horizontal curve has a special implication: it means that the x-variable and the y-variable are unrelated. Two variables are unrelated when a change in one variable (the independent variable) has no effect on the other variable (the dependent variable). Or to put it a slightly different way, two variables are unrelated when the dependent variable is constant regardless of the value of the independent variable. If, as is usual, the y-variable is the dependent variable, the curve is horizontal. If the dependent variable is the x-variable, the curve is vertical.

The Slope of a Nonlinear Curve

A **nonlinear curve** is one in which the slope changes as you move along it. Panels (a), (b), (c), and (d) of Figure 2A-4 show various nonlinear curves. Panels (a) and (b) show nonlinear curves whose slopes change as you move along them, but the slopes always remain positive. Although both curves tilt upward, the curve in panel (a) gets steeper as you move from left to right in contrast to the curve in panel (b), which gets flatter. A curve that is upward sloping and gets steeper, as in panel (a), is said to have *positive increasing* slope. A curve that is upward sloping but gets flatter, as in panel (b), is said to have *positive decreasing* slope.

When we calculate the slope along these nonlinear curves, we obtain different values for the slope at different points. How the slope changes along the curve determines the curve's shape. For example, in panel (a) of Figure 2A-4, the slope of the curve is a positive number that steadily increases as you move from left to right, whereas in panel (b), the slope is a positive number that steadily decreases.

The slopes of the curves in panels (c) and (d) are negative numbers. Economists often prefer to express a negative number as its **absolute value,** which is the value of the negative number without the minus sign. In general, we denote the absolute value of a number by two parallel bars around the number; for example, the absolute value of −4 is written as $|-4| = 4$. In panel (c), the absolute value of the slope steadily increases as you move from left to right. The curve therefore has *negative increasing* slope. And in panel (d), the absolute value of the slope of the curve steadily decreases along the curve. This curve therefore has *negative decreasing* slope.

Calculating the Slope Along a Nonlinear Curve

We've just seen that along a nonlinear curve, the value of the slope depends on where you are on that curve. So how do you calculate the slope of a nonlinear curve? We will focus on two methods: the *arc method* and the *point method.*

The Arc Method of Calculating the Slope An arc of a curve is some piece or segment of that curve. For example, panel (a) of Figure 2A-4 shows an arc consisting of the segment of the curve between points A and B. To calculate the slope along a nonlinear curve using the arc method, you draw a straight line between the two end-points of the arc. The slope of that straight line is a measure of the average slope of the curve between those two end-points. You can see from panel (a) of Figure 2A-4 that the straight line drawn between points A and B increases along the x-axis from 6 to 10 (so that $\Delta x = 4$) as it increases along the y-axis from 10 to 20 (so that $\Delta y = 10$). Therefore the slope of the straight line connecting points A and B is:

$$\frac{\Delta y}{\Delta x} = \frac{10}{4} = 2.5$$

This means that the average slope of the curve between points A and B is 2.5.

FIGURE 2A-4 Nonlinear Curves

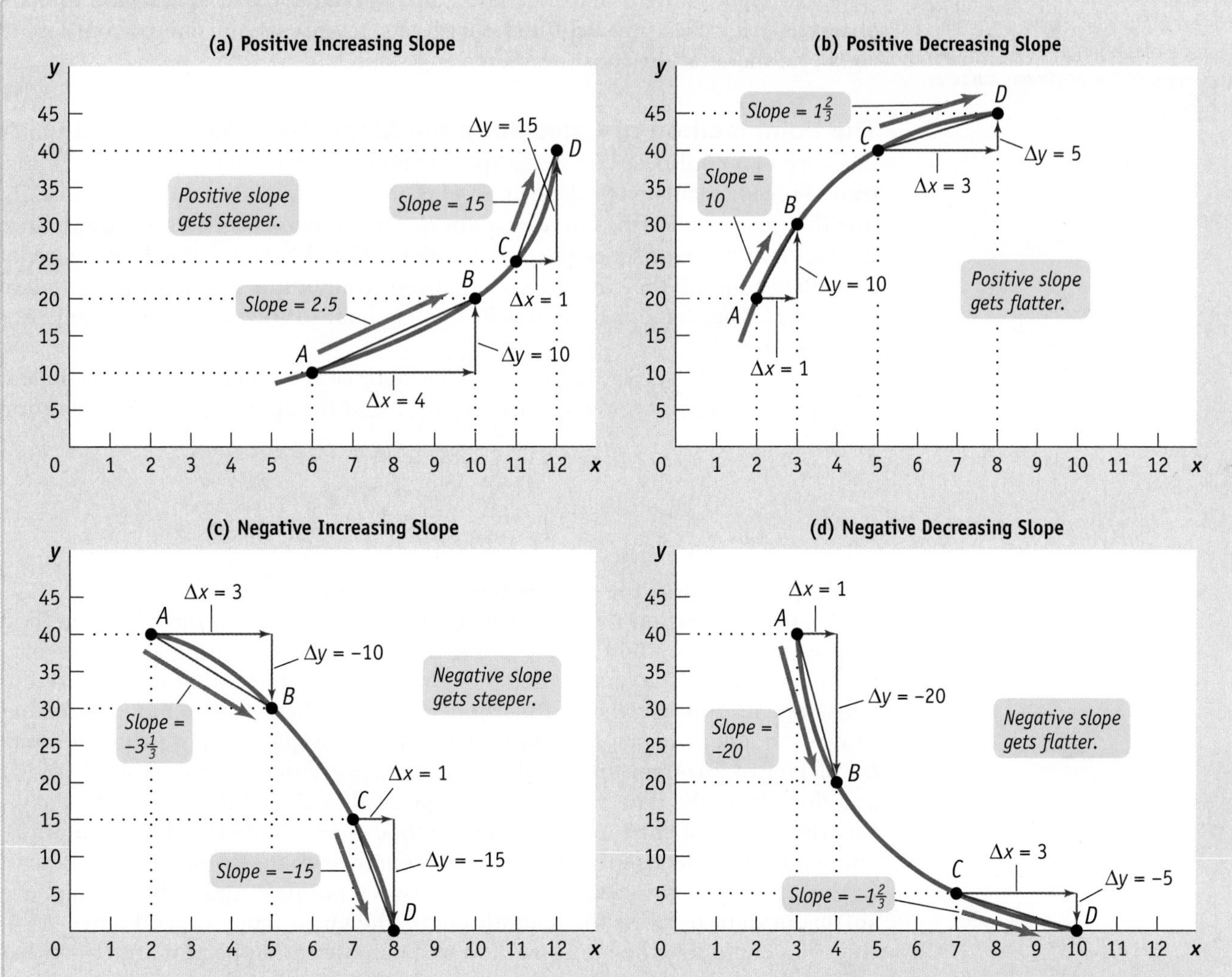

In panel (a) the slope of the curve from A to B is $\frac{y}{x} = \frac{10}{4} = 2.5$, and from C to D it is $\frac{\Delta y}{\Delta x} = \frac{15}{1} = 15$. The slope is positive and increasing; the curve gets steeper as you move to the right. In panel (b) the slope of the curve from A to B is $\frac{\Delta y}{\Delta x} = \frac{10}{1} = 10$, and from C to D it is $\frac{\Delta y}{\Delta x} = \frac{5}{3} = 1\frac{2}{3}$. The slope is positive and decreasing; the curve gets flatter as you move to the right. In panel (c) the slope from A to B is $\frac{\Delta y}{\Delta x} = \frac{-10}{3} = -3\frac{1}{3}$, and from C to D it is $\frac{\Delta y}{\Delta x} = \frac{-15}{1} = -15$. The slope is negative and increasing; the curve gets steeper as you move to the right. And in panel (d) the slope from A to B is $\frac{\Delta y}{\Delta x} = \frac{-20}{1} = -20$, and from C to D it is $\frac{\Delta y}{\Delta x} = \frac{-5}{3} = -1\frac{2}{3}$. The slope is negative and decreasing; the curve gets flatter as you move to the right. The slope in each case has been calculated by using the arc method—that is, by drawing a straight line connecting two points along a curve. The average slope between those two points is equal to the slope of the straight line between those two points.

Now consider the arc on the same curve between points C and D. A straight line drawn through these two points increases along the x-axis from 11 to 12 ($\Delta x = 1$) as it increases along the y-axis from 25 to 40 ($\Delta y = 15$). So the average slope between points C and D is:

$$\frac{\Delta y}{\Delta x} = \frac{15}{1} = 15$$

A **tangent line** is a straight line that just touches, or is tangent to, a nonlinear curve at a particular point. The slope of the tangent line is equal to the slope of the nonlinear curve at that point.

Therefore the average slope between points C and D is larger than the average slope between points A and B. These calculations verify what we have already observed—that this upward-tilted curve gets steeper as you move from left to right and therefore has positive increasing slope.

The Point Method of Calculating the Slope The point method calculates the slope of a nonlinear curve at a specific point on that curve. Figure 2A-5 illustrates how to calculate the slope at point B on the curve. First, we draw a straight line that just touches the curve at point B. Such a line is called a **tangent line:** the fact that it just touches the curve at point B and does not touch the curve at any other point on the curve means that the straight line is *tangent* to the curve at point B. The slope of this tangent line is equal to the slope of the nonlinear curve at point B.

You can see from Figure 2A-5 how the slope of the tangent line is calculated: from point A to point C, the change in y is 15 and the change in x is 5, generating a slope of:

$$\frac{\Delta y}{\Delta x} = \frac{15}{5} = 3$$

By the point method, the slope of the curve at point B is equal to 3.

A natural question to ask at this point is how to determine which method to use—the arc method or the point method—in calculating the slope of a nonlinear curve. The answer depends on the curve itself and the data used to construct it. You use the arc method when you don't have enough information to be able to draw a smooth curve. For example, suppose that in panel (a) of Figure 2A-4 you have only the data represented by points A, C, and D and don't have the data represented by point B or any of the rest of the curve. Clearly, then, you can't use the point method to calculate the slope at point B; you would have to use the arc method to approximate the slope of the curve in this area by drawing a straight line between points A and C. But if you have sufficient data to draw the smooth curve shown in panel (a) of Figure 2A-4, then you could use the point method to calculate the slope at point B—and at every other point along the curve as well.

FIGURE **2A-5** Calculating the Slope Using the Point Method

Here a tangent line has been drawn, a line that just touches the curve at point B. The slope of this line is equal to the slope of the curve at point B. The slope of the tangent line, measuring from A to C, is $\frac{\Delta y}{\Delta x} = \frac{15}{5} = 3$.

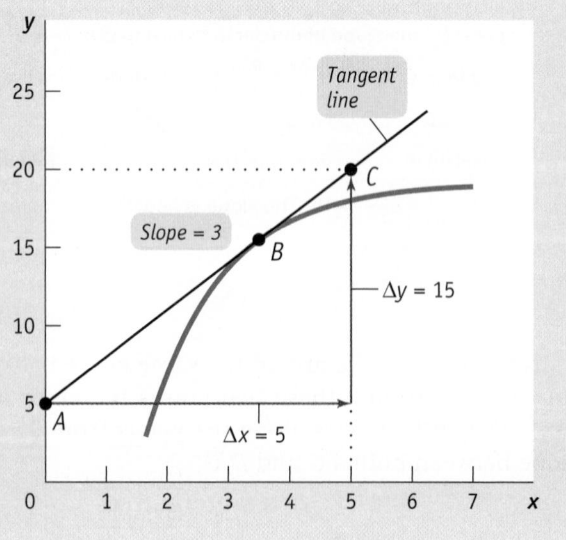

Maximum and Minimum Points

A nonlinear curve may have a **maximum** point, the highest point along the curve. At the maximum, the slope of the curve changes from positive to negative.

A nonlinear curve may have a **minimum** point, the lowest point along the curve. At the minimum, the slope of the curve changes from negative to positive.

The slope of a nonlinear curve can change from positive to negative or vice versa. When the slope of a curve changes from positive to negative, it creates what is called a *maximum* point of the curve. When the slope of a curve changes from negative to positive, it creates a *minimum* point.

Panel (a) of Figure 2A-6 illustrates a curve in which the slope changes from positive to negative as you move from left to right. When x is between 0 and 50, the slope of the curve is positive. At x equal to 50, the curve attains its highest point—the largest value of y along the curve. This point is called the **maximum** of the curve. When x exceeds 50, the slope becomes negative as the curve turns downward. Many important curves in economics, such as the curve that represents how the profit of a firm changes as it produces more output, are hill-shaped like this.

FIGURE 2A-6 Maximum and Minimum Points

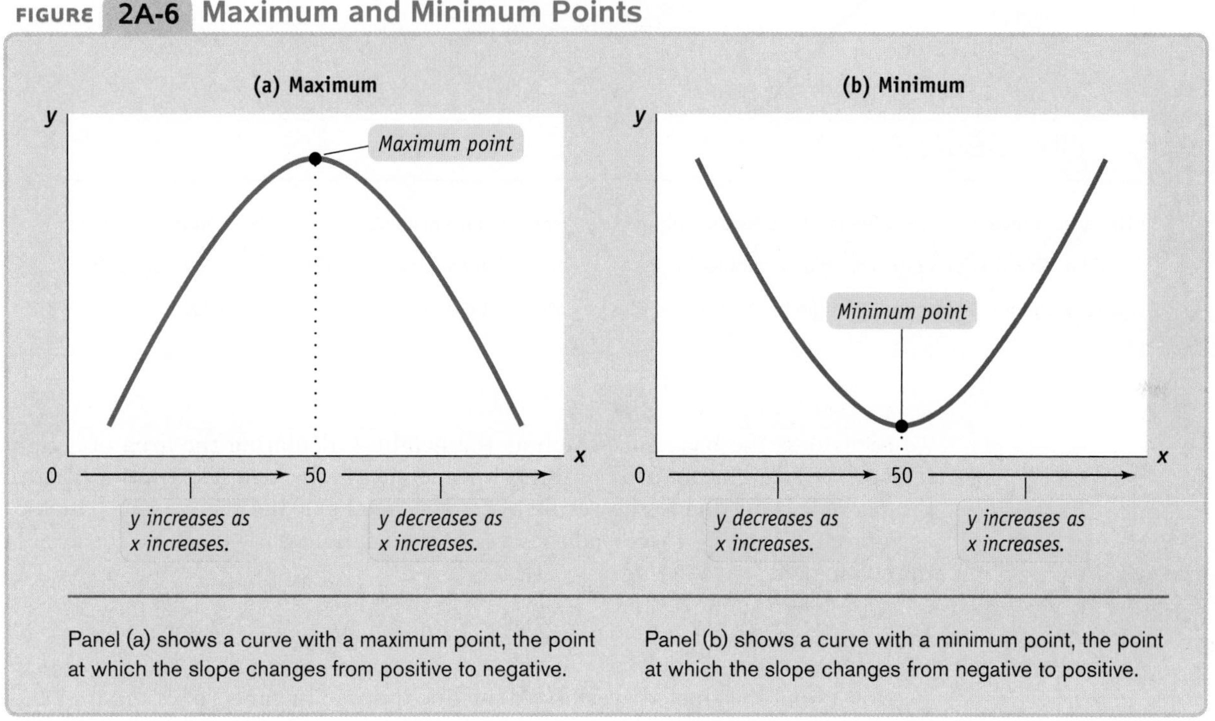

Panel (a) shows a curve with a maximum point, the point at which the slope changes from positive to negative.

Panel (b) shows a curve with a minimum point, the point at which the slope changes from negative to positive.

In contrast, the curve shown in panel (b) of Figure 2A-6 is U-shaped: it has a slope that changes from negative to positive. At x equal to 50, the curve reaches its lowest point—the smallest value of y along the curve. This point is called the **minimum** of the curve. Various important curves in economics, such as the curve that represents how per-unit the costs of some firms change as output increases, are U-shaped like this.

Calculating the Area Below or Above a Curve

Sometimes it is useful to be able to measure the size of the area below or above a curve. To keep things simple, we'll only calculate the area below or above a linear curve.

How large is the shaded area below the linear curve in panel (a) of Figure 2A-7? First note that this area has the shape of a right triangle. A right triangle is a triangle that has two sides that make a right angle with each other. We will refer to one of these sides as the *height* of the triangle and the other side as the *base* of the triangle. For our purposes, it doesn't matter which of these two sides

FIGURE 2A-7 Calculating the Area Below and Above a Linear Curve

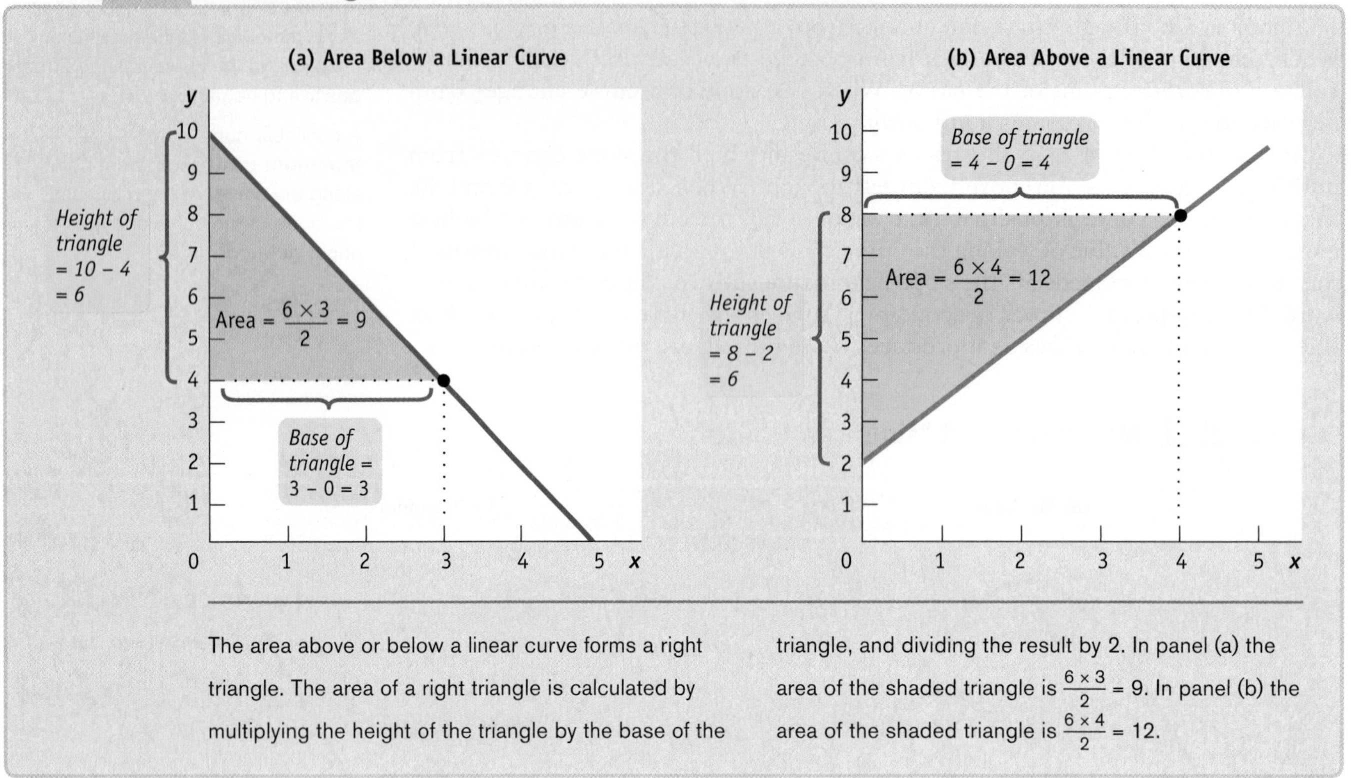

The area above or below a linear curve forms a right triangle. The area of a right triangle is calculated by multiplying the height of the triangle by the base of the triangle, and dividing the result by 2. In panel (a) the area of the shaded triangle is $\frac{6 \times 3}{2} = 9$. In panel (b) the area of the shaded triangle is $\frac{6 \times 4}{2} = 12$.

we refer to as the base and which as the height. Calculating the area of a right triangle is straightforward: multiply the height of the triangle by the base of the triangle, and divide the result by 2. The height of the triangle in panel (a) of Figure 2A-7 is 10 – 4 = 6. And the base of the triangle is 3 – 0 = 3. So the area of that triangle is

$$\frac{6 \times 3}{2} = 9$$

How about the shaded area above the linear curve in panel (b) of Figure 2A-7? We can use the same formula to calculate the area of this right triangle. The height of the triangle is 8 – 2 = 6. And the base of the triangle is 4 – 0 = 4. So the area of that triangle is

$$\frac{6 \times 4}{2} = 12$$

Graphs That Depict Numerical Information

Graphs can also be used as a convenient way to summarize and display data without assuming some underlying causal relationship. Graphs that simply display numerical information are called *numerical graphs*. Here we will consider four types of numerical graphs: *time-series graphs, scatter diagrams, pie charts,* and *bar graphs.* These are widely used to display real, empirical data about different economic variables because they often help economists and policy makers identify patterns or trends in the economy. But as we will also see, you must be careful not to misinterpret or draw unwarranted conclusions from numerical graphs. That is, you must be aware of both the usefulness and the limitations of numerical graphs.

FIGURE 2A-8 Time-Series Graph

Time-series graphs show successive dates on the *x*-axis and values for a variable on the *y*-axis. This time-series graph shows real gross domestic product per capita, a measure of a country's standard of living, in the United States from 1947 to late 2010.

Source: Bureau of Economic Analysis.

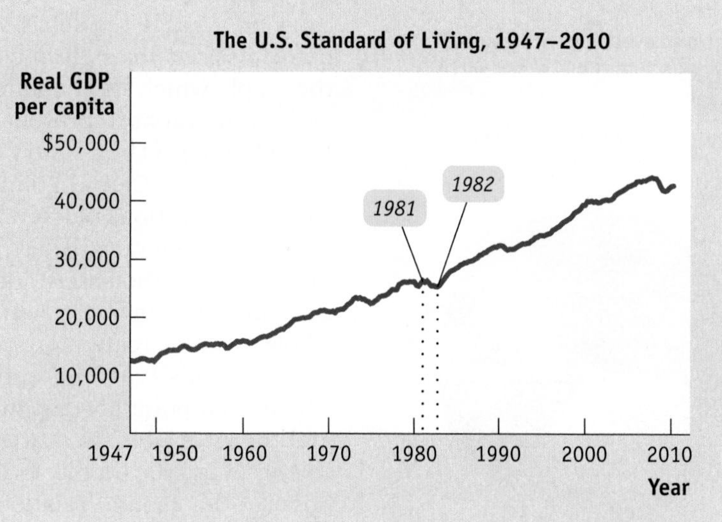

Types of Numerical Graphs

A **time-series graph** has dates on the horizontal axis and values of a variable that occurred on those dates on the vertical axis.

You have probably seen graphs in newspapers that show what has happened over time to economic variables such as the unemployment rate or stock prices. A **time-series graph** has successive dates on the horizontal axis and the values of a variable that occurred on those dates on the vertical axis. For example, Figure 2A-8 shows real gross domestic product (GDP) per capita—a rough measure of a country's standard of living—in the United States from 1947 to late 2010. A line connecting the points that correspond to real GDP per capita for each calendar quarter during those years gives a clear idea of the overall trend in the standard of living over these years.

Figure 2A-9 is an example of a different kind of numerical graph. It represents information from a sample of 184 countries on the standard of living,

FIGURE 2A-9 Scatter Diagram

In a scatter diagram, each point represents the corresponding values of the *x*- and *y*-variables for a given observation. Here, each point indicates the GDP per capita and the amount of carbon emissions per capita for a given country for a sample of 184 countries. The upward-sloping fitted line here is the best approximation of the general relationship between the two variables.

Source: World Bank.

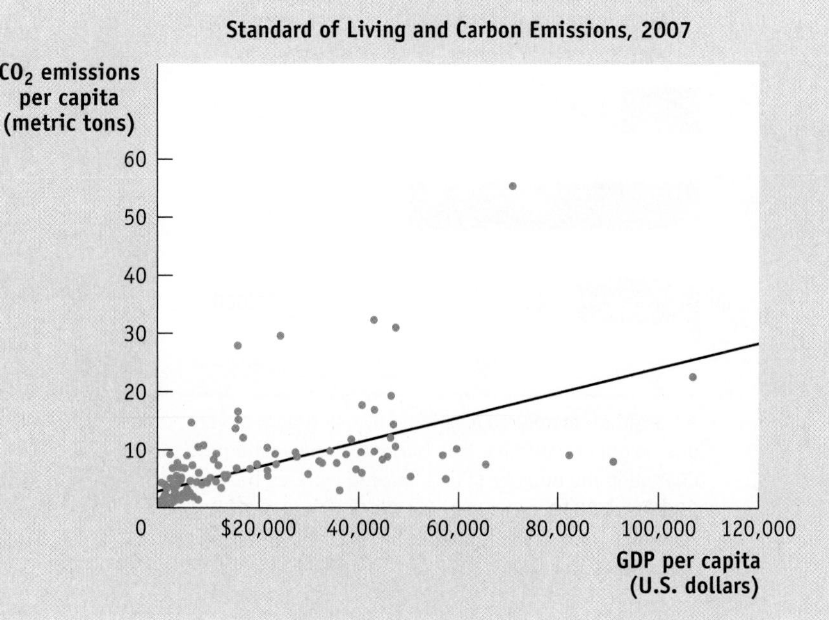

again measured by GDP per capita, and the amount of carbon emissions per capita, a measure of environmental pollution. Each point here indicates an average resident's standard of living and his or her annual carbon emissions for a given country. The points lying in the upper right of the graph, which show combinations of a high standard of living and high carbon emissions, represent economically advanced countries such as the United States. (The country with the highest carbon emissions, at the top of the graph, is Qatar.) Points lying in the bottom left of the graph, which show combinations of a low standard of living and low carbon emissions, represent economically less advanced countries such as Afghanistan and Sierra Leone. The pattern of points indicates that there is a positive relationship between living standard and carbon emissions per capita: on the whole, people create more pollution in countries with a higher standard of living. This type of graph is called a **scatter diagram,** a diagram in which each point corresponds to an actual observation of the x-variable and the y-variable. In scatter diagrams, a curve is typically fitted to the scatter of points; that is, a curve is drawn that approximates as closely as possible the general relationship between the variables. As you can see, the fitted line in Figure 2A-9 is upward sloping, indicating the underlying positive relationship between the two variables. Scatter diagrams are often used to show how a general relationship can be inferred from a set of data.

A **pie chart** shows the share of a total amount that is accounted for by various components, usually expressed in percentages. For example, Figure 2A-10 is a pie chart that depicts the education levels of workers who in 2011 were paid the federal minimum wage or less. As you can see, the majority of workers paid at or below the minimum wage had no college degree. Only 7% of workers who were paid at or below the minimum wage had a bachelor's degree or higher.

Bar graphs use bars of various heights or lengths to indicate values of a variable. In the bar graph in Figure 2A-11, the bars show the percent change in the number of unemployed workers in the United States from 2009 to 2010, separately for White, Black or African-American, and Asian workers. Exact values of the variable that is being measured may be written at the end of the bar, as in this figure. For instance, the number of unemployed Black or African-American workers in the United States increased by 9.4% between 2009 and 2010. But even without the precise values, comparing the heights or lengths of the bars can give useful insight into the relative magnitudes of the different values of the variable.

FIGURE 2A-10 Pie Chart

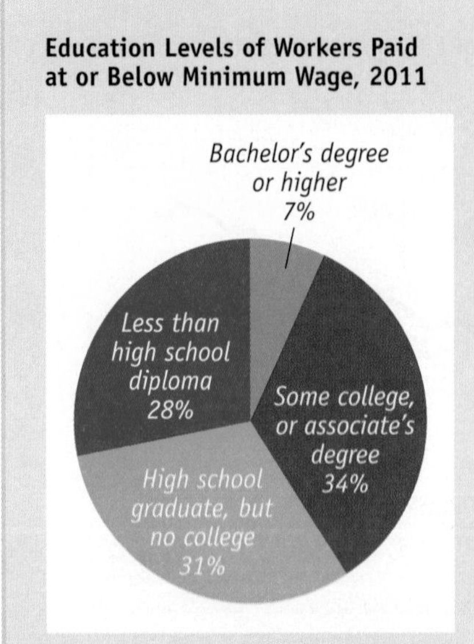

A pie chart shows the percentages of a total amount that can be attributed to various components. This pie chart shows the percentages of workers with given education levels who were paid at or below the federal minimum wage in 2011.
Source: Bureau of Labor Statistics.

FIGURE 2A-11 Bar Graph

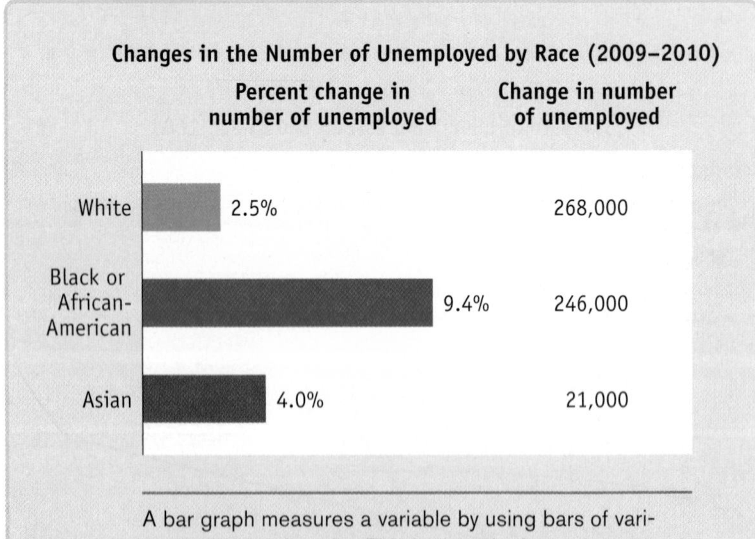

A bar graph measures a variable by using bars of various heights or lengths. This bar graph shows the percent change in the number of unemployed workers between 2009 and 2010, separately for White, Black or African-American, and Asian workers.
Source: Bureau of Labor Statistics.

Problems in Interpreting Numerical Graphs

Although the beginning of this appendix emphasized that graphs are visual images that make ideas or information easier to understand, graphs can be constructed (intentionally or unintentionally) in ways that are misleading and can lead to inaccurate conclusions. This section raises some issues that you should be aware of when you interpret graphs.

Features of Construction Before drawing any conclusions about what a numerical graph implies, you should pay attention to the scale, or size of increments, shown on the axes. Small increments tend to visually exaggerate changes in the variables, whereas large increments tend to visually diminish them. So the scale used in construction of a graph can influence your interpretation of the significance of the changes it illustrates—perhaps in an unwarranted way.

Take, for example, Figure 2A-12, which shows real GDP per capita in the United States from 1981 to 1982 using increments of $500. You can see that real GDP per capita fell from $26,208 to $25,189. A decrease, sure, but is it as enormous as the scale chosen for the vertical axis makes it seem? If you go back and reexamine Figure 2A-8, which shows real GDP per capita in the United States from 1947 to late 2010, you can see that this would be a misguided conclusion. Figure 2A-8 includes the same data shown in Figure 2A-12, but it is constructed with a scale having increments of $10,000 rather than $500. From it you can see that the fall in real GDP per capita from 1981 to 1982 was, in fact, relatively insignificant. In fact, the story of real GDP per capita in the United States is mostly a story of ups, not downs. This comparison shows that if you are not careful to factor in the choice of scale in interpreting a graph, you can arrive at very different, and possibly misguided, conclusions.

Related to the choice of scale is the use of *truncation* in constructing a graph. An axis is **truncated** when part of the range is omitted. This is indicated by two slashes (//) in the axis near the origin. You can see that the vertical axis of Figure 2A-12 has been truncated—some of the range of values from 0 to $25,000 have been omitted and a // appears in the axis. Truncation saves space in the presentation of a graph and allows smaller increments to be used in constructing it. As a result, changes in the variable depicted on a graph that has been truncated appear larger compared to a graph that has not been truncated and that uses larger increments.

You must also pay close attention to exactly what a graph is illustrating. For example, in Figure 2A-11, you should recognize that what is being shown here are percentage changes in the number of unemployed, not numerical changes. The unemployment rate for Black or African-American workers increased by the highest percentage, 9.4% in this example. If you confused numerical changes with percentage changes, you would erroneously conclude that the greatest number of newly unemployed workers were Black or African-American. But, in fact, a correct interpretation of Figure 2A-11 shows that the greatest number of newly unemployed workers were White: the total number of unemployed White

A **scatter diagram** shows points that correspond to actual observations of the *x*- and *y*-variables. A curve is usually fitted to the scatter of points.

A **pie chart** shows how some total is divided among its components, usually expressed in percentages.

A **bar graph** uses bars of varying height or length to show the comparative sizes of different observations of a variable.

An axis is **truncated** when some of the values on the axis are omitted, usually to save space.

FIGURE 2A-12 Interpreting Graphs: The Effect of Scale

Some of the same data for the years 1981 and 1982 used in Figure 2A-8 are represented here, except that here they are shown using increments of $500 rather than increments of $10,000. As a result of this change in scale, changes in the standard of living look much larger in this figure compared to Figure 2A-8.
Source: Bureau of Labor Statistics.

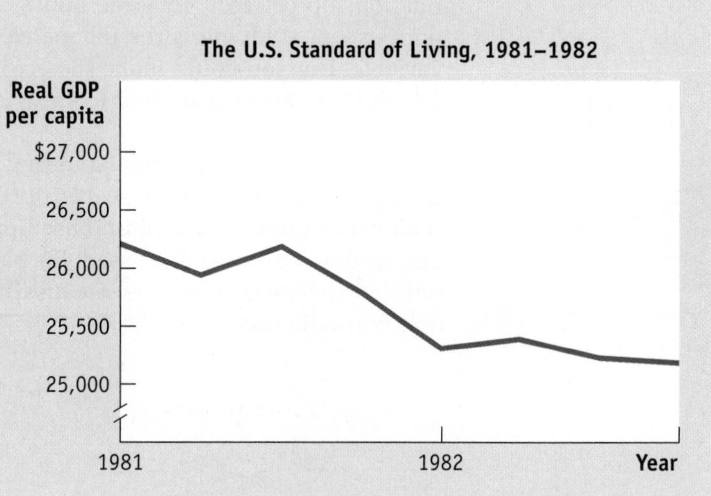

An **omitted variable** is an unobserved variable that, through its influence on other variables, creates the erroneous appearance of a direct causal relationship among those variables.

The error of **reverse causality** is committed when the true direction of causality between two variables is reversed.

workers grew by 268,000 workers, which is greater than the increase in the number of unemployed Black or African-American workers, which is 246,000 in this example. Although there was a higher percentage increase in the number of unemployed Black or African-American workers, the number of unemployed Black or African-American workers in the United States in 2009 was smaller than the number of unemployed White workers, leading to a smaller number of newly unemployed Black or African-American workers than White workers.

Omitted Variables From a scatter diagram that shows two variables moving either positively or negatively in relation to each other, it is easy to conclude that there is a causal relationship. But relationships between two variables are not always due to direct cause and effect. Quite possibly an observed relationship between two variables is due to the *unobserved* effect of a third variable on each of the other two variables. An unobserved variable that, through its influence on other variables, creates the erroneous appearance of a direct causal relationship among those variables is called an **omitted variable.** For example, in New England, a greater amount of snowfall during a given week will typically cause people to buy more snow shovels. It will also cause people to buy more de-icer fluid. But if you omitted the influence of the snowfall and simply plotted the number of snow shovels sold versus the number of bottles of de-icer fluid sold, you would produce a scatter diagram that showed an upward tilt in the pattern of points, indicating a positive relationship between snow shovels sold and de-icer fluid sold. To attribute a causal relationship between these two variables, however, is misguided; more snow shovels sold do not cause more de-icer fluid to be sold, or vice versa. They move together because they are both influenced by a third, determining, variable—the weekly snowfall, which is the omitted variable in this case. So before assuming that a pattern in a scatter diagram implies a cause-and-effect relationship, it is important to consider whether the pattern is instead the result of an omitted variable. Or to put it succinctly: correlation is not causation.

Reverse Causality Even when you are confident that there is no omitted variable and that there is a causal relationship between two variables shown in a numerical graph, you must also be careful that you don't make the mistake of **reverse causality**—coming to an erroneous conclusion about which is the dependent and which is the independent variable by reversing the true direction of causality between the two variables. For example, imagine a scatter diagram that depicts the grade point averages (GPAs) of 20 of your classmates on one axis and the number of hours that each of them spends studying on the other. A line fitted between the points will probably have a positive slope, showing a positive relationship between GPA and hours of studying. We could reasonably infer that hours spent studying is the independent variable and that GPA is the dependent variable. But you could make the error of reverse causality: you could infer that a high GPA causes a student to study more, whereas a low GPA causes a student to study less.

The significance of understanding how graphs can mislead or be incorrectly interpreted is not purely academic. Policy decisions, business decisions, and political arguments are often based on interpretation of the types of numerical graphs that we've just discussed. Problems of misleading features of construction, omitted variables, and reverse causality can lead to very important and undesirable consequences.

PROBLEMS

1. Study the four accompanying diagrams. Consider the following statements and indicate which diagram matches each statement. Which variable would appear on the horizontal and which on the vertical axis? In each of these statements, is the slope positive, negative, zero, or infinity?

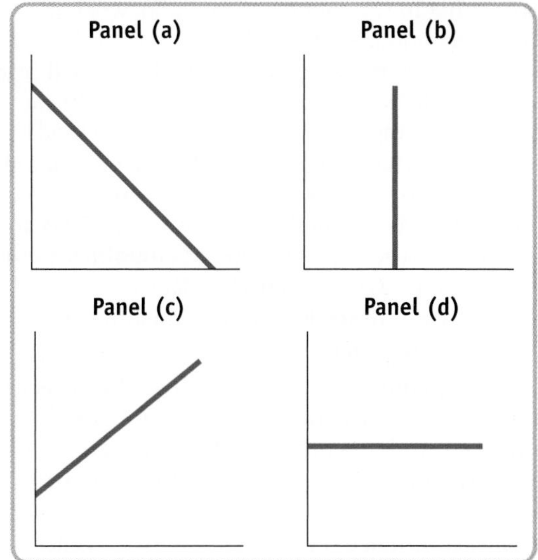

   a. If the price of movies increases, fewer consumers go to see movies.

   b. More experienced workers typically have higher incomes than less experienced workers.

   c. Whatever the temperature outside, Americans consume the same number of hot dogs per day.

   d. Consumers buy more frozen yogurt when the price of ice cream goes up.

   e. Research finds no relationship between the number of diet books purchased and the number of pounds lost by the average dieter.

   f. Regardless of its price, Americans buy the same quantity of salt.

2. During the Reagan administration, economist Arthur Laffer argued in favor of lowering income tax rates in order to increase tax revenues. Like most economists, he believed that at tax rates above a certain level, tax revenue would fall because high taxes would discourage some people from working and that people would refuse to work at all if they received no income after paying taxes. This relationship between tax rates and tax revenue is graphically summarized in what is widely known as the Laffer curve. Plot the Laffer curve relationship assuming that it has the shape of a nonlinear curve. The following questions will help you construct the graph.

   a. Which is the independent variable? Which is the dependent variable? On which axis do you therefore measure the income tax rate? On which axis do you measure income tax revenue?

   b. What would tax revenue be at a 0% income tax rate?

   c. The maximum possible income tax rate is 100%. What would tax revenue be at a 100% income tax rate?

   d. Estimates now show that the maximum point on the Laffer curve is (approximately) at a tax rate of 80%. For tax rates less than 80%, how would you describe the relationship between the tax rate and tax revenue, and how is this relationship reflected in the slope? For tax rates higher than 80%, how would you describe the relationship between the tax rate and tax revenue, and how is this relationship reflected in the slope?

3. In the accompanying figures, the numbers on the axes have been lost. All you know is that the units shown on the vertical axis are the same as the units on the horizontal axis.

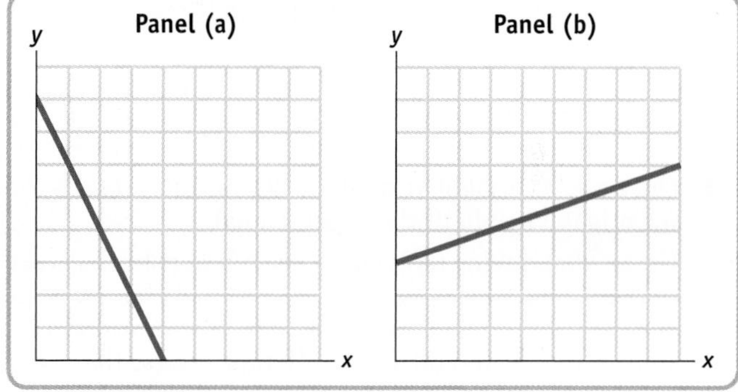

   a. In panel (a), what is the slope of the line? Show that the slope is constant along the line.

   b. In panel (b), what is the slope of the line? Show that the slope is constant along the line.

4. Answer each of the following questions by drawing a schematic diagram.

   a. Taking measurements of the slope of a curve at three points farther and farther to the right along the horizontal axis, the slope of the curve changes from –0.3, to –0.8, to –2.5, measured by the point method. Draw a schematic diagram of this curve. How would you describe the relationship illustrated in your diagram?

   b. Taking measurements of the slope of a curve at five points farther and farther to the right along the horizontal axis, the slope of the curve changes from 1.5, to 0.5, to 0, to –0.5, to –1.5, measured by the point method. Draw a schematic diagram of this curve. Does it have a maximum or a minimum?

5. For each of the accompanying diagrams, calculate the area of the shaded right triangle.

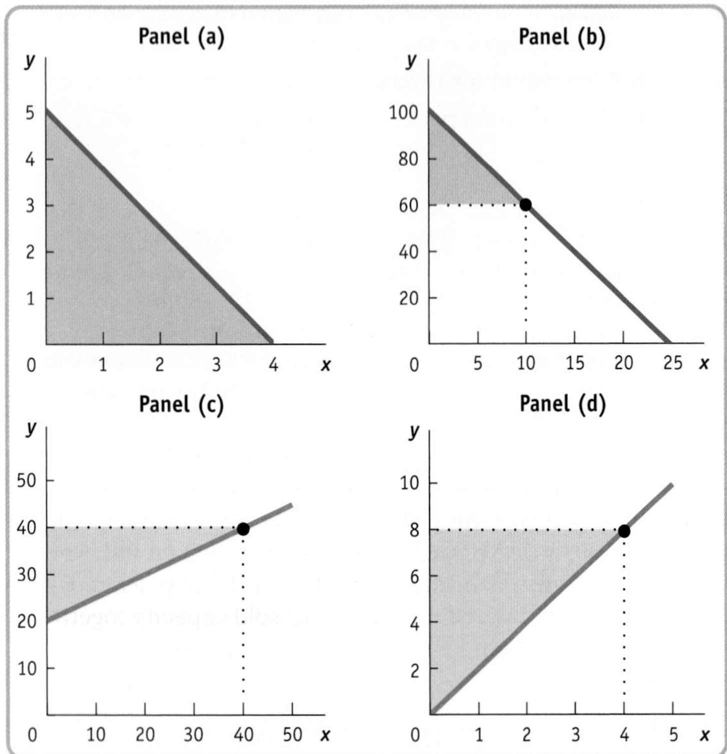

6. The base of a right triangle is 10, and its area is 20. What is the height of this right triangle?

7. The accompanying table shows the relationship between workers' hours of work per week and their hourly wage rate. Apart from the fact that they receive a different hourly wage rate and work different hours, these five workers are otherwise identical.

Name	Quantity of labor (hours per week)	Wage rate (per hour)
Athena	30	$15
Boris	35	30
Curt	37	45
Diego	36	60
Emily	32	75

a. Which variable is the independent variable? Which is the dependent variable?

b. Draw a scatter diagram illustrating this relationship. Draw a (nonlinear) curve that connects the points. Put the hourly wage rate on the vertical axis.

c. As the wage rate increases from $15 to $30, how does the number of hours worked respond according to the relationship depicted here? What is the average slope of the curve between Athena's and Boris's data points using the arc method?

d. As the wage rate increases from $60 to $75, how does the number of hours worked respond according to the relationship depicted here? What is the average slope of the curve between Diego's and Emily's data points using the arc method?

8. Studies have found a relationship between a country's yearly rate of economic growth and the yearly rate of increase in airborne pollutants. It is believed that a higher rate of economic growth allows a country's residents to have more cars and travel more, thereby releasing more airborne pollutants.

a. Which variable is the independent variable? Which is the dependent variable?

b. Suppose that in the country of Sudland, when the yearly rate of economic growth fell from 3.0% to 1.5%, the yearly rate of increase in airborne pollutants fell from 6% to 5%. What is the average slope of a nonlinear curve between these points using the arc method?

c. Now suppose that when the yearly rate of economic growth rose from 3.5% to 4.5%, the yearly rate of increase in airborne pollutants rose from 5.5% to 7.5%. What is the average slope of a nonlinear curve between these two points using the arc method?

d. How would you describe the relationship between the two variables here?

9. An insurance company has found that the severity of property damage in a fire is positively related to the number of firefighters arriving at the scene.

a. Draw a diagram that depicts this finding with number of firefighters on the horizontal axis and amount of property damage on the vertical axis. What is the argument made by this diagram? Suppose you reverse what is measured on the two axes. What is the argument made then?

b. In order to reduce its payouts to policyholders, should the insurance company therefore ask the city to send fewer firefighters to any fire?

10. The accompanying table illustrates annual salaries and income tax owed by five individuals. Apart from the fact that they receive different salaries and owe different amounts of income tax, these five individuals are otherwise identical.

Name	Annual salary	Annual income tax owed
Susan	$22,000	$3,304
Eduardo	63,000	14,317
John	3,000	454
Camila	94,000	23,927
Peter	37,000	7,020

a. If you were to plot these points on a graph, what would be the average slope of the curve between the points for Eduardo's and Camila's salaries and taxes using the arc method? How would you interpret this value for slope?

b. What is the average slope of the curve between the points for John's and Susan's salaries and taxes using the arc method? How would you interpret that value for slope?

c. What happens to the slope as salary increases? What does this relationship imply about how the level of income taxes affects a person's incentive to earn a higher salary?

BUSINESS CASE • How Priceline.com Revolutionized the Travel Industry

In 2001 and 2002, the travel industry was in deep trouble. After the terrorist attacks of September 11, 2001, many people simply stopped flying. As the economy went into a deep slump, airplanes sat empty on the tarmac and the airlines lost billions of dollars. When several major airlines spiraled toward bankruptcy and laid off 100,000 workers, Congress passed a $15 billion aid package that proved to be critical in stabilizing the airline industry.

This was also a particularly difficult time for Priceline.com, the online travel service. Just four years after its founding, Priceline.com was in danger of going under. The change in the company's fortunes had been dramatic. In 1999, one year after Priceline.com was formed, investors were so impressed by its potential for revolutionizing the travel industry that they valued the company at $9 billion dollars. But by 2002 investors had taken a decidedly dimmer view of the company, reducing its valuation by 95% to only $425 million.

To make matters worse, Priceline.com was losing several million dollars a year. Yet the company managed to survive; as of the time of writing in 2012, it was valued by investors at $31.74 billion. Not only has it survived, it has thrived.

So exactly how did Priceline.com bring such dramatic change to the travel industry? And what has allowed it to survive and prosper as a company in the face of dire economic conditions?

Priceline.com's success lies in its ability to spot exploitable opportunities for itself and its customers. The company understood that when a plane departs with empty seats or a hotel has empty beds, it bears a cost—the revenue that would have been earned if that seat or bed had been filled. And although some travelers like the security of booking their flights and hotels well in advance and are willing to pay for that, others are quite happy to wait until the last minute, risking not getting the flight or hotel they want but enjoying a lower price.

Customers specify the price they are willing to pay for a given trip or hotel location, and then Priceline.com presents them with a list of options from airlines or hotels that are willing to accept that price, with the price typically declining as the date of the trip nears. By bringing airlines and hotels with unsold capacity together with travelers who are willing to sacrifice some of their preferences for a lower price, Priceline.com made everyone better off—including itself, since it charged a small commission for each trade it facilitated.

Priceline.com was also quick on its feet when it saw its market challenged by newcomers Expedia and Orbitz. In response, it began aggressively moving more of its business toward hotel bookings and into Europe, where the online travel industry was still quite small. Its network was particularly valuable in the European hotel market, which is comprised of many more small hotels in comparison to the U.S. market, which is dominated by nationwide chains. The efforts paid off, and by 2003 Priceline.com had turned its first profit.

Priceline.com now operates within a network of more than 100,000 hotels in over 90 countries. As of September 2012, its revenues had grown at least 24% over each of the previous four years, even growing 34% during the 2008 recession.

Clearly, the travel industry will never be the same again.

QUESTION FOR THOUGHT

1. Explain how each of the twelve principles of economics is illustrated in this story.

BUSINESS CASE • Efficiency, Opportunity Cost, and the Logic of Lean Production

Corbis/Photolibrary

In the summer and fall of 2010, workers were rearranging the furniture in Boeing's final assembly plant in Everett, Washington, in preparation for the production of the Boeing 767. It was a difficult and time-consuming process, however, because the items of "furniture"—Boeing's assembly equipment—weighed on the order of 200 tons each. It was a necessary part of setting up a production system based on "lean manufacturing," also called "just-in-time" production. Lean manufacturing, pioneered by Toyota Motors of Japan, is based on the practice of having parts arrive on the factory floor just as they are needed for production. This reduces the amount of parts Boeing holds in inventory as well as the amount of the factory floor needed for production—in this case, reducing the square footage required for manufacture of the 767 by 40%.

Boeing had adopted lean manufacturing in 1999 in the manufacture of the 737, the most popular commercial airplane. By 2005, after constant refinement, Boeing had achieved a 50% reduction in the time it takes to produce a plane and a nearly 60% reduction in parts inventory. An important feature is a continuously moving assembly line, moving products from one assembly team to the next at a steady pace and eliminating the need for workers to wander across the factory floor from task to task or in search of tools and parts.

Toyota's lean production techniques have been the most widely adopted of all manufacturing techniques and have revolutionized manufacturing worldwide. In simple terms, lean production is focused on organization and communication. Workers and parts are organized so as to ensure a smooth and consistent workflow that minimizes wasted effort and materials. Lean production is also designed to be highly responsive to changes in the desired mix of output—for example, quickly producing more sedans and fewer minivans according to changes in customers' demands.

Toyota's lean production methods were so successful that they transformed the global auto industry and severely threatened once-dominant American automakers. Until the 1980s, the "Big Three"—Chrysler, Ford, and General Motors—dominated the American auto industry, with virtually no foreign-made cars sold in the United States. In the 1980s, however, Toyotas became increasingly popular in the United States due to their high quality and relatively low price—so popular that the Big Three eventually prevailed upon the U.S. government to protect them by restricting the sale of Japanese autos in the United States. Over time, Toyota responded by building assembly plants in the United States, bringing along its lean production techniques, which then spread throughout American manufacturing. Toyota's growth continued, and by 2008 it had eclipsed General Motors as the largest automaker in the world.

QUESTIONS FOR THOUGHT

1. What is the opportunity cost associated with having a worker wander across the factory floor from task to task or in search of tools and parts?
2. Explain how lean manufacturing improves the economy's efficiency in allocation.
3. Before lean manufacturing innovations, Japan mostly sold consumer electronics to the United States. How did lean manufacturing innovations alter Japan's comparative advantage vis-à-vis the United States?
4. Predict how the shift in the location of Toyota's production from Japan to the United States is likely to alter the pattern of comparative advantage in automaking between the two countries.

CHAPTER 3

Supply and Demand

BLUE JEAN BLUES

Ciaran Griffin/Thinkstock

How did flood-ravaged cotton crops in Pakistan lead to higher-priced blue jeans and more polyester in T-shirts?

WHAT YOU WILL LEARN IN THIS CHAPTER

- What a **competitive market** is and how it is described by the **supply and demand model**
- What the **demand curve** and the **supply curve** are
- The difference between **movements along a curve** and **shifts of a curve**
- How the supply and demand curves determine a market's **equilibrium price** and **equilibrium quantity**
- In the case of a **shortage** or **surplus**, how price moves the market back to equilibrium

IF YOU BOUGHT A PAIR OF BLUE jeans in 2011, you may have been shocked at the price. Or maybe not: fashions change, and maybe you thought you were paying the price for being fashionable. But you weren't—you were paying for cotton. Jeans are made of denim, which is a particular weave of cotton, and by late 2010, when jeans manufacturers were buying supplies for the coming year, cotton prices were more than triple their level just two years earlier. By December 2010, the price of a pound of cotton had hit a 140-year high, the highest cotton price since records began in 1870.

And why were cotton prices so high?

On one side, demand for clothing of all kinds was surging. In 2008–2009, as the world struggled with the effects of a financial crisis, nervous consumers cut back on clothing purchases. But by 2010, with the worst apparently over, buyers were back in force. On the supply side, severe weather events hit world cotton production. Most notably, Pakistan, the world's fourth-largest cotton producer, was hit by devastating floods that put one-fifth of the country underwater and virtually destroyed its cotton crop.

Fearing that consumers had limited tolerance for large increases in the price of cotton clothing, apparel makers began scrambling to find ways to reduce costs without offending consumers' fashion sense. They adopted changes like smaller buttons, cheaper linings, and—yes—polyester, doubting that consumers would be willing to pay more for cotton goods. In fact, some experts on the cotton market warned that the sky-high prices of cotton in 2010–2011 might lead to a permanent shift in tastes, with consumers becoming more willing to wear synthetics even when cotton prices came down.

At the same time, it was not all bad news for everyone connected with the cotton trade. In the United States, cotton producers had not been hit by bad weather and were relishing the higher prices. American farmers responded to sky-high cotton prices by sharply increasing the acreage devoted to the crop. None of this was enough, however, to produce immediate price relief.

Wait a minute: how, exactly, does flooding in Pakistan translate into higher jeans prices and more polyester in your T-shirts? It's a matter of supply and demand—but what does that mean? Many people use "supply and demand" as a sort of catchphrase to mean "the laws of the marketplace at work." To economists, however, the concept of supply and demand has a precise meaning: it is a *model of how a market behaves* that is extremely useful for understanding many—but not all—markets.

In this chapter, we lay out the pieces that make up the *supply and demand model*, put them together, and show how this model can be used to understand how many—but not all—markets behave.

A **competitive market** is a market in which there are many buyers and sellers of the same good or service, none of whom can influence the price at which the good or service is sold.

The **supply and demand model** is a model of how a competitive market behaves.

Supply and Demand: A Model of a Competitive Market

Cotton sellers and cotton buyers constitute a market—a group of producers and consumers who exchange a good or service for payment. In this chapter, we'll focus on a particular type of market known as a *competitive market*. Roughly, a **competitive market** is a market in which there are many buyers and sellers of the same good or service. More precisely, the key feature of a competitive market is that no individual's actions have a noticeable effect on the price at which the good or service is sold. It's important to understand, however, that this is not an accurate description of every market.

For example, it's not an accurate description of the market for cola beverages. That's because in the market for cola beverages, Coca-Cola and Pepsi account for such a large proportion of total sales that they are able to influence the price at which cola beverages are bought and sold. But it is an accurate description of the market for cotton. The global marketplace for cotton is so huge that even a jeans maker as large as Levi Strauss & Co. accounts for only a tiny fraction of transactions, making it unable to influence the price at which cotton is bought and sold.

It's a little hard to explain why competitive markets are different from other markets until we've seen how a competitive market works. So let's take a rain check—we'll return to that issue at the end of this chapter. For now, let's just say that it's easier to model competitive markets than other markets. When taking an exam, it's always a good strategy to begin by answering the easier questions. In this book, we're going to do the same thing. So we will start with competitive markets.

When a market is competitive, its behavior is well described by the **supply and demand model.** Because many markets are competitive, the supply and demand model is a very useful one indeed.

There are five key elements in this model:

- The *demand curve*
- The *supply curve*
- The set of factors that cause the demand curve to shift and the set of factors that cause the supply curve to shift
- The *market equilibrium*, which includes the *equilibrium price* and *equilibrium quantity*
- The way the market equilibrium changes when the supply curve or demand curve shifts

To understand the supply and demand model, we will examine each of these elements.

The Demand Curve

How many pounds of cotton, packaged in the form of blue jeans, do consumers around the world want to buy in a given year? You might at first think that we can answer this question by looking at the total number of pairs of blue jeans purchased around the world each day, multiply that number by the amount of cotton it takes to make a pair of jeans, and then multiply by 365. But that's not enough to answer the question, because how many pairs of jeans—in other words, how many pounds of cotton—consumers want to buy depends on the price of a pound of cotton.

When the price of cotton rises, as it did in 2010, some people will respond to the higher price of cotton clothing by buying fewer cotton garments or, perhaps, by switching completely to garments made from other materials, such as synthetics or linen. In general, the quantity of cotton clothing, or of any good or service that people want to buy, depends on the price. The higher the price, the less of the good or service people want to purchase; alternatively, the lower the price, the more they want to purchase.

So the answer to the question "How many pounds of cotton do consumers want to buy?" depends on the price of a pound of cotton. If you don't yet know what the price will be, you can start by making a table of how many pounds of cotton people would want to buy at a number of different prices. Such a table is known as a *demand schedule*. This, in turn, can be used to draw a *demand curve*, which is one of the key elements of the supply and demand model.

A **demand schedule** shows how much of a good or service consumers will want to buy at different prices.

The **quantity demanded** is the actual amount of a good or service consumers are willing to buy at some specific price.

The Demand Schedule and the Demand Curve

A **demand schedule** is a table showing how much of a good or service consumers will want to buy at different prices. At the right of Figure 3-1, we show a hypothetical demand schedule for cotton. It's hypothetical in that it doesn't use actual data on the world demand for cotton and it assumes that all cotton is of equal quality.

According to the table, if a pound of cotton costs $1, consumers around the world will want to purchase 10 billion pounds of cotton over the course of a year. If the price is $1.25 a pound, they will want to buy only 8.9 billion pounds; if the price is only $0.75 a pound, they will want to buy 11.5 billion pounds; and so on. The higher the price, the fewer pounds of cotton consumers will want to purchase. So, as the price rises, the **quantity demanded** of cotton—the actual amount consumers are willing to buy at some specific price—falls.

The graph in Figure 3-1 is a visual representation of the information in the table. (You might want to review the discussion of graphs in economics in the appendix to Chapter 2.) The vertical axis shows the price of a pound of cotton and the horizontal axis shows the quantity of cotton in pounds. Each point on the graph corresponds to one of the entries in the table. The curve that connects these points is a

FIGURE 3-1 The Demand Schedule and the Demand Curve

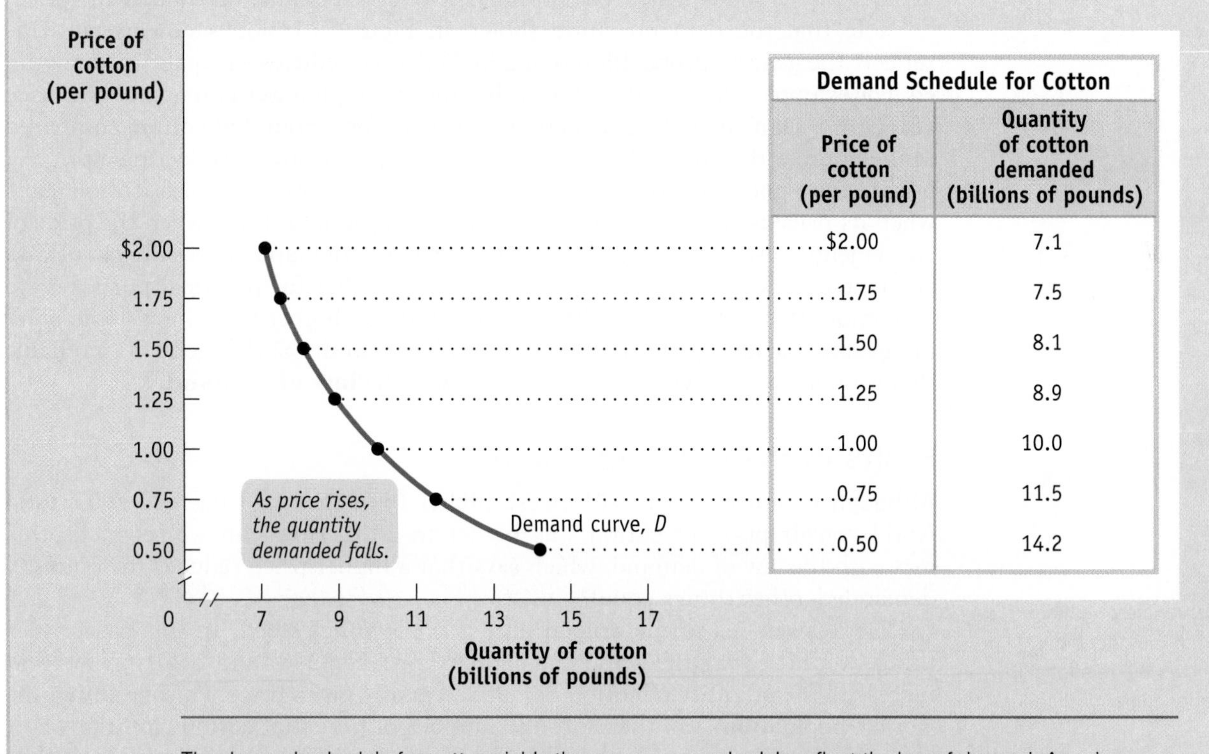

Demand Schedule for Cotton

Price of cotton (per pound)	Quantity of cotton demanded (billions of pounds)
$2.00	7.1
1.75	7.5
1.50	8.1
1.25	8.9
1.00	10.0
0.75	11.5
0.50	14.2

The demand schedule for cotton yields the corresponding demand curve, which shows how much of a good or service consumers want to buy at any given price. The demand curve and the demand schedule reflect the law of demand: As price rises, the quantity demanded falls. Similarly, a fall in price raises the quantity demanded. As a result, the demand curve is downward sloping.

PAY MORE, PUMP LESS

For a real-world illustration of the law of demand, consider how gasoline consumption varies according to the prices consumers pay at the pump. Because of high taxes, gasoline and diesel fuel are more than twice as expensive in most European countries as in the United States. According to the law of demand, this should lead Europeans to buy less gasoline than Americans—and they do. As you can see from the figure, per person, Europeans consume less than half as much fuel as Americans, mainly because they drive smaller cars with better mileage.

Prices aren't the only factor affecting fuel consumption, but they're probably the main cause of the difference between European and American fuel consumption per person.

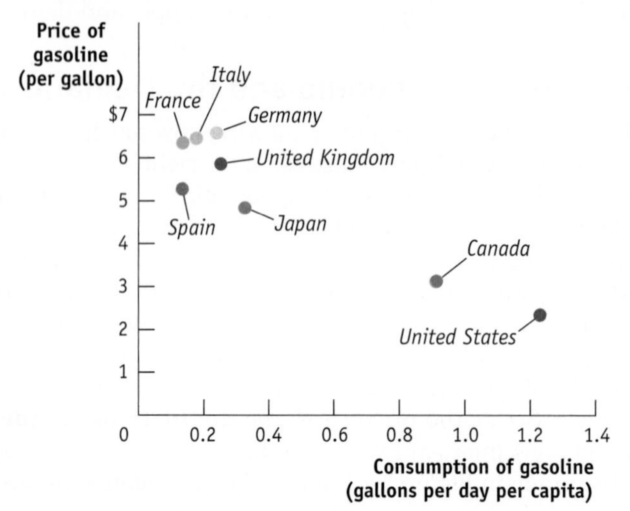

Source: U.S. Energy Information Administration, 2009.

demand curve. A demand curve is a graphical representation of the demand schedule, another way of showing the relationship between the quantity demanded and price.

Note that the demand curve shown in Figure 3-1 slopes downward. This reflects the general proposition that a higher price reduces the quantity demanded. For example, jeans-makers know that they will sell fewer pairs when the price of a pair of jeans is higher, reflecting a $2 price for a pound of cotton, compared to the number they will sell when the price of a pair is lower, reflecting a price of only $1 for a pound of cotton. Similarly, someone who buys a pair of cotton jeans when its price is relatively low will switch to synthetic or linen when the price of cotton jeans is relatively high. So in the real world, demand curves almost always *do* slope downward. (The exceptions are so rare that for practical purposes we can ignore them.) Generally, the proposition that a higher price for a good, *other things equal,* leads people to demand a smaller quantity of that good is so reliable that economists are willing to call it a "law"—the **law of demand.**

A **demand curve** is a graphical representation of the demand schedule. It shows the relationship between quantity demanded and price.

The **law of demand** says that a higher price for a good or service, other things equal, leads people to demand a smaller quantity of that good or service.

Shifts of the Demand Curve

Although cotton prices in 2010 were higher than they had been in 2007, total world consumption of cotton was higher in 2010. How can we reconcile this fact with the law of demand, which says that a higher price reduces the quantity demanded, other things equal?

The answer lies in the crucial phrase *other things equal.* In this case, other things weren't equal: the world had changed between 2007 and 2010, in ways that increased the quantity of cotton demanded at any given price. For one thing, the world's population, and therefore the number of potential cotton clothing wearers, increased. In addition, the growing popularity of cotton clothing, as well as higher incomes in countries like China that allowed people to buy more clothing than before, led to an increase in the quantity of cotton demanded at any given price. Figure 3-2 illustrates this phenomenon using the demand schedule and demand curve for cotton. (As before, the numbers in Figure 3-2 are hypothetical.)

FIGURE 3-2 An Increase in Demand

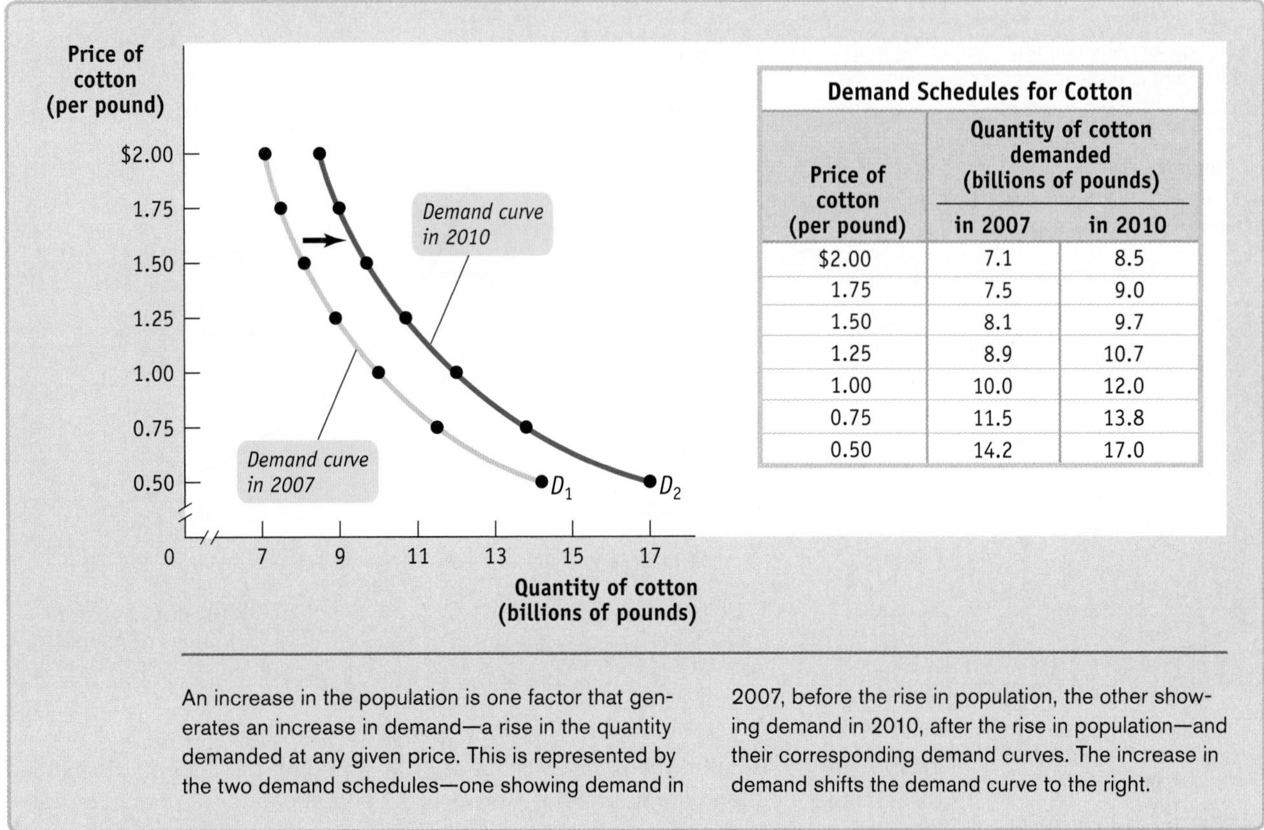

Demand Schedules for Cotton

Price of cotton (per pound)	Quantity of cotton demanded (billions of pounds) in 2007	in 2010
$2.00	7.1	8.5
1.75	7.5	9.0
1.50	8.1	9.7
1.25	8.9	10.7
1.00	10.0	12.0
0.75	11.5	13.8
0.50	14.2	17.0

An increase in the population is one factor that generates an increase in demand—a rise in the quantity demanded at any given price. This is represented by the two demand schedules—one showing demand in 2007, before the rise in population, the other showing demand in 2010, after the rise in population—and their corresponding demand curves. The increase in demand shifts the demand curve to the right.

The table in Figure 3-2 shows two demand schedules. The first is the demand schedule for 2007, the same as shown in Figure 3-1. The second is the demand schedule for 2010. It differs from the 2007 demand schedule due to factors such as a larger population and the increased popularity of cotton clothing, factors that led to an increase in the quantity of cotton demanded at any given price. So at each price the 2010 schedule shows a larger quantity demanded than the 2007 schedule. For example, the quantity of cotton consumers wanted to buy at a price of $1 per pound increased from 10 billion to 12 billion pounds per year, the quantity demanded at $1.25 per pound went from 8.9 billion to 10.7 billion, and so on.

What is clear from this example is that the changes that occurred between 2007 and 2010 generated a *new* demand schedule, one in which the quantity demanded was greater at any given price than in the original demand schedule. The two curves in Figure 3-2 show the same information graphically. As you can see, the demand schedule for 2010 corresponds to a new demand curve, D_2, that is to the right of the demand schedule for 2007, D_1. This **shift of the demand curve** shows the change in the quantity demanded at any given price, represented by the change in position of the original demand curve D_1 to its new location at D_2.

It's crucial to make the distinction between such shifts of the demand curve and **movements along the demand curve,** changes in the quantity demanded of a good arising from a change in that good's price. Figure 3-3 on the next page illustrates the difference.

The movement from point *A* to point *B* is a movement along the demand curve: the quantity demanded rises due to a fall in price as you move down D_1. Here, a fall in the price of cotton from $1.50 to $1 per pound generates a rise in the quantity demanded from 8.1 billion to 10 billion pounds per year. But the quantity demanded can also rise when the price is unchanged if there is an *increase in demand*—a rightward shift of the demand curve. This is illustrated in Figure 3-3 by the shift of the demand curve

A **shift of the demand curve** is a change in the quantity demanded at any given price, represented by the change of the original demand curve to a new position, denoted by a new demand curve.

A **movement along the demand curve** is a change in the quantity demanded of a good arising from a change in the good's price.

FIGURE 3-3 Movement Along the Demand Curve versus Shift of the Demand Curve

The rise in quantity demanded when going from point *A* to point *B* reflects a movement along the demand curve: it is the result of a fall in the price of the good. The rise in quantity demanded when going from point *A* to point *C* reflects a shift of the demand curve: it is the result of a rise in the quantity demanded at any given price.

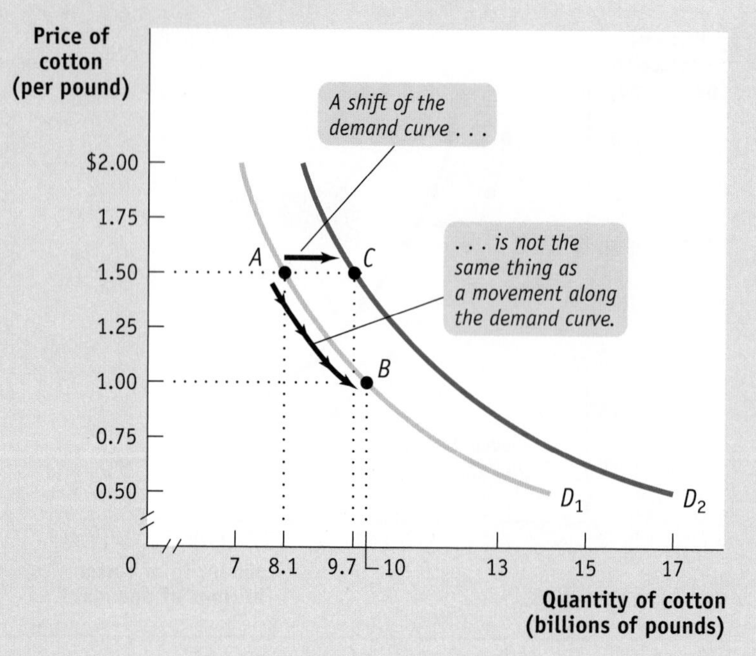

from D_1 to D_2. Holding the price constant at $1.50 a pound, the quantity demanded rises from 8.1 billion pounds at point *A* on D_1 to 9.7 billion pounds at point *C* on D_2.

When economists say "the demand for *X* increased" or "the demand for *Y* decreased," they mean that the demand curve for *X* or *Y* shifted—not that the quantity demanded rose or fell because of a change in the price.

PITFALLS

DEMAND VERSUS QUANTITY DEMANDED

When economists say "an increase in demand," they mean a rightward shift of the demand curve, and when they say "a decrease in demand," they mean a leftward shift of the demand curve—that is, when they're being careful. In ordinary speech most people, including professional economists, use the word *demand* casually. For example, an economist might say "the demand for air travel has doubled over the past 15 years, partly because of falling airfares" when he or she really means that the *quantity demanded* has doubled.

It's OK to be a bit sloppy in ordinary conversation. But when you're doing economic analysis, it's important to make the distinction between changes in the quantity demanded, which involve movements along a demand curve, and shifts of the demand curve (see Figure 3-3 for an illustration). Sometimes students end up writing something like this: "If demand increases, the price will go up, but that will lead to a fall in demand, which pushes the price down . . ." and then go around in circles. If you make a clear distinction between changes in *demand*, which mean shifts of the demand curve, and changes in *quantity demanded*, you can avoid a lot of confusion.

Understanding Shifts of the Demand Curve

Figure 3-4 illustrates the two basic ways in which demand curves can shift. When economists talk about an "increase in demand," they mean a *rightward* shift of the demand curve: at any given price, consumers demand a larger quantity of the good or service than before. This is shown by the rightward shift of the original demand curve D_1 to D_2. And when economists talk about a "decrease in demand," they mean a *leftward* shift of the demand curve: at any given price, consumers demand a smaller quantity of the good or service than before. This is shown by the leftward shift of the original demand curve D_1 to D_3.

What caused the demand curve for cotton to shift? We have already mentioned two reasons: changes in population and a change in the popularity of cotton

FIGURE 3-4 Shifts of the Demand Curve

Any event that increases demand shifts the demand curve to the right, reflecting a rise in the quantity demanded at any given price. Any event that decreases demand shifts the demand curve to the left, reflecting a fall in the quantity demanded at any given price.

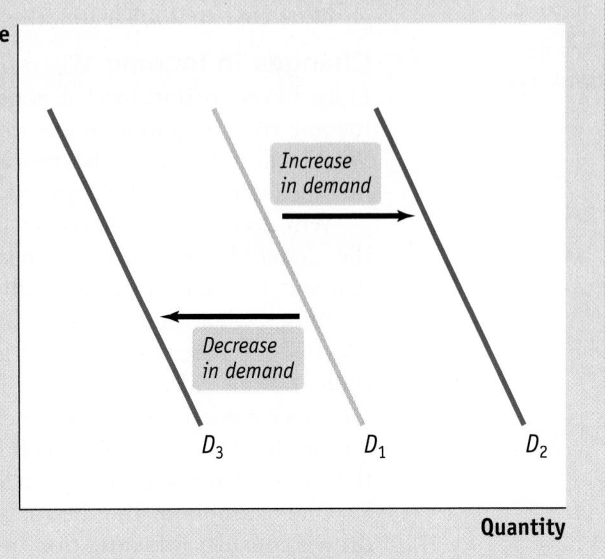

clothing. If you think about it, you can come up with other things that would be likely to shift the demand curve for cotton. For example, suppose that the price of polyester rises. This will induce some people who previously bought polyester clothing to buy cotton clothing instead, increasing the demand for cotton.

Economists believe that there are five principal factors that shift the demand curve for a good or service:

- Changes in the prices of related goods or services
- Changes in income
- Changes in tastes
- Changes in expectations
- Changes in the number of consumers

Although this is not an exhaustive list, it contains the five most important factors that can shift demand curves. So when we say that the quantity of a good or service demanded falls as its price rises, *other things equal*, we are in fact stating that the factors that shift demand are remaining unchanged. Let's now explore, in more detail, how those factors shift the demand curve.

Changes in the Prices of Related Goods or Services Although there's nothing quite like a comfortable pair of all-cotton blue jeans, for some purposes khakis—generally made from polyester blends—aren't a bad alternative. Khakis are what economists call a *substitute* for jeans. A pair of goods are **substitutes** if a rise in the price of one good (jeans) makes consumers more willing to buy the other good (khakis). Substitutes are usually goods that in some way serve a similar function: coffee and tea, muffins and doughnuts, train rides and air flights. A rise in the price of the alternative good induces some consumers to purchase the original good *instead* of it, shifting demand for the original good to the right.

But sometimes a rise in the price of one good makes consumers *less* willing to buy another good. Such pairs of goods are known as **complements.** Complements are usually goods that in some sense are consumed together: computers and software, cappuccinos and cookies, cars and gasoline. Because consumers like to consume a good and its complement together, a change in the price of one of the goods will affect the demand for its complement. In particular, when

Two goods are **substitutes** if a rise in the price of one of the goods leads to an increase in the demand for the other good.

Two goods are **complements** if a rise in the price of one good leads to a decrease in the demand for the other good.

When a rise in income increases the demand for a good—the normal case—it is a **normal good.**

When a rise in income decreases the demand for a good, it is an **inferior good.**

the price of one good rises, the demand for its complement decreases, shifting the demand curve for the complement to the left. So, for example, when the price of gasoline rose in 2007–2008, the demand for gas-guzzling cars fell.

Changes in Income When individuals have more income, they are normally more likely to purchase a good at any given price. For example, if a family's income rises, it is more likely to take that long-anticipated summer trip to Disney World—and therefore also more likely to buy plane tickets. So a rise in consumer incomes will cause the demand curves for most goods to shift to the right.

Why do we say "most goods," not "all goods"? Most goods are **normal goods**—the demand for them increases when consumer income rises. However, the demand for some products falls when income rises. Goods for which demand decreases when income rises are known as **inferior goods.** Usually an inferior good is one that is considered less desirable than more expensive alternatives—such as a bus ride versus a taxi ride. When they can afford to, people stop buying an inferior good and switch their consumption to the preferred, more expensive alternative. So when a good is inferior, a rise in income shifts the demand curve to the left. And, not surprisingly, a fall in income shifts the demand curve to the right.

One example of the distinction between normal and inferior goods that has drawn considerable attention in the business press is the difference between so-called casual-dining restaurants such as Applebee's or Olive Garden and fast-food chains such as McDonald's and KFC. When Americans' income rises, they tend to eat out more at casual-dining restaurants. However, some of this increased dining out comes at the expense of fast-food venues—to some extent, people visit McDonald's less once they can afford to move upscale. So casual dining is a normal good, whereas fast-food consumption appears to be an inferior good.

Changes in Tastes Why do people want what they want? Fortunately, we don't need to answer that question—we just need to acknowledge that people have certain preferences, or tastes, that determine what they choose to consume and that these tastes can change. Economists usually lump together changes in demand due to fads, beliefs, cultural shifts, and so on under the heading of changes in tastes or preferences.

For example, once upon a time men wore hats. Up until around World War II, a respectable man wasn't fully dressed unless he wore a dignified hat along with his suit. But the returning GIs adopted a more informal style, perhaps due to the rigors of the war. And President Eisenhower, who had been supreme commander of Allied Forces before becoming president, often went hatless. After World War II, it was clear that the demand curve for hats had shifted leftward, reflecting a decrease in the demand for hats.

Economists have relatively little to say about the forces that influence consumers' tastes. (Although marketers and advertisers have plenty to say about them!) However, a change in tastes has a predictable impact on demand. When tastes change in favor of a good, more people want to buy it at any given price, so the demand curve shifts to the right. When tastes change against a good, fewer people want to buy it at any given price, so the demand curve shifts to the left.

Changes in Expectations When consumers have some choice about when to make a purchase, current demand for a good is often affected by expectations about its future price. For example, savvy shoppers often wait for seasonal sales—say, buying next year's holiday gifts during the post-holiday markdowns. In this case, expectations of a future drop in price lead to a decrease in demand today. Alternatively, expectations of a future rise in price are likely to cause an increase in demand today. For example, as cotton prices began to rise in 2010, many textile mills began purchasing more cotton and stockpiling it in anticipation of further price increases.

Expected changes in future income can also lead to changes in demand: if you expect your income to rise in the future, you will typically borrow today and increase your demand for certain goods; if you expect your income to fall in the future, you are likely to save today and reduce your demand for some goods.

Changes in the Number of Consumers As we've already noted, one of the reasons for rising cotton demand between 2007 and 2010 was a growing world population. Because of population growth, overall demand for cotton would have risen even if the demand of each individual wearer of cotton clothing had remained unchanged.

An **individual demand curve** illustrates the relationship between quantity demanded and price for an individual consumer.

Let's introduce a new concept: the **individual demand curve,** which shows the relationship between quantity demanded and price for an individual consumer. For example, suppose that Darla is a consumer of cotton blue jeans; also suppose that all pairs of jeans are the same, so they sell for the same price. Panel (a) of Figure 3-5 shows how many pairs of jeans she will buy per year at any given price. Then D_{Darla} is Darla's individual demand curve.

FIGURE 3-5 Individual Demand Curves and the Market Demand Curve

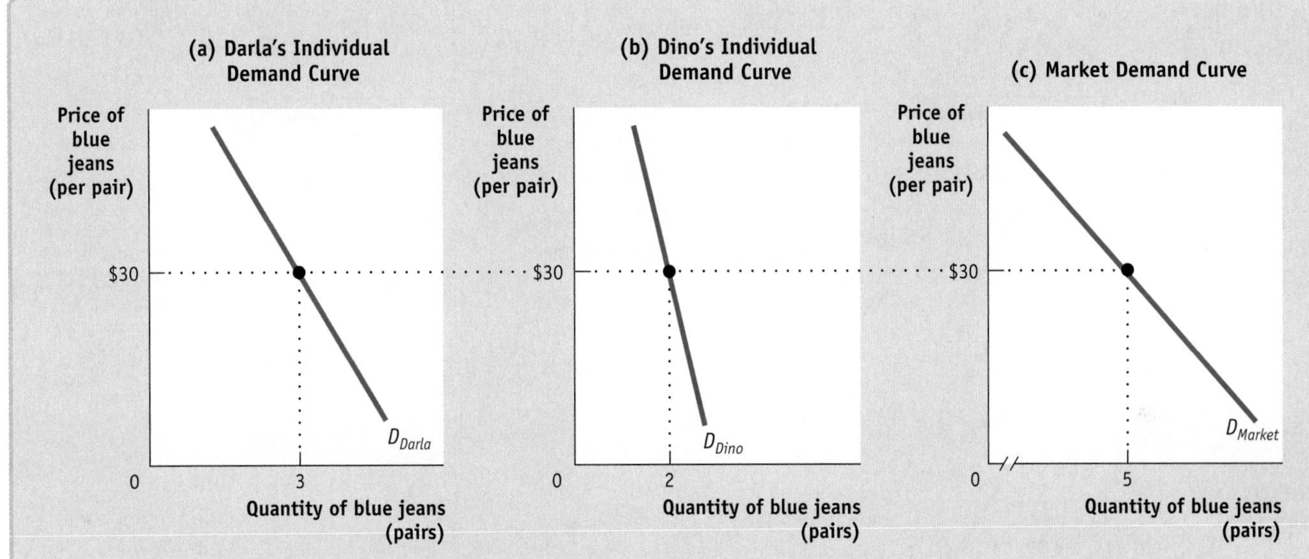

Darla and Dino are the only two consumers of blue jeans in the market. Panel (a) shows Darla's individual demand curve: the number of pairs of blue jeans she will buy per year at any given price. Panel (b) shows Dino's individual demand curve. Given that Darla and Dino are the only two consumers, the *market demand curve,* which shows the quantity of blue jeans demanded by all consumers at any given price, is shown in panel (c). The market demand curve is the *horizontal sum* of the individual demand curves of all consumers. In this case, at any given price, the quantity demanded by the market is the sum of the quantities demanded by Darla and Dino.

The *market demand curve* shows how the combined quantity demanded by all consumers depends on the market price of that good. (Most of the time, when economists refer to the demand curve, they mean the market demand curve.) The market demand curve is the *horizontal sum* of the individual demand curves of all consumers in that market. To see what we mean by the term *horizontal sum,* assume for a moment that there are only two consumers of blue jeans, Darla and Dino. Dino's individual demand curve, D_{Dino}, is shown in panel (b). Panel (c) shows the market demand curve. At any given price, the quantity demanded by the market is the sum of the quantities demanded by Darla and Dino. For example, at a price of $30 per pair, Darla demands 3 pairs of jeans per year and Dino demands 2 pairs per year. So the quantity demanded by the market is 5 pairs per year.

Clearly, the quantity demanded by the market at any given price is larger with Dino present than it would be if Darla were the only consumer. The quantity demanded at any given price would be even larger if we added a third consumer, then a fourth, and so on. So an increase in the number of consumers leads to an increase in demand.

For a review of the factors that shift demand, see Table 3-1.

TABLE 3-1 Factors That Shift Demand

When this happens . . .	. . . demand increases	But when this happens . . .	. . . demand decreases
When the price of a substitute rises . . .	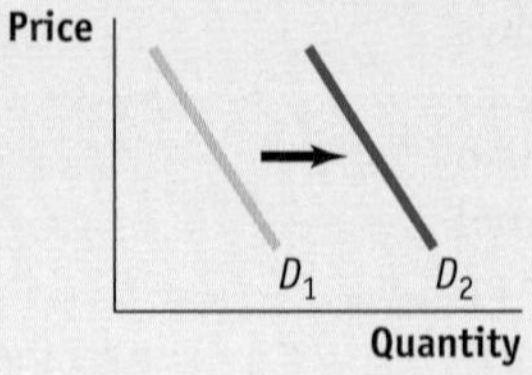 . . . demand for the original good increases.	When the price of a substitute falls . . .	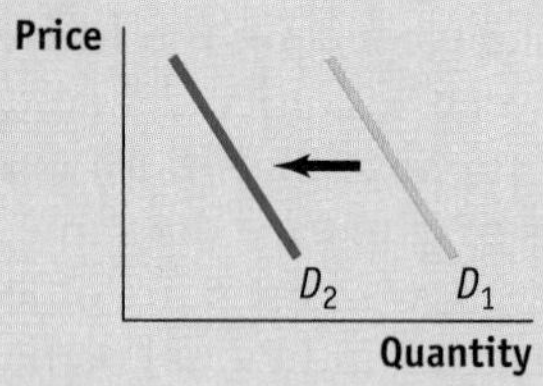 . . . demand for the original good decreases.
When the price of a complement falls . . .	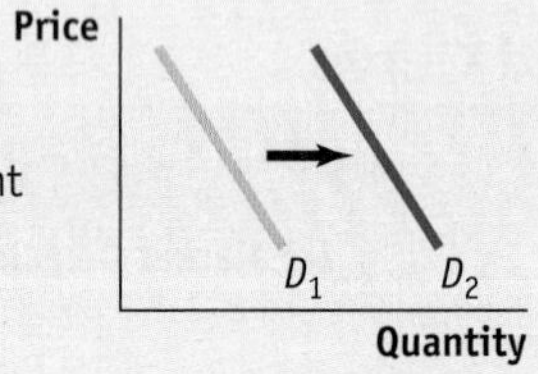 . . . demand for the original good increases.	When the price of a complement rises . . .	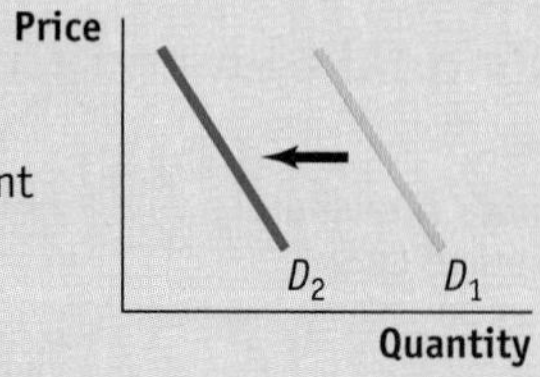 . . . demand for the original good decreases.
When income rises . . .	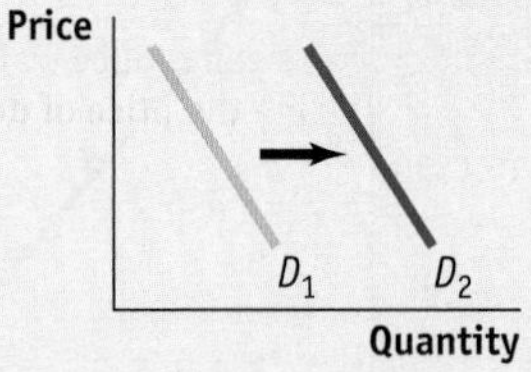 . . . demand for a normal good increases.	When income falls . . .	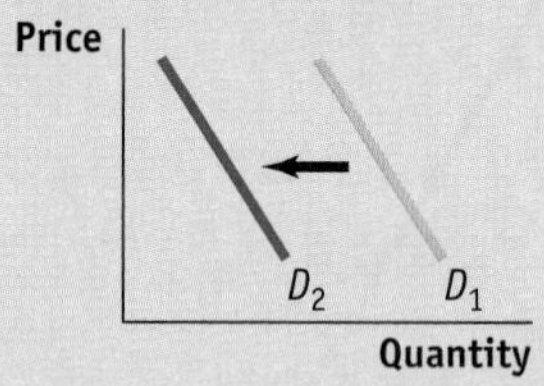 . . . demand for a normal good decreases.
When income falls . . .	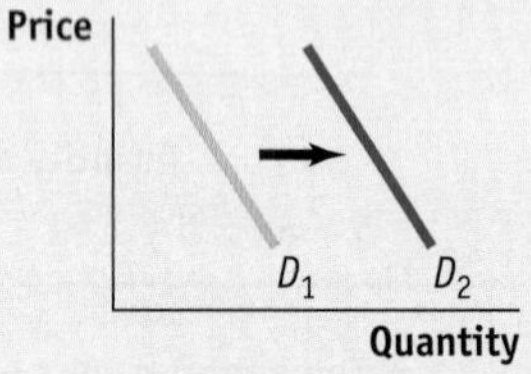 . . . demand for an inferior good increases.	When income rises . . .	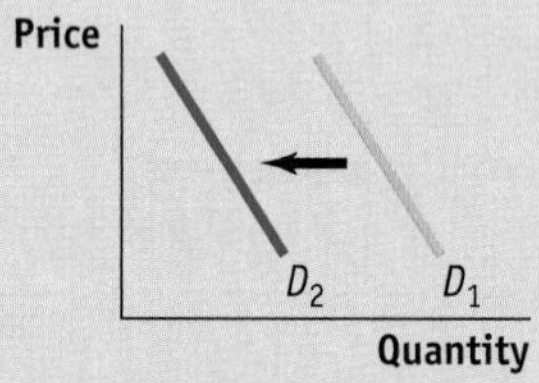 . . . demand for an inferior good decreases.
When tastes change in favor of a good . . .	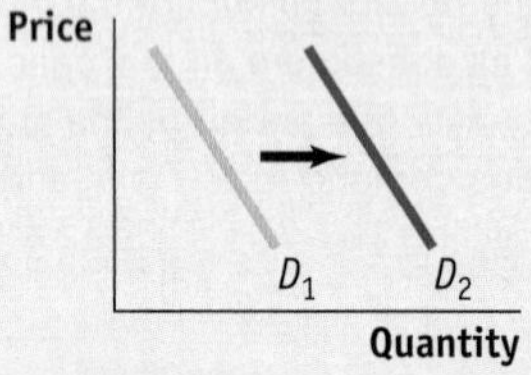 . . . demand for the good increases.	When tastes change against a good . . .	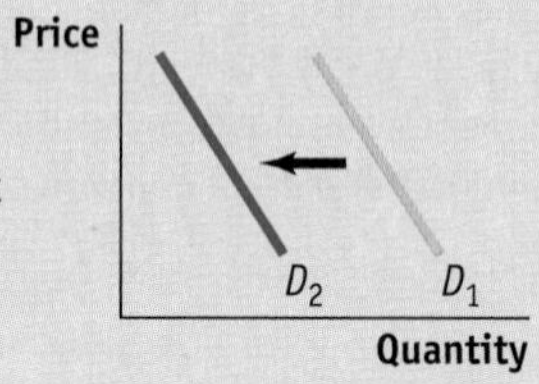 . . . demand for the good decreases.
When the price is expected to rise in the future . . .	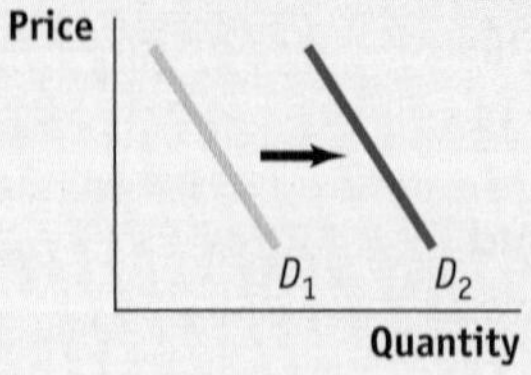 . . . demand for the good increases today.	When the price is expected to fall in the future . . .	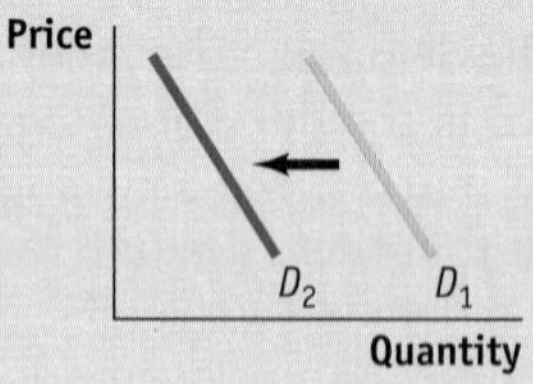 . . . demand for the good decreases today.
When the number of consumers rises . . .	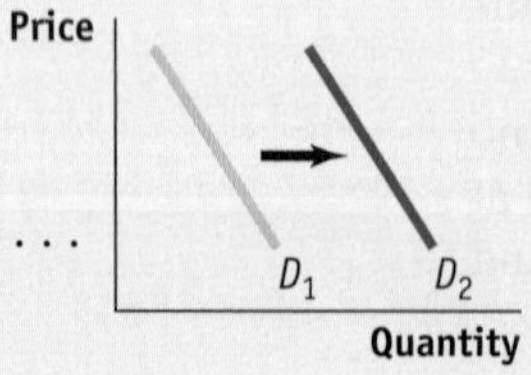 . . . market demand for the good increases.	When the number of consumers falls . . .	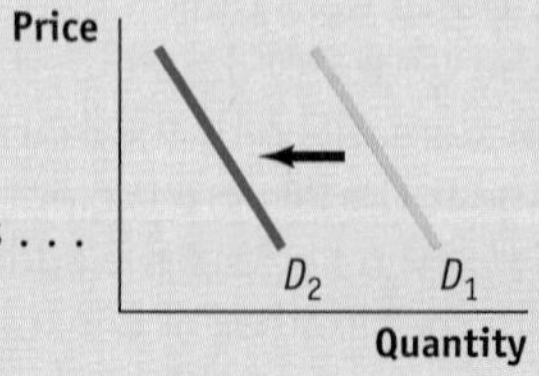 . . . market demand for the good decreases.

ECONOMICS ➤ IN ACTION

BEATING THE TRAFFIC

All big cities have traffic problems, and many local authorities try to discourage driving in the crowded city center. If we think of an auto trip to the city center as a good that people consume, we can use the economics of demand to analyze anti-traffic policies.

One common strategy is to reduce the demand for auto trips by lowering the prices of substitutes. Many metropolitan areas subsidize bus and rail service, hoping to lure commuters out of their cars. An alternative is to raise the price of complements: several major U.S. cities impose high taxes on commercial parking garages and impose short time limits on parking meters, both to raise revenue and to discourage people from driving into the city.

A few major cities—including Singapore, London, Oslo, Stockholm, and Milan—have been willing to adopt a direct and politically controversial approach: reducing congestion by raising the price of driving. Under "congestion pricing" (or "congestion charging" in the United Kingdom), a charge is imposed on cars entering the city center during business hours. Drivers buy passes, which are then debited electronically as they drive by monitoring stations. Compliance is monitored with automatic cameras that photograph license plates. Moscow is currently contemplating a congestion charge scheme to tackle the worst traffic jams of all major cities, with 40% of drivers reporting traffic jams exceeding three hours.

The current daily cost of driving in London ranges from £9 to £12 (about $14 to $19). And drivers who don't pay and are caught pay a fine of £120 (about $190) for each transgression.

Not surprisingly, studies have shown that after the implementation of congestion pricing, traffic does indeed decrease. In the 1990s, London had some of the worst traffic in Europe. The introduction of its congestion charge in 2003 immediately reduced traffic in the London city center by about 15%, with overall traffic falling by 21% between 2002 and 2006. And there was increased use of substitutes, such as public transportation, bicycles, motorbikes, and ride-sharing.

In the United States, the U.S. Department of Transportation has implemented pilot programs in five locations to study congestion pricing. Some transportation experts have even suggested using variable congestion prices, raising prices during peak commuting hours. So although congestion pricing may be controversial, it appears to be slowly gaining acceptance.

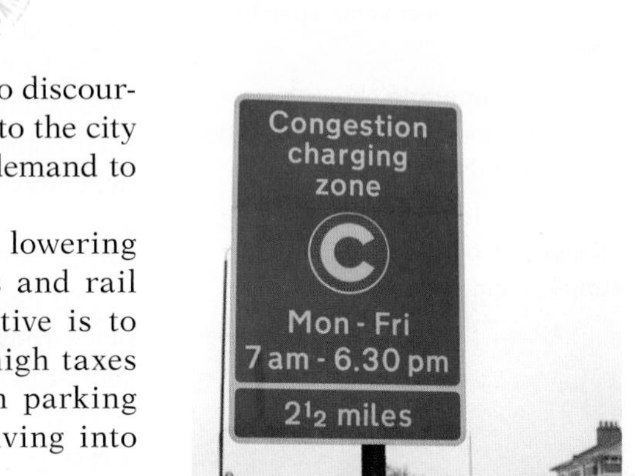

Global Warming Images/Alamy

Cities can reduce traffic congestion by raising the price of driving.

Quick Review

- The **supply and demand model** is a model of a **competitive market**—one in which there are many buyers and sellers of the same good or service.
- The **demand schedule** shows how the **quantity demanded** changes as the price changes. A **demand curve** illustrates this relationship.
- The **law of demand** asserts that a higher price reduces the quantity demanded. Thus, demand curves normally slope downward.
- An increase in demand leads to a rightward **shift of the demand curve:** the quantity demanded rises for any given price. A decrease in demand leads to a leftward shift: the quantity demanded falls for any given price. A change in price results in a change in the quantity demanded and a **movement along the demand curve.**
- The five main factors that can shift the demand curve are changes in (1) the price of a related good, such as a **substitute** or a **complement,** (2) income, (3) tastes, (4) expectations, and (5) the number of consumers.
- The market demand curve is the horizontal sum of the **individual demand curves** of all consumers in the market.

CHECK YOUR UNDERSTANDING 3-1

1. Explain whether each of the following events represents (i) a *shift of* the demand curve or (ii) a *movement along* the demand curve.
   a. A store owner finds that customers are willing to pay more for umbrellas on rainy days.
   b. When XYZ Telecom, a long-distance telephone service provider, offered reduced rates on weekends, its volume of weekend calling increased sharply.
   c. People buy more long-stem roses the week of Valentine's Day, even though the prices are higher than at other times during the year.
   d. A sharp rise in the price of gasoline leads many commuters to join carpools in order to reduce their gasoline purchases.

Solutions appear at back of book.

The **quantity supplied** is the actual amount of a good or service people are willing to sell at some specific price.

A **supply schedule** shows how much of a good or service would be supplied at different prices.

A **supply curve** shows the relationship between quantity supplied and price.

The Supply Curve

Some parts of the world are especially well suited to growing cotton, and the United States is one of those. But even in the United States, some land is better suited to growing cotton than other land. Whether American farmers restrict their cotton-growing to only the most ideal locations or expand it to less suitable land depends on the price they expect to get for their cotton. Moreover, there are many other areas in the world where cotton could be grown—such as Pakistan, Brazil, Turkey, and China. Whether farmers there actually grow cotton depends, again, on the price.

So just as the quantity of cotton that consumers want to buy depends on the price they have to pay, the quantity that producers are willing to produce and sell—the **quantity supplied**—depends on the price they are offered.

The Supply Schedule and the Supply Curve

The table in Figure 3-6 shows how the quantity of cotton made available varies with the price—that is, it shows a hypothetical **supply schedule** for cotton.

A supply schedule works the same way as the demand schedule shown in Figure 3-1: in this case, the table shows the number of pounds of cotton farmers are willing to sell at different prices. At a price of $0.50 per pound, farmers are willing to sell only 8 billion pounds of cotton per year. At $0.75 per pound, they're willing to sell 9.1 billion pounds. At $1, they're willing to sell 10 billion pounds, and so on.

In the same way that a demand schedule can be represented graphically by a demand curve, a supply schedule can be represented by a **supply curve,** as shown in Figure 3-6. Each point on the curve represents an entry from the table.

Suppose that the price of cotton rises from $1 to $1.25; we can see that the quantity that cotton farmers are willing to sell rises from 10 billion to 10.7 billion

FIGURE 3-6 The Supply Schedule and the Supply Curve

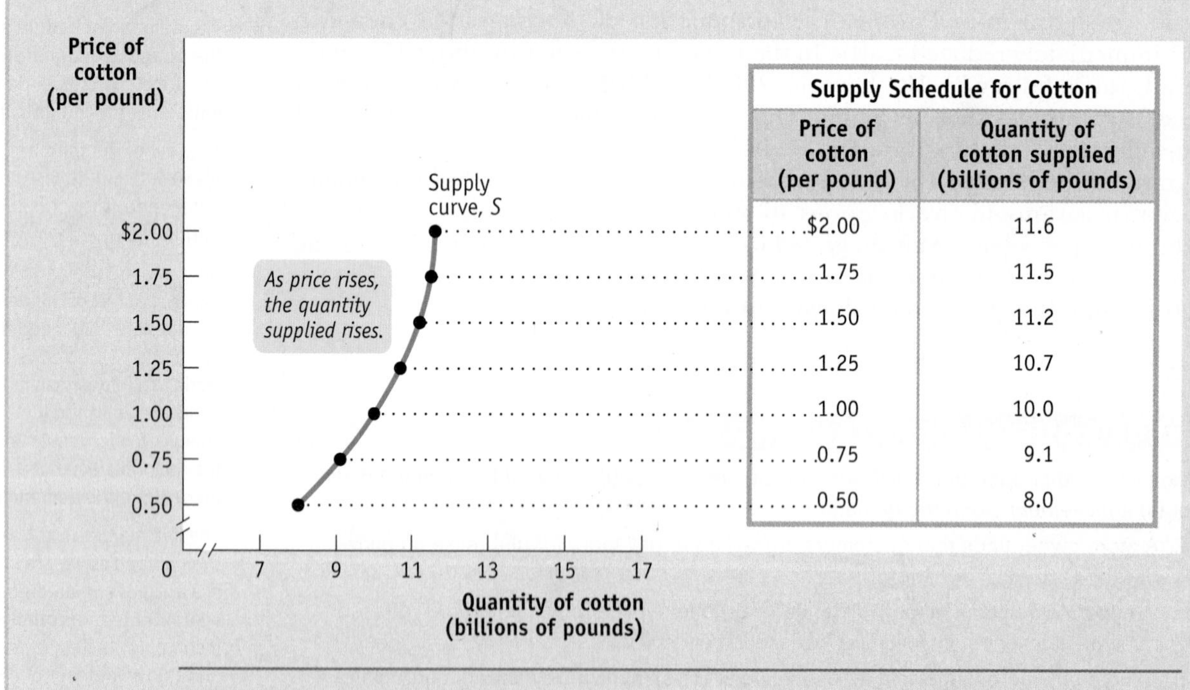

Supply Schedule for Cotton

Price of cotton (per pound)	Quantity of cotton supplied (billions of pounds)
$2.00	11.6
1.75	11.5
1.50	11.2
1.25	10.7
1.00	10.0
0.75	9.1
0.50	8.0

The supply schedule for cotton is plotted to yield the corresponding supply curve, which shows how much of a good producers are willing to sell at any given price. The supply curve and the supply schedule reflect the fact that supply curves are usually upward sloping: the quantity supplied rises when the price rises.

pounds. This is the normal situation for a supply curve, that a higher price leads to a higher quantity supplied. So just as demand curves normally slope downward, supply curves normally slope upward: the higher the price being offered, the more of any good or service producers will be willing to sell.

A **shift of the supply curve** is a change in the quantity supplied of a good or service at any given price. It is represented by the change of the original supply curve to a new position, denoted by a new supply curve.

A **movement along the supply curve** is a change in the quantity supplied of a good arising from a change in the good's price.

Shifts of the Supply Curve

Until recently, cotton remained relatively cheap over the past several decades. One reason is that the amount of land cultivated for cotton expanded over 35% from 1945 to 2007. However, the major factor accounting for cotton's relative cheapness was advances in the production technology, with output per acre more than quadrupling from 1945 to 2007. Figure 3-7 illustrates these events in terms of the supply schedule and the supply curve for cotton.

The table in Figure 3-7 shows two supply schedules. The schedule before improved cotton-growing technology was adopted is the same one as in Figure 3-6. The second schedule shows the supply of cotton *after* the improved technology was adopted. Just as a change in demand schedules leads to a shift of the demand curve, a change in supply schedules leads to a **shift of the supply curve**—a change in the quantity supplied at any given price. This is shown in Figure 3-7 by the shift of the supply curve before the adoption of new cotton-growing technology, S_1, to its new position after the adoption of new cotton-growing technology, S_2. Notice that S_2 lies to the right of S_1, a reflection of the fact that quantity supplied rises at any given price.

As in the analysis of demand, it's crucial to draw a distinction between such shifts of the supply curve and **movements along the supply curve**—changes in the quantity supplied arising from a change in price. We can see this difference in Figure 3-8. The movement from point A to point B is a movement along the supply curve: the quantity supplied rises along S_1 due to a rise in price. Here, a rise in price from \$1 to \$1.50 leads to a rise in the quantity supplied from 10 billion to 11.2 billion pounds of cotton. But the quantity supplied can also rise when

FIGURE 3-7 An Increase in Supply

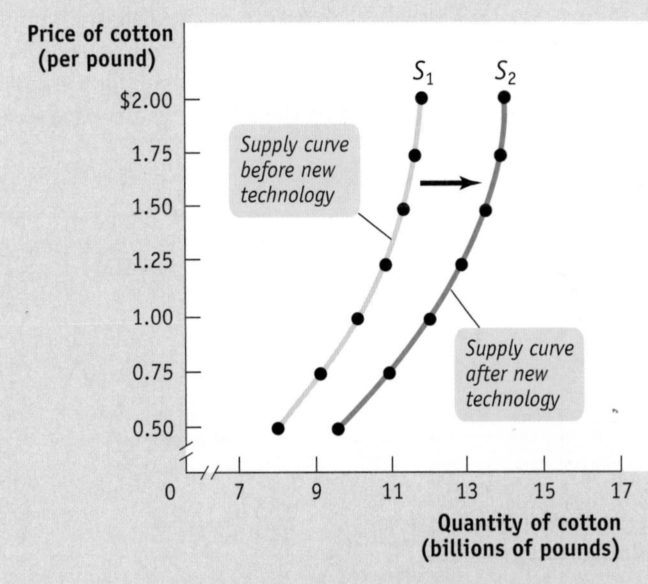

Supply Schedules for Cotton		
Price of cotton (per pound)	Quantity of cotton supplied (billions of pounds)	
	Before new technology	After new technology
\$2.00	11.6	13.9
1.75	11.5	13.8
1.50	11.2	13.4
1.25	10.7	12.8
1.00	10.0	12.0
0.75	9.1	10.9
0.50	8.0	9.6

The adoption of improved cotton-growing technology generated an increase in supply—a rise in the quantity supplied at any given price. This event is represented by the two supply schedules—one showing supply before the new technology was adopted, the other showing supply after the new technology was adopted—and their corresponding supply curves. The increase in supply shifts the supply curve to the right.

FIGURE 3-8 Movement Along the Supply Curve versus Shift of the Supply Curve

The increase in quantity supplied when going from point *A* to point *B* reflects a movement along the supply curve: it is the result of a rise in the price of the good. The increase in quantity supplied when going from point *A* to point *C* reflects a shift of the supply curve: it is the result of an increase in the quantity supplied at any given price.

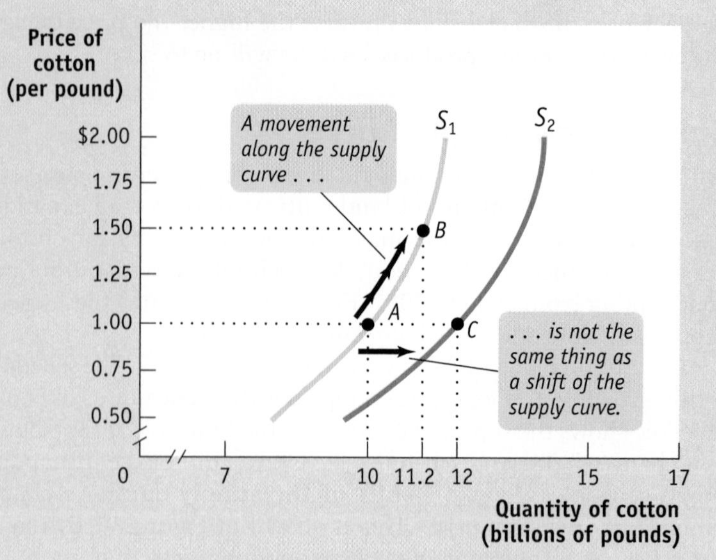

the price is unchanged if there is an increase in supply—a rightward shift of the supply curve. This is shown by the rightward shift of the supply curve from S_1 to S_2. Holding the price constant at $1, the quantity supplied rises from 10 billion pounds at point *A* on S_1 to 12 billion pounds at point *C* on S_2.

Understanding Shifts of the Supply Curve

Figure 3-9 illustrates the two basic ways in which supply curves can shift. When economists talk about an "increase in supply," they mean a *rightward* shift of the supply curve: at any given price, producers supply a larger quantity of the good than before. This is shown in Figure 3-9 by the rightward shift of the original supply curve S_1 to S_2. And when economists talk about a "decrease in supply," they mean a *leftward* shift of the supply curve: at any given price, producers supply a smaller quantity of the good than before. This is represented by the leftward shift of S_1 to S_3.

FIGURE 3-9 Shifts of the Supply Curve

Any event that increases supply shifts the supply curve to the right, reflecting a rise in the quantity supplied at any given price. Any event that decreases supply shifts the supply curve to the left, reflecting a fall in the quantity supplied at any given price.

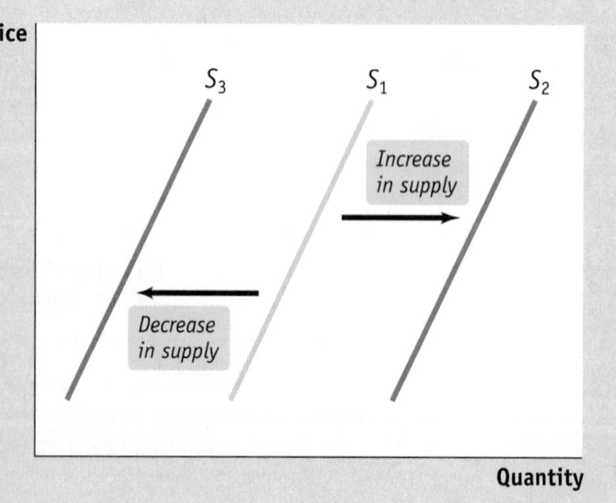

Economists believe that shifts of the supply curve for a good or service are mainly the result of five factors (though, as in the case of demand, there are other possible causes):

- Changes in input prices
- Changes in the prices of related goods or services
- Changes in technology
- Changes in expectations
- Changes in the number of producers

An **input** is a good or service that is used to produce another good or service.

Changes in Input Prices To produce output, you need inputs. For example, to make vanilla ice cream, you need vanilla beans, cream, sugar, and so on. An **input** is any good or service that is used to produce another good or service. Inputs, like outputs, have prices. And an increase in the price of an input makes the production of the final good more costly for those who produce and sell it. So producers are less willing to supply the final good at any given price, and the supply curve shifts to the left. For example, fuel is a major cost for airlines. When oil prices surged in 2007–2008, airlines began cutting back on their flight schedules and some went out of business. Similarly, a fall in the price of an input makes the production of the final good less costly for sellers. They are more willing to supply the good at any given price, and the supply curve shifts to the right.

Changes in the Prices of Related Goods or Services A single producer often produces a mix of goods rather than a single product. For example, an oil refinery produces gasoline from crude oil, but it also produces heating oil and other products from the same raw material. When a producer sells several products, the quantity of any one good it is willing to supply at any given price depends on the prices of its other co-produced goods.

This effect can run in either direction. An oil refiner will supply less gasoline at any given price when the price of heating oil rises, shifting the supply curve for gasoline to the left. But it will supply more gasoline at any given price when the price of heating oil falls, shifting the supply curve for gasoline to the right. This means that gasoline and other co-produced oil products are *substitutes in production* for refiners.

In contrast, due to the nature of the production process, other goods can be *complements in production*. For example, producers of crude oil—oil-well drillers—often find that oil wells also produce natural gas as a by-product of oil extraction. The higher the price at which a driller can sell its natural gas, the more oil wells it will drill and the more oil it will supply at any given price for oil. As a result, natural gas is a complement in production for crude oil.

Changes in Technology When economists talk about "technology," they don't necessarily mean high technology—they mean all the methods people can use to turn inputs into useful goods and services. In that sense, the whole complex sequence of activities that turn cotton from Pakistan into the pair of jeans hanging in your closet is technology.

Improvements in technology enable producers to spend less on inputs yet still produce the same output. When a better technology becomes available, reducing the cost of production, supply increases, and the supply curve shifts to the right. As we have already mentioned, improved technology enabled farmers to more than quadruple cotton output per acre planted over the past several decades. Improved technology is the main reason that, until recently, cotton remained relatively cheap even as worldwide demand grew.

Changes in Expectations Just as changes in expectations can shift the demand curve, they can also shift the supply curve. When suppliers have some choice about when they put their good up for sale, changes in the expected future price of the good can lead a supplier to supply less or more of the good today.

An **individual supply curve** illustrates the relationship between quantity supplied and price for an individual producer.

For example, consider the fact that gasoline and other oil products are often stored for significant periods of time at oil refineries before being sold to consumers. In fact, storage is normally part of producers' business strategy. Knowing that the demand for gasoline peaks in the summer, oil refiners normally store some of their gasoline produced during the spring for summer sale. Similarly, knowing that the demand for heating oil peaks in the winter, they normally store some of their heating oil produced during the fall for winter sale. In each case, there's a decision to be made between selling the product now versus storing it for later sale. Which choice a producer makes depends on a comparison of the current price versus the expected future price. This example illustrates how changes in expectations can alter supply: An increase in the anticipated future price of a good or service reduces supply today, a leftward shift of the supply curve. But a fall in the anticipated future price increases supply today, a rightward shift of the supply curve.

Changes in the Number of Producers Just as changes in the number of consumers affect the demand curve, changes in the number of producers affect the supply curve. Let's examine the **individual supply curve,** by looking at panel (a) in Figure 3-10. The individual supply curve shows the relationship between quantity supplied and price for an individual producer. For example, suppose that Mr. Silva is a Brazilian cotton farmer and that panel (a) of Figure 3-10 shows how many pounds of cotton he will supply per year at any given price. Then S_{Silva} is his individual supply curve.

The *market supply curve* shows how the combined total quantity supplied by all individual producers in the market depends on the market price of that good. Just as the market demand curve is the horizontal sum of the individual demand curves of all consumers, the market supply curve is the horizontal sum of the individual supply curves of all producers. Assume for a moment that there are only two producers of cotton, Mr. Silva and Mr. Liu, a Chinese cotton farmer. Mr. Liu's individual supply curve is shown in panel (b). Panel (c) shows the market supply curve. At any given price, the quantity supplied to the market is the sum of the quantities supplied by Mr. Silva and Mr. Liu. For example, at a price of $2 per pound, Mr. Silva supplies 3,000 pounds of cotton per year and Mr. Liu supplies 2,000 pounds per year, making the quantity supplied to the market 5,000 pounds.

FIGURE 3-10 The Individual Supply Curve and the Market Supply Curve

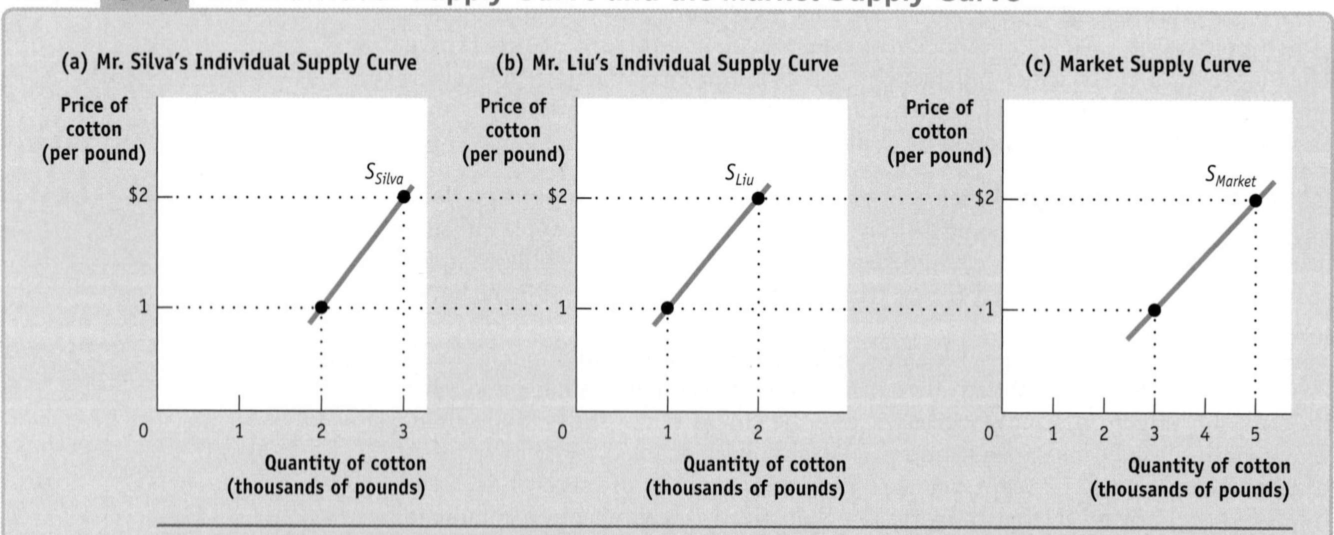

Panel (a) shows the individual supply curve for Mr. Silva, S_{Silva}, the quantity of cotton he will sell at any given price. Panel (b) shows the individual supply curve for Mr. Liu, S_{Liu}. The market supply curve, which shows the quantity of cotton supplied by all producers at any given price, is shown in panel (c). The market supply curve is the horizontal sum of the individual supply curves of all producers.

Clearly, the quantity supplied to the market at any given price is larger with Mr. Liu present than it would be if Mr. Silva were the only supplier. The quantity supplied at a given price would be even larger if we added a third producer, then a fourth, and so on. So an increase in the number of producers leads to an increase in supply and a rightward shift of the supply curve.

For a review of the factors that shift supply, see Table 3-2.

TABLE 3-2 Factors That Shift Supply

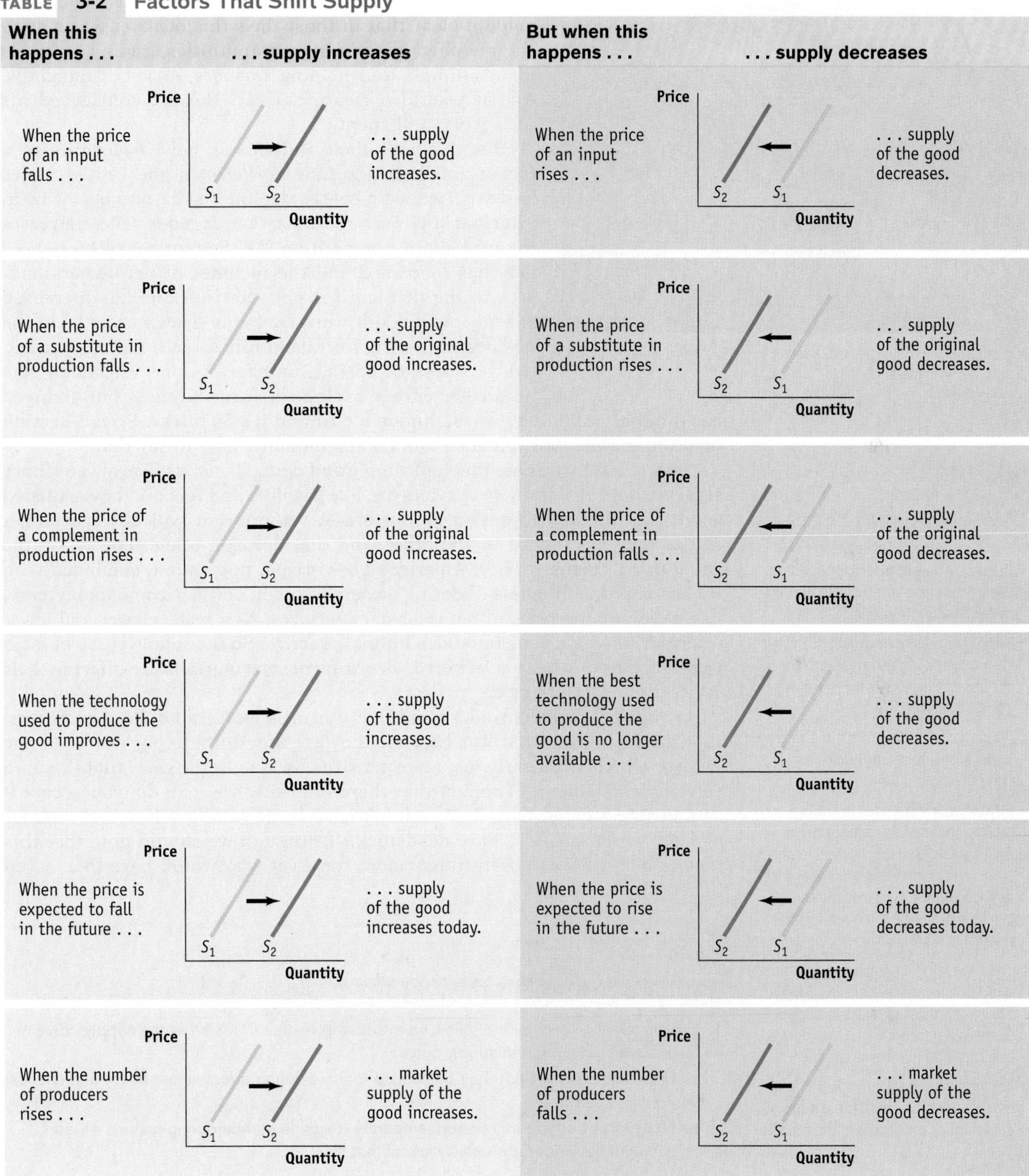

When this happens . . .	. . . supply increases	But when this happens . . .	. . . supply decreases
When the price of an input falls . . .	. . . supply of the good increases.	When the price of an input rises . . .	. . . supply of the good decreases.
When the price of a substitute in production falls . . .	. . . supply of the original good increases.	When the price of a substitute in production rises . . .	. . . supply of the original good decreases.
When the price of a complement in production rises . . .	. . . supply of the original good increases.	When the price of a complement in production falls . . .	. . . supply of the original good decreases.
When the technology used to produce the good improves . . .	. . . supply of the good increases.	When the best technology used to produce the good is no longer available . . .	. . . supply of the good decreases.
When the price is expected to fall in the future . . .	. . . supply of the good increases today.	When the price is expected to rise in the future . . .	. . . supply of the good decreases today.
When the number of producers rises . . .	. . . market supply of the good increases.	When the number of producers falls . . .	. . . market supply of the good decreases.

ECONOMICS ➤ IN ACTION

ONLY CREATURES SMALL AND PAMPERED

During the 1970s, British television featured a popular show titled *All Creatures Great and Small.* It chronicled the real life of James Herriot, a country veterinarian who tended to cows, pigs, sheep, horses, and the occasional house pet, often under arduous conditions, in rural England during the 1930s. The show made it clear that in those days the local vet was a critical member of farming communities, saving valuable farm animals and helping farmers survive financially. And it was also clear that Mr. Herriot considered his life's work well spent.

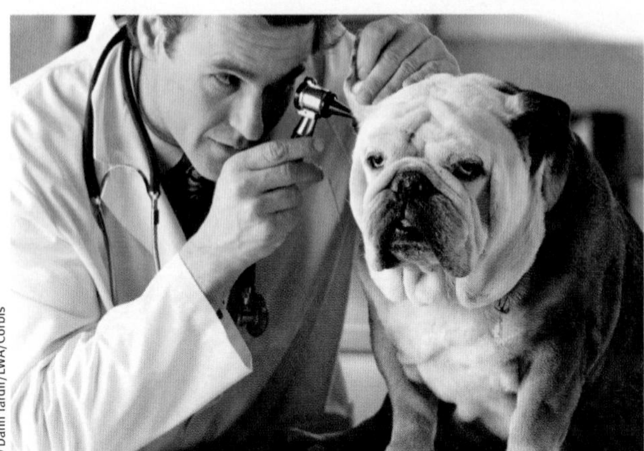

Higher spending on pets means fewer veterinarians are available to tend to farm animals.

But that was then and this is now. According to a recent article in the *New York Times,* the United States has experienced a severe decline in the number of farm veterinarians over the past two decades. The source of the problem is competition. As the number of household pets has increased and the incomes of pet owners have grown, the demand for pet veterinarians has increased sharply. As a result, vets are being drawn away from the business of caring for farm animals into the more lucrative business of caring for pets. As one vet stated, she began her career caring for farm animals but changed her mind after "doing a C-section on a cow and it's 50 bucks. Do a C-section on a Chihuahua and you get $300. It's the money. I hate to say that."

How can we translate this into supply and demand curves? Farm veterinary services and pet veterinary services are like gasoline and fuel oil: they're related goods that are substitutes in production. A veterinarian typically specializes in one type of practice or the other, and that decision often depends on the going price for the service. America's growing pet population, combined with the increased willingness of doting owners to spend on their companions' care, has driven up the price of pet veterinary services. As a result, fewer and fewer veterinarians have gone into farm animal practice. So the supply curve of farm veterinarians has shifted leftward—fewer farm veterinarians are offering their services at any given price.

In the end, farmers understand that it is all a matter of dollars and cents; they get fewer veterinarians because they are unwilling to pay more. As one farmer, who had recently lost an expensive cow due to the unavailability of a veterinarian, stated, "The fact that there's nothing you can do, you accept it as a business expense now. You didn't used to. If you have livestock, sooner or later you're going to have deadstock." (Although we should note that this farmer could have chosen to pay more for a vet who would have then saved his cow.)

Quick Review

- The **supply schedule** shows how the **quantity supplied** depends on the price. The **supply curve** illustrates this relationship.
- Supply curves are normally upward sloping: at a higher price, producers are willing to supply more of a good or service.
- A change in price results in a **movement along the supply curve** and a change in the quantity supplied.
- Increases or decreases in supply lead to **shifts of the supply curve.** An increase in supply is a rightward shift: the quantity supplied rises for any given price. A decrease in supply is a leftward shift: the quantity supplied falls for any given price.
- The five main factors that can shift the supply curve are changes in (1) **input** prices, (2) prices of related goods or services, (3) technology, (4) expectations, and (5) number of producers.
- The market supply curve is the horizontal sum of the **individual supply curves** of all producers in the market.

CHECK YOUR UNDERSTANDING 3-2

1. Explain whether each of the following events represents (i) a *shift of* the supply curve or (ii) a *movement along* the supply curve.
   a. More homeowners put their houses up for sale during a real estate boom that causes house prices to rise.
   b. Many strawberry farmers open temporary roadside stands during harvest season, even though prices are usually low at that time.

c. Immediately after the school year begins, fast-food chains must raise wages, which represent the price of labor, to attract workers.

d. Many construction workers temporarily move to areas that have suffered hurricane damage, lured by higher wages.

e. Since new technologies have made it possible to build larger cruise ships (which are cheaper to run per passenger), Caribbean cruise lines offer more cabins, at lower prices, than before.

Solutions appear at back of book.

A competitive market is in equilibrium when price has moved to a level at which the quantity of a good or service demanded equals the quantity of that good or service supplied. The price at which this takes place is the **equilibrium price,** also referred to as the **market-clearing price.** The quantity of the good or service bought and sold at that price is the **equilibrium quantity.**

Supply, Demand, and Equilibrium

We have now covered the first three key elements in the supply and demand model: the demand curve, the supply curve, and the set of factors that shift each curve. The next step is to put these elements together to show how they can be used to predict the actual price at which the good is bought and sold, as well as the actual quantity transacted.

What determines the price at which a good or service is bought and sold? What determines the quantity transacted of the good or service? In Chapter 1 we learned the general principle that *markets move toward equilibrium,* a situation in which no individual would be better off taking a different action. In the case of a competitive market, we can be more specific: a competitive market is in equilibrium when the price has moved to a level at which the quantity of a good demanded equals the quantity of that good supplied. At that price, no individual seller could make herself better off by offering to sell either more or less of the good and no individual buyer could make himself better off by offering to buy more or less of the good. In other words, at the market equilibrium, price has moved to a level that exactly matches the quantity demanded by consumers to the quantity supplied by sellers.

The price that matches the quantity supplied and the quantity demanded is the **equilibrium price;** the quantity bought and sold at that price is the **equilibrium quantity.** The equilibrium price is also known as the **market-clearing price:** it is the price that "clears the market" by ensuring that every buyer willing to pay that price finds a seller willing to sell at that price, and vice versa. So how do we find the equilibrium price and quantity?

Finding the Equilibrium Price and Quantity

The easiest way to determine the equilibrium price and quantity in a market is by putting the supply curve and the demand curve on the same diagram. Since the supply curve shows the quantity supplied at any given price and the demand curve shows the quantity demanded at any given price, the price at which the two

PITFALLS

BOUGHT AND SOLD?

We have been talking about the price at which a good or service is bought *and* sold, as if the two were the same. But shouldn't we make a distinction between the price received by sellers and the price paid by buyers? In principle, yes; but it is helpful at this point to sacrifice a bit of realism in the interest of simplicity—by assuming away the difference between the prices received by sellers and those paid by buyers.

In reality, there is often a middleman—someone who brings buyers and sellers together. The middleman buys from suppliers, then sells to consumers at a markup—for example, cotton brokers who buy from cotton farmers and sell to textile mills—which turn the cotton into clothing for you and me. The farmers generally receive less than the mills (who eventually buy their bales of cotton) pay. No mystery there: that difference is how cotton brokers or any other middlemen make a living. In many markets, however, the difference between the buying and selling price is quite small. So it's not a bad approximation to think of the price paid by buyers as being the *same* as the price received by sellers. And that is what we assume in this chapter.

FIGURE 3-11 Market Equilibrium

Market equilibrium occurs at point *E*, where the supply curve and the demand curve intersect. In equilibrium, the quantity demanded is equal to the quantity supplied. In this market, the equilibrium price is $1 per pound and the equilibrium quantity is 10 billion pounds per year.

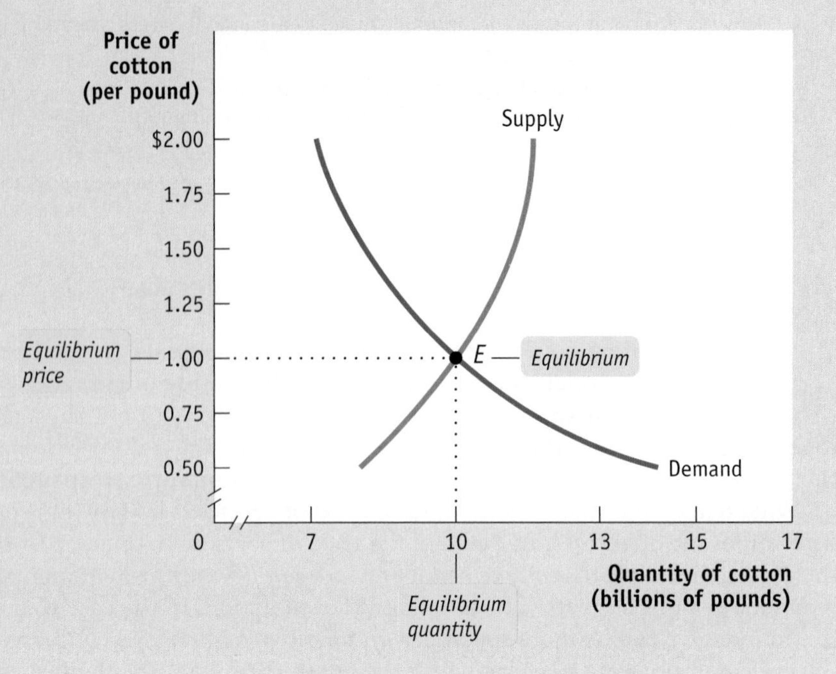

curves cross is the equilibrium price: the price at which quantity supplied equals quantity demanded.

Figure 3-11 combines the demand curve from Figure 3-1 and the supply curve from Figure 3-6. They *intersect* at point *E*, which is the equilibrium of this market; $1 is the equilibrium price and 10 billion pounds is the equilibrium quantity.

Dan Piraro, 1996 Dist. by Universal Press Syndicate

Let's confirm that point *E* fits our definition of equilibrium. At a price of $1 per pound, cotton farmers are willing to sell 10 billion pounds a year and cotton consumers want to buy 10 billion pounds a year. So at the price of $1 a pound, the quantity of cotton supplied equals the quantity demanded. Notice that at any other price the market would not clear: every willing buyer would not be able to find a willing seller, or vice versa. More specifically, if the price were more than $1, the quantity supplied would exceed the quantity demanded; if the price were less than $1, the quantity demanded would exceed the quantity supplied.

The model of supply and demand, then, predicts that given the demand and supply curves shown in Figure 3-11, 10 billion pounds of cotton would change hands at a price of $1 per pound. But how can we be sure that the market will arrive at the equilibrium price? We begin by answering three simple questions:

1. Why do all sales and purchases in a market take place at the same price?
2. Why does the market price fall if it is above the equilibrium price?
3. Why does the market price rise if it is below the equilibrium price?

Why Do All Sales and Purchases in a Market Take Place at the Same Price?

There are some markets where the same good can sell for many different prices, depending on who is selling or who is buying. For example, have you ever bought a souvenir in a "tourist trap" and then seen the same item on sale somewhere else (perhaps even in the shop next door) for a lower price? Because tourists don't know which shops offer the best deals and don't have time for comparison shopping, sellers in tourist areas can charge different prices for the same good.

But in any market where the buyers and sellers have both been around for some time, sales and purchases tend to converge at a generally uniform price, so we can safely talk about *the* market price. It's easy to see why. Suppose a seller offered a potential buyer a price noticeably above what the buyer knew other people to be paying. The buyer would clearly be better off shopping elsewhere—unless the seller were prepared to offer a better deal. Conversely, a seller would not be willing to sell for significantly less than the amount he knew most buyers were paying; he would be better off waiting to get a more reasonable customer. So in any well-established, ongoing market, all sellers receive and all buyers pay approximately the same price. This is what we call the *market price.*

There is a **surplus** of a good or service when the quantity supplied exceeds the quantity demanded. Surpluses occur when the price is above its equilibrium level.

Why Does the Market Price Fall if It Is Above the Equilibrium Price?

Suppose the supply and demand curves are as shown in Figure 3-11 but the market price is above the equilibrium level of $1—say, $1.50. This situation is illustrated in Figure 3-12. Why can't the price stay there?

As the figure shows, at a price of $1.50 there would be more pounds of cotton available than consumers wanted to buy: 11.2 billion pounds versus 8.1 billion pounds. The difference of 3.1 billion pounds is the **surplus**—also known as the *excess supply*—of cotton at $1.50.

This surplus means that some cotton farmers are frustrated: at the current price, they cannot find consumers who want to buy their cotton. The surplus offers an incentive for those frustrated would-be sellers to offer a lower price in order to poach business from other producers and entice more consumers

FIGURE 3-12 Price Above Its Equilibrium Level Creates a Surplus

The market price of $1.50 is above the equilibrium price of $1. This creates a surplus: at a price of $1.50, producers would like to sell 11.2 billion pounds but consumers want to buy only 8.1 billion pounds, so there is a surplus of 3.1 billion pounds. This surplus will push the price down until it reaches the equilibrium price of $1.

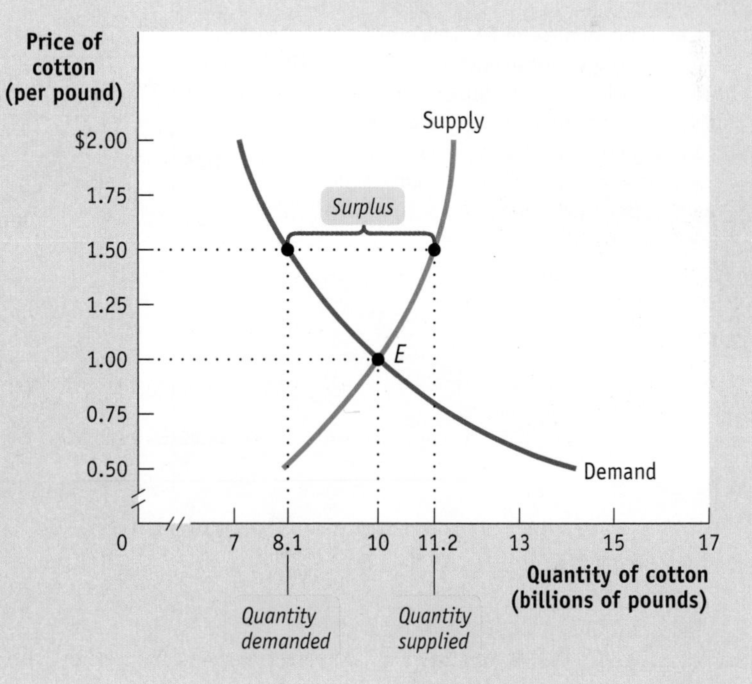

There is a **shortage** of a good or service when the quantity demanded exceeds the quantity supplied. Shortages occur when the price is below its equilibrium level.

to buy. The result of this price cutting will be to push the prevailing price down until it reaches the equilibrium price. So the price of a good will fall whenever there is a surplus—that is, whenever the market price is above its equilibrium level.

Why Does the Market Price Rise if It Is Below the Equilibrium Price?

Now suppose the price is below its equilibrium level—say, at $0.75 per pound, as shown in Figure 3-13. In this case, the quantity demanded, 11.5 billion pounds, exceeds the quantity supplied, 9.1 billion pounds, implying that there are would-be buyers who cannot find cotton: there is a **shortage,** also known as an *excess demand,* of 2.4 billion pounds.

When there is a shortage, there are frustrated would-be buyers—people who want to purchase cotton but cannot find willing sellers at the current price. In this situation, either buyers will offer more than the prevailing price or sellers will realize that they can charge higher prices. Either way, the result is to drive up the prevailing price. This bidding up of prices happens whenever there are shortages—and there will be shortages whenever the price is below its equilibrium level. So the market price will always rise if it is below the equilibrium level.

Using Equilibrium to Describe Markets

We have now seen that a market tends to have a single price, the equilibrium price. If the market price is above the equilibrium level, the ensuing surplus leads buyers and sellers to take actions that lower the price. And if the market price is below the equilibrium level, the ensuing shortage leads buyers and sellers to take actions that raise the price. So the market price always *moves toward* the equilibrium price, the price at which there is neither surplus nor shortage.

FIGURE 3-13 Price Below Its Equilibrium Level Creates a Shortage

The market price of $0.75 is below the equilibrium price of $1. This creates a shortage: consumers want to buy 11.5 billion pounds, but only 9.1 billion pounds are for sale, so there is a shortage of 2.4 billion pounds. This shortage will push the price up until it reaches the equilibrium price of $1.

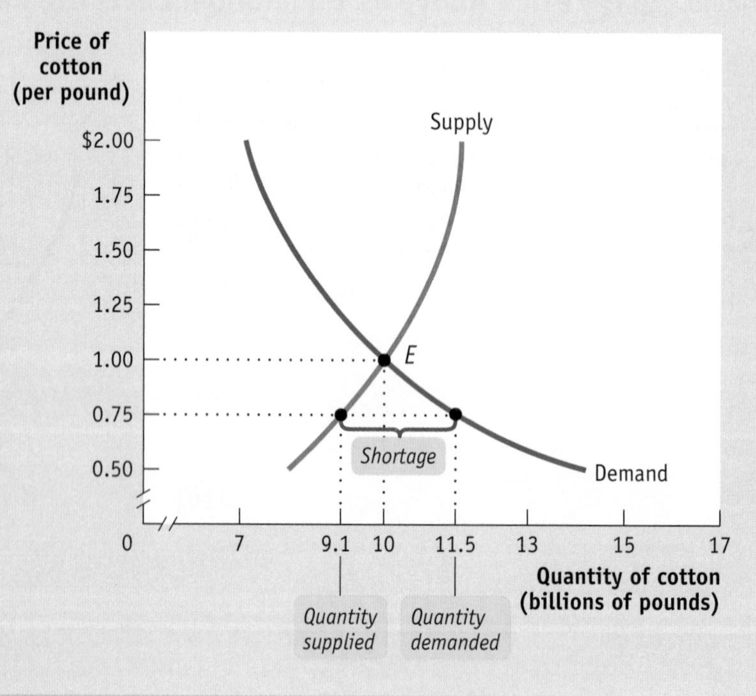

ECONOMICS ➤ IN ACTION

THE PRICE OF ADMISSION

The market equilibrium, so the theory goes, is pretty egalitarian because the equilibrium price applies to everyone. That is, all buyers pay the same price—the equilibrium price—and all sellers receive that same price. But is this realistic?

The market for concert tickets is an example that seems to contradict the theory—there's one price at the box office, and there's another price (typically much higher) for the same event on Internet sites where people who already have tickets resell them, such as StubHub.com or eBay. For example, compare the box office price for a Drake concert in Miami, Florida, to the StubHub.com price for seats in the same location: $88.50 versus $155.

Puzzling as this may seem, there is no contradiction once we take opportunity costs and tastes into account. For major events, buying tickets from the box office means waiting in very long lines. Ticket buyers who use Internet resellers have decided that the opportunity cost of their time is too high to spend waiting in line. And tickets for major events being sold at face value by online box offices often sell out within minutes. In this case, some people who want to go to the concert badly but have missed out on the opportunity to buy cheaper tickets from the online box office are willing to pay the higher Internet reseller price.

Claire R. Greenway/Getty Images

The competitive market model determines the price you pay for concert tickets.

Not only that—perusing the StubHub.com website, you can see that markets really do move to equilibrium. You'll notice that the prices quoted by different sellers for seats close to one another are also very close: $184.99 versus $185 for seats on the main floor of the Drake concert. As the competitive market model predicts, units of the same good end up selling for the same price. And prices move in response to demand and supply. According to an article in the *New York Times,* tickets on StubHub.com can sell for less than the face value for events with little appeal, but prices can skyrocket for events that are in high demand. (The article quotes a price of $3,530 for a Madonna concert.) Even StubHub.com's chief executive says his site is "the embodiment of supply-and-demand economics."

So the theory of competitive markets isn't just speculation. If you want to experience it for yourself, try buying tickets to a concert.

Quick Review

- Price in a competitive market moves to the **equilibrium price,** or **market-clearing price,** where the quantity supplied is equal to the quantity demanded. This quantity is the **equilibrium quantity.**
- All sales and purchases in a market take place at the same price. If the price is above its equilibrium level, there is a **surplus** that drives the price down to the equilibrium level. If the price is below its equilibrium level, there is a **shortage** that drives the price up to the equilibrium level.

CHECK YOUR UNDERSTANDING 3-3

1. In the following three situations, the market is initially in equilibrium. Explain the changes in either supply or demand that result from each event. After each event described below, does a surplus or shortage exist at the original equilibrium price? What will happen to the equilibrium price as a result?
   a. 2012 was a very good year for California wine-grape growers, who produced a bumper crop.
   b. After a hurricane, Florida hoteliers often find that many people cancel their upcoming vacations, leaving them with empty hotel rooms.
   c. After a heavy snowfall, many people want to buy second-hand snowblowers at the local tool shop.

Solutions appear at back of book.

Changes in Supply and Demand

The 2010 floods in Pakistan came as a surprise, but the subsequent increase in the price of cotton was no surprise at all. Suddenly there was a fall in supply: the quantity of cotton available at any given price fell. Predictably, a fall in supply raises the equilibrium price.

The flooding in Pakistan is an example of an event that shifted the supply curve for a good without having much effect on the demand curve. There are many such events. There are also events that shift the demand curve without shifting the supply curve. For example, a medical report that chocolate is good for you increases the demand for chocolate but does not affect the supply. Events often shift either the supply curve or the demand curve, but not both; it is therefore useful to ask what happens in each case.

We have seen that when a curve shifts, the equilibrium price and quantity change. We will now concentrate on exactly how the shift of a curve alters the equilibrium price and quantity.

What Happens When the Demand Curve Shifts

Cotton and polyester are substitutes: if the price of polyester rises, the demand for cotton will increase, and if the price of polyester falls, the demand for cotton will decrease. But how does the price of polyester affect the *market equilibrium* for cotton?

Figure 3-14 shows the effect of a rise in the price of polyester on the market for cotton. The rise in the price of polyester increases the demand for cotton. Point E_1 shows the equilibrium corresponding to the original demand curve, with P_1 the equilibrium price and Q_1 the equilibrium quantity bought and sold.

An increase in demand is indicated by a *rightward* shift of the demand curve from D_1 to D_2. At the original market price P_1, this market is no longer in equilibrium: a shortage occurs because the quantity demanded exceeds the quantity supplied. So the price of cotton rises and generates an increase in the quantity supplied, an upward *movement along the supply curve.* A new

FIGURE 3-14 Equilibrium and Shifts of the Demand Curve

The original equilibrium in the market for cotton is at E_1, at the intersection of the supply curve and the original demand curve, D_1. A rise in the price of polyester, a substitute, shifts the demand curve rightward to D_2. A shortage exists at the original price, P_1, causing both the price and quantity supplied to rise, a movement along the supply curve. A new equilibrium is reached at E_2, with a higher equilibrium price, P_2, and a higher equilibrium quantity, Q_2. When demand for a good or service increases, the equilibrium price and the equilibrium quantity of the good or service both rise.

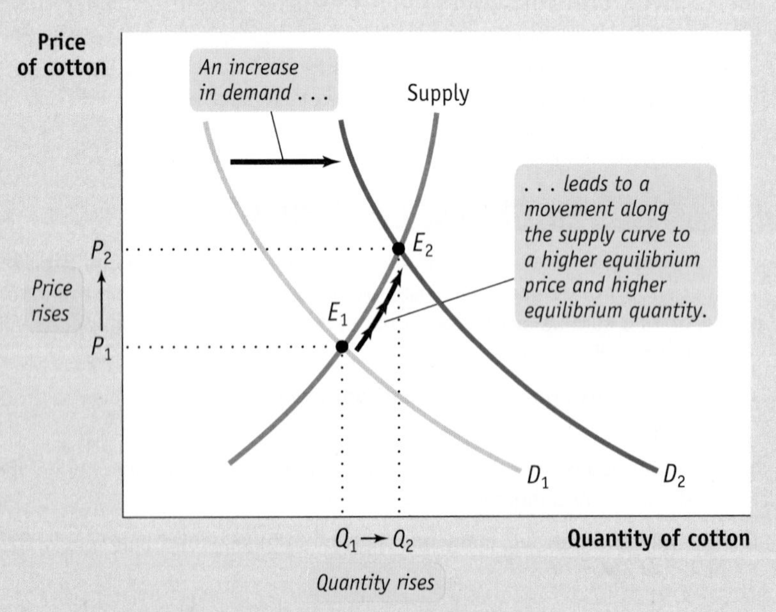

equilibrium is established at point E_2, with a higher equilibrium price, P_2, and higher equilibrium quantity, Q_2. This sequence of events reflects a general principle: *When demand for a good or service increases, the equilibrium price and the equilibrium quantity of the good or service both rise.*

What would happen in the reverse case, a fall in the price of polyester? A fall in the price of polyester reduces the demand for cotton, shifting the demand curve to the *left*. At the original price, a surplus occurs as quantity supplied exceeds quantity demanded. The price falls and leads to a decrease in the quantity supplied, resulting in a lower equilibrium price and a lower equilibrium quantity. This illustrates another general principle: *When demand for a good or service decreases, the equilibrium price and the equilibrium quantity of the good or service both fall.*

To summarize how a market responds to a change in demand: *An increase in demand leads to a rise in both the equilibrium price and the equilibrium quantity. A decrease in demand leads to a fall in both the equilibrium price and the equilibrium quantity.*

What Happens When the Supply Curve Shifts

In the real world, it is a bit easier to predict changes in supply than changes in demand. Physical factors that affect supply, like weather or the availability of inputs, are easier to get a handle on than the fickle tastes that affect demand. Still, with supply as with demand, what we can best predict are the *effects* of shifts of the supply curve.

As we mentioned in this chapter's opening story, devastating floods in Pakistan sharply reduced the supply of cotton in 2010. Figure 3-15 shows how this shift affected the market equilibrium. The original equilibrium is at E_1, the point of intersection of the original supply curve, S_1, and the demand curve, with an equilibrium price P_1 and equilibrium quantity Q_1. As a result of the bad weather, supply falls and S_1 shifts *leftward* to S_2. At the original price P_1, a shortage of cotton now exists and the market is no longer in equilibrium. The shortage causes a rise in price and a fall in quantity demanded, an upward movement along the demand curve. The new equilibrium is at E_2,

FIGURE 3-15 Equilibrium and Shifts of the Supply Curve

The original equilibrium in the market for cotton is at E_1. Bad weather in cotton-growing areas causes a fall in the supply of cotton and shifts the supply curve leftward from S_1 to S_2. A new equilibrium is established at E_2, with a higher equilibrium price, P_2, and a lower equilibrium quantity, Q_2.

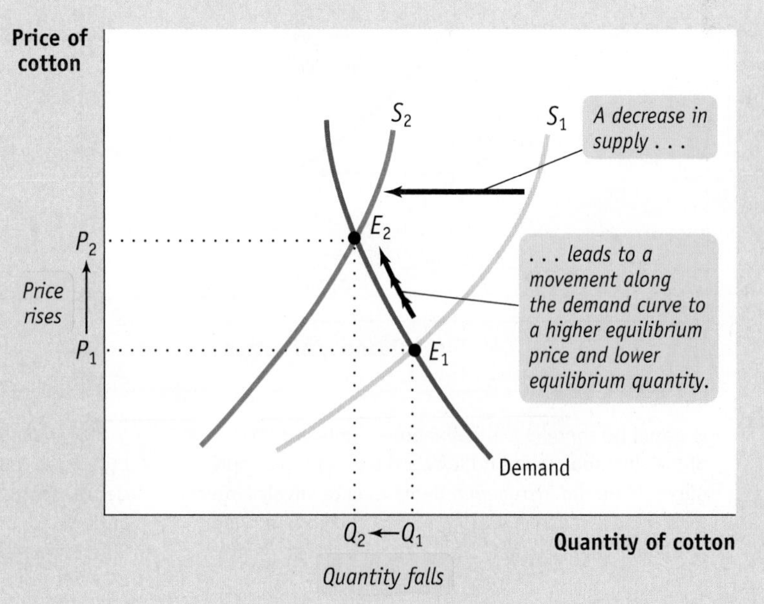

> **PITFALLS**
>
> **WHICH CURVE IS IT, ANYWAY?**
>
> When the price of some good or service changes, in general, we can say that this reflects a change in either supply or demand. But it is easy to get confused about which one. A helpful clue is the direction of change in the quantity. If the quantity sold changes in the *same* direction as the price—for example, if both the price and the quantity rise—this suggests that the demand curve has shifted. If the price and the quantity move in *opposite* directions, the likely cause is a shift of the supply curve.

with an equilibrium price P_2 and an equilibrium quantity Q_2. In the new equilibrium, E_2, the price is higher and the equilibrium quantity lower than before. This can be stated as a general principle: *When supply of a good or service decreases, the equilibrium price of the good or service rises and the equilibrium quantity of the good or service falls.*

What happens to the market when supply increases? An increase in supply leads to a *rightward* shift of the supply curve. At the original price, a surplus now exists; as a result, the equilibrium price falls and the quantity demanded rises. This describes what happened to the market for cotton as new technology increased cotton yields. We can formulate a general principle: *When supply of a good or service increases, the equilibrium price of the good or service falls and the equilibrium quantity of the good or service rises.*

To summarize how a market responds to a change in supply: *An increase in supply leads to a fall in the equilibrium price and a rise in the equilibrium quantity. A decrease in supply leads to a rise in the equilibrium price and a fall in the equilibrium quantity.*

Simultaneous Shifts of Supply and Demand Curves

Finally, it sometimes happens that events shift *both* the demand and supply curves at the same time. This is not unusual; in real life, supply curves and demand curves for many goods and services shift quite often because the economic environment continually changes. Figure 3-16 illustrates two examples of

FIGURE 3-16 Simultaneous Shifts of the Demand and Supply Curves

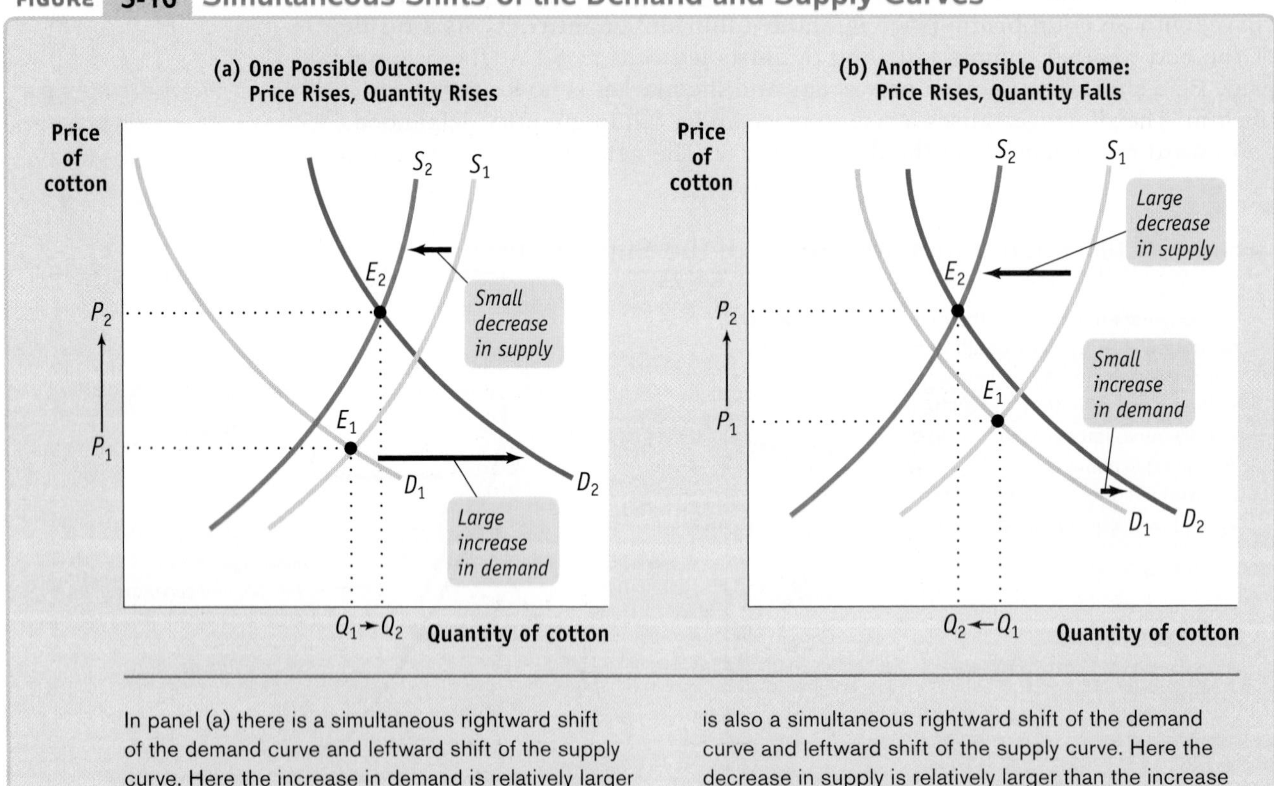

In panel (a) there is a simultaneous rightward shift of the demand curve and leftward shift of the supply curve. Here the increase in demand is relatively larger than the decrease in supply, so the equilibrium price and equilibrium quantity both rise. In panel (b) there is also a simultaneous rightward shift of the demand curve and leftward shift of the supply curve. Here the decrease in supply is relatively larger than the increase in demand, so the equilibrium price rises and the equilibrium quantity falls.

simultaneous shifts. In both panels there is an increase in demand—that is, a rightward shift of the demand curve, from D_1 to D_2—say, for example, representing an increase in the demand for cotton due to changing tastes. Notice that the rightward shift in panel (a) is larger than the one in panel (b): we can suppose that panel (a) represents a year in which many more people than usual choose to buy jeans and cotton T-shirts and panel (b) represents a normal year. Both panels also show a decrease in supply—that is, a leftward shift of the supply curve from S_1 to S_2. Also notice that the leftward shift in panel (b) is relatively larger than the one in panel (a): we can suppose that panel (b) represents the effect of particularly bad weather in Pakistan and panel (a) represents the effect of a much less severe weather event.

In both cases, the equilibrium price rises from P_1 to P_2, as the equilibrium moves from E_1 to E_2. But what happens to the equilibrium quantity, the quantity of cotton bought and sold? In panel (a) the increase in demand is large relative to the decrease in supply, and the equilibrium quantity rises as a result. In panel (b), the decrease in supply is large relative to the increase in demand, and the equilibrium quantity falls as a result. That is, when demand increases and supply decreases, the actual quantity bought and sold can go either way, depending on *how much* the demand and supply curves have shifted.

FOR INQUIRING MINDS

TRIBULATIONS ON THE RUNWAY

You probably don't spend much time worrying about the trials and tribulations of fashion models. Most of them don't lead glamorous lives; in fact, except for a lucky few, life as a fashion model today can be very trying and not very lucrative. And it's all because of supply and demand.

Consider the case of Bianca Gomez, a willowy 18-year-old from Los Angeles, with green eyes, honey-colored hair, and flawless skin, whose experience was detailed in a *Wall Street Journal* article. Bianca began modeling while still in high school, earning about $30,000 in modeling fees during her senior year. Having attracted the interest of some top designers in New York, she moved there after graduation, hoping to land jobs in leading fashion houses and photoshoots for leading fashion magazines.

But once in New York, Bianca entered the global market for fashion models. And it wasn't very pretty. Due to the ease of transmitting photos over the Internet and the relatively low cost of international travel, top fashion centers such as New York and Milan, Italy, are now deluged with beautiful young women from all over the world, eagerly trying to make it as models. Although Russians, other Eastern Europeans, and Brazilians are particularly numerous, some hail from places such as Kazakhstan and Mozambique. As one designer said, "There are so many models now. . . . There are just thousands every year."

Photo by Carlo Buscemi/WireImage

Bianca Gomez on the runway before intense global competition got her thinking about switching careers.

Returning to our (less glamorous) economic model of supply and demand, the influx of aspiring fashion models from around the world can be represented by a rightward shift of the supply curve in the market for fashion models, which would by itself tend to lower the price paid to models. And that wasn't the only change in the market. Unfortunately for Bianca and others like her, the tastes of many of those who hire models have changed as well. Over the past few years, fashion magazines have come to prefer using celebrities such as Angelina Jolie on their pages rather than anonymous models, believing that their readers connect better with a familiar face. This amounts to a leftward shift of the demand curve for models—again reducing the equilibrium price paid to them.

This was borne out in Bianca's experiences. After paying her rent, her transportation, all her modeling expenses, and 20% of her earnings to her modeling agency (which markets her to prospective clients and books her jobs), Bianca found that she was barely breaking even. Sometimes she even had to dip into savings from her high school years. To save money, she ate macaroni and hot dogs; she traveled to auditions, often four or five in one day, by subway. As the *Wall Street Journal* reported, Bianca was seriously considering quitting modeling altogether.

In general, when supply and demand shift in opposite directions, we can't predict what the ultimate effect will be on the quantity bought and sold. What we can say is that a curve that shifts a disproportionately greater distance than the other curve will have a disproportionately greater effect on the quantity bought and sold. That said, we can make the following prediction about the outcome when the supply and demand curves shift in opposite directions:

- When demand increases and supply decreases, the equilibrium price rises but the change in the equilibrium quantity is ambiguous.
- When demand decreases and supply increases, the equilibrium price falls but the change in the equilibrium quantity is ambiguous.

But suppose that the demand and supply curves shift in the same direction. Before 2010, this was the case in the global market for cotton, where both supply and demand had increased over the past decade. Can we safely make any predictions about the changes in price and quantity? In this situation, the change in quantity bought and sold can be predicted, but the change in price is ambiguous. The two possible outcomes when the supply and demand curves shift in the same direction (which you should check for yourself) are as follows:

- When both demand and supply increase, the equilibrium quantity rises but the change in equilibrium price is ambiguous.
- When both demand and supply decrease, the equilibrium quantity falls but the change in equilibrium price is ambiguous.

ECONOMICS ➤ *IN ACTION*

THE RICE RUN OF 2008

In April 2008, the price of rice exported from Thailand—a global benchmark for the price of rice traded in international markets—reached $950 per ton, up from $360 per ton at the beginning of 2008. Within hours, prices for rice at major rice-trading exchanges around the world were breaking record levels. The factors that lay behind the surge in rice prices were both demand-related and supply-related: growing incomes in China and India, traditionally large consumers of rice; drought in Australia; and pest infestation in Vietnam. But it was hoarding by farmers, panic buying by consumers, and an export ban by India, one of the largest exporters of rice, that explained the breathtaking speed of the rise in price.

In much of Asia, governments are major buyers of rice. They buy rice from their rice farmers, who are paid a government-set price, and then sell it to the poor at subsidized prices (prices lower than the market equilibrium price). In the past, the government-set price was better than anything farmers could get in the private market.

Now, even farmers in rural areas of Asia have access to the Internet and can see the price quotes on global rice exchanges. And as rice prices rose in response to changes in demand and supply, farmers grew dissatisfied with the government price and instead hoarded their rice in the belief that they would eventually get higher prices. This was a self-fulfilling belief, as the hoarding shifted the supply curve leftward and raised the price of rice even further.

At the same time, India, one of the largest growers of rice, banned Indian exports of rice in order to protect its domestic consumers, causing yet another leftward shift of the supply curve and pushing the price of rice even higher.

FIGURE 3-17 Rising Rice Prices in the United States, 2003–2011

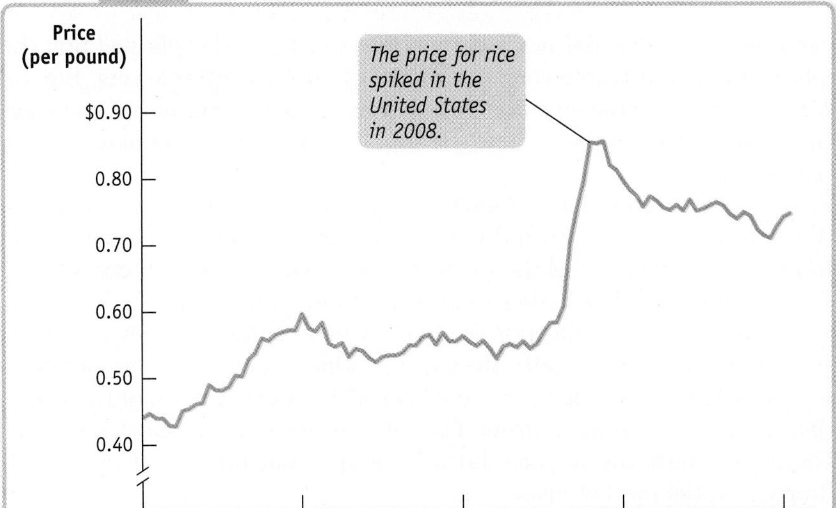

Source: U.S. Bureau of Labor Statistics.

As shown in Figure 3-17, the effects even spilled over to the United States, which had not suffered any fall in its rice production. American rice consumers grew alarmed when large retailers limited some bulk rice purchases by consumers in response to the turmoil in the global rice market.

Fearful of paying even higher prices in the future, panic buying set in. As one woman who was in the process of buying 30 pounds of rice said, "We don't even eat that much rice. But I read about it in the newspaper and decided to buy some." In San Francisco, some Asian markets reported runs on rice. And, predictably, this led to even higher prices as panic buying shifted the demand curve rightward, further feeding the buying frenzy. As one market owner said, "People are afraid. We tell them, 'There's no shortage yet' but it was crazy in here."

Quick Review

- Changes in the equilibrium price and quantity in a market result from shifts of the supply curve, the demand curve, or both.
- An increase in demand increases both the equilibrium price and the equilibrium quantity. A decrease in demand decreases both the equilibrium price and the equilibrium quantity.
- An increase in supply drives the equilibrium price down but increases the equilibrium quantity. A decrease in supply raises the equilibrium price but reduces the equilibrium quantity.
- Often fluctuations in markets involve shifts of both the supply and demand curves. When they shift in the same direction, the change in equilibrium quantity is predictable but the change in equilibrium price is not. When they shift in opposite directions, the change in equilibrium price is predictable but the change in equilibrium quantity is not. When there are simultaneous shifts of the demand and supply curves, the curve that shifts the greater distance has a greater effect on the change in equilibrium price and quantity.

CHECK YOUR UNDERSTANDING 3-4

1. In each of the following examples, determine (i) the market in question; (ii) whether a shift in demand or supply occurred, the direction of the shift, and what induced the shift; and (iii) the effect of the shift on the equilibrium price and the equilibrium quantity.
   - **a.** As the price of gasoline fell in the United States during the 1990s, more people bought large cars.
   - **b.** As technological innovation has lowered the cost of recycling used paper, fresh paper made from recycled stock is used more frequently.
   - **c.** When a local cable company offers cheaper on-demand films, local movie theaters have more unfilled seats.
2. When a new, faster computer chip is introduced, demand for computers using the older, slower chips decreases. Simultaneously, computer makers increase their production of computers containing the old chips in order to clear out their stocks of old chips.

   Draw two diagrams of the market for computers containing the old chips:
   - **a.** one in which the equilibrium quantity falls in response to these events and
   - **b.** one in which the equilibrium quantity rises. What happens to the equilibrium price in each diagram?

Solutions appear at back of book.

Competitive Markets—And Others

Early in this chapter, we defined a competitive market and explained that the supply and demand framework is a model of competitive markets. But we took a rain check on the question of why it matters whether or not a market is competitive. Now that we've seen how the supply and demand model works, we can offer some explanation.

To understand why competitive markets are different from other markets, compare the problems facing two individuals: a wheat farmer who must decide whether to grow more wheat and the president of a giant aluminum company—say, Alcoa—who must decide whether to produce more aluminum.

For the wheat farmer, the question is simply whether the extra wheat can be sold at a price high enough to justify the extra production cost. The farmer need not worry about whether producing more wheat will affect the price of the wheat he or she was already planning to grow. That's because the wheat market is competitive. There are thousands of wheat farmers, and no one farmer's decision will have any impact on the market price.

For the Alcoa executive, things are not that simple because the aluminum market is *not* competitive. There are only a few big producers, including Alcoa, and each of them is well aware that its actions *do* have a noticeable impact on the market price. This adds a whole new level of complexity to the decisions producers have to make. Alcoa can't decide whether or not to produce more aluminum just by asking whether the additional product will sell for more than it costs to make. The company also has to ask whether producing more aluminum will drive down the market price and reduce its *profit,* its net gain from producing and selling its output.

When a market is competitive, individuals can base decisions on less complicated analyses than those used in a noncompetitive market. This in turn means that it's easier for economists to build a model of a competitive market than of a noncompetitive market.

Don't take this to mean that economic analysis has nothing to say about noncompetitive markets. On the contrary, economists can offer some very important insights into how other kinds of markets work. But those insights require other models, which we will learn about later in this text.

WORKED PROBLEM

The Tortilla Price Stabilization Pact

"Thousands in Mexico City protest rising food prices." So read the headline in the *New York Times* on February 1, 2007. Specifically, the demonstrators were protesting a sharp rise in the price of tortillas, a staple food of Mexico's poor, which had gone from $0.25 a pound to between $0.35 and $0.45 a pound in just a few months.

Why were tortilla prices soaring? It was a classic example of what happens to equilibrium price when supply falls. Tortillas are made from corn; much of Mexico's corn is imported from the United States, with the price of corn in both countries basically set in the U.S. corn market. And U.S. corn prices were rising rapidly thanks to surging demand in a new market: the market for ethanol.

The Mexican government's response was the Tortilla Price Stabilization Pact, an agreement with Mexico's major tortilla producers to set the price of tortillas at 8.50 Mexican pesos per kilogram (about $0.78 per kilogram). The Pact aimed to address public concerns about rapidly rising tortilla prices.

This is a hypothetical supply and demand schedule for tortillas in Mexico:

	Quantity of tortillas (billions of kilos)	
Price of tortillas (per kilo in USD)	**Quantity demanded**	**Quantity supplied**
$1.40	1.6	2.8
1.30	1.7	2.6
1.20	1.8	2.4
1.10	1.9	2.2
1.00	2	2
0.90	2.1	1.8
0.80	2.2	1.6
0.70	2.3	1.4
0.60	2.4	1.2

Use a demand and supply graph to find the market equilibrium price and quantity. Show how a price of $0.80 creates a shortage of the good.

STEP 1: Draw and label supply and demand curves. Find the equilibrium quantity demanded.

Review the section "The Demand Schedule and the Demand Curve" (along with Figure 3-1) on pages 71–72, the section "The Supply Schedule and the Supply Curve" on pages 80–81 (including Figure 3-6), and the section "Finding the Equilibrium Price and Quantity" (and Figure 3-11) on pages 87–88.

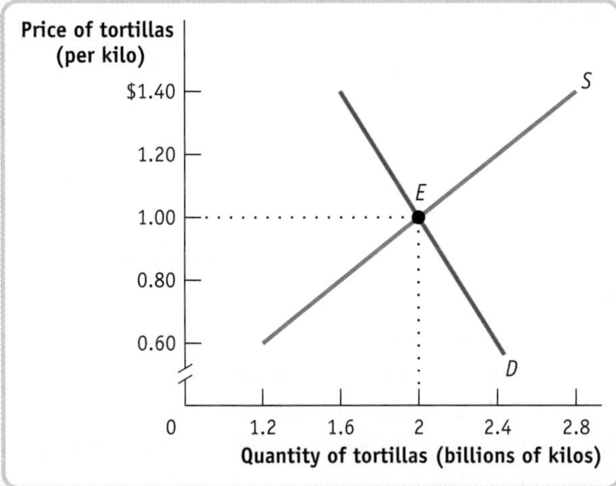

The equilibrium quantity demanded is at point *E*, the point at which quantity supplied equals quantity demanded. As shown both in the supply and demand schedule and in the figure above, this occurs at an equilibrium quantity of 2.0 billion kilos and an equilibrium price of $1.00. ■

STEP 2: Calculate the shortage of tortillas that would occur at a price of $0.80.

Review the section "Why Does the Market Price Rise if It is Below the Equilibrium Price?" on page 90. An example of a price below its equilibrium level that creates a shortage is given in Figure 3-13.

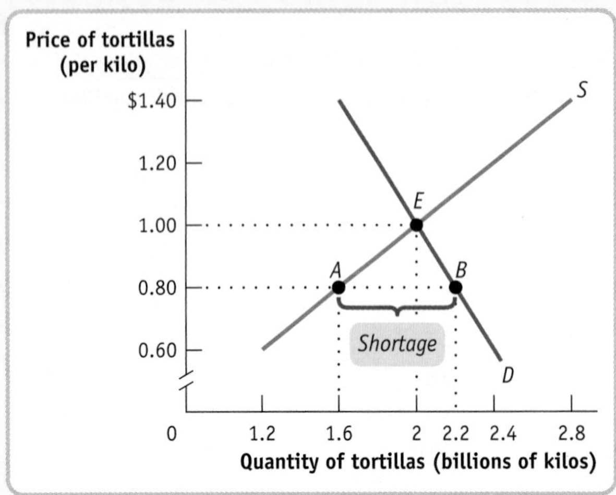

As shown above, a price of $0.80 corresponds to point *A* on the supply curve. The quantity supplied at a price of $0.80 can be found by starting at point *A* and following the dotted line down to the horizontal axis and observing that the quantity supplied is 1.6 billion kilos. Similarly, a price of $0.80 corresponds to point *B* on the demand curve. The quantity demanded at a price of $0.80 can be found by starting at point *B*, following the dotted line down to the horizontal axis, and observing that the quantity demanded is 2.2 billion kilos. The difference between the quantity demanded and the quantity supplied is 2.2 – 1.6 = 0.6 billion kilos. This difference can also be found from the supply and demand schedule. As shown in the schedule, at a price of $0.80, the quantity supplied (1.6 billion kilos) is less than the quantity demanded (2.2 billion kilos) by 0.6 billion kilos. ■

SUMMARY

1. The **supply and demand model** illustrates how a **competitive market,** one with many buyers and sellers, none of whom can influence the market price, works.
2. The **demand schedule** shows the **quantity demanded** at each price and is represented graphically by a **demand curve.** The **law of demand** says that demand curves slope downward; that is, a higher price for a good or service leads people to demand a smaller quantity, other things equal.
3. A **movement along the demand curve** occurs when a price change leads to a change in the quantity demanded. When economists talk of increasing or decreasing demand, they mean **shifts of the demand curve**—a change in the quantity demanded at any given price. An increase in demand causes a rightward shift of the demand curve. A decrease in demand causes a leftward shift.
4. There are five main factors that shift the demand curve:
   - A change in the prices of related goods or services, such as **substitutes** or **complements**
   - A change in income: when income rises, the demand for **normal goods** increases and the demand for **inferior goods** decreases.
   - A change in tastes
   - A change in expectations
   - A change in the number of consumers
5. The market demand curve for a good or service is the horizontal sum of the **individual demand curves** of all consumers in the market.
6. The **supply schedule** shows the **quantity supplied** at each price and is represented graphically by a **supply curve.** Supply curves usually slope upward.

7. A **movement along the supply curve** occurs when a price change leads to a change in the quantity supplied. When economists talk of increasing or decreasing supply, they mean **shifts of the supply curve**—a change in the quantity supplied at any given price. An increase in supply causes a rightward shift of the supply curve. A decrease in supply causes a leftward shift.

8. There are five main factors that shift the supply curve:
   - A change in **input** prices
   - A change in the prices of related goods and services
   - A change in technology
   - A change in expectations
   - A change in the number of producers

9. The market supply curve for a good or service is the horizontal sum of the **individual supply curves** of all producers in the market.

10. The supply and demand model is based on the principle that the price in a market moves to its **equilibrium price,** or **market-clearing price,** the price at which the quantity demanded is equal to the quantity supplied. This quantity is the **equilibrium quantity.** When the price is above its market-clearing level, there is a **surplus** that pushes the price down. When the price is below its market-clearing level, there is a **shortage** that pushes the price up.

11. An increase in demand increases both the equilibrium price and the equilibrium quantity; a decrease in demand has the opposite effect. An increase in supply reduces the equilibrium price and increases the equilibrium quantity; a decrease in supply has the opposite effect.

12. Shifts of the demand curve and the supply curve can happen simultaneously. When they shift in opposite directions, the change in equilibrium price is predictable but the change in equilibrium quantity is not. When they shift in the same direction, the change in equilibrium quantity is predictable but the change in equilibrium price is not. In general, the curve that shifts the greater distance has a greater effect on the changes in equilibrium price and quantity.

KEY TERMS

Competitive market, p. 70
Supply and demand model, p. 70
Demand schedule, p. 71
Quantity demanded, p. 71
Demand curve, p. 72
Law of demand, p. 72
Shift of the demand curve, p. 73
Movement along the demand curve, p. 73
Substitutes, p. 75
Complements, p. 75
Normal good, p. 76
Inferior good, p. 76
Individual demand curve, p. 77
Quantity supplied, p. 80
Supply schedule, p. 80
Supply curve, p. 80
Shift of the supply curve, p. 81
Movement along the supply curve, p. 81
Input, p. 83
Individual supply curve, p. 84
Equilibrium price, p. 87
Equilibrium quantity, p. 87
Market-clearing price, p. 87
Surplus, p. 89
Shortage, p. 90

PROBLEMS

1. A survey indicated that chocolate is Americans' favorite ice-cream flavor. For each of the following, indicate the possible effects on demand, supply, or both as well as equilibrium price and quantity of chocolate ice cream.
   a. A severe drought in the Midwest causes dairy farmers to reduce the number of milk-producing cattle in their herds by a third. These dairy farmers supply cream that is used to manufacture chocolate ice cream.
   b. A new report by the American Medical Association reveals that chocolate does, in fact, have significant health benefits.
   c. The discovery of cheaper synthetic vanilla flavoring lowers the price of vanilla ice cream.
   d. New technology for mixing and freezing ice cream lowers manufacturers' costs of producing chocolate ice cream.

2. In a supply and demand diagram, draw the shift of the demand curve for hamburgers in your hometown due to the following events. In each case, show the effect on equilibrium price and quantity.
   a. The price of tacos increases.
   b. All hamburger sellers raise the price of their french fries.
   c. Income falls in town. Assume that hamburgers are a normal good for most people.
   d. Income falls in town. Assume that hamburgers are an inferior good for most people.
   e. Hot dog stands cut the price of hot dogs.

3. The market for many goods changes in predictable ways according to the time of year, in response to events such as holidays, vacation times, seasonal changes in production, and so on. Using supply and demand, explain

the change in price in each of the following cases. Note that supply and demand may shift simultaneously.

a. Lobster prices usually fall during the summer peak lobster harvest season, despite the fact that people like to eat lobster during the summer more than at any other time of year.

b. The price of a Christmas tree is lower after Christmas than before but fewer trees are sold.

c. The price of a round-trip ticket to Paris on Air France falls by more than $200 after the end of school vacation in September. This happens despite the fact that generally worsening weather increases the cost of operating flights to Paris, and Air France therefore reduces the number of flights to Paris at any given price.

4. Show in a diagram the effect on the demand curve, the supply curve, the equilibrium price, and the equilibrium quantity of each of the following events.

a. The market for newspapers in your town

Case 1: The salaries of journalists go up.

Case 2: There is a big news event in your town, which is reported in the newspapers.

b. The market for St. Louis Rams cotton T-shirts

Case 1: The Rams win the Super Bowl.

Case 2: The price of cotton increases.

c. The market for bagels

Case 1: People realize how fattening bagels are.

Case 2: People have less time to make themselves a cooked breakfast.

d. The market for the Krugman and Wells economics textbook

Case 1: Your professor makes it required reading for all of his or her students.

Case 2: Printing costs for textbooks are lowered by the use of synthetic paper.

5. The U.S. Department of Agriculture reported that in 2004 each person in the United States consumed an average of 37 gallons of soft drinks (nondiet) at an average price of $2 per gallon. Assume that, at a price of $1.50 per gallon, each individual consumer would demand 50 gallons of soft drinks. The U.S. population in 2004 was 294 million. From this information about the individual demand schedule, calculate the market demand schedule for soft drinks for the prices of $1.50 and $2 per gallon.

6. Suppose that the supply schedule of Maine lobsters is as follows:

Price of lobster (per pound)	Quantity of lobster supplied (pounds)
$25	800
20	700
15	600
10	500
5	400

Suppose that Maine lobsters can be sold only in the United States. The U.S. demand schedule for Maine lobsters is as follows:

Price of lobster (per pound)	Quantity of lobster demanded (pounds)
$25	200
20	400
15	600
10	800
5	1,000

a. Draw the demand curve and the supply curve for Maine lobsters. What are the equilibrium price and quantity of lobsters?

Now suppose that Maine lobsters can be sold in France. The French demand schedule for Maine lobsters is as follows:

Price of lobster (per pound)	Quantity of lobster supplied (pounds)
$25	100
20	300
15	500
10	700
5	900

b. What is the demand schedule for Maine lobsters now that French consumers can also buy them? Draw a supply and demand diagram that illustrates the new equilibrium price and quantity of lobsters. What will happen to the price at which fishermen can sell lobster? What will happen to the price paid by U.S. consumers? What will happen to the quantity consumed by U.S. consumers?

7. Find the flaws in reasoning in the following statements, paying particular attention to the distinction between shifts of and movements along the supply and demand curves. Draw a diagram to illustrate what actually happens in each situation.

a. "A technological innovation that lowers the cost of producing a good might seem at first to result in a reduction in the price of the good to consumers. But a fall in price will increase demand for the good, and higher demand will send the price up again. It is not certain, therefore, that an innovation will really reduce price in the end."

b. "A study shows that eating a clove of garlic a day can help prevent heart disease, causing many consumers to demand more garlic. This increase in demand results in a rise in the price of garlic. Consumers, seeing that the price of garlic has gone up, reduce their demand for garlic. This causes the demand for garlic to decrease and the price of garlic to fall. Therefore, the ultimate effect of the study on the price of garlic is uncertain."

8. The following table shows a demand schedule for a normal good.

Price	Quantity demanded
$23	70
21	90
19	110
17	130

a. Do you think that the increase in quantity demanded (say, from 90 to 110 in the table) when price decreases (from $21 to $19) is due to a rise in consumers' income? Explain clearly (and briefly) why or why not.

b. Now suppose that the good is an inferior good. Would the demand schedule still be valid for an inferior good?

c. Lastly, assume you do not know whether the good is normal or inferior. Devise an experiment that would allow you to determine which one it was. Explain.

9. According to the *New York Times* (November 18, 2006), the number of car producers in China is increasing rapidly. The newspaper reports that "China has more car brands now than the United States. . . . But while car sales have climbed 38 percent in the first three quarters of this year, automakers have increased their output even faster, causing fierce competition and a slow erosion in prices." At the same time, Chinese consumers' incomes have risen. Assume that cars are a normal good. Use a diagram of the supply and demand curves for cars in China to explain what has happened in the Chinese car market.

10. Aaron Hank is a star hitter for the Bay City baseball team. He is close to breaking the major league record for home runs hit during one season, and it is widely anticipated that in the next game he will break that record. As a result, tickets for the team's next game have been a hot commodity. But today it is announced that, due to a knee injury, he will not in fact play in the team's next game. Assume that season ticket-holders are able to resell their tickets if they wish. Use supply and demand diagrams to explain the following.

a. Show the case in which this announcement results in a lower equilibrium price and a lower equilibrium quantity than before the announcement.

b. Show the case in which this announcement results in a lower equilibrium price and a higher equilibrium quantity than before the announcement.

c. What accounts for whether case a or case b occurs?

d. Suppose that a scalper had secretly learned before the announcement that Aaron Hank would not play in the next game. What actions do you think he would take?

11. In *Rolling Stone* magazine, several fans and rock stars, including Pearl Jam, were bemoaning the high price of concert tickets. One superstar argued, "It just isn't worth $75 to see me play. No one should have to pay that much to go to a concert." Assume this star sold out arenas around the country at an average ticket price of $75.

a. How would you evaluate the argument that ticket prices are too high?

b. Suppose that due to this star's protests, ticket prices were lowered to $50. In what sense is this price too low? Draw a diagram using supply and demand curves to support your argument.

c. Suppose Pearl Jam really wanted to bring down ticket prices. Since the band controls the supply of its services, what do you recommend they do? Explain using a supply and demand diagram.

d. Suppose the band's next CD was a total dud. Do you think they would still have to worry about ticket prices being too high? Why or why not? Draw a supply and demand diagram to support your argument.

e. Suppose the group announced their next tour was going to be their last. What effect would this likely have on the demand for and price of tickets? Illustrate with a supply and demand diagram.

12. The accompanying table gives the annual U.S. demand and supply schedules for pickup trucks.

Price of truck	Quantity of trucks demanded (millions)	Quantity of trucks supplied (millions)
$20,000	20	14
25,000	18	15
30,000	16	16
35,000	14	17
40,000	12	18

a. Plot the demand and supply curves using these schedules. Indicate the equilibrium price and quantity on your diagram.

b. Suppose the tires used on pickup trucks are found to be defective. What would you expect to happen in the market for pickup trucks? Show this on your diagram.

c. Suppose that the U.S. Department of Transportation imposes costly regulations on manufacturers that cause them to reduce supply by one-third at any given price. Calculate and plot the new supply schedule and indicate the new equilibrium price and quantity on your diagram.

13. After several years of decline, the market for handmade acoustic guitars is making a comeback. These guitars are usually made in small workshops employing relatively few highly skilled luthiers. Assess the impact on the equilibrium price and quantity of handmade acoustic guitars as a result of each of the following events. In your answers indicate which curve(s) shift(s) and in which direction.

a. Environmentalists succeed in having the use of Brazilian rosewood banned in the United States, forcing luthiers to seek out alternative, more costly woods.

b. A foreign producer reengineers the guitar-making process and floods the market with identical guitars.

c. Music featuring handmade acoustic guitars makes a comeback as audiences tire of heavy metal and alternative rock music.

d. The country goes into a deep recession and the income of the average American falls sharply.

14. Will Shakespeare is a struggling playwright in sixteenth-century London. As the price he receives for writing a play increases, he is willing to write more plays. For the following situations, use a diagram to illustrate how each event affects the equilibrium price and quantity in the market for Shakespeare's plays.

a. The playwright Christopher Marlowe, Shakespeare's chief rival, is killed in a bar brawl.

b. The bubonic plague, a deadly infectious disease, breaks out in London.

c. To celebrate the defeat of the Spanish Armada, Queen Elizabeth declares several weeks of festivities, which involves commissioning new plays.

15. The small town of Middling experiences a sudden doubling of the birth rate. After three years, the birth rate returns to normal. Use a diagram to illustrate the effect of these events on the following.

a. The market for an hour of babysitting services in Middling today

b. The market for an hour of babysitting services 14 years into the future, after the birth rate has returned to normal, by which time children born today are old enough to work as babysitters

c. The market for an hour of babysitting services 30 years into the future, when children born today are likely to be having children of their own

16. Use a diagram to illustrate how each of the following events affects the equilibrium price and quantity of pizza.

a. The price of mozzarella cheese rises.

b. The health hazards of hamburgers are widely publicized.

c. The price of tomato sauce falls.

d. The incomes of consumers rise and pizza is an inferior good.

e. Consumers expect the price of pizza to fall next week.

EXTEND YOUR UNDERSTANDING

17. *Demand twisters:* Sketch and explain the demand relationship in each of the following statements.

a. I would never buy a Britney Spears CD! You couldn't even give me one for nothing.

b. I generally buy a bit more coffee as the price falls. But once the price falls to $2 per pound, I'll buy out the entire stock of the supermarket.

c. I spend more on orange juice even as the price rises. (Does this mean that I must be violating the law of demand?)

d. Due to a tuition rise, most students at a college find themselves with less disposable income. Almost all of them eat more frequently at the school cafeteria and less often at restaurants, even though prices at the cafeteria have risen, too. (This one requires that you draw both the demand and the supply curves for school cafeteria meals.)

18. Although he was a prolific artist, Pablo Picasso painted only 1,000 canvases during his "Blue Period." Picasso is now dead, and all of his Blue Period works are currently on display in museums and private galleries throughout Europe and the United States.

a. Draw a supply curve for Picasso Blue Period works. Why is this supply curve different from ones you have seen?

b. Given the supply curve from part a, the price of a Picasso Blue Period work will be entirely dependent on what factor(s)? Draw a diagram showing how the equilibrium price of such a work is determined.

c. Suppose rich art collectors decide that it is essential to acquire Picasso Blue Period art for their collections. Show the impact of this on the market for these paintings.

19. Draw the appropriate curve in each of the following cases. Is it like or unlike the curves you have seen so far? Explain.

a. The demand for cardiac bypass surgery, given that the government pays the full cost for any patient

b. The demand for elective cosmetic plastic surgery, given that the patient pays the full cost

c. The supply of reproductions of Rembrandt paintings

CHAPTER 4

Price Controls and Quotas: Meddling with Markets

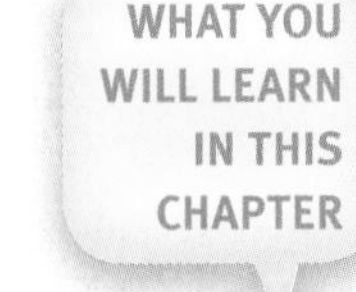

- The meaning of **consumer surplus** and its relationship to the demand curve
- The meaning of **producer surplus** and its relationship to the supply curve
- The meaning and importance of **total surplus** and how it can be used to measure the gains from trade
- How **price controls** and **quantity controls** create problems and can make a market inefficient
- What **deadweight loss** is
- Who benefits and who loses from market interventions, and why they are used despite their well-known problems

BIG CITY, NOT-SO-BRIGHT IDEAS

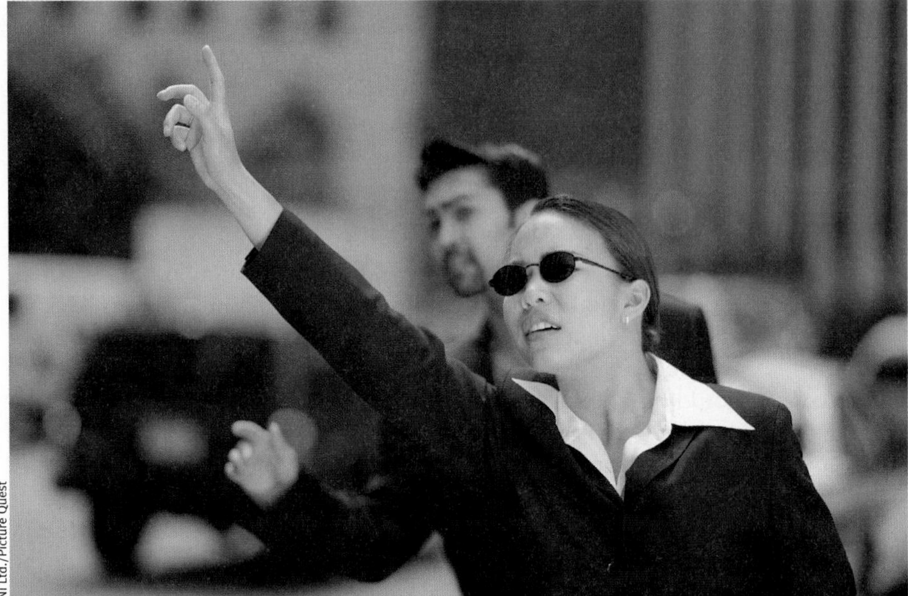

PNI Ltd./Picture Quest

New York City: an empty taxi is hard to find.

NEW YORK CITY IS A PLACE WHERE you can find almost anything—that is, almost anything, except a taxicab when you need one or a decent apartment at a rent you can afford. You might think that New York's notorious shortages of cabs and apartments are the inevitable price of big-city living. However, they are largely the product of government policies—specifically, of government policies that have, one way or another, tried to prevail over the market forces of supply and demand.

In Chapter 3, we learned the principle that a market moves to equilibrium—that the market price rises or falls to the level at which the quantity of a good that people are willing to supply is equal to the quantity that other people demand.

But sometimes governments try to defy that principle. Whenever a government tries to dictate either a market price or a market quantity that's different from the equilibrium price or quantity, the market strikes back in predictable ways. Our ability to predict what will happen when governments try to defy supply and demand shows the power and usefulness of supply and demand analysis itself.

The shortages of apartments and taxicabs in New York are particular examples that illuminate what happens when the logic of the market is defied. New York's housing shortage is the result of *rent control,* a law that prevents landlords from raising rents except when specifically given permission. Rent control was introduced during World War II to protect the interests of tenants, and it still remains in force. Many other American cities have had rent control at one time or another, but with the notable exceptions of New York and San Francisco, these controls have largely been done away with.

Similarly, New York's limited supply of taxis is the result of a licensing system introduced in the 1930s. New York taxi licenses are known as "medallions," and only taxis with medallions are allowed to pick up passengers. Although this system was originally intended to protect the interests of both drivers and customers, it has generated a shortage of taxis in the city. The number of medallions remained fixed for nearly 60 years, with no significant increase until 2004.

We begin this chapter by looking at *consumer surplus,* the benefit from being able to purchase a good or a service. We will then look at a corresponding measure, *producer surplus,* which shows the benefit sellers receive from being able to sell a good. We move on to examine what happens when governments try to control prices in a competitive market, keeping the price in a market either below its equilibrium level—a *price ceiling* such as rent control—or above it—a *price floor* such as the minimum wage paid to workers in many countries. We then turn to schemes such as taxi medallions that attempt to dictate the quantity of a good bought and sold. ■

A consumer's **willingness to pay** for a good is the maximum price at which he or she would buy that good.

Consumer Surplus and the Demand Curve

The market in used textbooks is a big business in terms of dollars and cents—approximately $2.9 billion in 2011. More importantly for us, it is a convenient starting point for developing the concepts of consumer and producer surplus. We'll use the concepts of consumer and producer surplus to understand exactly how buyers and sellers benefit from a competitive market and how big those benefits are. In addition, these concepts play important roles in analyzing what happens when competitive markets don't work well or there is interference in the market.

So let's begin by looking at the market for used textbooks, starting with the buyers. The key point, as we'll see in a minute, is that the demand curve is derived from their tastes or preferences—and that those same preferences also determine how much they gain from the opportunity to buy used books.

Willingness to Pay and the Demand Curve

A used book is not as good as a new book—it will be battered and coffee-stained, may include someone else's highlighting, and may not be completely up to date. How much this bothers you depends on your preferences. Some potential buyers would prefer to buy the used book even if it is only slightly cheaper than a new book, but others would buy the used book only if it is considerably cheaper. Let's define a potential buyer's **willingness to pay** as the maximum price at which he or she would buy a good, in this case a used textbook. An individual won't buy the book if it costs more than this amount but is eager to do so if it costs less. If the price is just equal to an individual's willingness to pay, he or she is indifferent between buying and not buying. For the sake of simplicity, we'll assume that the individual buys the good in this case.

Table 4-1 shows five potential buyers of a used book that costs $100 new, listed in order of their willingness to pay. At one extreme is Aleisha, who will buy a secondhand book even if the price is as high as $59. Brad is less willing to have a used book and will buy one only if the price is $45 or less. Claudia is willing to pay only $35; Darren, only $25. And Edwina, who really doesn't like the idea of a used book, will buy one only if it costs no more than $10.

How many of these five students will actually buy a used book? It depends on the price. If the price of a used book is $55, only Aleisha buys one; if the price is $40, Aleisha and Brad both buy used books, and so on. So the information in the table on willingness to pay also defines the *demand schedule* for used textbooks.

TABLE 4-1 Consumer Surplus When the Price of a Used Textbook Is $30

Potential buyer	Willingness to pay	Price paid	Individual consumer surplus = Willingness to pay − Price paid
Aleisha	$59	$30	$29
Brad	45	30	15
Claudia	35	30	5
Darren	25	—	—
Edwina	10	—	—
All buyers			**Total consumer surplus = $49**

Willingness to Pay and Consumer Surplus

Suppose that the campus bookstore makes used textbooks available at a price of $30. In that case Aleisha, Brad, and Claudia will buy books. Do they gain from their purchases, and if so, how much?

The answer, also shown in Table 4-1, is that each student who purchases a book does achieve a net gain but that the amount of the gain differs among students.

Aleisha would have been willing to pay $59, so her net gain is $59 — $30 = $29. Brad would have been willing to pay $45, so his net gain is $45 — $30 = $15. Claudia would have been willing to pay $35, so her net gain is $35 — $30 = $5. Darren and Edwina, however, won't be willing to buy a used book at a price of $30, so they neither gain nor lose.

The net gain that a buyer achieves from the purchase of a good is called that buyer's **individual consumer surplus.** What we learn from this example is that whenever a buyer pays a price less than his or her willingness to pay, the buyer achieves some individual consumer surplus.

The sum of the individual consumer surpluses achieved by all the buyers of a good is known as the **total consumer surplus** achieved in the market. In Table 4-1, the total consumer surplus is the sum of the individual consumer surpluses achieved by Aleisha, Brad, and Claudia: $29 + $15 + $5 = $49.

Economists often use the term **consumer surplus** to refer to both individual and total consumer surplus. We will follow this practice; it will always be clear in context whether we are referring to the consumer surplus achieved by an individual or by all buyers.

Total consumer surplus can be represented graphically. As we saw in Chapter 3, we can use the demand schedule to derive the market demand curve shown in Figure 4-1. Because we are considering only a small number of consumers, this curve doesn't look like the smooth demand curves of Chapter 3, where markets contained hundreds or thousands of consumers. This demand curve is stepped, with alternating horizontal and vertical segments. Each horizontal segment—each step—corresponds to one potential buyer's willingness to pay. Each step in that demand curve is one book wide and represents one consumer. For example, the height of Aleisha's step is $59, her willingness to pay. This step forms the top of a rectangle, with $30—the price she actually pays for a book—forming the bottom. The area of Aleisha's rectangle, ($59 — $30) × 1 = $29, is her consumer surplus from purchasing one book at $30. So the individual consumer surplus Aleisha gains is the *area of the dark blue rectangle* shown in Figure 4-1.

In addition to Aleisha, Brad and Claudia will also each buy a book when the price is $30. Like Aleisha, they benefit from their purchases, though not as much, because they each have a lower willingness to pay. Figure 4-1 also shows the consumer surplus gained by Brad and Claudia; again, this can be measured by the areas of the appropriate rectangles. Darren and Edwina, because they do not buy books at a price of $30, receive no consumer surplus.

Individual consumer surplus is the net gain to an individual buyer from the purchase of a good. It is equal to the difference between the buyer's willingness to pay and the price paid.

Total consumer surplus is the sum of the individual consumer surpluses of all the buyers of a good in a market.

The term **consumer surplus** is often used to refer to both individual and total consumer surplus.

FIGURE 4-1 Consumer Surplus in the Used-Textbook Market

At a price of $30, Aleisha, Brad, and Claudia each buy a book but Darren and Edwina do not. Aleisha, Brad, and Claudia receive individual consumer surpluses equal to the difference between their willingness to pay and the price, illustrated by the areas of the shaded rectangles. Both Darren and Edwina have a willingness to pay less than $30, so they are unwilling to buy a book in this market; they receive zero consumer surplus. The total consumer surplus is given by the entire shaded area—the sum of the individual consumer surpluses of Aleisha, Brad, and Claudia—equal to $29 + $15 + $5 = $49.

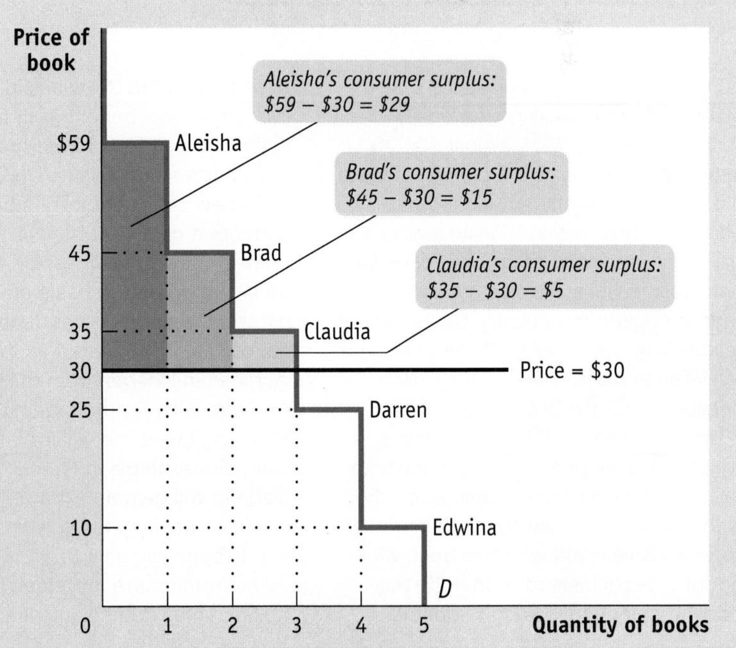

FIGURE 4-2 Consumer Surplus

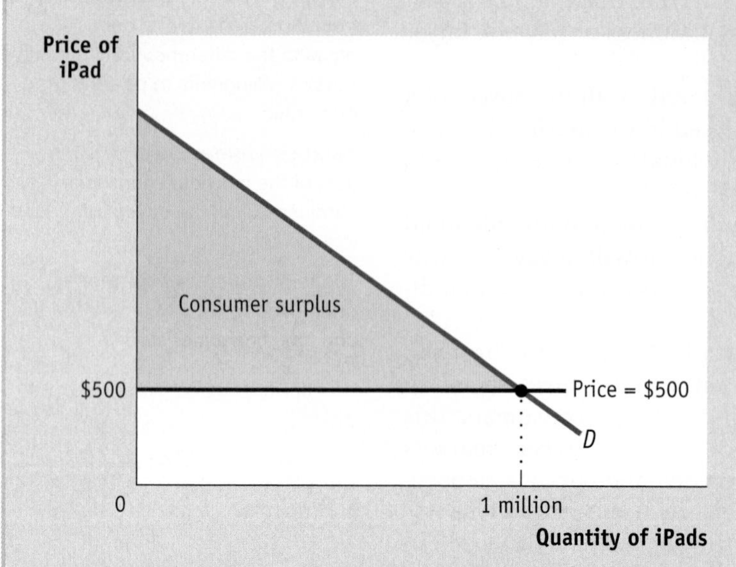

The demand curve for iPads is smooth because there are many potential buyers. At a price of $500, 1 million iPads are demanded. The consumer surplus at this price is equal to the shaded area: the area below the demand curve but above the price. This is the total net gain to consumers generated from buying and consuming iPads when the price is $500.

The total consumer surplus achieved in this market is just the sum of the individual consumer surpluses received by Aleisha, Brad, and Claudia. So total consumer surplus is equal to the combined area of the three rectangles—the entire shaded area in Figure 4-1. Another way to say this is that total consumer surplus is equal to the area below the demand curve but above the price.

Figure 4-1 illustrates the following general principle: *the total consumer surplus generated by purchases of a good at a given price is equal to the area below the demand curve but above that price.* The same principle applies regardless of the number of consumers.

When we consider large markets, this graphical representation becomes extremely helpful. Consider, for example, the sales of iPads to millions of potential buyers. Each potential buyer has a maximum price that he or she is willing to pay. With so many potential buyers, the demand curve will be smooth, like the one shown in Figure 4-2.

Suppose that at a price of $500, a total of 1 million iPads are purchased. How much do consumers gain from being able to buy those 1 million iPads? We could answer that question by calculating the consumer surplus of each individual buyer and then adding these numbers up to arrive at a total. But it is much easier just to look at Figure 4-2 and use the fact that the total consumer surplus is equal to the shaded area. As in our original example, consumer surplus is equal to the area below the demand curve but above the price. (You can refresh your memory on how to calculate the area of a right triangle by reviewing the appendix to Chapter 2.)

FOR INQUIRING MINDS

A MATTER OF LIFE AND DEATH

In 2010, over 3,900 people in the United States died while waiting for a kidney transplant. In early 2011, almost 90,000 were wait-listed. Since the number of those in need of a kidney far exceeds availability, what is the best way to allocate available organs? A market isn't feasible. For understandable reasons, the sale of human body parts is illegal in this country. So the task of establishing a protocol for these situations has fallen to the nonprofit group United Network for Organ Sharing (UNOS).

Under current UNOS guidelines, a donated kidney goes to the person who has been waiting the longest. According to this system, an available kidney would go to a 75-year-old who has been waiting for 2 years instead of to a 25-year-old who has been waiting 6 months, even though the 25-year-old will likely live longer and benefit from the transplanted organ for a longer period of time.

To address this issue, UNOS is devising a new set of guidelines based on a concept it calls "net benefit." According to these new guidelines, kidneys would be allocated on the basis of who will receive the greatest net benefit, where net benefit is measured as the expected increase in lifespan from the transplant. And age is by far the biggest predictor of how long someone will live after a transplant. For example, a typical 25-year-old diabetic will gain an extra 8.7 years of life from a transplant, but a typical 55-year-old diabetic will gain only 3.6 extra years.

Under the current system, based on waiting times, transplants lead to about 44,000 extra years of life for recipients; under the new system, that number would jump to 55,000 extra years. The share of kidneys going to those in their 20s would triple; the share going to those 60 and older would be halved.

What does this have to do with consumer surplus? As you may have guessed, the UNOS concept of "net benefit" is a lot like individual consumer surplus—the individual consumer surplus generated from getting a new kidney. In essence, UNOS has devised a system that allocates donated kidneys according to who gets the greatest individual consumer surplus. In terms of results, then, its proposed "net benefit" system operates a lot like a competitive market.

Producer Surplus and the Supply Curve

Just as some buyers of a good would have been willing to pay more for their purchase than the price they actually pay, some sellers of a good would have been willing to sell it for less than the price they actually receive. So just as there are consumers who receive consumer surplus from buying in a market, there are producers who receive producer surplus from selling in a market.

Cost and Producer Surplus

Consider a group of students who are potential sellers of used textbooks. Because they have different preferences, the various potential sellers differ in the price at which they are willing to sell their books. Table 4-2 shows the prices at which several different students would be willing to sell. Andrew is willing to sell the book as long as he can get at least $5; Betty won't sell unless she can get at least $15; Carlos, unless he can get $25; Donna, unless she can get $35; Engelbert, unless he can get $45.

TABLE 4-2 Producer Surplus When the Price of a Used Textbook Is $30

Potential seller	Cost	Price received	Individual producer surplus = Price received − Cost
Andrew	$5	$30	$25
Betty	15	30	15
Carlos	25	30	5
Donna	35	—	—
Engelbert	45	—	—
All sellers			**Total producer surplus = $45**

The lowest price at which a potential seller is willing to sell has a special name in economics: it is called the seller's **cost.** So Andrew's cost is $5, Betty's is $15, and so on.

Using the term *cost,* which people normally associate with the monetary cost of producing a good, may sound a little strange when applied to sellers of used textbooks. The students don't have to manufacture the books, so it doesn't cost the student who sells a book anything to make that book available for sale, does it?

Yes, it does. A student who sells a book won't have it later, as part of his or her personal collection. So there is an *opportunity cost* to selling a textbook, even if the owner has completed the course for which it was required. And remember that one of the basic principles of economics is that the true measure of the cost of doing something is always its opportunity cost. That is, the real cost of something is what you must give up to get it.

So it is good economics to talk of the minimum price at which someone will sell a good as the "cost" of selling that good, even if he or she doesn't spend any money to make the good available for sale. Of course, in most real-world markets the sellers are also those who produce the good and therefore do spend money to make the good available for sale. In this case the cost of making the good available for sale *includes* monetary costs, but it may also include other opportunity costs.

Getting back to the example, suppose that Andrew sells his book for $30. Clearly he has gained from the transaction: he would have been willing to sell for only $5, so he has gained $25. This net gain, the difference between the price he actually gets and his cost—the minimum price at which he would have been willing to sell—is known as his **individual producer surplus.**

As in the case of consumer surplus, we can add the individual producer surpluses of sellers to calculate the **total producer surplus,** the total net gain to all sellers in the market. Economists use the term **producer surplus** to refer to either total or individual producer surplus. Table 4-2 shows the net gain to each of the students who would sell a used book at a price of $30: $25 for Andrew, $15 for Betty, and $5 for Carlos. The total producer surplus is $25 + $15 + $5 = $45.

A seller's **cost** is the lowest price at which he or she is willing to sell a good.

Individual producer surplus is the net gain to an individual seller from selling a good. It is equal to the difference between the price received and the seller's cost.

Total producer surplus in a market is the sum of the individual producer surpluses of all the sellers of a good in a market.

Economists use the term **producer surplus** to refer to either total or individual producer surplus.

As with consumer surplus, the producer surplus gained by those who sell books can be represented graphically. Just as we derived the demand curve from the willingness to pay of different consumers, we first derive the supply curve from the cost of different producers. The step-shaped curve in Figure 4-3 shows the supply curve implied by the cost shown in Table 4-2. Each step in that supply curve is one book wide and represents one seller. The height of Andrew's step is $5, his cost. This forms the bottom of a rectangle, with $30, the price he actually receives for his book, forming the top. The area of this rectangle, ($30 – $5) × 1 = $25, is his producer surplus. So the producer surplus Andrew gains from selling his book is the *area of the dark red rectangle* shown in the figure.

Let's assume that the campus bookstore is willing to buy all the used copies of this book that students are willing to sell at a price of $30. Then, in addition to Andrew, Betty and Carlos will also sell their books. They will also benefit from their sales, though not as much as Andrew, because they have higher costs. Andrew, as we have seen, gains $25. Betty gains a smaller amount: since her cost is $15, she gains only $15. Carlos gains even less, only $5.

Again, as with consumer surplus, we have a general rule for determining the total producer surplus from sales of a good: *The total producer surplus from sales of a good at a given price is the area above the supply curve but below that price.*

This rule applies both to examples like the one shown in Figure 4-3, where there are a small number of producers and a step-shaped supply curve, and to more realistic examples, where there are many producers and the supply curve is more or less smooth.

Consider, for example, the supply of wheat. Figure 4-4 shows how producer surplus depends on the price per bushel. Suppose that, as shown in the figure, the price is $5 per bushel and farmers supply 1 million bushels. What is the benefit to the farmers from selling their wheat at a price of $5? Their producer surplus is equal to the shaded area in the figure—the area above the supply curve but below the price of $5 per bushel.

FIGURE 4-3 Producer Surplus in the Used-Textbook Market

At a price of $30, Andrew, Betty, and Carlos each sell a book but Donna and Engelbert do not. Andrew, Betty, and Carlos get individual producer surpluses equal to the difference between the price and their cost, illustrated here by the shaded rectangles. Donna and Engelbert each have a cost that is greater than the price of $30, so they are unwilling to sell a book and so receive zero producer surplus. The total producer surplus is given by the entire shaded area, the sum of the individual producer surpluses of Andrew, Betty, and Carlos, equal to $25 + $15 + $5 = $45.

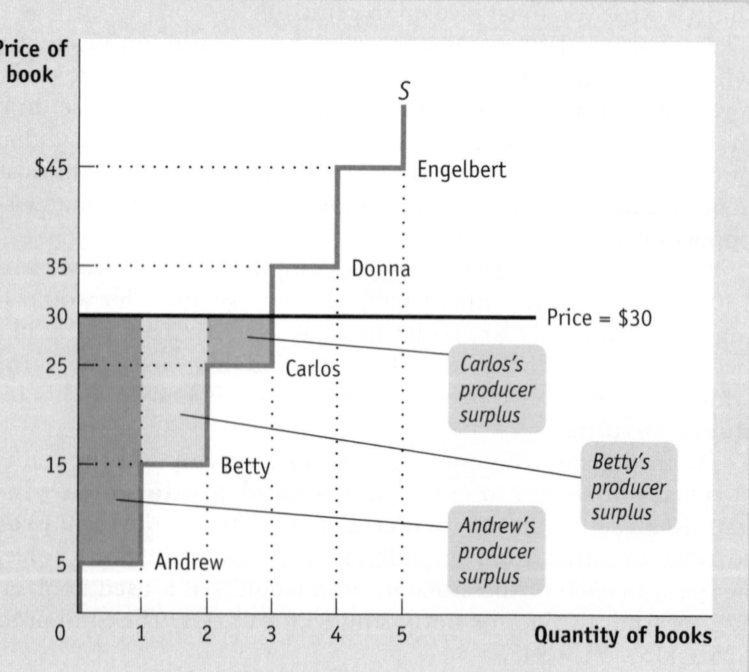

FIGURE 4-4 Producer Surplus

Here is the supply curve for wheat. At a price of $5 per bushel, farmers supply 1 million bushels. The producer surplus at this price is equal to the shaded area: the area above the supply curve but below the price. This is the total gain to producers—farmers in this case—from supplying their product when the price is $5.

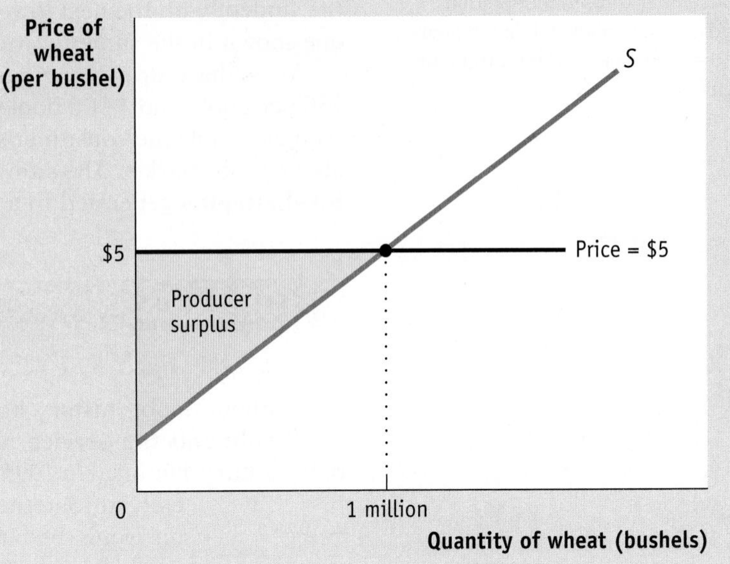

The Gains from Trade

Let's return to the market in used textbooks, but now consider a much bigger market—say, one at a large state university. There are many potential buyers and sellers, so the market is competitive. Let's line up incoming students who are potential buyers of a book in order of their willingness to pay, so that the entering student with the highest willingness to pay is potential buyer number 1, the student with the next highest willingness to pay is number 2, and so on. Then we can use their willingness to pay to derive a demand curve like the one in Figure 4-5.

FIGURE 4-5 Total Surplus

In the market for used textbooks, the equilibrium price is $30 and the equilibrium quantity is 1,000 books. Consumer surplus is given by the blue area, the area below the demand curve but above the price. Producer surplus is given by the red area, the area above the supply curve but below the price. The sum of the blue and the red areas is total surplus, the total benefit to society from the production and consumption of the good.

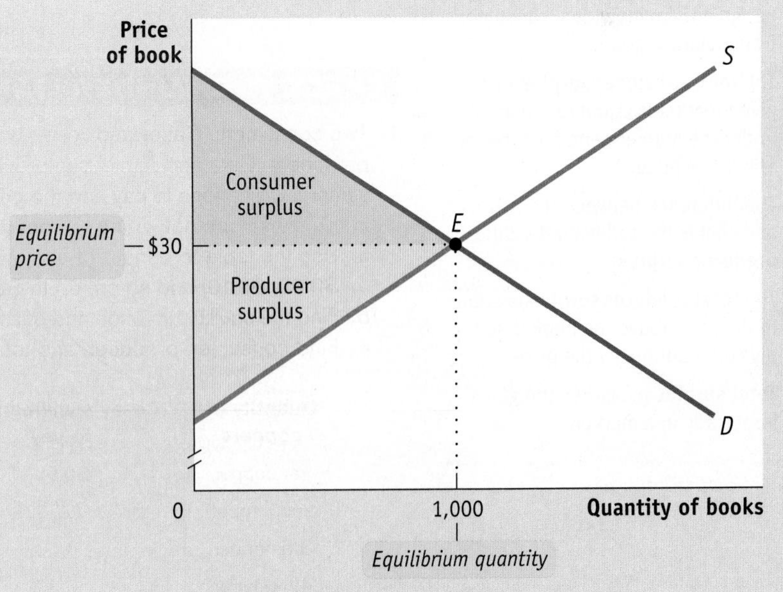

The **total surplus** generated in a market is the total net gain to consumers and producers from trading in the market. It is the sum of the consumer and the producer surplus.

Similarly, we can line up outgoing students, who are potential sellers of the book, in order of their cost—starting with the student with the lowest cost, then the student with the next lowest cost, and so on—to derive a supply curve like the one shown in the same figure.

As we have drawn the curves, the market reaches equilibrium at a price of $30 per book, and 1,000 books are bought and sold at that price. The two shaded triangles show the consumer surplus (blue) and the producer surplus (red) generated by this market. The sum of consumer and producer surplus is known as the **total surplus** generated in a market.

ECONOMICS ➤ IN ACTION

TAKE THE KEYS, PLEASE

Without doubt, history books (or digital readers) will one day cite eBay, the online auction service, as one of the great American innovations of the twentieth century. Founded in 1995, the company says that its mission is "to help practically anyone trade practically anything on earth." It provides a way for would-be buyers and would-be sellers—sometimes of unique or used items—to find one another. And the gains from trade accruing to eBay users were evidently large: in 2010, eBay reported $53.5 billion in goods bought and sold on its websites.

And the online matching hasn't stopped there. Websites are now popping up that allow people to rent out their personal possessions—items like cars, power tools, personal electronics, and spare bedrooms. Similar to what eBay did for buyers and sellers, these new websites provide a platform for renters and owners to find one another.

A recent *Business Week* article describes how one Boston couple used the website RelayRides to rent out a car that had been sitting around largely unused, earning enough to pay for its upkeep and insurance. And according to the founder of RelayRides, Shelby Clark, the average car renter on his website earns $250 per month. Judith Chevalier, a Yale School of Management economist says, "These companies let you wring a little bit of value out of . . . goods that are just sitting there."

RelayRides and companies like it are hoping that they can earn a nice return by helping you generate a little bit more surplus from your possessions.

"I got it from eBay"

Quick Review

- **Individual consumer surplus** is the net gain to an individual consumer from buying a good.
- The **total consumer surplus** in a given market is equal to the area under the market demand curve but above the price.
- The difference between the price and cost is the seller's **individual producer surplus.**
- The **total producer surplus** is equal to the area above the market supply curve but below the price.
- **Total surplus** measures the gains from trade in a market.

CHECK YOUR UNDERSTANDING 4-1

1. Two consumers, Casey and Josey, want cheese-stuffed jalapeno peppers for lunch. Two producers, Cara and Jamie, can provide them. The accompanying table shows the consumers' willingness to pay and the producers' costs. Note that consumers and producers in this market are not willing to consume or produce more than four peppers at any price.
   a. Use the table to construct a demand schedule and a supply schedule for prices of $0.00, $0.10, and so on, up to $0.90.
   b. Find the equilibrium price and quantity in the market for cheese-stuffed jalapeno peppers.
   c. Find consumer, producer, and total surplus in equilibrium in this market.

Quantity of peppers	Casey's willingness to pay	Josey's willingness to pay	Cara's cost	Jamie's cost
1st pepper	$0.90	$0.80	$0.10	$0.30
2nd pepper	0.70	0.60	0.10	0.50
3rd pepper	0.50	0.40	0.40	0.70
4th pepper	0.30	0.30	0.60	0.90

2. Suppose UNOS alters its guidelines for the allocation of donated kidneys. It will no longer rely solely on the concept of "net benefit" but also give preference to patients with young children. If "total surplus" in this case is defined as the total life span of kidney recipients, is this new guideline likely to reduce, increase, or leave total surplus unchanged? How might you justify this new guideline?

Solutions appear at back of book.

Price controls are legal restrictions on how high or low a market price may go. They can take two forms: a **price ceiling,** a maximum price sellers are allowed to charge for a good or service, or a **price floor,** a minimum price buyers are required to pay for a good or service.

Why Governments Control Prices

You learned in Chapter 3 that a market moves to equilibrium—that is, the market price moves to the level at which the quantity supplied equals the quantity demanded. But this equilibrium price does not necessarily please either buyers or sellers.

After all, buyers would always like to pay less if they could, and sometimes they can make a strong moral or political case that they should pay lower prices. For example, what if the equilibrium between supply and demand for apartments in a major city leads to rental rates that an average working person can't afford? In that case, a government might well be under pressure to impose limits on the rents landlords can charge.

Sellers, however, would always like to get more money for what they sell, and sometimes they can make a strong moral or political case that they should receive higher prices. For example, consider the labor market: the price for an hour of a worker's time is the wage rate. What if the equilibrium between supply and demand for less skilled workers leads to wage rates that yield an income below the poverty level? In that case, a government might well be pressured to require employers to pay a rate no lower than some specified minimum wage.

In other words, there is often a strong political demand for governments to intervene in markets. And powerful interests can make a compelling case that a market intervention favoring them is "fair." When a government intervenes to regulate prices, we say that it imposes **price controls.** These controls typically take the form either of an upper limit, a **price ceiling,** or a lower limit, a **price floor.**

Unfortunately, it's not that easy to tell a market what to do. As we will now see, when a government tries to legislate prices—whether it legislates them down by imposing a price ceiling or up by imposing a price floor—there are certain predictable and unpleasant side effects.

Price Ceilings

Aside from rent control, which you read about in the opening story, there are not many price ceilings in the United States today. But at times they have been widespread. Price ceilings are typically imposed during crises—wars, harvest failures, natural disasters—because these events often lead to sudden price increases that hurt many people but produce big gains for a lucky few. The U.S. government imposed ceilings on many prices during World War II: the war sharply increased demand for raw materials, such as aluminum and steel, and price controls prevented those with access to these raw materials from earning huge profits. Price controls on oil were imposed in 1973, when an embargo by Arab oil-exporting countries seemed likely to generate huge profits for U.S. oil companies. Price controls were imposed on California's wholesale electricity market in 2001, when a shortage created big profits for a few power-generating companies but led to higher electricity bills for consumers.

Rent control in New York is, believe it or not, a legacy of World War II: it was imposed because wartime production produced an economic boom, which increased demand for apartments at a time when the labor and raw materials that might have been used to build them were being used to win the war instead. Although most price controls were removed soon after the war ended, New York's rent limits were retained and gradually extended to buildings not previously covered, leading to some very strange situations.

You can rent a one-bedroom apartment in Manhattan on fairly short notice—if you are able and willing to pay several thousand dollars a month and live in a less-than-desirable area. Yet some people pay only a small fraction of this for comparable apartments, and others pay hardly more for bigger apartments in better locations.

Aside from producing great deals for some renters, however, what are the broader consequences of New York's rent-control system? To answer this question, we turn to the model we developed in Chapter 3: the supply and demand model.

Modeling a Price Ceiling

To see what can go wrong when a government imposes a price ceiling on an efficient market, consider Figure 4-6, which shows a simplified model of the market for apartments in New York. For the sake of simplicity, we imagine that all apartments are exactly the same and so would rent for the same price in an unregulated market. The table in the figure shows the demand and supply schedules; the demand and supply curves are shown on the left. We show the quantity of apartments on the horizontal axis and the monthly rent per apartment on the vertical axis. You can see that in an unregulated market the equilibrium would be at point *E*: 2 million apartments would be rented for $1,000 each per month.

FIGURE 4-6 The Market for Apartments in the Absence of Price Controls

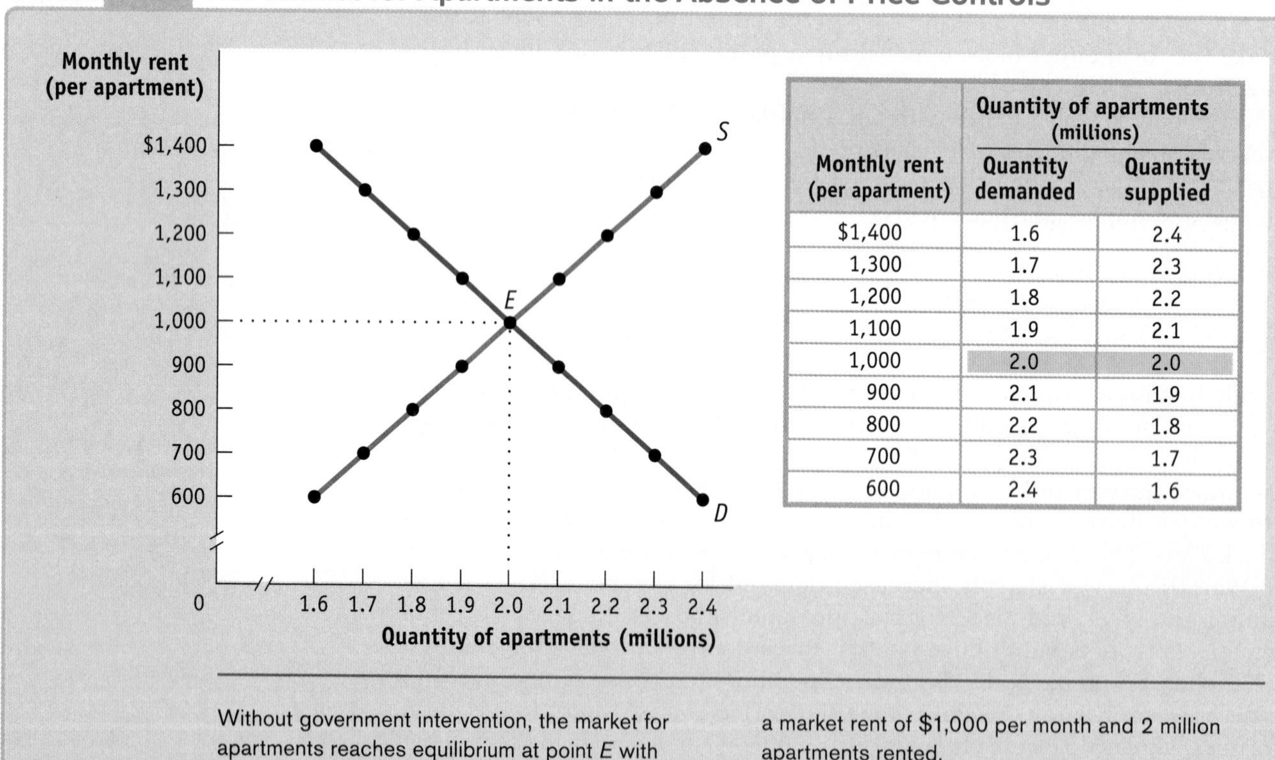

Monthly rent (per apartment)	Quantity of apartments (millions): Quantity demanded	Quantity supplied
$1,400	1.6	2.4
1,300	1.7	2.3
1,200	1.8	2.2
1,100	1.9	2.1
1,000	2.0	2.0
900	2.1	1.9
800	2.2	1.8
700	2.3	1.7
600	2.4	1.6

Without government intervention, the market for apartments reaches equilibrium at point *E* with a market rent of $1,000 per month and 2 million apartments rented.

The black horizontal line represents the government-imposed price ceiling on rents of $800 per month. This price ceiling reduces the quantity of apartments supplied to 1.8 million, point *A*, and increases the quantity demanded to 2.2 million, point *B*. This creates a persistent shortage of 400,000 units: 400,000 people who want apartments at the legal rent of $800 but cannot get them.

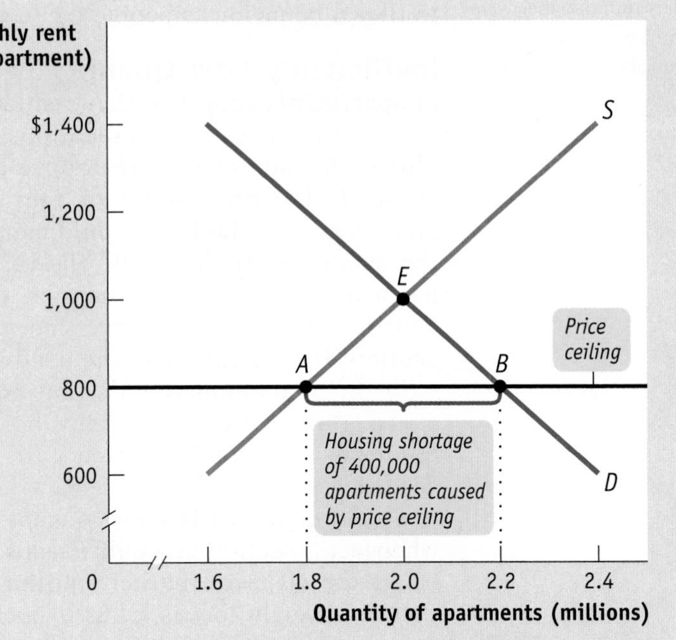

Now suppose that the government imposes a price ceiling, limiting rents to a price below the equilibrium price—say, no more than $800.

Figure 4-7 shows the effect of the price ceiling, represented by the line at $800. At the enforced rental rate of $800, landlords have less incentive to offer apartments, so they won't be willing to supply as many as they would at the equilibrium rate of $1,000. They will choose point *A* on the supply curve, offering only 1.8 million apartments for rent, 200,000 fewer than in the unregulated market. At the same time, more people will want to rent apartments at a price of $800 than at the equilibrium price of $1,000; as shown at point *B* on the demand curve, at a monthly rent of $800 the quantity of apartments demanded rises to 2.2 million, 200,000 more than in the unregulated market and 400,000 more than are actually available at the price of $800. So there is now a persistent shortage of rental housing: at that price, 400,000 more people want to rent than are able to find apartments.

Do price ceilings always cause shortages? No. If a price ceiling is set above the equilibrium price, it won't have any effect. Suppose that the equilibrium rental rate on apartments is $1,000 per month and the city government sets a ceiling of $1,200. Who cares? In this case, the price ceiling won't be *binding*—it won't actually constrain market behavior—and it will have no effect.

How a Price Ceiling Causes Inefficiency

The housing shortage shown in Figure 4-7 is not merely annoying: like any shortage induced by price controls, it can be seriously harmful because it leads to inefficiency. In other words, there are gains from trade that go unrealized. Rent control, like all price ceilings, creates inefficiency in at least four distinct ways. It reduces the quantity of apartments rented below the efficient level; it typically leads to misallocation of apartments among would-be renters; it leads to wasted time and effort as people search for

Deadweight loss is the loss in total surplus that occurs whenever an action or a policy reduces the quantity transacted below the efficient market equilibrium quantity.

apartments; and it leads landlords to maintain apartments in inefficiently low quality or condition. In addition to inefficiency, price ceilings give rise to illegal behavior as people try to circumvent them.

Inefficiently Low Quantity Because rent controls reduce the number of apartments supplied, they reduce the number of apartments rented, too. Figure 4-8 shows the implications for total surplus. Recall that total surplus is the sum of the area above the supply curve and below the demand curve. If the only effect of rent control was to reduce the number of apartments available, it would cause a loss of surplus equal to the area of the shaded triangle in the figure. The area represented by that triangle has a special name in economics, **deadweight loss:** the lost surplus associated with the transactions that no longer occur due to the market intervention. In this example, the deadweight loss is the lost surplus associated with the apartment rentals that no longer occur due to the price ceiling, a loss that is experienced by both disappointed renters and frustrated landlords. Economists often call triangles like the one in Figure 4-8 a *deadweight-loss triangle*.

Deadweight loss is a key concept in economics, one that we will encounter whenever an action or a policy leads to a reduction in the quantity transacted below the efficient market equilibrium quantity. It is important to realize that deadweight loss is a *loss to society*—it is a reduction in total surplus, a loss in surplus that accrues to no one as a gain. It is not the same as a loss in surplus to one person that then accrues as a gain to someone else, what an economist would call a *transfer* of surplus from one person to another. For an example of how a price ceiling can create deadweight loss as well as a transfer of surplus between renters and landlords, see the upcoming For Inquiring Minds.

FIGURE 4-8 A Price Ceiling Causes Inefficiently Low Quantity

A price ceiling reduces the quantity supplied below the market equilibrium quantity, leading to a deadweight loss. The area of the shaded triangle corresponds to the amount of total surplus lost due to the inefficiently low quantity transacted.

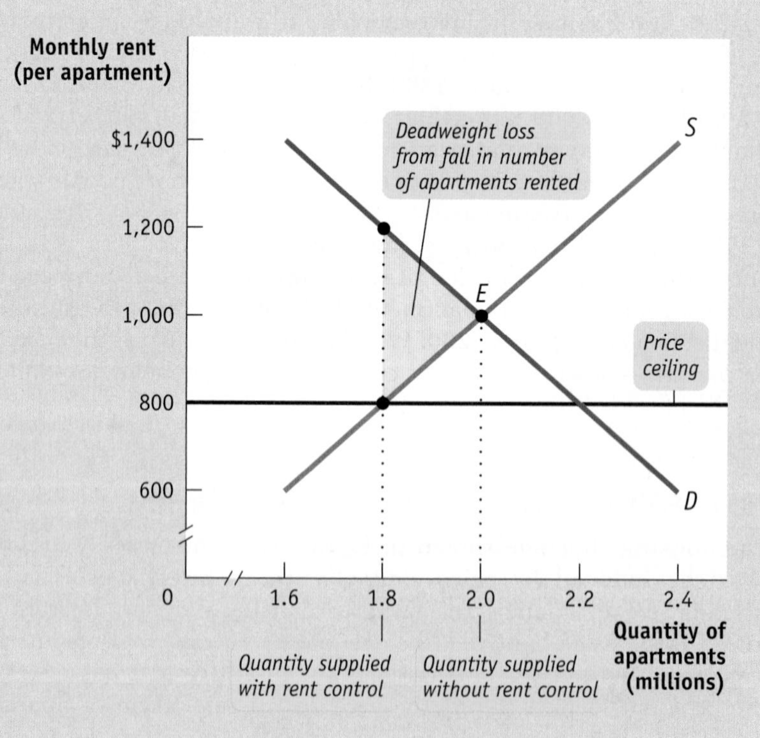

FOR INQUIRING MINDS

WINNERS, LOSERS, AND RENT CONTROL

Price controls create winners and losers: some people benefit from the policy but others are made worse off.

In New York City, some of the biggest beneficiaries of rent control are affluent tenants who have lived for decades in choice apartments that would now command very high rents. These winners include celebrities like actor Al Pacino and the pop singer Cyndi Lauper; Lauper pays only $989 a month for an apartment that would be worth $3,750 if unregulated. There is also the classic case of the actress Mia Farrow's apartment, which, when it lost its rent-control status, rose from the bargain rate of $2,900 per month to $8,000. Ironically, in cases like these, the losers are the working-class renters the system was intended to help.

We can use the concepts of consumer and producer surplus to graphically evaluate the winners and the losers from rent control. Panel (a) of Figure 4-9 shows the consumer surplus and producer surplus in the equilibrium of the unregulated market for apartments—before rent control. Recall that the consumer surplus, represented by the area below the demand curve and above the price, is the total net gain to consumers in the market equilibrium. Likewise, producer surplus, represented by the area above the supply curve and below the price, is the total net gain to producers in the market equilibrium.

Panel (b) of this figure shows the consumer and producer surplus in the market after the price ceiling of $800 has been imposed. As you can see, for consumers who can still obtain apartments under rent control, consumer surplus has increased. These renters are clearly winners: they obtain an apartment at $800, paying $200 less than the unregulated market price. These people receive a direct transfer of surplus from landlords in the form of lower rent. But not all renters win: there are fewer apartments to rent now than if the market had remained unregulated, making it hard, if not impossible, for some to find a place to call home.

Without direct calculation of the surpluses gained and lost, it is generally unclear whether renters as a whole are made better or worse off by rent control. What we can say is that the greater the deadweight loss—the larger the reduction in the quantity of apartments rented—the more likely it is that renters as a whole lose.

However, we can say unambiguously that landlords are worse off: producer surplus has clearly decreased. Landlords who continue to rent out their apartments get $200 a month less in rent, and others withdraw their apartments from the market altogether. The deadweight-loss triangle, shaded yellow in panel (b), represents the value lost to both renters and landlords from rentals that essentially vanish thanks to rent control.

FIGURE 4-9 Winners and Losers from Rent Control

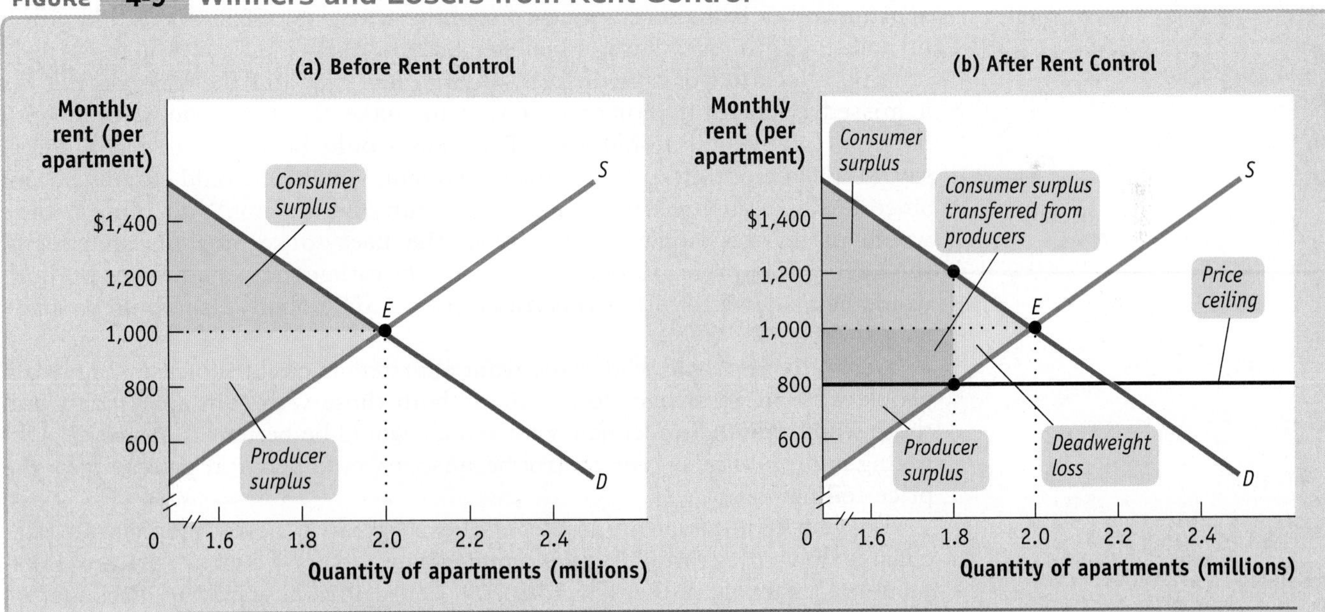

Panel (a) shows the consumer surplus and producer surplus in the equilibrium of the unregulated market for apartments—before rent control. Panel (b) shows the consumer and producer surplus in the market after a price ceiling of $800 has been imposed. As you can see, for those consumers who can still obtain apartments under rent control, consumer surplus has increased but producer surplus and total surplus have decreased.

Price ceilings often lead to inefficiency in the form of **inefficient allocation to consumers:** some people who want the good badly and are willing to pay a high price don't get it, and some who care relatively little about the good and are only willing to pay a low price do get it.

Deadweight loss is not the only type of inefficiency that arises from a price ceiling. The types of inefficiency created by rent control go beyond reducing the quantity of apartments available. These additional inefficiencies—inefficient allocation to consumers, wasted resources, and inefficiently low quality—lead to a loss of surplus over and above the deadweight loss.

Inefficient Allocation to Consumers Rent control doesn't just lead to too few apartments being available. It can also lead to misallocation of the apartments that are available: people who badly need a place to live may not be able to find an apartment, but some apartments may be occupied by people with much less urgent needs.

In the case shown in Figure 4-7, 2.2 million people would like to rent an apartment at $800 per month, but only 1.8 million apartments are available. Of those 2.2 million who are seeking an apartment, some want an apartment badly and are willing to pay a high price to get one. Others have a less urgent need and are only willing to pay a low price, perhaps because they have alternative housing. An efficient allocation of apartments would reflect these differences: people who really want an apartment will get one and people who aren't all that anxious to find an apartment won't. In an inefficient distribution of apartments, the opposite will happen: some people who are not especially anxious to find an apartment will get one and others who are very anxious to find an apartment won't.

Because people usually get apartments through luck or personal connections under rent control, it generally results in an **inefficient allocation to consumers** of the few apartments available.

To see the inefficiency involved, consider the plight of the Lees, a family with young children who have no alternative housing and would be willing to pay up to $1,500 for an apartment—but are unable to find one. Also consider George, a retiree who lives most of the year in Florida but still has a lease on the New York apartment he moved into 40 years ago. George pays $800 per month for this apartment, but if the rent were even slightly more—say, $850—he would give it up and stay with his children when he is in New York.

This allocation of apartments—George has one and the Lees do not—is a missed opportunity: there is a way to make the Lees and George both better off at no additional cost. The Lees would be happy to pay George, say, $1,200 a month to sublease his apartment, which he would happily accept since the apartment is worth no more than $849 a month to him. George would prefer the money he gets from the Lees to keeping his apartment; the Lees would prefer to have the apartment rather than the money. So both would be made better off by this transaction—and nobody else would be made worse off.

Generally, if people who really want apartments could sublease them from people who are less eager to live there, both those who gain apartments and those who trade their occupancy for money would be better off. However, subletting is illegal under rent control because it would occur at prices above the price ceiling.

The fact that subletting is illegal doesn't mean it never happens. In fact, chasing down illegal subletting is a major business for New York private investigators. An article in the *New York Times* described how private investigators use hidden cameras and other tricks to prove that the legal tenants in rent-controlled apartments actually live in the suburbs, or even in other states, and have sublet their apartments at two or three times the controlled rent. This subletting is a kind of illegal activity, which we will discuss shortly. For now, just note that landlords and legal agencies actively discourage the practice of illegal subletting. As a result, the problem of inefficient allocation of apartments remains.

Wasted Resources Another reason a price ceiling causes inefficiency is that it leads to **wasted resources:** people expend money, effort, and time to cope with the shortages caused by the price ceiling. Back in 1979, U.S. price controls on gasoline led to shortages that forced millions of Americans to spend hours each week waiting in lines at gas stations. The opportunity cost of the time spent in gas lines—the wages not earned, the leisure time not enjoyed—constituted wasted resources from the point of view of consumers and of the economy as a whole.

Because of rent control, the Lees will spend all their spare time for several months searching for an apartment, time they would rather have spent working or in family activities. That is, there is an opportunity cost to the Lees' prolonged search for an apartment—the leisure or income they had to forgo. If the market for apartments worked freely, the Lees would quickly find an apartment at the equilibrium rent of $1,000, leaving them time to earn more or to enjoy themselves—an outcome that would make them better off without making anyone else worse off. Again, rent control creates missed opportunities.

Price ceilings typically lead to inefficiency in the form of **wasted resources:** people expend money, effort, and time to cope with the shortages caused by the price ceiling.

Price ceilings often lead to inefficiency in that the goods being offered are of **inefficiently low quality:** sellers offer low-quality goods at a low price even though buyers would prefer a higher quality at a higher price.

A **black market** is a market in which goods or services are bought and sold illegally—either because it is illegal to sell them at all or because the prices charged are legally prohibited by a price ceiling.

Inefficiently Low Quality Yet another way a price ceiling creates inefficiency is by causing goods to be of inefficiently low quality. **Inefficiently low quality** means that sellers offer low-quality goods at a low price even though buyers would rather have higher quality and would be willing to pay a higher price for it.

Again, consider rent control. Landlords have no incentive to provide better conditions because they cannot raise rents to cover their repair costs but are able to find tenants easily. In many cases, tenants would be willing to pay much more for improved conditions than it would cost for the landlord to provide them—for example, the upgrade of an antiquated electrical system that cannot safely run air conditioners or computers. But any additional payment for such improvements would be legally considered a rent increase, which is prohibited. Indeed, rent-controlled apartments are notoriously badly maintained, rarely painted, subject to frequent electrical and plumbing problems, sometimes even hazardous to inhabit. As one former manager of Manhattan buildings described: "At unregulated apartments we'd do most things that the tenants requested. But on the rent-regulated units, we did absolutely only what the law required. . . . We had a perverse incentive to make those tenants unhappy."

This whole situation is a missed opportunity—some tenants would be happy to pay for better conditions, and landlords would be happy to provide them for payment. But such an exchange would occur only if the market were allowed to operate freely.

Black Markets And that leads us to a last aspect of price ceilings: the incentive they provide for illegal activities, specifically the emergence of **black markets.** We have already described one kind of black market activity—illegal subletting by tenants. But it does not stop there. Clearly, there is a temptation for a landlord to say to a potential tenant, "Look, you can have the place if you slip me an extra few hundred in cash each month"—and for the tenant to agree if he or she is one of those people who would be willing to pay much more than the maximum legal rent.

What's wrong with black markets? In general, it's a bad thing if people break any law, because it encourages disrespect for the law in general. Worse yet, in this case illegal activity worsens the position of those who are honest. If the Lees are scrupulous about upholding the rent-control law but other people—who may need an apartment less than the Lees—are willing to bribe landlords, the Lees may never find an apartment.

So Why Are There Price Ceilings?

We have seen three common results of price ceilings:

- A persistent shortage of the good
- Inefficiency arising from this persistent shortage in the form of inefficiently low quantity (deadweight loss), inefficient allocation of the good to consumers, resources wasted in searching for the good, and the inefficiently low quality of the good offered for sale
- The emergence of illegal, black market activity

Given these unpleasant consequences, why do governments still sometimes impose price ceilings? Why does rent control, in particular, persist in New York?

One answer is that although price ceilings may have adverse effects, they do benefit some people. In practice, New York's rent-control rules—which are more complex than our simple model—hurt most residents but give a small minority of renters much cheaper housing than they would get in an unregulated market. And those who benefit from the controls are typically better organized and more vocal than those who are harmed by them.

Also, when price ceilings have been in effect for a long time, buyers may not have a realistic idea of what would happen without them. In our previous example, the rental rate in an unregulated market (Figure 4-6) would be only 25% higher than in the regulated market (Figure 4-7): $1,000 instead of $800. But how would renters know that? Indeed, they might have heard about black market transactions at much higher prices—the Lees or some other family paying George $1,200 or more—and would not realize that these black market prices are much higher than the price that would prevail in a fully unregulated market.

A last answer is that government officials often do not understand supply and demand analysis! It is a great mistake to suppose that economic policies in the real world are always sensible or well informed.

ECONOMICS ➤ IN ACTION

HUNGER AND PRICE CONTROLS IN VENEZUELA

Something was rotten in the state of Venezuela—specifically, 30,000 tons of decomposing food in Puerto Cabello in June 2010. The discovery was particularly embarrassing for Venezuelan President Hugo Chávez. He was elected in 1998 on a platform denouncing the country's economic elite and promising policies favoring the poor and working classes. Among those policies were price controls on basic foodstuffs, which led to shortages that began in 2003 and had become severe by 2006.

AP Photo/Leslie Mazoch

Venezuela's food shortages offer a lesson in why price ceilings, however well intentioned, are usually never a good idea.

Generous government policies led to higher spending by consumers and sharply rising prices for goods that weren't subject to price controls or which were bought on the black market. The result was a big increase in the demand for price-controlled goods. But a sharp decline in the value of Venezuela's currency led to a fall in imports of foreign food, and the result was empty shelves in the nation's food stores.

As the shortages persisted and inflation of food prices worsened (in the first five months of 2010, the prices of food and drink rose by 21%), Chávez declared "economic war" on the private sector, berating it for "hoarding and smuggling." The government expropriated farms, food manufacturers and grocery stores, creating in their place government-owned ones, which were corrupt and inefficient—it was the government-owned food-distribution company, PDVAL, that left tens of thousands of tons of food to rot in Venezuelan ports. Food production also fell, forcing Venezuela to import 70% of its food.

Not surprisingly, the shelves were far more bare in government-run grocery stores than in those still in private hands. The food shortages were so severe that they greatly diminished Chávez's popularity among working-class Venezuelans and halted his expropriation plans. As an old Venezuelan saying has it, "Love with hunger doesn't last."

Quick Review

- **Price controls** take the form of either legal maximum prices—**price ceilings**—or legal minimum prices—**price floors.**
- A price ceiling below the equilibrium price benefits successful buyers but causes predictable adverse effects such as persistent shortages, which lead to four types of inefficiencies: **deadweight loss, inefficient allocation to consumers, wasted resources,** and **inefficiently low quality.**
- A deadweight loss is a loss of total surplus that occurs whenever a policy or action reduces the quantity transacted below the efficient market equilibrium level.
- Price ceilings also lead to **black markets,** as buyers and sellers attempt to evade the price controls.

CHECK YOUR UNDERSTANDING 4-2

1. On game days, homeowners near Middletown University's stadium used to rent parking spaces in their driveways to fans at a going rate of $11. A new town ordinance now sets a maximum parking fee of $7. Use the accompanying supply and demand diagram to explain how each of the following corresponds to a price-ceiling concept.
   a. Some homeowners now think it's not worth the hassle to rent out spaces.
   b. Some fans who used to car-pool to the game now drive alone.
   c. Some fans can't find parking and leave without seeing the game.

   Explain how each of the following adverse effects arises from the price ceiling.
   d. Some fans now arrive several hours early to find parking.
   e. Friends of homeowners near the stadium regularly attend games, even if they aren't big fans. But some serious fans have given up because of the parking situation.
   f. Some homeowners rent spaces for more than $7 but pretend that the buyers are nonpaying friends or family.

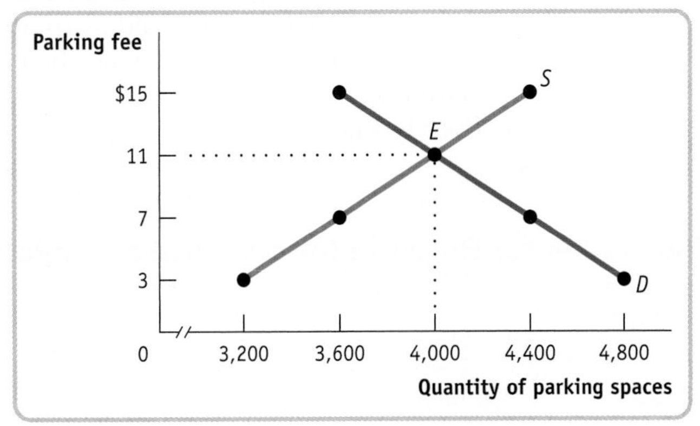

2. True or false? Explain your answer. A price ceiling below the equilibrium price of an otherwise efficient market does the following:
   a. Increases quantity supplied
   b. Makes some people who want to consume the good worse off
   c. Makes all producers worse off
3. Which of the following create deadweight loss? Which do not and are simply a transfer of surplus from one person to another? Explain your answer.
   a. You have been evicted from your rent-controlled apartment after the landlord discovered your pet boa constrictor. The apartment is quickly rented to someone else at the same price. You and the new renter do not necessarily have the same willingness to pay for the apartment.
   b. In a contest, you won a ticket to a jazz concert. But you can't go to the concert because of an exam, and the terms of the contest do not allow you to sell the ticket or give it to someone else. Would your answer to this question change if you could not sell the ticket but could give it to someone else?
   c. Your school's dean of students, who is a proponent of a low-fat diet, decrees that ice cream can no longer be served on campus.
   d. Your ice-cream cone falls on the ground and your dog eats it. (Take the liberty of counting your dog as a member of society, and assume that, if he could, your dog would be willing to pay the same amount for the ice-cream cone as you.)

Solutions appear at back of book.

The **minimum wage** is a legal floor on the wage rate, which is the market price of labor.

Price Floors

Sometimes governments intervene to push market prices up instead of down. *Price floors* have been widely legislated for agricultural products, such as wheat and milk, as a way to support the incomes of farmers. Historically, there were also price floors on such services as trucking and air travel, although these were phased out by the U.S. government in the 1970s. If you have ever worked in a fast-food restaurant, you are likely to have encountered a price floor: governments in the United States and many other countries maintain a lower limit on the hourly wage rate of a worker's labor; that is, a floor on the price of labor—called the **minimum wage.**

Just like price ceilings, price floors are intended to help some people but generate predictable and undesirable side effects. Figure 4-10 shows hypothetical supply and demand curves for butter. Left to itself, the market would move to equilibrium at point *E*, with 10 million pounds of butter bought and sold at a price of $1 per pound.

Now suppose that the government, in order to help dairy farmers, imposes a price floor on butter of $1.20 per pound. Its effects are shown in Figure 4-11, where the line at $1.20 represents the price floor. At a price of $1.20 per pound, producers would want to supply 12 million pounds (point *B* on the supply curve) but consumers would want to buy only 9 million pounds (point *A* on the demand curve). So the price floor leads to a persistent surplus of 3 million pounds of butter.

Does a price floor always lead to an unwanted surplus? No. Just as in the case of a price ceiling, the floor may not be binding—that is, it may be irrelevant. If the equilibrium price of butter is $1 per pound but the floor is set at only $0.80, the floor has no effect.

FIGURE 4-10 The Market for Butter in the Absence of Government Controls

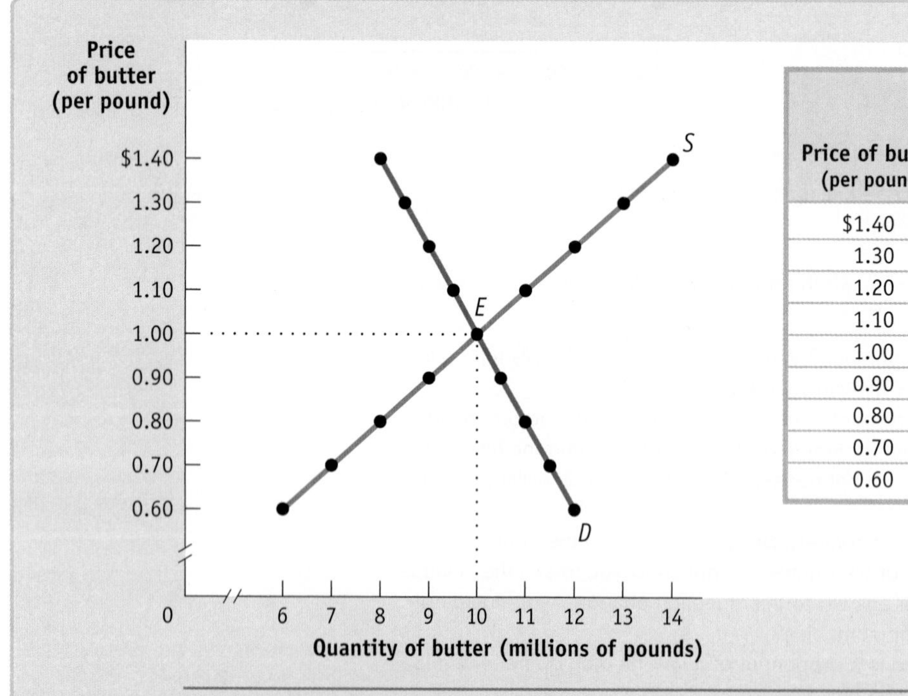

Price of butter (per pound)	Quantity of butter (millions of pounds)	
	Quantity demanded	Quantity supplied
$1.40	8.0	14.0
1.30	8.5	13.0
1.20	9.0	12.0
1.10	9.5	11.0
1.00	10.0	10.0
0.90	10.5	9.0
0.80	11.0	8.0
0.70	11.5	7.0
0.60	12.0	6.0

Without government intervention, the market for butter reaches equilibrium at a price of $1 per pound with 10 million pounds of butter bought and sold.

FIGURE 4-11 The Effects of a Price Floor

The black horizontal line represents the government-imposed price floor of $1.20 per pound of butter. The quantity of butter demanded falls to 9 million pounds, and the quantity supplied rises to 12 million pounds, generating a persistent surplus of 3 million pounds of butter.

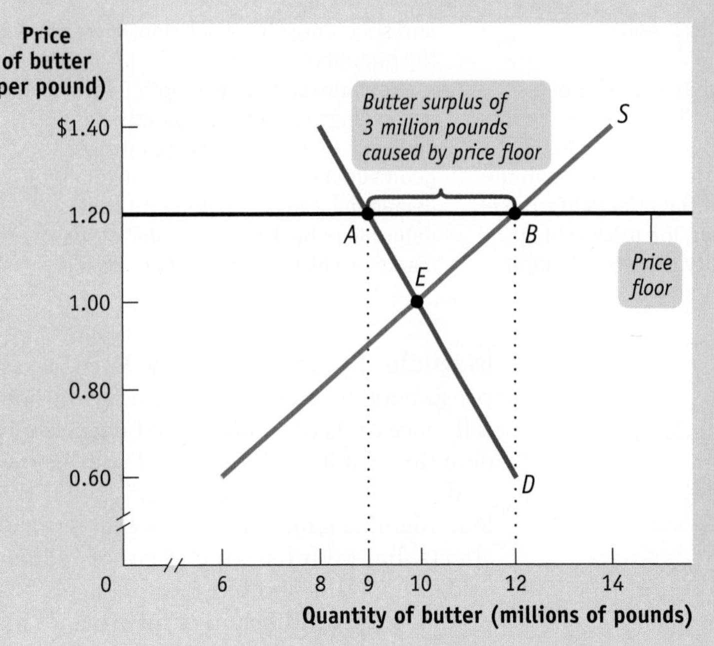

But suppose that a price floor is binding: what happens to the unwanted surplus? The answer depends on government policy. In the case of agricultural price floors, governments buy up unwanted surplus. As a result, the U.S. government has at times found itself warehousing thousands of tons of butter, cheese, and other farm products. (The European Commission, which administers price floors for a number of European countries, once found itself the owner of a so-called butter mountain, equal in weight to the entire population of Austria.) The government then has to find a way to dispose of these unwanted goods.

Some countries pay exporters to sell products at a loss overseas; this is standard procedure for the European Union. The United States gives surplus food away to schools, which use the products in school lunches. In some cases, governments have actually destroyed the surplus production. To avoid the problem of dealing with the unwanted surplus, the U.S. government typically pays farmers not to produce the products at all.

When the government is not prepared to purchase the unwanted surplus, a price floor means that would-be sellers cannot find buyers. This is what happens when there is a price floor on the wage rate paid for an hour of labor, the minimum wage: when the minimum wage is above the equilibrium wage rate, some people who are willing to work—that is, sell labor—cannot find buyers—that is, employers—willing to give them jobs.

How a Price Floor Causes Inefficiency

The persistent surplus that results from a price floor creates missed opportunities—inefficiencies—that resemble those created by the shortage that results from a price ceiling. These include deadweight loss from inefficiently low quantity, inefficient allocation of sales among sellers, wasted resources, inefficiently high quality, and the temptation to break the law by selling below the legal price.

PITFALLS

CEILINGS, FLOORS, AND QUANTITIES

A price ceiling pushes the price of a good *down*. A price floor pushes the price of a good *up*. So it's easy to assume that the effects of a price floor are the opposite of the effects of a price ceiling. In particular, if a price ceiling reduces the quantity of a good bought and sold, doesn't a price floor increase the quantity?

No, it doesn't. In fact, both floors and ceilings reduce the quantity bought and sold. Why? When the quantity of a good supplied isn't equal to the quantity demanded, the actual quantity sold is determined by the "short side" of the market—whichever quantity is less. If sellers don't want to sell as much as buyers want to buy, it's the sellers who determine the actual quantity sold, because buyers can't force unwilling sellers to sell. If buyers don't want to buy as much as sellers want to sell, it's the buyers who determine the actual quantity sold, because sellers can't force unwilling buyers to buy.

Inefficiently Low Quantity Because a price floor raises the price of a good to consumers, it reduces the quantity of that good demanded; because sellers can't sell more units of a good than buyers are willing to buy, a price floor reduces the quantity of a good bought and sold below the market equilibrium quantity and leads to a deadweight loss. Notice that this is the *same* effect as a price ceiling. You might be tempted to think that a price floor and a price ceiling have opposite effects, but both have the effect of reducing the quantity of a good bought and sold (see Pitfalls above).

Since the equilibrium of an efficient market maximizes the sum of consumer and producer surplus, a price floor that reduces the quantity below the equilibrium quantity reduces total surplus. Figure 4-12 shows the implications for total surplus of a price floor on the price of butter. Total surplus is the sum of the area above the supply curve and below the demand curve. By reducing the quantity of butter sold, a price floor causes a deadweight loss equal to the area of the shaded triangle in the figure. As in the case of a price ceiling, however, deadweight loss is only one of the forms of inefficiency that the price control creates.

FIGURE 4-12 A Price Floor Causes Inefficiently Low Quantity

A price floor reduces the quantity demanded below the market equilibrium quantity and leads to a deadweight loss.

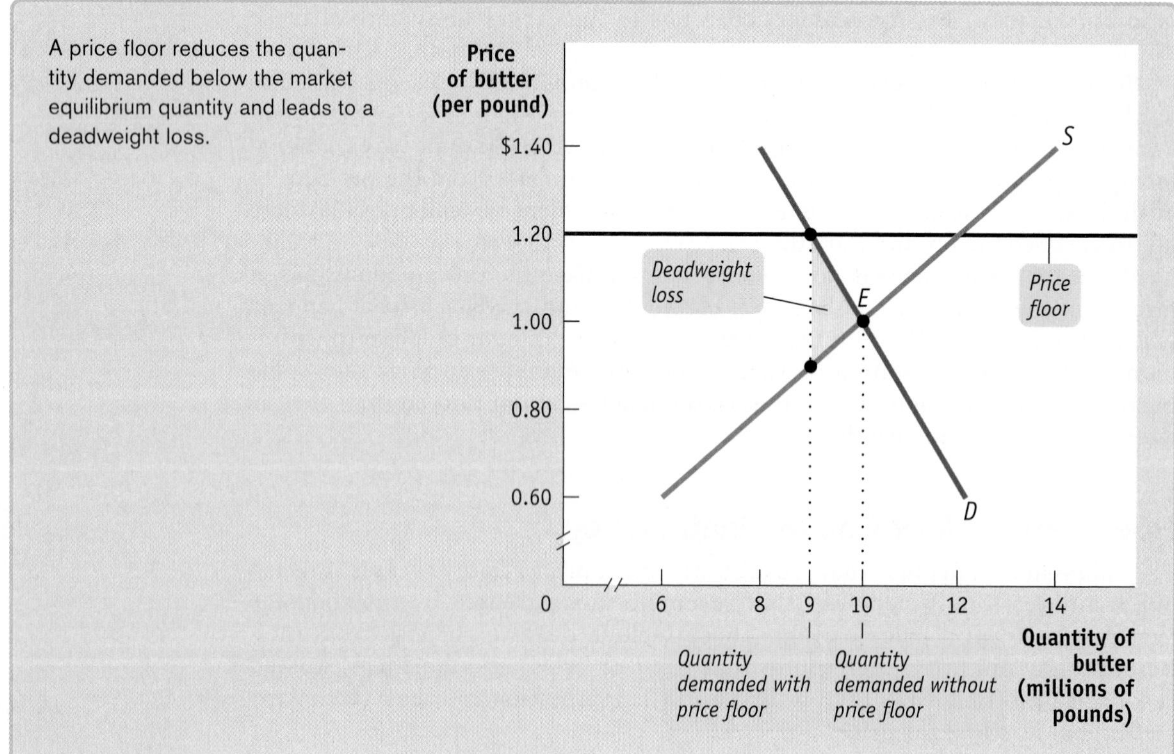

Inefficient Allocation of Sales Among Sellers Like a price ceiling, a price floor can lead to *inefficient allocation*—but in this case **inefficient allocation of sales among sellers** rather than inefficient allocation to consumers.

An episode from the Belgian movie *Rosetta*, a realistic fictional story, illustrates the problem of inefficient allocation of selling opportunities quite well. Like many European countries, Belgium has a high minimum wage, and jobs for young people are scarce. At one point Rosetta, a young woman who is very anxious to work, loses her job at a fast-food stand because the owner of the stand replaces her with his son—a very reluctant worker. Rosetta would be willing to work for less money, and with the money he would save, the owner could give his son an allowance and let him do something else. But to hire Rosetta for less than the minimum wage would be illegal.

Price floors lead to **inefficient allocation of sales among sellers:** those who would be willing to sell the good at the lowest price are not always those who actually manage to sell it.

Price floors often lead to inefficiency in that goods of **inefficiently high quality** are offered: sellers offer high-quality goods at a high price, even though buyers would prefer a lower quality at a lower price.

Wasted Resources Also like a price ceiling, a price floor generates inefficiency by *wasting resources*. The most graphic examples involve government purchases of the unwanted surpluses of agricultural products caused by price floors. The surplus production is sometimes destroyed, which is pure waste; in other cases, the stored produce goes, as officials euphemistically put it, "out of condition" and must be thrown away.

Price floors also lead to wasted time and effort. Consider the minimum wage. Would-be workers who spend many hours searching for jobs, or waiting in line in the hope of getting jobs, play the same role in the case of price floors as hapless families searching for apartments in the case of price ceilings.

Inefficiently High Quality Again like price ceilings, price floors lead to inefficiency in the quality of goods produced.

We saw that when there is a price ceiling, suppliers produce products that are of inefficiently low quality: buyers prefer higher-quality products and are willing to pay for them, but sellers refuse to improve the quality of their products because the price ceiling prevents their being compensated for doing so. This same logic applies to price floors, but in reverse: suppliers offer goods of **inefficiently high quality.**

How can this be? Isn't high quality a good thing? Yes, but only if it is worth the cost. Suppose that suppliers spend a lot to make goods of very high quality but that this quality isn't worth much to consumers, who would rather receive the money spent on that quality in the form of a lower price. This represents a missed opportunity: suppliers and buyers could make a mutually beneficial deal in which buyers got goods of lower quality for a much lower price.

A good example of the inefficiency of excessive quality comes from the days when transatlantic airfares were set artificially high by international treaty. Forbidden to compete for customers by offering lower ticket prices, airlines instead offered expensive services, like lavish in-flight meals that went largely uneaten. At one point the regulators tried to restrict this practice by defining maximum service standards—for example, that snack service should consist of no more than a sandwich. One airline then introduced what it called a "Scandinavian Sandwich," a towering affair that forced the convening of another conference to define *sandwich*. All of this was wasteful, especially considering that what passengers really wanted was less food and lower airfares.

Since the deregulation of U.S. airlines in the 1970s, American passengers have experienced a large decrease in ticket prices accompanied by a decrease in the quality of in-flight service—smaller seats, lower-quality food, and so on. Everyone complains about the service—but thanks to lower fares, the number of people flying on U.S. carriers has grown several hundred percent since airline deregulation.

Illegal Activity Finally, like price ceilings, price floors provide incentives for illegal activity. For example, in countries where the minimum wage is far above the equilibrium wage rate, workers desperate for jobs sometimes agree to work off the books for employers who conceal their employment from the government—or bribe the government inspectors. This practice, known in Europe as "black labor," is especially common in Southern European countries such as Italy and Spain (see the upcoming Economics in Action).

CHECK OUT OUR LOW, LOW WAGES!

The minimum wage rate in the United States, as you can see in this graph, is actually quite low compared with that in other rich countries. Since minimum wages are set in national currency—the British minimum wage is set in British pounds, the French minimum wage is set in euros, and so on—the comparison depends on the exchange rate on any given day. As of April 15, 2011, Australia had a minimum wage over twice as high as the U.S. rate, with France, Canada, and Ireland not far behind. You can see one effect of this difference in the supermarket checkout line. In the United States there is usually someone to bag your groceries—someone typically paid the minimum wage or at best slightly more. In Europe, where hiring a bagger is a lot more expensive, you're almost always expected to do the bagging yourself.

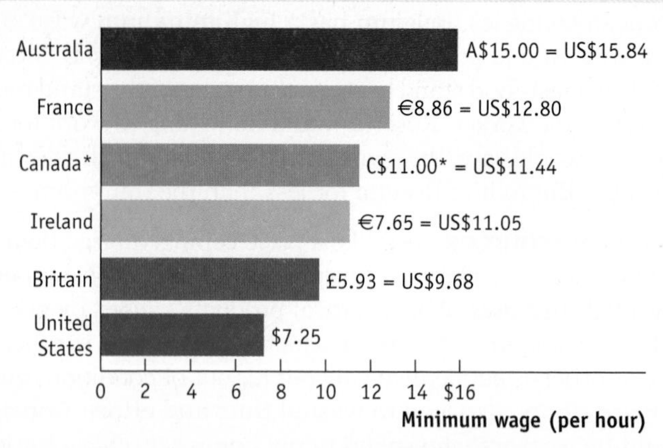

Source: National Employment Rights Authority (Ireland); Ministère du Travail, de l'Emploi et de la Santé (France); Fair Work Australia (Australia); Department for Business, Innovation and Skills (Britain); Human Resources and Skills Development Canada (Canada); Department of Labor (U.S.); Federal Reserve Bank of St. Louis (exchange rates as of 04/15/2011).

*The Canadian minimum wage varies by province from C$8.00 to C$11.00.

So Why Are There Price Floors?

To sum up, a price floor creates various negative side effects:

- A persistent surplus of the good
- Inefficiency arising from the persistent surplus in the form of inefficiently low quantity (deadweight loss), inefficient allocation of sales among sellers, wasted resources, and an inefficiently high level of quality offered by suppliers
- The temptation to engage in illegal activity, particularly bribery and corruption of government officials

So why do governments impose price floors when they have so many negative side effects? The reasons are similar to those for imposing price ceilings. Government officials often disregard warnings about the consequences of price floors either because they believe that the relevant market is poorly described by the supply and demand model or, more often, because they do not understand the model. Above all, just as price ceilings are often imposed because they benefit some influential buyers of a good, price floors are often imposed because they benefit some influential sellers.

ECONOMICS ➤ IN ACTION

"BLACK LABOR" IN SOUTHERN EUROPE

The best-known example of a price floor is the minimum wage. Most economists believe, however, that the minimum wage has relatively little effect on the job market in the United States, mainly because the floor is set so low. In 1964, the U.S. minimum wage was 53% of the average wage of blue-collar production workers; by 2012, despite several recent increases, it had fallen to about 37%.

The situation is different, however, in many European countries, where minimum wages have been set much higher than in the United States. This has happened despite the fact that workers in most European countries are somewhat less productive than their American counterparts, which means that the equilibrium wage in Europe—the wage that would clear the labor market—is probably lower in Europe than in the United States. Moreover, European countries often require employers to pay for health and retirement benefits, which are more extensive and so more costly than comparable American benefits. These mandated benefits make the actual cost of employing a European worker considerably more than the worker's paycheck.

Denis Doyle/Bloomberg via Getty Images

The generous minimum wage in many European countries has contributed to a high rate of unemployment and the flourishing of an illegal labor market.

The result is that in Europe the price floor on labor is definitely binding: the minimum wage is well above the wage rate that would make the quantity of labor supplied by workers equal to the quantity of labor demanded by employers.

The persistent surplus that results from this price floor appears in the form of high unemployment—millions of workers, especially young workers, seek jobs but cannot find them.

In countries where the enforcement of labor laws is lax, however, there is a second, entirely predictable result: widespread evasion of the law. In both Italy and Spain, officials believe there are hundreds of thousands, if not millions, of workers who are employed by companies that pay them less than the legal minimum, fail to provide the required health and retirement benefits, or both. In many cases the jobs are simply unreported: Spanish economists estimate that about a third of the country's reported unemployed are in the black labor market—working at unreported jobs. In fact, Spaniards waiting to collect checks from the unemployment office have been known to complain about the long lines that keep them from getting back to work!

Employers in these countries have also found legal ways to evade the wage floor. For example, Italy's labor regulations apply only to companies with 15 or more workers. This gives a big cost advantage to small Italian firms, many of which remain small in order to avoid paying higher wages and benefits. And sure enough, in some Italian industries there is an astonishing proliferation of tiny companies. For example, one of Italy's most successful industries is the manufacture of fine woolen cloth, centered in the Prato region. The average textile firm in that region employs only four workers!

Quick Review

- The most familiar price floor is the **minimum wage.** Price floors are also commonly imposed on agricultural goods.
- A price floor above the equilibrium price benefits successful sellers but causes predictable adverse effects such as a persistent surplus, which leads to four kinds of inefficiencies: deadweight loss from inefficiently low quantity, **inefficient allocation of sales among sellers,** wasted resources, and **inefficiently high quality.**
- Price floors encourage illegal activity, such as workers who work off the books, often leading to official corruption.

CHECK YOUR UNDERSTANDING 4-3

1. The state legislature mandates a price floor for gasoline of P_F per gallon. Assess the following statements and illustrate your answer using the figure provided.
   a. Proponents of the law claim it will increase the income of gas station owners. Opponents claim it will hurt gas station owners because they will lose customers.
   b. Proponents claim consumers will be better off because gas stations will provide better service. Opponents claim consumers will be generally worse off because they prefer to buy gas at cheaper prices.
   c. Proponents claim that they are helping gas station owners without hurting anyone else. Opponents claim that consumers are hurt and will end up doing things like buying gas in a nearby state or on the black market.

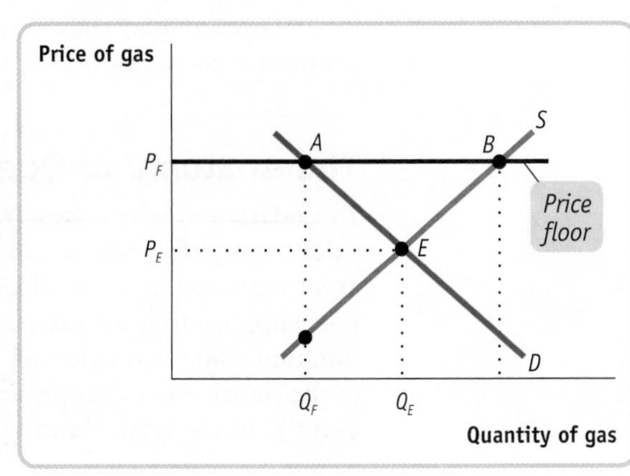

Solutions appear at back of book.

A **quantity control,** or **quota,** is an upper limit on the quantity of some good that can be bought or sold. The total amount of the good that can be legally transacted is the **quota limit.**

A **license** gives its owner the right to supply a good.

Controlling Quantities

In the 1930s, New York City instituted a system of licensing for taxicabs: only taxis with a "medallion" were allowed to pick up passengers. Because this system was intended to assure quality, medallion owners were supposed to maintain certain standards, including safety and cleanliness. A total of 11,787 medallions were issued, with taxi owners paying $10 for each medallion.

In 1995, there were still only 11,787 licensed taxicabs in New York, even though the city had meanwhile become the financial capital of the world, a place where hundreds of thousands of people in a hurry tried to hail a cab every day. (An additional 400 medallions were issued in 1995, and after several rounds of sales of additional medallions, today there are 13,128 medallions.)

The result of this restriction on the number of taxis was that a New York City taxi medallion became very valuable: if you wanted to operate a taxi in New York, you had to lease a medallion from someone else or buy one for a going price of several hundred thousand dollars.

It turns out that this story is not unique; other cities introduced similar medallion systems in the 1930s and, like New York, have issued few new medallions since. In San Francisco and Boston, as in New York, taxi medallions trade for six-figure prices.

A taxi medallion system is a form of **quantity control,** or **quota,** by which the government regulates the quantity of a good that can be bought and sold rather than the price at which it is transacted. The total amount of the good that can be transacted under the quantity control is called the **quota limit.** Typically, the government limits quantity in a market by issuing **licenses;** only people with a license can legally supply the good.

A taxi medallion is just such a license. The government of New York City limits the number of taxi rides that can be sold by limiting the number of taxis to only those who hold medallions. There are many other cases of quantity controls, ranging from limits on how much foreign currency (for instance, British pounds or Mexican pesos) people are allowed to buy to the quantity of clams New Jersey fishing boats are allowed to catch. Notice, by the way, that although there are price controls on both sides of the equilibrium price—price ceilings and price floors—in the real world, quantity controls always set an upper, not a lower, limit on quantities. After all, nobody can be forced to buy or sell more than they want to!

Some attempts to control quantities are undertaken for good economic reasons, some for bad ones. In many cases, as we will see, quantity controls introduced to address a temporary problem become politically hard to remove later because the beneficiaries don't want them abolished, even after the original reason for their existence is long gone. But whatever the reasons for such controls, they have certain predictable—and usually undesirable—economic consequences.

The Anatomy of Quantity Controls

To understand why a New York taxi medallion is worth so much money, we consider a simplified version of the market for taxi rides, shown in Figure 4-13. Just as we assumed in the analysis of rent control that all apartments are the same, we now suppose that all taxi rides are the same—ignoring the real-world complication that some taxi rides are longer, and so more expensive, than others. The table in the figure shows supply and demand schedules. The equilibrium—indicated by point *E* in the figure and by the shaded entries in the table—is a fare of $5 per

FIGURE 4-13 The Market for Taxi Rides in the Absence of Government Controls

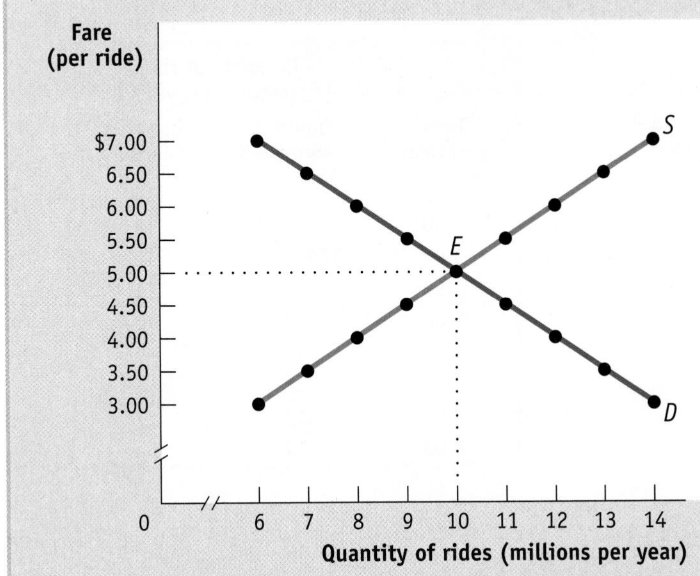

Fare (per ride)	Quantity of rides (millions per year) Quantity demanded	Quantity supplied
$7.00	6	14
6.50	7	13
6.00	8	12
5.50	9	11
5.00	10	10
4.50	11	9
4.00	12	8
3.50	13	7
3.00	14	6

Without government intervention, the market reaches equilibrium with 10 million rides taken per year at a fare of $5 per ride.

ride, with 10 million rides taken per year. (You'll see in a minute why we present the equilibrium this way.)

The New York medallion system limits the number of taxis, but each taxi driver can offer as many rides as he or she can manage. (Now you know why New York taxi drivers are so aggressive!) To simplify our analysis, however, we will assume that a medallion system limits the number of taxi rides that can legally be given to 8 million per year.

Until now, we have derived the demand curve by answering questions of the form: "How many taxi rides will passengers want to take if the price is $5 per ride?" But it is possible to reverse the question and ask instead: "At what price will consumers want to buy 10 million rides per year?" The price at which consumers want to buy a given quantity—in this case, 10 million rides at $5 per ride—is the **demand price** of that quantity. You can see from the demand schedule in Figure 4-13 that the demand price of 6 million rides is $7 per ride, the demand price of 7 million rides is $6.50 per ride, and so on.

Similarly, the supply curve represents the answer to questions of the form: "How many taxi rides would taxi drivers supply at a price of $5 each?" But we can also reverse this question to ask: "At what price will suppliers be willing to supply 10 million rides per year?" The price at which suppliers will supply a given quantity—in this case, 10 million rides at $5 per ride—is the **supply price** of that quantity. We can see from the supply schedule in Figure 4-13 that the supply price of 6 million rides is $3 per ride, the supply price of 7 million rides is $3.50 per ride, and so on.

Now we are ready to analyze a quota. We have assumed that the city government limits the quantity of taxi rides to 8 million per year. Medallions, each of which carries the right to provide a certain number of taxi rides per year, are made available to selected people in such a way that a total of 8 million rides will

The **demand price** of a given quantity is the price at which consumers will demand that quantity.

The **supply price** of a given quantity is the price at which producers will supply that quantity.

FIGURE 4-14 Effect of a Quota on the Market for Taxi Rides

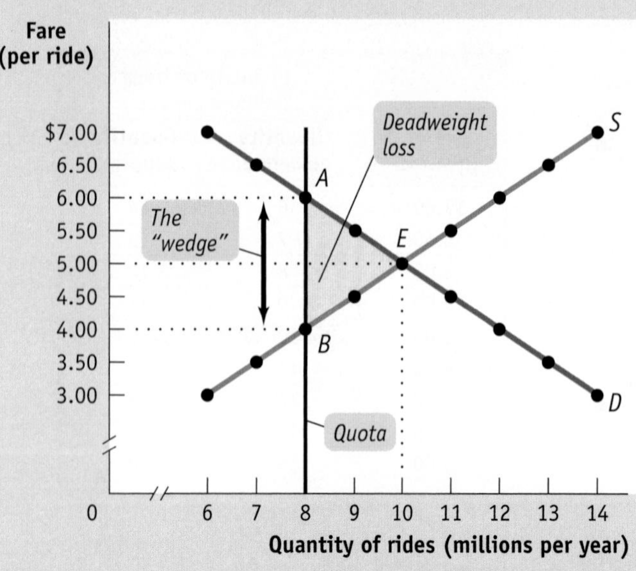

Fare (per ride)	Quantity of rides (millions per year) Quantity demanded	Quantity supplied
$7.00	6	14
6.50	7	13
6.00	8	12
5.50	9	11
5.00	10	10
4.50	11	9
4.00	12	8
3.50	13	7
3.00	14	6

The table shows the demand price and the supply price corresponding to each quantity: the price at which that quantity would be demanded and supplied, respectively. The city government imposes a quota of 8 million rides by selling licenses for only 8 million rides, represented by the black vertical line. The price paid by consumers rises to $6 per ride, the demand price of 8 million rides, shown by point *A*. The supply price of 8 million rides is only $4 per ride, shown by point *B*. The difference between these two prices is the quota rent per ride, the earnings that accrue to the owner of a license. The quota rent drives a wedge between the demand price and the supply price. And since the quota discourages mutually beneficial transactions, it creates a deadweight loss equal to the shaded triangle.

be provided. Medallion-holders may then either drive their own taxis or rent their medallions to others for a fee.

Figure 4-14 shows the resulting market for taxi rides, with the black vertical line at 8 million rides per year representing the quota limit. Because the quantity of rides is limited to 8 million, consumers must be at point *A* on the demand curve, corresponding to the shaded entry in the demand schedule: the demand price of 8 million rides is $6 per ride. Meanwhile, taxi drivers must be at point *B* on the supply curve, corresponding to the shaded entry in the supply schedule: the supply price of 8 million rides is $4 per ride.

But how can the price received by taxi drivers be $4 when the price paid by taxi riders is $6? The answer is that in addition to the market in taxi rides, there is also a market in medallions. Medallion-holders may not always want to drive their taxis: they may be ill or on vacation. Those who do not want to drive their own taxis will sell the right to use the medallion to someone else. So we need to consider two sets of transactions here, and so two prices: (1) the transactions in taxi rides and the price at which these will occur, and (2) the transactions in medallions and the price at which these will occur. It turns out that since we are looking at two markets, the $4 and $6 prices will both be right.

To see how this all works, consider two imaginary New York taxi drivers, Sunil and Harriet. Sunil has a medallion but can't use it because he's recovering from a severely sprained wrist. So he's looking to rent his medallion out to someone else. Harriet doesn't have a medallion but would like to rent one. Furthermore, at any point in time there are many other people like Harriet who would like to rent a medallion. Suppose Sunil agrees to rent his medallion to Harriet. To make things simple, assume that any driver can give only one ride per day and that Sunil is renting his medallion to Harriet for one day. What rental price will they agree on?

To answer this question, we need to look at the transactions from the viewpoints of both drivers. Once she has the medallion, Harriet knows she can make $6 per day—the demand price of a ride under the quota. And she is willing to rent the medallion only if she makes at least $4 per day—the supply price of a ride under the quota. So Sunil cannot demand a rent of more than $2—the difference between $6 and $4. And if Harriet offered Sunil less than $2—say, $1.50—there would be other eager drivers willing to offer him more, up to $2. So, in order to get the medallion, Harriet must offer Sunil at least $2. Since the rent can be no more than $2 and no less than $2, it must be exactly $2.

It is no coincidence that $2 is exactly the difference between $6, the demand price of 8 million rides, and $4, the supply price of 8 million rides. In every case in which the supply of a good is legally restricted, there is a **wedge** between the demand price of the quantity transacted and the supply price of the quantity transacted. This wedge, illustrated by the double-headed arrow in Figure 4-14, has a special name: the **quota rent.** It is the earnings that accrue to the license-holder from ownership of a valuable commodity, the license. In the case of Sunil and Harriet, the quota rent of $2 goes to Sunil because he owns the license, and the remaining $4 from the total fare of $6 goes to Harriet.

So Figure 4-14 also illustrates the quota rent in the market for New York taxi rides. The quota limits the quantity of rides to 8 million per year, a quantity at which the demand price of $6 exceeds the supply price of $4. The wedge between these two prices, $2, is the quota rent that results from the restrictions placed on the quantity of taxi rides in this market.

But wait a second. What if Sunil doesn't rent out his medallion? What if he uses it himself? Doesn't this mean that he gets a price of $6? No, not really. Even if Sunil doesn't rent out his medallion, he could have rented it out, which means that the medallion has an *opportunity cost* of $2: if Sunil decides to use his own medallion and drive his own taxi rather than renting his medallion to Harriet, the $2 represents his opportunity cost of not renting out his medallion. That is, the $2 quota rent is now the rental income he forgoes by driving his own taxi.

In effect, Sunil is in two businesses—the taxi-driving business and the medallion-renting business. He makes $4 per ride from driving his taxi and $2 per ride from renting out his medallion. It doesn't make any difference that in this particular case he has rented his medallion to himself! So regardless of whether the medallion owner uses the medallion himself or herself, or rents it to others, it is a valuable asset. And this is represented in the going price for a New York City taxi medallion: in June 2012, it was $704,000. According to Simon Greenbaum, a broker of New York taxi medallions, an owner of a medallion who leases it to a driver can expect to earn about $2,500 per month, or a 3% return—an attractive rate of return compared to other investments.

Notice, by the way, that quotas—like price ceilings and price floors—don't always have a real effect. If the quota were set at 12 million rides—that is, above the equilibrium quantity in an unregulated market—it would have no effect because it would not be binding.

A quantity control, or quota, drives a **wedge** between the demand price and the supply price of a good; that is, the price paid by buyers ends up being higher than that received by sellers.

The difference between the demand and supply price at the quota limit is the **quota rent,** the earnings that accrue to the license-holder from ownership of the right to sell the good. It is equal to the market price of the license when the licenses are traded.

The Costs of Quantity Controls

Like price controls, quantity controls can have some predictable and undesirable side effects. The first is the by-now-familiar problem of inefficiency due to missed opportunities: quantity controls create deadweight loss by preventing mutually beneficial transactions from occurring, transactions that would benefit both buyers and sellers. Looking back at Figure 4-14, you can see that starting at the quota limit of 8 million rides, New Yorkers would be willing to pay at least $5.50 per ride for an additional 1 million rides and that taxi drivers would be willing to provide those rides as long as they got at least $4.50 per ride. These are rides that would have taken place if there were no quota limit.

The same is true for the next 1 million rides: New Yorkers would be willing to pay at least $5 per ride when the quantity of rides is increased from 9 to 10 million, and taxi drivers would be willing to provide those rides as long as they got at least $5 per ride. Again, these rides would have occurred without the quota limit.

Only when the market has reached the unregulated market equilibrium quantity of 10 million rides are there no "missed-opportunity rides." The quota limit of 8 million rides has caused 2 million "missed-opportunity rides."

Generally, *as long as the demand price of a given quantity exceeds the supply price, there is a deadweight loss.* A buyer would be willing to buy the good at a price that the seller would be willing to accept, but such a transaction does not occur because it is forbidden by the quota. The deadweight loss arising from the 2 million in missed-opportunity rides is represented by the shaded triangle in Figure 4-14.

And because there are transactions that people would like to make but are not allowed to, quantity controls generate an incentive to evade them or even to break the law. New York's taxi industry again provides clear examples. Taxi regulation applies only to those drivers who are hailed by passengers on the street. A car service that makes prearranged pickups does not need a medallion. As a result, such hired cars provide much of the service that might otherwise be provided by taxis, as in other cities. In addition, there are substantial numbers of unlicensed cabs that simply defy the law by picking up passengers without a medallion. Because these cabs are illegal, their drivers are completely unregulated, and they generate a disproportionately large share of traffic accidents in New York City.

The Queens Ledger/Brooklyn Star Newspaper Group

Dangerous, unlicensed cabs are one cost of quantity controls.

In fact, in 2004 the hardships caused by the limited number of New York taxis led city leaders to authorize an increase in the number of licensed taxis. In a series of sales, the city sold 900 new medallions, to bring the total number up to the current 13,128 medallions—a move that certainly cheered New York riders.

But those who already owned medallions were less happy with the increase; they understood that the 900 new taxis would reduce or eliminate the shortage of taxis. As a result, taxi drivers anticipated a decline in their revenues because they would no longer always be assured of finding willing customers. And, in turn, the value of a medallion would fall. So to placate the medallion owners, city officials also raised taxi fares: by 25% in 2004, and again—by a smaller percentage—in 2006. Although taxis are now easier to find, a ride now costs more—and that price increase slightly diminished the newfound cheer of New York taxi riders.

In sum, quantity controls typically create the following undesirable side effects:

- Deadweight loss because some mutually beneficial transactions don't occur
- Incentives for illegal activities

ECONOMICS ➤ IN ACTION

THE CLAMS OF JERSEY SHORE

Forget the refineries along the Jersey Turnpike or reality TV shows; one industry that New Jersey *really* dominates is clam fishing. In 2009 the Garden State supplied 39% of the country's quahogs, which are used to make clam chowder, and 71% of the surf clams, whose tongues are used in fried-clam dinners.

Olivia Boinet for The Washington Post via Getty Images

Quotas helped to protect the clam beds of New Jersey but also transformed the clamming industry because boat owners found it more profitable to rent and sell licenses than to fish.

In the 1980s, however, excessive fishing threatened to wipe out New Jersey's clam beds. To save the resource, the U.S. government introduced a clam quota, which sets an overall limit on the number of bushels of clams that may be caught and allocates licenses to owners of fishing boats based on their historical catches.

Notice, by the way, that this is an example of a quota that is probably justified by broader economic and environmental considerations—unlike the New York taxicab quota, which has long since lost any economic rationale. Still, whatever its rationale, the New Jersey clam quota works the same way as any other quota.

Once the quota system was established, many boat owners stopped fishing for clams. They realized that rather than operate a boat part time, it was more profitable to sell or rent their licenses to someone else, who could then assemble enough licenses to operate a boat full time. Today, there are about 50 New Jersey boats fishing for clams; the license required to operate one is worth more than the boat itself.

▼ Quick Review

- **Quantity controls,** or **quotas,** are government-imposed limits on how much of a good may be bought or sold. The quantity allowed for sale is the **quota limit.** The government then issues a **license**—the right to sell a given quantity of a good under the quota.
- When the quota limit is smaller than the equilibrium quantity in an unregulated market, the **demand price** is higher than the **supply price**—there is a **wedge** between them at the quota limit.
- This wedge is the **quota rent,** the earnings that accrue to the license-holder from ownership of the right to sell the good—whether by actually supplying the good or by renting the license to someone else. The market price of a license equals the quota rent.
- Like price controls, quantity controls create deadweight loss and encourage illegal activity.

CHECK YOUR UNDERSTANDING 4-4

1. Suppose that the supply and demand for taxi rides is given by Figure 4-13 but the quota is set at 6 million rides instead of 8 million. Find the following and indicate them on Figure 4-13.
   a. The price of a ride
   b. The quota rent
   c. The deadweight loss
   d. Suppose the quota limit on taxi rides is increased to 9 million. What happens to the quota rent? To the deadweight loss?
2. Assume that the quota limit is 8 million rides. Suppose demand decreases due to a decline in tourism. What is the smallest parallel leftward shift in demand that would result in the quota no longer having an effect on the market? Illustrate your answer using Figure 4-13.

Solutions appear at back of book.

WORKED **PROBLEM**

The World's Most Expensive City

London is one of the most expensive places in the world to rent an apartment. If you have ever visited London, you might have noticed an area around the city known as the "Green Belt." Zoning laws make it nearly impossible to build new residential housing on land designated as the Green Belt. Consider the following hypothetical market for apartments in London in the absence of zoning controls.

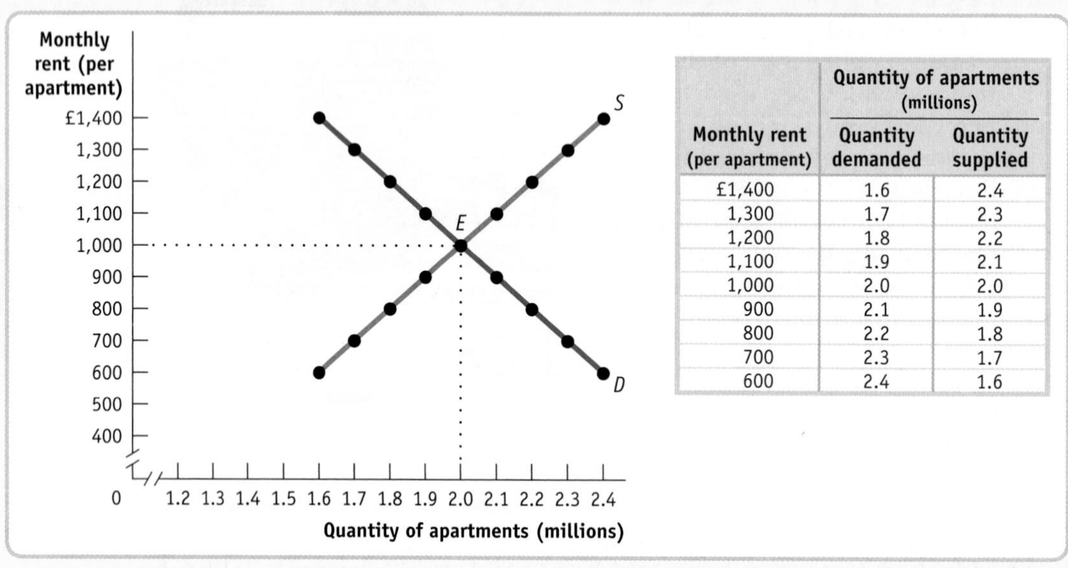

Monthly rent (per apartment)	Quantity of apartments (millions) Quantity demanded	Quantity supplied
£1,400	1.6	2.4
1,300	1.7	2.3
1,200	1.8	2.2
1,100	1.9	2.1
1,000	2.0	2.0
900	2.1	1.9
800	2.2	1.8
700	2.3	1.7
600	2.4	1.6

This figure should look familiar to you—it is Figure 4-6, but the currency is the British pound rather than the U.S. dollar. At the time of this writing, the British pound was worth about 1.6 dollars.

Now, let's go back to the reality of zoning controls in the Green Belt. Use a diagram to show the effect of a quota of 1.7 million apartments. What is the quota rent, and who gets it?

STEP 1: Use a diagram to show the effect of a quota of 1.7 million apartments.

Review the section "The Anatomy of Quantity Controls" beginning on page 128. Study carefully Figure 4-14 on page 130.

In the following figure, the black vertical line represents the quota limit of 1.7 million apartments. Because the quantity of apartments is limited, consumers must be at point A on the demand curve. The demand price of 1.7 million apartments is £1,300 each. The supply price, corresponding to point B on the diagram, of 1.7 million apartments is only £700 each, creating a "wedge" of £1300 – £700 = £600. ■

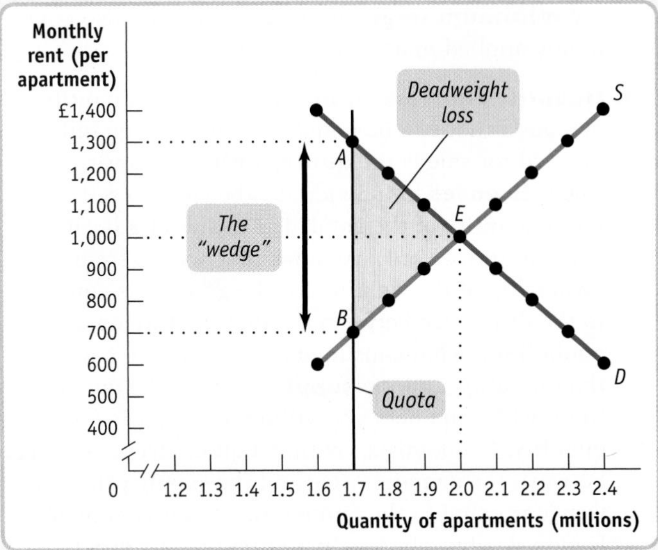

STEP 2: What is the quota rent in this case, and who gets it?

Review the second half of the section "The Anatomy of Quantity Controls," beginning on page 131.

In the case of taxis, the quota rent is the earnings that accrue to the license-holder from ownership of the right to sell the good. In the case of apartments inside the Green Belt in London, the quota rent is the "wedge" of £600 created by the difference in the demand price and the supply price. The wedge goes to current owners of property or flats in London. Current owners benefit from the strict application of zoning laws. ■

SUMMARY

1. The demand curve is determined by each individual consumer's **willingness to pay.** When price is less than or equal to the willingness to pay, the consumer purchases the good. The difference between willingness to pay and price is the net gain to the consumer, the **individual consumer surplus. Total consumer surplus** in a market, the sum of all individual consumer surpluses in a market, is equal to the area below the market demand curve but above the price.
2. The supply curve is determined by the cost to each potential producer—the lowest price at which the producer is willing to produce a unit of that good. If the price of a good is above the producer's cost, a sale generates a net gain to the producer, known as the **individual producer surplus. Total producer surplus** in a market is the sum of the individual producer surpluses. This is equal to the area above the market supply curve but below the price.
3. **Total surplus,** the total gain to society from the production and consumption of a good, is the sum of consumer and producer surpluses.
4. Even when a market is efficient, governments often intervene to pursue greater fairness or to please a powerful interest group. Interventions can take the form of **price controls** or quantity controls, both of which generate predictable and undesirable side effects consisting of various forms of inefficiency and illegal activity.
5. A **price ceiling,** a maximum market price below the equilibrium price, benefits successful buyers but creates persistent shortages. Because the price is maintained below the equilibrium price, the quantity

demanded is increased and the quantity supplied is decreased compared to the equilibrium quantity. This leads to predictable problems: inefficiencies in the form of **deadweight loss** from inefficiently low quantity, **inefficient allocation to consumers, wasted resources,** and **inefficiently low quality.** It also encourages illegal activity as people turn to **black markets** to get the good. Because of these problems, price ceilings have generally lost favor as an economic policy tool. But some governments continue to impose them either because they don't understand the effects or because the price ceilings benefit some influential group.

6. A **price floor,** a minimum market price above the equilibrium price, benefits successful sellers but creates persistent surplus. Because the price is maintained above the equilibrium price, the quantity demanded is decreased and the quantity supplied is increased compared to the equilibrium quantity. This leads to predictable problems: inefficiencies in the form of deadweight loss from inefficiently low quantity, **inefficient allocation of sales among sellers,** wasted resources, and **inefficiently high quality.** It also encourages illegal activity and black markets. The most well known kind of price floor is the **minimum wage,** but price floors are also commonly applied to agricultural products.

7. **Quantity controls,** or **quotas,** limit the quantity of a good that can be bought or sold. The quantity allowed for sale is the **quota limit.** The government issues **licenses** to individuals, the right to sell a given quantity of the good. The owner of a license earns a **quota rent,** earnings that accrue from ownership of the right to sell the good. It is equal to the difference between the **demand price** at the quota limit, what consumers are willing to pay for that quantity, and the **supply price** at the quota limit, what suppliers are willing to accept for that quantity. Economists say that a quota drives a **wedge** between the demand price and the supply price; this wedge is equal to the quota rent. Quantity controls lead to deadweight loss in addition to encouraging illegal activity.

KEY TERMS

Willingness to pay, p. 106
Individual consumer surplus, p. 107
Total consumer surplus, p. 107
Consumer surplus, p. 107
Cost, p. 109
Individual producer surplus, p. 109
Total producer surplus, p. 109
Producer surplus, p. 109
Total surplus, p. 112
Price controls, p. 113
Price ceiling, p. 113
Price floor, p. 113
Deadweight loss, p. 116
Inefficient allocation to consumers, p. 118
Wasted resources, p. 119
Inefficiently low quality, p. 119
Black markets, p. 119
Minimum wage, p. 122
Inefficient allocation of sales among sellers, p. 125
Inefficiently high quality, p. 125
Quantity control, p. 128
Quota, p. 128
Quota limit, p. 128
License, p. 128
Demand price, p. 129
Supply price, p. 129
Wedge, p. 131
Quota rent, p. 131

PROBLEMS

1. Determine the amount of consumer surplus generated in each of the following situations.
   a. Leon goes to the clothing store to buy a new T-shirt, for which he is willing to pay up to $10. He picks out one he likes with a price tag of exactly $10. When he is paying for it, he learns that the T-shirt has been discounted by 50%.
   b. Alberto goes to the CD store hoping to find a used copy of *Nirvana's Greatest Hits* for up to $10. The store has one copy selling for $10, which he purchases.
   c. After soccer practice, Stacey is willing to pay $2 for a bottle of mineral water. The 7-Eleven sells mineral water for $2.25 per bottle, so she declines to purchase it.

2. Determine the amount of producer surplus generated in each of the following situations.
   a. Gordon lists his old Lionel electric trains on eBay. He sets a minimum acceptable price, known as his reserve price, of $75. After five days of bidding, the final high bid is exactly $75. He accepts the bid.
   b. So-Hee advertises her car for sale in the used-car section of the student newspaper for $2,000, but she is willing to sell the car for any price higher than $1,500. The best offer she gets is $1,200, which she declines.
   c. Sanjay likes his job so much that he would be willing to do it for free. However, his annual salary is $80,000.

3. You are the manager of Fun World, a small amusement park. The accompanying diagram shows the demand curve of a typical customer at Fun World.

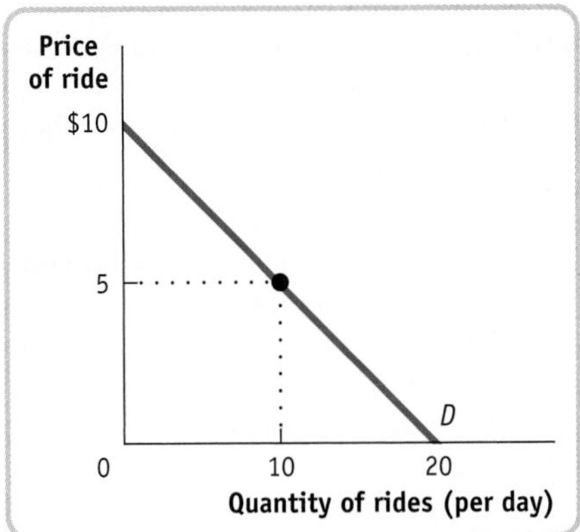

a. Suppose that the price of each ride is $5. At that price, how much consumer surplus does an individual consumer get? (Recall that the area of a right triangle is ½ × the height of the triangle × the base of the triangle.)

b. Suppose that Fun World considers charging an admission fee, even though it maintains the price of each ride at $5. What is the maximum admission fee it could charge? (Assume that all potential customers have enough money to pay the fee.)

c. Suppose that Fun World lowered the price of each ride to zero. How much consumer surplus does an individual consumer get? What is the maximum admission fee Fun World could charge?

4. The accompanying diagram illustrates a taxi driver's individual supply curve (assume that each taxi ride is the same distance).

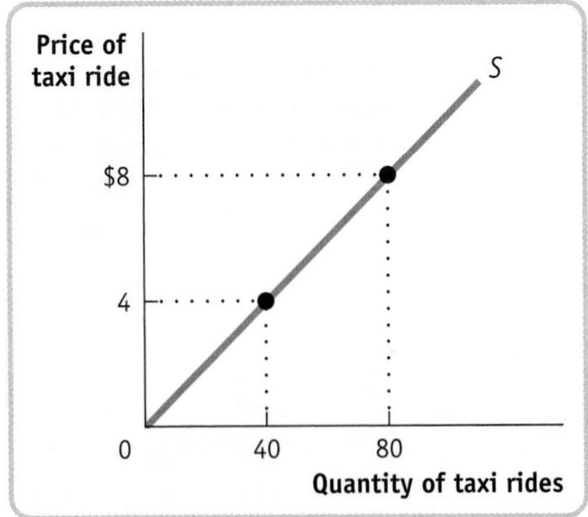

a. Suppose the city sets the price of taxi rides at $4 per ride, and at $4 the taxi driver is able to sell as many taxi rides as he desires. What is this taxi driver's producer surplus? (Recall that the area of a right triangle is ½ × the height of the triangle × the base of the triangle.)

b. Suppose that the city keeps the price of a taxi ride set at $4, but it decides to charge taxi drivers a "licensing fee." What is the maximum licensing fee the city could extract from this taxi driver?

c. Suppose that the city allowed the price of taxi rides to increase to $8 per ride. Again assume that, at this price, the taxi driver sells as many rides as he is willing to offer. How much producer surplus does an individual taxi driver now get? What is the maximum licensing fee the city could charge this taxi driver?

5. Suppose it is decided that rent control in New York City will be abolished and that market rents will now prevail. Assume that all rental units are identical and so are offered at the same rent. To address the plight of residents who may be unable to pay the market rent, an income supplement will be paid to all low-income households equal to the difference between the old controlled rent and the new market rent.

a. Use a diagram to show the effect on the rental market of the elimination of rent control. What will happen to the quality and quantity of rental housing supplied?

b. Use a second diagram to show the additional effect of the income-supplement policy on the market. What effect does it have on the market rent and quantity of rental housing supplied in comparison to your answers to part a?

c. Are tenants better or worse off as a result of these policies? Are landlords better or worse off? Is society as a whole better or worse off?

d. From a political standpoint, why do you think cities have been more likely to resort to rent control rather than a policy of income supplements to help low-income people pay for housing?

6. In order to ingratiate himself with voters, the mayor of Gotham City decides to lower the price of taxi rides. Assume, for simplicity, that all taxi rides are the same distance and therefore cost the same. The accompanying table shows the demand and supply schedules for taxi rides.

	Quantity of rides (millions per year)	
Fare (per ride)	Quantity demanded	Quantity supplied
$7.00	10	12
6.50	11	11
6.00	12	10
5.50	13	9
5.00	14	8
4.50	15	7

a. Assume that there are no restrictions on the number of taxi rides that can be supplied (there is no medallion system). Find the equilibrium price and quantity.

b. Suppose that the mayor sets a price ceiling at $5.50. How large is the shortage of rides? Illustrate with a diagram. Who loses and who benefits from this policy?

c. Suppose that the stock market crashes and, as a result, people in Gotham City are poorer. This reduces the quantity of taxi rides demanded by 6 million rides per year at any given price. What effect will the mayor's new policy have now? Illustrate with a diagram.

d. Suppose that the stock market rises and the demand for taxi rides returns to normal (that is, returns to the demand schedule given in the table). The mayor now decides to ingratiate himself with taxi drivers. He announces a policy in which operating licenses are given to existing taxi drivers; the number of licenses is restricted such that only 10 million rides per year can be given. Illustrate the effect of this policy on the market, and indicate the resulting price and quantity transacted. What is the quota rent per ride?

7. In the late eighteenth century, the price of bread in New York City was controlled, set at a predetermined price above the market price.

a. Draw a diagram showing the effect of the policy. Did the policy act as a price ceiling or a price floor?

b. What kinds of inefficiencies were likely to have arisen when the controlled price of bread was above the market price? Explain in detail.

One year during this period, a poor wheat harvest caused a leftward shift in the supply of bread and therefore an increase in its market price. New York bakers found that the controlled price of bread in New York was below the market price.

c. Draw a diagram showing the effect of the price control on the market for bread during this one-year period. Did the policy act as a price ceiling or a price floor?

d. What kinds of inefficiencies do you think occurred during this period? Explain in detail.

8. European governments tend to make greater use of price controls than does the U.S. government. For example, the French government sets minimum starting yearly wages for new hires who have completed *le bac*, certification roughly equivalent to a high school diploma. The demand schedule for new hires with *le bac* and the supply schedule for similarly credentialed new job seekers are given in the accompanying table. The price here—given in euros, the currency used in France—is the same as the yearly wage.

Wage (per year)	Quantity demanded (new job offers per year)	Quantity supplied (new job seekers per year)
€45,000	200,000	325,000
40,000	220,000	320,000
35,000	250,000	310,000
30,000	290,000	290,000
25,000	370,000	200,000

a. In the absence of government interference, what are the equilibrium wage and number of graduates hired per year? Illustrate with a diagram. Will there be anyone seeking a job at the equilibrium wage who is unable to find one—that is, will there be anyone who is involuntarily unemployed?

b. Suppose the French government sets a minimum yearly wage of €35,000. Is there any involuntary unemployment at this wage? If so, how much? Illustrate with a diagram. What if the minimum wage is set at €40,000? Also illustrate with a diagram.

c. Given your answer to part b and the information in the table, what do you think is the relationship between the level of involuntary unemployment and the level of the minimum wage? Who benefits from such a policy? Who loses? What is the missed opportunity here?

9. Until recently, the standard number of hours worked per week for a full-time job in France was 39 hours, just as in the United States. But in response to social unrest over high levels of involuntary unemployment, the French government instituted a 35-hour workweek—a worker could not work more than 35 hours per week even if both the worker and employer wanted it. The motivation behind this policy was that if current employees worked fewer hours, employers would be forced to hire more new workers. Assume that it is costly for employers to train new workers. French employers were greatly opposed to this policy and threatened to move their operations to neighboring countries that did not have such employment restrictions. Can you explain their attitude? Give an example of both an inefficiency and an illegal activity that are likely to arise from this policy.

10. The waters off the North Atlantic coast were once teeming with fish. But because of overfishing by the commercial fishing industry, the stocks of fish are seriously depleted. In 1991, the National Marine Fishery Service of the U.S. government implemented a quota to allow fish stocks to recover. The quota limited the amount of swordfish caught per year by all U.S.-licensed fishing boats to 7 million pounds. As soon as the U.S. fishing fleet had met the quota limit, the swordfish catch was closed down for the rest of the year. The accompanying table gives the hypothetical demand and supply schedules for swordfish caught in the United States per year.

Price of swordfish (per pound)	Quantity of swordfish (millions of pounds per year): Quantity demanded	Quantity supplied
$20	6	15
18	7	13
16	8	11
14	9	9
12	10	7

a. Use a diagram to show the effect of the quota on the market for swordfish in 1991. In your diagram, illustrate the deadweight loss from inefficiently low quantity.

b. How do you think fishermen will change how they fish in response to this policy?

11. In Maine, you must have a license to harvest lobster commercially; these licenses are issued yearly. The state of Maine is concerned about the dwindling supplies of lobsters found off its coast. The state fishery department has decided to place a yearly quota of 80,000 pounds of lobsters harvested in all Maine waters. It has also decided to give licenses this year only to those fishermen who had licenses last year. The accompanying diagram shows the demand and supply curves for Maine lobsters.

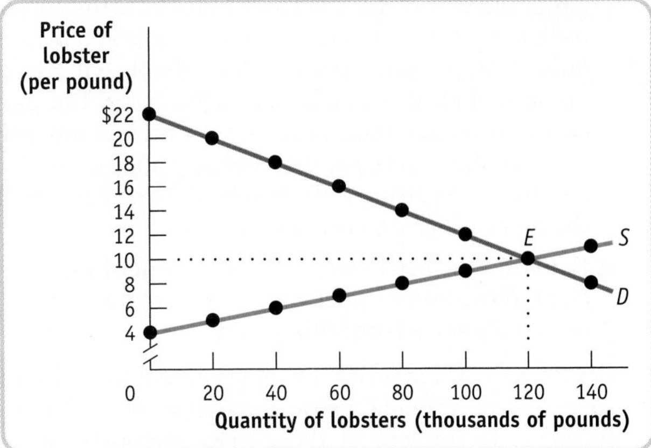

a. In the absence of government restrictions, what are the equilibrium price and quantity?

b. What is the *demand price* at which consumers wish to purchase 80,000 pounds of lobsters?

c. What is the *supply price* at which suppliers are willing to supply 80,000 pounds of lobsters?

d. What is the *quota rent* per pound of lobster when 80,000 pounds are sold? Illustrate the quota rent and the deadweight loss on the diagram.

e. Explain a transaction that benefits both buyer and seller but is prevented by the quota restriction.

12. The Venezuelan government has imposed a price ceiling on the retail price of roasted coffee beans. The accompanying diagram shows the market for coffee beans. In the absence of price controls, the equilibrium is at point *E*, with an equilibrium price of P_E and an equilibrium quantity bought and sold of Q_E.

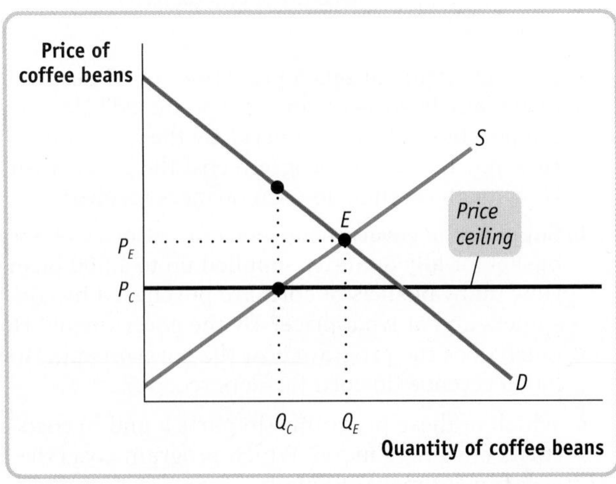

a. Show the consumer and producer surplus before the introduction of the price ceiling.

After the introduction of the price ceiling, the price falls to P_C and the quantity bought and sold falls to Q_C.

b. Show the consumer surplus after the introduction of the price ceiling (assuming that the consumers with the highest willingness to pay get to buy the available coffee beans; that is, assuming that there is no inefficient allocation to consumers).

c. Show the producer surplus after the introduction of the price ceiling (assuming that the producers with the lowest cost get to sell their coffee beans; that is, assuming that there is no inefficient allocation of sales among producers).

d. Using the diagram, show how much of what was producer surplus before the introduction of the price ceiling has been transferred to consumers as a result of the price ceiling.

e. Using the diagram, show how much of what was total surplus before the introduction of the price ceiling has been lost. That is, how great is the deadweight loss?

EXTEND YOUR UNDERSTANDING

13. According to the Bureau of Transportation Statistics, due to an increase in demand, the average domestic airline fare increased from $319.85 in the fourth quarter of 2009 to $328.12 in the first quarter of 2010, an increase of $8.27. The number of passenger tickets sold in the fourth quarter of 2009 was 151.4 million. Over the same period, the airlines' costs remained roughly the same: the price of jet fuel averaged around $2 per gallon in both quarters (Source: Energy Information Administration), and airline pilots' salaries remained roughly the same (according to the Bureau of Labor Statistics, they averaged $117,060 per year in 2009).

Can you determine precisely by how much producer surplus has increased as a result of the $8.27 increase in the average fare? If you cannot be precise, can you determine whether it will be less than, or more than, a specific amount?

14. The U.S. Department of Agriculture (USDA) administers the price floor for butter, which the 2008 Farm Bill set at $1.05 per pound. At that price, according to data from the USDA, the quantity of butter supplied in 2010 was 1.7 billion pounds, and the quantity demanded was 1.6 billion pounds. To support the price of butter at the price floor, the USDA therefore had to buy up 100 million pounds of butter. The accompanying diagram shows supply and demand curves illustrating the market for butter.

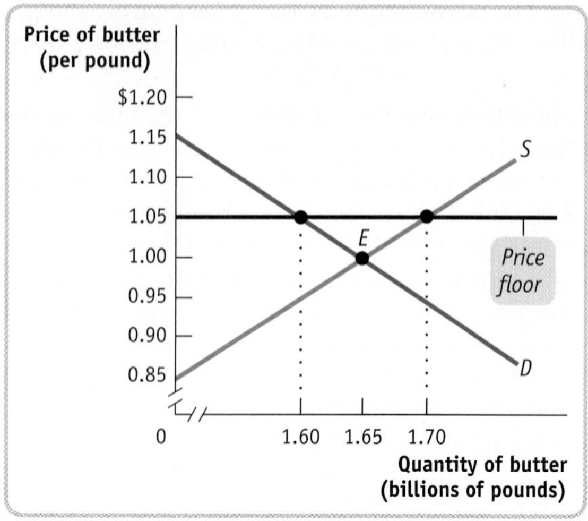

a. In the absence of a price floor, how much consumer surplus is created? How much producer surplus? What is the total surplus?

b. With the price floor at $1.05 per pound of butter, consumers buy 1.6 billion pounds of butter. How much consumer surplus is created now?

c. With the price floor at $1.05 per pound of butter, producers sell 1.7 billion pounds of butter (some to consumers and some to the USDA). How much producer surplus is created now?

d. How much money does the USDA spend on buying up surplus butter?

e. Taxes must be collected to pay for the purchases of surplus butter by the USDA. As a result, total surplus (producer plus consumer) is reduced by the amount the USDA spent on buying surplus butter. Using your answers for parts b–d, what is the total surplus when there is a price floor? How does this compare to the total surplus without a price floor from part a?

15. The accompanying table shows hypothetical demand and supply schedules for milk per year. The U.S. government decides that the incomes of dairy farmers should be maintained at a level that allows the traditional family dairy farm to survive. So it implements a price floor of $1 per pint by buying surplus milk until the market price is $1 per pint.

Price of milk (per pint)	Quantity of milk (millions of pints per year)	
	Quantity demanded	Quantity supplied
$1.20	550	850
1.10	600	800
1.00	650	750
0.90	700	700
0.80	750	650

a. In a diagram, show the deadweight loss from the inefficiently low quantity bought and sold.

b. How much surplus milk will be produced as a result of this policy?

c. What will be the cost to the government of this policy?

d. Since milk is an important source of protein and calcium, the government decides to provide the surplus milk it purchases to elementary schools at a price of only $0.60 per pint. Assume that schools will buy any amount of milk available at this low price. But parents now reduce their purchases of milk at any price by 50 million pints per year because they know their children are getting milk at school. How much will the dairy program now cost the government?

e. Explain how inefficiencies in the form of inefficient allocation of sales among sellers and wasted resources arise from this policy.

16. For the last 70 years the U.S. government has used price supports to provide income assistance to American farmers. To implement these price supports, at times the government has used price floors, which it maintains by buying up the surplus farm products. At other times, it has used target prices, a policy by which the government gives the farmer an amount equal to the difference between the market price and the target price for each unit sold. Consider the market for corn depicted in the accompanying diagram.

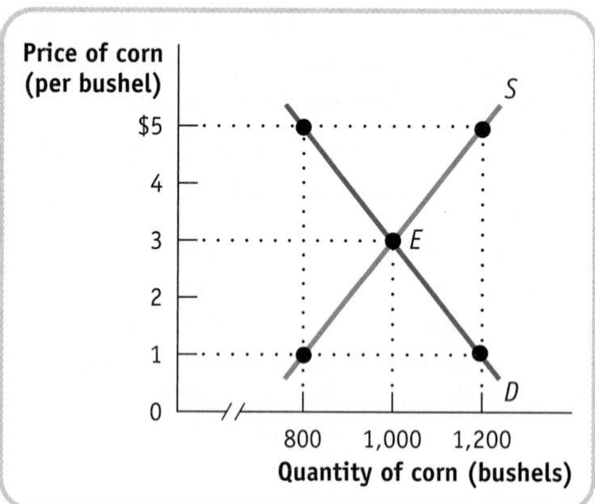

a. If the government sets a price floor of $5 per bushel, how many bushels of corn are produced? How many are purchased by consumers? By the government? How much does the program cost the government? How much revenue do corn farmers receive?

b. Suppose the government sets a target price of $5 per bushel for any quantity supplied up to 1,000 bushels. How many bushels of corn are purchased by consumers and at what price? By the government? How much does the program cost the government? How much revenue do corn farmers receive?

c. Which of these programs (in parts a and b) costs corn consumers more? Which program costs the government more? Explain.

d. Is one of these policies less inefficient than the other? Explain.

17. The accompanying diagram shows data from the U.S. Bureau of Labor Statistics on the average price of an airline ticket in the United States from 1975 until 1985, adjusted to eliminate the effect of *inflation* (the general increase in the prices of all goods over time). In 1978, the United States Airline Deregulation Act removed the price floor on airline fares, and it also allowed the airlines greater flexibility to offer new routes.

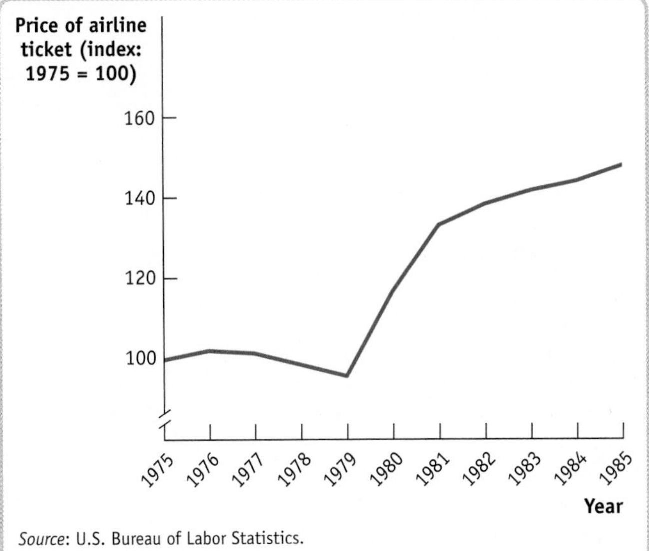

Source: U.S. Bureau of Labor Statistics.

a. Looking at the data on airline ticket prices in the diagram, do you think the price floor that existed before 1978 was binding or nonbinding? That is, do you think it was set above or below the equilibrium price? Draw a supply and demand diagram, showing where the price floor that existed before 1978 was in relation to the equilibrium price.

b. Most economists agree that the average airline ticket price per mile traveled actually *fell* as a result of the Airline Deregulation Act. How might you reconcile that view with what you see in the diagram?

Elasticity and Taxation

MORE PRECIOUS THAN A FLU SHOT

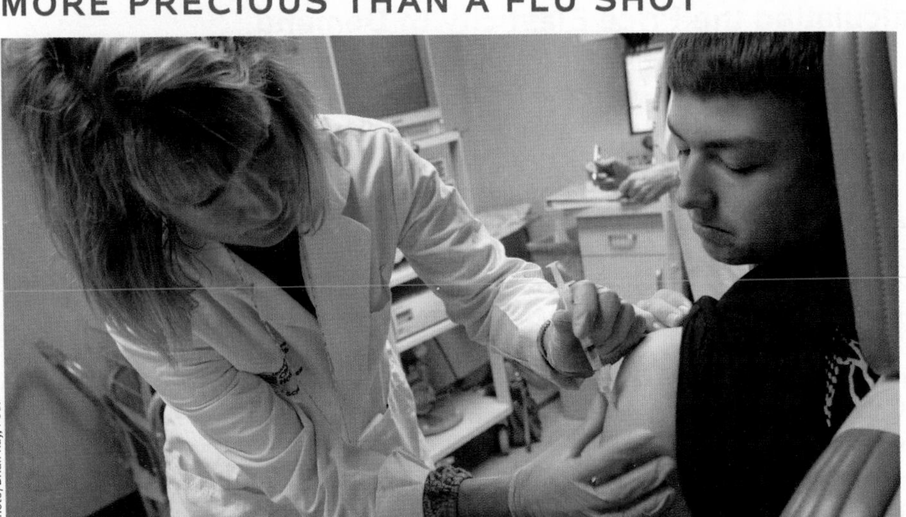

AP Photo/Brian Ray, Pool

Because consumers of flu shots are relatively unresponsive to the price of flu vaccine, availability of the vaccine will determine its price.

WHAT YOU WILL LEARN IN THIS CHAPTER

- Why economists use **elasticity** to measure responsiveness to changes in prices or incomes
- Why the **price elasticity of demand,** the **income elasticity of demand,** and the **cross-price elasticity of demand** are important indicators of consumer behavior in response to changes in prices and income
- Why the **price elasticity of supply** is an important indicator of producer behavior in response to changes in price
- What factors influence the size of these various elasticities
- How the price elasticities of supply and demand affect the costs and benefits of taxation

PANIC WAS THE ONLY WORD TO describe the situation at hospitals, clinics, and nursing homes across America in October 2004. Early that month, Chiron Corporation, one of only two suppliers of flu vaccine for the entire U.S. market, announced that contamination problems had forced the closure of its manufacturing plant. With that closure, the U.S. supply of vaccine for the 2004–2005 flu season was suddenly cut in half, from 100 million to 50 million doses.

Because making flu vaccine is a costly and time-consuming process, no more doses could be made to replace Chiron's lost output. And since every country jealously guards its supply of flu vaccine for its own citizens, none could be obtained from other countries.

If you've ever had a real case of the flu, you know just how unpleasant an experience it is. And it can be worse than unpleasant: every year the flu kills around 36,000 Americans and sends another 200,000 to the hospital. Victims are most commonly children, seniors, or those with compromised immune systems.

In 2004, as news of the flu vaccine shortfall spread, there was a rush to get the shots. People lined up in the middle of the night at the few locations that had somehow obtained the vaccine and were offering it at a reasonable price: the crowds included seniors with oxygen tanks, parents with sleeping children, and others in wheelchairs. Meanwhile, some pharmaceutical distributors—the companies that obtain vaccine from manufacturers and then distribute it to hospitals and pharmacies—detected a profit-making opportunity in the frenzy. One company, Med-Stat, which normally charged $8.50 for a dose, began charging $90, more than 10 times the normal price.

Although most people refused or were unable to pay such a high price for the vaccine, many others undoubtedly did. Med-Stat judged, correctly, that a significant number of consumers were *unresponsive* to price; that is, the large increase in the price of the vaccine left the quantity demanded by these consumers relatively unchanged.

Clearly, the demand for flu vaccine is unusual in this respect because getting vaccinated meant the difference between life and death. Let's consider a very different and less urgent scenario. Suppose, for example, that the supply of a particular type of breakfast cereal was halved due to manufacturing problems. It would be extremely unlikely, if not impossible, to find a consumer willing to pay 10 times the original price for a box of this particular cereal. In other words, consumers of breakfast cereal are much more responsive to price than consumers of flu vaccine.

But how do we define *responsiveness*? Economists measure responsiveness of consumers to price with a particular number, called the *price elasticity of demand.* In this chapter we will show how the price elasticity of demand is calculated and why it is the best measure of how the quantity demanded responds to changes in price. We will then see that the price elasticity of demand is only one of a family of related concepts, including the *income elasticity of demand, cross-price elasticity of demand,* and the *price elasticity of supply.*

We will finish our discussion of elasticities by looking at how the price elasticities of supply and demand influence the costs and benefits of taxation.

The **price elasticity of demand** is the ratio of the percent change in the quantity demanded to the percent change in the price as we move along the demand curve (dropping the minus sign).

Defining and Measuring Elasticity

In order for Flunomics, a hypothetical flu vaccine distributor, to know whether it could raise its revenue by significantly raising the price of its flu vaccine during the 2004 flu vaccine panic, it would have to know the *price elasticity of demand* for flu vaccinations.

Calculating the Price Elasticity of Demand

Figure 5-1 shows a hypothetical demand curve for flu vaccinations. At a price of \$20 per vaccination, consumers would demand 10 million vaccinations per year (point *A*); at a price of \$21, the quantity demanded would fall to 9.9 million vaccinations per year (point *B*).

Figure 5-1, then, tells us the change in the quantity demanded for a particular change in the price. But how can we turn this into a measure of price responsiveness? The answer is to calculate the *price elasticity of demand.*

The **price elasticity of demand** is the ratio of the *percent change in quantity demanded* to the *percent change in price* as we move along the demand curve. As we'll see later in this chapter, the reason economists use percent changes is to obtain a measure that doesn't depend on the units in which a good is measured (say, a child-size dose versus an adult-size dose of vaccine). But before we get to that, let's look at how elasticity is calculated.

To calculate the price elasticity of demand, we first calculate the *percent change in the quantity demanded* and the corresponding *percent change in the price* as we move along the demand curve. These are defined as follows:

$$\textbf{(5-1)}\ \%\ \text{change in quantity demanded} = \frac{\text{Change in quantity demanded}}{\text{Initial quantity demanded}} \times 100$$

and

$$\textbf{(5-2)}\ \%\ \text{change in price} = \frac{\text{Change in price}}{\text{Initial price}} \times 100$$

In Figure 5-1, we see that when the price rises from \$20 to \$21, the quantity demanded falls from 10 million to 9.9 million vaccinations, yielding a change in the quantity demanded of 0.1 million vaccinations. So the percent change in the quantity demanded is

$$\%\ \text{change in quantity demanded} = \frac{-0.1\ \text{million vaccinations}}{10\ \text{million vaccinations}} \times 100 = -1\%$$

The initial price is \$20 and the change in the price is \$1, so the percent change in price is

$$\%\ \text{change in price} = \frac{\$1}{\$20} \times 100 = 5\%$$

To calculate the price elasticity of demand, we find the ratio of the percent change in the quantity demanded to the percent change in the price:

$$\textbf{(5-3)}\ \text{Price elasticity of demand} = \frac{\%\ \text{change in quantity demanded}}{\%\ \text{change in price}}$$

In Figure 5-1, the price elasticity of demand is therefore

$$\text{Price elasticity of demand} = \frac{1\%}{5\%} = 0.2$$

The *law of demand* says that demand curves are downward sloping, so price and quantity demanded always move in opposite directions. In other words, a positive percent change in price (a rise in price) leads to a negative percent

FIGURE 5-1 The Demand for Vaccinations

At a price of $20 per vaccination, the quantity of vaccinations demanded is 10 million per year (point *A*). When price rises to $21 per vaccination, the quantity demanded falls to 9.9 million vaccinations per year (point *B*).

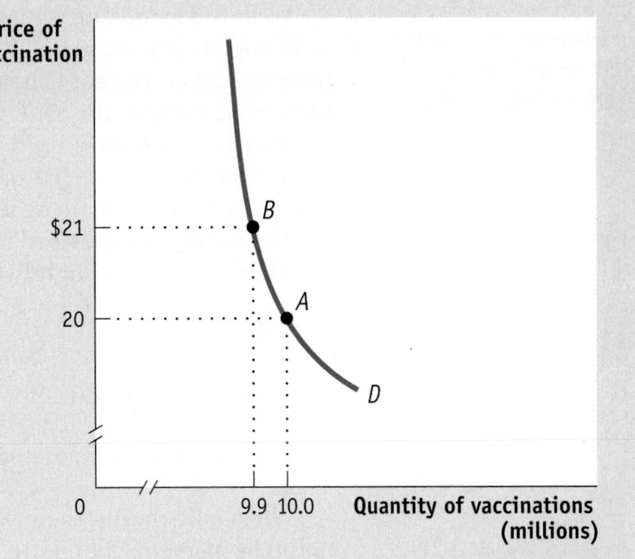

change in the quantity demanded; a negative percent change in price (a fall in price) leads to a positive percent change in the quantity demanded. This means that the price elasticity of demand is, in strictly mathematical terms, a negative number. However, it is inconvenient to repeatedly write a minus sign. So when economists talk about the price elasticity of demand, they usually drop the minus sign and report the absolute value of the price elasticity of demand. In this case, for example, economists would usually say "the price elasticity of demand is 0.2," taking it for granted that you understand they mean *minus* 0.2. We follow this convention here.

The larger the price elasticity of demand, the more responsive the quantity demanded is to the price. When the price elasticity of demand is large—when consumers change their quantity demanded by a large percentage compared with the percent change in the price—economists say that demand is highly elastic.

As we'll see shortly, a price elasticity of 0.2 indicates a small response of quantity demanded to price. That is, the quantity demanded will fall by a relatively small amount when price rises. This is what economists call *inelastic* demand. And inelastic demand was exactly what Flunomics needed for its strategy to increase revenue by raising the price of its flu vaccines.

An Alternative Way to Calculate Elasticities: The Midpoint Method

Price elasticity of demand compares the *percent change in quantity demanded* with the *percent change in price*. When we look at some other elasticities, which we will do shortly, we'll learn why it is important to focus on percent changes. But at this point we need to discuss a technical issue that arises when you calculate percent changes in variables.

The best way to understand the issue is with a real example. Suppose you were trying to estimate the price elasticity of demand for gasoline by comparing gasoline prices and consumption in different countries. Because of high taxes, gasoline usually costs about three times as much per gallon in Europe as it does

The **midpoint method** is a technique for calculating the percent change. In this approach, we calculate changes in a variable compared with the average, or midpoint, of the starting and final values.

in the United States. So what is the percent difference between American and European gas prices?

Well, it depends on which way you measure it. Because the price of gasoline in Europe is approximately three times higher than in the United States, it is 200 percent higher. Because the price of gasoline in the United States is one-third as high as in Europe, it is 66.7 percent lower.

This is a nuisance: we'd like to have a percent measure of the difference in prices that doesn't depend on which way you measure it. To avoid computing different elasticities for rising and falling prices we use the *midpoint method.*

The **midpoint method** replaces the usual definition of the percent change in a variable, X, with a slightly different definition:

(5-4) $$\% \text{ change in } X = \frac{\text{Change in } X}{\text{Average value of } X} \times 100$$

where the average value of X is defined as

$$\text{Average value of } X = \frac{\text{Starting value of } X + \text{Final value of } X}{2}$$

When calculating the price elasticity of demand using the midpoint method, both the percent change in the price and the percent change in the quantity demanded are found using this method. To see how this method works, suppose you have the following data for some good:

	Price	Quantity demanded
Situation A	$0.90	1,100
Situation B	$1.10	900

To calculate the percent change in quantity going from situation A to situation B, we compare the change in the quantity demanded—a fall of 200 units—with the *average* of the quantity demanded in the two situations. So we calculate

$$\% \text{ change in quantity demanded} = \frac{-200}{(1{,}100 + 900)/2} \times 100 = \frac{-200}{1{,}000} \times 100 = -20\%$$

In the same way, we calculate

$$\% \text{ change in price} = \frac{\$0.20}{(\$0.90 + \$1.10)/2} \times 100 = \frac{\$0.20}{\$1.00} \times 100 = 20\%$$

So in this case we would calculate the price elasticity of demand to be

$$\text{Price elasticity of demand} = \frac{\% \text{ change in quantity demanded}}{\% \text{ change in price}} = \frac{20\%}{20\%} = 1$$

again dropping the minus sign.

The important point is that we would get the same result, a price elasticity of demand of 1, whether we go up the demand curve from situation A to situation B or down from situation B to situation A.

To arrive at a more general formula for price elasticity of demand, suppose that we have data for two points on a demand curve. At point 1 the quantity demanded and price are (Q_1, P_1); at point 2 they are (Q_2, P_2). Then the formula for calculating the price elasticity of demand is:

(5-5) $$\text{Price elasticity of demand} = \frac{\dfrac{Q_2 - Q_1}{(Q_1 + Q_2)/2}}{\dfrac{P_2 - P_1}{(P_1 + P_2)/2}}$$

As before, when finding a price elasticity of demand calculated by the midpoint method, we drop the minus sign and use the absolute value.

ECONOMICS ➤ IN ACTION

ESTIMATING ELASTICITIES

You might think it's easy to estimate price elasticities of demand from real-world data: just compare percent changes in prices with percent changes in quantities demanded. Unfortunately, it's rarely that simple because changes in price aren't the only thing affecting changes in the quantity demanded: other factors—such as changes in income, changes in tastes, and changes in the prices of other goods—shift the demand curve, thereby changing the quantity demanded at any given price. To estimate price elasticities of demand, economists must use careful statistical analysis to separate the influence of these different factors, holding other things equal.

The most comprehensive effort to estimate price elasticities of demand was a mammoth study by the economists Hendrik S. Houthakker and Lester D. Taylor. Some of their results are summarized in Table 5-1. These estimates show a wide range of price elasticities. There are some goods, like eggs, for which demand hardly responds at all to changes in the price. There are other goods, most notably foreign travel, for which the quantity demanded is very sensitive to the price.

Notice that Table 5-1 is divided into two parts: inelastic and elastic demand. We'll explain in the next section the significance of that division.

TABLE 5-1 Some Estimated Price Elasticities of Demand

Good	Price elasticity of demand
Inelastic demand	
Eggs	0.1
Beef	0.4
Stationery	0.5
Gasoline	0.5
Elastic demand	
Housing	1.2
Restaurant meals	2.3
Airline travel	2.4
Foreign travel	4.1

Source note on copyright page.

Quick Review

- The **price elasticity of demand** is equal to the percent change in the quantity demanded divided by the percent change in the price as you move along the demand curve, and dropping any minus sign.
- In practice, percent changes are best measured using the **midpoint method,** in which the percent change in each variable is calculated using the average of starting and final values.

CHECK YOUR UNDERSTANDING 5-1

1. The price of strawberries falls from $1.50 to $1.00 per carton and the quantity demanded goes from 100,000 to 200,000 cartons. Use the midpoint method to find the price elasticity of demand.
2. At the present level of consumption, 4,000 movie tickets, and at the current price, $5 per ticket, the price elasticity of demand for movie tickets is 1. Using the midpoint method, calculate the percentage by which the owners of movie theaters must reduce price in order to sell 5,000 tickets.
3. The price elasticity of demand for ice-cream sandwiches is 1.2 at the current price of $0.50 per sandwich and the current consumption level of 100,000 sandwiches. Calculate the change in the quantity demanded when price rises by $0.05. Use Equations 5-1 and 5-2 to calculate percent changes and Equation 5-3 to relate price elasticity of demand to the percent changes.

Solutions appear at back of book.

Interpreting the Price Elasticity of Demand

Med-Stat and other pharmaceutical distributors believed they could sharply drive up flu vaccine prices in the face of a shortage because the price elasticity of vaccine demand was small. But what does that mean? How low does a price elasticity have to be for us to classify it as low? How big does it have to be for us to consider it high? And what determines whether the price elasticity of demand is high or low, anyway?

To answer these questions, we need to look more deeply at the price elasticity of demand.

Demand is **perfectly inelastic** when the quantity demanded does not respond at all to changes in the price. When demand is perfectly inelastic, the demand curve is a vertical line.

Demand is **perfectly elastic** when any price increase will cause the quantity demanded to drop to zero. When demand is perfectly elastic, the demand curve is a horizontal line.

How Elastic Is Elastic?

As a first step toward classifying price elasticities of demand, let's look at the extreme cases.

First, consider the demand for a good when people pay no attention to the price—say, snake anti-venom. Suppose that consumers will buy 1,000 doses of anti-venom per year regardless of the price. In this case, the demand curve for anti-venom would look like the curve shown in panel (a) of Figure 5-2: it would be a vertical line at 1,000 doses of anti-venom. Since the percent change in the quantity demanded is zero for *any* change in the price, the price elasticity of demand in this case is zero. The case of a zero price elasticity of demand is known as **perfectly inelastic demand.**

The opposite extreme occurs when even a tiny rise in the price will cause the quantity demanded to drop to zero or even a tiny fall in the price will cause the quantity demanded to get extremely large.

Panel (b) of Figure 5-2 shows the case of pink tennis balls; we suppose that tennis players really don't care what color their balls are and that other colors, such as neon green and vivid yellow, are available at $5 per dozen balls. In this case, consumers will buy no pink balls if they cost more than $5 per dozen but will buy only pink balls if they cost less than $5. The demand curve will therefore be a horizontal line at a price of $5 per dozen balls. As you move back and forth along this line, there is a change in the quantity demanded but no change in the price. Roughly speaking, when you divide a number by zero, you get infinity, denoted by the symbol ∞. So a horizontal demand curve implies an infinite price elasticity of demand. When the price elasticity of demand is infinite, economists say that demand is **perfectly elastic.**

The price elasticity of demand for the vast majority of goods is somewhere between these two extreme cases. Economists use one main criterion for classifying these intermediate cases: they ask whether the price elasticity of demand is greater

FIGURE 5-2 Two Extreme Cases of Price Elasticity of Demand

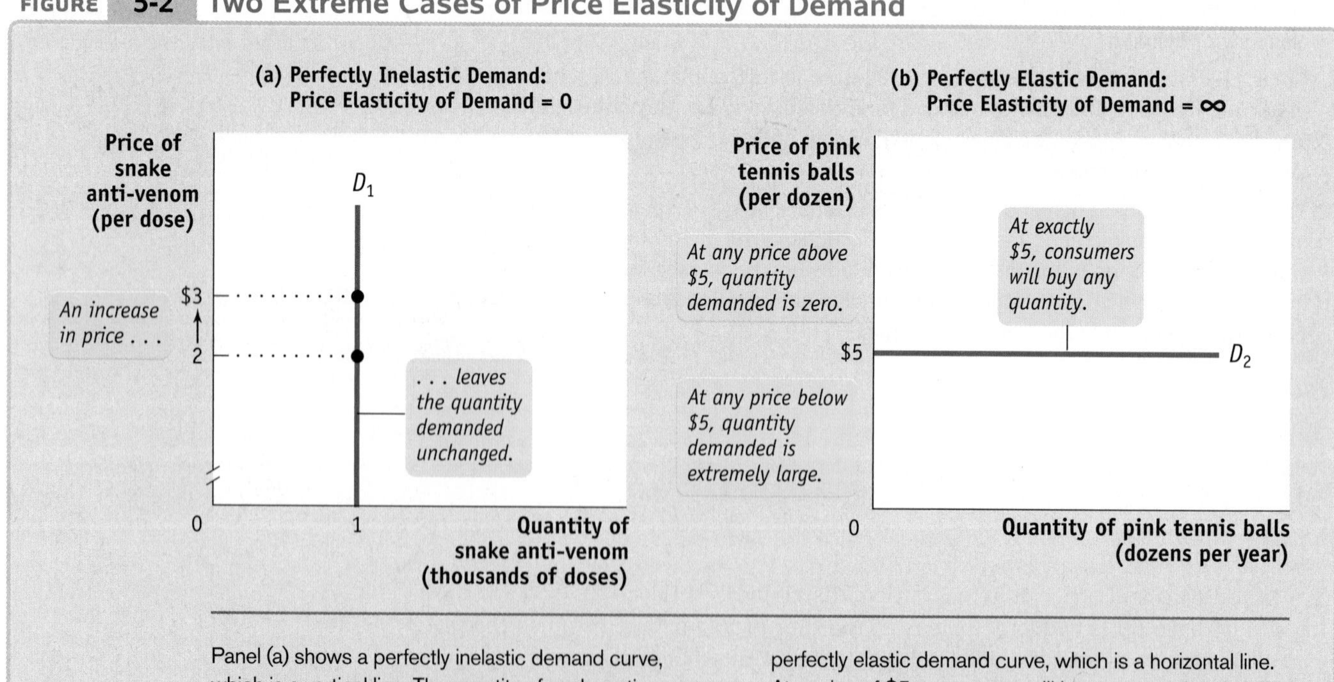

Panel (a) shows a perfectly inelastic demand curve, which is a vertical line. The quantity of snake anti-venom demanded is always 1,000 doses, regardless of price. As a result, the price elasticity of demand is zero—the quantity demanded is unaffected by the price. Panel (b) shows a perfectly elastic demand curve, which is a horizontal line. At a price of $5, consumers will buy any quantity of pink tennis balls, but they will buy none at a price above $5. If the price falls below $5, they will buy an extremely large number of pink tennis balls and none of any other color.

or less than 1. When the price elasticity of demand is greater than 1, economists say that demand is **elastic.** When the price elasticity of demand is less than 1, they say that demand is **inelastic.** The borderline case is **unit-elastic demand,** where the price elasticity of demand is—surprise—exactly 1.

Demand is **elastic** if the price elasticity of demand is greater than 1, **inelastic** if the price elasticity of demand is less than 1, and **unit-elastic** if the price elasticity of demand is exactly 1.

To see why a price elasticity of demand equal to 1 is a useful dividing line, let's consider a hypothetical example: a toll bridge operated by the state highway department. Other things equal, the number of drivers who use the bridge depends on the toll, the price the highway department charges for crossing the bridge: the higher the toll, the fewer the drivers who use the bridge.

Figure 5-3 shows three hypothetical demand curves—one in which demand is unit-elastic, one in which it is inelastic, and one in which it is elastic. In each case, point *A* shows the quantity demanded if the toll is \$0.90 and point *B* shows the quantity demanded if the toll is \$1.10. An increase in the toll from \$0.90 to \$1.10 is an increase of 20% if we use the midpoint method to calculate percent changes.

Panel (a) shows what happens when the toll is raised from \$0.90 to \$1.10 and the demand curve is unit-elastic. Here the 20% price rise leads to a fall in the quantity

FIGURE 5-3 Unit-Elastic Demand, Inelastic Demand, and Elastic Demand

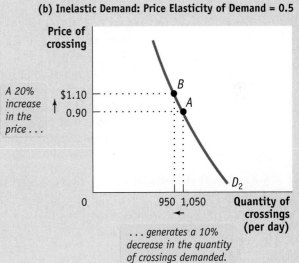

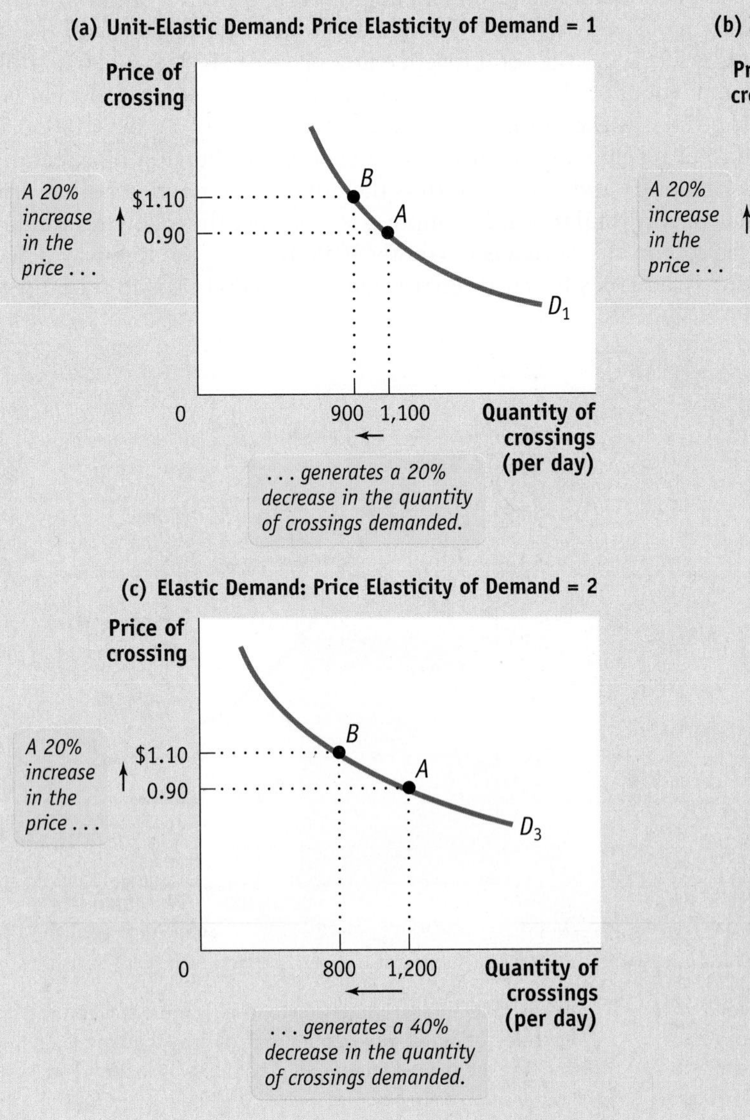

Panel (a) shows a case of unit-elastic demand: a 20% increase in price generates a 20% decline in quantity demanded, implying a price elasticity of demand of 1. Panel (b) shows a case of inelastic demand: a 20% increase in price generates a 10% decline in quantity demanded, implying a price elasticity of demand of 0.5. A case of elastic demand is shown in panel (c): a 20% increase in price causes a 40% decline in quantity demanded, implying a price elasticity of demand of 2. All percentages are calculated using the midpoint method.

The **total revenue** is the total value of sales of a good or service. It is equal to the price multiplied by the quantity sold.

of cars using the bridge each day from 1,100 to 900, which is a 20% decline (again using the midpoint method). So the price elasticity of demand is 20%/20% = 1.

Panel (b) shows a case of inelastic demand when the toll is raised from $0.90 to $1.10. The same 20% price rise reduces the quantity demanded from 1,050 to 950. That's only a 10% decline, so in this case the price elasticity of demand is 10%/20% = 0.5.

Panel (c) shows a case of elastic demand when the toll is raised from $0.90 to $1.10. The 20% price increase causes the quantity demanded to fall from 1,200 to 800—a 40% decline, so the price elasticity of demand is 40%/20% = 2.

Why does it matter whether demand is unit-elastic, inelastic, or elastic? Because this classification predicts how changes in the price of a good will affect the *total revenue* earned by producers from the sale of that good. In many real-life situations, such as the one faced by Med-Stat, it is crucial to know how price changes affect total revenue. **Total revenue** is defined as the total value of sales of a good or service, equal to the price multiplied by the quantity sold.

(5-6) Total revenue = Price × Quantity sold

Total revenue has a useful graphical representation that can help us understand why knowing the price elasticity of demand is crucial when we ask whether a price rise will increase or reduce total revenue. Panel (a) of Figure 5-4 shows the same demand curve as panel (a) of Figure 5-3. We see that 1,100 drivers will use the bridge if the toll is $0.90. So the total revenue at a price of $0.90 is $0.90 × 1,100 = $990. This value is equal to the area of the green rectangle, which is drawn with the bottom left corner at the point (0, 0) and the top right corner at (1,100, 0.90). In general, the total revenue at any given price is equal to the area of a rectangle whose height is the price and whose width is the quantity demanded at that price.

To get an idea of why total revenue is important, consider the following scenario. Suppose that the toll on the bridge is currently $0.90 but that the highway department must raise extra money for road repairs. One way to do this is to raise the toll

FIGURE 5-4 Total Revenue

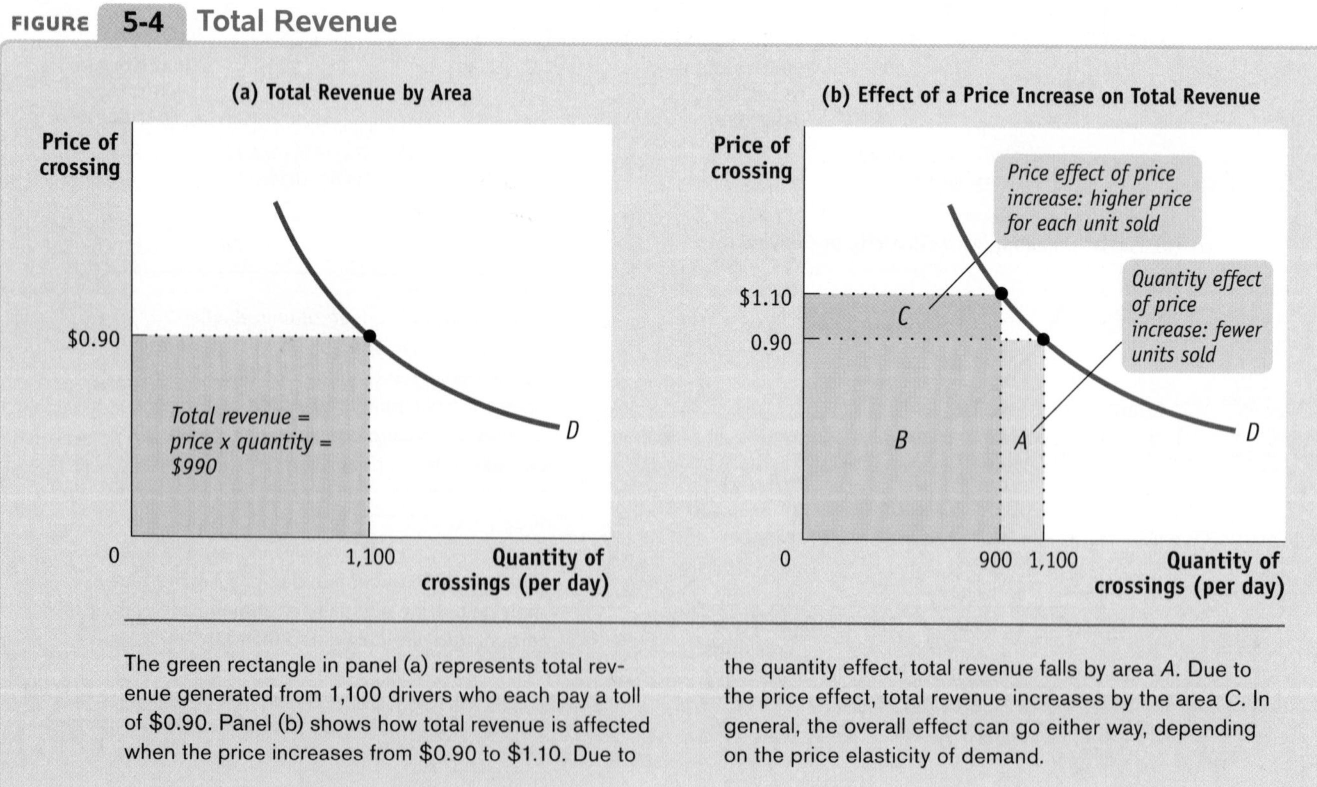

The green rectangle in panel (a) represents total revenue generated from 1,100 drivers who each pay a toll of $0.90. Panel (b) shows how total revenue is affected when the price increases from $0.90 to $1.10. Due to the quantity effect, total revenue falls by area *A*. Due to the price effect, total revenue increases by the area C. In general, the overall effect can go either way, depending on the price elasticity of demand.

on the bridge. But this plan might backfire, since a higher toll will reduce the number of drivers who use the bridge. And if traffic on the bridge dropped a lot, a higher toll would actually reduce total revenue instead of increasing it. So it's important for the highway department to know how drivers will respond to a toll increase.

We can see graphically how the toll increase affects total bridge revenue by examining panel (b) of Figure 5-4. At a toll of $0.90, total revenue is given by the sum of the areas *A* and *B*. After the toll is raised to $1.10, total revenue is given by the sum of areas *B* and *C*. So when the toll is raised, revenue represented by area *A* is lost but revenue represented by area *C* is gained.

These two areas have important interpretations. Area *C* represents the revenue gain that comes from the additional $0.20 paid by drivers who continue to use the bridge. That is, the 900 who continue to use the bridge contribute an additional $0.20 × 900 = $180 per day to total revenue, represented by area *C*. But 200 drivers who would have used the bridge at a price of $0.90 no longer do so, generating a loss to total revenue of $0.90 × 200 = $180 per day, represented by area *A*. (In this particular example, because demand is unit-elastic—the same as in panel (a) of Figure 5-3—the rise in the toll has no effect on total revenue; areas *A* and *C* are the same size.)

Except in the rare case of a good with perfectly elastic or perfectly inelastic demand, when a seller raises the price of a good, two countervailing effects are present:

- *A price effect:* After a price increase, each unit sold sells at a higher price, which tends to raise revenue.
- *A quantity effect:* After a price increase, fewer units are sold, which tends to lower revenue.

But then, you may ask, what is the ultimate net effect on total revenue: does it go up or down? The answer is that, in general, the effect on total revenue can go either way—a price rise may either increase total revenue or lower it. If the price effect, which tends to raise total revenue, is the stronger of the two effects, then total revenue goes up. If the quantity effect, which tends to reduce total revenue, is the stronger, then total revenue goes down. And if the strengths of the two effects are exactly equal—as in our toll bridge example, where a $180 gain offsets a $180 loss—total revenue is unchanged by the price increase.

The price elasticity of demand tells us what happens to total revenue when price changes: its size determines which effect—the price effect or the quantity effect—is stronger. Specifically:

- If demand for a good is *unit-elastic* (the price elasticity of demand is 1), an increase in price does not change total revenue. In this case, the quantity effect and the price effect exactly offset each other.
- If demand for a good is *inelastic* (the price elasticity of demand is less than 1), a higher price increases total revenue. In this case, the price effect is stronger than the quantity effect.
- If demand for a good is *elastic* (the price elasticity of demand is greater than 1), an increase in price reduces total revenue. In this case, the quantity effect is stronger than the price effect.

Table 5-2 shows how the effect of a price increase on total revenue depends on the price elasticity of demand, using the same data as in Figure 5-3. An increase in the price from $0.90 to $1.10 leaves total revenue unchanged at $990 when demand is unit-elastic. When demand is inelastic, the price effect dominates the quantity effect; the same price increase leads to an increase in total revenue from $945 to $1,045. And when demand is elastic, the quantity effect dominates the price effect; the price increase leads to a decline in total revenue from $1,080 to $880.

The price elasticity of demand also predicts the effect of a *fall* in price on total revenue. When the price falls, the same two countervailing effects are present, but they work in the opposite directions as compared to the case of a price rise. There

TABLE 5-2 Price Elasticity of Demand and Total Revenue

	Price of crossing = $0.90	Price of crossing = $1.10
Unit-elastic demand (price elasticity of demand = 1)		
Quantity demanded	1,100	900
Total revenue	$990	$990
Inelastic demand (price elasticity of demand = 0.5)		
Quantity demanded	1,050	950
Total revenue	$945	$1,045
Elastic demand (price elasticity of demand = 2)		
Quantity demanded	1,200	800
Total revenue	$1,080	$880

is the price effect of a lower price per unit sold, which tends to lower revenue. This is countered by the quantity effect of more units sold, which tends to raise revenue. Which effect dominates depends on the price elasticity. Here is a quick summary:

- When demand is *unit-elastic,* the two effects exactly balance; so a fall in price has no effect on total revenue.
- When demand is *inelastic,* the price effect dominates the quantity effect; so a fall in price reduces total revenue.
- When demand is *elastic,* the quantity effect dominates the price effect; so a fall in price increases total revenue.

Price Elasticity Along the Demand Curve

Suppose an economist says that "the price elasticity of demand for coffee is 0.25." What he or she means is that *at the current price* the elasticity is 0.25. In the previous discussion of the toll bridge, what we were really describing was the elasticity *at the price* of $0.90. Why this qualification? Because for the vast majority of demand curves, the price elasticity of demand at one point along the curve is different from the price elasticity of demand at other points along the same curve.

To see this, consider the table in Figure 5-5, which shows a hypothetical demand schedule. It also shows in the last column the total revenue generated at each price and quantity combination in the demand schedule. The upper panel of the graph in Figure 5-5 shows the corresponding demand curve. The lower panel illustrates the same data on total revenue: the height of a bar at each quantity demanded—which corresponds to a particular price—measures the total revenue generated at that price.

In Figure 5-5, you can see that when the price is low, raising the price increases total revenue: starting at a price of $1, raising the price to $2 increases total revenue from $9 to $16. This means that when the price is low, demand is inelastic. Moreover, you can see that demand is inelastic on the entire section of the demand curve from a price of $0 to a price of $5.

When the price is high, however, raising it further reduces total revenue: starting at a price of $8, raising the price to $9 reduces total revenue, from $16 to $9. This means that when the price is high, demand is elastic. Furthermore, you can see that demand is elastic over the section of the demand curve from a price of $5 to $10.

For the vast majority of goods, the price elasticity of demand changes along the demand curve. So whenever you measure a good's elasticity, you are really measuring it at a particular point or section of the good's demand curve.

FIGURE 5-5 The Price Elasticity of Demand Changes Along the Demand Curve

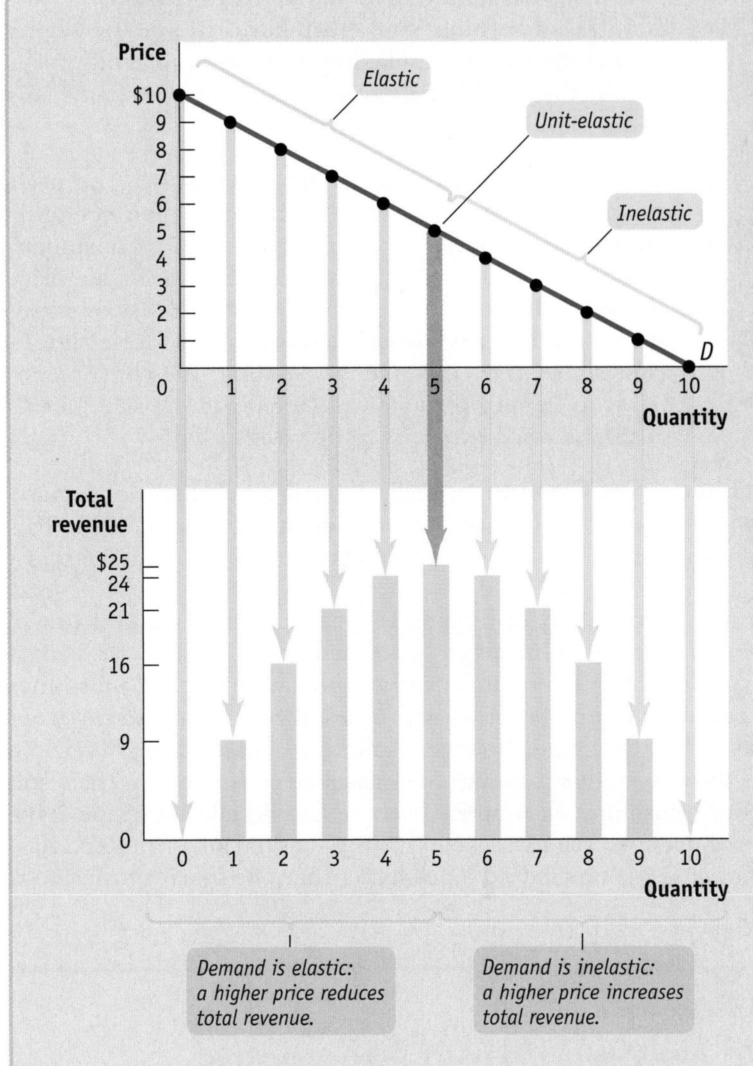

Demand Schedule and Total Revenue for a Linear Demand Curve

Price	Quantity demanded	Total revenue
$0	10	$0
1	9	9
2	8	16
3	7	21
4	6	24
5	5	25
6	4	24
7	3	21
8	2	16
9	1	9
10	0	0

The upper panel shows a demand curve corresponding to the demand schedule in the table. The lower panel shows how total revenue changes along that demand curve: at each price and quantity combination, the height of the bar represents the total revenue generated. You can see that at a low price, raising the price increases total revenue. So demand is inelastic at low prices. At a high price, however, a rise in price reduces total revenue. So demand is elastic at high prices.

What Factors Determine the Price Elasticity of Demand?

The flu vaccine shortfall of 2004–2005 allowed vaccine distributors to significantly raise their prices for two important reasons: substitutes were very difficult to obtain, and for many people the vaccine was a medical necessity.

People responded in various ways. Some paid the high prices, and some traveled to Canada and other countries to get vaccinated. Some simply did without (and over time often changed their habits to avoid catching the flu, such as eating out less often and avoiding mass transit). This experience illustrates the four main factors that determine elasticity: the availability of close substitutes, whether the good is a necessity or a luxury, the share of income a consumer spends on the good, and how much time has elapsed since the price change. We'll briefly examine each of these factors.

The Availability of Close Substitutes The price elasticity of demand tends to be high if there are other readily available goods that consumers regard as similar and would be willing to consume instead. The price elasticity of demand tends to be low if there are no close substitutes or they are very difficult to obtain.

David Sipress/The New Yorker Collection/www.cartoonbank.com

"Three hundred dollars' of regular."

Whether the Good Is a Necessity or a Luxury The price elasticity of demand tends to be low if a good is something you must have, like a life-saving medicine. The price elasticity of demand tends to be high if the good is a luxury—something you can easily live without.

Share of Income Spent on the Good The price elasticity of demand tends to be low when spending on a good accounts for a small share of a consumer's income. In that case, a significant change in the price of the good has little impact on how much the consumer spends. In contrast, when a good accounts for a significant share of a consumer's spending, the consumer is likely to be very responsive to a change in price. In this case, the price elasticity of demand is high.

Time Elapsed Since Price Change In general, the price elasticity of demand tends to increase as consumers have more time to adjust to a price change. This means that the long-run price elasticity of demand is often higher than the short-run elasticity.

A good illustration of the effect of time on the elasticity of demand is drawn from the 1970s, the first time gasoline prices increased dramatically in the United States. Initially, consumption fell very little because there were no close substitutes for gasoline and because driving their cars was necessary for people to carry out the ordinary tasks of life. Over time, however, Americans changed their habits in ways that enabled them to gradually reduce their gasoline consumption. The result was a steady decline in gasoline consumption over the next decade, even though the price of gasoline did not continue to rise, confirming that the long-run price elasticity of demand for gasoline was indeed much larger than the short-run elasticity.

ECONOMICS ➤ *IN ACTION*

RESPONDING TO YOUR TUITION BILL

College costs more than ever—and not just because of inflation. Tuition has been rising faster than the overall cost of living for years. But does rising tuition keep people from going to college? Two studies found that the answer depends on the type of college. Both studies assessed how responsive the decision to go to college is to a change in tuition.

Tony Avelar/The Christian Science Monitor/Getty Images

Students at two-year schools are more responsive to the price of tuition than students at four-year schools.

A 1988 study found that a 3% increase in tuition led to an approximately 2% fall in the number of students enrolled at four-year institutions, giving a price elasticity of demand of 0.67 (2%/3%). In the case of two-year institutions, the study found a significantly higher response: a 3% increase in tuition led to a 2.7% fall in enrollments, giving a price elasticity of demand of 0.9. In other words, the enrollment decision for students at two-year colleges was significantly more responsive to price than for students at four-year colleges. The result: students at two-year colleges are more likely to forgo getting a degree because of tuition costs than students at four-year colleges.

A 1999 study confirmed this pattern. In comparison to four-year colleges, it found that two-year college enrollment rates were significantly more responsive to changes in state financial aid (a decline in aid leading to a decline in enrollments), a predictable effect given these students' greater sensitivity to the cost of tuition. Another piece of evidence suggests that students at two-year colleges are more likely to be paying their own way and making a trade-off between attending college versus working: the study found that enrollments at two-year colleges are much more responsive to changes in the unemployment rate (an increase in the unemployment rate leading to an increase in enrollments) than enrollments at four-year colleges. So is the cost of tuition a barrier to getting a college degree in the United States? Yes, but more so at two-year colleges than for students at four-year colleges.

Interestingly, the 1999 study found that for both two-year and four-year colleges, price sensitivity of demand had fallen somewhat since the 1988 study. One possible explanation is that because the value of a college education has risen considerably over time, fewer people forgo college, even if tuition goes up. And the price elasticity of demand for education has remained low. A 2008 study estimates that the price elasticity of demand for education at four-year institutions may be as low as 0.11.

Quick Review

- Demand is **perfectly inelastic** if it is completely unresponsive to price. It is **perfectly elastic** if it is infinitely responsive to price.
- Demand is **elastic** if the price elasticity of demand is greater than 1. It is **inelastic** if the price elasticity of demand is less than 1. It is **unit-elastic** if the price elasticity of demand is exactly 1.
- When demand is elastic, the quantity effect of a price increase dominates the price effect and **total revenue** falls. When demand is inelastic, the price effect of a price increase dominates the quantity effect and total revenue rises.
- Because the price elasticity of demand can change along the demand curve, economists refer to a particular point on the demand curve when speaking of "the" price elasticity of demand.
- Ready availability of close substitutes makes demand for a good more elastic, as does the length of time elapsed since the price change. Demand for a necessity is less elastic, and demand for a luxury good is more elastic. Demand tends to be inelastic for goods that absorb a small share of a consumer's income and elastic for goods that absorb a large share of income.

CHECK YOUR UNDERSTANDING 5-2

1. For each case, choose the condition that characterizes demand: elastic demand, inelastic demand, or unit-elastic demand.
   a. Total revenue decreases when price increases.
   b. The additional revenue generated by an increase in quantity sold is exactly offset by revenue lost from the fall in price received per unit.
   c. Total revenue falls when output increases.
   d. Producers in an industry find they can increase their total revenues by coordinating a reduction in industry output.
2. For the following goods, what is the elasticity of demand? Explain. What is the shape of the demand curve?
   a. Demand for a blood transfusion by an accident victim
   b. Demand by students for green erasers

Solutions appear at back of book.

Other Demand Elasticities

The quantity of a good demanded depends not only on the price of that good but also on other variables. In particular, demand curves shift because of changes in the prices of related goods and changes in consumers' incomes. It is often important to have a measure of these other effects, and the best measures are—you guessed it—elasticities. Specifically, we can best measure how the demand for a good is affected by prices of other goods using a measure called the *cross-price elasticity of demand,* and we can best measure how demand is affected by changes in income using the *income elasticity of demand.*

The Cross-Price Elasticity of Demand

In Chapter 3 you learned that the demand for a good is often affected by the prices of other, related goods—goods that are substitutes or complements. There you saw that a change in the price of a related good shifts the demand curve of the original good, reflecting a change in the quantity demanded at any given price. The strength of such a "cross" effect on demand can be measured by the **cross-price elasticity of demand,** defined as the ratio of the percent change in the quantity demanded of one good to the percent change in the price of the other.

The **cross-price elasticity of demand** between two goods measures the effect of the change in one good's price on the quantity demanded of the other good. It is equal to the percent change in the quantity demanded of one good divided by the percent change in the other good's price.

The **income elasticity of demand** is the percent change in the quantity of a good demanded when a consumer's income changes divided by the percent change in the consumer's income.

(5-7) Cross-price elasticity of demand between goods A and B

$$= \frac{\text{\% change in quantity of A demanded}}{\text{\% change in price of B}}$$

When two goods are substitutes, like hot dogs and hamburgers, the cross-price elasticity of demand is positive: a rise in the price of hot dogs increases the demand for hamburgers—that is, it causes a rightward shift of the demand curve for hamburgers. If the goods are close substitutes, the cross-price elasticity will be positive and large; if they are not close substitutes, the cross-price elasticity will be positive and small. So when the cross-price elasticity of demand is positive, its size is a measure of how closely substitutable the two goods are.

When two goods are complements, like hot dogs and hot dog buns, the cross-price elasticity is negative: a rise in the price of hot dogs decreases the demand for hot dog buns—that is, it causes a leftward shift of the demand curve for hot dog buns. As with substitutes, the size of the cross-price elasticity of demand between two complements tells us how strongly complementary they are: if the cross-price elasticity is only slightly below zero, they are weak complements; if it is very negative, they are strong complements.

Note that in the case of the cross-price elasticity of demand, the sign (plus or minus) is very important: it tells us whether the two goods are complements or substitutes. So we cannot drop the minus sign as we did for the price elasticity of demand.

Our discussion of the cross-price elasticity of demand is a useful place to return to a point we made earlier: elasticity is a *unit-free* measure—that is, it doesn't depend on the units in which goods are measured.

To see the potential problem, suppose someone told you that "if the price of hot dog buns rises by $0.30, Americans will buy 10 million fewer hot dogs this year." If you've ever bought hot dog buns, you'll immediately wonder: is that a $0.30 increase in the price *per bun,* or is it a $0.30 increase in the price *per package* (buns are usually sold in packages of eight)? It makes a big difference what units we are talking about! However, if someone says that the cross-price elasticity of demand between buns and hot dogs is –0.3, it doesn't matter whether buns are sold individually or by the package. So elasticity is defined as a ratio of percent changes, as a way of making sure that confusion over units doesn't arise.

The Income Elasticity of Demand

The **income elasticity of demand** is a measure of how much the demand for a good is affected by changes in consumers' incomes. It allows us to determine whether a good is a normal or inferior good as well as to measure how intensely the demand for the good responds to changes in income.

(5-8) Income elasticity of demand $= \frac{\text{\% change in quantity demanded}}{\text{\% change in income}}$

Just as the cross-price elasticity of demand between two goods can be either positive or negative, depending on whether the goods are substitutes or complements, the income elasticity of demand for a good can also be either positive or negative. Recall from Chapter 3 that goods can be either *normal goods,* for which demand increases when income rises, or *inferior goods,* for which demand decreases when income rises. These definitions relate directly to the sign of the income elasticity of demand:

- When the income elasticity of demand is positive, the good is a normal good. In this case, the quantity demanded at any given price increases as income increases.
- When the income elasticity of demand is negative, the good is an inferior good. In this case, the quantity demanded at any given price decreases as income increases.

FOR INQUIRING MINDS

WILL CHINA SAVE THE U.S. FARMING SECTOR?

In the days of the Founding Fathers, the great majority of Americans lived on farms. As recently as the 1940s, one American in six—or approximately 17%—still did. But in 1991, the last year the U.S. government collected data on the population of farmers, the official number was 1.9%. Why do so few people now live and work on farms in the United States? There are two main reasons, both involving elasticities.

First, the income elasticity of demand for food is much less than 1—it is income-inelastic. As consumers grow richer, other things equal, spending on food rises less than income. As a result, as the U.S. economy has grown, the share of income it spends on food—and therefore the share of total U.S. income earned by farmers—has fallen.

Second, the demand for food is price-inelastic. This is important because technological advances in American agriculture have steadily raised yields over time and led to a long-term trend of lower U.S. food prices for most of the past century and a half. The combination of price inelasticity and falling prices led to falling total revenue for farmers. That's right: progress in farming has been good for American consumers but bad for American farmers.

The combination of these effects explains the long-term relative decline of farming in the United States. The low income elasticity of demand for food ensures that the income of farmers grows more slowly than the economy as a whole. And the combination of rapid technological progress in farming with price-inelastic demand for foodstuffs reinforces this effect, further reducing the growth of farm income.

That is, up until now. Starting in the mid-2000s, increased demand for foodstuffs from rapidly growing developing countries like China has pushed up the prices of agricultural products around the world. And American farmers have benefited, with U.S. farm income rising 47% in 2011 alone. Eventually, as the growth in developing countries tapers off and agricultural innovation continues to progress, it's likely that the agricultural sector will resume its downward trend. But for now and for the foreseeable future, American farmers are enjoying the sector's revival.

Economists often use estimates of the income elasticity of demand to predict which industries will grow most rapidly as the incomes of consumers grow over time. In doing this, they often find it useful to make a further distinction among normal goods, identifying which are *income-elastic* and which are *income-inelastic.*

The demand for a good is **income-elastic** if the income elasticity of demand for that good is greater than 1. When income rises, the demand for income-elastic goods rises *faster* than income. Luxury goods such as second homes and international

The demand for a good is **income-elastic** if the income elasticity of demand for that good is greater than 1.

FOOD'S BITE IN WORLD BUDGETS

If the income elasticity of demand for food is less than 1, we would expect to find that people in poor countries spend a larger share of their income on food than people in rich countries. And that's exactly what the data show. In this graph, we compare per capita income—a country's total income, divided by the population—with the share of income that is spent on food. (To make the graph a manageable size, per capita income is measured as a percentage of U.S. per capita income.) In very poor countries, like Sri Lanka, people spend most of their income on food. In middle-income countries, like Israel, the share of spending that goes to food is much lower. And it's even lower in rich countries, like the United States.

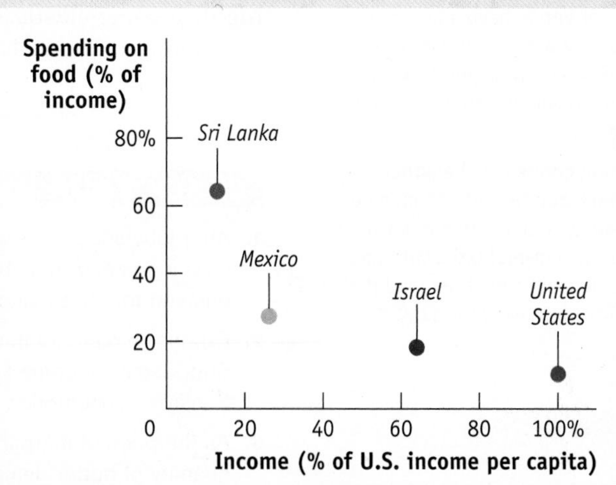

Source: Food shares from U.S. Department of Agriculture database. Income per capita from OECD, *The World Economy: Historical Statistics.*

The demand for a good is **income-inelastic** if the income elasticity of demand for that good is positive but less than 1.

travel tend to be income-elastic. The demand for a good is **income-inelastic** if the income elasticity of demand for that good is positive but less than 1. When income rises, the demand for income-inelastic goods rises, but more slowly than income. Necessities such as food and clothing tend to be income-inelastic.

ECONOMICS > IN ACTION

SPENDING IT

The U.S. Bureau of Labor Statistics carries out extensive surveys of how families spend their incomes. This is not just a matter of intellectual curiosity. Quite a few government benefit programs involve some adjustment for changes in the cost of living; to estimate those changes, the government must know how people spend their money. But an additional payoff to these surveys is data on the income elasticity of demand for various goods.

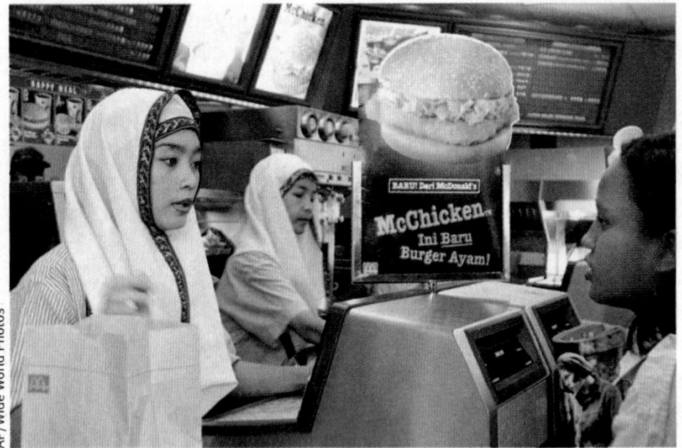

AP/Wide World Photos

Judging from the activity at this busy McDonald's, incomes are rising in Jakarta, Indonesia.

What stands out from these studies? The classic result is that the income elasticity of demand for "food eaten at home" is considerably less than 1: as a family's income rises, the share of its income spent on food consumed at home falls. Correspondingly, the lower a family's income, the higher the share of income spent on food consumed at home.

In poor countries, many families spend more than half their income on food consumed at home. Although the income elasticity of demand for "food eaten at home" is estimated at less than 0.5 in the United States, the income elasticity of demand for "food eaten away from home" (restaurant meals) is estimated to be much higher—close to 1.

Families with higher incomes eat out more often and at fancier places. In 1950, about 19% of U.S. income was spent on food consumed at home, a number that has dropped to 7% today. But over the same time period, the share of U.S. income spent on food consumed away from home has stayed constant at 5%. In fact, a sure sign of rising income levels in developing countries is the arrival of fast-food restaurants that cater to newly affluent customers. For example, McDonald's can now be found in Jakarta, Shanghai, and Mumbai.

There is one clear example of an inferior good found in the surveys: rental housing. Families with higher income actually spend less on rent than families with lower income, because they are much more likely to own their own homes. And the category identified as "other housing"—which basically means second homes—is highly income-elastic. Only higher-income families can afford a luxury like a vacation home, so "other housing" has an income elasticity of demand greater than 1.

Quick Review

- Goods are substitutes when the **cross-price elasticity of demand** is positive. Goods are complements when the cross-price elasticity of demand is negative.
- Inferior goods have a negative **income elasticity of demand.** Most goods are normal goods, which have a positive income elasticity of demand.
- Normal goods may be either **income-elastic,** with an income elasticity of demand greater than 1, or **income-inelastic,** with an income elasticity of demand that is positive but less than 1.

CHECK YOUR UNDERSTANDING 5-3

1. After Chelsea's income increased from $12,000 to $18,000 a year, her purchases of CDs increased from 10 to 40 CDs a year. Calculate Chelsea's income elasticity of demand for CDs using the midpoint method.
2. Expensive restaurant meals are income-elastic goods for most people, including Sanjay. Suppose his income falls by 10% this year. What can you predict about the change in Sanjay's consumption of expensive restaurant meals?
3. As the price of margarine rises by 20%, a manufacturer of baked goods increases its quantity of butter demanded by 5%. Calculate the cross-price elasticity of demand between butter and margarine. Are butter and margarine substitutes or complements for this manufacturer?

Solutions appear at back of book.

The Price Elasticity of Supply

In the wake of the flu vaccine shortfall of 2004, attempts by vaccine distributors to drive up the price of vaccines would have been much less effective if a higher price had induced a large increase in the output of flu vaccines by flu vaccine manufacturers other than Chiron. In fact, if the rise in price had precipitated a significant increase in flu vaccine production, the price would have been pushed back down. But that didn't happen because, as we mentioned earlier, it would have been far too costly and technically difficult to produce more vaccine for the 2004–2005 flu season. (In reality, the production of flu vaccine begins a year before distribution.)

This was another critical element in the ability of some flu vaccine distributors, like Med-Stat, to get significantly higher prices by restricting supply of their product: a low responsiveness in the quantity of output supplied to the higher price of flu vaccine by flu vaccine producers. To measure the response of producers to price changes, we need a measure parallel to the price elasticity of demand—the *price elasticity of supply.*

The **price elasticity of supply** is a measure of the responsiveness of the quantity of a good supplied to the price of that good. It is the ratio of the percent change in the quantity supplied to the percent change in the price as we move along the supply curve.

There is **perfectly inelastic supply** when the price elasticity of supply is zero, so that changes in the price of the good have no effect on the quantity supplied. A perfectly inelastic supply curve is a vertical line.

There is **perfectly elastic supply** when even a tiny increase or reduction in the price will lead to very large changes in the quantity supplied, so that the price elasticity of supply is infinite. A perfectly elastic supply curve is a horizontal line.

Measuring the Price Elasticity of Supply

The **price elasticity of supply** is defined the same way as the price elasticity of demand (although there is no minus sign to be eliminated here):

(5-9) $$\text{Price elasticity of supply} = \frac{\%\text{ change in quantity supplied}}{\%\text{ change in price}}$$

The only difference is that here we consider movements along the supply curve rather than movements along the demand curve.

Suppose that the price of tomatoes rises by 10%. If the quantity of tomatoes supplied also increases by 10% in response, the price elasticity of supply of tomatoes is 1 (10%/10%) and supply is unit-elastic. If the quantity supplied increases by 5%, the price elasticity of supply is 0.5 and supply is inelastic; if the quantity increases by 20%, the price elasticity of supply is 2 and supply is elastic.

As in the case of demand, the extreme values of the price elasticity of supply have a simple graphical representation. Panel (a) of Figure 5-6 shows the supply of cell phone frequencies, the portion of the radio spectrum that is suitable for sending and receiving cell phone signals. Governments own the right to sell the use of this part of the radio spectrum to cell phone operators inside their borders. But governments can't increase or decrease the number of cell phone frequencies that they have to offer—for technical reasons, the quantity of frequencies suitable for cell phone operation is a fixed quantity.

So the supply curve for cell phone frequencies is a vertical line, which we have assumed is set at the quantity of 100 frequencies. As you move up and down that curve, the change in the quantity supplied by the government is zero, whatever the change in price. So panel (a) illustrates a case in which the price elasticity of supply is zero. This is a case of **perfectly inelastic supply.**

Panel (b) shows the supply curve for pizza. We suppose that it costs $12 to produce a pizza, including all opportunity costs. At any price below $12, it would be unprofitable to produce pizza and all the pizza parlors in America would go out of business. Alternatively, there are many producers who could operate pizza parlors if they were profitable. The ingredients—flour, tomatoes, cheese—are plentiful. And if necessary, more tomatoes could be grown, more milk could be produced to make mozzarella, and so on. So any price above $12 would elicit an extremely large quantity of pizzas supplied. The implied supply curve is therefore a horizontal line at $12.

Since even a tiny increase in the price would lead to a huge increase in the quantity supplied, the price elasticity of supply would be more or less infinite. This is a case of **perfectly elastic supply.**

As our cell phone frequencies and pizza examples suggest, real-world instances of both perfectly inelastic and perfectly elastic supply are easy to find—much easier than their counterparts in demand.

FIGURE 5-6 Two Extreme Cases of Price Elasticity of Supply

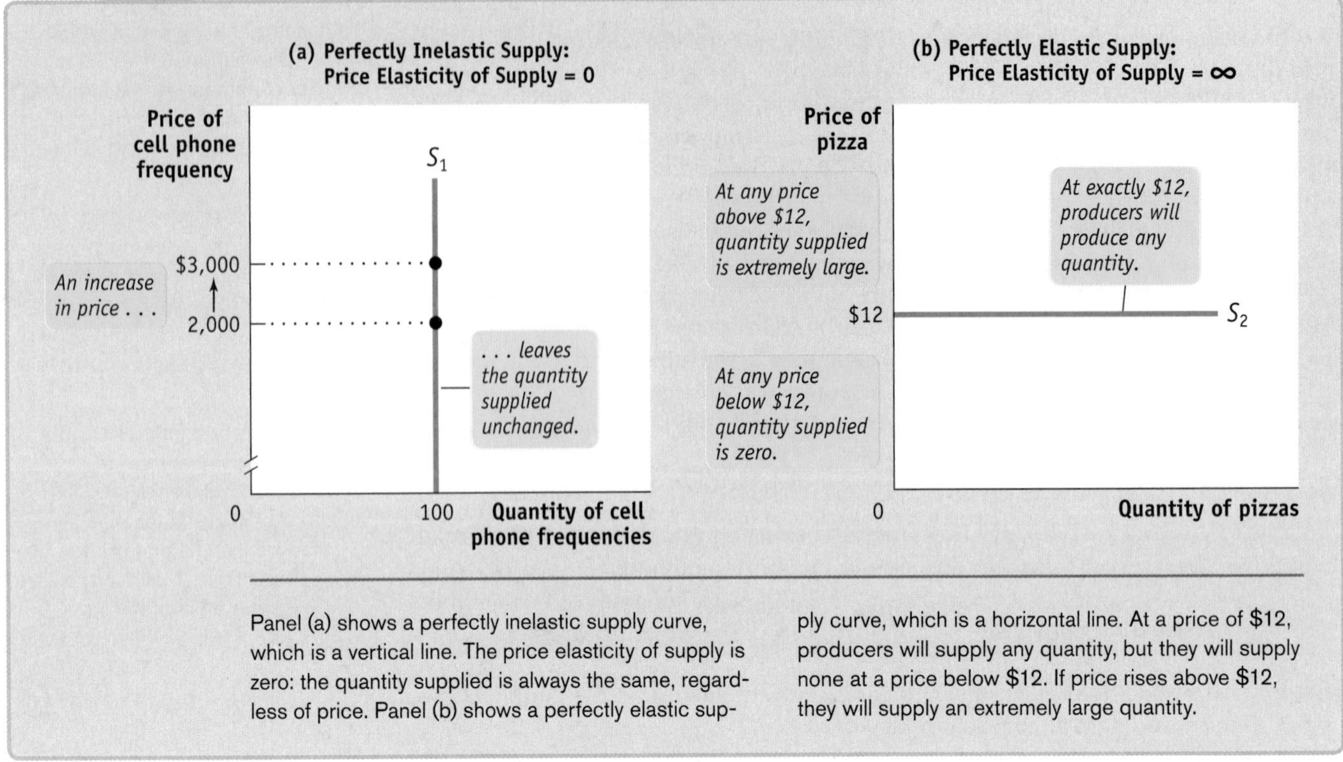

Panel (a) shows a perfectly inelastic supply curve, which is a vertical line. The price elasticity of supply is zero: the quantity supplied is always the same, regardless of price. Panel (b) shows a perfectly elastic supply curve, which is a horizontal line. At a price of $12, producers will supply any quantity, but they will supply none at a price below $12. If price rises above $12, they will supply an extremely large quantity.

What Factors Determine the Price Elasticity of Supply?

Our examples tell us the main determinant of the price elasticity of supply: the availability of inputs. In addition, as with the price elasticity of demand, time may also play a role in the price elasticity of supply. Here we briefly summarize the two factors.

The Availability of Inputs The price elasticity of supply tends to be large when inputs are readily available and can be shifted into and out of production at a relatively low cost. It tends to be small when inputs are difficult to obtain—and can be shifted into and out of production only at a relatively high cost.

Time The price elasticity of supply tends to grow larger as producers have more time to respond to a price change. This means that the long-run price elasticity of supply is often higher than the short-run elasticity. (In the case of the flu vaccine shortfall, time was the crucial element because flu vaccine must be grown in cultures over many months.)

The price elasticity of pizza supply is very high because the inputs needed to expand the industry are readily available. The price elasticity of cell phone frequencies is zero because an essential input—the radio spectrum—cannot be increased at all.

Many industries are like pizza production and have large price elasticities of supply: they can be readily expanded because they don't require any special or unique resources. In contrast, the price elasticity of supply is usually substantially less than perfectly elastic for goods that involve limited natural resources: minerals like gold or copper, agricultural products like coffee that flourish only on certain types of land, and renewable resources like ocean fish that can only be exploited up to a point without destroying the resource.

But given enough time, producers are often able to significantly change the amount they produce in response to a price change, even when production involves a limited natural resource. For example, consider again the effects of a surge in flu vaccine prices, but this time focus on the supply response. If the price were to rise to $90 per vaccination and stay there for a number of years, there would almost certainly be a substantial increase in flu vaccine production. Producers such as Chiron would eventually respond by increasing the size of their manufacturing plants, hiring more lab technicians, and so on. But significantly enlarging the capacity of a biotech manufacturing lab takes several years, not weeks or months or even a single year.

For this reason, economists often make a distinction between the short-run elasticity of supply, usually referring to a few weeks or months, and the long-run elasticity of supply, usually referring to several years. In most industries, the long-run elasticity of supply is larger than the short-run elasticity.

ECONOMICS ➤ IN ACTION

EUROPEAN FARM SURPLUSES

One of the policies we analyzed in Chapter 4 was the imposition of a *price floor,* a lower limit below which price of a good could not fall. We saw that price floors are often used by governments to support the incomes of farmers but create large unwanted surpluses of farm products. The most dramatic example of this is found in the European Union, where price floors have created a "butter mountain," a "wine lake," and so on.

Were European politicians unaware that their price floors would create huge surpluses? They probably knew that surpluses would arise but underestimated the price elasticity of agricultural supply. In fact, when the agricultural price supports were put in place, many analysts thought they were unlikely to lead to big increases in production. After all, European countries are densely populated and there is little new land available for cultivation.

What the analysts failed to realize, however, was how much farm production could expand by adding other resources, especially fertilizer and pesticides, which were readily available. So although European farm acreage didn't increase much in response to the imposition of price floors, European farm production did!

Quick Review

- The **price elasticity of supply** is the percent change in the quantity supplied divided by the percent change in the price.
- Under **perfectly inelastic supply,** the quantity supplied is completely unresponsive to price and the supply curve is a vertical line. Under **perfectly elastic supply,** the supply curve is horizontal at some specific price. If the price falls below that level, the quantity supplied is zero. If the price rises above that level, the quantity supplied is extremely large.
- The price elasticity of supply depends on the availability of inputs, the ease of shifting inputs into and out of alternative uses, and the period of time that has elapsed since the price change.

CHECK YOUR UNDERSTANDING 5-4

1. Using the midpoint method, calculate the price elasticity of supply for web-design services when the price per hour rises from $100 to $150 and the number of hours transacted increases from 300,000 to 500,000. Is supply elastic, inelastic, or unit-elastic?
2. True or false? If the demand for milk rose, then, in the long run, milk-drinkers would be better off if supply were elastic rather than inelastic.
3. True or false? Long-run price elasticities of supply are generally larger than short-run price elasticities of supply. As a result, the short-run supply curves are generally flatter than the long-run supply curves.
4. True or false? When supply is perfectly elastic, changes in demand have no effect on price.

Solutions appear at back of book.

An Elasticity Menagerie

We've just run through quite a few different elasticities. Keeping them all straight can be a challenge. So in Table 5-3 we provide a summary of all the elasticities we have discussed and their implications.

TABLE 5-3 An Elasticity Menagerie

Price elasticity of demand = $\frac{\text{\% change in quantity demanded}}{\text{\% change in price}}$ (dropping the minus sign)	
0	**Perfectly inelastic:** price has no effect on quantity demanded (vertical demand curve).
Between 0 and 1	**Inelastic:** a rise in price increases total revenue.
Exactly 1	**Unit-elastic:** changes in price have no effect on total revenue.
Greater than 1, less than ∞	**Elastic:** a rise in price reduces total revenue.
∞	**Perfectly elastic:** any rise in price causes quantity demanded to fall to 0. Any fall in price leads to an infinite quantity demanded (horizontal demand curve).
Cross-price elasticity of demand = $\frac{\text{\% change in quantity of one good demanded}}{\text{\% change in price of another good}}$	
Negative	**Complements:** quantity demanded of one good falls when the price of another rises.
Positive	**Substitutes:** quantity demanded of one good rises when the price of another rises.
Income elasticity of demand = $\frac{\text{\% change in quantity demanded}}{\text{\% change in income}}$	
Negative	**Inferior good:** quantity demanded falls when income rises.
Positive, less than 1	**Normal good, income-inelastic:** quantity demanded rises when income rises, but not as rapidly as income.
Greater than 1	**Normal good, income-elastic:** quantity demanded rises when income rises, and more rapidly than income.
Price elasticity of supply = $\frac{\text{\% change in quantity supplied}}{\text{\% change in price}}$	
0	**Perfectly inelastic:** price has no effect on quantity supplied (vertical supply curve).
Greater than 0, less than ∞	ordinary upward-sloping supply curve.
∞	**Perfectly elastic:** any fall in price causes quantity supplied to fall to 0. Any rise in price elicits an infinite quantity supplied (horizontal supply curve).

The Benefits and Costs of Taxation

When a government is considering whether to impose a tax or how to design a tax system, it has to weigh the benefits of a tax against its costs. We don't usually think of a tax as something that provides benefits, but governments need money to provide things people want, such as national defense and health care for those unable to afford it. The benefit of a tax is the revenue it raises for the government to pay for these services. Unfortunately, this benefit comes at a cost—a cost that is normally larger than the amount consumers and producers pay. Let's look first at what determines how much money a tax raises, then at the costs a tax imposes, both of which are dependent upon the elasticity of supply and demand. To understand the economics of taxes, it's helpful to look at a simple type of tax known as an **excise tax**—a tax charged on each unit of a good or service that is sold.

An **excise tax** is a tax on sales of a good or service.

The Revenue from an Excise Tax

Suppose that the supply and demand for hotel rooms in the city of Potterville are as shown in Figure 5-7. For simplicity, assume that all hotel rooms offer the same features. In the absence of taxes, the equilibrium price of a room is $80.00 per night and the equilibrium quantity of hotel rooms rented is 10,000 per night.

Now suppose that Potterville's city council imposes an excise tax of $40 per night on hotel rooms—that is, every time a room is rented for the night, the owner of the hotel must pay the city $40. For example, if a customer pays $80, $40 is collected as a tax, leaving the hotel owner with only $40.

How much revenue will the government collect from this excise tax? In this case, the revenue is equal to the area of the shaded rectangle in Figure 5-7.

To see why this area represents the revenue collected by a $40 tax on hotel rooms, notice that the height of the rectangle is $40, equal to the tax per room. It is also, as we've seen, the size of the wedge that the tax drives between the supply price (the price received by producers) and the demand price (the price paid by consumers). Meanwhile, the width of the rectangle is 5,000 rooms, equal to the equilibrium quantity of rooms given the $40 tax. With that information, we can make the following calculations.

The tax revenue collected is:

Tax revenue = $40 per room × 5,000 rooms = $200,000

The area of the shaded rectangle is:

Area = Height × Width = $40 per room × 5,000 rooms = $200,000

or

Tax revenue = Area of shaded rectangle

This is a general principle: *The revenue collected by an excise tax is equal to the area of the rectangle whose height is the tax wedge between the supply and demand curves and whose width is the quantity transacted under the tax.*

"What taxes would you like to see imposed on other people?"

FIGURE 5-7 The Revenue from an Excise Tax

The revenue from a $40 excise tax on hotel rooms is $200,000, equal to the tax rate, $40—the size of the wedge that the tax drives between the supply price and the demand price—multiplied by the number of rooms rented, 5,000. This is equal to the area of the shaded rectangle.

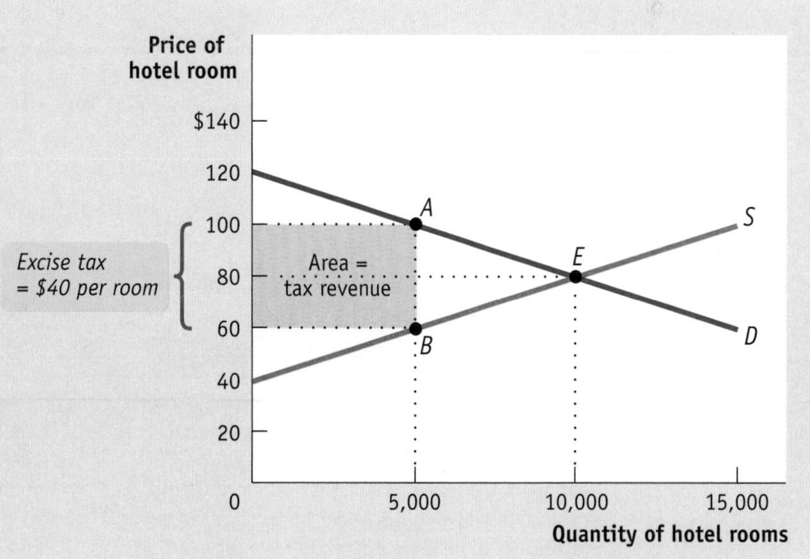

A **tax rate** is the amount of tax people are required to pay per unit of whatever is being taxed.

Tax Rates and Revenue

In Figure 5-7, $40 per room is the *tax rate* on hotel rooms. A **tax rate** is the amount of tax levied per unit of whatever is being taxed. Sometimes tax rates are defined in terms of dollar amounts per unit of a good or service; for example, $2.46 per pack of cigarettes sold. In other cases, they are defined as a percentage of the price; for example, the payroll tax is 15.3% of a worker's earnings up to $106,800.

There's obviously a relationship between tax rates and revenue. That relationship is not, however, one-for-one. In general, doubling the excise tax rate on a good or service won't double the amount of revenue collected, because the tax increase will reduce the quantity of the good or service transacted. And the relationship between the level of the tax and the amount of revenue collected may not even be positive: in some cases raising the tax rate actually *reduces* the amount of revenue the government collects.

We can illustrate these points using our hotel room example. Figure 5-7 showed the revenue the government collects from a $40 tax on hotel rooms. Figure 5-8 shows the revenue the government would collect from two alternative tax rates—a lower tax of only $20 per room and a higher tax of $60 per room.

Panel (a) of Figure 5-8 shows the case of a $20 tax, equal to half the tax rate illustrated in Figure 5-7. At this lower tax rate, 7,500 rooms are rented, generating tax revenue of:

Tax revenue = $20 per room × 7,500 rooms = $150,000

Recall that the tax revenue collected from a $40 tax rate is $200,000. So the revenue collected from a $20 tax rate, $150,000, is only 75% of the amount collected when the tax rate is twice as high ($150,000/$200,000 × 100 = 75%). To put

FIGURE 5-8 Tax Rates and Revenue

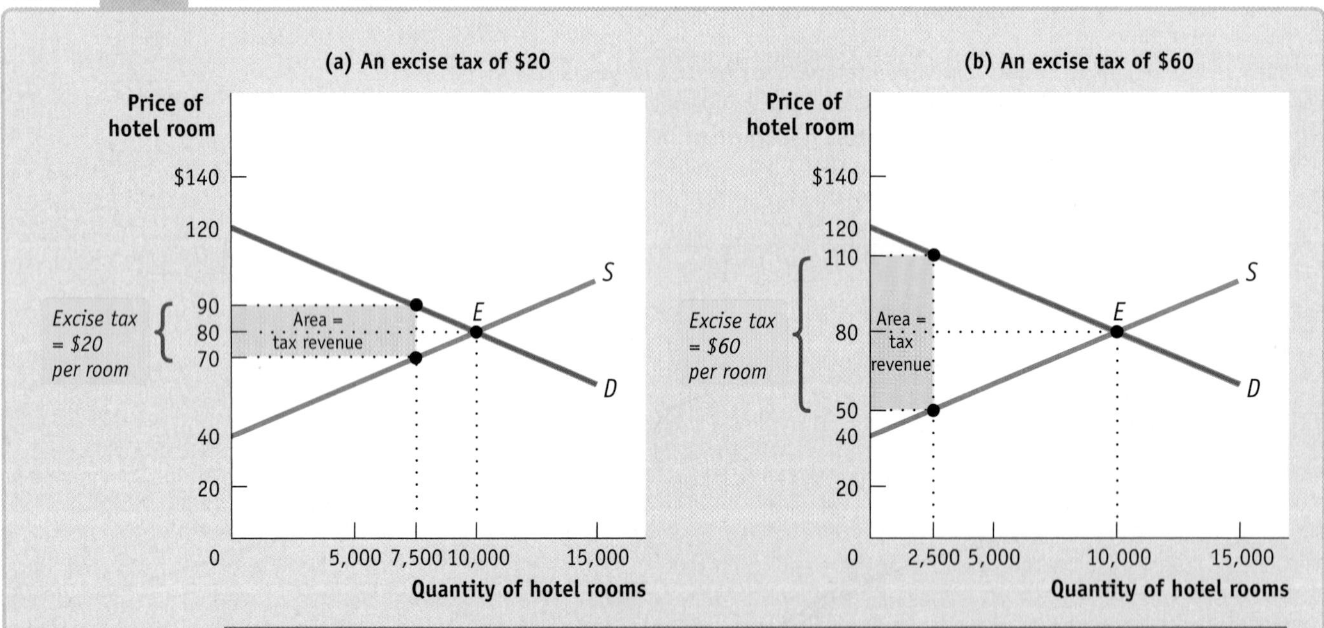

In general, doubling the excise tax rate on a good or service won't double the amount of revenue collected, because the tax increase will reduce the quantity of the good or service bought and sold. And the relationship between the level of the tax and the amount of revenue collected may not even be positive. Panel (a) shows the revenue raised by a tax rate of $20 per room, only half the tax rate in Figure 5-7. The tax revenue raised, equal to the area of the shaded rectangle, is $150,000, three-quarters as much as the revenue raised by a $40 tax rate. Panel (b) shows that the revenue raised by a $60 tax rate is also $150,000. So raising the tax rate from $40 to $60 actually reduces tax revenue.

it another way, a 100% increase in the tax rate from $20 to $40 per room leads to only a one-third, or 33.3%, increase in revenue, from $150,000 to $200,000 (($200,000 – $150,000)/$150,000 × 100 = 33.3%).

Panel (b) depicts what happens if the tax rate is raised from $40 to $60 per room, leading to a fall in the number of rooms rented from 5,000 to 2,500. The revenue collected at a $60 per room tax rate is:

Tax revenue = $60 per room × 2,500 rooms = $150,000

This is also *less* than the revenue collected by a $40 per room tax. So raising the tax rate from $40 to $60 actually reduces revenue. More precisely, in this case raising the tax rate by 50% (($60 – $40)/$40 × 100 = 50%) lowers the tax revenue by 25% (($150,000 – $200,000)/$200,000 × 100 = –25%). Why did this happen? It happened because the fall in tax revenue caused by the reduction in the number of rooms rented more than offset the increase in the tax revenue caused by the rise in the tax rate. In other words, setting a tax rate so high that it deters a significant number of transactions is likely to lead to a fall in tax revenue.

One way to think about the revenue effect of increasing an excise tax is that the tax increase affects tax revenue in two ways. On one side, the tax increase means that the government raises more revenue for each unit of the good sold, which other things equal would lead to a rise in tax revenue. On the other side, the tax increase reduces the quantity of sales, which other things equal would lead to a fall in tax revenue. The end result depends both on the price elasticities of supply and demand and on the initial level of the tax. If the price elasticities of both supply and demand are low, the tax increase won't reduce the quantity of the good sold very much, so tax revenue will definitely rise. If the price elasticities are high, the result is less certain; if they are high enough, the tax reduces the quantity sold so much that tax revenue falls. Also, if the initial tax rate is low, the government doesn't lose much revenue from the decline in the quantity of the good sold, so the tax increase will definitely increase tax revenue. If the initial tax rate is high, the result is again less certain. Tax revenue is likely to fall or rise very little from a tax increase only in cases where the price elasticities are high and there is already a high tax rate.

The possibility that a higher tax rate can reduce tax revenue, and the corresponding possibility that cutting taxes can increase tax revenue, is a basic principle of taxation that policy makers take into account when setting tax rates. That is, when considering a tax created for the purpose of raising revenue (in contrast to taxes created to discourage undesirable behavior, known as "sin taxes"), a

FOR INQUIRING MINDS

THE LAFFER CURVE

One afternoon in 1974, the economist Arthur Laffer got together in a cocktail lounge with Jude Wanniski, a writer for the *Wall Street Journal*, and Dick Cheney, who would later become vice president but at the time was the deputy White House chief of staff. During the course of their conversation, Laffer drew a diagram on a napkin that was intended to explain how tax cuts could sometimes lead to higher tax revenue. According to Laffer's diagram, raising tax rates initially increases tax revenue, but beyond a certain level revenue falls instead as tax rates continue to rise. That is, at some point tax rates are so high and reduce the number of transactions so greatly that tax revenues fall.

There was nothing new about this idea, but in later years that napkin became the stuff of legend. The editors of the *Wall Street Journal* began promoting the "Laffer curve" as a justification for tax cuts. And when Ronald Reagan took office in 1981, he used the Laffer curve to argue that his proposed cuts in income tax rates would not reduce the federal government's revenue.

So is there a Laffer curve? Yes—as a theoretical proposition it's definitely possible that tax rates could be so high that cutting taxes would increase tax revenue. But very few economists now believe that Reagan's tax cuts actually increased revenue, and real-world examples in which revenue and tax rates move in opposite directions are very hard to find. That's because it's rare to find an existing tax rate so high that reducing it leads to an increase in tax revenue.

well-informed policy maker won't impose a tax rate so high that cutting the tax would increase revenue. In the real world, policy makers aren't always well informed, but they usually aren't complete fools either. That's why it's very hard to find real-world examples in which raising a tax reduced revenue or cutting a tax increased revenue. Nonetheless, the theoretical possibility that a tax reduction increases tax revenue has played an important role in the folklore of American politics. As explained in For Inquiring Minds, on the Laffer curve, an economist who, in the 1970s, sketched on a napkin the figure of a revenue-increasing income tax reduction had a significant impact on the economic policies adopted in the United States in the 1980s.

The Costs of Taxation

What is the cost of a tax? You might be inclined to answer that it is the money taxpayers pay to the government. In other words, you might believe that the cost of a tax is the tax revenue collected. But suppose the government uses the tax revenue to provide services that taxpayers want. Or suppose that the government simply hands the tax revenue back to taxpayers. Would we say in those cases that the tax didn't actually cost anything?

No—because a tax, like a quota, prevents mutually beneficial transactions from occurring. Consider Figure 5-7 once more. Here, with a $40 tax on hotel rooms, guests pay $100 per room but hotel owners receive only $60 per room. Because of the wedge created by the tax, we know that some transactions don't occur that would have occurred without the tax. More specifically, we know from the supply and demand curves that there are some potential guests who would be willing to pay up to $90 per night and some hotel owners who would be willing to supply rooms if they received at least $70 per night. If these two sets of people were allowed to trade with each other without the tax, they would engage in mutually beneficial transactions—hotel rooms would be rented. But such deals would be illegal, because the $40 tax would not be paid. In our example, 5,000 potential hotel room rentals that would have occurred in the absence of the tax, to the mutual benefit of guests and hotel owners, do not take place because of the tax.

So an excise tax imposes costs over and above the tax revenue collected in the form of inefficiency, which occurs because the tax discourages mutually beneficial transactions. As we learned in Chapter 4, the cost to society of this kind of inefficiency—the value of the forgone mutually beneficial transactions—is called the deadweight loss. While all real-world taxes impose some deadweight loss, a badly designed tax imposes a larger deadweight loss than a well-designed one.

To measure the deadweight loss from a tax, we turn to the concepts of producer and consumer surplus. Figure 5-9 shows the effects of an excise tax on consumer and producer surplus. In the absence of the tax, the equilibrium is at E and the equilibrium price and quantity are P_E and Q_E, respectively. An excise tax drives a wedge equal to the amount of the tax between the price received by producers and the price paid by consumers, reducing the quantity sold. In this case, where the tax is T dollars per unit, the quantity sold falls to Q_T. The price paid by consumers rises to P_C, the demand price of the reduced quantity, Q_T, and the price received by producers falls to P_P, the supply price of that quantity. The difference between these prices, $P_C - P_P$, is equal to the excise tax, T.

The rise in the price paid by consumers causes a loss equal to the sum of the areas of a rectangle and a triangle: the dark blue rectangle labeled A and the area of the light blue triangle labeled B in Figure 5-9.

Meanwhile, the fall in the price received by producers leads to a fall in producer surplus. This, too, is equal to the sum of the areas of a rectangle and a triangle. The loss in producer surplus is the sum of the areas of the dark red rectangle labeled C and the light red triangle labeled F in Figure 5-9.

Of course, although consumers and producers are hurt by the tax, the government gains revenue. The revenue the government collects is equal to the tax per unit sold, T, multiplied by the quantity sold, Q_T. This revenue is equal to the

FIGURE 5-9 A Tax Reduces Consumer and Producer Surplus

Before the tax, the equilibrium price and quantity are P_E and Q_E, respectively. After an excise tax of T per unit is imposed, the price to consumers rises to P_C and consumer surplus falls by the sum of the dark blue rectangle, labeled A, and the light blue triangle, labeled B. The tax also causes the price to producers to fall to P_P; producer surplus falls by the sum of the dark red rectangle, labeled C, and the light red triangle, labeled F. The government receives revenue from the tax, $Q_T \times T$, which is given by the sum of the areas A and C. Areas B and F represent the losses to consumer and producer surplus that are not collected by the government as revenue; they are the deadweight loss to society of the tax.

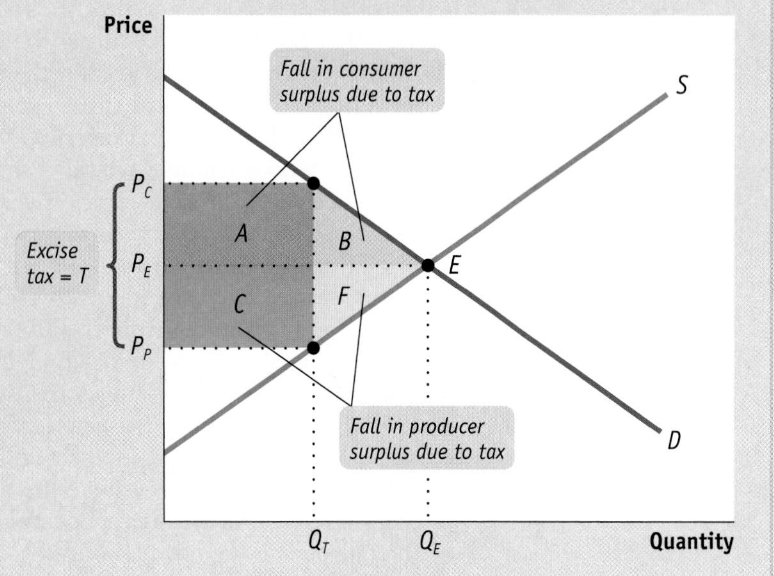

area of a rectangle Q_T wide and T high. And we already have that rectangle in the figure: it is the sum of rectangles A and C. So the government gains part of what consumers and producers lose from an excise tax.

But a portion of the loss to producers and consumers from the tax is not offset by a gain to the government—specifically, the two triangles B and F. The deadweight loss caused by the tax is equal to the combined area of these two triangles. It represents the total surplus lost to society because of the tax—that is, the amount of surplus that would have been generated by transactions that now do not take place because of the tax.

Figure 5-10 is a version of Figure 5-9 that leaves out rectangles A (the surplus shifted from consumers to the government) and C (the surplus shifted from

FIGURE 5-10 The Deadweight Loss of a Tax

A tax leads to a deadweight loss because it creates inefficiency: some mutually beneficial transactions never take place because of the tax—namely, the transactions $Q_E - Q_T$. The yellow area here represents the value of the deadweight loss: it is the total surplus that would have been gained from the $Q_E - Q_T$ transactions. If the tax had not discouraged transactions—had the number of transactions remained at Q_E—no deadweight loss would have been incurred.

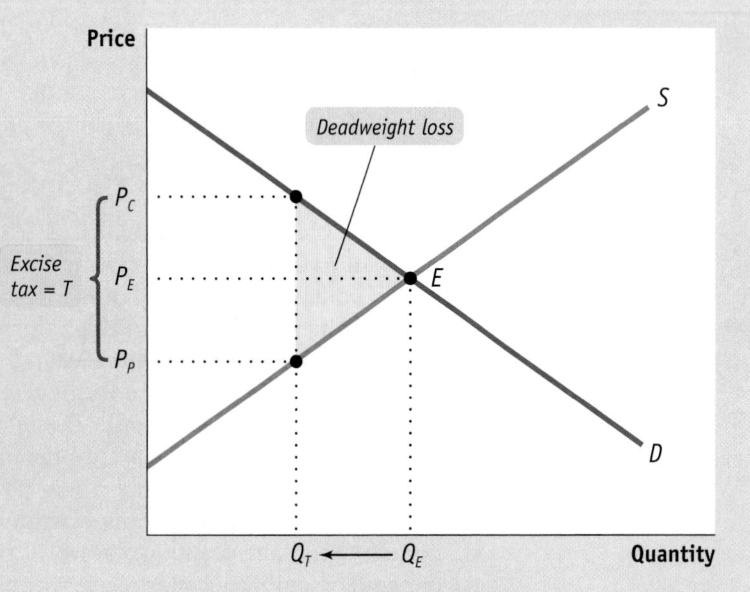

The **administrative costs** of a tax are the resources used by government to collect the tax, and by taxpayers to pay it, over and above the amount of the tax, as well as to evade it.

producers to the government) and shows only the deadweight loss, here drawn as a triangle shaded yellow. The base of that triangle is equal to the tax wedge, *T;* the height of the triangle is equal to the reduction in the quantity transacted due to the tax, $Q_E - Q_T$. Clearly, the larger the tax wedge and the larger the reduction in the quantity transacted, the greater the inefficiency from the tax. But also note an important, contrasting point: if the excise tax somehow *didn't* reduce the quantity bought and sold in this market—if Q_T remained equal to Q_E after the tax was levied—the yellow triangle would disappear and the deadweight loss from the tax would be zero. This observation is simply the flip-side of the principle found earlier in the chapter: a tax causes inefficiency because it discourages mutually beneficial transactions between buyers and sellers. So if a tax does not discourage transactions, it causes no deadweight loss. In this case, the tax simply shifts surplus straight from consumers and producers to the government.

Using a triangle to measure deadweight loss is a technique used in many economic applications. For example, triangles are used to measure the deadweight loss produced by types of taxes other than excise taxes. They are also used to measure the deadweight loss produced by monopoly, another kind of market distortion. And deadweight-loss triangles are often used to evaluate the benefits and costs of public policies besides taxation—such as whether to impose stricter safety standards on a product.

In considering the total amount of inefficiency caused by a tax, we must also take into account something not shown in Figure 5-10: the resources actually used by the government to collect the tax, and by taxpayers to pay it, over and above the amount of the tax. These lost resources are called the **administrative costs** of the tax. The most familiar administrative cost of the U.S. tax system is the time individuals spend filling out their income tax forms or the money they spend on accountants to prepare their tax forms for them. (The latter is considered an inefficiency from the point of view of society because accountants could instead be performing other, non-tax-related services.) Included in the administrative costs that taxpayers incur are resources used to evade the tax, both legally and illegally. The costs of operating the Internal Revenue Service, the arm of the federal government tasked with collecting the federal income tax, are actually quite small in comparison to the administrative costs paid by taxpayers.

So the total inefficiency caused by a tax is the sum of its deadweight loss and its administrative costs. The general rule for economic policy is that, other things equal, a tax system should be designed to minimize the total inefficiency it imposes on society. In practice, other considerations also apply, but this principle nonetheless gives valuable guidance. Administrative costs are usually well known, more or less determined by the current technology of collecting taxes (for example, filing paper returns versus filing electronically). But how can we predict the size of the deadweight loss associated with a given tax? Not surprisingly, as in our analysis of the incidence of a tax, the price elasticities of supply and demand play crucial roles in making such a prediction.

Elasticities and the Deadweight Loss of a Tax

We know that the deadweight loss from an excise tax arises because it prevents some mutually beneficial transactions from occurring. In particular, the producer and consumer surplus that is forgone because of these missing transactions is equal to the size of the deadweight loss itself. This means that the larger the number of transactions that are prevented by the tax, the larger the deadweight loss.

This fact gives us an important clue in understanding the relationship between elasticity and the size of the deadweight loss from a tax. Recall that when demand or supply is elastic, the quantity demanded or the quantity supplied is relatively responsive to changes in the price. So a tax imposed on a good for which either demand or supply, or both, is elastic will cause a relatively large decrease in the quantity transacted and a relatively large deadweight loss. And when we say that demand or supply is inelastic, we mean that the quantity demanded or the quantity supplied is relatively unresponsive to changes in the price. As a result, a tax imposed when demand or supply, or both, is inelastic will cause a relatively small decrease in the quantity transacted and a relatively small deadweight loss.

The four panels of Figure 5-11 illustrate the positive relationship between a good's price elasticity of either demand or supply and the deadweight loss from taxing that good. Each panel represents the same amount of tax imposed but on a different good; the size of the deadweight loss is given by the area of the shaded triangle. In panel (a), the deadweight-loss triangle is large because demand for this good is relatively elastic—a large number of transactions fail to occur

FIGURE 5-11 Deadweight Loss and Elasticities

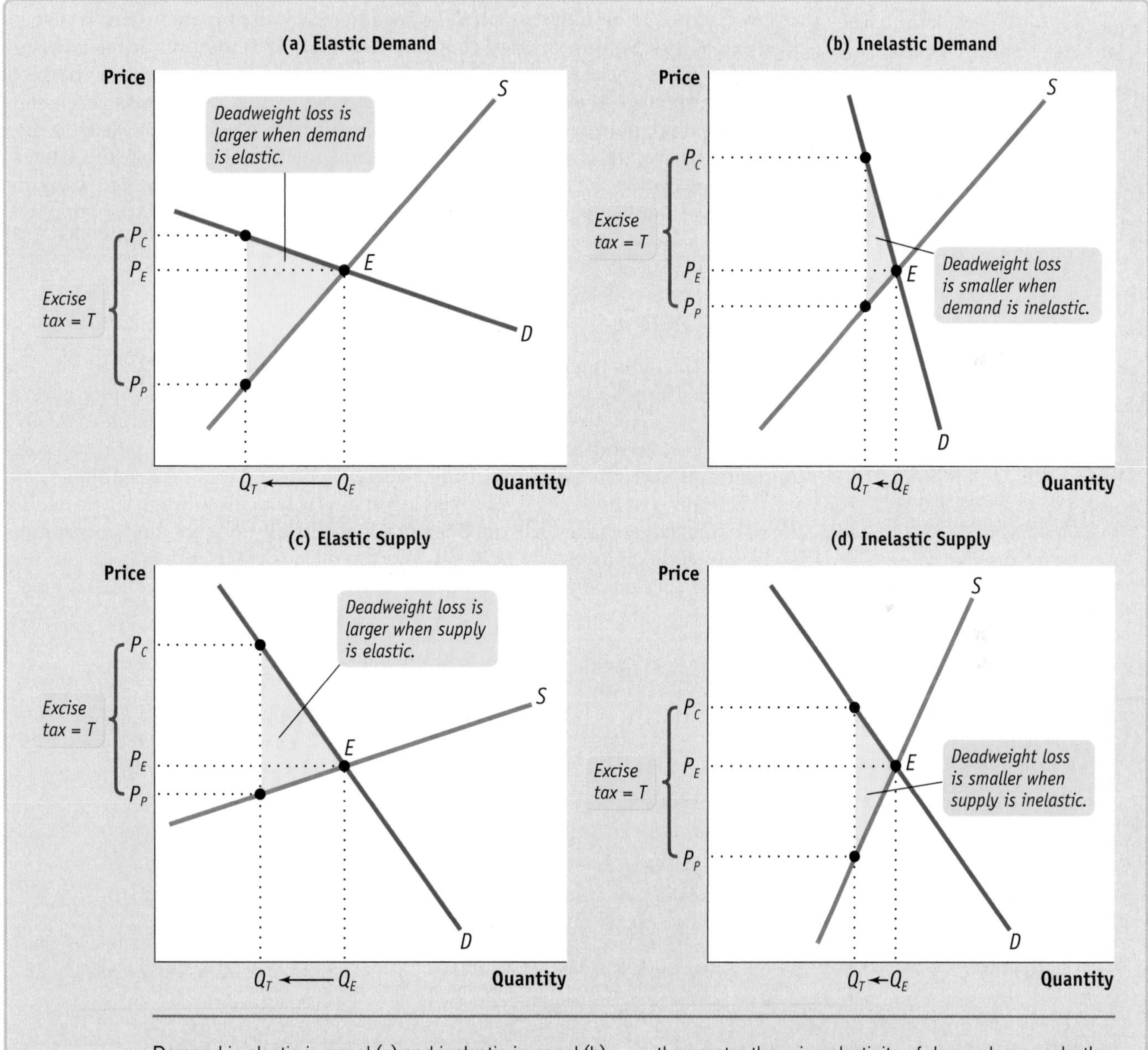

Demand is elastic in panel (a) and inelastic in panel (b), but the supply curves are the same. Supply is elastic in panel (c) and inelastic in panel (d), but the demand curves are the same. The deadweight losses are larger in panels (a) and (c) than in panels (b) and (d) because the greater the price elasticity of demand or supply, the greater the tax-induced fall in the quantity transacted. In contrast, the lower the price elasticity of demand or supply, the smaller the tax-induced fall in the quantity transacted and the smaller the deadweight loss.

because of the tax. In panel (b), the same supply curve is drawn as in panel (a), but demand for this good is relatively inelastic; as a result, the triangle is small because only a small number of transactions are forgone. Likewise, panels (c) and (d) contain the same demand curve but different supply curves. In panel (c), an elastic supply curve gives rise to a large deadweight-loss triangle, but in panel (d) an inelastic supply curve gives rise to a small deadweight-loss triangle.

The implication of this result is clear: if you want to minimize the efficiency costs of taxation, you should choose to tax only those goods for which demand or supply, or both, is relatively inelastic. For such goods, a tax has little effect on behavior because behavior is relatively unresponsive to changes in the price. In the extreme case in which demand is perfectly inelastic (a vertical demand curve), the quantity demanded is unchanged by the imposition of the tax. As a result, the tax imposes no deadweight loss. Similarly, if supply is perfectly inelastic (a vertical supply curve), the quantity supplied is unchanged by the tax and there is also no deadweight loss. So if the goal in choosing whom to tax is to minimize deadweight loss, then taxes should be imposed on goods and services that have the most inelastic response—that is, goods and services for which consumers or producers will change their behavior the least in response to the tax. (Unless they have a tendency to revolt, of course.) And this lesson carries a flip-side: using a tax to purposely decrease the amount of a harmful activity, such as underage drinking, will have the most impact when that activity is elastically demanded or supplied.

ECONOMICS ➤ IN ACTION

TAXING THE MARLBORO MAN

One of the most important excise taxes in the United States is the tax on cigarettes. The federal government imposes a tax of $1.01 a pack; state governments impose taxes that range from 7 cents a pack in South Carolina to $3.46 a pack in Rhode Island; and many cities impose further taxes. In general, tax rates on cigarettes have increased over time, because more and more governments have seen them not just as a source of revenue but as a way to discourage smoking. But the rise in cigarette taxes has not been gradual. Usually, once a state government decides to raise cigarette taxes, it raises them a lot—which provides economists with useful data on what happens when there is a big tax increase.

TABLE 5-4 Results of Increases in Cigarette Taxes

State	Year	Increase in tax (per pack)	New state tax (per pack)	Change in quantity transacted	Change in tax revenue
Utah	1997	$0.25	$0.52	−20.7%	+86.2%
Maryland	1999	0.30	0.66	−15.3	+52.6
California	1999	0.50	0.87	−18.9	+90.7
Michigan	1994	0.50	0.75	−20.8	+139.9
New York	2000	0.55	1.11	−20.2	+57.4

Source: M. C. Farrelly, C. T. Nimsch, and J. James, "State Cigarette Excise Taxes: Implications for Revenue and Tax Evasion," RTI International 2003.

Table 5-4 shows the results of big increases in cigarette taxes. In each case, sales fell, just as our analysis predicts. Although it's theoretically possible for tax revenue to fall after such a large tax increase, in reality tax revenue rose in each case. That's because cigarettes have a low price elasticity of demand.

▼ Quick Review

- An excise tax generates tax revenue equal to the **tax rate** times the number of units of the good or service transacted but reduces consumer and producer surplus.
- The government tax revenue collected is less than the loss in total surplus because the tax creates inefficiency by discouraging some mutually beneficial transactions.
- The difference between the tax revenue from an excise tax and the reduction in total surplus is the deadweight loss from the tax. The total amount of inefficiency resulting from a tax is equal to the deadweight loss plus the **administrative costs** of the tax.
- The larger the number of transactions prevented by a tax, the larger the deadweight loss. As a result, taxes on goods with a greater price elasticity of supply or demand, or both, generate higher deadweight losses. There is no deadweight loss when the number of transactions is unchanged by the tax.

CHECK YOUR UNDERSTANDING 5-5

Consumer	Willingness to pay	Producer	Cost
Ana	$0.70	Zhang	$0.10
Bernice	0.60	Yves	0.20
Chizuko	0.50	Xavier	0.30
Dagmar	0.40	Walter	0.40
Ella	0.30	Vern	0.50

1. The accompanying table shows five consumers' willingness to pay for one can of diet soda each as well as five producers' costs of selling one can of diet soda each. Each consumer buys at most one can of soda; each producer sells at most one can of soda. The government asks your advice about the effects of an excise tax of $0.40 per can of diet soda. Assume that there are no administrative costs from the tax.
   a. Without the excise tax, what is the equilibrium price and the equilibrium quantity of soda transacted?
   b. The excise tax raises the price paid by consumers post-tax to $0.60 and lowers the price received by producers post-tax to $0.20. With the excise tax, what is the quantity of soda transacted?
   c. Without the excise tax, how much individual consumer surplus does each of the consumers gain? How much with the tax? How much total consumer surplus is lost as a result of the tax?
   d. Without the excise tax, how much individual producer surplus does each of the producers gain? How much with the tax? How much total producer surplus is lost as a result of the tax?
   e. How much government revenue does the excise tax create?
   f. What is the deadweight loss from the imposition of this excise tax?
2. In each of the following cases, focus on the price elasticity of demand and use a diagram to illustrate the likely size—small or large—of the deadweight loss resulting from a tax. Explain your reasoning.
   a. Gasoline
   b. Milk chocolate bars

Solutions appear at back of book.

WORKED PROBLEM

Drive We Must

When the price of oil goes up, people decrease their consumption of gasoline. In the short run, consumers can quickly change their driving habits—they won't take as many summer road trips and they'll switch to public transportation. In the long run, people may also purchase more fuel-efficient vehicles, which will lead to a further decline in consumption. Thus, economists have to make different estimates of the demand for gasoline for the two time horizons, as individuals have a greater number of options in the long run. Specifically, economists have estimated the short-run elasticity of demand for gasoline to be about 0.25, and the long-run elasticity of demand for gasoline to be about 0.75.

Gasoline prices increased from about $3.00 per gallon in 2010 to about $4.00 per gallon in 2012. Using the above long- and short-run elasticities, what is the predicted percent change in consumption of gasoline in the short run and in the long run? Draw and label a demand curve that reflects the long-run elasticity, assuming that at $3.00 per gallon, motorists in the United States consume 10 million barrels per day of gasoline.

STEP 1: Find the percent change in the consumption of gasoline in the short run.

Review the section "Calculating the Price Elasticity of Demand" on pages 144–145. To solve the problem, begin with Equation 5-2,

% change in price = Change in price/Initial price × 100.

Looking at Equation 5-3, we see that

Price elasticity of demand = % change in quantity demanded/% change in price.

This equation can be rearranged as follows:

% change in quantity demanded = Price elasticity of demand × % change in price.

Using Equation 5-2, we can first find the percent change in price. Since price went from \$3.00 per gallon to \$4.00 per gallon, we divide the change in price, which is \$4.00 – \$3.00 = \$1.00, by the initial price, which is \$3.00. The percent change in price is therefore \$1.00/\$3.00 × 100 = 33%. By rearranging Equation 5-3 as above, we find that the percent change in quantity demanded is the short-run price elasticity of demand (0.25) multiplied by the percent change in price (33%) = 0.25 × 33.3% = 8.33%. ■

STEP 2: Find the percent change in the consumption of gasoline in the long run.

Use the same method as above to find the long-run percent change, but substitute 0.75 (the long-run elasticity) for 0.25 (the short-run elasticity).

As we found above, the percent change in price was 33%. We know that by rearranging Equation 5-3, we find that the percent change in quantity demanded is the long-run price elasticity of demand (0.75) multiplied by the percent change in price (33%) = 0.75 × 33% = 25%. ■

STEP 3: Draw and label a demand curve that reflects the long-run elasticity, assuming that at \$3.00 per gallon, motorists in the United States consume 10 million barrels per day of gasoline.

Use the next two steps to devise this curve. ■

STEP 4: Find the relevant numerical quantities for the horizontal axis by finding the amount demanded at \$4.00 per gallon.

Again, review the section on pages 144–145, "Calculating the Price Elasticity of Demand." Equation 5-1 relates the change in quantity demanded to the percent change in quantity demanded:

% change in quantity demanded =
Change in quantity demanded/Initial quantity demanded × 100

Rearranging, we find that the

Change in quantity demanded =
% change in quantity demanded × Initial quantity demanded/100.

From the question, we know that a price of \$3.00 corresponds to a quantity of 10 million barrels per day. If the price were to rise to \$4.00 and the elasticity is 0.75, we know from Step 2 that the percent change in consumption is 25%. Using the above rearranged equation, the change in quantity demanded = (25 × 10 million barrels)/100 = 2.5 million barrels. Hence, the new quantity at a price of \$4.00 equals the initial quantity minus the change in quantity demanded: 10 million barrels – 2.5 million barrels = 7.5 million barrels. ■

STEP 5: Draw and label the demand curve.

Review the section "How Elastic Is Elastic?" on pages 148–152. Carefully examine panel (b) of Figure 5-3 and consider how the figure would change if the elasticity were 0.75 rather than 0.5 as in the figure.

An elasticity of demand of 0.75 is slightly more elastic than an elasticity of demand of .50, so we would draw the curve to be slightly more horizontal than that of the figure. That is, we would rotate the curve slightly to the left, but not too much, as

0.75 still represents inelastic demand. As shown in the following figure, point A now corresponds to a price of $3.00 and a quantity of 10 million barrels per day, and point B now corresponds to a price of $4.00 and a quantity of 7.5 million barrels, as calculated in Step 4. ■

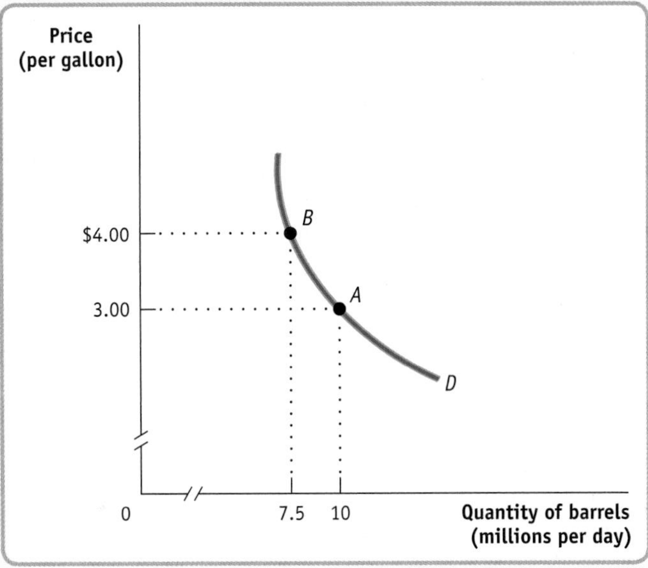

SUMMARY

1. Many economic questions depend on the size of consumer or producer responses to changes in prices or other variables. *Elasticity* is a general measure of responsiveness that can be used to answer such questions.
2. The **price elasticity of demand**—the percent change in the quantity demanded divided by the percent change in the price (dropping the minus sign)—is a measure of the responsiveness of the quantity demanded to changes in the price. In practical calculations, it is usually best to use the **midpoint method,** which calculates percent changes in prices and quantities based on the average of starting and final values.
3. The responsiveness of the quantity demanded to price can range from **perfectly inelastic demand,** where the quantity demanded is unaffected by the price, to **perfectly elastic demand,** where there is a unique price at which consumers will buy as much or as little as they are offered. When demand is perfectly inelastic, the demand curve is a vertical line; when it is perfectly elastic, the demand curve is a horizontal line.
4. The price elasticity of demand is classified according to whether it is more or less than 1. If it is greater than 1, demand is **elastic;** if it is less than 1, demand is **inelastic;** if it is exactly 1, demand is **unit-elastic.** This classification determines how **total revenue,** the total value of sales, changes when the price changes. If demand is elastic, total revenue falls when the price increases and rises when the price decreases. If demand is inelastic, total revenue rises when the price increases and falls when the price decreases.
5. The price elasticity of demand depends on whether there are close substitutes for the good in question, whether the good is a necessity or a luxury, the share of income spent on the good, and the length of time that has elapsed since the price change.
6. The **cross-price elasticity of demand** measures the effect of a change in one good's price on the quantity of another good demanded. The cross-price elasticity of demand can be positive, in which case the goods are substitutes, or negative, in which case they are complements.
7. The **income elasticity of demand** is the percent change in the quantity of a good demanded when a consumer's income changes divided by the percent change in income. The income elasticity of demand indicates how intensely the demand for a good responds to changes in income. It can be negative; in that case the good is an inferior good. Goods with positive income elasticities of demand are normal goods. If the income elasticity is greater than 1, a good

is **income-elastic;** if it is positive and less than 1, the good is **income-inelastic.**

8. The **price elasticity of supply** is the percent change in the quantity of a good supplied divided by the percent change in the price. If the quantity supplied does not change at all, we have an instance of **perfectly inelastic supply;** the supply curve is a vertical line. If the quantity supplied is zero below some price but infinite above that price, we have an instance of **perfectly elastic supply;** the supply curve is a horizontal line.
9. The price elasticity of supply depends on the availability of resources to expand production and on time. It is higher when inputs are available at relatively low cost and the longer the time elapsed since the price change.
10. The tax revenue generated by a tax depends on the **tax rate** and on the number of units transacted with the tax. Excise taxes cause inefficiency in the form of deadweight loss because they discourage some mutually beneficial transactions. Taxes also impose **administrative costs:** resources used to collect the tax, to pay it (over and above the amount of the tax), and to evade it.
11. An **excise tax** generates revenue for the government but lowers total surplus. The loss in total surplus exceeds the tax revenue, resulting in a deadweight loss to society. This deadweight loss is represented by a triangle, the area of which equals the value of the transactions discouraged by the tax. The greater the elasticity of demand or supply, or both, the larger the deadweight loss from a tax. If either demand or supply is perfectly inelastic, there is no deadweight loss from a tax.

KEY TERMS

Price elasticity of demand, p. 144
Midpoint method, p. 146
Perfectly inelastic demand, p. 148
Perfectly elastic demand, p. 148
Elastic demand, p. 149
Inelastic demand, p. 149
Unit-elastic demand, p. 149
Total revenue, p. 150
Cross-price elasticity of demand, p. 155
Income elasticity of demand, p. 156
Income-elastic demand, p. 157
Income-inelastic demand, p. 158
Price elasticity of supply, p. 159
Perfectly inelastic supply, p. 159
Perfectly elastic supply, p. 159
Excise tax, p. 162
Tax rate, p. 164
Administrative costs, p. 168

PROBLEMS

1. Nile.com, the online bookseller, wants to increase its total revenue. One strategy is to offer a 10% discount on every book it sells. Nile.com knows that its customers can be divided into two distinct groups according to their likely responses to the discount. The accompanying table shows how the two groups respond to the discount.

	Group A (sales per week)	Group B (sales per week)
Volume of sales before the 10% discount	1.55 million	1.50 million
Volume of sales after the 10% discount	1.65 million	1.70 million

   a. Using the midpoint method, calculate the price elasticities of demand for group A and group B.
   b. Explain how the discount will affect total revenue from each group.
   c. Suppose Nile.com knows which group each customer belongs to when he or she logs on and can choose whether or not to offer the 10% discount. If Nile.com wants to increase its total revenue, should discounts be offered to group A or to group B, to neither group, or to both groups?

2. Do you think the price elasticity of demand for Ford sport-utility vehicles (SUVs) will increase, decrease, or remain the same when each of the following events occurs? Explain your answer.
   a. Other car manufacturers, such as General Motors, decide to make and sell SUVs.
   b. SUVs produced in foreign countries are banned from the American market.
   c. Due to ad campaigns, Americans believe that SUVs are much safer than ordinary passenger cars.
   d. The time period over which you measure the elasticity lengthens. During that longer time, new models such as four-wheel-drive cargo vans appear.

3. In the United States, 2007 was a bad year for growing wheat. And as wheat supply decreased, the price of wheat rose dramatically, leading to a lower quantity demanded (a movement along the demand curve). The accompanying table describes what happened to prices and the quantity of wheat demanded.

	2006	2007
Quantity demanded (bushels)	2.2 billion	2.0 billion
Average price (per bushel)	$3.42	$4.26

a. Using the midpoint method, calculate the price elasticity of demand for winter wheat.

b. What is the total revenue for U.S. wheat farmers in 2006 and 2007?

c. Did the bad harvest increase or decrease the total revenue of U.S. wheat farmers? How could you have predicted this from your answer to part a?

4. The accompanying table gives part of the supply schedule for personal computers in the United States.

Price of computer	Quantity of computers supplied
$1,100	12,000
900	8,000

a. Calculate the price elasticity of supply when the price increases from $900 to $1,100 using the midpoint method.

b. Suppose firms produce 1,000 more computers at any given price due to improved technology. As price increases from $900 to $1,100, is the price elasticity of supply now greater than, less than, or the same as it was in part a?

c. Suppose a longer time period under consideration means that the quantity supplied at any given price is 20% higher than the figures given in the table. As price increases from $900 to $1,100, is the price elasticity of supply now greater than, less than, or the same as it was in part a?

5. What can you conclude about the price elasticity of demand in each of the following statements?

a. "The pizza delivery business in this town is very competitive. I'd lose half my customers if I raised the price by as little as 10%."

b. "I owned both of the two Jerry Garcia autographed lithographs in existence. I sold one on eBay for a high price. But when I sold the second one, the price dropped by 80%."

c. "My economics professor has chosen to use the Krugman/Wells textbook for this class. I have no choice but to buy this book."

d. "I always spend a total of exactly $10 per week on coffee."

6. The accompanying table shows the price and yearly quantity sold of souvenir T-shirts in the town of Crystal Lake according to the average income of the tourists visiting.

Price of T-shirt	Quantity of T-shirts demanded when average tourist income is $20,000	Quantity of T-shirts demanded when average tourist income is $30,000
$4	3,000	5,000
5	2,400	4,200
6	1,600	3,000
7	800	1,800

a. Using the midpoint method, calculate the price elasticity of demand when the price of a T-shirt rises from $5 to $6 and the average tourist income is $20,000. Also calculate it when the average tourist income is $30,000.

b. Using the midpoint method, calculate the income elasticity of demand when the price of a T-shirt is $4 and the average tourist income increases from $20,000 to $30,000. Also calculate it when the price is $7.

7. A recent study determined the following elasticities for Volkswagen Beetles:

Price elasticity of demand = 2
Income elasticity of demand = 1.5

The supply of Beetles is elastic. Based on this information, are the following statements true or false? Explain your reasoning.

a. A 10% increase in the price of a Beetle will reduce the quantity demanded by 20%.

b. An increase in consumer income will increase the price and quantity of Beetles sold. Since price elasticity of demand is greater than 1, total revenue will go down.

8. In each of the following cases, do you think the price elasticity of supply is (i) perfectly elastic; (ii) perfectly inelastic; (iii) elastic, but not perfectly elastic; or (iv) inelastic, but not perfectly inelastic? Explain using a diagram.

a. An increase in demand this summer for luxury cruises leads to a huge jump in the sales price of a cabin on the *Queen Mary 2*.

b. The price of a kilowatt of electricity is the same during periods of high electricity demand as during periods of low electricity demand.

c. Fewer people want to fly during February than during any other month. The airlines cancel about 10% of their flights as ticket prices fall about 20% during this month.

d. Owners of vacation homes in Maine rent them out during the summer. Due to the soft economy this year, a 30% decline in the price of a vacation rental leads more than half of homeowners to occupy their vacation homes themselves during the summer.

9. Use an elasticity concept to explain each of the following observations.

a. During economic booms, the number of new personal care businesses, such as gyms and tanning salons, is proportionately greater than the number of other new businesses, such as grocery stores.

b. Cement is the primary building material in Mexico. After new technology makes cement cheaper to produce, the supply curve for the Mexican cement industry becomes relatively flatter.

c. Some goods that were once considered luxuries, like a telephone, are now considered virtual necessities. As a result, the demand curve for telephone services has become steeper over time.

d. Consumers in a less developed country like Guatemala spend proportionately more of their income on equipment for producing things at home, like sewing machines, than consumers in a more developed country like Canada.

10. There is a debate about whether sterile hypodermic needles should be passed out free of charge in cities with high drug use. Proponents argue that doing so will reduce the incidence of diseases, such as HIV/AIDS, that are often spread by needle sharing among drug users. Opponents believe that doing so will encourage more drug use by reducing the risks of this behavior. As an economist asked to assess the policy, you must know the following: (i) how responsive the spread of diseases like HIV/AIDS is to the price of sterile needles and (ii) how responsive drug use is to the price of sterile needles. Assuming that you know these two things, use the concepts of price elasticity of demand for sterile needles and the cross-price elasticity between drugs and sterile needles to answer the following questions.

a. In what circumstances do you believe this is a beneficial policy?

b. In what circumstances do you believe this is a bad policy?

11. Worldwide, the average coffee grower has increased the amount of acreage under cultivation over the past few years. The result has been that the average coffee plantation produces significantly more coffee than it did 10 to 20 years ago. Unfortunately for the growers, however, this has also been a period in which their total revenues have plunged. In terms of an elasticity, what must be true for these events to have occurred? Illustrate these events with a diagram, indicating the quantity effect and the price effect that gave rise to these events.

12. According to data from the U.S. Department of Energy, sales of the fuel-efficient Toyota Prius hybrid fell from 158,574 vehicles sold in 2008 to 139,682 in 2009. Over the same period, according to data from the U.S. Energy Information Administration, the average price of regular gasoline fell from \$3.27 to \$2.35 per gallon. Using the midpoint method, calculate the cross-price elasticity of demand between Toyota Prii (the official plural of "Prius" is "Prii") and regular gasoline. According to your estimate of the cross-price elasticity, are the two goods complements or substitutes? Does your answer make sense?

13. The United States imposes an excise tax on the sale of domestic airline tickets. Let's assume that in 2010 the total excise tax was \$6.10 per airline ticket (consisting of the \$3.60 flight segment tax plus the \$2.50 September 11 fee). According to data from the Bureau of Transportation Statistics, in 2010, 630 million passengers traveled on domestic airline trips at an average price of \$337 per trip. The accompanying table shows the supply and demand schedules for airline trips. The quantity demanded at the average price of \$337 is actual data; the rest is hypothetical.

Price of trip	Quantity of trips demanded (millions)	Quantity of trips supplied (millions)
\$337.02	629	686
337.00	630	685
335.00	680	680
330.90	780	630
330.82	900	629

a. What is the government tax revenue in 2010 from the excise tax?

b. On January 1, 2011, the total excise tax increased to \$6.20 per ticket. What is the quantity of tickets transacted now? What is the average ticket price now? What is the 2011 government tax revenue?

c. Does this increase in the excise tax increase or decrease government tax revenue?

14. In 1990, the United States began to levy a tax on sales of luxury cars. For simplicity, assume that the tax was an excise tax of \$6,000 per car. The accompanying figure shows hypothetical demand and supply curves for luxury cars.

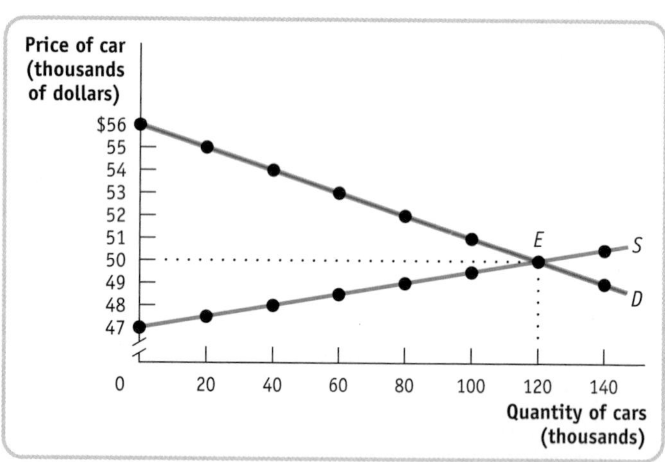

a. Under the tax, what is the price paid by consumers? What is the price received by producers? What is the government tax revenue from the excise tax?

Over time, the tax on luxury automobiles was slowly phased out (and completely eliminated in 2002). Suppose that the excise tax falls from \$6,000 per car to \$4,500 per car.

b. After the reduction in the excise tax from \$6,000 to \$4,500 per car, what is the price paid by consumers? What is the price received by producers? What is tax revenue now?

c. Compare the tax revenue created by the taxes in parts a and b. What accounts for the change in tax revenue from the reduction in the excise tax?

EXTEND YOUR UNDERSTANDING

15. The accompanying table lists the cross-price elasticities of demand for several goods, where the percent quantity change is measured for the first good of the pair, and the percent price change is measured for the second good.

Good	Cross-price elasticities of demand
Air-conditioning units and kilowatts of electricity	−0.34
Coke and Pepsi	+0.63
High-fuel-consuming sport-utility vehicles (SUVs) and gasoline	−0.28
McDonald's burgers and Burger King burgers	+0.82
Butter and margarine	+1.54

a. Explain the sign of each of the cross-price elasticities. What does it imply about the relationship between the two goods in question?

b. Compare the absolute values of the cross-price elasticities and explain their magnitudes. For example, why is the cross-price elasticity of McDonald's burgers and Burger King burgers less than the cross-price elasticity of butter and margarine?

c. Use the information in the table to calculate how a 5% increase in the price of Pepsi affects the quantity of Coke demanded.

d. Use the information in the table to calculate how a 10% decrease in the price of gasoline affects the quantity of SUVs demanded.

16. A recent report by the U.S. Centers for Disease Control and Prevention (CDC), published in the CDC's *Morbidity and Mortality Weekly Report,* studied the effect of an increase in the price of beer on the incidence of new cases of sexually transmitted disease in young adults. In particular, the researchers analyzed the responsiveness of gonorrhea cases to a tax-induced increase in the price of beer. The report concluded that "the . . . analysis suggested that a beer tax increase of $0.20 per six-pack could reduce overall gonorrhea rates by 8.9%." Assume that a six-pack costs $5.90 before the price increase. Use the midpoint method to determine the percent increase in the price of a six-pack, and then calculate the cross-price elasticity of demand between beer and incidence of gonorrhea. According to your estimate of this cross-price elasticity of demand, are beer and gonorrhea complements or substitutes?

17. All states impose excise taxes on gasoline. According to data from the Federal Highway Administration, the state of California imposes an excise tax of $0.18 per gallon of gasoline. In 2009, gasoline sales in California totaled 14.8 billion gallons. What was California's tax revenue from the gasoline excise tax? If California doubled the excise tax, would tax revenue double? Why or why not?

18. The U.S. government would like to help the American auto industry compete against foreign automakers that sell trucks in the United States. It can do this by imposing an excise tax on each foreign truck sold in the United States. The hypothetical pre-tax demand and supply schedules for imported trucks are given in the accompanying table.

Price of imported truck	Quantity of imported trucks (thousands)	
	Quantity demanded	Quantity supplied
$32,000	100	400
31,000	200	350
30,000	300	300
29,000	400	250
28,000	500	200
27,000	600	150

a. In the absence of government interference, what is the equilibrium price of an imported truck? The equilibrium quantity? Illustrate with a diagram.

b. Assume that the government imposes an excise tax of $3,000 per imported truck. Illustrate the effect of this excise tax in your diagram from part a. How many imported trucks are now purchased and at what price? How much does the foreign automaker receive per truck?

c. Calculate the government revenue raised by the excise tax in part b. Illustrate it on your diagram.

d. How does the excise tax on imported trucks benefit American automakers? Whom does it hurt? How does inefficiency arise from this government policy?

BUSINESS CASE • The Chicago Board of Trade

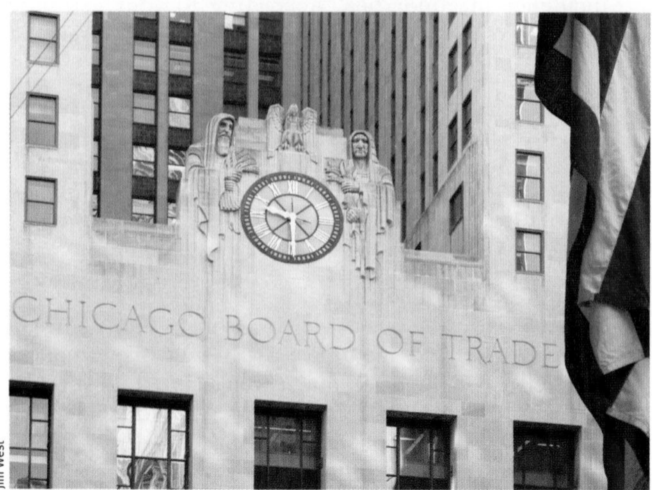

Jim West

Around the world, commodities are bought and sold on "exchanges," markets organized in a specific location, where buyers and sellers meet to trade. But it wasn't always like this.

The first modern commodity exchange was the Chicago Board of Trade, founded in 1848. At the time, the United States was already a major wheat producer. And St. Louis, not Chicago, was the leading city of the American West and the dominant location for wheat trading. But the St. Louis wheat market suffered from a major flaw: there was no central marketplace, no specific location where everyone met to buy and sell wheat. Instead, sellers would sell their grain from various warehouses or from stacked sacks of grain on the river levee. Buyers would wander around town, looking for the best price.

In Chicago, however, sellers had a better idea. The Chicago Board of Trade, an association of the city's leading grain dealers, created a much more efficient method for trading wheat. There, traders gathered in one place—the "pit"—where they called out offers to sell and accepted offers to buy. The Board guaranteed that these contracts would be fulfilled, removing the need for the wheat to be physically in place when a trade was agreed upon.

This system meant that buyers could very quickly find sellers and vice-versa, reducing the cost of doing business. It also ensured that everyone could see the latest price, leading the price to rise or fall quickly in response to market conditions. For example, news of bad weather in a wheat-growing area hundreds of miles away would send the price in the Chicago pit soaring in a matter of minutes.

The Chicago Board of Trade went on to become the world's most important trading center for wheat and many other agricultural commodities, a distinction it retains to this day. And the Board's rise helped the rise of Chicago, too. The city, as Carl Sandburg put it in his famous poem, "Chicago," became:

Hog Butcher for the World,
Tool Maker, Stacker of Wheat,
Player with Railroads and the Nation's Freight Handler;
Stormy, husky, brawling,
City of the Big Shoulders

By 1890, Chicago had more than a million people, second only to New York and far out-pacing St. Louis. Making a better market, it turned out, was very good business indeed.

QUESTIONS FOR THOUGHT

1. In Chapter 3 we mentioned how prices can vary in a tourist trap. Which market, St. Louis or Chicago, was more likely to behave like a tourist trap? Explain.
2. What was the advantage to buyers from buying their wheat in the Chicago pit instead of in St. Louis? What was the advantage to sellers?
3. Based on what you have learned from this case, explain why eBay is like the Chicago pit. Why has it been so successful as a marketplace for second-hand items compared to a market composed of various flea markets and dealers?

BUSINESS CASE • Medallion Financial: Cruising Right Along

Owaki/Kulla/Corbis

Back in 1937, before New York City froze its number of taxi medallions, Andrew Murstein's immigrant grandfather bought his first one for $10. Over time, the grandfather accumulated 500 medallions, which he rented to other drivers. Those 500 taxi medallions became the foundation for Medallion Financial: the company that would eventually pass to Andrew, its current president.

With a market value of over $250 million in late 2012, Medallion Financial has shifted its major line of business from renting out medallions to financing the purchase of new ones, lending money to those who want to buy a medallion but don't have the sizable amount of cash required to do so. Murstein believes that he is helping people who, like his Polish immigrant grandfather, want to buy a piece of the American dream.

Andrew Murstein carefully watches the value of a New York City taxi medallion: the more one costs, the more demand there is for loans from Medallion Financial, and the more interest the company makes on the loan. A loan from Medallion Financial is secured by the value of the medallion itself. If the borrower is unable to repay the loan, Medallion Financial takes possession of his or her medallion and resells it to offset the cost of the loan default. As of 2012, the value of a medallion has risen faster than stocks, oil, and gold. Over the past two decades, from 1990 through fall 2012, the value of a medallion rose 450% compared to 330% for an index of stocks.

But medallion prices can fluctuate dramatically, threatening profits. During periods of a very strong economy, such as 1999 and 2001, the price of New York taxi medallions fell as drivers found jobs in other sectors. When the New York economy tanked in the aftermath of 9/11, the price of a medallion fell to $180,000, its lowest level in 12 years. In 2004, medallion owners were concerned about the impending sale by the New York City Taxi and Limousine Commission of an additional 900 medallions. As Peter Hernandez, a worried New York cabdriver who financed his medallion with a loan from Medallion Financial, said at the time: "If they pump new taxis into the industry, it devalues my medallion. It devalues my daily income, too."

Yet Murstein has always been optimistic that medallions would hold their value. He believed that a 25% fare increase would offset potential losses in their value caused by the sale of new medallions. In addition, more medallions would mean more loans for his company. As of 2012, Murstein's optimism had been justified. Because of the financial crisis of 2007–2009, many New York companies cut back the limousine services they ordinarily provided to their employees, forcing them to take taxis instead. As a result, the price of a medallion rose to an astonishing $713,000 in August 2012. And investors have noticed the value in Medallion Financial's line of business: from August 2011 to August 2012, shares of Medallion Financial have risen 26%.

QUESTIONS FOR THOUGHT

1. How does Medallion Financial benefit from the restriction on the number of New York taxi medallions?
2. What will be the effect on Medallion Financial if New York companies resume widespread use of limousine services for their employees? What is the economic motivation that prompts companies to offer this perk to their employees? (Note that it is very difficult and expensive to own a personal car in New York City.)
3. Predict the effect on Medallion Financial's business if New York City eliminates restrictions on the number of taxis.

BUSINESS CASE • The Airline Industry: Fly Less, Charge More

Chris Sweda/Chicago Tribune/MCT via Getty Images

The recession that began in 2008 hit the airline industry very hard as both businesses and households cut back their travel plans. According to the International Air Transport Association, the industry lost $11 billion in 2008. However, by 2009, despite the fact that the economy was still extremely weak and airline traffic was still well below normal, the industry's profitability began to rebound. And by 2010, even in the midst of continued economic weakness, the airline industry's prospects had definitely recovered, with the industry achieving an $8.9 billion profit that year, with continued profitability in 2011. As Gary Kelly, CEO of Southwest Airlines said, "The industry is in the best position—certainly in a decade—to post profitability."

How did the airline industry achieve such a dramatic turnaround? Simple: fly less and charge more. In 2011, fares were 14% higher than they had been the previous year, and flights were more crowded than they had been in decades, with fewer than one in five seats empty on domestic flights.

In addition to cutting back on the number of flights—particularly money-losing ones—airlines implemented more extreme variations in ticket prices based on when a flight departed and when the ticket was purchased. For example, the cheapest day to fly is Wednesday, with Friday and Saturday the most expensive days to travel. The first flight of the morning (the one that requires you to get up at 4 A.M.) is cheaper than flights departing the rest of the day. And the cheapest time to buy a ticket is Tuesday at 3 P.M. Eastern Standard Time, with tickets purchased over the weekend carrying the highest prices.

And it doesn't stop there. As every beleaguered traveler knows, airlines have tacked on a wide variety of new fees and increased old ones—fees for food, for a blanket, for checked bags, for carry-on bags, for the right to board a flight first, for the right to choose your seat in advance, and so on. Airlines have also gotten more inventive in imposing fees that are hard for travelers to track in advance—such as claiming that fares have not risen during the holidays while imposing a "holiday surcharge." In 2011, airlines collected more than $22.6 billion from fees for checking baggage and changing tickets, up 66% from 2010.

But the question in the minds of industry analysts is whether airlines can manage to maintain their currently high levels of profitability. In the past, as travel demand picked up, airlines increased capacity—added seats—too quickly, leading to falling airfares. "The wild card is always capacity discipline," says William Swelbar, an airline industry researcher. "All it takes is one carrier to begin to add capacity aggressively, and then we follow and we undo all the good work that's been done."

QUESTIONS FOR THOUGHT

1. How would you describe the price elasticity of demand for airline flights given the information in this case? Explain.
2. Using the concept of elasticity, explain why airlines would create such great variations in the price of a ticket depending on when it is purchased and the day and time the flight departs. Assume that some people are willing to spend time shopping for deals as well as fly at inconvenient times, but others are not.
3. Using the concept of elasticity, explain why airlines have imposed fees on things such as checked bags. Why might they try to hide or disguise fees?
4. Use an elasticity concept to explain under what conditions the airline industry will be able to maintain its high profitability in the future. Explain.

CHAPTER 6

Behind the Supply Curve: Inputs and Costs

THE FARMER'S MARGIN

Terrance Klassen/AgeFotostock

How intensively an acre of land is worked—a decision at the margin—depends on the price of wheat a farmer faces.

WHAT YOU WILL LEARN IN THIS CHAPTER

- The importance of the firm's **production function,** the relationship between quantity of inputs and quantity of output
- Why production is often subject to **diminishing returns to inputs**
- The various types of costs a firm faces and how they generate the firm's marginal and average cost curves
- Why a firm's costs may differ in the **short run** versus the **long run**
- How the firm's technology of production can generate **increasing returns to scale**

"O BEAUTIFUL FOR SPACIOUS skies, for amber waves of grain." So begins the song "America the Beautiful." And those amber waves of grain are for real: though farmers are now only a small minority of America's population, our agricultural industry is immensely productive and feeds much of the world.

If you look at agricultural statistics, however, something may seem a bit surprising: when it comes to yield per acre, U.S. farmers are often nowhere near the top. For example, farmers in Western European countries grow about three times as much wheat per acre as their U.S. counterparts. Are the Europeans better at growing wheat than we are?

No: European farmers are very skillful, but no more so than Americans. They produce more wheat per acre because they employ more inputs—more fertilizer and, especially, more labor—per acre. Of course, this means that European farmers have higher costs than their American counterparts. But because of government policies, European farmers receive a much higher price for their wheat than American farmers. This gives them an incentive to use more inputs and to expend more effort at the margin to increase the crop yield per acre.

Notice our use of the phrase "at the margin." Like most decisions that involve a comparison of benefits and costs, decisions about inputs and production involve a comparison of marginal quantities—the marginal cost versus the marginal benefit of producing a bit more from each acre.

In this chapter and in Chapter 7, we will show how the *principle of marginal analysis* can be used to understand these output decisions—decisions that lie behind the supply curve. The first step in this analysis is to show how the relationship between a firm's inputs and its output—its *production function*—determines its *cost curves,* the relationship between cost and quantity of output produced. That is what we do in this chapter. In Chapter 7, we will use our understanding of the firm's cost curves to derive the individual and the market supply curves. ■

A **production function** is the relationship between the quantity of inputs a firm uses and the quantity of output it produces.

A **fixed input** is an input whose quantity is fixed for a period of time and cannot be varied.

A **variable input** is an input whose quantity the firm can vary at any time.

The **long run** is the time period in which all inputs can be varied.

The **short run** is the time period in which at least one input is fixed.

The **total product curve** shows how the quantity of output depends on the quantity of the variable input, for a given quantity of the fixed input.

The Production Function

A *firm* is an organization that produces goods or services for sale. To do this, it must transform inputs into output. The quantity of output a firm produces depends on the quantity of inputs; this relationship is known as the firm's **production function.** As we'll see, a firm's production function underlies its *cost curves.* As a first step, let's look at the characteristics of a hypothetical production function.

Inputs and Output

To understand the concept of a production function, let's consider a farm that we assume, for the sake of simplicity, produces only one output, wheat, and uses only two inputs, land and labor. This particular farm is owned by a couple named George and Martha. They hire workers to do the actual physical labor on the farm. Moreover, we will assume that all potential workers are of the same quality—they are all equally knowledgeable and capable of performing farmwork.

George and Martha's farm sits on 10 acres of land; no more acres are available to them, and they are currently unable to either increase or decrease the size of their farm by selling, buying, or leasing acreage. Land here is what economists call a **fixed input**—an input whose quantity is fixed for a period of time and cannot be varied. George and Martha are, however, free to decide how many workers to hire. The labor provided by these workers is called a **variable input**—an input whose quantity the firm can vary at any time.

In reality, whether or not the quantity of an input is really fixed depends on the time horizon. In the **long run**—that is, given that a long enough period of time has elapsed—firms can adjust the quantity of any input. For example, in the long run, George and Martha can vary the amount of land they farm by buying or selling land. So there are no fixed inputs in the long run. In contrast, the **short run** is defined as the time period during which at least one input is fixed. Later in this chapter, we'll look more carefully at the distinction between the short run and the long run. But for now, we will restrict our attention to the short run and assume that at least one input is fixed.

George and Martha know that the quantity of wheat they produce depends on the number of workers they hire. Using modern farming techniques, one worker can cultivate the 10-acre farm, albeit not very intensively. When an additional worker is added, the land is divided equally among all the workers: each worker has 5 acres to cultivate when 2 workers are employed, each cultivates 3⅓ acres when 3 are employed, and so on. So as additional workers are employed, the 10 acres of land are cultivated more intensively and more bushels of wheat are produced. The relationship between the quantity of labor and the quantity of output, for a given amount of the fixed input, constitutes the farm's production function. The production function for George and Martha's farm, where land is the fixed input and labor is a variable input, is shown in the first two columns of the table in Figure 6-1; the diagram there shows the same information graphically. The curve in Figure 6-1 shows how the quantity of output depends on the quantity of the variable input, for a given quantity of the fixed input; it is called the farm's **total product curve.** The physical quantity of output, bushels of wheat, is measured on the vertical axis; the quantity of the variable input, labor (that is, the number of workers employed), is measured on the horizontal axis. The total product curve here slopes upward, reflecting the fact that more bushels of wheat are produced as more workers are employed.

FIGURE 6-1 **Production Function and Total Product Curve for George and Martha's Farm**

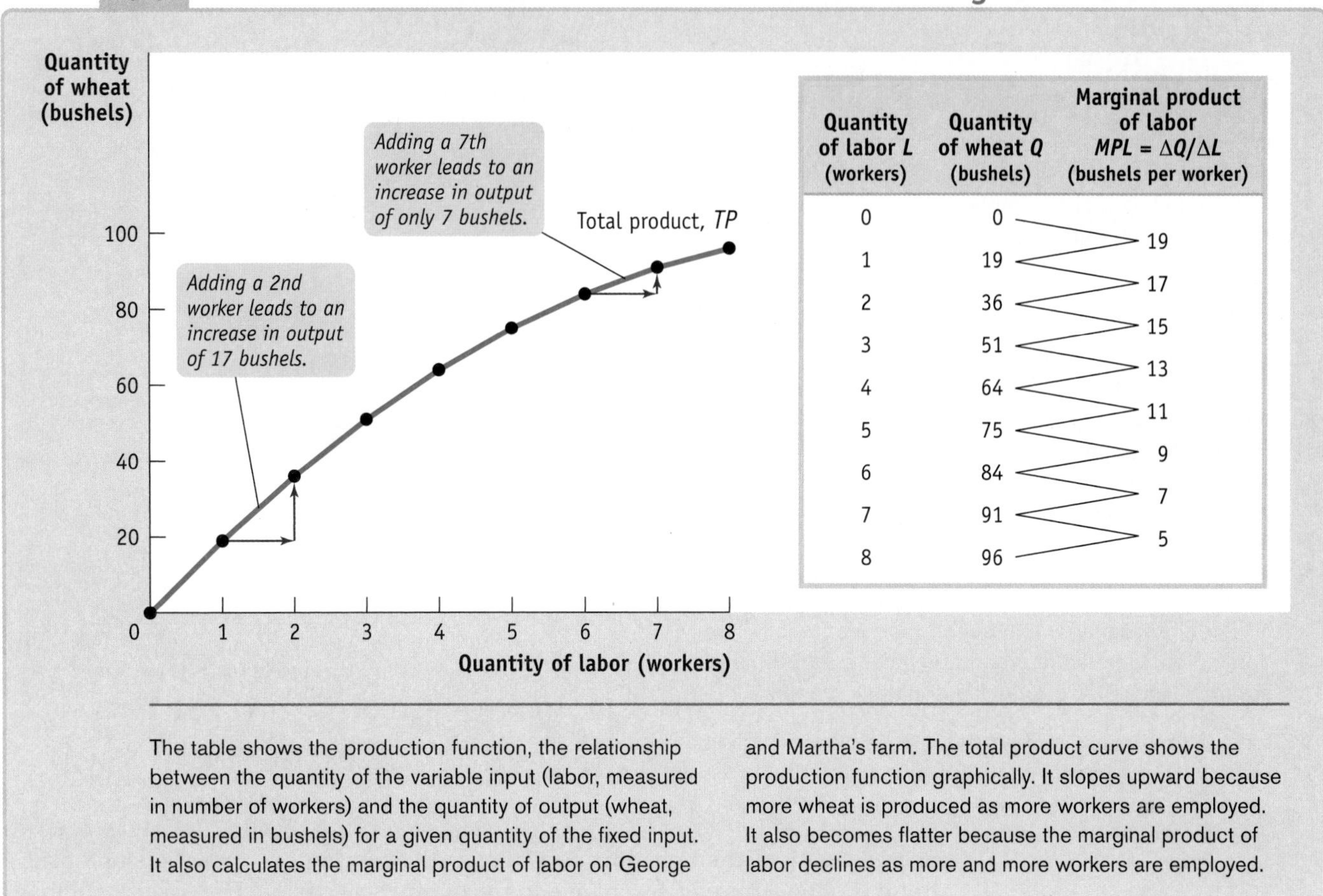

Quantity of labor L (workers)	Quantity of wheat Q (bushels)	Marginal product of labor $MPL = \Delta Q/\Delta L$ (bushels per worker)
0	0	
		19
1	19	
		17
2	36	
		15
3	51	
		13
4	64	
		11
5	75	
		9
6	84	
		7
7	91	
		5
8	96	

The table shows the production function, the relationship between the quantity of the variable input (labor, measured in number of workers) and the quantity of output (wheat, measured in bushels) for a given quantity of the fixed input. It also calculates the marginal product of labor on George and Martha's farm. The total product curve shows the production function graphically. It slopes upward because more wheat is produced as more workers are employed. It also becomes flatter because the marginal product of labor declines as more and more workers are employed.

Although the total product curve in Figure 6-1 slopes upward along its entire length, the slope isn't constant: as you move up the curve to the right, it flattens out. To understand why the slope changes, look at the third column of the table in Figure 6-1, which shows the *change in the quantity of output* that is generated by adding one more worker. This is called the *marginal product* of labor, or *MPL:* the additional quantity of output from using one more unit of labor (where one unit of labor is equal to one worker). In general, the **marginal product** of an input is the additional quantity of output that is produced by using one more unit of that input.

In this example, we have data on changes in output at intervals of 1 worker. Sometimes data aren't available in increments of 1 unit—for example, you might have information only on the quantity of output when there are 40 workers and when there are 50 workers. In this case, we use the following equation to calculate the marginal product of labor:

$$\text{(6-1)}\quad \begin{array}{l}\text{Marginal}\\ \text{product}\\ \text{of labor}\end{array} = \begin{array}{l}\text{Change in quantity of}\\ \text{output produced by one}\\ \text{additional unit of labor}\end{array} = \frac{\text{Change in quantity of output}}{\text{Change in quantity of labor}}$$

or

$$MPL = \frac{\Delta Q}{\Delta L}$$

In this equation, Δ, the Greek uppercase delta, represents the change in a variable.

Now we can explain the significance of the slope of the total product curve: it is equal to the marginal product of labor. The slope of a line is equal to "rise"

The **marginal product** of an input is the additional quantity of output that is produced by using one more unit of that input.

WHEAT YIELDS AROUND THE WORLD

Wheat yields differ substantially around the world. The disparity between France and the United States that you see in this graph is particularly striking, given that they are both wealthy countries with comparable agricultural technology. Yet the reason for that disparity is straightforward: differing government policies. In the United States, farmers receive payments from the government to supplement their incomes, but European farmers benefit from price floors. Since European farmers get higher prices for their output than American farmers, they employ more variable inputs and produce significantly higher yields. Interestingly, in poor countries like Uganda and Ethiopia, foreign aid can lead to significantly depressed yields. Foreign aid from wealthy countries has often taken the form of surplus food, which depresses local market prices, severely hurting the local agriculture that poor countries normally depend on. Charitable organizations like OXFAM have asked wealthy food-producing countries to modify their aid policies—principally, to give aid in cash rather than in food products except in the case of acute food shortages—to avoid this problem.

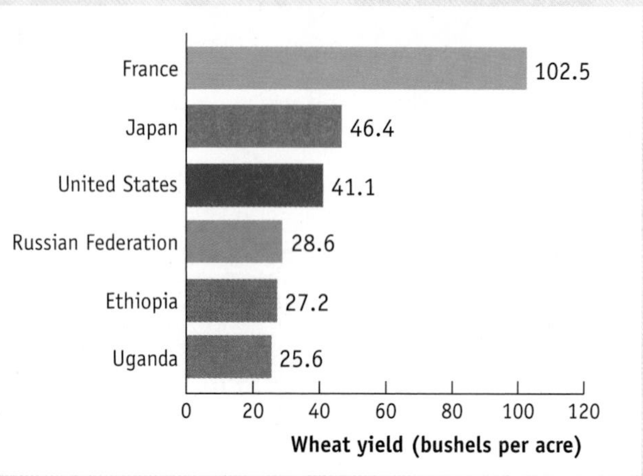

Source: Food and Agriculture Organization of the United Nations. Data are from 2010.

over "run" (see the appendix to Chapter 2). This implies that the slope of the total product curve is the change in the quantity of output (the "rise", ΔQ) divided by the change in the quantity of labor (the "run", ΔL). And this, as we can see from Equation 6-1, is simply the marginal product of labor. So in Figure 6-1, the fact that the marginal product of the first worker is 19 also means that the slope of the total product curve in going from 0 to 1 worker is 19. Similarly, the slope of the total product curve in going from 1 to 2 workers is the same as the marginal product of the second worker, 17, and so on.

In this example, the marginal product of labor steadily declines as more workers are hired—that is, each successive worker adds less to output than the previous worker. So as employment increases, the total product curve gets flatter.

Figure 6-2 shows how the marginal product of labor depends on the number of workers employed on the farm. The marginal product of labor, *MPL,* is measured on the vertical axis in units of physical output—bushels of wheat—produced per additional worker, and the number of workers employed is measured on the horizontal axis. You can see from the table in Figure 6-1 that if 5 workers are employed instead of 4, output rises from 64 to 75 bushels; in this case the marginal product of labor is 11 bushels—the same number found in Figure 6-2. To indicate that 11 bushels is the marginal product when employment rises from 4 to 5, we place the point corresponding to that information halfway between 4 and 5 workers.

There are **diminishing returns to an input** when an increase in the quantity of that input, holding the levels of all other inputs fixed, leads to a decline in the marginal product of that input.

In this example the marginal product of labor falls as the number of workers increases. That is, there are *diminishing returns to labor* on George and Martha's farm. In general, there are **diminishing returns to an input** when an increase in the quantity of that input, holding the quantity of all other inputs fixed, reduces that input's marginal product. Due to diminishing returns to labor, the *MPL* curve is negatively sloped.

FIGURE 6-2 Marginal Product of Labor Curve for George and Martha's Farm

The marginal product of labor curve plots each worker's marginal product, the increase in the quantity of output generated by each additional worker. The change in the quantity of output is measured on the vertical axis and the number of workers employed on the horizontal axis. The first worker employed generates an increase in output of 19 bushels, the second worker generates an increase of 17 bushels, and so on. The curve slopes downward due to diminishing returns to labor.

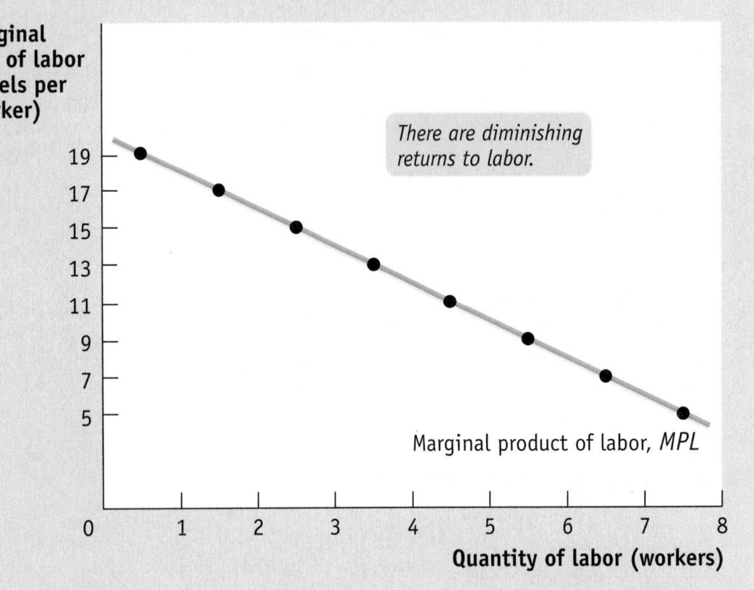

To grasp why diminishing returns can occur, think about what happens as George and Martha add more and more workers without increasing the number of acres of land. As the number of workers increases, the land is farmed more intensively and the number of bushels produced increases. But each additional worker is working with a smaller share of the 10 acres—the fixed input—than the previous worker. As a result, the additional worker cannot produce as much output as the previous worker. So it's not surprising that the marginal product of the additional worker falls.

The crucial point to emphasize about diminishing returns is that, like many propositions in economics, it is an "other things equal" proposition: each successive unit of an input will raise production by less than the last *if the quantity of all other inputs is held fixed.*

What would happen if the levels of other inputs were allowed to change? You can see the answer illustrated in Figure 6-3. Panel (a) shows two total product curves, TP_{10} and TP_{20}. TP_{10} is the farm's total product curve when its total area is 10 acres (the same curve as in Figure 6-1). TP_{20} is the total product curve when the farm has increased to 20 acres. Except when 0 workers are employed, TP_{20} lies everywhere above TP_{10} because with more acres available, any given number of workers produces more output. Panel (b) shows the corresponding marginal product of labor curves. MPL_{10} is the marginal product of labor curve given 10 acres to cultivate (the same curve as in Figure 6-2), and MPL_{20} is the marginal product of labor curve given 20 acres. Both curves slope downward because, in each case, the amount of land is fixed, albeit at different levels. But MPL_{20} lies everywhere above MPL_{10}, reflecting the fact that the marginal product of the same worker is higher when he or she has more of the fixed input to work with.

Figure 6-3 demonstrates a general result: the position of the total product curve of a given input depends on the quantities of other inputs. If you change the quantity of the other inputs, both the total product curve and the marginal product curve of the remaining input will shift.

PITFALLS

WHAT'S A UNIT?

The marginal product of labor (or any other input) is defined as the increase in the quantity of output when you increase the quantity of that input by one unit. But what do we mean by a "unit" of labor? Is it an additional hour of labor, an additional week, or a person-year?

The answer is that it doesn't matter, *as long as you are consistent.* One common source of error in economics is getting units confused—say, comparing the output added by an additional *hour* of labor with the cost of employing a worker for a *week.* Whatever units you use, always be careful that you use the same units throughout your analysis of any problem.

FIGURE 6-3 Total Product, Marginal Product, and the Fixed Input

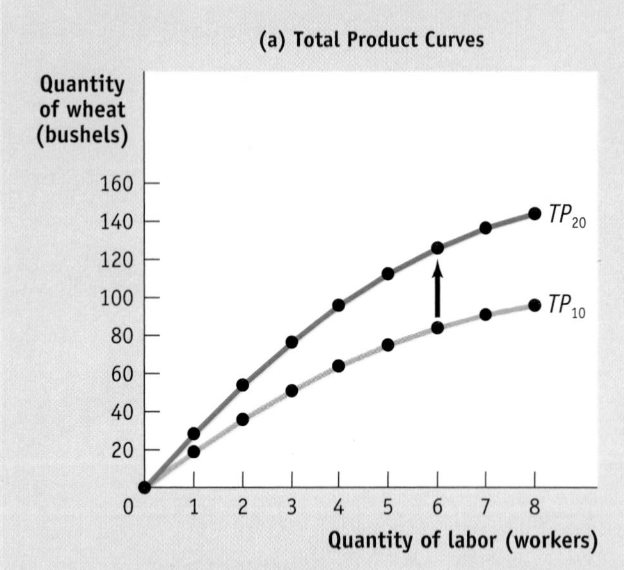

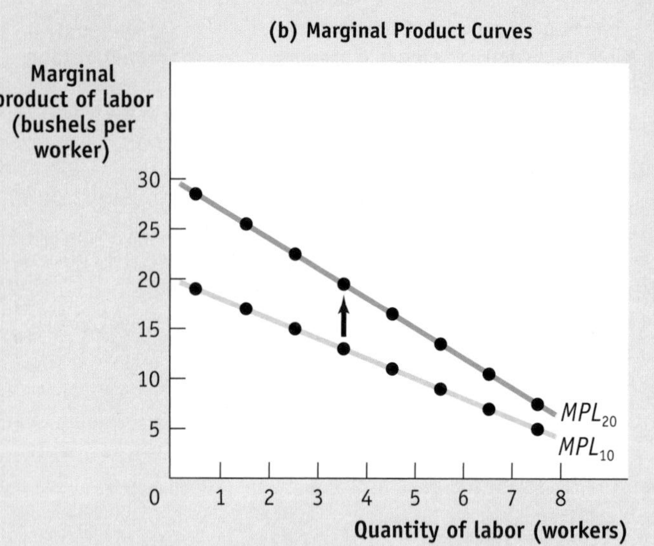

This figure shows how the quantity of output and the marginal product of labor depend on the level of the fixed input. Panel (a) shows two total product curves for George and Martha's farm, TP_{10} when their farm is 10 acres and TP_{20} when it is 20 acres. With more land, each worker can produce more wheat. So an increase in the fixed input shifts the total product curve up from TP_{10} to TP_{20}. This implies that the marginal product of each worker is higher when the farm is 20 acres than when it is 10 acres. Panel (b) shows the marginal product of labor curves. The increase in acreage also shifts the marginal product of labor curve up from MPL_{10} to MPL_{20}. Note that both marginal product of labor curves still slope downward due to diminishing returns to labor.

From the Production Function to Cost Curves

Once George and Martha know their production function, they know the relationship between inputs of labor and land and output of wheat. But if they want to maximize their profits, they need to translate this knowledge into information about the relationship between the quantity of output and cost. Let's see how they can do this.

To translate information about a firm's production function into information about its costs, we need to know how much the firm must pay for its inputs. We will assume that George and Martha face a cost of $400 for the use of the land. It is irrelevant whether George and Martha must rent the land for $400 from someone else or whether they own the land themselves and forgo earning $400 from renting it to someone else. Either way, they pay an opportunity cost of $400 by using the land to grow wheat. Moreover, since the land is a fixed input, the $400 George and Martha pay for it is a **fixed cost,** denoted by *FC*—a cost that does not depend on the quantity of output produced (in the short run). In business, fixed cost is often referred to as "overhead cost."

A **fixed cost** is a cost that does not depend on the quantity of output produced. It is the cost of the fixed input.

A **variable cost** is a cost that depends on the quantity of output produced. It is the cost of the variable input.

The **total cost** of producing a given quantity of output is the sum of the fixed cost and the variable cost of producing that quantity of output.

We also assume that George and Martha must pay each worker $200. Using their production function, George and Martha know that the number of workers they must hire depends on the amount of wheat they intend to produce. So the cost of labor, which is equal to the number of workers multiplied by $200, is a **variable cost,** denoted by *VC*—a cost that depends on the quantity of output produced. Adding the fixed cost and the variable cost of a given quantity of output gives the **total cost,** or *TC,* of that quantity of output. We can express the relationship among fixed cost, variable cost, and total cost as an equation:

(6-2) Total cost = Fixed cost + Variable cost

or

$$TC = FC + VC$$

The **total cost curve** shows how total cost depends on the quantity of output.

The table in Figure 6-4 shows how total cost is calculated for George and Martha's farm. The second column shows the number of workers employed, *L*. The third column shows the corresponding level of output, *Q*, taken from the table in Figure 6-1. The fourth column shows the variable cost, *VC*, equal to the number of workers multiplied by $200. The fifth column shows the fixed cost, *FC*, which is $400 regardless of how many workers are employed. The sixth column shows the total cost of output, *TC*, which is the variable cost plus the fixed cost.

The first column labels each row of the table with a letter, from *A* to *I*. These labels will be helpful in understanding our next step: drawing the **total cost curve,** a curve that shows how total cost depends on the quantity of output.

George and Martha's total cost curve is shown in the diagram in Figure 6-4, where the horizontal axis measures the quantity of output in bushels of wheat and the vertical axis measures total cost in dollars. Each point on the curve corresponds to one row of the table in Figure 6-4. For example, point *A* shows

FIGURE **6-4** Total Cost Curve for George and Martha's Farm

The table shows the variable cost, fixed cost, and total cost for various output quantities on George and Martha's 10-acre farm. The total cost curve shows how total cost (measured on the vertical axis) depends on the quantity of output (measured on the horizontal axis). The labeled points on the curve correspond to the rows of the table. The total cost curve slopes upward because the number of workers employed, and hence total cost, increases as the quantity of output increases. The curve gets steeper as output increases due to diminishing returns to labor.

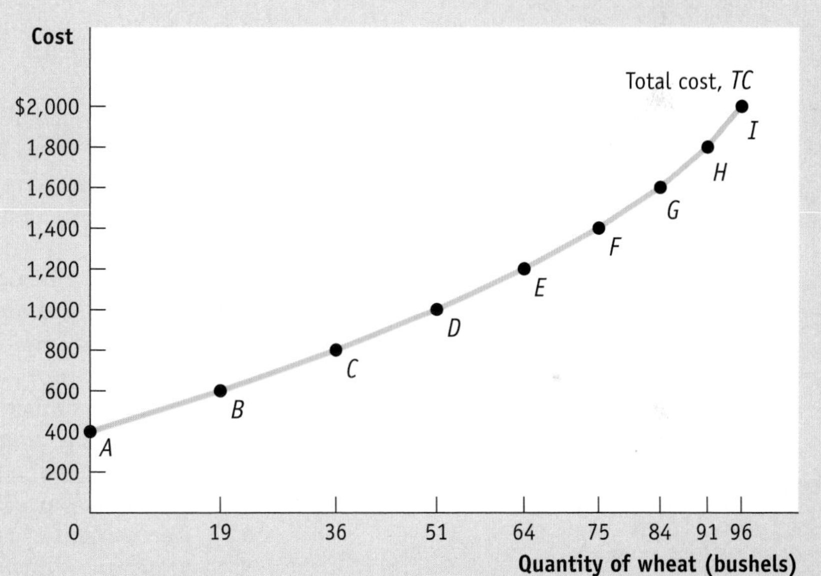

Point on graph	Quantity of labor *L* (workers)	Quantity of wheat *Q* (bushels)	Variable cost *VC*	Fixed cost *FC*	Total cost *TC = FC + VC*
A	0	0	$0	$400	$400
B	1	19	200	400	600
C	2	36	400	400	800
D	3	51	600	400	1,000
E	4	64	800	400	1,200
F	5	75	1,000	400	1,400
G	6	84	1,200	400	1,600
H	7	91	1,400	400	1,800
I	8	96	1,600	400	2,000

the situation when 0 workers are employed: output is 0, and total cost is equal to fixed cost, \$400. Similarly, point *B* shows the situation when 1 worker is employed: output is 19 bushels, and total cost is \$600, equal to the sum of \$400 in fixed cost and \$200 in variable cost.

Like the total product curve, the total cost curve slopes upward: due to the variable cost, the more output produced, the higher the farm's total cost. But unlike the total product curve, which gets flatter as employment rises, the total cost curve gets *steeper.* That is, the slope of the total cost curve is greater as the amount of output produced increases. As we will soon see, the steepening of the total cost curve is also due to diminishing returns to the variable input. Before we can understand this, we must first look at the relationships among several useful measures of cost.

ECONOMICS ➤ *IN ACTION*

THE MYTHICAL MAN-MONTH

The concept of diminishing returns to an input was first formulated by economists during the late eighteenth century. These economists, notably including Thomas Malthus, drew their inspiration from agricultural examples. Although still valid, examples drawn from agriculture can seem somewhat musty and old-fashioned in our modern economy.

However, the idea of diminishing returns to an input applies with equal force to the most modern of economic activities—such as, say, the design of software. In 1975 Frederick P. Brooks Jr., a project manager at IBM during the days when it dominated the computer business, published a book titled *The Mythical Man-Month* that soon became a classic—so much so that a special anniversary edition was published 20 years later.

The chapter that gave its title to the book is basically about diminishing returns to labor in the writing of software. Brooks observed that multiplying the number of programmers assigned to a project did not produce a proportionate reduction in the time it took to get the program written. A project that could be done by 1 programmer in 12 months could *not* be done by 12 programmers in 1 month—hence the "mythical man-month," the false notion that the number of lines of programming code produced was proportional to the number of code writers employed. In fact, above a certain number, adding another programmer on a project actually *increased* the time to completion.

FIGURE 6-5 The Mythical Man-Month

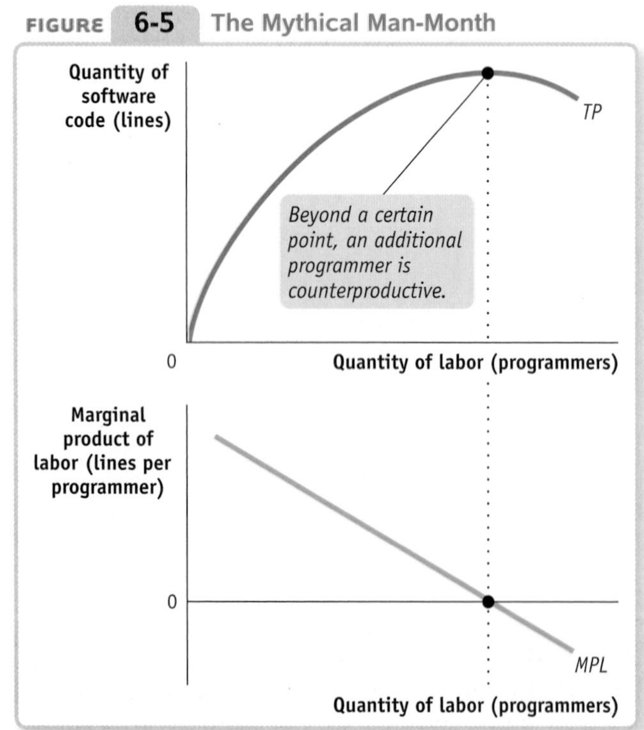

The argument of *The Mythical Man-Month* is summarized in Figure 6-5. The upper part of the figure shows how the quantity of the project's output, as measured by the number of lines of code produced per month, varies with the number of programmers. Each additional programmer accomplishes less than the previous one, and beyond a certain point an additional programmer is actually counterproductive. The lower part of the figure shows the marginal product of each successive programmer, which falls as more programmers are employed and eventually becomes negative. In other words, programming is subject to diminishing returns so severe that at some point more programmers actually have negative marginal product. The source of the diminishing returns lies in the nature of the production function for a programming project: each programmer must coordinate his or her work with that of all the other programmers on the project, leading to each person spending more and more time communicating with others as the number of programmers increases. In other words, other things equal, there are diminishing returns to labor. It is likely, however, that if fixed inputs devoted to programming projects are increased—say, installing a faster Wiki system—the problem of diminishing returns for additional programmers can be mitigated.

A reviewer of the reissued edition of *The Mythical Man-Month* summarized the reasons for these diminishing returns: "There is an inescapable overhead to yoking up programmers in parallel. The members of the team must 'waste time' attending meetings, drafting project plans, exchanging e-mail, negotiating interfaces, enduring performance reviews, and so on. . . . At Microsoft, there will be at least one team member that just designs T-shirts for the rest of the team to wear."

Quick Review

- The firm's **production function** is the relationship between quantity of inputs and output. The **total product curve** shows how the quantity of output depends on the quantity of the **variable input** for a given quantity of the **fixed input,** and its slope is equal to the **marginal product** of the variable input. In the **short run,** the fixed input cannot be varied; in the **long run** all inputs are variable.
- When the levels of all other inputs are fixed, **diminishing returns to an input** may arise, yielding a downward-sloping marginal product curve and a total product curve that becomes flatter as more output is produced.
- The **total cost** of a given quantity of output equals the **fixed cost** plus the **variable cost** of that output. The **total cost curve** becomes steeper as more output is produced due to diminishing returns to the variable input.

CHECK YOUR UNDERSTANDING 6-1

1. Bernie's ice-making company produces ice cubes using a 10-ton machine and electricity. The quantity of output, measured in terms of pounds of ice, is given in the accompanying table.
   a. What is the fixed input? What is the variable input?
   b. Construct a table showing the marginal product of the variable input. Does it show diminishing returns?
   c. Suppose a 50% increase in the size of the fixed input increases output by 100% for any given amount of the variable input. What is the fixed input now? Construct a table showing the quantity of output and marginal product in this case.

Quantity of electricity (kilowatts)	Quantity of ice (pounds)
0	0
1	1,000
2	1,800
3	2,400
4	2,800

Solutions appear at back of book.

Two Key Concepts: Marginal Cost and Average Cost

We've just learned how to derive a firm's total cost curve from its production function. Our next step is to take a deeper look at total cost by deriving two extremely useful measures: *marginal cost* and *average cost.* As we'll see, these two measures of the cost of production have a somewhat surprising relationship to each other. Moreover, they will prove to be vitally important in Chapter 7, where we will use them to analyze the firm's output decision and the market supply curve.

Marginal Cost

Marginal cost is the change in total cost generated by producing one more unit of output. We've already seen that the marginal product of an input is easiest to calculate if data on output are available in increments of one unit of that input. Similarly, marginal cost is easiest to calculate if data on total cost are available in increments of one unit of output. When the data come in less convenient increments, it's still possible to calculate marginal cost. But for the sake of simplicity, let's work with an example in which the data come in convenient one-unit increments.

Selena's Gourmet Salsas produces bottled salsa and Table 6-1 shows how its costs per day depend on the number of cases of salsa it produces per day. The firm has fixed cost of $108 per day, shown in the second column, which represents the daily cost of its food-preparation equipment. The third column shows the

The **marginal cost** of producing a good or service is the additional cost incurred by producing one more unit of that good or service.

TABLE 6-1 Costs at Selena's Gourmet Salsas

Quantity of salsa *Q* (cases)	Fixed cost *FC*	Variable cost *VC*	Total cost *TC* = *FC* + *VC*	Marginal cost of case *MC* = Δ*TC*/Δ*Q*
0	$108	$0	$108	
				$12
1	108	12	120	
				36
2	108	48	156	
				60
3	108	108	216	
				84
4	108	192	300	
				108
5	108	300	408	
				132
6	108	432	540	
				156
7	108	588	696	
				180
8	108	768	876	
				204
9	108	972	1,080	
				228
10	108	1,200	1,308	

variable cost, and the fourth column shows the total cost. Panel (a) of Figure 6-6 plots the total cost curve. Like the total cost curve for George and Martha's farm in Figure 6-4, this curve slopes upward, getting steeper as you move up it to the right.

The significance of the slope of the total cost curve is shown by the fifth column of Table 6-1, which calculates *marginal cost:* the additional cost of each additional unit. The general formula for marginal cost is:

$$\textbf{(6-3)}\ \text{Marginal cost} = \begin{array}{l}\text{Change in total cost}\\ \text{generated by one}\\ \text{additional unit of}\\ \text{output}\end{array} = \frac{\text{Change in total cost}}{\text{Change in quantity of output}}$$

or

$$MC = \frac{\Delta TC}{\Delta Q}$$

As in the case of marginal product, marginal cost is equal to "rise" (the increase in total cost) divided by "run" (the increase in the quantity of output). So just as marginal product is equal to the slope of the total product curve, marginal cost is equal to the slope of the total cost curve.

Now we can understand why the total cost curve gets steeper as we move up it to the right: as you can see in Table 6-1, marginal cost at Selena's Gourmet Salsas rises as output increases. Panel (b) of Figure 6-6 shows the marginal cost curve corresponding to the data in Table 6-1. Notice that, as in Figure 6-2, we plot the marginal cost for increasing output from 0 to 1 case of salsa halfway between 0 and 1, the marginal cost for increasing output from 1 to 2 cases of salsa halfway between 1 and 2, and so on.

Why does the marginal cost curve slope upward? Because there are diminishing returns to inputs in this example. As output increases, the marginal product of the variable input declines. This implies that more and more of the variable input must be used to produce each additional unit of output as the amount of output already produced rises. And since each unit of the variable input must be paid for, the additional cost per additional unit of output also rises.

In addition, recall that the flattening of the total product curve is also due to diminishing returns: the marginal product of an input falls as more of that input

FIGURE 6-6 Total Cost and Marginal Cost Curves for Selena's Gourmet Salsas

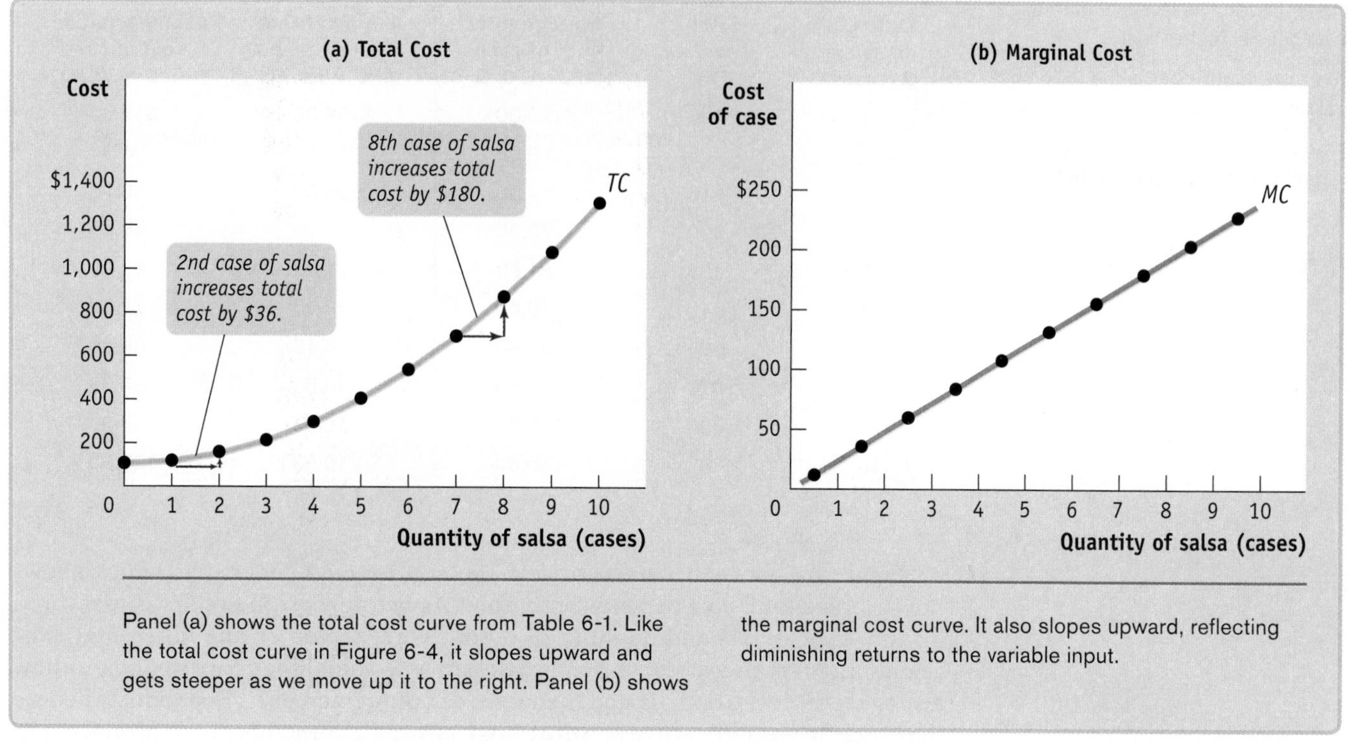

Panel (a) shows the total cost curve from Table 6-1. Like the total cost curve in Figure 6-4, it slopes upward and gets steeper as we move up it to the right. Panel (b) shows the marginal cost curve. It also slopes upward, reflecting diminishing returns to the variable input.

is used if the quantities of other inputs are fixed. The flattening of the total product curve as output increases and the steepening of the total cost curve as output increases are just flip-sides of the same phenomenon. That is, as output increases, the marginal cost of output also increases because the marginal product of the variable input decreases.

We will return to marginal cost in Chapter 7, when we consider the firm's profit-maximizing output decision. Our next step is to introduce another measure of cost: *average cost.*

Average Total Cost

In addition to total cost and marginal cost, it's useful to calculate another measure, **average total cost,** often simply called **average cost.** The average total cost is total cost divided by the quantity of output produced; that is, it is equal to total cost per unit of output. If we let *ATC* denote average total cost, the equation looks like this:

$$\textbf{(6-4)}\ ATC = \frac{\text{Total cost}}{\text{Quantity of output}} = \frac{TC}{Q}$$

Average total cost is important because it tells the producer how much the *average* or *typical* unit of output costs to produce. Marginal cost, meanwhile, tells the producer how much *one more* unit of output costs to produce. Although they may look very similar, these two measures of cost typically differ. And confusion between them is a major source of error in economics, both in the classroom and in real life, as illustrated by the upcoming Economics in Action.

Table 6-2 uses data from Selena's Gourmet Salsas to calculate average total cost. For example, the total cost of producing 4 cases of salsa is $300, consisting of $108 in fixed cost and $192 in variable cost (from Table 6-1). So the average total cost of producing 4 cases of salsa is $300/4 = $75. You can see from Table 6-2 that as quantity of output increases, average total cost first falls, then rises.

Average total cost, often referred to simply as **average cost,** is total cost divided by quantity of output produced.

A **U-shaped average total cost curve** falls at low levels of output, then rises at higher levels.

Average fixed cost is the fixed cost per unit of output.

Average variable cost is the variable cost per unit of output.

TABLE 6-2 Average Costs for Selena's Gourmet Salsas

Quantity of salsa Q (cases)	Total cost TC	Average total cost of case ATC = TC/Q	Average fixed cost of case AFC = FC/Q	Average variable cost of case AVC = VC/Q
1	$120	$120.00	$108.00	$12.00
2	156	78.00	54.00	24.00
3	216	72.00	36.00	36.00
4	300	75.00	27.00	48.00
5	408	81.60	21.60	60.00
6	540	90.00	18.00	72.00
7	696	99.43	15.43	84.00
8	876	109.50	13.50	96.00
9	1,080	120.00	12.00	108.00
10	1,308	130.80	10.80	120.00

Figure 6-7 plots that data to yield the *average total cost curve,* which shows how average total cost depends on output. As before, cost in dollars is measured on the vertical axis and quantity of output is measured on the horizontal axis. The average total cost curve has a distinctive U shape that corresponds to how average total cost first falls and then rises as output increases. Economists believe that such **U-shaped average total cost curves** are the norm for producers in many industries.

To help our understanding of why the average total cost curve is U-shaped, Table 6-2 breaks average total cost into its two underlying components, *average fixed cost* and *average variable cost.* **Average fixed cost,** or *AFC,* is fixed cost divided by the quantity of output, also known as the fixed cost per unit of output. For example, if Selena's Gourmet Salsas produces 4 cases of salsa, average fixed cost is $108/4 = $27 per case. **Average variable cost,** or *AVC,* is variable cost

FIGURE 6-7 Average Total Cost Curve for Selena's Gourmet Salsas

The average total cost curve at Selena's Gourmet Salsas is U-shaped. At low levels of output, average total cost falls because the "spreading effect" of falling average fixed cost dominates the "diminishing returns effect" of rising average variable cost. At higher levels of output, the opposite is true and average total cost rises. At point *M*, corresponding to an output of three cases of salsa per day, average total cost is at its minimum level, the minimum average total cost.

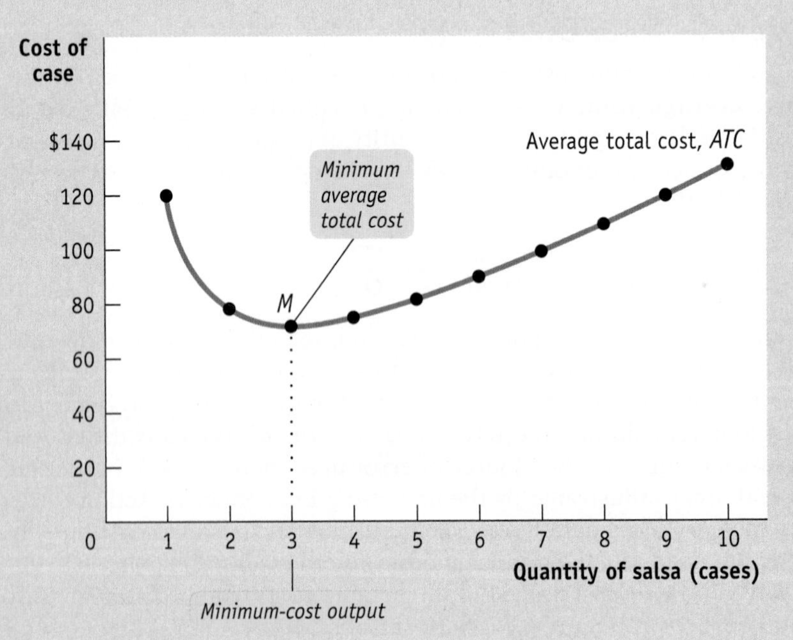

divided by the quantity of output, also known as variable cost per unit of output. At an output of 4 cases, average variable cost is $192/4 = $48 per case. Writing these in the form of equations:

(6-5) $$AFC = \frac{\text{Fixed cost}}{\text{Quantity of output}} = \frac{FC}{Q}$$

$$AVC = \frac{\text{Variable cost}}{\text{Quantity of output}} = \frac{VC}{Q}$$

Average total cost is the sum of average fixed cost and average variable cost. It has a U shape because these components move in opposite directions as output rises.

Average fixed cost falls as more output is produced because the numerator (the fixed cost) is a fixed number but the denominator (the quantity of output) increases as more is produced. Another way to think about this relationship is that, as more output is produced, the fixed cost is spread over more units of output; the end result is that the fixed cost *per unit of output*—the average fixed cost—falls. You can see this effect in the fourth column of Table 6-2: average fixed cost drops continuously as output increases.

Average variable cost, however, rises as output increases. As we've seen, this reflects diminishing returns to the variable input: each additional unit of output incurs more variable cost to produce than the previous unit. So variable cost rises at a faster rate than the quantity of output increases.

So increasing output has two opposing effects on average total cost—the "spreading effect" and the "diminishing returns effect":

- *The spreading effect.* The larger the output, the greater the quantity of output over which fixed cost is spread, leading to lower average fixed cost.
- *The diminishing returns effect.* The larger the output, the greater the amount of variable input required to produce additional units, leading to higher average variable cost.

At low levels of output, the spreading effect is very powerful because even small increases in output cause large reductions in average fixed cost. So at low levels of output, the spreading effect dominates the diminishing returns effect and causes the average total cost curve to slope downward. But when output is large, average fixed cost is already quite small, so increasing output further has only a very small spreading effect. Diminishing returns, however, usually grow increasingly important as output rises. As a result, when output is large, the diminishing returns effect dominates the spreading effect, causing the average total cost curve to slope upward. At the bottom of the U-shaped average total cost curve, point M in Figure 6-7, the two effects exactly balance each other. At this point average total cost is at its minimum level, the minimum average total cost.

Figure 6-8 brings together in a single picture four members of the family of cost curves that we have derived from the total cost curve for Selena's Gourmet Salsas: the marginal cost curve (MC), the average total cost curve (ATC), the average variable cost curve (AVC), and the average fixed cost curve (AFC). All are based on the information in Tables 6-1 and 6-2. As before, cost is measured on the vertical axis and the quantity of output is measured on the horizontal axis.

Let's take a moment to note some features of the various cost curves. First of all, marginal cost slopes upward—the result of diminishing returns that make an additional unit of output more costly to produce than the one before. Average variable cost also slopes upward—again, due to diminishing returns—but is flatter than the marginal cost curve. This is because the higher cost of an additional unit of output is averaged across all units, not just the additional units, in the average variable cost measure. Meanwhile, average fixed cost slopes downward because of the spreading effect.

FIGURE 6-8 Marginal Cost and Average Cost Curves for Selena's Gourmet Salsas

Here we have the family of cost curves for Selena's Gourmet Salsas: the marginal cost curve (*MC*), the average total cost curve (*ATC*), the average variable cost curve (*AVC*), and the average fixed cost curve (*AFC*). Note that the average total cost curve is U-shaped and the marginal cost curve crosses the average total cost curve at the bottom of the U, point *M*, corresponding to the minimum average total cost from Table 6-2 and Figure 6-7.

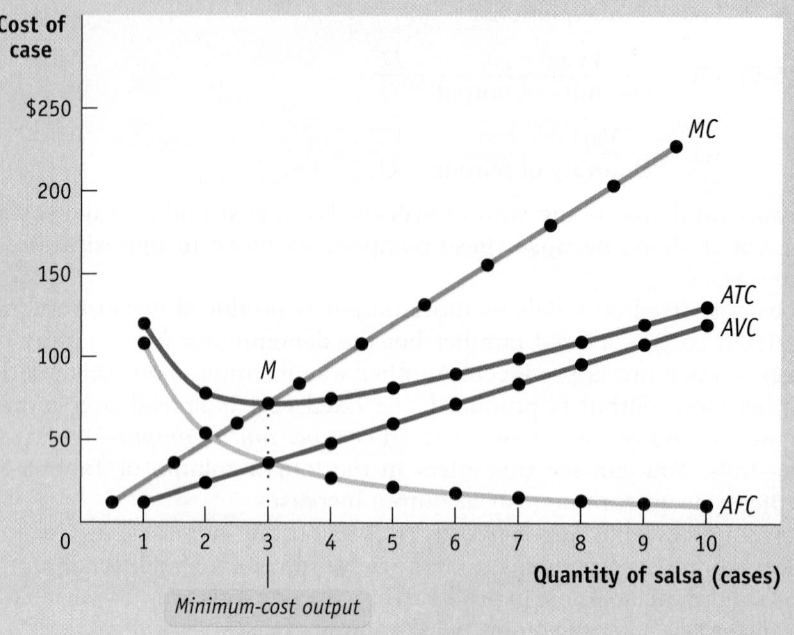

Finally, notice that the marginal cost curve intersects the average total cost curve from below, crossing it at its lowest point, point *M* in Figure 6-8. This last feature is our next subject of study.

Minimum Average Total Cost

For a U-shaped average total cost curve, average total cost is at its minimum level at the bottom of the U. Economists call the quantity of output that corresponds to the minimum average total cost the **minimum-cost output.** In the case of Selena's Gourmet Salsas, the minimum-cost output is three cases of salsa per day.

In Figure 6-8, the bottom of the U is at the level of output at which the marginal cost curve crosses the average total cost curve from below. Is this an accident? No—it reflects general principles that are always true about a firm's marginal cost and average total cost curves:

- At the minimum-cost output, average total cost *is equal to* marginal cost.
- At output less than the minimum-cost output, marginal cost *is less than* average total cost and average total cost is falling.
- At output greater than the minimum-cost output, marginal cost *is greater than* average total cost and average total cost is rising.

To understand these principles, think about how your grade in one course—say, a 3.0 in physics—affects your overall grade point average. If your GPA before receiving that grade was more than 3.0, the new grade lowers your average.

Similarly, if marginal cost—the cost of producing one more unit—is less than average total cost, producing that extra unit lowers average total cost. This is shown in Figure 6-9 by the movement from A_1 to A_2. In this case, the marginal cost of producing an additional unit of output is low, as indicated by the point MC_L on the marginal cost curve. When the cost of producing the next unit of output is less than average total cost, increasing production reduces average total cost. So any quantity of output at which marginal cost is less than average total cost must be on the downward-sloping segment of the U.

The **minimum-cost output** is the quantity of output at which average total cost is lowest—the bottom of the U-shaped average total cost curve.

FIGURE 6-9 The Relationship Between the Average Total Cost and the Marginal Cost Curves

To see why the marginal cost curve (*MC*) must cut through the average total cost curve at the minimum average total cost (point *M*), corresponding to the minimum-cost output, we look at what happens if marginal cost is different from average total cost. If marginal cost is *less* than average total cost, an increase in output must reduce average total cost, as in the movement from A_1 to A_2. If marginal cost is *greater* than average total cost, an increase in output must increase average total cost, as in the movement from B_1 to B_2.

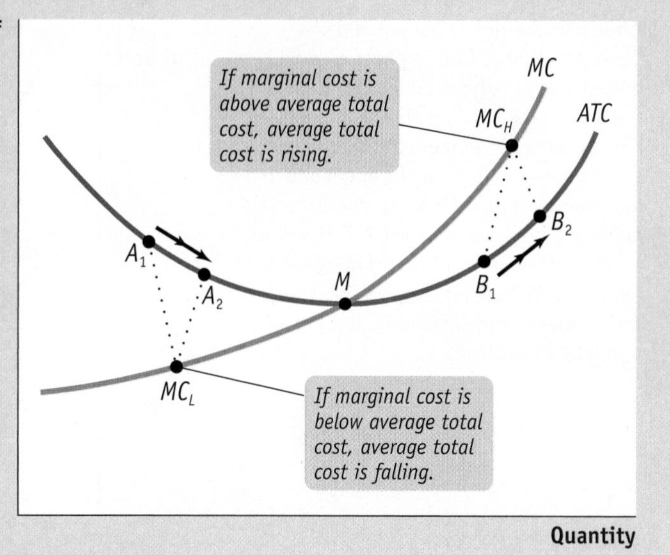
Cost of unit
If marginal cost is above average total cost, average total cost is rising.
MC
ATC
MC_H
B_2
A_1
A_2
M
B_1
MC_L
If marginal cost is below average total cost, average total cost is falling.
Quantity

But if your grade in physics is more than the average of your previous grades, this new grade raises your GPA. Similarly, if marginal cost is greater than average total cost, producing that extra unit raises average total cost. This is illustrated by the movement from B_1 to B_2 in Figure 6-9, where the marginal cost, MC_H, is higher than average total cost. So any quantity of output at which marginal cost is greater than average total cost must be on the upward-sloping segment of the U.

Finally, if a new grade is exactly equal to your previous GPA, the additional grade neither raises nor lowers that average—it stays the same. This corresponds to point *M* in Figure 6-9: when marginal cost equals average total cost, we must be at the bottom of the U, because only at that point is average total cost neither falling nor rising.

Does the Marginal Cost Curve Always Slope Upward?

Up to this point, we have emphasized the importance of diminishing returns, which lead to a marginal product curve that always slopes downward and a marginal cost curve that always slopes upward. In practice, however, economists believe that marginal cost curves often slope *downward* as a firm increases its production from zero up to some low level, sloping upward only at higher levels of production: they look like the curve *MC* in Figure 6-10.

This initial downward slope occurs because a firm often finds that, when it starts with only a very small number of workers, employing more workers and expanding output allows its workers to specialize in various tasks. This, in turn, lowers the firm's marginal cost as it expands output. For example, one individual producing salsa would have to perform all the tasks involved: selecting and preparing the ingredients, mixing the salsa, bottling and labeling it, packing it into cases, and so on. As more workers are employed, they can divide the tasks, with each worker specializing in one or a few aspects of salsa-making. This specialization leads to *increasing returns* to the hiring of additional workers and results in a marginal cost curve that initially slopes downward. But once there are enough workers to have completely exhausted the benefits of further specialization, diminishing returns to labor set in and the marginal cost curve changes direction and slopes upward. So typical marginal cost curves actually have the "swoosh" shape shown by *MC* in Figure 6-10. For the same reason, average variable cost

FIGURE 6-10 More Realistic Cost Curves

A realistic marginal cost curve has a "swoosh" shape. Starting from a very low output level, marginal cost often falls as the firm increases output. That's because hiring additional workers allows greater specialization of their tasks and leads to increasing returns. Once specialization is achieved, however, diminishing returns to additional workers set in and marginal cost rises. The corresponding average variable cost curve is now U-shaped, like the average total cost curve.

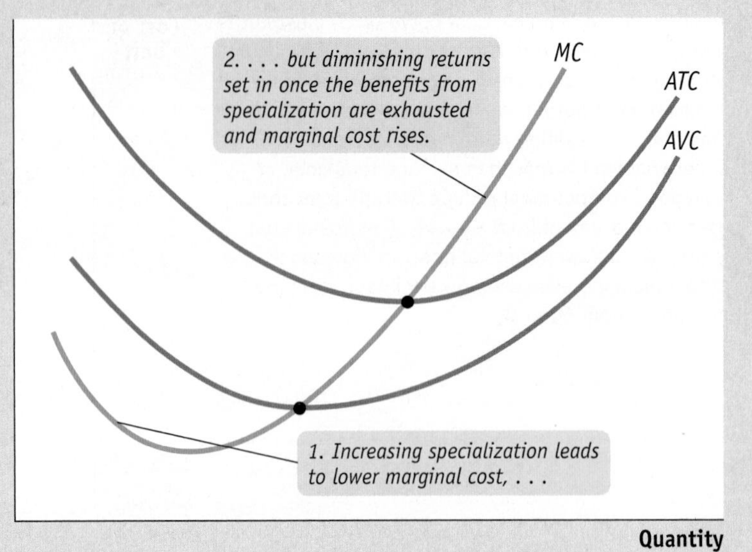

curves typically look like *AVC* in Figure 6-10: they are U-shaped rather than strictly upward sloping.

However, as Figure 6-10 also shows, the key features we saw from the example of Selena's Gourmet Salsas remain true: the average total cost curve is U-shaped, and the marginal cost curve passes through the point of minimum average total cost.

ECONOMICS ➤ *IN ACTION*

DON'T PUT OUT THE WELCOME MAT

Housing developments have traditionally been considered as American as apple pie. With our abundant supply of undeveloped land, real estate developers have long found it profitable to buy big parcels of land, build a large number of homes, and create entire new communities. But what is profitable for developers is not necessarily good for the existing residents.

In the past few years, real estate developers have encountered increasingly stiff resistance from local residents because of the additional costs—the marginal costs—imposed on existing homeowners from new developments. Let's look at why.

In the United States, a large percentage of the funding for local services comes from taxes paid by local homeowners. In a sense, the local township authority uses those taxes to "produce" municipal services for the town. The overall level of property taxes is set to reflect the costs of providing those services. The highest service cost by far, in most communities, is the cost of public education.

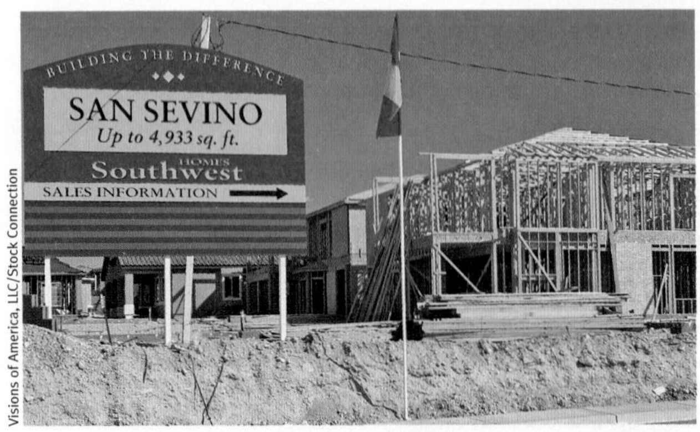

Visions of America, LLC/Stock Connection

New housing developments lead to higher taxes for everyone in the neighborhood.

The local tax rate that new homeowners pay on their new homes is the same as what existing homeowners pay on their older homes. That tax rate reflects the current total cost of services, and the taxes that an average homeowner pays reflect the average total cost of providing services to a household. The average total cost of providing services is based on the town's use of existing facilities, such as the existing school buildings, the existing number of teachers, the existing fleet of school buses, and so on.

But when a large development of homes is constructed, those facilities are no longer adequate: new schools must be built, new teachers hired, and so on. The quantity of output increases. So the *marginal cost* of providing municipal services per household associated with a new, large-scale development turns out to be much higher than the *average total cost* per household of existing homes. As a result, new developments and facilities cause everyone's local tax rate to go up, just as you would expect from Figure 6-9. A recent study in Massachusetts estimated that a $250,000 new home with one school-age child imposed an additional cost to the community of $5,527 per year over and above the taxes paid by the new homeowners. As a result, in many towns across America, potential new housing developments and newcomers are now facing a distinctly chilly reception.

Quick Review

- **Marginal cost**—the change in total cost with a change in output—is equal to the slope of the total cost curve. Diminishing returns cause the marginal cost curve to slope upward.
- **Average total cost** (or **average cost**) is equal to the sum of **average fixed cost** and **average variable cost.** When the **U-shaped average total cost curve** slopes downward, the spreading effect dominates: fixed cost is spread over more units of output. When it slopes upward, the diminishing returns effect dominates: an additional unit of output requires more variable inputs.
- Marginal cost is equal to average total cost at the **minimum-cost output.** At higher output levels, marginal cost is greater than average total cost and average total cost is rising. At lower output levels, marginal cost is lower than average total cost and average total cost is falling.
- At low levels of output there are often increasing returns to the variable input due to the benefits of specialization, making the marginal cost curve "swoosh"-shaped: initially sloping downward before sloping upward.

CHECK YOUR UNDERSTANDING 6-2

1. Alicia's Apple Pies is a roadside business. Alicia must pay $9.00 in rent each day. In addition, it costs her $1.00 to produce the first pie of the day, and each subsequent pie costs 50% more to produce than the one before. For example, the second pie costs $1.00 × 1.5 = $1.50 to produce, and so on.
   a. Calculate Alicia's marginal cost, variable cost, average total cost, average variable cost, and average fixed cost as her daily pie output rises from 0 to 6. (*Hint:* The variable cost of two pies is just the marginal cost of the first pie, plus the marginal cost of the second, and so on.)
   b. Indicate the range of pies for which the spreading effect dominates and the range for which the diminishing returns effect dominates.
   c. What is Alicia's minimum-cost output? Explain why making one more pie lowers Alicia's average total cost when output is lower than the minimum-cost output. Similarly, explain why making one more pie raises Alicia's average total cost when output is greater than the minimum-cost output.

Solutions appear at back of book.

Short-Run versus Long-Run Costs

Up to this point, we have treated fixed cost as completely outside the control of a firm because we have focused on the short run. But as we noted earlier, all inputs are variable in the long run: this means that in the long run fixed cost may also be varied. *In the long run, in other words, a firm's fixed cost becomes a variable it can choose.* For example, given time, Selena's Gourmet Salsas can acquire additional food-preparation equipment or dispose of some of its existing equipment. In this section, we will examine how a firm's costs behave in the short run and in the long run. We will also see that the firm will choose its fixed cost in the long run based on the level of output it expects to produce.

Let's begin by supposing that Selena's Gourmet Salsas is considering whether to acquire additional food-preparation equipment. Acquiring additional machinery will affect its total cost in two ways. First, the firm will have to either rent or buy the additional equipment; either way, that will mean higher fixed cost in the short run. Second, if the workers have more equipment, they will be more productive: fewer workers will be needed to produce any given output, so variable cost for any given output level will be reduced.

The table in Figure 6-11 shows how acquiring an additional machine affects costs. In our original example, we assumed that Selena's Gourmet Salsas had a fixed cost of $108. The left half of the table shows variable cost as well as total cost and average total cost assuming a fixed cost of $108. The average total cost curve for this level of fixed cost is given by ATC_1 in Figure 6-11. Let's compare that to a situation in which the firm buys additional food-preparation equipment,

FIGURE 6-11 Choosing the Level of Fixed Cost for Selena's Gourmet Salsas

There is a trade-off between higher fixed cost and lower variable cost for any given output level, and vice versa. ATC_1 is the average total cost curve corresponding to a fixed cost of $108; it leads to lower fixed cost and higher variable cost. ATC_2 is the average total cost curve corresponding to a higher fixed cost of $216 but lower variable cost. At low output levels, at 4 or fewer cases of salsa per day, ATC_1 lies below ATC_2: average total cost is lower with only $108 in fixed cost. But as output goes up, average total cost is lower with the higher amount of fixed cost, $216: at more than 4 cases of salsa per day, ATC_2 lies below ATC_1.

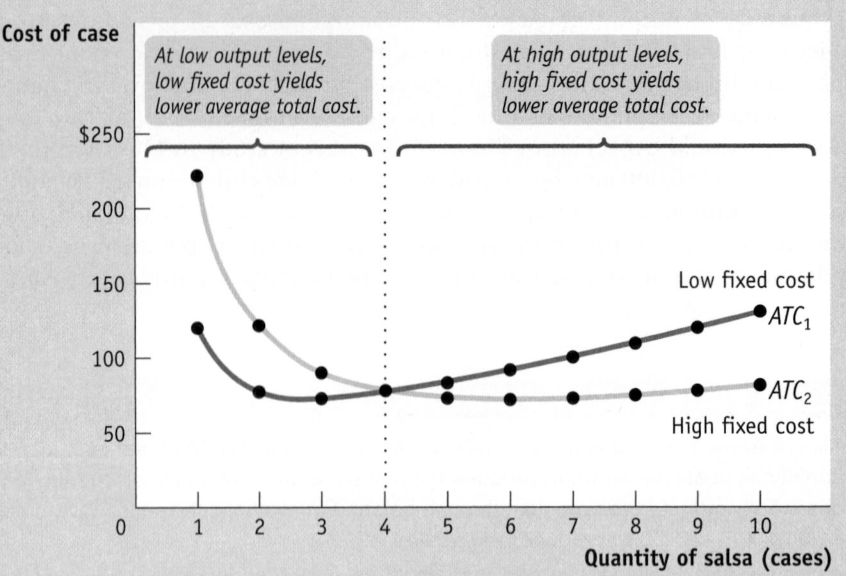

	Low fixed cost (FC = $108)			High fixed cost (FC = $216)		
Quantity of salsa (cases)	High variable cost	Total cost	Average total cost of case ATC_1	Low variable cost	Total cost	Average total cost of case ATC_2
1	$12	$120	$120.00	$6	$222	$222.00
2	48	156	78.00	24	240	120.00
3	108	216	72.00	54	270	90.00
4	192	300	75.00	96	312	78.00
5	300	408	81.60	150	366	73.20
6	432	540	90.00	216	432	72.00
7	588	696	99.43	294	510	72.86
8	768	876	109.50	384	600	75.00
9	972	1,080	120.00	486	702	78.00
10	1,200	1,308	130.80	600	816	81.60

doubling its fixed cost to $216 but reducing its variable cost at any given level of output. The right half of the table shows the firm's variable cost, total cost, and average total cost with this higher level of fixed cost. The average total cost curve corresponding to $216 in fixed cost is given by ATC_2 in Figure 6-11.

From the figure you can see that when output is small, 4 cases of salsa per day or fewer, average total cost is smaller when Selena forgoes the additional equipment and maintains the lower fixed cost of $108: ATC_1 lies below ATC_2. For example, at 3 cases per day, average total cost is $72 without the additional machinery and $90 with the additional machinery. But as output increases beyond 4 cases per day, the firm's average total cost is lower if it acquires the additional equipment, raising its fixed cost to $216. For example, at 9 cases of salsa per day, average total cost is $120 when fixed cost is $108 but only $78 when fixed cost is $216.

Why does average total cost change like this when fixed cost increases? When output is low, the increase in fixed cost from the additional equipment outweighs the reduction in variable cost from higher worker productivity—that is, there are too few units of output over which to spread the additional fixed cost. So if Selena plans to produce 4 or fewer cases per day, she would be better off choosing the lower level of fixed cost, \$108, to achieve a lower average total cost of production. When planned output is high, however, she should acquire the additional machinery.

In general, for each output level there is some choice of fixed cost that minimizes the firm's average total cost for that output level. So when the firm has a desired output level that it expects to maintain over time, it should choose the level of fixed cost optimal for that level—that is, the level of fixed cost that minimizes its average total cost.

Now that we are studying a situation in which fixed cost can change, we need to take time into account when discussing average total cost. All of the average total cost curves we have considered until now are defined for a given level of fixed cost—that is, they are defined for the short run, the period of time over which fixed cost doesn't vary. To reinforce that distinction, for the rest of this chapter we will refer to these average total cost curves as "short-run average total cost curves."

For most firms, it is realistic to assume that there are many possible choices of fixed cost, not just two. The implication: for such a firm, many possible short-run average total cost curves will exist, each corresponding to a different choice of fixed cost and so giving rise to what is called a firm's "family" of short-run average total cost curves.

At any given point in time, a firm will find itself on one of its short-run cost curves, the one corresponding to its current level of fixed cost; a change in output will cause it to move along that curve. If the firm expects that change in output level to be long-standing, then it is likely that the firm's current level of fixed cost is no longer optimal. Given sufficient time, it will want to adjust its fixed cost to a new level that minimizes average total cost for its new output level. For example, if Selena had been producing 2 cases of salsa per day with a fixed cost of \$108 but found herself increasing her output to 8 cases per day for the foreseeable future, then in the long run she should purchase more equipment and increase her fixed cost to a level that minimizes average total cost at the 8-cases-per-day output level.

Suppose we do a thought experiment and calculate the lowest possible average total cost that can be achieved for each output level if the firm were to choose its fixed cost for each output level. Economists have given this thought experiment a name: the *long-run average total cost curve.* Specifically, the **long-run average total cost curve,** or *LRATC,* is the relationship between output and average total cost when fixed cost has been chosen to minimize average total cost *for each level of output.* If there are many possible choices of fixed cost, the long-run average total cost curve will have the familiar, smooth U shape, as shown by *LRATC* in Figure 6-12.

The **long-run average total cost curve** shows the relationship between output and average total cost when fixed cost has been chosen to minimize average total cost for each level of output.

We can now draw the distinction between the short run and the long run more fully. In the long run, when a producer has had time to choose the fixed cost appropriate for its desired level of output, that producer will be at some point on the long-run average total cost curve. But if the output level is altered, the firm will no longer be on its long-run average total cost curve and will instead be moving along its current short-run average total cost curve. It will not be on its long-run average total cost curve again until it readjusts its fixed cost for its new output level.

Figure 6-12 illustrates this point. The curve ATC_3 shows short-run average total cost if Selena has chosen the level of fixed cost that minimizes average total cost at an output of 3 cases of salsa per day. This is confirmed by the fact that at 3 cases per day, ATC_3 touches *LRATC,* the long-run average total cost curve. Similarly, ATC_6 shows short-run average total cost if Selena has chosen the level of fixed cost that minimizes average total cost if her output is 6 cases per day. It touches *LRATC* at 6 cases per day. And ATC_9 shows short-run average total cost if Selena has chosen the level of fixed cost that minimizes average total cost if her output is 9 cases per day. It touches *LRATC* at 9 cases per day.

Suppose that Selena initially chose to be on ATC_6. If she actually produces 6 cases of salsa per day, her firm will be at point *C* on both its short-run and long-run average total cost curves. Suppose, however, that Selena ends up producing only 3 cases of salsa per day. In the short run, her average total cost is indicated by point *B* on ATC_6; it is no longer on *LRATC.* If Selena had known that she

FIGURE 6-12 Short-Run and Long-Run Average Total Cost Curves

Short-run and long-run average total cost curves differ because a firm can choose its fixed cost in the long run. If Selena has chosen the level of fixed cost that minimizes short-run average total cost at an output of 6 cases, and actually produces 6 cases, then she will be at point *C* on *LRATC* and ATC_6. But if she produces only 3 cases, she will move to point *B*. If she expects to produce only 3 cases for a long time, in the long run she will reduce her fixed cost and move to point *A* on ATC_3. Likewise, if she produces 9 cases (putting her at point *Y*) and expects to continue this for a long time, she will increase her fixed cost in the long run and move to point *X*.

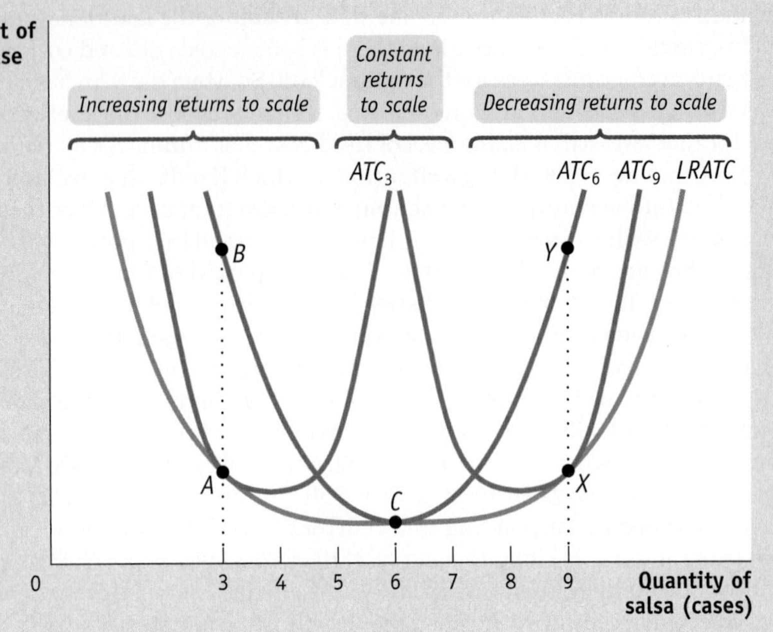

would be producing only 3 cases per day, she would have been better off choosing a lower level of fixed cost, the one corresponding to ATC_3, thereby achieving a lower average total cost. Then her firm would have found itself at point *A* on the long-run average total cost curve, which lies below point *B*.

Suppose, conversely, that Selena ends up producing 9 cases per day even though she initially chose to be on ATC_6. In the short run her average total cost is indicated by point *Y* on ATC_6. But she would be better off purchasing more equipment and incurring a higher fixed cost in order to reduce her variable cost and move to ATC_9. This would allow her to reach point *X* on the long-run average total cost curve, which lies below *Y*.

The distinction between short-run and long-run average total costs is extremely important in making sense of how real firms operate over time. A company that has to increase output suddenly to meet a surge in demand will typically find that in the short run its average total cost rises sharply because it is hard to get extra production out of existing facilities. But given time to build new factories or add machinery, short-run average total cost falls.

Returns to Scale

What determines the shape of the long-run average total cost curve? The answer is that *scale*, the size of a firm's operations, is often an important determinant of its long-run average total cost of production. Firms that experience scale effects in production find that their long-run average total cost changes substantially depending on the quantity of output they produce. There are **increasing returns to scale** (also known as *economies of scale*) when long-run average total cost declines as output increases. As you can see in Figure 6-12, Selena's Gourmet Salsas experiences increasing returns to scale over output levels ranging from 0 up to 5 cases of salsa per day—the output levels over which the long-run average total cost curve is declining. In contrast, there are **decreasing returns to scale** (also known as *diseconomies of scale*) when long-run average total cost increases as output increases. For Selena's Gourmet Salsas, decreasing returns to scale occur at output levels greater than 7 cases, the output levels over which its long-run average total cost curve is

There are **increasing returns to scale** when long-run average total cost declines as output increases.

There are **decreasing returns to scale** when long-run average total cost increases as output increases.

rising. There is also a third possible relationship between long-run average total cost and scale: firms experience **constant returns to scale** when long-run average total cost is constant as output increases. In this case, the firm's long-run average total cost curve is horizontal over the output levels for which there are constant returns to scale. As you can see in Figure 6-12, Selena's Gourmet Salsas has constant returns to scale when it produces anywhere from 5 to 7 cases of salsa per day.

There are **constant returns to scale** when long-run average total cost is constant as output increases.

A good is subject to a **network externality** when the value of the good to an individual is greater when a large number of other people also use that good.

What explains these scale effects in production? The answer ultimately lies in the firm's technology of production. Increasing returns often arise from the increased *specialization* that larger output levels allow—a larger scale of operation means that individual workers can limit themselves to more specialized tasks, becoming more skilled and efficient at doing them. Another source of increasing returns is very large initial setup cost; in some industries—such as auto manufacturing, electricity generating, or petroleum refining—incurring a high fixed cost in the form of plant and equipment is necessary to produce any output. A third source of increasing returns, found in certain high-tech industries such as software development, is known as a **network externality.** The classic example is computer operating systems. Worldwide, most personal computers run on Microsoft Windows. Although many believe that Apple has a superior operating system, the wider use of Windows in the early days of personal computers attracted more software development and technical support, giving it lasting dominance. As we'll see in Chapter 8, where we study monopoly, increasing returns have very important implications for how firms and industries interact and behave.

Decreasing returns—the opposite scenario—typically arise in large firms due to problems of coordination and communication: as the firm grows in size, it becomes ever more difficult and so more costly to communicate and to organize its activities. Although increasing returns induce firms to get larger, decreasing returns tend to limit their size. And when there are constant returns to scale, scale has no effect on a firm's long-run average total cost: it is the same regardless of whether the firm produces 1 unit or 100,000 units.

Summing Up Costs: The Short and Long of It

If a firm is to make the best decisions about how much to produce, it has to understand how its costs relate to the quantity of output it chooses to produce. Table 6-3 provides a quick summary of the concepts and measures of cost you have learned about.

TABLE 6-3 **Concepts and Measures of Cost**

	Measurement	Definition	Mathematical term
Short run	Fixed cost	Cost that does not depend on the quantity of output produced	FC
	Average fixed cost	Fixed cost per unit of output	$AFC = FC/Q$
Short run and long run	Variable cost	Cost that depends on the quantity of output produced	VC
	Average variable cost	Variable cost per unit of output	$AVC = VC/Q$
	Total cost	The sum of fixed cost (short run) and variable cost	$TC = FC$ (short run) $+ VC$
	Average total cost (average cost)	Total cost per unit of output	$ATC = TC/Q$
	Marginal cost	The change in total cost generated by producing one more unit of output	$MC = \Delta TC/\Delta Q$
Long run	Long-run average total cost	Average total cost when fixed cost has been chosen to minimize average total cost for each level of output	$LRATC$

AP/Wide World Photos

Cities with higher average annual snowfall maintain larger snowplow fleets.

ECONOMICS ➤ IN ACTION

THERE'S NO BUSINESS LIKE SNOW BUSINESS

Anyone who has lived both in a snowy city, like Chicago, and in a city that only occasionally experiences significant snowfall, like Washington, D.C., is aware of the differences in total cost that arise from making different choices about fixed cost.

In Washington, even a minor snowfall—say, an inch or two overnight—is enough to create chaos during the next morning's commute. The same snowfall in Chicago has hardly any effect at all. The reason is not that Washingtonians are wimps and Chicagoans are made of sterner stuff; it is that Washington, where it rarely snows, has only a fraction as many snowplows and other snowclearing equipment as cities where heavy snow is a fact of life.

In this sense Washington and Chicago are like two producers who expect to produce different levels of output, where the "output" is snow removal. Washington, which rarely has significant snow, has chosen a low level of fixed cost in the form of snow-clearing equipment. This makes sense under normal circumstances but leaves the city unprepared when major snow does fall. Chicago, which knows that it will face lots of snow, chooses to accept the higher fixed cost that leaves it in a position to respond effectively.

Quick Review

- In the long run, firms choose fixed cost according to expected output. Higher fixed cost reduces average total cost when output is high. Lower fixed cost reduces average total cost when output is low.
- There are many possible short-run average total cost curves, each corresponding to a different level of fixed cost. The **long-run average total cost curve, *LRATC*,** shows average total cost over the long run, when the firm has chosen fixed cost to minimize average total cost for each level of output.
- A firm that has fully adjusted its fixed cost for its output level will operate at a point that lies on both its current short-run and long-run average total cost curves. A change in output moves the firm along its current short-run average total cost curve. Once it has readjusted its fixed cost, the firm will operate on a new short-run average total cost curve and on the long-run average total cost curve.
- Scale effects arise from the technology of production. **Increasing returns to scale** tend to make firms larger. **Network externalities** are one reason for increasing returns to scale. **Decreasing returns to scale** tend to limit their size. With **constant returns to scale,** scale has no effect.

CHECK YOUR UNDERSTANDING 6-3

1. The accompanying table shows three possible combinations of fixed cost and average variable cost. Average variable cost is constant in this example (it does not vary with the quantity of output produced).
   a. For each of the three choices, calculate the average total cost of producing 12,000, 22,000, and 30,000 units. For each of these quantities, which choice results in the lowest average total cost?
   b. Suppose that the firm, which has historically produced 12,000 units, experiences a sharp, permanent increase in demand that leads it to produce 22,000 units. Explain how its average total cost will change in the short run and in the long run.
   c. Explain what the firm should do instead if it believes the change in demand is temporary.

Choice	Fixed cost	Average variable cost
1	$8,000	$1.00
2	12,000	0.75
3	24,000	0.25

2. In each of the following cases, explain what kind of scale effects you think the firm will experience and why.
   a. A telemarketing firm in which employees make sales calls using computers and telephones
   b. An interior design firm in which design projects are based on the expertise of the firm's owner
   c. A diamond-mining company
3. Draw a graph like Figure 6-12 and insert a short-run average total cost curve corresponding to a long-run output choice of 5 cases of salsa per day. Use the graph to show why Selena should change her fixed cost if she expects to produce only 4 cases per day for a long period of time.

Solutions appear at back of book.

Production Challenges for Tesla: The Model S

Tesla Motors, founded in 2003, exclusively produces electric cars and electric powertrains in a former Toyota factory in Fremont, California. The Tesla Roadster, a sports car, was the company's first design. Their newest design, available for 2012 delivery, is the Tesla Model S, a luxury sedan. The Model S uses no gasoline, has a range of up to 300 miles per charge, and has zero tailpipe emissions. Although demand for the car has been strong, production of the Model S at the Fremont plant is currently less than Tesla had anticipated.

Let's assume that Tesla engineers knew they needed to either build or buy a new factory in order to produce the new Model S. And, suppose that Tesla engineers and accountants estimated the following hypothetical cost structure per year based on full-year production at plants of different sizes.

	Total cost (hundreds of millions of U.S. dollars)		
Plant size	**10,000 cars sold**	**20,000 cars sold**	**30,000 cars sold**
A	$1.75	$3.25	$5.5
B	2.0	3.0	5.0
C	2.5	4.0	4.5

When Toyotas were built there, the Fremont plant produced about 80,000 vehicles per year. Suppose that Tesla equipped the plant with the hopes of producing 30,000 Tesla vehicles per year, yet in its first few years of production, Tesla predicted sales would be only 20,000 vehicles per year. But, by 2012, because of production delays, actual sales dropped to less than 10,000 cars per year. Using the table, find Tesla's average total cost of production per car at a size C plant if only 20,000 cars are built. At a size C plant, what is the average total cost of production if only 10,000 cars are built?

STEP 1: Find Tesla's total cost at this plant when producing 20,000 cars and when producing 10,000 cars.

Review the section "Short-Run versus Long-Run Costs" on pages 197–201. Compare Tesla's decision to the decision faced by Selena's Gourmet Salsas in Figure 6-11. By deciding to build a size C plant, Tesla has chosen the high fixed-cost, low variable-cost solution.

With production of 20,000 cars, the company's total cost of production is $400,000,000. When it falls to 10,000 cars, total production cost is $250,000,000. ■

STEP 2: Explain why the production cost with a size C plant is higher than it would be if Tesla could build a new plant that was best equipped to produce 10,000 vehicles.

Again, review the section "Short-Run versus Long-Run Costs," and especially the paragraphs discussing the long-run average total cost curve.

If Tesla were to build a new plant based on production of 10,000 vehicles, it would build a size A plant. Tesla would be able to adjust its fixed cost to a new level that minimizes average total cost for its new output level. If Tesla could easily change its plant size, it would always build the plant size that minimizes its average total cost on its long-run average total cost curve. However, if the size of the plant is fixed at size C, then it will be on its short-run average total cost curve based on a size C plant. ■

STEP 3: Find Tesla's average total cost of production at the various plant sizes and production levels.

Review the section "Average Total Cost" and especially Table 6-2 [on pages 191–194].

Average total cost is found by dividing total cost by the quantity of output. So, if Tesla has a total cost of $175,000,000 at an output of 10,000 cars we calculate $175,000,000/10,000 = $17,500. Average total cost for each plant size and production level from the previous table are given in the following table. ■

	Average Total Cost		
Plant size	10,000 cars sold	20,000 cars sold	30,000 cars sold
A	$17,500	$16,250	$18,333
B	$20,000	$15,000	$16,667
C	$25,000	$20,000	$15,000

SUMMARY

1. The relationship between inputs and output is a producer's **production function.** In the **short run,** the quantity of a **fixed input** cannot be varied but the quantity of a **variable input** can. In the **long run,** the quantities of all inputs can be varied. For a given amount of the fixed input, the **total product curve** shows how the quantity of output changes as the quantity of the variable input changes. We may also calculate the **marginal product** of an input, the increase in output from using one more unit of that input.
2. There are **diminishing returns to an input** when its marginal product declines as more of the input is used, holding the quantity of all other inputs fixed.
3. **Total cost,** represented by the **total cost curve,** is equal to the sum of **fixed cost,** which does not depend on output, and **variable cost,** which does depend on output. Due to diminishing returns, **marginal cost,** the increase in total cost generated by producing one more unit of output, normally increases as output increases.
4. **Average total cost** (also known as **average cost**), total cost divided by quantity of output, is the cost of the average unit of output, and marginal cost is the cost of one more unit produced. Economists believe that **U-shaped average total cost curves** are typical, because average total cost consists of two parts: **average fixed cost,** which falls when output increases (the spreading effect), and **average variable cost,** which rises with output (the diminishing returns effect).
5. When average total cost is U-shaped, the bottom of the U is the level of output at which average total cost is minimized, the point of **minimum-cost output.** This is also the point at which the marginal cost curve crosses the average total cost curve from below. Due to gains from specialization, the marginal cost curve may slope downward initially before sloping upward, giving it a "swoosh" shape.
6. In the long run, a producer can change its fixed input and its level of fixed cost. By accepting higher fixed cost, a firm can lower its variable cost for any given output level, and vice versa. The **long-run average total cost curve** shows the relationship between output and average total cost when fixed cost has been chosen to minimize average total cost at each level of output. A firm moves along its short-run average total cost curve as it changes the quantity of output, and it returns to a point on both its short-run and long-run average total cost curves once it has adjusted fixed cost to its new output level.
7. As output increases, there are **increasing returns to scale** if long-run average total cost declines; **decreasing returns to scale** if it increases; and **constant returns to scale** if it remains constant. **Network externalities** are a source of increasing returns to scale.

KEY TERMS

Production function, p. 182
Fixed input, p. 182
Variable input, p. 182
Long run, p. 182
Short run, p. 182
Total product curve, p. 182
Marginal product, p. 183
Diminishing returns to an input, p. 184
Fixed cost, p. 186
Variable cost, p. 186
Total cost, p. 186
Total cost curve, p. 187
Marginal cost, p. 189
Average total cost, p. 191
Average cost, p. 191
U-shaped average total cost curve, p. 192
Average fixed cost, p. 192
Average variable cost, p. 192
Minimum-cost output, p. 194
Long-run average total cost curve, p. 199
Increasing returns to scale, p. 200
Decreasing returns to scale, p. 200
Constant returns to scale, p. 201
Network externalities, p. 201

PROBLEMS

1. Marty's Frozen Yogurt is a small shop that sells cups of frozen yogurt in a university town. Marty owns three frozen-yogurt machines. His other inputs are refrigerators, frozen-yogurt mix, cups, sprinkle toppings, and, of course, workers. He estimates that his daily production function when he varies the number of workers employed (and at the same time, of course, yogurt mix, cups, and so on) is as shown in the accompanying table.

Quantity of labor (workers)	Quantity of frozen yogurt (cups)
0	0
1	110
2	200
3	270
4	300
5	320
6	330

a. What are the fixed inputs and variable inputs in the production of cups of frozen yogurt?

b. Draw the total product curve. Put the quantity of labor on the horizontal axis and the quantity of frozen yogurt on the vertical axis.

c. What is the marginal product of the first worker? The second worker? The third worker? Why does marginal product decline as the number of workers increases?

2. The production function for Marty's Frozen Yogurt is given in Problem 1. Marty pays each of his workers $80 per day. The cost of his other variable inputs is $0.50 per cup of yogurt. His fixed cost is $100 per day.

a. What is Marty's variable cost and total cost when he produces 110 cups of yogurt? 200 cups? Calculate variable and total cost for every level of output given in Problem 1.

b. Draw Marty's variable cost curve. On the same diagram, draw his total cost curve.

c. What is the marginal cost per cup for the first 110 cups of yogurt? For the next 90 cups? Calculate the marginal cost for all remaining levels of output.

3. The production function for Marty's Frozen Yogurt is given in Problem 1. The costs are given in Problem 2.

a. For each of the given levels of output, calculate the average fixed cost (*AFC*), average variable cost (*AVC*), and average total cost (*ATC*) per cup of frozen yogurt.

b. On one diagram, draw the *AFC*, *AVC*, and *ATC* curves.

c. What principle explains why the *AFC* declines as output increases? What principle explains why the *AVC* increases as output increases? Explain your answers.

d. How many cups of frozen yogurt are produced when average total cost is minimized?

4. The accompanying table shows a car manufacturer's total cost of producing cars.

Quantity of cars	*TC*
0	$500,000
1	540,000
2	560,000
3	570,000
4	590,000
5	620,000
6	660,000
7	720,000
8	800,000
9	920,000
10	1,100,000

a. What is this manufacturer's fixed cost?

b. For each level of output, calculate the variable cost (*VC*). For each level of output except zero output, calculate the average variable cost (*AVC*), average total cost (*ATC*), and average fixed cost (*AFC*). What is the minimum-cost output?

c. For each level of output, calculate this manufacturer's marginal cost (*MC*).

d. On one diagram, draw the manufacturer's *AVC*, *ATC*, and *MC* curves.

5. Magnificent Blooms is a florist specializing in floral arrangements for weddings, graduations, and other events. Magnificent Blooms has a fixed cost associated with space and equipment of $100 per day. Each worker is paid $50 per day. The daily production function for Magnificent Blooms is shown in the accompanying table.

Quantity of labor (workers)	Quantity of floral arrangements
0	0
1	5
2	9
3	12
4	14
5	15

a. Calculate the marginal product of each worker. What principle explains why the marginal product per worker declines as the number of workers employed increases?

b. Calculate the marginal cost of each level of output. What principle explains why the marginal cost per floral arrangement increases as the number of arrangements increases?

6. You have the information shown in the accompanying table about a firm's costs. Complete the missing data.

Quantity	*TC*	*MC*	*ATC*	*AVC*
0	$20		—	—
		$20		
1	?		?	?
		10		
2	?		?	?
		16		
3	?		?	?
		20		
4	?		?	?
		24		
5	?		?	?

7. Evaluate each of the following statements. If a statement is true, explain why; if it is false, identify the mistake and try to correct it.

a. A decreasing marginal product tells us that marginal cost must be rising.

b. An increase in fixed cost increases the minimum-cost output.

c. An increase in fixed cost increases marginal cost.

d. When marginal cost is above average total cost, average total cost must be falling.

8. Mark and Jeff operate a small company that produces souvenir footballs. Their fixed cost is $2,000 per month. They can hire workers for $1,000 per worker per month. Their monthly production function for footballs is as given in the accompanying table.

Quantity of labor (workers)	Quantity of footballs
0	0
1	300
2	800
3	1,200
4	1,400
5	1,500

a. For each quantity of labor, calculate average variable cost (*AVC*), average fixed cost (*AFC*), average total cost (*ATC*), and marginal cost (*MC*).

b. On one diagram, draw the *AVC*, *ATC*, and *MC* curves.

c. At what level of output is Mark and Jeff's average total cost minimized?

9. You produce widgets. Currently you produce 4 widgets at a total cost of $40.

a. What is your average total cost?

b. Suppose you could produce one more (the fifth) widget at a marginal cost of $5. If you do produce that fifth widget, what will your average total cost be? Has your average total cost increased or decreased? Why?

c. Suppose instead that you could produce one more (the fifth) widget at a marginal cost of $20. If you do produce that fifth widget, what will your average total cost be? Has your average total cost increased or decreased? Why?

10. In your economics class, each homework problem set is graded on the basis of a maximum score of 100. You have completed 9 out of 10 of the problem sets for the term, and your current average grade is 88. What range of grades for your 10th problem set will raise your overall average? What range will lower your overall average? Explain your answer.

11. Don owns a small concrete-mixing company. His fixed cost is the cost of the concrete-batching machinery and his mixer trucks. His variable cost is the cost of the sand, gravel, and other inputs for producing concrete; the gas and maintenance for the machinery and trucks; and his workers. He is trying to decide how many mixer trucks to purchase. He has estimated the costs shown in the accompanying table based on estimates of the number of orders his company will receive per week.

		VC		
Quantity of trucks	*FC*	20 orders	40 orders	60 orders
2	$6,000	$2,000	$5,000	$12,000
3	7,000	1,800	3,800	10,800
4	8,000	1,200	3,600	8,400

a. For each level of fixed cost, calculate Don's total cost for producing 20, 40, and 60 orders per week.

b. If Don is producing 20 orders per week, how many trucks should he purchase and what will his average total cost be? Answer the same questions for 40 and 60 orders per week.

12. Consider Don's concrete-mixing business described in Problem 11. Assume that Don purchased 3 trucks, expecting to produce 40 orders per week.

a. Suppose that, in the short run, business declines to 20 orders per week. What is Don's average total cost per order in the short run? What will his average total cost per order in the short run be if his business booms to 60 orders per week?

b. What is Don's long-run average total cost for 20 orders per week? Explain why his short-run average total cost of producing 20 orders per week when the number of trucks is fixed at 3 is greater than his long-run average total cost of producing 20 orders per week.

c. Draw Don's long-run average total cost curve. Draw his short-run average total cost curve if he owns 3 trucks.

13. True or false? Explain your reasoning.

a. The short-run average total cost can never be less than the long-run average total cost.

b. The short-run average variable cost can never be less than the long-run average total cost.

c. In the long run, choosing a higher level of fixed cost shifts the long-run average total cost curve upward.

14. Wolfsburg Wagon (WW) is a small automaker. The accompanying table shows WW's long-run average total cost.

Quantity of cars	*LRATC* of car
1	$30,000
2	20,000
3	15,000
4	12,000
5	12,000
6	12,000
7	14,000
8	18,000

a. For which levels of output does WW experience increasing returns to scale?

b. For which levels of output does WW experience decreasing returns to scale?

c. For which levels of output does WW experience constant returns to scale?

15. Changes in the prices of key commodities can have a significant impact on a company's bottom line. But, changes in the price of energy produced from oil, gas, and electricity are not the only concern for companies. According to an August 16, 2012, *Bloomberg* article, "ethanol requirements are aggravating the rise in food costs and spreading it to the price of gasoline, which is up almost 40 cents a gallon since the start of July." The U.S. government mandates that gasoline contain ethanol, which is derived from corn.

a. Explain how the cost of energy can be both a fixed cost and a variable cost for a company.

b. Suppose energy is a fixed cost and energy prices rise. What happens to the company's average total cost curve? What happens to its marginal cost curve? Illustrate your answer with a diagram.

c. Explain why the cost of corn is a variable cost but not a fixed cost for an ethanol producer.

d. When the cost of corn goes up, what happens to the average total cost curve of an ethanol producer? What happens to its marginal cost curve? Illustrate your answer with a diagram.

EXTEND YOUR UNDERSTANDING

16. Labor costs represent a large percentage of total costs for many firms. According to a July 29, 2011, *Wall Street Journal* article, U.S. labor costs were up 0.7% during the second quarter of 2011, compared to the first quarter of 2011.

a. When labor costs increase, what happens to average total cost and marginal cost? Consider a case in which labor costs are only variable costs and a case in which they are both variable and fixed costs.

An increase in labor productivity means each worker can produce more output. Recent data on productivity show that labor productivity in the U.S. nonfarm business sector grew by 1.7% between 1970 and 1999, by 2.6% between 2000 and 2010, and by 4.1% in 2010.

b. When productivity growth is positive, what happens to the total product curve and the marginal product of labor curve? Illustrate your answer with a diagram.

c. When productivity growth is positive, what happens to the marginal cost curve and the average total cost curve? Illustrate your answer with a diagram.

d. If labor costs are rising over time on average, why would a company want to adopt equipment and methods that increase labor productivity?

CHAPTER 7

Perfect Competition and the Supply Curve

DOING WHAT COMES NATURALLY

istockphoto/Thinkstock

Whether it's organic strawberries or satellites, how a good is produced determines its cost of production.

WHAT YOU WILL LEARN IN THIS CHAPTER

- What a **perfectly competitive market** is and the characteristics of a **perfectly competitive industry**
- How a **price-taking producer** determines its profit-maximizing quantity of output
- How to assess whether or not a producer is profitable and why an unprofitable producer may continue to operate in the short run
- Why industries behave differently in the short run and the long run
- What determines the **industry supply curve** in both the short run and the long run

FOOD CONSUMERS IN THE UNITED States are concerned about health issues. Demand for natural foods and beverages, such as bottled water and organically grown fruits and vegetables, increased rapidly over the past two decades, at an average growth rate of 20% per year. The small group of farmers who had pioneered organic farming techniques prospered thanks to higher prices.

But everyone knew that the high prices of organic produce were unlikely to persist even if the new, higher demand for naturally grown food continued: the supply of organic food, although relatively price-inelastic in the short run, was surely price-elastic in the long run. Over time, farms already producing organically would increase their capacity, and conventional farmers would enter the organic food business. So the increase in the quantity supplied in response to the increase in price would be much larger in the long run than in the short run.

Where does the supply curve come from? Why is there a difference between the short-run and the long-run supply curve? In this chapter we will use our understanding of costs, developed in Chapter 6, as the basis for an analysis of the supply curve. As we'll see, this will require that we understand the behavior both of individual firms and of an entire industry, composed of these many individual firms.

Our analysis in this chapter assumes that the industry in question is characterized by *perfect competition.* We begin by explaining the concept of perfect competition, providing a brief introduction to the conditions that give rise to a perfectly competitive industry. We then show how a producer under perfect competition decides how much to produce. Finally, we use the cost curves of the individual producers to derive the *industry supply curve* under perfect competition. By analyzing the way a competitive industry evolves over time, we will come to understand the distinction between the short-run and long-run effects of changes in demand on a competitive industry—such as, for example, the effect of America's new taste for organic food on the organic farming industry. We will conclude with a deeper discussion of the conditions necessary for an industry to be perfectly competitive.

A **price-taking producer** is a producer whose actions have no effect on the market price of the good or service it sells.

A **price-taking consumer** is a consumer whose actions have no effect on the market price of the good or service he or she buys.

A **perfectly competitive market** is a market in which all market participants are price-takers.

A **perfectly competitive industry** is an industry in which producers are price-takers.

Perfect Competition

Suppose that Yves and Zoe are neighboring farmers, both of whom grow organic tomatoes. Both sell their output to the same grocery store chains that carry organic foods; so, in a real sense, Yves and Zoe compete with each other.

Does this mean that Yves should try to stop Zoe from growing tomatoes or that Yves and Zoe should form an agreement to grow less? Almost certainly not: there are hundreds or thousands of organic tomato farmers, and Yves and Zoe are competing with all those other growers as well as with each other. Because so many farmers sell organic tomatoes, if any one of them produced more or less, there would be no measurable effect on market prices.

When people talk about business competition, the image they often have in mind is a situation in which two or three rival firms are intensely struggling for advantage. But economists know that when an industry consists of a few main competitors, it's actually a sign that competition is fairly limited. As the example of organic tomatoes suggests, when there is enough competition, it doesn't even make sense to identify your rivals: there are so many competitors that you cannot single out any one of them as a rival.

We can put it another way: Yves and Zoe are **price-taking producers.** A producer is a price-taker when its actions cannot affect the market price of the good or service it sells. As a result, a price-taking producer considers the market price as given. When there is enough competition—when competition is what economists call "perfect"—then every producer is a price-taker. And there is a similar definition for consumers: a **price-taking consumer** is a consumer who cannot influence the market price of the good or service by his or her actions. That is, the market price is unaffected by how much or how little of the good the consumer buys.

Defining Perfect Competition

In a **perfectly competitive market,** all market participants, both consumers and producers, are price-takers. That is, neither consumption decisions by individual consumers nor production decisions by individual producers affect the market price of the good.

The supply and demand model, which we introduced in Chapter 3 and have used repeatedly since then, is a model of a perfectly competitive market. It depends fundamentally on the assumption that no individual buyer or seller of a good, such as coffee beans or organic tomatoes, believes that it is possible to affect the price at which he or she can buy or sell the good.

As a general rule, consumers are indeed price-takers. Instances in which consumers are able to affect the prices they pay are rare. It is, however, quite common for producers to have a significant ability to affect the prices they receive, a phenomenon we'll address in Chapter 8. So the model of perfect competition is appropriate for some but not all markets. An industry in which producers are price-takers is called a **perfectly competitive industry.** Clearly, some industries aren't perfectly competitive; in later chapters we'll learn how to analyze industries that don't fit the perfectly competitive model.

Under what circumstances will all producers be price-takers? In the next section we will find that there are two necessary conditions for a perfectly competitive industry and that a third condition is often present as well.

Two Necessary Conditions for Perfect Competition

The markets for major grains, like wheat and corn, are perfectly competitive: individual wheat and corn farmers, as well as individual buyers of wheat and corn, take market prices as given. In contrast, the markets for some of the food items made from these grains—in particular, breakfast cereals—are by no means perfectly competitive. There is intense competition among cereal brands, but not *perfect* competition. To understand the difference between the market for wheat and the market for shredded wheat cereal is to understand the importance of the two necessary conditions for perfect competition.

First, for an industry to be perfectly competitive, it must contain many producers, none of whom has a large **market share.** A producer's market share is the fraction of the total industry output accounted for by that producer's output. The distribution of market share constitutes a major difference between the grain industry and the breakfast cereal industry. There are thousands of wheat farmers, none of whom accounts for more than a tiny fraction of total wheat sales.

The breakfast cereal industry, however, is dominated by four producers: Kellogg's, General Mills, Post Foods, and the Quaker Oats Company. Kellogg's alone accounts for about one-third of all cereal sales. Kellogg's executives know that if they try to sell more cornflakes, they are likely to drive down the market price of cornflakes. That is, they know that their actions influence market prices, simply because they are so large a part of the market that changes in their production will significantly affect the overall quantity supplied. It makes sense to assume that producers are price-takers only when an industry does *not* contain any large producers like Kellogg's.

Second, an industry can be perfectly competitive only if consumers regard the products of all producers as equivalent. This clearly isn't true in the breakfast cereal market: consumers don't consider Cap'n Crunch to be a good substitute for Wheaties. As a result, the maker of Wheaties has some ability to increase its price without fear that it will lose all its customers to the maker of Cap'n Crunch.

Contrast this with the case of a **standardized product,** which is a product that consumers regard as the same good even when it comes from different producers, sometimes known as a **commodity.** Because wheat is a standardized product, consumers regard the output of one wheat producer as a perfect substitute for that of another producer. Consequently, one farmer cannot increase the price for his or her wheat without losing all sales to other wheat farmers. *So the second necessary condition for a competitive industry is that the industry output is a standardized product* (see the upcoming For Inquiring Minds).

A producer's **market share** is the fraction of the total industry output accounted for by that producer's output.

A good is a **standardized product,** also known as a **commodity,** when consumers regard the products of different producers as the same good.

An industry has **free entry and exit** when new producers can easily enter into an industry and existing producers can easily leave that industry.

Free Entry and Exit

All perfectly competitive industries have many producers with small market shares, producing a standardized product. Most perfectly competitive industries are also characterized by one more feature: it is easy for new firms to enter the industry or for firms that are currently in the industry to leave. That is, no obstacles in the form of government regulations or limited access to key resources prevent new producers from entering the market. And no additional costs are associated with shutting down a company and leaving the industry. Economists refer to the arrival of new firms into an industry as *entry;* they refer to the departure of firms from an industry as *exit.* When there are no obstacles to entry into or exit from an industry, we say that the industry has **free entry and exit.**

Free entry and exit is not strictly necessary for perfect competition. In Chapter 4 we described the case of New Jersey clam fishing, where regulations limit the number of fishing boats, so entry into the industry is limited. Despite this, there are enough boats operating that the fishermen are price-takers. But free entry and exit is a key factor in most competitive industries. It ensures that the number of producers in an industry can adjust to changing market conditions. And, in particular, it ensures that producers in an industry cannot act to keep new firms out.

To sum up, then, perfect competition depends on two necessary conditions. First, the industry must contain many producers, each having a small

FOR INQUIRING MINDS

WHAT'S A STANDARDIZED PRODUCT?

A perfectly competitive industry must produce a standardized product. But is it enough for the products of different firms actually to be the same? No: people must also *think* that they are the same. And producers often go to great lengths to convince consumers that they have a distinctive, or *differentiated,* product, even when they don't.

Consider, for example, champagne—not the superexpensive premium champagnes but the more ordinary stuff. Most people cannot tell the difference between champagne actually produced in the Champagne region of France, where the product originated, and similar products from Spain or California. But the French government has sought and obtained legal protection for the winemakers of Champagne, ensuring that around the world only bubbly wine from that region can be called champagne. If it's from someplace else, all the seller can do is say that it was produced using the *méthode Champenoise.* This creates a differentiation in the minds of consumers and lets the champagne producers of Champagne charge higher prices.

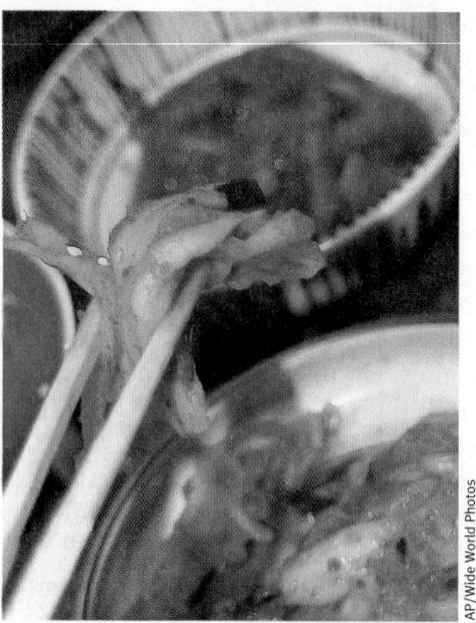
AP/Wide World Photos

In the end, only kimchi eaters can tell you if there is truly a difference between Korean-produced kimchi and the Japanese-produced variety.

Similarly, Korean producers of *kimchi,* the spicy fermented cabbage that is the Korean national side dish, are doing their best to convince consumers that the same product packaged by Japanese firms is just not the real thing. The purpose is, of course, to ensure higher prices for Korean *kimchi.*

So is an industry perfectly competitive if it sells products that are indistinguishable except in name but that consumers, for whatever reason, don't think are standardized? No. When it comes to defining the nature of competition, the consumer is always right.

market share. Second, the industry must produce a standardized product. In addition, perfectly competitive industries are normally characterized by free entry and exit.

How does an industry that meets these three criteria behave? As a first step toward answering that question, let's look at how an individual producer in a perfectly competitive industry maximizes profit.

ECONOMICS ➤ IN ACTION

THE PAIN OF COMPETITION

Sometimes it is possible to see an industry become perfectly competitive. In fact, it happens frequently in the case of pharmaceuticals when the patent on a popular drug expires.

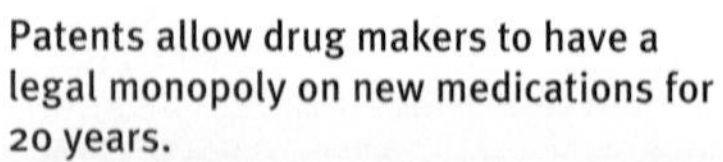
Patents allow drug makers to have a legal monopoly on new medications for 20 years.

© Todd Bennett/Journal Communications Inc.

When a company develops a new drug, it is usually able to receive a patent, which gives it a *legal monopoly*—the exclusive right to sell the drug—for 20 years from the date of filing. Legally, no one else can sell that drug without the patent owner's permission. When the patent expires, the market is open for other companies to sell their own versions of the drug, known collectively as *generics.* Generics are standardized products, much like aspirin, and are often sold by many producers.

The shift from a market with a single seller to perfect competition, not coincidentally, is accompanied by a sharp fall in the market price. For example, when the patent expired for the painkiller ibuprofen and generics were introduced, its price eventually fell by nearly 75%; the price of the painkiller naproxen fell by 90%. On average, drug prices are 40% lower after a generic enters the market.

Not surprisingly, the makers of patent-protected drugs are eager to forestall the entry of generic competitors and have tried a variety of strategies. One especially successful tactic is for the original drug maker to make an agreement with a potential generic competitor, essentially paying the competitor to delay its entry into the market. As a result, the original drug maker continues to charge high prices and reap high profits. These agreements have been fiercely contested by many government regulators, who view them as anti-competitive practices that hurt consumers. As of the time of writing, drug makers, consumers, and government officials were anticipating a review by the Supreme Court of the legality of these agreements.

Quick Review

- Neither the actions of a **price-taking producer** nor those of a **price-taking consumer** can influence the market price of a good.
- In a **perfectly competitive market** all producers and consumers are price-takers. Consumers are almost always price-takers, but this is often not true of producers. An industry in which producers are price-takers is a **perfectly competitive industry.**
- A perfectly competitive industry contains many producers, each of which produces a **standardized product** (also known as a **commodity**) but none of which has a large **market share.**
- Most perfectly competitive industries are also characterized by **free entry and exit.**

CHECK YOUR UNDERSTANDING 7-1

1. In each of the following situations, do you think the industry described will be perfectly competitive or not? Explain your answer.
   a. There are two producers of aluminum in the world; however, it is a good sold in many places.
   b. The price of natural gas is determined by global supply and demand. A small share of that global supply is produced by a handful of companies located in the North Sea.
   c. Dozens of designers sell high-fashion clothes. Each designer has a distinctive style and a loyal clientele.
   d. There are many baseball teams in the United States, one or two in each major city and each selling tickets to its hometown events.

Solutions appear at back of book.

Production and Profits

Consider Jennifer and Jason, who run an organic tomato farm. Suppose that the market price of organic tomatoes is $18 per bushel and that Jennifer and Jason are price-takers—they can sell as much as they like at that price. Then we can use the data in Table 7-1 to find their profit-maximizing level of output by direct calculation.

The first column shows the quantity of output in bushels, and the second column shows Jennifer and Jason's total revenue from their output: the market value of their output. Total revenue, *TR*, is equal to the market price multiplied by the quantity of output:

(7-1) $TR = P \times Q$

In this example, total revenue is equal to $18 per bushel times the quantity of output in bushels.

The third column of Table 7-1 shows Jennifer and Jason's total cost. The fourth column shows their profit, equal to total revenue minus total cost:

(7-2) Profit $= TR - TC$

TABLE 7-1 Profit for Jennifer and Jason's Farm When Market Price Is $18

Quantity of tomatoes Q (bushels)	Total revenue *TR*	Total cost *TC*	Profit *TR* – *TC*
0	$0	$14	–$14
1	18	30	–12
2	36	36	0
3	54	44	10
4	72	56	16
5	90	72	18
6	108	92	16
7	126	116	10

As indicated by the numbers in the table, profit is maximized at an output of 5 bushels, where profit is equal to $18. But we can gain more insight into the profit-maximizing choice of output by viewing it as a problem of marginal analysis, a task we'll do next.

The **marginal benefit** of a good or service is the additional benefit derived from producing one more unit of that good or service.

The **principle of marginal analysis** says that the optimal amount of an activity is the quantity at which marginal benefit equals marginal cost.

Marginal revenue is the change in total revenue generated by an additional unit of output.

According to the **optimal output rule,** profit is maximized by producing the quantity of output at which the marginal revenue of the last unit produced is equal to its marginal cost.

According to the **price-taking firm's optimal output rule,** a price-taking firm's profit is maximized by producing the quantity of output at which the market price is equal to the marginal cost of the last unit produced.

Using Marginal Analysis to Choose the Profit-Maximizing Quantity of Output

Recall from Chapter 6 the definition of *marginal cost:* the additional cost incurred by producing one more unit of that good or service. Similarly, the **marginal benefit** of a good or service is the additional benefit gained from producing one more unit of a good or service. We are now ready to use the **principle of marginal analysis,** which says that the optimal amount of an activity is the level at which marginal benefit is equal to marginal cost.

To apply this principle, consider the effect on a producer's profit of increasing output by one unit. The marginal benefit of that unit is the additional revenue generated by selling it; this measure has a name—it is called the **marginal revenue** of that unit of output. The general formula for marginal revenue is:

$$\textbf{(7-3)}\ \text{Marginal revenue} = \begin{array}{c}\text{Change in total revenue}\\ \text{generated by one}\\ \text{additional unit of output}\end{array} = \frac{\text{Change in total revenue}}{\text{Change in quantity of output}}$$

or

$$MR = \Delta TR/\Delta Q$$

So Jennifer and Jason maximize their profit by producing bushels up to the point at which the marginal revenue is equal to marginal cost. We can summarize this as the producer's **optimal output rule:** profit is maximized by producing the quantity at which the marginal revenue of the last unit produced is equal to its marginal cost. That is, $MR = MC$ at the optimal quantity of output.

We can learn how to apply the optimal output rule with the help of Table 7-2, which provides various short-run cost measures for Jennifer and Jason's farm. The second column contains the farm's variable cost, and the third column shows its total cost of output based on the assumption that the farm incurs a fixed cost of $14. The fourth column shows their marginal cost. Notice that, in this example, the marginal cost initially falls as output rises but then begins to increase. This gives the marginal cost curve the "swoosh" shape described in the Selena's Gourmet Salsas example in Chapter 6. (Shortly it will become clear that this shape has important implications for short-run production decisions.)

TABLE 7-2 Short-Run Costs for Jennifer and Jason's Farm

Quantity of tomatoes *Q* (bushels)	Variable cost *VC*	Total cost *TC*	Marginal cost of bushel $MC = \Delta TC/\Delta Q$	Marginal revenue of bushel *MR*	Net gain of bushel = *MR* − *MC*
0	$0	$14			
			$16	$18	$2
1	16	30			
			6	18	12
2	22	36			
			8	18	10
3	30	44			
			12	18	6
4	42	56			
			16	18	2
5	58	72			
			20	18	−2
6	78	92			
			24	18	−6
7	102	116			

The fifth column contains the farm's marginal revenue, which has an important feature: Jennifer and Jason's marginal revenue is constant at $18 for every output level. The sixth and final column shows the calculation of the net gain per bushel of tomatoes, which is equal to marginal revenue minus marginal cost—or, equivalently in this case, market price minus marginal cost. As you can see, it is positive for the 1st through 5th bushels; producing each of these bushels raises Jennifer and Jason's profit. For the 6th and 7th bushels, however, net gain is negative: producing them would decrease, not increase, profit. (You can verify this by examining Table 7-1.) So 5 bushels are Jennifer and Jason's profit-maximizing output; it is the level of output at which marginal cost is equal to the market price, $18.

This example, in fact, illustrates another general rule derived from marginal analysis—the **price-taking firm's optimal output rule,** which says that a price-taking firm's profit is maximized by producing the quantity of output at which the market price is equal to the marginal cost of the last unit produced. That is, $P = MC$ *at the price-taking firm's optimal quantity of output.* In fact, the price-taking firm's optimal output rule is just an application of the optimal output rule to the particular case of a price-taking firm. Why? Because *in the case of a price-taking firm, marginal revenue is equal to the market price.*

The **marginal revenue curve** shows how marginal revenue varies as output varies.

A price-taking firm cannot influence the market price by its actions. It always takes the market price as given because it cannot lower the market price by selling more or raise the market price by selling less. So, for a price-taking firm, the additional revenue generated by producing one more unit is always the market price. We will need to keep this fact in mind in future chapters, where we will learn that marginal revenue is not equal to the market price if the industry is not perfectly competitive. As a result, firms are not price-takers when an industry is not perfectly competitive.

For the remainder of this chapter, we will assume that the industry in question is like organic tomato farming, perfectly competitive. Figure 7-1 shows that Jennifer and Jason's profit-maximizing quantity of output is, indeed, the number of bushels at which the marginal cost of production is equal to price. The figure shows the marginal cost curve, *MC,* drawn from the data in the fourth column of Table 7-2. We plot the marginal cost of increasing output from 1 to 2 bushels halfway between 1 and 2, and so on. The horizontal line at $18 is Jennifer and Jason's **marginal revenue curve.**

Note that whenever a firm is a price-taker, its marginal revenue curve is a horizontal line at the market price: it can sell as much as it likes at the market price. Regardless of whether it sells more or less, the market price is unaffected. *In effect, the individual firm faces a horizontal, perfectly elastic demand curve for its output—an individual demand curve for its output that is equivalent to its marginal revenue curve.* The marginal cost curve crosses the marginal revenue curve at point *E.* Sure enough, the quantity of output at *E* is 5 bushels.

Does this mean that the price-taking firm's production decision can be entirely summed up as "produce up to the point where the marginal cost of

WHAT IF MARGINAL REVENUE AND MARGINAL COST AREN'T EXACTLY EQUAL?

The optimal output rule says that to maximize profit, you should produce the quantity at which marginal revenue is equal to marginal cost. But what do you do if there is no output level at which marginal revenue equals marginal cost? In that case, you produce the largest quantity for which marginal revenue exceeds marginal cost. This is the case in Table 7-2 at an output of 5 bushels. The simpler version of the optimal output rule applies when production involves large numbers, such as hundreds or thousands of units. In such cases marginal cost comes in small increments, and there is always a level of output at which marginal cost almost exactly equals marginal revenue.

FIGURE 7-1 The Price-Taking Firm's Profit-Maximizing Quantity of Output

At the profit-maximizing quantity of output, the market price is equal to marginal cost. It is located at the point where the marginal cost curve crosses the marginal revenue curve, which is a horizontal line at the market price. Here, the profit-maximizing point is at an output of 5 bushels of tomatoes, the output quantity at point *E*.

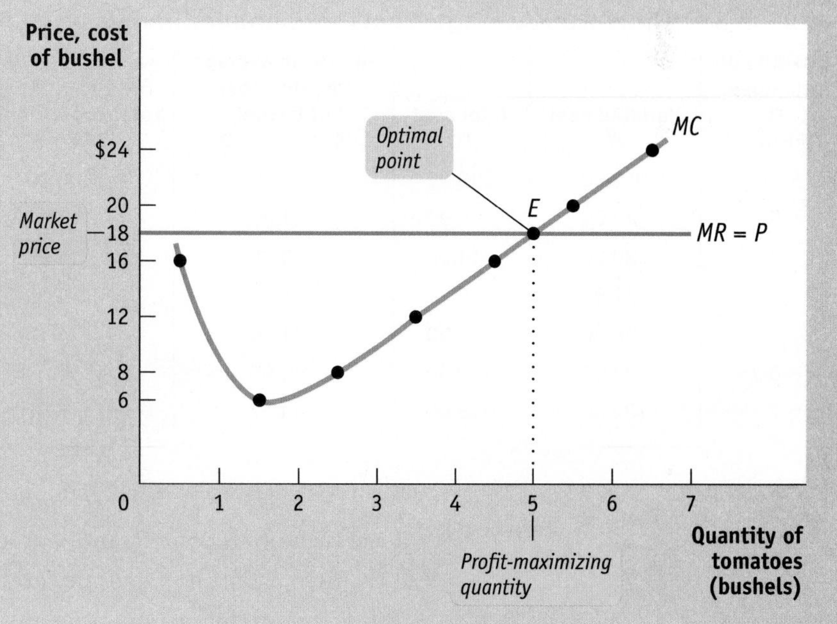

Economic profit is equal to revenue minus the opportunity cost of resources used.

An **explicit cost** is a cost that requires an outlay of money.

An **implicit cost** does not require an outlay of money; it is measured by the value, in dollar terms, of benefits that are forgone.

Accounting profit is equal to revenue minus explicit cost. It is usually larger than economic profit.

production is equal to the price"? No, not quite. Before applying the profit-maximizing principle of marginal analysis to determine how much to produce, a potential producer must as a first step answer an "either–or" question: should it produce at all? If the answer to that question is yes, it then proceeds to the second step—a "how much" decision: maximizing profit by choosing the quantity of output at which marginal cost is equal to price.

To understand why the first step in the production decision involves an "either–or" question, we need to ask how we determine whether it is profitable or unprofitable to produce at all.

When Is Production Profitable?

A firm's decision whether or not to stay in a given business depends on its **economic profit**—the firm's revenue minus the opportunity cost of its resources. To put it in a slightly different way: in the calculation of economic profit, a firm's total cost incorporates *explicit cost* and *implicit cost*. An **explicit cost** is a cost that involves actually laying out money. An **implicit cost** does not require an outlay of money; it is measured by the value, in dollar terms, of benefits that are forgone.

In contrast, **accounting profit** is profit calculated using only the explicit costs incurred by the firm. It is the firm's revenue minus the explicit cost and depreciation. This means that economic profit incorporates the opportunity cost of resources owned by the firm and used in the production of output, while accounting profit does not.

A firm may make positive accounting profit while making zero or even negative economic profit. It's important to understand clearly that a firm's decision to produce or not, to stay in business or to close down permanently, should be based on economic profit, not accounting profit.

We will assume that the cost numbers given in Tables 7-1 and 7-2 include all costs, implicit as well as explicit, and that the profit numbers in Table 7-1 are therefore economic profit. So what determines whether Jennifer and Jason's farm earns a profit or generates a loss? The answer is that, *given the farm's cost curves, whether or not it is profitable depends on the market price of tomatoes—specifically, whether the market price is more or less than the farm's minimum average total cost.*

In Table 7-3 we calculate short-run average variable cost and short-run average total cost for Jennifer and Jason's farm. These are short-run values because we take fixed cost as given. (We'll turn to the effects of changing fixed cost shortly.) The short-run average total cost curve, *ATC*, is shown in Figure 7-2, along with the marginal cost curve, *MC*, from Figure 7-1. As you can see, average total cost is minimized at point *C*, corresponding to an output of 4 bushels—the *minimum-cost output*—and an average total cost of $14 per bushel.

TABLE 7-3 Short-Run Average Costs for Jennifer and Jason's Farm

Quantity of tomatoes *Q* (bushels)	Variable cost *VC*	Total cost *TC*	Short-run average variable cost of bushel *AVC = VC/Q*	Short-run average total cost of bushel *ATC = TC/Q*
1	$16.00	$30.00	$16.00	$30.00
2	22.00	36.00	11.00	18.00
3	30.00	44.00	10.00	14.67
4	42.00	56.00	10.50	14.00
5	58.00	72.00	11.60	14.40
6	78.00	92.00	13.00	15.33
7	102.00	116.00	14.57	16.57

To see how these curves can be used to decide whether production is profitable or unprofitable, recall that profit is equal to total revenue minus total cost, *TR* – *TC*. This means:

- If the firm produces a quantity at which *TR* > *TC*, the firm is profitable.
- If the firm produces a quantity at which *TR* = *TC*, the firm breaks even.
- If the firm produces a quantity at which *TR* < *TC*, the firm incurs a loss.

FIGURE 7-2 Costs and Production in the Short Run

This figure shows the marginal cost curve, *MC*, and the short-run average total cost curve, *ATC*. When the market price is $14, output will be 4 bushels of tomatoes (the minimum-cost output), represented by point *C*. The price of $14, equal to the firm's minimum average total cost, is the firm's *break-even price*.

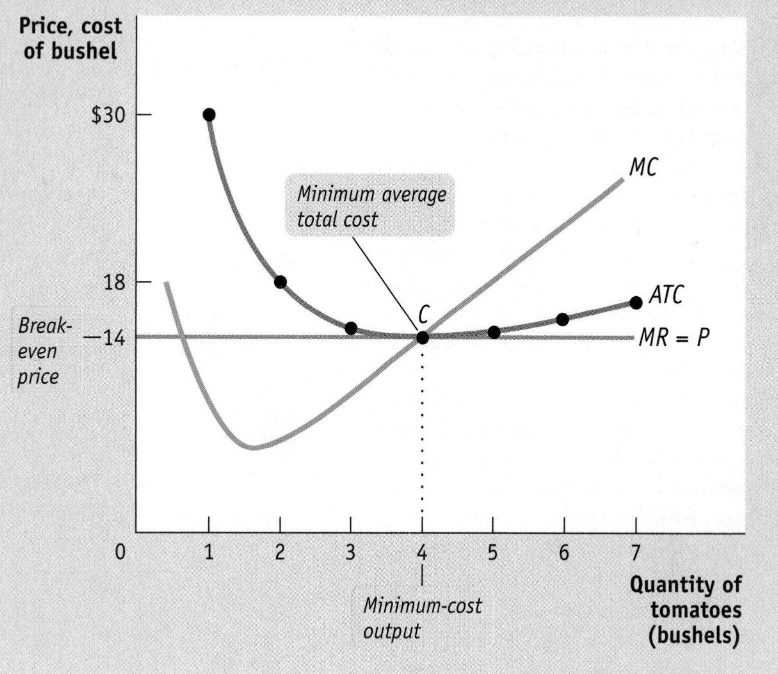

We can also express this idea in terms of revenue and cost per unit of output. If we divide profit by the number of units of output, *Q*, we obtain the following expression for profit per unit of output:

(7-4) $\text{Profit}/Q = TR/Q - TC/Q$

TR/Q is average revenue, which is the market price. *TC/Q* is average total cost. So a firm is profitable if the market price for its product is more than the average total cost of the quantity the firm produces; a firm loses money if the market price is less than average total cost of the quantity the firm produces. This means:

- If the firm produces a quantity at which $P > ATC$, the firm is profitable.
- If the firm produces a quantity at which $P = ATC$, the firm breaks even.
- If the firm produces a quantity at which $P < ATC$, the firm incurs a loss.

Figure 7-3 illustrates this result, showing how the market price determines whether a firm is profitable. It also shows how profits are depicted graphically. Each panel shows the marginal cost curve, *MC*, and the short-run average total cost curve, *ATC*. Average total cost is minimized at point *C*. Panel (a) shows the case we have already analyzed, in which the market price of tomatoes is $18 per bushel. Panel (b) shows the case in which the market price of tomatoes is lower, $10 per bushel.

In panel (a), we see that at a price of $18 per bushel the profit-maximizing quantity of output is 5 bushels, indicated by point *E*, where the marginal cost curve, *MC*, intersects the marginal revenue curve—which for a price-taking firm is a horizontal line at the market price. At that quantity of output, average total cost is $14.40 per bushel, indicated by point *Z*. Since the price per bushel exceeds average total cost per bushel, Jennifer and Jason's farm is profitable.

FIGURE 7-3 Profitability and the Market Price

In panel (a) the market price is $18. The farm is profitable because price exceeds minimum average total cost, the break-even price, $14. The farm's optimal output choice is indicated by point *E*, corresponding to an output of 5 bushels. The average total cost of producing 5 bushels is indicated by point *Z* on the *ATC* curve, corresponding to an amount of $14.40. The vertical distance between *E* and *Z* corresponds to the farm's per-unit profit, $18.00 – $14.40 = $3.60. Total profit is given by the area of the shaded rectangle, 5 × $3.60 = $18.00. In panel (b) the market price is $10; the farm is unprofitable because the price falls below the minimum average total cost, $14. The farm's optimal output choice when producing is indicated by point *A*, corresponding to an output of 3 bushels. The farm's per-unit loss, $14.67 – $10.00 = $4.67, is represented by the vertical distance between *A* and *Y*. The farm's total loss is represented by the shaded rectangle, 3 × $4.67 = $14.00 (adjusted for rounding error).

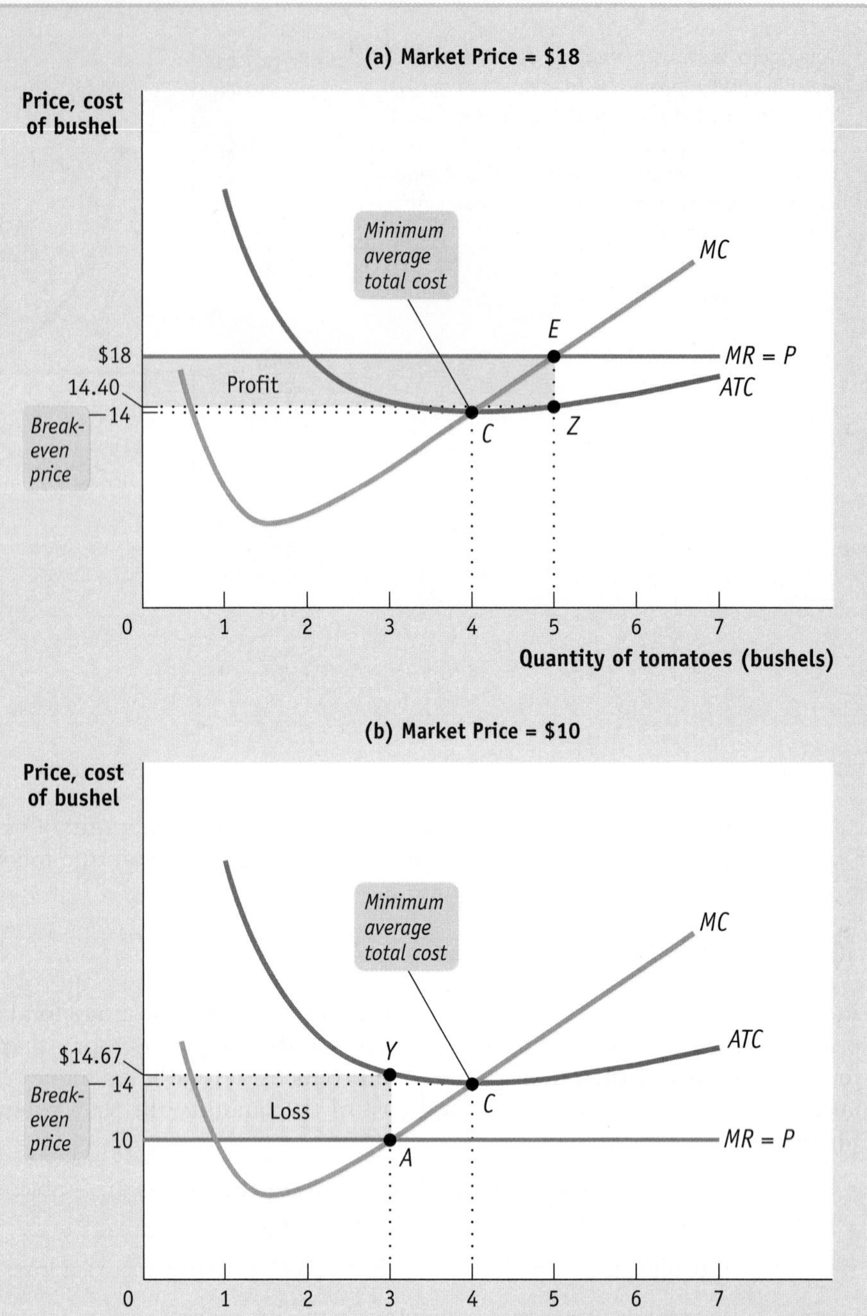

Jennifer and Jason's total profit when the market price is $18 is represented by the area of the shaded rectangle in panel (a). To see why, notice that total profit can be expressed in terms of profit per unit:

(7-5) Profit = $TR - TC = (TR/Q - TC/Q) \times Q$

or, equivalently,

$$\text{Profit} = (P - ATC) \times Q$$

since P is equal to TR/Q and ATC is equal to TC/Q. The height of the shaded rectangle in panel (a) corresponds to the vertical distance between points *E* and *Z*. It is equal to $P - ATC$ = \$18.00 – \$14.40 = \$3.60 per bushel. The shaded rectangle has a width equal to the output: Q = 5 bushels. So the area of that rectangle is equal to Jennifer and Jason's profit: 5 bushels × \$3.60 profit per bushel = \$18—the same number we calculated in Table 7-1.

What about the situation illustrated in panel (b)? Here the market price of tomatoes is \$10 per bushel. Setting price equal to marginal cost leads to a profit-maximizing output of 3 bushels, indicated by point *A*. At this output, Jennifer and Jason have an average total cost of \$14.67 per bushel, indicated by point *Y*. At their profit-maximizing output quantity—3 bushels—average total cost exceeds the market price. This means that Jennifer and Jason's farm generates a loss, not a profit.

How much do they lose by producing when the market price is \$10? On each bushel they lose $ATC - P$ = \$14.67 – \$10.00 = \$4.67, an amount corresponding to the vertical distance between points *A* and *Y*. And they would produce 3 bushels, which corresponds to the width of the shaded rectangle. So the total value of the losses is \$4.67 × 3 = \$14.00 (adjusted for rounding error), an amount that corresponds to the area of the shaded rectangle in panel (b).

But how does a producer know, in general, whether or not its business will be profitable? It turns out that the crucial test lies in a comparison of the market price to the producer's *minimum average total cost*. On Jennifer and Jason's farm, minimum average total cost, which is equal to \$14, occurs at an output quantity of 4 bushels, indicated by point *C*. Whenever the market price exceeds minimum average total cost, the producer can find some output level for which the average total cost is less than the market price. In other words, the producer can find a level of output at which the firm makes a profit. So Jennifer and Jason's farm will be profitable whenever the market price exceeds \$14. And they will achieve the highest possible profit by producing the quantity at which marginal cost equals the market price.

Conversely, if the market price is less than minimum average total cost, there is no output level at which price exceeds average total cost. As a result, the firm will be unprofitable at any quantity of output. As we saw, at a price of \$10—an amount less than minimum average total cost—Jennifer and Jason did indeed lose money. By producing the quantity at which marginal cost equals the market price, Jennifer and Jason did the best they could, but the best that they could do was a loss of \$14. Any other quantity would have increased the size of their loss.

The minimum average total cost of a price-taking firm is called its **break-even price,** the price at which it earns zero profit. (Recall that's *economic profit*.) A firm will earn positive profit when the market price is above the break-even price, and it will suffer losses when the market price is below the break-even price. Jennifer and Jason's break-even price of \$14 is the price at point *C* in Figures 7-2 and 7-3.

The **break-even price** of a price-taking firm is the market price at which it earns zero profit.

So the rule for determining whether a producer of a good is profitable depends on a comparison of the market price of the good to the producer's break-even price—its minimum average total cost:

- Whenever the market price exceeds minimum average total cost, the producer is profitable.
- Whenever the market price equals minimum average total cost, the producer breaks even.
- Whenever the market price is less than minimum average total cost, the producer is unprofitable.

The Short-Run Production Decision

You might be tempted to say that if a firm is unprofitable because the market price is below its minimum average total cost, it shouldn't produce any output. In the short run, however, this conclusion isn't right. In the short run, sometimes the firm should produce even if price falls below minimum average total cost. The reason is that total cost includes *fixed cost*—cost that does not depend on the amount of output produced and can only be altered in the long run. In the short run, fixed cost must still be paid, regardless of whether or not a firm produces. For example, if Jennifer and Jason have rented a tractor for the year, they have to pay the rent on the tractor regardless of whether they produce any tomatoes. *Since it cannot be changed in the short run, their fixed cost is irrelevant to their decision about whether to produce or shut down in the short run.*

Although fixed cost should play no role in the decision about whether to produce in the short run, other costs—variable costs—do matter. An example of variable costs is the wages of workers who must be hired to help with planting and harvesting. Variable costs can be saved by *not* producing; so they should play a role in determining whether or not to produce in the short run.

Let's turn to Figure 7-4: it shows both the short-run average total cost curve, *ATC*, and the short-run average variable cost curve, *AVC*, drawn from the information in Table 7-3. Recall that the difference between the two curves—the vertical distance between them—represents average fixed cost, the fixed cost per unit of output, *FC/Q*. Because the marginal cost curve has a "swoosh" shape—falling at first before rising—the short-run average variable cost curve is U-shaped: the initial fall in marginal cost causes average variable cost to fall as well, before rising marginal cost eventually pulls it up again. The short-run average variable cost curve reaches its minimum value of $10 at point *A*, at an output of 3 bushels.

We are now prepared to fully analyze the optimal production decision in the short run. We need to consider two cases:

- When the market price is below minimum average *variable* cost
- When the market price is greater than or equal to minimum average *variable* cost

When the market price is below minimum average variable cost, the price the firm receives per unit is not covering its variable cost per unit. A firm in this situation should cease production immediately. Why? Because there is no level of output at which the firm's total revenue covers its variable costs—the costs it can avoid by not operating. In this case the firm maximizes its profits by not producing at all—by, in effect, minimizing its losses. It will still incur a fixed cost in the short run, but it will no longer incur any variable cost. This means that the minimum

FIGURE 7-4 The Short-Run Individual Supply Curve

When the market price equals or exceeds Jennifer and Jason's *shut-down price* of $10, the minimum average variable cost indicated by point *A*, they will produce the output quantity at which marginal cost is equal to price. So at any price equal to or above the minimum average *variable* cost, the short-run individual supply curve is the firm's marginal cost curve; this corresponds to the upward-sloping segment of the individual supply curve. When market price falls below minimum average variable cost, the firm ceases operation in the short run. This corresponds to the vertical segment of the individual supply curve along the vertical axis.

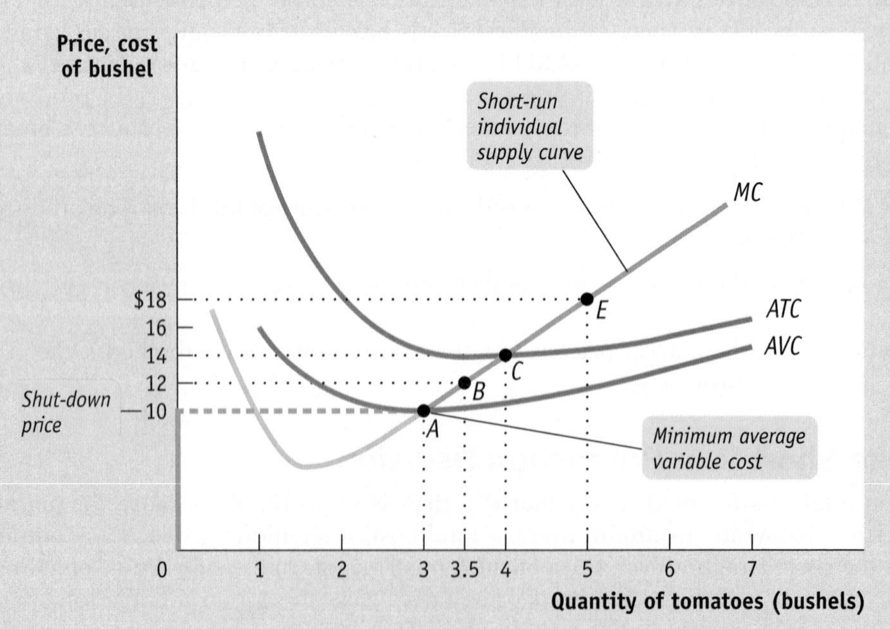

average variable cost is equal to the **shut-down price,** the price at which the firm ceases production in the short run.

When price is greater than minimum average variable cost, however, the firm should produce in the short run. In this case, the firm maximizes profit—or minimizes loss—by choosing the output quantity at which its marginal cost is equal to the market price. For example, if the market price of tomatoes is $18 per bushel, Jennifer and Jason should produce at point *E* in Figure 7-4, corresponding to an output of 5 bushels. Note that point *C* in Figure 7-4 corresponds to the farm's break-even price of $14 per bushel. Since *E* lies above *C*, Jennifer and Jason's farm will be profitable; they will generate a per-bushel profit of $18.00 – $14.40 = $3.60 when the market price is $18.

But what if the market price lies between the shut-down price and the break-even price—that is, between minimum average *variable* cost and minimum average *total* cost? In the case of Jennifer and Jason's farm, this corresponds to prices anywhere between $10 and $14—say, a market price of $12. At $12, Jennifer and Jason's farm is not profitable; since the market price is below minimum average total cost, the farm is losing the difference between price and average total cost per unit produced. Yet even if it isn't covering its total cost per unit, it is covering its variable cost per unit and some—but not all—of the fixed cost per unit. If a firm in this situation shuts down, it would incur no variable cost but would incur the *full* fixed cost. As a result, shutting down generates an even greater loss than continuing to operate.

This means that whenever price lies between minimum average total cost and minimum average variable cost, the firm is better off producing some output in the short run. The reason is that by producing, it can cover its variable cost per unit and at least some of its fixed cost, even though it is incurring a loss. In this case, the firm maximizes profit—that is, minimizes loss—by choosing the quantity of output at which its marginal cost is equal to the market price. So if Jennifer and Jason face a market price of $12 per bushel, their profit-maximizing output is given by point *B* in Figure 7-4, corresponding to an output of 3.5 bushels.

It's worth noting that the decision to produce when the firm is covering its variable costs but not all of its fixed cost is similar to the decision to ignore *sunk costs*. A **sunk cost** is a cost that has already been incurred and cannot be recouped; and because it cannot be changed, it should have no effect on any current decision. In the short-run production decision, fixed cost is, in effect, like a sunk cost—it has been spent, and it can't be recovered in the short run. This comparison also illustrates why variable cost does indeed matter in the short run: it can be avoided by not producing.

And what happens if market price is exactly equal to the shut-down price, minimum average variable cost? In this instance, the firm is indifferent between producing 3 units or 0 units. As we'll see shortly, this is an important point when looking at the behavior of an industry as a whole. For the sake of clarity, we'll assume that the firm, although indifferent, does indeed produce output when price is equal to the shut-down price.

Putting everything together, we can now draw the **short-run individual supply curve** of Jennifer and Jason's farm, the red line in Figure 7-4; it shows how the profit-maximizing quantity of output in the short run depends on the price. As you can see, the curve is in two segments. The upward-sloping red segment starting at point *A* shows the short-run profit-maximizing output when market price is equal to or above the shut-down price of $10 per bushel.

As long as the market price is equal to or above the shut-down price, Jennifer and Jason produce the quantity of output at which marginal cost is equal to the market price. That is, at market prices equal to or above the shut-down price, the firm's short-run supply curve corresponds to its marginal cost curve. But at any market price below minimum average variable cost—in this case, $10 per bushel—the firm shuts down and output drops to zero in the short run. This corresponds to the vertical segment of the curve that lies on top of the vertical axis.

A firm will cease production in the short run if the market price falls below the **shut-down price,** which is equal to minimum average variable cost.

A **sunk cost** is a cost that has already been incurred and is nonrecoverable. A sunk cost should be ignored in decisions about future actions.

The **short-run individual supply curve** shows how an individual producer's profit-maximizing output quantity depends on the market price, taking fixed cost as given.

Do firms really shut down temporarily without going out of business? Yes. In fact, in some businesses temporary shut-downs are routine. The most common examples are industries in which demand is highly seasonal, like outdoor amusement parks in climates with cold winters. Such parks would have to offer very low prices to entice customers during the colder months—prices so low that the owners would not cover their variable costs (principally wages and electricity). The wiser choice economically is to shut down until warm weather brings enough customers who are willing to pay a higher price.

Changing Fixed Cost

Although fixed cost cannot be altered in the short run, in the long run firms can acquire or get rid of machines, buildings, and so on. As we learned in Chapter 6, in the long run the level of fixed cost is a matter of choice. There we saw that a firm will choose the level of fixed cost that minimizes the average total cost for its desired output quantity. Now we will focus on an even bigger question facing a firm when choosing its fixed cost: whether to incur *any* fixed cost at all by remaining in its current business.

In the long run, a producer can always eliminate fixed cost by selling off its plant and equipment. If it does so, of course, it can't ever produce—it has exited the industry. In contrast, a potential producer can take on some fixed cost by acquiring machines and other resources, which puts it in a position to produce—it can enter the industry. In most perfectly competitive industries the set of producers, although fixed in the short run, changes in the long run as firms enter or exit the industry.

Consider Jennifer and Jason's farm once again. In order to simplify our analysis, we will sidestep the problem of choosing among several possible levels of fixed cost. Instead, we will assume from now on that Jennifer and Jason have only one possible choice of fixed cost if they operate, the amount of $14 that was the basis for the calculations in Tables 7-1, 7-2, and 7-3. (With this assumption, Jennifer and Jason's short-run average total cost curve and long-run average total cost curve are one and the same.) Alternatively, they can choose a fixed cost of zero if they exit the industry.

Suppose that the market price of organic tomatoes is consistently less than $14 over an extended period of time. In that case, Jennifer and Jason never fully cover their fixed cost: their business runs at a persistent loss. In the long run, then, they can do better by closing their business and leaving the industry. In other words, *in the long run* firms will exit an industry if the market price is consistently less than their break-even price—their minimum average total cost.

Conversely, suppose that the price of organic tomatoes is consistently above the break-even price, $14, for an extended period of time. Because their farm is profitable, Jennifer and Jason will remain in the industry and continue producing.

But things won't stop there. The organic tomato industry meets the criterion of *free entry*: there are many potential organic tomato producers because the necessary inputs are easy to obtain. And the cost curves of those potential producers are likely to be similar to those of Jennifer and Jason, since the technology used by other producers is likely to be very similar to that used by Jennifer and Jason. If the price is high enough to generate profits for existing producers, it will also attract some of these potential producers into the industry. So *in the long run* a price in excess of $14 should lead to entry: new producers will come into the organic tomato industry.

As we will see in the next section, exit and entry lead to an important distinction between the *short-run industry supply curve* and the *long-run industry supply curve.*

Summing Up: The Perfectly Competitive Firm's Profitability and Production Conditions

In this chapter, we've studied where the supply curve for a perfectly competitive, price-taking firm comes from. Every perfectly competitive firm makes its production decisions by maximizing profit, and these decisions determine the supply curve. Table 7-4 summarizes the perfectly competitive firm's profitability and production conditions. It also relates them to entry into and exit from the industry.

TABLE 7-4 Summary of the Perfectly Competitive Firm's Profitability and Production Conditions

Profitability condition (minimum *ATC* = break-even price)	Result
P > minimum *ATC*	Firm profitable. Entry into industry in the long run.
P = minimum *ATC*	Firm breaks even. No entry into or exit from industry in the long run.
P < minimum *ATC*	Firm unprofitable. Exit from industry in the long run.
Production condition (minimum *AVC* = shut-down price)	**Result**
P > minimum *AVC*	Firm produces in the short run. If *P* < minimum *ATC*, firm covers variable cost and some but not all of fixed cost. If *P* > minimum *ATC*, firm covers all variable cost and fixed cost.
P = minimum *AVC*	Firm indifferent between producing in the short run or not. Just covers variable cost.
P < minimum *AVC*	Firm shuts down in the short run. Does not cover variable cost.

ECONOMICS ➤ IN ACTION

PRICES ARE UP . . . BUT SO ARE COSTS

Because of the Energy Policy Act of 2005, 7.5 billion gallons of alternative fuel, mostly corn-based ethanol, was added to the American fuel supply to help reduce gasoline consumption. The unsurprising result of this mandate: the demand for corn skyrocketed, along with the price. In August 2012, a bushel of corn hit a high of $8.32, nearly quadruple the early January 2005 price of $2.09.

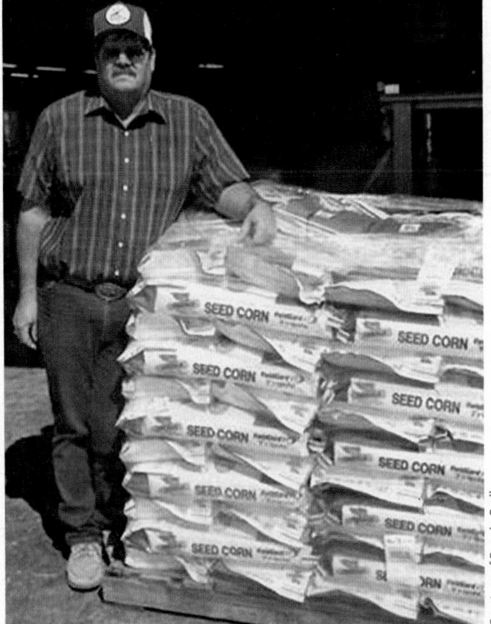

Courtesy of Ronnie Gerik.

Although Gerik was taking a big gamble when he cut the size of his cotton crop to plant more corn, his decision made good economic sense.

This sharp rise in the price of corn caught the eye of American farmers like Ronnie Gerik of Aquilla, Texas, who reduced the size of his cotton crop and increased his corn acreage by 40%. Overall, the U.S. corn acreage planted in 2011 was 9% more than the average planted over the previous decade, and 4% more corn was planted in 2012 than in 2011. Like Gerik, other farmers substituted corn production for the production of other crops; for example, in 2011, soybean acreage was down around 3% and decreased by another 1% in 2012.

Although this sounds like a sure way to make a profit, Gerik and farmers like him were taking a gamble. Consider the cost of an important input, fertilizer. Corn requires more fertilizer than other crops, and with more farmers planting corn, the increased demand for fertilizer led to a price increase. Prices for fertilizer produced from nitrogen nearly doubled from 2005 to 2012. Moreover, corn is more sensitive to the amount of rainfall than a crop like cotton. So farmers who plant corn in drought-prone places like Texas are increasing their risk of loss. Gerik had to incorporate into his calculations his best guess of what a dry spell would cost him.

Despite all this, what Gerik and other farmers did made complete economic sense. By planting more corn, each one moved up his or her individual short-run supply curve for corn production. And because the individual supply curve is the marginal cost curve, each farmer's costs also went up because of the need to apply more inputs—inputs that are now more expensive to obtain.

So the moral of the story is that farmers will increase their corn acreage until the marginal cost of producing corn is approximately equal to the market price of corn, which shouldn't come as a surprise because corn production satisfies all the requirements of a perfectly competitive industry.

Quick Review

- Per the **principle of marginal analysis,** the optimal amount of an activity is the quantity at which **marginal benefit** equals marginal cost.
- A producer chooses output according to the **optimal output rule.** For a price-taking firm, **marginal revenue** is equal to price and it chooses output according to the **price-taking firm's optimal output rule.**
- The **economic profit** of a company includes **explicit costs** and **implicit costs.** It isn't necessarily equal to the **accounting profit.**
- A firm is profitable whenever price exceeds its **break-even price,** equal to its minimum average total cost. Below that price it is unprofitable. It breaks even when price is equal to its break-even price.
- Fixed cost is irrelevant to the firm's optimal short-run production decision. When price exceeds its **shut-down price,** minimum average variable cost, the price-taking firm produces the quantity of output at which marginal cost equals price. When price is lower than its shut-down price, it ceases production. Like **sunk costs,** fixed costs are irrelevant to the firm's short-run production decisions. These decisions define the firm's **short-run individual supply curve.**
- Over time, fixed cost matters. If price consistently falls below minimum average total cost, a firm will exit the industry. If price exceeds minimum average total cost, the firm is profitable and will remain in the industry; other firms will enter the industry in the long run.

CHECK YOUR UNDERSTANDING 7-2

1. Draw a short-run diagram showing a U-shaped average total cost curve, a U-shaped average variable cost curve, and a "swoosh"-shaped marginal cost curve. On it, indicate the range of output and the range of price for which the following actions are optimal.
   a. The firm shuts down immediately.
   b. The firm operates in the short run despite sustaining a loss.
   c. The firm operates while making a profit.
2. The state of Maine has a very active lobster industry, which harvests lobsters during the summer months. During the rest of the year, lobsters can be obtained from other parts of the world but at a much higher price. Maine is also full of "lobster shacks," roadside restaurants serving lobster dishes that are open only during the summer. Explain why it is optimal for lobster shacks to operate only during the summer.

Solutions appear at back of book.

The Industry Supply Curve

Why will an increase in the demand for organic tomatoes lead to a large price increase at first but a much smaller increase in the long run? The answer lies in the behavior of the **industry supply curve**—the relationship between the price and the total output of an industry as a whole. The industry supply curve is what we referred to in earlier chapters as *the* supply curve or the market supply curve. But here we take some extra care to distinguish between the *individual supply curve* of a single firm and the supply curve of the industry as a whole.

As you might guess from the previous section, the industry supply curve must be analyzed in somewhat different ways for the short run and the long run. Let's start with the short run.

The **industry supply curve** shows the relationship between the price of a good and the total output of the industry as a whole.

The Short-Run Industry Supply Curve

Recall that in the short run the number of producers in an industry is fixed—there is no entry or exit. And you may also remember from Chapter 3 that the industry supply curve is the horizontal sum of the individual supply curves of all producers—

you find it by summing the total output across all suppliers at every given price. We will do that exercise here under the assumption that all the producers are alike—an assumption that makes the derivation particularly simple. So let's assume that there are 100 organic tomato farms, each with the same costs as Jennifer and Jason's farm.

Each of these 100 farms will have an individual short-run supply curve like the one in Figure 7-4. At a price below $10, no farms will produce. At a price of more than $10, each farm will produce the quantity of output at which its marginal cost is equal to the market price. As you can see from Figure 7-4, this will lead each farm to produce 4 bushels if the price is $14 per bushel, 5 bushels if the price is $18, and so on. So if there are 100 organic tomato farms and the price of organic tomatoes is $18 per bushel, the industry as a whole will produce 500 bushels, corresponding to 100 farms × 5 bushels per farm, and so on. The result is the **short-run industry supply curve,** shown as *S* in Figure 7-5. This curve shows the quantity that producers will supply at each price, *taking the number of producers as given.*

The demand curve *D* in Figure 7-5 crosses the short-run industry supply curve at E_{MKT}, corresponding to a price of $18 and a quantity of 500 bushels. Point E_{MKT} is a **short-run market equilibrium:** the quantity supplied equals the quantity demanded, taking the number of producers as given. But the long run may look quite different, because in the long run farms may enter or exit the industry.

The **short-run industry supply curve** shows how the quantity supplied by an industry depends on the market price given a fixed number of producers.

There is a **short-run market equilibrium** when the quantity supplied equals the quantity demanded, taking the number of producers as given.

FIGURE 7-5 The Short-Run Market Equilibrium

The short-run industry supply curve, *S*, is the industry supply curve taking the number of producers—here, 100—as given. It is generated by adding together the individual supply curves of the 100 producers. Below the shut-down price of $10, no producer wants to produce in the short run. Above $10, the short-run industry supply curve slopes upward, as each producer increases output as price increases. It intersects the demand curve, *D*, at point E_{MKT}, the point of short-run market equilibrium, corresponding to a market price of $18 and a quantity of 500 bushels.

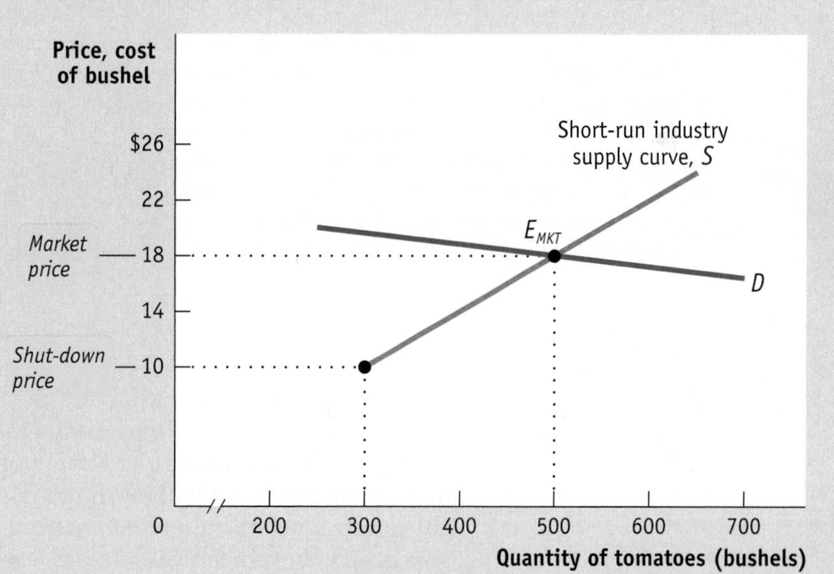

The Long-Run Industry Supply Curve

Suppose that in addition to the 100 farms currently in the organic tomato business, there are many other potential producers. Suppose also that each of these potential producers would have the same cost curves as existing producers like Jennifer and Jason if it entered the industry.

When will additional producers enter the industry? Whenever existing producers are making a profit—that is, whenever the market price is above the break-even price of $14 per bushel, the minimum average total cost of production. For example, at a price of $18 per bushel, new firms will enter the industry.

What will happen as additional producers enter the industry? Clearly, the quantity supplied at any given price will increase. The short-run industry supply curve will shift to the right. This will, in turn, alter the market equilibrium and result in a lower market price. Existing firms will respond to the lower market

FIGURE 7-6 The Long-Run Market Equilibrium

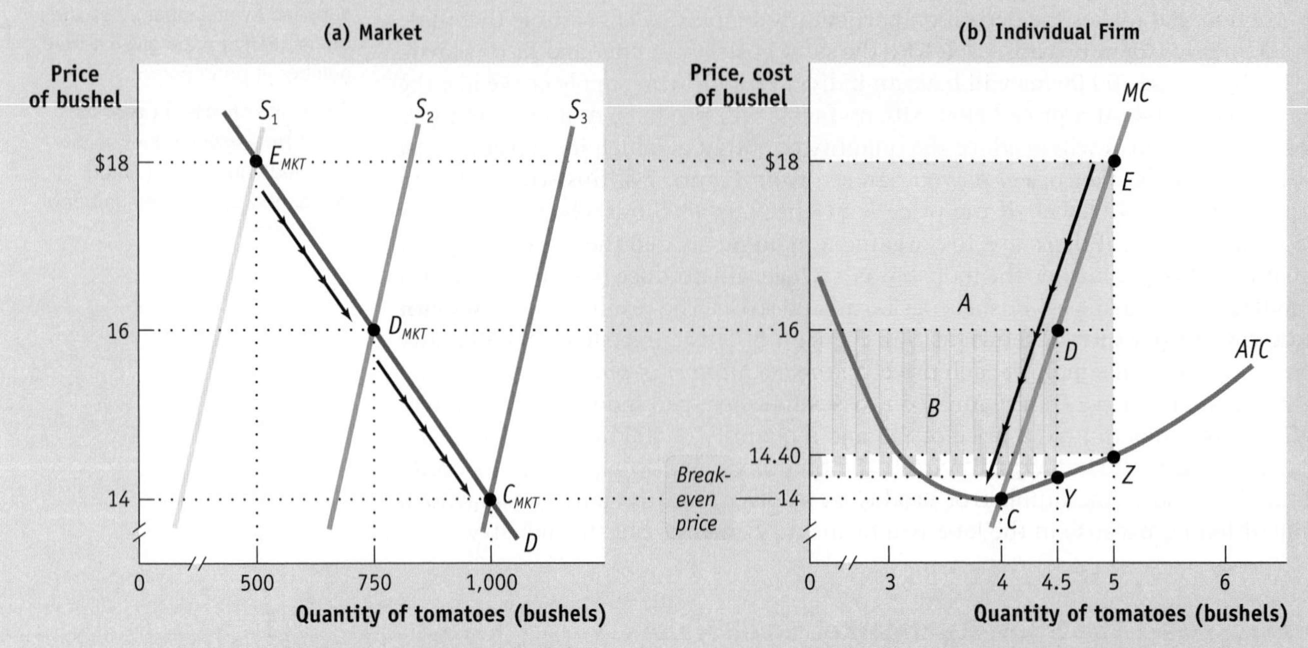

Point E_{MKT} of panel (a) shows the initial short-run market equilibrium. Each of the 100 existing producers makes an economic profit, illustrated in panel (b) by the green rectangle labeled *A*, the profit of an existing firm. Profits induce entry by additional producers, shifting the short-run industry supply curve outward from S_1 to S_2 in panel (a), resulting in a new short-run equilibrium at point D_{MKT}, at a lower market price of $16 and higher industry output. Existing firms reduce output and profit falls to the area given by the striped rectangle labeled *B* in panel (b). Entry continues to shift out the short-run industry supply curve, as price falls and industry output increases yet again. Entry ceases at point C_{MKT} on supply curve S_3 in panel (a). Here market price is equal to the break-even price; existing producers make zero economic profits, and there is no incentive for entry or exit. So C_{MKT} is also a long-run market equilibrium.

price by reducing their output, but the total industry output will increase because of the larger number of firms in the industry.

Figure 7-6 illustrates the effects of this chain of events on an existing firm and on the market; panel (a) shows how the market responds to entry, and panel (b) shows how an individual existing firm responds to entry. (Note that these two graphs have been rescaled in comparison to Figures 7-4 and 7-5 to better illustrate how profit changes in response to price.) In panel (a), S_1 is the initial short-run industry supply curve, based on the existence of 100 producers. The initial short-run market equilibrium is at E_{MKT}, with an equilibrium market price of $18 and a quantity of 500 bushels. At this price existing producers are profitable, which is reflected in panel (b): an existing firm makes a total profit represented by the green-shaded rectangle labeled *A* when market price is $18.

These profits will induce new producers to enter the industry, shifting the short-run industry supply curve to the right. For example, the short-run industry supply curve when the number of producers has increased to 167 is S_2. Corresponding to this supply curve is a new short-run market equilibrium labeled D_{MKT}, with a market price of $16 and a quantity of 750 bushels. At $16, each firm produces 4.5 bushels, so that industry output is 167 × 4.5 = 750 bushels (rounded). From panel (b) you can see the effect of the entry of 67 new producers on an existing firm: the fall in price causes it to reduce its output, and its profit falls to the area represented by the striped rectangle labeled *B*.

Although diminished, the profit of existing firms at D_{MKT} means that entry will continue and the number of firms will continue to rise. If the number of producers rises to 250, the short-run industry supply curve shifts out again to S_3, and the market equilibrium is at C_{MKT}, with a quantity supplied and demanded of 1,000 bushels and a market price of $14 per bushel.

A market is in **long-run market equilibrium** when the quantity supplied equals the quantity demanded, given that sufficient time has elapsed for entry into and exit from the industry to occur.

Like E_{MKT} and D_{MKT}, C_{MKT} is a short-run equilibrium. But it is also something more. Because the price of $14 is each firm's break-even price, an existing producer makes zero economic profit—neither a profit nor a loss, earning only the opportunity cost of the resources used in production—when producing its profit-maximizing output of 4 bushels. At this price there is no incentive either for potential producers to enter or for existing producers to exit the industry. So C_{MKT} corresponds to a **long-run market equilibrium**—a situation in which quantity supplied equals the quantity demanded given that sufficient time has elapsed for producers to either enter or exit the industry. In a long-run market equilibrium, all existing and potential producers have fully adjusted to their optimal long-run choices; as a result, no producer has an incentive to either enter or exit the industry.

To explore further the significance of the difference between short-run and long-run equilibrium, consider the effect of an increase in demand on an industry with free entry that is initially in long-run equilibrium. Panel (b) in Figure 7-7 shows the market adjustment; panels (a) and (c) show how an existing individual firm behaves during the process.

FIGURE 7-7 The Effect of an Increase in Demand in the Short Run and the Long Run

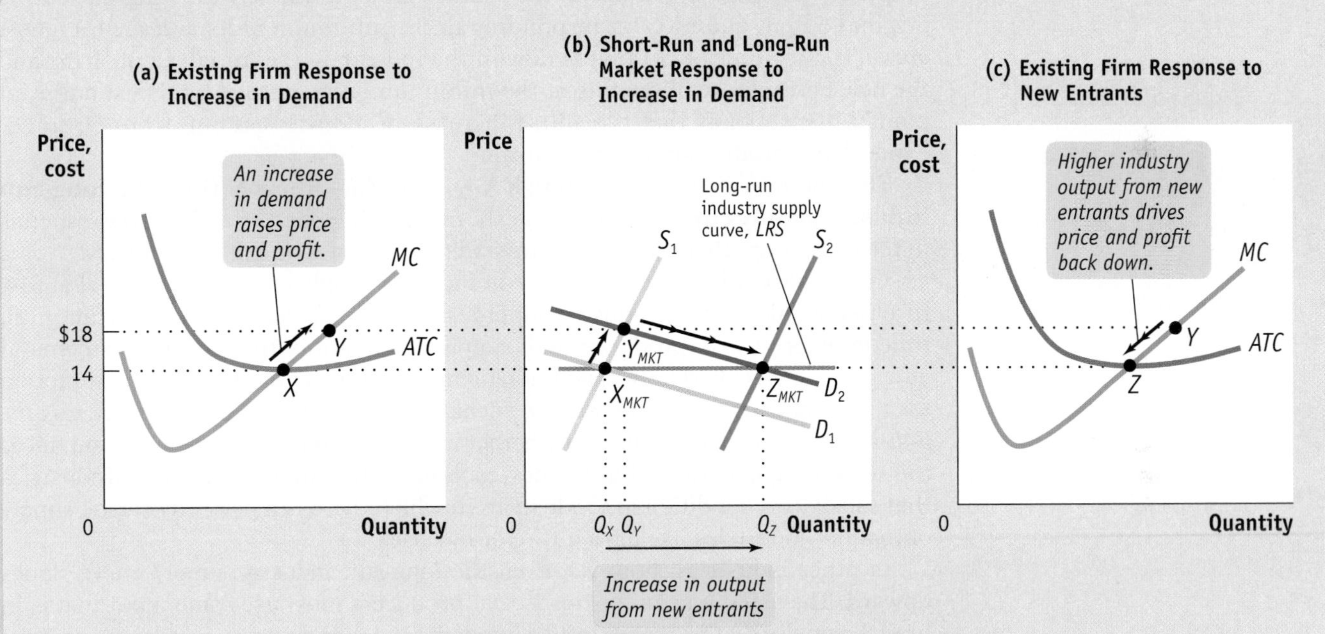

Panel (b) shows how an industry adjusts in the short and long run to an increase in demand; panels (a) and (c) show the corresponding adjustments by an existing firm. Initially the market is at point X_{MKT} in panel (b), a short-run and long-run equilibrium at a price of $14 and industry output of Q_X. An existing firm makes zero economic profit, operating at point X in panel (a) at minimum average total cost. Demand increases as D_1 shifts rightward to D_2 in panel (b), raising the market price to $18. Existing firms increase their output, and industry output moves along the short-run industry supply curve S_1 to a short-run equilibrium at Y_{MKT}. Correspondingly, the existing firm in panel (a) moves from point X to point Y. But at a price of $18 existing firms are profitable. As shown in panel (b), in the long run new entrants arrive and the short-run industry supply curve shifts rightward, from S_1 to S_2. There is a new equilibrium at point Z_{MKT}, at a lower price of $14 and higher industry output of Q_Z. An existing firm responds by moving from Y to Z in panel (c), returning to its initial output level and zero economic profit. Production by new entrants accounts for the total increase in industry output, $Q_Z - Q_X$. Like X_{MKT}, Z_{MKT} is also a short-run and long-run equilibrium: with existing firms earning zero economic profit, there is no incentive for any firms to enter or exit the industry. The horizontal line passing through X_{MKT} and Z_{MKT}, *LRS*, is the long-run industry supply curve: at the break-even price of $14, producers will produce any amount that consumers demand in the long run.

The **long-run industry supply curve** shows how the quantity supplied responds to the price once producers have had time to enter or exit the industry.

In panel (b) of Figure 7-7, D_1 is the initial demand curve and S_1 is the initial short-run industry supply curve. Their intersection at point X_{MKT} is both a short-run and a long-run market equilibrium because the equilibrium price of $14 leads to zero economic profit—and therefore neither entry nor exit. It corresponds to point *X* in panel (a), where an individual existing firm is operating at the minimum of its average total cost curve.

Now suppose that the demand curve shifts out for some reason to D_2. As shown in panel (b), in the short run, industry output moves along the short-run industry supply curve S_1 to the new short-run market equilibrium at Y_{MKT}, the intersection of S_1 and D_2. The market price rises to $18 per bushel, and industry output increases from Q_X to Q_Y. This corresponds to an existing firm's movement from *X* to *Y* in panel (a) as the firm increases its output in response to the rise in the market price.

But we know that Y_{MKT} is not a long-run equilibrium, because $18 is higher than minimum average total cost, so existing producers are making economic profits. This will lead additional firms to enter the industry. Over time entry will cause the short-run industry supply curve to shift to the right. In the long run, the short-run industry supply curve will have shifted out to S_2, and the equilibrium will be at Z_{MKT}—with the price falling back to $14 per bushel and industry output increasing yet again, from Q_Y to Q_Z. Like X_{MKT} before the increase in demand, Z_{MKT} is both a short-run and a long-run market equilibrium.

The effect of entry on an existing firm is illustrated in panel (c), in the movement from *Y* to *Z* along the firm's individual supply curve. The firm reduces its output in response to the fall in the market price, ultimately arriving back at its original output quantity, corresponding to the minimum of its average total cost curve. In fact, every firm that is now in the industry—the initial set of firms and the new entrants—will operate at the minimum of its average total cost curve, at point *Z*. This means that the entire increase in industry output, from Q_X to Q_Z, comes from production by new entrants.

The line *LRS* that passes through X_{MKT} and Z_{MKT} in panel (b) is the **long-run industry supply curve.** It shows how the quantity supplied by an industry responds to the price given that producers have had time to enter or exit the industry.

In this particular case, the long-run industry supply curve is horizontal at $14. In other words, in this industry supply is *perfectly elastic* in the long run: given time to enter or exit, producers will supply any quantity that consumers demand at a price of $14. Perfectly elastic long-run supply is actually a good assumption for many industries. In this case we speak of there being *constant costs across the industry*: each firm, regardless of whether it is an incumbent or a new entrant, faces the same cost structure (that is, they each have the same cost curves). Industries that satisfy this condition are industries in which there is a perfectly elastic supply of inputs—industries like agriculture or bakeries.

In other industries, however, even the long-run industry supply curve slopes upward. The usual reason for this is that producers must use some input that is in limited supply (that is, inelastically supplied). As the industry expands, the price of that input is driven up. Consequently, later entrants in the industry find that they have a higher cost structure than early entrants. An example is beachfront resort hotels, which must compete for a limited quantity of prime beachfront property. Industries that behave like this are said to have *increasing costs across the industry.*

It is possible for the long-run industry supply curve to slope downward. This can occur when an industry faces increasing returns to scale, in which average costs fall as output rises. Notice we said that the *industry* faces increasing returns. However, when increasing returns apply at the level of the individual firm, the industry usually ends up dominated by a small number of firms (an *oligopoly*) or a single firm (a *monopoly*). In some cases, the advantages of large scale for an entire industry accrue to all firms in that industry. For example, the costs of new technologies such as solar panels tend to fall as the industry grows because that growth leads to improved knowledge, a larger pool of workers with the right skills, and so on.

Regardless of whether the long-run industry supply curve is horizontal or upward sloping or even downward sloping, the long-run price elasticity of supply

FIGURE 7-8 Comparing the Short-Run and Long-Run Industry Supply Curves

The long-run industry supply curve may slope upward, but it is always flatter—more elastic—than the short-run industry supply curve. This is because of entry and exit: a higher price attracts new entrants in the long run, resulting in a rise in industry output and a fall in price; a lower price induces existing producers to exit in the long run, generating a fall in industry output and an eventual rise in price.

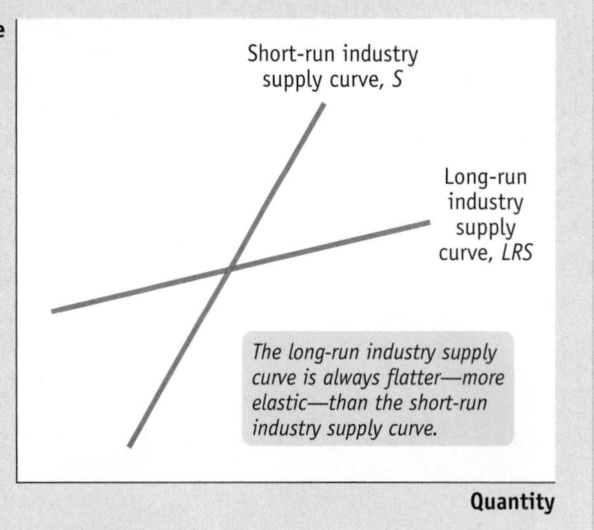

is *higher* than the short-run price elasticity whenever there is free entry and exit. As shown in Figure 7-8, the long-run industry supply curve is always flatter than the short-run industry supply curve. The reason is entry and exit: a high price caused by an increase in demand attracts entry by new producers, resulting in a rise in industry output and an eventual fall in price; a low price caused by a decrease in demand induces existing firms to exit, leading to a fall in industry output and an eventual increase in price.

The distinction between the short-run industry supply curve and the long-run industry supply curve is very important in practice. We often see a sequence of events like that shown in Figure 7-7: an increase in demand initially leads to a large price increase, but prices return to their initial level once new firms have entered the industry. Or we see the sequence in reverse: a fall in demand reduces prices in the short run, but they return to their initial level as producers exit the industry.

The Cost of Production and Efficiency in Long-Run Equilibrium

Our analysis leads us to three conclusions about the cost of production and efficiency in the long-run equilibrium of a perfectly competitive industry. These results will be important in our discussion in Chapter 8 of how monopoly gives rise to inefficiency.

First, in a perfectly competitive industry in equilibrium, the value of marginal cost is the same for all firms. That's because all firms produce the quantity of output at which marginal cost equals the market price, and as price-takers they all face the same market price.

Second, in a perfectly competitive industry with free entry and exit, each firm will have zero economic profit in long-run equilibrium. Each firm produces the quantity of output that minimizes its average total cost—corresponding to point *Z* in panel (c) of Figure 7-7. So the total cost of production of the industry's output is minimized in a perfectly competitive industry. (The exception is an industry with increasing costs across the industry. Given a sufficiently high market price, early entrants make positive economic profits, but the last entrants do not. Costs are minimized for later entrants, but not necessarily for the early ones.)

The third and final conclusion is that the long-run market equilibrium of a perfectly competitive industry is efficient: no mutually beneficial transactions go unexploited. All consumers who have a willingness to pay greater than or equal to sellers' costs actually get the good.

ECONOMIC PROFIT, AGAIN

Some readers may wonder why a firm would want to enter an industry if the market price is only slightly greater than the break-even price. Wouldn't a firm prefer to go into another business that yields a higher profit?

The answer is that here, as always, when we calculate cost, we mean *opportunity cost*—that is, cost that includes the return a firm could get by using its resources elsewhere. And so the profit that we calculate is *economic profit;* if the market price is above the break-even level, no matter how slightly, the firm can earn more in this industry than they could elsewhere.

So in the long-run equilibrium of a perfectly competitive industry, production is efficient: costs are minimized and no resources are wasted. In addition, the allocation of goods to consumers is efficient: every consumer willing to pay the cost of producing a unit of the good gets it. Indeed, no mutually beneficial transaction is left unexploited. Moreover, this condition tends to persist over time as the environment changes: the force of competition makes producers responsive to changes in consumers' desires and to changes in technology.

ECONOMICS ➤ IN ACTION

BALING IN, BAILING OUT

REUTERS/Stringer Shanghai

King Cotton's reign will inevitably end as new producers, seeking to profit from the crop's success, enter the market and bring prices down.

"King Cotton is back," proclaimed a 2010 article in the *Los Angeles Times*, describing a cotton boom that had "turned great swaths of Central California a snowy white during harvest season." Cotton prices were soaring: they more than tripled between early 2010 and early 2011. And farmers responded by planting more cotton.

What was behind the price rise? As we learned in Chapter 3, it was partly caused by temporary factors, notably severe floods in Pakistan that destroyed much of that nation's cotton crop. But there was also a big rise in demand, especially from China, whose burgeoning textile and clothing industries demanded ever more raw cotton to weave into cloth. And all indications were that higher demand was here to stay.

So is cotton farming going to be a highly profitable business from now on? The answer is no, because when an industry becomes highly profitable, it draws in new producers, and that brings prices down. And the cotton industry was following the standard script.

For it wasn't just the Central Valley of California that had turned "snowy white." Farmers around the world were moving into cotton growing. "This summer, cotton will stretch from Queensland through northern NSW [New South Wales] all the way down to the Murrumbidgee valley in southern NSW," declared an Australian report.

And by 2012 the entry of all these new producers was having a big effect. By the summer of 2012, cotton prices were only about a third of their peak in early 2011. It was clear that the cotton boom had reached its limit—and that at some point in the not too distant future some of the farmers who had rushed into the industry would leave it again.

▼ Quick Review

- The **industry supply curve** corresponds to the supply curve of earlier chapters. In the short run, the time period over which the number of producers is fixed, the **short-run market equilibrium** is given by the intersection of the **short-run industry supply curve** and the demand curve. In the long run, the time period over which producers can enter or exit the industry, the **long-run market equilibrium** is given by the intersection of the **long-run industry supply curve** and the demand curve. In the long-run market equilibrium, no producer has an incentive to enter or exit the industry.
- The long-run industry supply curve is often horizontal, although it may slope upward when a necessary input is in limited supply. It is always more elastic than the short-run industry supply curve.
- In the long-run market equilibrium of a perfectly competitive industry, each firm produces at the same marginal cost, which is equal to the market price, and the total cost of production of the industry's output is minimized. It is also efficient.

CHECK YOUR UNDERSTANDING 7-3

1. Which of the following events will induce firms to enter an industry? Which will induce firms to exit? When will entry or exit cease? Explain your answer.
   - **a.** A technological advance lowers the fixed cost of production of every firm in the industry.
   - **b.** The wages paid to workers in the industry go up for an extended period of time.
   - **c.** A permanent change in consumer tastes increases demand for the good.
   - **d.** The price of a key input rises due to a long-term shortage of that input.
2. Assume that the egg industry is perfectly competitive and is in long-run equilibrium with a perfectly elastic long-run industry supply curve. Health concerns about cholesterol then lead to a decrease in demand. Construct a figure similar to Figure 7-7, showing the short-run behavior of the industry and how long-run equilibrium is reestablished.

Solutions appear at back of book.

WORKED PROBLEM

Is There a Catch?

New York's Fulton Fish Market, now located in Hunts Point in the Bronx, has been in operation since 1822. One of the more popular fish sold at the market is whiting, a white fish that can end up in fast-food sandwiches or on a plate at your favorite sit-down seafood restaurant. Whiting are "boxed at sea," that is, they are packaged on location. Consider the following hypothetical daily costs for a fisherman who runs a boat that fishes primarily for whiting. His quantity, or catch, is represented in boxes, approximately 60 pounds per box. Each day begins with the decision of whether to take out the boat, given the price he expects to receive at the fish market. Whether he goes out or not, he incurs fixed costs such as dockage, licensing, and mortgage on the boat. In addition to fixed costs, he incurs a variable cost for each box brought back to port. So, he must also decide how much to catch.

Using the following table, find the break-even price per box of fish. If the market price falls to $14.00 a box, how many boxes will the fisherman bring to market?

Quantity of fish (boxes) Q	Variable cost VC	Total cost TC
30	$280	$680
40	320	720
50	440	840
60	600	1,000
70	840	1,240
80	1,160	1,560
90	1,560	1,960
100	2,040	2,440

STEP 1: Find the average variable cost, average total cost, and marginal cost of a box of fish. You will need each of these costs in order to answer the question.

Read the section "Two Key Concepts: Marginal Cost and Average Cost" on pages 189–197 in Chapter 6. These costs are defined in Equations 6-3, 6-4, and 6-5.

The average variable cost is equal to the variable cost divided by the quantity (VC/Q), the average total cost is equal to the total cost divided by the quantity (TC/Q), and the marginal cost is the change in the total cost divided by the change in the quantity (ΔTC/ΔQ). These costs are calculated for each box in the following table. ■

Quantity of fish (boxes) Q	Variable cost VC	Total cost TC	Marginal cost MC = ΔTC/ΔQ	Average variable cost AVC = VC/Q	Average total cost ATC = TQ/Q
30	$280	$680		$9.33	$22.67
			$4.00		
40	320	720		8.00	18.00
			12.00		
50	440	840		8.80	16.80
			16.00		
60	600	1,000		10.00	16.67
			24.00		
70	840	1,240		12.00	17.71
			32.00		
80	1,160	1,560		14.50	19.50
			40.00		
90	1,560	1,960		17.33	21.78
			48.00		
100	2,040	2,440		20.40	24.40

STEP 2: Find the break-even price per box of fish.

Read the section "When Is Production Profitable?" on pages 216–219, and study Figure 7-2, including the caption.

To find the break-even price, we need to find the minimum average total cost of production. In the table, the minimum average total cost occurs at 60 boxes of fish. Thus, the break-even price is $16.67 per box of fish. ■

STEP 3: If the market price falls to $14.00 per box, how many boxes will be brought to market?

Read the section "Using Marginal Analysis to Choose the Profit-Maximizing Quantity of Output"on pages 214–216, and concentrate on the ***price-taking firm's optimal output rule*** *and the "Pitfalls" box on page 215.*

In the case of the price-taking firm, the marginal revenue is equal to the market price. So, to find the optimal quantity, we need to find the point where P = MC. If there is not a point on the table at which P = MC, then the fisherman will want to produce the largest quantity for which P exceeds MC. Going from 40 to 50 boxes, the MC is $12.00, but going from 50 to 60 boxes, the MC is $16.00. Hence, the largest quantity for which P exceeds MC is 50 boxes. Although price is less than average total cost, he will still fish because the price is greater than his average variable cost. ■

SUMMARY

1. In a **perfectly competitive market** all producers are **price-taking producers** and all consumers are **price-taking consumers**—no one's actions can influence the market price. Consumers are normally price-takers, but producers often are not. In a **perfectly competitive industry,** all producers are price-takers.
2. There are two necessary conditions for a perfectly competitive industry: there are many producers, none of whom have a large **market share,** and the industry produces a **standardized product** or **commodity**—goods that consumers regard as equivalent. A third condition is often satisfied as well: **free entry and exit** into and from the industry.
3. The **marginal benefit** of a good or service is the additional benefit derived from producing one more unit of that good or service. The **principle of marginal analysis** says that the optimal amount of an activity is the level at which marginal benefit equals marginal cost.
4. A producer chooses output according to the **optimal output rule:** produce the quantity at which **marginal revenue** equals marginal cost. For a price-taking firm, marginal revenue is equal to price and its **marginal revenue curve** is a horizontal line at the market price. It chooses output according to the **price-taking firm's optimal output rule:** produce the quantity at which price equals marginal cost. However, a firm that produces the optimal quantity may not be profitable.
5. Companies should base decisions on **economic profit,** which takes into account **explicit costs** that involve an actual outlay of cash as well as **implicit costs** that do not require an outlay of cash, but are measured by the value, in dollar terms, of benefits that are forgone. The **accounting profit** is often considerably larger than the economic profit because it includes only explicit costs and depreciation, not implicit costs.
6. A firm is profitable if total revenue exceeds total cost or, equivalently, if the market price exceeds its **break-even price**—minimum average total cost. If market price exceeds the break-even price, the firm is profitable; if it is less, the firm is unprofitable; if it is equal, the firm breaks even. When profitable, the firm's per-unit profit is $P - ATC$; when unprofitable, its per-unit loss is $ATC - P$.
7. Fixed cost is irrelevant to the firm's optimal short-run production decision, which depends on its **shut-down price**—its minimum average variable cost—and the market price. The decision to ignore fixed costs is similar to the decision to ignore **sunk costs,** nonrecoverable costs that have already been incurred. When the market price is equal to or exceeds the shut-down price, the firm produces the output quantity where marginal cost equals the market price. When the market price falls below the shut-down price, the firm ceases production in the short run. This generates the firm's **short-run individual supply curve.**

8. Fixed cost matters over time. If the market price is below minimum average total cost for an extended period of time, firms will exit the industry in the long run. If above, existing firms are profitable and new firms will enter the industry in the long run.

9. The **industry supply curve** depends on the time period. The **short-run industry supply curve** is the industry supply curve given that the number of firms is fixed. The **short-run market equilibrium** is given by the intersection of the short-run industry supply curve and the demand curve.

10. The **long-run industry supply curve** is the industry supply curve given sufficient time for entry into and exit from the industry. In the **long-run market equilibrium**—given by the intersection of the long-run industry supply curve and the demand curve—no producer has an incentive to enter or exit. The long-run industry supply curve is often horizontal. It may slope upward if there is limited supply of an input, resulting in increasing costs across the industry. It may even slope downward, the case of decreasing costs across the industry. But it is always more elastic than the short-run industry supply curve.

11. In the long-run market equilibrium of a competitive industry, profit maximization leads each firm to produce at the same marginal cost, which is equal to market price. Free entry and exit means that each firm earns zero economic profit—producing the output corresponding to its minimum average total cost. So the total cost of production of an industry's output is minimized. The outcome is efficient because every consumer with a willingness to pay greater than or equal to marginal cost gets the good.

KEY TERMS

Price-taking producer, p. 210
Price-taking consumer, p. 210
Perfectly competitive market, p. 210
Perfectly competitive industry, p. 210
Market share, p. 211
Standardized product, p. 211
Commodity, p. 211
Free entry and exit, p. 211
Marginal benefit, p. 214
Principle of marginal analysis, p. 214
Marginal revenue, p. 214
Optimal output rule, p. 214
Price-taking firm's optimal output rule, p. 214
Marginal revenue curve, p. 215
Economic profit, p. 216
Explicit cost, p. 216
Implicit cost, p. 216
Accounting profit, p. 216
Break-even price, p. 219
Shut-down price, p. 221
Sunk cost, p. 221
Short-run individual supply curve, p. 221
Industry supply curve, p. 224
Short-run industry supply curve, p. 225
Short-run market equilibrium, p. 225
Long-run market equilibrium, p. 227
Long-run industry supply curve, p. 228

PROBLEMS

1. For each of the following, is the business a price-taking producer? Explain your answers.
   a. A cappuccino café in a university town where there are dozens of very similar cappuccino cafés
   b. The makers of Pepsi-Cola
   c. One of many sellers of zucchini at a local farmers' market

2. For each of the following, is the industry perfectly competitive? Referring to market share, standardization of the product, and/or free entry and exit, explain your answers.
   a. Aspirin
   b. Alicia Keys concerts
   c. SUVs

3. Kate's Katering provides catered meals, and the catered meals industry is perfectly competitive. Kate's machinery costs $100 per day and is the only fixed input. Her variable cost consists of the wages paid to the cooks and the food ingredients. The variable cost per day associated with each level of output is given in the accompanying table.

Quantity of meals	*VC*
0	0
10	2
20	4
30	10
40	10
50	10

   a. Calculate the total cost, the average variable cost, the average total cost, and the marginal cost for each quantity of output.
   b. What is the break-even price? What is the shut-down price?
   c. Suppose that the price at which Kate can sell catered meals is $21 per meal. In the short run, will Kate earn a profit? In the short run, should she produce or shut down?
   d. Suppose that the price at which Kate can sell catered meals is $17 per meal. In the short run, will Kate earn a profit? In the short run, should she produce or shut down?

e. Suppose that the price at which Kate can sell catered meals is $13 per meal. In the short run, will Kate earn a profit? In the short run, should she produce or shut down?

4. Bob produces DVD movies for sale, which requires a building and a machine that copies the original movie onto a DVD. Bob rents a building for $30,000 per month and rents a machine for $20,000 a month. Those are his fixed costs. His variable cost per month is given in the accompanying table.

Quantity of DVDs	*VC*
0	$0
1,000	5,000
2,000	8,000
3,000	9,000
4,000	14,000
5,000	20,000
6,000	33,000
7,000	49,000
8,000	72,000
9,000	99,000
10,000	150,000

a. Calculate Bob's average variable cost, average total cost, and marginal cost for each quantity of output.

b. There is free entry into the industry, and anyone who enters will face the same costs as Bob. Suppose that currently the price of a DVD is $25. What will Bob's profit be? Is this a long-run equilibrium? If not, what will the price of DVD movies be in the long run?

5. Consider Bob's DVD company described in Problem 4. Assume that DVD production is a perfectly competitive industry. For each of the following questions, explain your answers.

a. What is Bob's break-even price? What is his shut-down price?

b. Suppose the price of a DVD is $2. What should Bob do in the short run?

c. Suppose the price of a DVD is $7. What is the profit-maximizing quantity of DVDs that Bob should produce? What will his total profit be? Will he produce or shut down in the short run? Will he stay in the industry or exit in the long run?

d. Suppose instead that the price of DVDs is $20. Now what is the profit-maximizing quantity of DVDs that Bob should produce? What will his total profit be now? Will he produce or shut down in the short run? Will he stay in the industry or exit in the long run?

6. Consider again Bob's DVD company described in Problem 4.

a. Draw Bob's marginal cost curve.

b. Over what range of prices will Bob produce no DVDs in the short run?

c. Draw Bob's individual supply curve.

7. a. A profit-maximizing business incurs an economic loss of $10,000 per year. Its fixed cost is $15,000 per year. Should it produce or shut down in the short run? Should it stay in the industry or exit in the long run?

b. Suppose instead that this business has a fixed cost of $6,000 per year. Should it produce or shut down in the short run? Should it stay in the industry or exit in the long run?

8. The first sushi restaurant opens in town. Initially people are very cautious about eating tiny portions of raw fish, as this is a town where large portions of grilled meat have always been popular. Soon, however, an influential health report warns consumers against grilled meat and suggests that they increase their consumption of fish, especially raw fish. The sushi restaurant becomes very popular and its profit increases.

a. What will happen to the short-run profit of the sushi restaurant? What will happen to the number of sushi restaurants in town in the long run? Will the first sushi restaurant be able to sustain its short-run profit over the long run? Explain your answers.

b. Local steakhouses suffer from the popularity of sushi and start incurring losses. What will happen to the number of steakhouses in town in the long run? Explain your answer.

9. A perfectly competitive firm has the following short-run total cost:

Quantity	*TC*
0	$5
1	10
2	13
3	18
4	25
5	34
6	45

Market demand for the firm's product is given by the following market demand schedule:

Price	Quantity demanded
$12	300
10	500
8	800
6	1,200
4	1,800

a. Calculate this firm's marginal cost and, for all output levels except zero, the firm's average variable cost and average total cost.

b. There are 100 firms in this industry that all have costs identical to those of this firm. Draw the short-run industry supply curve. In the same diagram, draw the market demand curve.

c. What is the market price, and how much profit will each firm make?

10. Evaluate each of the following statements. If a statement is true, explain why; if it is false, identify the mistake and try to correct it.

a. A profit-maximizing firm in a perfectly competitive industry should select the output level at which the difference between the market price and marginal cost is greatest.

b. An increase in fixed cost lowers the profit-maximizing quantity of output produced in the short run.

EXTEND YOUR UNDERSTANDING

11. A new vaccine against a deadly disease has just been discovered. Presently, 55 people die from the disease each year. The new vaccine will save lives, but it is not completely safe. Some recipients of the shots will die from adverse reactions. The projected effects of the inoculation are given in the accompanying table:

Percent of population inoculated	Total deaths due to disease	Total deaths due to inoculation	Marginal benefit of inoculation	Marginal cost of inoculation	"Profit" of inoculation
0	55	0			
			—	—	—
10	45	0			
			—	—	—
20	36	1			
			—	—	—
30	28	3			
			—	—	—
40	21	6			
			—	—	—
50	15	10			
			—	—	—
60	10	15			
			—	—	—
70	6	20			
			—	—	—
80	3	25			
			—	—	—
90	1	30			
			—	—	—
100	0	35			

a. What are the interpretations of "marginal benefit" and "marginal cost" here? Calculate marginal benefit and marginal cost per each 10% increase in the rate of inoculation. Write your answers in the table.

b. What proportion of the population should optimally be inoculated?

c. What is the interpretation of "profit" here? Calculate the profit for all levels of inoculation.

12. The production of agricultural products like wheat is one of the few examples of a perfectly competitive industry. In this question, we analyze results from a study released by the U.S. Department of Agriculture about wheat production in the United States in 1998.

a. The average variable cost per acre planted with wheat was $107 per acre. Assuming a yield of 50 bushels per acre, calculate the average variable cost per bushel of wheat.

b. The average price of wheat received by a farmer in 1998 was $2.65 per bushel. Do you think the average farm would have exited the industry in the short run? Explain.

c. With a yield of 50 bushels of wheat per acre, the average total cost per farm was $3.80 per bushel. The harvested acreage for rye (a type of wheat) in the United States fell from 418,000 acres in 1998 to 274,000 in 2006. Using the information on prices and costs here and in parts a and b, explain why this might have happened.

d. Using the above information, do you think the prices of wheat were higher or lower prior to 1998? Why?

13. The accompanying table presents prices for washing and ironing a man's shirt taken from a survey of California dry cleaners.

Dry Cleaner	City	Price
A-1 Cleaners	Santa Barbara	$1.50
Regal Cleaners	Santa Barbara	1.95
St. Paul Cleaners	Santa Barbara	1.95
Zip Kleen Dry Cleaners	Santa Barbara	1.95
Effie the Tailor	Santa Barbara	2.00
Magnolia Too	Goleta	2.00
Master Cleaners	Santa Barbara	2.00
Santa Barbara Cleaners	Goleta	2.00
Sunny Cleaners	Santa Barbara	2.00
Casitas Cleaners	Carpinteria	2.10
Rockwell Cleaners	Carpinteria	2.10
Norvelle Bass Cleaners	Santa Barbara	2.15
Ablitt's Fine Cleaners	Santa Barbara	2.25
California Cleaners	Goleta	2.25
Justo the Tailor	Santa Barbara	2.25
Pressed 4 Time	Goleta	2.50
King's Cleaners	Goleta	2.50

a. What is the average price per shirt washed and ironed in Goleta? In Santa Barbara?

b. Draw typical marginal cost and average total cost curves for California Cleaners in Goleta, assuming it is a perfectly competitive firm but is making a profit on each shirt in the short run. Mark the short-run equilibrium point and shade the area that corresponds to the profit made by the dry cleaner.

c. Assume $2.25 is the short-run equilibrium price in Goleta. Draw a typical short-run demand and supply curve for the market. Label the equilibrium point.

d. Observing profits in the Goleta area, another dry cleaning service, Diamond Cleaners, enters the market. It charges $1.95 per shirt. What is the new average price of washing and ironing a shirt in Goleta? Illustrate the effect of entry on the average Goleta price by a shift of the short-run supply curve, the demand curve, or both.

e. Assume that California Cleaners now charges the new average price and just breaks even (that is, makes zero economic profit) at this price. Show the likely effect of the entry on your diagram in part b.

f. If the dry cleaning industry is perfectly competitive, what does the average difference in price between Goleta and Santa Barbara imply about costs in the two areas?

BUSINESS CASE • Kiva Systems' Robots versus Humans: The Challenge of Holiday Order Fulfillment

Courtesy Kiva Systems

For those who like to procrastinate when it comes to holiday shopping, the rise of e-commerce has been a welcome phenomenon. Amazon.com boasts that in 2012, customers living in 11 cities in the United States could receive same-day delivery for orders placed on the day before Christmas.

E-commerce retailers like Amazon.com and CrateandBarrel.com can see their sales quadruple for the holidays. With advances in order fulfillment technology that get customers' orders to them quickly, e-commerce sellers have been able to capture an ever-greater share of sales from brick-and-mortar retailers. Holiday sales at e-commerce sites grew by over 13% from 2011 to 2012.

Behind these technological advances, however, lies an intense debate: people versus robots. Amazon has relied on a large staff of temporary human workers to get it through the previous holiday seasons, often quadrupling its staff and operating 24 hours a day. In contrast, Crate and Barrel only doubled its workforce, thanks to a cadre of orange robots that allows each worker to do the work of six people.

But, Amazon is set to increase its robotic work force in the future. In May of 2012, Amazon bought Kiva Systems, the leader in order fulfillment robotics, for $775 million, with the hope of tailoring Kiva's systems to best fit Amazon's warehouse and fulfillment needs.

Although many retailers—Staples, Gap, Saks Fifth Avenue, and Walgreens, for example—also use Kiva equipment, installation of a robotic system can be expensive, with some installations costing as much as $20 million. Yet hiring workers has a cost, too: during the 2010 holiday season, before it had installed an extensive robotic system, Amazon hired some 12,500 temporary workers at its 20 distribution centers around the United States.

As one industry analyst noted, an obstacle to the purchase of a robotic system for many e-commerce retailers is that it often doesn't make economic sense: it's too expensive to buy sufficient robots for the busiest time of the year because they would be idle at other times. Before Amazon's purchase, Kiva was testing a program to rent out its robots seasonally so that retailers could "hire" enough robots to handle their holiday orders just like Amazon used to hire more humans.

QUESTIONS FOR THOUGHT

1. Assume that a firm can sell a robot, but that the sale takes time and the firm is likely to get less than what it paid. Other things equal, which system, human-based or robotic, will have a higher fixed cost? Which will have a higher variable cost? Explain.
2. Predict the pattern of off-holiday sales versus holiday sales that would induce a retailer to keep a human-based system. Predict the pattern that would induce a retailer to move to a robotic system.
3. How would a "robot-for-hire" program affect your answer to Question 2? Explain.

BUSINESS CASE • TheFind Finds the Cheapest Price

Courtesy of TheFind, Inc.

Recently in Sunnyvale, California, Tri Trang walked into a Best Buy and found the perfect gift for his girlfriend: a $184.85 Garmin GPS system. A year earlier, he would have put the item in his cart and purchased it. Instead, he whipped out his Android phone; using an app that instantly compared Best Buy's price to those of other retailers, he found the same item on Amazon.com for $106.75, with no shipping charges and no sales tax. Trang proceeded to buy it from Amazon, right there on the spot.

It doesn't stop there. TheFind, the most popular of the price-comparison sites, will also provide a map to the store with the best price, identify coupon codes and shipping deals, and supply other tools to help users organize their purchases. *Terror* has been the word used to describe the reaction of brick-and-mortar retailers.

Before the advent of apps like TheFind's, a retailer could lure customers into its store with enticing specials, and reasonably expect them to buy other, more profitable things, too—with some prompting from salespeople. But those days are disappearing. A recent study by the consulting firm Accenture found that 73% of customers with mobile devices prefer to shop by phone rather than talk to a salesperson. Best Buy recently settled a lawsuit alleging that it posted web prices at in-store kiosks faster than the ones customers saw on their home computers, a maneuver that would have been quickly discovered by users of TheFind's app.

Not surprisingly, use of TheFind's app has increased at an extremely fast clip. The number of people making purchases on their mobile phone nearly doubled between 2011 and 2012. Indeed, retailers are expecting even more shoppers to use their phones to make purchases in the coming years. The accompanying figure illustrates their projections for dramatic growth in cell phone sales through 2016. On TheFind, the most frequently searched items in stores are iPhones, iPads, video games, and other electronics.

According to e-commerce experts, U.S. retailers have begun to alter their selling strategies in response. One strategy involves stocking products that manufacturers have slightly modified for the retailer, which allows the retailer to be their exclusive seller. In addition, some retailers, when confronted by an in-store customer wielding a lower price on a mobile device, will lower their price to avoid losing the sale.

Yet retailers are clearly frightened. As one analyst said, "Only a couple of retailers can play the lowest-price game. This is going to accelerate the demise of retailers who do not have either competitive pricing or stand-out store experience."

Expected Growth in Cell Phone Purchases in the United States, 2010–2016

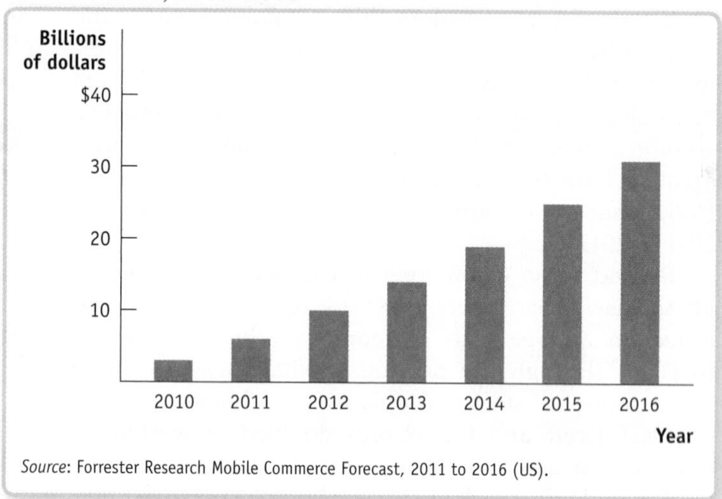

Source: Forrester Research Mobile Commerce Forecast, 2011 to 2016 (US).

QUESTIONS FOR THOUGHT

1. From the evidence in the case, what can you infer about whether or not the retail market for electronics satisfied the conditions for perfect competition before the advent of mobile-device comparison shopping? What was the most important impediment to competition?
2. What effect will the introduction of TheFind's and similar apps have on competition in the retail market for electronics? On the profitability of brick-and-mortar retailers like Best Buy? What, on average, will be the effect on the consumer surplus of purchasers of these items?
3. Why are some retailers responding by having manufacturers make exclusive versions of products for them? Is this trend likely to increase or diminish?

Monopoly, Oligopoly, and Monopolistic Competition

WHAT YOU WILL LEARN IN THIS CHAPTER

- The significance of **monopoly,** where a single **monopolist** is the only producer of a good
- How a monopolist determines its profit-maximizing output and price
- The prevalence of **oligopoly** and why **oligopolists** have an incentive to act in ways that reduce their combined profits
- How policy makers address the problems posed by monopoly and oligopoly
- The meaning of monopolistic competition and why **monopolistically competitive** firms differentiate their products

EVERYBODY MUST GET STONES

Corbis

"Got stones?"

A FEW YEARS AGO DE BEERS, THE world's main supplier of diamonds, ran an ad urging men to buy their wives diamond jewelry. "She married you for richer, for poorer," read the ad. "Let her know how it's going."

Crass? Yes. Effective? No question. For generations diamonds have been a symbol of luxury, valued not only for their appearance but also for their rarity.

But geologists will tell you that diamonds aren't all that rare. In fact, according to the *Dow Jones-Irwin Guide to Fine Gems and Jewelry,* diamonds are "more common than any other gem-quality colored stone. They only seem rarer . . ."

Why do diamonds seem rarer than other gems? Part of the answer is a brilliant marketing campaign. But mainly diamonds seem rare because De Beers *makes* them rare: the company controls most of the world's diamond mines and limits the quantity of diamonds supplied to the market.

Up to now we have concentrated exclusively on perfectly competitive markets—markets in which the producers are perfect competitors. But De Beers isn't like the producers we've studied so far: it is a *monopolist,* the sole (or almost sole) producer of a good. Monopolists behave differently from producers in perfectly competitive industries: whereas perfect competitors take the price at which they can sell their output as given, monopolists know that their actions affect market prices and take that effect into account when deciding how much to produce.

Monopoly is one type of market structure in which firms have the ability to raise prices. *Oligopoly* and *monopolistic competition* are two other types of market structures in which firms can also take actions that affect market prices. We begin this chapter with a brief overview of the types of market structures and a system of classifying markets and industries into two main dimensions. This will help us understand monopoly, oligopoly, and monopolistic competition on a deeper level and see why producers in these markets behave quite differently.

Types of Market Structure

In the real world, there is a mind-boggling array of different markets. We observe widely different behavior patterns by producers across markets: in some markets producers are extremely competitive; in others, they seem somehow to coordinate their actions to avoid competing with one another; and, as we have just described, some markets are monopolies in which there is no competition at all. In order to develop principles and make predictions about markets and how producers will behave in them, economists have developed four principal models of market structure: *perfect competition, monopoly, oligopoly,* and *monopolistic competition*.

This system of market structures is based on two dimensions:

- The number of producers in the market (one, few, or many)
- Whether the goods offered are identical or *differentiated*

Differentiated goods are goods that are different but considered somewhat substitutable by consumers (think Coke versus Pepsi).

Figure 8-1 provides a simple visual summary of the types of market structure classified according to the two dimensions. In *monopoly,* a single producer sells a single, undifferentiated product. In *oligopoly,* a few producers—more than one but not a large number—sell products that may be either identical or differentiated. In *monopolistic competition,* many producers each sell a differentiated product (think of producers of economics textbooks). And finally, as we know, in *perfect competition* many producers each sell an identical product.

You might wonder what determines the number of firms in a market: whether there is one (monopoly), a few (oligopoly), or many (perfect competition and monopolistic competition). We won't answer that question here because it will be covered in detail later in this chapter. We will just briefly note that in the long run it depends on whether there are conditions that make it difficult for new firms to enter the market, such as control of necessary resources or inputs, increasing returns to scale in production, technological superiority, a network externality, or government regulations. When these conditions are present, industries tend to be monopolies or oligopolies; when they are not present, industries tend to be perfectly competitive or monopolistically competitive.

FIGURE 8-1 Types of Market Structure

The behavior of any given firm and the market it occupies are analyzed using one of four models of market structure—monopoly, oligopoly, perfect competition, or monopolistic competition. This system for categorizing market structure is based on two dimensions: (1) whether products are differentiated or identical, and (2) the number of producers in the industry—one, a few, or many.

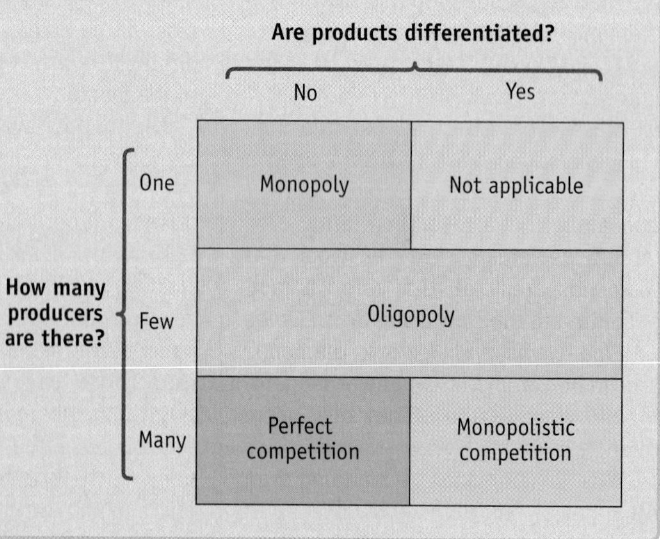

Are products differentiated?
No
Yes
How many producers are there?
One
Few
Many
Monopoly
Not applicable
Oligopoly
Perfect competition
Monopolistic competition

In the next section, we will define *monopoly* and review the conditions that make it possible. We will see how a monopolist can increase profit by limiting the quantity supplied to a market—behavior that is good for the producer but bad for consumers. We then turn to two other forms of market structure, *oligopoly* and *monopolistic competition*. The same conditions that, in less extreme form, give rise to monopoly also give rise to oligopoly, and certain characteristics of monopoly are relevant for both oligopoly and monopolistic competition. Finally, we will take a look at how monopolistic competition gives rise to product differentiation.

A **monopolist** is a firm that is the only producer of a good that has no close substitutes. An industry controlled by a monopolist is known as a **monopoly.**

The Meaning of Monopoly

The De Beers monopoly of South Africa was created in the 1880s by Cecil Rhodes, a British businessman. By 1880 mines in South Africa already dominated the world's supply of diamonds. There were, however, many mining companies, all competing with each other. During the 1880s Rhodes bought the great majority of those mines and consolidated them into a single company, De Beers. By 1889 De Beers controlled almost all of the world's diamond production.

De Beers, in other words, became a **monopolist.** A producer is a monopolist if it is the sole supplier of a good that has no close substitutes. When a firm is a monopolist, the industry is a **monopoly.**

Monopoly: Our First Departure from Perfect Competition

As we saw in the Chapter 7 section "Defining Perfect Competition," the supply and demand model of a market is not universally valid. Instead, it's a model of perfect competition, which is only one of several different types of market structure. Back in Chapter 7 we learned that a market will be perfectly competitive only if there are many producers, all of whom produce the same good. Monopoly is the most extreme departure from perfect competition.

In practice, true monopolies are hard to find in the modern American economy, partly because of legal obstacles. A contemporary entrepreneur who tried to consolidate all the firms in an industry the way that Rhodes did would soon find himself in court, accused of breaking *antitrust* laws, which are intended to prevent monopolies from emerging. Oligopoly, a market structure in which there is a small number of large producers, is much more common. In fact, most of the goods you buy, from autos to airline tickets, are supplied by oligopolies.

Monopolies do, however, play an important role in some sectors of the economy, such as pharmaceuticals. Furthermore, our analysis of monopoly will provide a foundation for our analysis of other departures from perfect competition, such as oligopoly and monopolistic competition.

What Monopolists Do

Why did Rhodes want to consolidate South African diamond producers into a single company? What difference did it make to the world diamond market?

Figure 8-2 offers a preliminary view of the effects of monopoly. It shows an industry in which the supply curve under perfect competition intersects the demand curve at C, leading to the price P_C and the output Q_C.

Suppose that this industry is consolidated into a monopoly. The monopolist *moves up the demand curve* by reducing quantity supplied to a point like M, at which the quantity produced, Q_M, is lower and the price, P_M, is higher than under perfect competition.

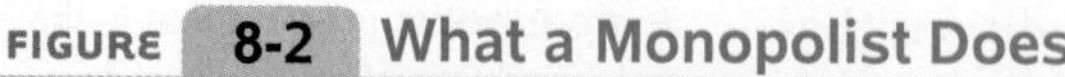

FIGURE 8-2 What a Monopolist Does

Under perfect competition, the price and quantity are determined by supply and demand. Here, the competitive equilibrium is at *C*, where the price is P_C and the quantity is Q_C. A monopolist reduces the quantity supplied to Q_M and moves up the demand curve from *C* to *M*, raising the price to P_M.

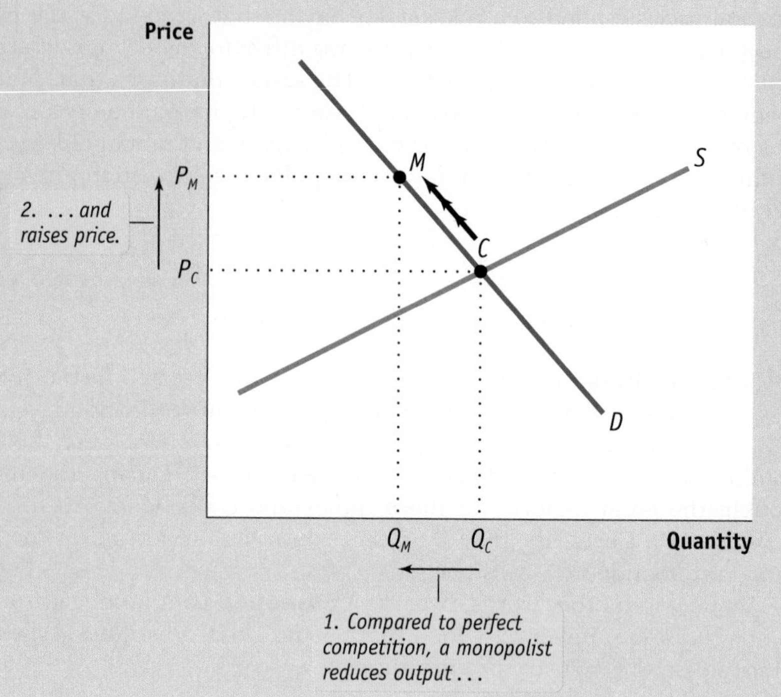

The ability of a monopolist to raise its price above the competitive level by reducing output is known as **market power.** And market power is what monopoly is all about. A wheat farmer who is one of 100,000 wheat farmers has no market power: he or she must sell wheat at the going market price. Your local water utility company, though, does have market power: it can raise prices and still keep many (though not all) of its customers, because they have nowhere else to go. In short, it's a monopolist.

The reason a monopolist reduces output and raises price compared to the perfectly competitive industry levels is to increase profit. Cecil Rhodes consolidated the diamond producers into De Beers because he realized that the whole would be worth more than the sum of its parts—the monopoly would generate more profit than the sum of the profits of the individual competitive firms. As we saw in Chapter 7, under perfect competition economic profits normally vanish in the long run as competitors enter the market. Under monopoly the profits don't go away—a monopolist is able to continue earning economic profits in the long run.

In fact, monopolists are not the only types of firms that possess market power. Later in this chapter we will study *oligopolists,* firms that can have market power as well. Under certain conditions, oligopolists can earn positive economic profits in the long run by restricting output like monopolists do.

But why don't profits get competed away? What allows monopolists to be monopolists?

Why Do Monopolies Exist?

A monopolist making profits will not go unnoticed by others. (Recall that this is "economic profit," revenue over and above the opportunity costs of the firm's resources.) But won't other firms crash the party, grab a piece of the action, and drive down prices and profits in the long run? For a profitable monopoly

Market power is the ability of a firm to raise prices.

to persist, something must keep others from going into the same business; that "something" is known as a **barrier to entry.** There are five principal types of barriers to entry: control of a scarce resource or input, increasing returns to scale, technological superiority, a network externality, and a government-created barrier to entry.

To earn economic profits, a monopolist must be protected by a **barrier to entry**—something that prevents other firms from entering the industry.

A **natural monopoly** exists when increasing returns to scale provide a large cost advantage to a single firm that produces all of an industry's output.

1. Control of a Scarce Resource or Input A monopolist that controls a resource or input crucial to an industry can prevent other firms from entering its market. Cecil Rhodes created the De Beers monopoly by establishing control over the mines that produced the great bulk of the world's diamonds.

2. Increasing Returns to Scale Many Americans have natural gas piped into their homes, for cooking and heating. Invariably, the local gas company is a monopolist. But why don't rival companies compete to provide gas?

In the early nineteenth century, when the gas industry was just starting up, companies did compete for local customers. But this competition didn't last long; soon local gas supply became a monopoly in almost every town because of the large fixed costs involved in providing a town with gas lines. The cost of laying gas lines didn't depend on how much gas a company sold, so a firm with a larger volume of sales had a cost advantage: because it was able to spread the fixed costs over a larger volume, it had lower average total costs than smaller firms.

Local gas supply is an industry in which average total cost falls as output increases. As we learned in Chapter 6, this phenomenon is called *increasing returns to scale.* There we learned that when average total cost falls as output increases, firms tend to grow larger. In an industry characterized by increasing returns to scale, larger companies are more profitable and drive out smaller ones. For the same reason, established companies have a cost advantage over any potential entrant—a potent barrier to entry. So increasing returns to scale can both give rise to and sustain monopoly.

A monopoly created and sustained by increasing returns to scale is called a **natural monopoly.** The defining characteristic of a natural monopoly is that it possesses increasing returns to scale over the range of output that is relevant for the industry. This is illustrated in Figure 8-3, showing the firm's average

FIGURE **8-3** Increasing Returns to Scale Create Natural Monopoly

A natural monopoly can arise when fixed costs required to operate are very high. When this occurs, the firm's *ATC* curve declines over the range of output at which price is greater than or equal to average total cost. This gives the firm increasing returns to scale over the entire range of output at which the firm would at least break even in the long run. As a result, a given quantity of output is produced more cheaply by one large firm than by two or more smaller firms.

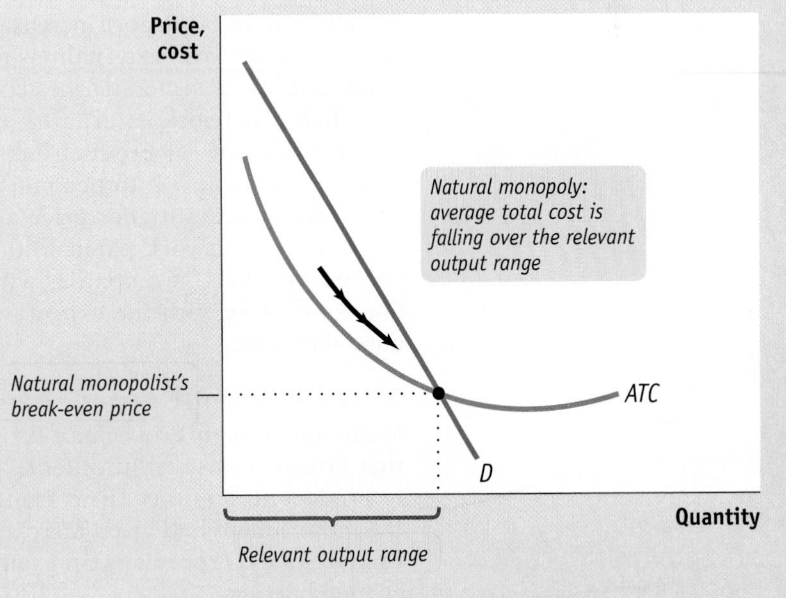

total cost curve and the market demand curve, *D*. Here we can see that the natural monopolist's *ATC* curve declines over the output levels at which price is greater than or equal to average total cost. So the natural monopolist has increasing returns to scale over the entire range of output for which any firm would want to remain in the industry—the range of output at which the firm would at least break even in the long run. The source of this condition is large fixed costs: when large fixed costs are required to operate, a given quantity of output is produced at lower average total cost by one large firm than by two or more smaller firms.

The most visible natural monopolies in the modern economy are local utilities—water, gas, and sometimes electricity. As we'll see later in this chapter, natural monopolies pose a special challenge to public policy.

3. Technological Superiority A firm that maintains a consistent technological advantage over potential competitors can establish itself as a monopolist. For example, from the 1970s through the 1990s the chip manufacturer Intel was able to maintain a consistent advantage over potential competitors in both the design and production of microprocessors, the chips that run computers. But technological superiority is typically not a barrier to entry over the longer term: over time competitors will invest in upgrading their technology to match that of the technology leader. In fact, in the last few years Intel found its technological superiority eroded by a competitor, Advanced Micro Devices (also known as AMD), which now produces chips approximately as fast and as powerful as Intel chips.

We should note, however, that in certain high-tech industries, technological superiority is not a guarantee of success against competitors because of *network externalities.*

4. Network Externality If you were the only person in the world with an Internet connection, what would that connection be worth to you? The answer, of course, is nothing. Your Internet connection is valuable only because other people are also connected. And, in general, the more people who are connected, the more valuable your connection is. As we learned in Chapter 6, this phenomenon, whereby the value of a good or service to an individual is greater when many others use the same good or service, is called a *network externality*—its value derives from enabling its users to participate in a network of other users.

The earliest form of network externalities arose in transportation, where the value of a road or airport increased as the number of people who had access to it rose. But network externalities are especially prevalent in the technology and communications sectors of the economy.

When a network externality exists, the firm with the largest network of customers using its product has an advantage in attracting new customers, one that may allow it to become a monopolist. At a minimum, the dominant firm can charge a higher price and so earn higher profits than competitors. Moreover, a network externality gives an advantage to the firm with the "deepest pockets." Companies with the most money on hand can sell the most goods at a loss with the expectation that doing so will give them the largest customer base.

5. Government-Created Barrier In 1998 the pharmaceutical company Merck introduced Propecia, a drug effective against baldness. Despite the fact that Propecia was very profitable and other drug companies had the know-how to produce it, no other firms challenged Merck's monopoly. That's because the U.S. government had given Merck the sole legal right to produce the drug in the United States. Propecia is an example of a monopoly protected by government-created barriers.

The most important legally created monopolies today arise from *patents* and *copyrights*. A **patent** gives an inventor the sole right to make, use, or sell that invention for a period that in most countries lasts between 16 and 20 years. Patents are given to the creators of new products, such as drugs or devices. Similarly, a **copyright** gives the creator of a literary or artistic work the sole rights to profit from that work, usually for a period equal to the creator's lifetime plus 70 years.

A **patent** gives an inventor a temporary monopoly in the use or sale of an invention.

A **copyright** gives the creator of a literary or artistic work sole rights to profit from that work.

The justification for patents and copyrights is a matter of incentives. If inventors are not protected by patents, they would gain little reward from their efforts: as soon as a valuable invention was made public, others would copy it and sell products based on it. And if inventors could not expect to profit from their inventions, then there would be no incentive to incur the costs of invention in the first place. Likewise for the creators of literary or artistic works. So the law gives a temporary monopoly that encourages invention and creation by imposing temporary property rights.

Patents and copyrights are temporary because the law strikes a compromise. The higher price for the good that holds while the legal protection is in effect compensates inventors for the cost of invention; conversely, the lower price that results once the legal protection lapses and competition emerges benefits consumers and increases economic efficiency.

Because the length of the temporary monopoly cannot be tailored to specific cases, this system is imperfect and leads to some missed opportunities. In some cases there can be significant welfare issues. For example, the violation of American drug patents by pharmaceutical companies in poor countries has been a major source of controversy, pitting the needs of poor patients who cannot afford retail drug prices against the interests of drug manufacturers that have incurred high research costs to discover these drugs. To solve this problem, some American drug companies and poor countries have negotiated deals in which the patents are honored but the American companies sell their drugs at deeply discounted prices.

How a Monopolist Maximizes Profit

As we've suggested, once Cecil Rhodes consolidated the competing diamond producers of South Africa into a single company, the industry's behavior changed: the quantity supplied fell and the market price rose. In this section, we will learn how a monopolist increases its profit by reducing output. And we will see the crucial role that market demand plays in leading a monopolist to behave differently from a perfectly competitive industry. (Remember that profit here is economic profit, not accounting profit.)

The Monopolist's Demand Curve and Marginal Revenue In Chapter 7 we derived the firm's optimal output rule: a profit-maximizing firm produces the quantity of output at which the marginal cost of producing the last unit of output equals marginal revenue—the change in total revenue generated by that last unit of output. That is, $MR = MC$ at the profit-maximizing quantity of output. Although the optimal output rule holds for all firms, we will see shortly that its application leads to different profit-maximizing output levels for a monopolist compared to a firm in a perfectly competitive industry—that is, a price-taking firm. The source of that difference lies in the comparison of the demand curve faced by a monopolist to the demand curve faced by an individual perfectly competitive firm.

In addition to the optimal output rule, we also learned in Chapter 7 that even though the market demand curve always slopes downward, each of the firms that make up a perfectly competitive industry faces a *perfectly elastic* demand curve that is horizontal at the market price, like D_C in panel (a) of

FIGURE 8-4 Comparing the Demand Curves of a Perfectly Competitive Producer and a Monopolist

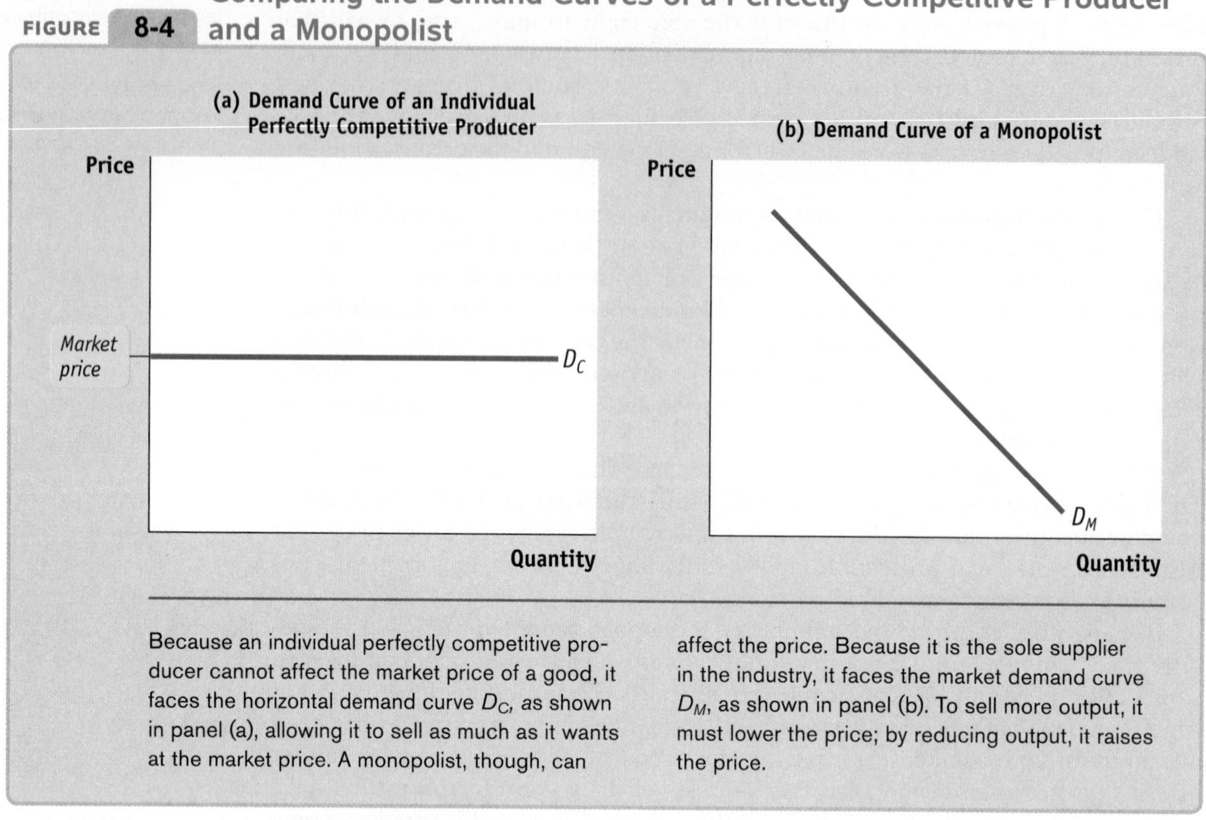

Because an individual perfectly competitive producer cannot affect the market price of a good, it faces the horizontal demand curve D_C, as shown in panel (a), allowing it to sell as much as it wants at the market price. A monopolist, though, can affect the price. Because it is the sole supplier in the industry, it faces the market demand curve D_M, as shown in panel (b). To sell more output, it must lower the price; by reducing output, it raises the price.

Figure 8-4. Any attempt by an individual firm in a perfectly competitive industry to charge more than the going market price will cause it to lose all its sales. It can, however, sell as much as it likes at the market price. As we saw in Chapter 7, the marginal revenue of a perfectly competitive producer is simply the market price. As a result, the price-taking firm's optimal output rule is to produce the output level at which the marginal cost of the last unit produced is equal to the market price.

A monopolist, in contrast, is the sole supplier of its good. So its demand curve is simply the market demand curve, which slopes downward, like D_M in panel (b) of Figure 8-4. This downward slope creates a "wedge" between the price of the good and the marginal revenue of the good—the change in revenue generated by producing one more unit.

Table 8-1 shows this wedge between price and marginal revenue for a monopolist, by calculating the monopolist's total revenue and marginal revenue schedules from its demand schedule.

The first two columns of Table 8-1 show a hypothetical demand schedule for De Beers diamonds. For the sake of simplicity, we assume that all diamonds are exactly alike. And to make the arithmetic easy, we suppose that the number of diamonds sold is far smaller than is actually the case. For instance, at a price of $500 per diamond, we assume that only 10 diamonds are sold. The demand curve implied by this schedule is shown in panel (a) of Figure 8-5.

The third column of Table 8-1 shows De Beers's total revenue from selling each quantity of diamonds—the price per diamond multiplied by the number of diamonds sold. The last column calculates marginal revenue, the change in total revenue from producing and selling another diamond.

Clearly, after the 1st diamond, the marginal revenue a monopolist receives from selling one more unit is less than the price at which that unit is sold. For example, if De Beers sells 10 diamonds, the price at which the 10th diamond is sold is \$500. But the marginal revenue—the change in total revenue in going from 9 to 10 diamonds—is only \$50.

Why is the marginal revenue from that 10th diamond less than the price? It is less than the price because an increase in production by a monopolist has two opposing effects on revenue:

- *A quantity effect.* One more unit is sold, increasing total revenue by the price at which the unit is sold.
- *A price effect.* In order to sell the last unit, the monopolist must cut the market price on *all* units sold. This decreases total revenue.

The quantity effect and the price effect when the monopolist goes from selling 9 diamonds to 10 diamonds are illustrated by the two shaded areas in panel (a) of Figure 8-5. Increasing diamond sales from 9 to 10 means moving down the demand curve from *A* to *B*, reducing the price per diamond from \$550 to \$500. The green-shaded area represents the quantity effect: De Beers sells the 10th diamond at a price of \$500. This is offset, however, by the price effect, represented by the orange-shaded area. In order to sell that 10th diamond, De Beers must reduce the price on all its diamonds from \$550 to \$500. So it loses 9 × \$50 = \$450 in revenue, the orange-shaded area. As point *C* indicates, the total effect on revenue of selling one more diamond—the marginal revenue—derived from an increase in diamond sales from 9 to 10 is only \$50.

Point *C* lies on the monopolist's marginal revenue curve, labeled *MR* in panel (a) of Figure 8-5 and taken from the last column of Table 8-1. The crucial point about the monopolist's marginal revenue curve is that it is always *below* the demand curve. That's because of the price effect: a monopolist's marginal revenue from selling an additional unit is always less than the price the monopolist receives for the previous unit. It is the price effect that creates the wedge between the monopolist's marginal revenue curve and the demand curve: in order to sell an additional diamond, De Beers must cut the market price on all units sold.

TABLE 8-1 Demand, Total Revenue, and Marginal Revenue for the De Beers Monopoly

Price of diamond P	Quantity of diamonds Q	Total revenue $TR = P \times Q$	Marginal revenue $MR = \Delta TR/\Delta Q$
\$1,000	0	\$0	
			\$950
950	1	950	
			850
900	2	1,800	
			750
850	3	2,550	
			650
800	4	3,200	
			550
750	5	3,750	
			450
700	6	4,200	
			350
650	7	4,550	
			250
600	8	4,800	
			150
550	9	4,950	
			50
500	10	5,000	
			−50
450	11	4,950	
			−150
400	12	4,800	
			−250
350	13	4,550	
			−350
300	14	4,200	
			−450
250	15	3,750	
			−550
200	16	3,200	
			−650
150	17	2,550	
			−750
100	18	1,800	
			−850
50	19	950	
			−950
0	20	0	

In fact, this wedge exists for any firm that possesses market power, such as an oligopolist as well as a monopolist. Having market power means that the firm faces a downward-sloping demand curve. As a result, there will always be a price effect from an increase in its output. So for a firm with market power, the marginal revenue curve always lies below its demand curve.

Take a moment to compare the monopolist's marginal revenue curve with the marginal revenue curve for a perfectly competitive firm, one without market power. For such a firm there is no price effect from an increase in output: its marginal revenue curve is simply its horizontal demand curve. So for a perfectly competitive firm, market price and marginal revenue are always equal.

To emphasize how the quantity and price effects offset each other for a firm with market power, De Beers's total revenue curve is shown in panel (b) of Figure 8-5. Notice that it is hill-shaped: as output rises from 0 to 10 diamonds, total revenue increases. This reflects the fact that at *low levels of output, the quantity effect is stronger than the price effect:* as the monopolist

FIGURE 8-5 A Monopolist's Demand, Total Revenue, and Marginal Revenue Curves

Panel (a) shows the monopolist's demand and marginal revenue curves for diamonds from Table 8-1. The marginal revenue curve lies below the demand curve. To see why, consider point *A* on the demand curve, where 9 diamonds are sold at $550 each, generating total revenue of $4,950. To sell a 10th diamond, the price on all 10 diamonds must be cut to $500, as shown by point B. As a result, total revenue increases by the green area (the quantity effect: +$500) but decreases by the orange area (the price effect: −$450). So the marginal revenue from the 10th diamond is $50 (the difference between the green and orange areas), which is much lower than its price, $500. Panel (b) shows the monopolist's total revenue curve for diamonds. As output goes from 0 to 10 diamonds, total revenue increases. It reaches its maximum at 10 diamonds—the level at which marginal revenue is equal to 0—and declines thereafter. The quantity effect dominates the price effect when total revenue is rising; the price effect dominates the quantity effect when total revenue is falling.

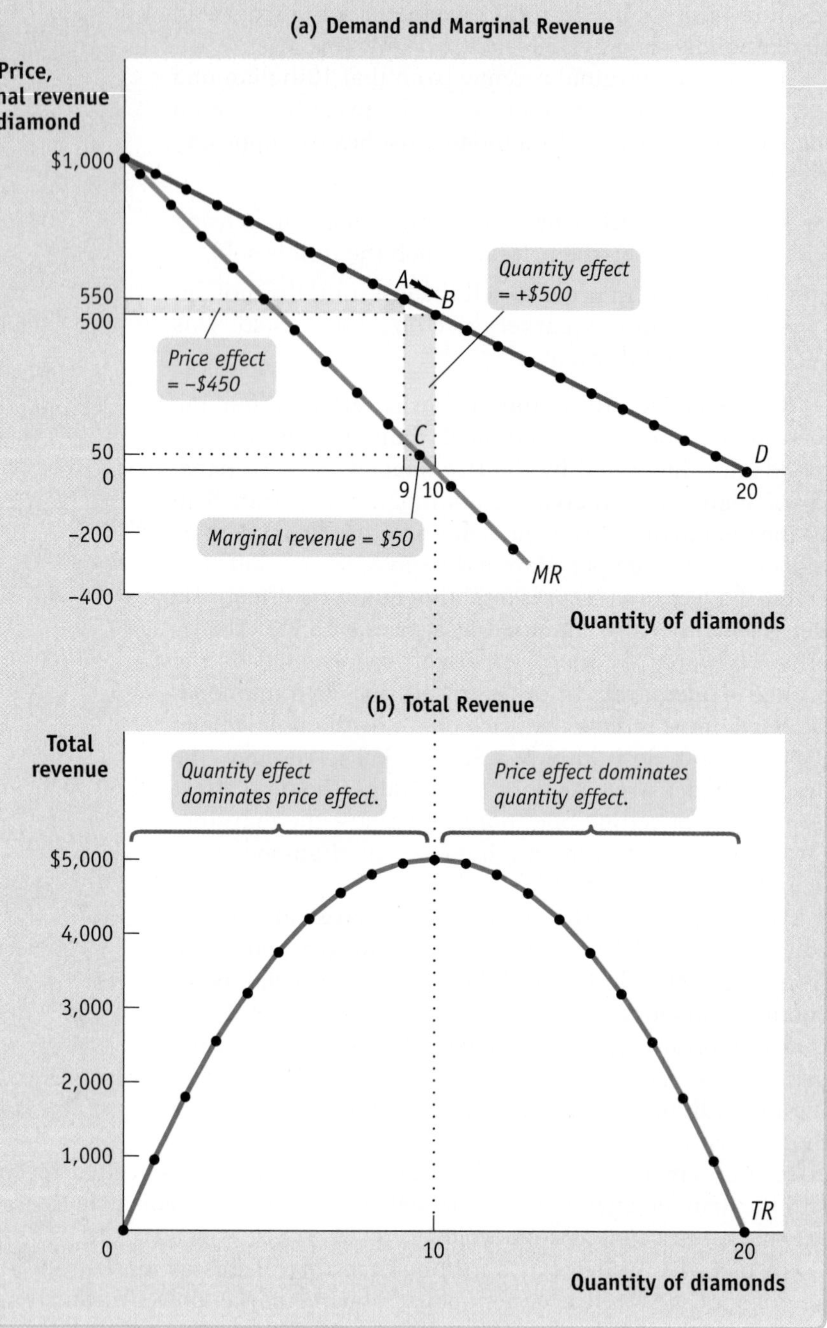

sells more, it has to lower the price on only very few units, so the price effect is small. As output rises beyond 10 diamonds, total revenue actually falls. This reflects the fact that *at high levels of output, the price effect is stronger than the quantity effect:* as the monopolist sells more, it now has to lower the price on many units of output, making the price effect very large. Correspondingly, the marginal revenue curve lies below zero at output levels above 10 diamonds. For example, an increase in diamond production from 11 to 12 yields only $400 for the 12th diamond, simultaneously reducing the revenue from diamonds 1 through 11 by $550. As a result, the marginal revenue of the 12th diamond is −$150.

The Monopolist's Profit-Maximizing Output and Price To complete the story of how a monopolist maximizes profit, we now bring in the monopolist's marginal cost. Let's assume that there is no fixed cost of production; we'll also assume that the marginal cost of producing an additional diamond is constant at $200, no matter how many diamonds De Beers produces. Then marginal cost will always equal average total cost, and the marginal cost curve (and the average total cost curve) is a horizontal line at $200, as shown in Figure 8-6.

To maximize profit, the monopolist compares marginal cost with marginal revenue. If marginal revenue exceeds marginal cost, De Beers increases profit by producing more; if marginal revenue is less than marginal cost, De Beers increases profit by producing less. So the monopolist maximizes its profit by using the optimal output rule:

(8-1) $MR = MC$ at the monopolist's profit-maximizing quantity of output

The monopolist's optimal point is shown in Figure 8-6. At *A*, the marginal cost curve, *MC*, crosses the marginal revenue curve, *MR*. The corresponding output level, 8 diamonds, is the monopolist's profit-maximizing quantity of output, Q_M. The price at which consumers demand 8 diamonds is $600, so the monopolist's price, P_M, is $600—corresponding to point *B*. The average total cost of producing each diamond is $200, so the monopolist earns a profit of $600 – $200 = $400 per diamond, and total profit is 8 × $400 = $3,200, as indicated by the shaded area.

Monopoly versus Perfect Competition When Cecil Rhodes consolidated many independent diamond producers into De Beers, he converted a perfectly competitive industry into a monopoly. We can now use our analysis to see the effects of such a consolidation.

PITFALLS

FINDING THE MONOPOLY PRICE

In order to find the *profit-maximizing quantity of output* for a monopolist, you look for the point where the marginal revenue curve crosses the marginal cost curve. Point *A* in Figure 8-6 is an example.

However, it's important not to fall into a common error: imagining that point *A* also shows the *price* at which the monopolist sells its output. It doesn't: it shows the *marginal revenue* received by the monopolist, which we know is less than the price.

To find the monopoly price, you have to go up vertically from *A* to the demand curve. There you find the price at which consumers demand the profit-maximizing quantity. So the profit-maximizing price–quantity combination is always a point on the demand curve, like *B* in Figure 8-6.

FIGURE 8-6 The Monopolist's Profit-Maximizing Output and Price

This figure shows the demand, marginal revenue, and marginal cost curves. Marginal cost per diamond is constant at $200, so the marginal cost curve is horizontal at $200. According to the optimal output rule, the profit-maximizing quantity of output for the monopolist is at *MR* = *MC*, shown by point *A*, where the marginal cost and marginal revenue curves cross at an output of 8 diamonds. The price De Beers can charge per diamond is found by going to the point on the demand curve directly above point *A*, which is point *B* here—a price of $600 per diamond. It makes a profit of $400 × 8 = $3,200. A perfectly competitive industry produces the output level at which *P* = *MC*, given by point *C*, where the demand curve and marginal cost curves cross. So a competitive industry produces 16 diamonds, sells at a price of $200, and makes zero profit.

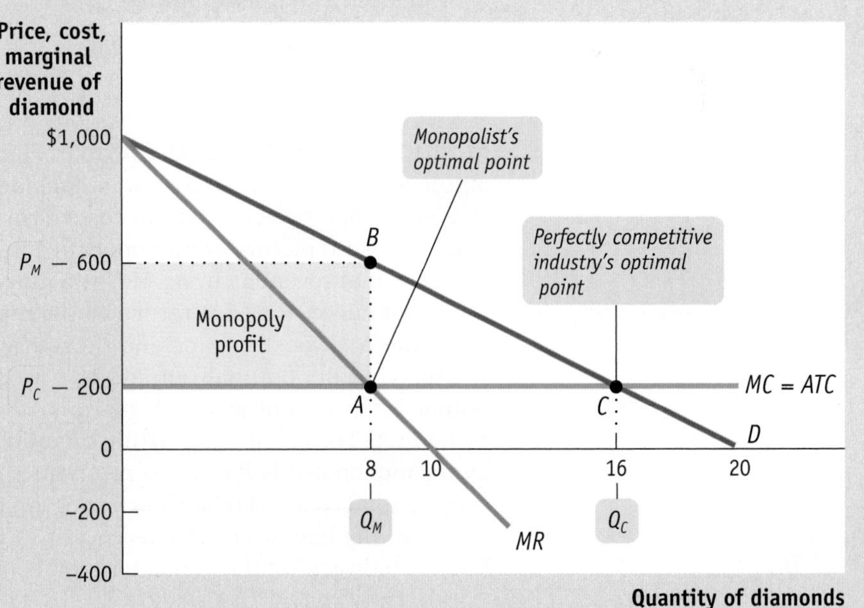

PITFALLS

IS THERE A MONOPOLY SUPPLY CURVE?

Given how a monopolist applies its optimal output rule, you might be tempted to ask what this implies for the supply curve of a monopolist. But this is a meaningless question: *monopolists don't have supply curves.*

Remember that a supply curve shows the quantity that producers are willing to supply for any given market price. A monopolist, however, does not take the price as given; it chooses a profit-maximizing quantity, taking into account its own ability to influence the price.

Let's look again at Figure 8-6 and ask how this same market would work if, instead of being a monopoly, the industry were perfectly competitive. We will continue to assume that there is no fixed cost and that marginal cost is constant, so average total cost and marginal cost are equal.

If the diamond industry consists of many perfectly competitive firms, each of those producers takes the market price as given. That is, each producer acts as if its marginal revenue is equal to the market price. So each firm within the industry uses the price-taking firm's optimal output rule:

(8-2) $P = MC$ at the perfectly competitive firm's profit-maximizing quantity of output

In Figure 8-6, this would correspond to producing at *C*, where the price per diamond, P_C, is \$200, equal to the marginal cost of production. So the profit-maximizing output of an industry under perfect competition, Q_C, is 16 diamonds.

But does the perfectly competitive industry earn any profits at *C*? No: the price of \$200 is equal to the average total cost per diamond. So there are no economic profits for this industry when it produces at the perfectly competitive output level.

We've already seen that once the industry is consolidated into a monopoly, the result is very different. The monopolist's calculation of marginal revenue takes the price effect into account, so that marginal revenue is less than the price. That is,

(8-3) $P > MR = MC$ at the monopolist's profit-maximizing quantity of output

As we've already seen, the monopolist produces less than the competitive industry—8 diamonds rather than 16. The price under monopoly is \$600, compared with only \$200 under perfect competition. The monopolist earns a positive profit, but the competitive industry does not.

So, just as we suggested earlier, we see that compared with a competitive industry, a monopolist does the following:

- Produces a smaller quantity: $Q_M < Q_C$
- Charges a higher price: $P_M > P_C$
- Earns a profit

Monopoly: The General Picture Figure 8-6 involved specific numbers and assumed that marginal cost was constant, that there was no fixed cost, and, therefore, that the average total cost curve was a horizontal line. Figure 8-7 shows a more general picture of monopoly in action: *D* is the market demand curve; *MR*, the marginal revenue curve; *MC*, the marginal cost curve; and *ATC*, the average total cost curve. Here we return to the usual assumption that the marginal cost curve has a "swoosh" shape and the average total cost curve is U-shaped.

Applying the optimal output rule, we see that the profit-maximizing level of output is the output at which marginal revenue equals marginal cost, indicated by point *A*. The profit-maximizing quantity of output is Q_M, and the price charged by the monopolist is P_M. At the profit-maximizing level of output, the monopolist's average total cost is ATC_M, shown by point *C*.

Recalling how we calculated profit in Equation 7-5, profit is equal to the difference between total revenue and total cost. So we have:

(8-4)
$$\begin{aligned} \text{Profit} &= TR - TC \\ &= (P_M \times Q_M) - (ATC_M \times Q_M) \\ &= (P_M - ATC_M) \times Q_M \end{aligned}$$

FIGURE 8-7 The Monopolist's Profit

In this case, the marginal cost curve has a "swoosh" shape and the average total cost curve is U-shaped. The monopolist maximizes profit by producing the level of output at which $MR = MC$, given by point A, generating quantity Q_M. It finds its monopoly price, P_M, from the point on the demand curve directly above point A, point B here. The average total cost of Q_M is shown by point C. Profit is given by the area of the shaded rectangle.

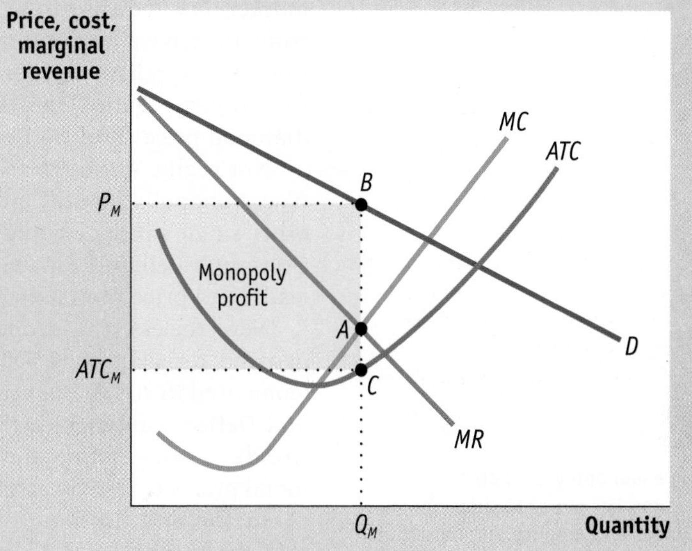

Profit is equal to the area of the shaded rectangle in Figure 8-7, with a height of $P_M - ATC_M$ and a width of Q_M.

In Chapter 7 we learned that a perfectly competitive industry can have profits in the *short run but not in the long run.* In the short run, price can exceed average total cost, allowing a perfectly competitive firm to make a profit. But we also know that this cannot persist. In the long run, any profit in a perfectly competitive industry will be competed away as new firms enter the market. In contrast, barriers to entry allow a monopolist to make profits in *both the short run and the long run.*

ECONOMICS ➤ IN ACTION

NEWLY EMERGING MARKETS: A DIAMOND MONOPOLIST'S BEST FRIEND

When Cecil Rhodes created the De Beers monopoly, it was a particularly opportune moment. The new diamond mines in South Africa dwarfed all previous sources, so almost all of the world's diamond production was concentrated in a few square miles.

Until recently, De Beers was able to extend its control of resources even as new mines opened. De Beers either bought out new producers or entered into agreements with local governments that controlled some of the new mines, effectively making them part of the De Beers monopoly. The most remarkable of these was an agreement with the former Soviet Union, which ensured that Russian diamonds would be marketed through De Beers, preserving its ability to control retail prices. De Beers also went so far as to stockpile a year's supply of diamonds in its London vaults so that when demand dropped, newly mined stones would be stored rather than sold, restricting retail supply until demand and prices recovered.

L. Lartigue/USAID

An increase in demand for diamonds in emerging markets has led to increased depletion of the world's diamond mines and higher prices.

However, over the past few years the De Beers monopoly has been under assault. Government regulators have forced De Beers to loosen its control of the market. For the first time, De Beers has competition: a number of independent companies have begun mining for diamonds in other African countries. In addition, high-quality, inexpensive synthetic diamonds have become an alternative to real gems, eating into De Beers's profits. So does this mean an end to high diamond prices and De Beers's high profits?

Not really. Although today's De Beers is more of a "near-monopolist" than a true monopolist, it still mines more of the world's supply of diamonds than any other single producer. And it has been benefiting from newly emerging markets. Consumer demand for diamonds has soared in countries like China and India, leading to price increases.

Nevertheless, the economic crisis of 2009 put a serious dent in worldwide demand for diamonds. DeBeers responded by cutting 2011 production by 20% (compared to 2008). But affluent Chinese continue to be heavy buyers of diamonds, and DeBeers anticipates that Asian demand will accelerate the depletion of the world's existing diamond mines. As a result, diamond analysts predict rough diamond prices to rise by at least 5% per year for the next five years.

In the end, although a diamond monopoly may not be forever, a near-monopoly with rising demand in newly emerging markets may be just as profitable.

Quick Review

- In a **monopoly,** a single firm uses its **market power** to charge higher prices and produce less output than a competitive industry, generating profits in the short and long run.
- Profits will not persist in the long run unless there is a **barrier to entry.** A **natural monopoly** arises when average total cost is declining over the output range relevant for the industry. This creates a barrier to entry because an established monopolist has lower average total cost than an entrant.
- **Patents** and **copyrights,** government-created barriers, are a source of temporary monopoly.
- The crucial difference between a firm with market power, such as a monopolist, and a firm in a perfectly competitive industry is that perfectly competitive firms are price-takers that face horizontal demand curves, but a firm with market power faces a downward-sloping demand curve.
- Due to the price effect of an increase in output, the marginal revenue curve of a firm with market power always lies below its demand curve. So a profit-maximizing monopolist chooses the output level at which marginal cost is equal to marginal revenue—*not* to price.
- As a result, the monopolist produces less and sells its output at a higher price than a perfectly competitive industry would. It earns profits in the short run and the long run.

CHECK YOUR UNDERSTANDING 8-1

1. Currently, Texas Tea Oil Co. is the only local supplier of home heating oil in Frigid, Alaska. This winter residents were shocked that the price of a gallon of heating oil had doubled and believed that they were the victims of market power. Explain which of the following pieces of evidence support or contradict that conclusion.

a. There is a national shortage of heating oil, and Texas Tea could procure only a limited amount.

b. Last year, Texas Tea and several other competing local oil-supply firms merged into a single firm.

c. The cost to Texas Tea of purchasing heating oil from refineries has gone up significantly.

d. Recently, some nonlocal firms have begun to offer heating oil to Texas Tea's regular customers at a price much lower than Texas Tea's.

e. Texas Tea has acquired an exclusive government license to draw oil from the only heating oil pipeline in the state.

2. Use the accompanying total revenue schedule of Emerald, Inc., a monopoly producer of 10-carat emeralds, to calculate the answers to parts a–d. Then answer part e.

a. The demand schedule

b. The marginal revenue schedule

c. The quantity effect component of marginal revenue per output level

d. The price effect component of marginal revenue per output level

e. What additional information is needed to determine Emerald, Inc.'s profit-maximizing output?

Quantity of emeralds demanded	Total revenue
1	$100
2	186
3	252
4	280
5	250

3. Use Figure 8-6 to show what happens to the following when the marginal cost of diamond production rises from $200 to $400.

a. Marginal cost curve

b. Profit-maximizing price and quantity

c. Profit of the monopolist

d. Perfectly competitive industry profits

Solutions appear at back of book.

The Meaning of Oligopoly

An **oligopoly** is an industry with only a small number of producers. A producer in such an industry is known as an **oligopolist.**

When no one firm has a monopoly, but producers nonetheless realize that they can affect market prices, an industry is characterized by **imperfect competition.**

What we have learned about both perfect competition and monopoly is relevant to oligopoly. But, oligopoly also raises some entirely new issues. Among other things, firms in an oligopoly are often tempted to engage in the kind of behavior that gets them into trouble with the law. A classic example is the case of the Archer Daniels Midland Corporation (ADM) and its Japanese competitor Ajinomoto.

On October 25, 1993, executives from ADM and Ajinomoto met at the Marriott Hotel in Irvine, California, to discuss the market for lysine, an additive used in animal feed. In this and subsequent meetings, the two companies joined with several other competitors to set targets for the market price of lysine, a behavior called *price-fixing.* Each company agreed to limit its production in order to achieve those targets. What the participants in the meeting didn't know was that the FBI had bugged the room and was filming them with a hidden camera.

What these companies were doing was illegal. To understand why it was illegal and why the companies were doing it anyway, we need to examine the issues posed by industries in which there are only a few sellers, otherwise known as an **oligopoly.** A firm in such an industry is known as an **oligopolist.**

The Prevalence of Oligopoly

Oligopolists obviously compete with one another for sales. But neither ADM nor Ajinomoto were like a firm in a perfectly competitive industry, which takes the price at which it can sell its product as given. Each of these firms knew that its decision about how much to produce would affect the market price. That is, like monopolists, each of the firms had some *market power.* So the competition in this industry wasn't "perfect."

Economists refer to a situation in which firms compete but also possess market power—which enables them to affect market prices—as **imperfect competition.** There are actually two important forms of imperfect competition: oligopoly and *monopolistic competition.* Of these, oligopoly is probably the more important in practice.

Although lysine is a multibillion-dollar business, it is not exactly a product familiar to most consumers. However, many familiar goods and services are supplied by only a few competing sellers, which means the industries in question are oligopolies. For example, most air routes are served by only two or three airlines: in recent years, regularly scheduled shuttle service between New York and either Boston or Washington, D.C., has been provided only by Delta and US Airways. Three firms—Chiquita, Dole, and Del Monte, which own huge banana plantations in Central America—control 65% of world banana exports. Most cola beverages are sold by Coca-Cola and Pepsi. This list could go on for many pages.

It's important to realize that an oligopoly isn't necessarily made up of large firms. What matters isn't size per se; the question is how many competitors there are. When a small town has only two grocery stores, grocery service there is just as much an oligopoly as air shuttle service between New York and Washington.

Why are oligopolies so prevalent? Essentially, oligopoly is the result of the same factors that sometimes produce monopoly, but in somewhat weaker form. Probably the most important source of oligopoly is the existence of *increasing returns to scale,* which give bigger producers a cost advantage over smaller ones. When these effects are very strong, they lead to monopoly; when they are not that strong, they lead to an industry with a small number of firms. For example, larger grocery stores typically have lower costs than smaller ones. But the advantages of

An oligopoly consisting of only two firms is a **duopoly.** Each firm is known as a **duopolist.**

Sellers engage in **collusion** when they cooperate to raise their joint profits. A **cartel** is an agreement among several producers to obey output restrictions in order to increase their joint profits.

large scale taper off once grocery stores are reasonably large, which is why two or three stores often survive in small towns.

If oligopoly is so common, why has most of this book focused on competition in industries where the number of sellers is very large? And why did we study monopoly, which is relatively uncommon, first? The answer has two parts.

First, much of what we learn from the study of perfectly competitive markets—about costs, entry and exit, and efficiency—remains valid despite the fact that many industries are not perfectly competitive. Second, the analysis of oligopoly turns out to present some puzzles for which there are no easy solutions. It is almost always a good idea—in exams and in life in general—first to deal with the questions you can answer, then to puzzle over the harder ones. We have simply followed the same strategy, developing the relatively clear-cut theories of perfect competition and monopoly first, and only then turning to the puzzles presented by oligopoly.

Understanding Oligopoly

How much will a firm produce? Up to this point, we have always answered: the quantity that maximizes its profit. Together with its cost curves, the assumption that a firm maximizes profit is enough to determine its output when it is a perfect competitor or a monopolist.

When it comes to oligopoly, however, we run into some difficulties. Indeed, economists often describe the behavior of oligopolistic firms as a "puzzle."

A Duopoly Example Let's begin looking at the puzzle of oligopoly with the simplest version, an industry in which there are only two producing firms—a **duopoly**—and each is known as a **duopolist.**

Going back to our opening story, imagine that ADM and Ajinomoto are the only two producers of lysine. To make things even simpler, suppose that once a company has incurred the fixed cost needed to produce lysine, the marginal cost of producing another pound is zero. So the companies are concerned only with the revenue they receive from sales.

Table 8-2 shows a hypothetical demand schedule for lysine and the total revenue of the industry at each price–quantity combination.

If this were a perfectly competitive industry, each firm would have an incentive to produce more as long as the market price was above marginal cost. Since the marginal cost is assumed to be zero, this would mean that at equilibrium lysine would be provided free. Firms would produce until price equals zero, yielding a total output of 120 million pounds and zero revenue for both firms.

However, surely the firms would not be that stupid. With only two firms in the industry, each would realize that by producing more, it drives down the market price. So each firm would, like a monopolist, realize that profits would be higher if it and its rival limited their production.

So how much will the two firms produce?

One possibility is that the two companies will engage in **collusion**—they will cooperate to raise their joint profits. The strongest form of collusion is a **cartel,** an arrangement between producers that determines how much each is allowed to produce. The world's most famous cartel is the Organization of Petroleum Exporting Countries (OPEC). As its name indicates, it's actually an agreement among governments rather than

TABLE 8-2 Demand Schedule for Lysine

Price of lysine (per pound)	Quantity of lysine demanded (millions of pounds)	Total revenue (millions)
$12	0	$0
11	10	110
10	20	200
9	30	270
8	40	320
7	50	350
6	60	360
5	70	350
4	80	320
3	90	270
2	100	200
1	110	110
0	120	0

firms. There's a reason this most famous of cartels is an agreement among governments: cartels among firms are illegal in the United States and many other jurisdictions. But let's ignore the law for a moment (which is, of course, what ADM and Ajinomoto did in real life—to their own detriment).

So suppose that ADM and Ajinomoto were to form a cartel and that this cartel decided to act as if it were a monopolist, maximizing total industry profits. It's obvious from Table 8-2 that in order to maximize the combined profits of the firms, this cartel should set total industry output at 60 million pounds of lysine, which would sell at a price of $6 per pound, leading to revenue of $360 million, the maximum possible. Then the only question would be how much of that 60 million pounds each firm gets to produce. A "fair" solution might be for each firm to produce 30 million pounds with revenues for each firm of $180 million.

But even if the two firms agreed on such a deal, they might have a problem: each of the firms would have an incentive to break its word and produce more than the agreed-upon quantity.

Collusion and Competition Suppose that the presidents of ADM and Ajinomoto were to agree that each would produce 30 million pounds of lysine over the next year. Both would understand that this plan maximizes their combined profits. And both would have an incentive to cheat.

To see why, consider what would happen if Ajinomoto honored its agreement, producing only 30 million pounds, but ADM ignored its promise and produced 40 million pounds. This increase in total output would drive the price down from $6 to $5 per pound, the price at which 70 million pounds are demanded. The industry's total revenue would fall from $360 million ($6 × 60 million pounds) to $350 million ($5 × 70 million pounds). However, ADM's revenue would *rise*, from $180 million to $200 million. Since we are assuming a marginal cost of zero, this would mean a $20 million increase in ADM's profits.

But Ajinomoto's president might make exactly the same calculation. And if both firms were to produce 40 million pounds of lysine, the price would drop to $4 per pound. So each firm's profits would fall, from $180 million to $160 million.

Why do individual firms have an incentive to produce more than the quantity that maximizes their joint profits? Because neither firm has as strong an incentive to limit its output as a true monopolist would.

Let's go back for a minute to the theory of monopoly. We know that a profit-maximizing monopolist sets marginal cost (which in this case is zero) equal to marginal revenue. But what is marginal revenue? Recall that producing an additional unit of a good has two effects:

1. A positive *quantity* effect: one more unit is sold, increasing total revenue by the price at which that unit is sold.
2. A negative *price* effect: in order to sell one more unit, the monopolist must cut the market price on *all* units sold.

The negative price effect is the reason marginal revenue for a monopolist is less than the market price. In the case of oligopoly, when considering the effect of increasing production, a firm is concerned only with the price effect on its *own* units of output, not those of its fellow oligopolists. Both ADM and Ajinomoto suffer a negative price effect if ADM decides to produce extra lysine and so drives down the price. But ADM cares only about the negative price effect on the units it produces, not about the loss to Ajinomoto.

This tells us that an individual firm in an oligopolistic industry faces a smaller price effect from an additional unit of output than does a monopolist; therefore, the marginal revenue that such a firm calculates is higher. So it

When firms ignore the effects of their actions on each others' profits, they engage in **noncooperative behavior.**

will seem to be profitable for any one company in an oligopoly to increase production, even if that increase reduces the profits of the industry as a whole. But if everyone thinks that way, the result is that everyone earns a lower profit!

Until now, we have been able to analyze producer behavior by asking what a producer should do to maximize profits. But even if ADM and Ajinomoto are both trying to maximize profits, what does this predict about their behavior? Will they engage in collusion, reaching and holding to an agreement that maximizes their combined profits? Or will they engage in **noncooperative behavior,** with each firm acting in its own self-interest, even though this has the effect of driving down everyone's profits? Both strategies sound like profit maximization. Which will actually describe their behavior?

Now you see why oligopoly presents a puzzle: there are only a small number of players, making collusion a real possibility. If there were dozens or hundreds of firms, it would be safe to assume they would behave noncooperatively. Yet when there are only a handful of firms in an industry, it's hard to determine whether collusion will actually materialize.

Since collusion is ultimately more profitable than noncooperative behavior, firms have an incentive to collude if they can. One way to do so is to formalize it—sign an agreement (maybe even make a legal contract) or establish some financial incentives for the companies to set their prices high. But in the United States and many other nations, you can't do that—at least not legally. Companies cannot make a legal contract to keep prices high: not only is the contract unenforceable, but writing it is a one-way ticket to jail. Neither can they sign an informal "gentlemen's agreement," which lacks the force of law but perhaps rests on threats of retaliation—that's illegal, too.

In fact, executives from rival companies rarely meet without lawyers present, who make sure that the conversation does not stray into inappropriate territory. Even hinting at how nice it would be if prices were higher can bring you an unwelcome interview with the Justice Department or the Federal Trade Commission. For example, in 2003 the Justice Department launched a price-fixing case against Monsanto and other large producers of genetically modified seed. The Justice Department was alerted by a series of meetings held between Monsanto and Pioneer Hi-Bred International, two companies that account for 60% of the U.S. market in maize and soybean seed. The two companies, parties to a licensing agreement involving genetically modified seed, claimed that no illegal discussions of price-fixing occurred in those meetings. But the fact that the two firms discussed prices as part of the licensing agreement was enough to ensure action by the Justice Department.

Sometimes, as we've seen, oligopolistic firms just ignore the rules. But more often they find ways to achieve collusion without a formal agreement, as we'll discuss later in the chapter.

ECONOMICS ➤ IN ACTION

BITTER CHOCOLATE?

Millions of chocolate lovers around the world have been spending more and more to satisfy their cravings, and regulators in Germany, Canada, and the United States have become suspicious. They are investigating whether the seven leading chocolate companies—including Mars, Kraft Foods, Nestle, Hershey, and Cadbury—have been colluding to raise prices. The amount of money involved could well run into the billions of dollars.

Many of the nation's largest grocery stores and snack retailers are convinced that they have been the victims of collusion. They claim that the chocolate industry has responded to stagnant consumer sales by price-fixing, an allegation the chocolate makers have vigorously denied.

In 2010, one of those stores, Supervalu, filed a lawsuit against Mars, Hershey, Nestle, and Cadbury, who together control about 76% of the U.S. chocolate market. Supervalu claimed that the confectioners had been fixing prices since 2002, regularly increasing prices by mid-single to double-digit amounts. Supervalu also claimed that grocers who resisted or refused to raise prices were systematically penalized with delayed or insufficient product deliveries. In 2012, the Associated Wholesale Grocers, a retailer-owned co-op, filed a similar suit, alleging these firms colluded on three occasions between 2002 and 2008 by artificially raising chocolate prices.

istockphoto/thinkstock

Are chocolate makers engaging in price-fixing?

What's clear is that chocolate candy prices have been soaring. Chocolate makers defend their actions, contending that they were simply passing on increases in their costs. The price of cocoa, the main ingredient in chocolate, more than doubled between 2005 and early 2011. While cocoa prices then fell in 2011 and stabilized in 2012, chocolate manufacturers continued to push through price increases. Furthermore, critics claim that the price of cocoa was stable from 2003 to 2007 and that sugar prices were similarly stable during that time, except for a brief spike in 2005, a time period in which chocolate prices were rising.

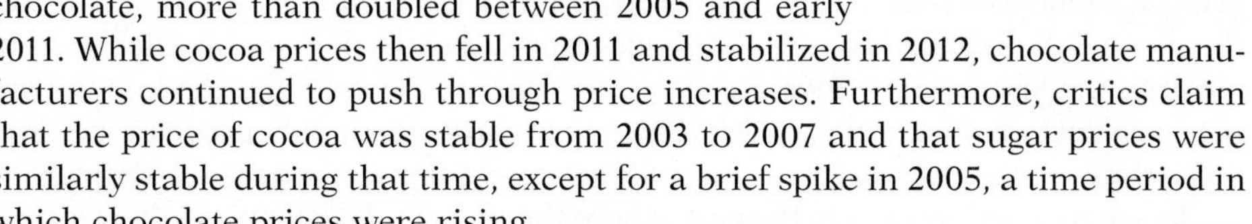

But, as antitrust experts point out, price collusion is often very difficult to prove because it is not illegal for businesses to increase their prices at the same time. To prove collusion, there must be some evidence of conversations or written agreements.

Such evidence has emerged in our chocolate case. According to the Canadian press, 13 Cadbury executives voluntarily provided information to the courts about contacts between the companies, including a 2005 episode in which a Nestle executive handed over a brown envelope containing details about a forthcoming price hike to a Cadbury employee. And, according to affidavits submitted to a Canadian court, top executives at Hershey, Mars, and Nestle met secretly in coffee shops, in restaurants, and at conventions to set prices.

Critics of the chocolate makers may soon get some sweet vindication.

Quick Review

- **Oligopoly** is a common market structure, one in which there are only a few firms, called **oligopolists,** in the industry.
- Oligopoly is a form of **imperfect competition** and arises from the same forces that lead to monopoly, except in weaker form.
- Some of the key issues in oligopoly can be understood by looking at the simplest case, a **duopoly**—an industry containing only two firms, called **duopolists.**
- By acting as if they were a single monopolist, oligopolists can maximize their combined profits. So there is an incentive to form a **cartel.**
- However, each firm has an incentive to cheat—to produce more than it is supposed to under the cartel agreement. So there are two principal outcomes: successful **collusion** or behaving **noncooperatively** by cheating.

CHECK YOUR UNDERSTANDING 8-2

1. Explain why each of the following industries is an oligopoly, not a perfectly competitive industry.
   a. The world oil industry, where a few countries near the Persian Gulf control much of the world's oil reserves
   b. The microprocessor industry, where two firms, Intel and its bitter rival AMD, dominate the technology
   c. The wide-body passenger jet industry, composed of the American firm Boeing and the European firm Airbus, where production is characterized by extremely large fixed cost
2. Which of the following factors increase the likelihood that an oligopolist will collude with other firms in the industry? The likelihood that an oligopolist will act noncooperatively and raise output? Explain your answers.
   a. The firm's initial market share is small. (*Hint:* Think about the price effect.)
   b. The firm has a cost advantage over its rivals.
   c. The firm's customers face additional costs when they switch from the use of one firm's product to another firm's product.
   d. The oligopolist has a lot of unused production capacity but knows that its rivals are operating at their maximum production capacity and cannot increase the amount they produce.

Solutions appear at back of book.

Monopoly, Oligopoly, and Public Policy

It's good to be a monopolist, but it's not so good to be a monopolist's customer. A monopolist, by reducing output and raising prices, benefits at the expense of consumers. But buyers and sellers always have conflicting interests. Is the conflict of interest under monopoly any different than it is under perfect competition?

The answer is yes, because monopoly is a source of inefficiency: the losses to consumers from monopoly behavior are larger than the gains to the monopolist. Because monopoly leads to net losses for the economy, governments often try either to prevent the emergence of monopolies or to limit their effects. In this section, we will see why monopoly leads to inefficiency and examine the policies governments adopt in an attempt to prevent this inefficiency.

Welfare Effects of Monopoly

By restricting output below the level at which marginal cost is equal to the market price, a monopolist increases its profit but hurts consumers. To assess whether this is a net benefit or loss to society, we must compare the monopolist's gain in profit to the loss in consumer surplus. And what we learn is that the loss in consumer surplus is larger than the monopolist's gain. Monopoly causes a net loss for society.

To see why, let's return to the case where the marginal cost curve is horizontal, as shown in the two panels of Figure 8-8. Here the marginal cost curve is *MC*, the demand curve is *D*, and, in panel (b), the marginal revenue curve is *MR*.

Panel (a) shows what happens if this industry is perfectly competitive. Equilibrium output is Q_C; the price of the good, P_C, is equal to marginal cost, and marginal cost is also equal to average total cost because there is no fixed cost and marginal cost is constant. Each firm is earning exactly its average

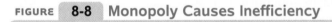

FIGURE 8-8 Monopoly Causes Inefficiency

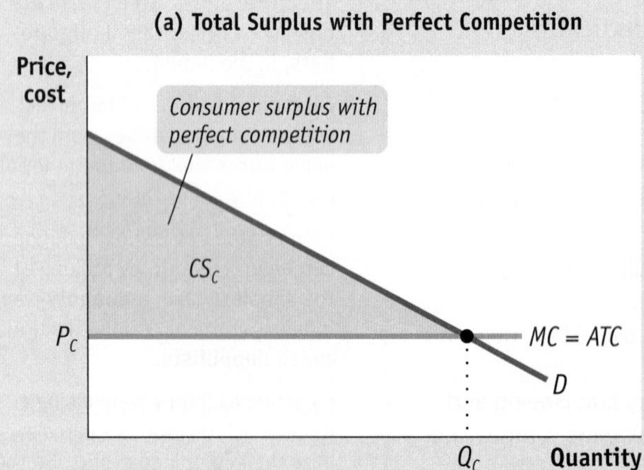

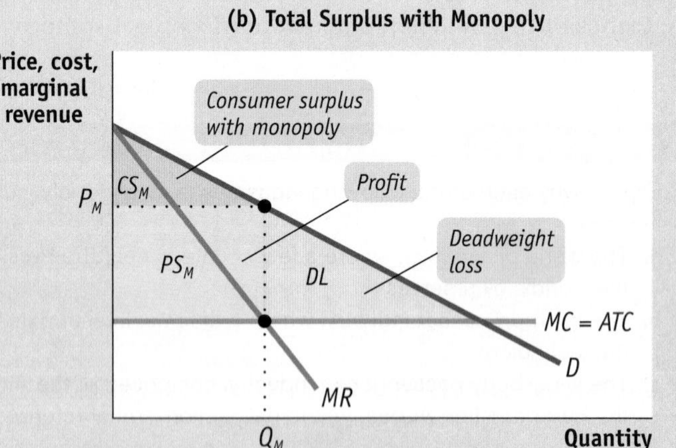

Panel (a) depicts a perfectly competitive industry: output is Q_C, and market price, P_C, is equal to *MC*. Since price is exactly equal to each producer's average total cost of production per unit, there is no profit and no producer surplus. So total surplus is equal to consumer surplus, the entire shaded area. Panel (b) depicts the industry under monopoly: the monopolist decreases output to Q_M and charges P_M. Consumer surplus (blue area) has shrunk: a portion of it has been captured as profit (green area), and a portion of it has been lost to deadweight loss (yellow area), the value of mutually beneficial transactions that do not occur because of monopoly behavior. As a result, total surplus falls.

total cost per unit of output, so there is no profit and no producer surplus in this equilibrium. The consumer surplus generated by the market is equal to the area of the blue-shaded triangle CS_C shown in panel (a). Since there is no producer surplus when the industry is perfectly competitive, CS_C also represents the total surplus.

Panel (b) shows the results for the same market, but this time assuming that the industry is a monopoly. The monopolist produces the level of output Q_M, at which marginal cost is equal to marginal revenue, and it charges the price P_M. The industry now earns profit—which is also the producer surplus—equal to the area of the green rectangle, PS_M. Note that this profit is surplus that has been captured from consumers as consumer surplus shrinks to the area of the blue triangle, CS_M.

By comparing panels (a) and (b), we see that in addition to the redistribution of surplus from consumers to the monopolist, another important change has occurred: the sum of profit and consumer surplus—total surplus—is *smaller* under monopoly than under perfect competition. That is, the sum of CS_M and PS_M in panel (b) is less than the area CS_C in panel (a). In Chapter 5, we analyzed how taxes generated *deadweight loss* to society. Here we show that monopoly creates a deadweight loss to society equal to the area of the yellow triangle, *DL*. So monopoly produces a net loss for society.

This net loss arises because some mutually beneficial transactions do not occur. There are people for whom an additional unit of the good is worth more than the marginal cost of producing it but who don't consume it because they are not willing to pay P_M.

If you recall our discussion of the deadweight loss from taxes in Chapter 5 you will notice that the deadweight loss from monopoly looks quite similar. Indeed, by driving a wedge between price and marginal cost, monopoly acts much like a tax on consumers and produces the same kind of inefficiency.

So monopoly hurts the welfare of society as a whole and is a source of market failure. Is there anything government policy can do about it?

Preventing Monopoly

Policy toward monopoly depends crucially on whether or not the industry in question is a natural monopoly, one in which increasing returns to scale ensure that a bigger producer has lower average total cost. If the industry is not a natural monopoly, the best policy is to prevent monopoly from arising or break it up if it already exists. Let's focus on that case first, then turn to the more difficult problem of dealing with natural monopoly.

The De Beers monopoly on diamonds didn't have to happen. Diamond production is not a natural monopoly: the industry's costs would be no higher if it consisted of a number of independent, competing producers (as is the case, for example, in gold production).

So if the South African government had been worried about how a monopoly would have affected consumers, it could have blocked Cecil Rhodes in his drive to dominate the industry or broken up his monopoly after the fact. Today, governments often try to prevent monopolies from forming and break up existing ones.

De Beers is a rather unique case: for complicated historical reasons, it was allowed to remain a monopoly. But over the last century, most similar monopolies have been broken up. The most celebrated example in the United States is Standard Oil, founded by John D. Rockefeller in 1870. By 1878 Standard Oil controlled almost all U.S. oil refining; but in 1911 a court order broke the company into a number of smaller units, including the companies that later became Exxon and Mobil (and more recently merged to become ExxonMobil).

In **public ownership** of a monopoly, the good is supplied by the government or by a firm owned by the government.

Price regulation limits the price that a monopolist is allowed to charge.

The government policies used to prevent or eliminate monopolies are known as *antitrust policy,* which we will discuss shortly.

Natural Monopoly

Breaking up a monopoly that isn't natural is clearly a good idea: the gains to consumers outweigh the loss to the producer. But it's not so clear whether a natural monopoly, one in which a large producer has lower average total costs than small producers, should be broken up, because this would raise average total cost. For example, a town government that tried to prevent a single company from dominating local gas supply—which, as we've discussed, is almost surely a natural monopoly—would raise the cost of providing gas to its residents.

Yet even in the case of a natural monopoly, a profit-maximizing monopolist acts in a way that causes inefficiency—it charges consumers a price that is higher than marginal cost and, by doing so, prevents some potentially beneficial transactions. Also, it can seem unfair that a firm that has managed to establish a monopoly position earns a large profit at the expense of consumers.

What can public policy do about this? There are two common answers.

Public Ownership In many countries, the preferred answer to the problem of natural monopoly has been **public ownership.** Instead of allowing a private monopolist to control an industry, the government establishes a public agency to provide the good and protect consumers' interests. In Britain, for example, telephone service was provided by the state-owned British Telecom before 1984, and airline travel was provided by the state-owned British Airways before 1987. (These companies still exist, but they have been privatized, competing with other firms in their respective industries.)

There are some examples of public ownership in the United States. Passenger rail service is provided by the public company Amtrak; regular mail delivery is provided by the U.S. Postal Service; some cities, including Los Angeles, have publicly owned electric power companies.

Regulation In the United States, the more common answer has been to leave the industry in private hands but subject it to regulation. In particular, most local utilities like electricity, land line telephone service, natural gas, and so on are covered by **price regulation** that limits the prices they can charge.

We saw in Chapter 4 that imposing a *price ceiling* on a competitive industry is a recipe for shortages, black markets, and other nasty side effects. Doesn't imposing a limit on the price that, say, a local gas company can charge have the same effects?

Not necessarily: a price ceiling on a monopolist need not create a shortage—in the absence of a price ceiling, a monopolist would charge a price that is higher than its marginal cost of production. So even if forced to charge a lower price—as long as that price is above *MC* and the monopolist at least breaks even on total output—the monopolist still has an incentive to produce the quantity demanded at that price.

Oligopoly: The Legal Framework

To understand oligopoly pricing in practice, we must be familiar with the legal constraints under which oligopolistic firms operate. In the United States, oligopoly first became an issue during the second half of the nineteenth century, when the growth of railroads—themselves an oligopolistic industry—created a national market for many goods. Large firms producing oil, steel, and many other products soon emerged. The industrialists quickly realized that profits would be higher if they could limit price competition. So many industries formed cartels—that is, they signed formal agreements to limit production and raise prices. Until

1890, when the first federal legislation against such cartels was passed, this was perfectly legal.

Antitrust policy consists of efforts undertaken by the government to prevent oligopolistic industries from becoming or behaving like monopolies.

However, although these cartels were legal, they weren't legally *enforceable*—members of a cartel couldn't ask the courts to force a firm that was violating its agreement to reduce its production. And firms often did violate their agreements, for the reason already suggested by our duopoly example: there is always a temptation for each firm in a cartel to produce more than it is supposed to.

In 1881 clever lawyers at John D. Rockefeller's Standard Oil Company came up with a solution—the so-called trust. In a trust, shareholders of all the major companies in an industry placed their shares in the hands of a board of trustees who controlled the companies. This, in effect, merged the companies into a single firm that could then engage in monopoly pricing. In this way, the Standard Oil Trust established what was essentially a monopoly of the oil industry, and it was soon followed by trusts in sugar, whiskey, lead, cottonseed oil, and linseed oil.

Eventually there was a public backlash, driven partly by concern about the economic effects of the trust movement, partly by fear that the owners of the trusts were simply becoming too powerful. The result was the Sherman Antitrust Act of 1890, which was intended both to prevent the creation of more monopolies and to break up existing ones. At first this law went largely unenforced. But over the decades that followed, the federal government became increasingly committed to making it difficult for oligopolistic industries either to become monopolies or to behave like them. Such efforts are known to this day as **antitrust policy.**

One of the most striking early actions of antitrust policy was the breakup of Standard Oil in 1911. (Its components formed the nuclei of many of today's large oil companies—Standard Oil of New Jersey became Exxon, Standard Oil of New York became Mobil, and so on.) In the 1980s a long-running case led to the breakup of Bell Telephone, which once had a monopoly of both local and long-distance phone service in the United States. As we mentioned earlier, the Justice Department reviews proposed mergers between companies in the same industry and will bar mergers that it believes will reduce competition.

Sidney Harris/Cartoonstock.com

"Frankly, I'm dubious about amalgamated smelting and refining pleading innocent to their anti-trust violation due to insanity."

Among advanced countries, the United States is unique in its long tradition of antitrust policy. Until recently, other advanced countries did not have policies against price-fixing, and some had even supported the creation of cartels, believing that it would help their own firms against foreign rivals. But the situation has changed radically over the past 25 years, as the European Union (EU)—a supranational body tasked with enforcing antitrust policy for its member countries—has converged toward U.S. practices. Today, EU and U.S. regulators often target the same firms because price-fixing has "gone global" as international trade has expanded.

During the early 1990s, the United States instituted an amnesty program in which a price-fixer receives a much-reduced penalty if it informs on its co-conspirators. In addition, Congress substantially increased maximum fines levied upon conviction. These two new policies clearly made informing on your cartel partners a dominant strategy, and it has paid off: in recent years, executives from Belgium, Britain, Canada, France, Germany, Italy, Mexico, the Netherlands, South Korea, and Switzerland, as well as from the United States, have been convicted in U.S. courts of cartel crimes. As one lawyer commented, "you get a race to the courthouse" as each conspirator seeks to be the first to come clean.

Life has gotten much tougher over the past few years if you want to operate a cartel. So what's an oligopolist to do?

When firms limit production and raise prices in a way that raises one anothers' profits, even though they have not made any formal agreement, they are engaged in **tacit collusion**.

Tacit Collusion and Price Wars

If a real industry were as simple as our lysine example, it probably wouldn't be necessary for the company presidents to meet or do anything that could land them in jail. Both firms would realize that it was in their mutual interest to restrict output to 30 million pounds each and that any short-term gains to either firm from producing more would be much less than the later losses as the other firm retaliated. Despite the fact that firms have no way of making an enforceable agreement to limit output and raise prices (and are in legal jeopardy if they even discuss prices), they manage to act "as if" they had such an agreement. When this happens, we say that firms engage in **tacit collusion.** So even without any explicit agreement, the firms would probably achieve the tacit collusion needed to maximize their combined profits.

Real industries are nowhere near that simple. Nonetheless, in most oligopolistic industries, most of the time, the sellers do appear to succeed in keeping prices above their noncooperative level. Tacit collusion, in other words, is the normal state of oligopoly.

Although tacit collusion is common, it rarely allows an industry to push prices all the way up to their monopoly level; collusion is usually far from perfect. As we discuss next, a variety of factors make it hard for an industry to coordinate on high prices.

Less Concentration In a less concentrated industry, the typical firm will have a smaller market share than in a more concentrated industry. This tilts firms toward noncooperative behavior because when a smaller firm cheats and increases its output, it gains for itself all of the profit from the higher output. And if its rivals should retaliate by increasing their output, the firm's losses are limited because of its relatively modest market share. A less concentrated industry is often an indication that there are low barriers to entry.

Complex Products and Pricing Schemes In our lysine example the two firms produce only one product. In reality, however, oligopolists often sell thousands or even tens of thousands of different products. Under these circumstances, keeping track of what other firms are producing and what prices they are charging is difficult. This makes it hard to determine whether a firm is cheating on the tacit agreement.

Differences in Interests In the lysine example, a tacit agreement for the firms to split the market equally is a natural outcome, probably acceptable to both firms. In real industries, however, firms often differ both in their perceptions about what is fair and in their real interests.

For example, suppose that Ajinomoto was a long-established lysine producer and ADM a more recent entrant to the industry. Ajinomoto might feel that it deserved to continue producing more than ADM, but ADM might feel that it was entitled to 50% of the business. (A disagreement along these lines was one of the contentious issues in those meetings the FBI was filming.)

Alternatively, suppose that ADM's marginal costs were lower than Ajinomoto's. Even if they could agree on market shares, they would then disagree about the profit-maximizing level of output.

Bargaining Power of Buyers Often oligopolists sell not to individual consumers but to large buyers—other industrial enterprises, nationwide chains of stores, and so on. These large buyers are in a position to bargain for lower prices from the oligopolists: they can ask for a discount from an oligopolist and warn that they will go to a competitor if they don't get it. An important reason large retailers like Walmart are able to offer lower prices to customers than small retailers is precisely their ability to use their size to extract lower prices from their suppliers.

A **price war** occurs when tacit collusion breaks down and prices collapse.

These difficulties in enforcing tacit collusion have sometimes led companies to defy the law and create illegal cartels. We've already examined the cases of the lysine industry and the chocolate industry. An older, classic example was the U.S. electrical equipment conspiracy of the 1950s, which led to the indictment of and jail sentences for some executives. The industry was one in which tacit collusion was especially difficult because of all the reasons just mentioned. There were many firms—40 companies were indicted. They produced a very complex array of products, often more or less custom-built for particular clients. They differed greatly in size, from giants like General Electric to family firms with only a few dozen employees. And the customers in many cases were large buyers like electrical utilities, which would normally try to force suppliers to compete for their business. Tacit collusion just didn't seem practical—so executives met secretly and illegally to decide who would bid what price for which contract.

Because tacit collusion is often hard to achieve, most oligopolies charge prices that are well below what the same industry would charge if it were controlled by a monopolist—or what they would charge if they were able to collude explicitly. In addition, sometimes collusion breaks down and there is a **price war.** A price war sometimes involves simply a collapse of prices to their noncooperative level. Sometimes they even go *below* that level, as sellers try to put each other out of business or at least punish what they regard as cheating.

ECONOMICS ➤ IN ACTION

THE PRICE WARS OF CHRISTMAS

During the last several holiday seasons, the toy aisles of American retailers have been the scene of cutthroat competition: During the 2012 Christmas shopping season, Amazon cut prices on toys earlier than usual. In response, Target, Toys "R" Us, and Best Buy offered price-match guarantees on identical products that were advertised at online stores, including Amazon. So extreme is the price-cutting that since 2003 three toy retailers—KB Toys, FAO Schwartz, and Zany Brainy—have been forced into bankruptcy.

Bloomberg via Getty Images

The price wars of Christmas, which traditionally began after Thanksgiving, now arrive earlier each year.

What is happening? The turmoil can be traced back to trouble in the toy industry itself as well as to changes in toy retailing. Every year for several years, overall toy sales have fallen a few percentage points as children increasingly turn to video games and the Internet. There have also been new entrants into the toy business: Walmart and Target have expanded their number of stores and have been aggressive price-cutters. The result is much like a story of tacit collusion sustained by repeated interaction run in reverse: because the overall industry is in a state of decline and there are new entrants, the future payoff from collusion is shrinking. The predictable outcome is a price war.

Since retailers depend on holiday sales for nearly half of their annual sales, the holidays are a time of particularly intense price-cutting. Traditionally, the biggest shopping day of the year has been "Black Friday," the day after Thanksgiving. But in an effort to expand sales and undercut rivals, retailers—particularly Walmart—have now begun their price-cutting earlier in the fall. Now it begins in early November, well before Thanksgiving. In 2012, Amazon offered new deals every hour leading up to Black Friday, starting the Monday *before* Thanksgiving.

With other retailers feeling as if they have no choice but to follow this pattern, we have the phenomenon known as "creeping Christmas": the price wars of Christmas arrive earlier each year.

Quick Review

- By reducing output and raising price above marginal cost, a monopolist captures some of the consumer surplus as profit and causes deadweight loss. To avoid deadweight loss, government policy attempts to curtail monopoly behavior.
- Natural monopoly poses a harder policy problem. Two solutions are **public ownership** and **price regulation.**
- Oligopolies operate under legal restrictions in the form of **antitrust policy.** But many succeed in achieving tacit collusion.
- **Tacit collusion** is limited by a number of factors, including large numbers of firms, complex products and pricing, differences in interests among firms, and bargaining power of buyers. When collusion breaks down, there is a **price war.**

CHECK YOUR UNDERSTANDING 8-3

1. What policy should the government adopt in the following cases? Explain.
   a. Internet service in Anytown, Ohio, is provided by cable. Customers feel they are being overcharged, but the cable company claims it must charge prices that let it recover the costs of laying cable.
   b. The only two airlines that currently fly to Alaska need government approval to merge. Other airlines wish to fly to Alaska but need government-allocated landing slots to do so.
2. True or false? Explain your answer.
   a. Society's welfare is lower under monopoly because some consumer surplus is transformed into profit for the monopolist.
   b. A monopolist causes inefficiency because there are consumers who are willing to pay a price greater than or equal to marginal cost but less than the monopoly price.

Solutions appear at back of book.

The Meaning of Monopolistic Competition

Leo manages the Wonderful Wok stand in the food court of a big shopping mall. He offers the only Chinese food there, but there are more than a dozen alternatives, from Bodacious Burgers to Pizza Paradise. When deciding what to charge for a meal, Leo knows that he must take those alternatives into account: even people who normally prefer stir-fry won't order a $15 lunch from Leo when they can get a burger, fries, and drink for $4.

But Leo also knows that he won't lose all his business even if his lunches cost a bit more than the alternatives. Chinese food isn't the same thing as burgers or pizza. Some people will really be in the mood for Chinese that day, and they will buy from Leo even if they could dine more cheaply on burgers. Of course, the reverse is also true: even if Chinese is a bit cheaper, some people will choose burgers instead. In other words, Leo does have some market power: he has *some* ability to set his own price.

So how would you describe Leo's situation? He definitely isn't a price-taker, so he isn't in a situation of perfect competition. But you wouldn't exactly call him a monopolist, either. Although he's the only seller of Chinese food in that food court, he does face competition from other food vendors.

Yet it would also be wrong to call him an oligopolist. Oligopoly, remember, involves competition among a small number of interdependent firms in an industry protected by some—albeit limited—barriers to entry and whose profits are highly interdependent. Because their profits are highly interdependent, oligopolists have an incentive to collude, tacitly or explicitly. But in Leo's case there are *lots* of vendors in the shopping mall, too many to make tacit collusion feasible.

Monopolistic competition is a market structure in which there are many competing producers in an industry, each producer sells a differentiated product, and there is free entry into and exit from the industry in the long run.

Economists describe Leo's situation as one of **monopolistic competition.** Monopolistic competition is particularly common in service industries like restaurants and gas stations, but it also exists in some manufacturing industries. It involves three conditions: large numbers of competing producers, differentiated products, and free entry into and exit from the industry in the long run. In a monopolistically competitive industry, each producer has some ability to set the price of her differentiated product. But exactly how high she can set it is limited by the competition she faces from other existing and potential producers that produce close, but not identical, products.

Product differentiation is an attempt by a firm to convince buyers that its product is different from the products of other firms in the industry.

Large Numbers

In a monopolistically competitive industry, there are many producers. Such an industry does not look either like a monopoly, where the firm faces no competition, or an oligopoly, where each firm has only a few rivals. Instead, each seller has many competitors. For example, there are many vendors in a big food court, many gas stations along a major highway, and many hotels at a popular beach resort.

Free Entry and Exit in the Long Run

In monopolistically competitive industries, new producers, with their own distinct products, can enter the industry freely in the long run. For example, other food vendors would open outlets in the food court if they thought it would be profitable to do so. In addition, firms will exit the industry if they find they are not covering their costs in the long run.

Differentiated Products

In a monopolistically competitive industry, each producer has a product that consumers view as somewhat distinct from the products of competing firms; at the same time, though, consumers see these competing products as close substitutes. If Leo's food court contained 15 vendors selling exactly the same kind and quality of food, there would be perfect competition: any seller who tried to charge a higher price would have no customers. But suppose that Wonderful Wok is the only Chinese food vendor, Bodacious Burgers is the only hamburger stand, and so on. The result of this differentiation is that each seller has some ability to set his own price: each producer has some—albeit limited—market power.

Product differentiation—an attempt by a firm to create the perception that its product is different—is the only way that monopolistically competitive firms can acquire some market power. How do firms in the same industry—such as fast-food vendors, gas stations, or chocolate makers—differentiate their products? Sometimes the difference is mainly in the minds of consumers rather than in the products themselves. In general, however, firms differentiate their products by—surprise!—actually making them different.

The key to product differentiation is that consumers have different preferences and are willing to pay somewhat more to satisfy those preferences. Each producer can carve out a market niche by producing something that caters to the particular preferences of some group of consumers better than the products of other firms. There are three important forms of product differentiation: differentiation by style or type, differentiation by location, and differentiation by quality.

Differentiation by Style or Type The sellers in Leo's food court offer different types of fast food: hamburgers, pizza, Chinese food, Mexican food, and so on. Each consumer arrives at the food court with some preference for one or another of these offerings. This preference may depend on the consumer's mood, her diet, or what she has already eaten that day. These preferences will not make consumers indifferent to price: if Wonderful Wok were to charge $15 for an egg roll, everybody would go to Bodacious Burgers or Pizza Paradise instead. But some people will choose a more expensive meal if that type of food is closer to their preference. So the products of the different vendors are substitutes, but they aren't *perfect* substitutes—they are *imperfect substitutes.*

Vendors in a food court aren't the only sellers that differentiate their offerings by type. Clothing stores concentrate on women's or men's clothes, on business attire or sportswear, on trendy or classic styles, and so on. Auto manufacturers offer sedans, minivans, sport-utility vehicles, and sports cars, each type aimed at drivers with different needs and tastes.

Books offer yet another example of differentiation by type and style. Mysteries are differentiated from romances; among mysteries, we can differentiate among hard-boiled detective stories, whodunits, and police procedurals. And no two writers of hard-boiled detective stories are exactly alike: Raymond Chandler and Sue Grafton each have their devoted fans.

In fact, product differentiation is characteristic of most consumer goods. As long as people differ in their tastes, producers find it possible and profitable to produce a range of varieties.

Differentiation by Location Gas stations along a road offer differentiated products. True, the gas may be exactly the same. But the location of the stations is different, and location matters to consumers: it's more convenient to stop for gas near your home, near your workplace, or near wherever you are when the gas gauge gets low.

In fact, many monopolistically competitive industries supply goods differentiated by location. This is especially true in service industries, from dry cleaners to hairdressers, where customers often choose the seller who is closest rather than cheapest.

Differentiation by Quality Do you have a craving for chocolate? How much are you willing to spend on it? You see, there's chocolate and then there's chocolate: although ordinary chocolate may not be very expensive, gourmet chocolate can cost several dollars per bite.

With chocolate, as with many goods, there is a range of possible qualities. You can get a usable bicycle for less than \$100; you can get a much fancier bicycle for 10 times as much. It all depends on how much the additional quality matters to you and how much you will miss the other things you could have purchased with that money.

Because consumers vary in what they are willing to pay for higher quality, producers can differentiate their products by quality—some offering lower-quality, inexpensive products and others offering higher-quality products at a higher price.

Product differentiation, then, can take several forms. Whatever form it takes, however, there are two important features of industries with differentiated products: *competition among sellers* and *value in diversity*.

Competition among sellers means that even though sellers of differentiated products are not offering identical goods, they are to some extent competing for a limited market. If more businesses enter the market, each will find that it sells less quantity at any given price. For example, if a new gas station opens along a road, each of the existing gas stations will sell a bit less.

Value in diversity refers to the gain to consumers from the proliferation of differentiated products. A food court with eight vendors makes consumers happier than one with only six vendors, even if the prices are the same, because some customers will get a meal that is closer to what they had in mind. A road on which there is a gas station every two miles is more convenient for motorists than a road where gas stations are five miles apart. When a product is available in many different qualities, fewer people are forced to pay for more quality than they need or to settle for lower quality than they want. There are, in other words, benefits to consumers from a greater diversity of available products.

Monopolistic competition differs from the three market structures we have examined so far. It's not the same as perfect competition: firms have some power to set prices. It's not pure monopoly: firms face some competition. And it's not the same as oligopoly: because there are many firms and free entry, the potential for collusion so important in oligopoly no longer exists.

ECONOMICS ➤ IN ACTION

ANY COLOR, SO LONG AS IT'S BLACK

The early history of the auto industry offers a classic illustration of the power of product differentiation.

The modern automobile industry was created by Henry Ford, who first introduced assembly-line production. This technique made it possible for him to offer the famous Model T at a far lower price than anyone else was charging for a car; by 1920, Ford dominated the automobile business.

Ford's strategy was to offer just one style of car, which maximized his economies of scale in production but made no concessions to differences in consumers' tastes. He supposedly declared that customers could get the Model T in "any color, so long as it's black."

Ford's Model T in basic black.

Science and Society/Superstock

This strategy was challenged by Alfred P. Sloan, who had merged a number of smaller automobile companies into General Motors. Sloan's strategy was to offer a range of car types, differentiated by quality and price. Chevrolets were basic cars that directly challenged the Model T, Buicks were bigger and more expensive, and so on up to Cadillacs. And you could get each model in several different colors.

By the 1930s the verdict was clear: customers preferred a range of styles, and General Motors, not Ford, became the dominant auto manufacturer for the rest of the twentieth century.

Quick Review

- In **monopolistic competition** there are many competing producers, each with a differentiated product, and free entry and exit in the long run.
- **Product differentiation** takes three main forms: by style or type, by location, or by quality. The products of competing sellers are considered imperfect substitutes.
- Producers compete for the same market, so entry by more producers reduces the quantity each existing producer sells at any given price. In addition, consumers gain from the increased diversity of products.

CHECK YOUR UNDERSTANDING 8-4

1. Each of the following goods and services is a differentiated product. Which are differentiated as a result of monopolistic competition and which are not? Explain your answers.
   a. Ladders
   b. Soft drinks
   c. Department stores
   d. Steel
2. You must determine which of two types of market structure better describes an industry, but you are allowed to ask only one question about the industry. What question should you ask to determine if an industry is:
   a. Perfectly competitive or monopolistically competitive?
   b. A monopoly or monopolistically competitive?

Solutions appear at back of book.

WORKED PROBLEM

The Ups (and Downs) of Oil Prices

Call it a cartel that does not need to meet in secret. The Organization of Petroleum Exporting Countries, usually referred to as OPEC, includes 12 national governments (Algeria, Angola, Ecuador, Iran, Iraq, Kuwait, Libya, Nigeria, Qatar, Saudi Arabia, the United Arab Emirates, and Venezuela), and it controls 40% of the world's oil exports and 80% of its proven resources. Two other oil-exporting countries, Norway and Mexico, are not formally part of the cartel but act as if they were. (Russia, also an important oil exporter, has not yet become part of the club.) Unlike corporations, which are often legally prohibited by governments from reaching agreements about production and prices, national governments can talk about whatever they like. OPEC members routinely meet to set targets for production.

The following table gives a hypothetical demand schedule for the OPEC cartel.

Price of oil (dollars per barrel)	Quantity of oil demand (millions of barrels per day)
$120	40
100	56
80	72
60	88
40	104
20	120

Suppose that, with current technology, the marginal cost of extracting a barrel of oil from the ground is $30. If the cartel colludes and acts as a monopolist, how many barrels of oil should it sell in total, and at what price? If the members of the cartel split production equally, how much oil would each of the 12 members produce, and what is each producer's profit [assuming no fixed costs]?

STEP 1: In order to find the cartel's optimal quantity and price, we first need to find the marginal revenue schedule for the cartel.

Study the section, "The Monopolist's Demand Curve and Marginal Revenue," beginning on p. 245. (Pay close attention to Table 8-1 on page 247).

The total revenue is found by multiplying price and quantity (TR = P × Q). The marginal revenue is the change in total revenue divided by the change in quantity (MR = ΔTR/ΔQ). Thus, in the table below, the total revenue ($4,800) on the first line is found by multiplying $120 by 40. The first entry for marginal revenue in the last column is ($5,600 – $4,800)/(56 – 40) = $50. ■

Price of oil (dollars per barrel)	Quantity of oil demanded (millions of barrels per day)	Total revenue (millions of dollars) TR = P × Q	Marginal revenue per barrel (dollars) MR = ΔTR/ΔQ
$120	40	$4,800	
			$50.00
100	56	5,600	
			10.00
80	72	5,760	
			−30.00
60	88	5,280	
			−70.00
40	104	4,160	
			−110.00
20	120	2,400	

STEP 2: How many barrels of oil should the cartel sell in total and at what price?

Study the section, "The Monopolist's Profit-Maximizing Output and Price," beginning on p. 249.

We need to find the quantity and price where marginal revenue (MR) = marginal cost (MC). As we can see from the table above, OPEC's profit will be maximized when the cartel sells 56 million barrels of oil per day, since for the first 56 barrels, its marginal revenue exceeds its marginal cost of $30 per barrel, and after that, its marginal revenue is less than its marginal cost. OPEC will charge $100 per barrel. ■

STEP 3: If the members of the cartel split production equally, how much oil would each of the 12 members produce, and what is each producer's profit?

This situation is similar to the example discussed in the section "A Duopoly Example," on page 254, except that in this case there are 12 producers, each of which produces 1/12 of the cartel's output.

Each producer produces 1/12 of the cartel's output. So, each member produces 4.67 million barrels for a profit of 4.67 million × ($100 – $30) = $326.67 million, assuming no fixed costs. ■

SUMMARY

1. There are four main types of market structure based on the number of firms in the industry and product differentiation: perfect competition, monopoly, oligopoly, and monopolistic competition.
2. A **monopolist** is a producer who is the sole supplier of a good without close substitutes. An industry controlled by a monopolist is a **monopoly.**
3. The key difference between a monopoly and a perfectly competitive industry is that a single perfectly competitive firm faces a horizontal demand curve but a monopolist faces a downward-sloping demand curve. This gives the monopolist **market power,** the ability to raise the market price by reducing output compared to a perfectly competitive firm.
4. To persist, a monopoly must be protected by a **barrier to entry.** This can take the form of control of a natural resource or input, increasing returns to scale that give rise to **natural monopoly,** technological superiority, a network externality, or government rules that prevent entry by other firms, such as **patents** or **copyrights.**
5. At the monopolist's profit-maximizing output level, marginal cost equals marginal revenue, which is less than market price. At the perfectly competitive firm's profit-maximizing output level, marginal cost equals the market price. So in comparison to perfectly competitive industries, monopolies produce less, charge higher prices, and earn profits in both the short run and the long run. A monopoly creates deadweight losses by charging a price above marginal cost: the loss in consumer surplus exceeds the monopolist's profit.
6. Natural monopolies can still cause deadweight losses. To limit these losses, governments sometimes impose **public ownership** and at other times impose **price regulation.**
7. Many industries are **oligopolies:** there are only a few sellers. In particular, a **duopoly** has only two sellers. Oligopolies exist for more or less the same reasons that monopolies exist, but in weaker form. They are characterized by **imperfect competition:** firms compete but possess market power.
8. Predicting the behavior of **oligopolists** poses something of a puzzle. The firms in an oligopoly could maximize their combined profits by acting as a **cartel,** setting output levels for each firm as if they were a single monopolist; to the extent that firms manage to do this, they engage in **collusion.**
9. In order to limit the ability of oligopolists to collude and act like monopolists, most governments pursue an **antitrust policy** designed to make collusion more difficult. In practice, however, tacit collusion is widespread. A variety of factors make tacit collusion difficult: large numbers of firms, complex products and pricing, differences in interests, and bargaining power of buyers. When tacit collusion breaks down, there is a **price war.**
10. **Monopolistic competition** is a market structure in which there are many competing producers, each producing a differentiated product, and there is free entry and exit in the long run. **Product differentiation** takes three main forms: by style or type, by location, or by quality. Products of competing sellers are considered imperfect substitutes, and each firm has its own downward-sloping demand curve and marginal revenue curve.

KEY TERMS

Monopolist, p. 241
Monopoly, p. 241
Market power, p. 242
Barrier to entry, p. 243
Natural monopoly, p. 243
Patent, p. 245
Copyright, p. 245
Oligopoly, p. 253
Oligopolist, p. 253

Imperfect competition, p. 253
Duopoly, p. 254
Duopolist, p. 254
Collusion, p. 254
Cartel, p. 254
Noncooperative behavior, p. 256
Public ownership, p. 260
Price regulation, p. 260
Antitrust policy, p. 261
Tacit collusion, p. 262
Price war, p. 263
Monopolistic competition, p. 264
Product differentiation, p. 265

PROBLEMS

1. Each of the following firms possesses market power. Explain its source.

a. Merck, the producer of the patented cholesterol-lowering drug Zetia

b. WaterWorks, a provider of piped water

c. Chiquita, a supplier of bananas and owner of most banana plantations

d. The Walt Disney Company, the creators of Mickey Mouse

2. Skyscraper City has a subway system, for which a one-way fare is \$1.50. There is pressure on the mayor to reduce the fare by one-third, to \$1.00. The mayor is dismayed, thinking that this will mean Skyscraper City is losing one-third of its revenue from sales of subway tickets. The mayor's economic adviser reminds her that she is focusing only on the price effect and ignoring the quantity effect. Explain why the mayor's estimate of a one-third loss of revenue is likely to be an overestimate. Illustrate with a diagram.

3. Consider an industry with the demand curve (*D*) and marginal cost curve (*MC*) shown in the accompanying diagram. There is no fixed cost. If the industry is a monopoly, the monopolist's marginal revenue curve would be *MR*. Answer the following questions by naming the appropriate points or areas.

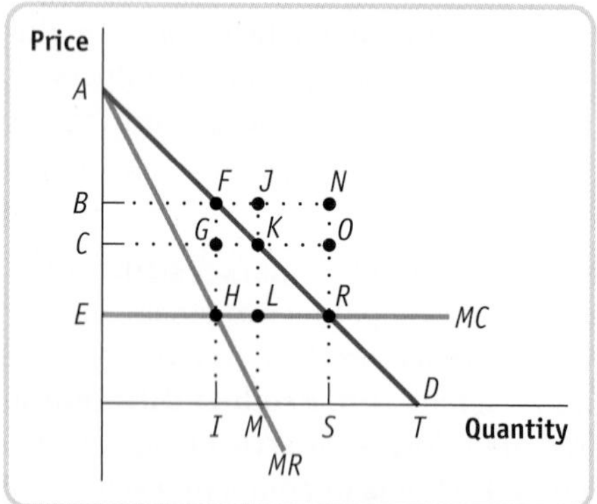

a. If the industry is perfectly competitive, what will be the total quantity produced? At what price?

b. Which area reflects consumer surplus under perfect competition?

c. If the industry is a monopoly, what quantity will the monopolist produce? Which price will it charge?

d. Which area reflects the monopolist's profit?

e. Which area reflects consumer surplus under monopoly?

f. Which area reflects the deadweight loss to society from monopoly?

4. Bob, Bill, Ben, and Brad Baxter have just made a documentary movie about their basketball team. They are thinking about making the movie available for download on the Internet, and they can act as a monopolist if they choose to. Each time the movie is downloaded, their Internet service provider charges them a fee of \$4. The Baxter brothers are arguing about which price to charge customers per download. The accompanying table shows the demand schedule for their film.

Price of download	Quantity of downloads demanded
\$10	0
8	1
6	3
4	6
2	10
0	15

a. Calculate the total revenue and the marginal revenue per download.

b. Bob is proud of the film and wants as many people as possible to download it. Which price would he choose? How many downloads would be sold?

c. Bill wants as much total revenue as possible. Which price would he choose? How many downloads would be sold?

d. Ben wants to maximize profit. Which price would he choose? How many downloads would be sold?

e. Brad wants to charge the efficient price. Which price would he choose? How many downloads would be sold?

5. Jimmy has a room that overlooks, from some distance, a major league baseball stadium. He decides to rent a telescope for \$50.00 a week and charge his friends and classmates to use it to peep at the game for 30 seconds. He can act as a monopolist for renting out "peeps." For each person who takes a 30-second peep, it costs Jimmy \$0.20 to clean the eyepiece. The accompanying table shows the information Jimmy has gathered about the demand for the service in a given week.

Price of peep	Quantity of peeps demanded
$1.20	0
1.00	100
0.90	150
0.80	200
0.70	250
0.60	300
0.50	350
0.40	400
0.30	450
0.20	500
0.10	550

a. For each price in the table, calculate the total revenue from selling peeps and the marginal revenue per peep.

b. At what quantity will Jimmy's profit be maximized? What price will he charge? What will his total profit be?

c. Jimmy's landlady complains about all the visitors coming into the building and tells Jimmy to stop selling peeps. Jimmy discovers, however, that if he gives the landlady $0.20 for every peep he sells, she will stop complaining. What effect does the $0.20-per-peep bribe have on Jimmy's marginal cost per peep? What is the new profit-maximizing quantity of peeps? What effect does the $0.20-per-peep bribe have on Jimmy's total profit?

6. Suppose that De Beers is a monopolist in the market for diamonds. De Beers has five potential customers: Raquel, Jackie, Joan, Mia, and Sophia. Each of these customers will buy at most one diamond—and only if the price is just equal to, or lower than, her willingness to pay. Raquel's willingness to pay is $400; Jackie's, $300; Joan's, $200; Mia's, $100; and Sophia's, $0. De Beers's marginal cost per diamond is $100. This leads to the demand schedule for diamonds shown in the accompanying table.

Price of diamond	Quantity of diamonds demanded
$500	0
400	1
300	2
200	3
100	4
0	5

a. Calculate De Beers's total revenue and its marginal revenue. From your calculation, draw the demand curve and the marginal revenue curve.

b. Explain why De Beers faces a downward-sloping demand curve.

c. Explain why the marginal revenue from an additional diamond sale is less than the price of the diamond.

d. Suppose De Beers currently charges $200 for its diamonds. If it lowers the price to $100, how large is the price effect? How large is the quantity effect?

e. Add the marginal cost curve to your diagram from part a and determine which quantity maximizes De Beers's profit and which price De Beers will charge.

7. Use the demand schedule for diamonds given in Problem 6. The marginal cost of producing diamonds is constant at $100. There is no fixed cost.

a. If De Beers charges the monopoly price, how large is the individual consumer surplus that each buyer experiences? Calculate total consumer surplus by summing the individual consumer surpluses. How large is producer surplus?

Suppose that upstart Russian and Asian producers enter the market and the market becomes perfectly competitive.

b. What is the perfectly competitive price? What quantity will be sold in this perfectly competitive market?

c. At the competitive price and quantity, how large is the consumer surplus that each buyer experiences? How large is total consumer surplus? How large is producer surplus?

d. Compare your answer to part c to your answer to part a. How large is the deadweight loss associated with monopoly in this case?

8. Download Records decides to release an album by the group Mary and the Little Lamb. It produces the album with no fixed cost, but the total cost of downloading an album to a CD and paying Mary her royalty is $6 per album. Download Records can act as a monopolist. Its marketing division finds that the demand schedule for the album is as shown in the accompanying table.

Price of album	Quantity of albums demanded
$22	0
20	1,000
18	2,000
16	3,000
14	4,000
12	5,000
10	6,000
8	7,000

a. Calculate the total revenue and the marginal revenue per album.

b. The marginal cost of producing each album is constant at $6. To maximize profit, what level of output should Download Records choose, and which price should it charge for each album?

c. Mary renegotiates her contract and now needs to be paid a higher royalty per album. So the marginal cost rises to be constant at $14. To maximize profit, what level of output should Download Records now choose, and which price should it charge for each album?

9. The accompanying diagram illustrates your local electricity company's natural monopoly. The diagram shows the demand curve for kilowatt-hours (kWh) of electricity, the company's marginal revenue (*MR*) curve, its marginal cost (*MC*) curve, and its average total cost (*ATC*) curve. The government wants to regulate the monopolist by imposing a price ceiling.

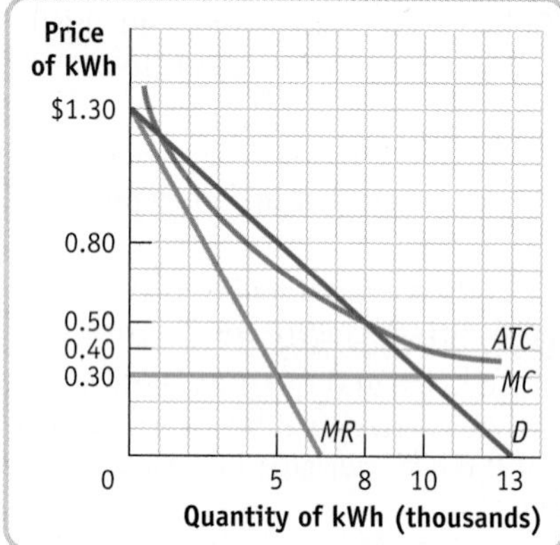

a. If the government does not regulate this monopolist, which price will it charge? Illustrate the inefficiency this creates by shading the deadweight loss from monopoly.

b. If the government imposes a price ceiling equal to the marginal cost, $0.30, will the monopolist make profits or lose money? Shade the area of profit (or loss) for the monopolist. If the government does impose this price ceiling, do you think the firm will continue to produce in the long run?

c. If the government imposes a price ceiling of $0.50, will the monopolist make a profit, lose money, or break even?

10. A monopolist knows that in order to expand the quantity of output it produces from 8 to 9 units it must lower the price of its output from $2 to $1. Calculate the quantity effect and the price effect. Use these results to calculate the monopolist's marginal revenue of producing the 9th unit. The marginal cost of producing the 9th unit is positive. Is it a good idea for the monopolist to produce the 9th unit?

11. In the United States, the Federal Trade Commission (FTC) is charged with promoting competition and challenging mergers that would likely lead to higher prices. Several years ago, Staples and Office Depot, two of the largest office supply superstores, announced their agreement to merge.

a. Some critics of the merger argued that, in many parts of the country, a merger between the two companies would create a monopoly in the office supply superstore market. Based on the FTC's argument and its mission to challenge mergers that would likely lead to higher prices, do you think it allowed the merger?

b. Staples and Office Depot argued that, while in some parts of the country they might create a monopoly in the office supply superstore market, the FTC should consider the larger market for all office supplies, which includes many smaller stores that sell office supplies (such as grocery stores and other retailers). In that market, Staples and Office Depot would face competition from many other, smaller stores. If the market for all office supplies is the relevant market that the FTC should consider, would it make the FTC more or less likely to allow the merger?

12. The accompanying table shows the demand schedule for vitamin D. Suppose that the marginal cost of producing vitamin D is zero.

Price of vitamin D (per ton)	Quantity of vitamin D demanded (tons)
$8	0
7	10
6	20
5	30
4	40
3	50
2	60
1	70

a. Assume that BASF is the only producer of vitamin D and acts as a monopolist. It currently produces 40 tons of vitamin D at $4 per ton. If BASF were to produce 10 more tons, what would be the price effect for BASF? What would be the quantity effect? Would BASF have an incentive to produce those 10 additional tons?

b. Now assume that Roche enters the market by also producing vitamin D and the market is now a duopoly. BASF and Roche agree to produce 40 tons of vitamin D in total, 20 tons each. BASF cannot be punished for deviating from the agreement with Roche. If BASF, on its own, were to deviate from that agreement and produce 10 more tons, what would be the price effect for BASF? What would be the quantity effect for BASF? Would BASF have an incentive to produce those 10 additional tons?

13. Suppose you are an economist working for the Antitrust Division of the Department of Justice. In each of the following cases you are given the task of determining whether the behavior warrants an antitrust investigation for possible illegal acts or is just an example of undesirable, but not illegal, tacit collusion. Explain your reasoning.

a. Two companies dominate the industry for industrial lasers. Several people sit on the boards of directors of both companies.

b. Three banks dominate the market for banking in a given state. Their profits have been going up recently as they add new fees for customer transactions. Advertising among the banks is fierce, and new branches are springing up in many locations.

c. The two oil companies that produce most of the petroleum for the western half of the United States have decided to forgo building their own pipelines and to share a common pipeline, the only means of transporting petroleum products to that market.

d. The two major companies that dominate the market for herbal supplements have each created a subsidiary that sells the same product as the parent company in large quantities but with a generic name.

e. The two largest credit card companies, Passport and OmniCard, have required all retailers who accept their cards to agree to limit their use of rival credit cards.

14. Use the three conditions for monopolistic competition discussed in the chapter to decide which of the following firms are likely to be operating as monopolistic competitors. If they are not monopolistically competitive firms, are they monopolists, oligopolists, or perfectly competitive firms?

a. A local band that plays for weddings, parties, and so on

b. Minute Maid, a producer of individual-serving juice boxes

c. Your local dry cleaner

d. A farmer who produces soybeans

15. You are thinking of setting up a coffee shop. The market structure for coffee shops is monopolistic competition. There are three Starbucks shops and two other coffee shops very much like Starbucks in your town already. In order for you to have some degree of market power, you may want to differentiate your coffee shop. Thinking about the three different ways in which products can be differentiated, explain how you would decide whether you should copy Starbucks or whether you should sell coffee in a completely different way.

EXTEND YOUR UNDERSTANDING

16. Prior to the late 1990s, the same company that generated your electricity also distributed it to you over high-voltage lines. Since then, 16 states and the District of Columbia have begun separating the generation from the distribution of electricity, allowing competition between electricity generators and between electricity distributors.

a. Assume that the market for electricity distribution was and remains a natural monopoly. Use a graph to illustrate the market for electricity distribution if the government sets price equal to average total cost.

b. Assume that deregulation of electricity generation creates a perfectly competitive market. Also assume that electricity generation does not exhibit the characteristics of a natural monopoly. Use a graph to illustrate the cost curves in the long-run equilibrium for an individual firm in this industry.

17. The market for olive oil in New York City is controlled by two families, the Sopranos and the Contraltos. Both families will ruthlessly eliminate any other family that attempts to enter the New York City olive oil market. The marginal cost of producing olive oil is constant and equal to $40 per gallon. There is no fixed cost. The accompanying table gives the market demand schedule for olive oil.

Price of olive oil (per gallon)	Quantity of olive oil demanded (gallons)
$100	1,000
90	1,500
80	2,000
70	2,500
60	3,000
50	3,500
40	4,000
30	4,500
20	5,000
10	5,500

a. Suppose the Sopranos and the Contraltos form a cartel. For each of the quantities given in the table, calculate the total revenue for their cartel and the marginal revenue for each additional gallon. How many gallons of olive oil would the cartel sell in total and at what price? The two families share the market equally (each produces half of the total output of the cartel). How much profit does each family make?

b. Uncle Junior, the head of the Soprano family, breaks the agreement and sells 500 more gallons of olive oil than under the cartel agreement. Assuming the Contraltos maintain the agreement, how does this affect the price for olive oil and the profit earned by each family?

c. Anthony Contralto, the head of the Contralto family, decides to punish Uncle Junior by increasing his sales by 500 gallons as well. How much profit does each family earn now?

CHAPTER 9

Externalities and Public Goods

THE GREAT STINK

UPPA/Topham/The Image Works

London's River Thames then . . .

Corbis

. . . and the same river now, thanks to government intervention.

WHAT YOU WILL LEARN IN THIS CHAPTER

- What **externalities** are and why they can lead to inefficiency and government intervention in the market
- The difference between **negative** and **positive externalities**
- The importance of the **Coase theorem,** which explains how private individuals can sometimes remedy externalities
- Why some government policies to deal with externalities, like **emissions taxes, tradable emissions permits,** or **Pigouvian subsidies,** are efficient and others, like **environmental standards,** are not
- The difference between **private goods,** which can be efficiently provided by markets, and **public goods,** which markets fail to supply

BY THE MIDDLE OF THE NINETEENTH century, London had become the world's largest city, with close to 2.5 million inhabitants. Unfortunately, all those people produced a lot of waste—and there was no place for it to go except into the Thames, the river flowing through the city. Nobody with a working nose could ignore the results. And the river didn't just smell bad—it carried dangerous waterborne diseases like cholera and typhoid. London neighborhoods close to the Thames had death rates from cholera more than six times greater than the neighborhoods farthest away. And the great majority of Londoners drew their drinking water from the Thames.

The hot summer of 1858 brought what came to be known as the Great Stink, which was so bad that one health journal reported "men struck down with the stench." Even the privileged and powerful suffered: Parliament met in a building next to the river and unsuccesfully attempted to stop the smell by covering the windows with chemical-soaked curtains. Parliament finally approved a plan for an immense system of sewers and pumping stations to direct sewage away from the city. The system, opened in 1865, brought dramatic improvement in the city's quality of life.

By dumping waste into the Thames, individuals imposed costs on all of the residents of London. When individuals impose costs on or provide benefits for others, but don't have an economic incentive to take those costs or benefits into account, economists say that *externalities* are generated. In this chapter, we'll examine the economics of externalities, seeing how they can get in the way of economic efficiency and lead to market failure, why they provide a reason for government intervention in markets, and how economic analysis can be used to guide government policy.

The story of the Great Stink also illustrates an important reason for government intervention in the economy. London's new sewage system was a clear example of a public good—a good that benefits many people, whether or not they have paid for it, and whose benefits to any one individual do not depend on how many others also benefit. As we will see, public goods differ in important ways from the private goods we have studied so far—and these differences mean that public goods cannot be efficiently supplied by the market. ■

The **marginal social cost of pollution** is the additional cost imposed on society as a whole by an additional unit of pollution.

The **marginal social benefit of pollution** is the additional gain to society as a whole from an additional unit of pollution.

The **socially optimal quantity of pollution** is the quantity of pollution that society would choose if all the costs and benefits of pollution were fully accounted for.

The Economics of Pollution

Pollution is a bad thing. Yet most pollution is a side effect of activities that provide us with good things: our air is polluted by power plants generating the electricity that lights our cities, and our rivers are damaged by fertilizer runoff from farms that grow our food. Why shouldn't we accept a certain amount of pollution as the cost of a good life?

Actually, we do. Even highly committed environmentalists don't think that we can or should completely eliminate pollution—even an environmentally conscious society would accept *some* pollution as the cost of producing useful goods and services. What environmentalists argue is that unless there is a strong and effective environmental policy, our society will generate *too much* pollution—too much of a bad thing. And the great majority of economists agree.

To see why, we need a framework that lets us think about how much pollution a society *should* have. We'll then be able to see why a market economy, left to itself, will produce more pollution than it should. We'll start by adopting the simplest framework to study the problem—assuming that the amount of pollution emitted by a polluter is directly observable and controllable.

Costs and Benefits of Pollution

How much pollution should society allow? We learned in Chapter 7 that "how much" decisions always involve comparing the marginal benefit from an additional unit of something with the marginal cost of that additional unit. The same is true of pollution.

The **marginal social cost of pollution** is the additional cost imposed on society as a whole by an additional unit of pollution. For example, acid rain damages fisheries, crops, and forests, and each additional ton of sulfur dioxide released into the atmosphere increases the damage.

The **marginal social benefit of pollution**—the additional benefit to society from an additional unit of pollution—may seem like a confusing concept. What's good about pollution? However, avoiding pollution requires using scarce resources that could have been used to produce other goods and services. For example, to reduce the quantity of sulfur dioxide they emit, power companies must either buy expensive low-sulfur coal or install special scrubbers to remove sulfur from their emissions. The more sulfur dioxide they are allowed to emit, the lower these extra costs. Suppose we could calculate how much money the power industry would save if it were allowed to emit an additional ton of sulfur dioxide. That savings would be the marginal benefit to society of emitting an extra ton of sulfur dioxide.

PITFALLS

SO HOW DO YOU MEASURE THE MARGINAL SOCIAL COST OF POLLUTION?

It might be confusing to think of marginal *social* cost—after all, we have up to this point always defined marginal cost as being incurred by an individual or a firm, not society as a whole. But it is easily understandable once we link it to the familiar concept of willingness to pay: the marginal social cost of a unit of pollution is equal to the *sum of the willingness to pay among all members of society* to avoid that unit of pollution. It's the sum because, in general, more than one person is affected by the pollution.

But calculating the true cost to society of pollution—marginal or average—is a difficult matter, requiring a great deal of scientific knowledge, as the upcoming Economics in Action on smoking illustrates. As a result, society often underestimates the true marginal social cost of pollution.

Using hypothetical numbers, Figure 9-1 shows how we can determine the **socially optimal quantity of pollution**—the quantity of pollution society would choose if all its costs and benefits were fully accounted for. The upward-sloping marginal social cost curve, *MSC,* shows how the marginal cost to society of an additional ton of pollution emissions varies with the quantity of emissions. (An upward slope is likely because nature can often safely handle low levels of pollution but is increasingly harmed as pollution reaches high levels.) The marginal social benefit curve, *MSB,* is downward

FIGURE 9-1 The Socially Optimal Quantity of Pollution

Pollution yields both costs and benefits. Here the curve *MSC* shows how the marginal cost to society as a whole from emitting one more ton of pollution emissions depends on the quantity of emissions. The curve *MSB* shows how the marginal benefit to society as a whole of emitting an additional ton of pollution emissions depends on the quantity of pollution emissions. The socially optimal quantity of pollution is Q_{OPT}; at that quantity, the marginal social benefit of pollution is equal to the marginal social cost, corresponding to $200.

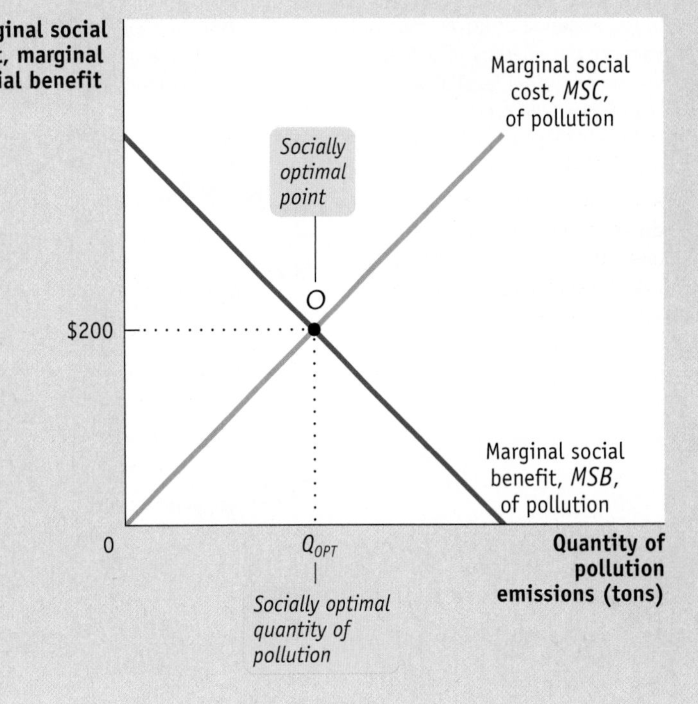

sloping because it is progressively harder, and therefore more expensive, to achieve a further reduction in pollution as the total amount of pollution falls—increasingly more expensive technology must be used. As a result, as total pollution falls, the cost savings to a polluter of being allowed to emit one more ton rises.

The socially optimal quantity of pollution in this example isn't zero. It's Q_{OPT}, the quantity corresponding to point *O*, where *MSB* crosses *MSC*. At Q_{OPT}, the marginal social benefit from an additional ton of emissions and its marginal social cost are equalized at $200.

But will a market economy, left to itself, arrive at the socially optimal quantity of pollution? No, it won't.

PITFALLS

SO HOW DO YOU MEASURE THE MARGINAL SOCIAL BENEFIT OF POLLUTION?

Similar to the problem of measuring the marginal social cost of pollution, the concept of willingness to pay helps us understand the marginal social benefit of pollution in contrast to the marginal benefit to an individual or firm. The marginal social benefit of a unit of pollution is simply equal to the highest willingness to pay for the right to emit that unit measured across all polluters. But unlike the marginal social cost of pollution, the value of the marginal social benefit of pollution is a number likely to be known—to polluters, that is.

Pollution: An External Cost

Pollution yields both benefits and costs to society. But in a market economy without government intervention, those who benefit from pollution—like the owners of power companies—decide how much pollution occurs. They have no incentive to take into account the costs of pollution that they impose on others.

To see why, remember the nature of the benefits and costs from pollution. For polluters, the benefits take the form of monetary savings: by emitting an extra ton of sulfur dioxide, any given polluter saves the cost of buying expensive, low-sulfur coal or installing pollution-control equipment. So the benefits of pollution accrue directly to the polluters.

The costs of pollution, though, fall on people who have no say in the decision about how much pollution takes place: for example, people who fish in northeastern lakes do not control the decisions of power plants.

FIGURE 9-2 Why a Market Economy Produces Too Much Pollution

In the absence of government intervention, the quantity of pollution will be Q_{MKT}, the level at which the marginal social benefit of pollution is zero. This is an inefficiently high quantity of pollution: the marginal social cost, $400, greatly exceeds the marginal social benefit, $0. An optimal Pigouvian tax of $200, the value of the marginal social cost of pollution when it equals the marginal social benefit of pollution, can move the market to the socially optimal quantity of pollution, Q_{OPT}.

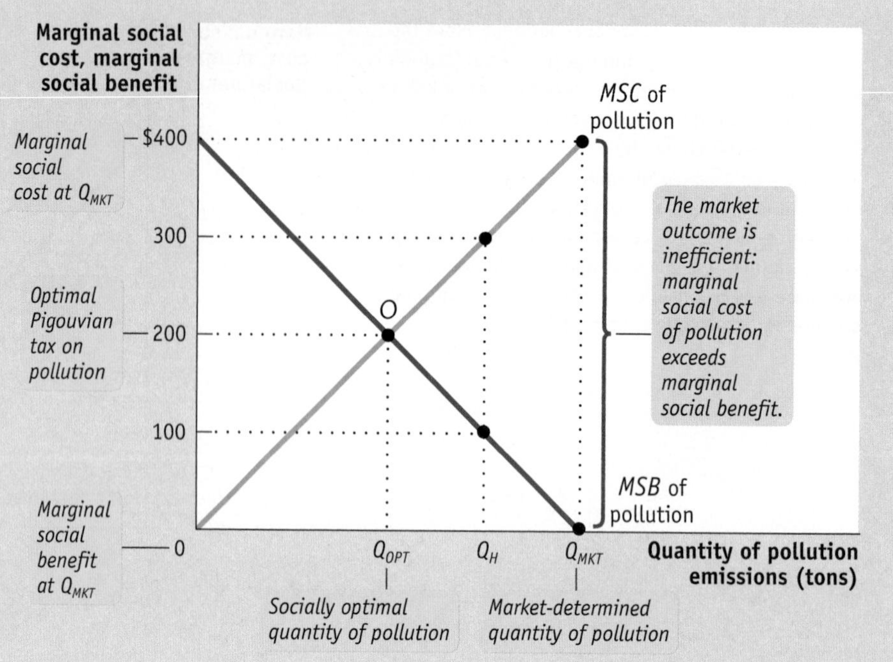

Figure 9-2 shows the result of this asymmetry between who reaps the benefits and who pays the costs. In a market economy without government intervention to protect the environment, only the benefits of pollution are taken into account in choosing the quantity of pollution. So the quantity of emissions won't be the socially optimal quantity Q_{OPT}; it will be Q_{MKT}, the quantity at which the marginal social benefit of an additional ton of pollution is zero, but the marginal social cost of that additional ton is much larger—$400. The quantity of pollution in a market economy without government intervention will be higher than its socially optimal quantity. (The Pigouvian tax noted in Figure 9-2 will be explained shortly.)

The reason is that in the absence of government intervention, those who derive the benefits from pollution—in this case, the owners of power plants—don't have to compensate those who bear the costs. So the marginal cost of pollution to any given polluter is zero: polluters have no incentive to limit the amount of emissions. For example, before the Clean Air Act of 1970, midwestern power plants used the cheapest type of coal available, despite the fact that cheap coal generated more pollution, and they did nothing to scrub their emissions.

An **external cost** is an uncompensated cost that an individual or firm imposes on others.

An **external benefit** is a benefit that an individual or firm confers on others without receiving compensation.

External costs and benefits are known as **externalities.** External costs are **negative externalities,** and external benefits are **positive externalities.**

The environmental costs of pollution are the best-known and most important example of an **external cost**—an uncompensated cost that an individual or firm imposes on others. There are many other examples of external costs besides pollution. Another important, and certainly very familiar, external cost is traffic congestion—an individual who chooses to drive during rush hour increases congestion and so increases the travel time of other drivers.

We'll see later in this chapter that there are also important examples of **external benefits,** benefits that individuals or firms confer on others without receiving compensation. External costs and benefits are jointly known as **externalities,** with external costs called **negative externalities** and external benefits called **positive externalities.**

FOR INQUIRING MINDS

TALKING, TEXTING, AND DRIVING

Why is that woman in the car in front of us driving so erratically? Is she drunk? No, she's talking on her cell phone or texting.

Traffic safety experts take the risks posed by driving while using a cell phone very seriously: Using data from 2010, the National Safety Council estimated that almost a quarter of all traffic accidents involve distracted drivers who are either talking or texting on their cell phones. This translates to 1.1 million crashes caused by talking on cell phones, and 160,000 crashes that involve texting. Other estimates suggest that talking on cell phones while driving may be responsible for 3,000 or more traffic deaths each year. And using hands-free, voice-activated phones to make a call doesn't seem to help much because the main danger is distraction. As one traffic consultant put it, "It's not where your eyes are; it's where your head is."

The National Safety Council urges people not to use phones while driving. Most states have some restrictions on talking on a cell phone while driving. But in response to a growing number of accidents, several states have banned cell phone use behind the wheel altogether. In 39 states and the District of Columbia, it is illegal to text and drive. Cell phone use while driving is illegal in many other countries as well, including Japan and Israel.

Stephen M. Wallace

"It's not where your eyes are; it's where your head is."

Why not leave the decision up to the driver? Because the risk posed by driving while using a cell phone isn't just a risk to the driver; it's also a safety risk to others—to a driver's passengers, pedestrians, and people in other cars. Even if you decide that the benefit to you of using your cell phone while driving is worth the cost, you aren't taking into account the cost to other people. Driving while using a cell phone, in other words, generates a serious—and sometimes fatal—negative externality.

As we've already suggested, externalities can lead to individual decisions that are not optimal for society as a whole. Let's take a closer look at why.

The Inefficiency of Excess Pollution

We have just shown that in the absence of government action, the quantity of pollution will be *inefficient:* polluters will pollute up to the point at which the marginal social benefit of pollution is zero, as shown by the pollution quantity, Q_{MKT}, in Figure 9-2.

Because the marginal social benefit of pollution is zero at Q_{MKT}, reducing the quantity of pollution by one ton would subtract very little from the total social benefit from pollution. In other words, the benefit to polluters from that last unit of pollution is very low—virtually zero. Meanwhile, the marginal social cost imposed on the rest of society of that last ton of pollution at Q_{MKT} is quite high—\$400. In other words, by reducing the quantity of pollution at Q_{MKT} by one ton, the total social cost of pollution falls by \$400, but total social benefit falls by virtually zero. So total surplus rises by approximately \$400 if the quantity of pollution at Q_{MKT} is reduced by one ton.

If the quantity of pollution is reduced further, there will be more gains in total surplus, though they will be smaller. For example, if the quantity of pollution is Q_H in Figure 9-2, the marginal social benefit of a ton of pollution is \$100, but the marginal social cost is still \$300. In other words, reducing the quantity of pollution by one ton leads to a net gain in total surplus of approximately \$300 – \$100 = \$200. This tells us that Q_H is still an inefficiently high quantity of pollution. Only if the quantity of pollution is reduced to Q_{OPT}, where the marginal social cost and the marginal social benefit of an additional ton of pollution are both \$200, is the outcome efficient.

According to the **Coase theorem,** even in the presence of externalities an economy can always reach an efficient solution as long as **transaction costs**—the costs to individuals of making a deal—are sufficiently low.

When individuals take external costs or benefits into account, they **internalize the externality.**

Private Solutions to Externalities

Can the private sector solve the problem of externalities without government intervention? Bear in mind that when an outcome is inefficient, there is potentially a deal that makes people better off. Why don't individuals find a way to make that deal?

In an influential 1960 article, the economist and Nobel laureate Ronald Coase pointed out that in an ideal world the private sector could indeed deal with all externalities. According to the **Coase theorem,** even in the presence of externalities an economy can always reach an efficient solution provided that the costs of making a deal are sufficiently low. The costs of making a deal are known as **transaction costs.**

To get a sense of Coase's argument, imagine two neighbors, Mick and Christina, who both like to barbecue in their backyards on summer afternoons. Mick likes to play golden oldies on his boombox while barbecuing, but this annoys Christina, who can't stand that kind of music.

Who prevails? You might think that it depends on the legal rights involved in the case: if the law says that Mick has the right to play whatever music he wants, Christina just has to suffer; if the law says that Mick needs Christina's consent to play music in his backyard, Mick has to live without his favorite music while barbecuing.

But as Coase pointed out, the outcome need not be determined by legal rights, because Christina and Mick can make a private deal. Even if Mick has the right to play his music, Christina could pay him not to. Even if Mick can't play the music without an OK from Christina, he can offer to pay her to give that OK. These payments allow them to reach an efficient solution, regardless of who has the legal upper hand. If the benefit of the music to Mick exceeds its cost to Christina, the music will go on; if the benefit to Mick is less than the cost to Christina, there will be silence.

The implication of Coase's analysis is that externalities need not lead to inefficiency because individuals have an incentive to make mutually beneficial deals—deals that lead them to take externalities into account when making decisions. When individuals *do* take externalities into account when making decisions, economists say that they **internalize the externality.** If externalities are fully internalized, the outcome is efficient even without government intervention.

Why can't individuals always internalize externalities? Our barbecue example implicitly assumes the transaction costs are low enough for Mick and Christina to be able to make a deal. In many situations involving externalities, however, transaction costs prevent individuals from making efficient deals. Examples of transaction costs include the following:

- *The costs of communication among the interested parties.* Such costs may be very high if many people are involved.
- *The costs of making legally binding agreements.* Such costs may be high if expensive legal services are required.
- *Costly delays involved in bargaining.* Even if there is a potentially beneficial deal, both sides may hold out in an effort to extract more favorable terms, leading to increased effort and forgone benefit.

In some cases, people do find ways to reduce transaction costs, allowing them to internalize externalities. For example, a house with a junk-filled yard and peeling paint imposes a negative externality on the neighboring houses, diminishing their value in the eyes of potential house buyers. So many people live in private communities that set rules for home maintenance and behavior, making bargaining between neighbors unnecessary. But in many other cases, transaction costs are too high to make it possible to deal with externalities through private action. For example, tens of millions of people are adversely affected by acid rain. It would be prohibitively expensive to try to make a deal among all those people and all those power companies.

When transaction costs prevent the private sector from dealing with externalities, it is time to look for government solutions. We turn to public policy in the next section.

ECONOMICS ➤ IN ACTION

THANK YOU FOR NOT SMOKING

New Yorkers call them the "shiver-and-puff people"—the smokers who stand outside their workplaces, even in the depths of winter, to take a cigarette break. Over the past couple of decades, rules against smoking in spaces shared by others have become ever stricter. This is partly a matter of personal dislike—nonsmokers really don't like to smell other people's cigarette smoke—but it also reflects concerns over the health risks of second-hand smoke. As the Surgeon General's warning on many packs says, "Smoking causes lung cancer, heart disease, emphysema, and may complicate pregnancy." And there's no question that being in the same room as someone who smokes exposes you to at least some health risk.

Rubberball/Mike Kemp/Getty Images

The external costs of second-hand smoke rise considerably when the impact on smokers' families is taken into account.

Second-hand smoke, then, is clearly an example of a negative externality. But how important is it? Putting a dollar-and-cents value on it—that is, measuring the marginal social cost of cigarette smoke—requires not only estimating the health effects but putting a value on these effects. Despite the difficulty, economists have tried. A paper published in 1993 in the *Journal of Economic Perspectives* surveyed the research on the external costs of both cigarette smoking and alcohol consumption.

According to this paper, valuing the health costs of cigarettes depends on whether you count the costs imposed on members of smokers' families, including unborn children, in addition to costs borne by smokers. If you don't, the external costs of second-hand smoke have been estimated at about only $0.19 per pack smoked. (Using this method of calculation, $0.19 corresponds to the *average* social cost of smoking per pack at the current level of smoking in society.) A 2005 study raised this estimate to $0.52 per pack smoked. If you include effects on smokers' families, the number rises considerably—family members who live with smokers are exposed to a lot more smoke. (They are also exposed to the risk of fires, which alone is estimated at $0.09 per pack.) If you include the effects of smoking by pregnant women on their unborn children's future health, the cost is immense—$4.80 per pack, which is more than twice the wholesale price charged by cigarette manufacturers.

Quick Review

- There are costs as well as benefits to reducing pollution, so the optimal quantity of pollution isn't zero. Instead, the **socially optimal quantity of pollution** is the quantity at which the **marginal social cost of pollution** is equal to the **marginal social benefit of pollution.**
- Left to itself, a market economy will typically generate an inefficiently high level of pollution because polluters have no incentive to take into account the costs they impose on others.
- External costs and benefits are known as **externalities.** Pollution is an example of an **external cost,** or **negative externality;** in contrast, some activities can give rise to **external benefits,** or **positive externalities.**
- According to the **Coase theorem,** the private sector can sometimes resolve externalities on its own: if **transaction costs** aren't too high, individuals can reach a deal to **internalize the externality.** When transaction costs are too high, government intervention may be warranted.

CHECK YOUR UNDERSTANDING 9-1

1. Wastewater runoff from large poultry farms adversely affects their neighbors. Explain the following:
   a. The nature of the external cost imposed
   b. The outcome in the absence of government intervention or a private deal
   c. The socially optimal outcome
2. According to Yasmin, any student who borrows a book from the university library and fails to return it on time imposes a negative externality on other students. She claims that rather than charging a modest fine for late returns, the library should charge a huge fine so that borrowers will never return a book late. Is Yasmin's economic reasoning correct?

Solutions appear at back of book.

Environmental standards are rules that protect the environment by specifying actions by producers and consumers.

An **emissions tax** is a tax that depends on the amount of pollution a firm produces.

Policies Toward Pollution

Before 1970, there were no rules governing the amount of sulfur dioxide power plants in the United States could emit—which is why acid rain got to be such a problem. After 1970, the Clean Air Act set rules about sulfur dioxide emissions—and the acidity of rainfall declined significantly. Economists argued, however, that a more flexible system of rules that exploited the effectiveness of markets could achieve lower pollution at less cost. In 1990 this theory was put into effect with a modified version of the Clean Air Act. And guess what? The economists were right!

In this section we'll look at the policies governments use to deal with pollution and at how economic analysis has been used to improve those policies.

Environmental Standards

The most serious external costs in the modern world are surely those associated with actions that damage the environment—air pollution, water pollution, habitat destruction, and so on. Protection of the environment has become a major role of government in all advanced nations. In the United States, the Environmental Protection Agency is the principal enforcer of environmental policies at the national level, supported by the actions of state and local governments.

How does a country protect its environment? At present the main policy tools are **environmental standards,** rules that protect the environment by specifying actions by producers and consumers. A familiar example is the law that requires almost all vehicles to have catalytic converters, which reduce the emission of chemicals that can cause smog and lead to health problems. Other rules require communities to treat their sewage or factories to avoid or limit certain kinds of pollution, and so on.

Environmental standards came into widespread use in the 1960s and 1970s, and they have had considerable success in reducing pollution. For example, since the United States passed the Clean Air Act in 1970, overall emission of pollutants into the air has fallen by more than a third, even though the population has grown by a third and the size of the economy has more than doubled. Even in Los Angeles, still famous for its smog, the air has improved dramatically: in 1976 ozone levels in the South Coast Air Basin exceeded federal standards on 194 days; in 2010, on only 7 days.

Despite these successes, economists believe that when regulators can control a polluter's emissions directly, there are more efficient ways than environmental standards to deal with pollution. By using methods grounded in economic analysis, society can achieve a cleaner environment at lower cost. Most current environmental standards are inflexible and don't allow reductions in pollution to be achieved at minimum cost. For example, two power plants—plant A and plant B—might be ordered to reduce pollution by the same percentage, even if their costs of achieving that objective are very different.

How does economic theory suggest that pollution should be directly controlled? There are actually two approaches: taxes and tradable permits. As we'll see, either approach can achieve the efficient outcome at the minimum feasible cost.

Emissions Taxes

One way to deal with pollution directly is to charge polluters an **emissions tax.** Emissions taxes are taxes that depend on the amount of pollution a firm produces. For example, power plants might be charged $200 for every ton of sulfur dioxide they emit.

Look again at Figure 9-2, which shows that the socially optimal quantity of pollution is Q_{OPT}. At that quantity of pollution, the marginal social benefit and

ECONOMIC GROWTH AND GREENHOUSE GASES IN SIX COUNTRIES

At first glance, a comparison of the per capita greenhouse gas emissions of various countries, shown in panel (a) of this graph, suggests that Australia, Canada, and the United States are the worst offenders. The average American is responsible for 23.4 tonnes of greenhouse gas emissions (measured in CO_2 equivalents)—the pollution that causes global warming—compared to only 6.9 tonnes for the average Uzbek, 5.5 tonnes for the average Chinese, and 1.7 tonnes for the average Indian. (A tonne, also called a metric ton, equals 1.10 ton.)

Such a conclusion, however, ignores an important factor in determining the level of a country's greenhouse gas emissions: its gross domestic product, or GDP—the total value of a country's domestic output. Output typically cannot be produced without more energy, and more energy usage typically results in more pollution. In fact, some have argued that criticizing a country's level of greenhouse gases without taking account of its level of economic development is misguided. It would be equivalent to faulting a country for being at a more advanced stage of economic development.

A more meaningful way to compare pollution across countries is to measure emissions per $1 million of a country's GDP, as shown in panel (b). On this basis, the United States, Canada, India, and Australia are now "green" countries, but China and Uzbekistan are not. What explains the reversal once GDP is accounted for? The answer: both economics and government behavior.

First, there is the issue of economics. Countries that are poor and have begun to industrialize, such as China and Uzbekistan, often view money spent to reduce pollution as better spent on other things. From their perspective, they are still too poor to afford as clean an environment as wealthy advanced countries. They claim that to impose a wealthy country's environmental standards on them would jeopardize their economic growth.

Second, there is the issue of government behavior—or more precisely, whether or not a government possesses the tools necessary to effectively control pollution. China is a good illustration of this problem. The Chinese government lacks sufficient regulatory power to enforce its own environmental rules, promote energy conservation, or encourage pollution reduction. To produce $1 of GDP, China spends three times the world average on energy—far more than Indonesia, for example, which is also a poor country. The case of China illustrates just how important government intervention is in improving society's welfare in the presence of externalities.

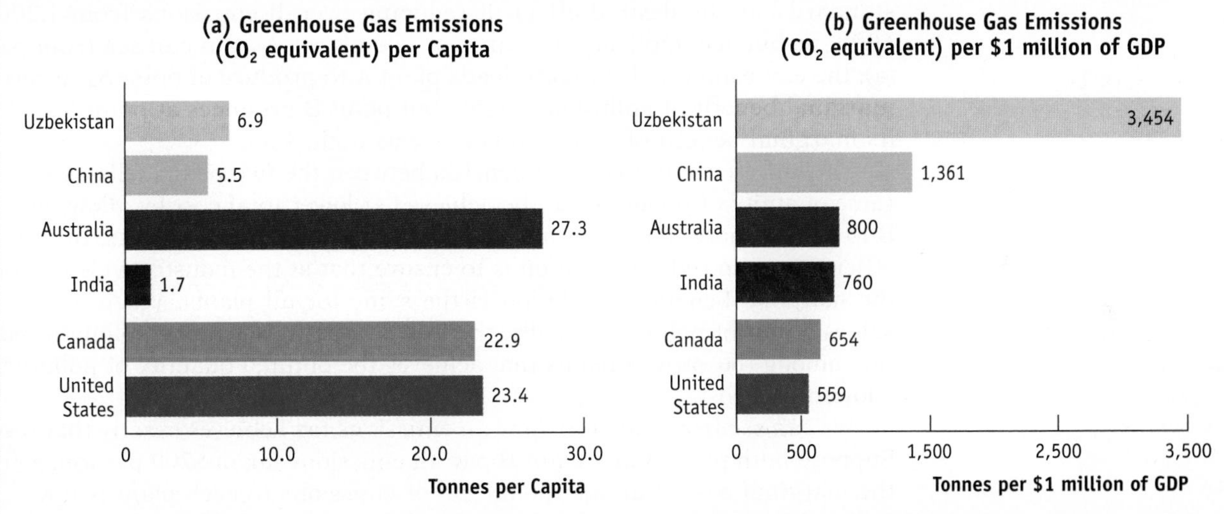

Source: World Resources Institute.

marginal social cost of an additional ton of emissions are equal at $200. But in the absence of government intervention, power companies have no incentive to limit pollution to the socially optimal quantity, Q_{OPT}; instead, they will push pollution up to the quantity Q_{MKT}, at which marginal social benefit is zero.

It's now easy to see how an emissions tax can solve the problem. If power companies are required to pay a tax of $200 per ton of emissions, they now face a marginal cost of $200 per ton and have an incentive to reduce emissions to Q_{OPT}, the socially optimal quantity. This illustrates a general result: an emissions

Taxes designed to reduce external costs are known as **Pigouvian taxes.**

tax equal to the marginal social cost at the socially optimal quantity of pollution induces polluters to internalize the externality—to take into account the true costs to society of their actions.

Why is an emissions tax an efficient way (that is, a cost-minimizing way) to reduce pollution but environmental standards generally are not? Because an emissions tax ensures that the marginal benefit of pollution is equal for all sources of pollution, but an environmental standard does not. Figure 9-3 shows a hypothetical industry consisting of only two plants, plant A and plant B. We'll assume that plant A uses newer technology than plant B and so has a lower cost of reducing pollution. Reflecting this difference in costs, plant A's marginal benefit of pollution curve, MB_A, lies below plant B's marginal benefit of pollution curve, MB_B. Because it is more costly for plant B to reduce its pollution at any output quantity, an additional ton of pollution is worth more to plant B than to plant A.

In the absence of government action, we know that polluters will pollute until the marginal social benefit of an additional unit of emissions is equal to zero. Recall that the marginal social benefit of pollution is the cost savings, at the margin, to polluters of an additional unit of pollution. As a result, without government intervention each plant will pollute until its own marginal benefit of pollution is equal to zero. This corresponds to an emissions quantity of 600 tons each for plants A and B—the quantity of pollution at which MB_A and MB_B are each equal to zero. So although plant A and plant B value a ton of emissions differently, without government action they will each choose to emit the same amount of pollution.

Now suppose that the government decides that overall pollution from this industry should be cut in half, from 1,200 tons to 600 tons. Panel (a) of Figure 9-3 shows how this might be achieved with an environmental standard that requires each plant to cut its emissions in half, from 600 to 300 tons. The standard has the desired effect of reducing overall emissions from 1,200 to 600 tons but accomplishes it in an inefficient way. As you can see from panel (a), the environmental standard leads plant A to produce at point S_A, where its marginal benefit of pollution is \$150, but plant B produces at point S_B, where its marginal benefit of pollution is twice as high, \$300.

This difference in marginal benefits between the two plants tells us that the same quantity of pollution can be achieved at lower total cost by allowing plant B to pollute more than 300 tons but inducing plant A to pollute less. In fact, the efficient way to reduce pollution is to ensure that at the industry-wide outcome, the marginal benefit of pollution is the same for all plants. When each plant values a unit of pollution equally, there is no way to rearrange pollution reduction among the various plants that achieves the optimal quantity of pollution at a lower total cost.

We can see from panel (b) how an emissions tax achieves exactly that result. Suppose both plant A and plant B pay an emissions tax of \$200 per ton, so that the marginal cost of an additional ton of emissions to each plant is now \$200 rather than zero. As a result, plant A produces at T_A and plant B produces at T_B. So plant A reduces its pollution more than it would under an inflexible environmental standard, cutting its emissions from 600 to 200 tons; meanwhile, plant B reduces its pollution less, going from 600 to 400 tons. In the end, total pollution—600 tons—is the same as under the environmental standard, but total surplus is higher. That's because the reduction in pollution has been achieved efficiently, allocating most of the reduction to plant A, the plant that can reduce emissions at lower cost.

The term *emissions tax* may convey the misleading impression that taxes are a solution to only one kind of external cost, pollution. In fact, taxes can be used to discourage any activity that generates negative externalities, such as driving during rush hour or operating a noisy bar in a residential area. In general, taxes designed to reduce external costs are known as **Pigouvian taxes,** after the

FIGURE 9-3 Environmental Standards versus Emissions Taxes

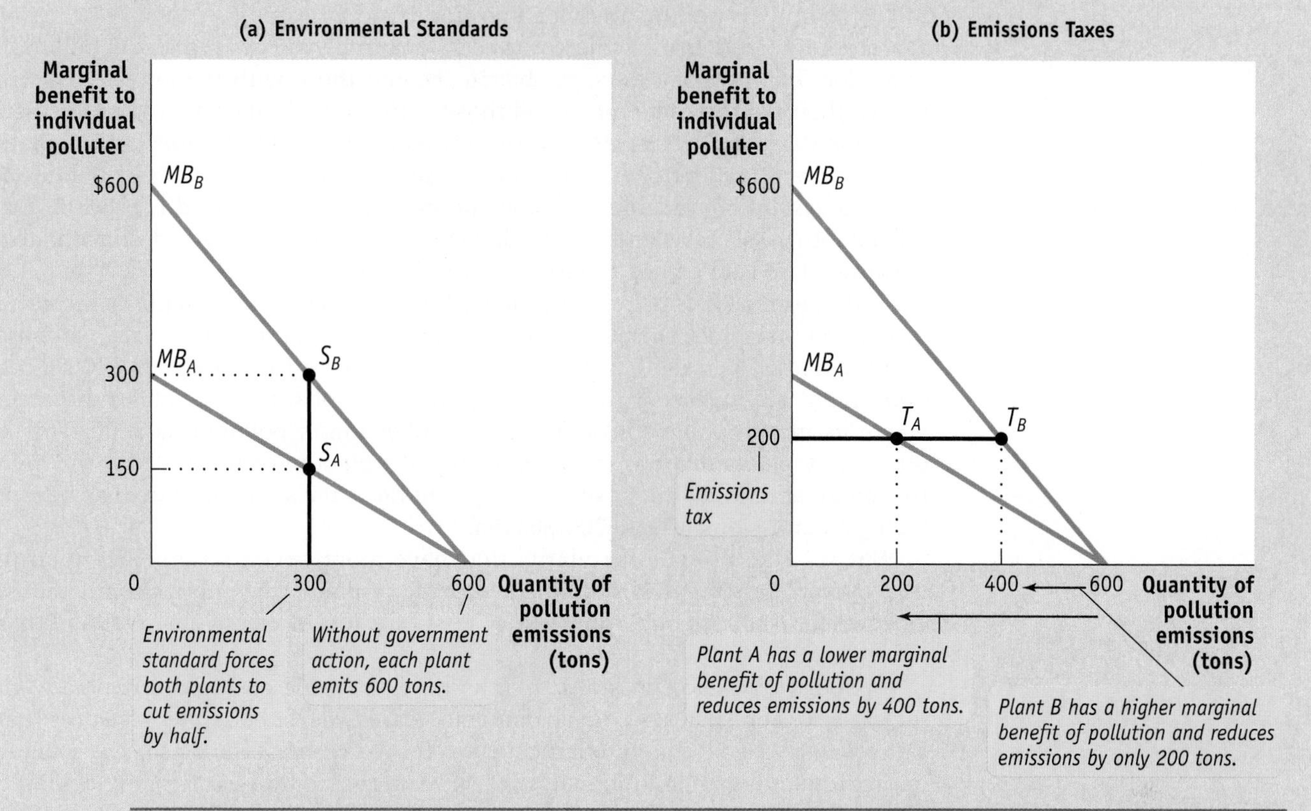

In both panels, MB_A shows the marginal benefit of pollution to plant A and MB_B shows the marginal benefit of pollution to plant B. In the absence of government intervention, each plant would emit 600 tons. However, the cost of reducing emissions is lower for plant A, as shown by the fact that MB_A lies below MB_B. Panel (a) shows the result of an environmental standard that requires both plants to cut emissions in half; this is inefficient, because it leaves the marginal benefit of pollution higher for plant B than for plant A. Panel (b) shows that an emissions tax achieves the same quantity of overall pollution efficiently: faced with an emissions tax of $200 per ton, each plant reduces pollution to the point where its marginal benefit is $200.

economist A. C. Pigou, who emphasized their usefulness in his classic 1920 book, *The Economics of Welfare*. In our example, the optimal Pigouvian tax is $200; as you can see from Figure 9-2, this corresponds to the marginal social cost of pollution at the optimal output quantity, Q_{OPT}.

Are there any problems with emissions taxes? The main concern is that in practice government officials usually aren't sure how high the tax should be set. If they set the tax too low, there will be too little improvement in the environment; if they set it too high, emissions will be reduced by more than is efficient. This uncertainty cannot be eliminated, but the nature of the risks can be changed by using an alternative strategy, issuing tradable emissions permits.

Tradable Emissions Permits

Tradable emissions permits are licenses to emit limited quantities of pollutants that can be bought and sold by polluters. They are usually issued to polluting firms according to some formula reflecting their history. For example, each power plant might be issued permits equal to 50% of its emissions before the system went into effect. The more important point, however, is that these permits

Tradable emissions permits are licenses to emit limited quantities of pollutants that can be bought and sold by polluters.

are *tradable*. Firms with differing costs of reducing pollution can now engage in mutually beneficial transactions: those that find it easier to reduce pollution will sell some of their permits to those that find it more difficult.

In other words, firms will use transactions in permits to reallocate pollution reduction among themselves, so that in the end those with the lowest cost will reduce their pollution the most, and those with the highest cost will reduce their pollution the least. Assume that the government issues 300 licenses each to plant A and plant B, where one license allows the emission of one ton of pollution. Under a system of tradable emissions permits, plant A will find it profitable to sell 100 of its 300 government-issued licenses to plant B. The effect of a tradable permit system is to create a market in rights to pollute.

Just like emissions taxes, tradable permits provide polluters with an incentive to take the marginal social cost of pollution into account. To see why, suppose that the market price of a permit to emit one ton of sulfur dioxide is $200. Then every plant has an incentive to limit its emissions of sulfur dioxide to the point where its marginal benefit of emitting another ton of pollution is $200. This is obvious for plants that buy rights to pollute: if a plant must pay $200 for the right to emit an additional ton of sulfur dioxide, it faces the same incentives as a plant facing an emissions tax of $200 per ton.

But it's equally true for plants that have more permits than they plan to use: by *not* emitting a ton of sulfur dioxide, a plant frees up a permit that it can sell for $200, so the opportunity cost of a ton of emissions to the plant's owner is $200.

In short, tradable emissions permits have the same cost-minimizing advantage as emissions taxes over environmental standards: either system ensures that those who can reduce pollution most cheaply are the ones who do so. The socially optimal quantity of pollution shown in Figure 9-2 could be efficiently achieved either way: by imposing an emissions tax of $200 per ton of pollution or by issuing tradable permits to emit Q_{OPT} tons of pollution. If regulators choose to issue Q_{OPT} permits, where one permit allows the release of one ton of emissions, then the equilibrium market price of a permit among polluters will indeed be $200. Why? You can see from Figure 9-2 that at Q_{OPT}, only polluters with a marginal benefit of pollution of $200 or more will buy a permit. And the last polluter who buys—who has a marginal benefit of exactly $200—sets the market price.

It's important to realize that emissions taxes and tradable permits do more than induce polluting industries to reduce their output. Unlike rigid environmental standards, emissions taxes and tradable permits provide incentives to create and use technology that emits less pollution—new technology that lowers the socially optimal level of pollution. The main effect of the permit system for sulfur dioxide has been to change *how* electricity is produced rather than to reduce the nation's electricity output. For example, power companies have shifted to the use of alternative fuels such as low-sulfur coal and natural gas; they have also installed scrubbers that take much of the sulfur dioxide out of a power plant's emissions.

The main problem with tradable emissions permits is the flip-side of the problem with emissions taxes: because it is difficult to determine the optimal quantity of pollution, governments can find themselves either issuing too many permits (that is, they don't reduce pollution enough) or issuing too few (that is, they reduce pollution too much).

After first relying on environmental standards, the U.S. government has turned to a system of tradable permits to control acid rain. Current proposals would extend the system to other major sources of pollution. And in 2005 the European Union created the largest emissions-trading scheme, with the purpose of controlling emissions of carbon dioxide, also known as greenhouse gases. The EU scheme is part of a larger global market for the trading of greenhouse gas permits. The Economics in Action that follows describes these two systems.

ECONOMICS > IN ACTION

CAP AND TRADE

The tradable emissions permit systems for both acid rain in the United States and greenhouse gases in the European Union are examples of *cap and trade systems:* the government sets a *cap* (a maximum amount of pollutant that can be emitted), issues tradable emissions permits, and enforces a yearly rule that a polluter must hold a number of permits equal to the amount of pollutant emitted. The goal is to set the cap low enough to generate environmental benefits, while giving polluters flexibility in meeting environmental standards and motivating them to adopt new technologies that will lower the cost of reducing pollution.

In 1994 the United States began a cap and trade system for the sulfur dioxide emissions that cause acid rain by issuing permits to power plants based on their historical consumption of coal. Thanks to the system, air pollutants in the United States decreased by more than 40% from 1990 to 2008, and 2010 acid rain levels dropped to approximately 50% of their 1980 levels. Economists who have analyzed the sulfur dioxide cap and trade system point to another reason for its success: it would have been a lot more expensive—80% more to be exact—to reduce emissions by this much using a non-market-based regulatory policy.

Companies like Terrapass help individuals and companies manage their carbon emissions.

The EU cap and trade scheme, covering all 27 member nations of the European Union, is the world's only mandatory trading scheme for greenhouse gases. It is scheduled to achieve a 21% reduction in greenhouse gases by 2020 compared to 2005 levels.

Other countries, like Australia and New Zealand, have adopted less comprehensive trading schemes for greenhouse gases. According to the World Bank, the worldwide market for greenhouse gases—also called *carbon trading*—has grown rapidly, from $11 billion in permits traded in 2005 to $142 billion in 2010. In New Zealand, famous for its sheep and lamb industry, farmers are busy converting grazing land into forests so that they can sell permits beginning in 2015, when companies will be required to pay for their emissions.

Despite all this good news, however, cap and trade systems are not silver bullets for the world's pollution problems. Although they are appropriate for pollution that's geographically dispersed, like sulfur dioxide and greenhouse gases, they don't work for pollution that's localized, like mercury or lead contamination. In addition, the amount of overall reduction in pollution depends on the level of the cap. Under industry pressure, regulators run the risk of issuing too many permits, effectively eliminating the cap. Finally, there must be vigilant monitoring of compliance if the system is to work. Without oversight of how much a polluter is actually emitting, there is no way to know for sure that the rules are being followed.

Quick Review

- Governments often limit pollution with **environmental standards.** Generally, such standards are an inefficient way to reduce pollution because they are inflexible.
- When the quantity of pollution emitted can be directly observed and controlled, environmental goals can be achieved efficiently in two ways: **emissions taxes** and **tradable emissions permits.** These methods are efficient because they are flexible, allocating more pollution reduction to those who can do it more cheaply. They also motivate polluters to adopt new pollution-reducing technology.
- An emissions tax is a form of **Pigouvian tax.** The optimal Pigouvian tax is equal to the marginal social cost of pollution at the socially optimal quantity of pollution.

CHECK YOUR UNDERSTANDING 9-2

1. Some opponents of tradable emissions permits object to them on the grounds that polluters that sell their permits benefit monetarily from their contribution to polluting the environment. Assess this argument.

2. Explain the following.
   a. Why an emissions tax smaller than or greater than the marginal social cost at Q_{OPT} leads to a smaller total surplus compared to the total surplus generated if the emissions tax had been set optimally
   b. Why a system of tradable emissions permits that sets the total quantity of allowable pollution higher or lower than Q_{OPT} leads to a smaller total surplus compared to the total surplus generated if the number of permits had been set optimally

Solutions appear at back of book.

Positive Externalities

New Jersey is the most densely populated state in the country, lying along the northeastern corridor, an area of almost continuous development stretching from Washington, D.C., to Boston. Yet a drive through New Jersey reveals a surprising feature: acre upon acre of farmland, growing everything from corn to pumpkins to the famous Jersey tomatoes. This situation is no accident: starting in 1961, New Jerseyans have voted in a series of measures that subsidize farmers to permanently preserve their farmland rather than sell it to developers. By 2012, the Green Acres Program, administered by the state, had preserved almost 650,000 acres of open space.

Why have New Jersey citizens voted to raise their own taxes to subsidize the preservation of farmland? Because they believe that preserved farmland in an already heavily developed state provides external benefits, such as natural beauty, access to fresh food, and the conservation of wild bird populations. In addition, preservation alleviates the external costs that come with more development, such as pressure on roads, water supplies, and municipal services—and, inevitably, more pollution.

In this section we'll explore the topics of external benefits and positive externalities. They are, in many ways, the mirror images of external costs and negative externalities. Left to its own, the market will produce too little of a good (in this case, preserved New Jersey farmland) that confers external benefits on others. But society as a whole is better off when policies are adopted that increase the supply of such a good.

Preserved Farmland: An External Benefit

Preserved farmland yields both benefits and costs to society. In the absence of government intervention, the farmer who wants to sell his land incurs all the costs of preservation—namely, the forgone profit to be made from selling the farmland to a developer. But the benefits of preserved farmland accrue not to the farmer but to neighboring residents, who have no right to influence how the farmland is disposed of.

Figure 9-4 illustrates society's problem. The marginal social cost of preserved farmland, shown by the *MSC* curve, is the additional cost imposed on society by an additional acre of such farmland. This represents the forgone profits that would have accrued to farmers if they had sold their land to developers. The line is upward-sloping because when very few acres are preserved and there is plenty of land available for development, the profit that could be made from selling an acre to a developer is small. But as the number of preserved acres increases and few are left for development, the amount a developer is willing to pay for them, and therefore the forgone profit, increases as well.

The *MSB* curve represents the marginal social benefit of preserved farmland. It is the additional benefit that accrues to society—in this case, the farmer's neighbors—when an additional acre of farmland is preserved. The curve is downward sloping because as more farmland is preserved, the benefit to society of preserving another acre falls. As Figure 9-4 shows, the socially optimal point, *O*, occurs when the marginal social cost and the marginal social benefit are equalized—here, at a price of $10,000 per acre. At the socially optimum point, Q_{OPT} acres of farmland are preserved.

FIGURE 9-4 Why a Market Economy Preserves Too Little Farmland

Without government intervention, the quantity of preserved farmland will be zero, the level at which the marginal social cost of preservation is zero. This is an inefficiently low quantity of preserved farmland: the marginal social benefit is $20,000, but the marginal social cost is zero. An optimal Pigouvian subsidy of $10,000, the value of the marginal social benefit of preservation when it equals the marginal social cost, can move the market to the socially optimal level of preservation, Q_{OPT}.

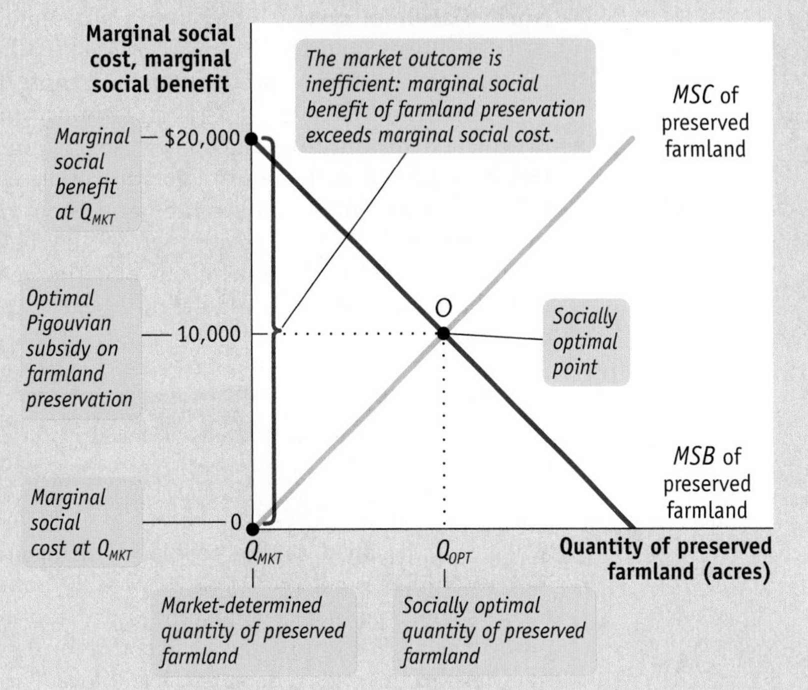

The market alone will not provide Q_{OPT} acres of preserved farmland. Instead, in the market outcome no acres will be preserved; the level of preserved farmland, Q_{MKT}, is equal to zero. That's because farmers will set the marginal social cost of preservation—their forgone profits—at zero and sell all their acres to developers. Because farmers bear the entire cost of preservation but gain none of the benefits, an inefficiently low quantity of acres will be preserved in the market outcome.

This is clearly inefficient because at zero acres preserved, the marginal social benefit of preserving an acre of farmland is $20,000. So how can the economy be induced to produce Q_{OPT} acres of preserved farmland, the socially optimal level? The answer is a **Pigouvian subsidy:** a payment designed to encourage activities that yield external benefits. The optimal Pigouvian subsidy, as shown in Figure 9-4, is equal to the marginal social benefit of preserved farmland at the socially optimal level, Q_{OPT}—that is, $10,000 per acre.

So New Jersey voters are indeed implementing the right policy to raise their social welfare—taxing themselves in order to provide subsidies for farmland preservation.

Positive Externalities in the Modern Economy

In the overall U.S. economy, the most important single source of external benefits is the creation of knowledge. In high-tech industries such as semiconductors, software design, green technology, and bioengineering, innovations by one firm are quickly emulated and improved upon by rival firms. Such spreading of knowledge across individuals and firms is known as a **technology spillover.** In the modern economy, the greatest sources of technology spillovers are major universities and research institutes.

In technologically advanced countries such as the United States, Japan, the United Kingdom, Germany, France, and Israel, there is an ongoing exchange of people and ideas among private industries, major universities, and research institutes located in close proximity. The dynamic interplay that occurs in these *research clusters* spurs innovation and competition, theoretical advances, and practical applications. (See the Business Case at the end of Part 4 for more on research clusters.)

A **Pigouvian subsidy** is a payment designed to encourage activities that yield external benefits.

A **technology spillover** is an external benefit that results when knowledge spreads among individuals and firms.

One of the best known and most successful research clusters is the Research Triangle in North Carolina, anchored by Duke University and the University of North Carolina, several other universities and hospitals, and companies such as IBM, Pfizer, and Qualcomm. Ultimately, these areas of technology spillover increase the economy's productivity and raise living standards.

But research clusters don't appear out of thin air. Except in a few instances in which firms have funded basic research on a long-term basis, research clusters have grown up around major universities. And like farmland preservation in New Jersey, major universities and their research activities are subsidized by government. In fact, government policy makers in advanced countries have long understood that the external benefits generated by knowledge, stemming from basic education to high-tech research, are key to the economy's growth over time.

ECONOMICS ➤ IN ACTION

THE IMPECCABLE ECONOMIC LOGIC OF EARLY-CHILDHOOD INTERVENTION PROGRAMS

One of the most vexing problems facing any society is how to break what researchers call the "cycle of poverty": children who grow up in disadvantaged socioeconomic circumstances are far more likely to remain trapped in poverty as adults, even after we account for differences in ability. They are more likely to be unemployed or underemployed, to engage in crime, and to suffer chronic health problems.

© Michael Newman/PhotoEdit

Early-childhood intervention programs focusing on education and health offer many external benefits to society.

Early-childhood intervention has offered some hope of breaking the cycle. A 2006 study by the RAND Corporation found that high-quality early-childhood programs that focus on education and health care lead to significant social, intellectual, and financial advantages for kids who would otherwise be at risk of dropping out of high school and of engaging in criminal behavior. Children in programs like Head Start were less likely to engage in such destructive behaviors and more likely to end up with a job and to earn a high salary later in life.

Another study by researchers at the University of Pittsburgh in 2003 looked at early-childhood intervention programs from a dollars-and-cents perspective, finding from $4 to $7 in benefits for every $1 spent on early-childhood intervention programs, while a RAND study put the figure as high as $17 per $1 spent. The Pittsburgh study also pointed to one program whose participants, by age 20, were 26% more likely to have finished high school, 35% less likely to have been charged in juvenile court, and 40% less likely to have repeated a grade compared to individuals of similar socioeconomic background who did not attend preschool.

The observed external benefits to society of these programs are so large that the Brookings Institution predicts that providing high-quality preschool education to every American child would result in an increase in GDP, the total value of a country's domestic output, by almost 2%, representing over 3 million more jobs.

▼ Quick Review

- When there are positive externalities, or external benefits, a market economy, left to itself, will typically produce too little of the good or activity. The socially optimal quantity of the good or activity can be achieved by an optimal **Pigouvian subsidy.**
- The most important example of external benefits in the economy is the creation of knowledge through **technology spillover.**

CHECK YOUR UNDERSTANDING 9-3

1. In 2012, the U.S. Department of Education spent over $40 billion on college student aid. Explain why this can be an optimal policy to encourage the creation of knowledge.

2. In each of the following cases, determine whether an external cost or an external benefit is imposed and what an appropriate policy response would be.
   a. Trees planted in urban areas improve air quality and lower summer temperatures.
   b. Water-saving toilets reduce the need to pump water from rivers and aquifers. The cost of a gallon of water to homeowners is virtually zero.
   c. Old computer monitors contain toxic materials that pollute the environment when improperly disposed of.

Solutions appear at back of book.

A good is **excludable** if the supplier of that good can prevent people who do not pay from consuming it.

A good is **rival in consumption** if the same unit of the good cannot be consumed by more than one person at the same time.

A good that is both excludable and rival in consumption is a **private good.**

When a good is **nonexcludable,** the supplier cannot prevent consumption by people who do not pay for it.

Public Goods

The opening story described the Great Stink of 1858, a negative externality created by individuals dumping waste into the Thames.

What the city needed, said reformers at the time, was a sewage system that would carry waste away from the river. Yet no private individual was willing to build such a system, and influential people were opposed to the idea that the government should take responsibility for the problem. For example, the magazine *The Economist* weighed in against proposals for a government-built sewage system, declaring that "suffering and evil are nature's admonitions—they cannot be got rid of."

As we saw in the story, Parliament approved a plan for an immense system of sewers and pumping stations with the result that cholera and typhoid epidemics, which had been regular occurrences, completely disappeared. The Thames was turned from the filthiest to the cleanest metropolitan river in the world, and the sewage system's principal engineer, Sir Joseph Bazalgette, was lauded as having "saved more lives than any single Victorian public official." It was estimated at the time that Bazalgette's sewer system added 20 years to the life span of the average Londoner.

So, what's the difference between installing a new bathroom in a house and building a municipal sewage system? What's the difference between growing wheat and fishing in the open ocean?

These aren't trick questions. In each case there is a basic difference in the characteristics of the goods involved. Bathroom fixtures and wheat have the characteristics necessary to allow markets to work efficiently. Public sewage systems and fish in the sea do not.

Let's look at these crucial characteristics and why they matter.

Characteristics of Goods

Goods like bathroom fixtures or wheat have two characteristics that, as we'll soon see, are essential if a good is to be efficiently provided by a market economy.

- They are **excludable:** suppliers of the good can prevent people who don't pay from consuming it.
- They are **rival in consumption:** the same unit of the good cannot be consumed by more than one person at the same time.

When a good is both excludable and rival in consumption, it is called a **private good.** Wheat is an example of a private good. It is *excludable*: the farmer can sell a bushel to one consumer without having to provide wheat to everyone in the county. And it is *rival in consumption*: if I eat bread baked with a farmer's wheat, that wheat cannot be consumed by someone else.

But not all goods possess these two characteristics. Some goods are **nonexcludable**—the supplier cannot prevent consumption of the good by people who do not pay for it. Fire protection is one example: a fire department that puts out fires before they spread protects the whole city, not just people who have made contributions to the Firemen's Benevolent Association. An improved environment is another: the city of London couldn't have ended the Great Stink for some residents while leaving the river Thames foul for others.

FIGURE 9-5 Four Types of Goods

	Rival in consumption	Nonrival in consumption
Excludable	**Private goods** • Wheat • Bathroom fixtures	**Artificially scarce goods** • On-demand movies • Computer software
Non-excludable	**Common resources** • Clean water • Biodiversity	**Public goods** • Public sanitation • National defense

There are four types of goods. The type of a good depends on (1) whether or not it is excludable—whether a producer can prevent someone from consuming it; and (2) whether or not it is rival in consumption—whether it is impossible for the same unit of a good to be consumed by more than one person at the same time.

Nor are all goods rival in consumption. Goods are **nonrival in consumption** if more than one person can consume the same unit of the good at the same time. TV programs are nonrival in consumption: your decision to watch a show does not prevent other people from watching the same show.

Because goods can be either excludable or nonexcludable, rival or nonrival in consumption, there are four types of goods, illustrated by the matrix in Figure 9-5:

- *Private goods,* which are excludable and rival in consumption, like wheat
- *Public goods,* which are nonexcludable and nonrival in consumption, like a public sewer system
- *Common resources,* which are nonexcludable but rival in consumption, like clean water in a river
- *Artificially scarce goods,* which are excludable but nonrival in consumption, like on-demand movies on DirecTV

There are, of course, many other characteristics that distinguish between types of goods—necessities versus luxuries, normal versus inferior, and so on. Why focus on whether goods are excludable and rival in consumption?

Why Markets Can Supply Only Private Goods Efficiently

As we learned in earlier chapters, markets are typically the best means for a society to deliver goods and services to its members; that is, markets are efficient except in the case of the well-defined problems of market power, externalities, or other instances of market failure. But there is yet another condition that must be met, one rooted in the nature of the good itself: markets cannot supply goods and services efficiently unless they are private goods—excludable and rival in consumption.

To see why excludability is crucial, suppose that a farmer had only two choices: either produce no wheat or provide a bushel of wheat to every resident of the county who wants it, whether or not that resident pays for it. It seems unlikely that anyone would grow wheat under those conditions.

Yet the operator of a municipal sewage system faces pretty much the same problem as our hypothetical farmer. A sewage system makes the whole city cleaner and healthier—but that benefit accrues to all the city's residents, whether or not they pay the system operator. That's why no private entrepreneur came forward with a plan to end London's Great Stink.

The general point is that if a good is nonexcludable, self-interested consumers won't be willing to pay for it—they will take a "free ride" on anyone who *does* pay. So there is a **free-rider problem.** Examples of the free-rider problem are familiar from daily life. One example you may have encountered happens when students are required to do a group project. There is often a tendency of some group members to shirk, relying on others in the group to get the work done. The shirkers *free-ride* on someone else's effort.

A good is **nonrival in consumption** if more than one person can consume the same unit of the good at the same time.

Goods that are nonexcludable suffer from the **free-rider problem:** many individuals are unwilling to pay for their own consumption and instead will take a "free ride" on anyone who does pay.

Because of the free-rider problem, the forces of self-interest alone do not lead to an efficient level of production for a nonexcludable good. Even though consumers would benefit from increased production of the good, no one individual is willing to pay for more, and so no producer is willing to supply it. The result is that nonexcludable goods suffer from *inefficiently low production* in a market economy. In fact, in the face of the free-rider problem, self-interest may not ensure that any amount of the good—let alone the efficient quantity—is produced.

Goods that are excludable and nonrival in consumption, like on-demand movies, suffer from a different kind of inefficiency. As long as a good is excludable, it is possible to earn a profit by making it available only to those who pay. Therefore, producers are willing to supply an excludable good. But the marginal cost of letting an additional viewer watch an on-demand movie is zero because it is nonrival in consumption. So the efficient price to the consumer is also zero—or, to put it another way, individuals should watch movies up to the point where their marginal benefit is zero.

But if DirecTV actually charges viewers $4, viewers will consume the good only up to the point where their marginal benefit is $4. When consumers must pay a price greater than zero for a good that is nonrival in consumption, the price they pay is higher than the marginal cost of allowing them to consume that good, which is zero. So in a market economy goods that are nonrival in consumption suffer from *inefficiently low consumption.*

Now we can see why private goods are the only goods that can be efficiently produced and consumed in a competitive market. (That is, a private good will be efficiently produced and consumed in a market free of market power, externalities, or other instances of market failure.) Because private goods are excludable, producers can charge for them and so have an incentive to produce them. And because they are also rival in consumption, it is efficient for consumers to pay a positive price—a price equal to the marginal cost of production. If one or both of these characteristics are lacking, a market economy will not lead to efficient production and consumption of the good.

Fortunately for the market system, most goods are private goods. Food, clothing, shelter, and most other desirable things in life are excludable and rival in consumption, so markets can provide us with most things. Yet there are crucial goods that don't meet these criteria—and in most cases, that means that the government must step in.

PITFALLS

MARGINAL COST OF WHAT EXACTLY?
In the case of a good that is nonrival in consumption, it's easy to confuse the marginal cost of *producing* a unit of the good with the marginal cost of *allowing* a unit of the good *to be consumed.* For example, DirecTV incurs a marginal cost in making a movie available to its subscribers that is equal to the cost of the resources it uses to produce and broadcast that movie. However, *once that movie is being broadcast,* no marginal cost is incurred by letting an additional family watch it. In other words, no costly resources are "used up" when one more family consumes a movie that has already been produced and is being broadcast.

This complication does not arise, however, when a good is rival in consumption. In that case, the resources used to produce a unit of the good are "used up" by a person's consumption of it—they are no longer available to satisfy someone else's consumption. So when a good is rival in consumption, the marginal cost to society of allowing an individual to consume a unit is equal to the resource cost of producing that unit—that is, equal to the marginal cost of producing it.

Providing Public Goods

A **public good** is the exact opposite of a private good: it is a good that is both nonexcludable and nonrival in consumption. A public sewer system is an example of a public good: you can't keep a river clean without making it clean for everyone who lives near its banks, and my protection from great stinks does not come at my neighbor's expense.

Here are some other examples of public goods:

- *Disease prevention.* When doctors act to stamp out the beginnings of an epidemic before it can spread, they protect people around the world.
- *National defense.* A strong military protects all citizens.
- *Scientific research.* More knowledge benefits everyone.

Because these goods are nonexcludable, they suffer from the free-rider problem, so no private firm would be willing to produce them. And because they are nonrival in consumption, it would be inefficient to charge people for consuming them. As a result, society must find nonmarket methods for providing these goods.

Public goods are provided through a variety of means. The government doesn't always get involved—in many cases a nongovernmental solution has been found for the free-rider problem. But these solutions are usually imperfect in some way.

A **public good** is both nonexcludable and nonrival in consumption.

Some public goods are supplied through voluntary contributions. For example, private donations support a considerable amount of scientific research. But private donations are insufficient to finance huge, socially important projects like basic medical research.

Some public goods are supplied by self-interested individuals or firms because those who produce them are able to make money in an indirect way. The classic example is broadcast television, which in the United States is supported entirely by advertising. The downside of such indirect funding is that it skews the nature and quantity of the public goods that are supplied, as well as imposing additional costs on consumers. TV stations show the programs that yield the most advertising revenue (that is, programs best suited for selling prescription drugs, hair-loss remedies, antihistamines, and the like to the segment of the population that buys them), which are not necessarily the programs people most want to see. And viewers must also endure many commercials.

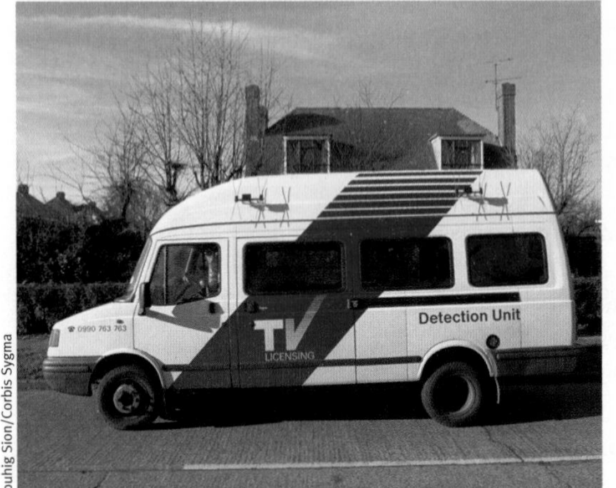

Touhig Sion/Corbis Sygma

On the prowl: a British TV detection van at work.

Some potentially public goods are deliberately made excludable and therefore subject to charge, like on-demand movies. In the United Kingdom, where most television programming is paid for by a yearly license fee assessed on every television owner (£145.50, or about $233 in 2012), television viewing is made artificially excludable by the use of "television detection vans": vans that roam neighborhoods in an attempt to detect televisions in nonlicensed households and fine them. However, as noted earlier, when suppliers charge a price greater than zero for a nonrival good, consumers will consume an inefficiently low quantity of that good.

In small communities, a high level of social encouragement or pressure can be brought to bear on people to contribute money or time to provide the efficient level of a public good. Volunteer fire departments, which depend both on the volunteered services of the firefighters themselves and on contributions from local residents, are a good example. But as communities grow larger and more anonymous, social pressure is increasingly difficult to apply, compelling larger towns and cities to tax residents to provide salaried firefighters for fire protection services.

As this last example suggests, when these other solutions fail, it is up to the government to provide public goods. Indeed, the most important public goods—national defense, the legal system, disease control, fire protection in large cities, and so on—are provided by government and paid for by taxes. Economic theory tells us that the provision of public goods is one of the crucial roles of government.

How Much of a Public Good Should Be Provided?

In some cases, provision of a public good is an "either–or" decision: London would either have a sewage system—or not. But in most cases, governments must decide not only whether to provide a public good but also *how much* of that public good to provide. For example, street cleaning is a public good—but how often should the streets be cleaned? Once a month? Twice a month? Every other day?

Imagine a city in which there are only two residents, Ted and Alice. Assume that the public good in question is street cleaning and that Ted and Alice truthfully tell the government how much they value a unit of the public good, where a unit is equal to one street cleaning per month. Specifically, each of them tells the government *his or her willingness to pay for another unit of the public good supplied*—an amount that corresponds to that *individual's marginal benefit* of another unit of the public good.

Using this information plus information on the cost of providing the good, the government can use marginal analysis to find the efficient level of providing the public good: the level at which the *marginal social benefit* of the public good is equal to the marginal cost of producing it. Recall from the first section of this chapter that the marginal social benefit of a good is the benefit that accrues to society as a whole from the consumption of one additional unit of the good.

But what is the marginal social benefit of another unit of a public good—a unit that generates utility for *all* consumers, not just one consumer, because it is nonexcludable and nonrival in consumption? This question leads us to an important principle: *In the special case of a public good, the marginal social benefit of a unit of the good is equal to the sum of the individual marginal benefits that are enjoyed by all consumers of that unit.* Or to consider it from a slightly different angle, if a consumer could be compelled to pay for a unit before consuming it (the good is made excludable), then the marginal social benefit of a unit is equal to the *sum* of each consumer's willingness to pay for that unit. Using this principle, the marginal social benefit of an additional street cleaning per month is equal to Ted's individual marginal benefit from that additional cleaning *plus* Alice's individual marginal benefit.

Why? Because a public good is nonrival in consumption—Ted's benefit from a cleaner street does not diminish Alice's benefit from that same clean street, and vice versa. Because people can all simultaneously consume the same unit of a public good, the marginal social benefit of an additional unit of that good is the *sum* of the individual marginal benefits of all who enjoy the public good. And the efficient quantity of a public good is the quantity at which the marginal social benefit is equal to the marginal cost of providing it.

Figure 9-6 illustrates the efficient provision of a public good, showing three marginal benefit curves. Panel (a) shows Ted's individual marginal benefit curve from street cleaning, MB_T: he would be willing to pay \$25 for the city to clean its streets once a month, an additional \$18 to have it done a second time, and so on. Panel (b) shows Alice's individual marginal benefit curve from street cleaning, MB_A. Panel (c) shows the marginal social benefit curve from street cleaning, *MSB:* it is the vertical sum of Ted's and Alice's individual marginal benefit curves, MB_T and MB_A.

To maximize society's welfare, the government should clean the street up to the level at which the marginal social benefit of an additional cleaning is no longer greater than the marginal cost. Suppose that the marginal cost of street cleaning is \$6 per cleaning. Then the city should clean its streets 5 times per month, because the marginal social benefit of going from 4 to 5 cleanings is \$8, but going from 5 to 6 cleanings would yield a marginal social benefit of only \$2.

Figure 9-6 can help reinforce our understanding of why we cannot rely on individual self-interest to yield provision of an efficient quantity of public goods. Suppose that the city did one fewer street cleaning than the efficient quantity and that either Ted or Alice was asked to pay for the last cleaning. Neither one would be willing to pay for it! Ted would personally gain only the equivalent of \$3 in utility from adding one more street cleaning—so he wouldn't be willing to pay the \$6 marginal cost of another cleaning. Alice would personally gain the equivalent of \$5 in utility—so she wouldn't be willing to pay either. The point is that the marginal social benefit of one more unit of a public good is always greater than the individual marginal benefit to any one individual. That is why no individual is willing to pay for the efficient quantity of the good.

Does this description of the public-good problem, in which the marginal social benefit of an additional unit of the public good is greater than any individual's marginal benefit, sound a bit familiar? It should: we encountered a somewhat similar situation in our discussion of *positive externalities.* Remember that in the case of a positive externality, the marginal social benefit accruing to all consumers of another unit of the good is greater than the price that the producer receives for that unit; as a result, the market produces too little of

FIGURE 9-6 A Public Good

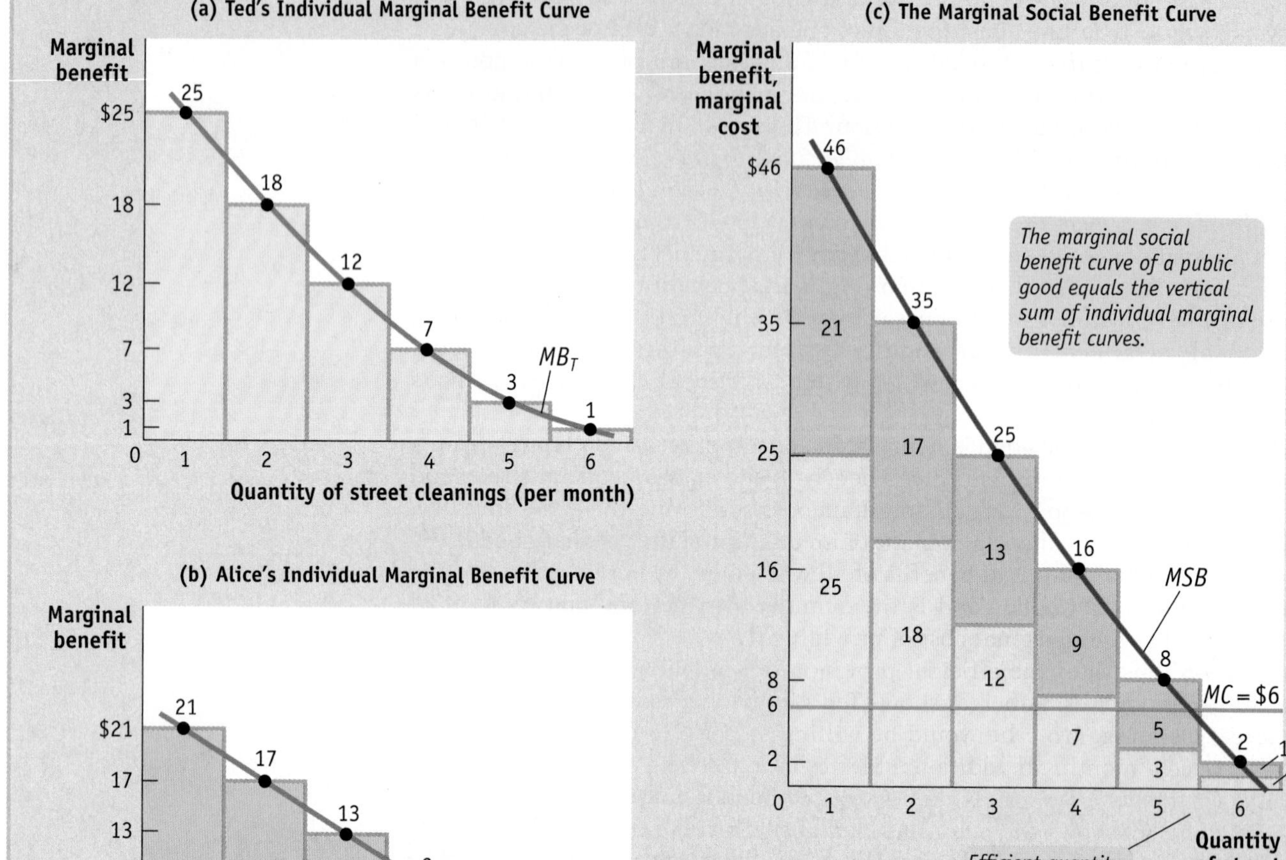

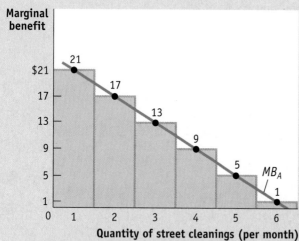

Panel (a) shows Ted's individual marginal benefit curve of street cleanings per month, MB_T, and panel (b) shows Alice's individual marginal benefit curve, MB_A. Panel (c) shows the marginal social benefit of the public good, equal to the sum of the individual marginal benefits to all consumers (in this case, Ted and Alice). The marginal social benefit curve, *MSB*, is the vertical sum of the individual marginal benefit curves MB_T and MB_A. At a constant marginal cost of $6, there should be 5 street cleanings per month, because the marginal social benefit of going from 4 to 5 cleanings is $8 ($3 for Ted plus $5 for Alice), but the marginal social benefit of going from 5 to 6 cleanings is only $2.

the good. In the case of a public good, the individual marginal benefit of a consumer plays the same role as the price received by the producer in the case of positive externalities: both cases create insufficient incentive to provide an efficient amount of the good.

The problem of providing public goods is very similar to the problem of dealing with positive externalities; in both cases there is a market failure that calls for government intervention. One basic rationale for the existence of government is that it provides a way for citizens to tax themselves in order to provide public goods—particularly a vital public good like national defense.

Of course, if society really consisted of only two individuals, they would probably manage to strike a deal to provide the good. But imagine a city with a million residents, each of whose individual marginal benefit from provision of the good is only a tiny fraction of the marginal social benefit. It would be impossible for people to reach a voluntary agreement to pay for the efficient level of street cleaning—the potential for free-riding makes it too difficult to make and enforce an agreement among so many people. But they could and would vote to tax themselves to pay for a citywide sanitation department.

Cost-benefit analysis is the estimation and comparison of the social costs and social benefits of providing a public good.

Cost-Benefit Analysis

How do governments decide in practice how much of a public good to provide? Sometimes policy makers just guess—or do whatever they think will get them reelected. However, responsible governments try to estimate and compare both the social benefits and the social costs of providing a public good, a process known as **cost-benefit analysis.**

It's straightforward to estimate the cost of supplying a public good. Estimating the benefit is harder. In fact, it is a very difficult problem.

Now you might wonder why governments can't figure out the marginal social benefit of a public good just by asking people their willingness to pay for it (their individual marginal benefit). But it turns out that it's hard to get an honest answer.

This is not a problem with private goods: we can determine how much an individual is willing to pay for one more unit of a private good by looking at his or her actual choices. But because people don't actually pay for public goods, the question of willingness to pay is always hypothetical.

Worse yet, it's a question that people have an incentive not to answer truthfully. People naturally want more rather than less. Because they cannot be made to pay for whatever quantity of the public good they use, people are apt to overstate their true feelings when asked how much they desire a public good. For example, if street cleaning were scheduled according to the stated wishes of homeowners alone, the streets would be cleaned every day—an inefficient level of provision.

So governments must be aware that they cannot simply rely on the public's statements when deciding how much of a public good to provide—if they do, they are likely to provide too much. In contrast, relying on the public to indicate how much of the public good they want through voting has problems as well—and is likely to lead to too little of the public good being provided.

ECONOMICS ➤ IN ACTION

OLD MAN RIVER

It just keeps rolling along—but now and then it decides to roll in a different direction. In fact, the Mississippi River changes its course every few hundred years. Sediment carried downstream gradually clogs the river's route to the sea, and eventually the river breaches its banks and opens a new channel. Over the millennia, the mouth of the Mississippi has swung back and forth along an arc some 200 miles wide.

So when is the Mississippi due to change course again? Oh, about 40 years ago.

The Mississippi currently runs to the sea past New Orleans; but by 1950 it was apparent that the river was about to shift course, taking a new route to the sea. If the Army Corps of Engineers hadn't gotten involved, the shift would probably have happened by 1970.

A shift in the Mississippi would have severely damaged the Louisiana economy. A major industrial area would have lost good

Jim Wark/Air Photo

The Old River Control Structure helps to keep the Mississippi on course.

access to the ocean, and salt water would have contaminated much of its water supply. So the Army Corps of Engineers has kept the Mississippi in its place with a huge complex of dams, walls, and gates known as the Old River Control Structure. At times the amount of water released by this control structure is five times the flow at Niagara Falls.

The Old River Control Structure is a dramatic example of a public good. No individual would have had an incentive to build it, yet it protects many billions of dollars' worth of private property. The history of the Army Corps of Engineers, which handles water-control projects across the United States, illustrates a persistent problem associated with government provision of public goods. That is, everyone wants a project that benefits his or her own property—if other people are going to pay for it. So there is a systematic tendency for potential beneficiaries of Corps projects to overstate the benefits. And the Corps has become notorious for undertaking expensive projects that cannot be justified with any reasonable cost-benefit analysis.

The flip-side of the problem of overfunding of public projects is chronic underfunding. A tragic illustration of this problem was the devastation of New Orleans by Hurricane Katrina in 2005.

Although it was well understood from the time of its founding that New Orleans was at risk for severe flooding because it sits below sea level, very little was done to shore up the crucial system of levees and pumps that protects the city. More than 50 years of inadequate funding for construction and maintenance, coupled with inadequate supervision, left the system weakened and unable to cope with the onslaught from Katrina. The catastrophe was compounded by the failure of local and state government to develop an evacuation plan in the event of a hurricane. In the end, because of this neglect of a public good, 1,464 people in and around New Orleans lost their lives and the city suffered economic losses totaling billions of dollars.

▼ Quick Review

- Goods can be classified according to two attributes: whether they are **excludable** and whether they are **rival in consumption.**
- Goods that are both excludable and rival in consumption are **private goods.** Private goods can be efficiently produced and consumed in a competitive market.
- When goods are **nonexcludable,** there is a **free-rider problem:** consumers will not pay producers, leading to inefficiently low production.
- When goods are **nonrival in consumption,** the efficient price for consumption is zero.
- A **public good** is both nonexcludable and nonrival in consumption.
- Although governments should rely on **cost-benefit analysis** to determine how much of a public good to supply, doing so is problematic because individuals tend to overstate the good's value to them.

CHECK YOUR UNDERSTANDING 9-4

1. Classify each of the following goods according to whether they are excludable and whether they are rival in consumption. What kind of good is each?
   a. Use of a public space such as a park
   b. A cheese burrito
   c. Information from a website that is password-protected
   d. Publicly announced information on the path of an incoming hurricane
2. The town of Centreville, population 16, has two types of residents, Homebodies and Revelers. Using the accompanying table, the town must decide how much to spend on its New Year's Eve party. No individual resident expects to directly bear the cost of the party.
   a. Suppose there are 10 Homebodies and 6 Revelers. Determine the marginal social benefit schedule of money spent on the party. What is the efficient level of spending?
   b. Suppose there are 6 Homebodies and 10 Revelers. How do your answers to part a change? Explain.
   c. Suppose that the individual marginal benefit schedules are known but no one knows the true proportion of Homebodies versus Revelers. Individuals are asked their preferences. What is the likely outcome if each person assumes that others will pay for any additional amount of the public good? Why is it likely to result in an inefficiently high level of spending? Explain.

Money spent on party	Individual marginal benefit of additional $1 spent on party	
	Homebody	Reveler
$0		
	$0.05	$0.13
1		
	0.04	0.11
2		
	0.03	0.09
3		
	0.02	0.07
4		

Solutions appear at back of book.

WORKED PROBLEM

Reducing Greenhouse Gases

In July 2009, the House of Representatives passed the American Clean Energy and Security Act. Part of the bill provides for a cap and trade program for greenhouse gases. In a cap and trade program, the government sets a legal limit (a cap) on the amount of pollutant that can be emitted. In order to identify the cap, the government should apply the principle of marginal analysis, setting the marginal social cost of pollution equal to the marginal social benefit of pollution. But how can pollution have a marginal social benefit?

As we saw earlier in the chapter, avoiding pollution requires using scarce resources that could have been used to produce other goods and services. Take the example of carbon dioxide. The more carbon dioxide factories are allowed to emit, the lower the extra costs imposed on these companies in terms of installing special equipment to reduce those emissions. The social benefit from pollution is the money that does not have to be spent on reducing it. Generally, the costs of reducing pollution decrease with the amount of pollution that is allowed, so the marginal social benefit decreases as pollution increases. Suppose that scientists have estimated the marginal social costs and marginal social benefits of carbon dioxide emissions. The table below shows these costs at various levels of emissions.

Marginal Social Cost and Benefit of Carbon Dioxide Emissions

Quantity of carbon dioxide emissions (millions of tons)	Marginal social benefit ($ per ton)	Marginal social cost ($ per ton)
0	$800	$ 0
1	720	80
2	640	160
3	560	240
4	480	320
5	400	400
6	320	480
7	240	560
8	160	640
9	80	720
10	0	800

Graph the marginal social cost and marginal social benefit of carbon dioxide emissions. What is the market-determined quantity of emissions? What is the social gain from reducing the market-determined quantity of emissions by one ton?

STEP 1: Draw and label marginal social benefit and marginal social cost curves. Find the optimal level of pollution.

Review the section "Costs and Benefits of Pollution" on pp. 276–277. Label the x-axis the "quantity of carbon dioxide emissions," and label the y-axis "marginal social cost, marginal social benefit," as in Figure 9-1. At each level of carbon dioxide emissions, graph the corresponding marginal social benefit of emissions and the corresponding marginal social cost of emissions. Find the point where the two curves intersect.

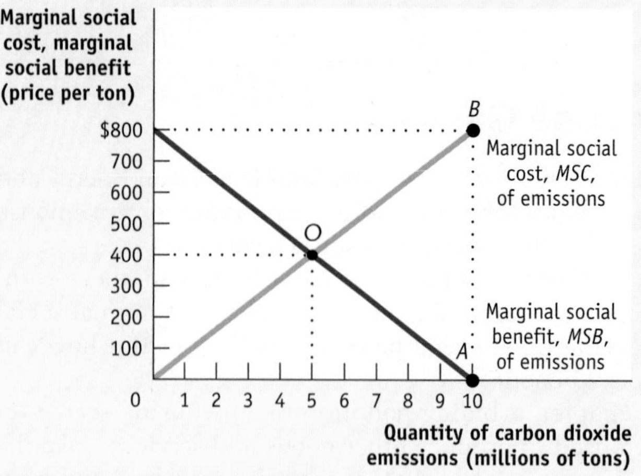

The optimal social quantity of pollution is at the point where the marginal social benefit of polluting equals the marginal social cost of polluting. As shown in the accompanying figure, this occurs at point O, the intersection of the marginal social cost curve and the marginal social benefit curve. At point O, the optimal quantity of emissions is 5 million tons and the marginal social benefit of emissions, which equals the marginal social cost of emissions, is $400 per ton. ■

STEP 2: Find the market-determined quantity of pollution.

Review the section "Pollution: An External Cost" on pp. 277–279. In a market economy without government intervention to protect the environment, only the benefits of pollution are taken into account. Polluters will continue to pollute until there are no further benefits—when the marginal benefit of polluting is zero.

The market-determined quantity of pollution will be at the point where the marginal benefits to polluters are zero. As there are no marginal social benefits to pollution beyond the cost savings realized by the polluters themselves, the market-determined quantity will be at the point where the marginal social benefit of pollution is zero. This occurs at a carbon dioxide emissions level of 10 million tons, as shown at point A on the figure. ■

STEP 3: Find the social gain from reducing the quantity of pollution by one ton from the market-determined level.

Review the section "The Inefficiency of Excess Pollution" on p. 279. Find the marginal social cost of a ton of emissions at 10 million tons. Find the marginal social benefit of a ton of emissions at 10 million tons. The difference between these two numbers is the social gain.

Moving up from point A to point B in the figure, we can see that the marginal social cost of polluting at the market-determined level of 10 million tons is high at $800 per ton. The marginal social benefit at point A is zero. As the marginal cost per ton of polluting at a level of 10 million tons is $800 per ton and the marginal social benefit per ton of polluting at that level is zero, reducing the quantity of pollution by one ton leads to a net gain in total surplus of approximately $800 – 0 = $800. ■

SUMMARY

1. When pollution can be directly observed and controlled, government policies should be geared directly to producing the **socially optimal quantity of pollution,** the quantity at which the **marginal social cost of pollution** is equal to the **marginal social benefit of pollution.** In the absence of government intervention, a market produces too much pollution because polluters take only their benefit from polluting into account, not the costs imposed on others.
2. The costs to society of pollution are an example of an **external cost;** in some cases, however, economic activities yield **external benefits.** External costs and benefits are jointly known as **externalities,** with external costs called **negative externalities** and external benefits called **positive externalities.**
3. According to the **Coase theorem,** individuals can find a way to **internalize the externality,** making government intervention unnecessary, as long as **transaction costs**—the costs of making a deal—are sufficiently low. However, in many cases transaction costs are too high to permit such deals.
4. Governments often deal with pollution by imposing **environmental standards,** a method, economists argue, that is usually an inefficient way to reduce pollution. Two efficient (cost-minimizing) methods for reducing pollution are **emissions taxes,** a form of **Pigouvian tax,** and **tradable emissions permits.** The optimal Pigouvian tax on pollution is equal to its marginal social cost at the socially optimal quantity of pollution. These methods also provide incentives for the creation and adoption of production technologies that cause less pollution.
5. When a good or activity yields external benefits, or positive externalities, such as **technology spillovers,** then an optimal **Pigouvian subsidy** to producers moves the market to the socially optimal quantity of production.
6. Goods may be classified according to whether or not they are **excludable** and whether or not they are **rival in consumption.**
7. Free markets can deliver efficient levels of production and consumption for **private goods,** which are both excludable and rival in consumption. When goods are nonexcludable or nonrival in consumption, or both, free markets cannot achieve efficient outcomes.
8. When goods are **nonexcludable,** there is a **free-rider problem:** some consumers will not pay for the good, consuming what others have paid for and leading to inefficiently low production. When goods are **nonrival in consumption,** they should be free, and any positive price leads to inefficiently low consumption.
9. A **public good** is nonexcludable and nonrival in consumption. In most cases a public good must be supplied by the government. The marginal social benefit of a public good is equal to the sum of the individual marginal benefits to each consumer. The efficient quantity of a public good is the quantity at which marginal social benefit equals the marginal cost of providing the good. Like a positive externality, marginal social benefit is greater than any one individual's marginal benefit, so no individual is willing to provide the efficient quantity.
10. One rationale for the presence of government is that it allows citizens to tax themselves in order to provide public goods. Governments use **cost-benefit analysis** to determine the efficient provision of a public good. Such analysis is difficult, however, because individuals have an incentive to overstate the good's value to them.

KEY TERMS

PROBLEMS

1. What type of externality (positive or negative) is present in each of the following examples? Is the marginal social benefit of the activity greater than or equal to the marginal benefit to the individual? Is the marginal social cost of the activity greater than or equal to the marginal cost to the individual? Without intervention, will there be too little or too much (relative to what would be socially optimal) of this activity?
   a. Mr. Chau plants lots of colorful flowers in his front yard.
   b. Your next-door neighbor likes to build bonfires in his backyard, and sparks often drift onto your house.
   c. Maija, who lives next to an apple orchard, decides to keep bees to produce honey.
   d. Justine buys a large SUV that consumes a lot of gasoline.

2. The loud music coming from the sorority next to your dorm is a negative externality that can be directly quantified. The accompanying table shows the marginal social benefit and the marginal social cost per decibel (dB, a measure of volume) of music.

Volume of music (dB)	Marginal social benefit of dB	Marginal social cost of dB
90		
	$36	$0
91		
	30	2
92		
	24	4
93		
	18	6
94		
	12	8
95		
	6	10
96		
	0	12
97		

   a. Draw the marginal social benefit curve and the marginal social cost curve. Use your diagram to determine the socially optimal volume of music.
   b. Only the members of the sorority benefit from the music, and they bear none of the cost. Which volume of music will they choose?
   c. The college imposes a Pigouvian tax of $3 per decibel of music played. From your diagram, determine the volume of music the sorority will now choose.

3. Many dairy farmers in California are adopting a new technology that allows them to produce their own electricity from methane gas captured from animal wastes. (One cow can produce up to 2 kilowatts a day.) This practice reduces the amount of methane gas released into the atmosphere. In addition to reducing their own utility bills, the farmers are allowed to sell any electricity they produce at favorable rates.
   a. Explain how the ability to earn money from capturing and transforming methane gas behaves like a Pigouvian tax on methane gas pollution and can lead dairy farmers to emit the efficient amount of methane gas pollution.
   b. Suppose some dairy farmers have lower costs of transforming methane into electricity than others. Explain how this system leads to an efficient allocation of emissions reduction among farmers.

4. According to a report from the U.S. Census Bureau, "the average [lifetime] earnings of a full-time, year round worker with a high school education are about $1.2 million compared with $2.1 million for a college graduate." This indicates that there is a considerable benefit to a graduate from investing in his or her own education. Tuition at most state universities covers only about two-thirds to three-quarters of the cost, so the state applies a Pigouvian subsidy to college education.
   If a Pigouvian subsidy is appropriate, is the externality created by a college education a positive or a negative externality? What does this imply about the differences between the costs and benefits to students compared to social costs and benefits? What are some reasons for the differences?

5. The city of Falls Church, Virginia, subsidizes trees planted in homeowners' front yards when they are within 15 feet of the street.
   a. Using concepts in the chapter, explain why a municipality would subsidize trees planted on private property, but near the street.
   b. Draw a diagram similar to Figure 9-4 that shows the marginal social benefit, the marginal social cost, and the optimal Pigouvian subsidy on trees.

6. Fishing for sablefish has been so intensive that sablefish were threatened with extinction. After several years of banning such fishing, the government is now proposing to introduce tradable vouchers, each of which entitles its holder to a catch of a certain size. Explain how fishing generates a negative externality and how the voucher scheme may overcome the inefficiency created by this externality.

7. The two dry-cleaning companies in Collegetown, College Cleaners and Big Green Cleaners, are a major source of air pollution. Together they currently produce 350 units of air pollution, which the town wants to reduce to 200 units. The accompanying table shows the current pollution level produced by each company and each company's marginal cost of reducing its pollution. The marginal cost is constant.

Companies	Initial pollution level (units)	Marginal cost of reducing pollution (per unit)
College Cleaners	230	$5
Big Green Cleaners	120	$2

a. Suppose that Collegetown passes an environmental standards law that limits each company to 100 units of pollution. What would be the total cost to the two companies of each reducing its pollution emissions to 100 units?

Suppose instead that Collegetown issues 100 pollution vouchers to each company, each entitling the company to one unit of pollution, and that these vouchers can be traded.

b. How much is each pollution voucher worth to College Cleaners? To Big Green Cleaners? (That is, how much would each company, at most, be willing to pay for one more voucher?)

c. Who will sell vouchers and who will buy them? How many vouchers will be traded?

d. What is the total cost to the two companies of the pollution controls under this voucher system?

8. The government is involved in providing many goods and services. For each of the goods or services listed, determine whether it is rival or nonrival in consumption and whether it is excludable or nonexcludable. What type of good is it? Without government involvement, would the quantity provided be efficient, inefficiently low, or inefficiently high?

a. Street signs

b. Amtrak rail service

c. Regulations limiting pollution

d. A congested interstate highway without tolls

e. A lighthouse on the coast

9. An economist gives the following advice to a museum director: "You should introduce 'peak pricing.' At times when the museum has few visitors, you should admit visitors for free. And at times when the museum has many visitors, you should charge a higher admission fee."

a. When the museum is quiet, is it rival or nonrival in consumption? Is it excludable or nonexcludable? What type of good is the museum at those times? What would be the efficient price to charge visitors during that time, and why?

b. When the museum is busy, is it rival or nonrival in consumption? Is it excludable or nonexcludable? What type of good is the museum at those times? What would be the efficient price to charge visitors during that time, and why?

10. In many planned communities, various aspects of community living are subject to regulation by a homeowners' association. These rules can regulate house architecture; require snow removal from sidewalks; exclude outdoor equipment, such as backyard swimming pools; require appropriate conduct in shared spaces such as the community clubhouse; and so on. Suppose there has been some conflict in one such community because some homeowners feel that some of the regulations mentioned above are overly intrusive. You have been called in to mediate. Using what you have learned about public goods and common resources, how would you decide what types of regulations are warranted and what types are not?

11. A residential community has 100 residents who are concerned about security. The accompanying table gives the total cost of hiring a 24-hour security service as well as each individual resident's total benefit.

Quantity of security guards	Total cost	Total individual benefit to each resident
0	$0	$0
1	150	10
2	300	16
3	450	18
4	600	19

a. Explain why the security service is a public good for the residents of the community.

b. Calculate the marginal cost, the individual marginal benefit for each resident, and the marginal social benefit.

c. If an individual resident were to decide about hiring and paying for security guards on his or her own, how many guards would that resident hire?

d. If the residents act together, how many security guards will they hire?

12. The accompanying table shows Tanisha's and Ari's individual marginal benefit of different amounts of street cleanings per month. Suppose that the marginal cost of street cleanings is constant at $9 each.

Quantity of street cleanings per month	Tanisha's individual marginal benefit	Ari's individual marginal benefit
0		
	$10	$8
1		
	6	4
2		
	2	1
3		

a. If Tanisha had to pay for street cleaning on her own, how many street cleanings would there be?

b. Calculate the marginal social benefit of street cleaning. What is the optimal number of street cleanings?

c. Consider the optimal number of street cleanings. The last street cleaning of that number costs $9. Is Tanisha willing to pay for that last cleaning on her own? Is Ari willing to pay for that last cleaning on his own?

EXTEND YOUR UNDERSTANDING

13. Voluntary environmental programs were extremely popular in the United States, Europe, and Japan in the 1990s. Part of their popularity stems from the fact that these programs do not require legislative authority, which is often hard to obtain. The 33/50 program started by the Environmental Protection Agency (EPA) is an example of such a program. With this program, the EPA attempted to reduce industrial emissions of 17 toxic chemicals by providing information on relatively inexpensive methods of pollution control. Companies were asked to voluntarily commit to reducing emissions from their 1988 levels by 33% by 1992 and by 50% by 1995. The program actually met its second target by 1994.

a. As in Figure 9-3, draw marginal benefit curves for pollution generated by two plants, A and B, in 1988. Assume that without government intervention, each plant emits the same amount of pollution, but that at all levels of pollution less than this amount, plant A's marginal benefit of polluting is less than that of plant B. Label the vertical axis "Marginal benefit to individual polluter" and the horizontal axis "Quantity of pollution emissions." Mark the quantity of pollution each plant produces without government action.

b. Do you expect the total quantity of pollution before the program was put in place to have been less than or more than the optimal quantity of pollution? Why?

c. Suppose the plants whose marginal benefit curves you depicted in part a were participants in the 33/50 program. In a replica of your graph from part a, mark targeted levels of pollution in 1995 for the two plants. Which plant was required to reduce emissions more? Was this solution necessarily efficient?

d. What kind of environmental policy does the 33/50 program most closely resemble? What is the main shortcoming of such a policy? Compare it to two other types of environmental policy discussed in this chapter.

14. In developing a vaccine for the SARS virus, a pharmaceutical company incurs a very high fixed cost. The marginal cost of delivering the vaccine to patients, however, is negligible (consider it to be equal to zero). The pharmaceutical company holds the exclusive patent to the vaccine. You are a regulator who must decide what price the pharmaceutical company is allowed to charge.

a. Draw a diagram that shows the price for the vaccine that would arise if the company is unregulated, and label it P_M. What is the efficient price for the vaccine? Show the deadweight loss that arises from the price P_M.

b. On another diagram, show the lowest price that the regulator can enforce that would still induce the pharmaceutical company to develop the vaccine. Label it P^*. Show the deadweight loss that arises from this price. How does it compare to the deadweight loss that arises from the price P_M?

c. Suppose you have accurate information about the pharmaceutical company's fixed cost. How could you use price regulation of the pharmaceutical company, combined with a subsidy to the company, to have the efficient quantity of the vaccine provided at the lowest cost to the government?

BUSINESS CASE • Virgin Atlantic Blows the Whistle . . . or Blows It?

Carl Court/AFP/Getty Images

Ian Waldie/Getty Images

The United Kingdom is home to two long-haul airline carriers (carriers that fly between continents): British Airways and its rival, Virgin Atlantic. Although British Airways is the dominant company, with a market share generally between 50% and 100% on routes between London and various American cities, Virgin has been a tenacious competitor.

The rivalry between the two has ranged from relatively peaceable to openly hostile over the years. In the 1990s, British Airways lost a court case alleging it had engaged in "dirty tricks" to drive Virgin out of business. In April 2010, however, British Airways may well have wondered if the tables had been turned.

It all began in mid-July 2004, when oil prices were rising (long-haul airlines are especially vulnerable to oil price hikes). British prosecutors alleged that the two airlines had plotted to levy fuel surcharges on passengers. For the next two years, according to the prosecutors, the rivals had established a cartel through which they coordinated increases in surcharges. British Airways first introduced a £5 ($8.25) surcharge on long-haul flights when a barrel of oil traded at about $38. It increased the surcharge six times, so that by 2006, when oil was trading at about $69 a barrel, the surcharge was £70 ($115). At the same time, Virgin Atlantic also levied a £70 fee. These surcharges increased within days of each other.

Eventually, three Virgin executives decided to blow the whistle in exchange for immunity from prosecution. British Airways immediately suspended its executives under suspicion and paid fines of nearly $500 million to U.S. and U.K. authorities. And in 2010 four British Airways executives were prosecuted by British authorities for their alleged role in the conspiracy.

The lawyers for the executives argued that although the two airlines had swapped information, this was not proof of a criminal conspiracy. In fact, they argued, Virgin was so fearful of American regulators that it had admitted to criminal behavior before confirming that it had indeed committed an offense. One of the defense lawyers, Clare Montgomery, argued that because U.S. laws against anti-competitive behavior are much tougher than those in the United Kingdom, companies may be compelled to blow the whistle to avoid investigation. "It's a race," she said. "If you don't get to them and confess first, you can't get immunity. The only way to protect yourself is to go to the authorities, even if you haven't [done anything]." The result was that the Virgin executives were given immunity in both the United States and the United Kingdom, but the British Airways executives were subject to prosecution (and possible multiyear jail terms) in both countries.

In late 2011 the case came to a shocking end—shocking, that is, for Virgin Atlantic and U.K. authorities. Citing e-mails that Virgin had finally been forced by the court to turn over, the judge found insufficient evidence that there had ever been a conspiracy between the two airlines. The court was incensed enough to threaten to rescind the immunity granted to the three Virgin executives.

QUESTIONS FOR THOUGHT

1. Explain why Virgin Atlantic and British Airlines might collude in response to increased oil prices. Was the market conducive to collusion or not?
2. How would you determine whether illegal behavior actually occurred? What might explain these events other than illegal behavior?
3. Explain the dilemma facing the two airlines as well as their individual executives.

BUSINESS CASE: A Tale of Two Research Clusters

Courtesy Silicon Maps

Silicon Valley in California and Route 128 in Massachusetts are the preeminent high-tech clusters in the world. Silicon Valley dates back to the early 1930s, when Stanford University encouraged its electrical engineering graduates to stay in the area and start companies.

In the early 1950s Stanford created the Stanford Industrial Park, leasing university land to high-tech companies that worked closely with its engineering school. In the mid-1950s, defense contractors such as Lockheed brought dollars to the area. By the late 1960s, a critical mass of such talent had accumulated. For example, in 1968, eight young engineers left their employer over a disagreement; over the next 20 years, they founded 65 new companies, including Intel Corporation, which later created the microprocessor chip, the brain of personal computers.

This pattern repeated: one researcher estimated that in small and medium-sized firms, 35% of the workforce would, on average, turn over in a year. Silicon Valley became a fertile location for startups, with dozens sprouting every year—everything from firms specializing in hardware and software to network firms like eBay, Facebook, and Google. It also became home to investors who specialize in financing new high-tech companies. Silicon Valley's compact geographical location allowed people to form close social and research bonds even while working for rival firms.

On the other side of the country, a high-tech cluster known as Route 128 lies on a 65-mile highway surrounding Boston and Cambridge. It owes its beginnings to the Massachusetts Institute of Technology (MIT), the top engineering university in the world, as well as funding from the U.S. military, NASA, and the National Science Foundation. In the 1950s Route 128 dominated Silicon Valley, with three times the employment.

But early on Route 128 differed from Silicon Valley in significant ways. Geographically, Route 128 was more spread out than Silicon Valley. Its firms were larger, reflecting the needs of defense contractors during the Cold War. And MIT extended little help to Route 128 firms.

Another major difference between the two clusters lay in how firms were organized. Route 128 firms tended to be "vertically integrated," combining the entire chain of production from research to design to production in the same firm. Silicon Valley firms focused exclusively on research and design, contracting production out to specialized firms that achieved economies of scale. In contrast to the fluidity of employees and ideas across companies in Silicon Valley, Route 128 firms emphasized a commitment to lifetime employment and closely guarded their innovations to remain competitive.

The 1970s and 1980s were harsh for Route 128. Military spending dried up, and it lost its edge in minicomputers when Apollo Computers lost its preeminence to an aggressive Silicon Valley firm, Sun Microsystems. By 1980, electronics employment in Silicon Valley was three times that of Route 128. Over time, Route 128 ceded the advantage to Silicon Valley in electronics and networking. Today its niche is in biotechnology, genetics, materials engineering, and finance.

QUESTIONS FOR THOUGHT

1. What positive externalities were common to both Silicon Valley and Route 128? What positive externalities were not common to both? Explain.
2. What factors made Silicon Valley such a fertile place for startups? How did these factors interact with one another? What inhibited startups in Route 128?
3. In hindsight, what could Apollo Computers have done to maintain its advantage in minicomputers? What does this tell you generally about research clusters?

Macroeconomics: The Big Picture

WHAT YOU WILL LEARN IN THIS CHAPTER

- What makes macroeconomics different from microeconomics
- What a **business cycle** is and why policy makers seek to diminish the severity of business cycles
- How **long-run economic growth** determines a country's standard of living
- The meaning of **inflation** and **deflation** and why **price stability** is preferred
- The importance of **open-economy macroeconomics** and how economies interact through **trade deficits** and **trade surpluses**

HOOVERVILLES

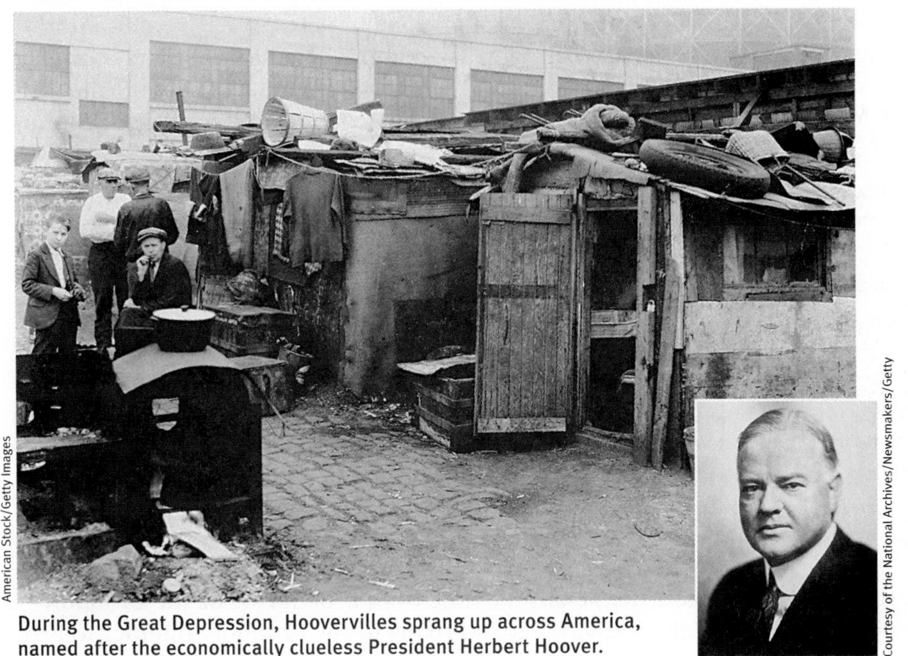

American Stock/Getty Images

Courtesy of the National Archives/Newsmakers/Getty

During the Great Depression, Hoovervilles sprang up across America, named after the economically clueless President Herbert Hoover.

TODAY MANY PEOPLE ENJOY walking, biking, and horseback riding in New York's Central Park. But in 1932 there were also many people living there: Central Park contained one of the "Hoovervilles"—shantytowns—that had sprung up all across America as a result of a catastrophic economic slump that started in 1929, leaving millions of workers out of work, reduced to standing in breadlines or selling apples on street corners. The U.S. economy would stage a partial recovery beginning in 1933, but joblessness stayed high throughout the 1930s. The whole period would come to be known as the Great Depression.

Why Hoovervilles? The shantytowns got their derisive name from Herbert Hoover, who had been elected president in 1928—and who lost his bid for reelection because many Americans blamed him for the Depression. Hoover began his career as an engineer, and until he became president he had a reputation as a can-do, highly competent manager. But when the Depression struck, neither he nor his economic advisers had any idea what to do.

Hoover's cluelessness was no accident. At the time of the Great Depression, *microeconomics,* which is concerned with the consumption and production decisions of individual consumers and producers and with the allocation of scarce resources among industries, was already a well-developed branch of economics. But *macroeconomics,* which focuses on the behavior of the economy as a whole, was still in its infancy.

What happened between 1929 and 1933, and on a smaller scale on many other occasions (most recently between 2007 and 2009), was a blow to the economy as a whole. At any given moment there are always some industries laying off workers. For example, the number of independent record stores in America fell almost 30% between 2003 and 2007, as consumers turned to online purchases. But workers who lost their jobs at record stores had a good chance of finding new jobs elsewhere, because other industries were expanding even as record stores shut their doors. In the early 1930s, however, there were no expanding industries: everything was headed downward.

Macroeconomics came into its own as a branch of economics during the Great Depression. Economists realized that they needed to understand the nature of the catastrophe that had overtaken the United States and much of the rest of the world in order to extricate themselves as well as to learn how to avoid such catastrophes in the future. To this day, the effort to understand economic slumps and find ways to prevent them is at the core of macroeconomics. Over time, however, macroeconomics has broadened its reach to encompass a number of other subjects, such as *long-run economic growth, inflation,* and *open-economy macroeconomics.*

This chapter offers an overview of macroeconomics. We start with a general description of the difference between macroeconomics and microeconomics, then briefly describe some of the field's major concerns. ■

The Nature of Macroeconomics

What makes macroeconomics different from microeconomics? The distinguishing feature of macroeconomics is that it focuses on the behavior of the economy as a whole.

Macroeconomic Questions

Table 10-1 lists some typical questions that involve economics. A microeconomic version of the question appears on the left paired with a similar macroeconomic question on the right. By comparing the questions, you can begin to get a sense of the difference between microeconomics and macroeconomics.

TABLE 10-1 Microeconomic versus Macroeconomic Questions

Microeconomic Questions	Macroeconomic Questions
Should I go to business school or take a job right now?	How many people are employed in the economy as a whole this year?
What determines the salary offered by Citibank to Cherie Camajo, a new MBA?	What determines the overall salary levels paid to workers in a given year?
What determines the cost to a university or college of offering a new course?	What determines the overall level of prices in the economy as a whole?
What government policies should be adopted to make it easier for low-income students to attend college?	What government policies should be adopted to promote employment and growth in the economy as a whole?
What determines whether Citibank opens a new office in Shanghai?	What determines the overall trade in goods, services, and financial assets between the United States and the rest of the world?

As these questions illustrate, microeconomics focuses on how decisions are made by individuals and firms and the consequences of those decisions. For example, we use microeconomics to determine how much it would cost a university or college to offer a new course, which includes the instructor's salary, the cost of class materials, and so on. The school can then decide whether or not to offer the course by weighing the costs and benefits. Macroeconomics, in contrast, examines the *overall* behavior of the economy—how the actions of all the individuals and firms in the economy interact to produce a particular economy-wide level of economic performance. For example, macroeconomics is concerned with the general level of prices in the economy and how high or how low it is relative to prices last year, rather than with the price of one particular good or service.

You might imagine that macroeconomic questions can be answered simply by adding up microeconomic answers. For example, the model of supply and demand we introduced in Chapter 3 tells us how the equilibrium price of an individual good or service is determined in a competitive market. So you might think that applying supply and demand analysis to every good and service in the economy, then summing the results, is the way to understand the overall level of prices in the economy as a whole.

But that turns out not to be right: although basic concepts such as supply and demand are as essential to macroeconomics as they are to microeconomics, answering macroeconomic questions requires an additional set of tools and an expanded frame of reference.

Macroeconomics: The Whole Is Greater Than the Sum of Its Parts

If you occasionally drive on a highway, you probably know what a rubber-necking traffic jam is and why it is so annoying. Someone pulls over to the side of the road for something minor, such as changing a flat tire, and, pretty soon, a long traffic jam occurs as drivers slow down to take a look. What makes it so annoying is that the length of the traffic jam is greatly out of proportion to the minor event that precipitated it. Because some drivers hit their brakes in order to rubber-neck, the drivers behind them must also hit their brakes, those behind them must do the same, and so on. The accumulation of all the individual hitting of brakes eventually leads to a long, wasteful traffic jam as each driver slows down a little bit more than the driver in front of him or her. In other words, each person's response leads to an amplified response by the next person.

In a **self-regulating economy,** problems such as unemployment are resolved without government intervention, through the working of the invisible hand.

According to **Keynesian economics,** economic slumps are caused by inadequate spending, and they can be mitigated by government intervention.

Understanding a rubber-necking traffic jam gives us some insight into one very important way in which macroeconomics is different from microeconomics: many thousands or millions of individual actions compound upon one another to produce an outcome that isn't simply the sum of those individual actions.

Consider, for example, what macroeconomists call the *paradox of thrift:* when families and businesses are worried about the possibility of economic hard times, they prepare by cutting their spending. This reduction in spending depresses the economy as consumers spend less and businesses react by laying off workers. As a result, families and businesses may end up worse off than if they hadn't tried to act responsibly by cutting their spending. This is a paradox because seemingly virtuous behavior—preparing for hard times by saving more—ends up harming everyone. And there is a flip-side to this story: when families and businesses are feeling optimistic about the future, they spend more today. This stimulates the economy, leading businesses to hire more workers, which further expands the economy. Seemingly profligate behavior leads to good times for all.

Or consider what happens when something causes the quantity of cash circulating through the economy to rise. An individual with more cash on hand is richer. But if everyone has more cash, the long-run effect is simply to push the overall level of prices higher, taking the purchasing power of the total amount of cash in circulation right back to where it was before.

A key insight of macroeconomics, then, is that the combined effect of individual decisions can have results that are very different from what any one individual intended, results that are sometimes perverse. The behavior of the macroeconomy is, indeed, greater than the sum of individual actions and market outcomes.

Matthias Clamer/Getty Images

The behavior of the macroeconomy is greater than the sum of individual actions and market outcomes.

Macroeconomics: Theory and Policy

To a much greater extent than microeconomists, macroeconomists are concerned with questions about *policy,* about what the government can do to make macroeconomic performance better. This policy focus was strongly shaped by history, in particular by the Great Depression of the 1930s.

Before the 1930s, economists tended to regard the economy as **self-regulating:** they believed that problems such as unemployment would be corrected through the working of the invisible hand and that government attempts to improve the economy's performance would be ineffective at best—and would probably make things worse.

The Great Depression changed all that. The sheer scale of the catastrophe, which left a quarter of the U.S. workforce without jobs and threatened the political stability of many countries—the Depression is widely believed to have been a major factor in the Nazi takeover of Germany—created a demand for action. It also led to a major effort on the part of economists to understand economic slumps and find ways to prevent them.

In 1936 the British economist John Maynard Keynes (pronounced "canes") published *The General Theory of Employment, Interest, and Money,* a book that transformed macroeconomics. According to **Keynesian economics,** a depressed economy is the result of inadequate spending. In addition, Keynes

Monetary policy uses changes in the quantity of money to alter interest rates and affect overall spending.

Fiscal policy uses changes in government spending and taxes to affect overall spending.

argued that government intervention can help a depressed economy through *monetary policy* and *fiscal policy*. **Monetary policy** uses changes in the quantity of money to alter interest rates, which in turn affect the level of overall spending. **Fiscal policy** uses changes in taxes and government spending to affect overall spending.

In general, Keynes established the idea that managing the economy is a government responsibility. Keynesian ideas continue to have a strong influence on both economic theory and public policy: in 2008 and 2009, Congress, the White House, and the Federal Reserve (a quasi-governmental agency that manages U.S. monetary policy) took steps to fend off an economic slump that were clearly Keynesian in spirit, as described in the following Economics in Action.

ECONOMICS ➤ IN ACTION

FENDING OFF DEPRESSION

In 2008 the world economy experienced a severe financial crisis that was all too reminiscent of the early days of the Great Depression. Major banks teetered on the edge of collapse; world trade slumped. In the spring of 2009, the economic historians Barry Eichengreen and Kevin O'Rourke, reviewing the available data, pointed out that "globally we are tracking or even doing worse than the Great Depression."

But the worst did not, in the end, come to pass. Figure 10-1 shows one of Eichengreen and O'Rourke's measures of economic activity, world industrial production, during the Great Depression and during "the Great Recession," the now widely used term for the slump that followed the 2008 financial crisis. During the first year the two crises were indeed comparable. But this time, fortunately, world production leveled off and turned around. Why?

FIGURE 10-1 Measures of Economic Activity and World Industrial Production During the Great Depression and the Great Recession

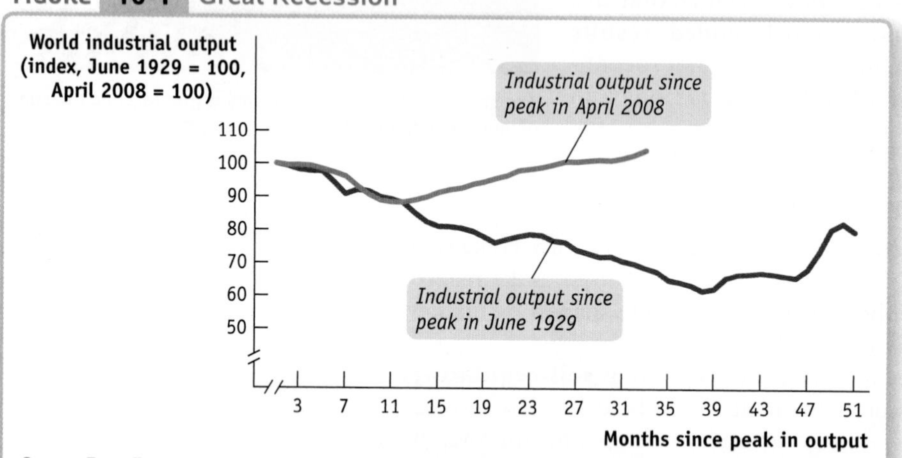

Source: Barry Eichengreen and Kevin O'Rourke (2009), "A Tale of Two Depressions." © VoxEU.org; CPB Netherlands Bureau for Economic Policy Analysis World Trade Monitor.

At least part of the answer is that policy makers responded very differently. During the Great Depression, it was widely argued that the slump should simply be allowed to run its course. Any attempt to mitigate the ongoing catastrophe, declared Joseph Schumpeter—the Austrian-born Harvard economist now famed for his work on innovation—would "leave the work of depression undone." In the early 1930s, some countries' monetary authorities actually raised interest rates in the face of the slump, while governments cut spending and raised taxes—actions that, as we'll see in later chapters, deepened the recession.

In the aftermath of the 2008 crisis, by contrast, interest rates were slashed, and a number of countries, the United States included, used temporary increases in spending and reductions in taxes in an attempt to sustain spending. Governments also moved to shore up their banks with loans, aid, and guarantees.

Many of these measures were controversial, to say the least. But most economists believe that by responding actively to the Great Recession—and doing so using the knowledge gained from the study of macroeconomics—governments helped avoid a global economic catastrophe.

Quick Review

- Microeconomics focuses on decision making by individuals and firms and the consequences of the decisions made. Macroeconomics focuses on the overall behavior of the economy.
- The combined effect of individual actions can have unintended consequences and lead to worse or better macroeconomic outcomes for everyone.
- Before the 1930s, economists tended to regard the economy as **self-regulating.** After the Great Depression, **Keynesian economics** provided the rationale for government intervention through **monetary policy** and **fiscal policy** to help a depressed economy.

CHECK YOUR UNDERSTANDING 10-1

1. Which of the following questions involve microeconomics, and which involve macroeconomics? In each case, explain your answer.
   a. Why did consumers switch to smaller cars in 2008?
   b. Why did overall consumer spending slow down in 2008?
   c. Why did the standard of living rise more rapidly in the first generation after World War II than in the second?
   d. Why have starting salaries for students with geology degrees risen sharply of late?
   e. What determines the choice between rail and road transportation?
   f. Why has salmon gotten cheaper over the past 20 years?
   g. Why did inflation fall in the 1990s?
2. In 2008, problems in the financial sector led to a drying up of credit around the country: home-buyers were unable to get mortgages, students were unable to get student loans, car buyers were unable to get car loans, and so on.
   a. Explain how the drying up of credit can lead to compounding effects throughout the economy and result in an economic slump.
   b. If you believe the economy is self-regulating, what would you advocate that policy makers do?
   c. If you believe in Keynesian economics, what would you advocate that policy makers do?

Solutions appear at back of book.

The Business Cycle

The Great Depression was by far the worst economic crisis in U.S. history. But although the economy managed to avoid catastrophe for the rest of the twentieth century, it has experienced many ups and downs.

It's true that the ups have consistently been bigger than the downs: a chart of any of the major numbers used to track the U.S. economy shows a strong upward trend over time. For example, panel (a) of Figure 10-2 shows total U.S. private-sector employment (the total number of jobs offered by private businesses) measured along the left vertical axis, with the data from 1988 to 2011 given by the purple line. The graph also shows the index of industrial production (a measure of the total output of U.S. factories) measured along the right vertical axis, with the data from 1988 to 2011 given by the red line. Both private-sector employment and industrial production were much higher at the end of this period than at the beginning, and in most years both measures rose.

But they didn't rise steadily. As you can see from the figure, there were three periods—in the early 1990s, in the early 2000s, and again beginning in late 2007—when both employment and industrial output stumbled. Panel (b) emphasizes these stumbles by showing the *rate of change* of employment and industrial production over the previous year. For example, the percent change in employment for December 2007 was 0.7, because employment in December 2007 was 0.7% higher than it had been in December 2006. The three big downturns stand out clearly. What's more, a detailed look at the data makes it clear that in each period the stumble wasn't confined to only a few industries: in each downturn, just about every sector of the U.S. economy cut back on production and on the number of people employed.

FIGURE 10-2 Growth, Interrupted, 1988–2011

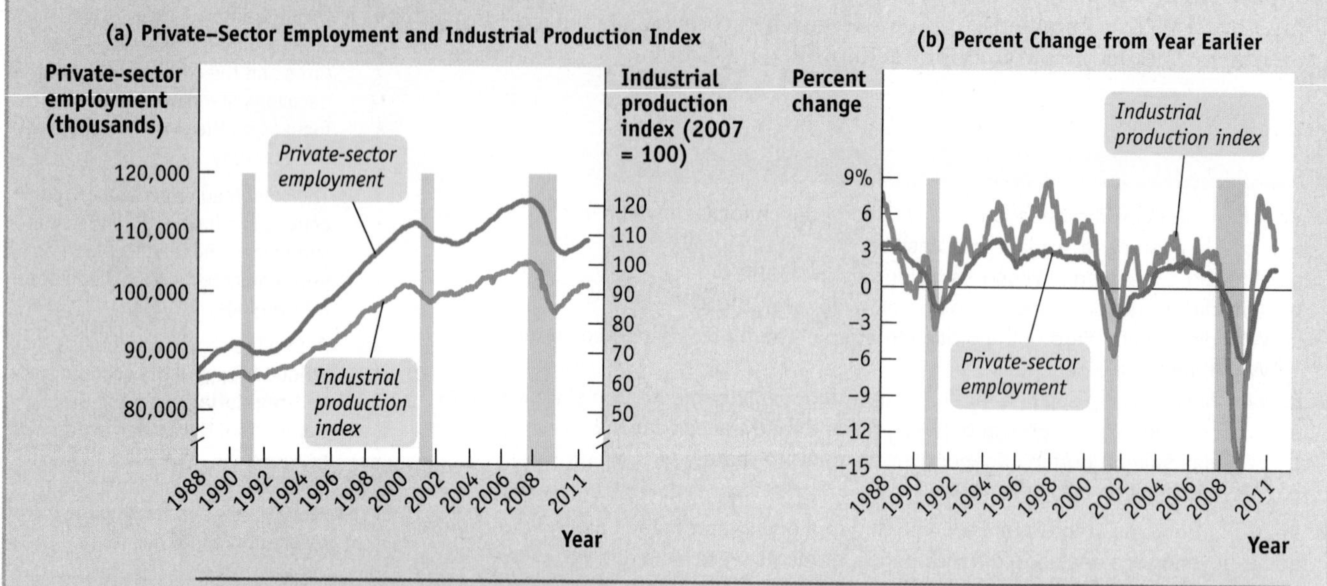

Panel (a) shows two important economic numbers, the industrial production index and total private-sector employment. Both numbers grew substantially from 1988 to 2011, but they didn't grow steadily. Instead, both suffered from three downturns associated with *recessions,* which are indicated by the shaded areas in the figure. Panel (b) emphasizes those downturns by showing the annual rate of change of industrial production and employment, that is, the percentage increase over the past year. The simultaneous downturns in both numbers during the three recessions are clear.

Source: Federal Reserve Bank of St. Louis.

The economy's forward march, in other words, isn't smooth. And the uneven pace of the economy's progress, its ups and downs, is one of the main preoccupations of macroeconomics.

Charting the Business Cycle

Figure 10-3 shows a stylized representation of the way the economy evolves over time. The vertical axis shows either employment or an indicator of how much the economy is producing, such as industrial production or *real gross domestic product (real GDP),* a measure of the economy's overall output that we'll learn about in the next chapter. As the data in Figure 10-2 suggest, these two measures tend to move together. Their common movement is the starting point for a major theme of macroeconomics: the economy's alternation between short-run downturns and upturns.

Recessions, or contractions, are periods of economic downturn when output and employment are falling.

Expansions, or recoveries, are periods of economic upturn when output and employment are rising.

The **business cycle** is the short-run alternation between recessions and expansions.

The point at which the economy turns from expansion to recession is a **business-cycle peak.**

The point at which the economy turns from recession to expansion is a **business-cycle trough.**

"Please stand by for a series of tones. The first indicates the official end of the recession, the second indicates prosperity, and the third the return of the recession."

A broad-based downturn, in which output and employment fall in

FIGURE 10-3 The Business Cycle

This is a stylized picture of the business cycle. The vertical axis measures either employment or total output in the economy. Periods when these two variables turn down are *recessions;* periods when they turn up are *expansions.* The point at which the economy turns down is a *business-cycle peak;* the point at which it turns up again is a *business-cycle trough.*

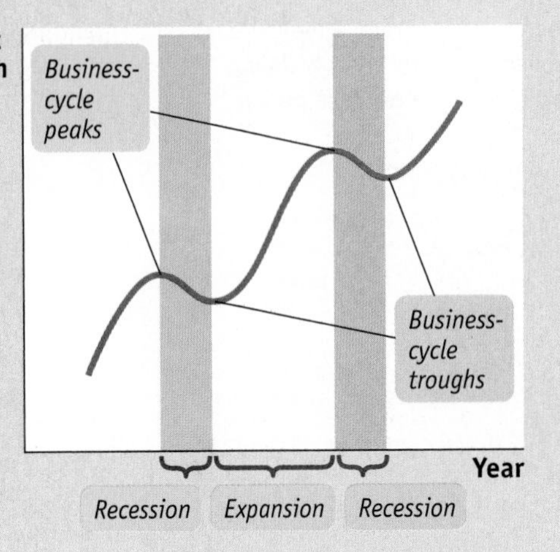

many industries, is called a **recession** (sometimes referred to as a *contraction*). Recessions, as officially declared by the National Bureau of Economic Research, or NBER (see the upcoming For Inquiring Minds), are indicated by the shaded areas in Figure 10-2. When the economy isn't in a recession, when most economic numbers are following their normal upward trend, the economy is said to be in an **expansion** (sometimes referred to as a *recovery*). The alternation between recessions and expansions is known as the **business cycle.** The point in time at which the economy shifts from expansion to recession is known as a **business-cycle peak;** the point at which the economy shifts from recession to expansion is known as a **business-cycle trough.**

The business cycle is an enduring feature of the economy. Table 10-2 shows the official list of business-cycle peaks and troughs. As you can see, there have been recessions and expansions for at least the past 155 years. Whenever there is a prolonged expansion, as there was in the 1960s and again in the 1990s, books and articles come out proclaiming the end of the business cycle. Such proclamations have always proved wrong: The cycle always comes back. But why does it matter?

TABLE 10-2 The History of the Business Cycle

Business-Cycle Peak	Business-Cycle Trough
no prior data available	December 1854
June 1857	December 1858
October 1860	June 1861
April 1865	December 1867
June 1869	December 1870
October 1873	March 1879
March 1882	May 1885
March 1887	April 1888
July 1890	May 1891
January 1893	June 1894
December 1895	June 1897
June 1899	December 1900
September 1902	August 1904
May 1907	June 1908
January 1910	January 1912
January 1913	December 1914
August 1918	March 1919
January 1920	July 1921
May 1923	July 1924
October 1926	November 1927
August 1929	March 1933
May 1937	June 1938
February 1945	October 1945
November 1948	October 1949
July 1953	May 1954
August 1957	April 1958
April 1960	February 1961
December 1969	November 1970
November 1973	March 1975
January 1980	July 1980
July 1981	November 1982
July 1990	March 1991
March 2001	November 2001
December 2007	June 2009

Source: National Bureau of Economic Research.

The Pain of Recession

Not many people complain about the business cycle when the economy is expanding. Recessions, however, create a great deal of pain.

The most important effect of a recession is its effect on the ability of workers to find and hold jobs. The most widely used indicator of conditions in the labor market is the *unemployment rate*. We'll explain how that rate is calculated in Chapter 12, but for now it's enough to say that a high unemployment rate tells us that jobs are scarce and a low unemployment rate tells us that jobs are easy to find.

FIGURE 10-4 The U.S. Unemployment Rate, 1988–2011

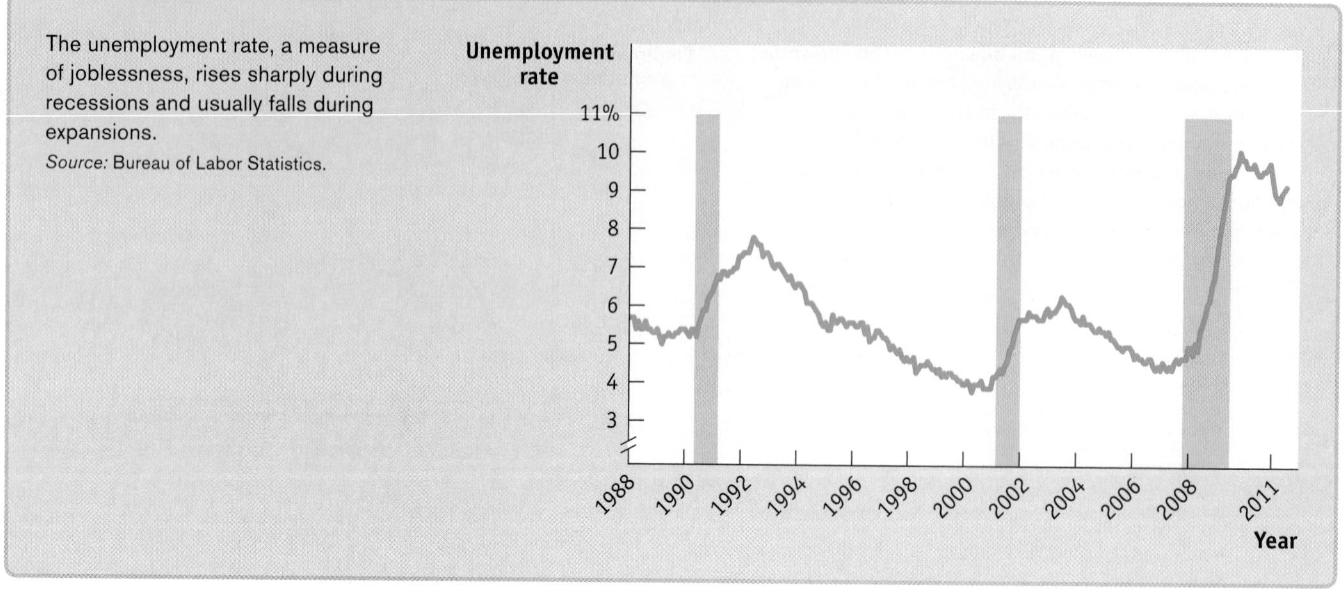

The unemployment rate, a measure of joblessness, rises sharply during recessions and usually falls during expansions.
Source: Bureau of Labor Statistics.

Figure 10-4 shows the unemployment rate from 1988 to 2011. As you can see, the U.S. unemployment rate surged during and after each recession but eventually fell during periods of expansion. The rising unemployment rate in 2008 was a sign that a new recession might be under way, which was later confirmed by the NBER to have begun in December 2007.

Because recessions cause many people to lose their jobs and also make it hard to find new ones, recessions hurt the standard of living of many families. Recessions are usually associated with a rise in the number of people living below the poverty line, an increase in the number of people who lose their houses because they can't afford the mortgage payments, and a fall in the percentage of Americans with health insurance coverage.

FOR INQUIRING MINDS

DEFINING RECESSIONS AND EXPANSIONS

Some readers may be wondering exactly how recessions and expansions are defined. The answer is that there is no exact definition!

In many countries, economists adopt the rule that a recession is a period of at least two consecutive quarters (a quarter is three months) during which the total output of the economy shrinks. The two-consecutive-quarters requirement is designed to avoid classifying brief hiccups in the economy's performance, with no lasting significance, as recessions.

Sometimes, however, this definition seems too strict. For example, an economy that has three months of sharply declining output, then three months of slightly positive growth, then another three months of rapid decline, should surely be considered to have endured a nine-month recession.

In the United States, we try to avoid such misclassifications by assigning the task of determining when a recession begins and ends to an independent panel of experts at the National Bureau of Economic Research (NBER). This panel looks at a variety of economic indicators, with the main focus on employment and production. But, ultimately, the panel makes a judgment call.

Sometimes this judgment is controversial. In fact, there is lingering controversy over the 2001 recession. According to the NBER, that recession began in March 2001 and ended in November 2001 when output began rising. Some critics argue, however, that the recession really began several months earlier, when industrial production began falling. Other critics argue that the recession didn't really end in 2001 because employment continued to fall and the job market remained weak for another year and a half.

You should not think, however, that workers are the only group that suffers during a recession. Recessions are also bad for firms: like employment and wages, profits suffer during recessions, with many small businesses failing, and do well during expansions.

All in all, then, recessions are bad for almost everyone. Can anything be done to reduce their frequency and severity?

Taming the Business Cycle

Modern macroeconomics largely came into being as a response to the worst recession in history—the 43-month downturn that began in 1929 and continued into 1933, ushering in the Great Depression. The havoc wreaked by the 1929–1933 recession spurred economists to search both for understanding and for solutions: they wanted to know how such things could happen and how to prevent them.

As we explained earlier in this chapter, the work of John Maynard Keynes, published during the Great Depression, suggested that monetary and fiscal policies could be used to mitigate the effects of recessions, and to this day governments turn to Keynesian policies when recession strikes. Later work, notably that of another great macroeconomist, Milton Friedman, led to a consensus that it's important to rein in booms as well as to fight slumps. So modern policy makers try to "smooth out" the business cycle. They haven't been completely successful, as a look at Figure 10-2 makes clear. It's widely believed, however, that policy guided by macroeconomic analysis has helped make the economy more stable.

Although the business cycle is one of the main concerns of macroeconomics and historically played a crucial role in fostering the development of the field, macroeconomists are also concerned with other issues. We turn next to the question of long-run growth.

INTERNATIONAL BUSINESS CYCLES

This figure shows the annual rate of growth in industrial production—the percent change since the same month the previous year—for three economies from 1991 to 2011: the United States, Japan, and the euro area, the group of European countries that have adopted the euro as their common currency. Do other economies have business cycles similar to those in the United States?

The answer, which is clear from the figure, is yes. Furthermore, business cycles in different economies are often, although not always, synchronized. The U.S. recession of 2001 was paralleled by recessions in both the euro area and Japan; the Great Recession of 2007–2009 was a severe slump around the world, not just in America. But not all business cycles are international phenomena. Japan suffered a fairly severe recession in 1998, even as the United States and European economies continued to expand.

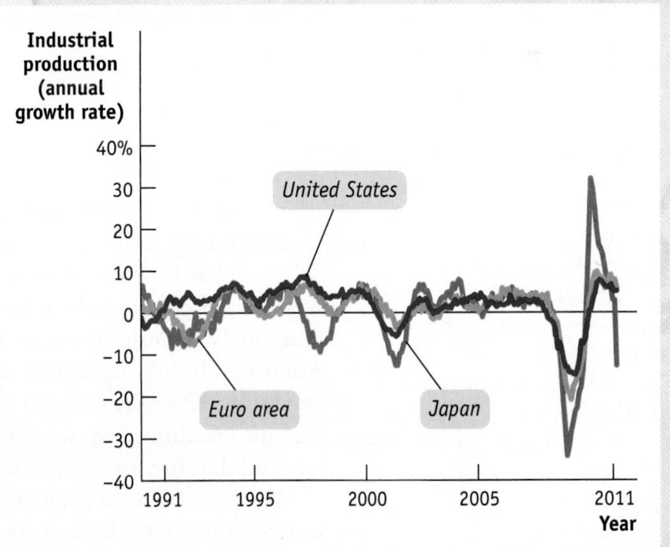

Sources: OECD; Eurostat.

ECONOMICS ➤ IN ACTION

COMPARING RECESSIONS

The alternation of recessions and expansions seems to be an enduring feature of economic life. However, not all business cycles are created equal. In particular, some recessions have been much worse than others.

FIGURE 10-5 Two Recessions

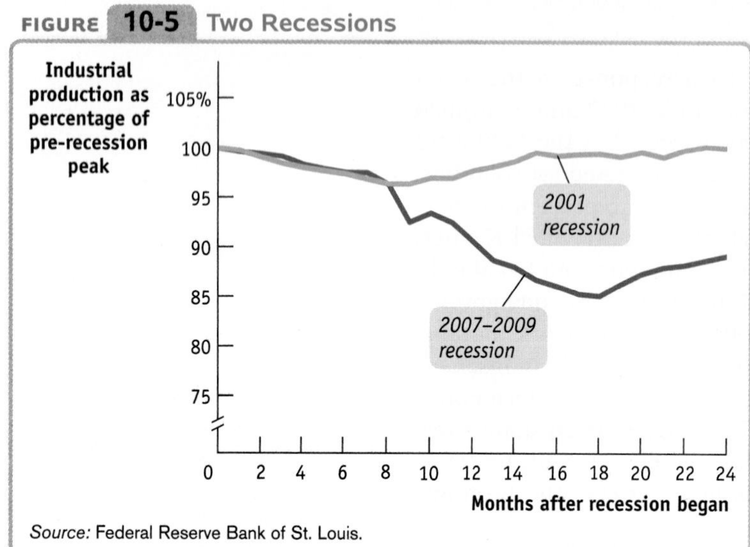

Source: Federal Reserve Bank of St. Louis.

Let's compare the two most recent recessions: the 2001 recession and the Great Recession of 2007–2009. These recessions differed in duration: the first lasted only eight months, the second more than twice as long. Even more important, however, they differed greatly in depth.

In Figure 10-5 we compare the depth of the recessions by looking at what happened to industrial production over the months after the recession began. In each case, production is measured as a percentage of its level at the recession's start. Thus the line for the 2007–2009 recession shows that industrial production eventually fell to about 85% of its initial level.

Clearly, the 2007–2009 recession hit the economy vastly harder than the 2001 recession. Indeed, by comparison to many recessions, the 2001 slump was very mild.

Of course, this was no consolation to the millions of American workers who lost their jobs, even in that mild recession.

▼ Quick Review

- The **business cycle,** the short-run alternation between **recessions** and **expansions,** is a major concern of modern macroeconomics.
- The point at which expansion shifts to recession is a **business-cycle peak.** The point at which recession shifts to expansion is a **business-cycle trough.**

CHECK YOUR UNDERSTANDING 10-2

1. Why do we talk about business cycles for the economy as a whole, rather than just talking about the ups and downs of particular industries?
2. Describe who gets hurt in a recession, and how.

Solutions appear at back of book.

Long-Run Economic Growth

In 1955, Americans were delighted with the nation's prosperity. The economy was expanding, consumer goods that had been rationed during World War II were available for everyone to buy, and most Americans believed, rightly, that they were better off than the citizens of any other nation, past or present. Yet by today's standards, Americans were quite poor in 1955. Figure 10-6 shows the percentage of American homes equipped with a variety of appliances in 1905, 1955, and 2005: in 1955 only 37% of American homes contained washing machines and hardly anyone had air conditioning. And if we turn the clock back another half-century, to 1905, we find that life for many Americans was startlingly primitive by today's standards.

Why are the vast majority of Americans today able to afford conveniences that many Americans lacked in 1955? The answer is **long-run economic growth,** the sustained rise in the quantity of goods and services the economy produces. Figure 10-7 shows the growth since 1900 in real GDP per capita, a measure of total output per person in the economy. The severe recession of 1929–1933 stands out, but business cycles between World War II and 2007 are almost invisible,

Long-run economic growth is the sustained upward trend in the economy's output over time.

FIGURE 10-6 The Fruits of Long-Run Growth in America

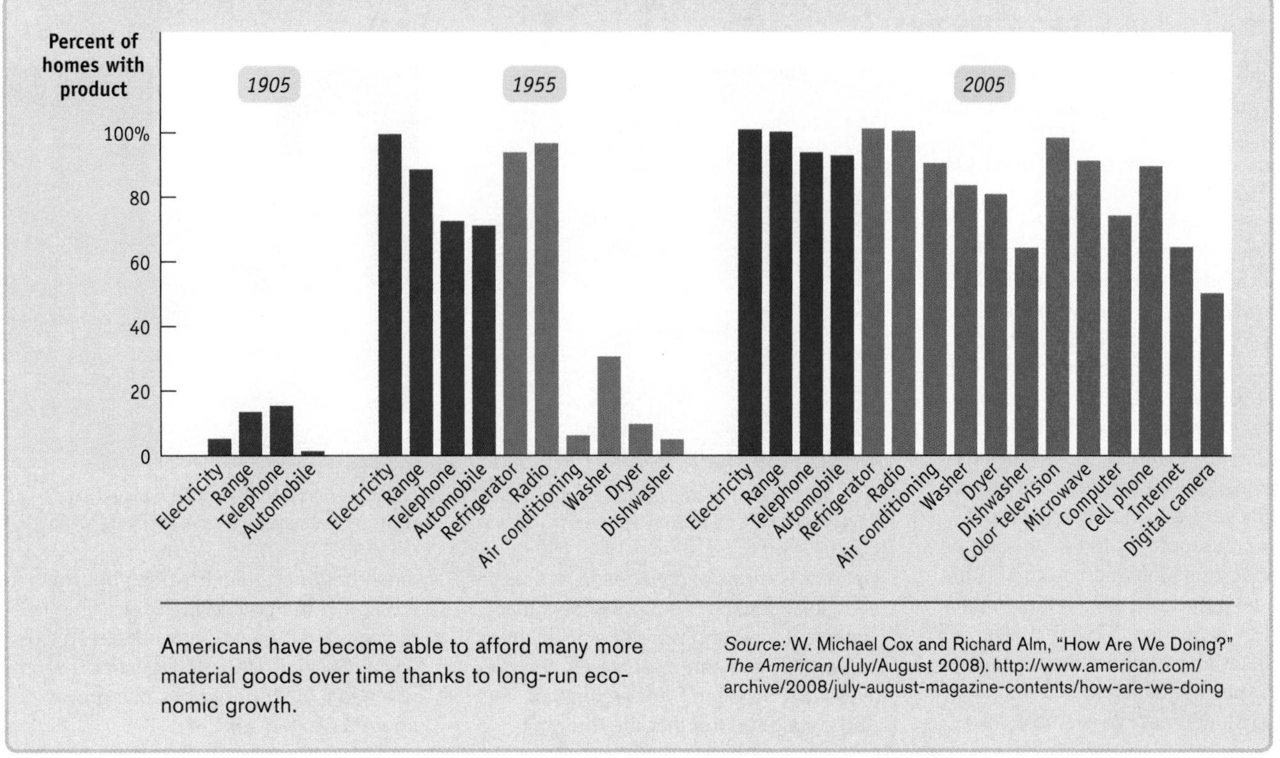

Americans have become able to afford many more material goods over time thanks to long-run economic growth.

Source: W. Michael Cox and Richard Alm, "How Are We Doing?" *The American* (July/August 2008). http://www.american.com/archive/2008/july-august-magazine-contents/how-are-we-doing

dwarfed by the strong upward trend. Part of the long-run increase in output is accounted for by the fact that we have a growing population and workforce. But the economy's overall production has increased by much more than the population. On average, in 2011 the U.S. economy produced about $48,000 worth of goods and services per person, about twice as much as in 1971, about three times as much as in 1951, and almost eight times as much as in 1900.

Long-run economic growth is fundamental to many of the most pressing economic questions today. Responses to key policy questions, like the country's ability to bear the future costs of government programs such as Social Security and Medicare,

FIGURE 10-7 Growth, the Long View

Over the long run, growth in real GDP per capita has dwarfed the ups and downs of the business cycle. Except for the recession that began the Great Depression, recessions are almost invisible until 2007.

Sources: Angus Maddison, *Statistics on World Population, GDP, and Per Capita GDP, 1–2008AD*, http://www.ggdc.net/MADDISON/oriindex.htm; Bureau of Economic Analysis.

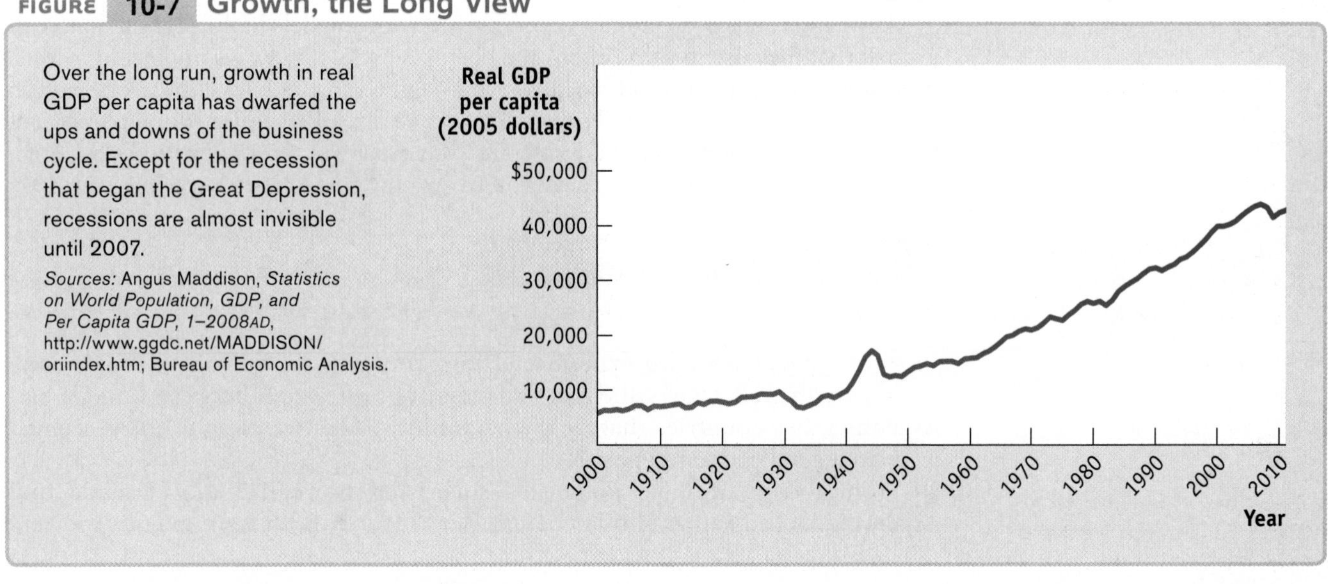

FOR INQUIRING MINDS

WHEN DID LONG-RUN GROWTH START?

Today, the United States is much richer than it was in 1955; in 1955 it was much richer than it had been in 1905. But how did 1855 compare with 1805? Or 1755? How far back does long-run economic growth go?

The answer is that long-run growth is a relatively modern phenomenon. The U.S. economy was already growing steadily by the mid-nineteenth century—think railroads. But if you go back to the period before 1800, you find a world economy that grew extremely slowly by today's standards. Furthermore, the population grew almost as fast as the economy, so there was very little increase in output per person. According to the economic historian Angus Maddison, from 1000 to 1800, real aggregate output around the world grew less than 0.2% per year, with population rising at about the same rate.

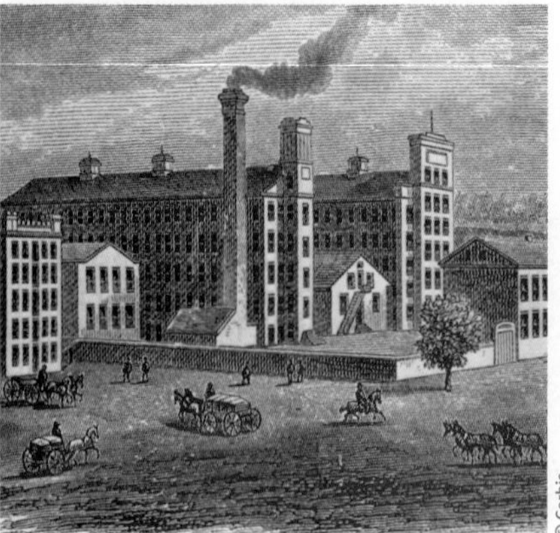

© Corbis

Thinkstock

Economic stagnation and unchanging living standards prevailed for centuries until the Industrial Revolution in the mid-1800s ushered in a new era of wealth and sustained increases in living standards.

Economic stagnation meant unchanging living standards. For example, information on prices and wages from sources such as monastery records shows that workers in England weren't significantly better off in the early eighteenth century than they had been five centuries earlier. And it's a good bet that they weren't much better off than Egyptian peasants in the age of the pharaohs. However, long-run economic growth has increased significantly since 1800. In the last 50 years or so, real GDP per capita has grown about 3.5% per year.

depend in part on how fast the U.S. economy grows over the next few decades. More broadly, the public's sense that the country is making progress depends crucially on success in achieving long-run growth. When growth slows, as it did in the 1970s, it can help feed a national mood of pessimism. In particular, *long-run growth per capita*—a sustained upward trend in output per person—is the key to higher wages and a rising standard of living. A major concern of macroeconomics—and the theme of Chapter 13—is trying to understand the forces behind long-run growth.

Long-run growth is an even more urgent concern in poorer, less developed countries. In these countries, which would like to achieve a higher standard of living, the question of how to accelerate long-run growth is the central concern of economic policy.

As we'll see, macroeconomists don't use the same models to think about long-run growth that they use to think about the business cycle. It's always important to keep both sets of models in mind, because what is good in the long run can be bad in the short run, and vice versa. For example, we've already mentioned the paradox of thrift: an attempt by households to increase their savings can cause a recession. But a higher level of savings plays a crucial role in encouraging long-run economic growth.

ECONOMICS ➤ IN ACTION

A TALE OF TWO COUNTRIES

Many countries have experienced long-run growth, but not all have done equally well. One of the most informative contrasts is between Canada and Argentina, two countries that, at the beginning of the twentieth century, seemed to be in a good economic position.

From today's vantage point, it's surprising to realize that Canada and Argentina looked rather similar before World War I. Both were major exporters of agricultural products; both attracted large numbers of European immigrants; both also attracted large amounts of European investment, especially in the railroads that opened up their agricultural hinterlands. Economic historians believe that the average level of per capita income was about the same in the two countries as late as the 1930s.

After World War II, however, Argentina's economy performed poorly, largely due to political instability and bad macroeconomic policies. (Argentina experienced several periods of extremely high inflation, during which the cost of living soared.) Meanwhile, Canada made steady progress. Thanks to the fact that Canada has achieved sustained long-run growth since 1930, but Argentina has not, Canada today has almost as high a standard of living as the United States—and is about three times as high as Argentina's.

Quick Review

- Because the U.S. economy has achieved **long-run economic growth,** Americans live much better than they did a half-century or more ago.
- Long-run economic growth is crucial for many economic concerns, such as a higher standard of living or financing government programs. It's especially crucial for poorer countries.

CHECK YOUR UNDERSTANDING 10-3

1. Many poor countries have high rates of population growth. What does this imply about the long-run growth rates of overall output that they must achieve in order to generate a higher standard of living per person?
2. Argentina used to be as rich as Canada; now it's much poorer. Does this mean that Argentina is poorer than it was in the past? Explain.

Solutions appear at back of book.

Inflation and Deflation

In January 1980 the average production worker in the United States was paid $6.57 an hour. By June 2011, the average hourly earnings for such a worker had risen to $19.41 an hour. Three cheers for economic progress!

But wait. American workers were paid much more in 2011, but they also faced a much higher cost of living. In early 1980, a dozen eggs cost only about $0.88; by June 2011, that was up to $1.68. The price of a loaf of white bread went from about $0.50 to $1.49. And the price of a gallon of gasoline rose from just $1.11 to $3.75. Figure 10-8 compares the percentage increase

FIGURE 10-8 Rising Prices

Between 1980 and 2011, American workers' hourly earnings rose by 195%. But the prices of just about all the goods bought by workers also rose, some by more, some by less. Overall, the rising cost of living offset most of the rise in the average U.S. worker's wage.
Source: Bureau of Labor Statistics.

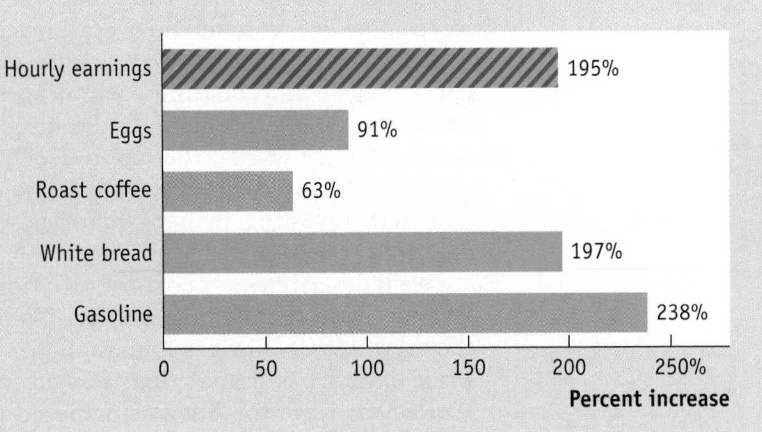

A rising overall level of prices is **inflation.**

A falling overall level of prices is **deflation.**

The economy has **price stability** when the overall level of prices changes slowly or not at all.

in hourly earnings between 1980 and 2011 with the increases in the prices of some standard items: the average worker's paycheck went further in terms of some goods, but less far in terms of others. Overall, the rise in the cost of living wiped out many, if not all, of the wage gains of the typical worker from 1980 to 2011. In other words, once inflation is taken into account, the living standard of the typical U.S. worker has stagnated from 1980 to the present.

The point is that between 1980 and 2011 the economy experienced substantial **inflation:** a rise in the overall level of prices. Understanding the causes of inflation and its opposite, **deflation**—a fall in the overall level of prices—is another main concern of macroeconomics.

The Causes of Inflation and Deflation

You might think that changes in the overall level of prices are just a matter of supply and demand. For example, higher gasoline prices reflect the higher price of crude oil, and higher crude oil prices reflect such factors as the exhaustion of major oil fields, growing demand from China and other emerging economies as more people grow rich enough to buy cars, and so on. Can't we just add up what happens in each of these markets to find out what happens to the overall level of prices?

The answer is no, we can't. Supply and demand can only explain why a particular good or service becomes more expensive *relative to other goods and services.* It can't explain why, for example, the price of chicken has risen over time in spite of the facts that chicken production has become more efficient (you don't want to know) and that chicken has become substantially cheaper compared to other goods.

What causes the overall level of prices to rise or fall? As we'll learn in Chapter 12, in the short run, movements in inflation are closely related to the business cycle. When the economy is depressed and jobs are hard to find, inflation tends to fall; when the economy is booming, inflation tends to rise. For example, prices of most goods and services fell sharply during the terrible recession of 1929–1933.

In the long run, by contrast, the overall level of prices is mainly determined by changes in the *money supply,* the total quantity of assets that can be readily used to make purchases.

The Pain of Inflation and Deflation

Both inflation and deflation can pose problems for the economy. Here are two examples: inflation discourages people from holding onto cash, because cash loses value over time if the overall price level is rising. That is, the amount of goods and services you can buy with a given amount of cash falls. In extreme cases, people stop holding cash altogether and turn to barter. Deflation can cause the reverse problem. If the price level is falling, cash gains value over time. In other words, the amount of goods and sevices you can buy with a given amount of cash increases. So holding on to it can become more attractive than investing in new factories and other productive assets. This can deepen a recession.

We'll describe other costs of inflation and deflation in Chapter 12. For now, let's just note that, in general, economists regard **price stability**—in which the overall level of prices is changing, if at all, only slowly—as a desirable goal. Price stability is a goal that seemed far out of reach for much of the post–World War II period but was achieved to most macroeconomists' satisfaction in the 1990s.

ECONOMICS ➤ IN ACTION

A FAST (FOOD) MEASURE OF INFLATION

The original McDonald's opened in 1954. It offered fast service—it was, indeed, the original fast-food restaurant. And it was also very inexpensive: hamburgers cost $0.15, $0.25 with fries. By 2012, a hamburger at a typical McDonald's cost just over 6 times as much, about $0.95. Has McDonald's lost touch with its fast-food roots? Have burgers become luxury cuisine?

No—in fact, compared with other consumer goods, a burger is a better bargain today than it was in 1954. Burger prices were about 6.3 times as high in 2012 as they were in 1954. But the consumer price index, the most widely used measure of the cost of living, was 8.5 times as high in 2012 as it was in 1954.

Everett Collection/Alamy

Even though a burger costs 6 times more than it did in 1954 when McDonald's first opened, it's still a good bargain compared to other consumer goods.

Quick Review

- A dollar today doesn't buy what it did in 1971, because the prices of most goods have risen. This rise in the overall price level has wiped out most if not all of the wage increases received by the typical American worker over the past 30 years.
- One area of macroeconomic study is in the overall level of prices. Because either **inflation** or **deflation** can cause problems for the economy, economists typically advocate maintaining **price stability.**

CHECK YOUR UNDERSTANDING 10-4

1. Which of these sound like inflation, which sound like deflation, and which are ambiguous?
   a. Gasoline prices are up 10%, food prices are down 20%, and the prices of most services are up 1–2%.
   b. Gas prices have doubled, food prices are up 50%, and most services seem to be up 5% or 10%.
   c. Gas prices haven't changed, food prices are way down, and services have gotten cheaper, too.

Solutions appear at back of book.

International Imbalances

The United States is an **open economy:** an economy that trades goods and services with other countries. There have been times when that trade was more or less balanced—when the United States sold about as much to the rest of the world as it bought. But this isn't one of those times.

In 2010, the United States ran a big **trade deficit**—that is, the value of the goods and services U.S. residents bought from the rest of the world was a lot larger than the value of the goods and services American producers sold to customers abroad. Meanwhile, some other countries were in the opposite position, selling much more to foreigners than they bought. Figure 10-9 shows the exports and imports of goods for several important economies in 2010. As you can see, the United States imported much more than it exported, but Germany, China, and Saudi Arabia did the reverse: they each ran a **trade surplus.** A country runs a trade surplus when the value of the goods and services it buys from the rest of the world is smaller than the value of the goods and services it sells abroad. Was America's trade deficit a sign that something was wrong with our economy—that we weren't able to make things that people in other countries wanted to buy?

No, not really. Trade deficits and their opposite, trade surpluses, are macroeconomic phenomena. They're the result of situations in which the whole is very different from the sum of its parts. You might think that countries

An **open economy** is an economy that trades goods and services with other countries.

A country runs a **trade deficit** when the value of goods and services bought from foreigners is more than the value of goods and services it sells to them. It runs a **trade surplus** when the value of goods and services bought from foreigners is less than the value of the goods and services it sells to them.

FIGURE 10-9 Unbalanced Trade

In 2010, the goods and services the United States bought from other countries were worth considerably more than the goods and services we sold abroad. Germany, China, and Saudi Arabia were in the reverse position. Trade deficits and trade surpluses reflect macroeconomic forces, especially differences in savings and investment spending.

Source: World Trade Organization.

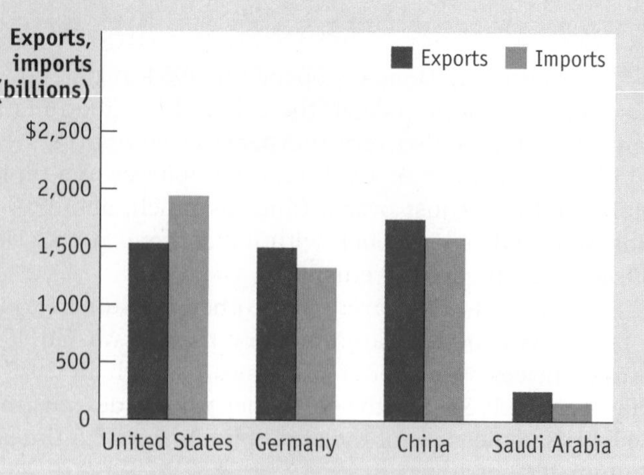

with highly productive workers or widely desired products and services to sell run trade surpluses but countries with unproductive workers or poor-quality products and services run deficits. But the reality is that there's no simple relationship between the success of an economy and whether it runs trade surpluses or deficits.

Microeconomic analysis tells us why countries trade but not why they run trade surpluses or deficits. In Chapter 2 we learned that international trade is the result of comparative advantage: countries export goods they're relatively good at producing and import goods they're not as good at producing. That's why the United States exports wheat and imports coffee. One important thing the concept of comparative advantage doesn't explain, however, is why the value of a country's imports is sometimes much larger than the value of its exports, or vice versa.

So what does determine whether a country runs a trade surplus or a trade deficit? In Chapter 19 we'll learn the surprising answer: the determinants of the overall balance between exports and imports lie in decisions about savings and investment spending—spending on goods like machinery and factories that are in turn used to produce goods and services for consumers. Countries with high investment spending relative to savings run trade deficits; countries with low investment spending relative to savings run trade surpluses.

ECONOMICS ➤ IN ACTION

BALTIC BALANCING ACT

The Soviet Union, once second only to the United States as a world power, broke up into 15 independent countries in 1991. Many of these countries have had a hard time finding a new place in the world, both politically and economically. However, the three small nations of Estonia, Latvia, and Lithuania—often referred to as the "Baltics" because they all have coastlines on the Baltic Sea—were quick both to establish democratic institutions and to move to market economies, building strong ties to the democratic market economies of Western Europe.

What has this meant for their international trade? Figure 10-10 shows the current account balances of the three countries—a broad definition of their trade balances—from 2000 to 2010. As you can see, in the middle years of that decade all three countries began running sizable deficits (amounting in each case to more than 10% of the total value of goods and services they produced.) Then, after 2008, all three suddenly moved into surplus.

Does this mean that these economies were doing badly around 2005 or 2006 and that they rapidly improved late in the decade? Actually, it was the opposite. During the period from 2000 to 2007, financial markets were extremely optimistic about the economic prospects of the Baltic nations and poured money into the countries, allowing them to engage in high rates of investment spending and, correspondingly, to run large trade deficits. When the world plunged into financial crisis, this inflow of funds dried up, forcing the Baltics to move into trade surplus. The adjustment was hard on the three countries, all of which saw unemployment rates rise to Depression-era levels.

FIGURE 10-10 Baltic Current Account Balances, 2000–2010

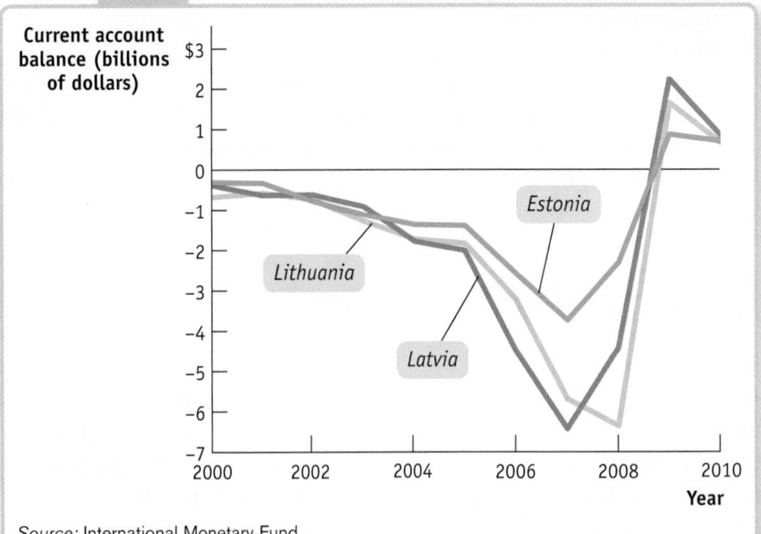

Source: International Monetary Fund.

Quick Review

- Comparative advantage can explain why an **open economy** exports some goods and services and imports others, but it can't explain why a country imports more than it exports, or vice versa.
- **Trade deficits** and **trade surpluses** are macroeconomic phenomena, determined by decisions about investment spending and savings.

CHECK YOUR UNDERSTANDING 10-5

1. Which of the following reflect comparative advantage, and which reflect macroeconomic forces?
   a. Thanks to the development of huge oil sands in the province of Alberta, Canada has become an exporter of oil and an importer of manufactured goods.
   b. Like many consumer goods, the Apple iPod is assembled in China, although many of the components are made in other countries.
   c. Since 2002, Germany has been running huge trade surpluses, exporting much more than it imports.
   d. The United States, which had roughly balanced trade in the early 1990s, began running large trade deficits later in the decade, as the technology boom took off.

Solutions appear at back of book.

SUMMARY

1. Macroeconomics is the study of the behavior of the economy as a whole, which can be different from the sum of its parts. Macroeconomics differs from microeconomics in the type of questions it tries to answer. Macroeconomics also has a strong policy focus: **Keynesian economics,** which emerged during the Great Depression, advocates the use of **monetary policy** and **fiscal policy** to fight economic slumps. Prior to the Great Depression, the economy was thought to be **self-regulating.**
2. One key concern of macroeconomics is the **business cycle,** the short-run alternation between **recessions,** periods of falling employment and output, and **expansions,** periods of rising employment and output. The point at which expansion turns to recession is a **business-cycle peak.** The point at which recession turns to expansion is a **business-cycle trough.**
3. Another key area of macroeconomic study is **long-run economic growth,** the sustained upward trend in the economy's output over time. Long-run economic growth rce behind long-term increases in living standards and is important for financing some economic programs. It is especially important for poorer countries.
4. When the prices of most goods and services are rising, so that the overall level of prices is going up, the economy experiences **inflation.** When the overall level

of prices is going down, the economy is experiencing **deflation.** In the short run, inflation and deflation are closely related to the business cycle. In the long run, prices tend to reflect changes in the overall quantity of money. Because both inflation and deflation can cause problems, economists and policy makers generally aim for **price stability.**

5. Although comparative advantage explains why **open economies** export some things and import others, macroeconomic analysis is needed to explain why countries run **trade surpluses** or **trade deficits.** The determinants of the overall balance between exports and imports lie in decisions about savings and investment spending.

KEY TERMS

Self-regulating economy, p. 309
Keynesian economics, p. 309
Monetary policy, p. 310
Fiscal policy, p. 310
Recession, p. 312
Expansion, p. 312
Business cycle, p. 312
Business-cycle peak, p. 312
Business-cycle trough, p. 312
Long-run economic growth, p. 316
Inflation, p. 320
Deflation, p. 320
Price stability, p. 320
Open economy, p. 321
Trade deficit, p. 321
Trade surplus, p. 321

PROBLEMS

1. Which of the following questions are relevant for the study of macroeconomics and which for microeconomics?
   a. How will Ms. Martin's tips change when a large manufacturing plant near the restaurant where she works closes?
   b. What will happen to spending by consumers when the economy enters a downturn?
   c. How will the price of oranges change when a late frost damages Florida's orange groves?
   d. How will wages at a manufacturing plant change when its workforce is unionized?
   e. What will happen to U.S. exports as the dollar becomes less expensive in terms of other currencies?
   f. What is the relationship between a nation's unemployment rate and its inflation rate?
2. When one person saves more, that person's wealth is increased, meaning that he or she can consume more in the future. But when everyone saves more, everyone's income falls, meaning that everyone must consume less today. Explain this seeming contradiction.
3. Before the Great Depression, the conventional wisdom among economists and policy makers was that the economy is largely self-regulating.
   a. Is this view consistent or inconsistent with Keynesian economics? Explain.
   b. What effect did the Great Depression have on conventional wisdom?
   c. Contrast the response of policy makers during the 2007–2009 recession to the actions of policy makers during the Great Depression. What would have been the likely outcome of the 2007–2009 recession if policy makers had responded in the same fashion as policy makers during the Great Depression?
4. How do economists in the United States determine when a recession begins and when it ends? How do other countries determine whether or not a recession is occurring?
5. The U.S. Department of Labor reports statistics on employment and earnings that are used as key indicators by many economists to gauge the health of the economy. Figure 10-4 in the text plots historical data on the unemployment rate each month. Noticeably, the numbers were high during the recessions in the early 1990s, in 2001, and in 2007–2009.
   a. Locate the latest data on the national unemployment rate. (*Hint:* Go to the website of the Bureau of Labor Statistics, www.bls.gov, and locate the latest release of the Employment Situation.)
   b. Compare the current numbers with the recessions in the early 1990s, in 2001, and in 2007–2009 as well as with the periods of relatively high economic growth just before the recessions. Are the current numbers indicative of a recessionary trend?

6. The accompanying figure shows the annual rate of growth in employment for the United Kingdom and Japan from 1991 to 2010. (The annual growth rate is the percent change in each year's employment over the previous year.)

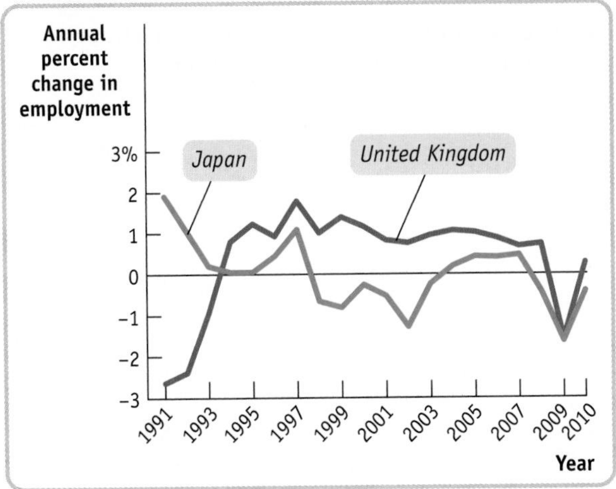

a. Comment on the business cycles of these two economies. Are their business cycles similar or dissimilar?

b. Use the accompanying figure and the figure in the Global Comparison on international business cycles in the chapter to compare the business cycles of each of these two economies with those of the United States and the euro area.

7. a. What three measures of the economy tend to move together during the business cycle? Which way do they move during an upturn? During a downturn?

b. Who in the economy is hurt during a recession? How?

c. How did Milton Friedman alter the consensus that had developed in the aftermath of the Great Depression on how the economy should be managed? What is the current goal of policy makers in managing the economy?

8. Why do we consider a business-cycle expansion different from long-run economic growth? Why do we care about the size of the long-run growth rate of real GDP versus the size of the growth rate of the population?

9. In 1798, Thomas Malthus's *Essay on the Principle of Population* was published. In it, he wrote: "Population, when unchecked, increases in a geometrical ratio. Subsistence increases only in an arithmetical ratio. . . . This implies a strong and constantly operating check on population from the difficulty of subsistence." Malthus was saying that the growth of the population is limited by the amount of food available to eat; people will live at the subsistence level forever. Why didn't Malthus's description apply to the world after 1800?

10. College tuition has risen significantly in the last few decades. From the 1979–1980 academic year to the 2009–2010 academic year, total tuition, room, and board paid by full-time undergraduate students went from $2,327 to $15,041 at public institutions and from $5,013 to $35,061 at private institutions. This is an average annual tuition increase of 6.4% at public institutions and 6.7% at private institutions. Over the same time, average personal income after taxes rose from $7,956 to $35,088 per year, which is an average annual rate of growth of personal income of 5.0%. Have these tuition increases made it more difficult for the average student to afford college tuition?

11. Each year, *The Economist* publishes data on the price of the Big Mac in different countries and exchange rates. The accompanying table shows some data used for the index from 2007 and 2011. Use this information to answer the following questions.

	2007		2011	
Country	**Price of Big Mac (in local currrency)**	**Price of Big Mac (in U.S. dollars)**	**Price of Big Mac (in local currency)**	**Price of Big Mac (in U.S. dollars)**
Argentina	peso8.25	$2.65	peso20.0	$4.84
Canada	C$3.63	$3.08	C$4.73	$5.00
Euro area	€2.94	$3.82	€3.44	$4.93
Japan	¥280	$2.31	¥320	$4.08
United States	$3.22	$3.22	$4.07	$4.07

a. Where was it cheapest to buy a Big Mac in U.S. dollars in 2007?

b. Where was it cheapest to buy a Big Mac in U.S. dollars in 2011?

c. Using the increase in the local currency price of the Big Mac in each country to measure the percent change in the overall price level from 2007 to 2011, which nation experienced the most inflation? Did any of the nations experience deflation?

12. The accompanying figure illustrates the trade deficit of the United States since 1987. The United States has been consistently and, on the whole, increasingly importing more goods than it has been exporting. One of the countries it runs a trade deficit with is China. Which of the following statements are valid possible explanations of this fact? Explain.

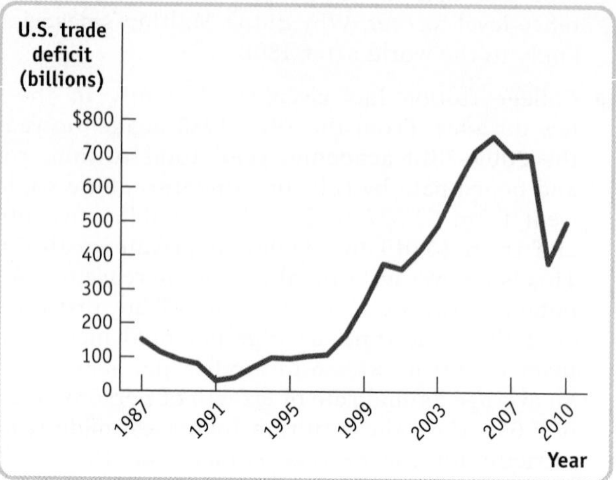

a. Many products, such as televisions, that were formerly manufactured in the United States are now manufactured in China.

b. The wages of the average Chinese worker are far lower than the wages of the average American worker.

c. Investment spending in the United States is high relative to its level of savings.

CHAPTER 11

GDP and the CPI: Tracking the Macroeconomy

WHAT YOU WILL LEARN IN THIS CHAPTER

- How economists use aggregate measures to track the performance of the economy
- What **gross domestic product, or GDP,** is and the three ways of calculating it
- The difference between **real GDP** and **nominal GDP** and why real GDP is the appropriate measure of real economic activity
- What a **price index** is and how it is used to calculate the **inflation rate**

THE NEW #2

REUTERS/Aly Song

The 2010 economic data showed that China had become an economic superpower, surpassing Japan.

"CHINA PASSES JAPAN AS Second-Largest Economy." That was the headline in the *New York Times* on August 15, 2010. Citing economic data suggesting that Japan's economy was weakening while China's was roaring ahead, the article predicted—correctly, as it turned out—that 2010 would mark the first year in which the surging Chinese economy finally overtook Japan's, taking second place to the United States on the world economic stage. "The milestone," wrote the *Times,* "though anticipated for some time, is the most striking evidence yet that China's ascendance is for real and that the rest of the world will have to reckon with a new economic superpower."

But wait a minute—what does it mean to say that China's economy is larger than Japan's? The two economies are, after all, producing very different mixes of goods. Despite its rapid advance, China is still a fairly poor country whose greatest strength is in relatively low-tech production. Japan, by contrast, is very much a high-tech nation, and it dominates world output of some sophisticated goods, like electronic sensors for automobiles. That's why the 2011 earthquake in northeastern Japan, which put many factories out of action, temporarily caused major production disruptions for auto factories around the world.

How can you compare the sizes of two economies when they aren't producing the same things?

The answer is that comparisons of national economies are based on the *value* of their production. When news reports declared that China's economy had overtaken Japan's, they meant that China's *gross domestic product,* or *GDP*—a measure of the overall value of goods and services produced—had surpassed Japan's GDP.

GDP is one of the most important measures used to track the macroeconomy—that is, to quantify movements in the overall level of output and prices. Measures like GDP and *price indexes* play an important role in formulating economic policy, since policy makers need to know what's going on, and anecdotes are no substitute for hard data. They're also important for business decisions—to such an extent that, as the business case at the end of the chapter illustrates, corporations and other players are willing to pay for early reads on what official economic measurements are likely to find.

In this chapter, we explain how macroeconomists measure key aspects of the economy. We first explore ways to measure the economy's total output and total income. We then turn to the problem of how to measure the level of prices and the change in prices in the economy.

The **national income and product accounts,** or **national accounts,** keep track of the flows of money between different sectors of the economy.

Final goods and services are goods and services sold to the final, or end, user.

Intermediate goods and services are goods and services—bought from one firm by another firm—that are inputs for production of final goods and services.

Gross domestic product, or **GDP,** is the total value of all final goods and services produced in the economy during a given year.

Measuring the Macroeconomy

Almost all countries calculate a set of numbers known as the *national income and product accounts.* In fact, the accuracy of a country's accounts is a remarkably reliable indicator of its state of economic development—in general, the more reliable the accounts, the more economically advanced the country. When international economic agencies seek to help a less developed country, typically the first order of business is to send a team of experts to audit and improve the country's accounts.

In the United States, these numbers are calculated by the Bureau of Economic Analysis, a division of the U.S. government's Department of Commerce. The **national income and product accounts,** often referred to simply as the **national accounts,** keep track of the spending of consumers, sales of producers, business investment spending, government purchases, and a variety of other flows of money between different sectors of the economy.

Economists use the national accounts to measure the overall market value of the goods and services the economy produces. That measure has a name: it's a country's *gross domestic product.* But before we can formally define gross domestic product, or GDP, we have to examine an important distinction between classes of goods and services: the difference between *final goods and services* versus *intermediate goods and services.*

Gross Domestic Product

A consumer's purchase of a new car from a dealer is one example of a sale of **final goods and services:** goods and services sold to the final, or end, user. But an automobile manufacturer's purchase of steel from a steel foundry or glass from a glassmaker is an example of purchasing **intermediate goods and services:** goods and services that are inputs for production of final goods and services. In the case of intermediate goods and services, the purchaser—another firm—is *not* the final user.

Gross domestic product, or **GDP,** is the total value of all *final goods and services* produced in an economy during a given period, usually a year. In 2011 the GDP of the United States was $15,321 billion, or about $48,960 per person. If you are an economist trying to construct a country's national accounts, *one way to calculate GDP is to calculate it directly: survey firms and add up the total value of their production of final goods and services.* We'll explain in detail in the next section why intermediate goods, and some other types of goods as well, are not included in the calculation of GDP.

"You wouldn't think there'd be much money in potatoes, chickens, and woodchopping, but it all adds up."

But adding up the total value of final goods and services produced is only one of three ways of calculating GDP. A second way is based on total spending on final goods and services. This second method adds aggregate spending on domestically produced final goods and services in the economy. The third way of calculating GDP is based on total income earned in the economy. Firms and the factors of production that they employ are owned by households. So firms must ultimately pay out what they earn to households. And so, a third way of calculating GDP is to sum the total factor income earned by households from firms in the economy.

Calculating GDP

We've just explained that there are in fact three methods for calculating GDP:

1. adding up total value of all final goods and services produced
2. adding up spending on all domestically produced goods and services
3. adding to total factor income earned by households from firms in the economy

Government statisticians use all three methods. To illustrate how these three methods work, we will consider a hypothetical economy, shown in Figure 11-1. This economy consists of three firms—American Motors, Inc., which produces one car per year; American Steel, Inc., which produces the steel that goes into the car; and American Ore, Inc., which mines the iron ore that goes into the steel. So GDP is $21,500, the value of the one car per year the economy produces. Let's look at how the three different methods of calculating GDP yield the same result.

The **value added** of a producer is the value of its sales minus the value of its purchases of intermediate goods and services.

Measuring GDP as the Value of Production of Final Goods and Services The first method for calculating GDP is to add up the value of all the final goods and services produced in the economy—a calculation that excludes the value of intermediate goods and services. Why are intermediate goods and services excluded? After all, don't they represent a very large and valuable portion of the economy?

To understand why only final goods and services are included in GDP, look at the simplified economy described in Figure 11-1. Should we measure the GDP of this economy by adding up the total sales of the iron ore producer, the steel producer, and the auto producer? If we did, we would in effect be counting the value of the steel twice—once when it is sold by the steel plant to the auto plant, and again when the steel auto body is sold to a consumer as a finished car. And we would be counting the value of the iron ore *three* times—once when it is mined and sold to the steel company, a second time when it is made into steel and sold to the auto producer, and a third time when the steel is made into a car and sold to the consumer.

So counting the full value of each producer's sales would cause us to count the same items several times and artificially inflate the calculation of GDP. For example, in Figure 11-1, the total value of all sales, intermediate and final, is $34,700: $21,500 from the sale of the car, plus $9,000 from the sale of the steel, plus $4,200 from the sale of the iron ore. Yet we know that GDP is only $21,500. The way we avoid double-counting is to count only each producer's **value added** in the calculation of GDP: the difference between the value of its sales and the value of the intermediate goods and services it purchases from other businesses.

FIGURE 11-1 Calculating GDP

In this hypothetical economy consisting of three firms, GDP can be calculated in three different ways: 1) measuring GDP as the value of production of final goods and services, by summing each firm's value added; 2) measuring GDP as aggregate spending on domestically produced final goods and services; and 3) measuring GDP as factor income earned by households from firms in the economy.

2. Aggregate spending on domestically produced final goods and services = $21,500

	American Ore, Inc.	American Steel, Inc.	American Motors, Inc.	Total factor income
Value of sales	$4,200 (ore)	$9,000 (steel)	$21,500 (car)	
Intermediate goods	0	4,200 (iron ore)	9,000 (steel)	
Wages	2,000	3,700	10,000	$15,700
Interest payments	1,000	600	1,000	2,600
Rent	200	300	500	1,000
Profit	1,000	200	1,000	2,200
Total expenditure by firm	4,200	9,000	21,500	
Value added per firm = Value of sales − Cost of intermediate goods	4,200	4,800	12,500	

3. Total payments to factors = $21,500

1. Value of production of final goods and services, sum of value added = $21,500

That is, at each stage of the production process we subtract the cost of inputs—the intermediate goods—at that stage. In this case, the value added of the auto producer is the dollar value of the cars it manufactures *minus* the cost of the steel it buys, or $12,500. The value added of the steel producer is the dollar value of the steel it produces *minus* the cost of the ore it buys, or $4,800. Only the ore producer, which we have assumed doesn't buy any inputs, has value added equal to its total sales, $4,200. The sum of the three producers' value added is $21,500, equal to GDP.

Measuring GDP as Spending on Domestically Produced Final Goods and Services Another way to calculate GDP is by adding up aggregate spending on domestically produced final goods and services. That is, GDP can be measured by the flow of funds into firms. Like the method that estimates GDP as the value of domestic production of final goods and services, this measurement must be carried out in a way that avoids double-counting. In terms of our steel and auto example, we don't want to count both consumer spending on a car (represented in Figure 11-1 by $12,500, the sales price of the car) and the auto producer's spending on steel (represented in Figure 11-1 by $9,000, the price of a car's worth of steel). If we counted both, we would be counting the steel embodied in the car twice. We solve this problem by counting only the value of sales to *final buyers,* such as consumers, firms that purchase investment goods, the government, or foreign buyers. In other words, in order to avoid double-counting of spending, we omit sales of inputs from one business to another when estimating GDP using spending data. You can see from Figure 11-1 that aggregate spending on final goods and services—the finished car—is $21,500.

As we've already pointed out, the national accounts *do* include investment spending by firms as a part of final spending. That is, an auto company's purchase of steel to make a car isn't considered a part of final spending, but the company's purchase of new machinery for its factory *is* considered a part of final spending. What's the difference? Steel is an input that is used up in production; machinery will last for a number of years. Since purchases of capital goods that will last for a considerable time aren't closely tied to current production, the national accounts consider such purchases a form of final sales.

FOR INQUIRING MINDS

OUR IMPUTED LIVES

An old line says that when a person marries the household cook, GDP falls. And it's true: when someone provides services for pay, those services are counted as a part of GDP. But the services family members provide to each other are not. Some economists have produced alternative measures that try to "impute" the value of household work—that is, assign an estimate of what the market value of that work would have been if it had been paid for. But the standard measure of GDP doesn't contain that imputation.

GDP estimates do, however, include an imputation for the value of "owner-occupied housing." That is, if you buy the home you were formerly renting, GDP does not go down. It's true that because you no longer pay rent to your landlord, the landlord no longer sells a service to you—namely, use of the house or apartment. But the statisticians make an estimate of what you would have paid if you rented whatever you live in, whether it's an apartment or a house. For the purposes of the statistics, it's as if you were renting your dwelling from yourself.

If you think about it, this makes a lot of sense. In a home-owning country like the United States, the pleasure we derive from our houses is an important part of the standard of living. So to be accurate, estimates of GDP must take into account the value of housing that is occupied by owners as well as the value of rental housing.

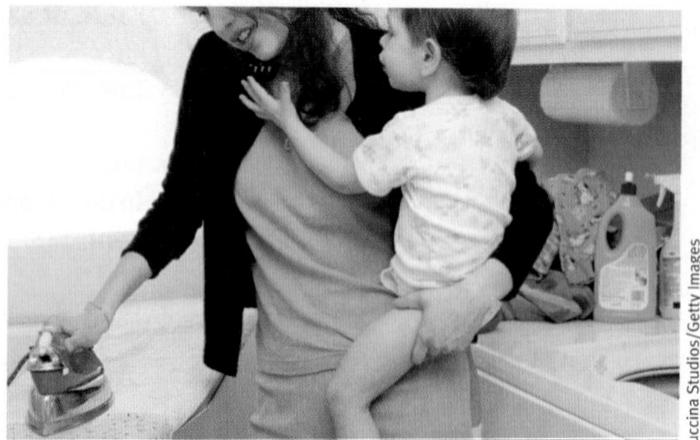

Buccina Studios/Getty Images

The value of the services that family members provide to each other is not counted as part of GDP.

Measuring GDP as Factor Income Earned from Firms in the Economy

A final way to calculate GDP is to add up all the income earned by factors of production from firms in the economy—the wages earned by labor; the interest paid to those who lend their savings to firms and the government; the rent earned by those who lease their land or structures to firms; and dividends, the profits paid to the shareholders, the owners of the firms' physical capital. This is a valid measure because the money firms earn by selling goods and services must go somewhere; whatever isn't paid as wages, interest, or rent is profit. Ultimately, profits are paid out to shareholders as dividends.

Figure 11-1 shows how this calculation works for our simplified economy. The shaded column at the far right shows the total wages, interest, and rent paid by all these firms as well as their total profit. Summing up all of these yields total factor income of $21,500—again, equal to GDP.

We won't emphasize factor income as much as the other two methods of calculating GDP. It's important to keep in mind, however, that all the money spent on domestically produced goods and services generates factor income to households.

What GDP Tells Us

Now we've seen the various ways that gross domestic product is calculated. But what does the measurement of GDP tell us?

The most important use of GDP is as a measure of the size of the economy, providing us a scale against which to measure the economic performance of other years or to compare the economic performance of other countries. For example, suppose you want to compare the economies of different nations. A natural approach is to compare their GDPs. In 2011, as we've seen, U.S. GDP was $15,321 billion, Japan's GDP was $5,866 billion, and the combined GDP of the 27 countries that make up the European Union was $17,578 billion. This comparison tells us that Japan, although it has the world's second-largest national economy, carries considerably less economic weight than does the United States. When taken in aggregate, Europe is America's equal or superior.

Still, one must be careful when using GDP numbers, especially when making comparisons over time. That's because part of the increase in the value of GDP over time represents increases in the *prices* of goods and services rather than an increase in output. For example, U.S. GDP was $7,415 billion in 1995 and had more than doubled to $15,321 billion by 2011. But the U.S. economy didn't actually double in size over that period. To measure actual changes in aggregate output, we need a modified version of GDP that is adjusted for price changes, known as *real GDP*. We'll see next how real GDP is calculated.

ECONOMICS > *IN ACTION*

CREATING THE NATIONAL ACCOUNTS

The national accounts, like modern macroeconomics, owe their creation to the Great Depression. As the economy plunged into depression, government officials found their ability to respond crippled not only by the lack of adequate economic theories but also by the lack of adequate information. All they had were scattered statistics: railroad freight car loadings, stock prices, and incomplete indexes of industrial production. They could only guess at what was happening to the economy as a whole.

In response to this perceived lack of information, the Department of Commerce commissioned Simon Kuznets, a young Russian-born economist, to develop a set of national income accounts. (Kuznets later won the Nobel Prize in economics for his work.) The first version of these accounts was presented to Congress in 1937 and in a research report titled *National Income, 1929–35*.

Quick Review

- A country's **national income and product accounts,** or **national accounts,** track flows of money among economic sectors.
- **Gross domestic product,** or **GDP,** can be calculated in three different ways: add up the **value added** by all firms; add up all spending on domestically produced **final goods and services,** or add up all factor income paid by firms. **Intermediate goods and services** are not included in the calculation of GDP.

Kuznets's initial estimates fell short of the full modern set of accounts because they focused on income, not production. The push to complete the national accounts came during World War II, when policy makers were in even more need of comprehensive measures of the economy's performance. The federal government began issuing estimates of gross domestic product and gross national product in 1942.

In January 2000, in its publication *Survey of Current Business,* the Department of Commerce ran an article titled "GDP: One of the Great Inventions of the 20th Century." This may seem a bit over the top, but national income accounting, invented in the United States, has since become a tool of economic analysis and policy making around the world.

CHECK YOUR UNDERSTANDING 11-1

1. Explain why the three methods of calculating GDP produce the same estimate of GDP.
2. Consider Figure 11-1 and suppose you mistakenly believed that total value added was $30,500, the sum of the sales price of a car and a car's worth of steel. What items would you be counting twice?

Solutions appear at back of book.

Real GDP: A Measure of Aggregate Output

In this chapter's opening story, we described how China passed Japan as the world's second-largest economy in 2010. At the time, Japan's economy was weakening: during the second quarter of 2010, output declined by an annual rate of 6.3%. Oddly, however, GDP was up. In fact, Japan's GDP measured in yen, its national currency, rose by an annual rate of 4.8% during the quarter. How was that possible? The answer is that Japan was experiencing inflation at the time. As a result, the yen value of Japan's GDP rose although output actually fell.

The moral of this story is that the commonly cited GDP number is an interesting and useful statistic, one that provides a good way to compare the size of different economies, but it's not a good measure of the economy's growth over time. GDP can grow because the economy grows, but it can also grow simply because of inflation. Even if an economy's output doesn't change, GDP will go up if the prices of the goods and services the economy produces have increased. Likewise, GDP can fall either because the economy is producing less or because prices have fallen.

In order to accurately measure the economy's growth, we need a measure of **aggregate output:** the total quantity of final goods and services the economy produces. The measure that is used for this purpose is known as *real GDP.* By tracking real GDP over time, we avoid the problem of changes in prices distorting the value of changes in production of goods and services over time. Let's look first at how real GDP is calculated, then at what it means.

Calculating Real GDP

To understand how real GDP is calculated, imagine an economy in which only two goods, apples and oranges, are produced and in which both goods are sold only to final consumers. The outputs and prices of the two fruits for two consecutive years are shown in Table 11-1.

Aggregate output is the economy's total quantity of output of final goods and services.

The first thing we can say about these data is that the value of sales increased from year 1 to year 2. In the first year, the total value of sales was (2,000 billion ×

TABLE 11-1 Calculating GDP and Real GDP in a Simple Economy

	Year 1	Year 2
Quantity of apples (billions)	2,000	2,200
Price of apple	$0.25	$0.30
Quantity of oranges (billions)	1,000	1,200
Price of orange	$0.50	$0.70
GDP (billions of dollars)	$1,000	$1,500
Real GDP (billions of year 1 dollars)	$1,000	$1,150

Real GDP is the total value of all final goods and services produced in the economy during a given year, calculated using the prices of a selected base year.

Nominal GDP is the value of all final goods and services produced in the economy during a given year, calculated using the prices current in the year in which the output is produced.

$0.25) + (1,000 billion × $0.50) = $1,000 billion; in the second it was (2,200 billion × $0.30) + (1,200 billion × $0.70) = $1,500 billion, which is 50% larger. But it is also clear from the table that this increase in the dollar value of GDP overstates the real growth in the economy. Although the quantities of both apples and oranges increased, the prices of both apples and oranges also rose. So part of the 50% increase in the dollar value of GDP from year 1 to year 2 simply reflects higher prices, not higher production of output.

To estimate the true increase in aggregate output produced, we have to ask the following question: how much would GDP have gone up if prices had *not* changed? To answer this question, we need to find the value of output in year 2 expressed in year 1 prices. In year 1 the price of apples was $0.25 each and the price of oranges $0.50 each. So year 2 output *at year 1 prices* is (2,200 billion × $0.25) + (1,200 billion × $0.50) = $1,150 billion. And output in year 1 at year 1 prices was $1,000 billion. So in this example GDP measured in year 1 prices rose 15%—from $1,000 billion to $1,150 billion.

Now we can define **real GDP:** it is the total value of final goods and services produced in the economy during a year, calculated as if prices had stayed constant at the level of some given base year. A real GDP number always comes with information about what the base year is.

A GDP number that has not been adjusted for changes in prices is calculated using the prices in the year in which the output is produced. Economists call this measure **nominal GDP,** GDP at current prices. If we had used nominal GDP to measure the true change in output from year 1 to year 2 in our apples and oranges example, we would have overstated the true growth in output: we would have claimed it to be 50%, when in fact it was only 15%. By comparing output in the two years using a common set of prices—the year 1 prices in this example—we are able to focus solely on changes in the quantity of output by eliminating the influence of changes in prices.

Table 11-2 shows a real-life version of our apples and oranges example. The second column shows nominal GDP in 1995, 2005, and 2010. The third column shows real GDP for each year in 2005 dollars. For 2005 the two numbers are the same. But real GDP in 1995 expressed in 2005 dollars was higher than nominal GDP in 1995, reflecting the fact that prices were in general higher in 2005 than in 1995. Real GDP in 2010 expressed in 2005 dollars, however, was less than nominal GDP in 2010 because prices in 2005 were lower than in 2010.

TABLE 11-2 Nominal versus Real GDP in 1995, 2005, and 2010

	Nominal GDP (billions of current dollars)	Real GDP (billions of 2005 dollars)
1995	$7,415	$9,086
2005	12,623	12,623
2010	14,527	13,088

You might have noticed that there is an alternative way to calculate real GDP using the data in Table 11-1. Why not measure it using the prices of year 2 rather than year 1 as the base-year prices? This procedure seems equally valid. According to that calculation, real GDP in year 1 at year 2 prices is (2,000 billion × $0.30) + (1,000 billion × $0.70) = $1,300 billion; real GDP in year 2 at year 2 prices is $1,500

Chained dollars is the method of calculating changes in real GDP using the average between the growth rate calculated using an early base year and the growth rate calculated using a late base year.

billion, the same as nominal GDP in year 2. So using year 2 prices as the base year, the growth rate of real GDP is equal to ($1,500 billion – $1,300 billion)/$1,300 billion = 0.154, or 15.4%. This is slightly higher than the figure we got from the previous calculation, in which year 1 prices were the base-year prices. In that calculation, we found that real GDP increased by 15%. Neither answer, 15.4% versus 15%, is more "correct" than the other.

In reality, the government economists who put together the U.S. national accounts have adopted a method to measure the change in real GDP known as chain-linking, which uses the average between the GDP growth rate calculated using an early base year and the GDP growth rate calculated using a late base year. As a result, U.S. statistics on real GDP are always expressed in **chained dollars.**

What Real GDP Doesn't Measure

GDP, nominal or real, is a measure of a country's aggregate output. Other things equal, a country with a larger population will have higher GDP simply because there are more people working. So if we want to compare GDP across countries

GDP AND THE MEANING OF LIFE

"I've been rich and I've been poor," the actress Mae West famously declared. "Believe me, rich is better." But is the same true for countries?

This figure shows two pieces of information for a number of countries: how rich they are, as measured by GDP per capita, and how people assess their well-being. Well-being was measured by a Gallup world survey that asked people to rate their lives at the current time and their expectations for the next five years. The graph shows the percentage of people who rated their well-being as "thriving." The figure seems to tell us three things:

1. *Rich is better.* Richer countries on average have higher well-being than poor countries.
2. *Money matters less as you grow richer.* The gain in life satisfaction as you go from GDP per capita of $5,000 to $20,000 is greater than the gain as you go from $20,000 to $35,000.
3. *Money isn't everything.* Israelis, though rich by world standards, are poorer than Americans—but they seem more satisfied with their lives. Japan is richer than most other nations, but by and large, quite miserable.

These results are consistent with the observation that high GDP per capita makes it easier to achieve a good life but that countries aren't equally successful in taking advantage of that possibility.

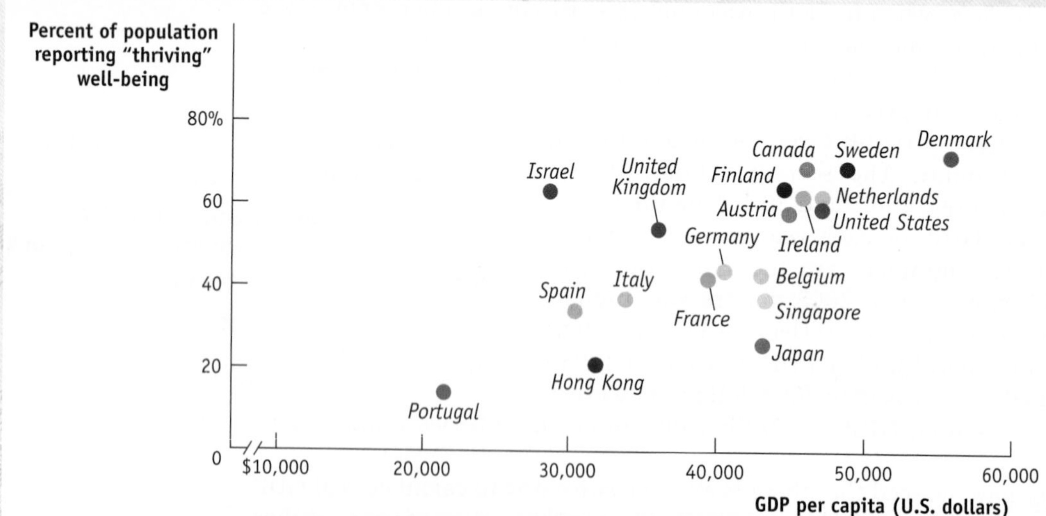

Source: Gallup; World Bank.

but want to eliminate the effect of differences in population size, we use the measure **GDP per capita**—GDP divided by the size of the population, equivalent to the average GDP per person.

GDP per capita is GDP divided by the size of the population; it is equivalent to the average GDP per person.

Real GDP per capita can be a useful measure in some circumstances, such as in a comparison of labor productivity between countries. However, despite the fact that it is a rough measure of the average real output per person, real GDP per capita has well-known limitations as a measure of a country's living standards. Every once in a while economists are accused of believing that growth in real GDP per capita is the only thing that matters—that is, thinking that increasing real GDP per capita is a goal in itself. In fact, economists rarely make that mistake; the idea that economists care only about real GDP per capita is a sort of urban legend. Let's take a moment to be clear about why a country's real GDP per capita is not a sufficient measure of human welfare in that country and why growth in real GDP per capita is not an appropriate policy goal in itself.

One way to think about this issue is to say that an increase in real GDP means an expansion in the economy's production possibility frontier. Because the economy has increased its productive capacity, there are more things that society can achieve. But whether society actually makes good use of that increased potential to improve living standards is another matter. To put it in a slightly different way, your income may be higher this year than last year, but whether you use that higher income to actually improve your quality of life is your choice.

So let's say it again: real GDP per capita is a measure of an economy's average aggregate output per person—and so of what it *can* do. It is not a sufficient goal in itself because it doesn't address how a country uses that output to affect living standards. A country with a high GDP can afford to be healthy, to be well educated, and in general to have a good quality of life. But there is not a one-to-one match between GDP and the quality of life.

ECONOMICS ➤ *IN ACTION*

MIRACLE IN VENEZUELA?

The South American nation of Venezuela has a distinction that may surprise you: in recent years, it has had one of the world's fastest-growing nominal GDPs. Between 2000 and 2010, Venezuelan nominal GDP grew by an average of 29% each year—much faster than nominal GDP in the United States or even in booming economies like China.

So is Venezuela experiencing an economic miracle? No, it's just suffering from unusually high inflation. Figure 11-2 shows Venezuela's nominal and real GDP from 2000 to 2010, with real GDP measured in 1997 prices. Real GDP did

FIGURE 11-2 Real Versus Nominal GDP in Venezuela

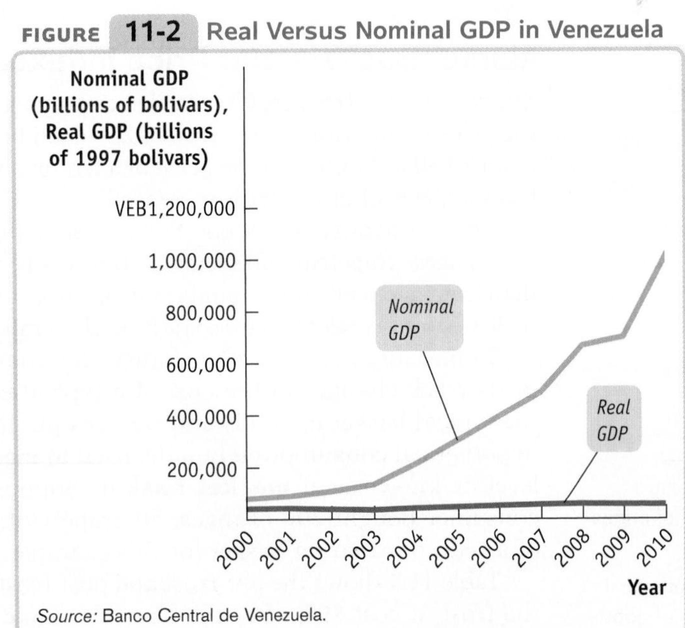

Source: Banco Central de Venezuela.

grow over the period, but at an annual rate of only 3%. That's about twice the U.S. growth rate over the same period, but it is far short of China's 10% growth.

▼ Quick Review

- To determine the actual growth in **aggregate output,** we calculate **real GDP** using prices from some given base year. In contrast, **nominal GDP** is the value of aggregate output calculated with current prices. U.S. statistics on real GDP are always expressed in **chained dollars.**
- Real **GDP per capita** is a measure of the average aggregate output per person. But it is not a sufficient measure of human welfare, nor is it an appropriate goal in itself, because it does not reflect important aspects of living standards within an economy.

CHECK YOUR UNDERSTANDING 11-2

1. Assume there are only two goods in the economy, french fries and onion rings. In 2011, 1,000,000 servings of french fries were sold at $0.40 each and 800,000 servings of onion rings at $0.60 each. From 2011 to 2012, the price of french fries rose by 25% and the servings sold fell by 10%; the price of onion rings fell by 15% and the servings sold rose by 5%.
   a. Calculate nominal GDP in 2011 and 2012. Calculate real GDP in 2012 using 2011 prices.
   b. Why would an assessment of growth using nominal GDP be misguided?
2. From 2005 to 2010, the price of electronic equipment fell dramatically and the price of housing rose dramatically. What are the implications of this in deciding whether to use 2005 or 2010 as the base year in calculating 2012 real GDP?

Solutions appear at back of book.

Price Indexes and the Aggregate Price Level

In 2011 and 2012, Americans faced sticker shock at the gas pump: the price of a gallon of regular gasoline had risen from an average of $1.61 at the end of December 2008 to close to $4. Many other prices were also up. Some prices, like those for electronics, though, were heading down. Yet practically everyone felt that the overall cost of living was rising. But how fast?

Clearly, there was a need for a single number summarizing what was happening to consumer prices. Just as macroeconomists find it useful to have a single number representing the overall level of output, they also find it useful to have a single number representing the overall level of prices: the **aggregate price level.** Yet a huge variety of goods and services are produced and consumed in the economy. How can we summarize the prices of all these goods and services with a single number? The answer lies in the concept of a *price index*—a concept best introduced with an example.

Market Baskets and Price Indexes

Suppose that a frost in Florida destroys most of the citrus harvest. As a result, the price of an orange rises from $0.20 each to $0.40, the price of grapefruit rises from $0.60 to $1.00, and the price of a lemon rises from $0.25 to $0.45. How much has the price of citrus fruit increased?

One way to answer that question is to state three numbers—the changes in prices for oranges, grapefruit, and lemons. But this is a very cumbersome method. Rather than having to recite three numbers in an effort to track changes in the prices of citrus fruit, we would prefer to have some kind of overall measure of the *average* price change.

To measure average price changes for consumer goods and services, economists track changes in the cost of a typical consumer's *consumption bundle*—the typical basket of goods and services purchased before the price changes. A hypothetical consumption bundle, used to measure changes in the overall price level, is known as a **market basket.** Suppose that before the frost a typical consumer bought 200 oranges, 50 grapefruit, and 100 lemons over the course of a year, our market basket for this example.

The **aggregate price level** is a measure of the overall level of prices in the economy.

A **market basket** is a hypothetical set of consumer purchases of goods and services.

Table 11-3 shows the pre-frost and post-frost cost of this market basket. Before the frost, it cost $95; after the frost, the same bundle of goods cost $175. Since $175/$95 = 1.842, the post-frost basket costs 1.842 times the cost of the pre-frost

TABLE 11-3 Calculating the Cost of a Market Basket

	Pre-frost	Post-frost
Price of orange	$0.20	$0.40
Price of grapefruit	0.60	1.00
Price of lemon	0.25	0.45
Cost of market basket (200 oranges, 50 grapefruit, 100 lemons)	(200 × $0.20) + (50 × $0.60) + (100 × $0.25) = $95.00	(200 × $0.40) + (50 × $1.00) + (100 × $0.45) = $175.00

A **price index** measures the cost of purchasing a given market basket in a given year, where that cost is normalized so that it is equal to 100 in the selected base year.

The **inflation rate** is the percent change per year in a price index—typically the consumer price index.

The **consumer price index,** or **CPI,** measures the cost of the market basket of a typical urban American family.

basket, a cost increase of 84.2%. In this example, the average price of citrus fruit has increased 84.2% since the base year as a result of the frost, where the base year is the initial year used in the measurement of the price change.

Economists use the same method to measure changes in the overall price level: they track changes in the cost of buying a given market basket. In addition, they perform another simplification in order to avoid having to keep track of the information that the market basket cost, for example, $95 in such-and-such a year. They *normalize* the measure of the aggregate price level, which means that they set the cost of the market basket equal to 100 in the chosen base year. Working with a market basket and a base year, and after performing normalization, we obtain what is known as a **price index,** a normalized measure of the overall price level. It is always cited along with the year for which the aggregate price level is being measured and the base year. A price index can be calculated using the following formula:

$$\textbf{(11-1)}\ \text{Price index in a given year} = \frac{\text{Cost of market basket in a given year}}{\text{Cost of market basket in base year}} \times 100$$

In our example, the citrus fruit market basket cost $95 in the base year, the year before the frost. So by Equation 11-1 we define the price index for citrus fruit as (cost of market basket in current year/$95) × 100, yielding an index of 100 for the period before the frost and 184.2 after the frost. You should note that the price index for the base year always results in a price index equal to 100. This is because the price index in the base year is equal to: (cost of market basket in base year/cost of market basket in base year) × 100 = 100.

Thus, the price index makes it clear that the average price of citrus has risen 84.2% as a consequence of the frost. Because of its simplicity and intuitive appeal, the method we've just described is used to calculate a variety of price indexes to track average price changes among a variety of different groups of goods and services. For example, the *consumer price index,* which we'll discuss shortly, is the most widely used measure of the aggregate price level, the overall price level of final consumer goods and services across the economy.

Price indexes are also the basis for measuring inflation. The **inflation rate** is the annual percent change in an official price index. The inflation rate from year 1 to year 2 is calculated using the following formula, where we assume that year 1 and year 2 are consecutive years.

$$\textbf{(11-2)}\ \text{Inflation rate} = \frac{\text{Price index in year 2} - \text{Price index in year 1}}{\text{Price index in year 1}} \times 100$$

Typically, a news report that cites "the inflation rate" is referring to the annual percent change in the consumer price index.

The Consumer Price Index

The most widely used measure of prices in the United States is the **consumer price index** (often referred to simply as the **CPI**), which is intended to show how the cost of all purchases by a typical urban family has changed

FIGURE 11-3 The Makeup of the Consumer Price Index in 2011

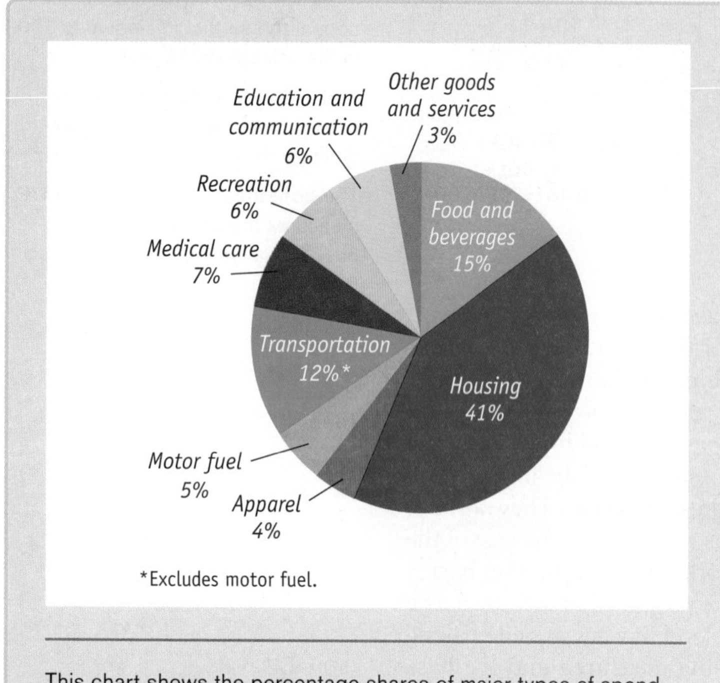

This chart shows the percentage shares of major types of spending in the CPI as of December 2011. Housing, food, transportation, and motor fuel made up about 73% of the CPI market basket. (Numbers don't add to 100% due to rounding.)
Source: Bureau of Labor Statistics.

over time. It is calculated by surveying market prices for a market basket that is constructed to represent the consumption of a typical family of four living in a typical American city. The base period for the index is currently 1982–1984; that is, the index is calculated so that the average of consumer prices in 1982–1984 is 100.

The market basket used to calculate the CPI is far more complex than the three-fruit market basket we described above. In fact, to calculate the CPI, the Bureau of Labor Statistics sends its employees out to survey supermarkets, gas stations, hardware stores, and so on—some 23,000 retail outlets in 87 cities. Every month it tabulates about 80,000 prices, on everything from romaine lettuce to a medical check-up. Figure 11-3 shows the weight of major categories in the consumer price index as of December 2011. For example, motor fuel, mainly gasoline, accounted for 5% of the CPI in December 2011. So when gas prices rose 150%, from about $1.61 a gallon in late 2008 to $3.96 a gallon in May 2011, the effect was to increase the CPI by about 1.5 times 5%—that is, around 7.5%.

Figure 11-4 shows how the CPI has changed since measurement began in 1913. Since 1940, the CPI has risen steadily, although its annual percent increases in recent years have been much smaller than those of the 1970s and early 1980s. A logarithmic scale is used so that equal percent changes in the CPI have the same slope.

FIGURE 11-4 The CPI, 1913–2011

Since 1940, the CPI has risen steadily. But the annual percentage increases in recent years have been much smaller than those of the 1970s and early 1980s. (The vertical axis is measured on a logarithmic scale so that equal percent changes in the CPI have the same slope.)
Source: Bureau of Labor Statistics.

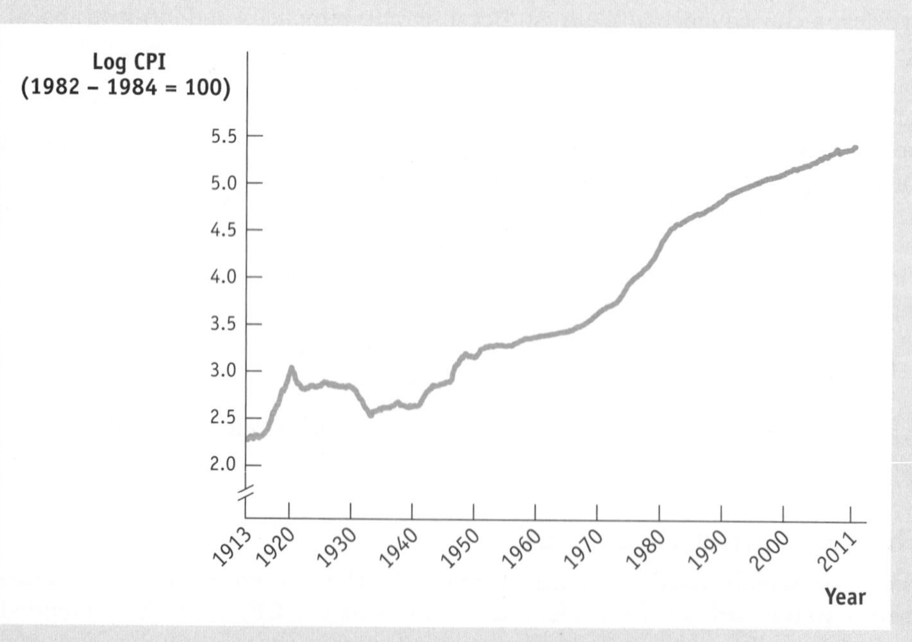

The United States is not the only country that calculates a consumer price index. In fact, nearly every country has one. As you might expect, the market baskets that make up these indexes differ quite a lot from country to country. In poor countries, where people must spend a high proportion of their income just to feed themselves, food makes up a large share of the price index. Among high-income countries, differences in consumption patterns lead to differences in the price indexes: the Japanese price index puts a larger weight on raw fish and a smaller weight on beef than ours does, and the French price index puts a larger weight on wine.

The **producer price index,** or **PPI,** measures changes in the prices of goods purchased by producers.

The **GDP deflator** for a given year is 100 times the ratio of nominal GDP to real GDP in that year.

Other Price Measures

There are two other price measures that are also widely used to track economy-wide price changes. One is the **producer price index** (or **PPI,** which used to be known as the *wholesale price index*). As its name suggests, the producer price index measures the cost of a typical basket of goods and services—containing raw commodities such as steel, electricity, coal, and so on—purchased by producers. Because commodity producers are relatively quick to raise prices when they perceive a change in overall demand for their goods, the PPI often responds to inflationary or deflationary pressures more quickly than the CPI. As a result, the PPI is often regarded as an "early warning signal" of changes in the inflation rate.

The other widely used price measure is the *GDP deflator;* it isn't exactly a price index, although it serves the same purpose. Recall how we distinguished between nominal GDP (GDP in current prices) and real GDP (GDP calculated using the prices of a base year). The **GDP deflator** for a given year is equal to 100 times the ratio of nominal GDP for that year to real GDP for that year. Since real GDP is currently expressed in 2005 dollars, the GDP deflator for 2005 is equal to 100. If nominal GDP doubles but real GDP does not change, the GDP deflator indicates that the aggregate price level doubled.

Perhaps the most important point about the different inflation rates generated by these three measures of prices is that they usually move closely together (although the producer price index tends to fluctuate more than either of the other two measures). Figure 11-5 shows the annual percent changes in the three indexes since 1930. By all three measures, the U.S. economy experienced

FIGURE 11-5 The CPI, the PPI, and the GDP Deflator

As the figure shows, the three different measures of inflation, the PPI (orange), the CPI (green), and the GDP deflator (purple), usually move closely together. Each reveals a drastic acceleration of inflation during the 1970s and a return to relative price stability in the 1990s.

Sources: Bureau of Labor Statistics; Bureau of Economic Analysis.

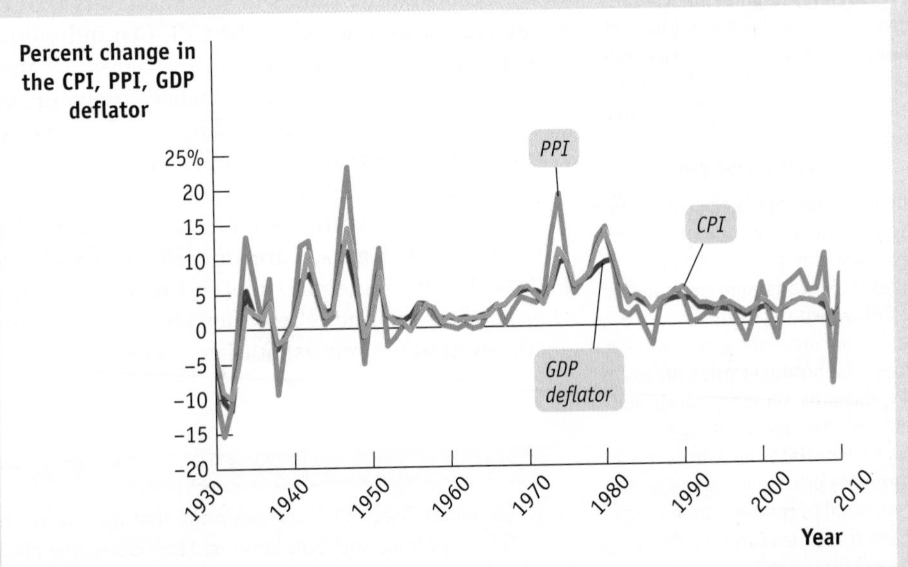

deflation during the early years of the Great Depression, inflation during World War II, accelerating inflation during the 1970s, and a return to relative price stability in the 1990s. Notice, by the way, the dramatic ups and downs in producer prices from 2000 to 2010 on the graph; this reflects large swings in energy and food prices, which play a much bigger role in the PPI than they do in either the CPI or the GDP deflator.

ECONOMICS ➤ IN ACTION

INDEXING TO THE CPI

Although GDP is a very important number for shaping economic policy, official statistics on GDP don't have a direct effect on people's lives. The CPI, by contrast, has a direct and immediate impact on millions of Americans. The reason is that many payments are tied, or "indexed," to the CPI—the amount paid rises or falls when the CPI rises or falls.

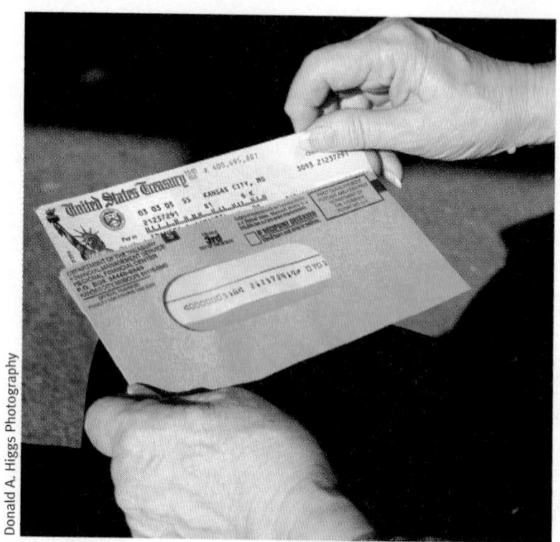

Donald A. Higgs Photography

A small change in the CPI has large consequences for those dependent on Social Security payments.

The practice of indexing payments to consumer prices goes back to the dawn of the United States as a nation. In 1780 the Massachusetts State Legislature recognized that the pay of its soldiers fighting the British needed to be increased because of inflation that occurred during the Revolutionary War. The legislature adopted a formula that made a soldier's pay proportional to the cost of a market basket, consisting of 5 bushels of corn, 68⁴⁄₇ pounds of beef, 10 pounds of sheep's wool, and 16 pounds of sole leather.

Today, 54 million people, most of them old or disabled, receive payments from Social Security, a national retirement program that accounts for almost a quarter of current total federal spending—more than the defense budget. The amount of an individual's Social Security payment is determined by a formula that reflects his or her previous payments into the system as well as other factors. In addition, all Social Security payments are adjusted each year to offset any increase in consumer prices over the previous year. The CPI is used to calculate the official estimate of the inflation rate used to adjust these payments yearly. So every percentage point added to the official estimate of the rate of inflation adds 1% to the checks received by tens of millions of individuals.

Other government payments are also indexed to the CPI. In addition, income tax brackets, the bands of income levels that determine a taxpayer's income tax rate, are also indexed to the CPI. (An individual in a higher income bracket pays a higher income tax rate in a progressive tax system like ours.) Indexing also extends to the private sector, where many private contracts, including some wage settlements, contain cost-of-living allowances (called COLAs) that adjust payments in proportion to changes in the CPI.

Because the CPI plays such an important and direct role in people's lives, it's a politically sensitive number. The Bureau of Labor Statistics, which calculates the CPI, takes great care in collecting and interpreting price and consumption data. It uses a complex method in which households are surveyed to determine what they buy and where they shop, and a carefully selected sample of stores are surveyed to get representative prices.

▼ Quick Review

- Changes in the **aggregate price level** are measured by the cost of buying a particular **market basket** during different years. A **price index** for a given year is the cost of the market basket in that year normalized so that the price index equals 100 in a selected base year.
- The **inflation rate** is calculated as the percent change in a price index. The most commonly used price index is the **consumer price index,** or **CPI,** which tracks the cost of a basket of consumer goods and services. The **producer price index,** or **PPI,** does the same for goods and services used as inputs by firms. The **GDP deflator** measures the aggregate price level as the ratio of nominal to real GDP times 100. These three measures normally behave quite similarly.

CHECK YOUR UNDERSTANDING 11-3

1. Consider Table 11-3 but suppose that the market basket is composed of 100 oranges, 50 grapefruit, and 200 lemons. How does this change the pre-frost and post-frost price indexes? Explain. Generalize your explanation to how the construction of the market basket affects the price index.

2. For each of the following events, how would an economist using a 10-year-old market basket create a bias in measuring the change in the cost of living today?
   a. A typical family owns more cars than it would have a decade ago. Over that time, the average price of a car has increased more than the average prices of other goods.
   b. Virtually no households had broadband Internet access a decade ago. Now many households have it, and the price has regularly fallen each year.
3. The consumer price index in the United States (base period 1982–1984) was 218.056 in 2010 and 224.939 in 2011. Calculate the inflation rate from 2010 to 2011.

Solutions appear at back of book.

WORKED PROBLEM

A Change in Fortune?

In Figure 11-2 on page 335, we compare real versus nominal GDP in Venezuela for the period 2000 to 2010. The accompanying table shows the underlying data on nominal GDP (in billions of bolivars), real GDP (in billions of 1997 bolivars), and population (in thousands) for the years 2000, 2002, 2004, 2006, 2008, and 2010. For each period, 2000–2002, 2002–2004, 2004–2006, 2006–2008, and 2008–2010, calculate the real growth rate in GDP per capita.

Year	Nominal GDP (billions of bolivars)	Real GDP (billions of 1997 bolivars)	Population (thousands)
2000	VEB79,655.69	VEB41,013.29	24,765
2002	107,840.17	38,650.11	25,220
2004	212,683.08	42,172.34	26,127
2006	393,926.24	51,116.53	27,031
2008	677,593.64	58,525.07	27,935
2010	1,016,834.75	55,807.51	28,834

STEP 1: Calculate real GDP per capita (in bolivars) for each year in the table.

Read the section "What Real GDP Doesn't Measure," beginning on page 334. Real GDP per capita is GDP divided by the size of the population and is equivalent to average GDP per person.

Real GDP per capita for each of the years is listed in the table below. For 2000, real GDP per capita is calculated by multiplying VEB41,013.29 by 1 billion, and then dividing by 24,765 multiplied by 1,000: (VEB41,013.29 × 1,000,000,000)/(24,765 × 1,000). Multiplying the numerator by 1 billion and multiplying the denominator by 1,000 is done to correct for the fact that real GDP is expressed in billions of bolivars and the population is expressed in thousands of people. ■

Year	Real GDP (billions of 1997 bolivars)	Population (thousands)	Real GDP per capita (thousands of 1997 bolivars)
2000	VEB41,013.29	24,765	VEB1,656
2002	38,650.11	25,220	1,533
2004	42,172.34	26,127	1,614
2006	51,116.53	27,031	1,891
2008	58,525.07	27,935	2,095
2010	55,807.51	28,834	1,935

STEP 2: Calculate the change in real GDP per capita for the periods 2000–2002, 2002–2004, 2004–2006, 2006–2008, and 2008–2010.

The percent change in real GDP per capita between year 1 and year 2 is calculated using the following formula:

$$\%\ \textit{change in real GDP per capita} = \frac{\textit{Real GDP per capita in year 2} - \textit{Real GDP per capita in year 1}}{\textit{Real GDP per capita in year 1}} \times 100$$

Note the similarity between this equation and Equation 11-2 on page 337. They are similar because both measures calculate rates of change.

The percent change in real GDP per capita for each of the periods is presented in the second column of the table.

Year	% Change in real GDP per capita
2000–2002	−7.43%
2002–2004	5.28%
2004–2006	17.16%
2006–2008	10.79%
2008–2010	−7.64%

The percent change in real GDP per capita for 2000–2002 is calculated by subtracting real GDP per capita in 2000 from real GDP per capita in 2002, dividing by real GDP per capita in 2000, and then multiplying this expression by 100:

$$\frac{\text{VEB1,533} - \text{VEB1,656}}{\text{VEB1,656}} \times 100 = -7.43\% \ ■$$

SUMMARY

1. Economists keep track of the flows of money between sectors with the **national income and product accounts,** or **national accounts.**
2. **Gross domestic product,** or **GDP,** measures the value of all **final goods and services** produced in the economy. It does not include the value of **intermediate goods and services.** It can be calculated in three ways: add up the **value added** by all producers; add up all spending on domestically produced final goods and services; or add up all the income paid by domestic firms to factors of production. These three methods are equivalent because in the economy as a whole, total income paid by domestic firms to factors of production must equal total spending on domestically produced final goods and services.
3. **Real GDP** is the value of the final goods and services produced calculated using the prices of a selected base year. Except in the base year, real GDP is not the same as **nominal GDP,** the value of **aggregate output** calculated using current prices. Analysis of the growth rate of aggregate output must use real GDP because doing so eliminates any change in the value of aggregate output due solely to price changes. Real **GDP per capita** is a measure of average aggregate output per person but is not in itself an appropriate policy goFal. U.S. statistics on real GDP are always expressed in **chained dollars.**
4. To measure the **aggregate price level,** economists calculate the cost of purchasing a **market basket.** A **price index** is the ratio of the current cost of that market basket to the cost in a selected base year, multiplied by 100.
5. The **inflation rate** is the yearly percent change in a price index, typically based on the **consumer price index,** or **CPI,** the most common measure of the aggregate price level. A similar index for goods and services purchased by firms is the **producer price index,** or **PPI.** Finally, economists also use the **GDP deflator,** which measures the price level by calculating the ratio of nominal to real GDP times 100.

KEY TERMS

National income and product accounts (national accounts), p. 328
Final goods and services, p. 328
Intermediate goods and services, p. 328
Gross domestic product (GDP), p. 328
Value added, p. 329
Aggregate output, p. 332
Real GDP, p. 333
Nominal GDP, p. 333
Chained dollars, p. 334
GDP per capita, p. 335
Aggregate price level, p. 336
Market basket, p. 336
Price index, p. 337
Inflation rate, p. 337
Consumer price index (CPI), p. 337
Producer price index (PPI), p. 339
GDP deflator, p. 339

PROBLEMS

1. The small economy of Pizzania produces three goods (bread, cheese, and pizza), each produced by a separate company. The bread and cheese companies produce all the inputs they need to make bread and cheese, respectively. The pizza company uses the bread and cheese from the other companies to make its pizzas. All three companies employ labor to help produce their goods, and the difference between the value of goods sold and the sum of labor and input costs is the firm's profit. The accompanying table summarizes the activities of the three companies when all the bread and cheese produced are sold to the pizza company as inputs in the production of pizzas.

	Bread company	Cheese company	Pizza company
Cost of inputs	$0	$0	$50 (bread) 35 (cheese)
Wages	15	20	75
Value of output	50	35	200

a. Calculate GDP as the value added in production.

b. Calculate GDP as spending on final goods and services.

c. Calculate GDP as factor income.

2. In the economy of Pizzania (from Problem 1), bread and cheese produced are sold both to the pizza company for inputs in the production of pizzas and to consumers as final goods. The accompanying table summarizes the activities of the three companies.

	Bread company	Cheese company	Pizza company
Cost of inputs	$0	$0	$50 (bread) 35 (cheese)
Wages	25	30	75
Value of output	100	60	200

a. Calculate GDP as the value added in production.

b. Calculate GDP as spending on final goods and services.

c. Calculate GDP as factor income.

3. Which of the following transactions will be included in GDP for the United States?

a. Coca-Cola builds a new bottling plant in the United States.

b. Delta sells one of its existing airplanes to Korean Air.

c. Ms. Moneybags buys an existing share of Disney stock.

d. A California winery produces a bottle of Chardonnay and sells it to a customer in Montreal, Canada.

e. An American buys a bottle of French perfume in Tulsa.

f. A book publisher produces too many copies of a new book; the books don't sell this year, so the publisher adds the surplus books to inventories.

4. The economy of Britannica produces three goods: computers, DVDs, and pizza. The accompanying table shows the prices and output of the three goods for the years 2010, 2011, and 2012.

	Computers		DVDs		Pizzas	
Year	Price	Quantity	Price	Quantity	Price	Quantity
2010	$900	10	$10	100	$15	2
2011	1,000	10.5	12	105	16	2
2012	1,050	12	14	110	17	3

a. What is the percent change in production of each of the goods from 2010 to 2011 and from 2011 to 2012?

b. What is the percent change in prices of each of the goods from 2010 to 2011 and from 2011 to 2012?

c. Calculate nominal GDP in Britannica for each of the three years. What is the percent change in nominal GDP from 2010 to 2011 and from 2011 to 2012?

d. Calculate real GDP in Britannica using 2010 prices for each of the three years. What is the percent change in real GDP from 2010 to 2011 and from 2011 to 2012?

5. The accompanying table shows data on nominal GDP (in billions of dollars), real GDP (in billions of 2005 dollars), and population (in thousands) of the United States in 1960, 1970, 1980, 1990, 2000, and

2010. The U.S. price level rose consistently over the period 1960–2010.

Year	Nominal GDP (billions of dollars)	Real GDP (billions of 2005 dollars)	Population (thousands)
1960	$526.4	$2,828.5	180,760
1970	1,038.5	4,266.3	205,089
1980	2,788.1	5,834.0	227,726
1990	5,800.5	8,027.1	250,181
2000	9,951.5	11,216.4	282,418
2010	14,526.5	13,088.0	310,106

a. Why is real GDP greater than nominal GDP for all years until 2000 and lower for 2010?

b. Calculate the percent change in real GDP from 1960 to 1970, 1970 to 1980, 1980 to 1990, 1990 to 2000, and 2000 to 2010. Which period had the highest growth rate?

c. Calculate real GDP per capita for each of the years in the table.

d. Calculate the percent change in real GDP per capita from 1960 to 1970, 1970 to 1980, 1980 to 1990, 1990 to 2000, and 2000 to 2010. Which period had the highest growth rate?

e. How do the percent change in real GDP and the percent change in real GDP per capita compare? Which is larger? Do we expect them to have this relationship?

6. Eastland College is concerned about the rising price of textbooks that students must purchase. To better identify the increase in the price of textbooks, the dean asks you, the Economics Department's star student, to create an index of textbook prices. The average student purchases three English, two math, and four economics textbooks per year. The prices of these books are given in the accompanying table.

	2010	2011	2012
English textbook	$50	$55	$57
Math textbook	70	72	74
Economics textbook	80	90	100

a. What is the percent change in the price of an English textbook from 2010 to 2012?

b. What is the percent change in the price of a math textbook from 2010 to 2012?

c. What is the percent change in the price of an economics textbook from 2010 to 2012?

d. Using 2010 as a base year, create a price index for these books for all years.

e. What is the percent change in the price index from 2010 to 2012?

7. The consumer price index, or CPI, measures the cost of living for a typical urban household by multiplying the price for each category of expenditure (housing, food, and so on) times a measure of the importance of that expenditure in the average consumer's market basket and summing over all categories. However, using data from the consumer price index, we can see that changes in the cost of living for different types of consumers can vary a great deal. Let's compare the cost of living for a hypothetical retired person and a hypothetical college student. Let's assume that the market basket of a retired person is allocated in the following way: 10% on housing, 15% on food, 5% on transportation, 60% on medical care, 0% on education, and 10% on recreation. The college student's market basket is allocated as follows: 5% on housing, 15% on food, 20% on transportation, 0% on medical care, 40% on education, and 20% on recreation. The accompanying table shows the September 2012 CPI for each of the relevant categories.

	CPI September 2012
Housing	223.9
Food	234.2
Transportation	221.7
Medical care	418.0
Education	134.6
Recreation	115.0

Calculate the overall CPI for the retired person and for the college student by multiplying the CPI for each of the categories by the relative importance of that category to the individual and then summing each of the categories. The CPI for all items in September 2012 was 231.4. How do your calculations for a CPI for the retired person and the college student compare to the overall CPI?

8. Each month the Bureau of Labor Statistics releases the Consumer Price Index Summary for the previous month. Go to the Bureau of Labor Statistics home page at www.bls.gov. Place the cursor over the "Economic Releases" tab and then click on "Major Economic Indicators" in the drop-down menu that appears. Once on the "Major Economic Indicators" page, click on "Consumer Price Index." Use the "not seasonally adjusted" figures. On that page, under "Table of Contents," click on "Consumer Price Index Summary." What was the CPI for the previous month? How did it change from the previous month? How does the CPI compare to the same month one year ago?

9. The accompanying table provides the annual real GDP (in billions of 2005 dollars) and nominal GDP (in billions of dollars) for the United States.

	2007	2008	2009	2010	2011
Real GDP (billions of 2005 dollars)	13,206.4	13,161.9	12,703.1	13,088.0	13,299.1
Nominal GDP (billions of dollars)	14,028.7	14,291.5	13,939.0	14,526.5	15,075.7

a. Calculate the GDP deflator for each year.

b. Use the GDP deflator to calculate the inflation rate for all years except 2007.

10. The accompanying table contains two price indexes for the years 2009, 2010, and 2011: the GDP deflator and the CPI. For each price index, calculate the inflation rate from 2009 to 2010 and from 2010 to 2011.

Year	GDP deflator	CPI
2009	109.729	214.537
2010	110.992	218.056
2011	113.359	224.939

EXTEND YOUR UNDERSTANDING

11. The cost of a college education in the United States is rising at a rate faster than inflation. The table below shows the average cost of a college education in the United States during the academic year that began in 2009 and the academic year that began in 2010 for public and private colleges. Assume the costs listed in the table are the only costs experienced by the various college students in a single year.

a. Calculate the cost of living for an average college student in each category for 2009 and 2010.

b. Calculate an inflation rate for each type of college student between 2009 and 2010.

	Cost of college education during academic year beginning 2009 (averages in 2009 dollars)				
	Tuition and fees	Room and board	Books and supplies	Transportation	Other expenses
Two-year public college: commuter	$2,544	$7,202	$1,098	$1,445	$1,996
Four-year public college: in-state, on-campus	7,020	8,193	1,122	1,079	1,974
Four-year public college: out-of-state, on-campus	18,548	8,193	1,122	1,079	1,974
Four-year private college: on-campus	26,273	9,363	1,116	849	1,427
	Cost of college education during academic year beginning 2010 (averages in 2010 dollars)				
	Tuition and fees	Room and board	Books and supplies	Transportation	Other expenses
Two-year public college: commuter	$2,713	$7,259	$1,133	$1,491	$2,041
Four-year public college: in-state, on-campus	7,605	8,535	1,137	1,073	1,989
Four-year public college: out-of-state, on-campus	19,595	8,535	1,137	1,073	1,989
Four-year private college: on-campus	27,293	9,700	1,181	862	1,440

Unemployment and Inflation

A VERY BRITISH DILEMMA

Alex Segre/Alamy

Through good times and bad, the Old Lady of Threadneedle Street has been managing Great Britain's money supply for over 300 years.

David Levenson/Alamy

WHAT YOU WILL LEARN IN THIS CHAPTER

- How **unemployment** is measured and how the **unemployment rate** is calculated
- The significance of the unemployment rate for the economy
- The relationship between the unemployment rate and economic growth
- The factors that determine the **natural rate of unemployment**
- The economic costs of inflation
- How inflation and deflation create winners and losers
- Why policy makers try to maintain a stable rate of inflation

THE BANK OF ENGLAND IS A venerable institution—so venerable that it makes the Federal Reserve, its American counterpart, look like a youthful upstart. The Old Lady of Threadneedle Street, as the Bank is sometimes known, has been managing Great Britain's money supply for three centuries—pumping up the money supply when the economy needs a boost, putting on the brakes when inflation looms.

But in early 2011, it wasn't at all clear what the Bank should do. British inflation was rising: in February 2011 consumer prices were 4.4 percent higher than they had been a year earlier, a rate of increase far above the Bank's comfort level. At the same time, the British economy was still suffering the aftereffects of a severe recession, and unemployment, especially among young people, was disturbingly high. So should the Bank have focused on fighting inflation, or should it have kept trying to bring down unemployment?

Opinion was sharply divided. The Bank faced "a genuine problem of credibility," declared Patrick Minford, a professor at Cardiff University, who urged the Bank to fight inflation by raising interest rates. The rise in inflation reflected temporary factors and would soon reverse course, countered Adam Posen, a member of the Bank's Policy Committee, who argued that any tightening would risk putting Britain into a prolonged slump.

Whoever was right, the dispute highlighted the key concerns of macroeconomic policy. Unemployment and inflation are the two great evils of macroeconomics. So the two principal goals of macroeconomic policy are low unemployment and price stability, usually defined as a low but positive rate of inflation. Unfortunately, those goals sometimes appear to be in conflict with each other: economists often warn that policies intended to fight unemployment run the risk of increasing inflation; conversely, policies intended to bring down inflation can raise unemployment.

The nature of the trade-off between low unemployment and low inflation, along with the policy dilemma it creates, is a topic reserved for later chapters. This chapter provides an overview of the basic facts about unemployment and inflation: how they're measured, how they affect consumers and firms, and how they change over time.

Employment is the number of people currently employed in the economy, either full time or part time.

Unemployment is the number of people who are actively looking for work but aren't currently employed.

The Unemployment Rate

Britain had an unemployment rate of 7.7 percent in early 2011, up from just 5.7 percent in 2008. That was bad. But the U.S. unemployment rate was even worse. Figure 12-1 shows the U.S. unemployment rate from 1948 to mid-2011; as you can see, unemployment soared during the 2007–2009 recession and had fallen only modestly by 2011. What did the rise in the unemployment rate mean, and why was it such a big factor in people's lives? To understand why policy makers pay so much attention to employment and unemployment, we need to understand how they are both defined and measured.

FIGURE 12-1 The U.S. Unemployment Rate, 1948–2011

The unemployment rate has fluctuated widely over time. It always rises during recessions, which are shown by the shaded bars. It usually, but not always, falls during periods of economic expansion.

Sources: Bureau of Labor Statistics; National Bureau of Economic Research.

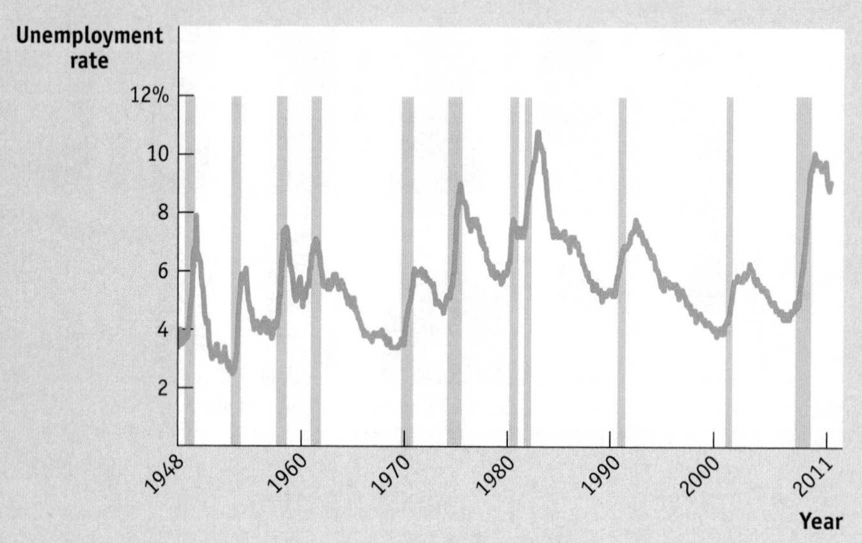

Defining and Measuring Unemployment

It's easy to define employment: you're employed if and only if you have a job. **Employment** is the total number of people currently employed, either full time or part time.

Unemployment, however, is a more subtle concept. Just because a person isn't working doesn't mean that we consider that person unemployed. For example, as of September 2012, there were 38.2 million retired workers in the United States receiving Social Security checks. Most of them were probably happy that they were no longer working, so we wouldn't consider someone who has settled into a comfortable, well-earned retirement to be unemployed. There were also 7.9 million disabled U.S. workers receiving benefits because they were unable to work. Again, although they weren't working, we wouldn't normally consider them to be unemployed.

The U.S. Census Bureau, the federal agency tasked with collecting data on unemployment, considers the unemployed to be those who are "jobless, looking for jobs, and available for work." Retired people don't count because they aren't looking for jobs; the disabled don't count because they aren't available for work. More specifically, an individual is considered unemployed if he or she doesn't currently have a job and has been actively seeking a job during the past four weeks. So **unemployment** is defined as the total number of people who are actively looking for work but aren't currently employed.

A country's **labor force** is the sum of employment and unemployment—that is, of people who are currently working and people who are currently looking for work, respectively. The **labor force participation rate,** defined as the share of the working-age population that is in the labor force, is calculated as follows:

The **labor force** is equal to the sum of employment and unemployment.

The **labor force participation rate** is the percentage of the population aged 16 or older that is in the labor force.

The **unemployment rate** is the percentage of the total number of people in the labor force who are unemployed.

$$\textbf{(12-1)}\ \text{Labor force participation rate} = \frac{\text{Labor force}}{\text{Population age 16 and older}} \times 100$$

The **unemployment rate,** defined as the percentage of the total number of people in the labor force who are unemployed, is calculated as follows:

$$\textbf{(12-2)}\ \text{Unemployment rate} = \frac{\text{Number of unemployed workers}}{\text{Labor force}} \times 100$$

To estimate the numbers that go into calculating the unemployment rate, the U.S. Census Bureau carries out a monthly survey called the Current Population Survey, which involves interviewing a random sample of 60,000 American families. People are asked whether they are currently employed. If they are not employed, they are asked whether they have been looking for a job during the past four weeks. The results are then scaled up, using estimates of the total population, to estimate the total number of employed and unemployed Americans.

The Significance of the Unemployment Rate

In general, the unemployment rate is a good indicator of how easy or difficult it is to find a job given the current state of the economy. When the unemployment rate is low, nearly everyone who wants a job can find one. In 2000, when the unemployment rate averaged 4%, jobs were so abundant that employers spoke of a "mirror test" for getting a job: if you were breathing (therefore your breath would fog a mirror), you could find work. By contrast, in 2010, with the unemployment rate above 9% all year, it was very hard to find work. In fact, there were almost five times as many Americans seeking work as there were job openings.

Although the unemployment rate is a good indicator of current labor market conditions, it's not a literal measure of the percentage of people who want a job but can't find one. That's because in some ways the unemployment rate exaggerates the difficulty people have in finding jobs. But in other ways, the opposite is true—a low unemployment rate can conceal deep frustration over the lack of job opportunities.

How the Unemployment Rate Can Overstate the True Level of Unemployment If you are searching for work, it's normal to take at least a few weeks to find a suitable job. Yet a worker who is quite confident of finding a job, but has not yet accepted a position, is counted as unemployed. As a consequence, the unemployment rate never falls to zero, even in boom times when jobs are plentiful. Even in the buoyant labor market of 2000, when it was easy to find work, the unemployment rate was still 4%. Later in this chapter, we'll discuss in greater depth the reasons that measured unemployment persists even when jobs are abundant.

How the Unemployment Rate Can Understate the True Level of Unemployment Frequently, people who would like to work but aren't working still don't get counted as unemployed. In particular, an individual who has given up looking for a job for the time being because there are no jobs available—say, a laid-off steelworker in a deeply depressed steel town—isn't counted as unemployed because he or she has not been searching for a job during the previous four weeks. Individuals who want to work but have told government researchers that they aren't currently searching because they see little prospect of finding a job given the state of the job market are called

Discouraged workers are nonworking people who are capable of working but have given up looking for a job given the state of the job market.

Marginally attached workers would like to be employed and have looked for a job in the recent past but are not currently looking for work.

Underemployment is the number of people who work part time because they cannot find full-time jobs.

discouraged workers. Because it does not count discouraged workers, the measured unemployment rate may understate the percentage of people who want to work but are unable to find jobs.

Discouraged workers are part of a larger group—**marginally attached workers.** These are people who say they would like to have a job and have looked for work in the recent past but are not currently looking for work. They, too, are not included when calculating the unemployment rate.

Finally, another category of workers who are frustrated in their ability to find work but aren't counted as unemployed are the **underemployed:** workers who would like to find full-time jobs but are currently working part time "for economic reasons"—that is, they can't find a full-time job. Again, they aren't counted in the unemployment rate.

The Bureau of Labor Statistics is the federal agency that calculates the official unemployment rate. It also calculates broader "measures of labor underutilization" that include the three categories of frustrated workers. Figure 12-2 shows what happens to the measured unemployment rate once discouraged workers, other marginally attached workers, and the underemployed are counted. The broadest measure of unemployment and underemployment, known as U-6, is the sum of these three measures plus the unemployed. It is substantially higher than the rate usually quoted by the news media. But U-6 and the unemployment rate move very much in parallel, so changes in the unemployment rate remain a good guide to what's happening in the overall labor market, including frustrated workers.

Finally, it's important to realize that the unemployment rate varies greatly among demographic groups. Other things equal, jobs are generally easier to find for more experienced workers and for workers during their "prime" working years, from ages 25 to 54. For younger workers, as well as workers nearing retirement age, jobs are typically harder to find, other things equal.

Figure 12-3 shows unemployment rates for different groups in December 2007, when the overall unemployment rate of 5.0% was low by historical standards. As you can see, at this time the unemployment rate for African-American workers was much higher than the national average; the unemployment rate for White teenagers (ages 16–19) was almost three times the national average; and the unemployment rate for African-American teenagers, at 33.1%, was over six times the national average. (Bear in mind that a teenager isn't considered unemployed,

FIGURE 12-2 Alternative Measures of Unemployment, 1994–2011

The unemployment number usually quoted in the news media counts someone as unemployed only if he or she has been looking for work during the past four weeks. Broader measures also count discouraged workers, marginally attached workers, and the underemployed. These broader measures show a higher unemployment rate, but they move closely in parallel with the standard rate.
Source: Bureau of Labor Statistics.

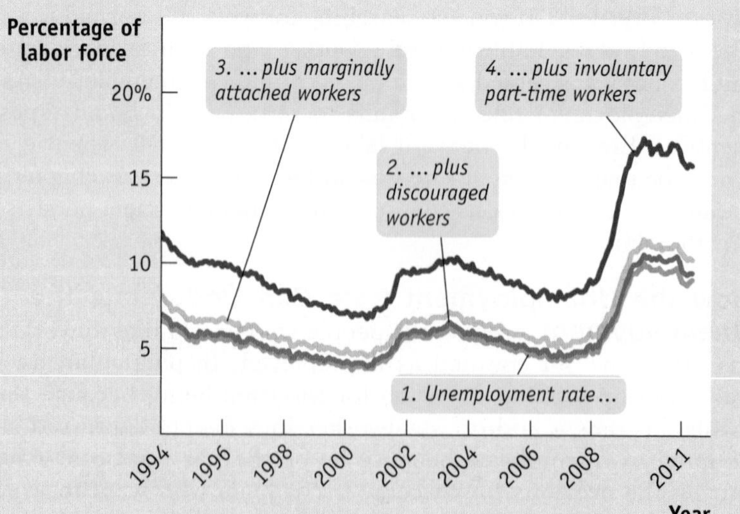

FIGURE **12-3** Unemployment Rates of Different Groups, 2007

Unemployment rates vary greatly among different demographic groups. For example, although the overall unemployment rate in December 2007 was 5.0%, the unemployment rate among African-American teenagers was 33.1%. As a result, even during periods of low overall unemployment, unemployment remains a serious problem for some groups.

Source: Bureau of Labor Statistics.

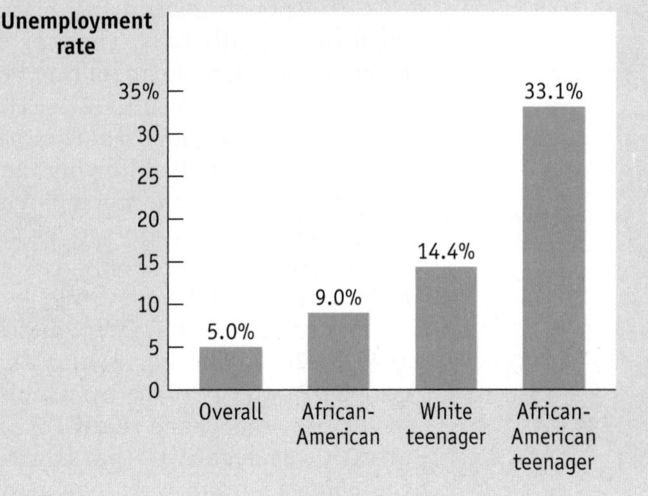

even if he or she isn't working, unless that teenager is looking for work but can't find it.) So even at a time when the overall unemployment rate was relatively low, jobs were hard to find for some groups.

So you should interpret the unemployment rate as an indicator of overall labor market conditions, not as an exact, literal measure of the percentage of people unable to find jobs. The unemployment rate is, however, a very good indicator: its ups and downs closely reflect economic changes that have a significant impact on people's lives. Let's turn now to the causes of these fluctuations.

Growth and Unemployment

Compared to Figure 12-1, Figure 12-4 shows the U.S. unemployment rate over a somewhat shorter period, the 33 years from 1978 to 2011. The shaded bars represent periods of recession. As you can see, during every recession, without exception,

FIGURE **12-4** Unemployment and Recessions, 1978–2011

This figure shows a close-up of the unemployment rate for the past three decades, with the shaded bars indicating recessions. It's clear that unemployment always rises during recessions and *usually* falls during expansions. But in both the early 1990s and the early 2000s, unemployment continued to rise for some time after the recession was officially declared over.

Sources: Bureau of Labor Statistics; National Bureau of Economic Research.

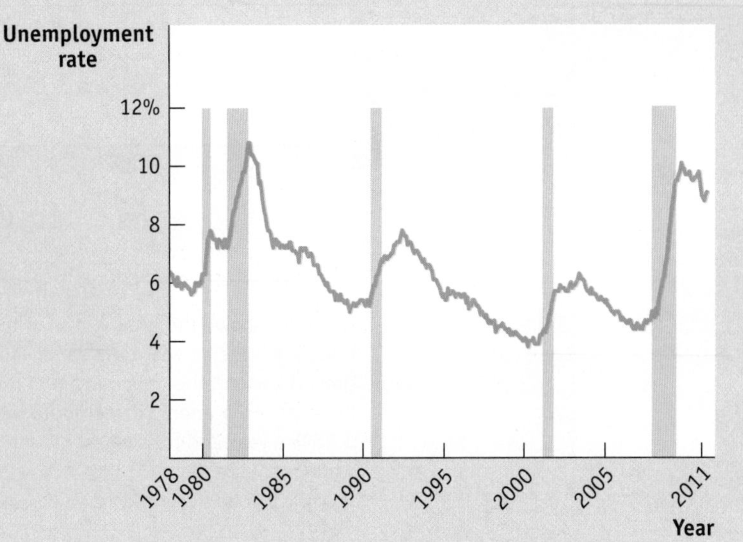

the unemployment rate rose. The severe recession of 2007–2009, like the earlier one of 1981–1982, led to a huge rise in unemployment.

Correspondingly, during periods of economic expansion the unemployment rate usually falls. The long economic expansion of the 1990s eventually brought the unemployment rate below 4%, and the expansion of the mid-2000s brought the rate down to 4.7%. However, it's important to recognize that *economic expansions aren't always periods of falling unemployment*. Look at the periods immediately following the recessions of 1990–1991 and 2001 in Figure 12-4. In each case the unemployment rate continued to rise for more than a year after the recession was officially over. The explanation in both cases is that although the economy was growing, it was not growing fast enough to reduce the unemployment rate.

Figure 12-5 is a scatter diagram showing U.S. data for the period from 1949 to 2010. The horizontal axis measures the annual rate of growth in real GDP—the percent by which each year's real GDP changed compared to the previous year's real GDP. (Notice that there were nine years in which growth was negative—that is, real GDP shrank.) The vertical axis measures the *change* in the unemployment rate over the previous year in percentage points. Each dot represents the observed growth rate of real GDP and change in the unemployment rate for a given year. For example, in 2000 the average unemployment rate fell to 4.0% from 4.2% in 1999; this is shown as a value of −0.2 along the vertical axis for the year 2000. Over the same period, real GDP grew by 3.7%; this is the value shown along the horizontal axis for the year 2000.

FIGURE 12-5 Growth and Changes in Unemployment, 1949–2010

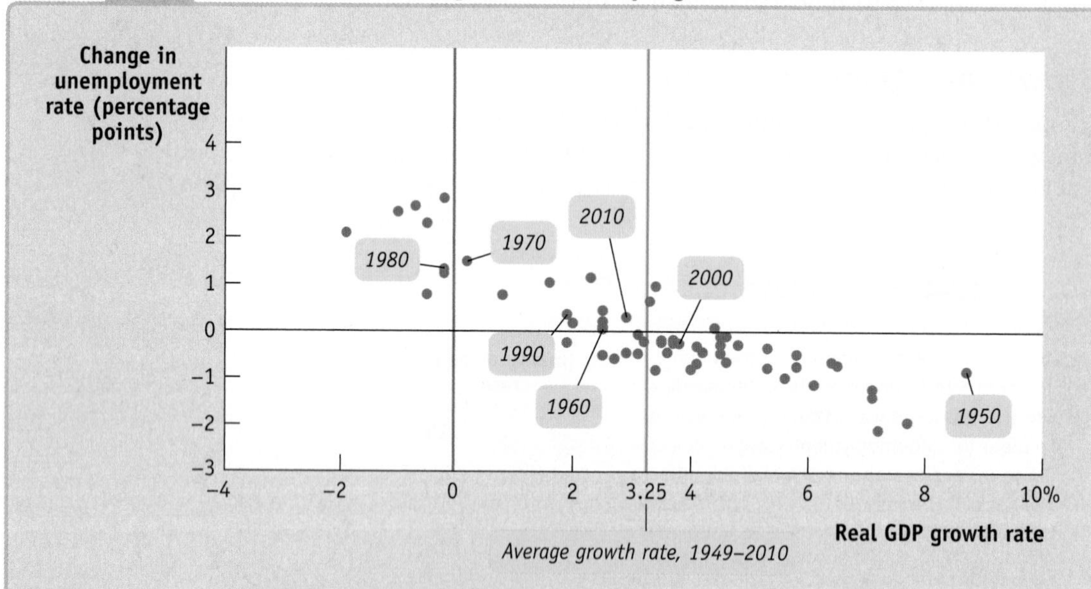

Each dot shows the growth rate of the economy and the change in the unemployment rate for a specific year between 1949 and 2010. For example, in 2000 the economy grew 3.7% and the unemployment rate fell 0.2 percentage point, from 4.2% to 4.0%. In general, the unemployment rate fell when growth was above its average rate of 3.25% a year and rose when growth was below average. Unemployment always rose when real GDP fell.

Sources: Bureau of Labor Statistics; Bureau of Economic Analysis.

The downward trend of the scatter diagram in Figure 12-5 shows that there is a generally strong negative relationship between growth in the economy and the rate of unemployment. Years of high growth in real GDP were also years in which the unemployment rate fell, and years of low or negative growth in real GDP were years in which the unemployment rate rose.

The green vertical line in Figure 12-5 at the value of 3.25% indicates the average growth rate of real GDP over the period from 1949 to 2010. Points lying to the right of the vertical line are years of above-average growth. In these years, the value on the vertical axis is usually negative, meaning that the unemployment rate fell. That is, years of above-average growth were usually years in which the unemployment rate was falling. Conversely, points lying to the left of the green vertical line were years of below-average growth. In these years, the value on the vertical axis is usually positive, meaning that the unemployment rate rose. That is, years of below-average growth were usually years in which the unemployment rate was rising.

A period in which real GDP is growing at a below-average rate and unemployment is rising is called a **jobless recovery** or a "growth recession." Since 1990, there have been three recessions, all of which have been followed by jobless recoveries. But true recessions, periods when real GDP falls, are especially painful for workers. As illustrated by the points to the left of the purple vertical line in Figure 12-5 (representing years in which the real GDP growth rate is negative), falling real GDP is always associated with a rising rate of unemployment, causing a great deal of hardship to families.

A **jobless recovery** is a period in which the real GDP growth rate is positive but the unemployment rate is still rising.

ECONOMICS ➤ IN ACTION

FAILURE TO LAUNCH

In March 2010, when the U.S. job situation was near its worst, the *Harvard Law Record* published a brief note titled "Unemployed law student will work for $160K plus benefits." In a self-mocking tone, the author admitted to having graduated from Harvard Law School the previous year but not landing a job offer. "What mark on our résumé is so bad that it outweighs the crimson H?" the note asked.

The answer, of course, is that it wasn't about the résumé—it was about the economy. Times of high unemployment are especially hard on new graduates, who often find it hard to get any kind of full-time job.

How bad was it in March 2010, around the time that note was written? Researchers at the San Francisco Fed analyzed the employment experience of college graduates, ages 21–23, and their findings are in Figure 12-6.

Although the overall unemployment rate for college graduates 25 and older, even at its peak, was only about 5 percent, unemployment among recent graduates aged 21–23 peaked in 2010 at 10.7 percent. And many of those who *were* employed had been able to get only part-time jobs. In December 2007, at the beginning of the 2007–2009 recession, 83 percent of college graduates under the age of 24 who weren't still in school were employed full time. By December 2009, that number was down to just 72 percent. Quite simply, many college graduates were having a hard time getting their working lives started.

FIGURE 12-6 Unemployment Rate for Recent College Graduates, 1995–2010

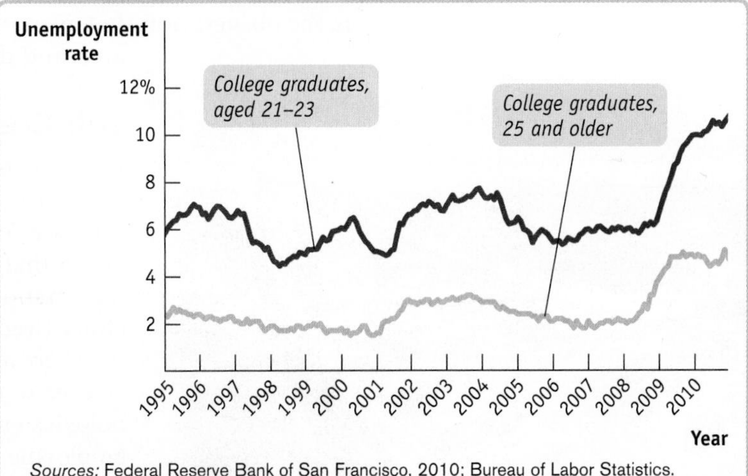

Sources: Federal Reserve Bank of San Francisco, 2010; Bureau of Labor Statistics.

A year later, the situation was starting to improve, but slowly: in December 2010, 74 percent of recent graduates had full-time jobs. The U.S. labor market had a long way to go before being able to offer college graduates—and young people in general—the kinds of opportunities they deserved.

Quick Review

- The **labor force,** equal to **employment** plus **unemployment,** does not include discouraged workers. Nor do labor statistics contain data on **underemployment.** The **labor force participation rate** is the percentage of the population age 16 and over in the labor force.
- The **unemployment rate** is an indicator of the state of the labor market, not an exact measure of the percentage of workers who can't find jobs. It can overstate the true level of unemployment because workers often spend time searching for a job even when jobs are plentiful. But it can also understate the true level of unemployment because it excludes **discouraged workers, marginally attached workers,** and **underemployed** workers.
- There is a strong negative relationship between growth in real GDP and changes in the unemployment rate. When growth is above average, the unemployment rate generally falls. When growth is below average, the unemployment rate generally rises—a period called a **jobless recovery** that typically follows a deep recession.

CHECK YOUR UNDERSTANDING 12-1

1. Suppose that the advent of employment websites enables job-seekers to find suitable jobs more quickly. What effect will this have on the unemployment rate over time? Also suppose that these websites encourage job-seekers who had given up their searches to begin looking again. What effect will this have on the unemployment rate?
2. In which of the following cases is a worker counted as unemployed? Explain.
   a. Rosa, an older worker who has been laid off and who gave up looking for work months ago
   b. Anthony, a schoolteacher who is not working during his three-month summer break
   c. Grace, an investment banker who has been laid off and is currently searching for another position
   d. Sergio, a classically trained musician who can only find work playing for local parties
   e. Natasha, a graduate student who went back to school because jobs were scarce
3. Which of the following are consistent with the observed relationship between growth in real GDP and changes in the unemployment rate? Which are not?
   a. A rise in the unemployment rate accompanies a fall in real GDP.
   b. An exceptionally strong business recovery is associated with a greater percentage of the labor force being employed.
   c. Negative real GDP growth is associated with a fall in the unemployment rate.

Solutions appear at back of book.

The Natural Rate of Unemployment

Fast economic growth tends to reduce the unemployment rate. So how low can the unemployment rate go? You might be tempted to say zero, but that isn't feasible. Over the past half-century, the national unemployment rate has never dropped below 2.9%.

How can there be so much unemployment even when many businesses are having a hard time finding workers? To answer this question, we need to examine the nature of labor markets and why they normally lead to substantial measured unemployment even when jobs are plentiful. Our starting point is the observation that even in the best of times, jobs are constantly being created and destroyed.

"At this point, I'm just happy to still have a job"

Job Creation and Job Destruction

Even during good times, most Americans know someone who has lost his or her job. In July 2007, the U.S. unemployment rate was only 4.7%, relatively low by historical standards. Yet in that month there were 4.5 million "job separations"—terminations of employment that occur because a worker is either fired or quits voluntarily.

There are many reasons for such job loss. One is structural change in the economy: industries rise and fall as new technologies emerge and consumers' tastes change. For example, employment in high-tech industries such as telecommunications surged in the late 1990s but slumped severely after 2000. However, structural change also brings the creation of new jobs: after 2000, the number of jobs in the American healthcare sector surged as new medical technologies and the aging of the population increased the demand for medical care. Poor management performance or bad luck at individual companies also leads to job loss for their employees. For example, in 2005 General Motors announced plans to eliminate 30,000 jobs after several years of lagging sales, even as Japanese companies such as Toyota announced plans to open new plants in North America to meet growing demand for their cars.

Workers who spend time looking for employment are engaged in **job search.**

Frictional unemployment is unemployment due to the time workers spend in job search.

Continual job creation and destruction are a feature of modern economies, making a naturally occurring amount of unemployment inevitable. Within this naturally occurring amount, there are two types of unemployment—*frictional* and *structural.*

Frictional Unemployment

When a worker loses a job involuntarily due to job destruction, he or she often doesn't take the first new job offered. For example, suppose a skilled programmer, laid off because her software company's product line was unsuccessful, sees a help-wanted ad for clerical work online. She might respond to the ad and get the job—but that would be foolish. Instead, she should take the time to look for a job that takes advantage of her skills and pays accordingly. In addition, individual workers are constantly leaving jobs voluntarily, typically for personal reasons—family moves, dissatisfaction, and better job prospects elsewhere.

Economists say that workers who spend time looking for employment are engaged in **job search.** If all workers and all jobs were alike, job search wouldn't be necessary; if information about jobs and workers was perfect, job search would be very quick. In practice, however, it's normal for a worker who loses a job, or a young worker seeking a first job, to spend at least a few weeks searching.

Frictional unemployment is unemployment due to the time workers spend in job search. A certain amount of frictional unemployment is inevitable due to the constant process of economic change. Thus even in 2007, a year of low unemployment, there were 62 million "job separations," in which workers left or lost their jobs. Total employment grew because these separations were more than offset by more than 63 million hires. Inevitably, some of the workers who left or lost their jobs spent at least some time unemployed, as did some of the workers newly entering the labor force.

Figure 12-7 shows the 2007 average monthly flows of workers among three states: employed, unemployed, and not in the labor force. What the figure suggests is how much churning is constantly taking place in the labor market. An inevitable consequence of that churning is a significant number of workers who haven't yet found their next job—that is, frictional unemployment.

FIGURE 12-7 Labor Market Flows in an Average Month in 2007

Even in 2007, a low-unemployment year, large numbers of workers moved into and out of both employment and unemployment each month. On average, each month in 2007, 1.781 million unemployed became employed, and 1.929 million employed became unemployed.
Source: Bureau of Labor Statistics.

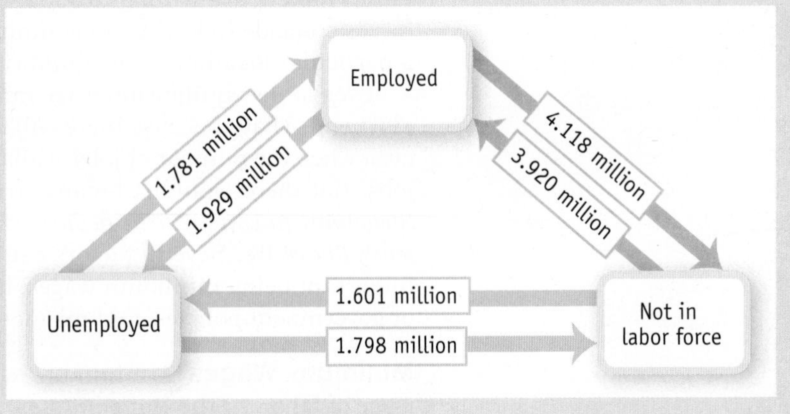

In **structural unemployment,** more people are seeking jobs in a particular labor market than there are jobs available at the current wage rate, even when the economy is at the peak of the business cycle.

A limited amount of frictional unemployment is relatively harmless and may even be a good thing. The economy is more productive if workers take the time to find jobs that are well matched to their skills and workers who are unemployed for a brief period while searching for the right job don't experience great hardship. In fact, when there is a low unemployment rate, periods of unemployment tend to be quite short, suggesting that much of the unemployment is frictional.

FIGURE 12-8 Distribution of the Unemployed by Duration of Unemployment, 2007

In years when the unemployment rate is low, most unemployed workers are unemployed for only a short period. In 2007, a year of low unemployment, 36% of the unemployed had been unemployed for less than 5 weeks and 67% for less than 15 weeks. The short duration of unemployment for most workers suggests that most unemployment in 2007 was frictional.
Source: Bureau of Labor Statistics.

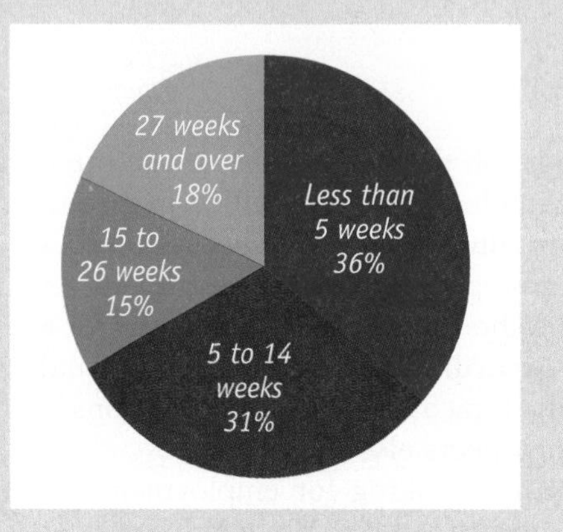

Figure 12-8 shows the composition of unemployment for all of 2007, when the unemployment rate was only 4.6%. Thirty-six percent of the unemployed had been unemployed for less than 5 weeks, and only 33% had been unemployed for 15 or more weeks. Only about one in six unemployed workers were considered to be "long-term unemployed"—unemployed for 27 or more weeks.

In periods of higher unemployment, however, workers tend to be jobless for longer periods of time, suggesting that a smaller share of unemployment is frictional. By 2010, the fraction of unemployed workers considered "long-term unemployed" had jumped to 43%.

Structural Unemployment

Frictional unemployment exists even when the number of people seeking jobs is equal to the number of jobs being offered—that is, the existence of frictional unemployment doesn't mean that there is a surplus of labor. Sometimes, however, there is a *persistent surplus* of job-seekers in a particular labor market, even when the economy is at the peak of the business cycle. There may be more workers with a particular skill than there are jobs available using that skill, or there may be more workers in a particular geographic region than there are jobs available in that region. **Structural unemployment** is unemployment that results when there are more people seeking jobs in a particular labor market than there are jobs available at the current wage rate.

The supply and demand model tells us that the price of a good, service, or factor of production tends to move toward an equilibrium level that matches the quantity supplied with the quantity demanded. This is equally true, in general, of labor markets.

Figure 12-9 shows a typical market for labor. The labor demand curve indicates that when the price of labor—the wage rate—increases, employers demand less labor. The labor supply curve indicates that when the price of labor increases, more workers are willing to supply labor at the prevailing wage rate. These two forces coincide to lead to an equilibrium wage rate for any given type of labor in a particular location. That equilibrium wage rate is shown as W_E.

Even at the equilibrium wage rate W_E, there will still be some frictional unemployment. That's because there will always be some workers engaged in job search even when the number of jobs available is equal to the number of workers seeking jobs. But there wouldn't be any structural unemployment in this labor market. *Structural unemployment occurs when the wage rate is, for some reason, persistently above* W_E. Several factors can lead to a wage rate in excess of W_E, the most important being minimum wages, labor unions, *efficiency wages,* the side effects of government policies, and mismatches between employees and employers.

Minimum Wages A minimum wage is a government-mandated floor on the price of labor. In the United States, the national minimum wage in late 2012 was $7.25 an hour. For many American workers, the minimum wage is irrelevant; the

FIGURE 12-9 The Effect of a Minimum Wage on a Labor Market

When the government sets a minimum wage, W_F, that exceeds the market equilibrium wage rate in that market, W_E, the number of workers, Q_S, who would like to work at that minimum wage is greater than the number of workers, Q_D, demanded at that wage rate. This surplus of labor is structural unemployment.

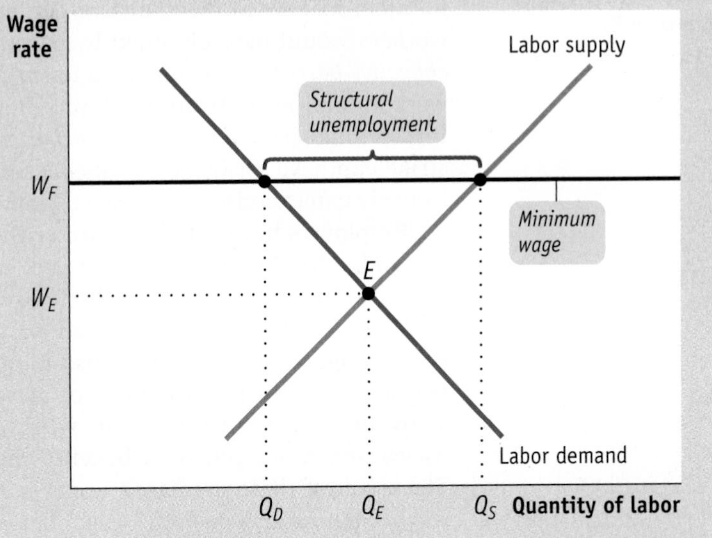

market equilibrium wage for these workers is well above this price floor. But for less-skilled workers, the minimum wage may be binding—it affects the wages that people are actually paid and can lead to structural unemployment in particular markets for labor. Other wealthy countries have higher minimum wages; for example, in 2012 the French minimum wage was 9.22 euros an hour, or around \$11.90. In these countries, the range of workers for whom the minimum wage is binding is larger.

Figure 12-9 shows the effect of a binding minimum wage. In this market, there is a legal floor on wages, W_F, which is above the equilibrium wage rate, W_E. This leads to a persistent surplus in the labor market: the quantity of labor supplied, Q_S, is larger than the quantity demanded, Q_D. In other words, more people want to work than can find jobs at the minimum wage, leading to structural unemployment.

Given that minimum wages—that is, binding minimum wages—generally lead to structural unemployment, you might wonder why governments impose them. The rationale is to help ensure that people who work can earn enough income to afford at least a minimally comfortable lifestyle. However, this may come at a cost, because it may eliminate the opportunity to work for some workers who would have willingly worked for lower wages. As illustrated in Figure 12-9, not only are there more sellers of labor than there are buyers, but there are also fewer people working at a minimum wage (Q_D) than there would have been with no minimum wage at all (Q_E).

Although economists broadly agree that a high minimum wage has the employment-reducing effects shown in Figure 12-9, there is some question about whether this is a good description of how the U.S. minimum wage actually works. The minimum wage in the United States is quite low compared with that in other wealthy countries. For three decades, from the 1970s to the mid-2000s, the American minimum wage was so low that it was not binding for the vast majority of workers.

In addition, some researchers have produced evidence that increases in the minimum wage actually lead to higher employment when, as was the case in the United States at one time, the minimum wage is low compared to average wages. They argue that firms that employ low-skilled workers sometimes restrict their hiring in order to keep wages low and that, as a result, the minimum wage can sometimes be increased without any loss of jobs. Most economists, however, agree that a sufficiently high minimum wage *does* lead to structural unemployment.

Efficiency wages are wages that employers set above the equilibrium wage rate as an incentive for better employee performance.

Labor Unions The actions of *labor unions* can have effects similar to those of minimum wages, leading to structural unemployment. By bargaining collectively for all of a firm's workers, unions can often win higher wages from employers than workers would have obtained by bargaining individually. This process, known as *collective bargaining,* is intended to tip the scales of bargaining power more toward workers and away from employers. Labor unions exercise bargaining power by threatening firms with a *labor strike,* a collective refusal to work. The threat of a strike can have serious consequences for firms. In such cases, workers acting collectively can exercise more power than they could if acting individually.

Employers have acted to counter the bargaining power of unions by threatening and enforcing lockouts—periods in which union workers are locked out and rendered unemployed—while hiring replacement workers.

When workers have increased bargaining power, they tend to demand and receive higher wages. Unions also bargain over benefits, such as health care and pensions, which we can think of as additional wages. Indeed, economists who study the effects of unions on wages find that unionized workers earn higher wages and more generous benefits than non-union workers with similar skills. The result of these increased wages can be the same as the result of a minimum wage: labor unions push the wage that workers receive above the equilibrium wage. Consequently, there are more people willing to work at the wage being paid than there are jobs available. Like a binding minimum wage, this leads to structural unemployment. In the United States, however, due to a low level of unionization, the amount of unemployment generated by union demands is likely to be very small.

Efficiency Wages Actions by firms can contribute to structural unemployment. Firms may choose to pay **efficiency wages**—wages that employers set above the equilibrium wage rate as an incentive for their workers to perform better.

Employers may feel the need for such incentives for several reasons. For example, employers often have difficulty observing directly how hard an employee works. They can, however, elicit more work effort by paying above-market wages: employees receiving these higher wages are more likely to work harder to ensure that they aren't fired, which would cause them to lose their higher wages.

When many firms pay efficiency wages, the result is a pool of workers who want jobs but can't find them. So the use of efficiency wages by firms leads to structural unemployment.

Side Effects of Government Policies In addition, government policies designed to help workers who lose their jobs can lead to structural unemployment as an unintended side effect. Most economically advanced countries provide benefits to laid-off workers as a way to tide them over until they find a new job. In the United States, these benefits typically replace only a small fraction of a worker's income and expire after 26 weeks. (This was extended in some cases to 99 weeks when the period of high unemployment began in 2009. As of December 2012, in all cases, benefits expire after 73 weeks.). In other countries, particularly in Europe, benefits are more generous and last longer. The drawback to this generosity is that it reduces a worker's incentive to quickly find a new job. Generous unemployment benefits in some European countries are often argued to be one of the causes of "Eurosclerosis," the persistent high unemployment that afflicts a number of European economies.

Mismatches between Employees and Employers It takes time for workers and firms to adjust to shifts in the economy. The result can be a mismatch between what employees have to offer and what employers are looking for. A skills mismatch is one form; for example, in the aftermath of the housing bust of 2009, there were more construction workers looking for jobs than were available. Another form is geographic as in Michigan, which has had a long-standing surplus of workers after its auto industry declined. Until the mismatch is resolved through a big enough fall in wages of the surplus workers that induces retraining or relocation, there will be structural unemployment.

The Natural Rate of Unemployment

Because some frictional unemployment is inevitable and because many economies also suffer from structural unemployment, a certain amount of unemployment is normal, or "natural." Actual unemployment fluctuates around this normal level. The **natural rate of unemployment** is the normal unemployment rate around which the actual unemployment rate fluctuates. It is the rate of unemployment that arises from the effects of frictional plus structural unemployment. **Cyclical unemployment** is the deviation of the actual rate of unemployment from the natural rate; that is, it is the difference between the actual and natural rates of unemployment. As the name suggests, cyclical unemployment is the share of unemployment that arises from the downturns of the business cycle.

The **natural rate of unemployment** is the unemployment rate that arises from the effects of frictional plus structural unemployment.

Cyclical unemployment is the deviation of the actual rate of unemployment from the natural rate due to downturns in the business cycle.

We can summarize the relationships between the various types of unemployment as follows:

(12-3) Natural unemployment =
Frictional unemployment + Structural unemployment

(12-4) Actual unemployment =
Natural unemployment + Cyclical unemployment

NATURAL UNEMPLOYMENT AROUND THE OECD

The Organization for Economic Cooperation and Development (OECD) is an association of relatively wealthy countries, in Europe and North America but also including Japan, Korea, New Zealand, and Australia. Among other activities, the OECD collects data on unemployment rates for member nations. The figure shows average unemployment, which is a rough estimate of the natural rate of unemployment, for select OECD members, from 2000–2010. The purple bar in the middle shows the average across all the OECD countries.

The U.S. natural rate of unemployment appears to be somewhat below average; those of many European countries (including the major economies of Germany, Italy, and France) are above average. Many economists think that persistently high European unemployment rates are the result of government policies, such as high minimum wages and generous unemployment benefits, which discourage employers from offering jobs and discourage workers from accepting jobs, leading to high rates of structural unemployment.

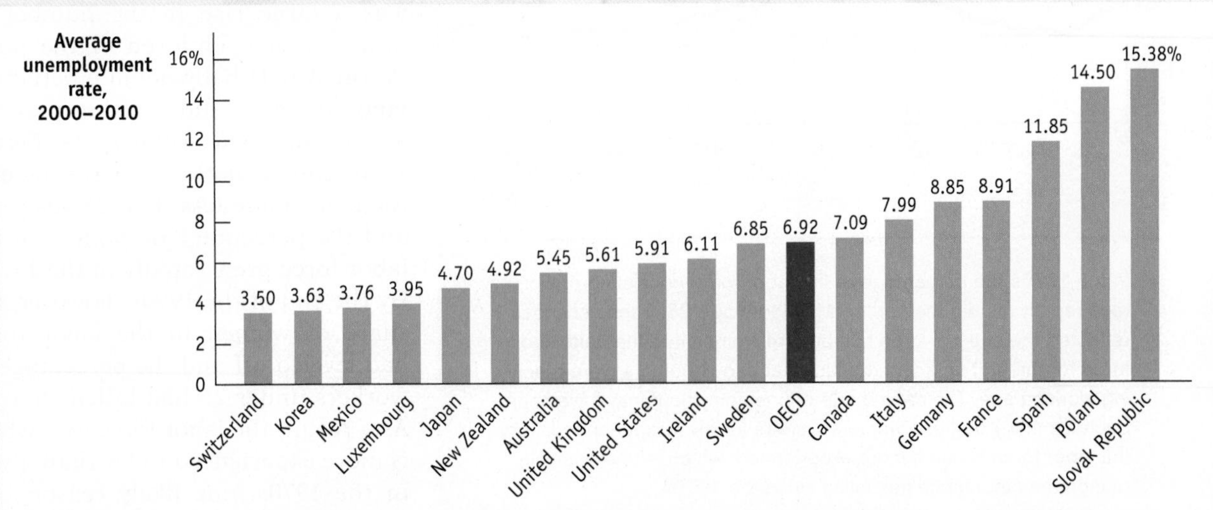

Source: OECD.

Perhaps because of its name, people often imagine that the natural rate of unemployment is a constant that doesn't change over time and can't be affected by government policy. Neither proposition is true. Let's take a moment to stress two facts: the natural rate of unemployment changes over time, and it can be affected by government policies.

Changes in the Natural Rate of Unemployment

Private-sector economists and government agencies need estimates of the natural rate of unemployment both to make forecasts and to conduct policy analyses. Almost all these estimates show that the U.S. natural rate rises and falls over time. For example, the Congressional Budget Office, the independent agency that conducts budget and economic analyses for Congress, believes that the U.S. natural rate of unemployment was 5.3% in 1950, rose to 6.3% by the end of the 1970s, but has fallen to 5.2% today. European countries have experienced even larger swings in their natural rates of unemployment.

What causes the natural rate of unemployment to change? The most important factors are changes in labor force characteristics, changes in labor market institutions, and changes in government policies. Let's look briefly at each factor.

Changes in Labor Force Characteristics In 2007 the overall rate of unemployment in the United States was 4.6%. Young workers, however, had much higher unemployment rates: 15.7% for teenagers and 8.2% for workers aged 20 to 24. Workers aged 25 to 54 had an unemployment rate of only 3.7%.

In general, unemployment rates tend to be lower for experienced than for inexperienced workers. Because experienced workers tend to stay in a given job longer than do inexperienced ones, they have lower frictional unemployment. Also, because older workers are more likely than young workers to be family breadwinners, they have a stronger incentive to find and keep jobs.

One reason the natural rate of unemployment rose during the 1970s was a large rise in the number of new workers—children of the post–World War II baby boom entered the labor force, as did a rising percentage of married women. As Figure 12-10 shows, both the percentage of the labor force less than 25 years old and the percentage of women in the labor force grew rapidly in the 1970s. By the end of the 1990s, however, the share of women in the labor force had leveled off and the percentage of workers under 25 had fallen sharply. As a result, the labor force as a whole is more experienced today than it was in the 1970s, one likely reason that the natural rate of unemployment is lower today than in the 1970s.

FIGURE 12-10 The Changing Makeup of the U.S. Labor Force, 1948–2011

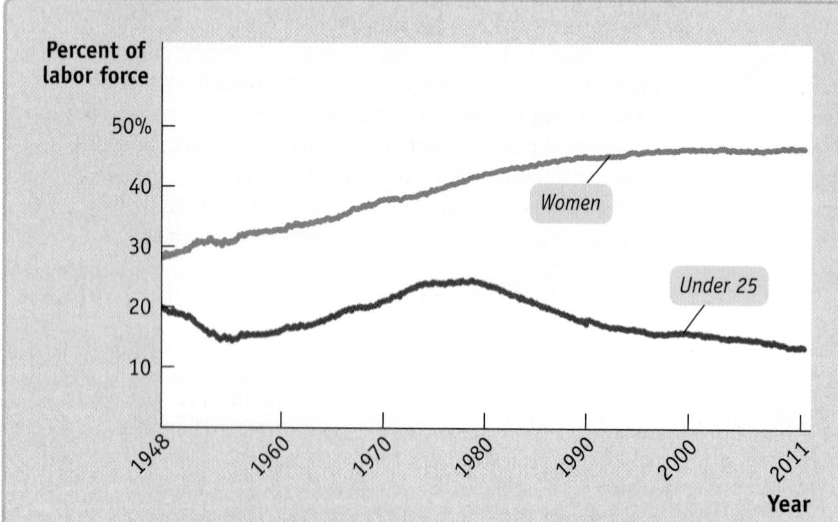

In the 1970s the percentage of the labor force consisting of women rose rapidly, as did the percentage under age 25. These changes reflected the entry of large numbers of women into the paid labor force for the first time and the fact that baby boomers were reaching working age. The natural rate of unemployment may have risen because many of these workers were relatively inexperienced. Today, the labor force is much more experienced, which is one possible reason the natural rate has fallen since the 1970s.

Source: Bureau of Labor Statistics.

Changes in Labor Market Institutions As we pointed out earlier, unions that negotiate wages above the equilibrium level can be a source of structural unemployment. Some economists believe that strong labor unions are one reason for the high natural rate of unemployment in Europe, discussed in the Global Comparison. In the United States, a sharp fall in union membership after 1980 may have been one reason the natural rate of unemployment fell between the 1970s and the 1990s.

Other institutional changes may also be at work. For example, some labor economists believe that temporary employment agencies, which have proliferated in recent years, have reduced frictional unemployment by helping match workers to jobs. Furthermore, as discussed in the Business Case at the end of the chapter, Internet websites such as Monster.com may have reduced frictional unemployment.

Technological change, coupled with labor market institutions, can also affect the natural rate of unemployment. Technological change tends to increase the demand for skilled workers who are familiar with the relevant technology and a reduction in the demand for unskilled workers. Economic theory predicts that wages should increase for skilled workers and decrease for unskilled workers. But if wages for unskilled workers cannot go down—say, due to a binding minimum wage—increased structural unemployment, and therefore a higher natural rate of unemployment, will result.

Changes in Government Policies A high minimum wage can cause structural unemployment. Generous unemployment benefits can increase both structural and frictional unemployment. So government policies intended to help workers can have the undesirable side effect of raising the natural rate of unemployment.

Some government policies, however, may reduce the natural rate. Two examples are job training and employment subsidies. Job-training programs are supposed to provide unemployed workers with skills that widen the range of jobs they can perform. Employment subsidies are payments either to workers or to employers that provide a financial incentive to accept or offer jobs.

ECONOMICS ➤ IN ACTION

STRUCTURAL UNEMPLOYMENT IN EAST GERMANY

In one of the most dramatic events in world history, a spontaneous popular uprising in 1989 overthrew the communist dictatorship in East Germany. Citizens quickly tore down the wall that had divided Berlin, and in short order East and West Germany united into one democratic nation.

Then the trouble started.

After reunification, employment in East Germany plunged and the unemployment rate soared. This high unemployment rate has persisted: despite receiving massive aid from the federal German government, the economy of the former East Germany has remained persistently depressed, with an unemployment rate of 10.3% percent in July 2012, compared to an unemployment rate of only 5.9% in West Germany. Other parts of formerly communist Eastern Europe have done much better. For example, the Czech Republic, which was often cited along with East Germany as a relatively successful communist economy, had an unemployment rate of 8.1% in July 2012. What went wrong in East Germany?

Robert Wallis/Corbis

After reunification in 1989, East Germany found itself suffering from severe structural unemployment that continues to this day.

The answer is that, through nobody's fault, East Germany found itself suffering from severe structural unemployment. When Germany was reunified, it became clear that workers in East Germany were much less productive than their cousins in the west. Yet unions initially demanded and received wage rates equal to those in West Germany. These wage rates have been slow to come down because East German workers objected to being treated as inferior to their West German counterparts. Meanwhile, productivity in the former East Germany has remained well below West German levels, in part because of decades of misguided investment under the former dictatorship. The result has been a persistently large mismatch between the number of workers demanded and the number of those seeking jobs, and persistently high structural unemployment in the former East Germany.

Quick Review

- **Frictional unemployment** occurs because unemployed workers engage in **job search,** making some amount of unemployment inevitable.
- A variety of factors—minimum wages, unions, **efficiency wages,** the side effects of government policies such as unemployment benefits, and mismatches between employees and employers—lead to **structural unemployment.**
- Frictional plus structural unemployment equals natural unemployment, yielding **a natural rate of unemployment.** In contrast, **cyclical unemployment** changes with the business cycle. Actual unemployment is equal to the sum of natural unemployment and cyclical unemployment.
- The natural rate of unemployment can shift over time, due to changes in labor force characteristics and institutions. Government policies designed to help workers are believed to be one reason for high natural rates of unemployment in Europe.

CHECK YOUR UNDERSTANDING 12-2

1. Explain the following.
   a. Frictional unemployment is higher when the pace of technological advance quickens.
   b. Structural unemployment is higher when the pace of technological advance quickens.
   c. Frictional unemployment accounts for a larger share of total unemployment when the unemployment rate is low.
2. Why does collective bargaining have the same general effect on unemployment as a minimum wage? Illustrate your answer with a diagram.
3. Suppose that at the peak of the business cycle the United States dramatically increases benefits for unemployed workers. Explain what will happen to the natural rate of unemployment.

Solutions appear at back of book.

Inflation and Deflation

As we mentioned in the opening story, in early 2011 British officials were worried about two things: the unemployment rate was high and so was inflation. And there was a fierce debate about which concern should take priority.

Why is inflation something to worry about? Why do policy makers even now get anxious when they see the inflation rate moving upward? The answer is that inflation can impose costs on the economy—but not in the way most people think.

The Level of Prices Doesn't Matter . . .

The most common complaint about inflation, an increase in the price level, is that it makes everyone poorer—after all, a given amount of money buys less. But inflation does not make everyone poorer. To see why, it's helpful to imagine what would happen if the United States did something other countries have done from time to time—replacing the dollar with a new currency.

An example of this kind of currency conversion happened in 2002, when France, like a number of other European countries, replaced its national currency, the franc, with the new pan-European currency, the euro. People turned in their franc coins and notes, and received euro coins and notes in exchange, at a rate of precisely 6.55957 francs per euro. At the same time, all contracts were restated in euros at the same rate of exchange. For example, if a French citizen had a home mortgage debt of 500,000 francs, this became a debt of 500,000/6.55957 = 76,224.51 euros. If a worker's contract specified that he or she should be paid 100 francs per hour, it became a contract specifying a wage of 100/6.55957 = 5.2449 euros per hour, and so on.

You could imagine doing the same thing here, replacing the dollar with a "new dollar" at a rate of exchange of, say, 7 to 1. If you owed $140,000 on your home, that would become a debt of 20,000 new dollars. If you had a wage rate of $14 an hour, it would become 2 new dollars an hour, and so on. This would bring the overall U.S. price level back to about what it was in 1962, when John F. Kennedy was president.

So would everyone be richer as a result because prices would be only one-seventh as high? Of course not. Prices would be lower, but so would wages and incomes in general. If you cut a worker's wage to one-seventh of its previous value, but also cut all prices to one-seventh of their previous level, the worker's **real wage**—the wage rate divided by the price level—hasn't changed. In fact, bringing the overall price level back to what it was during the Kennedy administration would have no effect on overall purchasing power because doing so would reduce income exactly as much as it reduced prices.

Conversely, the rise in prices that has actually taken place since the early 1960s hasn't made America poorer because it has also raised incomes by the same amount: **real incomes**—incomes divided by the price level—haven't been affected by the rise in overall prices.

The moral of this story is that the *level* of prices doesn't matter: the United States would be no richer than it is now if the overall level of prices was still as low as it was in 1961; conversely, the rise in prices over the past 50 years hasn't made us poorer.

The **real wage** is the wage rate divided by the price level.

Real income is income divided by the price level.

. . . But the Rate of Change of Prices Does

The conclusion that the level of prices doesn't matter might seem to imply that the inflation rate doesn't matter either. But that's not true.

To see why, it's crucial to distinguish between the *level of prices* and the *inflation rate:* the percent increase in the overall level of prices per year. Recall from Chapter 11 that the inflation rate is defined as follows:

$$\text{Inflation rate} = \frac{\text{Price index in year 2} - \text{Price index in year 1}}{\text{Price index in year 1}} \times 100$$

Figure 12-11 highlights the difference between the price level and the inflation rate in the United States over the last half-century, with the price level measured along the left vertical axis and the inflation rate measured along

FIGURE 12-11 The Price Level versus the Inflation Rate, 1960–2011

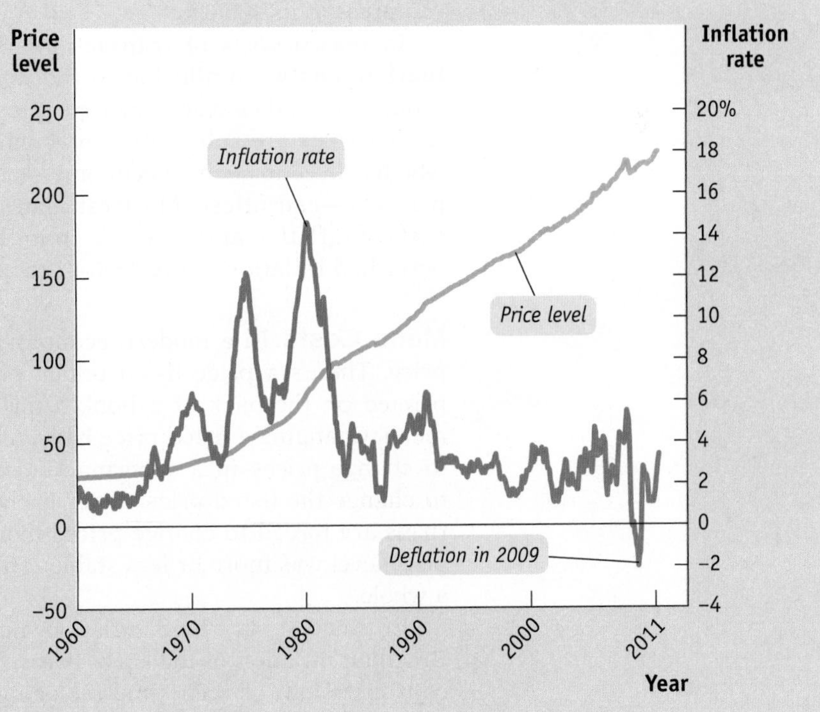

With the exception of 2009, over the past half-century the consumer price index has continuously increased. But the *inflation rate*—the rate at which consumer prices are rising—has had both ups and downs. And in 2009, the inflation rate briefly turned negative, a phenomenon called *deflation*.

Source: Bureau of Labor Statistics.

Shoe-leather costs are the increased costs of transactions caused by inflation.

The **menu cost** is the real cost of changing a listed price.

the right vertical axis. In the 2000s, the overall level of prices in America was much higher than it had been in 1960—but that, as we've learned, didn't matter. The inflation rate in the 2000s, however, was much lower than in the 1970s—and that almost certainly made the economy richer than it would have been if high inflation had continued.

Economists believe that high rates of inflation impose significant economic costs. The most important of these costs are *shoe-leather costs, menu costs,* and *unit-of-account costs.* We'll discuss each in turn.

Shoe-Leather Costs People hold money—cash in their wallets and bank deposits on which they can write checks—for convenience in making transactions. A high inflation rate, however, discourages people from holding money because the purchasing power of the cash in your wallet and the funds in your bank account steadily erodes as the overall level of prices rises. This leads people to search for ways to reduce the amount of money they hold, often at considerable economic cost.

The Economics in Action at the end of this section describes how Israelis spent a lot of time at the bank during the periods of high inflation rates that afflicted Israel in 1984–1985. During the most famous of all inflations, the German *hyperinflation* of 1921–1923, merchants employed runners to take their cash to the bank many times a day to convert it into something that would hold its value, such as a stable foreign currency. In each case, in an effort to avoid having the purchasing power of their money eroded, people used up valuable resources, such as time for Israeli citizens and the labor of those German runners that could have been used productively elsewhere. During the German hyperinflation, so many banking transactions were taking place that the number of employees at German banks nearly quadrupled—from around 100,000 in 1913 to 375,000 in 1923.

More recently, Brazil experienced hyperinflation during the early 1990s; during that episode, the Brazilian banking sector grew so large that it accounted for 15% of GDP, more than twice the size of the financial sector in the United States measured as a share of GDP. The large increase in the Brazilian banking sector needed to cope with the consequences of inflation represented a loss of real resources to its society.

Increased costs of transactions caused by inflation are known as **shoe-leather costs,** an allusion to the wear and tear caused by the extra running around that takes place when people are trying to avoid holding money. Shoe-leather costs are substantial in economies with very high inflation, as anyone who has lived in such an economy—say, one suffering inflation of 100% or more per year—can attest. Most estimates suggest, however, that the shoe-leather costs of inflation at the rates seen in the United States—which in peacetime has never had inflation above 15%—are quite small.

Menu Costs In a modern economy, most of the things we buy have a listed price. There's a price listed under each item on a supermarket shelf, a price printed on the back of a book, a price listed for each dish on a restaurant's menu. Changing a listed price has a real cost, called a **menu cost.** For example, to change prices in a supermarket requires sending clerks through the store to change the listed price under each item. In the face of inflation, of course, firms are forced to change prices more often than they would if the aggregate price level was more or less stable. This means higher costs for the economy as a whole.

In times of very high inflation, menu costs can be substantial. During the Brazilian inflation of the early 1990s, for instance, supermarket workers reportedly spent half of their time replacing old price stickers with new ones. When inflation is high, merchants may decide to stop listing prices in terms of the local currency and use either an artificial unit—in effect, measuring prices relative to one another—or a more stable currency, such as the U.S. dollar. This is exactly what the Israeli real estate market began doing in the mid-1980s: prices were quoted in U.S. dollars, even though payment was made in Israeli shekels. And this is also what happened in Zimbabwe when, in May 2008, official estimates of the inflation rate reached 1,694,000%. By 2009, the government had suspended the Zimbabwean dollar, allowing Zimbabweans to buy and sell goods using foreign currencies.

100000000000000 RESERVE BANK OF ZIMBABWE 100000000000000
I promise to pay the bearer on demand
ONE HUNDRED TRILLION DOLLARS
for the Reserve Bank of Zimbabwe
100 000 000 000 000 HARARE 2008
AA4067304

When trillion-dollar bills are in circulation as they were in Zimbabwe, menu costs are substantial.

Menu costs are also present in low-inflation economies, but they are not severe. In low-inflation economies, businesses might update their prices only sporadically—not daily or even more frequently, as is the case in high-inflation or hyperinflation economies. Also, with technological advances, menu costs are becoming less and less important, since prices can be changed electronically and fewer merchants attach price stickers to merchandise.

Unit-of-Account Costs In the Middle Ages, contracts were often specified "in kind": a tenant might, for example, be obliged to provide his landlord with a certain number of cattle each year (the phrase *in kind* actually comes from an ancient word for *cattle*). This may have made sense at the time, but it would be an awkward way to conduct modern business. Instead, we state contracts in monetary terms: a renter owes a certain number of dollars per month, a company that issues a bond promises to pay the bondholder the dollar value of the bond when it comes due, and so on. We also tend to make our economic calculations in dollars: a family planning its budget, or a small business owner trying to figure out how well the business is doing, makes estimates of the amount of money coming in and going out.

This role of the dollar as a basis for contracts and calculation is called the *unit-of-account* role of money. It's an important aspect of the modern economy. Yet it's a role that can be degraded by inflation, which causes the purchasing power of a dollar to change over time—a dollar next year is worth less than a dollar this year. The effect, many economists argue, is to reduce the quality of economic decisions: the economy as a whole makes less efficient use of its resources because of the uncertainty caused by changes in the unit of account, the dollar. The **unit-of-account costs** of inflation are the costs arising from the way inflation makes money a less reliable unit of measurement.

Unit-of-account costs may be particularly important in the tax system because inflation can distort the measures of income on which taxes are collected. Here's an example: Assume that the inflation rate is 10%, so the overall level of prices rises 10% each year. Suppose that a business buys an asset, such as a piece of land, for $100,000, then resells it a year later for $110,000. In a fundamental sense, the business didn't make a profit on the deal: in real terms, it got no more for the land than it paid for it. But U.S. tax law would say that the business made a capital gain of $10,000, and it would have to pay taxes on that phantom gain.

During the 1970s, when the United States had relatively high inflation, the distorting effects of inflation on the tax system were a serious problem. Some businesses were discouraged from productive investment spending because they

Unit-of-account costs arise from the way inflation makes money a less reliable unit of measurement.

The **interest rate** on a loan is the price, calculated as a percentage of the amount borrowed, that a lender charges a borrower for the use of their savings for one year.

The **nominal interest rate** is the interest rate expressed in dollar terms.

The **real interest rate** is the nominal interest rate minus the rate of inflation.

found themselves paying taxes on phantom gains. Meanwhile, some unproductive investments became attractive because they led to phantom losses that reduced tax bills. When inflation fell in the 1980s—and tax rates were reduced—these problems became much less important.

Winners and Losers from Inflation

As we've just learned, a high inflation rate imposes overall costs on the economy. In addition, inflation can produce winners and losers within the economy. The main reason inflation sometimes helps some people while hurting others is that economic transactions often involve contracts that extend over a period of time, such as loans, and these contracts are normally specified in nominal—that is, in dollar—terms.

In the case of a loan, the borrower receives a certain amount of funds at the beginning, and the loan contract specifies the *interest rate* on the loan and when it must be paid off. The **interest rate** is the return a lender receives for allowing borrowers the use of their savings for one year, calculated as a percentage of the amount borrowed.

But what that dollar is worth in real terms—that is, in terms of purchasing power—depends greatly on the rate of inflation over the intervening years of the loan. Economists summarize the effect of inflation on borrowers and lenders by distinguishing between the *nominal* interest rate and the *real* interest rate. The **nominal interest rate** is the interest rate in dollar terms—for example, the interest rate on a student loan. The **real interest rate** is the nominal interest rate minus the rate of inflation. For example, if a loan carries an interest rate of 8%, but there is 5% inflation, the real interest rate is 8% – 5% = 3%.

When a borrower and a lender enter into a loan contract, the contract is normally written in dollar terms—that is, the interest rate it specifies is a nominal interest rate. (And in later chapters, when we say the interest rate we will mean the nominal interest rate unless noted otherwise.) But each party to a loan contract has an expectation about the future rate of inflation and therefore an expectation about the real interest rate on the loan. If the actual inflation rate is *higher* than expected, borrowers gain at the expense of lenders: borrowers will repay their loans with funds that have a lower real value than had been expected. Conversely, if the inflation rate is *lower* than expected, lenders will gain at the expense of borrowers: borrowers must repay their loans with funds that have a higher real value than had been expected.

Historically, the fact that inflation creates winners and losers has sometimes been a major source of political controversy. In 1896 William Jennings Bryan electrified the Democratic presidential convention with a speech in which he declared, "You shall not crucify mankind on a cross of gold." What he was actually demanding was an inflationary policy. At the time, the U.S. dollar had a fixed value in terms of gold. Bryan wanted to abandon that gold standard and have the U.S. government print more money, which would have raised the level of prices. The reason he wanted inflation was to help farmers, many of whom were deeply in debt.

In modern America, home mortgages are the most important source of gains and losses from inflation. Americans who took out mortgages in the early 1970s quickly found their real payments reduced by higher-than-expected inflation: by 1983, the purchasing power of a dollar was only 45% of what it had been in 1973. Those who took out mortgages in the early 1990s were not so lucky, because the inflation rate fell to lower-than-expected levels in the following years: in 2003 the purchasing power of a dollar was 78% of what it had been in 1993.

Because gains for some and losses for others result from inflation that is either higher or lower than expected, yet another problem arises: uncertainty about the future inflation rate discourages people from entering into any form of long-term contract. This is an additional cost of high inflation, because

high rates of inflation are usually unpredictable. In countries with high and uncertain inflation, long-term loans are rare, which makes it difficult in many cases to make long-term investments.

One last point: unexpected *deflation*—a surprise fall in the price level—creates winners and losers, too. Between 1929 and 1933, as the U.S. economy plunged into the Great Depression, the consumer price index fell by 35%. This meant that debtors, including many farmers and homeowners, saw a sharp rise in the real value of their debts, which led to widespread bankruptcy and helped create a banking crisis, as lenders found their customers unable to pay back their loans. And as you can see in Figure 12-11, deflation occurred again in 2009, when the inflation rate fell to –2% at the trough of a deep recession. Like the Great Depression (but to a much lesser extent), the unexpected deflation of 2009 imposed heavy costs on debtors.

Disinflation is the process of bringing the inflation rate down.

Inflation Is Easy; Disinflation Is Hard

There is not much evidence that a rise in the inflation rate from, say, 2% to 5% would do a great deal of harm to the economy. Still, policy makers generally move forcefully to bring inflation back down when it creeps above 2% or 3%. Why? Because experience shows that bringing the inflation rate down—a process called **disinflation**—is very difficult and costly once a higher rate of inflation has become well established in the economy.

Figure 12-12 shows what happened during two major episodes of disinflation in the United States, in the mid-1970s and in the early 1980s. The horizontal axis shows the unemployment rate. The vertical axis shows "core" inflation over the previous year, a measure that excludes volatile food and energy prices and is widely considered a better measure of underlying inflation than overall consumer prices. Each marker represents the inflation rate and the unemployment rate for one month. In each episode, unemployment and inflation followed a sort of clockwise spiral, with high inflation gradually falling in the face of an extended period of very high unemployment.

According to many economists, these periods of high unemployment that temporarily depressed the economy were necessary to reduce inflation that had become deeply embedded in the economy. The best way to avoid having to put the economy through a wringer to reduce inflation, however, is to avoid having a

FIGURE 12-12 The Cost of Disinflation

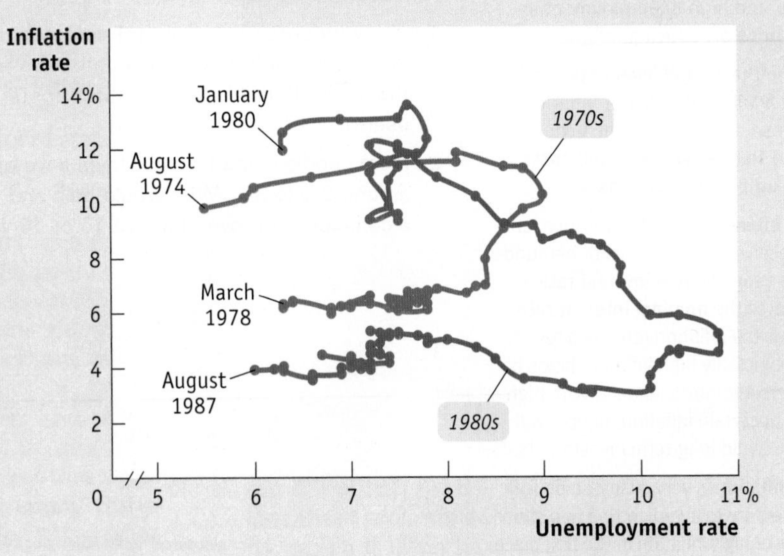

There were two major periods of disinflation in modern U.S. history, in the mid-1970s and the early 1980s. This figure shows the track of the unemployment rate and the "core" inflation rate, which excludes food and energy, during these two episodes. In each case bringing inflation down required a temporary but very large increase in the unemployment rate, demonstrating the high cost of disinflation.

Source: Bureau of Labor Statistics.

serious inflation problem in the first place. So policy makers respond forcefully to signs that inflation may be accelerating as a form of preventive medicine for the economy.

ECONOMICS ➤ IN ACTION

ISRAEL'S EXPERIENCE WITH INFLATION

It's often hard to see the costs of inflation clearly because serious inflation problems are often associated with other problems that disrupt economic life, notably war or political instability (or both). In the mid-1980s, however, Israel experienced a "clean" inflation: there was no war, the government was stable, and there was order in the streets. Yet a series of policy errors led to very high inflation, with prices often rising more than 10% a month.

Ricki Rosen/Corbis Saba

The shoe-leather costs of inflation in Israel: when the inflation rate hit 500% in 1985, people spent a lot of time in line at banks.

As it happens, one of the authors spent a month visiting at Tel Aviv University at the height of the inflation, so we can give a first-hand account of the effects.

First, the shoe-leather costs of inflation were substantial. At the time, Israelis spent a lot of time in lines at the bank, moving money in and out of accounts that provided high enough interest rates to offset inflation. People walked around with very little cash in their wallets; they had to go to the bank whenever they needed to make even a moderately large cash payment. Banks responded by opening a lot of branches, a costly business expense.

Second, although menu costs weren't that visible to a visitor, what you could see were the efforts businesses made to minimize them. For example, restaurant menus often didn't list prices. Instead, they listed numbers that you had to multiply by another number, written on a chalkboard and changed every day, to figure out the price of a dish.

Finally, it was hard to make decisions because prices changed so much and so often. It was a common experience to walk out of a store because prices were 25% higher than at one's usual shopping destination, only to discover that prices had just been increased 25% there, too.

CHECK YOUR UNDERSTANDING 12-3

1. The widespread use of technology has revolutionized the banking industry, making it much easier for customers to access and manage their assets. Does this mean that the shoe-leather costs of inflation are higher or lower than they used to be?
2. Most people in the United States have grown accustomed to a modest inflation rate of around 2% to 3%. Who would gain and who would lose if inflation unexpectedly came to a complete stop over the next 15 or 20 years?

Solutions appear at back of book.

▼ Quick Review

- The **real wage** and **real income** are unaffected by the level of prices.
- Inflation, like unemployment, is a major concern of policy makers—so much so that in the past they have accepted high unemployment as the price of reducing inflation.
- While the overall level of prices is irrelevant, high rates of inflation impose real costs on the economy: **shoe-leather costs, menu costs,** and **unit-of-account costs.**
- The **interest rate** is the return a lender receives for use of his or her funds for a year. The **real interest rate** is equal to the **nominal interest rate** minus the inflation rate. As a result, unexpectedly high inflation helps borrowers and hurts lenders. With high and uncertain inflation, people will often avoid long-term investments.
- **Disinflation** is very costly, so policy makers try to avoid getting into situations of high inflation in the first place.

WORKED PROBLEM

The Current Population Survey

Every month, the U.S. Census Bureau surveys about 60,000 American households to gather information about the U.S. labor force for the Bureau of Labor Statistics. The survey, known as the Current Population Survey (CPS), provides information about employment, unemployment, earnings, work hours, and more. Once these data are collected, researchers at the Bureau of Labor Statistics publish a number of tables describing their findings. Please complete the table below and analyze the trend in the unemployment rate, the employment-population rate, and the participation rate from September 2011 through September 2012. Then determine whether the unemployment rate in September 2012 is high or low by historical standards.

	Sept. 2011 (thousands)	May 2012 (thousands)	June 2012 (thousands)	July 2012 (thousands)	August 2012 (thousands)	Sept. 2012 (thousands)
Civilian noninstitutional population	240,071	242,966	243,155	243,354	243,566	243,772
Civilian labor force	154,004	155,007	155,163	155,013	154,645	155,063
Participation rate	?	?	?	?	?	?
Employed	140,107	142,287	142,415	142,220	142,101	142,974
Employment-population ratio	?	?	?	?	?	?
Unemployed	13,897	12,720	12,749	12,794	12,544	12,088
Unemployment rate	?	?	?	?	?	?
Not in labor force	86,067	87,959	87,992	88,341	88,921	88,709
Persons who currently want a job . . .	5,929	6,291	6,520	6,554	6,957	6,727

STEP 1: Complete the table.

Read the section "Defining and Measuring Unemployment" on pages 348–349. Equations 12-1 and 12-2 demonstrate how to calculate the participation rate and the unemployment rate. The employment-population ratio is calculated as follows:

$$\textit{Employment-Population Ratio} = \frac{\textit{Employed}}{\textit{Civilian noninstitutional population}} \times 100$$

The completed table is shown below.

	Sept. 2011 (thousands)	May 2012 (thousands)	June 2012 (thousands)	July 2012 (thousands)	August 2012 (thousands)	Sept. 2012 (thousands)
Civilian noninstitutional population	240,071	242,966	243,155	243,354	243,566	243,772
Civilian labor force	154,004	155,007	155,163	155,013	154,645	155,063
Participation rate	64.1%	63.8%	63.8%	63.7%	63.5%	63.6%
Employed	140,107	142,287	142,415	142,220	142,101	142,974
Employment-population ratio	58.4%	58.6%	58.6%	58.4%	58.3%	58.7%
Unemployed	13,897	12,720	12,749	12,794	12,544	12,088
Unemployment rate	9.0%	8.2%	8.2%	8.3%	8.1%	7.8%
Not in labor force	86,067	87,959	87,992	88,341	88,921	88,709
Persons who currently want a job . . .	5,929	6,291	6,520	6,554	6,957	6,727

As shown in Equation 12-1 on page 349, the participation rate is calculated by dividing the civilian labor force by the civilian noninstitutional population and then multiplying by 100. The September 2011 participation rate is therefore $\frac{154{,}004{,}000}{240{,}071{,}000} \times 100 = 64.1\%$. As shown in Equation 12-2 on page 349, the unemployment rate is calculated by dividing the unemployed by the civilian labor force and then multiplying by 100. The September 2011 unemployment rate is therefore $\frac{13{,}897}{154{,}004{,}000} \times 100 = 9.0\%$. The employment-population ratio is calculated by dividing the employed by the civilian noninstitutional population and then multiplying by 100. The September 2011 employment-population ratio is therefore $\frac{140{,}107{,}000}{240{,}071{,}000} = 58.4\%$. ■

STEP 2: Analyze the trend in the unemployment rate, the employment-population rate, and the participation rate from September 2011 through September 2012. Is the unemployment rate in September 2012 high or low by historical standards?

Read the section "The Significance of the Unemployment Rate" beginning on page 349, and study Figure 12-1 on page 348.

The unemployment rate is broadly decreasing over this period. Both the participation rate and the employment-population ratio are decreasing as well. By historical standards, as indicated in Figure 12-1, an unemployment rate of 7.8% is high. ■

SUMMARY

1. Inflation and unemployment are the twin evils of macroeconomics and the main concerns of macroeconomic policy.
2. **Employment** is the number of people employed; **unemployment** is the number of people unemployed and actively looking for work. Their sum is equal to the **labor force,** and the **labor force participation rate** is the percentage of the population age 16 or older that is in the labor force.
3. The **unemployment rate,** the percentage of the labor force that is unemployed and actively looking for work, can both overstate and understate the true level of unemployment. It can overstate because it counts as unemployed those who are continuing to search for a job despite having been offered one. It can understate because it ignores frustrated workers, such as **discouraged workers, marginally attached workers,** and the **underemployed.** In addition, the unemployment rate varies greatly among different groups in the population; it is typically higher for younger workers and for workers near retirement age than for workers in their prime working years.
4. The unemployment rate is affected by the business cycle. The unemployment rate generally falls when the growth rate of real GDP is above average and generally increases when the growth rate of real GDP is below average. A **jobless recovery,** a period in which real GDP is growing but unemployment rises, often follows recessions.
5. Job creation and destruction, as well as voluntary job separations, lead to **job search** and **frictional unemployment.** In addition, a variety of factors such as minimum wages, unions, **efficiency wages,** government policies designed to help laid-off workers, and mismatch between employees and employers result in a situation in which there is a surplus of labor at the market wage rate, creating **structural unemployment.** As a result, the **natural rate of unemployment,** the sum of frictional and structural employment, is well above zero, even when jobs are plentiful.
6. The actual unemployment rate is equal to the natural rate of unemployment, the share of unemployment that is independent of the business cycle, plus **cyclical unemployment,** the share of

unemployment that depends on fluctuations in the business cycle.

7. The natural rate of unemployment changes over time, largely in response to changes in labor force characteristics, labor market institutions, and government policies.

8. Inflation does not, as many assume, make everyone poorer by raising the level of prices. That's because wages and incomes are adjusted to take into account a rising price level, leaving **real wages** and **real income** unaffected. However, a high inflation rate imposes overall costs on the economy: **shoe-leather costs, menu costs,** and **unit-of-account costs.**

9. Inflation can produce winners and losers within the economy, because long-term contracts are generally written in dollar terms. The **interest rate** specified in a loan is typically a **nominal interest rate,** which differs from the **real interest rate** due to inflation. A higher-than-expected inflation rate is good for borrowers and bad for lenders. A lower-than-expected inflation rate is good for lenders and bad for borrowers.

10. Many believe policies that depress the economy and produce high unemployment are necessary to reduce embedded inflation. Because **disinflation** is very costly, policy makers try to prevent inflation from becoming excessive in the first place.

KEY TERMS

PROBLEMS

1. Each month, usually on the first Friday of the month, the Bureau of Labor Statistics releases the Employment Situation Summary for the previous month. Go to www.bls.gov and find the latest report. On the Bureau of Labor Statistics home page, at the top of the page, select the "Subject Areas" tab, find "Unemployment," and select "National Unemployment Rate." You will find the Employment Situation Summary under "CPS News Releases" on the left side of the page. How does the unemployment rate compare to the rate one month earlier? How does the unemployment rate compare to the rate one year earlier?

2. In general, how do changes in the unemployment rate vary with changes in real GDP? After several quarters of a severe recession, explain why we might observe a decrease in the official unemployment rate. Explain why we could see an increase in the official unemployment rate after several quarters of a strong expansion.

3. In each of the following situations, what type of unemployment is Melanie facing?
   a. After completing a complex programming project, Melanie is laid off. Her prospects for a new job requiring similar skills are good, and she has signed up with a programmer placement service. She has passed up offers for low-paying jobs.
   b. When Melanie and her co-workers refused to accept pay cuts, her employer outsourced their programming tasks to workers in another country. This phenomenon is occurring throughout the programming industry.
   c. Due to the current slump, Melanie has been laid off from her programming job. Her employer promises to rehire her when business picks up.

4. Part of the information released in the Employment Situation Summary concerns how long individuals have been unemployed. Go to www.bls.gov to find the latest report. Use the same technique as in Problem 1 to find the Employment Situation Summary. Near the end of the Employment Situation, click on Table A-12, titled "Unemployed persons by duration of unemployment." Use the seasonally adjusted numbers to answer the following questions.
   a. How many workers were unemployed less than 5 weeks? What percentage of all unemployed workers do these workers represent? How do these numbers compare to the previous month's data?
   b. How many workers were unemployed for 27 or more weeks? What percentage of all unemployed workers do these workers represent? How do these numbers compare to the previous month's data?
   c. How long has the average worker been unemployed (average duration, in weeks)? How does

this compare to the average for the previous month's data?

d. Comparing the latest month for which there are data with the previous month, has the problem of long-term unemployment improved or deteriorated?

5. There is only one labor market in Profunctia. All workers have the same skills, and all firms hire workers with these skills. Use the accompanying diagram, which shows the supply of and demand for labor, to answer the following questions. Illustrate each answer with a diagram.

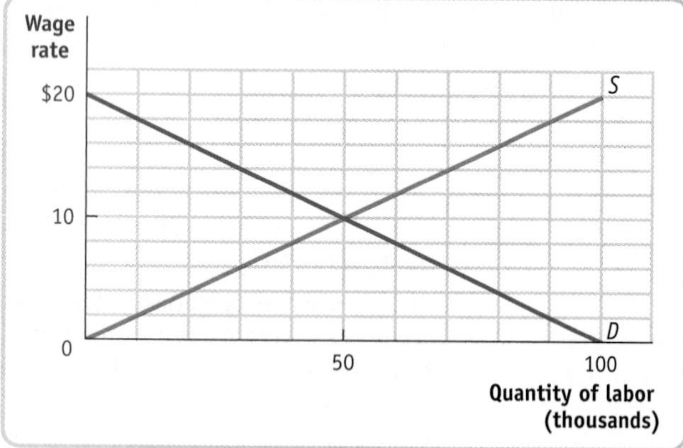

a. What is the equilibrium wage rate in Profunctia? At this wage rate, what are the level of employment, the size of the labor force, and the unemployment rate?

b. If the government of Profunctia sets a minimum wage equal to $12, what will be the level of employment, the size of the labor force, and the unemployment rate?

c. If unions bargain with the firms in Profunctia and set a wage rate equal to $14, what will be the level of employment, the size of the labor force, and the unemployment rate?

d. If the concern for retaining workers and encouraging high-quality work leads firms to set a wage rate equal to $16, what will be the level of employment, the size of the labor force, and the unemployment rate?

6. A country's labor force is the sum of the number of employed and unemployed workers. The accompanying table provides data on the size of the labor force and the number of unemployed workers for different regions of the United States.

	Labor force (thousands)		Unemployed (thousands)	
Region	May 2010	May 2011	May 2010	May 2011
Northeast	28,303.7	28,201.9	2,482.7	2,254.1
South	55,223.5	55,544.1	5,126.3	4,896.6
Midwest	34,520.2	34,430.0	3,305.7	2,803.7
West	35,827.2	35,613.0	3,954.0	3,664.4

Source: Bureau of Labor Statistics.

a. Calculate the number of workers employed in each of the regions in May 2010 and May 2011. Use your answers to calculate the change in the total number of workers employed between May 2010 and May 2011.

b. For each region, calculate the growth in the labor force from May 2010 to May 2011.

c. Compute unemployment rates in the different regions of the country in May 2010 and May 2011.

d. What can you infer about the fall in unemployment rates over this period? Was it caused by a net gain in the number of jobs or by a large fall in the number of people seeking jobs?

7. In which of the following cases is it more likely for efficiency wages to exist? Why?

a. Jane and her boss work as a team selling ice cream.

b. Jane sells ice cream without any direct supervision by her boss.

c. Jane speaks Korean and sells ice cream in a neighborhood in which Korean is the primary language. It is difficult to find another worker who speaks Korean.

8. How will the following changes affect the natural rate of unemployment?

a. The government reduces the time during which an unemployed worker can receive unemployment benefits.

b. More teenagers focus on their studies and do not look for jobs until after college.

c. Greater access to the Internet leads both potential employers and potential employees to use the Internet to list and find jobs.

d. Union membership declines.

9. With its tradition of a job for life for most citizens, Japan once had a much lower unemployment rate than that of the United States; from 1960 to 1995, the unemployment rate in Japan exceeded 3% only once. However, since the crash of its stock market in 1989 and slow economic growth in the 1990s, the job-for-life system has broken down and unemployment rose to more than 5% in 2003.

a. Explain the likely effect of the breakdown of the job-for-life system in Japan on the Japanese natural rate of unemployment.

b. As the accompanying diagram shows, the rate of growth of real GDP picked up in Japan after 2001 and before the global economic crisis of 2007–2009. Explain the likely effect of this increase in real GDP growth on the unemployment rate. Was the likely cause of the change in the unemployment rate during this period a change in the natural rate of unemployment or a change in the cyclical unemployment rate?

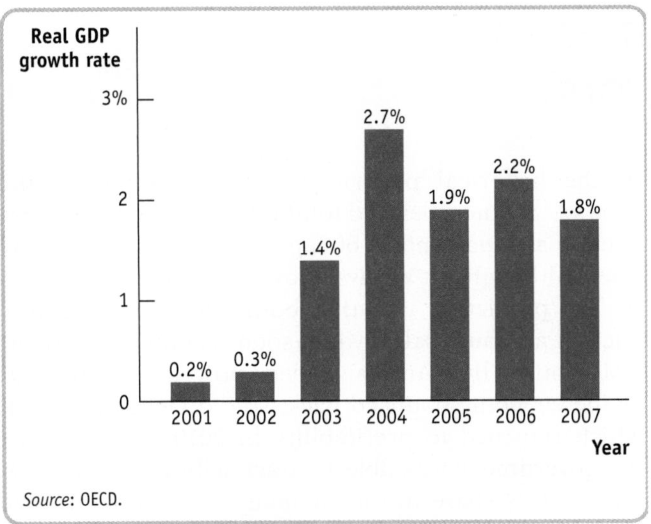

Source: OECD.

10. In the following examples, is inflation creating winners and losers at no net cost to the economy or is inflation imposing a net cost on the economy? If a net cost is being imposed, which type of cost is involved?
   a. When inflation is expected to be high, workers get paid more frequently and make more trips to the bank.
   b. Lanwei is reimbursed by her company for her work-related travel expenses. Sometimes, however, the company takes a long time to reimburse her. So when inflation is high, she is less willing to travel for her job.
   c. Hector Homeowner has a mortgage with a fixed nominal 6% interest rate that he took out five years ago. Over the years, the inflation rate has crept up unexpectedly to its present level of 7%.
   d. In response to unexpectedly high inflation, the manager of Cozy Cottages of Cape Cod must reprint and resend expensive color brochures correcting the price of rentals this season.

11. The accompanying diagram shows the interest rate on one-year loans and inflation during 1995–2010 in the economy of Albernia. When would one-year loans have been especially attractive and why?

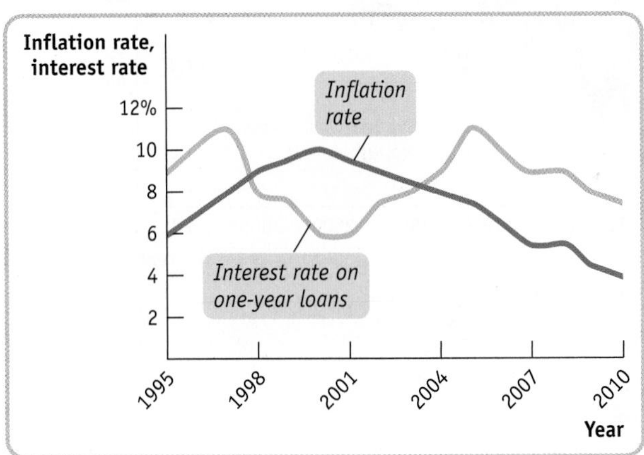

12. The accompanying table provides the inflation rate in the year 2000 and the average inflation rate over the period 2001–2010 for seven different countries.

Country	Inflation rate in 2000	Average inflation rate in 2001–2010
Brazil	7.06%	6.70%
China	0.4	2.16
France	1.83	1.86
Indonesia	3.77	8.55
Japan	−0.78	−0.25
Turkey	55.03	18.51
United States	3.37	2.40

Source: IMF.

   a. Given the expected relationship between average inflation and menu costs, rank the countries in descending order of menu costs using average inflation over the period 2001–2010.
   b. Rank the countries in order of inflation rates that most favored borrowers with ten-year loans that were taken out in 2000. Assume that the loans were agreed upon with the expectation that the inflation rate for 2001 to 2010 would be the same as the inflation rate in 2000.
   c. Did borrowers who took out ten-year loans in Japan gain or lose overall versus lenders? Explain.

13. The accompanying diagram shows the inflation rate in the United Kingdom from 1980 to 2010.

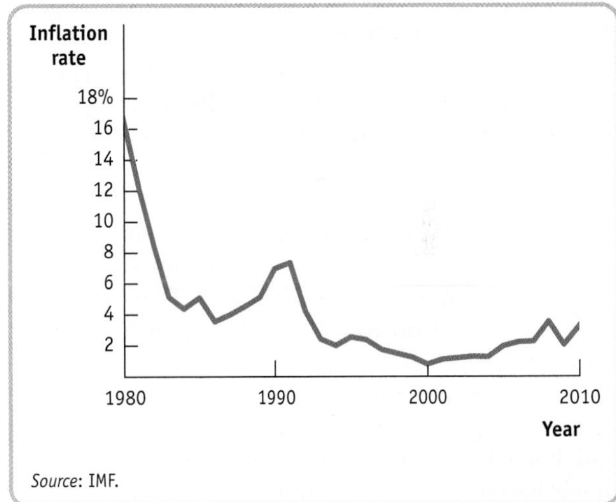

Source: IMF.

   a. Between 1980 and 1985, policy makers in the United Kingdom worked to lower the inflation rate. What would you predict happened to unemployment between 1980 and 1985?
   b. Policy makers in the United Kingdom react forcefully when the inflation rate rises above a target rate of 2%. Why would it be harmful if inflation rose from 3.4% (the level in 2010) to, say, a level of 5%?

BUSINESS CASE • Is What's Good for America Good for General Motors?

AP Photo/Paul Sancya, file

On June 1, 2009, General Motors filed for bankruptcy. It was a sad comedown for a company that had once been the very symbol of American economic success—so much so that in 1953 the company's CEO declared that the company's interests and those of the nation were identical: "For years I thought that what was good for the country was good for General Motors, and vice versa."

The 2009 bankruptcy didn't mean that GM shut down; the company was able to continue operating thanks to almost $50 billion in federal aid. In return for that aid, the government received stock in the restructured company. The government's intention was to sell off that stock later, once the company was profitable again.

But why did government officials believe that GM had a reasonable prospect of returning to profitability? Their case was based on an observation and a prediction.

The observation was that GM's troubles weren't unique. To be sure, the company had been badly run and needed both to make better cars and to reduce its costs. But all U.S. automakers were in trouble: overall car sales had slumped and, beyond that, overall manufacturing production had slumped. The association of weak auto sales with a general manufacturing slump fit the historical pattern. The accompanying figure shows U.S. auto sales and total U.S. manufacturing production as a percentage of capacity; the two series have often, although not always, moved together.

The prediction was that both manufacturing production and auto sales would soon rebound, improving GM's bottom line. And this indeed proved to be the case: as the economy bounced back, so did General Motors, which returned to profitability in 2010. By late 2010, the government was able to start selling off its stock, reducing its share in the company from about 60% to about 30%. As of December 2012, the government had not completely sold its 30% stake, but General Motors remained profitable.

So far, at least, the old line still applies: what is good for America is indeed good for General Motors, and vice versa.

QUESTIONS FOR THOUGHT

1. Why do overall manufacturing production and auto sales tend to move together?
2. Why was it reasonable in June 2009 to predict that auto sales would improve in the near future?
3. Why was the Obama administration especially lucky that it stepped in to rescue GM in June 2009 rather than, say, six months earlier?

U.S. Auto Sales and Total Manufacturing Production, 1976–2011

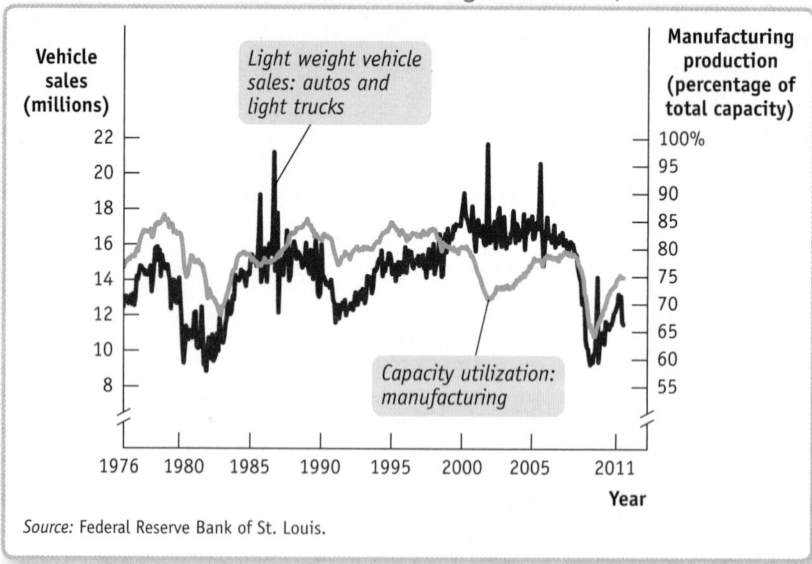

Source: Federal Reserve Bank of St. Louis.

BUSINESS CASE • Getting a Jump on GDP

REUTERS/Lucas Jackson

GDP matters. Investors and business leaders are always anxious to get the latest numbers. When the Bureau of Economic Analysis releases its first estimate of each quarter's GDP, normally on the 27th or 28th day of the month after the quarter ends, it's invariably a big news story.

In fact, many companies and other players in the economy are so eager to know what's happening to GDP that they don't want to wait for the official estimate. So a number of organizations produce numbers that can be used to predict what the official GDP number will say. Let's talk about two of those organizations, the economic consulting firm Macroeconomic Advisers and the nonprofit Institute of Supply Management.

Macroeconomic Advisers takes a direct approach: it produces its own estimates of GDP based on raw data from the U.S. government. But whereas the Bureau of Economic Analysis estimates GDP only on a quarterly basis, Macroeconomic Advisers produces monthly estimates. This means that clients can, for example, look at the estimates for January and February and make a pretty good guess at what first-quarter GDP, which also includes March, will turn out to be. The monthly estimates are derived by looking at a number of monthly measures that track purchases, such as car and truck sales, new housing construction, and exports.

The Institute for Supply Management (ISM) takes a very different approach. It relies on monthly surveys of purchasing managers—that is, executives in charge of buying supplies—who are basically asked whether their companies are increasing or reducing production. (We say "basically" because the ISM asks a longer list of questions.) Responses to the surveys are released in the form of indexes showing the percentage of companies that are expanding. Obviously, these indexes don't directly tell you what is happening to GDP. But historically, the ISM indexes have been strongly correlated with the rate of growth of GDP, and this historical relationship can be used to translate ISM data into "early warning" GDP estimates.

So if you just can't wait for those quarterly GDP numbers, you're not alone. The private sector has responded to demand, and you can get your data fix every month.

QUESTIONS FOR THOUGHT

1. Why do businesses care about GDP to such an extent that they want early estimates?
2. How do the methods of Macroeconomic Advisers and the Institute of Supply Management fit into the three different ways to calculate GDP?
3. If private firms are producing GDP estimates, why do we need the Bureau of Economic Analysis?

BUSINESS CASE • A Monster Slump

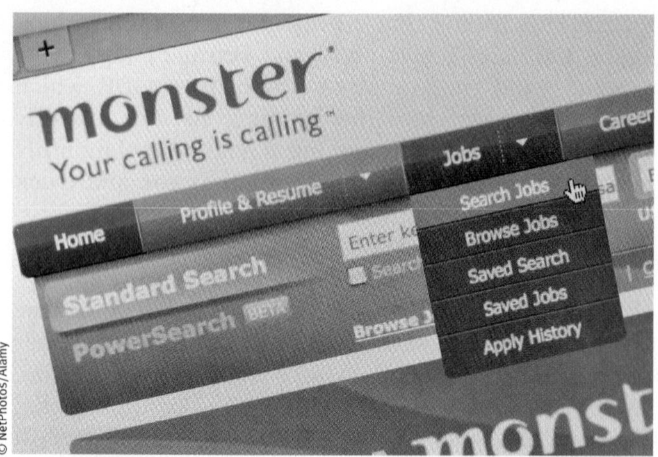

© NetPhotos/Alamy

The 1990s were famously an era of business hype, a decade when numerous Internet-based companies were created, then sold their stock at incredibly high prices, and, in the end, went bust. Some of the dot-coms, however, turned out to have workable business models and have endured. Among them is Monster.com, a job-search company that, along with its competitors, has helped replace traditional help-wanted ads in newspapers with online listings.

Monster Worldwide (the company's current name) and its competitors sell services to both employers seeking workers and workers seeking jobs. The employers place job listings, to which workers can respond; in addition to responding to these listings, job-seekers can pay for premium services such as résumé-writing and priority listing of their résumés.

The growing importance of online job listings was brought home in 2007 when The Conference Board, a business group that has long tracked the economy by producing an index of help-wanted ads, added an index of online help-wanted ads. As the accompanying figure shows, a plunge in online help-wanted ads heralded the surge in unemployment in 2008–2009; when online ads began to recover, unemployment stabilized and began a slow decline.

In the late 1990s, when the U.S. economy was experiencing unusually low unemployment, some economists suggested that Monster Worldwide and other Internet job services might be partly responsible, by making it easier for workers to get new jobs without a prolonged intervening period of unemployment. The evidence for this effect is, however, inconclusive.

You might have thought that the 2007–2009 recession, in which many laid-off workers were desperately seeking new jobs, would have been good for Monster. And the company did, in fact, receive a lot more business from workers wanting to post their résumés. But the company makes much more money from employer job listings, and these were sharply lower during the slump, hurting Monster's bottom line.

By late 2010, the economy seemed to be on the road to recovery, but online job listings were losing ground to Twitter and social networks. In fact, by the end of 2012, Monster had lost 90% of its value, primarily due to the rise of LinkedIn and other professional and social networking sites.

QUESTIONS FOR THOUGHT

1. Use the flows shown in Figure 12-7 to explain the potential role of online job listings in the economy.
2. In light of our discussion of the determinants of the unemployment rate, how could improved matching of job-seekers and employers through online job listings help?
3. What does the fact that Monster did badly during the 2008–2009 surge in unemployment suggest about the nature of that surge?

A Plunge in Online Help-Wanted Ads Heralds a Surge in Unemployment, 2008–2009

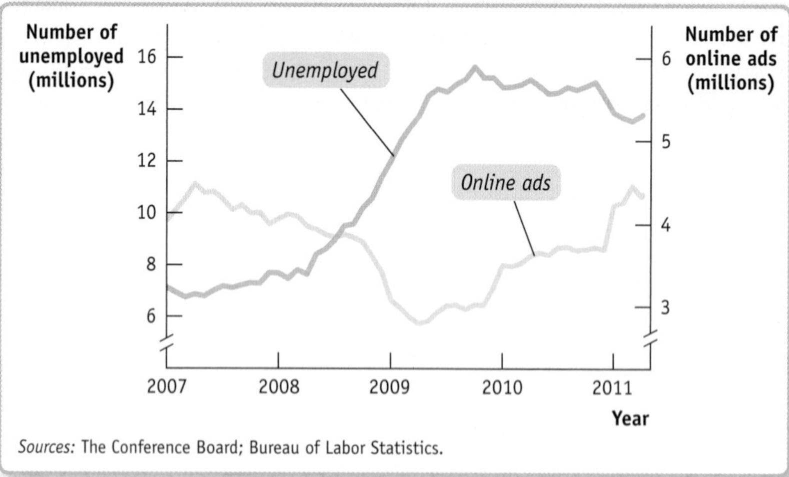

Sources: The Conference Board; Bureau of Labor Statistics.

Long-Run Economic Growth

WHAT YOU WILL LEARN IN THIS CHAPTER

- Why long-run economic growth is measured as the increase in real GDP per capita, how real GDP per capita has changed over time, and how it varies across countries
- Why **productivity** is the key to long-run economic growth and how productivity is driven by **physical capital, human capital,** and technological progress
- The factors that explain why long-run growth rates differ so much among countries
- How growth has varied among several important regions of the world and why the **convergence hypothesis** applies to economically advanced countries
- The question of **sustainability** and the challenges to growth posed by scarcity of natural resources and environmental degradation

TALL TALES

Yann Layma/Getty Images

As China illustrates, there is a positive relationship between a country's rate of long-run economic growth and its average population height.

CHINA IS GROWING—AND SO are the Chinese. According to official statistics, children in China are almost 2½ inches taller now than they were 30 years ago. The average Chinese citizen is still a lot shorter than the average American, but at the current rate of growth the difference may be largely gone in a couple of generations.

If that does happen, China will be following in Japan's footsteps. Older Americans tend to think of the Japanese as short, but today young Japanese men are more than 5 inches taller on average than they were in 1900, which makes them almost as tall as their American counterparts.

There's no mystery about why the Japanese grew taller—it's because they grew richer. In the early twentieth century, Japan was a relatively poor country in which many families couldn't afford to give their children adequate nutrition. As a result, their children grew up to be short adults. However, since World War II, Japan has become an economic powerhouse in which food is ample and young adults are much taller than before.

The same phenomenon is now happening in China. Although it is still a relatively poor country, China has made great economic strides over the past 30 years. Its recent history is probably the world's most dramatic example of long-run economic growth—a sustained increase in output per capita. Yet despite its impressive performance, China is currently playing catch-up with economically advanced countries like the United States and Japan. It's still a relatively poor country because these other nations began their own processes of long-run economic growth many decades ago—and in the case of the United States and European countries, more than a century ago.

Many economists have argued that long-run economic growth—why it happens and how to achieve it—is the single most important issue in macroeconomics. In this chapter, we present some facts about long-run growth, look at the factors that economists believe determine the pace at which long-run growth takes place, examine how government policies can help or hinder growth, and address questions about the environmental sustainability of long-run growth.

Comparing Economies Across Time and Space

Before we analyze the sources of long-run economic growth, it's useful to have a sense of just how much the U.S. economy has grown over time and how large the gaps are between wealthy countries like the United States and countries that have yet to achieve comparable growth. So let's take a look at the numbers.

Real GDP per Capita

The key statistic used to track economic growth is *real GDP per capita*—real GDP divided by the population size. We focus on GDP because, as we learned in Chapter 11, GDP measures the total value of an economy's production of final goods and services as well as the income earned in that economy in a given year. We use *real* GDP because we want to separate changes in the quantity of goods and services from the effects of a rising price level. We focus on real GDP *per capita* because we want to isolate the effect of changes in the population. For example, other things equal, an increase in the population lowers the standard of living for the average person—there are now more people to share a given amount of real GDP. An increase in real GDP that only matches an increase in population leaves the average standard of living unchanged.

Although we also learned in Chapter 11 that growth in real GDP per capita should not be a policy goal in and of itself, it does serve as a very useful summary measure of a country's economic progress over time. Figure 13-1 shows real GDP per capita for the United States, India, and China, measured in 1990 dollars, from 1900 to 2010. (We'll talk about India and China in a moment.) The vertical axis is drawn on a logarithmic scale so that equal percent changes in real GDP per capita across countries are the same size in the graph.

To give a sense of how much the U.S. economy grew during the last century, Table 13-1 shows real GDP per capita at selected years, expressed two ways: as a percentage of the 1900 level and as a percentage of the 2010 level. In 1920, the U.S.

FIGURE 13-1 Economic Growth in the United States, India, and China over the Past Century

Real GDP per capita from 1900 to 2010, measured in 1990 dollars, is shown for the United States, India, and China. Equal percent changes in real GDP per capita are drawn the same size. As the steeper slopes of the lines representing China and India show, since 1980 India and China had a much higher growth rate than the United States. In 2000, China attained the standard of living achieved in the United States in 1900. In 2010, India was still poorer than the United States was in 1900. (Break in China data from 1940 to 1950 is due to war.)

Sources: Angus Maddison, *Statistics on World Population, GDP, and Per Capita GDP, 1–2008AD*, http://www.ggdc.net/maddison; International Monetary Fund.

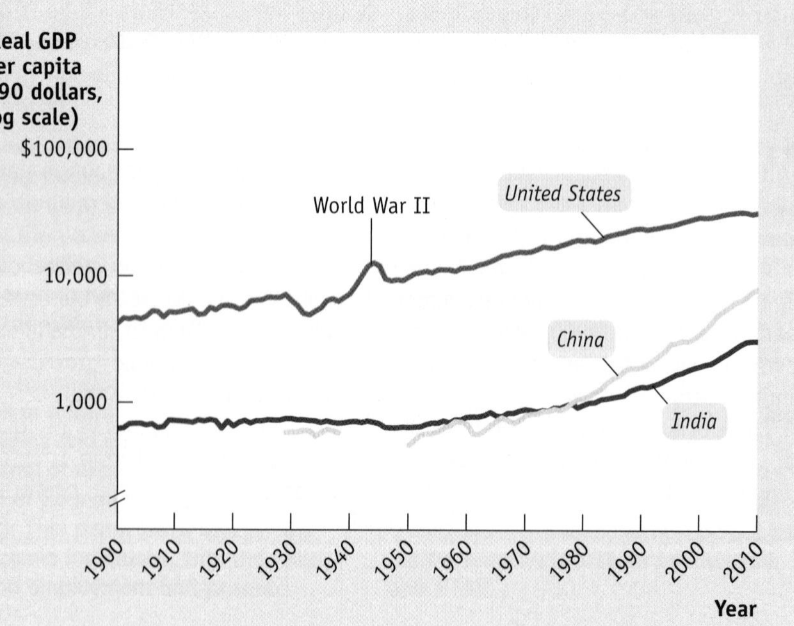

economy already produced 136% as much per person as it did in 1900. In 2010, it produced 758% as much per person as it did in 1900, a more than sevenfold increase. Alternatively, in 1900 the U.S. economy produced only 13% as much per person as it did in 2010.

The income of the typical family normally grows more or less in proportion to per capita income. For example, a 1% increase in real GDP per capita corresponds, roughly, to a 1% increase in the income of the median or typical family—a family at the center of the income distribution. In 2010, the median American household had an income of about $50,000. Since Table 13-1 tells us that real GDP per capita in 1900 was only 13% of its 2010 level, a typical family in 1900 probably had a purchasing power only 13% as large as the purchasing power of a typical family in 2010. That's around $6,100 in today's dollars, representing a standard of living that we would now consider severe poverty. Today's typical American family, if transported back to the United States of 1900, would feel quite a lot of deprivation.

TABLE 13-1 U.S. Real GDP per Capita

Year	Percentage of 1900 real GDP per capita	Percentage of 2010 real GDP per capita
1900	100%	13%
1920	136	18
1940	171	23
1980	454	60
2000	696	92
2010	758	100

Sources: Angus Maddison, *Statistics on World Population, GDP, and Per Capita GDP, 1–2008AD*, http://www.ggdc.net/maddison; Bureau of Economic Analysis.

Yet many people in the world have a standard of living equal to or lower than that of the United States at the beginning of the last century. That's the message about China and India in Figure 13-1: despite dramatic economic growth in China over the last three decades and the less dramatic acceleration of economic growth in India, China has only recently exceeded the standard of living that the United States enjoyed in the early twentieth century, while India is still poorer than the United States was at that time. And much of the world today is poorer than China or India.

You can get a sense of how poor much of the world remains by looking at Figure 13-2, a map of the world in which countries are classified according to their 2010 levels of GDP per capita, in U.S. dollars. As you can see, large parts of the world have very low incomes. Generally speaking, the countries of Europe and North America, as well as a few in the Pacific, have high incomes. The rest of the world, containing most of its population, is dominated by countries with GDP

FIGURE 13-2 Incomes Around the World, 2010

Although the countries of Europe and North America—along with a few in the Pacific—have high incomes, much of the world is still very poor. Today, about 50% of the world's population lives in countries with a lower standard of living than the United States had a century ago.

Source: International Monetary Fund.

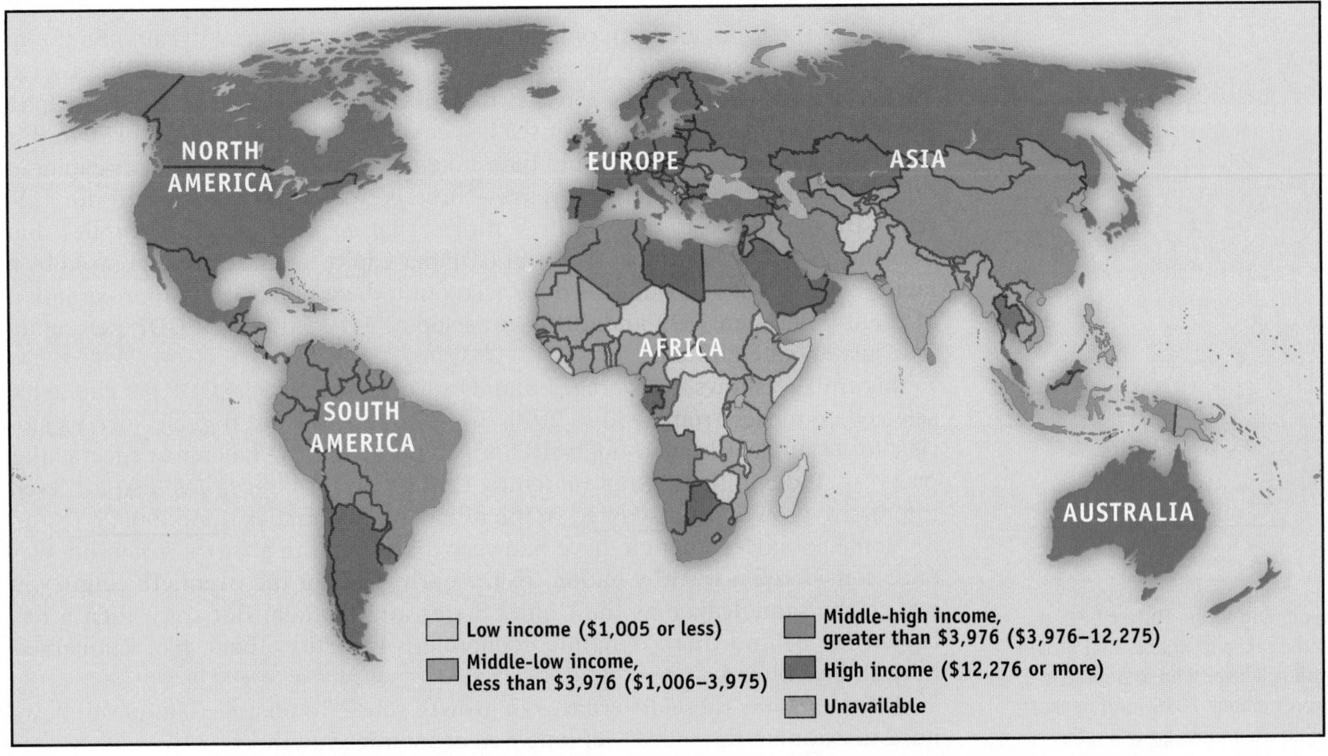

CHANGE IN LEVELS VERSUS RATE OF CHANGE

When studying economic growth, it's vitally important to understand the difference between a change in level and a rate of change. When we say that real GDP "grew," we mean that the level of real GDP increased. For example, we might say that U.S. real GDP grew during 2010 by $385 billion.

If we knew the level of U.S. real GDP in 2009, we could also represent the amount of 2010 growth in terms of a rate of change. For example, if U.S. real GDP in 2009 was $12,703 billion, then U.S. real GDP in 2010 was $12,703 billion + $385 billion = $13,088 billion. We could calculate the rate of change, or the growth rate, of U.S. real GDP during 2010 as: (($13,088 billion − $12,703 billion)/$12,703 billion) × 100 = ($385 billion/$12,703 billion) × 100 = 3.03%. Statements about economic growth over a period of years almost always refer to changes in the growth rate.

When talking about growth or growth rates, economists often use phrases that appear to mix the two concepts and so can be confusing. For example, when we say that "U.S. growth fell during the 1970s," we are really saying that the U.S. growth rate of real GDP was lower in the 1970s in comparison to the 1960s. When we say that "growth accelerated during the early 1990s," we are saying that the growth rate increased year after year in the early 1990s—for example, going from 3% to 3.5% to 4%.

less than $3,976 per capita—and often much less. In fact, today about 50% of the world's people live in countries with a lower standard of living than the United States had a century ago.

Growth Rates

How did the United States manage to produce over seven times as much per person in 2010 than in 1900? A little bit at a time. Long-run economic growth is normally a gradual process in which real GDP per capita grows at most a few percent per year. From 1900 to 2010, real GDP per capita in the United States increased an average of 1.9% each year.

To have a sense of the relationship between the annual growth rate of real GDP per capita and the long-run change in real GDP per capita, it's helpful to keep in mind the **Rule of 70,** a mathematical formula that tells us how long it takes real GDP per capita, or any other variable that grows gradually over time, to double. The approximate answer is:

(13-1) $$\text{Number of years for variable to double} = \frac{70}{\text{Annual growth rate of variable}}$$

(Note that the Rule of 70 can only be applied to a positive growth rate.) So if real GDP per capita grows at 1% per year, it will take 70 years to double. If it grows at 2% per year, it will take only 35 years to double. In fact, U.S. real GDP per capita rose on average 1.9% per year over the last century. Applying the Rule of 70 to this information implies that it should have taken 37 years for real GDP per capita to double; it would have taken 111 years—three periods of 37 years each—for U.S. real GDP per capita to double three times. That is, the Rule of 70 implies that over the course of 111 years, U.S. real GDP per capita should have increased by a factor of 2 × 2 × 2 = 8. And this does turn out to be a pretty good approximation of reality. Between 1899 and 2010—a period of 111 years—real GDP per capita rose just about eightfold.

Figure 13-3 shows the average annual rate of growth of real GDP per capita for selected countries from 1980 to 2010. Some countries were notable success stories: for example, China, though still quite a poor country, has made spectacular progress. India, although not matching China's performance, has also achieved impressive growth, as discussed in the following Economics in Action.

Some countries, though, have had very disappointing growth. Argentina was once considered a wealthy nation. In the early years of the twentieth century, it was in the same league as the United States and Canada. But since then it has lagged far behind more dynamic economies. And still others, like Zimbabwe, have slid backward.

According to the **Rule of 70,** the time it takes a variable that grows gradually over time to double is approximately 70 divided by that variable's annual growth rate.

What explains these differences in growth rates? To answer that question, we need to examine the sources of long-run economic growth.

FIGURE 13-3 Comparing Recent Growth Rates

The average annual rate of growth of real GDP per capita from 1980 to 2010 is shown here for selected countries. China and, to a lesser extent, India and Ireland achieved impressive growth. The United States and France had moderate growth. Once considered an economically advanced country, Argentina had more sluggish growth. Still others, such as Zimbabwe, slid backward.

Source: International Monetary Fund.

*Data for Zimbabwe is average annual growth rate 2000–2010 due to data limitations.

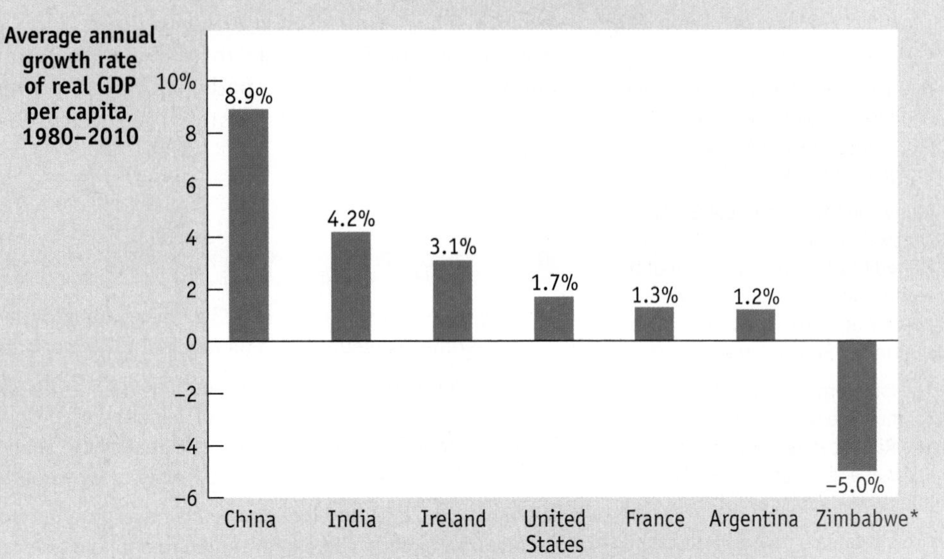

ECONOMICS ➤ IN ACTION

INDIA TAKES OFF

India achieved independence from Great Britain in 1947, becoming the world's most populous democracy—a status it has maintained to this day. For more than three decades after independence, however, this happy political story was partly overshadowed by economic disappointment. Despite ambitious economic development plans, India's performance was consistently sluggish. In 1980, India's real GDP per capita was only about 50% higher than it had been in 1947; the gap between Indian living standards and those in wealthy countries like the United States had been growing rather than shrinking.

Since then, however, India has done much better. As Figure 13-3 shows, real GDP per capita has grown at an average rate of 4.2% a year, more than tripling between 1980 and 2010. India now has a large and rapidly growing middle class. And yes, the well-fed children of that middle class are much taller than their parents.

What went right in India after 1980? Many economists point to policy reforms. For decades after independence, India had a tightly controlled, highly regulated economy. Today, things are very different: a series of reforms opened the economy to international trade and freed up domestic competition. Some economists, however, argue that this can't be the main story because the big policy reforms weren't adopted until 1991, yet growth accelerated around 1980.

Regardless of the explanation, India's economic rise has transformed it into a major new economic power—and allowed hundreds of millions of people to have a much better life, better than their grandparents could have dreamed.

Martin Harvey/Getty Images

India's high rate of economic growth since 1980 has raised living standards and led to the emergence of a rapidly growing middle class.

▼ Quick Review

- Economic growth is measured using real GDP per capita.
- In the United States, real GDP per capita increased over sevenfold since 1900, resulting in a large increase in living standards.
- Many countries have real GDP per capita much lower than that of the United States. More than half of the world's population has living standards worse than those existing in the United States in the early 1900s.
- The long-term rise in real GDP per capita is the result of gradual growth. The **Rule of 70** tells us how many years at a given annual rate of growth it takes to double real GDP per capita.
- Growth rates of real GDP per capita differ substantially among nations.

The big question now is whether this growth can continue. Skeptics argue that there are important bottlenecks in the Indian economy that may constrain future growth. They point in particular to the still low education level of much of India's population and inadequate infrastructure—that is, the poor quality and limited capacity of the country's roads, railroads, power supplies, and so on. But India's economy has defied the skeptics for several decades and the hope is that it can continue doing so.

CHECK YOUR UNDERSTANDING 13-1

1. Why do economists use real GDP per capita to measure economic progress rather than some other measure, such as nominal GDP per capita or real GDP?
2. Apply the Rule of 70 to the data in Figure 13-3 to determine how long it will take each of the countries listed there (except Zimbabwe) to double its real GDP per capita. Would India's real GDP per capita exceed that of the United States in the future if growth rates remain as shown in Figure 13-3? Why or why not?
3. Although China and India currently have growth rates much higher than the U.S. growth rate, the typical Chinese or Indian household is far poorer than the typical American household. Explain why.

Solutions appear at back of book.

The Sources of Long-Run Growth

Long-run economic growth depends almost entirely on one ingredient: rising *productivity*. However, a number of factors affect the growth of productivity. Let's look first at why productivity is the key ingredient and then examine what affects it.

The Crucial Importance of Productivity

Sustained economic growth occurs only when the amount of output produced by the average worker increases steadily. The term **labor productivity,** or **productivity** for short, is used to refer either to output per worker or, in some cases, to output per hour. (The number of hours worked by an average worker differs to some extent across countries, although this isn't an important factor in the difference between living standards in, say, India and the United States.) In this book we'll focus on output per worker. For the economy as a whole, productivity—output per worker—is simply real GDP divided by the number of people working.

You might wonder why we say that higher productivity is the only source of long-run growth. Can't an economy also increase its real GDP per capita by putting more of the population to work? The answer is, yes, but . . . . For short periods of time, an economy can experience a burst of growth in output per capita by putting a higher percentage of the population to work. That happened in the United States during World War II, when millions of women who previously worked only in the home entered the paid workforce. The percentage of adult civilians employed outside the home rose from 50% in 1941 to 58% in 1944, and you can see the resulting bump in real GDP per capita during those years in Figure 13-1.

Over the longer run, however, the rate of employment growth is never very different from the rate of population growth. Over the course of the twentieth century, for example, the population of the United States rose at an average rate of 1.3% per year and employment rose 1.5% per year. Real GDP per capita rose 1.9% per year; of that, 1.7%—that is, almost 90% of the total—was the result of rising

Labor productivity, often referred to simply as **productivity,** is output per worker.

productivity. In general, overall real GDP can grow because of population growth, but any large increase in real GDP *per capita* must be the result of increased output *per worker*. That is, it must be due to higher productivity.

So increased productivity is the key to long-run economic growth. But what leads to higher productivity?

Physical capital consists of human-made resources such as buildings and machines.

Human capital is the improvement in labor created by the education and knowledge embodied in the workforce.

Technological progress is an advance in the technical means of the production of goods and services.

Explaining Growth in Productivity

There are three main reasons why the average U.S. worker today produces far more than his or her counterpart a century ago. First, the modern worker has far more *physical capital,* such as machinery and office space, to work with. Second, the modern worker is much better educated and so possesses much more *human capital.* Finally, modern firms have the advantage of a century's accumulation of technical advancements reflecting a great deal of *technological progress.*

Let's look at each of these factors in turn.

Increase in Physical Capital Economists define **physical capital** as manufactured resources such as buildings and machines. Physical capital makes workers more productive. For example, a worker operating a backhoe can dig a lot more feet of trench per day than one equipped only with a shovel.

The average U.S. private-sector worker today is backed up by more than $150,000 worth of physical capital—far more than a U.S. worker had 100 years ago and far more than the average worker in most other countries has today.

Increase in Human Capital It's not enough for a worker to have good equipment—he or she must also know what to do with it. **Human capital** refers to the improvement in labor created by the education and knowledge embodied in the workforce.

The human capital of the United States has increased dramatically over the past century. A century ago, although most Americans were able to read and write, very few had an extensive education. In 1910, only 13.5% of Americans over 25 had graduated from high school and only 3% had four-year college degrees. By 2010, the percentages were 87% and 30%, respectively. It would be impossible to run today's economy with a population as poorly educated as that of a century ago.

Analyses based on *growth accounting,* described later in this chapter, suggest that education—and its effect on productivity—is an even more important determinant of growth than increases in physical capital.

Technological Progress Probably the most important driver of productivity growth is **technological progress,** which is broadly defined as an advance in the technical means of the production of goods and services. We'll see shortly how economists measure the impact of technology on growth.

Workers today are able to produce more than those in the past, even with the same amount of physical and human capital, because technology has advanced over time. It's important to realize that economically important technological progress need not be flashy or rely on cutting-edge science. Historians have noted that past economic growth has been driven not only by major inventions, such as the railroad or the semiconductor chip, but also by thousands of modest innovations, such as the flat-bottomed paper bag, patented in 1870, which made packing groceries and many other goods much easier, and the Post-it® note, introduced in 1981, which has had surprisingly large benefits for office productivity. Experts attribute much of the productivity

The **aggregate production function** is a hypothetical function that shows how productivity (real GDP per worker) depends on the quantities of physical capital per worker and human capital per worker as well as the state of technology.

An aggregate production function exhibits **diminishing returns to physical capital** when, holding the amount of human capital per worker and the state of technology fixed, each successive increase in the amount of physical capital per worker leads to a smaller increase in productivity.

surge that took place in the United States late in the twentieth century to new technology adopted by retail companies like Walmart rather than to high-technology companies.

Accounting for Growth: The Aggregate Production Function

Productivity is higher, other things equal, when workers are equipped with more physical capital, more human capital, better technology, or any combination of the three. But can we put numbers to these effects? To do this, economists make use of estimates of the **aggregate production function,** which shows how productivity depends on the quantities of physical capital per worker and human capital per worker as well as the state of technology. In general, all three factors tend to rise over time, as workers are equipped with more machinery, receive more education, and benefit from technological advances. What the aggregate production function does is allow economists to disentangle the effects of these three factors on overall productivity.

An example of an aggregate production function applied to real data comes from a comparative study of Chinese and Indian economic growth by the economists Barry Bosworth and Susan Collins of the Brookings Institution. They used the following aggregate production function:

$$\text{GDP per worker} = T \times (\text{Physical capital per worker})^{0.4} \times (\text{Human capital per worker})^{0.6}$$

where T represented an estimate of the level of technology and they assumed that each year of education raises workers' human capital by 7%. Using this function, they tried to explain why China grew faster than India between 1978 and 2004. About half the difference, they found, was due to China's higher levels of investment spending, which raised its level of physical capital per worker faster than India's. The other half was due to faster Chinese technological progress.

In analyzing historical economic growth, economists have discovered a crucial fact about the estimated aggregate production function: it exhibits **diminishing returns to physical capital.** That is, when the amount of human capital per worker and the state of technology are held fixed, each successive increase in the amount of physical capital per worker leads to a smaller increase in productivity. Figure 13-4 and the table to its right give a hypothetical example of how the level of physical capital per worker might affect the level of real GDP per worker, holding human capital per worker and the state of technology fixed. In this example, we measure the quantity of physical capital in dollars.

To see why the relationship between physical capital per worker and productivity exhibits diminishing returns, think about how having farm equipment affects the productivity of farmworkers. A little bit of equipment makes a big difference: a worker equipped with a tractor can do much more than a worker without one. And a worker using more expensive equipment will, other things equal, be more productive: a worker with a $40,000 tractor will normally be able to cultivate more farmland in a given amount of time than a worker with a $20,000 tractor because the more expensive machine will be more powerful, perform more tasks, or both.

But will a worker with a $40,000 tractor, holding human capital and technology constant, be twice as productive as a worker with a $20,000 tractor? Probably not: there's a huge difference between not having a tractor at all and having even an inexpensive tractor; there's much less difference between having an inexpensive tractor and having a better tractor. And we can be sure that a worker with a $200,000 tractor won't be 10 times as productive: a tractor can be improved only so much. Because the same is true of other kinds of equipment, the aggregate production function shows diminishing returns to physical capital.

Diminishing returns to physical capital imply a relationship between physical capital per worker and output per worker like the one shown in Figure 13-4. As

FIGURE 13-4 Physical Capital and Productivity

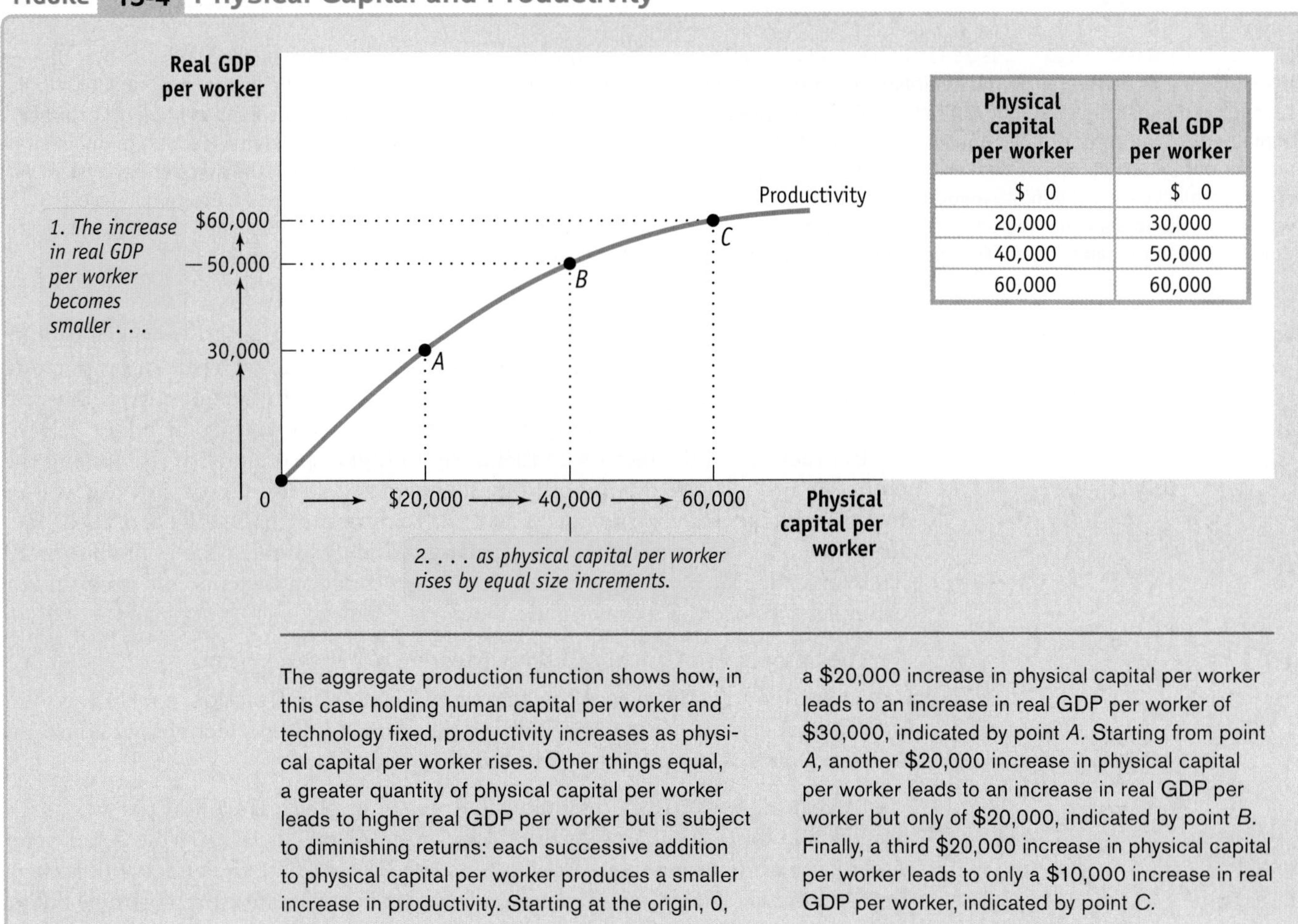

Physical capital per worker	Real GDP per worker
$ 0	$ 0
20,000	30,000
40,000	50,000
60,000	60,000

The aggregate production function shows how, in this case holding human capital per worker and technology fixed, productivity increases as physical capital per worker rises. Other things equal, a greater quantity of physical capital per worker leads to higher real GDP per worker but is subject to diminishing returns: each successive addition to physical capital per worker produces a smaller increase in productivity. Starting at the origin, 0, a $20,000 increase in physical capital per worker leads to an increase in real GDP per worker of $30,000, indicated by point *A*. Starting from point *A*, another $20,000 increase in physical capital per worker leads to an increase in real GDP per worker but only of $20,000, indicated by point *B*. Finally, a third $20,000 increase in physical capital per worker leads to only a $10,000 increase in real GDP per worker, indicated by point *C*.

the productivity curve for physical capital and the accompanying table illustrate, more physical capital per worker leads to more output per worker. But each $20,000 increment in physical capital per worker adds less to productivity. As you can see from the table, there is a big payoff for the first $20,000 of physical capital: real GDP per worker rises by $30,000. The second $20,000 of physical capital also raises productivity, but not by as much: real GDP per worker goes up by only $20,000. The third $20,000 of physical capital raises real GDP per worker by only $10,000. By comparing points along the curve you can also see that as physical capital per worker rises, output per worker also rises—but at a diminishing rate. Going from the origin at 0 to point *A*, a $20,000 increase in physical capital per worker, leads to an increase of $30,000 in real GDP per worker. Going from point *A* to point *B*, a second $20,000 increase in physical capital per worker, leads to an increase of only $20,000 in real GDP per worker. And from point *B* to point *C*, a $20,000 increase in physical capital per worker increased real GDP per worker by only $10,000.

It's important to realize that diminishing returns to physical capital is an "other things equal" phenomenon: additional amounts of physical capital are less productive *when the amount of human capital per worker and the technology are held fixed.* Diminishing returns may disappear if we increase the amount of human capital per worker, or improve the technology, or both at the same time the amount of physical capital per worker is increased.

For example, a worker with a $40,000 tractor who has also been trained in the most advanced cultivation techniques may in fact be more than twice as productive as a worker with only a $20,000 tractor and no additional human capital. But

PITFALLS

IT MAY BE DIMINISHED . . . BUT IT'S STILL POSITIVE

It's important to understand what diminishing returns to physical capital means and what it doesn't mean. As we've already explained, it's an "other things equal" statement: holding the amount of human capital per worker and the technology fixed, each successive increase in the amount of physical capital per worker results in a smaller increase in real GDP per worker. But this doesn't mean that real GDP per worker eventually falls as more and more physical capital is added. It's just that the *increase* in real GDP per worker gets smaller and smaller, albeit remaining at or above zero. So an increase in physical capital per worker will never reduce productivity. But due to diminishing returns, at some point increasing the amount of physical capital per worker no longer produces an economic payoff: at some point the increase in output is so small that it is not worth the cost of the additional physical capital.

diminishing returns to any one input—regardless of whether it is physical capital, human capital, or number of workers—is a pervasive characteristic of production. Typical estimates suggest that in practice a 1% increase in the quantity of physical capital per worker increases output per worker by only one-third of 1%, or 0.33%.

In practice, all the factors contributing to higher productivity rise during the course of economic growth: both physical capital and human capital per worker increase, and technology advances as well. To disentangle the effects of these factors, economists use **growth accounting,** which estimates the contribution of each major factor in the aggregate production function to economic growth. For example, suppose the following are true:

- The amount of physical capital per worker grows 3% a year.
- According to estimates of the aggregate production function, each 1% rise in physical capital per worker, holding human capital and technology constant, raises output per worker by one-third of 1%, or 0.33%.

In that case, we would estimate that growing physical capital per worker is responsible for 3% × 0.33 = 1 percentage point of productivity growth per year. A similar but more complex procedure is used to estimate the effects of growing human capital. The procedure is more complex because there aren't simple dollar measures of the quantity of human capital.

Growth accounting allows us to calculate the effects of greater physical and human capital on economic growth. But how can we estimate the effects of technological progress? We do so by estimating what is left over after the effects of physical and human capital have been taken into account. For example, let's imagine that there was no increase in human capital per worker so that we can focus on changes in physical capital and in technology.

In Figure 13-5, the lower curve shows the same hypothetical relationship between physical capital per worker and output per worker shown in Figure 13-4. Let's assume that this was the relationship given the technology available in 1940. The upper curve also shows a relationship between physical capital per worker and productivity, but this time given the technology available in 2010. (We've chosen a 70-year stretch to allow us to use the Rule of 70.) The 2010 curve is shifted up compared to the 1940 curve because technologies developed over the previous 70 years make it possible to produce more output for a given amount of physical capital per worker than was possible with the technology available in 1940. (Note that the two curves are measured in constant dollars.)

Let's assume that between 1940 and 2010 the amount of physical capital per worker rose from $20,000 to $60,000. If this increase in physical capital per worker had taken place without any technological progress, the economy would have moved from *A* to *C:* output per worker would have risen, but only from $30,000 to $60,000, or 1% per year (using the Rule of 70 tells us that a 1% growth rate over 70 years doubles output). In fact, however, the economy moved from *A* to *D:* output rose from $30,000 to $120,000, or 2% per year. There was an increase in both physical capital per worker and technological progress, which shifted the aggregate production function.

Growth accounting estimates the contribution of each major factor in the aggregate production function to economic growth.

FIGURE 13-5 Technological Progress and Productivity Growth

Technological progress raises productivity at any given level of physical capital per worker, and therefore shifts the aggregate production function upward. Here we hold human capital per worker fixed. We assume that the lower curve (the same curve as in Figure 13-4) reflects technology in 1940 and the upper curve reflects technology in 2010. Holding technology and human capital fixed, tripling physical capital per worker from $20,000 to $60,000 leads to a doubling of real GDP per worker, from $30,000 to $60,000. This is shown by the movement from point *A* to point *C*, reflecting an approximately 1% per year rise in real GDP per worker. In reality, technological progress raised productivity at any given level of physical capital—shown here by the upward shift of the curve—and the actual rise in real GDP per worker is shown by the movement from point *A* to point *D*. Real GDP per worker grew 2% per year, leading to a quadrupling during the period. The extra 1% in growth of real GDP per worker is due to higher total factor productivity.

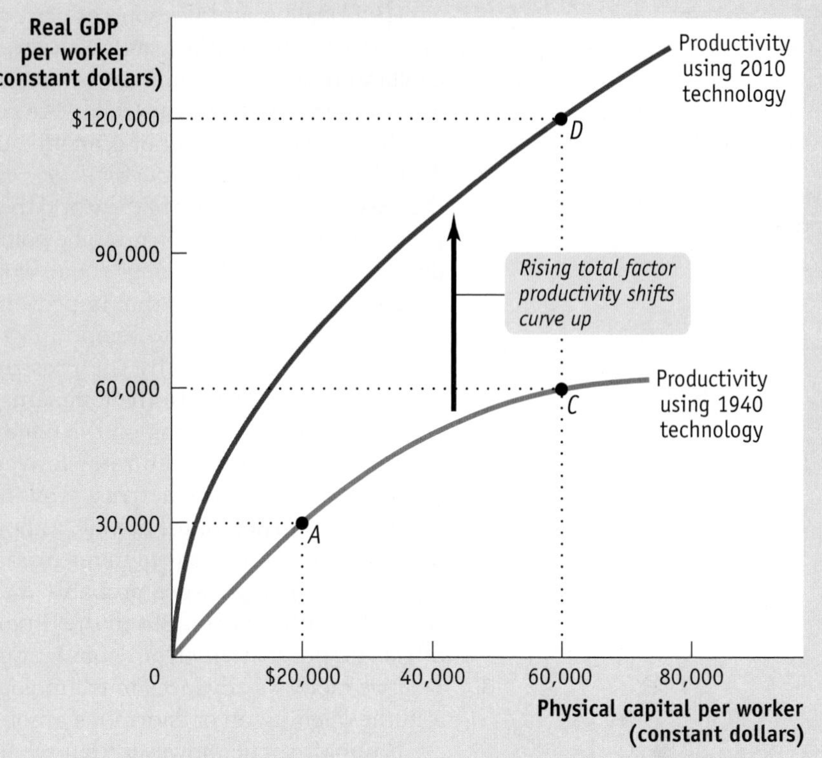

In this case, 50% of the annual 2% increase in productivity—that is, 1% in annual productivity growth—is due to higher **total factor productivity,** the amount of output that can be produced with a given amount of factor inputs. So when total factor productivity increases, the economy can produce more output with the same quantity of physical capital, human capital, and labor.

Most estimates find that increases in total factor productivity are central to a country's economic growth. We believe that observed increases in total factor productivity in fact measure the economic effects of technological progress. All of this implies that technological change is crucial to economic growth. The Bureau of Labor Statistics estimates the growth rate of both labor productivity and total factor productivity for nonfarm business in the United States. According to the Bureau's estimates, over the period from 1948 to 2010 American labor productivity rose 2.3% per year. Only 49% of that rise is explained by increases in physical and human capital per worker; the rest is explained by rising total factor productivity—that is, by technological progress.

What About Natural Resources?

In our discussion so far, we haven't mentioned natural resources, which certainly have an effect on productivity. Other things equal, countries that are abundant in valuable natural resources, such as highly fertile land or rich mineral deposits, have higher real GDP per capita than less fortunate countries. The most obvious modern example is the Middle East, where enormous oil deposits have made a few sparsely populated countries very rich. For example, Kuwait has about the same level of real GDP per capita as Germany, but Kuwait's wealth is based on oil, not manufacturing, the source of Germany's high output per worker.

But other things are often not equal. In the modern world, natural resources are a much less important determinant of productivity than human or physical capital for the great majority of countries. For example, some nations with very high real

Total factor productivity is the amount of output that can be achieved with a given amount of factor inputs.

GDP per capita, such as Japan, have very few natural resources. Some resource-rich nations, such as Nigeria (which has sizable oil deposits), are very poor.

Historically, natural resources played a much more prominent role in determining productivity. In the nineteenth century, the countries with the highest real GDP per capita were those abundant in rich farmland and mineral deposits: the United States, Canada, Argentina, and Australia. As a consequence, natural resources figured prominently in the development of economic thought. In a famous book published in 1798, *An Essay on the Principle of Population,* the English economist Thomas Malthus made the fixed quantity of land in the world the basis of a pessimistic prediction about future productivity. As population grew, he pointed out, the amount of land per worker would decline. And this, other things equal, would cause productivity to fall.

His view, in fact, was that improvements in technology or increases in physical capital would lead only to temporary improvements in productivity because they would always be offset by the pressure of rising population and more workers on the supply of land. In the long run, he concluded, the great majority of people were condemned to living on the edge of starvation. Only then would death rates be high enough and birth rates low enough to prevent rapid population growth from outstripping productivity growth.

It hasn't turned out that way, although many historians believe that Malthus's prediction of falling or stagnant productivity was valid for much of human history. Population pressure probably did prevent large productivity increases until the eighteenth century. But in the time since Malthus wrote his book, any negative effects on productivity from population growth have been far outweighed by other, positive factors—advances in technology, increases in human and physical capital, and the opening up of enormous amounts of cultivatable land in the New World.

It remains true, however, that we live on a finite planet, with limited supplies of resources such as oil and limited ability to absorb environmental damage. We address the concerns these limitations pose for economic growth in the final section of this chapter.

ECONOMICS ➤ IN ACTION

THE INFORMATION TECHNOLOGY PARADOX

From the early 1970s through the mid-1990s, the United States went through a slump in total factor productivity growth. Figure 13-6 shows Bureau of Labor Statistics estimates of annual total factor productivity growth, averaged for each 10-year period from 1948 to 2010. As you can see, there was a large fall in the total factor productivity growth rate beginning in the early 1970s. Because higher total factor productivity plays such a key role in long-run growth, the economy's overall growth was also disappointing, leading to a widespread sense that economic progress had ground to a halt.

FIGURE 13-6 The U.S. Productivity Growth Slowdown and Recovery

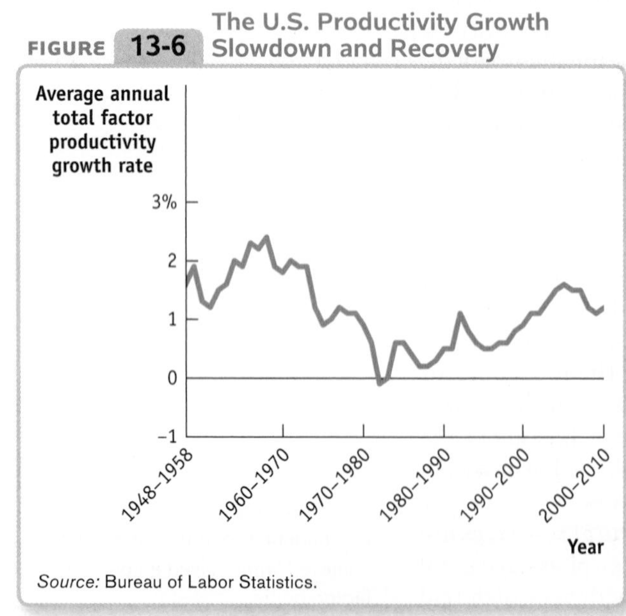

Source: Bureau of Labor Statistics.

Many economists were puzzled by the slowdown in total factor productivity growth after 1973, since in other ways the era seemed to be one of rapid technological progress. Modern information technology really began with the development of the first microprocessor—a computer on a chip—in 1971. In the 25 years that followed, a series of inventions that seemed revolutionary became standard equipment in the business world: fax machines, desktop computers, cell phones, and e-mail. Yet the rate of growth of total factor productivity remained stagnant. In a famous remark, MIT economics professor and Nobel laureate Robert Solow, a pioneer in the analysis of economic growth, declared that the information technology revolution could be seen everywhere except in the economic statistics.

Why didn't information technology show large rewards? Paul David, a Stanford University economic historian, offered a theory and a prediction. He pointed out that 100 years earlier another miracle technology—electric power—had spread through the economy, again with surprisingly little impact on productivity growth at first. The reason, he suggested, was that a new technology doesn't yield its full potential if you use it in old ways.

For example, a traditional factory around 1900 was a multistory building, with the machinery tightly crowded together and designed to be powered by a steam engine in the basement. This design had problems: it was very difficult to move people and materials around. Yet owners who electrified their factories initially maintained the multistory, tightly packed layout. Only with the switch to spread-out, one-story factories that took advantage of the flexibility of electric power—most famously Henry Ford's auto assembly line—did productivity take off.

David suggested that the same phenomenon was happening with information technology. Productivity, he predicted, would take off when people really changed their way of doing business to take advantage of the new technology—such as replacing letters and phone calls with e-mail. Sure enough, productivity growth accelerated dramatically in the second half of the 1990s as companies like Walmart discovered how to effectively use information technology.

Quick Review

- Long-run increases in living standards arise almost entirely from growing **labor productivity,** often simply referred to as **productivity.**
- An increase in **physical capital** is one source of higher productivity, but it is subject to **diminishing returns to physical capital.**
- **Human capital** and **technological progress** are also sources of increases in productivity.
- The **aggregate production function** is used to estimate the sources of increases in productivity. **Growth accounting** has shown that rising **total factor productivity,** interpreted as the effect of technological progress, is central to long-run economic growth.
- Natural resources are less important today than physical and human capital as sources of productivity growth in most economies.

CHECK YOUR UNDERSTANDING 13-2

1. Predict the effect of each of the following events on the growth rate of productivity.
   a. The amounts of physical and human capital per worker are unchanged, but there is significant technological progress.
   b. The amount of physical capital per worker grows at a steady pace, but the level of human capital per worker and technology are unchanged.
2. Output in the economy of Erewhon has grown 3% per year over the past 30 years. The labor force has grown at 1% per year, and the quantity of physical capital has grown at 4% per year. The average education level hasn't changed. Estimates by economists say that each 1% increase in physical capital per worker, other things equal, raises productivity by 0.3%. (*Hint:* % change in (X/Y) = % change in X – % change in Y.)
   a. How fast has productivity in Erewhon grown?
   b. How fast has physical capital per worker grown?
   c. How much has growing physical capital per worker contributed to productivity growth? What percentage of productivity growth is that?
   d. How much has technological progress contributed to productivity growth? What percentage of productivity growth is that?
3. Multinomics, Inc., is a large company with many offices around the country. It has just adopted a new computer system that will affect virtually every function performed within the company. Why might a period of time pass before employees' productivity is improved by the new computer system? Why might there be a temporary decrease in employees' productivity?

Solutions appear at back of book.

Why Growth Rates Differ

In 1820, according to estimates by the economic historian Angus Maddison, Mexico had somewhat higher real GDP per capita than Japan. Today, Japan has higher real GDP per capita than most European nations and Mexico is a poor country, though by no means among the poorest. The difference? Over the long run—since 1820—real GDP per capita grew at 1.9% per year in Japan but at only 1.3% per year in Mexico.

As this example illustrates, even small differences in growth rates have large consequences over the long run. So why do growth rates differ across countries and across periods of time?

Explaining Differences in Growth Rates

As one might expect, economies with rapid growth tend to be economies that add physical capital, increase their human capital, or experience rapid technological progress. Striking economic success stories, like Japan in the 1950s and 1960s or China today, tend to be countries that do all three: that rapidly add to their physical capital through high savings and investment spending, upgrade their educational level, and make fast technological progress. Evidence also points to the importance of government policies, property rights, political stability, and good governance in fostering the sources of growth.

Savings and Investment Spending One reason for differences in growth rates between countries is that some countries are increasing their stock of physical capital much more rapidly than others, through high rates of investment spending. In the 1960s, Japan was the fastest-growing major economy; it also spent a much higher share of its GDP on investment goods than did other major economies. Today, China is the fastest-growing major economy, and it similarly spends a very large share of its GDP on investment goods. In 2010, investment spending was 38% of China's GDP, compared with only 16% in the United States.

Where does the money for high investment spending come from? Investment spending must be paid for either out of savings from domestic households or by savings from foreign households—that is, an inflow of foreign capital.

Foreign capital has played an important role in the long-run economic growth of some countries, including the United States, which relied heavily on foreign funds during its early industrialization. For the most part, however, countries that invest a large share of their GDP are able to do so because they have high domestic savings. In fact, China in 2010 saved an even higher percentage of its GDP than it invested at home. The extra savings were invested abroad, largely in the United States.

One reason for differences in growth rates, then, is that countries add different amounts to their stocks of physical capital because they have different rates of savings and investment spending.

Education Just as countries differ substantially in the rate at which they add to their physical capital, there have been large differences in the rate at which countries add to their human capital through education.

A case in point is the comparison between Argentina and China. In both countries the average educational level has risen steadily over time, but it has risen much faster in China. Figure 13-7 shows the average years of education of adults in China, which we have highlighted as a spectacular example of long-run growth, and in Argentina, a country whose growth has been disappointing. Compared to China sixty years ago, Argentina had a much more educated population, while many Chinese were still illiterate. Today, the average educational level in China is still slightly below that in Argentina—but that's mainly because there are still many elderly adults who never received basic education. In terms of secondary and tertiary education, China has outstripped once-rich Argentina.

Research and Development The advance of technology is a key force behind economic growth. What drives technological progress?

Scientific advances make new technologies possible. To take the most spectacular example in today's world, the semiconductor chip—which is the basis for all modern information technology—could not have been developed without the theory of quantum mechanics in physics.

FIGURE 13-7 China's Students Are Catching Up

In both China and Argentina, the average educational level—measured by the number of years the average adult aged 25 or older has spent in school—has risen over time. Although China is still lagging behind Argentina, it is catching up—and China's success at adding human capital is one key to its spectacular long-run growth.

Source: Robert Barro and Jong-Wha Lee, "A New Data Set of Educational Attainment in the World, 1950–2010," NBER Working Paper No. 15902 (April 2010).

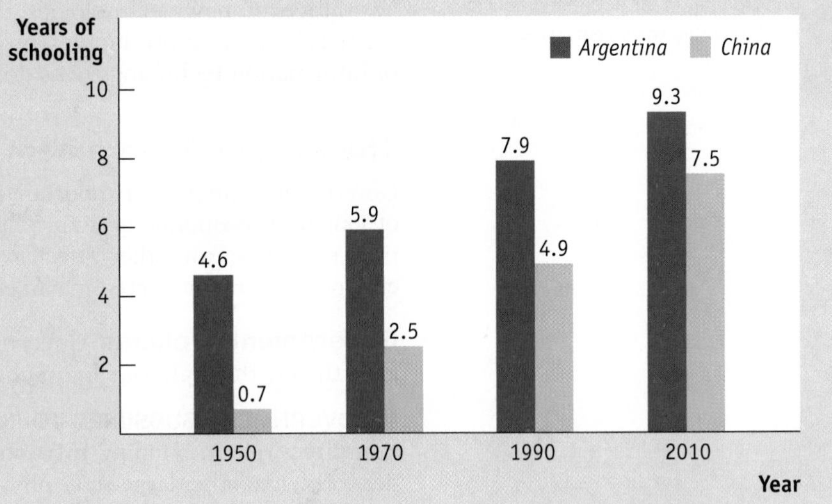

But science alone is not enough: scientific knowledge must be translated into useful products and processes. And that often requires devoting a lot of resources to **research and development,** or **R&D,** spending to create new technologies and apply them to practical use.

Research and development, or **R&D,** is spending to create and implement new technologies.

Although some research and development is conducted by governments, much R&D is paid for by the private sector, as discussed below. The United States became the world's leading economy in large part because American businesses were among the first to make systematic research and development a part of their operations. The upcoming For Inquiring Minds describes how Thomas Edison created the first modern industrial research laboratory.

FOR INQUIRING MINDS

INVENTING R&D

Thomas Edison is best known as the inventor of the lightbulb and the phonograph. But his biggest invention may surprise you: he invented research and development.

Before Edison's time, there had, of course, been many inventors. Some of them worked in teams. But in 1875 Edison created something new: his Menlo Park, New Jersey, laboratory. It employed 25 men full time to generate new products and processes for business. In other words, he did not set out to pursue a particular idea and then cash in. He created an organization whose purpose was to create new ideas year after year.

Edison's Menlo Park lab is now a museum. "To name a few of the products that were developed in Menlo Park," says the museum's website, "we can list the following: the carbon button mouthpiece for the telephone, the phonograph, the incandescent light bulb and the electrical distribution system, the electric train, ore separation, the Edison effect bulb, early experiments in wireless, the grasshopper telegraph, and improvements in telegraphic transmission."

You could say that before Edison's lab, technology just sort of happened: people came up with ideas, but businesses didn't plan to make continuous technological progress. Now R&D operations, often much bigger than Edison's original team, are standard practice throughout the business world.

Dennis MacDonald/Alamy

Roads, power lines, ports, information networks, and other underpinnings for economic activity are known as **infrastructure.**

Developing new technology is one thing; applying it is another. There have often been notable differences in the pace at which different countries take advantage of new technologies. As this chapter's Global Comparison shows, America's surge in productivity growth after 1995, as firms learned to make use of information technology, was at least initially not matched in Europe.

The Role of Government in Promoting Economic Growth

Governments can play an important role in promoting—or blocking—all three sources of long-term economic growth: physical capital, human capital, and technological progress. They can either affect growth directly through subsidies to factors that enhance growth, or by creating an environment that either fosters or hinders growth.

Government Policies Government policies can increase the economy's growth rate through four main channels.

1. GOVERNMENT SUBSIDIES TO INFRASTRUCTURE Governments play an important direct role in building **infrastructure:** roads, power lines, ports, information networks, and other large-scale physical capital projects that provide a foundation for economic activity. Although some infrastructure is provided by private companies, much of it is either provided by the government or requires a great deal of government regulation and support. Ireland is often cited as an example of the importance of government-provided infrastructure. After the government invested in an excellent telecommunications infrastructure in the 1980s, Ireland became a favored location for high-technology companies from abroad and its economy took off in the 1990s.

Poor infrastructure, such as a power grid that frequently fails and cuts off electricity, is a major obstacle to economic growth in many countries. To provide

OLD EUROPE AND NEW TECHNOLOGY

The United States experienced a burst of productivity growth after 1995, probably because businesses finally figured out how to use modern information technology effectively. As we'll see in the Business Case on the "Walmart effect" that follows Chapter 14, the acceleration of technological progress was especially dramatic in distribution—that is, in the business of getting goods to consumers. But did the rest of the world experience a similar takeoff?

The answer is, not everywhere. This figure shows 5-year average rates of growth in labor productivity in the United States and in the four big economies of Western Europe—France, Germany, Italy, and the United Kingdom—from 1971 to 2010. Up until the mid-1990s, Europe consistently achieved higher productivity growth than did the United States. But in the years that followed, European growth declined as U.S. growth surged for a decade. By the mid-2000s, the U.S. productivity growth rate had reverted to the pre-information technology boom levels.

There is great dispute both about why much of Europe didn't share in the productivity takeoff and about whether it will soon catch up to the United States. Some economists argue that high levels of government regulation made it hard for European businesses to reorganize themselves to take advantage of new technology. What is clear is that for at least a decade Europe lagged behind.

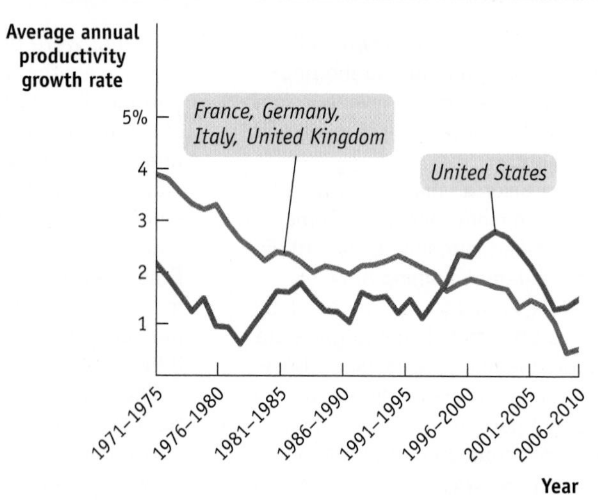

Source: OECD.

good infrastructure, an economy must not only be able to afford it, but it must also have the political discipline to maintain it.

Perhaps the most crucial infrastructure is something we, in an advanced country, rarely think about: basic public health measures in the form of a clean water supply and disease control. As we'll see in the next section, poor health infrastructure is a major obstacle to economic growth in poor countries, especially those in Africa.

2. GOVERNMENT SUBSIDIES TO EDUCATION In contrast to physical capital, which is mainly created by private investment spending, much of an economy's human capital is the result of government spending on education. Government pays for the great bulk of primary and secondary education. And it pays for a significant share of higher education: 75% of students attend public colleges and universities, and government significantly subsidizes research performed at private colleges and universities. As a result, differences in the rate at which countries add to their human capital largely reflect government policy. As we saw in Figure 13-7, educational levels in China are increasing much more rapidly than in Argentina. This isn't because China is richer than Argentina; until recently, China was, on average, poorer than Argentina. Instead, it reflects the fact that the Chinese government has made education of the population a high priority.

3. GOVERNMENT SUBSIDIES TO R&D Technological progress is largely the result of private initiative. But in the more advanced countries, important R&D is done by government agencies as well. In the upcoming Economics in Action, we describe Brazil's agricultural boom, which was made possible by government researchers who made discoveries that expanded the amount of arable land in Brazil, as well as developing new varieties of crops that flourish in Brazil's climate.

4. MAINTAINING A WELL-FUNCTIONING FINANCIAL SYSTEM Governments play an important indirect role in making high rates of private investment spending possible. Both the amount of savings and the ability of an economy to direct savings into productive investment spending depend on the economy's institutions, especially its financial system. In particular, a well-regulated and well-functioning financial system is very important for economic growth because in most countries it is the principal way in which savings are channeled into investment spending.

If a country's citizens trust their banks, they will place their savings in bank deposits, which the banks will then lend to their business customers. But if people don't trust their banks, they will hoard gold or foreign currency, keeping their savings in safe deposit boxes or under the mattress, where it cannot be turned into productive investment spending. As we'll discuss later, a well-functioning financial system requires appropriate government regulation to assure depositors that their funds are protected from loss.

Protection of Property Rights *Property rights* are the rights of owners of valuable items to dispose of those items as they choose. A subset, *intellectual property rights,* are the rights of an innovator to accrue the rewards of her innovation. The state of property rights generally, and intellectual property rights in particular, are important factors in explaining differences in growth rates across economies. Why? Because no one would bother to spend the effort and resources required to innovate if someone else could appropriate that innovation and capture the rewards. So, for innovation to flourish, intellectual property rights must receive protection.

Sometimes this is accomplished by the nature of the innovation: it may be too difficult or expensive to copy. But, generally, the government has to protect intellectual property rights. A *patent* is a government-created temporary monopoly given to an innovator for the use or sale of his or her innovation. It's a temporary rather than permanent monopoly because while it's in society's interests to give an innovator an incentive to invent, it's also in society's interests to eventually encourage competition.

Political Stability and Good Governance There's not much point in investing in a business if rioting mobs are likely to destroy it, or saving your money if someone with political connections can steal it. Political stability and good governance

FOR INQUIRING MINDS

THE NEW GROWTH THEORY

Until the 1990s, economic models of technological progress assumed that what drove innovation was a mystery—unknown and unpredictable. In the words of economists, the sources of technological progress were *exogenous*—they were outside the models of economics and assumed to "just happen." Then, in a series of influential papers written in the 1980s and 1990s, Paul Romer founded what we now call "the New Growth Theory." In Romer's model, technological progress was explainable because it was in fact *endogenous*—the outcome of economic variables and incentives. And because technological progress was endogenous, policies could be adopted to foster its growth.

At any point in time, an economy has a stock of knowledge capital—the accumulated knowledge generated by past investments in research and development, education, and skill enhancement, as well as knowledge acquired from other economies. And that stock of knowledge capital is spread throughout the economy, so all firms benefit from it. According to the New Growth Theory, a rising stock of knowledge capital creates the foundation for further technological progress as innovation, shared by firms throughout the economy, makes further innovation possible. For example, touchscreen technology—developed in the 1970s and 1980s—became the basis for later developments such as smartphones and tablet computers.

Yet, as Romer pointed out, there is a severe wrinkle in this story: because knowledge is shared throughout the economy, it may be very difficult for an innovator to capture the rewards of his or her innovation as others exploit the innovation for their own interests. So in the New Growth Theory, government protection of intellectual property rights is critical to furthering technological progress. In addition, governments, institutions, and firms can enhance technological progress by subsidizing investments in education and research and development, which, in turn, can increase the stock of knowledge capital.

By giving us a better model of where technological progress comes from, the New Growth Theory makes clear how important the policies of government, institutions, and firms are in fostering it.

(including the protection of property rights) are essential ingredients in fostering economic growth in the long run.

Long-run economic growth in successful economies, like that of the United States, has been possible because there are good laws, institutions that enforce those laws, and a stable political system that maintains those institutions. The law must say that your property is really yours so that someone else can't take it away. The courts and the police must be honest so that they can't be bribed to ignore the law. And the political system must be stable so that laws don't change capriciously.

Americans take these preconditions for granted, but they are by no means guaranteed. Aside from the disruption caused by war or revolution, many countries find that their economic growth suffers due to corruption among the government officials who should be enforcing the law. For example, until 1991 the Indian government imposed many bureaucratic restrictions on businesses, which often had to bribe government officials to get approval for even routine activities—a tax on business, in effect. Economists have argued that a reduction in this burden of corruption is one reason Indian growth has been much faster in recent years.

Even when the government isn't corrupt, excessive government intervention can be a brake on economic growth. If large parts of the economy are supported by government subsidies, protected from imports, subject to unnecessary monopolization, or otherwise insulated from competition, productivity tends to suffer because of a lack of incentives. As we'll see in the next section, excessive government intervention is one often-cited explanation for slow growth in Latin America.

ECONOMICS ➤ IN ACTION

THE BRAZILIAN BREADBASKET

A wry Brazilian joke says that "Brazil is the country of the future—and always will be." The world's fifth most populous country has often been considered as a possible major economic power yet has never fulfilled that promise.

In recent years, however, Brazil's economy has made a better showing, especially in agriculture. This success depends on exploiting a natural resource, the tropical savanna land known as the *cerrado*. Until a quarter-century ago, the land was considered unsuitable for farming. A combination of three factors changed that: technological progress due to research and development, improved economic policies, and greater physical capital.

The Brazilian Enterprise for Agricultural and Livestock Research, a government-run agency, developed the crucial technologies. It showed that adding lime and phosphorus made *cerrado* land productive, and it developed breeds of cattle and varieties of soybeans suited for the climate. (Now they're working on wheat.) Also, until the 1980s, Brazilian international trade policies discouraged exports, as did an overvalued exchange rate that made the country's goods more expensive to foreigners. After economic reform, investing in Brazilian agriculture became much more profitable and companies began putting in place the farm machinery, buildings, and other forms of physical capital needed to exploit the land.

LatinStock Collection/Alamy

In Brazil, government-funded R&D has resulted in crucial agricultural technologies and economic reforms that turn unusable land into profitable farmland.

What still limits Brazil's growth? Infrastructure. According to a report in the *New York Times*, Brazilian farmers are "concerned about the lack of reliable highways, railways and barge routes, which adds to the cost of doing business." Recognizing this, the Brazilian government is investing in infrastructure, and Brazilian agriculture is continuing to expand. The country has already overtaken the United States as the world's largest beef exporter and may not be far behind in soybeans.

Quick Review

- Countries differ greatly in their growth rates of real GDP per capita due to differences in the rates at which they accumulate physical capital and human capital as well as differences in technological progress. A prime cause of differences in growth rates is differences in rates of domestic savings and investment spending as well as differences in education levels, and **research and development,** or **R&D,** levels. R&D largely drives technological progress.
- Government actions can promote or hinder the sources of long-term growth.
- Government policies that directly promote growth are subsidies to **infrastructure,** particularly public health infrastructure, subsidies to education, subsidies to R&D, and the maintenance of a well-functioning financial system.
- Governments improve the environment for growth by protecting property rights (particularly intellectual property rights through patents), by providing political stability, and through good governance. Poor governance includes corruption and excessive government intervention.

CHECK YOUR UNDERSTANDING 13-3

1. Explain the link between a country's growth rate, its investment spending as a percent of GDP, and its domestic savings.
2. U.S. centers of academic biotechnology research have closer connections with private biotechnology companies than do their European counterparts. What effect might this have on the pace of creation and development of new drugs in the United States versus Europe?
3. During the 1990s in the former U.S.S.R., a lot of property was seized and controlled by those in power. How might this have affected the country's growth rate at that time? Explain.

Solutions appear at back of book.

Success, Disappointment, and Failure

As we've seen, rates of long-run economic growth differ quite a lot around the world. Now let's look at three regions of the world that have had quite different experiences with economic growth over the last few decades.

Figure 13-8 shows trends since 1960 in real GDP per capita in 2000 dollars for three countries: Argentina, Nigeria, and South Korea. (As in Figure 13-1, the vertical axis is drawn in logarithmic scale.) We have chosen these countries because each is a particularly striking example of what has happened in its region. South Korea's amazing rise is part of a broad "economic miracle"

FIGURE 13-8 Success and Disappointment

Real GDP per capita from 1960 to 2010, measured in 2000 dollars, is shown for Argentina, South Korea, and Nigeria, using a logarithmic scale. South Korea and some other East Asian countries have been highly successful at achieving economic growth. Argentina, like much of Latin America, has had several setbacks, slowing its growth. Nigeria's standard of living in 2010 was only barely higher than it had been in 1960, an experience shared by many African countries. Neither Argentina nor Nigeria exhibited much growth over the 50-year period, although both have had significantly higher growth in recent years.
Source: World Bank.

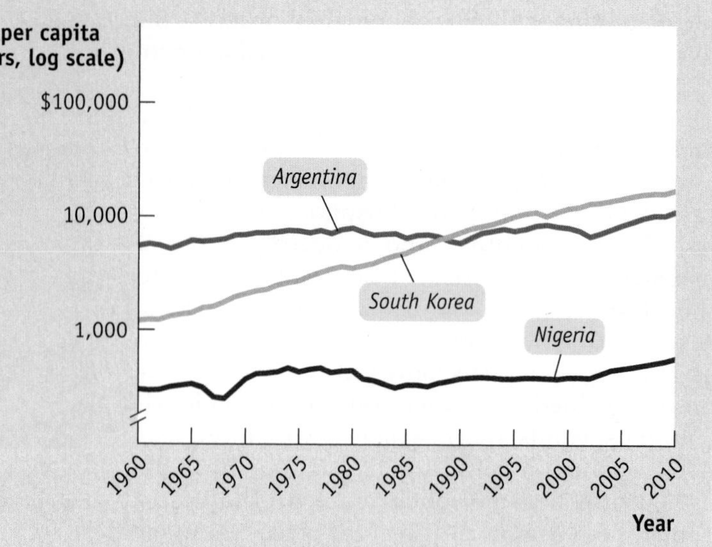

in East Asia. Argentina's slow progress, interrupted by repeated setbacks, is more or less typical of the disappointing growth that has characterized Latin America. And Nigeria's unhappy story until very recently—with little growth in real GDP until after 2000 —was, unfortunately, an experience shared by many African countries.

East Asia's Miracle

In 1960 South Korea was a very poor country. In fact, in 1960 its real GDP per capita was lower than that of India today. But, as you can see from Figure 13-8, beginning in the early 1960s South Korea began an extremely rapid economic ascent: real GDP per capita grew about 7% per year for more than 30 years. Today South Korea, though still somewhat poorer than Europe or the United States, looks very much like an economically advanced country.

South Korea's economic growth is unprecedented in history: it took the country only 35 years to achieve growth that required centuries elsewhere. Yet South Korea is only part of a broader phenomenon, often referred to as the East Asian economic miracle. High growth rates first appeared in South Korea, Taiwan, Hong Kong, and Singapore but then spread across the region, most notably to China. Since 1975, the whole region has increased real GDP per capita by 6% per year, more than three times America's historical rate of growth.

How have the Asian countries achieved such high growth rates? The answer is that all of the sources of productivity growth have been firing on all cylinders. Very high savings rates, the percentage of GDP that is saved nationally in any given year, have allowed the countries to significantly increase the amount of physical capital per worker. Very good basic education has permitted a rapid improvement in human capital. And these countries have experienced substantial technological progress.

Why didn't any economy achieve this kind of growth in the past? Most economic analysts think that East Asia's growth spurt was possible because of its *relative* backwardness. That is, by the time that East Asian economies began to move into the modern world, they could benefit from adopting the technological advances that had been generated in technologically advanced countries such as the United States.

In 1900, the United States could not have moved quickly to a modern level of productivity because much of the technology that powers the modern economy, from jet planes to computers, hadn't been invented yet. In 1970, South Korea probably still had lower labor productivity than the United States had in 1900, but it could rapidly upgrade its productivity by adopting technology that had been developed in the United States, Europe, and Japan over the previous century. This was aided by a huge investment in human capital through widespread schooling.

The East Asian experience demonstrates that economic growth can be especially fast in countries that are playing catch-up to other countries with higher GDP per capita. On this basis, many economists have suggested a general principle known as the **convergence hypothesis.** It says that differences in real GDP per capita among countries tend to narrow over time because countries that start with lower real GDP per capita tend to have higher growth rates. We'll look at the evidence on the convergence hypothesis in the Economics in Action at the end of this section.

According to the **convergence hypothesis**, international differences in real GDP per capita tend to narrow over time.

Even before we get to that evidence, however, we can say right away that starting with a relatively low level of real GDP per capita is no guarantee of rapid growth, as the examples of Latin America and Africa both demonstrate.

Latin America's Disappointment

In 1900, Latin America was not considered an economically backward region. Natural resources, including both minerals and cultivatable land, were abundant. Some countries, notably Argentina, attracted millions of immigrants from Europe in search of a better life. Measures of real GDP per capita in Argentina, Uruguay, and southern Brazil were comparable to those in economically advanced countries.

Since about 1920, however, growth in Latin America has been disappointing. As Figure 13-8 shows in the case of Argentina, growth has been disappointing for many decades, until 2000 when it finally began to increase. The fact that South Korea is now much richer than Argentina would have seemed inconceivable a few generations ago.

Why did Latin America stagnate? Comparisons with East Asian success stories suggest several factors. The rates of savings and investment spending in Latin America have been much lower than in East Asia, partly as a result of irresponsible government policy that has eroded savings through high inflation, bank failures, and other disruptions. Education—especially broad basic education—has been underemphasized: even Latin American nations rich in natural resources often failed to channel that wealth into their educational systems. And political instability, leading to irresponsible economic policies, has taken a toll.

In the 1980s, many economists came to believe that Latin America was suffering from excessive government intervention in markets. They recommended opening the economies to imports, selling off government-owned companies, and, in general, freeing up individual initiative. The hope was that this would produce an East Asian–type economic surge. So far, however, only one Latin American nation, Chile, has achieved sustained rapid growth. It now seems that pulling off an economic miracle is harder than it looks, although in recent years Brazil and Argentina have seen their growth rates increase significantly as they exported large amounts of commodities to the advanced countries and rapidly developing China.

Africa's Troubles and Promise

Africa south of the Sahara is home to about 780 million people, more than 2½ times the population of the United States. On average, they are very poor, nowhere close to U.S. living standards 100 or even 200 years ago. And economic progress has been both slow and uneven, as the example of Nigeria, the most populous nation in the region, suggests. In fact, real GDP per capita in sub-Saharan Africa actually fell 13 percent from 1980 to 1994, although it has recovered since then. The consequence of this poor growth performance has been intense and continuing poverty.

This is a very disheartening story. What explains it?

Several factors are probably crucial. Perhaps first and foremost is the problem of political instability. In the years since 1975, large parts of Africa have experienced savage civil wars (often with outside powers backing rival sides) that have killed millions of people and made productive investment spending impossible. The threat of war and general anarchy has also inhibited other important preconditions for growth, such as education and provision of necessary infrastructure.

Property rights are also a major problem. The lack of legal safeguards means that property owners are often subject to extortion because of government corruption, making them averse to owning property or improving it. This is especially damaging in a country that is very poor.

While many economists see political instability and government corruption as the leading causes of underdevelopment in Africa, some—most notably Jeffrey Sachs of Columbia University and the United Nations—believe the opposite. They argue that Africa is politically unstable because Africa is poor. And Africa's poverty, they go on to claim, stems from its extremely unfavorable geographic conditions—much of the continent is landlocked, hot, infested with tropical diseases, and cursed with poor soil.

Sachs, along with economists from the World Health Organization, has highlighted the importance of health problems in Africa. In poor countries, worker productivity is often severely hampered by malnutrition and disease. In particular, tropical diseases such as malaria can only be controlled with an effective public health infrastructure, something that is lacking in much of Africa. At the time of writing, economists are studying certain regions of Africa to determine whether modest amounts of aid given directly to residents for the purposes of increasing crop yields, reducing malaria, and increasing school attendance can produce self-sustaining gains in living standards.

Although the example of African countries represents a warning that long-run economic growth cannot be taken for granted, there are some signs of hope. As we noted in Figure 13-8, Nigeria's per capita GDP, after decades of stagnation, turned upward after 2000, achieving a 5.5% real GDP per capita growth rate in 2010. The same is true for sub-Saharan African economies as a whole. In 2011, real GDP per capita growth rates averaged around 5.5% across sub-Saharan African countries and are projected to be nearly 6% in 2012. Rising prices for their exports are part of the reason for recent success, but there is growing optimism among development experts that a period of relative peace and better government is ushering in a new era for Africa's economies.

ECONOMICS ➤ *IN ACTION*

ARE ECONOMIES CONVERGING?

In the 1950s, much of Europe seemed quaint and backward to American visitors, and Japan seemed very poor. Today, a visitor to Paris or Tokyo sees a city that looks about as rich as New York. Although real GDP per capita is still somewhat higher in the United States, the differences in the standards of living among the United States, Europe, and Japan are relatively small.

Many economists have argued that this convergence in living standards is normal; the convergence hypothesis says that relatively poor countries should have higher rates of growth of real GDP per capita than relatively rich countries. And if we look at today's relatively well-off countries, the convergence hypothesis seems to be true. Panel (a) of Figure 13-9 shows data for a number of today's wealthy economies measured in 1990 dollars. On the horizontal axis is real GDP per capita in 1960; on the vertical axis is the average annual growth rate of real GDP per capita from 1960 to 2008. There is a clear negative relationship as can be seen from the line fitted through the points. The United States was the richest country in this group in 1960 and had the slowest rate of growth. Japan and Spain were the poorest countries in 1960 and had the fastest rates of growth. These data suggest that the convergence hypothesis is true.

But economists who looked at similar data realized that these results depend on the countries selected. If you look at successful economies that have a high standard of living today, you find that real GDP per capita has converged. But

FIGURE 13-9 Do Economies Converge?

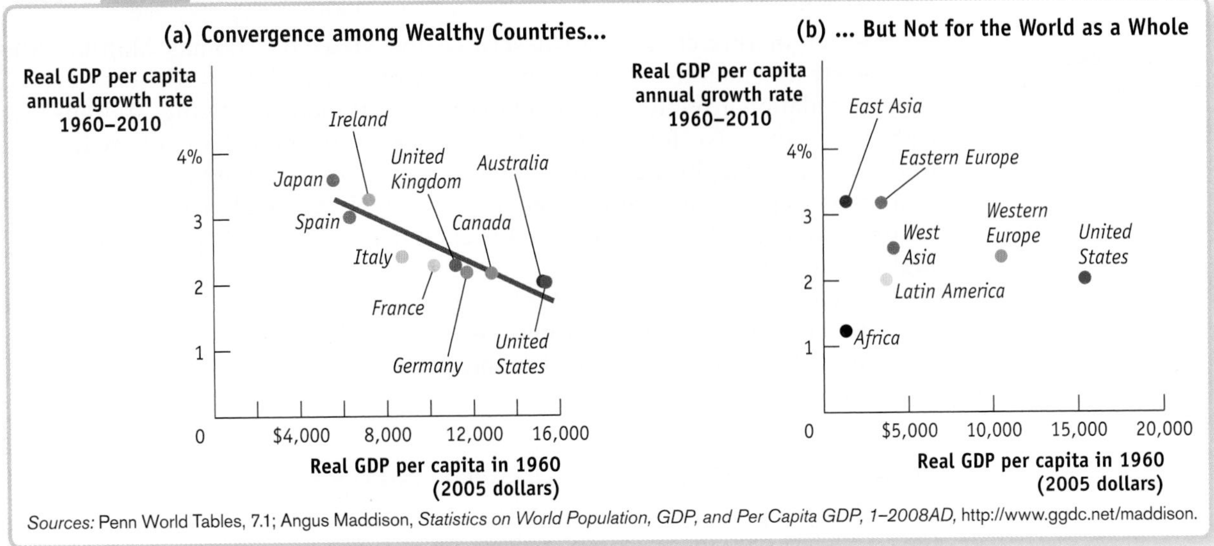

Sources: Penn World Tables, 7.1; Angus Maddison, *Statistics on World Population, GDP, and Per Capita GDP, 1–2008AD*, http://www.ggdc.net/maddison.

looking across the world as a whole, including countries that remain poor, there is little evidence of convergence. Panel (b) of Figure 13-9 illustrates this point using data for regions rather than individual countries (other than the United States). In 1960, East Asia and Africa were both very poor regions. Over the next 55 years, the East Asian regional economy grew quickly, as the convergence hypothesis would have predicted, but the African regional economy grew very slowly. In 1960, Western Europe had substantially higher real GDP per capita than Latin America. But, contrary to the convergence hypothesis, the Western European regional economy grew more quickly over the next 55 years, widening the gap between the regions.

So is the convergence hypothesis all wrong? No: economists still believe that countries with relatively low real GDP per capita tend to have higher rates of growth than countries with relatively high real GDP per capita, *other things equal.* But other things—education, infrastructure, rule of law, and so on—are often not equal. Statistical studies find that when you adjust for differences in these other factors, poorer countries do tend to have higher growth rates. This result is known as *conditional convergence.*

Because other factors differ, however, there is no clear tendency toward convergence in the world economy as a whole. Western Europe, North America, and parts of Asia are becoming more similar in real GDP per capita, but the gap between these regions and the rest of the world is growing.

Quick Review

- East Asia's spectacular growth was generated by high savings and investment spending rates, emphasis on education, and adoption of technological advances from other countries.
- Poor education, political instability, and irresponsible government policies are major factors in the slow growth of Latin America.
- In sub-Saharan Africa, severe instability, war, and poor infrastructure—particularly affecting public health—resulted in a catastrophic failure of growth. But economic performance in recent years has been much better than in preceding years.
- The **convergence hypothesis** seems to hold only when other things that affect economic growth—such as education, infrastructure, property rights, and so on—are held equal.

CHECK YOUR UNDERSTANDING 13-4

1. Some economists think the high rates of growth of productivity achieved by many Asian economies cannot be sustained. Why might they be right? What would have to happen for them to be wrong?
2. Consider Figure 13-9, panel (b). Based on the data there, which regions support the convergence hypothesis? Which do not? Explain.
3. Some economists think the best way to help African countries is for wealthier countries to provide more funds for basic infrastructure. Others think this policy will have no long-run effect unless African countries have the financial and political means to maintain this infrastructure. What policies would you suggest?

Solutions appear at back of book.

Sustainable long-run economic growth is long-run growth that can continue in the face of the limited supply of natural resources and the impact of growth on the environment.

Is World Growth Sustainable?

Earlier in this chapter we described the views of Thomas Malthus, the early-nineteenth-century economist who warned that the pressure of population growth would tend to limit the standard of living. Malthus was right about the past: for around 58 centuries, from the origins of civilization until his own time, limited land supplies effectively prevented any large rise in real incomes per capita. Since then, however, technological progress and rapid accumulation of physical and human capital have allowed the world to defy Malthusian pessimism.

But will this always be the case? Some skeptics have expressed doubt about whether **sustainable long-run economic growth** is possible—whether it can continue in the face of the limited supply of natural resources and the impact of growth on the environment.

Natural Resources and Growth, Revisited

In 1972 a group of scientists called The Club of Rome made a big splash with a book titled *The Limits to Growth,* which argued that long-run economic growth wasn't sustainable due to limited supplies of nonrenewable resources such as oil and natural gas. These "neo-Malthusian" concerns at first seemed to be validated by a sharp rise in resource prices in the 1970s, then came to seem foolish when resource prices fell sharply in the 1980s. After 2005, however, resource prices rose sharply again, leading to renewed concern about resource limitations to growth. Figure 13-10 shows the real price of oil—the price of oil adjusted for inflation in the rest of the economy. The rise, fall, and rise of concern about resource-based limits to growth have more or less followed the rise, fall, and rise of oil prices shown in the figure.

Differing views about the impact of limited natural resources on long-run economic growth turn on the answers to three questions:

- How large are the supplies of key natural resources?
- How effective will technology be at finding alternatives to natural resources?
- Can long-run economic growth continue in the face of resource scarcity?

FIGURE 13-10 The Real Price of Oil, 1949–2010

The real price of natural resources, like oil, rose dramatically in the 1970s and then fell just as dramatically in the 1980s. Since 2005, however, the real prices of natural resources have soared.
Source: Energy Information Administration.

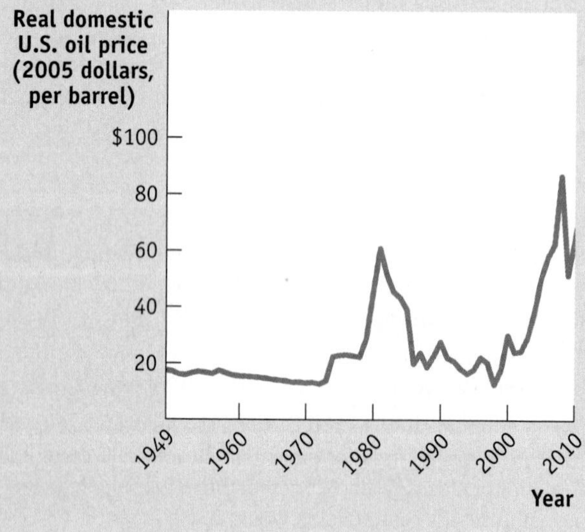

It's mainly up to geologists to answer the first question. Unfortunately, there's wide disagreement among the experts, especially about the prospects for future oil production. Some analysts believe that there is enough untapped oil in the ground that world oil production can continue to rise for several decades. Others, including a number of oil company executives, believe that the growing difficulty of finding new oil fields will cause oil production to plateau—that is, stop growing and eventually begin a gradual decline—in the fairly near future. Some analysts believe that we have already reached that plateau.

The answer to the second question, whether there are alternatives to natural resources, has to come from engineers. There's no question that there are many alternatives to the natural resources currently being depleted, some of which are already being exploited. For example, "unconventional" oil extracted from Canadian tar sands is already making a significant contribution to world oil supplies, and electricity generated by wind turbines is rapidly becoming big business.

The third question, whether economies can continue to grow in the face of resource scarcity, is mainly a question for economists. And most, though not all, economists are optimistic: they believe that modern economies can find ways to work around limits on the supply of natural resources. One reason for this optimism is the fact that resource scarcity leads to high resource prices. These high prices in turn provide strong incentives to conserve the scarce resource and to find alternatives.

For example, after the sharp oil price increases of the 1970s, American consumers turned to smaller, more fuel-efficient cars, and U.S. industry also greatly intensified its efforts to reduce energy bills. The result is shown in Figure 13-11, which compares U.S. real GDP per capita and oil consumption before and after the 1970s energy crisis. In the United States before 1973, there seemed to be a more or less one-to-one relationship between economic growth and oil consumption. But after 1973 the U.S. economy continued to deliver growth in real GDP per capita even as it substantially reduced the use of oil. This move toward conservation paused after 1990, as low real oil prices encouraged consumers to shift back to gas-greedy larger cars and SUVs. But a sharp

FIGURE **13-11** U.S. Oil Consumption and Growth over Time

Until 1973, the real price of oil was relatively cheap and there was a more or less one-to-one relationship between economic growth and oil consumption. Conservation efforts increased sharply after the spike in the real price of oil in the mid-1970s. Yet the U.S. economy was still able to deliver growth despite cutting back on oil consumption.

Sources: Energy Information Administration; Bureau of Economic Analysis.

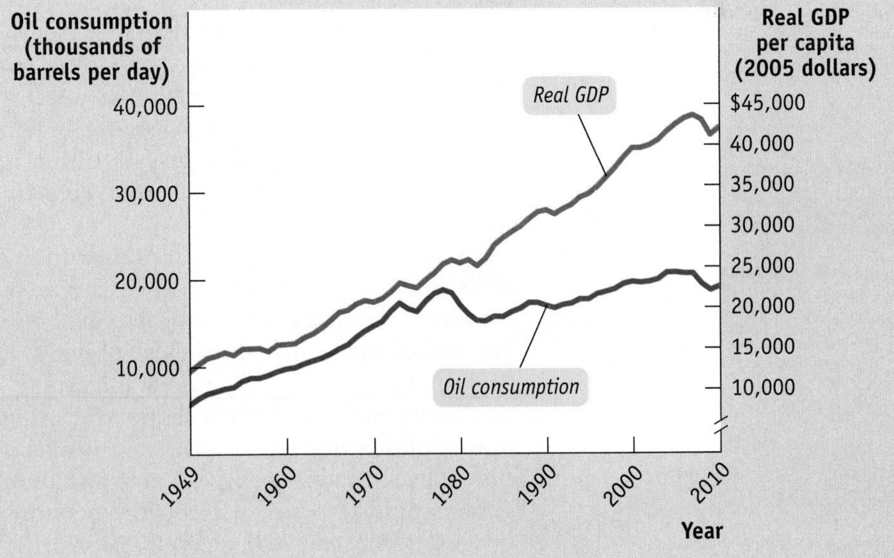

rise in oil prices from 2005 to 2008, and again in 2010, encouraged renewed shifts toward oil conservation.

Given such responses to prices, economists generally tend to see resource scarcity as a problem that modern economies handle fairly well, and so not a fundamental limit to long-run economic growth. Environmental issues, however, pose a more difficult problem because dealing with them requires effective political action.

Economic Growth and the Environment

Economic growth, other things equal, tends to increase the human impact on the environment. For example, China's spectacular economic growth has also brought a spectacular increase in air pollution in that nation's cities.

It's important to realize, however, that other things aren't necessarily equal: countries can and do take action to protect their environments. In fact, air and water quality in today's advanced countries is generally much better than it was a few decades ago. London's famous "fog"—actually a form of air pollution, which killed 4,000 people during a two-week episode in 1952—is gone, thanks to regulations that virtually eliminated the use of coal heat. The equally famous smog of Los Angeles, although not extinguished, is far less severe than it was in the 1960s and early 1970s, again thanks to pollution regulations.

Despite these past environmental success stories, there is widespread concern today about the environmental impacts of continuing economic growth, reflecting a change in the scale of the problem. Environmental success stories have mainly involved dealing with *local* impacts of economic growth, such as the effect of widespread car ownership on air quality in the Los Angeles basin. Today, however, we are faced with *global* environmental issues—the adverse impacts on the environment of the Earth as a whole by worldwide economic growth. The biggest of these issues involves the impact of fossil-fuel consumption on the world's climate.

Burning coal and oil releases carbon dioxide into the atmosphere. There is broad scientific consensus that rising levels of carbon dioxide and other gases are causing a greenhouse effect on the Earth, trapping more of the sun's energy and raising the planet's overall temperature. And rising temperatures may impose high human and economic costs: rising sea levels may flood coastal areas; changing climate may disrupt agriculture, especially in poor countries; and so on.

The problem of climate change is clearly linked to economic growth. Figure 13-12 shows carbon dioxide emissions from the United States, Europe, and China since 1980. Historically, the wealthy nations have been responsible for the bulk of these emissions because they have consumed far more energy per person than poorer countries. As China and other emerging economies have grown, however, they have begun to consume much more energy and emit much more carbon dioxide.

Is it possible to continue long-run economic growth while curbing the emissions of greenhouse gases? The answer, according to most economists who have studied the issue, is yes. It should be possible to reduce greenhouse gas emissions in a wide variety of ways, ranging from the use of non-fossil-fuel energy sources such as wind, solar, and nuclear power; to preventive measures such as carbon sequestration (capturing the carbon dioxide from power plants and storing it); to simpler things like designing buildings so that they're easier to keep warm in winter and cool in summer. Such measures would impose costs on the economy, but the best available estimates suggest that even a large reduction in greenhouse gas emissions over the

FIGURE 13-12 Climate Change and Growth

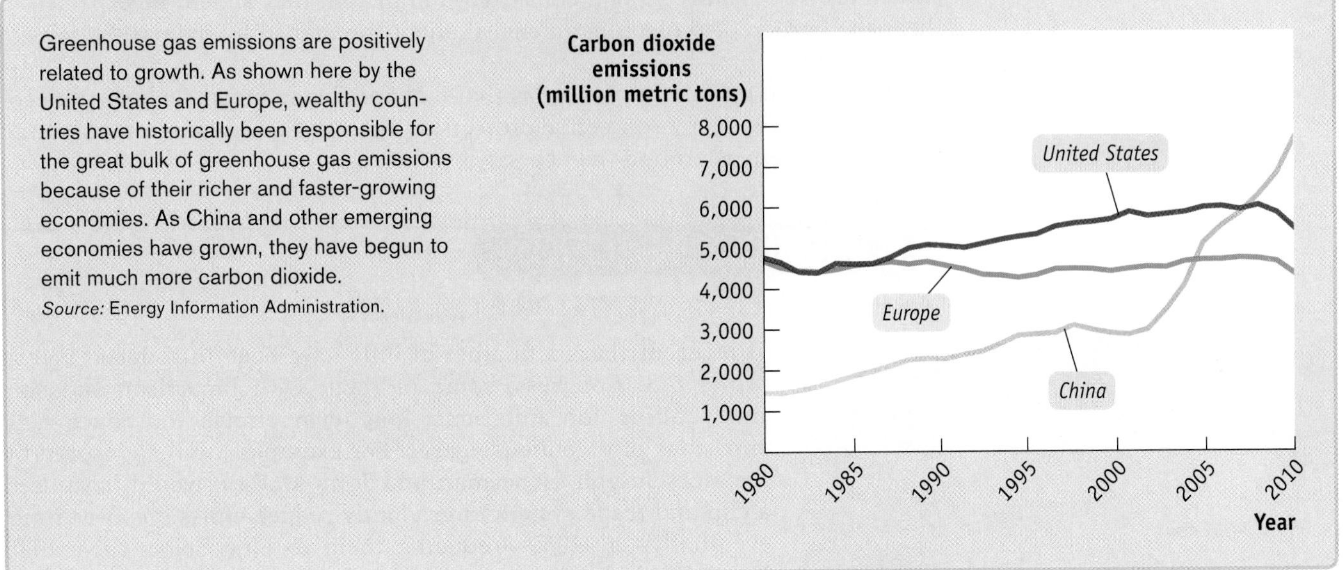

Greenhouse gas emissions are positively related to growth. As shown here by the United States and Europe, wealthy countries have historically been responsible for the great bulk of greenhouse gas emissions because of their richer and faster-growing economies. As China and other emerging economies have grown, they have begun to emit much more carbon dioxide.
Source: Energy Information Administration.

next few decades would only modestly dent the long-term rise in real GDP per capita.

The problem is how to make all of this happen. Unlike resource scarcity, environmental problems don't automatically provide incentives for changed behavior. Pollution is an example of a *negative externality,* a cost that individuals or firms impose on others without having to offer compensation. In the absence of government intervention, individuals and firms have no incentive to reduce negative externalities, which is why it took regulation to reduce air pollution in America's cities. And as Nicholas Stern, the author of an influential report on climate change, put it, greenhouse gas emissions are "the mother of all externalities."

So there is a broad consensus among economists—although there are some dissenters—that government action is needed to deal with climate change. There is also broad consensus that this action should take the form of market-based incentives, either in the form of a carbon tax—a tax per unit of carbon emitted—or a cap and trade system in which the total amount of emissions is capped, and producers must buy licenses to emit greenhouse gases. There is, however, considerable dispute about how much action is appropriate, reflecting both uncertainty about the costs and benefits and scientific uncertainty about the pace and extent of climate change.

There are also several aspects of the climate change problem that make it much more difficult to deal with than, say, smog in Los Angeles. One is the problem of taking the long view. The impact of greenhouse gas emissions on the climate is very gradual: carbon dioxide put into the atmosphere today won't have its full effect on the climate for several generations. As a result, there is the political problem of persuading voters to accept pain today in return for gains that will benefit their children, grandchildren, or even great-grandchildren.

There is also a difficult problem of international burden sharing. As Figure 13-12 shows, today's rich economies have historically been responsible for most greenhouse gas emissions, but newly emerging economies like China are responsible for most of the recent growth. Inevitably, rich countries are reluctant to pay the price of reducing emissions only to have their efforts frustrated by rapidly growing emissions from new players. On the other hand, countries like China, which are still relatively poor, consider it unfair that they should be expected to bear the burden of protecting an environment threatened by the past actions of rich nations.

The general moral of this story is that it is possible to reconcile long-run economic growth with environmental protection. The main question is one of getting political consensus around the necessary policies.

ECONOMICS ➤ IN ACTION

THE COST OF CLIMATE PROTECTION

AP Photo/Adam Rountree

Reducing U.S. emissions of greenhouse gases over the long run would have few economic costs and many health benefits.

In recent years a number of bills have been introduced before the U.S. Congress, some of them with bipartisan sponsorship, calling for ambitious, long-term efforts to reduce U.S. emissions of greenhouse gases. For example, a bill sponsored by Senators Joseph Lieberman and John McCain would have used a cap and trade system to gradually reduce emissions over time, eventually—by 2050—reducing them to 60% below their 1990 level. Another bill, sponsored by Senators Barbara Boxer and Bernie Sanders, called for an 80% reduction by 2050.

Would implementing these bills, or others like them, put a stop to long-run economic growth? Not according to a comprehensive study by a team at MIT, which found that reducing emissions would impose significant but not overwhelming costs. Using an elaborate model of the interaction between environmental policy and the economy, the MIT group estimated that the Lieberman–McCain proposal would reduce real GDP per capita in 2050 by 1.11% and the more stringent Sanders–Boxer proposal would reduce real GDP per capita by 1.79%.

These may sound like big numbers—they would amount to between $200 billion and $250 billion today—but they would hardly make a dent in the economy's long-run growth rate. Remember that over the long run the U.S. economy has on average seen real GDP per capita rise by almost 2% a year. If the MIT group's estimates are correct, even a strong policy to avert climate change would, in effect, require that we give up less than one year's growth over the next four decades.

▼ Quick Review

- There's wide disagreement about whether it is possible to have **sustainable long-run economic growth.** However, economists generally believe that modern economies can find ways to alleviate limits to growth from natural resource scarcity through the price response that promotes conservation and the creation of alternatives.
- Overcoming the limits to growth arising from environmental degradation is more difficult because it requires effective government intervention. Limiting the emission of greenhouse gases would require only a modest reduction in the growth rate.
- There is broad consensus that government action to address climate change and greenhouse gases should be in the form of market-based incentives, like a carbon tax or a cap and trade system. It will also require rich and poor countries to come to some agreement on how the cost of emissions reductions will be shared.

CHECK YOUR UNDERSTANDING 13-5

1. Are economists typically more concerned about the limits to growth imposed by environmental degradation or those imposed by resource scarcity? Explain, noting the role of negative externalities in your answer.
2. What is the link between greenhouse gas emissions and growth? What is the expected effect on growth from emissions reduction? Why is international burden sharing of greenhouse gas emissions reduction a contentious problem?

Solutions appear at back of book.

WORKED PROBLEM

Fluctuations and Economic Growth

Between 1985 and 1995, the economic climate in the United Kingdom, and especially in central London, fluctuated quite a bit. At the end of the 1980s, the economy was booming. People were purchasing closet-sized apartments in central London for outrageously expensive prices, and traffic in central London was impossible. The wait time for reservations at top restaurants could be three months or longer. However, that all changed by the early 1990s. Flats—the British word for apartments—were suddenly affordable again, traffic eased considerably, and it was very easy to get a table at those top restaurants—all signs of a troubled economy. But then the economic situation changed again. By 1995, London experienced another boom, with rapidly rising property prices, lots of traffic, and bustling restaurants.

By comparing the economy in the United Kingdom across time from 1985 to 1995, show that the change in the economic environment in London in the early 1990s reflected changes in the overall economic environment in the United Kingdom over the same period. What was the long-run growth rate in the United Kingdom during this 10-year period? At this growth rate, approximately how long should it take for GDP to double in the United Kingdom?

STEP 1: Compare the economy in the United Kingdom across time from 1985 to 1995. (Hint: the OECD Internet site http://stats.oecd.org provides statistics over time on real GDP per capita for various countries.)

Read the section "Comparing Economies Across Time and Space" beginning on page 378, and especially note the first paragraph under "Real GDP per Capita." Go to the Internet site http://stats.oecd.org. On the menu labeled "Data by theme" on the left-hand side of the page, find and click on "National Accounts." Then click on "Annual National Accounts," then "Main Aggregates," then "Gross Domestic Product." Finally, click on the selection that starts with "GDP per head, US$, Constant Prices." In the top, dark-blue section of the table, click on "Frequency," choose "Select date range," "Annual," and then select 1985 for the first drop-down list and 1995 for the second. Click on "View Data." Scroll down to the row "United Kingdom," and copy the numbers from 1985 to 1995.

Real GDP per capita in the United Kingdom from the OECD site in constant U.S. dollars (reference year 2005) is as follows:

Year	Real GDP per capita
1985	$20,073
1986	20,830
1987	21,734
1988	22,783
1989	23,237
1990	23,352
1991	22,947
1992	22,922
1993	23,379
1994	24,317
1995	24,987

■

STEP 2: Using the numbers in the table above, find the growth rate in real GDP in the United Kingdom for this same period, and discuss the difference in growth rates in the early 1990s with growth rates during other years.

Read carefully the Pitfalls box, "Change in Levels versus Rate of Change," on page 380.

The rate of change, or growth rate, in real GDP per capita between year 1 and year 2 is calculated using the following formula:

$$\left(\frac{\text{(real GDP per capita in year 2 − real GDP per capita in year 1)}}{\text{(real GDP per capita in year 1)}}\right) \times 100$$

Thus, the growth rate below between 1985 and 1986 is calculated as follows:

$$\left(\frac{(\$20{,}830 - \$20{,}073)}{\$20{,}073}\right) \times 100 = 3.8\%$$

Year	Growth Rate
1986	3.8%
1987	4.3
1988	4.8
1989	2.0
1990	0.5
1991	−1.7
1992	−0.1
1993	2.0
1994	4.0
1995	2.8

As you can see from the numbers in this table, the United Kingdom experienced negative growth in 1991 and 1992, but strong and positive growth in most other years. ■

STEP 3: What was the average long-run growth rate during this period, and how long should it take for UK GDP to double if growth continues at this rate?

Read the section "Growth Rates," beginning on page 380. Pay close attention to the Rule of 70 as stated in Equation 13-1.

Summing the above growth rates and then dividing by 10, we find an average growth rate of 2.2%. According to the Rule of 70, it would take 70/2.2 = 31.8 years for GDP to double in the United Kingdom at this growth rate. ■

SUMMARY

1. Growth is measured as changes in real GDP per capita in order to eliminate the effects of changes in the price level and changes in population size. Levels of real GDP per capita vary greatly around the world: more than half of the world's population lives in countries that are still poorer than the United States was in 1900. Over the course of the twentieth century, real GDP per capita in the United States increased more than fivefold.

2. Growth rates of real GDP per capita also vary widely. According to the **Rule of 70,** the number of years it takes for real GDP per capita to double is equal to 70 divided by the annual growth rate of real GDP per capita.

3. The key to long-run economic growth is rising **labor productivity,** or just **productivity,** which is output per worker. Increases in productivity arise from increases in **physical capital** per worker and **human capital** per worker as well as **technological progress.** The **aggregate production function** shows how real GDP per worker depends on these three factors. Other things equal, there are **diminishing returns to physical capital:** holding human capital per worker and technology fixed, each successive addition to physical capital per worker yields a smaller increase in productivity than the one before. Equivalently, more physical capital per worker results in a lower, but still positive, increase in productivity. **Growth accounting,** which estimates the contribution of each factor to a country's economic growth, has shown that rising **total factor productivity,** the amount of output produced from a given amount of factor inputs, is key to long-run growth. It is usually interpreted as the effect of technological progress. In contrast to earlier times, natural resources are a less significant source of productivity growth in most countries today.

4. The large differences in countries' growth rates are largely due to differences in their rates of accumulation of physical and human capital as well as differences in technological progress. Although inflows of foreign savings from abroad help, a prime factor is differences in domestic savings and investment spending rates, since most countries that have high investment spending in physical capital finance it by high domestic savings. Technological progress is largely a result of **research and development,** or **R&D.**

5. Governments can help or hinder growth. Government policies that directly foster growth are subsidies to **infrastructure,** particularly public health infrastructure, subsidies to education, subsidies to R&D, and maintenance of a well-functioning financial system that channels savings into investment spending, education, and R&D. Governments can enhance the environment for growth by protecting property rights (particularly intellectual property rights through patents), by being politically stable, and by providing good governance. Poor governance includes corruption and excessive government intervention.

6. The world economy contains examples of success and failure in the effort to achieve long-run economic growth. East Asian economies have done many things right and achieved very high growth rates. The low growth rates of Latin American and African economies over many years led economists to believe that the **convergence hypothesis,** the claim that differences in real GDP per capita across countries narrow over time, fits the data only when factors that affect growth, such as education, infrastructure, and favorable government policies and institutions, are held equal across countries. In recent years, there has been an uptick in growth among some Latin American and sub-Saharan African countries, largely due to a boom in commodity exports.

7. Economists generally believe that environmental degradation poses a greater challenge to **sustainable long-run economic growth** than does natural resource scarcity. Addressing environmental degradation requires effective governmental intervention, but the problem of natural resource scarcity is often well handled by the market price response.

8. The emission of greenhouse gases is clearly linked to growth, and limiting them will require some reduction in growth. However, the best available estimates suggest that a large reduction in emissions would require only a modest reduction in the growth rate.

9. There is broad consensus that government action to address climate change and greenhouse gases should be in the form of market-based incentives, like a carbon tax or a cap and trade system. It will also require rich and poor countries to come to some agreement on how the cost of emissions reductions will be shared.

KEY TERMS

Rule of 70, p. 380
Labor productivity, p. 382
Productivity, p. 382
Physical capital, p. 383
Human capital, p. 383
Technological progress, p. 383
Aggregate production function, p. 384
Diminishing returns to physical capital, p. 384
Growth accounting, p. 386
Total factor productivity, p. 387
Research and development (R&D), p. 391
Infrastructure, p. 392
Convergence hypothesis, p. 397
Sustainable long-run economic growth, p. 400

PROBLEMS

1. The accompanying table shows data from the Penn World Table, Version 7.0, for real GDP per capita in 2005 U.S. dollars for Argentina, Ghana, South Korea, and the United States for 1960, 1970, 1980, 1990, 2000, and 2009.

   a. Complete the table by expressing each year's real GDP per capita as a percentage of its 1960 and 2009 levels.

   b. How does the growth in living standards from 1960 to 2009 compare across these four nations? What might account for these differences?

	Argentina			Ghana			South Korea			United States		
Year	Real GDP per capita (2005 dollars)	Percentage of 1960 real GDP per capita	Percentage of 2009 real GDP per capita	Real GDP per capita (2005 dollars)	Percentage of 1960 real GDP per capita	Percentage of 2009 real GDP per capita	Real GDP per capita (2005 dollars)	Percentage of 1960 real GDP per capita	Percentage of 2009 real GDP per capita	Real GDP per capita (2005 dollars)	Percentage of 1960 real GDP per capita	Percentage of 2009 real GDP per capita
1960	$6,243	?	?	$603	?	?	$1,782	?	?	$15,438	?	?
1970	$7,810	?	?	$939	?	?	$3,018	?	?	$20,480	?	?
1980	$8,638	?	?	$807	?	?	$5,339	?	?	$25,090	?	?
1990	$6,823	?	?	$844	?	?	$11,437	?	?	$31,637	?	?
2000	$9,172	?	?	$887	?	?	$18,926	?	?	$39,175	?	?
2009	$11,961	?	?	$1,239	?	?	$25,029	?	?	$41,102	?	?

2. The accompanying table shows the average annual growth rate in real GDP per capita for Argentina, Ghana, and South Korea using data from the Penn World Table, Version 6.2, for the past few decades.

	Average annual growth rate of real GDP per capita		
Years	Argentina	Ghana	South Korea
1960–1970	2.53%	15.54%	7.50%
1970–1980	1.12	0.85	7.62
1980–1990	−2.50	0.10	11.33
1990–2000	3.83	2.08	6.37

   a. For each decade and for each country, use the Rule of 70 where possible to calculate how long it would take for that country's real GDP per capita to double.

   b. Suppose that the average annual growth rate that each country achieved over the period 1990–2000 continues indefinitely into the future. Starting from 2000, use the Rule of 70 to calculate, where possible, the year in which a country will have doubled its real GDP per capita.

3. The accompanying table provides approximate statistics on per capita income levels and growth rates for regions defined by income levels. According to the Rule of 70, starting in 2010 the high-income countries are projected to double their per capita GDP in approximately 78 years, in 2088. Throughout this question, assume constant growth rates for each of the regions that are equal to their average value between 2000 and 2010.

Region	GDP per capita (2010)	Average annual growth rate of real GDP per capita (2000–2010)
High-income countries	$38,293	0.9%
Middle-income countries	3,980	4.8
Low-income countries	507	3.0

Source: World Bank.

   a. Calculate the ratio of per capita GDP in 2010 of the following:

      i. Middle-income to high-income countries

      ii. Low-income to high-income countries

      iii. Low-income to middle-income countries

   b. Calculate the number of years it will take the low-income and middle-income countries to double their per capita GDP.

   c. Calculate the per capita GDP of each of the regions in 2088. (*Hint:* How many times does their per capita GDP double in 78 years, the number of years from 2010 to 2088?)

   d. Repeat part a with the projected per capita GDP in 2088.

   e. Compare your answers to parts a and d. Comment on the change in economic inequality between the regions.

4. You are hired as an economic consultant to the countries of Albernia and Brittania. Each country's

current relationship between physical capital per worker and output per worker is given by the curve labeled "Productivity$_1$" in the accompanying diagram. Albernia is at point *A* and Brittania is at point *B*.

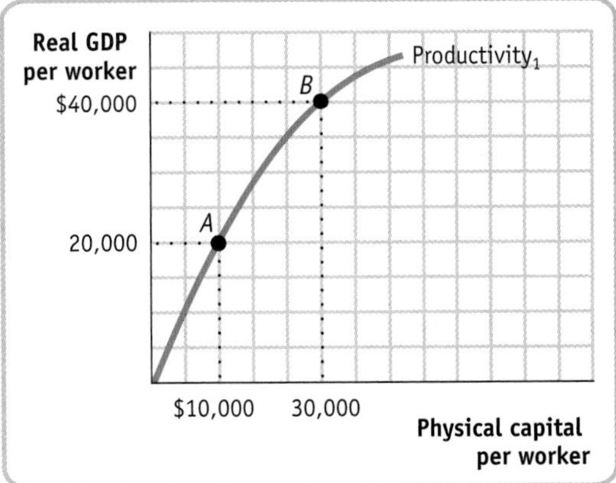

a. In the relationship depicted by the curve Productivity$_1$, what factors are held fixed? Do these countries experience diminishing returns to physical capital per worker?

b. Assuming that the amount of human capital per worker and the technology are held fixed in each country, can you recommend a policy to generate a doubling of real GDP per capita in Albernia?

c. How would your policy recommendation change if the amount of human capital per worker could be changed? Assume that an increase in human capital doubles the output per worker when physical capital per worker equals $10,000. Draw a curve on the diagram that represents this policy for Albernia.

5. The country of Androde is currently using Method 1 for its production function. By chance, scientists stumble onto a technological breakthrough that will enhance Androde's productivity. This technological breakthrough is reflected in another production function, Method 2. The accompanying table shows combinations of physical capital per worker and output per worker for both methods, assuming that human capital per worker is fixed.

Method 1		Method 2	
Physical capital per worker	Real GDP per worker	Physical capital per worker	Real GDP per worker
0	0.00	0	0.00
50	35.36	50	70.71
100	50.00	100	100.00
150	61.24	150	122.47
200	70.71	200	141.42
250	79.06	250	158.11
300	86.60	300	173.21
350	93.54	350	187.08
400	100.00	400	200.00
450	106.07	450	212.13
500	111.80	500	223.61

a. Using the data in the accompanying table, draw the two production functions in one diagram. Androde's current amount of physical capital per worker is 100. In your figure, label that point *A*.

b. Starting from point *A*, over a period of 70 years, the amount of physical capital per worker in Androde rises to 400. Assuming Androde still uses Method 1, in your diagram, label the resulting point of production *B*. Using the Rule of 70, calculate by how many percent per year output per worker has grown.

c. Now assume that, starting from point *A*, over the same period of 70 years, the amount of physical capital per worker in Androde rises to 400, but that during that time period, Androde switches to Method 2. In your diagram, label the resulting point of production *C*. Using the Rule of 70, calculate by how many percent per year output per worker has grown now.

d. As the economy of Androde moves from point *A* to point *C*, what share of the annual productivity growth is due to higher total factor productivity?

6. The Bureau of Labor Statistics regularly releases the "Productivity and Costs" report for the previous month. Go to www.bls.gov and find the latest report. (On the Bureau of Labor Statistics home page, from the tab "Subject Areas," select the link to "Productivity: Labor Productivity & Costs"; then, from the heading "LPC News Releases," find the most recent "Productivity and Costs" report.) What were the percent changes in business and nonfarm business productivity for the previous quarter? How does the percent change in that quarter's productivity compare to the percent change from the same quarter a year ago?

7. What roles do physical capital, human capital, technology, and natural resources play in influencing long-run economic growth of aggregate output per capita?

8. How have U.S. policies and institutions influenced the country's long-run economic growth?

9. Over the next 100 years, real GDP per capita in Groland is expected to grow at an average annual rate of 2.0%. In Sloland, however, growth is expected to be somewhat slower, at an average annual growth rate of 1.5%. If both countries have a real GDP per capita today of $20,000, how will their real GDP per capita differ in 100 years? [*Hint:* A country that has a real GDP today of $\$x$ and grows at $y\%$ per year will achieve a real GDP of $\$x \times (1 + (y/100))^z$ in z years. We assume that $0 \leq y < 10$.]

10. The accompanying table shows data from the Penn World Table, Version 7.0, for real GDP per capita (2005 U.S. dollars) in France, Japan, the United Kingdom, and the United States in 1950 and 2009. Complete the table. Have these countries converged economically?

	1950		2009	
	Real GDP per capita (2005 dollars)	Percentage of U.S. real GDP per capita	Real GDP per capita (2005 dollars)	Percentage of U.S. real GDP per capita
France	$7,112	?	$30,821	?
Japan	3,118	?	31,958	?
United Kingdom	10,401	?	33,386	?
United States	13,183	?	41,102	?

11. The accompanying table shows data from the Penn World Table, Version 7.0, for real GDP per capita (2005 U.S. dollars) for Argentina, Ghana, South Korea, and the United States in 1960 and 2009. Complete the table. Have these countries converged economically?

	1960		2009	
	Real GDP per capita (2005 dollars)	Percentage of U.S. real GDP per capita	Real GDP per capita (2005 dollars)	Percentage of U.S. real GDP per capita
Argentina	$6,243	?	$11,961	?
Ghana	603	?	1,239	?
South Korea	1,782	?	25,029	?
United States	15,438	?	41,102	?

12. Why would you expect real GDP per capita in California and Pennsylvania to exhibit convergence but not in California and Baja California, a state of Mexico that borders the United States? What changes would allow California and Baja California to converge?

13. According to the *Oil & Gas Journal,* the proven oil reserves existing in the world in 2009 consisted of 1,342 billion barrels. In that year, the U.S. Energy Information Administration reported that the world daily oil production was 72.26 million barrels a day.

a. At this rate, for how many years will the proven oil reserves last? Discuss the Malthusian view in the context of the number you just calculated.

b. In order to do the calculations in part a, what did you assume about the total quantity of oil reserves over time? About oil prices over time? Are these assumptions consistent with the Malthusian view on resource limits?

c. Discuss how market forces may affect the amount of time the proven oil reserves will last, assuming that no new oil reserves are discovered and that the demand curve for oil remains unchanged.

14. The accompanying table shows the annual growth rate for the years 2000–2009 in per capita emissions of carbon dioxide (CO_2) and the annual growth rate in real GDP per capita for selected countries.

	2000–2009 average annual growth rate of:	
Country	Real GDP per capita	CO_2 emissions per capita
Argentina	2.81%	1.01%
Bangladesh	4.17	5.47
Canada	0.68	−1.46
China	9.85	11.11
Germany	0.59	−1.23
Ireland	1.05	−2.10
Japan	0.29	−1.03
South Korea	3.48	1.68
Mexico	0.18	0.44
Nigeria	6.07	−2.46
Russia	5.22	0.52
South Africa	2.39	0.80
United Kingdom	0.88	−1.35
United States	0.58	−1.78

Sources: Energy Information Administration; International Monetary Fund.

a. Rank the countries in terms of their growth in CO_2 emissions, from highest to lowest. What five countries have the highest growth rate in emissions? What five countries have the lowest growth rate in emissions?

b. Now rank the countries in terms of their growth in real GDP per capita, from highest to lowest. What five countries have the highest growth rate? What five countries have the lowest growth rate?

c. Would you infer from your results that CO_2 emissions are linked to growth in output per capita?

d. Do high growth rates necessarily lead to high CO_2 emissions?

Aggregate Demand and Aggregate Supply

SHOCKS TO THE SYSTEM

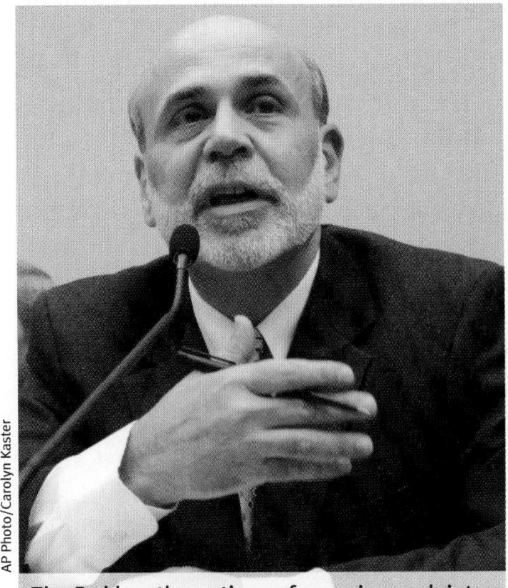
AP Photo/Carolyn Kaster

The Fed has the options of pumping cash into the economy to fight unemployment or pulling cash out of the economy to fight inflation.

WHAT YOU WILL LEARN IN THIS CHAPTER

- How the **aggregate demand curve** illustrates the relationship between the aggregate price level and the quantity of aggregate output demanded in the economy
- How the **aggregate supply curve** illustrates the relationship between the aggregate price level and the quantity of aggregate output supplied in the economy
- Why the aggregate supply curve is different in the short run compared to the long run
- How the ***AD–AS* model** is used to analyze economic fluctuations
- How monetary policy and fiscal policy can stabilize the economy

SOMETIMES IT'S NOT EASY BEING BEN.

In 2008 Ben Bernanke, a distinguished former Princeton economics professor, was chairman of the Federal Reserve—the institution that sets U.S. *monetary policy,* along with regulating the financial sector. The Federal Reserve's job is to help the economy avoid the twin evils of high inflation and high unemployment. It does this, loosely speaking, either by pumping cash into the economy to fight unemployment or by pulling cash out of the economy to fight inflation.

When the U.S. economy went into a recession in 2001, the Fed rushed cash into the system. It was an easy choice: unemployment was rising, and inflation was low and falling. In fact, for much of 2002 the Fed was actually worried about the possibility of *deflation.*

For much of 2008, however, Bernanke faced a much more difficult problem. In fact, he faced the problem people in his position dread most: a combination of unacceptably high inflation and rising unemployment, often referred to as *stagflation.* Stagflation was the scourge of the 1970s: the two deep recessions of 1973–1975 and 1979–1982 were both accompanied by soaring inflation. And in the first half of 2008, the threat of stagflation seemed to be back.

Why did the economic difficulties of early 2008 look so different from those of 2001? Because they had a different cause. The lesson of stagflation in the 1970s was that recessions can have different causes and that the appropriate policy response depends on the cause. Many recessions, from the great slump of 1929–1933 to the much milder recession of 2001, have been caused by a fall in investment and consumer spending. In these recessions high inflation isn't a threat. In fact, the 1929–1933 slump was accompanied by a sharp fall in the aggregate price level. And because inflation isn't a problem in such recessions, policy makers know what they must do: pump cash in, to fight rising unemployment.

The recessions of the 1970s, however, were largely caused by events in the Middle East that led to sharp cuts in world oil production and soaring prices for oil and other fuels. Not coincidentally, soaring oil prices also contributed to the economic difficulties of early 2008. In both periods, high energy prices led to a combination of unemployment and high inflation. They also created a dilemma: should the Fed fight the slump by pumping cash *into* the economy, or should it fight inflation by pulling cash *out* of the economy?

It's worth noting, by the way, that in 2011 the Fed faced some of the same problems it faced in 2008, as rising oil and food prices led to rising inflation despite high unemployment. In 2011, however, the Fed was fairly sure that demand was the main problem.

In this chapter, we'll develop a model that shows us how to distinguish between different types of short-run economic fluctuations—*demand shocks,* like those of the Great Depression and the 2001 recession, and *supply shocks,* like those of the 1970s and 2008.

To develop this model, we'll proceed in three steps. First, we'll develop the concept of *aggregate demand.* Then we'll turn to the parallel concept of *aggregate supply.* Finally, we'll put them together in the *AD–AS model.*

The **aggregate demand curve** shows the relationship between the aggregate price level and the quantity of aggregate output demanded by households, businesses, the government, and the rest of the world.

Aggregate Demand

The Great Depression, the great majority of economists agree, was the result of a massive negative demand shock. What does that mean? In Chapter 3 we explained that when economists talk about a fall in the demand for a particular good or service, they're referring to a leftward shift of the demand curve. Similarly, when economists talk about a negative demand shock to the economy as a whole, they're referring to a leftward shift of the **aggregate demand curve,** a curve that shows the relationship between the aggregate price level and the quantity of aggregate output demanded by households, firms, the government, and the rest of the world.

Figure 14-1 shows what the aggregate demand curve may have looked like in 1933, at the end of the 1929–1933 recession. The horizontal axis shows the total quantity of domestic goods and services demanded, measured in 2005 dollars. We use real GDP to measure aggregate output and will often use the two terms interchangeably. The vertical axis shows the aggregate price level, measured by the GDP deflator. With these variables on the axes, we can draw a curve, *AD,* showing how much aggregate output would have been demanded at any given aggregate price level. Since *AD* is meant to illustrate aggregate demand in 1933, one point on the curve corresponds to actual data for 1933, when the aggregate price level was 7.9 and the total quantity of domestic final goods and services purchased was $716 billion in 2005 dollars.

As drawn in Figure 14-1, the aggregate demand curve is downward sloping, indicating a negative relationship between the aggregate price level and the quantity of aggregate output demanded. A higher aggregate price level, other things equal, reduces the quantity of aggregate output demanded; a lower aggregate price level, other things equal, increases the quantity of aggregate output demanded. According to Figure 14-1, if the price level in 1933 had been 4.2 instead of 7.9, the total quantity of domestic final goods and services demanded would have been $1,000 billion in 2005 dollars instead of $716 billion.

The first key question about the aggregate demand curve is: why should the curve be downward sloping?

FIGURE 14-1 The Aggregate Demand Curve

The aggregate demand curve shows the relationship between the aggregate price level and the quantity of aggregate output demanded. The curve is downward sloping due to the wealth effect of a change in the aggregate price level and the interest rate effect of a change in the aggregate price level. Corresponding to the actual 1933 data, here the total quantity of goods and services demanded at an aggregate price level of 7.9 is $716 billion in 2005 dollars. According to our hypothetical curve, however, if the aggregate price level had been only 4.2, the quantity of aggregate output demanded would have risen to $1,000 billion.

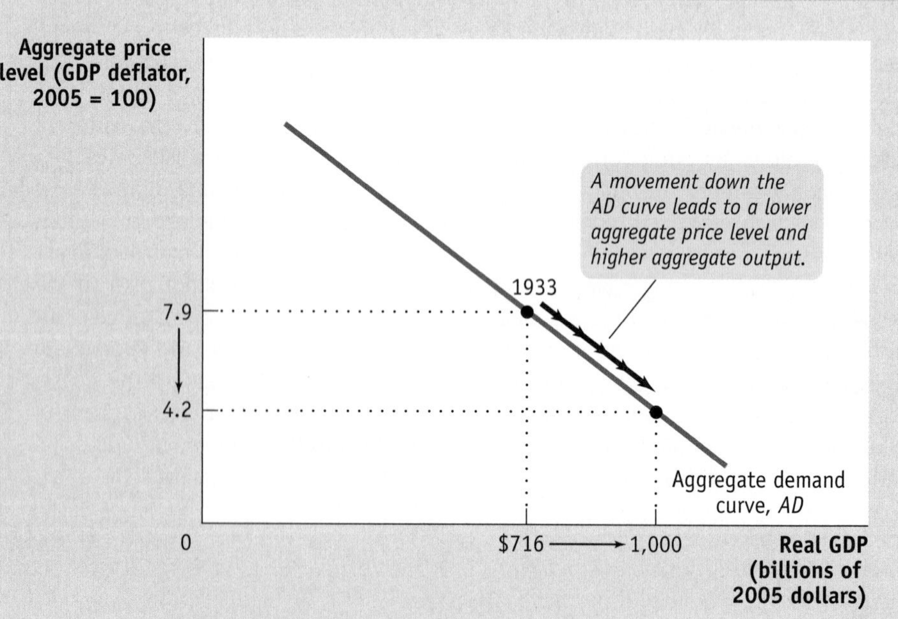

Why Is the Aggregate Demand Curve Downward Sloping?

In Figure 14-1, the curve *AD* is downward sloping. Why? To understand why, you'll need to learn the basic equation of national income accounting:

(14-1) $\text{GDP} = C + I + G + X - IM$

where *C* is consumer spending, *I* is investment spending, *G* is government purchases of goods and services, *X* is exports to other countries, and *IM* is imports. If we measure these variables in constant dollars—that is, in prices of a base year—then $C + I + G + X - IM$ is the quantity of domestically produced final goods and services demanded during a given period. *G* is decided by the government, but the other variables are private-sector decisions. To understand why the aggregate demand curve slopes downward, we need to understand why a rise in the aggregate price level reduces *C, I,* and $X - IM$.

You might think that the downward slope of the aggregate demand curve is a natural consequence of the *law of demand* we defined back in Chapter 3. That is, since the demand curve for any one good is downward sloping, isn't it natural that the demand curve for aggregate output is also downward sloping? This turns out, however, to be a misleading parallel. The demand curve for any individual good shows how the quantity demanded depends on the price of that good, *holding the prices of other goods and services constant.* The main reason the quantity of a good demanded falls when the price of that good rises—that is, the quantity of a good demanded falls as we move up the demand curve—is that people switch their consumption to other goods and services.

But when we consider movements up or down the aggregate demand curve, we're considering *a simultaneous change in the prices of all final goods and services.* Furthermore, changes in the composition of goods and services in consumer spending aren't relevant to the aggregate demand curve: if consumers decide to buy fewer clothes but more cars, this doesn't necessarily change the total quantity of final goods and services they demand.

Why, then, does a rise in the aggregate price level lead to a fall in the quantity of all domestically produced final goods and services demanded? There are two main reasons: the *wealth effect* and the *interest rate effect* of a change in the aggregate price level.

The Wealth Effect An increase in the aggregate price level, other things equal, reduces the purchasing power of many assets. Consider, for example, someone who has \$5,000 in a bank account. If the aggregate price level were to rise by 25%, what used to cost \$5,000 would now cost \$6,250, and would no longer be affordable. And what used to cost \$4,000 would now cost \$5,000, so that the \$5,000 in the bank account would now buy only as much as \$4,000 would have bought previously. With the loss in purchasing power, the owner of that bank account would probably scale back his or her consumption plans. Millions of other people would respond the same way, leading to a fall in spending on final goods and services, because a rise in the aggregate price level reduces the purchasing power of everyone's bank account. Correspondingly, a fall in the aggregate price level increases the purchasing power of consumers' assets and leads to more consumer demand. The **wealth effect of a change in the aggregate price level** is the effect on consumer spending caused by the effect of a change in the aggregate price level on the purchasing power of consumers' assets. Because of the wealth effect, consumer spending, *C,* falls when the aggregate price level rises, leading to a downward-sloping aggregate demand curve.

The **wealth effect of a change in the aggregate price level** is the effect on consumer spending caused by the effect of a change in the aggregate price level on the purchasing power of consumers' assets.

The Interest Rate Effect Economists use the term *money* in its narrowest sense to refer to cash and bank deposits on which people can write checks. People and firms hold money because it reduces the cost and inconvenience of making transactions. An increase in the aggregate price level, other things equal, reduces the purchasing power of a given amount of money holdings. To purchase the same basket of goods and services as before, people and firms now need to hold more money. So, in response to an increase in the aggregate price level, the public tries to increase its money holdings,

The **interest rate effect of a change in the aggregate price level** is the effect on consumer spending and investment spending caused by the effect of a change in the aggregate price level on the purchasing power of consumers' and firms' money holdings.

either by borrowing more or by selling assets such as bonds. This reduces the funds available for lending to other borrowers and drives interest rates up.

A rise in the interest rate reduces investment spending because it makes the cost of borrowing higher. It also reduces consumer spending because households save more of their disposable income. So a rise in the aggregate price level depresses investment spending, *I*, and consumer spending, *C*, through its effect on the purchasing power of money holdings, an effect known as the **interest rate effect of a change in the aggregate price level.** This also leads to a downward-sloping aggregate demand curve.

We'll have a lot more to say about money and interest rates in Chapter 17 on monetary policy. For now, the important point is that the aggregate demand curve is downward sloping due to both the wealth effect and the interest rate effect of a change in the aggregate price level.

Shifts of the Aggregate Demand Curve

In Chapter 3, where we introduced the analysis of supply and demand in the market for an individual good, we stressed the importance of the distinction between *movements along* the demand curve and *shifts of* the demand curve. The same distinction applies to the aggregate demand curve. Figure 14-1 shows a *movement along* the aggregate demand curve, a change in the aggregate quantity of goods and services demanded as the aggregate price level changes.

But there can also be *shifts of* the aggregate demand curve, changes in the quantity of goods and services demanded at any given price level, as shown in Figure 14-2. When we talk about an increase in aggregate demand, we mean a shift of the aggregate demand curve to the right, as shown in panel (a) by the shift from AD_1 to AD_2. A rightward shift occurs when the quantity of aggregate output demanded increases at any given aggregate price level. A decrease in aggregate demand means that the AD curve shifts to the left, as in panel (b). A leftward shift implies that the quantity of aggregate output demanded falls at any given aggregate price level.

FIGURE 14-2 Shifts of the Aggregate Demand Curve

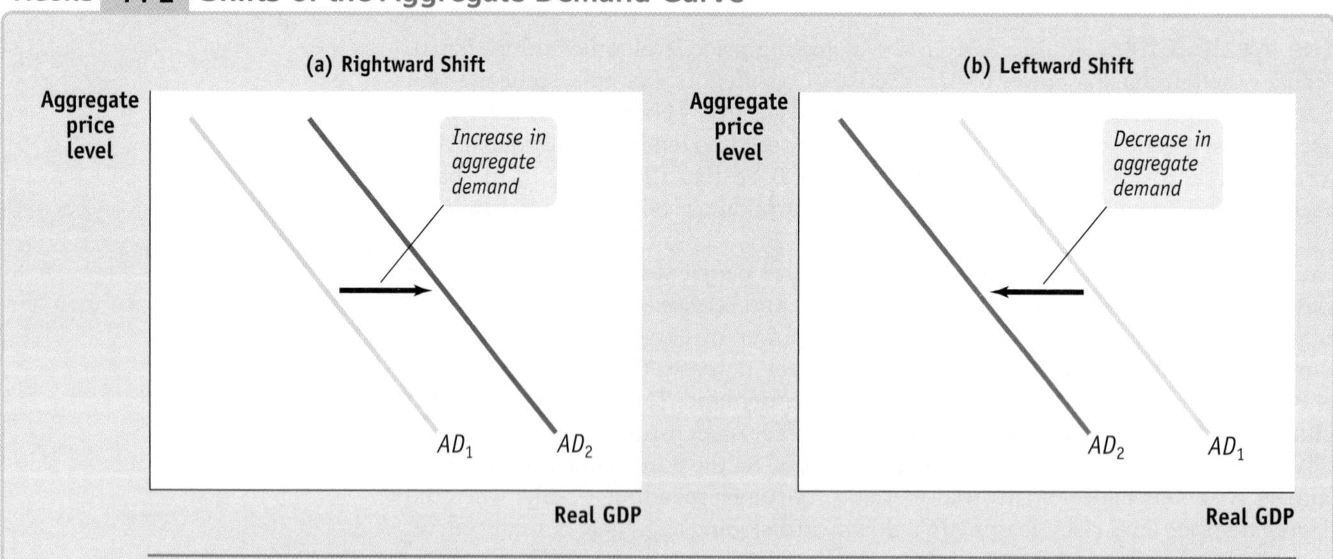

Panel (a) shows the effect of events that increase the quantity of aggregate output demanded at any given aggregate price level, such as improvements in business and consumer expectations or increased government spending. Such changes shift the aggregate demand curve to the right, from AD_1 to AD_2. Panel (b) shows the effect of events that decrease the quantity of aggregate output demanded at any given aggregate price level, such as a fall in wealth caused by a stock market decline. This shifts the aggregate demand curve leftward from AD_1 to AD_2.

A number of factors can shift the aggregate demand curve. Among the most important factors are changes in expectations, changes in wealth, and the size of the existing stock of physical capital. In addition, both fiscal and monetary policy can shift the aggregate demand curve. We'll now examine each of these factors in detail. For an overview of factors that shift the aggregate demand curve, see Table 14-1.

TABLE 14-1 Factors That Shift Aggregate Demand

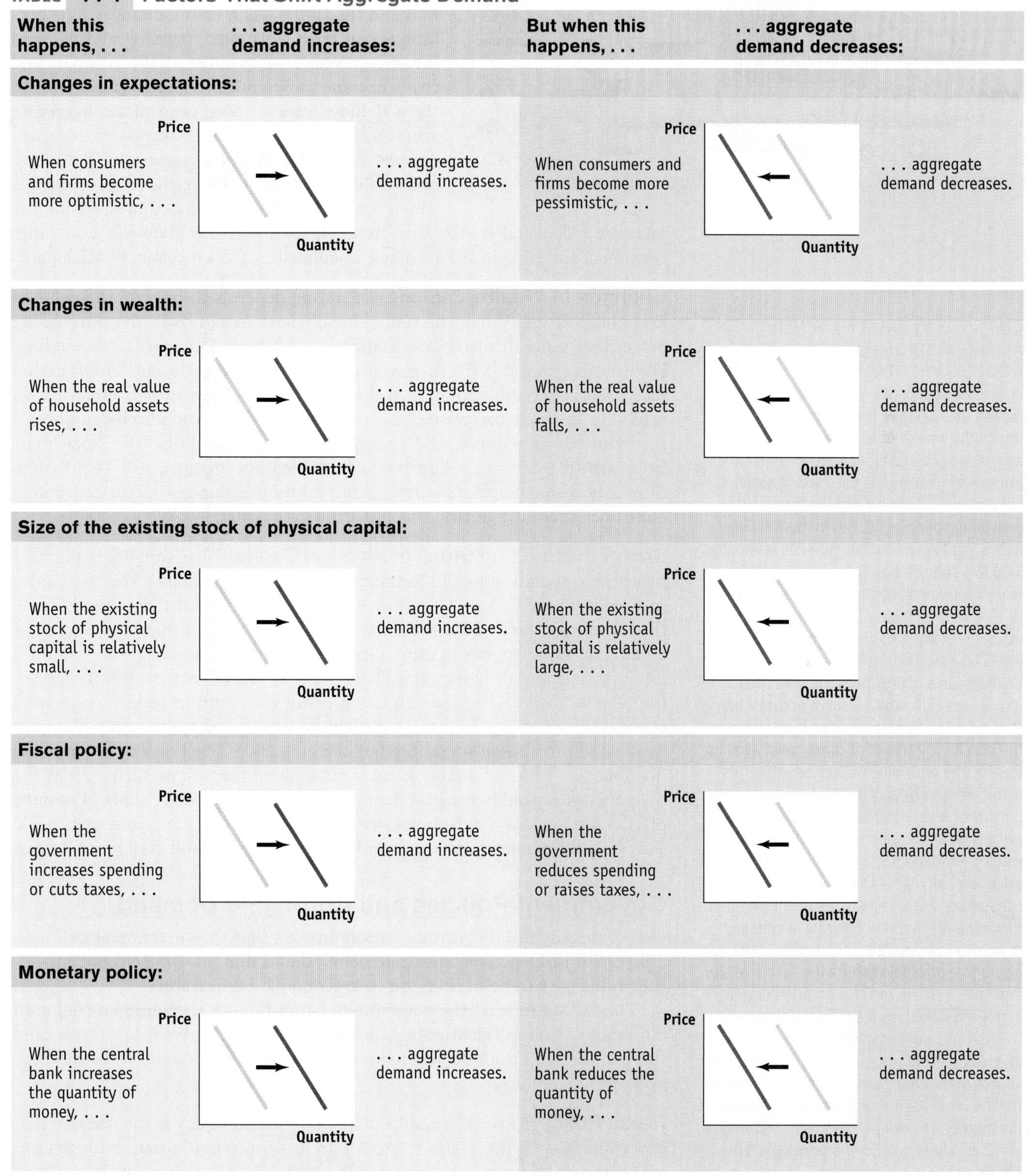

When this happens, . . .	. . . aggregate demand increases:	But when this happens, . . .	. . . aggregate demand decreases:
Changes in expectations:			
When consumers and firms become more optimistic, . . .	. . . aggregate demand increases.	When consumers and firms become more pessimistic, . . .	. . . aggregate demand decreases.
Changes in wealth:			
When the real value of household assets rises, . . .	. . . aggregate demand increases.	When the real value of household assets falls, . . .	. . . aggregate demand decreases.
Size of the existing stock of physical capital:			
When the existing stock of physical capital is relatively small, . . .	. . . aggregate demand increases.	When the existing stock of physical capital is relatively large, . . .	. . . aggregate demand decreases.
Fiscal policy:			
When the government increases spending or cuts taxes, . . .	. . . aggregate demand increases.	When the government reduces spending or raises taxes, . . .	. . . aggregate demand decreases.
Monetary policy:			
When the central bank increases the quantity of money, . . .	. . . aggregate demand increases.	When the central bank reduces the quantity of money, . . .	. . . aggregate demand decreases.

Jim Borgman

"CONSUMER CONFIDENCE CRISIS IN AISLE 3!"

Changes in Expectations Both consumer spending and planned investment spending depend in part on people's expectations about the future. Consumers base their spending not only on the income they have now but also on the income they expect to have in the future. Firms base their planned investment spending not only on current conditions but also on the sales they expect to make in the future. As a result, changes in expectations can push consumer spending and planned investment spending up or down. If consumers and firms become more optimistic, aggregate spending rises; if they become more pessimistic, aggregate spending falls. In fact, short-run economic forecasters pay careful attention to surveys of consumer and business sentiment. In particular, forecasters watch the Consumer Confidence Index, a monthly measure calculated by the Conference Board, and the Michigan Consumer Sentiment Index, a similar measure calculated by the University of Michigan.

Changes in Wealth Consumer spending depends in part on the value of household assets. When the real value of these assets rises, the purchasing power they embody also rises, leading to an increase in aggregate spending. For example, in the 1990s there was a significant rise in the stock market that increased aggregate demand. And when the real value of household assets falls—for example, because of a stock market crash—the purchasing power they embody is reduced and aggregate demand also falls. The stock market crash of 1929 was a significant factor leading to the Great Depression. Similarly, a sharp decline in real estate values was a major factor depressing consumer spending during the 2007–2009 recession.

Size of the Existing Stock of Physical Capital Firms engage in planned investment spending to add to their stock of physical capital. Their incentive to spend depends in part on how much physical capital they already have: the more they have, the less they will feel a need to add more, other things equal. The same applies to other types of investment spending—for example, if a large number of houses have been built in recent years, this will depress the demand for new houses and as a result also tend to reduce residential investment spending. In fact, that's part of the reason for the deep slump in residential investment spending that began in 2006. The housing boom of the previous few years had created an oversupply of houses: by spring 2009, the inventory of unsold houses on the market was equal to more than 14 months of sales, and prices of new homes had fallen more than 25% from their peak. This gave the construction industry little incentive to build even more homes.

PITFALLS

CHANGES IN WEALTH: A MOVEMENT ALONG VERSUS A SHIFT OF THE AGGREGATE DEMAND CURVE

In the last section we explained that one reason the *AD* curve is downward sloping is due to the wealth effect of a change in the aggregate price level: a higher aggregate price level reduces the purchasing power of households' assets and leads to a fall in consumer spending, *C*. But in this section we've just explained that changes in wealth lead to a shift of the *AD* curve. Aren't those two explanations contradictory? Which one is it—does a change in wealth move the economy along the *AD* curve or does it shift the *AD* curve? The answer is both: it depends on the *source* of the change in wealth. A movement along the *AD* curve occurs when a change in the aggregate price level changes the purchasing power of consumers' existing wealth (the real value of their assets). This is the *wealth effect of a change in the aggregate price level*—a change in the aggregate price level is the source of the change in wealth. For example, a fall in the aggregate price level increases the purchasing power of consumers' assets and leads to a movement down the *AD* curve. In contrast, a change in wealth *independent of a change in the aggregate price level* shifts the *AD* curve. For example, a rise in the stock market or a rise in real estate values leads to an increase in the real value of consumers' assets at any given aggregate price level. In this case, the source of the change in wealth is a change in the values of assets without any change in the aggregate price level—that is, a change in asset values holding the prices of all final goods and services constant.

Government Policies and Aggregate Demand

One of the key insights of macroeconomics is that the government can have a powerful influence on aggregate demand and that, in some circumstances, this influence can be used to improve economic performance.

The two main ways the government can influence the aggregate demand curve are through fiscal policy and monetary policy. We'll briefly discuss their influence on aggregate demand, leaving a full-length discussion for upcoming chapters.

Fiscal Policy As we learned in Chapter 10, fiscal policy is the use of either government spending—government purchases of final goods and services and government transfers—or tax policy to stabilize the economy. In practice, governments often respond to recessions by increasing spending, cutting taxes, or both. They often respond to inflation by reducing spending or increasing taxes.

The effect of government purchases of final goods and services, *G*, on the aggregate demand curve is *direct* because government purchases are themselves a component of aggregate demand. So an increase in government purchases shifts the aggregate demand curve to the right and a decrease shifts it to the left. History's most dramatic example of how increased government purchases affect aggregate demand was the effect of wartime government spending during World War II. Because of the war, U.S. federal purchases surged 400%. This increase in purchases is usually credited with ending the Great Depression. In the 1990s Japan used large public works projects—such as government-financed construction of roads, bridges, and dams—in an effort to increase aggregate demand in the face of a slumping economy. Similarly, in 2009, the United States began spending more than $100 billion on infrastructure projects such as improving highways, bridges, public transportation, and more, to stimulate overall spending.

In contrast, changes in either tax rates or government transfers influence the economy *indirectly* through their effect on disposable income. A lower tax rate means that consumers get to keep more of what they earn, increasing their disposable income. An increase in government transfers also increases consumers' disposable income. In either case, this increases consumer spending and shifts the aggregate demand curve to the right. A higher tax rate or a reduction in transfers reduces the amount of disposable income received by consumers. This reduces consumer spending and shifts the aggregate demand curve to the left.

Monetary Policy We opened this chapter by talking about the problems faced by the Federal Reserve, which controls monetary policy—the use of changes in the quantity of money or the interest rate to stabilize the economy. We've just discussed how a rise in the aggregate price level, by reducing the purchasing power of money holdings, causes a rise in the interest rate. That, in turn, reduces both investment spending and consumer spending.

But what happens if the quantity of money in the hands of households and firms changes? In modern economies, the quantity of money in circulation is largely determined by the decisions of a *central bank* created by the government. As we'll learn in Chapter 16, the Federal Reserve, the U.S. central bank, is a special institution that is neither exactly part of the government nor exactly a private institution. When the central bank increases the quantity of money in circulation, households and firms have more money, which they are willing to lend out. The effect is to drive the interest rate down at any given aggregate price level, leading to higher investment spending and higher consumer spending. That is, increasing the quantity of money shifts the aggregate demand curve to the right. Reducing the quantity of money has the opposite effect: households and firms have less money holdings than before, leading them to borrow more and lend less. This raises the interest rate, reduces investment spending and consumer spending, and shifts the aggregate demand curve to the left.

ECONOMICS ➤ *IN ACTION*

MOVING ALONG THE AGGREGATE DEMAND CURVE, 1979–1980

When looking at data, it's often hard to distinguish between changes in spending that represent *movements along* the aggregate demand curve and *shifts of* the aggregate demand curve. One telling exception, however, is what happened right after the oil crisis of 1979, which we mentioned in this chapter's opening story. Faced with a sharp increase in the aggregate price level—the rate of consumer

Glow Images/SuperStock

The interest rate effect of a rise in the aggregate price level leads to a drop in consumer and investment spending.

price inflation reached 14.8% in March of 1980—the Federal Reserve stuck to a policy of increasing the quantity of money slowly. The aggregate price level was rising steeply, but the quantity of money circulating in the economy was growing slowly. The net result was that the purchasing power of the quantity of money in circulation fell.

This led to an increase in the demand for borrowing and a surge in interest rates. The *prime rate,* which is the interest rate banks charge their best customers, climbed above 20%. High interest rates, in turn, caused both consumer spending and investment spending to fall: in 1980 purchases of durable consumer goods like cars fell by 5.3% and real investment spending fell by 8.9%.

In other words, in 1979–1980 the economy responded just as we'd expect if it were moving upward along the aggregate demand curve from right to left: due to the wealth effect and the interest rate effect of a change in the aggregate price level, the quantity of aggregate output demanded fell as the aggregate price level rose. This does not explain, of course, why the aggregate price level rose. But as we'll see in the section "The *AD–AS* Model," the answer to that question lies in the behavior of the *short-run aggregate supply curve.*

Quick Review

- The **aggregate demand curve** is downward sloping because of the **wealth effect of a change in the aggregate price level** and the **interest rate effect of a change in the aggregate price level.**
- The aggregate demand curve shows how income–expenditure equilibrium GDP changes when the aggregate price level changes.
- Changes in consumer spending caused by changes in wealth and expectations about the future shift the aggregate demand curve. Changes in investment spending caused by changes in expectations and by the size of the existing stock of physical capital also shift the aggregate demand curve.
- Fiscal policy affects aggregate demand directly through government purchases and indirectly through changes in taxes or government transfers. Monetary policy affects aggregate demand indirectly through changes in the interest rate.

CHECK YOUR UNDERSTANDING 14-1

1. Determine the effect on aggregate demand of each of the following events. Explain whether it represents a movement along the aggregate demand curve (up or down) or a shift of the curve (leftward or rightward).
   a. A rise in the interest rate caused by a change in monetary policy
   b. A fall in the real value of money in the economy due to a higher aggregate price level
   c. News of a worse-than-expected job market next year
   d. A fall in tax rates
   e. A rise in the real value of assets in the economy due to a lower aggregate price level
   f. A rise in the real value of assets in the economy due to a surge in real estate values

Solutions appear at back of book.

Aggregate Supply

Between 1929 and 1933, there was a sharp fall in aggregate demand—a reduction in the quantity of goods and services demanded at any given price level. One consequence of the economy-wide decline in demand was a fall in the prices of most goods and services. By 1933, the GDP deflator (one of the price indexes we defined in Chapter 11) was 26% below its 1929 level, and other indexes were down by similar amounts. A second consequence was a decline in the output of most goods and services: by 1933, real GDP was 27% below its 1929 level. A third consequence, closely tied to the fall in real GDP, was a surge in the unemployment rate from 3% to 25%.

The association between the plunge in real GDP and the plunge in prices wasn't an accident. Between 1929 and 1933, the U.S. economy was moving down its **aggregate supply curve,** which shows the relationship between the economy's aggregate price level (the overall price level of final goods and services in the economy) and the total quantity of final goods and services, or aggregate output, producers are willing to supply. (As you will recall, we use real GDP to measure aggregate output. So we'll often use the two terms interchangeably.) More specifically, between 1929 and 1933 the U.S. economy moved down its *short-run aggregate supply curve.*

The **aggregate supply curve** shows the relationship between the aggregate price level and the quantity of aggregate output supplied in the economy.

The Short-Run Aggregate Supply Curve

The period from 1929 to 1933 demonstrated that there is a positive relationship in the short run between the aggregate price level and the quantity of aggregate output supplied. That is, a rise in the aggregate price level is associated with a rise in the quantity of aggregate output supplied, other things equal; a fall in the aggregate price level is associated with a fall in the quantity of aggregate output supplied, other things equal. To understand why this positive relationship exists, consider the most basic question facing a producer: is producing a unit of output profitable or not? Let's define profit per unit:

(14-2) Profit per unit of output =
Price per unit of output – Production cost per unit of output

Thus, the answer to the question depends on whether the price the producer receives for a unit of output is greater or less than the cost of producing that unit of output. At any given point in time, many of the costs producers face are fixed per unit of output and can't be changed for an extended period of time. Typically, the largest source of inflexible production cost is the wages paid to workers. *Wages* here refers to all forms of worker compensation, such as employer-paid health care and retirement benefits in addition to earnings.

Wages are typically an inflexible production cost because the dollar amount of any given wage paid, called the **nominal wage,** is often determined by contracts that were signed some time ago. And even when there are no formal contracts, there are often informal agreements between management and workers, making companies reluctant to change wages in response to economic conditions. For example, companies usually will not reduce wages during poor economic times—unless the downturn has been particularly long and severe—for fear of generating worker resentment. Correspondingly, they typically won't raise wages during better economic times—until they are at risk of losing workers to competitors—because they don't want to encourage workers to routinely demand higher wages.

As a result of both formal and informal agreements, then, the economy is characterized by **sticky wages:** nominal wages that are slow to fall even in the face of high unemployment and slow to rise even in the face of labor shortages. It's important to note, however, that nominal wages cannot be sticky forever: ultimately, formal contracts and informal agreements will be renegotiated to take into account changed economic circumstances. As the Pitfalls at the end of this section explains, how long it takes for nominal wages to become flexible is an integral component of what distinguishes the short run from the long run.

To understand how the fact that many costs are fixed in nominal terms gives rise to an upward-sloping short-run aggregate supply curve, it's helpful to know that prices are set somewhat differently in different kinds of markets. In *perfectly competitive markets,* producers take prices as given; in *imperfectly competitive markets,* producers have some ability to choose the prices they charge. In both kinds of markets, there is a short-run positive relationship between prices and output, but for slightly different reasons.

Let's start with the behavior of producers in perfectly competitive markets; remember, they take the price as given. Imagine that, for some reason, the aggregate price level falls, which means that the price received by the typical producer of a final good or service falls. Because many production costs are fixed in the short run, production cost per unit of output doesn't fall by the same proportion as the fall in the price of output. So the profit per unit of output declines, leading perfectly competitive producers to reduce the quantity supplied in the short run.

On the other hand, suppose that for some reason the aggregate price level rises. As a result, the typical producer receives a higher price for its final good or service. Again, many production costs are fixed in the short run, so production cost per unit of output doesn't rise by the same proportion as the rise in the price

The **nominal wage** is the dollar amount of the wage paid.

Sticky wages are nominal wages that are slow to fall even in the face of high unemployment and slow to rise even in the face of labor shortages.

The **short-run aggregate supply curve** shows the relationship between the aggregate price level and the quantity of aggregate output supplied that exists in the short run, the time period when many production costs can be taken as fixed.

of a unit. And since the typical perfectly competitive producer takes the price as given, profit per unit of output rises and output increases.

Now consider an imperfectly competitive producer that is able to set its own price. If there is a rise in the demand for this producer's product, it will be able to sell more at any given price. Given stronger demand for its products, it will probably choose to increase its prices as well as its output, as a way of increasing profit per unit of output. In fact, industry analysts often talk about variations in an industry's "pricing power": when demand is strong, firms with pricing power are able to raise prices—and they do.

Conversely, if there is a fall in demand, firms will normally try to limit the fall in their sales by cutting prices.

Both the responses of firms in perfectly competitive industries and those of firms in imperfectly competitive industries lead to an upward-sloping relationship between aggregate output and the aggregate price level. The positive relationship between the aggregate price level and the quantity of aggregate output producers are willing to supply during the time period when many production costs, particularly nominal wages, can be taken as fixed is illustrated by the **short-run aggregate supply curve.** The positive relationship between the aggregate price level and aggregate output in the short run gives the short-run aggregate supply curve its upward slope.

Figure 14-3 shows a hypothetical short-run aggregate supply curve, *SRAS*, which matches actual U.S. data for 1929 and 1933. On the horizontal axis is aggregate output (or, equivalently, real GDP)—the total quantity of final goods and services supplied in the economy—measured in 2005 dollars. On the vertical axis is the aggregate price level as measured by the GDP deflator, with the value for the year 2005 equal to 100. In 1929, the aggregate price level was 10.6 and real GDP was $976 billion. In 1933, the aggregate price level was 7.9 and real GDP was only $716 billion. The movement down the *SRAS* curve corresponds to the deflation and fall in aggregate output experienced over those years.

FIGURE 14-3 The Short-Run Aggregate Supply Curve

The short-run aggregate supply curve shows the relationship between the aggregate price level and the quantity of aggregate output supplied in the short run, the period in which many production costs such as nominal wages are fixed. It is upward sloping because a higher aggregate price level leads to higher profit per unit of output and higher aggregate output given fixed nominal wages. Here we show numbers corresponding to the Great Depression, from 1929 to 1933: when deflation occurred and the aggregate price level fell from 10.6 (in 1929) to 7.9 (in 1933), firms responded by reducing the quantity of aggregate output supplied from $976 billion to $716 billion measured in 2005 dollars.

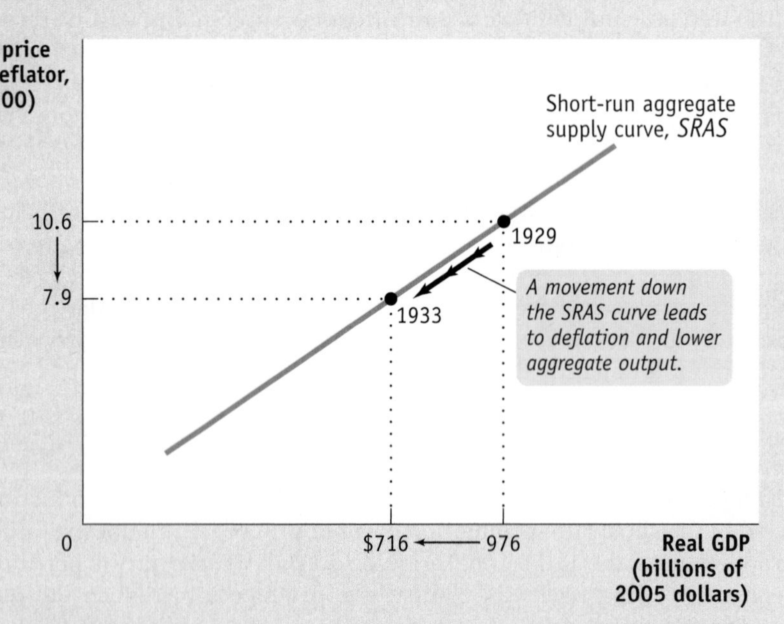

FOR INQUIRING MINDS

WHAT'S TRULY FLEXIBLE, WHAT'S TRULY STICKY

Most macroeconomists agree that the basic picture shown in Figure 14-3 is correct: there is, other things equal, a positive short-run relationship between the aggregate price level and aggregate output. But many would argue that the details are a bit more complicated.

So far we've stressed a difference in the behavior of the aggregate price level and the behavior of nominal wages. That is, we've said that the aggregate price level is flexible but nominal wages are sticky in the short run. Although this assumption is a good way to explain why the short-run aggregate supply curve is upward sloping, empirical data on wages and prices don't wholly support a sharp distinction between flexible prices of final goods and services and sticky nominal wages.

On one side, some nominal wages are in fact flexible even in the short run because some workers are not covered by a contract or informal agreement with their employers. Since some nominal wages are sticky but others are flexible, we observe that the *average nominal wage*—the nominal wage averaged over all workers in the economy—falls when there is a steep rise in unemployment. For example, nominal wages fell substantially in the early years of the Great Depression.

On the other side, some prices of final goods and services are sticky rather than flexible. For example, some firms, particularly the makers of luxury or name-brand goods, are reluctant to cut prices even when demand falls. Instead they prefer to cut output even if their profit per unit hasn't declined.

These complications, as we've said, don't change the basic picture. When the aggregate price level falls, some producers cut output because the nominal wages they pay are sticky. And some producers don't cut their prices in the face of a falling aggregate price level, preferring instead to reduce their output. In both cases, the positive relationship between the aggregate price level and aggregate output is maintained. So, in the end, the short-run aggregate supply curve is still upward sloping.

Shifts of the Short-Run Aggregate Supply Curve

Figure 14-3 shows a *movement along* the short-run aggregate supply curve, as the aggregate price level and aggregate output fell from 1929 to 1933. But there can also be *shifts of* the short-run aggregate supply curve, as shown in Figure 14-4. Panel (a) shows a *decrease in short-run aggregate supply*—a leftward shift of the short-run aggregate supply curve. Aggregate supply decreases when producers reduce the quantity of aggregate output they are willing to supply at any given aggregate price level. Panel (b)

FIGURE 14-4 Shifts of the Short-Run Aggregate Supply Curve

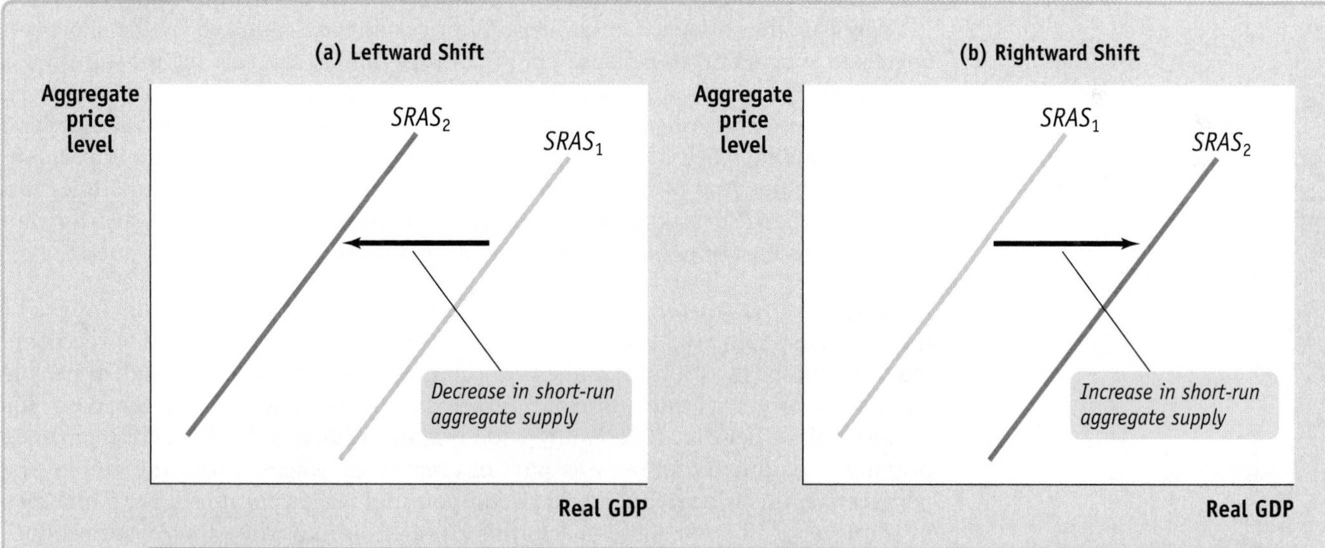

Panel (a) shows a decrease in short-run aggregate supply: the short-run aggregate supply curve shifts leftward from $SRAS_1$ to $SRAS_2$, and the quantity of aggregate output supplied at any given aggregate price level falls.

Panel (b) shows an increase in short-run aggregate supply: the short-run aggregate supply curve shifts rightward from $SRAS_1$ to $SRAS_2$, and the quantity of aggregate output supplied at any given aggregate price level rises.

shows an *increase in short-run aggregate supply*—a rightward shift of the short-run aggregate supply curve. Aggregate supply increases when producers increase the quantity of aggregate output they are willing to supply at any given aggregate price level.

To understand why the short-run aggregate supply curve can shift, it's important to recall that producers make output decisions based on their profit per unit of output. The short-run aggregate supply curve illustrates the relationship between the aggregate price level and aggregate output: because some production costs are fixed in the short run, a change in the aggregate price level leads to a change in producers' profit per unit of output and, in turn, leads to a change in aggregate output. But other factors besides the aggregate price level can affect profit per unit and, in turn, aggregate output. It is changes in these other factors that will shift the short-run aggregate supply curve.

To develop some intuition, suppose that something happens that raises production costs—say, an increase in the price of oil. At any given price of output, a producer now earns a smaller profit per unit of output. As a result, producers reduce the quantity supplied at any given aggregate price level, and the short-run aggregate supply curve shifts to the left. If, in contrast, something happens that lowers production costs—say, a fall in the nominal wage—a producer now earns a higher profit per unit of output at any given price of output. This leads producers to increase the quantity of aggregate output supplied at any given aggregate price level, and the short-run aggregate supply curve shifts to the right.

Now we'll discuss some of the important factors that affect producers' profit per unit and so can lead to shifts of the short-run aggregate supply curve.

Changes in Commodity Prices In this chapter's opening story, we described how a surge in the price of oil caused problems for the U.S. economy in the 1970s, early in 2008, and again in 2011. Oil is a commodity, a standardized input bought and sold in bulk quantities. An increase in the price of a commodity—oil—raised production costs across the economy and reduced the quantity of aggregate output supplied at any given aggregate price level, shifting the short-run aggregate supply curve to the left. Conversely, a decline in commodity prices reduces production costs, leading to an increase in the quantity supplied at any given aggregate price level and a rightward shift of the short-run aggregate supply curve.

Why isn't the influence of commodity prices already captured by the short-run aggregate supply curve? Because commodities—unlike, say, soft drinks—are not a final good, their prices are not included in the calculation of the aggregate price level. Further, commodities represent a significant cost of production to most suppliers, just like nominal wages do. So changes in commodity prices have large impacts on production costs. And in contrast to noncommodities, the prices of commodities can sometimes change drastically due to industry-specific shocks to supply—such as wars in the Middle East or rising Chinese demand that leaves less oil for the United States.

Changes in Nominal Wages At any given point in time, the dollar wages of many workers are fixed because they are set by contracts or informal agreements made in the past. Nominal wages can change, however, once enough time has passed for contracts and informal agreements to be renegotiated. Suppose, for example, that there is an economy-wide rise in the cost of health care insurance premiums paid by employers as part of employees' wages. From the employers' perspective, this is equivalent to a rise in nominal wages because it is an increase in employer-paid compensation. So this rise in nominal wages increases production costs and shifts the short-run aggregate supply curve to the left. Conversely, suppose there is an economy-wide fall in the cost of such premiums. This is equivalent to a fall in nominal wages from the point of view of employers; it reduces production costs and shifts the short-run aggregate supply curve to the right.

An important historical fact is that during the 1970s the surge in the price of oil had the indirect effect of also raising nominal wages. This "knock-on" effect occurred because many wage contracts included *cost-of-living allowances* that automatically raised the nominal wage when consumer prices increased. Through this channel, the surge in the price of oil—which led to an increase in overall consumer prices—ultimately caused a rise in nominal wages. So the economy, in the end, experienced two leftward shifts of the aggregate supply curve: the first generated by the initial surge in the price of oil, the second generated by the induced increase in nominal wages. The negative effect on the economy of rising oil prices was greatly magnified through the cost-of-living allowances in wage contracts. Today, cost-of-living allowances in wage contracts are rare.

Changes in Productivity An increase in productivity means that a worker can produce more units of output with the same quantity of inputs. For example, the introduction of bar-code scanners in retail stores greatly increased the ability of a single worker to stock, inventory, and resupply store shelves. As a result, the cost to a store of "producing" a dollar of sales fell and profit rose. And, correspondingly, the quantity supplied increased. (Think of Walmart and the increase in the number of its stores as an increase in aggregate supply.) So a rise in productivity, whatever the source, increases producers' profits and shifts the short-run aggregate supply curve to the right. Conversely, a fall in productivity—say, due to new regulations that require workers to spend more time filling out forms—reduces the number of units of output a worker can produce with the same quantity of inputs. Consequently, the cost per unit of output rises, profit falls, and quantity supplied falls. This shifts the short-run aggregate supply curve to the left.

For a summary of the factors that shift the short-run aggregate supply curve, see Table 14-2.

TABLE 14-2 Factors That Shift Aggregate Supply

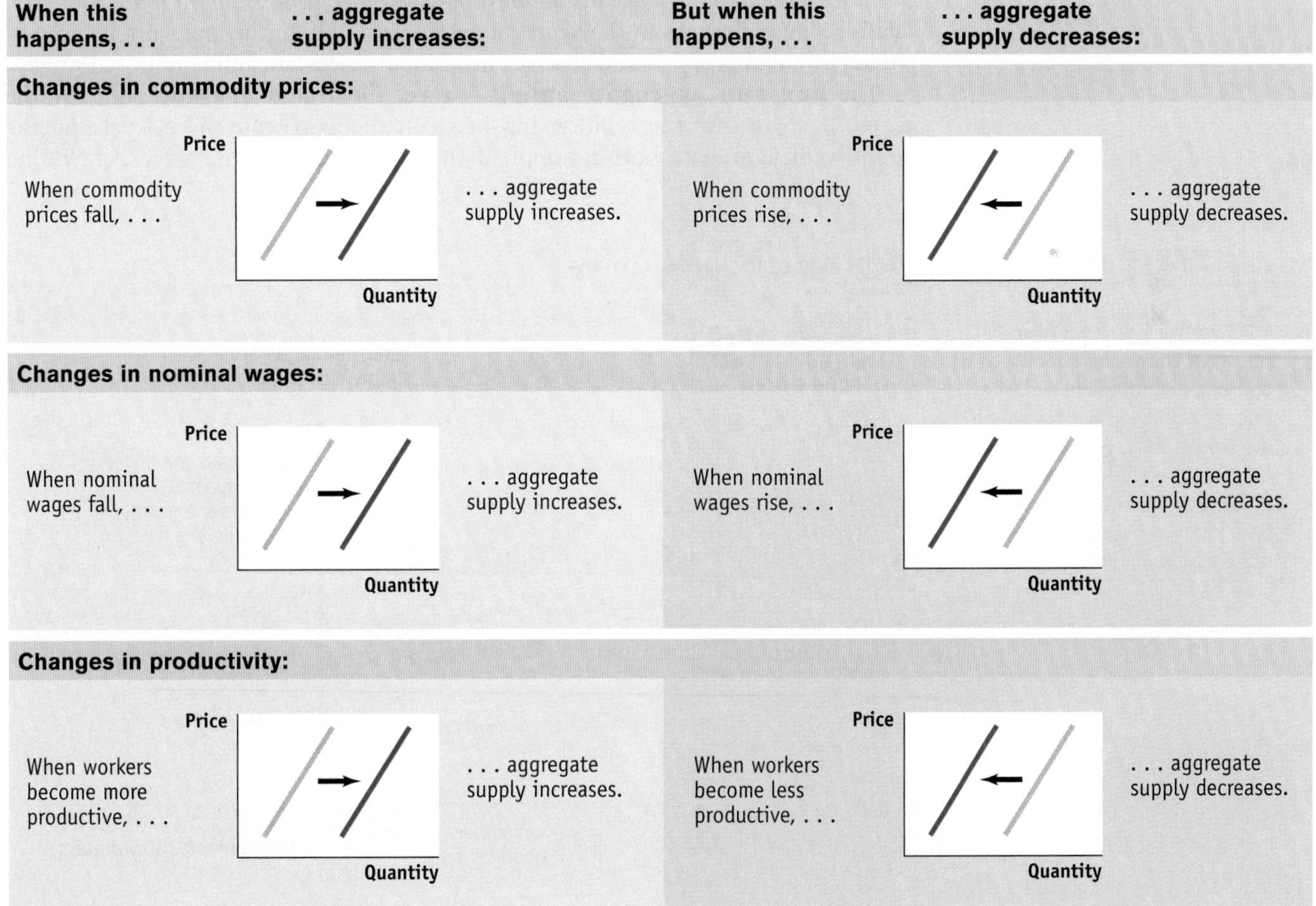

When this happens, . . .	. . . aggregate supply increases:	But when this happens, . . .	. . . aggregate supply decreases:
Changes in commodity prices:			
When commodity prices fall, . . .	. . . aggregate supply increases.	When commodity prices rise, . . .	. . . aggregate supply decreases.
Changes in nominal wages:			
When nominal wages fall, . . .	. . . aggregate supply increases.	When nominal wages rise, . . .	. . . aggregate supply decreases.
Changes in productivity:			
When workers become more productive, . . .	. . . aggregate supply increases.	When workers become less productive, . . .	. . . aggregate supply decreases.

The **long-run aggregate supply curve** shows the relationship between the aggregate price level and the quantity of aggregate output supplied that would exist if all prices, including nominal wages, were fully flexible.

The Long-Run Aggregate Supply Curve

We've just seen that in the short run a fall in the aggregate price level leads to a decline in the quantity of aggregate output supplied because nominal wages are sticky in the short run. But, as we mentioned earlier, contracts and informal agreements are renegotiated in the long run. So in the long run, nominal wages—like the aggregate price level—are flexible, not sticky. This fact greatly alters the long-run relationship between the aggregate price level and aggregate supply. In fact, in the long run the aggregate price level has *no* effect on the quantity of aggregate output supplied.

To see why, let's conduct a thought experiment. Imagine that you could wave a magic wand—or maybe a magic bar-code scanner—and cut *all prices* in the economy in half at the same time. By "all prices" we mean the prices of all inputs, including nominal wages, as well as the prices of final goods and services. What would happen to aggregate output, given that the aggregate price level has been halved and all input prices, including nominal wages, have been halved?

The answer is: nothing. Consider Equation 14-2 again: each producer would receive a lower price for its product, but costs would fall by the same proportion. As a result, every unit of output profitable to produce before the change in prices would still be profitable to produce after the change in prices. So a halving of *all* prices in the economy has no effect on the economy's aggregate output. In other words, changes in the aggregate price level now have no effect on the quantity of aggregate output supplied.

In reality, of course, no one can change all prices by the same proportion at the same time. But now, we'll consider the *long run, the period of time over which all prices are fully flexible.* In the long run, inflation or deflation has the same effect as someone changing all prices by the same proportion. *As a result, changes in the aggregate price level do not change the quantity of aggregate output supplied in the long run.* That's because changes in the aggregate price level will, in the long run, be accompanied by equal proportional changes in *all* input prices, including nominal wages.

The **long-run aggregate supply curve,** illustrated in Figure 14-5 by the curve *LRAS*, shows the relationship between the aggregate price level and the quantity of aggregate output supplied that would exist if all prices, including

FIGURE **14-5** The Long-Run Aggregate Supply Curve

The long-run aggregate supply curve shows the quantity of aggregate output supplied when all prices, including nominal wages, are flexible. It is vertical at potential output, Y_P, because in the long run a change in the aggregate price level has no effect on the quantity of aggregate output supplied.

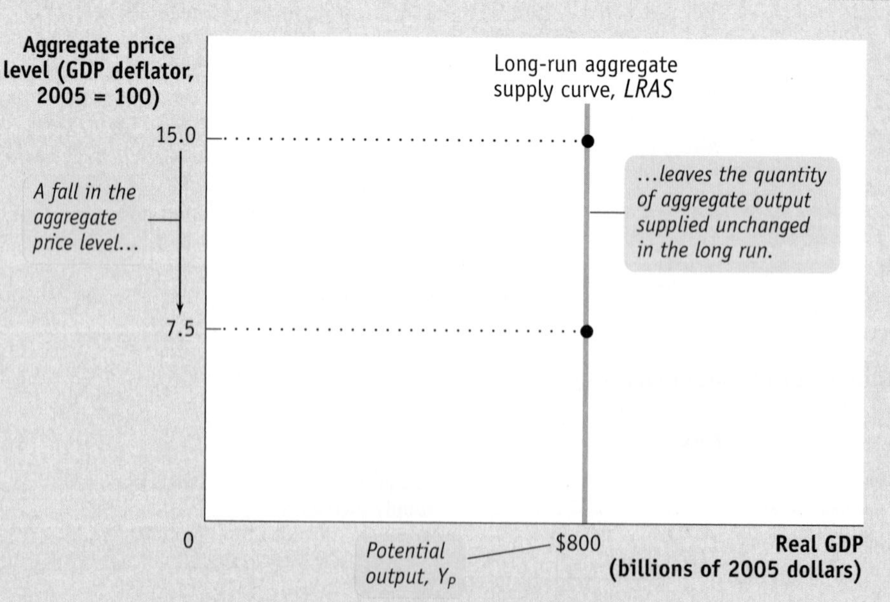

nominal wages, were fully flexible. The long-run aggregate supply curve is vertical because changes in the aggregate price level have *no* effect on aggregate output in the long run. At an aggregate price level of 15.0, the quantity of aggregate output supplied is $800 billion in 2005 dollars. If the aggregate price level falls by 50% to 7.5, the quantity of aggregate output supplied is unchanged in the long run at $800 billion in 2005 dollars.

Potential output is the level of real GDP the economy would produce if all prices, including nominal wages, were fully flexible.

It's important to understand not only that the *LRAS* curve is vertical but also that its position along the horizontal axis represents a significant measure. The horizontal intercept in Figure 14-5, where *LRAS* touches the horizontal axis ($800 billion in 2005 dollars), is the economy's **potential output,** Y_P: the level of real GDP the economy would produce if all prices, including nominal wages, were fully flexible.

In reality, the actual level of real GDP is almost always either above or below potential output. We'll see why later in this chapter, when we discuss the *AD–AS* model. Still, an economy's potential output is an important number because it defines the trend around which actual aggregate output fluctuates from year to year.

In the United States, the Congressional Budget Office, or CBO, estimates annual potential output for the purpose of federal budget analysis. In Figure 14-6, the CBO's estimates of U.S. potential output from 1990 to 2011 are represented by the orange line and the actual values of U.S. real GDP over the same period are represented by the blue line. Years shaded purple on the horizontal axis correspond to periods in which actual aggregate output fell short of potential output, years shaded green to periods in which actual aggregate output exceeded potential output.

FIGURE 14-6 Actual and Potential Output from 1990 to 2011

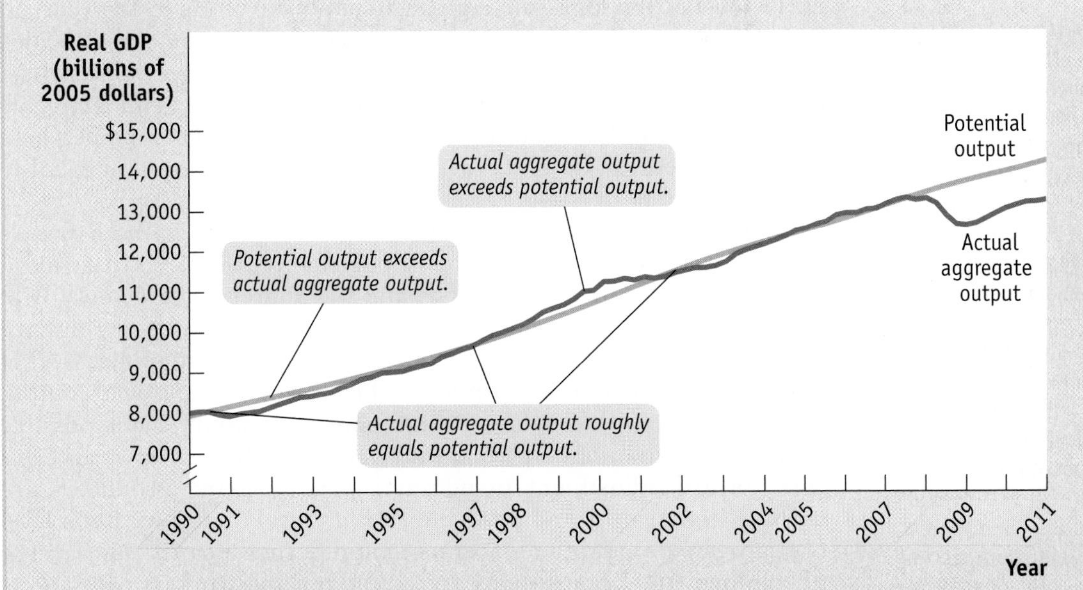

This figure shows the performance of actual and potential output in the United States from 1990 to 2011. The orange line shows estimates of U.S. potential output, produced by the Congressional Budget Office, and the blue line shows actual aggregate output. The purple-shaded years are periods in which actual aggregate output fell below potential output, and the green-shaded years are periods in which actual aggregate output exceeded potential output. As shown, significant shortfalls occurred in the recessions of the early 1990s and after 2000. Actual aggregate output was significantly above potential output in the boom of the late 1990s, and a huge shortfall occurred after the recession of 2007–2009.

Sources: Congressional Budget Office; Bureau of Economic Analysis.

As you can see, U.S. potential output has risen steadily over time—implying a series of rightward shifts of the *LRAS* curve. What has caused these rightward shifts? The answer lies in the factors related to long-run growth that we discussed in Chapter 13, such as increases in physical capital and human capital as well as technological progress. Over the long run, as the size of the labor force and the productivity of labor both rise, the level of real GDP that the economy is capable of producing also rises. Indeed, one way to think about long-run economic growth is that it is the growth in the economy's potential output. We generally think of the long-run aggregate supply curve as shifting to the right over time as an economy experiences long-run growth.

From the Short Run to the Long Run

As you can see in Figure 14-6, the economy normally produces more or less than potential output: actual aggregate output was below potential output in the early 1990s, above potential output in the late 1990s, below potential output for most of the 2000s, and significantly below potential output after the recession of 2007–2009. So the economy is normally on its short-run aggregate supply curve—but not on its long-run aggregate supply curve. So why is the long-run curve relevant? Does the economy ever move from the short run to the long run? And if so, how?

The first step to answering these questions is to understand that the economy is always in one of only two states with respect to the short-run and long-run aggregate supply curves. It can be on both curves simultaneously by being at a point where the curves cross (as in the few years in Figure 14-6 in which actual aggregate output and potential output roughly coincided). Or it can be on the short-run aggregate supply curve but not the long-run aggregate supply curve (as in the years in which actual aggregate output and potential output *did not* coincide). But that is not the end of the story. If the economy is on the short-run but not the long-run aggregate supply curve, the short-run aggregate supply curve will shift over time until the economy is at a point where both curves cross—a point where actual aggregate output is equal to potential output.

PITFALLS

ARE WE THERE YET? WHAT THE LONG RUN REALLY MEANS

We've used the term *long run* in two different contexts. In an earlier chapter we focused on *long-run economic growth:* growth that takes place over decades. In this chapter we introduced the *long-run aggregate supply curve,* which depicts the economy's potential output: the level of aggregate output that the economy would produce if all prices, including nominal wages, were fully flexible. It might seem that we're using the same term, *long run,* for two different concepts. But we aren't: these two concepts are really the same thing.

Because the economy always tends to return to potential output in the long run, actual aggregate output *fluctuates around* potential output, rarely getting too far from it. As a result, the economy's rate of growth over long periods of time—say, decades—is very close to the rate of growth of potential output. And potential output growth is determined by the factors we analyzed in the chapter on long-run economic growth. So that means that the "long run" of long-run growth and the "long run" of the long-run aggregate supply curve coincide.

Figure 14-7 illustrates how this process works. In both panels *LRAS* is the long-run aggregate supply curve, $SRAS_1$ is the initial short-run aggregate supply curve, and the aggregate price level is at P_1. In panel (a) the economy starts at the initial production point, A_1, which corresponds to a quantity of aggregate output supplied, Y_1, that is higher than potential output, Y_P. Producing an aggregate output level (such as Y_1) that is higher than potential output (Y_P) is possible only because nominal wages haven't yet fully adjusted upward. Until this upward adjustment in nominal wages occurs, producers are earning high profits and producing a high level of output. But a level of aggregate output higher than potential output means a low level of unemployment. Because jobs are abundant and workers are scarce, nominal wages will rise over time, gradually shifting the short-run aggregate supply curve leftward. Eventually it will be in a new position, such as $SRAS_2$. (Later in this chapter, we'll show where the short-run aggregate supply curve ends up. As we'll see, that depends on the aggregate demand curve as well.)

In panel (b), the initial production point, A_1, corresponds to an aggregate output level, Y_1, that is lower than potential output, Y_P. Producing an aggregate output level (such as Y_1) that is lower than potential output (Y_P) is possible only because nominal wages haven't yet fully adjusted downward. Until this downward adjustment occurs, producers are earning low (or negative) profits and producing a low level of output. An aggregate output level lower than potential output means high unemployment. Because workers are abundant and jobs

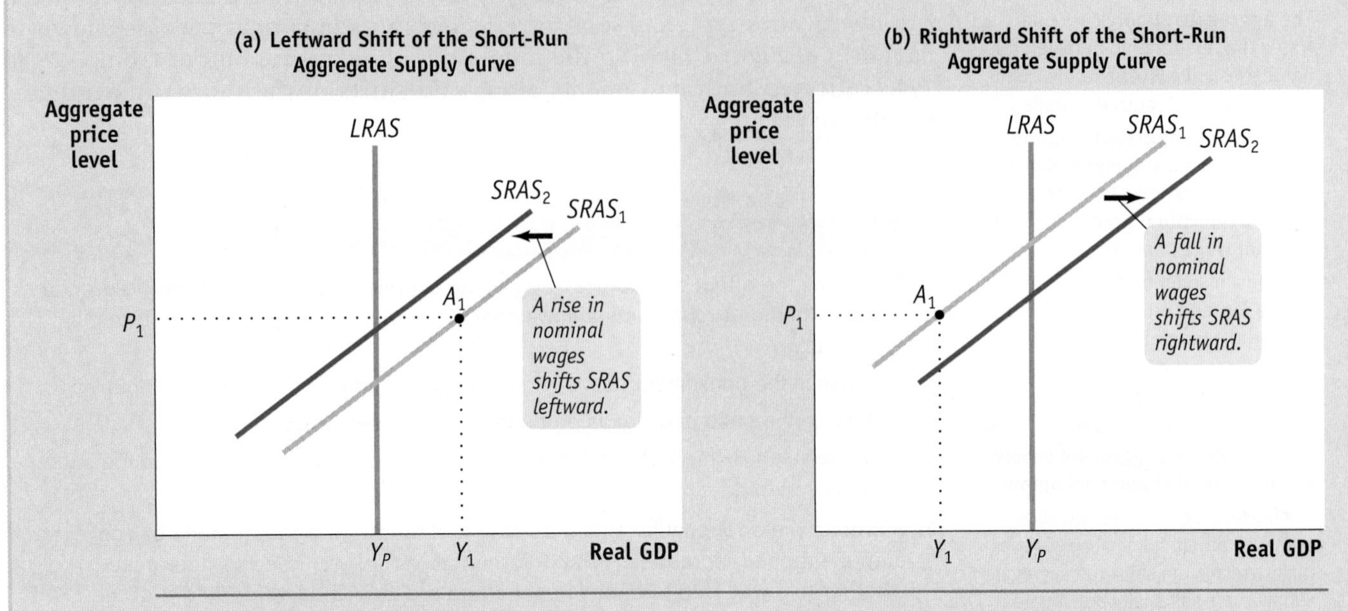

In panel (a), the initial short-run aggregate supply curve is $SRAS_1$. At the aggregate price level, P_1, the quantity of aggregate output supplied, Y_1, exceeds potential output, Y_P. Eventually, low unemployment will cause nominal wages to rise, leading to a leftward shift of the short-run aggregate supply curve from $SRAS_1$ to $SRAS_2$. In panel (b), the reverse happens: at the aggregate price level, P_1, the quantity of aggregate output supplied is less than potential output. High unemployment eventually leads to a fall in nominal wages over time and a rightward shift of the short-run aggregate supply curve.

are scarce, nominal wages will fall over time, shifting the short-run aggregate supply curve gradually to the right. Eventually it will be in a new position, such as $SRAS_2$.

We'll see shortly that these shifts of the short-run aggregate supply curve will return the economy to potential output in the long run.

ECONOMICS ➤ IN ACTION

PRICES AND OUTPUT DURING THE GREAT DEPRESSION

Figure 14-8 shows the actual track of the aggregate price level, as measured by the GDP deflator, and real GDP, from 1929 to 1942. As you can see, aggregate output and the aggregate price level fell together from 1929 to 1933 and rose together from 1933 to 1937. This is what we'd expect to see if the economy were moving down the short-run aggregate supply curve from 1929 to 1933 and moving up it (with a brief reversal in 1937–1938) thereafter.

But even in 1942 the aggregate price level was still lower than it was in 1929; yet real GDP was much higher. What happened?

The answer is that the short-run aggregate supply curve shifted to the right over time. This shift partly reflected rising productivity—a rightward shift of the underlying long-run aggregate supply curve.

FIGURE 14-8 Prices and Output During the Great Depression

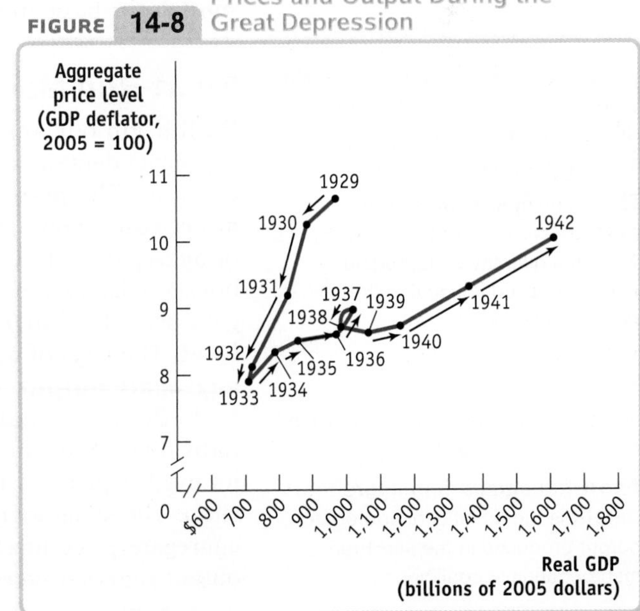

But since the U.S. economy was producing below potential output and had high unemployment during this period, the rightward shift of the short-run aggregate supply curve also reflected the adjustment process shown in panel (b) of Figure 14-7. So the movement of aggregate output from 1929 to 1942 reflected both movements along and shifts of the short-run aggregate supply curve.

Quick Review

- The **aggregate supply curve** illustrates the relationship between the aggregate price level and the quantity of aggregate output supplied.
- The **short-run aggregate supply curve** is upward sloping: a higher aggregate price level leads to higher aggregate output given that **nominal wages** are **sticky.**
- Changes in commodity prices, nominal wages, and productivity shift the short-run aggregate supply curve.
- In the long run, all prices are flexible, and changes in the aggregate price level have no effect on aggregate output. The **long-run aggregate supply curve** is vertical at **potential output.**
- If actual aggregate output exceeds potential output, nominal wages eventually rise and the short-run aggregate supply curve shifts leftward. If potential output exceeds actual aggregate output, nominal wages eventually fall and the short-run aggregate supply curve shifts rightward.

CHECK YOUR UNDERSTANDING 14-2

1. Determine the effect on short-run aggregate supply of each of the following events. Explain whether it represents a movement along the *SRAS* curve or a shift of the *SRAS* curve.
   a. A rise in the consumer price index (CPI) leads producers to increase output.
   b. A fall in the price of oil leads producers to increase output.
   c. A rise in legally mandated retirement benefits paid to workers leads producers to reduce output.
2. Suppose the economy is initially at potential output and the quantity of aggregate output supplied increases. What information would you need to determine whether this was due to a movement along the *SRAS* curve or a shift of the *LRAS* curve?

Solutions appear at back of book.

The *AD–AS* Model

From 1929 to 1933, the U.S. economy moved down the short-run aggregate supply curve as the aggregate price level fell. In contrast, from 1979 to 1980 the U.S. economy moved up the aggregate demand curve as the aggregate price level rose. In each case, the cause of the movement along the curve was a shift of the other curve. In 1929–1933, it was a leftward shift of the aggregate demand curve—a major fall in consumer spending. In 1979–1980, it was a leftward shift of the short-run aggregate supply curve—a dramatic fall in short-run aggregate supply caused by the oil price shock.

So to understand the behavior of the economy, we must put the aggregate supply curve and the aggregate demand curve together. The result is the ***AD–AS* model,** the basic model we use to understand economic fluctuations.

In the ***AD–AS* model,** the aggregate supply curve and the aggregate demand curve are used together to analyze economic fluctuations.

The economy is in **short-run macroeconomic equilibrium** when the quantity of aggregate output supplied is equal to the quantity demanded.

The **short-run equilibrium aggregate price level** is the aggregate price level in the short-run macroeconomic equilibrium.

Short-run equilibrium aggregate output is the quantity of aggregate output produced in the short-run macroeconomic equilibrium.

Short-Run Macroeconomic Equilibrium

We'll begin our analysis by focusing on the short run. Figure 14-9 shows the aggregate demand curve and the short-run aggregate supply curve on the same diagram. The point at which the *AD* and *SRAS* curves intersect, E_{SR}, is the **short-run macroeconomic equilibrium:** the point at which the quantity of aggregate output supplied is equal to the quantity demanded by domestic households, businesses, the government, and the rest of the world. The aggregate price level at E_{SR}, P_E, is the **short-run equilibrium aggregate price level.** The level of aggregate output at E_{SR}, Y_E, is the **short-run equilibrium aggregate output.**

In the supply and demand model of Chapter 3 we saw that a shortage of any individual good causes its market price to rise but a surplus of the good causes its market price to fall. These forces ensure that the market reaches equilibrium. The same logic applies to short-run macroeconomic equilibrium. If the aggregate price level is above its equilibrium level, the quantity of aggregate output supplied exceeds the quantity of aggregate output demanded. This leads

FIGURE 14-9 The *AD–AS* Model

The *AD–AS* model combines the aggregate demand curve and the short-run aggregate supply curve. Their point of intersection, E_{SR}, is the point of short-run macroeconomic equilibrium where the quantity of aggregate output demanded is equal to the quantity of aggregate output supplied. P_E is the short-run equilibrium aggregate price level, and Y_E is the short-run equilibrium level of aggregate output.

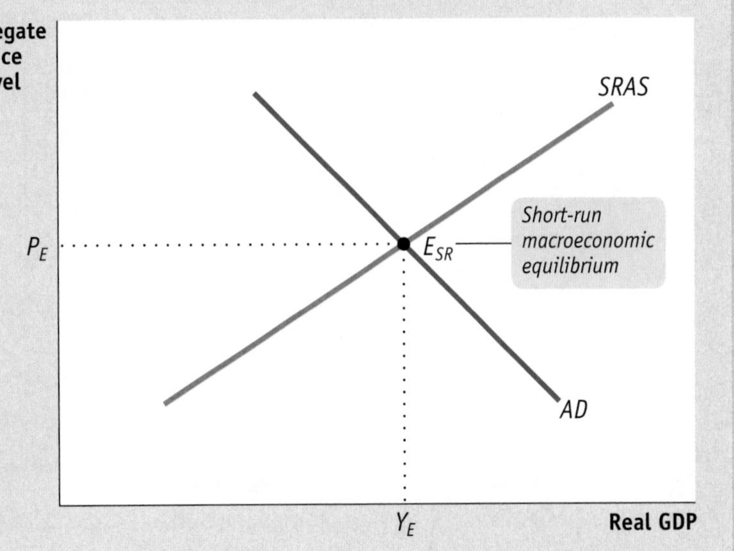

to a fall in the aggregate price level and pushes it toward its equilibrium level. If the aggregate price level is below its equilibrium level, the quantity of aggregate output supplied is less than the quantity of aggregate output demanded. This leads to a rise in the aggregate price level, again pushing it toward its equilibrium level. In the discussion that follows, we'll assume that the economy is always in short-run macroeconomic equilibrium.

We'll also make another important simplification based on the observation that in reality there is a long-term upward trend in both aggregate output and the aggregate price level. We'll assume that a fall in either variable really means a fall compared to the long-run trend. For example, if the aggregate price level normally rises 4% per year, a year in which the aggregate price level rises only 3% would count, for our purposes, as a 1% decline. In fact, since the Great Depression there have been very few years in which the aggregate price level of any major nation actually declined—Japan's period of deflation since 1995 is one of the few exceptions. There have, however, been many cases in which the aggregate price level fell relative to the long-run trend.

Short-run equilibrium aggregate output and the short-run equilibrium aggregate price level can change either because of shifts of the *AD* curve or because of shifts of the *SRAS* curve. Let's look at each case in turn.

Shifts of Aggregate Demand: Short-Run Effects

An event that shifts the aggregate demand curve, such as a change in expectations or wealth, the effect of the size of the existing stock of physical capital, or the use of fiscal or monetary policy, is known as a **demand shock.** The Great Depression was caused by a negative demand shock, the collapse of wealth and of business and consumer confidence that followed the stock market crash of 1929 and the banking crisis of 1930–1931. The Depression was ended by a positive demand shock—the huge increase in government purchases during World War II. In 2008 the U.S. economy experienced another significant negative demand shock as the housing market turned from boom to bust, leading consumers and firms to scale back their spending.

Figure 14-10 shows the short-run effects of negative and positive demand shocks. A negative demand shock shifts the aggregate demand curve, *AD*, to the

An event that shifts the aggregate demand curve is a **demand shock.**

FIGURE 14-10 Demand Shocks

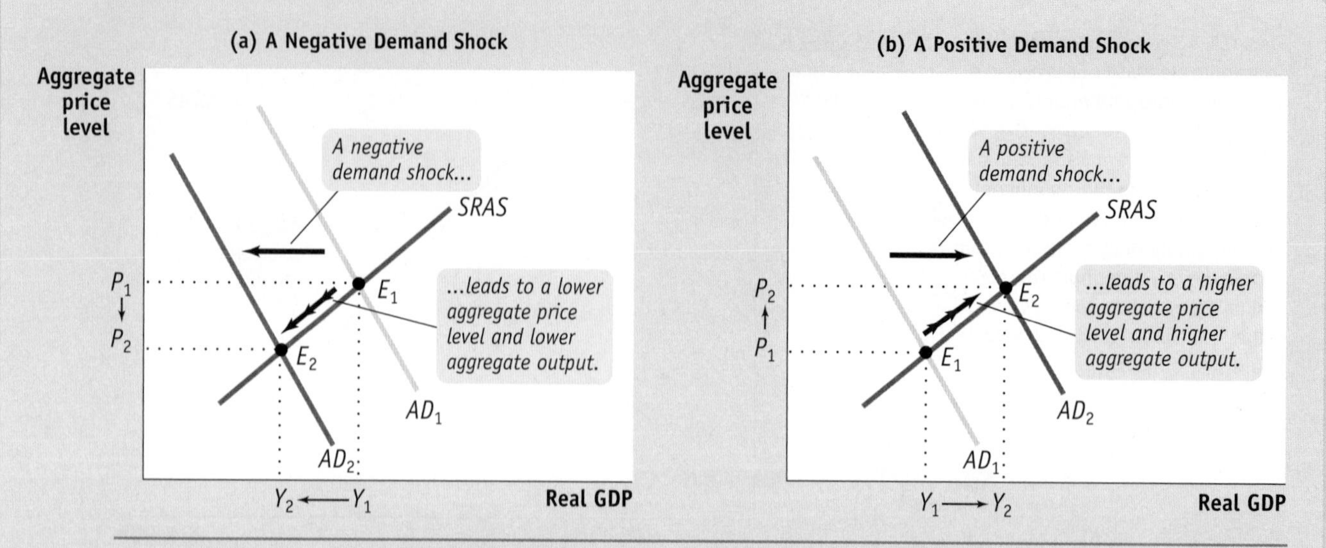

A demand shock shifts the aggregate demand curve, moving the aggregate price level and aggregate output in the same direction. In panel (a), a negative demand shock shifts the aggregate demand curve leftward from AD_1 to AD_2, reducing the aggregate price level from P_1 to P_2 and aggregate output from Y_1 to Y_2. In panel (b), a positive demand shock shifts the aggregate demand curve rightward, increasing the aggregate price level from P_1 to P_2 and aggregate output from Y_1 to Y_2.

left, from AD_1 to AD_2, as shown in panel (a). The economy moves down along the *SRAS* curve from E_1 to E_2, leading to lower short-run equilibrium aggregate output and a lower short-run equilibrium aggregate price level. A positive demand shock shifts the aggregate demand curve, *AD*, to the right, as shown in panel (b). Here, the economy moves up along the *SRAS* curve, from E_1 to E_2. This leads to higher short-run equilibrium aggregate output and a higher short-run equilibrium aggregate price level. Demand shocks cause aggregate output and the aggregate price level to move in the same direction.

Shifts of the *SRAS* Curve

An event that shifts the short-run aggregate supply curve, such as a change in commodity prices, nominal wages, or productivity, is known as a **supply shock.** A *negative* supply shock raises production costs and reduces the quantity producers are willing to supply at any given aggregate price level, leading to a leftward shift of the short-run aggregate supply curve. The U.S. economy experienced severe negative supply shocks following disruptions to world oil supplies in 1973 and 1979. In contrast, a *positive* supply shock reduces production costs and increases the quantity supplied at any given aggregate price level, leading to a rightward shift of the short-run aggregate supply curve. The United States experienced a positive supply shock between 1995 and 2000, when the increasing use of the Internet and other information technologies caused productivity growth to surge.

An event that shifts the short-run aggregate supply curve is a **supply shock.**

The effects of a negative supply shock are shown in panel (a) of Figure 14-11. The initial equilibrium is at E_1, with aggregate price level P_1 and aggregate output Y_1. The disruption in the oil supply causes the short-run aggregate supply curve to shift to the left, from $SRAS_1$ to $SRAS_2$. As a consequence, aggregate output falls and the aggregate price level rises, an upward movement along the *AD* curve. At the new equilibrium, E_2, the short-run equilibrium aggregate price

FIGURE 14-11 Supply Shocks

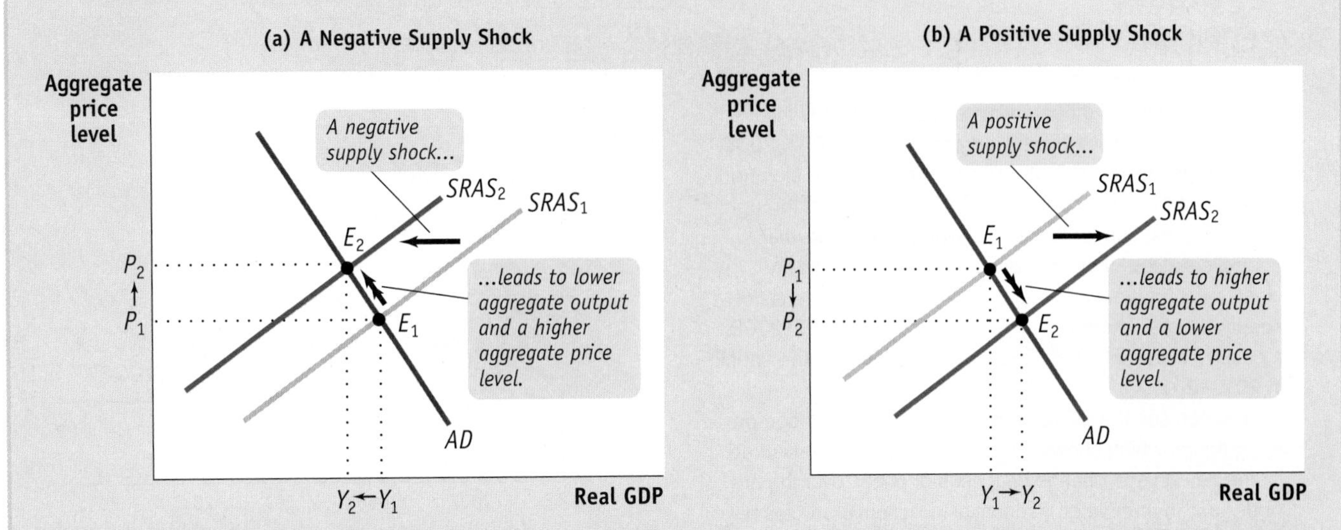

A supply shock shifts the short-run aggregate supply curve, moving the aggregate price level and aggregate output in opposite directions. Panel (a) shows a negative supply shock, which shifts the short-run aggregate supply curve leftward and causes stagflation—lower aggregate output and a higher aggregate price level. Here the short-run aggregate supply curve shifts from $SRAS_1$ to $SRAS_2$, and the economy moves from E_1 to E_2. The aggregate price level rises from P_1 to P_2, and aggregate output falls from Y_1 to Y_2. Panel (b) shows a positive supply shock, which shifts the short-run aggregate supply curve rightward, generating higher aggregate output and a lower aggregate price level. The short-run aggregate supply curve shifts from $SRAS_1$ to $SRAS_2$, and the economy moves from E_1 to E_2. The aggregate price level falls from P_1 to P_2, and aggregate output rises from Y_1 to Y_2.

level, P_2, is higher, and the short-run equilibrium aggregate output level, Y_2, is lower than before.

Stagflation is the combination of inflation and falling aggregate output.

The combination of inflation and falling aggregate output shown in panel (a) has a special name: **stagflation,** for "stagnation plus inflation." When an economy experiences stagflation, it's very unpleasant: falling aggregate output leads to rising unemployment, and people feel that their purchasing power is squeezed by rising prices. Stagflation in the 1970s led to a mood of national pessimism. It also, as we'll see shortly, poses a dilemma for policy makers.

A positive supply shock, shown in panel (b), has exactly the opposite effects. A rightward shift of the *SRAS* curve from $SRAS_1$ to $SRAS_2$ results in a rise in aggregate output and a fall in the aggregate price level, a downward movement along the *AD* curve. The favorable supply shocks of the late 1990s led to a combination of full employment and declining inflation. That is, the aggregate price level fell compared with the long-run trend. This combination produced, for a time, a great wave of national optimism.

The distinctive feature of supply shocks, both negative and positive, is that, unlike demand shocks, they cause the aggregate price level and aggregate output to move in *opposite* directions.

There's another important contrast between supply shocks and demand shocks. As we've seen, monetary policy and fiscal policy enable the government to shift the *AD* curve, meaning that governments

AP Photo/Mark Lennihan

As you can see from the faces of these job seekers, pessimism prevails during stagflation as unemployment and prices rise.

SUPPLY SHOCKS OF THE TWENTY-FIRST CENTURY

The price of oil and other raw materials has been highly unstable in recent years, with surging prices in 2007–2008, plunging prices in 2008–2009, and another surge starting in 2010–2011, with prices remaining at a high level through 2012. The reasons for these wild swings are somewhat controversial, but their macroeconomic implications are clear: much of the world has been subjected to a series of supply shocks. There was a negative shock in 2007–2008, a positive shock in 2008–2009, and another negative shock in 2010–2011.

You can see the effect of these shocks in the accompanying figure, which shows the rate of inflation, as measured by the percentage change in consumer prices over the previous year, in three large economies. Economic policies have been quite different in the United States, Germany (which shares a currency with many other European countries), and China. Yet in all three inflation rose sharply in 2007–2008, fell dramatically thereafter, and rose sharply again in 2011.

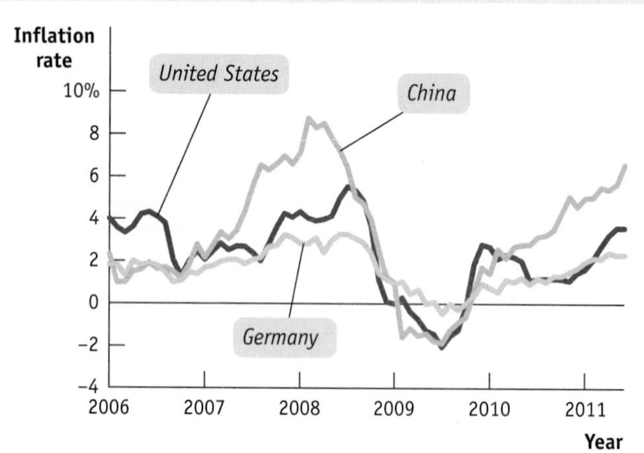

Source: Federal Reserve Bank of St. Louis.

are in a position to create the kinds of shocks shown in Figure 14-10. It's much harder for governments to shift the *AS* curve. Are there good policy reasons to shift the *AD* curve? We'll turn to that question soon. First, however, let's look at the difference between short-run macroeconomic equilibrium and long-run macroeconomic equilibrium.

Long-Run Macroeconomic Equilibrium

Figure 14-12 combines the aggregate demand curve with both the short-run and long-run aggregate supply curves. The aggregate demand curve, *AD,* crosses the short-run aggregate supply curve, *SRAS,* at E_{LR}. Here we assume that enough time has elapsed that the economy is also on the long-run aggregate supply curve, *LRAS.* As a result, E_{LR} is at the intersection of all three curves—*SRAS, LRAS,* and *AD.* So short-run equilibrium aggregate output is equal to potential output, Y_P. Such a situation, in which the point of short-run macroeconomic equilibrium is on the long-run aggregate supply curve, is known as **long-run macroeconomic equilibrium.**

To see the significance of long-run macroeconomic equilibrium, let's consider what happens if a demand shock moves the economy away from long-run macroeconomic equilibrium. In Figure 14-13, we assume that the initial aggregate demand curve is AD_1 and the initial short-run aggregate supply curve is $SRAS_1$. So the initial macroeconomic equilibrium is at E_1, which lies on the long-run aggregate supply curve, *LRAS.* The economy, then, starts from a point of short-run and long-run macroeconomic equilibrium, and short-run equilibrium aggregate output equals potential output at Y_1.

Now suppose that for some reason—such as a sudden worsening of business and consumer expectations—aggregate demand falls and the aggregate demand curve shifts leftward to AD_2. This results in a lower equilibrium aggregate price level at P_2 and a lower equilibrium aggregate output level at Y_2 as the economy settles in the short run at E_2. The short-run effect of such a fall in aggregate

The economy is in **long-run macroeconomic equilibrium** when the point of short-run macroeconomic equilibrium is on the long-run aggregate supply curve.

There is a **recessionary gap** when aggregate output is below potential output.

FIGURE 14-12 Long-Run Macroeconomic Equilibrium

Here the point of short-run macroeconomic equilibrium also lies on the long-run aggregate supply curve, *LRAS*. As a result, short-run equilibrium aggregate output is equal to potential output, Y_P. The economy is in long-run macroeconomic equilibrium at E_{LR}.

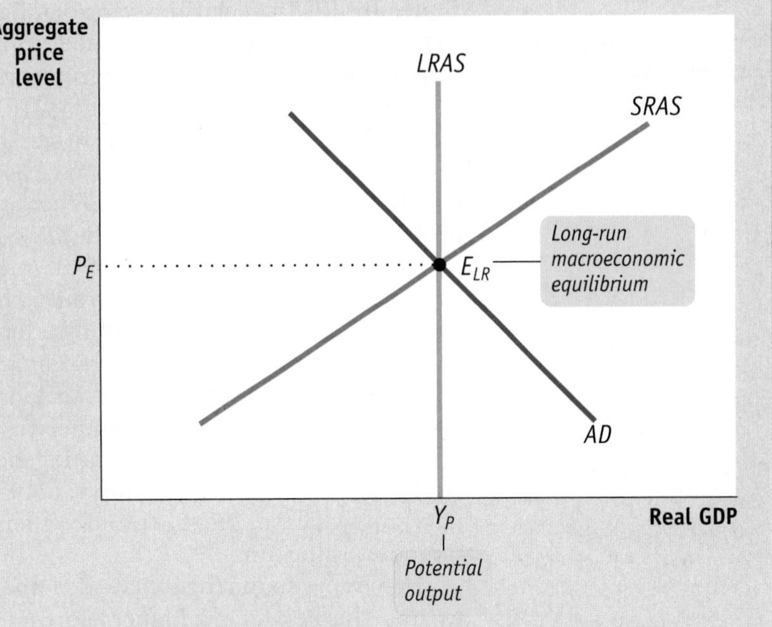

demand is what the U.S. economy experienced in 1929–1933: a falling aggregate price level and falling aggregate output.

Aggregate output in this new short-run equilibrium, E_2, is below potential output. When this happens, the economy faces a **recessionary gap.** A

FIGURE 14-13 Short-Run versus Long-Run Effects of a Negative Demand Shock

In the long run the economy is self-correcting: demand shocks have only a short-run effect on aggregate output. Starting at E_1, a negative demand shock shifts AD_1 leftward to AD_2. In the short run the economy moves to E_2 and a recessionary gap arises: the aggregate price level declines from P_1 to P_2, aggregate output declines from Y_1 to Y_2, and unemployment rises. But in the long run nominal wages fall in response to high unemployment at Y_2, and $SRAS_1$ shifts rightward to $SRAS_2$. Aggregate output rises from Y_2 to Y_1, and the aggregate price level declines again, from P_2 to P_3. Long-run macroeconomic equilibrium is eventually restored at E_3.

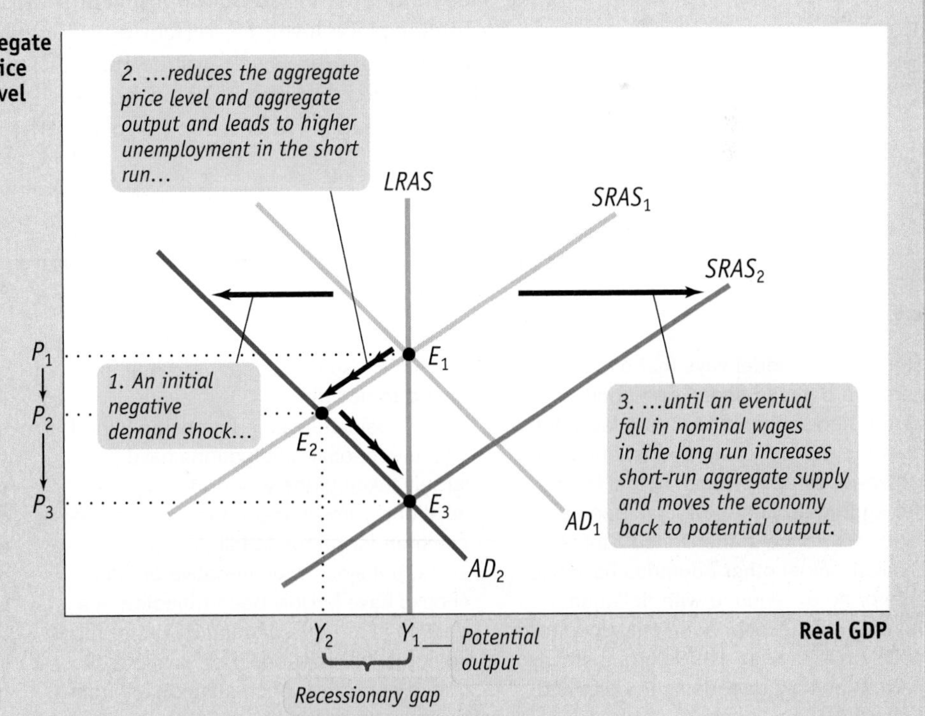

There is an **inflationary gap** when aggregate output is above potential output.

The **output gap** is the percentage difference between actual aggregate output and potential output.

recessionary gap inflicts a great deal of pain because it corresponds to high unemployment. The large recessionary gap that had opened up in the United States by 1933 caused intense social and political turmoil. And the devastating recessionary gap that opened up in Germany at the same time played an important role in Hitler's rise to power.

But this isn't the end of the story. In the face of high unemployment, nominal wages eventually fall, as do any other sticky prices, ultimately leading producers to increase output. As a result, a recessionary gap causes the short-run aggregate supply curve to gradually shift to the right over time. This process continues until $SRAS_1$ reaches its new position at $SRAS_2$, bringing the economy to equilibrium at E_3, where AD_2, $SRAS_2$, and *LRAS* all intersect. At E_3, the economy is back in long-run macroeconomic equilibrium; it is back at potential output Y_1 but at a lower aggregate price level, P_3, reflecting a long-run fall in the aggregate price level. In the end, the economy is *self-correcting* in the long run.

What if, instead, there was an increase in aggregate demand? The results are shown in Figure 14-14, where we again assume that the initial aggregate demand curve is AD_1 and the initial short-run aggregate supply curve is $SRAS_1$, so that the initial macroeconomic equilibrium, at E_1, lies on the long-run aggregate supply curve, *LRAS*. Initially, then, the economy is in long-run macroeconomic equilibrium.

Now suppose that aggregate demand rises, and the *AD* curve shifts rightward to AD_2. This results in a higher aggregate price level, at P_2, and a higher aggregate output level, at Y_2, as the economy settles in the short run at E_2. Aggregate output in this new short-run equilibrium is above potential output, and unemployment is low in order to produce this higher level of aggregate output. When this happens, the economy experiences an **inflationary gap.**

As in the case of a recessionary gap, this isn't the end of the story. In the face of low unemployment, nominal wages will rise, as will other sticky prices. An inflationary gap causes the short-run aggregate supply curve to shift gradually to the left as producers reduce output in the face of rising nominal wages. This process continues until $SRAS_1$ reaches its new position at $SRAS_2$, bringing the economy to equilibrium at E_3, where AD_2, $SRAS_2$, and *LRAS* all intersect. At E_3, the economy is back in long-run macroeconomic equilibrium. It is back at potential output, but at a higher price level, P_3, reflecting a long-run rise in the aggregate price level. Again, the economy is self-correcting in the long run.

To summarize the analysis of how the economy responds to recessionary and inflationary gaps, we can focus on the **output gap,** the percentage difference

FOR INQUIRING MINDS

WHERE'S THE DEFLATION?

The *AD–AS* model says that either a negative demand shock or a positive supply shock should lead to a fall in the aggregate price level—that is, deflation. However, since 1949, an actual fall in the aggregate price level has been a rare occurrence in the United States. Similarly, most other countries have had little or no experience with deflation. Japan, which experienced sustained mild deflation in the late 1990s and the early part of the next decade, is the big (and much discussed) exception. What happened to deflation?

The basic answer is that since World War II economic fluctuations have largely taken place around a long-run inflationary trend. Before the war, it was common for prices to fall during recessions, but since then negative demand shocks have largely been reflected in a *decline in the rate of inflation* rather than an actual fall in prices. For example, the rate of consumer price inflation fell from more than 3% at the beginning of the 2001 recession to 1.1% a year later, but it never went below zero.

All of this changed during the recession of 2007–2009. The negative demand shock that followed the 2008 financial crisis was so severe that, for most of 2009, consumer prices in the United States indeed fell. But the deflationary period didn't last long: beginning in 2010, prices again rose, at a rate of between 1% and 4% per year.

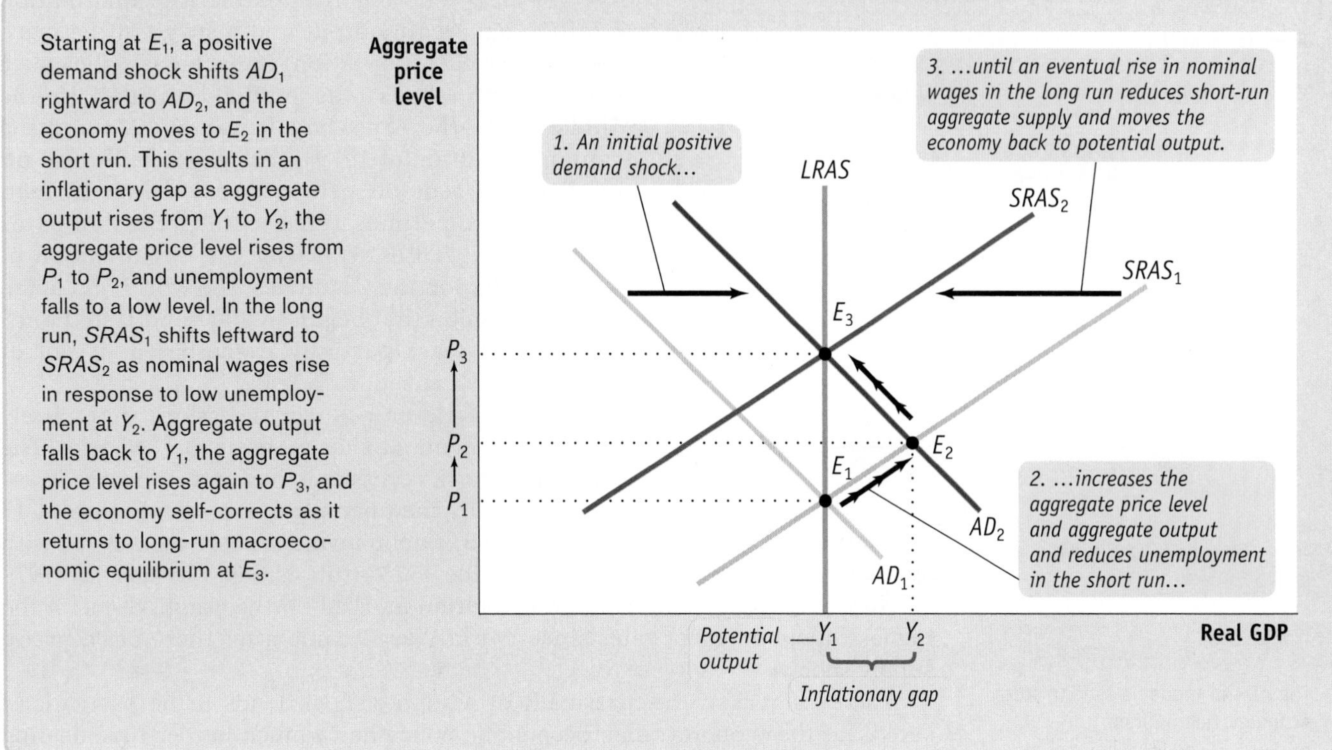

FIGURE 14-14 Short-Run versus Long-Run Effects of a Positive Demand Shock

Starting at E_1, a positive demand shock shifts AD_1 rightward to AD_2, and the economy moves to E_2 in the short run. This results in an inflationary gap as aggregate output rises from Y_1 to Y_2, the aggregate price level rises from P_1 to P_2, and unemployment falls to a low level. In the long run, $SRAS_1$ shifts leftward to $SRAS_2$ as nominal wages rise in response to low unemployment at Y_2. Aggregate output falls back to Y_1, the aggregate price level rises again to P_3, and the economy self-corrects as it returns to long-run macroeconomic equilibrium at E_3.

between actual aggregate output and potential output. The output gap is calculated as follows:

$$\textbf{(14-3)}\ \text{Output gap} = \frac{\text{Actual aggregate output} - \text{Potential output}}{\text{Potential output}} \times 100$$

Our analysis says that the output gap always tends toward zero.

If there is a recessionary gap, so that the output gap is negative, nominal wages eventually fall, moving the economy back to potential output and bringing the output gap back to zero. If there is an inflationary gap, so that the output gap is positive, nominal wages eventually rise, also moving the economy back to potential output and again bringing the output gap back to zero. So in the long run the economy is **self-correcting:** shocks to aggregate demand affect aggregate output in the short run but not in the long run.

ECONOMICS ➤ IN ACTION

SUPPLY SHOCKS VERSUS DEMAND SHOCKS IN PRACTICE

How often do supply shocks and demand shocks, respectively, cause recessions? The verdict of most, though not all, macroeconomists is that recessions are mainly caused by demand shocks. But when a negative supply shock does happen, the resulting recession tends to be particularly severe.

Let's get specific. Officially there have been twelve recessions in the United States since World War II. However, two of these, in 1979–1980 and 1981–1982, are often treated as a single "double-dip" recession, bringing the total number down to eleven. Of these eleven recessions, only two—the

The economy is **self-correcting** when shocks to aggregate demand affect aggregate output in the short run, but not the long run.

FIGURE 14-15 Negative Supply Shocks Are Relatively Rare but Nasty

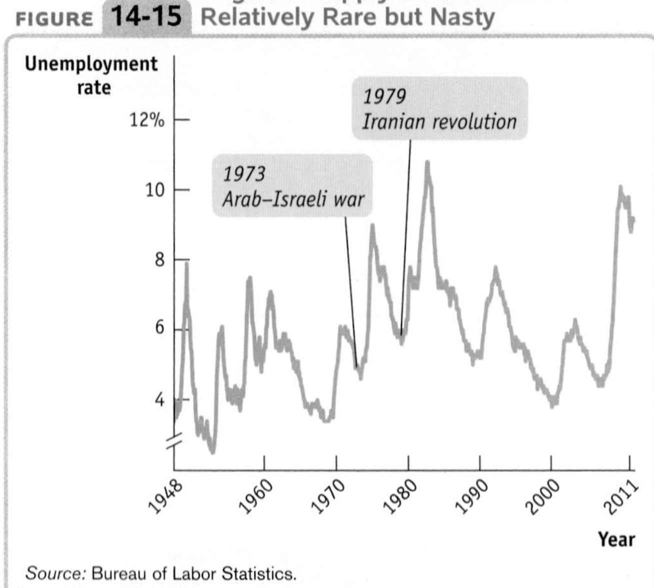

Source: Bureau of Labor Statistics.

recession of 1973–1975 and the double-dip recession of 1979–1982—showed the distinctive combination of falling aggregate output and a surge in the price level that we call stagflation. In each case, the cause of the supply shock was political turmoil in the Middle East—the Arab–Israeli war of 1973 and the Iranian revolution of 1979—that disrupted world oil supplies and sent oil prices skyrocketing. In fact, economists sometimes refer to the two slumps as "OPEC I" and "OPEC II," after the Organization of Petroleum Exporting Countries, the world oil cartel. A third recession that began in 2007 and lasted until 2009 was at least partially exacerbated, if not at least partially caused, by a spike in oil prices.

So eight of eleven postwar recessions were purely the result of demand shocks, not supply shocks. The few supply-shock recessions, however, were the worst as measured by the unemployment rate. Figure 14-15 shows the U.S. unemployment rate since 1948, with the dates of the 1973 Arab–Israeli war and the 1979 Iranian revolution marked on the graph. Some of the highest unemployment rates since World War II came after these big negative supply shocks.

There's a reason the aftermath of a supply shock tends to be particularly severe for the economy: macroeconomic policy has a much harder time dealing with supply shocks than with demand shocks. Indeed, the reason the Federal Reserve was having a hard time in 2008, as described in the opening story, was the fact that in early 2008 the U.S. economy was in a recession partially caused by a supply shock (although it was also facing a demand shock). We'll see in a moment why supply shocks present such a problem.

Quick Review

- The ***AD–AS* model** is used to study economic fluctuations.
- **Short-run macroeconomic equilibrium** occurs at the intersection of the short-run aggregate supply and aggregate demand curves. This determines the **short-run equilibrium aggregate price level** and the level of **short-run equilibrium aggregate output.**
- A **demand shock,** a shift of the *AD* curve, causes the aggregate price level and aggregate output to move in the same direction. A **supply shock,** a shift of the *SRAS* curve, causes them to move in opposite directions. **Stagflation** is the consequence of a negative supply shock.
- A fall in nominal wages occurs in response to a **recessionary gap,** and a rise in nominal wages occurs in response to an **inflationary gap.** Both move the economy to **long-run macroeconomic equilibrium,** where the *AD, SRAS,* and *LRAS* curves intersect.
- The **output gap** always tends toward zero because the economy is **self-correcting** in the long run.

CHECK YOUR UNDERSTANDING 14-3

1. Describe the short-run effects of each of the following shocks on the aggregate price level and on aggregate output.
   a. The government sharply increases the minimum wage, raising the wages of many workers.
   b. Solar energy firms launch a major program of investment spending.
   c. Congress raises taxes and cuts spending.
   d. Severe weather destroys crops around the world.
2. A rise in productivity increases potential output, but some worry that demand for the additional output will be insufficient even in the long run. How would you respond?

Solutions appear at back of book.

Macroeconomic Policy

We've just seen that the economy is self-correcting in the long run: it will eventually trend back to potential output. Most macroeconomists believe, however, that the process of self-correction typically takes a decade or more. In particular, if aggregate output is below potential output, the economy can suffer an extended period of depressed aggregate output and high unemployment before it returns to normal.

This belief is the background to one of the most famous quotations in economics: John Maynard Keynes's declaration, "In the long run we are all dead." We explain the context in which he made this remark in the accompanying For Inquiring Minds.

Economists usually interpret Keynes as having recommended that governments not wait for the economy to correct itself. Instead, it is argued by many economists, but not all, that the government should use monetary and fiscal policy to get the economy back to potential output in the aftermath of a shift of the aggregate demand curve. This is the rationale for an active **stabilization policy,** which is the use of government policy to reduce the severity of recessions and rein in excessively strong expansions.

Stabilization policy is the use of government policy to reduce the severity of recessions and rein in excessively strong expansions.

FOR INQUIRING MINDS

KEYNES AND THE LONG RUN

The British economist Sir John Maynard Keynes (1883–1946), probably more than any other single economist, created the modern field of macroeconomics. One of his lasting contributions was a famous quote on the meaning of the long run.

In 1923 Keynes published *A Tract on Monetary Reform,* a small book on the economic problems of Europe after World War I. In it he decried the tendency of many of his colleagues to focus on how things work out in the long run—as in the long-run macroeconomic equilibrium we have just analyzed—while ignoring the often very painful and possibly disastrous things that can happen along the way. Here's a fuller version of the quote:

> This *long run* is a misleading guide to current affairs. *In the long run* we are all dead. Economists set themselves too easy, too useless a task if in tempestuous seasons they can only tell us that when the storm is long past the sea is flat again.

Keynes focused the attention of economists of his day on the short run.

Can stabilization policy improve the economy's performance? If we reexamine Figure 14-6, the answer certainly appears to be yes. Under active stabilization policy, the U.S. economy returned to potential output in 1996 after an approximately five-year recessionary gap. Likewise, in 2001 it also returned to potential output after an approximately four-year inflationary gap. These periods are much shorter than the decade or more that economists believe it would take for the economy to self-correct in the absence of active stabilization policy. However, as we'll see shortly, the ability to improve the economy's performance is not always guaranteed. It depends on the kinds of shocks the economy faces.

Policy in the Face of Demand Shocks

Imagine that the economy experiences a negative demand shock, like the one shown in Figure 14-13. As we've discussed in this chapter, monetary and fiscal policy shift the aggregate demand curve. If policy makers react quickly to the fall in aggregate demand, they can use monetary or fiscal policy to shift the aggregate demand curve back to the right. And if policy were able to perfectly anticipate shifts of the aggregate demand curve, it could short-circuit the whole process shown in Figure 14-13. Instead of going through a period of low aggregate output and falling prices, the government could manage the economy so that it would stay at E_1.

Why might a policy that short-circuits the adjustment shown in Figure 14-13 and maintains the economy at its original equilibrium be desirable? For two reasons. First, the temporary fall in aggregate output that would happen without policy intervention is a bad thing, particularly because such a decline is associated with high unemployment. Second, as we explained in Chapter 12, *price stability* is generally regarded as a desirable goal. So preventing deflation—a fall in the aggregate price level—is a good thing.

Does this mean that policy makers should always act to offset declines in aggregate demand? Not necessarily. As we'll see in later chapters, some policy measures to increase aggregate demand, especially those that increase budget deficits, may have long-term costs in terms of lower long-run growth. Furthermore, in the real world policy makers aren't perfectly informed, and the effects of their policies aren't perfectly predictable. This creates the danger that stabilization policy will do more harm than good; that is, attempts to stabilize the economy may end up creating more instability. Despite these qualifications, most economists believe that a good case can be made for using macroeconomic policy to offset major negative shocks to the *AD* curve.

Should policy makers also try to offset positive shocks to aggregate demand? It may not seem obvious that they should. After all, even though inflation may be a bad thing, isn't more output and lower unemployment a good thing? Not necessarily. Most economists now believe that any short-run gains from an inflationary gap must be paid back later. So policy makers today usually try to offset positive as well as negative demand shocks. For reasons we'll explain in Chapter 17, attempts to eliminate recessionary gaps and inflationary gaps usually rely on monetary rather than fiscal policy. In 2007 and 2008 the Federal Reserve sharply cut interest rates in an attempt to head off a rising recessionary gap; earlier in the decade, when the U.S. economy seemed headed for an inflationary gap, it raised interest rates to generate the opposite effect.

But how should macroeconomic policy respond to supply shocks?

Responding to Supply Shocks

We've now come full circle to the story that began this chapter. We can now explain why people in Ben Bernanke's position dread stagflation.

Back in panel (a) of Figure 14-11 we showed the effects of a negative supply shock: in the short run such a shock leads to lower aggregate output but a higher aggregate price level. As we've noted, policy makers can respond to a negative *demand* shock by using monetary and fiscal policy to return aggregate demand to its original level. But what can or should they do about a negative *supply* shock?

In contrast to the aggregate demand curve, there are no easy policies that shift the short-run aggregate supply curve. That is, there is no government policy that can easily affect producers' profitability and so compensate for shifts of the shortrun aggregate supply curve. So the policy response to a negative supply shock cannot aim to simply push the curve that shifted back to its original position.

And if you consider using monetary or fiscal policy to shift the aggregate demand curve in response to a supply shock, the right response isn't obvious. Two bad things are happening simultaneously: a fall in aggregate output, leading to a rise in unemployment, *and* a rise in the aggregate price level. Any policy that shifts the aggregate demand curve helps one problem only by making the other worse. If the government acts to increase aggregate demand and limit the rise in unemployment, it reduces the decline in output but causes even more inflation. If it acts to reduce aggregate demand, it curbs inflation but causes a further rise in unemployment.

It's a trade-off with no good answer. In the end, the United States and other economically advanced nations suffering from the supply shocks of the 1970s eventually chose to stabilize prices even at the cost of higher unemployment. But being an economic policy maker in the 1970s, or in early 2008, meant facing even harder choices than usual.

ECONOMICS ➤ IN ACTION

IS STABILIZATION POLICY STABILIZING?

We've described the theoretical rationale for stabilization policy as a way of responding to demand shocks. But does stabilization policy actually stabilize the economy? One way we might try to answer this question is to look at the long-term historical record. Before World War II, the U.S. government didn't really have a stabilization policy, largely because macroeconomics as we know it didn't exist, and there was no consensus about what to do. Since World War II, and especially since 1960, active stabilization policy has become standard practice.

So here's the question: has the economy actually become more stable since the government began trying to stabilize it? The answer is a qualified yes. It's qualified for two reasons. One is that data from the pre–World War II era are less reliable than more modern data. The other is that the severe and protracted slump that began in 2007 has shaken confidence in the effectiveness of government policy. Still, there seems to have been a reduction in the size of fluctuations.

Figure 14-16 shows the number of unemployed as a percentage of the nonfarm labor force since 1890. (We focus on nonfarm workers because farmers, though they often suffer economic hardship, are rarely reported as unemployed.) Even ignoring the huge spike in unemployment during the Great Depression, unemployment seems to have varied a lot more before World War II than after. It's also worth noticing that the peaks in postwar unemployment, in 1975, 1982, and, as we described earlier, to some extent in 2010, corresponded to major supply shocks—the kind of shock for which stabilization policy has no good answer.

It's possible that the greater stability of the economy reflects good luck rather than policy. But on the face of it, the evidence suggests that stabilization policy is indeed stabilizing.

FIGURE 14-16 Has Stabilization Policy Been Stabilizing?

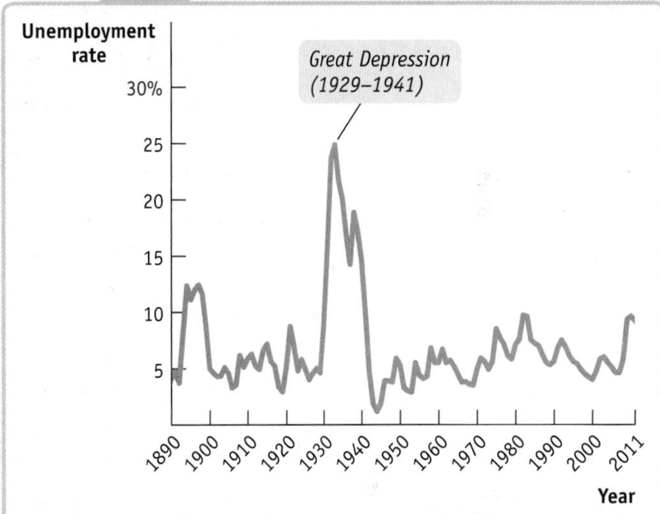

Sources: Christina Romer, "Spurious Volatility in Historical Unemployment Data." *Journal of Political Economy* 94, no. 1 (1986): 1–37 (years 1890–1928); Bureau of Labor Statistics (years 1929–2011).

Quick Review

- **Stabilization policy** is the use of fiscal or monetary policy to offset demand shocks. There can be drawbacks, however. Such policies may lead to a long-term rise in the budget deficit and lower long-run growth because of crowding out. And, due to incorrect predictions, a misguided policy can increase economic instability.
- Negative supply shocks pose a policy dilemma because fighting the slump in aggregate output worsens inflation and fighting inflation worsens the slump.

CHECK YOUR UNDERSTANDING 14-4

1. Suppose someone says, "Using monetary or fiscal policy to pump up the economy is counterproductive—you get a brief high, but then you have the pain of inflation."
   a. Explain what this means in terms of the *AD–AS* model.
   b. Is this a valid argument against stabilization policy? Why or why not?
2. In 2008, in the aftermath of the collapse of the housing bubble and a sharp rise in the price of commodities, particularly oil, there was much internal disagreement within the Fed about how to respond, with some advocating lowering interest rates and others contending that this would set off a rise in inflation. Explain the reasoning behind each one of these views in terms of the *AD–AS* model.

Solutions appear at back of book.

WORKED PROBLEM

A Shocking Analysis

During the financial crisis in autumn 2008, the financial system delivered a sobering shock to the economy when the stock market lost about half of its value. Soon afterward, consumer spending came to a screeching halt. Within six months of the crash, GDP fell by 2.5% and the price level fell by 2.8%. Show how an analysis of aggregate demand and aggregate supply could have predicted this short-run effect on aggregate output and the aggregate price level. Assuming no government intervention, what would you have predicted in the long run?

STEP 1: Draw and label the aggregate demand curve and the short-run aggregate supply curve. Find and label the initial equilibrium point, the initial price level, and the initial output level.

Read the section "Short-Run Macroeconomic Equilibrium" beginning on page 428. Study Figure 14-9. Label the horizontal axis "Real GDP," the vertical axis "Aggregate price level," and the initial equilibrium point E_1. The initial price level and output levels should be labeled P_1 and Y_1, respectively.

The aggregate demand curve and the short-run aggregate supply curve are shown in the diagram below. The initial equilibrium point is labeled E_1, the initial price level is labeled P_1, and the initial output level is labeled Y_1. ■

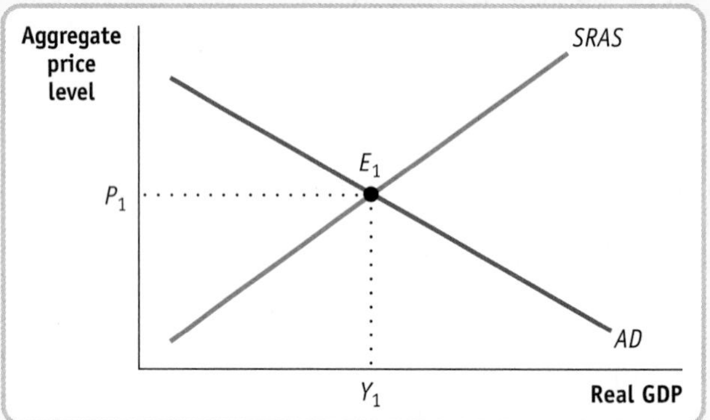

STEP 2: Using your figure from Step 1, analyze the short-run effect of the stock market fall on aggregate demand and aggregate supply by drawing a new curve representing aggregate demand after the stock market fall.

Read the section "Shifts of the Aggregate Demand Curve" beginning on page 414. A fall in the stock market represents a fall in the real value of household assets. Then read the section, "Shifts of Aggregate Demand: Short-Run Effects" beginning on page 429. Study panel (a) of Figure 14-10. Label the initial aggregate demand curve "AD_1," and the aggregate demand curve after the stock market fall "AD_2."

A decrease in household wealth will reduce consumer spending. Beginning at the equilibrium point, E_1 in the accompanying diagram, the aggregate demand curve will shift from AD_1 to AD_2. The economy will be in short-run macroeconomic equilibrium at point E_2. The aggregate price level will be lower than at P_1, and aggregate output will be lower than output at the original equilibrium point. ■

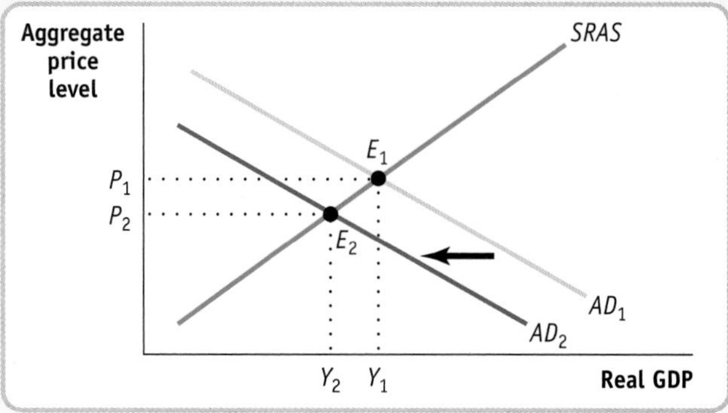

STEP 3: Draw the long-run aggregate supply curve through the initial equilibrium point E_1, and label the recessionary gap.

Read the first part of the section "Long-Run Macroeconomic Equilibrium" beginning on page 432. Study Figures 14-12 and 14-13 on page 433.

The long-run aggregate supply curve is drawn in the diagram below. The economy now faces a recessionary gap between Y_1 and Y_2. ■

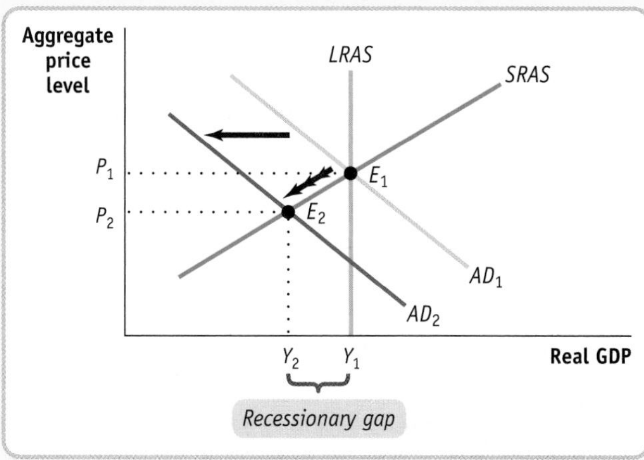

STEP 4: What would you predict in the long run?

Read the section, "Long-Run Macroeconomic Equilibrium" beginning on page 432. Study Figure 14-13 on page 433.

As wage contracts are renegotiated, nominal wages will fall and the short-run aggregate supply curve will shift gradually to the right over time until it reaches

$SRAS_2$ and intersects AD_2 at point E_3. At E_3, the economy is back at its potential output but at a much lower aggregate price level. ■

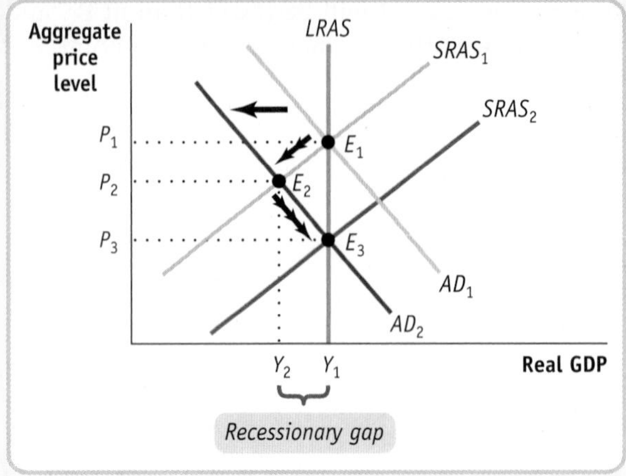

SUMMARY

1. The **aggregate demand curve** shows the relationship between the aggregate price level and the quantity of aggregate output demanded.

2. The aggregate demand curve is downward sloping for two reasons. The first is the **wealth effect of a change in the aggregate price level**—a higher aggregate price level reduces the purchasing power of households' wealth and reduces consumer spending. The second is the **interest rate effect of a change in the aggregate price level**—a higher aggregate price level reduces the purchasing power of households' and firms' money holdings, leading to a rise in interest rates and a fall in investment spending and consumer spending.

3. The aggregate demand curve shifts because of changes in expectations, changes in wealth not due to changes in the aggregate price level, and the effect of the size of the existing stock of physical capital. Policy makers can use fiscal policy and monetary policy to shift the aggregate demand curve.

4. The **aggregate supply curve** shows the relationship between the aggregate price level and the quantity of aggregate output supplied.

5. The **short-run aggregate supply curve** is upward sloping because **nominal wages** are **sticky** in the short run: a higher aggregate price level leads to higher profit per unit of output and increased aggregate output in the short run.

6. Changes in commodity prices, nominal wages, and productivity lead to changes in producers' profits and shift the short-run aggregate supply curve.

7. In the long run, all prices, including nominal wages, are flexible and the economy produces at its **potential output.** If actual aggregate output exceeds potential output, nominal wages will eventually rise in response to low unemployment and aggregate output will fall. If potential output exceeds actual aggregate output, nominal wages will eventually fall in response to high unemployment and aggregate output will rise. So the **long-run aggregate supply curve** is vertical at potential output.

8. In the ***AD–AS* model,** the intersection of the short-run aggregate supply curve and the aggregate demand curve is the point of **short-run macroeconomic equilibrium.** It determines the **short-run equilibrium aggregate price level** and the level of **short-run equilibrium aggregate output.**

9. Economic fluctuations occur because of a shift of the aggregate demand curve (a *demand shock*) or the short-run aggregate supply curve (a *supply shock*). A **demand shock** causes the aggregate price level and aggregate output to move in the same direction as the economy moves along the short-run aggregate supply curve. A **supply shock** causes them to move in opposite directions as the economy moves along the aggregate demand curve. A particularly nasty occurrence is **stagflation**—inflation and falling aggregate output—which is caused by a negative supply shock.

10. Demand shocks have only short-run effects on aggregate output because the economy is **self-correcting** in the long run. In a **recessionary gap,** an eventual fall in nominal wages moves the economy to **long-run macroeconomic equilibrium,** where aggregate output is equal to potential output. In an **inflationary gap,** an eventual rise in nominal wages moves the economy to long-run macroeconomic equilibrium. We can use the **output gap,** the percentage difference between actual aggregate output and potential output, to summarize how the economy responds to recessionary and inflationary gaps. Because the economy tends to be self-correcting in the long run, the output gap always tends toward zero.

11. The high cost—in terms of unemployment—of a recessionary gap and the future adverse consequences of an inflationary gap lead many economists to advocate active **stabilization policy:** using fiscal or monetary policy to offset demand shocks. There can be drawbacks, however, because such policies may contribute to a long-term rise in the budget deficit and crowding out of private investment, leading to lower long-run growth. Also, poorly timed policies can increase economic instability.

12. Negative supply shocks pose a policy dilemma: a policy that counteracts the fall in aggregate output by increasing aggregate demand will lead to higher inflation, but a policy that counteracts inflation by reducing aggregate demand will deepen the output slump.

KEY TERMS

Aggregate demand curve, p. 412
Wealth effect of a change in the aggregate price level, p. 413
Interest rate effect of a change in the aggregate price level, p. 414
Aggregate supply curve, p. 418
Nominal wage, p. 419
Sticky wages, p. 419
Short-run aggregate supply curve, p. 420
Long-run aggregate supply curve, p. 424
Potential output, p. 425
AD–AS model, p. 428
Short-run macroeconomic equilibrium, p. 428
Short-run equilibrium aggregate price level, p. 428
Short-run equilibrium aggregate output, p. 428
Demand shock, p. 429
Supply shock, p. 430
Stagflation, p. 431
Long-run macroeconomic equilibrium, p. 432
Recessionary gap, p. 432
Inflationary gap, p. 434
Output gap, p. 434
Self-correcting, p. 435
Stabilization policy, p. 437

PROBLEMS

1. A fall in the value of the dollar against other currencies makes U.S. final goods and services cheaper to foreigners even though the U.S. aggregate price level stays the same. As a result, foreigners demand more American aggregate output. Your study partner says that this represents a movement down the aggregate demand curve because foreigners are demanding more in response to a lower price. You, however, insist that this represents a rightward shift of the aggregate demand curve. Who is right? Explain.

2. Your study partner is confused by the upward-sloping short-run aggregate supply curve and the vertical long-run aggregate supply curve. How would you explain this?

3. Suppose that in Wageland all workers sign annual wage contracts each year on January 1. No matter what happens to prices of final goods and services during the year, all workers earn the wage specified in their annual contract. This year, prices of final goods and services fall unexpectedly after the contracts are signed. Answer the following questions using a diagram and assume that the economy starts at potential output.

   a. In the short run, how will the quantity of aggregate output supplied respond to the fall in prices?

   b. What will happen when firms and workers renegotiate their wages?

4. In each of the following cases, in the short run, determine whether the events cause a shift of a curve or a movement along a curve. Determine which curve is involved and the direction of the change.

   a. As a result of an increase in the value of the dollar in relation to other currencies, American producers now pay less in dollar terms for foreign steel, a major commodity used in production.

   b. An increase in the quantity of money by the Federal Reserve increases the quantity of money that people wish to lend, lowering interest rates.

   c. Greater union activity leads to higher nominal wages.

   d. A fall in the aggregate price level increases the purchasing power of households' and firms' money holdings. As a result, they borrow less and lend more.

5. The economy is at point A in the accompanying diagram. Suppose that the aggregate price level rises from P_1 to P_2. How will aggregate supply adjust in the short run and in the long run to the increase in the aggregate price level? Illustrate with a diagram.

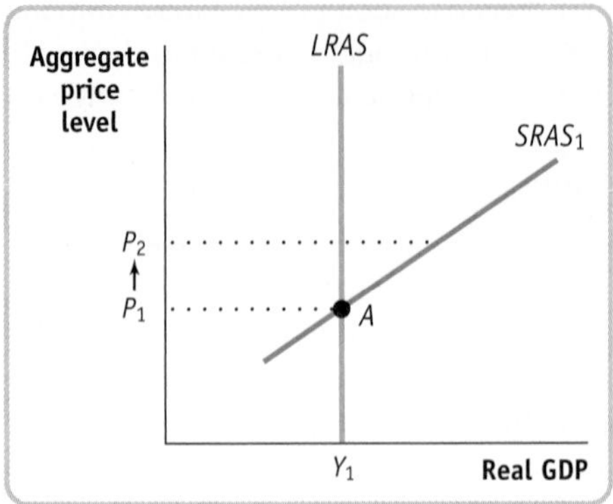

6. Suppose that all households hold all their wealth in assets that automatically rise in value when the aggregate price level rises (an example of this is what is called an "inflation-indexed bond"—a bond whose interest rate, among other things, changes one-for-one with the inflation rate). What happens to the wealth effect of a change in the aggregate price level as a result of this allocation of assets? What happens to the slope of the aggregate demand curve? Will it still slope downward? Explain.

7. Suppose that the economy is currently at potential output. Also suppose that you are an economic policy maker and that a college economics student asks you to rank, if possible, your most preferred to least preferred type of shock: positive demand shock, negative demand shock, positive supply shock, negative supply shock. How would you rank them and why?

8. Explain whether the following government policies affect the aggregate demand curve or the short-run aggregate supply curve and how.

a. The government reduces the minimum nominal wage.

b. The government increases Temporary Assistance to Needy Families (TANF) payments, government transfers to families with dependent children.

c. To reduce the budget deficit, the government announces that households will pay much higher taxes beginning next year.

d. The government reduces military spending.

9. In Wageland, all workers sign an annual wage contract each year on January 1. In late January, a new computer operating system is introduced that increases labor productivity dramatically. Explain how Wageland will move from one short-run macroeconomic equilibrium to another. Illustrate with a diagram.

10. The Conference Board publishes the Consumer Confidence Index (CCI) every month based on a survey of 5,000 representative U.S. households. It is used by many economists to track the state of the economy. A press release by the Board on June 28, 2011 stated: "The Conference Board Consumer Confidence Index, which had declined in May, decreased again in June. The Index now stands at 58.5 (1985 = 100), down from 61.7 in May."

a. As an economist, is this news encouraging for economic growth?

b. Explain your answer to part a with the help of the *AD–AS* model. Draw a typical diagram showing two equilibrium points (E_1) and (E_2). Label the vertical axis "Aggregate price level" and the horizontal axis "Real GDP." Assume that all other major macroeconomic factors remain unchanged.

c. How should the government respond to this news? What are some policy measures that could be used to help neutralize the effect of falling consumer confidence?

11. There were two major shocks to the U.S. economy in 2007, leading to the severe recession of 2007–2009. One shock was related to oil prices; the other was the slump in the housing market. This question analyzes the effect of these two shocks on GDP using the *AD–AS* framework.

a. Draw typical aggregate demand and short-run aggregate supply curves. Label the horizontal axis "Real GDP" and the vertical axis "Aggregate price level." Label the equilibrium point E_1, the equilibrium quantity Y_1, and equilibrium price P_1.

b. Data taken from the Department of Energy indicate that the average price of crude oil in the world increased from \$54.63 per barrel on January 5, 2007, to \$92.93 on December 28, 2007. Would an increase in oil prices cause a demand shock or a supply shock? Redraw the diagram from part a to illustrate the effect of this shock by shifting the appropriate curve.

c. The Housing Price Index, published by the Office of Federal Housing Enterprise Oversight, calculates that U.S. home prices fell by an average of 3.0% in the 12 months between January 2007 and January 2008. Would the fall in home prices cause a supply shock or demand shock? Redraw the diagram from part b to illustrate the effect of this shock by shifting the appropriate curve. Label the new equilibrium point E_3, the equilibrium quantity Y_3, and equilibrium price P_3.

d. Compare the equilibrium points E_1 and E_3 in your diagram for part c. What was the effect of the two shocks on real GDP and the aggregate price level (increase, decrease, or indeterminate)?

EXTEND YOUR UNDERSTANDING

12. Using aggregate demand, short-run aggregate supply, and long-run aggregate supply curves, explain the process by which each of the following economic events will move the economy from one long-run macroeconomic equilibrium to another. Illustrate with diagrams. In each case, what are the short-run and long-run effects on the aggregate price level and aggregate output?

a. There is a decrease in households' wealth due to a decline in the stock market.

b. The government lowers taxes, leaving households with more disposable income, with no corresponding reduction in government purchases.

13. Using aggregate demand, short-run aggregate supply, and long-run aggregate supply curves, explain the process by which each of the following government policies will move the economy from one long-run macroeconomic equilibrium to another. Illustrate with diagrams. In each case, what are the short-run and long-run effects on the aggregate price level and aggregate output?

a. There is an increase in taxes on households.

b. There is an increase in the quantity of money.

c. There is an increase in government spending.

14. The economy is in short-run macroeconomic equilibrium at point E_1 in the accompanying diagram. Based on the diagram, answer the following questions.

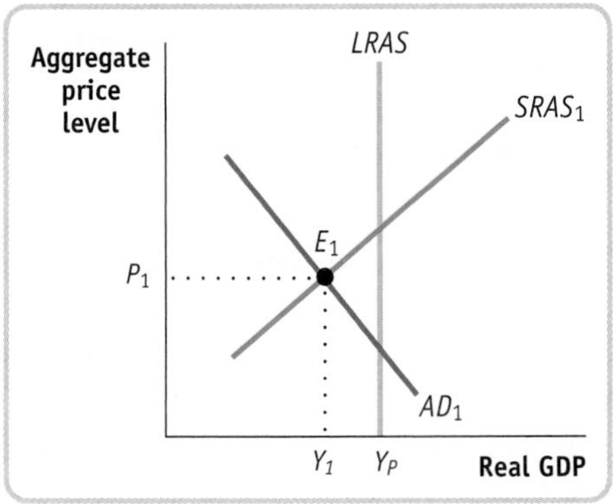

a. Is the economy facing an inflationary or a recessionary gap?

b. What policies can the government implement that might bring the economy back to long-run macroeconomic equilibrium? Illustrate with a diagram.

c. If the government did not intervene to close this gap, would the economy return to long-run macroeconomic equilibrium? Explain and illustrate with a diagram.

d. What are the advantages and disadvantages of the government implementing policies to close the gap?

15. In the accompanying diagram, the economy is in long-run macroeconomic equilibrium at point E_1 when an oil shock shifts the short-run aggregate supply curve to $SRAS_2$. Based on the diagram, answer the following questions.

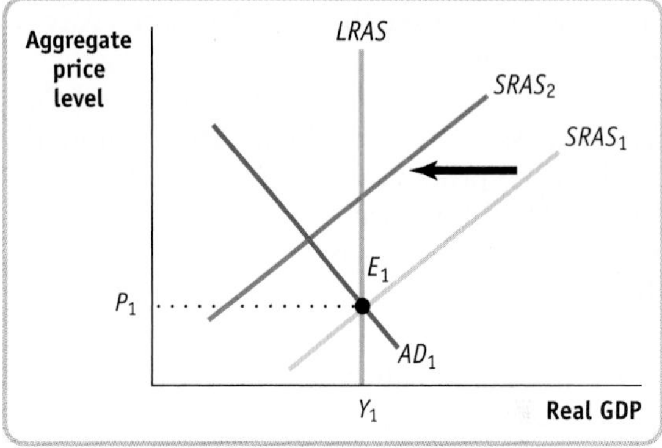

a. How do the aggregate price level and aggregate output change in the short run as a result of the oil shock? What is this phenomenon known as?

b. What fiscal or monetary policies can the government use to address the effects of the supply shock? Use a diagram that shows the effect of policies chosen to address the change in real GDP. Use another diagram to show the effect of policies chosen to address the change in the aggregate price level.

c. Why do supply shocks present a dilemma for government policy makers?

16. The late 1990s in the United States was characterized by substantial economic growth with low inflation; that is, real GDP increased with little, if any, increase in the aggregate price level. Explain this experience using aggregate demand and aggregate supply curves. Illustrate with a diagram.

BUSINESS CASE • Big Box Boom

AP Photo/Morry Gash

After 20 years of being sluggish, U.S. productivity growth accelerated sharply in the late 1990s; that is, productivity began to grow at a much faster rate than previously. What caused that acceleration? Was it the rise of the Internet?

Not according to analysts at McKinsey and Co., the famous business consulting firm. They found that a major source of productivity improvement after 1995 was a surge in output per worker in retailing—stores were selling much more merchandise per worker.

Other analysts agree. The accompanying figure shows the result of an analysis of total factor productivity growth in France, Germany, and the United States between 1995 and 2004, the decade of the U.S. productivity surge. As you can see, the United States did considerably better than either European nation. The key to the surge was very fast growth in the productivity of the distribution sector, that is, in wholesale and retail trade.

U.S. and European Productivity Growth, 1995–2004

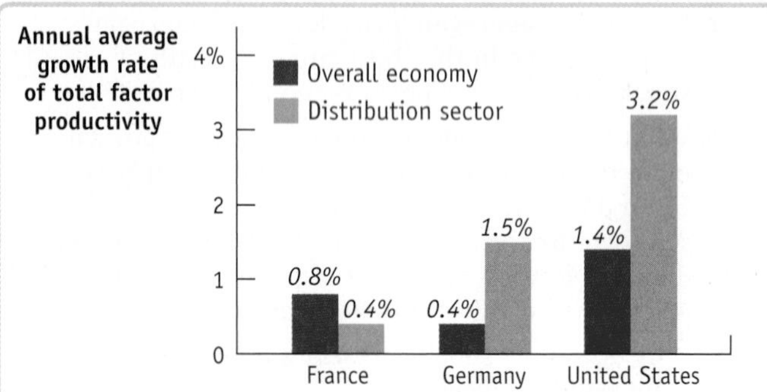

Source: Bart Van Ark, "Productivity, Sources of Growth and Potential Output in the Euro Area and the United States," *Intereconomics* 45, no. 1 (2010). Brussels: Center for European Policy Studies.

Why did productivity surge in retailing in the United States? "The reason can be explained in just two syllables: Walmart," wrote McKinsey.

Walmart is famed in the business world for its successful focus on the unglamorous but crucial area of *logistics*: getting stuff where it was needed, when it was needed. For example, it was one of the first companies to use computers to track inventory, to use bar-code scanners, to establish direct electronic links with suppliers, and so on. These practices gave it a huge advantage over competitors, leading to high profits and rapid expansion. Other firms, observing Walmart's success, have emulated its business practices, spreading productivity gains through the economy as a whole.

There are two lessons from the "Walmart effect," as McKinsey calls it. One is that how you apply a technology makes all the difference: everyone in the retail business knew about computers, but Walmart figured out what to do with them. The other is that a lot of economic growth comes from everyday improvements rather than flashy new technologies.

QUESTIONS FOR THOUGHT

1. In Chapter 13 we described several sources of productivity growth. Which of these sources corresponds to the "Walmart effect"?
2. How does our description of Walmart's role tie in with the New Growth Theory?
3. How does the Walmart story relate to the "information technology paradox"?

BUSINESS CASE • United in Pain

Bayne Stanley/Alamy

The airline industry is notoriously cyclical. That is, instead of making profits all through the business cycle, it tends to plunge into losses during recessions, only regaining profitability sometime after recovery begins. Mainly this is because airlines have large fixed costs that remain high even if ticket sales slump. The cost of operating a flight from one city to another is pretty much the same whether the flight is fully booked or two-thirds empty, so when business slumps for whatever reason, even highly profitable routes quickly become money-losers. It's true that airlines can to some extent adapt to a decline in business by switching to smaller planes, consolidating flights, and so on, but this process takes time and still tends to leave costs per passenger higher than before.

But some recessions are worse for airlines than for other businesses, because operating costs rise even as demand falls. This was very much the case in early 2008. In the spring of that year, the so-called Great Recession of 2007–2009 was still in its early stages, with unemployment just starting to rise. Yet airlines were already, as an article in the *Los Angeles Times* put it, in a "sea of red ink." The article highlighted the case of United Airlines, which had suddenly plunged into large losses and was planning large layoffs.

Why was United in so much trouble? Business travel had started to slacken, but at that point leisure travel, such as flights to Disney World, was still holding up. What was hurting United and its sister airlines was the cost of fuel, which soared in late 2007 and early 2008.

Fuel prices fell back down in late 2008. But by that time United was suffering from a sharp drop in ticket sales. The airline finally returned to profitability in 2010, which was also the year it agreed to merge with Continental. In 2011, United Continental earned $840 million in profits, offsetting high fuel prices with increased revenue. But the news was far more bleak in 2012 when the airline, faced with operational and other problems, lost over $700 million.

QUESTIONS FOR THOUGHT

1. How did United's problems in early 2008 relate to our analysis of the causes of recessions?
2. Ben Bernanke had to make a choice between fighting two evils in early 2008. How would that choice affect United compared with, say, a company producing a service without expensive raw-material inputs, like health care?
3. In early 2008, business travel was beginning to slacken, but leisure travel was still holding up. Given the situation the overall economy was in, what would you expect to happen to leisure travel as the economy moved further into recession?

Fiscal Policy

TO STIMULATE OR NOT TO STIMULATE?

WHAT YOU WILL LEARN IN THIS CHAPTER

- What fiscal policy is and why it is an important tool in managing economic fluctuations
- Which policies constitute an **expansionary fiscal policy** and which constitute a **contractionary fiscal policy**
- Why fiscal policy has a **multiplier** effect and how this effect is influenced by **automatic stabilizers**
- Why governments calculate the **cyclically adjusted budget balance**
- Why a large **public debt** may be a cause for concern
- Why **implicit liabilities** of the government are also a cause for concern

ON FEBRUARY 17, 2009, PRESIDENT Obama signed the American Recovery and Reinvestment Act, a $787 billion package of spending, aid, and tax cuts intended to help the struggling U.S. economy reverse a severe recession that began in December 2007. A week earlier, as the bill neared final passage in Congress, Obama hailed the measure: "It is the right size; it is the right scope. Broadly speaking it has the right priorities to create jobs that will jumpstart our economy and transform it for the twenty-first century."

Others weren't so sure. Some argued that the government should be cutting spending, not increasing it, at a time when American families were suffering. "It's time for government to tighten their belts and show the American people that we 'get' it," said John Boehner, the leader of Republicans in the House of Representatives. Some economic analysts warned that the stimulus bill, as the Recovery Act was commonly called, would drive up interest rates and increase the burden of national debt.

Others had the opposite complaint—that the stimulus was too small given the economy's troubles. For example, Joseph Stiglitz, the 2001 recipient of the Nobel Prize in economics, stated about the stimulus, "First of all that it was not enough should be pretty apparent from what I just said: It is trying to offset the deficiency in aggregate demand and it is just too small."

Nor did the passage of time resolve these disputes. True, some predictions were proved false. On one side, Obama's hope that the bill would "jumpstart" the economy fell short: although the recession officially ended in June 2009, unemployment remained high through 2011 and into 2012, by which time the stimulus had largely run its course. On the other side, the soaring interest rates predicted by stimulus opponents failed to materialize, as U.S. borrowing costs remained low by historical standards. But the net effect of the stimulus remained controversial, with opponents arguing that it had failed to help the economy and defenders arguing that things would have been much worse without the bill.

Whatever the verdict—and this is one of those issues that economists and historians will probably be arguing about for decades to come—the Recovery Act of 2009 was a classic example of *fiscal policy*, the use of government spending and taxes to manage aggregate demand. In this chapter we'll see how fiscal policy fits into the models of economic fluctuations we studied in Chapter 14. We'll also see why budget deficits and government debt can be a problem and how short-run and long-run concerns can pull fiscal policy in different directions.

Social insurance programs are government programs intended to protect families against economic hardship.

Fiscal Policy: The Basics

Let's begin with the obvious: modern governments in economically advanced countries spend a great deal of money and collect a lot in taxes. Figure 15-1 shows government spending and tax revenue as percentages of GDP for a selection of high-income countries in 2007. (We focus on 2007, rather than a more recent year, because it was a largely "normal" year. The numbers for later years were very much affected by the financial crisis of 2008 and its aftermath.) As you can see, the Swedish government sector is relatively large, accounting for more than half of the Swedish economy. The government of the United States plays a smaller role in the economy than those of Canada or most European countries. But that role is still sizable, with the government playing a major role in the U.S. economy. As a result, changes in the federal budget—changes in government spending or in taxation—can have large effects on the American economy.

FIGURE 15-1 Government Spending and Tax Revenue for Some High-Income Countries in 2007

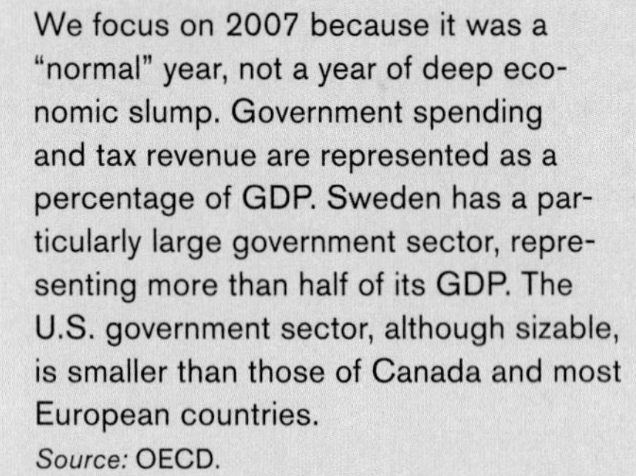
We focus on 2007 because it was a "normal" year, not a year of deep economic slump. Government spending and tax revenue are represented as a percentage of GDP. Sweden has a particularly large government sector, representing more than half of its GDP. The U.S. government sector, although sizable, is smaller than those of Canada and most European countries.
Source: OECD.

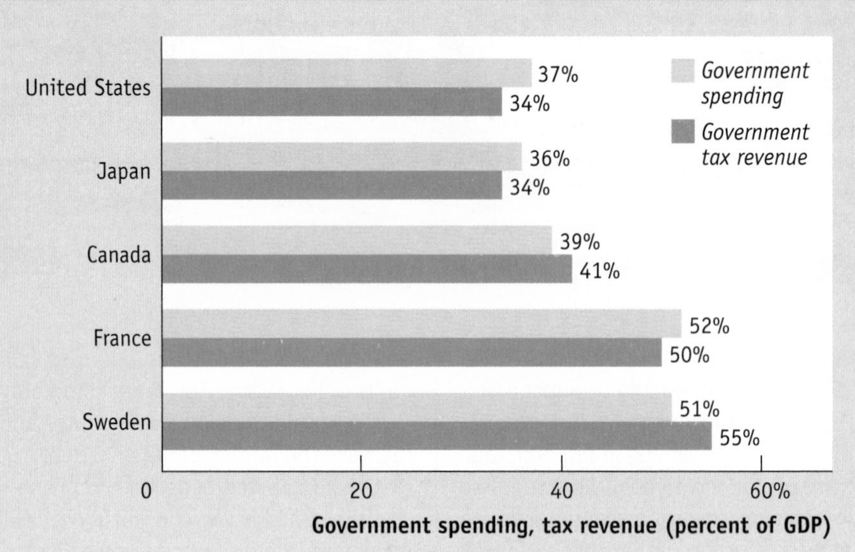

To analyze these effects, we begin by showing how taxes and government spending affect the economy's flow of income. Then we can see how changes in spending and tax policy affect aggregate demand.

Taxes, Purchases of Goods and Services, Government Transfers, and Borrowing

What kinds of taxes do Americans pay, and where does the money go? Figure 15-2 shows the composition of U.S. tax revenue in 2007. Taxes, of course, are required payments to the government. In the United States, taxes are collected at the national level by the federal government; at the state level by each state government; and at local levels by counties, cities, and towns. At the federal level, the taxes that generate the greatest revenue are income taxes on both personal income and corporate profits as well as *social insurance* taxes, which we'll explain shortly. At the state and local levels, the picture is more complex:

these governments rely on a mix of sales taxes, property taxes, income taxes, and fees of various kinds. Overall, taxes on personal income and corporate profits accounted for 48% of total government revenue in 2007; social insurance taxes accounted for 25%; and a variety of other taxes, collected mainly at the state and local levels, accounted for the rest.

Figure 15-3 shows the composition of total U.S. government spending in 2007, which takes two broad forms. One form is purchases of goods and services. This includes everything from ammunition for the military to the salaries of public school teachers (who are treated in the national accounts as providers of a service—education). The big items here are national defense and education. The large category labeled "Other goods and services" consists mainly of state and local spending on a variety of services, from police and firefighters to highway construction and maintenance.

The other form of government spending is government transfers, which are payments by the government to households for which no good or service is provided in return. In the modern United States, as well as in Canada and Europe, government transfers represent a very large proportion of the budget. Most U.S. government spending on transfer payments is accounted for by three big programs:

- Social Security, which provides guaranteed income to older Americans, disabled Americans, and the surviving spouses and dependent children of deceased or retired beneficiaries
- Medicare, which covers much of the cost of health care for Americans over age 65
- Medicaid, which covers much of the cost of health care for Americans with low incomes

The term **social insurance** is used to describe government programs that are intended to protect families against economic hardship. These include Social Security, Medicare, and Medicaid, as well as smaller programs such as unemployment insurance and food stamps. In the United States, social insurance programs are largely paid for with special, dedicated taxes on wages—the social insurance taxes we mentioned earlier.

But how do tax policy and government spending affect the economy? The answer is that taxation and government spending have a strong effect on total aggregate spending in the economy.

The Government Budget and Total Spending

Let's recall the basic equation of national income accounting:

(15-1) $GDP = C + I + G + X - IM$

The left-hand side of this equation is GDP, the value of all final goods and services produced in the economy. The

FIGURE **15-2** Sources of Tax Revenue in the United States, 2007

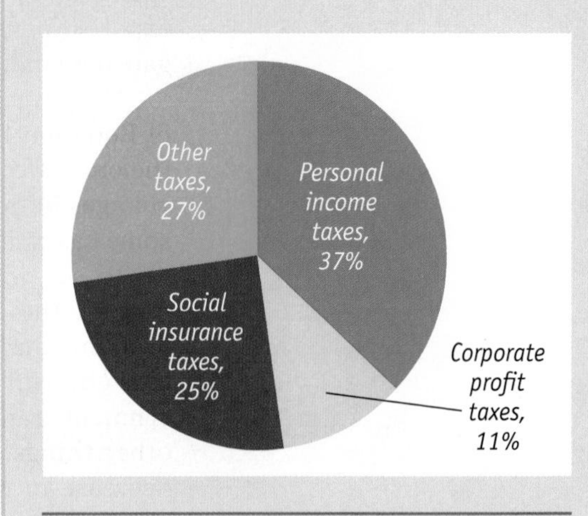

Personal income taxes, taxes on corporate profits, and social insurance taxes account for most government tax revenue. The rest is a mix of property taxes, sales taxes, and other sources of revenue.
Source: Bureau of Economic Analysis.

FIGURE **15-3** Government Spending in the United States, 2007

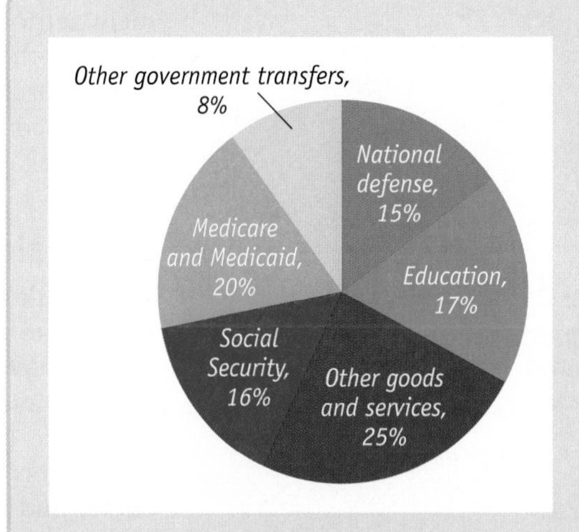

The two types of government spending are purchases of goods and services and government transfers. The big items in government purchases are national defense and education. The big items in government transfers are Social Security and the Medicare and Medicaid health care programs. (Numbers do not add to 100% due to rounding.)
Source: Bureau of Economic Analysis.

Expansionary fiscal policy is fiscal policy that increases aggregate demand.

right-hand side is aggregate spending, total spending on final goods and services produced in the economy. It is the sum of consumer spending (C), investment spending (I), government purchases of goods and services (G), and the value of exports (X) minus the value of imports (IM). It includes all the sources of aggregate demand.

The government directly controls one of the variables on the right-hand side of Equation 15-1: government purchases of goods and services (G). But that's not the only effect fiscal policy has on aggregate spending in the economy. Through changes in taxes and transfers, it also influences consumer spending (C) and, in some cases, investment spending (I).

To see why the budget affects consumer spending, recall that *disposable income,* the total income households have available to spend, is equal to the total income they receive from wages, dividends, interest, and rent, *minus* taxes, *plus* government transfers. So either an increase in taxes or a reduction in government transfers *reduces* disposable income. And a fall in disposable income, other things equal, leads to a fall in consumer spending. Conversely, either a decrease in taxes or an increase in government transfers *increases* disposable income. And a rise in disposable income, other things equal, leads to a rise in consumer spending.

The government's ability to affect investment spending is a more complex story, which we won't discuss in detail. The important point is that the government taxes profits, and changes in the rules that determine how much a business owes can increase or reduce the incentive to spend on investment goods.

Because the government itself is one source of spending in the economy, and because taxes and transfers can affect spending by consumers and firms, the government can use changes in taxes or government spending to *shift the aggregate demand curve.* And as we saw in Chapter 14, there are sometimes good reasons to shift the aggregate demand curve. In early 2009, as this chapter's opening story explained, the Obama administration believed it was crucial that the U.S. government act to increase aggregate demand—that is, to move the aggregate demand curve to the right of where it would otherwise be. The 2009 stimulus package was a classic example of *fiscal policy:* the use of taxes, government transfers, or government purchases of goods and services to stabilize the economy by shifting the aggregate demand curve.

Expansionary and Contractionary Fiscal Policy

Why would the government want to shift the aggregate demand curve? Because it wants to close either a recessionary gap, created when aggregate output falls below potential output, or an inflationary gap, created when aggregate output exceeds potential output.

Figure 15-4 shows the case of an economy facing a recessionary gap. *SRAS* is the short-run aggregate supply curve, *LRAS* is the long-run aggregate supply curve, and AD_1 is the initial aggregate demand curve. At the initial short-run macroeconomic equilibrium, E_1, aggregate output is Y_1, below potential output, Y_P. What the government would like to do is increase aggregate demand, shifting the aggregate demand curve rightward to AD_2. This would increase aggregate output, making it equal to potential output. Fiscal policy that increases aggregate demand, called **expansionary fiscal policy,** normally takes one of three forms:

- An increase in government purchases of goods and services
- A cut in taxes
- An increase in government transfers

The 2009 American Recovery and Reinvestment Act or simply, the Recovery Act, was a combination of all three: a direct increase in federal spending and aid

FIGURE 15-4 Expansionary Fiscal Policy Can Close a Recessionary Gap

The economy is in short-run macroeconomic equilibrium at E_1, where the aggregate demand curve, AD_1, intersects the *SRAS* curve. However, it is not in long-run macroeconomic equilibrium. At E_1, there is a recessionary gap of $Y_P - Y_1$. An expansionary fiscal policy—an increase in government purchases of goods and services, a reduction in taxes, or an increase in government transfers—shifts the aggregate demand curve rightward. It can close the recessionary gap by shifting AD_1 to AD_2, moving the economy to a new short-run macroeconomic equilibrium, E_2, which is also a long-run macroeconomic equilibrium.

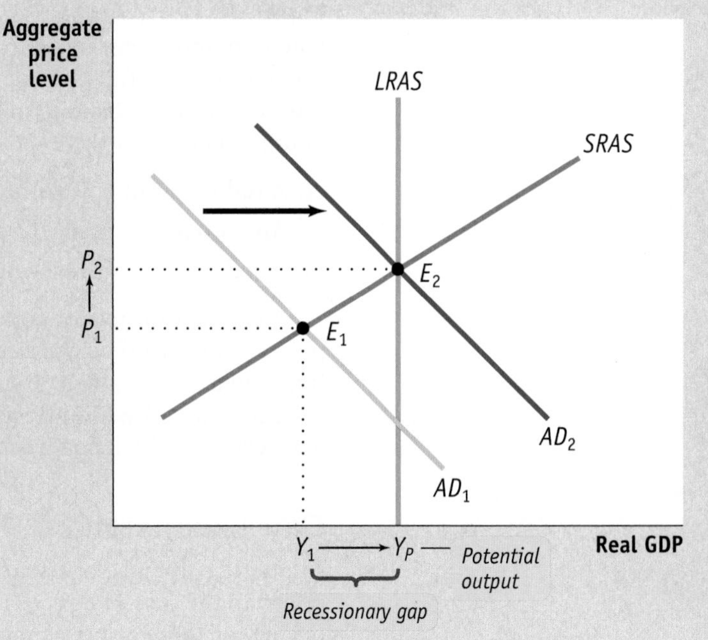

to state governments to help them maintain spending, tax cuts for most families, and increased aid to the unemployed.

Figure 15-5 shows the opposite case—an economy facing an inflationary gap. Again, *SRAS* is the short-run aggregate supply curve, *LRAS* is the long-run aggregate supply curve, and AD_1 is the initial aggregate demand curve. At the initial equilibrium, E_1, aggregate output is Y_1, above potential output, Y_P.

FIGURE 15-5 Contractionary Fiscal Policy Can Close an Inflationary Gap

The economy is in short-run macroeconomic equilibrium at E_1, where the aggregate demand curve, AD_1, intersects the *SRAS* curve. But it is not in long-run macroeconomic equilibrium. At E_1, there is an inflationary gap of $Y_1 - Y_P$. A contractionary fiscal policy—such as reduced government purchases of goods and services, an increase in taxes, or a reduction in government transfers—shifts the aggregate demand curve leftward. It closes the inflationary gap by shifting AD_1 to AD_2, moving the economy to a new short-run macroeconomic equilibrium, E_2, which is also a long-run macroeconomic equilibrium.

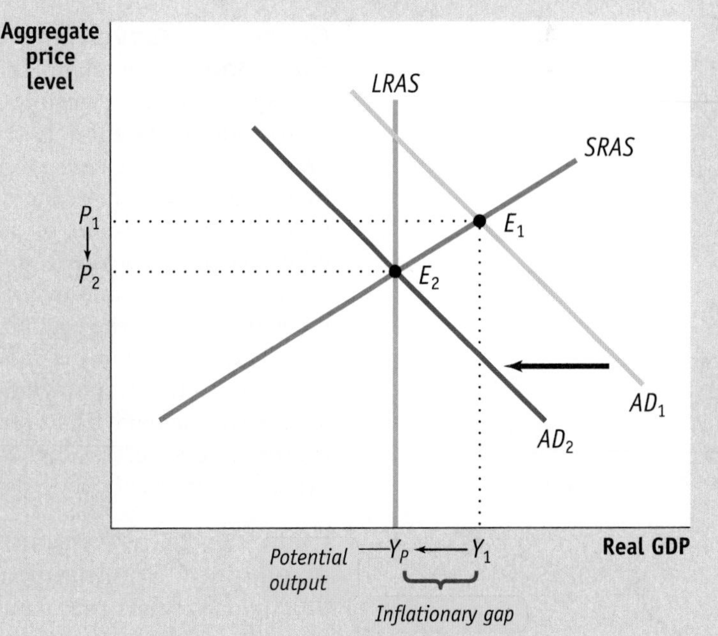

Contractionary fiscal policy is fiscal policy that reduces aggregate demand.

As we'll explain in later chapters, policy makers often try to head off inflation by eliminating inflationary gaps. To eliminate the inflationary gap shown in Figure 15-5, fiscal policy must reduce aggregate demand and shift the aggregate demand curve leftward to AD_2. This reduces aggregate output and makes it equal to potential output. Fiscal policy that reduces aggregate demand, called **contractionary fiscal policy,** is the opposite of expansionary fiscal policy. It is implemented in three possible ways:

1. A reduction in government purchases of goods and services
2. An increase in taxes
3. A reduction in government transfers

A classic example of contractionary fiscal policy occurred in 1968, when U.S. policy makers grew worried about rising inflation. President Lyndon Johnson imposed a temporary 10% surcharge on taxable income—everyone's income taxes were increased by 10%. He also tried to scale back government purchases of goods and services, which had risen dramatically because of the cost of the Vietnam War.

Can Expansionary Fiscal Policy Actually Work?

In practice, the use of fiscal policy—in particular, the use of expansionary fiscal policy in the face of a recessionary gap—is often controversial. We'll examine the origins of these controversies in detail in Chapter 18. But for now, let's quickly summarize the major points of the debate over expansionary fiscal policy, so we can understand when the critiques are justified and when they are not.

Broadly speaking, there are three arguments against the use of expansionary fiscal policy.

- Government spending always crowds out private spending
- Government borrowing always crowds out private investment spending
- Government budget deficits lead to reduced private spending

The first of these claims is wrong in principle, but it has nonetheless played a prominent role in public debates. The second is valid under some, but not all, circumstances. The third argument, although it raises some important issues, isn't a good reason to believe that expansionary fiscal policy doesn't work.

Claim 1: "Government Spending Always Crowds Out Private Spending" Some claim that expansionary fiscal policy can never raise aggregate spending and therefore can never raise aggregate income, with reasons that go something like this: "Every dollar that the government spends is a dollar taken away from the private sector. So any rise in government spending must be offset by an equal fall in private spending." In other words, every dollar spent by the government *crowds out,* or displaces, a dollar of private spending. So what's wrong with this view? The answer is that the statement is wrong because it assumes that resources in the economy are always fully employed and, as a result, the aggregate income earned in the economy is always a fixed sum—which isn't true. In particular, when the economy is suffering from a recessionary gap, there are unemployed resources in the economy and output, and therefore income, is below its potential level. Expansionary fiscal policy during these periods puts unemployed resources to work and generates higher spending and higher income. So the argument that expansionary fiscal policy always crowds out private spending is wrong in principle.

Claim 2: "Government Borrowing Always Crowds Out Private Investment Spending" How valid is the argument that government borrowing uses funds that would have otherwise been used for private investment spending—that is, it crowds out private investment spending?

The answer is "it depends." Specifically, it depends upon whether the economy is depressed or not. If the economy is not depressed, then increased government borrowing, by increasing the demand for loanable funds, can raise interest rates and crowd out private investment spending. However, what if the economy is depressed? In that case, crowding out is much less likely. When the economy is at far less than full employment, a fiscal expansion will lead to higher incomes, which in turn leads to increased savings at any given interest rate. This larger pool of savings allows the government to borrow without driving up interest rates. The Recovery Act of 2009 was a case in point: despite high levels of government borrowing, U.S. interest rates stayed near historic lows.

Claim 3: "Government Budget Deficits Lead to Reduced Private Spending" Other things equal, expansionary fiscal policy leads to a larger budget deficit and greater government debt. And higher debt will eventually require the government to raise taxes to pay it off. So, according to the third argument against expansionary fiscal policy, consumers, anticipating that they must pay higher taxes in the future to pay off today's government debt, will cut their spending today in order to save money. This argument, first made by the nineteenth-century economist David Ricardo, is known as *Ricardian equivalence.* It is an argument often taken to imply that expansionary fiscal policy will have no effect on the economy because far-sighted consumers will undo any attempts at expansion by the government. (And will also undo any contractionary fiscal policy, for that matter.)

In reality, however, it's doubtful that consumers behave with such foresight and budgeting discipline. Most people, when provided with extra cash (generated by the fiscal expansion), will spend at least some of it. So even fiscal policy that takes the form of temporary tax cuts or transfers of cash to consumers probably does have an expansionary effect.

Moreover, it's possible to show that even with Ricardian equivalence, a temporary rise in government spending that involves direct purchases of goods and services—such as a program of road construction—would still lead to a boost in total spending in the near term. That's because even if consumers cut back their current spending in anticipation of higher future taxes, their reduced spending will take place over an extended period as consumers save over time to pay the future tax bill. Meanwhile, the additional government spending will be concentrated in the near future, when the economy needs it. So although the effects emphasized by Ricardian equivalence may reduce the impact of fiscal expansion, the claim that it makes fiscal expansion completely ineffective is neither consistent with how consumers actually behave nor a reason to believe that increases in government spending have no effect. So, in the end, it's not a valid argument against expansionary fiscal policy.

In sum, then, the extent to which we should expect expansionary fiscal policy to work depends upon the circumstances. When the economy has a recessionary gap—as it did when the 2009 Recovery Act was passed—economics tells us that this is just the kind of situation in which expansionary fiscal policy helps the economy. However, when the economy is already at full employment, expansionary fiscal policy is the wrong policy and will lead to crowding out, an overheated economy, and higher inflation.

A Cautionary Note: Lags in Fiscal Policy

Looking back at Figures 15-4 and 15-5, it may seem obvious that the government should actively use fiscal policy—always adopting an expansionary fiscal policy when the economy faces a recessionary gap and always adopting a contractionary fiscal policy when the economy faces an inflationary gap. But many economists caution against an extremely active stabilization policy, arguing that a government that tries too hard to stabilize the economy—through either fiscal policy or monetary policy—can end up making the economy less stable.

We'll leave discussion of the warnings associated with monetary policy to Chapter 17. In the case of fiscal policy, one key reason for caution is that there are important *time lags* between when the policy is decided upon and when it is implemented. To understand the nature of these lags, think about what has to happen before the government increases spending to fight a recessionary gap. First, the government has to realize that the recessionary gap exists: economic data take time to collect and analyze, and recessions are often recognized only months after they have begun. Second, the government has to develop a spending plan, which can itself take months, particularly if politicians take time debating how the money should be spent and passing legislation. Finally, it takes time to spend money. For example, a road construction project begins with activities such as surveying that don't involve spending large sums. It may be quite some time before the big spending begins.

Because of these lags, an attempt to increase spending to fight a recessionary gap may take so long to get going that the economy has already recovered on its own. In fact, the recessionary gap may have turned into an inflationary gap by the time the fiscal policy takes effect. In that case, the fiscal policy will make things worse instead of better.

This doesn't mean that fiscal policy should never be actively used. In early 2009 there was good reason to believe that the slump facing the U.S. economy would be both deep and long and that a fiscal stimulus designed to arrive over the next year or two would almost surely push aggregate demand in the right direction. In fact, as we'll see later in this chapter, the 2009 stimulus arguably faded out too soon, leaving the economy still deeply depressed. But the problem of lags makes the actual use of both fiscal and monetary policy harder than you might think from a simple analysis like the one we have just given.

ECONOMICS ➤ IN ACTION

WHAT WAS IN THE RECOVERY ACT?

As we've just learned, fiscal stimulus can take three forms: increased government purchases of goods and services, increased transfer payments, and tax cuts. So what form did the Recovery Act take? The answer is that it's a bit complicated.

Figure 15-6 shows the composition of the budget impact of the Recovery Act, a measure that adds up the dollar value of tax cuts, transfer payments, and government spending. Here, the numbers are broken down into *four* categories, not three. "Infrastructure and other spending" means spending on roads, bridges, and schools as well as "nontraditional" infrastructure like research and development, all of which fall under government purchases of goods and services. "Tax cuts" are self-explanatory. "Transfer payments to persons" mostly took the form of expanded benefits for the unemployed. But a fourth category, "transfers to state and local governments," accounted for roughly a third of the funds. Why this fourth category?

FIGURE 15-6 The American Recovery and Reinvestment Act of 2009 (Billions of Dollars)

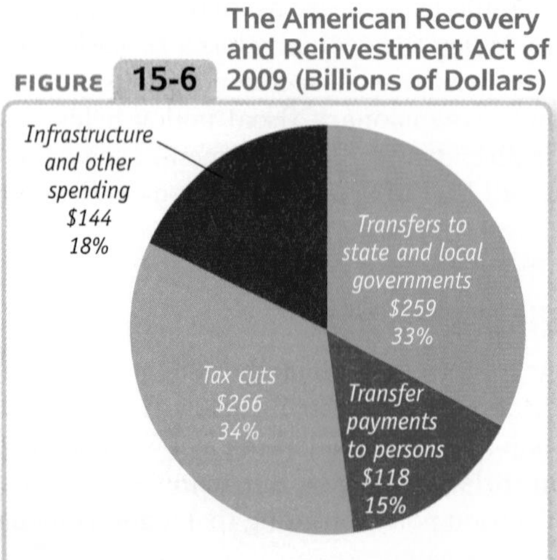

Because America has multiple levels of government. Two of the authors live in Princeton Township, which has its own budget, which is part of Mercer County, which has its own budget, which is part of the state of New Jersey, which has its own budget, which is part of the United States. One effect of the recession was a sharp drop in revenues at the state and local levels, which in turn forced these lower levels of government to cut spending. Federal aid—those transfers to state and local governments—was intended to mitigate these spending cuts.

Perhaps the most surprising aspect of the Recovery Act was how little direct federal spending on goods and services was involved. The great bulk of the program involved giving money to other people, one way or another, in the hope that they would spend it.

Quick Review

- The main channels of fiscal policy are taxes and government spending. Government spending takes the form of purchases of goods and services as well as transfers.
- In the United States, most government transfers are accounted for by **social insurance** programs designed to alleviate economic hardship—principally Social Security, Medicare, and Medicaid.
- The government controls *G* directly and influences *C* and *I* through taxes and transfers.
- **Expansionary fiscal policy** is implemented by an increase in government spending, a cut in taxes, or an increase in government transfers. **Contractionary fiscal policy** is implemented by a reduction in government spending, an increase in taxes, or a reduction in government transfers.
- Arguments against the effectiveness of expansionary fiscal policy based upon crowding out are valid only when the economy is at full employment. The argument that expansionary fiscal policy won't work because of Ricardian equivalence—that consumers will cut back spending today to offset expected future tax increases—appears to be untrue in practice. What is clearly true is that time lags can reduce the effectiveness of fiscal policy, and potentially render it counterproductive.

CHECK YOUR UNDERSTANDING 15-1

1. In each of the following cases, determine whether the policy is an expansionary or contractionary fiscal policy.
   a. Several military bases around the country, which together employ tens of thousands of people, are closed.
   b. The number of weeks an unemployed person is eligible for unemployment benefits is increased.
   c. The federal tax on gasoline is increased.
2. Explain why federal disaster relief, which quickly disburses funds to victims of natural disasters such as hurricanes, floods, and large-scale crop failures, will stabilize the economy more effectively after a disaster than relief that must be legislated.
3. Is the following statement true or false? Explain. "When the government expands, the private sector shrinks; when the government shrinks, the private sector expands."

Solutions appear at back of book.

Fiscal Policy and the Multiplier

An expansionary fiscal policy, like the 2009 U.S. stimulus, pushes the aggregate demand curve to the right. A contractionary fiscal policy, like Lyndon Johnson's tax surcharge, pushes the aggregate demand curve to the left. For policy makers, however, knowing the direction of the shift isn't enough: they need estimates of *how much* a given policy will shift the aggregate demand curve. To get these estimates, they use the concept of the *multiplier*.

Multiplier Effects of an Increase in Government Purchases of Goods and Services

Suppose that a government decides to spend $50 billion building bridges and roads. The government's purchases of goods and services will directly increase total spending on final goods and services by $50 billion. But there will also be an indirect effect: the government's purchases will start a chain reaction throughout the economy.

The firms that produce the goods and services purchased by the government earn revenues that flow to households in the form of wages, profits, interest, and rent. This increase in disposable income leads to a rise in consumer spending. The rise in consumer spending, in turn, induces firms to increase output, leading to a further rise in disposable income, which leads to another round of consumer spending increases, and so on. In this case, the *multiplier* is the ratio of the total change in real GDP caused by the change in the government's purchases of goods and services. More generally, real GDP can change with any *autonomous change in aggregate spending,* not just a change in consumer spending. An **autonomous change in aggregate spending** is the initial rise or fall in the desired level of spending by firms, households, or government at a given level of GDP. Formally, the **multiplier**

An **autonomous change in aggregate spending** is an initial change in the desired level of spending by firms, households, or government at a given level of real GDP. The **multiplier** is the ratio of the total change in real GDP caused by an autonomous change in aggregate spending to the size of that autonomous change.

The **marginal propensity to consume,** or ***MPC,*** is the increase in consumer spending when disposable income rises by $1.

is the ratio of the total change in real GDP caused by an autonomous change in aggregate spending to the size of that autonomous change.

If we sum the effect from all these rounds of consumer spending increases, how large is the total effect on aggregate output? To answer this question, we need to introduce the concept of the **marginal propensity to consume,** or ***MPC:*** the increase in consumer spending when disposable income rises by $1. When consumer spending changes because of a rise or fall in disposable income, *MPC* is that change in consumer spending divided by the change in disposable income:

$$\textbf{(15-2)}\ MPC = \frac{\Delta \text{ Consumer spending}}{\Delta \text{ Disposable income}}$$

where the symbol Δ (delta) means "change in." For example, if consumer spending goes up by $5 billion when disposable income goes up by $10 billion, *MPC* is $5 billion/$10 billion = 0.5.

Now, consider a simple case in which there are no taxes or international trade, so that any change in GDP accrues entirely to households. Also assume that the aggregate price level is fixed, so that any increase in nominal GDP is also a rise in real GDP, and assume that the interest rate is fixed. In this case, the multiplier is 1/(1 – *MPC*). So, if the marginal propensity to consume is 0.5, the multiplier is 1/(1 – 0.5) = 1/0.5 = 2. Given a multiplier of 2, a $50 billion increase in government purchases of goods and services would increase real GDP by $100 billion. Of that $100 billion, $50 billion is the initial effect from the increase in *G*, and the remaining $50 billion is the subsequent effect arising from the increase in consumer spending.

What happens if government purchases of goods and services are instead reduced? The math is exactly the same, except that there's a minus sign in front: if government purchases of goods and services fall by $50 billion and the marginal propensity to consume is 0.5, real GDP falls by $100 billion.

Multiplier Effects of Changes in Government Transfers and Taxes

Expansionary or contractionary fiscal policy need not take the form of changes in government purchases of goods and services. Governments can also change transfer payments or taxes. In general, however, a change in government transfers or taxes shifts the aggregate demand curve by *less* than an equal-sized change in government purchases, resulting in a smaller effect on real GDP.

To see why, imagine that instead of spending $50 billion on building bridges, the government simply hands out $50 billion in the form of government transfers. In this case, there is no direct effect on aggregate demand, as there was with government purchases of goods and services. Real GDP goes up only because households spend some of that $50 billion—and they probably won't spend it all.

Table 15-1 shows a hypothetical comparison of two expansionary fiscal policies assuming an *MPC* equal to 0.5 and a multiplier equal to 2: one in which the government directly purchases $50 billion in goods and services and one in which the government makes transfer payments instead, sending out $50 billion in checks to consumers. In each case there is a first-round effect on real GDP, either from purchases by the government or from purchases by the consumers who received the checks, followed by a series of additional rounds as rising real GDP raises disposable income.

TABLE 15-1 Hypothetical Effects of a Fiscal Policy with Multiplier of 2

Effect on real GDP	$50 billion rise in government purchases of goods and services	$50 billion rise in government transfer payments
First round	$50 billion	$25 billion
Second round	$25 billion	$12.5 billion
Third round	$12.5 billion	$6.25 billion
•	•	•
•	•	•
•	•	•
Eventual effect	$100 billion	$50 billion

Lump-sum taxes are taxes that don't depend on the taxpayer's income.

However, the first-round effect of the transfer program is smaller; because we have assumed that the *MPC* is 0.5, only $25 billion of the $50 billion is spent, with the other $25 billion saved. And as a result, all the further rounds are smaller, too. In the end, the transfer payment increases real GDP by only $50 billion. In comparison, a $50 billion increase in government purchases produces a $100 billion increase in real GDP.

Overall, when expansionary fiscal policy takes the form of a rise in transfer payments, real GDP may rise by either more or less than the initial government outlay—that is, the multiplier may be either more or less than 1 depending upon the size of the *MPC*. In Table 15-1, with an *MPC* equal to 0.5, the multiplier is exactly 1: a $50 billion rise in transfer payments increases real GDP by $50 billion. If the *MPC* is less than 0.5, so that a smaller share of the initial transfer is spent, the multiplier on that transfer is *less* than 1. If a larger share of the initial transfer is spent, the multiplier is *more* than 1.

A tax cut has an effect similar to the effect of a transfer. It increases disposable income, leading to a series of increases in consumer spending. But the overall effect is smaller than that of an equal-sized increase in government purchases of goods and services: the autonomous increase in aggregate spending is smaller because households save part of the amount of the tax cut.

We should also note that taxes introduce a further complication—they typically change the size of the multiplier. That's because in the real world governments rarely impose **lump-sum taxes,** in which the amount of tax a household owes is independent of its income. With lump-sum taxes there is no change in the multiplier. Instead, the great majority of tax revenue is raised via taxes that are not lump-sum, and so tax revenue depends upon the level of real GDP.

In practice, economists often argue that the size of the multiplier determines *who* among the population should get tax cuts or increases in government transfers. For example, compare the effects of an increase in unemployment benefits with a cut in taxes on profits distributed to shareholders as dividends. Consumer surveys suggest that the average unemployed worker will spend a higher share of any increase in his or her disposable income than would the average recipient of dividend income. That is, people who are unemployed tend to have a higher *MPC* than people who own a lot of stocks because the latter tend to be wealthier and tend to save more of any increase in disposable income. If that's true, a dollar spent on unemployment benefits increases aggregate demand more than a dollar's worth of dividend tax cuts.

How Taxes Affect the Multiplier

The increase in government tax revenue when real GDP rises isn't the result of a deliberate decision or action by the government. It's a consequence of the way the tax laws are written, which causes most sources of government revenue to increase *automatically* when real GDP goes up. For example, income tax receipts increase when real GDP rises because the amount each individual owes in taxes depends positively on his or her income, and households' taxable income rises when real GDP rises. Sales tax receipts increase when real GDP rises because people with more income spend more on goods and services. And corporate profit tax receipts increase when real GDP rises because profits increase when the economy expands.

The effect of these automatic increases in tax revenue is to reduce the size of the multiplier. Remember, the multiplier is the result of a chain reaction in which higher real GDP leads to higher disposable income, which leads to higher consumer spending, which leads to further increases in real GDP. The fact that the government siphons off some of any increase in real GDP means that at each stage of this process, the increase in consumer spending is smaller

Automatic stabilizers are government spending and taxation rules that cause fiscal policy to be automatically expansionary when the economy contracts and automatically contractionary when the economy expands.

Discretionary fiscal policy is fiscal policy that is the result of deliberate actions by policy makers rather than rules.

than it would be if taxes weren't part of the picture. The result is to reduce the multiplier.

Many macroeconomists believe it's a good thing that in real life taxes reduce the multiplier. In Chapter 14 we argued that most, though not all, recessions are the result of negative demand shocks. The same mechanism that causes tax revenue to increase when the economy expands causes it to decrease when the economy contracts. Since tax receipts decrease when real GDP falls, the effects of these negative demand shocks are smaller than they would be if there were no taxes. The decrease in tax revenue reduces the adverse effect of the initial fall in aggregate demand.

The automatic decrease in government tax revenue generated by a fall in real GDP—caused by a decrease in the amount of taxes households pay—acts like an automatic expansionary fiscal policy implemented in the face of a recession. Similarly, when the economy expands, the government finds itself automatically pursuing a contractionary fiscal policy—a tax increase. Government spending and taxation rules that cause fiscal policy to be automatically expansionary when the economy contracts and automatically contractionary when the economy expands, without requiring any deliberate action by policy makers, are called **automatic stabilizers.**

The rules that govern tax collection aren't the only automatic stabilizers, although they are the most important ones. Some types of government transfers also play a stabilizing role. For example, more people receive unemployment insurance when the economy is depressed than when it is booming. The same is true of Medicaid and food stamps. So transfer payments tend to rise when the economy is contracting and fall when the economy is expanding. Like changes in tax revenue, these automatic changes in transfers tend to reduce the size of the multiplier because the total change in disposable income that results from a given rise or fall in real GDP is smaller.

A historical example of discretionary fiscal policy was the Works Progress Administration (WPA), a relief measure established during the Great Depression that put millions of unemployed Americans to work building bridges, roads, buildings, and parks.

As in the case of government tax revenue, many macroeconomists believe that it's a good thing that government transfers reduce the multiplier. Expansionary and contractionary fiscal policies that are the result of automatic stabilizers are widely considered helpful to macroeconomic stabilization because they blunt the extremes of the business cycle.

But what about fiscal policy that *isn't* the result of automatic stabilizers? **Discretionary fiscal policy** is fiscal policy that is the direct result of deliberate actions by policy makers rather than automatic adjustment. For example, during a recession, the government may pass legislation that cuts taxes and increases government spending in order to stimulate the economy. In general, economists tend to support the use of discretionary fiscal policy only in special circumstances, such as an especially severe recession.

ECONOMICS ➤ *IN ACTION*

MULTIPLIERS AND THE OBAMA STIMULUS

The American Recovery and Reinvestment Act, also known as the Obama stimulus, was the largest example of discretionary fiscal expansion in U.S. history. The total stimulus was $787 billion, although not all of that was spent at once: only about half, or roughly $400 billion, of the stimulus arrived in 2010, the year of peak impact. Still, even that was a lot—roughly 2.7% of GDP. But was that enough? From the beginning, there were doubts.

The first description of the planned stimulus and its expected effects came in early January 2009, from two of the incoming administration's top economists—Christina Romer, who would head the Council of Economic Advisers, and Jared Bernstein, who would serve as the vice president's chief economist. Romer and Bernstein were explicit about the assumed multipliers: based on models developed at the Federal Reserve and elsewhere, they assumed that government spending would have a multiplier of 1.57 and that tax cuts would have a multiplier of 0.99.

These assumptions yielded an overall multiplier for the stimulus of almost 1.4, implying that the stimulus would, at its peak in 2010, add about 3.7% to real GDP. It would also, they estimated, reduce unemployment by about 1.8 percentage points relative to what it would otherwise have been.

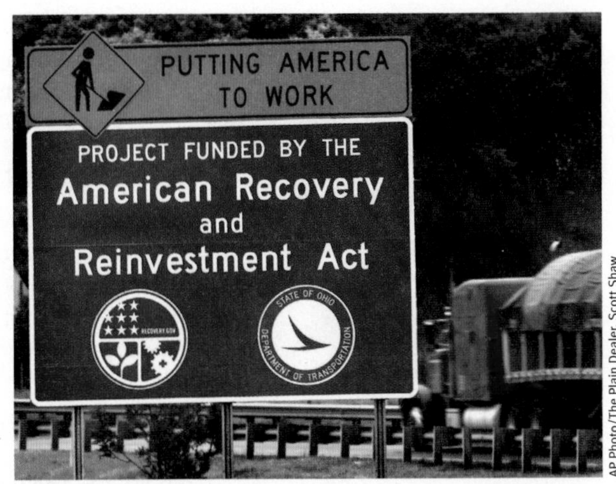

AP Photo/The Plain Dealer, Scott Shaw

The Obama stimulus, although too small to significantly lower unemployment, did create jobs and added about 3.7% to real GDP.

But here's the problem: the slump the Obama stimulus was intended to fight was brought on by a major financial crisis—and such crises tend to produce very deep, prolonged slumps. Shortly before Romer and Bernstein released their analysis, another team of economists—Carmen Reinhart of the University of Maryland and Kenneth Rogoff of Harvard—circulated a paper titled "The Aftermath of Financial Crises," based on historical episodes. Reinhart and Rogoff found that major crises are followed, on average, by a 7-percentage-point rise in the unemployment rate and that it takes years before unemployment falls to anything like normal levels.

Compared with the economy's problems, then, the Obama stimulus was actually small: it cut only 1.8 points off the unemployment rate in 2010 and faded out rapidly thereafter. And given its small size relative to the problem, the failure of the stimulus to avert persistently high unemployment should not have come as a surprise.

Quick Review

- The **multiplier** is the ratio of the total change in real GDP caused by an **autonomous change in aggregate spending** to the size of that autonomous change. The multiplier is determined by the **marginal propensity to consume (*MPC*).**
- Changes in taxes and government transfers also move real GDP, but by less than equal-sized changes in government purchases.
- Taxes reduce the size of the multiplier unless they are **lump-sum taxes.**
- Taxes and some government transfers act as **automatic stabilizers** as tax revenue responds positively to changes in real GDP and some government transfers respond negatively to changes in real GDP. Many economists believe that it is a good thing that they reduce the size of the multiplier. In contrast, the use of **discretionary fiscal policy** is more controversial.

CHECK YOUR UNDERSTANDING 15-2

1. Explain why a $500 million increase in government purchases of goods and services will generate a larger rise in real GDP than a $500 million increase in government transfers.
2. Explain why a $500 million reduction in government purchases of goods and services will generate a larger fall in real GDP than a $500 million reduction in government transfers.
3. The country of Boldovia has no unemployment insurance benefits and a tax system using only lump-sum taxes. The neighboring country of Moldovia has generous unemployment benefits and a tax system in which residents must pay a percentage of their income. Which country will experience greater variation in real GDP in response to demand shocks, positive and negative? Explain.

Solutions appear at back of book.

The Budget Balance

Headlines about the government's budget tend to focus on just one point: whether the government is running a surplus or a deficit and, in either case, how big. People usually think of surpluses as good: when the federal government ran a record surplus in 2000, many people regarded it as a cause for celebration. Conversely, people usually think of deficits as bad: when the U.S. federal government ran record deficits in 2009 and 2010, many people regarded it as a cause for concern.

How do surpluses and deficits fit into the analysis of fiscal policy? Are deficits ever a good thing and surpluses a bad thing? To answer those questions, let's look at the causes and consequences of surpluses and deficits.

The Budget Balance as a Measure of Fiscal Policy

What do we mean by surpluses and deficits? The budget balance is the difference between the government's revenue, in the form of tax revenue, and its spending, both on goods and services and on government transfers, in a given year. That is, the budget balance—savings by government—is defined by Equation 15-3:

$$\textbf{(15-3)}\ S_{Government} = T - G - TR$$

where T is the value of tax revenues, G is government purchases of goods and services, and TR is the value of government transfers. A budget surplus is a positive budget balance and a budget deficit is a negative budget balance.

Other things equal, expansionary fiscal policies—increased government purchases of goods and services, higher government transfers, or lower taxes—reduce the budget balance for that year. That is, expansionary fiscal policies make a budget surplus smaller or a budget deficit bigger. Conversely, contractionary fiscal policies—reduced government purchases of goods and services, lower government transfers, or higher taxes—increase the budget balance for that year, making a budget surplus bigger or a budget deficit smaller.

You might think this means that changes in the budget balance can be used to measure fiscal policy. In fact, economists often do just that: they use changes in the budget balance as a "quick-and-dirty" way to assess whether current fiscal policy is expansionary or contractionary. But they always keep in mind two reasons this quick-and-dirty approach is sometimes misleading:

1. Two different changes in fiscal policy that have equal-sized effects on the budget balance may have quite unequal effects on the economy. As we have already seen, changes in government purchases of goods and services have a larger effect on real GDP than equal-sized changes in taxes and government transfers.
2. Often, changes in the budget balance are themselves the result, not the cause, of fluctuations in the economy.

To understand the second point, we need to examine the effects of the business cycle on the budget.

The Business Cycle and the Cyclically Adjusted Budget Balance

Historically there has been a strong relationship between the federal government's budget balance and the business cycle. The budget tends to move into deficit when the economy experiences a recession, but deficits tend to get smaller or even turn into surpluses when the economy is expanding. Figure 15-7 shows the federal budget deficit as a percentage of GDP from 1970 to 2011. Shaded areas indicate recessions; unshaded areas indicate expansions. As you can see, the federal budget deficit increased around the time of each recession and usually declined during expansions. In fact, in the late stages of the long expansion from 1991 to 2000, the deficit actually became negative—the budget deficit became a budget surplus.

The relationship between the business cycle and the budget balance is even clearer if we compare the budget deficit as a percentage of GDP with the

FIGURE 15-7 The U.S. Federal Budget Deficit and the Business Cycle, 1970–2011

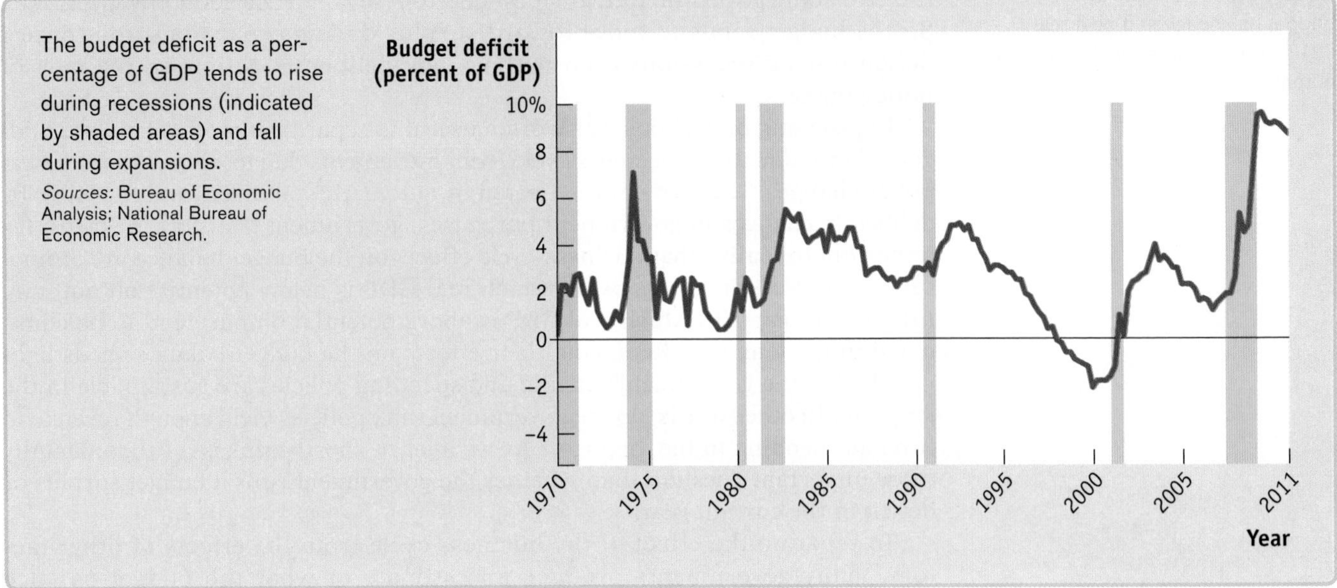

The budget deficit as a percentage of GDP tends to rise during recessions (indicated by shaded areas) and fall during expansions.

Sources: Bureau of Economic Analysis; National Bureau of Economic Research.

unemployment rate, as we do in Figure 15-8. The budget deficit almost always rises when the unemployment rate rises and falls when the unemployment rate falls.

Is this relationship between the business cycle and the budget balance evidence that policy makers engage in discretionary fiscal policy, using expansionary fiscal policy during recessions and contractionary fiscal policy during expansions? Not necessarily. To a large extent the relationship in Figure 15-8 reflects automatic stabilizers at work. As we learned in the discussion of automatic stabilizers, government tax revenue tends to rise and some government transfers, like unemployment benefit payments, tend to

FIGURE 15-8 The U.S. Federal Budget Deficit and the Unemployment Rate

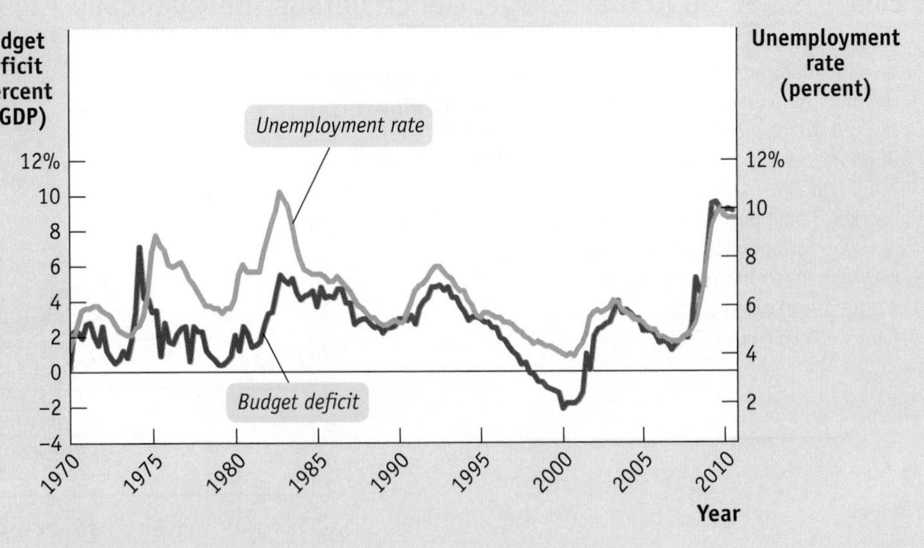

There is a close relationship between the budget balance and the business cycle: a recession moves the budget balance toward deficit, but an expansion moves it toward surplus. Here, the unemployment rate serves as an indicator of the business cycle, and we should expect to see a higher unemployment rate associated with a higher budget deficit. This is confirmed by the figure: the budget deficit as a percentage of GDP moves closely in tandem with the unemployment rate.

Sources: Bureau of Economic Analysis; Bureau of Labor Statistics.

The **cyclically adjusted budget balance** is an estimate of what the budget balance would be if real GDP were exactly equal to potential output.

fall when the economy expands. Conversely, government tax revenue tends to fall and some government transfers tend to rise when the economy contracts. So the budget tends to move toward surplus during expansions and toward deficit during recessions even without any deliberate action on the part of policy makers.

In assessing budget policy, it's often useful to separate movements in the budget balance due to the business cycle from movements due to discretionary fiscal policy changes. The former are affected by automatic stabilizers and the latter by deliberate changes in government purchases, government transfers, or taxes. It's important to realize that business-cycle effects on the budget balance are temporary: both recessionary gaps (in which real GDP is below potential output) and inflationary gaps (in which real GDP is above potential output) tend to be eliminated in the long run. Removing their effects on the budget balance sheds light on whether the government's taxing and spending policies are sustainable in the long run. In other words, do the government's tax policies yield enough revenue to fund its spending in the long run? As we'll learn shortly, this is a fundamentally more important question than whether the government runs a budget surplus or deficit in the current year.

To separate the effect of the business cycle from the effects of other factors, many governments produce an estimate of what the budget balance would be if there were neither a recessionary nor an inflationary gap. The **cyclically adjusted budget balance** is an estimate of what the budget balance would be if real GDP were exactly equal to potential output. It takes into account the extra tax revenue the government would collect and the transfers it would save if a recessionary gap were eliminated—or the revenue the government would lose and the extra transfers it would make if an inflationary gap were eliminated.

Figure 15-9 shows the actual budget deficit and the Congressional Budget Office estimate of the cyclically adjusted budget deficit, both as a percentage of GDP, from 1970 to 2011. As you can see, the cyclically adjusted budget deficit doesn't fluctuate as much as the actual budget deficit. In particular, large actual deficits, such as those of 1975, 1983, and 2009 are usually caused in part by a depressed economy.

FIGURE 15-9 The Actual Budget Deficit versus the Cyclically Adjusted Budget Deficit

The cyclically adjusted budget deficit is an estimate of what the budget deficit would be if the economy was at potential output. It fluctuates less than the actual budget deficit because years of large budget deficits also tend to be years when the economy has a large recessionary gap.

Sources: Congressional Budget Office; Bureau of Economic Analysis.

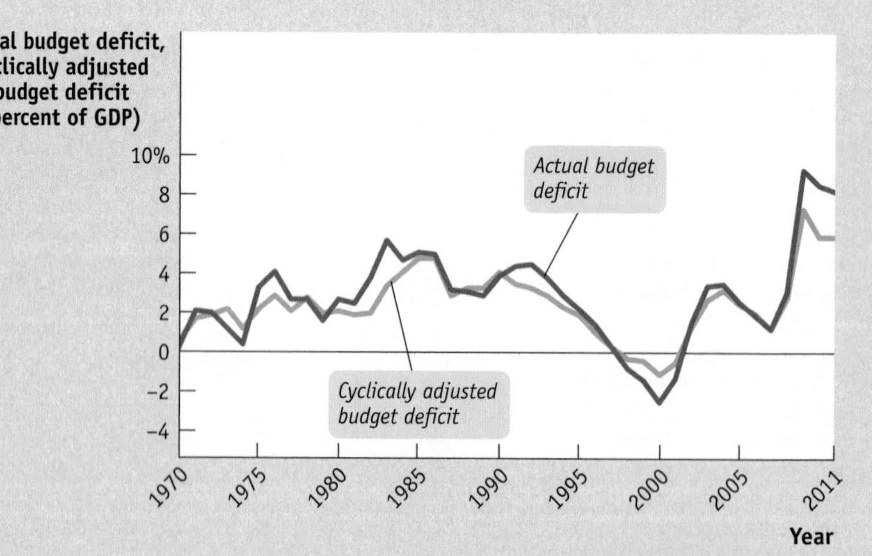

Should the Budget Be Balanced?

As we'll see in the next section, persistent budget deficits can cause problems for both the government and the economy. Yet politicians are always tempted to run deficits because this allows them to cater to voters by cutting taxes without cutting spending or by increasing spending without increasing taxes. As a result, there are occasional attempts by policy makers to force fiscal discipline by introducing legislation—even a constitutional amendment—forbidding the government from running budget deficits. This is usually stated as a requirement that the budget be "balanced"—that revenues at least equal spending each fiscal year. Would it be a good idea to require a balanced budget annually?

Most economists don't think so. They believe that the government should only balance its budget on average—that it should be allowed to run deficits in bad years, offset by surpluses in good years. They don't believe the government should be forced to run a balanced budget *every year* because this would undermine the role of taxes and transfers as automatic stabilizers. As we learned earlier in this chapter, the tendency of tax revenue to fall and transfers to rise when the economy contracts helps to limit the size of recessions. But falling tax revenue and rising transfer payments generated by a downturn in the economy push the budget toward deficit. If constrained by a balanced-budget rule, the government would have to respond to this deficit with contractionary fiscal policies that would tend to deepen a recession.

Yet policy makers concerned about excessive deficits sometimes feel that rigid rules prohibiting—or at least setting an upper limit on—deficits are necessary. As the following Economics in Action explains, Europe has had a lot of trouble reconciling rules to enforce fiscal responsibility with the challenges of short-run fiscal policy.

ECONOMICS ➤ IN ACTION

EUROPE'S SEARCH FOR A FISCAL RULE

In 1999 a group of European nations took a momentous step when they adopted a common currency, the euro, to replace their various national currencies, such as the French franc, the German mark, and the Italian lira. Along with the introduction of the euro came the creation of the European Central Bank, which sets monetary policy for the whole region.

As part of the agreement creating the new currency, governments of member countries signed on to the European "stability pact." This agreement required each government to keep its budget deficit—its actual deficit, not a cyclically adjusted number—below 3% of the country's GDP or face fines. The pact was intended to prevent irresponsible deficit spending arising from political pressure that might eventually undermine the new currency. The stability pact, however, had a serious downside: in principle, it would force countries to slash spending and/or raise taxes whenever an economic downturn pushed their deficits above the critical level. This would turn fiscal policy into a force that worsens recessions instead of fighting them.

Nonetheless, the stability pact proved impossible to enforce: European nations, including France and even Germany, with its reputation for fiscal probity, simply ignored the rule during the 2001 recession and its aftermath.

In 2011 the Europeans tried again, this time against the background of a severe debt crisis. In the wake of the 2008

Image source photography/Veer

Although several European nations have adopted a common currency—the euro—they struggle to establish effective fiscal policy.

financial crisis, Greece, Ireland, Portugal, Spain, and Italy all lost the confidence of investors, who were worried about their ability and/or willingness to repay all their debt—and the efforts of these nations to reduce their deficits seemed likely to push Europe back into recession. Yet a return to the old stability pact didn't seem to make sense. Among other things, it was clear that the stability pact's rule on the size of budget deficits would not have done much to prevent the crisis—in 2007 all of the problem debtors except Greece were running deficits under 3% of GDP, with Ireland and Spain actually running surpluses.

So the agreement reached in December 2011 was framed in terms of the "structural" budget balance, more or less corresponding to the cyclically adjusted budget balance as defined in the text. According to the new rule, the structural budget balance of each country should be very nearly zero, with deficits not to exceed 0.5% of GDP. This seemed like a much better rule than the old stability pact.

Yet big problems remained. One was the question of how reliable were the estimates of the structural budget balances. Also, the new rule seemed to ban any use of discretionary fiscal policy, under any circumstances. Was this wise?

Before patting themselves on the back over the superiority of their own fiscal rules, Americans should note that the United States has its own version of the original, flawed European stability pact. The federal government's budget acts as an automatic stabilizer, but 49 of the 50 states are required by their state constitutions to balance their budgets every year. When recession struck in 2008, most states were forced to—guess what?—slash spending and raise taxes in the face of a recession, exactly the wrong thing from a macroeconomic point of view.

Quick Review

- The budget deficit tends to rise during recessions and fall during expansions. This reflects the effect of the business cycle on the budget balance.
- The **cyclically adjusted budget balance** is an estimate of what the budget balance would be if the economy were at potential output. It varies less than the actual budget deficit.
- Most economists believe that governments should run budget deficits in bad years and budget surpluses in good years. A rule requiring a balanced budget would undermine the role of automatic stabilizers.

CHECK YOUR UNDERSTANDING 15-3

1. Why is the cyclically adjusted budget balance a better measure of whether government policies are sustainable in the long run than the actual budget balance?
2. Explain why states required by their constitutions to balance their budgets are likely to experience more severe economic fluctuations than states not held to that requirement.

Solutions appear at back of book.

Long-Run Implications of Fiscal Policy

In 2009 the government of Greece ran into a financial wall. Like most other governments in Europe (and the U.S. government, too), the Greek government was running a large budget deficit, which meant that it needed to keep borrowing more funds, both to cover its expenses and to pay off existing loans as they came due. But governments, like companies or individuals, can only borrow if lenders believe there's a good chance they are willing or able to repay their debts. By 2009 most investors, having lost confidence in Greece's financial future, were no longer willing to lend to the Greek government. Those few who were willing to lend demanded very high interest rates to compensate them for the risk of loss.

Figure 15-10 compares interest rates on 10-year bonds issued by the governments of Greece and Germany. At the beginning of 2007, Greece could borrow at almost the same rate as Germany, widely considered a very safe borrower. By the end of 2011, however, Greece was having to pay an interest rate around 10 times the rate Germany paid.

Why was Greece having these problems? Largely because investors had become deeply worried about the level of its debt (in part because it became

FIGURE 15-10 Greek and German Long-Term Interest Rates

As late as 2008, the government of Greece could borrow at interest rates only slightly higher than those facing Germany, widely considered a very safe borrower. But in early 2009, as it became clear that both Greek debt and Greek deficits were larger than previously reported, investors lost confidence, sending Greek borrowing costs sky-high.
Source: European Central Bank.

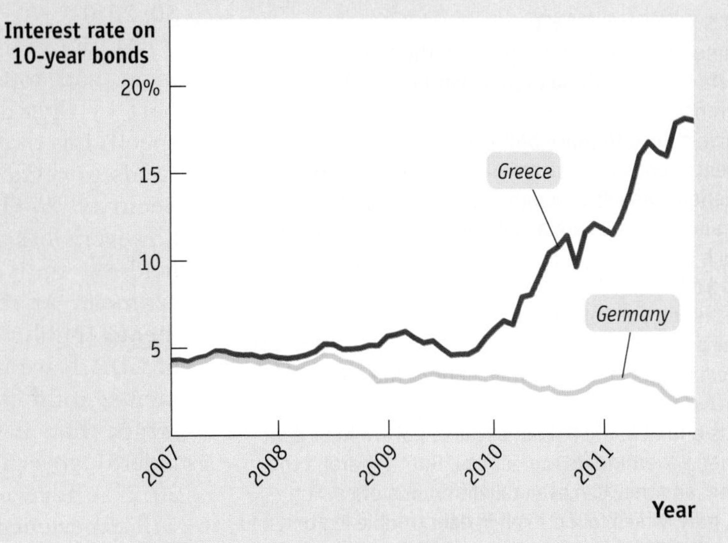

clear that the Greek government had been using creative accounting to hide just how much debt it had already taken on). Government debt is, after all, a promise to make future payments to lenders. By 2009 it seemed likely that the Greek government had already promised more than it could possibly deliver.

The result was that Greece found itself unable to borrow more from private lenders; it received emergency loans from other European nations and the International Monetary Fund, but these loans came with the requirement that the Greek government make severe spending cuts, which wreaked havoc with its economy, imposed severe economic hardship on Greeks, and led to massive social unrest.

No discussion of fiscal policy is complete if it doesn't take into account the long-run implications of government budget surpluses and deficits, especially the implications for government debt. We now turn to those long-run implications.

Aris Messinis/AFP/Getty Images

Greeks angered by their government's harsh austerity measures took to the streets in protest.

Deficits, Surpluses, and Debt

When a family spends more than it earns over the course of a year, it has to raise the extra funds either by selling assets or by borrowing. And if a family borrows year after year, it will eventually end up with a lot of debt.

The same is true for governments. With a few exceptions, governments don't raise large sums by selling assets such as national parkland. Instead, when a government spends more than the tax revenue it receives—when it runs a budget deficit—it almost always borrows the extra funds. And governments that run persistent budget deficits end up with substantial debts.

To interpret the numbers that follow, you need to know a slightly peculiar feature of federal government accounting. For historical reasons, the U.S. government does not keep books by calendar years. Instead, budget totals are kept by **fiscal years,** which run from October 1 to September 30 and are labeled

A **fiscal year** runs from October 1 to September 30 and is labeled according to the calendar year in which it ends.

DEFICITS VERSUS DEBT

One common mistake—it happens all the time in newspaper reports—is to confuse *deficits* with *debt.* Let's review the difference.

A *deficit* is the difference between the amount of money a government spends and the amount it receives in taxes over a given period—usually, though not always, a year. Deficit numbers always come with a statement about the time period to which they apply, as in "the U.S. budget deficit *in fiscal 2012* was $1.1 trillion."

A *debt* is the sum of money a government owes at a particular point in time. Debt numbers usually come with a specific date, as in "U.S. public debt *at the end of fiscal 2012* was $11.3 trillion."

Deficits and debt are linked, because government debt grows when governments run deficits. But they aren't the same thing, and they can even tell different stories. For example, Italy, which found itself in debt trouble in 2011, had a fairly small deficit by historical standards, but it had very high debt, a legacy of past policies.

by the calendar year in which they end. For example, fiscal 2010 began on October 1, 2009, and ended on September 30, 2010.

At the end of fiscal 2012, the U.S. federal government had total debt equal to $16.1 trillion. However, part of that debt represented special accounting rules specifying that the federal government as a whole owes funds to certain government programs, especially Social Security. We'll explain those rules shortly. For now, however, let's focus on **public debt:** government debt held by individuals and institutions outside the government. At the end of fiscal 2012, the federal government's public debt was "only" $11.3 trillion, or 72% of GDP. If we include the debts of state and local governments, total public debt at the end of fiscal 2012 was larger than it was at the end of fiscal 2011 because the federal government ran a budget deficit during fiscal 2012. A government that runs persistent budget deficits will experience a rising level of public debt. Why is this a problem?

THE AMERICAN WAY OF DEBT

How does the public debt of the United States stack up internationally? In dollar terms, we're number one—but this isn't very informative, since the U.S. economy and so the government's tax base are much larger than those of any other nation. A more informative comparison is the ratio of public debt to GDP.

The figure shows the *net public debt* of a number of rich countries as a percentage of GDP at the end of 2011. Net public debt is government debt minus any assets governments may have—an adjustment that can make a big difference. What you see here is that the United States is more or less in the middle of the pack.

It may not surprise you that Greece heads the list, and most of the other high net debt countries are European nations that have been making headlines for their debt problems. Interestingly, however, Japan is also high on the list because it used massive public spending to prop up its economy in the 1990s. Investors, however, still consider Japan a reliable government, so its borrowing costs remain low despite high net debt.

In contrast to the other countries, Norway has a large *negative* net public debt. What's going on in Norway? In a word, oil. Norway is the world's third-largest oil exporter, thanks to large offshore deposits in the North Sea. Instead of spending its oil revenues immediately, the government of Norway has used them to build up an investment fund for future needs following the lead of traditional oil producers like Saudi Arabia. As a result, Norway has a huge stock of government assets rather than a large government debt.

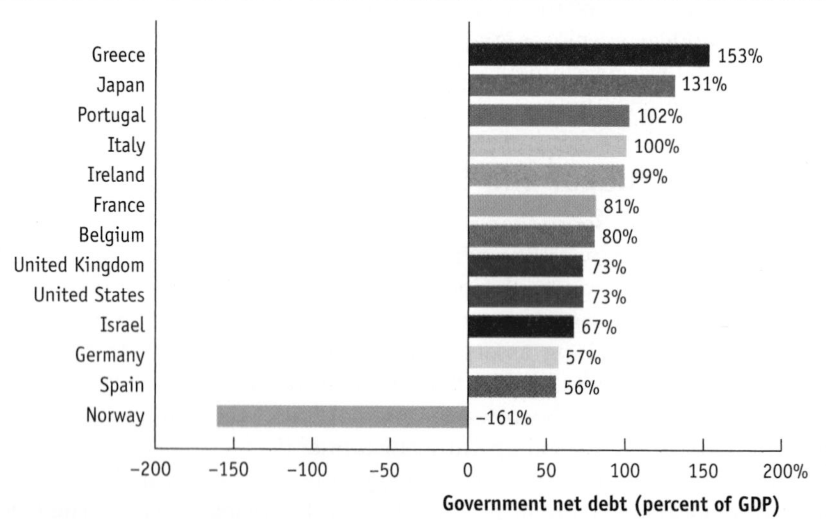

Source: International Monetary Fund.

Problems Posed by Rising Government Debt

Public debt is government debt held by individuals and institutions outside the government.

There are two reasons to be concerned when a government runs persistent budget deficits. When the economy is at full employment and the government borrows funds in the financial markets, it is competing with firms that plan to borrow funds for investment spending. As a result, the government's borrowing may crowd out private investment spending, increasing interest rates and reducing the economy's long-run rate of growth.

But there's a second reason: today's deficits, by increasing the government's debt, place financial pressure on future budgets. The impact of current deficits on future budgets is straightforward. Like individuals, governments must pay their bills, including interest payments on their accumulated debt. When a government is deeply in debt, those interest payments can be substantial. In fiscal 2011, the U.S. federal government paid 1.8% of GDP—$266 billion—in interest on its debt. The more heavily indebted government of Italy paid interest of 4.7% of its GDP in 2011.

Other things equal, a government paying large sums in interest must raise more revenue from taxes or spend less than it would otherwise be able to afford—or it must borrow even more to cover the gap. And a government that borrows to pay interest on its outstanding debt pushes itself even deeper into debt. This process can eventually push a government to the point where lenders question its ability to repay. Like a consumer who has maxed out his or her credit cards, it will find that lenders are unwilling to lend any more funds. The result can be that the government defaults on its debt—it stops paying what it owes. Default is often followed by deep financial and economic turmoil.

Americans aren't used to the idea of government default, but such things do happen. In the 1990s Argentina, a relatively high-income developing country, was widely praised for its economic policies—and it was able to borrow large sums from foreign lenders. By 2001, however, Argentina's interest payments were spiraling out of control, and the country stopped paying the sums that were due. In the end, it reached a settlement with most of its lenders under which it paid less than a third of the amount originally due. By late 2011 investors were placing a fairly high probability on Argentine-type default by several European countries—namely, Greece, Ireland, and Portugal—and were seriously worried about Italy and Spain. Each one was forced to pay high interest rates on its debt by nervous lenders, exacerbating the risk of default.

Default creates havoc in a country's financial markets and badly shakes public confidence in both the government and the economy. Argentina's debt default was accompanied by a crisis in the country's banking system and a very severe recession. And even if a highly indebted government avoids default, a heavy debt burden typically forces it to slash spending or raise taxes, politically unpopular measures that can also damage the economy. In some cases, "austerity" measures intended to reassure lenders that the government can indeed pay end up depressing the economy so much that lender confidence continues to fall—a process we'll look at more closely in the Economics in Action that follows this section.

Some may ask why can't a government that has trouble borrowing just print money to pay its bills? Yes, it can if it has its own currency (which the troubled European nations don't). But printing money to pay the government's bills can lead to another problem: inflation. In fact, budget problems are the main cause of very severe inflation. The point for now is that governments do not want to find themselves in a position where the choice is between defaulting on their debts and inflating those debts away by printing money.

Concerns about the long-run effects of deficits need not rule out the use of expansionary fiscal policy to stimulate the economy when it is depressed.

The **debt–GDP ratio** is the government's debt as a percentage of GDP.

However, these concerns do mean that governments should try to offset budget deficits in bad years with budget surpluses in good years. In other words, governments should run a budget that is approximately balanced over time. Have they actually done so?

Deficits and Debt in Practice

Figure 15-11 shows how the U.S. federal government's budget deficit and its debt evolved from 1940 to 2011. Panel (a) shows the federal deficit as a percentage of GDP. As you can see, the federal government ran huge deficits during World War II. It briefly ran surpluses after the war, but it has normally run deficits ever since, especially after 1980. This seems inconsistent with the advice that governments should offset deficits in bad times with surpluses in good times.

However, panel (b) of Figure 15-11 shows that for most of the period these persistent deficits didn't lead to runaway debt. To assess the ability of governments to pay their debt, we use the **debt–GDP ratio,** the government's debt as a percentage of GDP. We use this measure, rather than simply looking at the size of the debt, because GDP, which measures the size of the economy as a whole, is a good indicator of the potential taxes the government can collect. If the government's debt grows more slowly than GDP, the burden of paying that debt is actually falling compared with the government's potential tax revenue.

What we see from panel (b) is that although the federal debt grew in almost every year, the debt–GDP ratio fell for 30 years after the end of World War II. This shows that the debt–GDP ratio can fall, even when debt is rising, as long as GDP grows faster than debt. For Inquiring Minds, which focuses on the large debt the U.S. government ran up during World War II, explains how growth and inflation sometimes allow a government that runs persistent budget deficits to nevertheless have a declining debt–GDP ratio.

FIGURE 15-11 U.S. Federal Deficits and Debt

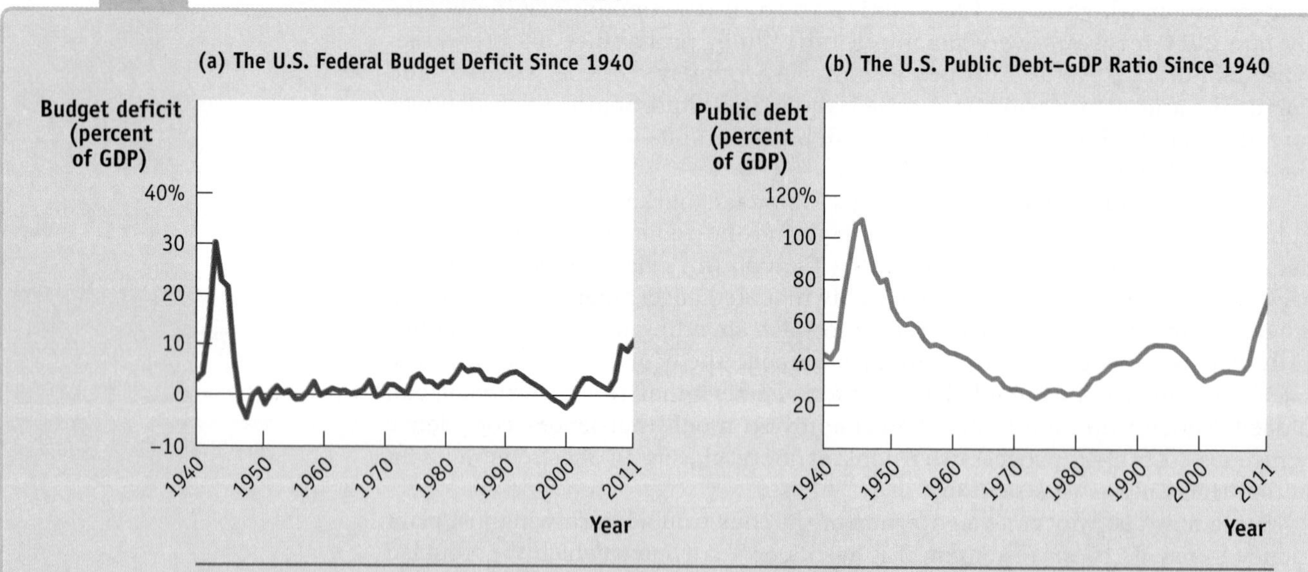

Panel (a) shows the U.S. federal budget deficit as a percentage of GDP from 1940 to 2011. The U.S. government ran huge deficits during World War II and has run smaller deficits ever since. Panel (b) shows the U.S. debt–GDP ratio. Comparing panels (a) and (b), you can see that in many years the debt–GDP ratio has declined in spite of government deficits. This seeming paradox reflects the fact that the debt–GDP ratio can fall, even when debt is rising, as long as GDP grows faster than debt.
Source: Office of Management and Budget.

FOR INQUIRING MINDS

WHAT HAPPENED TO THE DEBT FROM WORLD WAR II?

As you can see from Figure 15-11, the U.S. government paid for World War II by borrowing on a huge scale. By the war's end, the public debt was more than 100% of GDP, and many people worried about how it could ever be paid off.

The truth is that it never was paid off. In 1946 public debt was $242 billion; that number dipped slightly in the next few years, as the United States ran postwar budget surpluses, but the government budget went back into deficit in 1950 with the start of the Korean War. By 1962 the public debt was back up to $248 billion.

But by that time nobody was worried about the fiscal health of the U.S. government because the debt–GDP ratio had fallen by more than half. The reason? Vigorous economic growth, plus mild inflation, had led to a rapid rise in GDP. The experience was a clear lesson in the peculiar fact that modern governments can run deficits forever, as long as they aren't too large.

Still, a government that runs persistent *large* deficits will have a rising debt–GDP ratio when debt grows faster than GDP. In the aftermath of the financial crisis of 2008, the U.S. government began running deficits much larger than anything seen since World War II, and the debt–GDP ratio began rising sharply. Similar surges in the debt–GDP ratio could be seen in a number of other countries in 2008. Economists and policy makers agreed that this was not a sustainable trend, that governments would need to get their spending and revenues back in line. But *when* to bring spending in line with revenue was a source of great disagreement. Some argued for fiscal tightening right away; others argued that this tightening should be postponed until the major economies had recovered from their slump.

Implicit Liabilities

Looking at Figure 15-11, you might be tempted to conclude that until the 2008 crisis struck, the U.S. federal budget was in fairly decent shape: the return to budget deficits after 2001 caused the debt–GDP ratio to rise a bit, but that ratio was still low compared with both historical experience and some other wealthy countries. In fact, however, experts on long-run budget issues view the situation of the United States (and other countries such as Japan and Italy) with alarm. The reason is the problem of *implicit liabilities.* **Implicit liabilities** are spending promises made by governments that are effectively a debt despite the fact that they are not included in the usual debt statistics.

The largest implicit liabilities of the U.S. government arise from two transfer programs that principally benefit older Americans: Social Security and Medicare. The third-largest implicit liability, Medicaid, benefits low-income families. In each of these cases, the government has promised to provide transfer payments to future as well as current beneficiaries. So these programs represent a future debt that must be honored, even though the debt does not currently show up in the usual statistics. Together, these three programs currently account for almost 40% of federal spending.

The implicit liabilities created by these transfer programs worry fiscal experts. Figure 15-12 shows why. It shows actual spending on Social Security and on Medicare, Medicaid, and CHIP (a program that provides health care coverage to uninsured children) as percentages of GDP from 2000 to 2010, together with Congressional Budget Office projections of spending through 2085. According to these projections, spending on Social Security will rise substantially over the next few decades and spending on the three health care programs will soar. Why?

In the case of Social Security, the answer is demography. Social Security is a "pay-as-you-go" system: current workers pay payroll taxes that fund the benefits of current retirees. So the ratio of the number of retirees drawing benefits to the number of workers paying into Social Security has a major impact on the system's finances. There was a huge surge in the U.S. birth rate between 1946 and 1964, the years of

Implicit liabilities are spending promises made by governments that are effectively a debt despite the fact that they are not included in the usual debt statistics.

FIGURE 15-12 Future Demands on the Federal Budget

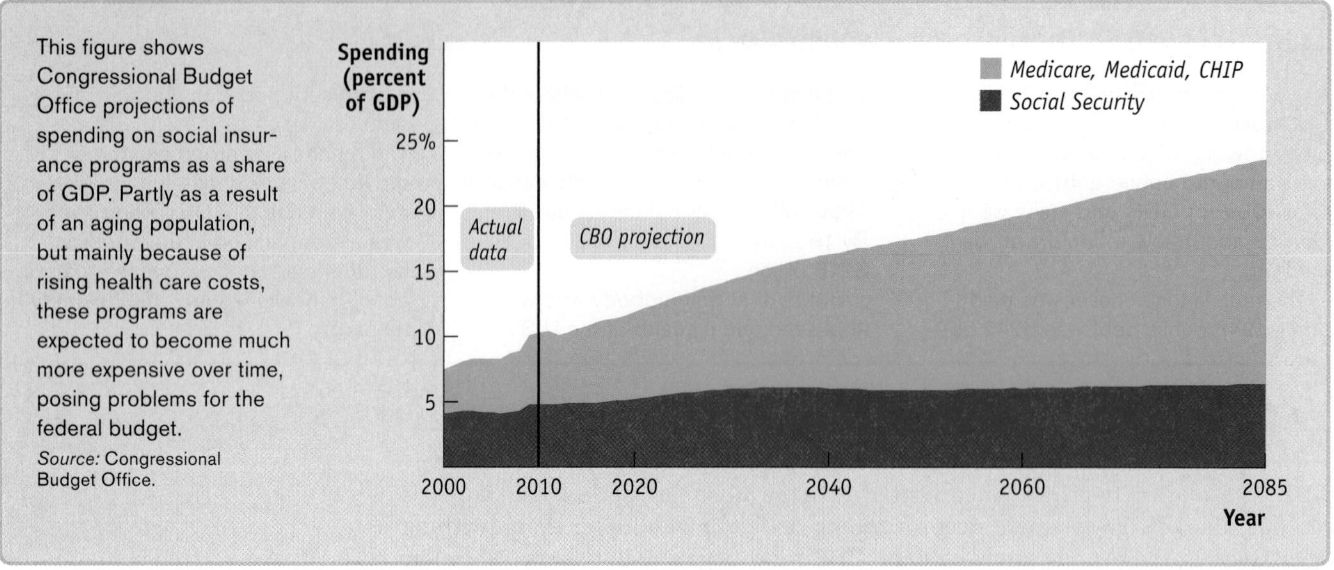

This figure shows Congressional Budget Office projections of spending on social insurance programs as a share of GDP. Partly as a result of an aging population, but mainly because of rising health care costs, these programs are expected to become much more expensive over time, posing problems for the federal budget.
Source: Congressional Budget Office.

what is commonly called the "baby boom." Most baby boomers are currently of working age—which means they are paying taxes, not collecting benefits. But some are starting to retire, and as more and more of them do so, they will stop earning taxable income and start collecting benefits. As a result, the ratio of retirees receiving benefits to workers paying into the Social Security system will rise. In 2010 there were 34 retirees receiving benefits for every 100 workers paying into the system. By 2030, according to the Social Security Administration, that number will rise to 46; by 2050, it will rise to 48; and by 2080, that number will be 51. So as baby boomers move into retirement, benefit payments will continue to rise relative to the size of the economy.

The aging of the baby boomers, by itself, poses only a moderately sized long-run fiscal problem. The projected rise in Medicare and Medicaid spending is a much more serious concern. The main story behind projections of higher Medicare and Medicaid spending is the long-run tendency of health care spending to rise faster than overall spending, both for government-funded and for privately funded health care.

To some extent, the implicit liabilities of the U.S. government are already reflected in debt statistics. We mentioned earlier that the government had a total debt of \$16.1 trillion at the end of fiscal 2012 but that only \$11.3 trillion of that total was owed to the public. The main explanation for that discrepancy is that both Social Security and part of Medicare (the hospital insurance program) are supported by *dedicated taxes:* their expenses are paid out of special taxes on wages. At times, these dedicated taxes yield more revenue than is needed to pay current benefits. In particular, since the mid-1980s the Social Security system has been taking in more revenue than it currently needs in order to prepare for the retirement of the baby boomers. This surplus in the Social Security system has been used to accumulate a *Social Security trust fund,* which was about \$3 trillion at the end of fiscal 2012.

The money in the trust fund is held in the form of U.S. government bonds, which are included in the \$16.1 trillion in total debt. You could say that there's something funny about counting bonds in the Social Security trust fund as part of government debt. After all, these bonds are owed by one part of the government (the government outside the Social Security system) to another part of the government (the Social Security system itself). But the debt corresponds to a real, if implicit, liability: promises by the government to pay future retirement benefits. So many economists argue that the gross debt of \$16.1 trillion, the sum of public debt and government debt held by Social Security and other trust funds, is a more accurate indication of the government's fiscal health than the smaller amount owed to the public alone.

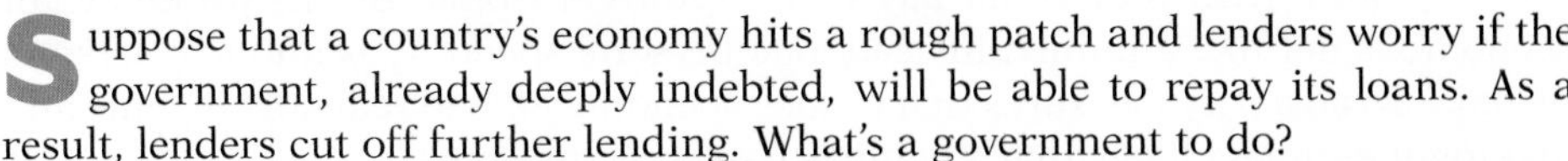

AUSTERITY DILEMMAS

Suppose that a country's economy hits a rough patch and lenders worry if the government, already deeply indebted, will be able to repay its loans. As a result, lenders cut off further lending. What's a government to do?

The usual prescription has been fiscal austerity: cut government spending and raise taxes, to both reduce the need to borrow more funds and to demonstrate to lenders the ability and determination to do what's necessary to honor its debts. But besides being painful and politically unpopular, does fiscal austerity really work to extricate a country from a crisis of lender confidence? Both economics and history indicate that the likely answer is no.

Fiscal austerity means contractionary fiscal policy. And we know from our earlier analysis that if an economy is already depressed, contractionary fiscal policy will depress it further. Moreover, the experiences of Argentina and Ireland show that the worsened state of an economy arising from austerity can further undermine the lender confidence that it was supposed to support.

Argentina presents a clear picture of the dynamic. Starting in the 1990s, Argentina was a favorite of foreign lenders and borrowed freely from abroad. But its debts accumulated, and by the late 2000s when the economy hit a downturn, lenders began to get worried. From 1997 to 2001, Argentina tried to reassure lenders that it was credit-worthy by repeatedly raising taxes and cutting government spending. But each round of austerity so weakened the economy that the government was unable to balance its budget. Finally, facing massive popular protests, the government collapsed and defaulted on its debts.

Since 2009, Ireland has gone through a similar experience, although the origins of its troubles were different. Until 2008, Ireland's government ran a more or less balanced budget. But during the 2000s, the Irish economy had a massive real estate bubble, fueled by excessive bank lending to real estate developers. When the bubble burst, Irish banks were left with massive losses. In order to prop them up, the Irish government guaranteed the banks' losses, making Irish taxpayers responsible for paying off the banks' debts. But, as it turns out, these debts were so large that the government's own solvency came into question, and the interest rate at which it had to borrow rose abruptly. This result can be seen in Figure 15-13, which shows how the interest rate spread between Irish government bonds and German government bonds (which are considered very safe) jumped in late 2008 and early 2009.

In an attempt to regain lender confidence, Ireland imposed severe austerity, even though the economy had already fallen into recession. For example, the government adopted a policy of reducing its workforce by 25,000; calculated as a percentage of the population, this was equivalent to a loss of 2.5 million jobs in the United States.

By mid-2010, the Irish austerity policy appeared to be working, as rates on Irish bonds stabilized and even fell a bit from 2009 to 2010. But by 2011, it all fell apart as the size of the banks' losses continued to mushroom and it became clear that the austerity policies were pushing the economy deeper into a recession. By late 2010, Irish GDP was 12% lower than it had been at the end of 2007, with very little growth in 2011 or 2012. The weaknesses of the Irish economy were depressing tax revenues, undoing much of the direct effect of austerity. Simultaneously, the decline in GDP had contributed to a surge in the debt–GDP ratio.

FIGURE 15-13 Interest Rates on Irish and German Bonds

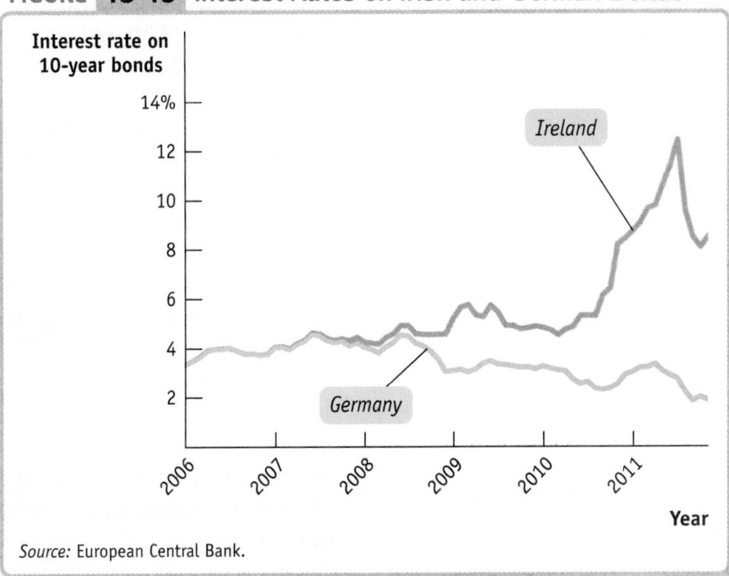

Source: European Central Bank.

So why do lenders advocate, and indebted countries adopt, such self-defeating austerity measures? Because they make the mistake of thinking that an economy is like a household: if the family would just cut back on their spending, so the thinking goes, then they could pay their credit card bills. But as we know, an economy is not like a family; instead, one person's spending is another person's income. So austerity measures that reduce spending end up reducing income and making it even less likely that a country can repay its debts.

Quick Review

- Persistent budget deficits lead to increases in **public debt.**
- Rising public debt can lead to government default. In less extreme cases, it can crowd out investment spending, reducing long-run growth. This suggests that budget deficits in bad **fiscal years** should be offset with budget surpluses in good fiscal years.
- A widely used indicator of fiscal health is the **debt–GDP ratio.** A country with rising GDP can have a stable or falling debt–GDP ratio even if it runs budget deficits if GDP is growing faster than the debt.
- In addition to their official public debt, modern governments have implicit liabilities. The U.S. government has large **implicit liabilities** in the form of Social Security, Medicare, and Medicaid.

CHECK YOUR UNDERSTANDING 15-4

1. Explain how each of the following events would affect the public debt or implicit liabilities of the U.S. government, other things equal. Would the public debt or implicit liabilities be greater or smaller?
   a. A higher growth rate of real GDP
   b. Retirees live longer
   c. A decrease in tax revenue
   d. Government borrowing to pay interest on its current public debt
2. Suppose the economy is in a slump and the current public debt is quite large. Explain the trade-off of short-run versus long-run objectives that policy makers face when deciding whether or not to engage in deficit spending.
3. Explain how a policy of fiscal austerity can make it more likely that a government is unable to pay its debts.

Solutions appear at back of book.

WORKED PROBLEM

Mind the Gap

The Congressional Budget Office is an independent federal agency founded in 1974 to provide Congress with nonpartisan and timely economic data on budgetary matters. One of its tasks is to produce estimates of GDP and potential GDP and then make projections about recessionary or inflationary gaps. Congress then uses this information to make decisions about the need for expansionary or contractionary fiscal policies. In June of 2009, the Congressional Budget Office estimated that actual U.S. GDP was $14.22 trillion and potential GDP was $14.44 trillion for 2008. Knowing this, what was the size of the recessionary gap in 2008? Assuming that the marginal propensity to consume is 0.5, what is the change in government purchases of goods and services necessary to increase GDP by this amount if there are no price changes?

As you have learned, in February 2009 Congress passed the American Recovery and Reinvestment Act that provided for a nominal stimulus of $787 billion. By March 2010, only $62 billion of the nominal stimulus had actually been spent. Based on our assumptions above, by how much would this amount of government spending be expected to increase nominal GDP?

STEP 1: Find the size of the recessionary gap in 2008.

Read the section "The Business Cycle and the Cyclically Adjusted Budget Balance" beginning on page 462. A recessionary gap is when real GDP is below potential output.

As potential GDP is valued in 2008 dollars, the size of the recessionary gap in 2008 dollars was $14.44 trillion – $14.22 trillion = $0.22 trillion, or 220 billion dollars. ■

STEP 2: Find the multiplier.

Read the section "Multiplier Effects of an Increase in Government Purchases of Goods and Services" beginning on page 457.

The multiplier is equal to 1/(1 – *MPC*), so in this case, the multiplier is 1/(1 – 0.5) = 2. ■

STEP 3: Find the change in government purchases of goods and services necessary to close the gap with a multiplier of 2.

Again, read the section "Multiplier Effects of an Increase in Government Purchases of Goods and Services," beginning on page 457.

With no price changes and a multiplier of 2, government purchases of goods and services need to increase by $110 billion in order to close a recessionary gap of $220 billion. Without a change in the aggregate price level, a shift of the aggregate demand curve results in an equivalent change in equilibrium GDP. This assumption has the same effect as assuming that the short-run aggregate supply curve is horizontal. ■

STEP 4: By how much would $62 billion of government spending be expected to increase nominal GDP?

Use the multiplier from Step 2.

With a multiplier of 2, $62 billion of government spending would be expected to increase nominal GDP by $124 billion. Through the first half of 2009, the recessionary gap continued to widen, reaching an estimated $1.07 trillion during the second quarter of 2009—much larger than the estimated recessionary gap of $220 billion in 2008. During the last half of 2009 and the first quarter of 2010, the recessionary gap began to narrow, but slowly. The gap was still $996 billion at the end of 2011. Stimulus spending in 2009 and the first quarter of 2010 was not enough to quickly and significantly narrow a very wide recessionary gap. ■

SUMMARY

1. The government plays a large role in the economy, collecting a large share of GDP in taxes and spending a large share both to purchase goods and services and to make transfer payments, largely for **social insurance.** *Fiscal policy* is the use of taxes, government transfers, or government purchases of goods and services to shift the aggregate demand curve.
2. Government purchases of goods and services directly affect aggregate demand, and changes in taxes and government transfers affect aggregate demand indirectly by changing households' disposable income. **Expansionary fiscal policy** shifts the aggregate demand curve rightward; **contractionary fiscal policy** shifts the aggregate demand curve leftward.
3. Only when the economy is at full employment is there potential for crowding out of private spending and private investment spending by expansionary fiscal policy. The argument that expansionary fiscal policy won't work because of Ricardian equivalence—that consumers will cut back spending today to offset expected future tax increases—appears to be untrue in practice. What is clearly true is that very active fiscal policy may make the economy less stable due to time lags in policy formulation and implementation.
4. Fiscal policy has a multiplier effect on the economy, the size of which depends on the fiscal policy and the **marginal propensity to consume (*MPC*).** The *MPC* determines the size of the **multiplier,** the ratio of the total change in real GDP caused by an **autonomous change in aggregate spending** to the size of that autonomous change. Except in the case of lump-sum taxes, taxes reduce the size of the multiplier. Expansionary fiscal policy leads to an increase in real GDP, and contractionary fiscal policy leads to a reduction in real GDP. Because part of any change in taxes or transfers is absorbed by savings in the first round of spending, changes in government purchases of goods and services have a more powerful effect on the economy than equal-sized changes in taxes or transfers.
5. Rules governing taxes—with the exception of **lump-sum taxes**—and some transfers act as **automatic stabilizers,** reducing the size of the multiplier and

automatically reducing the size of fluctuations in the business cycle. In contrast, **discretionary fiscal policy** arises from deliberate actions by policy makers rather than from the business cycle.

6. Some of the fluctuations in the budget balance are due to the effects of the business cycle. In order to separate the effects of the business cycle from the effects of discretionary fiscal policy, governments estimate the **cyclically adjusted budget balance,** an estimate of the budget balance if the economy were at potential output.

7. U.S. government budget accounting is calculated on the basis of **fiscal years.** Persistent budget deficits have long-run consequences because they lead to an increase in **public debt.** This can be a problem for two reasons. Public debt may crowd out investment spending, which reduces long-run economic growth. And in extreme cases, rising debt may lead to government default, resulting in economic and financial turmoil.

8. A widely used measure of fiscal health is the **debt–GDP ratio.** This number can remain stable or fall even in the face of moderate budget deficits if GDP rises over time. However, a stable debt–GDP ratio may give a misleading impression that all is well because modern governments often have large **implicit liabilities.** The largest implicit liabilities of the U.S. government come from Social Security, Medicare, and Medicaid, the costs of which are increasing due to the aging of the population and rising medical costs.

KEY TERMS

PROBLEMS

1. The accompanying diagram shows the current macroeconomic situation for the economy of Albernia. You have been hired as an economic consultant to help the economy move to potential output, Y_P.

   a. Is Albernia facing a recessionary or inflationary gap?

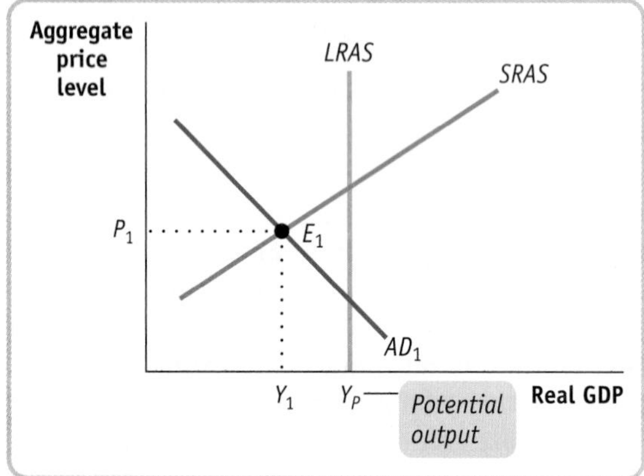

   b. Which type of fiscal policy—expansionary or contractionary—would move the economy of Albernia to potential output, Y_P? What are some examples of such policies?

   c. Illustrate the macroeconomic situation in Albernia with a diagram after the successful fiscal policy has been implemented.

2. The accompanying diagram shows the current macroeconomic situation for the economy of Brittania; real GDP is Y_1, and the aggregate price level is P_1. You have been hired as an economic consultant to help the economy move to potential output, Y_P.

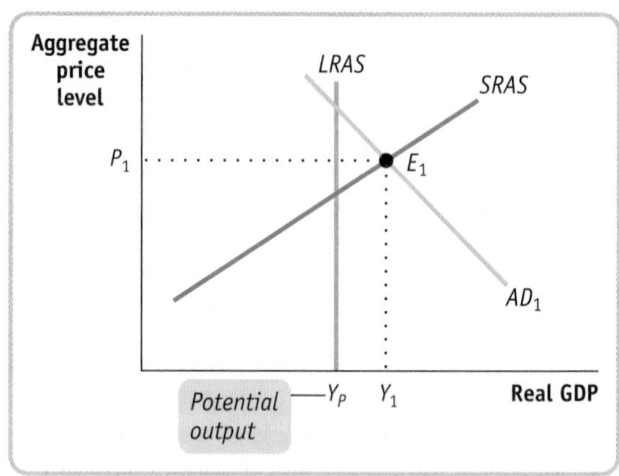

   a. Is Brittania facing a recessionary or inflationary gap?

   b. Which type of fiscal policy—expansionary or contractionary—would move the economy of Brittania to potential output, Y_P? What are some examples of such policies?

   c. Illustrate the macroeconomic situation in Brittania with a diagram after the successful fiscal policy has been implemented.

3. An economy is in long-run macroeconomic equilibrium when each of the following aggregate demand shocks occurs. What kind of gap—inflationary or recessionary—will the economy face after the shock, and what type of fiscal policies would help move the economy back to potential output? How would your recommended fiscal policy shift the aggregate demand curve?

a. A stock market boom increases the value of stocks held by households.

b. Firms come to believe that a recession in the near future is likely.

c. Anticipating the possibility of war, the government increases its purchases of military equipment.

d. The quantity of money in the economy declines and interest rates increase.

4. Show why a $10 billion reduction in government purchases of goods and services will have a larger effect on real GDP than a $10 billion reduction in government transfers by completing the accompanying table for an economy with a marginal propensity to consume (*MPC*) of 0.6. The first and second rows of the table are filled in for you: on the left side of the table, in the first row, the $10 billion reduction in government purchases decreases real GDP and disposable income, *YD*, by $10 billion, leading to a reduction in consumer spending of $6 billion (*MPC* × change in disposable income) in row 2. However, on the right side of the table, the $10 billion reduction in transfers has no effect on real GDP in round 1 but does lower *YD* by $10 billion, resulting in a decrease in consumer spending of $6 billion in round 2.

	Decrease in G = −$10 billion			Decrease in *TR* = −$10 billion		
	Billions of dollars			Billions of dollars		
Rounds	Change in G or C	Change in real GDP	Change in *YD*	Change in *TR* or C	Change in real GDP	Change in *YD*
1	ΔG = −$10.00	−$10.00	−$10.00	Δ*TR* = −$10.00	$0.00	−$10.00
2	ΔC = −6.00	−6.00	−6.00	ΔC = −6.00	−6.00	−6.00
3	ΔC = ?	?	?	ΔC = ?	?	?
4	ΔC = ?	?	?	ΔC = ?	?	?
5	ΔC = ?	?	?	ΔC = ?	?	?
6	ΔC = ?	?	?	ΔC = ?	?	?
7	ΔC = ?	?	?	ΔC = ?	?	?
8	ΔC = ?	?	?	ΔC = ?	?	?
9	ΔC = ?	?	?	ΔC = ?	?	?
10	ΔC = ?	?	?	ΔC = ?	?	?

a. When government purchases decrease by $10 billion, what is the sum of the changes in real GDP after the 10 rounds?

b. When the government reduces transfers by $10 billion, what is the sum of the changes in real GDP after the 10 rounds?

c. Using the formula for the multiplier for changes in government purchases and for changes in transfers, calculate the total change in real GDP due to the $10 billion decrease in government purchases and the $10 billion reduction in transfers. What explains the difference? (*Hint:* The multiplier for government purchases of goods and services is 1/(1 − *MPC*). But since each $1 change in government transfers only leads to an initial change in real GDP of *MPC* × $1, the multiplier for government transfers is *MPC*/(1 − *MPC*).)

5. In each of the following cases, either a recessionary or inflationary gap exists. Assume that the aggregate supply curve is horizontal, so that the change in real GDP arising from a shift of the aggregate demand curve equals the size of the shift of the curve. Calculate both the change in government purchases of goods and services and the change in government transfers necessary to close the gap.
   a. Real GDP equals $100 billion, potential output equals $160 billion, and the marginal propensity to consume is 0.75.
   b. Real GDP equals $250 billion, potential output equals $200 billion, and the marginal propensity to consume is 0.5.
   c. Real GDP equals $180 billion, potential output equals $100 billion, and the marginal propensity to consume is 0.8.

6. Most macroeconomists believe it is a good thing that taxes act as automatic stabilizers and lower the size of the multiplier. However, a smaller multiplier means that the change in government purchases of goods and services, government transfers, or taxes needed to close an inflationary or recessionary gap is larger. How can you explain this apparent inconsistency?

7. The accompanying table shows how consumers' marginal propensities to consume in a particular economy are related to their level of income.

Income range	Marginal propensity to consume
$0–$20,000	0.9
$20,001–$40,000	0.8
$40,001–$60,000	0.7
$60,001–$80,000	0.6
Above $80,000	0.5

   a. Suppose the government engages in increased purchases of goods and services. For each of the income groups in the table, what is the value of the multiplier—that is, what is the "bang for the buck" from each dollar the government spends on government purchases of goods and services in each income group?
   b. If the government needed to close a recessionary or inflationary gap, at which group should it primarily aim its fiscal policy of changes in government purchases of goods and services?

8. The government's budget surplus in Macroland has risen consistently over the past five years. Two government policy makers disagree as to why this has happened. One argues that a rising budget surplus indicates a growing economy; the other argues that it shows that the government is using contractionary fiscal policy. Can you determine which policy maker is correct? If not, why not?

9. Figure 15-9 shows the actual budget deficit and the cyclically adjusted budget deficit as a percentage of GDP in the United States from 1970 to 2011. Assuming that potential output was unchanged, use this figure to determine which of the years from 1990 to 2009 the government used expansionary fiscal policy and in which years it used contractionary fiscal policy.

10. You are an economic adviser to a candidate for national office. She asks you for a summary of the economic consequences of a balanced-budget rule for the federal government and for your recommendation on whether she should support such a rule. How do you respond?

11. Your study partner argues that the distinction between the government's budget deficit and debt is similar to the distinction between consumer savings and wealth. He also argues that if you have large budget deficits, you must have a large debt. In what ways is your study partner correct and in what ways is he incorrect?

12. In which of the following cases does the size of the government's debt and the size of the budget deficit indicate potential problems for the economy?
    a. The government's debt is relatively low, but the government is running a large budget deficit as it builds a high-speed rail system to connect the major cities of the nation.
    b. The government's debt is relatively high due to a recently ended deficit-financed war, but the government is now running only a small budget deficit.
    c. The government's debt is relatively low, but the government is running a budget deficit to finance the interest payments on the debt.

13. How did or would the following affect the current public debt and implicit liabilities of the U.S. government?
    a. In 2003, Congress passed and President Bush signed the Medicare Modernization Act, which provides seniors and individuals with disabilities with a prescription drug benefit. Some of the benefits under this law took effect immediately, but others will not begin until sometime in the future.
    b. The age at which retired persons can receive full Social Security benefits is raised to age 70 for future retirees.
    c. Social Security benefits for future retirees are limited to those with low incomes.
    d. Because the cost of health care is increasing faster than the overall inflation rate, annual increases in Social Security benefits are increased by the annual increase in health care costs rather than the overall inflation rate.

EXTEND YOUR UNDERSTANDING

14. In 2012, the policy makers of the economy of Eastlandia projected the debt–GDP ratio and the ratio of the budget deficit to GDP for the economy for the next 10 years under different scenarios for growth in the government's

deficit. Real GDP is currently $1,000 billion per year and is expected to grow by 3% per year, the public debt is $300 billion at the beginning of the year, and the deficit is $30 billion in 2012.

Year	Real GDP (billions of dollars)	Debt (billions) of dollars)	Budget deficit (billions of dollars)	Debt (percent of real GDP)	Budget deficit (percent of real GDP)
2012	$1,000	$300	$30	?	?
2013	1,030	?	?	?	?
2014	1,061	?	?	?	?
2015	1,093	?	?	?	?
2016	1,126	?	?	?	?
2017	1,159	?	?	?	?
2018	1,194	?	?	?	?
2019	1,230	?	?	?	?
2020	1,267	?	?	?	?
2021	1,305	?	?	?	?
2022	1,344	?	?	?	?

a. Complete the accompanying table to show the debt–GDP ratio and the ratio of the budget deficit to GDP for the economy if the government's budget deficit remains constant at $30 billion over the next 10 years. (Remember that the government's debt will grow by the previous year's deficit.)

b. Redo the table to show the debt–GDP ratio and the ratio of the budget deficit to GDP for the economy if the government's budget deficit grows by 3% per year over the next 10 years.

c. Redo the table again to show the debt–GDP ratio and the ratio of the budget deficit to GDP for the economy if the government's budget deficit grows by 20% per year over the next 10 years.

d. What happens to the debt–GDP ratio and the ratio of the budget deficit to GDP for the economy over time under the three different scenarios?

15. Unlike households, governments are often able to sustain large debts. For example, in 2011, the U.S. government's total debt reached $14.8 trillion, approximately equal to 102.7% of GDP. At the time, according to the U.S. Treasury, the average interest rate paid by the government on its debt was 2.2%. However, running budget deficits becomes hard when very large debts are outstanding.

a. Calculate the dollar cost of the annual interest on the government's total debt assuming the interest rate and debt figures cited above.

b. If the government operates on a balanced budget before interest payments are taken into account, at what rate must GDP grow in order for the debt–GDP ratio to remain unchanged?

c. Calculate the total increase in national debt if the government incurs a deficit of $600 billion in 2012.

d. At what rate would GDP have to grow in order for the debt–GDP ratio to remain unchanged when the deficit in 2012 is $600 billion?

e. Why is the debt–GDP ratio the preferred measure of a country's debt rather than the dollar value of the debt? Why is it important for a government to keep this number under control?

16. During an interview in 2008, the German Finance Minister Peer Steinbrueck said, "We have to watch out that in Europe and beyond, nothing like a combination of downward economic [growth] and high inflation rates emerges—something that experts call stagflation." Such a situation can be depicted by the movement of the short-run aggregate supply curve from its original position, $SRAS_1$, to its new position, $SRAS_2$, with the new equilibrium point E_2 in the accompanying figure. In this question, we try to understand why stagflation is particularly hard to fix using fiscal policy.

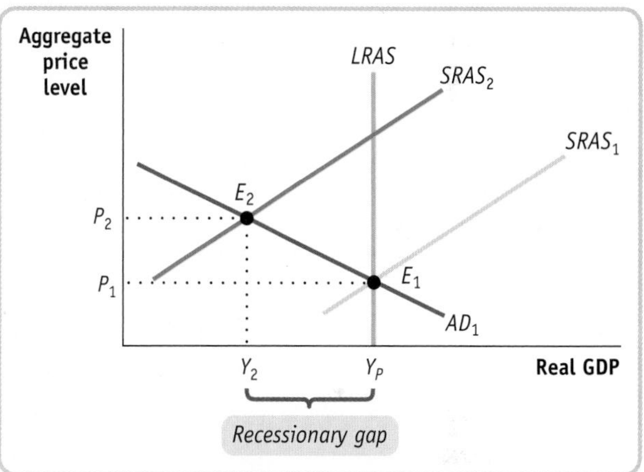

a. What would be the appropriate fiscal policy response to this situation if the primary concern of the government was to maintain economic growth? Illustrate the effect of the policy on the equilibrium point and the aggregate price level using the diagram.

b. What would be the appropriate fiscal policy response to this situation if the primary concern of the government was to maintain price stability? Illustrate the effect of the policy on the equilibrium point and the aggregate price level using the diagram.

c. Discuss the effectiveness of the policies in parts a and b in fighting stagflation.

CHAPTER 16

Money, Banking, and the Federal Reserve System

FUNNY MONEY

© Anna Delaw/Alamy

Money is the essential channel that links the various parts of the modern economy.

WHAT YOU WILL LEARN IN THIS CHAPTER

- The various roles **money** plays and the many forms it takes in the economy
- How the actions of private banks and the Federal Reserve determine the **money supply**
- How the Federal Reserve uses **open-market operations** to change the **monetary base**

ON OCTOBER 2, 2004, FBI AND Secret Service agents seized a shipping container that had just arrived in Newark, New Jersey, on a ship from China. Inside the container, under cardboard boxes containing plastic toys, they found what they were looking for: more than $300,000 in counterfeit $100 bills. Two months later, another shipment with $3 million in counterfeit bills was intercepted. Government and law enforcement officials began alleging publicly that these bills—high-quality fakes that were very hard to tell from the real thing—were being produced by the government of North Korea.

The funny thing is that elaborately decorated pieces of paper have little or no intrinsic value. Indeed, a $100 bill printed with blue or orange ink literally wouldn't be worth the paper it was printed on. But if the ink on that decorated piece of paper is just the right shade of green, people will think that it's money and will accept it as payment for very real goods and services. Why? Because they believe, correctly, that they can do the same thing: exchange that piece of green paper for real goods and services.

In fact, here's a riddle: if a fake $100 bill from North Korea enters the United States, and nobody ever realizes it's fake, who gets hurt? Accepting a fake $100 bill isn't like buying a car that turns out to be a lemon or a meal that turns out to be inedible; as long as the bill's counterfeit nature remains undiscovered, it will pass from hand to hand just like a real $100 bill. The answer to the riddle, as we'll learn later in this chapter, is that the real victims of North Korean counterfeiting are U.S. taxpayers, because counterfeit dollars reduce the revenues available to pay for the operations of the U.S. government. Accordingly, the Secret Service diligently monitors the integrity of U.S. currency, promptly investigating any reports of counterfeit dollars.

The efforts of the Secret Service attest to the fact that money isn't like ordinary goods and services. It plays a unique role in the economy as the essential channel that links the various parts of the modern economy. In this chapter, we'll look at the role money plays, then look at how a modern monetary system works and at the institutions that sustain and regulate it. This topic is important in itself, and it's also essential background for the understanding of monetary policy, which we will examine in the next chapter. ■

Money is any asset that can easily be used to purchase goods and services.

An asset is **liquid** if it can be quickly converted into cash without much loss of value.

Currency in circulation is cash held by the public.

Checkable bank deposits are bank accounts on which people can write checks.

The **money supply** is the total value of financial assets in the economy that are considered money.

The Meaning of Money

In everyday conversation, people often use the word *money* to mean "wealth." If you ask, "How much money does Bill Gates have?" the answer will be something like, "Oh, $50 billion or so, but who's counting?" That is, the number will include the value of the stocks, bonds, real estate, and other assets he owns.

But the economist's definition of money doesn't include all forms of wealth. The dollar bills in your wallet are money; other forms of wealth—such as cars, houses, and stock certificates—aren't money. What, according to economists, distinguishes money from other forms of wealth?

What Is Money?

Money is defined in terms of what it does: **money** is any asset that can easily be used to purchase goods and services. An asset is **liquid** if it can easily be converted into cash without much loss of value. Money consists of cash itself, which is liquid by definition, as well as other assets that are highly liquid.

You can see the distinction between money and other assets by asking yourself how you pay for groceries. The person at the cash register will accept dollar bills in return for milk and frozen pizza—but he or she won't accept stock certificates or a collection of vintage baseball cards. If you want to convert stock certificates or vintage baseball cards into groceries, you have to sell them—trade them for money—and then use the money to buy groceries.

Of course, many stores allow you to write a check on your bank account in payment for goods (or to pay with a debit card that is linked to your bank account). Does that make your bank account money, even if you haven't converted it into cash? Yes. **Currency in circulation**—actual cash in the hands of the public—is considered money. So are **checkable bank deposits**—bank accounts on which people can write checks.

Are currency and checkable bank deposits the only assets that are considered money? It depends. As we'll see later, there are two widely used definitions of the **money supply,** the total value of financial assets in the economy that are considered money. The narrower definition considers only the most liquid assets to be money: currency in circulation, traveler's checks, and checkable bank deposits. The broader definition includes these three categories plus other assets that are "almost" checkable, such as savings account deposits that can be transferred into a checking account with a phone call or a mouse click. Both definitions of the money supply, however, make a distinction between those assets that can easily be used to purchase goods and services and those that can't.

Money plays a crucial role in generating *gains from trade* because it makes indirect exchange possible. Think of what happens when a cardiac surgeon buys a new refrigerator. The surgeon has valuable services to offer—namely, heart operations. The owner of the store has valuable goods to offer—refrigerators and other appliances. It would be extremely difficult for both parties if, instead of using money, they had to directly barter the goods and services they sell. In a barter system, a cardiac surgeon and an appliance store owner could trade only if the store owner happened to want a heart operation and the surgeon happened to want a new refrigerator.

This is known as the problem of finding a "double coincidence of wants": in a barter system, two parties can trade only when each wants what the other has to offer. Money solves this problem: individuals can trade what they have to offer for money and trade money for what they want.

Because the ability to make transactions with money rather than relying on bartering makes it easier to achieve gains from trade, the existence of money increases welfare, even though money does not directly produce anything. As Adam Smith put it, money "may very properly be compared to a highway, which, while it circulates and carries to market all the grass and corn of the country, produces itself not a single pile of either."

Let's take a closer look at the roles money plays in the economy.

A **medium of exchange** is an asset that individuals acquire for the purpose of trading goods and services rather than for their own consumption.

A **store of value** is a means of holding purchasing power over time.

Roles of Money

Money plays three main roles in any modern economy: it is a *medium of exchange*, a *store of value*, and a *unit of account*.

1. Medium of Exchange Our cardiac surgeon/refrigerator example illustrates the role of money as a **medium of exchange**—an asset that individuals use to trade for goods and services rather than for consumption. People can't eat dollar bills; rather, they use dollar bills to trade for edible goods and their accompanying services.

In normal times, the official money of a given country—the dollar in the United States, the peso in Mexico, and so on—is also the medium of exchange in virtually all transactions in that country. During troubled economic times, however, other goods or assets often play that role instead. For example, during economic turmoil people often turn to other countries' moneys as the medium of exchange: U.S. dollars have played this role in troubled Latin American countries, as have euros in troubled Eastern European countries. In a famous example, cigarettes functioned as the medium of exchange in World War II prisoner-of-war camps: even nonsmokers traded goods and services for cigarettes because the cigarettes could in turn be easily traded for other items. During the extreme German inflation of 1923, goods such as eggs and lumps of coal became, briefly, mediums of exchange.

2. Store of Value In order to act as a medium of exchange, money must also be a **store of value**—a means of holding purchasing power over time. To see why this is necessary, imagine trying to operate an economy in which

THE BIG MONEYS

Americans tend to think of the dollar as the world's leading currency—and it does remain the currency most likely to be accepted in payment around the globe. But there are other important currencies, too. One simple measure of a currency's importance is the value of the quantity of that currency in circulation. This figure shows the value, in billions of dollars, of the quantity of four major currencies in circulation at the end of 2010. The dollar, it turns out, is only number 2, behind the euro. The euro's prominence isn't that surprising, since the combined economies of the countries using the euro, the eurozone, are about as big as the U.S. economy. And despite the fact that its economy is much smaller, Japan is closely behind the United States, largely because the Japanese make much more use of cash, as opposed to checks and credit cards, than either Europeans or Americans. And China, with its rapidly growing economy, is moving up the charts.

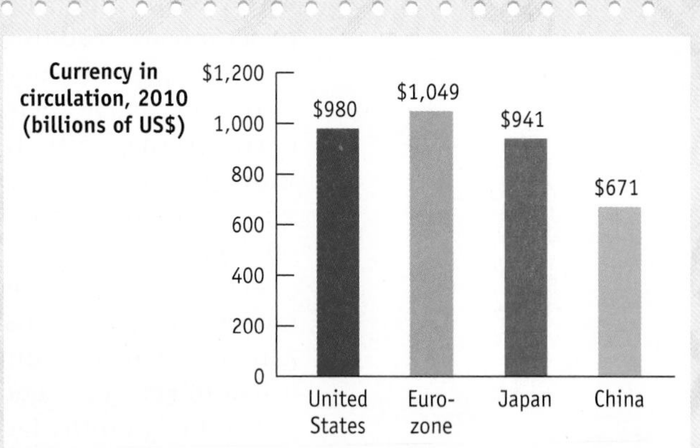

Sources: Federal Reserve Bank of St. Louis; European Central Bank; Bank of Japan; The People's Bank of China.

A **unit of account** is a measure used to set prices and make economic calculations.

Commodity money is a good used as a medium of exchange that has intrinsic value in other uses.

Commodity-backed money is a medium of exchange with no intrinsic value whose ultimate value is guaranteed by a promise that it can be converted into valuable goods.

ice-cream cones were the medium of exchange. Such an economy would quickly suffer from, well, monetary meltdown: your medium of exchange would often turn into a sticky puddle before you could use it to buy something else. Of course, money is by no means the only store of value. Any asset that holds its purchasing power over time is a store of value. So the store-of-value role is a necessary but not distinctive feature of money.

3. Unit of Account Finally, money normally serves as the **unit of account**—the commonly accepted measure individuals use to set prices and make economic calculations. To understand the importance of this role, consider a historical fact: during the Middle Ages, peasants typically were required to provide landowners with goods and labor rather than money. A peasant might, for example, be required to work on the lord's land one day a week and hand over one-fifth of his harvest.

Today, rents, like other prices, are almost always specified in money terms. That makes things much clearer: imagine how hard it would be to decide which apartment to rent if modern landlords followed medieval practice. Suppose, for example, that Mr. Smith says he'll let you have a place if you clean his house twice a week and bring him a pound of steak every day, whereas Ms. Jones wants you to clean her house just once a week but wants four pounds of chicken every day. Who's offering the better deal? It's hard to say. If, instead, Smith wants $600 a month and Jones wants $700, the comparison is easy. In other words, without a commonly accepted measure, the terms of a transaction are harder to determine, making it more difficult to make transactions and achieve gains from trade.

Types of Money

In some form or another, money has been in use for thousands of years. For most of that period, people used **commodity money:** the medium of exchange was a good, normally gold or silver, that had intrinsic value in other uses. These alternative uses gave commodity money value independent of its role as a medium of exchange. For example, cigarettes, which served as money in World War II prisoner of war camps, were also valuable because many prisoners smoked. Gold was valuable because it was used for jewelry and ornamentation, aside from the fact that it was minted into coins.

By 1776, the year in which the United States declared independence and Adam Smith published *The Wealth of Nations,* there was widespread use of paper money in addition to gold or silver coins. Unlike modern dollar bills, however, this paper money consisted of notes issued by private banks, which promised to exchange their notes for gold or silver coins on demand. So the paper currency that initially replaced commodity money was **commodity-backed money,** a medium of exchange with no intrinsic value whose ultimate value was guaranteed by a promise that it could always be converted into valuable goods on demand.

The big advantage of commodity-backed money over simple commodity money, like gold and silver coins, was that it tied up fewer valuable resources. Although a note-issuing bank still had to keep some gold and silver on hand, it had to keep only enough to satisfy demands for redemption of its notes. And it could rely on the fact that on a normal day only a fraction of its paper notes would be redeemed. So the bank needed to keep only a portion of the total value of its notes in circulation in the form of gold and silver in its vaults. It could lend out the remaining gold and silver to those who wished to use it. This allowed society to use the remaining gold and silver for other purposes, all with no loss in the ability to achieve gains from trade.

In a famous passage in *The Wealth of Nations,* Adam Smith described paper money as a "waggon-way through the air." Smith was making an analogy between money and an imaginary highway that did not absorb valuable land beneath it. An actual highway provides a useful service but at a cost: land that could be used to grow crops is instead paved over. If the highway could be built through the air, it wouldn't destroy useful land. As Smith understood, when banks replaced gold and silver money with paper notes, they accomplished a similar feat: they reduced the amount of real resources used by society to provide the functions of money.

At this point you may ask: why make any use at all of gold and silver in the monetary system, even to back paper money? In fact, today's monetary system goes even further than the system Smith admired, having eliminated any role for gold and silver. A U.S. dollar bill isn't commodity money, and it isn't even commodity-backed. Rather, its value arises entirely from the fact that it is generally accepted as a means of payment, a role that is ultimately decreed by the U.S. government. Money whose value derives entirely from its official status as a means of exchange is known as **fiat money** because it exists by government fiat, a historical term for a policy declared by a ruler.

Fiat money has two major advantages over commodity-backed money. First, it is even more of a "waggon-way through the air"—creating it doesn't use up any real resources beyond the paper it's printed on. Second, the supply of money can be adjusted based on the needs of the economy, instead of being determined by the amount of gold and silver prospectors happen to discover.

Fiat money, though, poses some risks. In this chapter's opening story, we described one such risk—counterfeiting. Counterfeiters usurp a privilege of the U.S. government, which has the sole legal right to print dollar bills. And the benefit that counterfeiters get by exchanging fake bills for real goods and services comes at the expense of the U.S. federal government, which covers a small but nontrivial part of its own expenses by issuing new currency to meet a growing demand for money.

The larger risk is that governments that can create money whenever they feel like it will be tempted to abuse the privilege.

Fiat money is a medium of exchange whose value derives entirely from its official status as a means of payment.

A **monetary aggregate** is an overall measure of the money supply.

Near-moneys are financial assets that can't be directly used as a medium of exchange but can be readily converted into cash or checkable bank deposits.

Measuring the Money Supply

The Federal Reserve (an institution we'll talk about shortly) calculates the size of two **monetary aggregates,** overall measures of the money supply, which differ in how strictly money is defined. The two aggregates are known, rather cryptically, as M1 and M2. (There used to be a third aggregate named—you guessed it—M3, but in 2006 the Federal Reserve concluded that measuring it was no longer useful.)

M1, the narrowest definition, contains only currency in circulation (also known as cash), traveler's checks, and checkable bank deposits. M2 adds several other kinds of assets, often referred to as **near-moneys**—financial assets that aren't directly usable as a medium of exchange but can be readily converted into cash or checkable bank deposits, such as savings accounts. Examples are time deposits such as small-denomination CDs, which aren't checkable but can be withdrawn at any time before their

WHAT'S NOT IN THE MONEY SUPPLY

Are financial assets like stocks and bonds part of the money supply? No, not under any definition, because they're not liquid enough.

M1 consists, roughly speaking, of assets you can use to buy groceries: currency, traveler's checks, and checkable deposits (which work as long as your grocery store accepts either checks or debit cards). M2 is broader, because it includes things like savings accounts that can easily and quickly be converted into M1. Normally, for example, you can switch funds between your savings and checking accounts with a click of a mouse or a call to an automated phone service.

By contrast, converting a stock or a bond into cash requires selling the stock or bond—something that usually takes some time and also involves paying a broker's fee. That makes these assets much less liquid than bank deposits. So stocks and bonds, unlike bank deposits, aren't considered money.

FIGURE 16-1 Monetary Aggregates, September 2011

The Federal Reserve uses two definitions of the money supply, M1 and M2. As panel (a) shows, more than half of M1 consists of checkable bank deposits with currency in circulation making up virtually all of the rest. M2, as panel (b) shows, has a much broader definition: it includes M1 plus a range of other deposits and deposit-like assets, making it almost five times as large.

Source: Federal Reserve Bank of St. Louis.

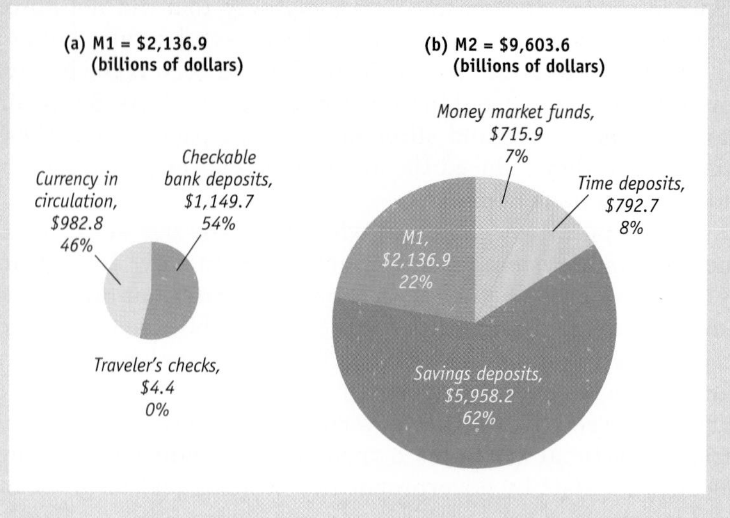

maturity date by paying a penalty. Because currency and checkable deposits are directly usable as a medium of exchange, M1 is the most liquid measure of money.

Figure 16-1 shows the actual composition of M1 and M2 in September 2011, in billions of dollars. M1 was valued at $2,136.9 billion, with just under half accounted for by currency in circulation, almost all the rest accounted for by checkable bank deposits, and a tiny slice accounted for by traveler's checks. In turn, M1 made up 22% of M2, valued at $9,603.6 billion. M2 consists of M1 plus other types of assets: two types of bank deposits, known as savings deposits and time deposits, both of which are considered noncheckable, plus money market funds, which are mutual funds that invest only in liquid assets and bear a close resemblance to bank deposits. These near-moneys pay interest although cash (currency in circulation) does not, and they typically pay higher interest rates than any offered on checkable bank deposits.

FOR INQUIRING MINDS

WHAT'S WITH ALL THE CURRENCY?

Alert readers may be a bit startled at one of the numbers in the money supply: almost $1,000 billion of currency in circulation. That's just over $3,000 in cash for every man, woman, and child in the United States. How many people do you know who carry $3,000 in their wallets? Not many. So where is all that cash?

Part of the answer is that it isn't in individuals' wallets—it's in cash registers. Businesses as well as individuals need to hold cash.

Economists believe that cash also plays an important role in transactions that people want to keep hidden. Small businesses and the self-employed sometimes prefer to be paid in cash so they can avoid paying taxes by hiding income from the Internal Revenue Service. Also, drug dealers and other criminals obviously don't want bank records of their dealings. In fact, some analysts have tried to infer the amount of illegal activity in the economy from the total amount of cash holdings held by the public.

The most important reason for those huge currency holdings, however, is foreign use of dollars. The Federal Reserve estimates that 60% of U.S. currency is actually held outside the United States—largely in countries in which residents are so distrustful of their national currencies that the U.S. dollar has become a widely accepted medium of exchange.

ECONOMICS ➤ IN ACTION

THE HISTORY OF THE DOLLAR

U.S. dollar bills are pure fiat money: they have no intrinsic value, and they are not backed by anything that does. But American money wasn't always like that. In the early days of European settlement, the colonies that would become the United States used commodity money, partly consisting of gold and silver coins minted in Europe. But such coins were scarce on this side of the Atlantic, so the colonists relied on a variety of other forms of commodity money. For example, settlers in Virginia used tobacco as money and settlers in the Northeast used "wampum," a type of clamshell.

Later in American history, commodity-backed paper money came into widespread use. But this wasn't paper money as we now know it, issued by the U.S. government and bearing the signature of the Secretary of the Treasury. Before the Civil War, the U.S. government didn't issue any paper money. Instead, dollar bills were issued by private banks, which promised that their bills could be redeemed for silver coins on demand. These promises weren't always credible because banks sometimes failed, leaving holders of their bills with worthless pieces of paper. Understandably, people were reluctant to accept currency from any bank rumored to be in financial trouble. In this private money system, some dollars were less valuable than others.

A curious legacy of that time was notes issued by the Citizens' Bank of Louisiana, based in New Orleans, that became among the most widely used bank notes in the southern states. These notes were printed in English on one side and French on the other. (At the time, many people in New Orleans, originally a colony of France, spoke French.) Thus, the $10 bill read *Ten* on one side and *Dix,* the French word for "ten," on the other. These $10 bills became known as "dixies," probably the source of the nickname of the U.S. South.

Reuters/Corbis

Not until the Civil War did the U.S. government issue official paper money.

The U.S. government began issuing official paper money, called "greenbacks," during the Civil War, as a way to help pay for the war. At first greenbacks had no fixed value in terms of commodities. After 1873, the U.S. government guaranteed the value of a dollar in terms of gold, effectively turning dollars into commodity-backed money.

In 1933, when President Franklin D. Roosevelt broke the link between dollars and gold, his own federal budget director—who feared that the public would lose confidence in the dollar if it wasn't ultimately backed by gold—declared ominously, "This will be the end of Western civilization." It wasn't. The link between the dollar and gold was restored a few years later, then dropped again—seemingly for good—in August 1971. Despite the warnings of doom, the U.S. dollar went on to become the world's most widely used currency. (Now it is the second-most widely used, after the euro.)

▼ Quick Review

- **Money** is any asset that can easily be used to purchase goods and services. Money consists of cash, which is **liquid** by definition, as well as other highly liquid assets. **Currency in circulation** and **checkable bank deposits** are both part of the **money supply.**
- Money plays three roles: a **medium of exchange,** a **store of value,** and a **unit of account.**
- Historically, money took the form first of **commodity money,** then of **commodity-backed money.** Today the dollar is pure **fiat money.**
- The money supply is measured by two **monetary aggregates:** M1 and M2. M1 consists of currency in circulation, checkable bank deposits, and traveler's checks. M2 consists of M1 plus various kinds of **near-moneys.**

CHECK YOUR UNDERSTANDING 16-1

1. Suppose you hold a gift certificate, good for certain products at participating stores. Is this gift certificate money? Why or why not?
2. Although most bank accounts pay some interest, depositors can get a higher interest rate by buying a certificate of deposit, or CD. The difference between a CD and a checking account is that the depositor pays a penalty for withdrawing the money before the CD comes due—a period of months or even years. Small CDs are counted in M2 but not in M1. Explain why they are not part of M1.
3. Explain why a system of commodity-backed money uses resources more efficiently than a system of commodity money.

Solutions appear at back of book.

Bank reserves are the currency banks hold in their vaults plus their deposits at the Federal Reserve.

A **T-account** is a tool for analyzing a business's financial position by showing, in a single table, the business's assets (on the left) and liabilities (on the right).

The Monetary Role of Banks

Roughly half of M1, the narrowest definition of the money supply, consists of currency in circulation—$1 bills, $5 bills, and so on. It's obvious where currency comes from: it's printed by the U.S. Treasury. But the rest of M1 consists of bank deposits, and deposits account for the great bulk of M2, the broader definition of the money supply. By either measure, then, bank deposits are a major component of the money supply. And this fact brings us to our next topic: the monetary role of banks.

What Banks Do

A bank uses liquid assets in the form of bank deposits to finance the illiquid investments of borrowers. Banks can create liquidity because it isn't necessary for a bank to keep all of the funds deposited with it in the form of highly liquid assets. Except in the case of a *bank run*—which we'll get to shortly—all of a bank's depositors won't want to withdraw their funds at the same time. So a bank can provide its depositors with liquid assets yet still invest much of the depositors' funds in illiquid assets, such as mortgages and business loans.

Banks can't, however, lend out all the funds placed in their hands by depositors because they have to satisfy any depositor who wants to withdraw his or her funds. In order to meet these demands, a bank must keep substantial quantities of liquid assets on hand. In the modern U.S. banking system, these assets take the form either of currency in the bank's vault or deposits held in the bank's own account at the Federal Reserve. As we'll see shortly, the latter can be converted into currency more or less instantly. Currency in bank vaults and bank deposits held at the Federal Reserve are called **bank reserves.** Because bank reserves are in bank vaults and at the Federal Reserve, not held by the public, they are not part of currency in circulation.

To understand the role of banks in determining the money supply, we start by introducing a simple tool for analyzing a bank's financial position: a **T-account.** A business's T-account summarizes its financial position by showing, in a single table, the business's assets and liabilities, with assets on the left and liabilities on the right.

Figure 16-2 shows the T-account for a hypothetical business that *isn't* a bank—Samantha's Smoothies. According to Figure 16-2, Samantha's Smoothies owns a building worth $30,000 and has $15,000 worth of smoothie-making equipment. These are assets, so they're on the left side of the table. To finance its opening, the business borrowed $20,000 from a local bank. That's a liability, so the loan is on the right side of the table. By looking at the T-account, you can immediately see what Samantha's Smoothies owns and what it owes. Oh, and it's called a T-account because the lines in the table make a T-shape.

Samantha's Smoothies is an ordinary, nonbank business. Now let's look at the T-account for a hypothetical bank, First Street Bank, which is the repository of $1 million in bank deposits.

FIGURE 16-2 A T-Account for Samantha's Smoothies

A T-account summarizes a business's financial position. Its assets, in this case consisting of a building and some smoothie-making machinery, are on the left side. Its liabilities, consisting of the money it owes to a local bank, are on the right side.

Assets		Liabilities	
Building	$30,000	Loan from bank	$20,000
Smoothie-making machines	$15,000		

FIGURE 16-3 Assets and Liabilities of First Street Bank

First Street Bank's assets consist of $1,200,000 in loans and $100,000 in reserves. Its liabilities consist of $1,000,000 in deposits—money owed to people who have placed funds in First Street's hands.

Assets		Liabilities	
Loans	$1,200,000	Deposits	$1,000,000
Reserves	$100,000		

Figure 16-3 shows First Street Bank's financial position. The loans First Street Bank has made are on the left side because they're assets: they represent funds that those who have borrowed from the bank are expected to repay. The bank's only other assets, in this simplified example, are its reserves, which, as we've learned, can take the form either of cash in the bank's vault or deposits at the Federal Reserve. On the right side we show the bank's liabilities, which in this example consist entirely of deposits made by customers at First Street Bank. These are liabilities because they represent funds that must ultimately be repaid to depositors.

Notice, by the way, that in this example First Street Bank's assets are larger than its liabilities. That's the way it's supposed to be! In fact, as we'll see shortly, banks are required by law to maintain assets larger by a specific percentage than their liabilities.

In this example, First Street Bank holds reserves equal to 10% of its customers' bank deposits. The fraction of bank deposits that a bank holds as reserves is its **reserve ratio.** In the modern American system, the Federal Reserve—which, among other things, regulates banks operating in the United States—sets a minimum required reserve ratio that banks are required to maintain. To understand why banks are regulated, let's consider a problem banks can face: bank runs.

The Problem of Bank Runs

A bank can lend out most of the funds deposited in its care because in normal times only a small fraction of its depositors want to withdraw their funds on any given day. But what would happen if, for some reason, all or at least a large fraction of its depositors did try to withdraw their funds during a short period of time, such as a couple of days?

If a significant share of its depositors demand their money back at the same time, the bank wouldn't be able to raise enough cash to meet those demands. The reason is that banks convert most of their depositors' funds into loans made to borrowers; that's how banks earn revenue—by charging interest on loans.

Bank loans, however, are illiquid: they can't easily be converted into cash on short notice. To see why, imagine that First Street Bank has lent $100,000 to Drive-A-Peach Used Cars, a local dealership. To raise cash to meet demands for withdrawals, First Street Bank can sell its loan to Drive-A-Peach to someone else—another bank or an individual investor. But if First Street Bank tries to sell the loan quickly, potential buyers will be wary: they will suspect that First Street Bank wants to sell the loan because there is something wrong and the loan might not be repaid. As a result, First Street Bank can sell the loan quickly only by offering it for sale at a deep discount—say, a discount of 40%, for a sale price of $60,000.

The upshot is that if a significant number of First Street Bank's depositors suddenly decided to withdraw their funds, the bank's efforts to raise the necessary cash quickly would force it to sell off its assets very cheaply. Inevitably, this leads to a *bank failure:* the bank would be unable to pay off its depositors in full.

The **reserve ratio** is the fraction of bank deposits that a bank holds as reserves.

A **bank run** is a phenomenon in which many of a bank's depositors try to withdraw their funds due to fears of a bank failure.

Deposit insurance guarantees that a bank's depositors will be paid even if the bank can't come up with the funds, up to a maximum amount per account.

What might start this whole process? That is, what might lead First Street Bank's depositors to rush to pull their money out? A plausible answer is a spreading rumor that the bank is in financial trouble. Even if depositors aren't sure the rumor is true, they are likely to play it safe and get their money out while they still can. And it gets worse: a depositor who simply thinks that *other* depositors are going to panic and try to get their money out will realize that this could "break the bank." So he or she joins the rush. In other words, fear about a bank's financial condition can be a self-fulfilling prophecy: depositors who believe that other depositors will rush to the exit will rush to the exit themselves.

A **bank run** is a phenomenon in which many of a bank's depositors try to withdraw their funds due to fears of a bank failure. Moreover, bank runs aren't bad only for the bank in question and its depositors. Historically, they have often proved contagious, with a run on one bank leading to a loss of faith in other banks, causing additional bank runs. The upcoming Economics in Action describes an actual case of just such a contagion, the wave of bank runs that swept across the United States in the early 1930s. In response to that experience and similar experiences in other countries, the United States and most other modern governments have established a system of bank regulations that protect depositors and prevent most bank runs. We'll encounter bank runs again in Chapter 18, which contains an in-depth analysis of financial crises and their aftermath.

Bank Regulation

Should you worry about losing money in the United States due to a bank run? No. After the banking crises of the 1930s, the United States and most other countries put into place a system designed to protect depositors and the economy as a whole against bank runs. This system has four main features: *deposit insurance, capital requirements, reserve requirements,* and, in addition, banks have access to the *discount window,* a source of cash when it's needed.

1. Deposit Insurance Almost all banks in the United States advertise themselves as a "member of the FDIC"—the Federal Deposit Insurance Corporation. The FDIC provides **deposit insurance,** a guarantee that depositors will be paid even if the bank can't come up with the funds, up to a maximum amount per account. The FDIC currently guarantees the first $250,000 per depositor, per insured bank.

It's important to realize that deposit insurance doesn't just protect depositors if a bank actually fails. The insurance also eliminates the main reason for bank runs: since depositors know their funds are safe even if a bank fails, they have no incentive to rush to pull them out because of a rumor that the bank is in trouble.

2. Capital Requirements Deposit insurance, although it protects the banking system against bank runs, creates a well-known incentive problem. Because depositors are protected from loss, they have no incentive to monitor their bank's financial health, allowing risky behavior by the bank to go undetected. At the same time, the owners of banks have an incentive to engage in overly risky investment behavior, such as making questionable loans at high interest rates. That's because if all goes well, the owners profit; if things go badly, the government covers the losses through federal deposit insurance.

To reduce the incentive for excessive risk taking, regulators require that the owners of banks hold substantially more assets than the value of bank deposits. That way, the bank will still have assets larger than its deposits even if some of its loans go bad, and losses will accrue against the bank owners' assets, not the government. The excess of a bank's assets over its bank deposits and other liabilities is called the *bank's capital*. For example, First Street Bank has capital of $300,000, equal to $300,000/($1,200,000 + $100,000) = 23% of the total value of its assets. In practice, banks' capital is required to equal at least 7% of the value of their assets.

Reserve requirements are rules set by the Federal Reserve that determine the minimum reserve ratio for banks.

The **discount window** is an arrangement in which the Federal Reserve stands ready to lend money to banks in trouble.

3. Reserve Requirements Another regulation used to reduce the risk of bank runs is **reserve requirements,** rules set by the Federal Reserve that specify the minimum reserve ratio for banks. For example, in the United States, the minimum reserve ratio for checkable bank deposits is 10%.

4. The Discount Window One final protection against bank runs is the fact that the Federal Reserve, which we'll discuss more thoroughly later in this chapter, stands ready to lend money to banks in trouble, an arrangement known as the **discount window.** The ability to borrow money means a bank can avoid being forced to sell its assets at fire-sale prices in order to satisfy the demands of a sudden rush of depositors demanding cash. Instead, it can turn to the Fed and borrow the funds it needs to pay off depositors.

ECONOMICS ➤ IN ACTION

IT'S A WONDERFUL BANKING SYSTEM

Next Christmastime, it's a sure thing that at least one TV channel will show the 1946 film *It's a Wonderful Life,* featuring Jimmy Stewart as George Bailey, a small-town banker whose life is saved by an angel. The movie's climactic scene is a run on Bailey's bank, as fearful depositors rush to take their funds out.

When the movie was made, such scenes were still fresh in Americans' memories. There was a wave of bank runs in late 1930, a second wave in the spring of 1931, and a third wave in early 1933. By the end, more than a third of the nation's banks had failed. To bring the panic to an end, on March 6, 1933, the newly inaugurated president, Franklin Delano Roosevelt, declared a national "bank holiday," closing all banks for a week to give bank regulators time to close unhealthy banks and certify healthy ones.

Since then, regulation has protected the United States and other wealthy countries against most bank runs. In fact, the scene in *It's a Wonderful Life* was already out of date when the movie was made. But recent decades have seen several waves of bank runs in developing countries. For example, bank runs played a role in an economic crisis that swept Southeast Asia in 1997–1998 and in the severe economic crisis in Argentina that began in late 2001. And as you will see in Chapter 18, a "panic" with strong resemblance to a wave of bank runs swept world financial markets in 2008.

In July 2008, panicky IndyMac depositors lined up to pull their money out of the troubled California bank.

Notice that we said "most bank runs." There are some limits on deposit insurance; in particular, in the United States currently only the first $250,000 of an individual depositor's funds in an insured bank is covered. As a result, there can still be a run on a bank perceived as troubled. In fact, that's exactly what happened in July 2008 to IndyMac, a Pasadena-based lender that had made a large number of questionable home loans. As questions about IndyMac's financial soundness were raised, depositors began pulling out funds, forcing federal regulators to step in and close the bank. In Britain the limits on deposit insurance are much lower, which exposed the bank Northern Rock to a classic bank run that same year. Unlike in the bank runs of the 1930s, however, most depositors at both IndyMac and Northern Rock got all their funds back—and the panics at these banks didn't spread to other institutions.

Quick Review

- A **T-account** is used to analyze a bank's financial position. A bank holds **bank reserves**—currency in its vaults plus deposits held in its account at the Federal Reserve. The **reserve ratio** is the ratio of bank reserves to customers' bank deposits.
- Because bank loans are illiquid, but a bank is obligated to return depositors' funds on demand, **bank runs** are a potential problem. Although they took place on a massive scale during the 1930s, they have been largely eliminated in the United States through bank regulation in the form of **deposit insurance,** capital requirements, and **reserve requirements,** as well as through the availability of the **discount window.**

CHECK YOUR UNDERSTANDING 16-2

1. Suppose you are a depositor at First Street Bank. You hear a rumor that the bank has suffered serious losses on its loans. Every depositor knows that the rumor isn't true, but each thinks that most other depositors believe the rumor. Why, in the absence of deposit insurance, could this lead to a bank run? How does deposit insurance change the situation?
2. A con artist has a great idea: he'll open a bank without investing any capital and lend all the deposits at high interest rates to real estate developers. If the real estate market booms, the loans will be repaid and he'll make high profits. If the real estate market goes bust, the loans won't be repaid and the bank will fail—but he will not lose any of his own wealth. How would modern bank regulation frustrate his scheme?

Solutions appear at back of book.

Determining the Money Supply

Without banks, there would be no checkable deposits, so the quantity of currency in circulation would equal the money supply. In that case, the money supply would be solely determined by whoever controls government minting and printing presses. But banks do exist, and through their creation of checkable bank deposits they affect the money supply in two ways. First, banks remove some currency from circulation: dollar bills that are sitting in bank vaults, as opposed to sitting in people's wallets, aren't part of the money supply. Second, and much more importantly, banks create money by accepting deposits and making loans—that is, they make the money supply larger than just the value of currency in circulation. Our next topic is how banks create money and what determines the amount of money they create.

How Banks Create Money

To see how banks create money, let's examine what happens when someone decides to deposit currency in a bank. Consider the example of Silas, a miser, who keeps a shoebox full of cash under his bed. Suppose Silas realizes that it would be safer, as well as more convenient, to deposit that cash in the bank and to use his debit card when shopping. Assume that he deposits $1,000 into a checkable account at First Street Bank. What effect will Silas's actions have on the money supply?

Panel (a) of Figure 16-4 shows the initial effect of his deposit. First Street Bank credits Silas with $1,000 in his account, so the economy's checkable bank deposits rise by $1,000. Meanwhile, Silas's cash goes into the vault, raising First Street's reserves by $1,000 as well.

This initial transaction has no effect on the money supply. Currency in circulation, part of the money supply, falls by $1,000; checkable bank deposits, also part of the money supply, rise by the same amount.

But this is not the end of the story because First Street Bank can now lend out part of Silas's deposit. Assume that it holds 10% of Silas's deposit—$100—in reserves and lends the rest out in cash to Silas's neighbor, Maya. The effect of this second stage is shown in panel (b). First Street's deposits remain unchanged, and so does the value of its assets. But the composition of its assets changes: by

FIGURE 16-4 Effect on the Money Supply of Turning Cash into a Checkable Deposit at First Street Bank

(a) Initial Effect Before Bank Makes a New Loan

Assets		Liabilities	
Loans	No change	Checkable deposits	+$1,000
Reserves	+$1,000		

(b) Effect When Bank Makes a New Loan

Assets		Liabilities
Loans	+$900	No change
Reserves	−$900	

When Silas deposits $1,000 (which had been stashed under his bed) into a checkable bank account, there is initially no effect on the money supply: currency in circulation falls by $1,000, but checkable bank deposits rise by $1,000. The corresponding entries on the bank's T-account, depicted in panel (a), show deposits initially rising by $1,000 and the bank's reserves initially rising by $1,000. In the second stage, depicted in panel (b), the bank holds 10% of Silas's deposit ($100) as reserves and lends out the rest ($900) to Maya. As a result, its reserves fall by $900 and its loans increase by $900. Its liabilities, including Silas's $1,000 deposit, are unchanged. The money supply, the sum of checkable bank deposits and currency in circulation, has now increased by $900—the $900 now held by Maya.

making the loan, it reduces its reserves by $900, so that they are only $100 larger than they were before Silas made his deposit. In the place of the $900 reduction in reserves, the bank has acquired an IOU, its $900 cash loan to Maya.

So by putting $900 of Silas's cash back into circulation by lending it to Maya, First Street Bank has, in fact, increased the money supply. That is, the sum of currency in circulation and checkable bank deposits has risen by $900 compared to what it had been when Silas's cash was still under his bed. Although Silas is still the owner of $1,000, now in the form of a checkable deposit, Maya has the use of $900 in cash from her borrowings.

And this may not be the end of the story. Suppose that Maya uses her cash to buy a television and a DVD player from Acme Merchandise. What does Anne Acme, the store's owner, do with the cash? If she holds on to it, the money supply doesn't increase any further. But suppose she deposits the $900 into a checkable bank deposit—say, at Second Street Bank. Second Street Bank, in turn, will keep only part of that deposit in reserves, lending out the rest, creating still more money.

Assume that Second Street Bank, like First Street Bank, keeps 10% of any bank deposit in reserves and lends out the rest. Then it will keep $90 in reserves and lend out $810 of Anne's deposit to another borrower, further increasing the money supply.

Table 16-1 shows the process of money creation we have described so far. At first the money supply consists only of Silas's $1,000. After he deposits the cash into a checkable bank deposit and the bank makes a loan, the money supply rises to $1,900. After the second deposit and the second loan, the money supply rises to $2,710. And the process will, of course, continue from there. (Although we have considered the case in which Silas places his cash in a checkable bank deposit, the results would be the same if he put it into any type of near-money.)

This process of money creation may sound familiar. In Chapter 15 we described the *multiplier process:* an initial increase in real GDP leads to a rise

TABLE 16-1 How Banks Create Money

	Currency in circulation	Checkable bank deposits	Money supply
First stage: Silas keeps his cash under his bed.	$1,000	$0	$1,000
Second stage: Silas deposits cash in First Street Bank, which lends out $900 to Maya, who then pays it to Anne Acme.	900	1,000	1,900
Third stage: Anne Acme deposits $900 in Second Street Bank, which lends out $810 to another borrower.	810	1,900	2,710

Excess reserves are a bank's reserves over and above its required reserves.

in consumer spending, which leads to a further rise in real GDP, which leads to a further rise in consumer spending, and so on. What we have here is another kind of multiplier—the *money multiplier.* Next, we'll learn what determines the size of this multiplier.

Reserves, Bank Deposits, and the Money Multiplier

In tracing out the effect of Silas's deposit in Table 16-1, we assumed that the funds a bank lends out always end up being deposited either in the same bank or in another bank—so funds disbursed as loans come back to the banking system, even if not to the lending bank itself.

In reality, some of these loaned funds may be held by borrowers in their wallets and not deposited in a bank, meaning that some of the loaned amount "leaks" out of the banking system. Such leaks reduce the size of the money multiplier.

But let's set that complication aside for a moment and consider how the money supply is determined in a "checkable-deposits-only" monetary system, where funds are always deposited in bank accounts and none are held in wallets as currency. That is, in our checkable-deposits-only monetary system, any and all funds borrowed from a bank are immediately deposited into a checkable bank account. We'll assume that banks are required to satisfy a minimum reserve ratio of 10% and that every bank lends out all of its **excess reserves,** reserves over and above the amount needed to satisfy the minimum reserve ratio.

Now suppose that for some reason a bank suddenly finds itself with \$1,000 in excess reserves. What happens? The answer is that the bank will lend out that \$1,000, which will end up as a checkable bank deposit somewhere in the banking system, launching a money multiplier process very similar to the process shown in Table 16-1.

In the first stage, the bank lends out its excess reserves of \$1,000, which becomes a checkable bank deposit somewhere. The bank that receives the \$1,000 deposit keeps 10%, or \$100, as reserves and lends out the remaining 90%, or \$900, which again becomes a checkable bank deposit somewhere. The bank receiving this \$900 deposit again keeps 10%, which is \$90, as reserves and lends out the remaining \$810. The bank receiving this \$810 keeps \$81 in reserves and lends out the remaining \$729, and so on. As a result of this process, the total increase in checkable bank deposits is equal to a sum that looks like:

$$\$1{,}000 + \$900 + \$810 + \$729 + \ldots$$

We'll use the symbol rr for the reserve ratio. More generally, the total increase in checkable bank deposits that is generated when a bank lends out \$1,000 in excess reserves is:

(16-1) Increase in checkable bank deposits from \$1,000 in excess reserves =
$$\$1{,}000 + (\$1{,}000 \times (1 - rr)) + (\$1{,}000 \times (1 - rr)^2) + (\$1{,}000 \times (1 - rr)^3) + \ldots$$

An infinite series of this form can be simplified to:

(16-2) Increase in checkable bank deposits from \$1,000 in excess reserves =
$$\$1{,}000/rr$$

Given a reserve ratio of 10%, or 0.1, a $1,000 increase in excess reserves will increase the total value of checkable bank deposits by $1,000/0.1 = $10,000. In fact, in a checkable-deposits-only monetary system, the total value of checkable bank deposits will be equal to the value of bank reserves divided by the reserve ratio. Or to put it a different way, if the reserve ratio is 10%, each $1 of reserves held by a bank supports $\$1/rr = \$1/0.1 = \$10$ of checkable bank deposits.

The **monetary base** is the sum of currency in circulation and bank reserves.

The Money Multiplier in Reality

In reality, the determination of the money supply is more complicated than our simple model suggests because it depends not only on the ratio of reserves to bank deposits but also on the fraction of the money supply that individuals choose to hold in the form of currency. In fact, we already saw this in our example of Silas depositing the cash under his bed: when he chose to hold a checkable bank deposit instead of currency, he set in motion an increase in the money supply.

To define the money multiplier in practice, it's important to recognize that the Federal Reserve controls the *sum* of bank reserves and currency in circulation, called the *monetary base,* but it does not control the allocation of that sum between bank reserves and currency in circulation. Consider Silas and his deposit one more time: by taking the cash from under his bed and depositing it in a bank, he reduced the quantity of currency in circulation but increased bank reserves by an equal amount—leaving the *monetary base,* on net, unchanged. The **monetary base,** which is the quantity the monetary authorities control, is the sum of currency in circulation and reserves held by banks.

The monetary base is different from the money supply in two ways. First, bank reserves, which are part of the monetary base, aren't considered part of the money supply. A $1 bill in someone's wallet is considered money because it's available for an individual to spend, but a $1 bill held as bank reserves in a bank vault or deposited at the Federal Reserve isn't considered part of the money supply because it's not available for spending. Second, checkable bank deposits, which are part of the money supply because they are available for spending, aren't part of the monetary base.

Figure 16-5 shows the two concepts schematically. The circle on the left represents the monetary base, consisting of bank reserves plus currency

FIGURE 16-5 The Monetary Base and the Money Supply

The monetary base is equal to bank reserves plus currency in circulation. It is different from the money supply, consisting mainly of checkable or near-checkable bank deposits plus currency in circulation. Each dollar of bank reserves backs several dollars of bank deposits, making the money supply larger than the monetary base.

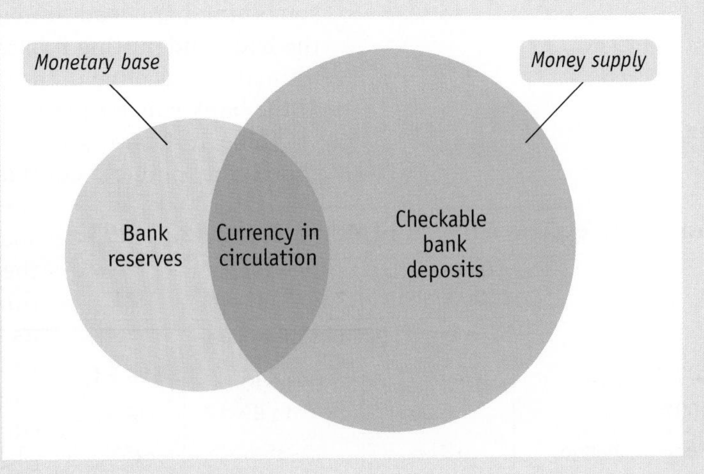

The **money multiplier** is the ratio of the money supply to the monetary base.

in circulation. The circle on the right in Figure 16-5 represents the money supply, consisting mainly of currency in circulation plus checkable or near-checkable bank deposits. As the figure indicates, currency in circulation is part of both the monetary base and the money supply. But bank reserves aren't part of the money supply, and checkable or near-checkable bank deposits aren't part of the monetary base. In practice, most of the monetary base actually consists of currency in circulation, which also makes up about half of the money supply.

Now we can formally define the **money multiplier:** it's the ratio of the money supply to the monetary base. In normal times the money multiplier in the United States, using M1 as our measure of money, has fluctuated between 3.0 and 1.5. During the recession of 2007–2009, it fell to about 0.7. Even in normal times, that's a lot smaller than 1/0.1 = 10, the money multiplier in a checkable-deposits-only system with a reserve ratio of 10% (the minimum required ratio for most checkable deposits in the United States). The reason the actual money multiplier is so small arises from the fact that people hold significant amounts of cash, and a dollar of currency in circulation, unlike a dollar in reserves, doesn't support multiple dollars of the money supply. In fact, currency in circulation normally accounts for more than 90% of the monetary base. However, in January 2012, currency in circulation was $1,069 billion, compared with a monetary base of $2,659 billion—just about 40%. What had happened?

Notice that earlier we said "in normal times." As explained later in this chapter, a very abnormal situation developed after Lehman Brothers, a key financial institution, failed in September 2008. Banks, seeing few opportunities for safe, profitable lending, began parking large sums at the Federal Reserve in the form of deposits—deposits that counted as part of the monetary base. As a result, currency in circulation in January 2012 made up only 40% of the monetary base, and in 2011 the monetary base was actually larger than M1, with the money multiplier therefore less than 1.

ECONOMICS ➤ IN ACTION

MULTIPLYING MONEY DOWN

In our hypothetical example illustrating how banks create money, we described Silas the miser taking the currency from under his bed and turning it into a checkable bank deposit. This led to an increase in the money supply, as banks engaged in successive waves of lending backed by Silas's funds. It follows that if something happened to make Silas revert to old habits, taking his money out of the bank and putting it back under his bed, the result would be less lending and, ultimately, a decline in the money supply. That's exactly what happened as a result of the bank runs of the 1930s.

Table 16-2 shows what happened between 1929 and 1933, as bank failures shook the public's confidence in the banking system. The second column shows the public's holdings of currency. This increased sharply, as many Americans decided that money under the bed was safer than money in the bank after all. The third column shows the value of checkable bank deposits. This fell sharply, through the multiplier process we have just analyzed, when individuals pulled their cash out of banks. Loans also fell because banks that survived the waves of bank runs increased their excess reserves, just in case another wave began. The fourth column shows the value of M1, the first of the monetary

TABLE 16-2 The Effects of Bank Runs, 1929–1933

	Currency in circulation	Checkable bank deposits	M1
	(billions of dollars)		
1929	$3.90	$22.74	$26.64
1933	5.09	14.82	19.91
Percent change	+31%	−35%	−25%

Source: U.S. Census Bureau (1975), *Historical Statistics of the United States.*

aggregates we described earlier. It fell sharply because the total reduction in checkable or near-checkable bank deposits was much larger than the increase in currency in circulation.

CHECK YOUR UNDERSTANDING 16-3

1. Assume that total reserves are equal to $200 and total checkable bank deposits are equal to $1,000. Also assume that the public does not hold any currency. Now suppose that the required reserve ratio falls from 20% to 10%. Trace out how this leads to an expansion in bank deposits.
2. Take the example of Silas depositing his $1,000 in cash into First Street Bank and assume that the required reserve ratio is 10%. But now assume that each time someone receives a bank loan, he or she keeps half the loan in cash. Trace out the resulting expansion in the money supply.

Solutions appear at back of book.

Quick Review

- Banks create money when they lend out **excess reserves,** generating a multiplier effect on the money supply.
- In a checkable-deposits-only system, the money supply would be equal to bank reserves divided by the reserve ratio. In reality, however, the public holds some funds as cash rather than in checkable deposits, which reduces the size of the multiplier.
- The **monetary base,** equal to bank reserves plus currency in circulation, overlaps but is not equal to the money supply. The **money multiplier** is equal to the money supply divided by the monetary base.

The Federal Reserve System

Who's in charge of ensuring that banks maintain enough reserves? Who decides how large the monetary base will be? The answer, in the United States, is an institution known as the Federal Reserve (or, informally, as "the Fed"). The Federal Reserve is a **central bank**—an institution that oversees and regulates the banking system and controls the monetary base. Other central banks include the Bank of England, the Bank of Japan, and the European Central Bank, or ECB. The ECB acts as a common central bank for 17 European countries: Austria, Belgium, Cyprus, Estonia, Finland, France, Germany, Greece, Ireland, Italy, Luxembourg, Malta, the Netherlands, Portugal, Slovakia, Slovenia, and Spain. The world's oldest central bank, by the way, is Sweden's Sveriges Rijksbank, which awards the Nobel Prize in economics.

The Structure of the Fed

The legal status of the Fed, which was created in 1913, is unusual: it is not exactly part of the U.S. government, but it is not really a private institution either. Strictly speaking, the Federal Reserve system consists of two parts: the Board of Governors and the 12 regional Federal Reserve Banks.

The Board of Governors, which oversees the entire system from its offices in Washington, D.C., is constituted like a government agency: its seven members are appointed by the president and must be approved by the Senate. However, they are appointed for 14-year terms, to insulate them from political pressure in their conduct of monetary policy. Although the chairman is appointed more frequently—every four years—it's traditional for chairmen to be reappointed and serve much longer terms. For example, William McChesney Martin was chairman of the Fed from 1951 until 1970. Alan Greenspan, appointed in 1987, served as the Fed's chairman until 2006.

The 12 Federal Reserve Banks each serve a region of the country, providing various banking and supervisory services. One of their jobs, for example, is to audit the books of private-sector banks to ensure their financial health. Each regional bank is run by a board of directors chosen from the local banking and business community. The Federal Reserve Bank of New York plays a special role: it carries out *open-market operations,* usually the main

A **central bank** is an institution that oversees and regulates the banking system and controls the monetary base.

FIGURE 16-6
The Federal Reserve System

The Federal Reserve system consists of the Board of Governors in Washington, D.C., plus 12 regional Federal Reserve Banks. This map shows each of the 12 Federal Reserve districts.

Source: Board of Governors of the Federal Reserve System.

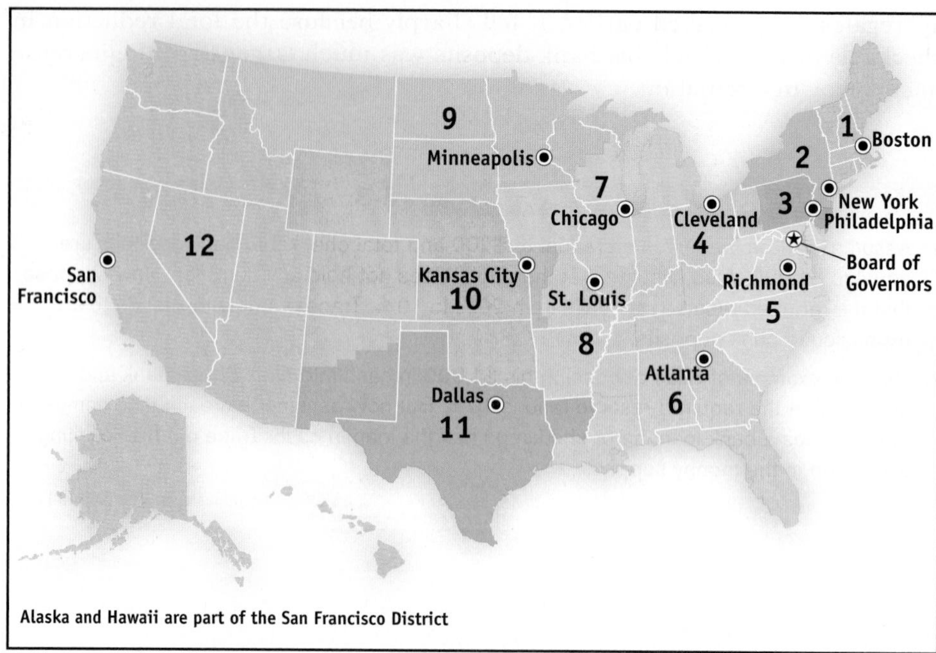

tool of monetary policy. Figure 16-6 shows the 12 Federal Reserve districts and the city in which each regional Federal Reserve Bank is located.

Decisions about monetary policy are made by the Federal Open Market Committee, which consists of the Board of Governors plus five of the regional bank presidents. The president of the Federal Reserve Bank of New York is always on the committee, and the other four seats rotate among the 11 other regional bank presidents. The chairman of the Board of Governors normally also serves as the chairman of the Open Market Committee.

The effect of this complex structure is to create an institution that is ultimately accountable to the voting public because the Board of Governors is chosen by the president and confirmed by the Senate, all of whom are themselves elected officials. But the long terms served by board members, as well as the indirectness of their appointment process, largely insulate them from short-term political pressures.

What the Fed Does: Reserve Requirements and the Discount Rate

The Fed has three main policy tools at its disposal: *reserve requirements,* the *discount rate,* and, most importantly, *open-market operations.*

In our discussion of bank runs, we noted that the Fed sets a minimum reserve ratio requirement, currently equal to 10% for checkable bank deposits. Banks that fail to maintain at least the required reserve ratio on average over a two-week period face penalties.

What does a bank do if it looks as if it has insufficient reserves to meet the Fed's reserve requirement? Normally, it borrows additional reserves from other banks via the **federal funds market,** a financial market that allows banks that fall short of the reserve requirement to borrow reserves (usually just overnight) from banks that are holding excess reserves. The interest rate in this market is determined by supply and demand—but the supply and demand for bank reserves are both strongly affected by Federal Reserve actions. As we'll see in the next chapter, the **federal funds rate,** the interest rate at which funds are borrowed and lent in the federal funds market, plays a key role in modern monetary policy.

The **federal funds market** allows banks that fall short of the reserve requirement to borrow funds from banks with excess reserves.

The **federal funds rate** is the interest rate determined in the federal funds market.

Alternatively, banks in need of reserves can borrow from the Fed itself via the *discount window*. The **discount rate** is the rate of interest the Fed charges on those loans. Normally, the discount rate is set 1 percentage point above the federal funds rate in order to discourage banks from turning to the Fed when they are in need of reserves. Beginning in the fall of 2007, however, the Fed reduced the spread between the federal funds rate and the discount rate as part of its response to an ongoing financial crisis, described in the upcoming Economics in Action. As a result, by the spring of 2008 the discount rate was only 0.25 percentage point above the federal funds rate. And by January 2012 the discount rate was still only 0.65 percentage point above the federal funds rate.

The **discount rate** is the rate of interest the Fed charges on loans to banks.

An **open-market operation** is a purchase or sale of government debt by the Fed.

In order to alter the money supply, the Fed can change reserve requirements, the discount rate, or both. If the Fed reduces reserve requirements, banks will lend a larger percentage of their deposits, leading to more loans and an increase in the money supply via the money multiplier. Alternatively, if the Fed increases reserve requirements, banks are forced to reduce their lending, leading to a fall in the money supply via the money multiplier. If the Fed reduces the spread between the discount rate and the federal funds rate, the cost to banks of being short of reserves falls; banks respond by increasing their lending, and the money supply increases via the money multiplier. If the Fed increases the spread between the discount rate and the federal funds rate, bank lending falls—and so will the money supply via the money multiplier.

Under current practice, however, the Fed doesn't use changes in reserve requirements to actively manage the money supply. The last significant change in reserve requirements was in 1992. The Fed normally doesn't use the discount rate either, although, as we mentioned earlier, there was a temporary surge in lending through the discount window beginning in 2007 in response to a financial crisis. Ordinarily, normal monetary policy is conducted almost exclusively using the Fed's third policy tool: open-market operations.

Open-Market Operations

Like the banks it oversees, the Federal Reserve has assets and liabilities. The Fed's assets normally consist of holdings of debt issued by the U.S. government, mainly short-term U.S. government bonds with a maturity of less than one year, known as U.S. Treasury bills. Remember, the Fed isn't exactly part of the U.S. government, so U.S. Treasury bills held by the Fed are a liability of the government but an asset of the Fed. The Fed's liabilities consist of currency in circulation and bank reserves. Figure 16-7 summarizes the normal assets and liabilities of the Fed in the form of a T-account.

In an **open-market operation** the Federal Reserve buys or sells U.S. Treasury bills, normally through a transaction with *commercial banks*—banks that mainly make business loans, as opposed to home loans. The Fed never buys U.S. Treasury bills directly from the federal government. There's a good reason for this: when a central bank buys government debt directly from the government, it is lending directly to the government—in effect, the central

FIGURE 16-7 The Federal Reserve's Assets and Liabilities

The Federal Reserve holds its assets mostly in short-term government bonds called U.S. Treasury bills. Its liabilities are the monetary base—currency in circulation plus bank reserves.

Assets	Liabilities
Government debt (Treasury bills)	Monetary base (currency in circulation + bank reserves)

bank is printing money to finance the government's budget deficit. This has historically been a formula for disastrously high levels of inflation.

The two panels of Figure 16-8 show the changes in the financial position of both the Fed and commercial banks that result from open-market operations. When the Fed buys U.S. Treasury bills from a commercial bank, it pays by crediting the bank's reserve account by an amount equal to the value of the Treasury bills. This is illustrated in panel (a): the Fed buys $100 million of U.S. Treasury bills from commercial banks, which increases the monetary base by $100 million because it increases bank reserves by $100 million. When the Fed sells U.S. Treasury bills to commercial banks, it debits the banks' accounts, reducing their reserves. This is shown in panel (b), where the Fed sells $100 million of U.S. Treasury bills. Here, bank reserves and the monetary base decrease.

You might wonder where the Fed gets the funds to purchase U.S. Treasury bills from banks. The answer is that it simply creates them with a stroke of the pen—or, these days, a click of the mouse—that credits the banks' accounts with extra reserves. (The Fed prints money to pay for Treasury bills only when banks want the additional reserves in the form of currency.) Remember, the modern dollar is fiat money, which isn't backed by anything. So the Fed can create additional monetary base at its own discretion.

The change in bank reserves caused by an open-market operation doesn't directly affect the money supply. Instead, it starts the money multiplier in motion. After the $100 million increase in reserves shown in panel (a) of Figure 16-8, commercial banks would lend out their additional reserves, immediately increasing the money supply by $100 million. Some of those loans would be deposited back into the banking system, increasing reserves again and permitting a further round of loans, and so on, leading to a rise

FIGURE 16-8 Open-Market Operations by the Federal Reserve

(a) An Open-Market Purchase of $100 Million

	Assets		Liabilities	
Federal Reserve	Treasury bills	+$100 million	Monetary base	+$100 million

	Assets		Liabilities
Commercial banks	Treasury bills	−$100 million	No change
	Reserves	+$100 million	

(b) An Open-Market Sale of $100 Million

	Assets		Liabilities	
Federal Reserve	Treasury bills	−$100 million	Monetary base	−$100 million

	Assets		Liabilities
Commercial banks	Treasury bills	+$100 million	No change
	Reserves	−$100 million	

In panel (a), the Federal Reserve increases the monetary base by purchasing U.S. Treasury bills from private commercial banks in an open-market operation. Here, a $100 million purchase of U.S. Treasury bills by the Federal Reserve is paid for by a $100 million addition to private bank reserves, generating a $100 million increase in the monetary base. This will ultimately lead to an increase in the money supply via the money multiplier as banks lend out some of these new reserves. In panel (b), the Federal Reserve reduces the monetary base by selling U.S. Treasury bills to private commercial banks in an open-market operation. Here, a $100 million sale of U.S. Treasury bills leads to a $100 million reduction in private bank reserves, resulting in a $100 million decrease in the monetary base. This will ultimately lead to a fall in the money supply via the money multiplier as banks reduce their loans in response to a fall in their reserves.

FOR INQUIRING MINDS

WHO GETS THE INTEREST ON THE FED'S ASSETS?

As we've just learned, the Fed owns a lot of assets—Treasury bills—that it bought from commercial banks in exchange for monetary base in the form of credits to banks' reserve accounts. These assets pay interest. Yet the Fed's liabilities consist mainly of the monetary base, liabilities on which the Fed normally *doesn't* pay interest. So the Fed is, in effect, an institution that has the privilege of borrowing funds at a zero interest rate and lending them out at a positive interest rate. That sounds like a pretty profitable business. Who gets the profits?

The answer is, you do—or rather, U.S. taxpayers do. The Fed keeps some of the interest it receives to finance its operations but turns most of it over to the U.S. Treasury. For example, in 2010 the Federal Reserve system received $79.301 billion in interest income (most of it in interest on its holdings of Treasury bills and on government-sponsored mortgage-backed securities), of which $79.268 billion was returned to the Treasury.

We can now finish the chapter's opening story—the impact of those forged $100 bills allegedly printed in North Korea. When a fake $100 bill enters circulation, it has the same economic effect as a real $100 bill printed by the U.S. government. That is, as long as nobody catches the forgery, the fake bill serves, for all practical purposes, as part of the monetary base.

Meanwhile, the Fed decides on the size of the monetary base based on economic considerations—in particular, the Fed doesn't let the monetary base get too large because that can cause higher inflation. So every fake $100 bill that enters circulation basically means that the Fed prints one less real $100 bill. When the Fed prints a $100 bill legally, however, it gets Treasury bills in return—and the interest on those bills helps pay for the U.S. government's expenses. So a counterfeit $100 bill reduces the amount of Treasury bills the Fed can acquire and thereby reduces the interest payments going to the Fed and the U.S. Treasury. Taxpayers, then, bear the real cost of counterfeiting.

in the money supply. An open-market sale has the reverse effect: bank reserves fall, requiring banks to reduce their loans, leading to a fall in the money supply.

Economists often say, loosely, that the Fed controls the money supply—checkable deposits plus currency in circulation. In fact, it controls only the monetary base—bank reserves plus currency in circulation. But by increasing or reducing the monetary base, the Fed can exert a powerful influence on both the money supply and interest rates. This influence is the basis of monetary policy, the subject of our next chapter.

The European Central Bank

As we noted earlier, the Fed is only one of a number of central banks around the world, and it's much younger than Sweden's Sveriges Rijksbank and Britain's Bank of England. In general, other central banks operate in much the same way as the Fed. That's especially true of the only other central bank that rivals the Fed in terms of importance to the world economy: the European Central Bank.

The European Central Bank, known as the ECB, was created in January 1999 when 11 European nations abandoned their national currencies and adopted the euro as their common currency and placed their joint monetary policy in the ECB's hands. (Six more countries have joined since 1999.) The ECB instantly became an extremely important institution: although no single European nation has an economy anywhere near as large as that of the United States, the combined economies of the eurozone, the group of countries that have adopted the euro as their currency, are roughly as big as the U.S. economy. As a result, the ECB and the Fed are the two giants of the monetary world.

Like the Fed, the ECB has a special status: it's not a private institution, but it's not exactly a government agency either. In fact, it can't be a government agency because there is no pan-European government! Luckily for puzzled Americans, there are strong analogies between European central banking and the Federal Reserve system.

First of all, the ECB, which is located in the German city of Frankfurt, isn't really the counterpart of the whole Federal Reserve system: it's the equivalent of the Board of Governors in Washington. The European counterparts of the regional Federal Reserve Banks are Europe's national central banks: the Bank of France, the Bank of Italy, and so on. Until 1999, each of these national banks was its country's equivalent to the Fed. For example, the Bank of France controlled the French monetary base.

Today these national banks, like regional Feds, provide various financial services to local banks and businesses and conduct open-market operations, but the making of monetary policy has moved upstream to the ECB. Still, the various European national central banks aren't small institutions: in total, they employ more than 50,000 people; in December 2010, the ECB employed only 1,607.

In the eurozone, each country chooses who runs its own national central bank. The ECB's Executive Board is the counterpart of the Fed's Board of Governors; its members are chosen by unanimous consent of the eurozone national governments. The counterpart of the Federal Open Market Committee is the ECB's Governing Council. Just as the Fed's Open Market Committee consists of the Board of Governors plus a rotating group of regional Fed presidents, the ECB's Governing Council consists of the Executive Board plus the heads of the national central banks.

Like the Fed, the ECB is ultimately answerable to voters but given the fragmentation of political forces across national boundaries, it appears to be even more insulated than the Fed from short-term political pressures.

ECONOMICS ➤ *IN ACTION*

THE FED'S BALANCE SHEET, NORMAL AND ABNORMAL

Figure 16-7 showed a simplified version of the Fed's balance sheet. Here, liabilities consisted entirely of the monetary base and assets consisted entirely of Treasury bills. This is an oversimplification because the Fed's operations are more complicated in reality and its balance sheet contains a number of additional things. But, in normal times, Figure 16-7 is a reasonable approximation: the monetary base typically accounts for 90% of the Fed's liabilities, and 90% of its assets are in the form of claims on the U.S. Treasury (as in Treasury bills).

But in late 2007 it became painfully clear that we were no longer in normal times. The source of the turmoil was the bursting of a huge housing bubble, which led to massive losses for financial institutions that had made mortgage loans or held mortgage-related assets. This led to a widespread loss of confidence in the financial system.

As we'll describe in more detail in the next section, not only standard deposit-taking banks were in trouble, but also non-depository financial institutions—financial institutions that did not accept customer deposits. Because they carried a lot of debt, faced huge losses from the collapse of the housing bubble, and held illiquid assets, panic hit these "nonbank banks." Within hours the financial system was frozen as financial institutions experienced what were essentially bank runs. For example, in 2008, many investors became worried about the health of Bear Stearns, a Wall Street non-depository financial institution that engaged in complex financial deals, buying and selling financial assets with borrowed funds. When confidence in Bear Stearns dried up, the firm found itself unable to raise the funds it needed to deliver on its end of these deals and it quickly spiraled into collapse.

The Fed sprang into action to contain what was becoming a meltdown across the entire financial sector. It greatly expanded its discount window—making huge loans to deposit-taking banks as well as nondepository financial institutions such as Wall Street financial firms. This gave financial institutions the liquidity that the financial market had now denied them. And as these firms took advantage of the ability to borrow cheaply from the Fed, they pledged their assets on hand as collateral—a motley collection of real estate loans, business loans, and so on.

FIGURE 16-9 The Federal Reserve's Assets

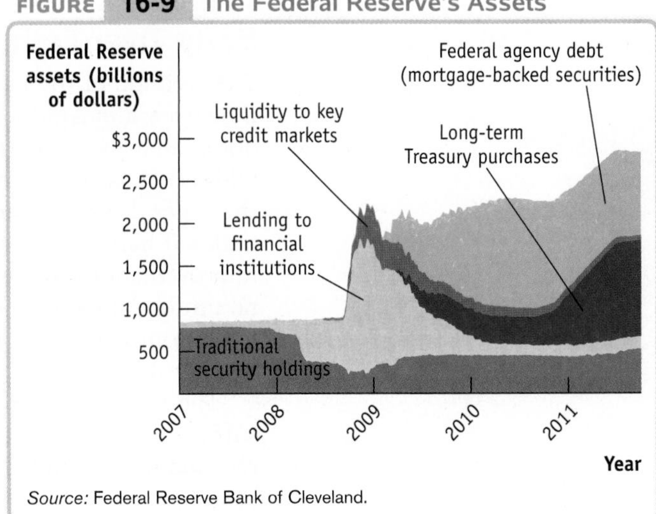

Source: Federal Reserve Bank of Cleveland.

Examining Figure 16-9, we see that starting in mid-2008, the Fed sharply reduced its holdings of traditional securities like Treasury bills, as its lending to financial institutions skyrocketed. "Lending to financial institutions" refers to discount window lending, but also loans the Fed made directly to firms like Bear Stearns. "Liquidity to key credit markets" covers purchases by the Fed of assets like corporate bonds, which was necessary to keep interest rates on loans to firms from soaring. Finally, "Federal agency debt" is the debt of Fannie Mae and Freddie Mac, the government-sponsored home mortgage agencies, which the Fed was also compelled to buy in order to prevent collapse in the mortgage market.

As the crisis subsided in late 2009, the Fed didn't return to its traditional asset holdings. Instead, it shifted into long-term Treasury bills and increased its purchases of Federal agency debt. The whole episode was very unusual—a major departure from the way in which the Fed normally conducts business, but one that it deemed necessary to stave off financial and economic collapse. It was also a graphic illustration of the fact that the Fed does much more than just determine the size of the monetary base.

CHECK YOUR UNDERSTANDING 16-4

1. Assume that any money lent by a bank is always deposited back in the banking system as a checkable deposit and that the reserve ratio is 10%. Trace out the effects of a $100 million open-market purchase of U.S. Treasury bills by the Fed on the value of checkable bank deposits. What is the size of the money multiplier?

Solution appears at back of book.

Quick Review

- The Federal Reserve is America's **central bank,** overseeing banking and making monetary policy.
- The Fed sets the required reserve ratio. Banks borrow and lend reserves in the **federal funds market.** The interest rate determined in this market is the **federal funds rate.** Banks can also borrow from the Fed at the **discount rate.**
- Although the Fed can change reserve requirements or the discount rate, in practice, monetary policy is conducted using **open-market operations.**
- An open-market purchase of Treasury bills increases the monetary base and therefore the money supply. An open-market sale reduces the monetary base and the money supply.

The Evolution of the American Banking System

Up to this point, we have been describing the U.S. banking system and how it works. To fully understand that system, however, it is helpful to understand how and why it was created—a story that is closely intertwined with the story of how and when things went wrong. For the key elements of twenty-first-century U.S. banking weren't created out of thin air: efforts to change both the regulations that govern banking and the Federal Reserve system that began in 2008 have propelled financial reform to the forefront. This reform promises to continue reshaping the financial system well into future years.

The Crisis in American Banking in the Early Twentieth Century

The creation of the Federal Reserve system in 1913 marked the beginning of the modern era of American banking. From 1864 until 1913, American banking was dominated by a federally regulated system of national banks. They alone were allowed to issue currency, and the currency notes they issued were printed by the federal government with uniform size and design. How much currency a national bank could issue depended on its capital. Although this system was an improvement on the earlier period in which banks issued their own notes with no uniformity and virtually no regulation, the national banking regime still suffered numerous bank failures and major financial crises—at least one and often two per decade.

The main problem afflicting the system was that the money supply was not sufficiently responsive: it was difficult to shift currency around the country to respond quickly to local economic changes. (In particular, there was often a tug-of-war between New York City banks and rural banks for adequate amounts of currency.) Rumors that a bank had insufficient currency to satisfy demands for withdrawals would quickly lead to a bank run. A bank run would then spark a contagion, setting off runs at other nearby banks, sowing widespread panic and devastation in the local economy. In response, bankers in some locations pooled their resources to create local clearinghouses that would jointly guarantee a member's liabilities in the event of a panic, and some state governments began offering deposit insurance on their banks' deposits.

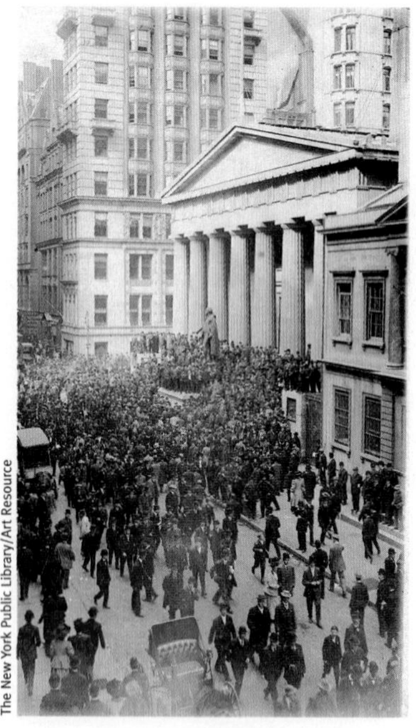
The New York Public Library/Art Resource

In both the Panic of 1907 and the financial crisis of 2008, large losses from risky speculation destabilized the banking system.

However, the cause of the Panic of 1907 was different from those of previous crises; in fact, its cause was eerily similar to the roots of the 2008 crisis. Ground zero of the 1907 panic was New York City, but the consequences devastated the entire country, leading to a deep four-year recession.

The crisis originated in institutions in New York known as trusts, bank-like institutions that accepted deposits but that were originally intended to manage only inheritances and estates for wealthy clients. Because these trusts were supposed to engage only in low-risk activities, they were less regulated, had lower reserve requirements, and had lower cash reserves than national banks.

However, as the American economy boomed during the first decade of the twentieth century, trusts began speculating in real estate and the stock market, areas of speculation forbidden to national banks. Less regulated than national banks, trusts were able to pay their depositors higher returns. Yet trusts took a free ride on national banks' reputation for soundness, with depositors considering them equally safe. As a result, trusts grew rapidly: by 1907, the total assets of trusts in New York City were as large as those of national banks. Meanwhile, the trusts declined to join the New York Clearinghouse, a consortium of New York City national banks that guaranteed one anothers' soundness; that would have required the trusts to hold higher cash reserves, reducing their profits.

The Panic of 1907 began with the failure of the Knickerbocker Trust, a large New York City trust that failed when it suffered massive losses in unsuccessful stock market speculation. Quickly, other New York trusts came under pressure, and frightened depositors began queuing in long lines to withdraw their funds. The New York Clearinghouse declined to step in and lend to the trusts, and even healthy trusts came under serious assault. Within two days, a dozen major trusts had gone under. Credit markets froze, and the stock market fell dramatically as stock traders were unable to get credit to finance their trades and business confidence evaporated.

Fortunately, New York City's wealthiest man, the banker J. P. Morgan, quickly stepped in to stop the panic. Understanding that the crisis was spreading and would soon engulf healthy institutions, trusts and banks alike, he worked with other bankers, wealthy men such as John D. Rockefeller, and the U.S. Secretary of the Treasury to shore up the reserves of banks and trusts so they could withstand the onslaught of withdrawals. Once people were assured that they could withdraw their money, the panic ceased. Although the panic itself lasted little more than a week, it and the stock market collapse decimated the economy. A four-year recession ensued, with production falling 11% and unemployment rising from 3% to 8%.

Responding to Banking Crises: The Creation of the Federal Reserve

Concerns over the frequency of banking crises and the unprecedented role of J. P. Morgan in saving the financial system prompted the federal government to initiate banking reform. In 1913 the national banking system was eliminated and the Federal Reserve system was created as a way to compel all deposit-taking institutions to hold adequate reserves and to open their accounts to inspection by regulators. The Panic of 1907 convinced many that the time for centralized control of bank reserves had come. In addition, the Federal Reserve was given the sole right to issue currency in order to make the money supply sufficiently responsive to satisfy economic conditions around the country.

Although the new regime standardized and centralized the holding of bank reserves, it did not eliminate the potential for bank runs because banks' reserves were still less than the total value of their deposits. The potential for more bank runs became a reality during the Great Depression. Plunging commodity prices hit American farmers particularly hard, precipitating a series of bank runs in 1930, 1931, and 1933, each of which started at midwestern banks and then spread throughout the country.

After the failure of a particularly large bank in 1930, federal officials realized that the economy-wide effects compelled them to take a less hands-off approach and to intervene more vigorously. In 1932, the Reconstruction Finance Corporation (RFC) was established and given the authority to make loans to banks in order to stabilize the banking sector. Also, the Glass-Steagall Act of 1932, which created federal deposit insurance and increased the ability of banks to borrow from the Federal Reserve system, was passed. A loan to a leading Chicago bank from the Federal Reserve appears to have stopped a major banking crisis in 1932. However, the beast had not yet been tamed. Banks became fearful of borrowing from the RFC because doing so signaled weakness to the public.

During the catastrophic bank run of 1933, the new president, Franklin Delano Roosevelt, was inaugurated. He immediately declared a "bank holiday," closing all banks until regulators could get a handle on the problem.

In March 1933, emergency measures were adopted that gave the RFC extraordinary powers to stabilize and restructure the banking industry by providing capital to banks through either loans or outright purchases of bank shares. With the new rules, regulators closed nonviable banks and recapitalized viable ones by allowing the RFC to buy preferred shares in banks (shares that gave the U.S. government more rights than regular shareholders) and by greatly expanding banks' ability to borrow from the Federal Reserve. By 1933, the RFC had invested over $16.2 billion (2010 dollars) in bank capital—one-third of the total capital of all banks in the United States at that time—and purchased shares in almost one-half of all banks. The RFC loaned more than $32.4 billion (2010 dollars) to banks during this period.

Economic historians uniformly agree that the banking crises of the early 1930s greatly exacerbated the severity of the Great Depression, rendering

Official White House Photo by Pete Souza

Like FDR, President Obama, shown here meeting with economic advisers, was faced with a major financial crisis upon taking office.

monetary policy ineffective as the banking sector broke down and currency, withdrawn from banks and stashed under beds, reduced the money supply.

Although the powerful actions of the RFC stabilized the banking industry, new legislation was needed to prevent future banking crises. The Glass-Steagall Act of 1933 separated banks into two categories, **commercial banks,** depository banks that accepted deposits and were covered by deposit insurance, and **investment banks,** which engaged in creating and trading financial assets such as stocks and corporate bonds but were not covered by deposit insurance because their activities were considered more risky.

Regulation Q prevented commercial banks from paying interest on checking accounts in the belief that this would promote unhealthy competition between banks. In addition, investment banks were much more lightly regulated than commercial banks. The most important measure for the prevention of bank runs, however, was the adoption of federal deposit insurance (with an original limit of $2,500 per deposit).

These measures were clearly successful, and the United States enjoyed a long period of financial and banking stability. As memories of the bad old days dimmed, Depression-era bank regulations were lifted. In 1980, Regulation Q was eliminated; by 1999, the Glass-Steagall Act had been so weakened that offering services like trading financial assets was no longer off-limits to commercial banks.

The Savings and Loan Crisis of the 1980s

Along with banks, the banking industry also included **savings and loans** (also called S&Ls or **thrifts**), institutions designed to accept savings and turn them into long-term mortgages for home-buyers. S&Ls were covered by federal deposit insurance and were tightly regulated for safety. However, trouble hit in the 1970s, as high inflation led savers to withdraw their funds from low-interest-paying S&L accounts and put them into higher-interest-paying money market accounts. In addition, the high inflation rate severely eroded the value of the S&Ls' assets, the long-term mortgages they held on their books.

In order to improve S&Ls' competitive position vis-à-vis banks, Congress eased regulations to allow S&Ls to undertake much more risky investments in addition to long-term home mortgages. However, the new freedom did not bring with it increased oversight, leaving S&Ls with less oversight than banks. Not surprisingly, during the real estate boom of the 1970s and 1980s, S&Ls engaged in overly risky real estate lending. Also, corruption occurred as some S&L executives used their institutions as private piggy banks.

Unfortunately, during the late 1970s and early 1980s, political interference from Congress kept insolvent S&Ls open when a bank in a comparable situation would have been quickly shut down by bank regulators. By the early 1980s, a large number of S&Ls had failed. Because accounts were covered by federal deposit insurance, the liabilities of a failed S&L were now liabilities of the federal government, and depositors had to be paid from taxpayer funds. From 1986 through 1995, the federal government closed over 1,000 failed S&Ls, costing U.S. taxpayers over $124 billion dollars.

A **commercial bank** accepts deposits and is covered by deposit insurance.

An **investment bank** trades in financial assets and is not covered by deposit insurance.

A **savings and loan (thrift)** is another type of deposit-taking bank, usually specialized in issuing home loans.

In a classic case of shutting the barn door after the horse has escaped, in 1989 Congress put in place comprehensive oversight of S&L activities. It also empowered Fannie Mae and Freddie Mac to take over much of the home mortgage lending previously done by S&Ls. Fannie Mae and Freddie Mac are quasi-governmental agencies created during the Great Depression to make homeownership more affordable for low- and moderate-income households. It has been calculated that the S&L crisis helped cause a steep slowdown in the finance and real estate industries, leading to the recession of the early 1990s.

A financial institution engages in **leverage** when it finances its investments with borrowed funds.

The **balance sheet effect** is the reduction in a firm's net worth due to falling asset prices.

A **vicious cycle of deleveraging** takes place when asset sales to cover losses produce negative balance sheet effects on other firms and force creditors to call in their loans, forcing sales of more assets and causing further declines in asset prices.

Back to the Future: The Financial Crisis of 2008

The financial crisis of 2008 shared features of previous crises. Like the Panic of 1907 and the S&L crisis, it involved institutions that were not as strictly regulated as deposit-taking banks as well as excessive speculation. Like the crises of the early 1930s, it involved a U.S. government that was reluctant to take aggressive action until the scale of the devastation became clear. In addition, by the late 1990s, advances in technology and financial innovation had created yet another systemic weakness that played a central role in 2008. The story of Long-Term Capital Management, or LTCM, highlights these problems.

Long-Term Capital (Mis)Management Created in 1994, LTCM was a hedge fund, a private investment partnership open only to wealthy individuals and institutions. Hedge funds are virtually unregulated, allowing them to make much riskier investments than mutual funds, which are open to the average investor. Using vast amounts of **leverage**—that is, borrowed money—in order to increase its returns, LTCM used sophisticated computer models to make money by taking advantage of small differences in asset prices in global financial markets to buy at a lower price and sell at a higher price. In one year, LTCM made a return as high as 40%.

LTCM was also heavily involved in derivatives, complex financial instruments that are constructed—derived—from the obligations of more basic financial assets. Derivatives are popular investment tools because they are cheaper to trade than basic financial assets and can be constructed to suit a buyer's or seller's particular needs. Yet their complexity can make it extremely hard to measure their value. LTCM believed that its computer models allowed it to accurately gauge the risk in the huge bets that it was undertaking in derivatives using borrowed money.

However, LTCM's computer models hadn't factored in a series of financial crises in Asia and in Russia during 1997 and 1998. Through its large borrowing, LTCM had become such a big player in global financial markets that attempts to sell its assets depressed the prices of what it was trying to sell. As the markets fell around the world and LTCM's panic-stricken investors demanded the return of their funds, LTCM's losses mounted as it tried to sell assets to satisfy those demands. Quickly, its operations collapsed because it could no longer borrow money and other parties refused to trade with it. Financial markets around the world froze in panic.

The Federal Reserve realized that allowing LTCM's remaining assets to be sold at panic-stricken prices presented a grave risk to the entire financial system through the **balance sheet effect:** as sales of assets by LTCM depressed asset prices all over the world, other firms would see the value of their balance sheets fall as assets held on these balance sheets declined in value. Moreover, falling asset prices meant the value of assets held by borrowers on their balance sheets would fall below a critical threshold, leading to a default on the terms of their credit contracts and forcing creditors to call in their loans. This in turn would lead to more sales of assets as borrowers tried to raise cash to repay their loans, more credit defaults, and more loans called in, creating a **vicious cycle of deleveraging.**

The Federal Reserve Bank of New York arranged a \$3.625 billion bailout of LTCM in 1998, in which other private institutions took on shares of LTCM's assets and obligations, liquidated them in an orderly manner, and eventually

Subprime lending is lending to home-buyers who don't meet the usual criteria for being able to afford their payments.

In **securitization,** a pool of loans is assembled and shares of that pool are sold to investors.

turned a small profit. Quick action by the Federal Reserve Bank of New York prevented LTCM from sparking a contagion, yet virtually all of LTCM's investors were wiped out.

Subprime Lending and the Housing Bubble After the LTCM crisis, U.S. financial markets stabilized. They remained more or less stable even as stock prices fell sharply from 2000 to 2002 and the U.S. economy went into recession. During the recovery from the 2001 recession, however, the seeds for another financial crisis were planted.

The story begins with low interest rates: by 2003, U.S. interest rates were at historically low levels, partly because of Federal Reserve policy and partly because of large inflows of capital from other countries, especially China. These low interest rates helped cause a boom in housing, which in turn led the U.S. economy out of recession. As housing boomed, however, financial institutions began taking on growing risks—risks that were not well understood.

Traditionally, people were only able to borrow money to buy homes if they could show that they had sufficient income to meet the mortgage payments. Home loans to people who don't meet the usual criteria for borrowing, called **subprime lending,** were only a minor part of overall lending. But in the booming housing market of 2003–2006, subprime lending started to seem like a safe bet. Since housing prices kept rising, borrowers who couldn't make their mortgage payments could always pay off their mortgages, if necessary, by selling their homes. As a result, subprime lending exploded.

Who was making these subprime loans? For the most part, it wasn't traditional banks lending out depositors' money. Instead, most of the loans were made by "loan originators," who quickly sold mortgages to other investors. These sales were made possible by a process known as **securitization:** financial institutions assembled pools of loans and sold shares in the income from these pools. These shares were considered relatively safe investments, since it was considered unlikely that large numbers of home-buyers would default on their payments at the same time.

"Honey, we're homeless."

But that's exactly what happened. The housing boom turned out to be a bubble, and when home prices started falling in late 2006, many subprime borrowers were unable either to meet their mortgage payments or sell their houses for enough to pay off their mortgages. As a result, investors in securities backed by subprime mortgages started taking heavy losses. Many of the mortgage-backed assets were held by financial institutions, including banks and other institutions playing bank-like roles. Like the trusts that played a key role in the Panic of 1907, these "nonbank banks" were less regulated than commercial banks, which allowed them to offer higher returns to investors but left them extremely vulnerable in a crisis. Mortgage-related losses, in turn, led to a collapse of trust in the financial system.

Figure 16-10 shows one measure of this loss of trust: the TED spread, which is the difference between the interest rate on three-month loans that banks make to each other and the interest rate the federal government pays on three-month bonds. Since government bonds are considered extremely safe, the TED spread shows how much risk banks think they're taking on when lending to each other. Normally the spread is around a quarter of a percentage point, but it shot up in August 2007 and surged to an unprecedented 4.58 percentage points in October 2008, before returning to more normal levels in mid-2009.

Crisis and Response The collapse of trust in the financial system, combined with the large losses suffered by financial firms, led to a severe cycle of deleveraging and a credit crunch for the economy as a whole. Firms found it difficult to

FIGURE 16-10 The TED Spread

The TED spread is the difference between the interest rate at which banks lend to each other and the interest rate on U.S. government debt. It's widely used as a measure of financial stress. The TED spread soared as a result of the financial crisis of 2007–2008.

Sources: British Bankers' Association; Federal Reserve Bank of St. Louis.

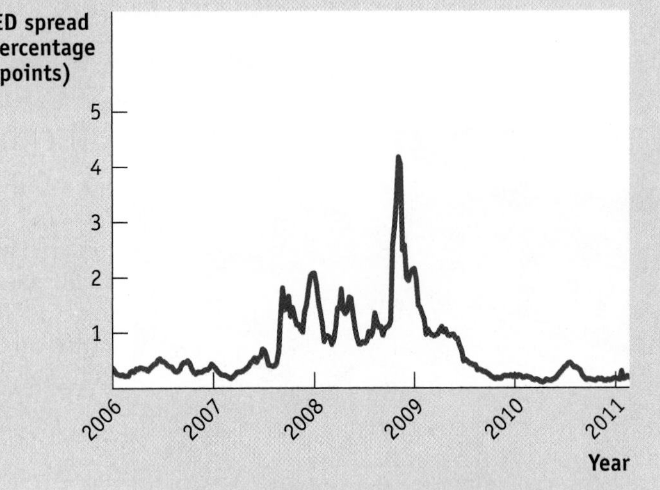

borrow, even for short-term operations; individuals found home loans unavailable and credit card limits reduced.

Overall, the negative economic effect of the financial crisis bore a distinct and troubling resemblance to the effects of the banking crisis of the early 1930s, which helped cause the Great Depression. Policy makers noticed the resemblance and tried to prevent a repeat performance. Beginning in August 2007, the Federal Reserve engaged in a series of efforts to provide cash to the financial system, lending funds to a widening range of institutions and buying private-sector debt. The Fed and the Treasury Department also stepped in to rescue individual firms that were deemed too crucial to be allowed to fail, such as the investment bank Bear Stearns and the insurance company AIG.

In September 2008, however, policy makers decided that one major investment bank, Lehman Brothers, could be allowed to fail. They quickly regretted the decision. Within days of Lehman's failure, widespread panic gripped the financial markets, as illustrated by the surge in the TED spread shown in Figure 16-10. In response to the intensified crisis, the U.S. government intervened further to support the financial system, as the U.S. Treasury began "injecting" capital into banks. Injecting capital, in practice, meant that the U.S. government would supply cash to banks in return for shares—in effect, partially nationalizing the financial system.

By the fall of 2010, the financial system appeared to be stabilized, and major institutions had repaid much of the money the federal government had injected during the crisis. It was generally expected that taxpayers would end up losing little if any money. However, the recovery of the banks was not matched by a successful turnaround for the overall economy: although the recession that began in December 2007 officially ended in June 2009, unemployment remained stubbornly high.

The Federal Reserve responded to this troubled situation with novel forms of open-market operations. Conventional open-market operations are limited to short-term government debt, but the Fed believed that this was no longer enough. It provided massive liquidity through discount window lending, as well as buying large quantities of other assets, mainly long-term government debt and debt of Fannie Mae and Freddie Mac, government-sponsored agencies that support home lending. This explains the surge in Fed assets after September 2008 visible in Figure 16-9.

Like earlier crises, the crisis of 2008 led to changes in banking regulation, most notably the Dodd-Frank financial regulatory reform bill enacted in 2010. We describe that bill briefly in the Economics in Action that follows.

ECONOMICS ➤ IN ACTION

REGULATION AFTER THE 2008 CRISIS

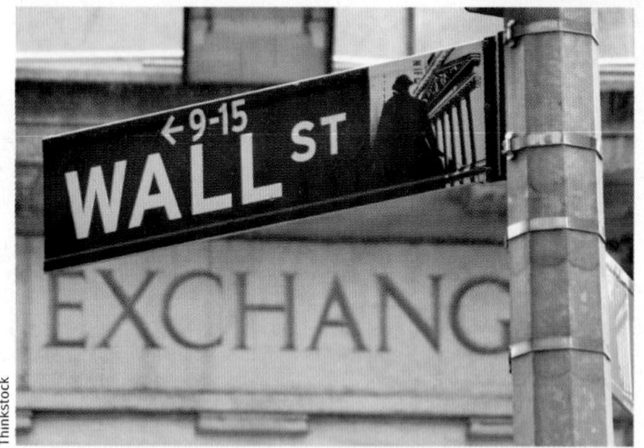

Thinkstock

The Wall Street Reform and Consumer Protection Act of 2010 was an attempt to extend the spirit of old-fashioned bank regulation to today's more complex financial system.

In July 2010, President Obama signed the Wall Street Reform and Consumer Protection Act—generally known as Dodd-Frank, after its sponsors in the Senate and House, respectively—into law. It was the biggest financial reform enacted since the 1930s—not surprising given that the nation had just gone through the worst financial crisis since the 1930s. How did it change regulation?

For the most part, it left regulation of traditional deposit-taking banks more or less as it was. The main change these banks would face was the creation of a new agency, the Bureau of Consumer Financial Protection, whose mission was to protect borrowers from being exploited through seemingly attractive financial deals they didn't understand.

The major changes came in the regulation of financial institutions other than banks—institutions that, as the fall of Lehman Brothers showed, could trigger banking crises. The new law gave a special government committee, the Financial Stability Oversight Council, the right to designate certain institutions as "systemically important" even if they weren't ordinary deposit-taking banks. These systemically important institutions would be subjected to bank-style regulation, including relatively high capital requirements and limits on the kinds of risks they could take. In addition, the federal government would acquire "resolution authority," meaning the right to seize troubled financial institutions in much the same way that it routinely takes over troubled banks.

Beyond this, the law established new rules on the trading of derivatives, those complex financial instruments that sank LTCM and played an important role in the 2008 crisis as well: most derivatives would henceforth have to be bought and sold on exchanges, where everyone could observe their prices and the volume of transactions. The idea was to make the risks taken by financial institutions more transparent.

Overall, Dodd-Frank is probably best seen as an attempt to extend the spirit of old-fashioned bank regulation to the more complex financial system of the twenty-first century. Will it succeed in heading off future banking crises? Stay tuned.

▼ Quick Review

- The Federal Reserve system was created in response to the Panic of 1907.
- Widespread bank runs in the early 1930s resulted in greater bank regulation and the creation of federal deposit insurance. Banks were separated into two categories: **commercial** (covered by deposit insurance) and **investment** (not covered).
- In the **savings and loan (thrift)** crisis of the 1970s and 1980s, insufficiently regulated S&Ls incurred huge losses from risky speculation.
- During the mid-1990s, the hedge fund LTCM used huge amounts of **leverage** to speculate in global markets, incurred massive losses, and collapsed. In selling assets to cover its losses, LTCM caused **balance sheet effects** for firms around the world. To prevent a **vicious cycle of deleveraging,** the New York Fed coordinated a private bailout.
- In the mid-2000s, loans from **subprime lending** spread through the financial system via **securitization,** leading to a financial crisis. The Fed responded by injecting cash into financial institutions and buying private debt.
- In 2010, the Dodd-Frank bill revised financial regulation in an attempt to prevent repeats of the 2008 crisis.

CHECK YOUR UNDERSTANDING 16-5

1. What are the similarities between the Panic of 1907, the S&L crisis, and the crisis of 2008?
2. Why did the creation of the Federal Reserve fail to prevent the bank runs of the Great Depression? What measures stopped the bank runs?
3. Describe the balance sheet effect. Describe the vicious cycle of deleveraging. Why is it necessary for the government to step in to halt a vicious cycle of deleveraging?

Solutions appear at back of book.

WORKED PROBLEM

Multiplying Money

As part of the Economic Stimulus Act of 2008, the U.S. government issued tax rebate checks to eligible households. On average, rebate checks totaled $950.00.

Economists have estimated that each household initially spent about $450.00 of the rebate. Since the public holds about 50% of M1 in the form of currency, the average household deposited about $250.00 of the remaining $500.00 and held the other $250.00 in cash. In light of this data, approximately how much will the money supply increase in response to the average household's deposit? (*Hint:* Create a table that shows the change in the money supply for ten rounds.) Assume that banks lend out the full amount of any excess reserves.

STEP 1: Find the required reserve ratio in the United States.

In order to find and understand the U.S. required reserve ratio, read the section "The Monetary Role of Banks," beginning on page 488. Pay close attention to the subsections, "What Banks Do," beginning on page 488, and "Bank Regulation," beginning on page 490.

The required reserve ratio in the United States is 10%. ■

STEP 2: Make a table that shows on line 1 the initial deposit, the required reserves, the excess reserves, the loans that a bank makes, and the amount held in currency from the initial loans made by the bank.

Read the subsection, "Bank Regulation," beginning on page 490, and the section, "Reserves, Bank Deposits, and the Money Multiplier," beginning on page 494, to help determine the required reserves, excess reserves, and the loans made. The amount held in currency from the initial loans made by the bank is the amount in the loan that "leaks" out of the banking system, which is also discussed in the section, "Reserves, Bank Deposits, and the Money Multiplier."

The first line of this table is shown here.

Round	Deposits	Required reserves	Excess reserves	Loans	Held as currency
1	$250.00	$25.00	$225.00	$225.00	$112.50

The deposit amount is $250.00. As determined in Step 1, the required reserves are 10% of this deposit amount: 10% × $250.00 = $25.00. The excess reserves are therefore $250.00 – $25.00 = $225.00. We have assumed that banks loan out all of their excess reserves, so they loan out $225.00. Of this amount, the public will hold 50% in currency: 50% × $225.00 = $112.50. ■

STEP 3: Extend this table for 10 rounds.

If, after the first round, the public has held $112.50 of $225.00 in loans as currency, then the second round will begin with a deposit of $112.50 = $225.00 – $112.50. Each round begins with the difference between the loan amount and the amount held in currency from the previous round.

The extended table is shown below.

Round	Deposits	Required reserves	Excess reserves	Loans	Held as currency
1	$250.00	$25.00	$225.00	$225.00	$112.50
2	112.50	11.25	101.50	101.25	50.63
3	50.63	5.06	45.56	45.56	22.78
4	22.78	2.28	20.50	20.50	10.25
5	10.25	1.03	9.23	9.23	4.61
6	4.61	0.46	4.15	4.15	2.08
7	2.08	0.21	1.87	1.87	0.93
8	0.93	0.09	0.84	0.84	0.42
9	0.42	0.04	0.38	0.38	0.19
10	0.19	0.02	0.17	0.17	0.09
Total after 10 rounds	$454.39	$45.44	$408.95	$408.95	$204.48

Round 2 is constructed in the same manner as Round 1 above. The round begins with a deposit of $112.50. The bank holds $11.25 of this as reserves, and so the excess reserves and the amount loaned out is $112.50 – $11.25 = $101.25. Of this, the public keeps $50.63 in currency. ■

STEP 4: Determine the increase in the money supply that results from the average household deposit.

Read the section "How Banks Create Money" beginning on page 492. The amount of the increase in the money supply is the total amount that banks have been able to loan out in response to the first deposit.

The approximate increase in the money supply from the average household deposit is $408.95. ■

SUMMARY

1. **Money** is any asset that can easily be used to purchase goods and services. Money consists of cash, which is **liquid** by definition, as well as other highly liquid assets. **Currency in circulation** and **checkable bank deposits** are both considered part of the **money supply.** Money plays three roles: it is a **medium of exchange** used for transactions, a **store of value** that holds purchasing power over time, and a **unit of account** in which prices are stated.
2. Over time, **commodity money,** which consists of goods possessing value aside from their role as money, such as gold and silver coins, was replaced by **commodity-backed money,** such as paper currency backed by gold. Today the dollar is pure **fiat money,** whose value derives solely from its official role.
3. The Federal Reserve calculates two measures of the money supply. M1 is the narrowest **monetary aggregate,** containing only currency in circulation, traveler's checks, and checkable bank deposits. M2 includes a wider range of assets called **near-moneys,** mainly other forms of bank deposits, that can easily be converted into checkable bank deposits.
4. Banks allow depositors immediate access to their funds, but they also lend out most of the funds deposited in their care. To meet demands for cash, they maintain **bank reserves** composed of both currency held in vaults and deposits at the Federal Reserve. The **reserve ratio** is the ratio of bank reserves to bank deposits. A **T-account** summarizes a bank's financial position, with loans and reserves counted as assets and deposits counted as liabilities.

5. Banks have sometimes been subject to **bank runs,** most notably in the early 1930s. To avert this danger, depositors are now protected by **deposit insurance,** bank owners face capital requirements that reduce the incentive to make overly risky loans with depositors' funds, and banks must satisfy **reserve requirements.**

6. When currency is deposited in a bank, it starts a multiplier process in which banks lend out **excess reserves,** leading to an increase in the money supply—so banks create money. If the entire money supply consisted of checkable bank deposits, the money supply would be equal to the value of reserves divided by the reserve ratio. In reality, much of the **monetary base** consists of currency in circulation, and the **money multiplier** is the ratio of the money supply to the monetary base.

7. The monetary base is controlled by the Federal Reserve, the **central bank** of the United States. The Fed regulates banks and sets reserve requirements. To meet those requirements, banks borrow and lend reserves in the **federal funds market** at the **federal funds rate.** Through the **discount window** facility, banks can borrow from the Fed at the **discount rate.**

8. **Open-market operations** by the Fed are the principal tool of monetary policy: the Fed can increase or reduce the monetary base by buying U.S. Treasury bills from banks or selling U.S. Treasury bills to banks.

9. In response to the Panic of 1907, the Fed was created to centralize the holding of reserves, inspect banks' books, and make the money supply sufficiently responsive to varying economic conditions.

10. The Great Depression sparked widespread bank runs in the early 1930s, which greatly worsened and lengthened it. Federal deposit insurance was created, and the government recapitalized banks by lending to them and by buying shares of banks. By 1933, banks had been separated into two categories: **commercial banks** (covered by deposit insurance) and **investment banks** (not covered). Public acceptance of deposit insurance finally stopped the bank runs of the Great Depression.

11. The **savings and loan (thrift)** crisis of the 1980s arose because insufficiently regulated S&Ls engaged in overly risky speculation and incurred huge losses. Depositors in failed S&Ls were compensated with taxpayer funds because they were covered by deposit insurance. The crisis caused steep losses in the financial and real estate sectors, resulting in a recession in the early 1990s.

12. During the mid-1990s, the hedge fund LTCM used huge amounts of **leverage** to speculate in global financial markets, incurred massive losses, and collapsed. LTCM was so large that, in selling assets to cover its losses, it caused **balance sheet effects** for firms around the world, leading to the prospect of a **vicious cycle of deleveraging.** As a result, credit markets around the world froze. The New York Fed coordinated a private bailout of LTCM and revived world credit markets.

13. **Subprime lending** during the U.S. housing bubble of the mid-2000s spread through the financial system via **securitization.** When the bubble burst, massive losses by banks and nonbank financial institutions led to widespread collapse in the financial system. To prevent another Great Depression, the Fed and the U.S. Treasury expanded lending to bank and nonbank institutions, provided capital through the purchase of bank shares, and purchased private debt. Because much of the crisis originated in nontraditional bank institutions, the crisis of 2008 indicated that a wider safety net and broader regulation are needed in the financial sector. The 2010 Dodd-Frank bill, the biggest financial reform since the 1930s, is an attempt to prevent another crisis.

KEY TERMS

Money, p. 482
Liquid, p. 482
Currency in circulation, p. 482
Checkable bank deposits, p. 482
Money supply, p. 482
Medium of exchange, p. 483
Store of value, p. 483
Unit of account, p. 484
Commodity money, p. 484
Commodity-backed money, p. 484
Fiat money, p. 485
Monetary aggregate, p. 485
Near-moneys, p. 485
Bank reserves, p. 488
T-account, p. 488
Reserve ratio, p. 489
Bank run, p. 490
Deposit insurance, p. 490
Reserve requirements, p. 491
Discount window, p. 491
Excess reserves, p. 494
Monetary base, p. 495
Money multiplier, p. 496
Central bank, p. 497
Federal funds market, p. 498
Federal funds rate, p. 498
Discount rate, p. 499
Open-market operation, p. 499
Commercial bank, p. 506
Investment bank, p. 506
Savings and loan (thrift), p. 506
Leverage, p. 507
Balance sheet effect, p. 507
Vicious cycle of deleveraging, p. 507
Subprime lending, p. 508
Securitization, p. 508

PROBLEMS

1. For each of the following transactions, what is the initial effect (increase or decrease) on M1? On M2?
   a. You sell a few shares of stock and put the proceeds into your savings account.
   b. You sell a few shares of stock and put the proceeds into your checking account.
   c. You transfer money from your savings account to your checking account.
   d. You discover $0.25 under the floor mat in your car and deposit it in your checking account.
   e. You discover $0.25 under the floor mat in your car and deposit it in your savings account.
2. There are three types of money: commodity money, commodity-backed money, and fiat money. Which type of money is used in each of the following situations?
   a. Bottles of rum were used to pay for goods in colonial Australia.
   b. Salt was used in many European countries as a medium of exchange.
   c. For a brief time, Germany used paper money (the "Rye Mark") that could be redeemed for a certain amount of rye, a type of grain.
   d. The town of Ithaca, New York, prints its own currency, the Ithaca HOURS, which can be used to purchase local goods and services.
3. The table below shows the components of M1 and M2 in billions of dollars for the month of December in the years 2000 to 2010 as published in the 2011 Economic Report of the President. Complete the table by calculating M1, M2, currency in circulation as a percentage of M1, and currency in circulation as a percentage of M2. What trends or patterns about M1, M2, currency in circulation as a percentage of M1, and currency in circulation as a percentage of M2 do you see? What might account for these trends?

Year	Currency in circulation	Traveler's checks	Checkable deposits	Savings deposits	Time deposits	Money market funds	M1	M2	Currency in circulation as a percentage of M1	Currency in circulation as a percentage of M2
2000	$531.2	$8.3	$547.7	$1,878.0	$1,046.0	$902.0	?	?	?	?
2001	581.1	8.0	592.9	2,309.5	974.5	962.5	?	?	?	?
2002	626.2	7.8	585.7	2,773.4	894.5	887.5	?	?	?	?
2003	662.5	7.7	636.2	3,162.8	817.8	777.0	?	?	?	?
2004	697.7	7.6	671.1	3,508.8	827.9	694.7	?	?	?	?
2005	724.1	7.2	643.5	3,606.0	993.1	699.4	?	?	?	?
2006	749.6	6.7	610.0	3,694.6	1,205.3	799.0	?	?	?	?
2007	759.7	6.3	607.6	3,872.6	1,275.0	972.7	?	?	?	?
2008	815.0	5.5	782.1	4,106.1	1,455.7	1,080.5	?	?	?	?
2009	861.5	5.1	827.0	4,836.9	1,177.4	820.8	?	?	?	?
2010	915.7	4.7	911.7	5,357.6	926.6	700.0	?	?	?	?

Source: 2011 Economic Report of the President.

4. Indicate whether each of the following is part of M1, M2, or neither:
   a. $95 on your campus meal card
   b. $0.55 in the change cup of your car
   c. $1,663 in your savings account
   d. $459 in your checking account
   e. 100 shares of stock worth $4,000
   f. A $1,000 line of credit on your Sears credit card
5. Tracy Williams deposits $500 that was in her sock drawer into a checking account at the local bank.
   a. How does the deposit initially change the T-account of the local bank? How does it change the money supply?
   b. If the bank maintains a reserve ratio of 10%, how will it respond to the new deposit?
   c. If every time the bank makes a loan, the loan results in a new checkable bank deposit in a different bank equal to the amount of the loan, by how much could the total money supply in the economy expand in response to Tracy's initial cash deposit of $500?
   d. If every time the bank makes a loan, the loan results in a new checkable bank deposit in a different bank equal to the amount of the loan and the bank maintains a reserve ratio of 5%, by how much could the money supply expand in response to Tracy's initial cash deposit of $500?

6. Ryan Cozzens withdraws $400 from his checking account at the local bank and keeps it in his wallet.

a. How will the withdrawal change the T-account of the local bank and the money supply?

b. If the bank maintains a reserve ratio of 10%, how will it respond to the withdrawal? Assume that the bank responds to insufficient reserves by reducing the amount of deposits it holds until its level of reserves satisfies its required reserve ratio. The bank reduces its deposits by calling in some of its loans, forcing borrowers to pay back these loans by taking cash from their checking deposits (at the same bank) to make repayment.

c. If every time the bank decreases its loans, checkable bank deposits fall by the amount of the loan, by how much will the money supply in the economy contract in response to Ryan's withdrawal of $400?

d. If every time the bank decreases its loans, checkable bank deposits fall by the amount of the loan and the bank maintains a reserve ratio of 20%, by how much will the money supply contract in response to a withdrawal of $400?

7. The government of Eastlandia uses measures of monetary aggregates similar to those used by the United States, and the central bank of Eastlandia imposes a required reserve ratio of 10%. Given the following information, answer the questions below.

Bank deposits at the central bank = $200 million

Currency held by public = $150 million

Currency in bank vaults = $100 million

Checkable bank deposits = $500 million

Traveler's checks = $10 million

a. What is M1?

b. What is the monetary base?

c. Are the commercial banks holding excess reserves?

d. Can the commercial banks increase checkable bank deposits? If yes, by how much can checkable bank deposits increase?

8. In Westlandia, the public holds 50% of M1 in the form of currency, and the required reserve ratio is 20%. Estimate how much the money supply will increase in response to a new cash deposit of $500 by completing the accompanying table. (*Hint:* The first row shows that the bank must hold $100 in minimum reserves—20% of the $500 deposit—against this deposit, leaving $400 in excess reserves that can be loaned out. However, since the public wants to hold 50% of the loan in currency, only $400 × 0.5 = $200 of the loan will be deposited in round 2 from the loan granted in round 1.) How does your answer compare to an economy in which the total amount of the loan is deposited in the banking system and the public doesn't hold any of the loan in currency? What does this imply about the relationship between the public's desire for holding currency and the money multiplier?

Round	Deposits	Required reserves	Excess reserves	Loans	Held as currency
1	$500.00	$100.00	$400.00	$400.00	$200.00
2	200.00	?	?	?	?
3	?	?	?	?	?
4	?	?	?	?	?
5	?	?	?	?	?
6	?	?	?	?	?
7	?	?	?	?	?
8	?	?	?	?	?
9	?	?	?	?	?
Total after 10 rounds	?	?	?	?	?

9. What will happen to the money supply under the following circumstances in a checkable-deposits-only system?

a. The required reserve ratio is 25%, and a depositor withdraws $700 from his checkable bank deposit.

b. The required reserve ratio is 5%, and a depositor withdraws $700 from his checkable bank deposit.

c. The required reserve ratio is 20%, and a customer deposits $750 to her checkable bank deposit.

d. The required reserve ratio is 10%, and a customer deposits $600 to her checkable bank deposit.

10. Although the U.S. Federal Reserve doesn't use changes in reserve requirements to manage the money supply, the central bank of Albernia does. The commercial banks of Albernia have $100 million in reserves and $1,000 million in checkable deposits; the initial required reserve ratio is 10%. The commercial banks follow a policy of holding no excess reserves. The public holds no currency, only checkable deposits in the banking system.

a. How will the money supply change if the required reserve ratio falls to 5%?

b. How will the money supply change if the required reserve ratio rises to 25%?

11. Using Figure 16-6, find the Federal Reserve district in which you live. Go to http://www.federalreserve.gov/bios/pres.htm and click on your district to identify the president of the Federal Reserve Bank in your district. Go to http://www.federalreserve.gov/fomc/ and determine if the president of the regional Federal Reserve bank in your district is currently a voting member of the Federal Open Market Committee (FOMC).

12. The Congressional Research Service estimates that at least $45 million of counterfeit U.S. $100 notes produced by the North Korean government are in circulation.

a. Why do U.S. taxpayers lose because of North Korea's counterfeiting?

b. As of November 2012, the interest rate earned on one-year U.S. Treasury bills was 0.18%. At a 0.18% rate of interest, what is the amount of money U.S. taxpayers are losing per year because of these $45 million in counterfeit notes?

13. As shown in Figure 16-9, the portion of the Federal Reserve's assets made up of U.S. Treasury bills has declined since 2007. Go to www.federalreserve.gov. Under "Select Statistical Releases," click on "All Statistical Releases." Under the heading "Money Stock and Reserve Balances," click on "Factors Affecting Reserve Balances." Click on the date of the current release.

a. Under "Statement of Condition of Each Federal Reserve Bank," look in the "Total" column. What is the amount displayed next to "Total assets"? What is the amount displayed next to "U.S. Treasury securities"? What percentage of the Federal Reserve's total assets are currently made up of U.S. Treasury bills?

b. Do the Federal Reserve's assets consist primarily of U.S. Treasury securities, as they did in January 2007, the beginning of the graph in Figure 16-9, or does the Fed still own a large number of other assets, as it did in mid-2011, the end of the graph in Figure 16-9?

14. The accompanying figure shows new U.S. housing starts, in thousands of units per month, between January 1980 and August 2011. The graph shows a large drop in new housing starts in 1984–1991 and 2006–2009. New housing starts are related to the availability of mortgages.

a. What caused the drop in new housing starts in 1984–1991?

b. What caused the drop in new housing starts in 2006–2009?

c. How could better regulation of financial institutions have prevented these two instances?

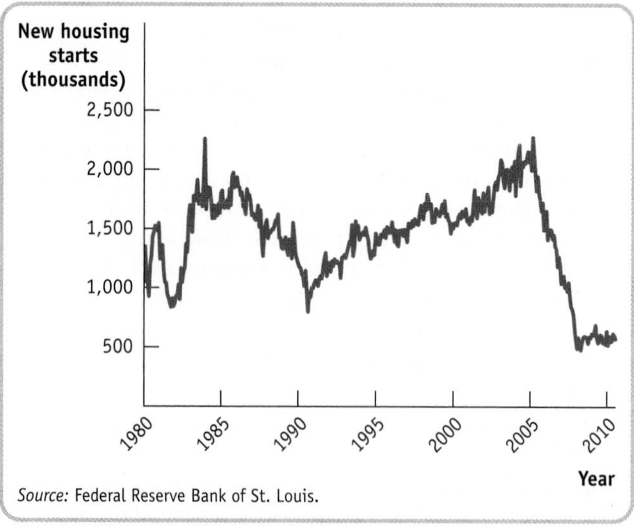

Source: Federal Reserve Bank of St. Louis.

EXTEND YOUR UNDERSTANDING

15. Show the changes to the T-accounts for the Federal Reserve and for commercial banks when the Federal Reserve buys $50 million in U.S. Treasury bills. If the public holds a fixed amount of currency (so that all loans create an equal amount of deposits in the banking system), the minimum reserve ratio is 10%, and banks hold no excess reserves, by how much will deposits in the commercial banks change? By how much will the money supply change? Show the final changes to the T-account for commercial banks when the money supply changes by this amount.

16. Show the changes to the T-accounts for the Federal Reserve and for commercial banks when the Federal Reserve sells $30 million in U.S. Treasury bills. If the public holds a fixed amount of currency (so that all new loans create an equal amount of checkable bank deposits in the banking system) and the minimum reserve ratio is 5%, by how much will checkable bank deposits in the commercial banks change? By how much will the money supply change? Show the final changes to the T-account for the commercial banks when the money supply changes by this amount.

CHAPTER 17

Monetary Policy

WHAT YOU WILL LEARN IN THIS CHAPTER

- What the **money demand curve** is
- Why the **liquidity preference model** determines the interest rate in the short run
- How the Federal Reserve implements monetary policy, moving the interest rate to affect aggregate output
- Why monetary policy is the main tool for stabilizing the economy
- How the behavior of the Federal Reserve compares to that of other central banks
- Why economists believe in **monetary neutrality**—that monetary policy affects only the price level, not aggregate output, in the long run

PERSON OF THE YEAR

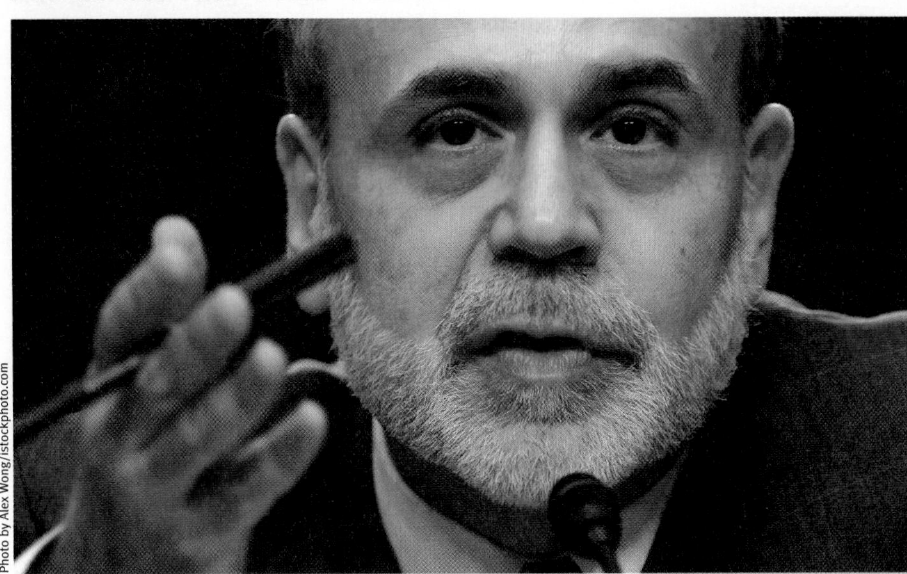

Photo by Alex Wong/istockphoto.com

As Fed chairman, Ben Bernanke has more influence over the economy's ups and downs than the president.

"A BALD MAN WITH A GRAY beard and tired eyes is sitting in his oversize Washington office, talking about the economy. He doesn't have a commanding presence. He isn't a mesmerizing speaker. He has none of the look-at-me swagger or listen-to-me charisma so common among men with oversize Washington offices. His arguments aren't partisan or ideological; they're methodical, grounded in data and the latest academic literature. When he doesn't know something, he doesn't bluster or bluff. He's professorial, which makes sense, because he spent most of his career as a professor."

So began *Time* magazine's profile of Ben Bernanke, whom the magazine named Person of the Year for 2009. Who is this mild-mannered man, and why does he matter so much? The answer is that Bernanke is the chairman of the Board of Governors of the Federal Reserve System—the body that controls *monetary policy.*

People sometimes say that Bernanke decides how much money to print. That's not quite true: for one thing, the Fed doesn't literally print money, and beyond that, monetary decisions are actually made by a committee rather than by one man. But as we learned in Chapter 16, the Federal Reserve can use open-market operations and other actions, such as changes in reserve requirements, to alter the money supply—and Ben Bernanke has more influence over these actions than anyone else in America.

And these actions matter a lot. Roughly half of the recessions the United States has experienced since World War II can be attributed, at least in part, to the decisions of the Federal Reserve to tighten policy to fight inflation. In a number of other cases, the Fed has played a key role in fighting slumps and promoting recovery. The financial crisis of 2008 put the Fed at center stage. Bernanke's aggressive response to the crisis, which, as we saw in Chapter 16, included a tripling of the monetary base, inspired both praise (including his designation as Person of the Year) and condemnation.

In this chapter we'll learn how monetary policy works—how actions by the Federal Reserve can have a powerful effect on the economy. We'll start by looking at the *demand for money* from households and firms. Then we'll see how the Fed's ability to change the *supply of money* allows it to move interest rates in the short run and thereby affect real GDP. We'll look at U.S. monetary policy in practice and compare it to the monetary policy of other central banks. We'll conclude by examining the long-run effects of monetary policy.

The Demand for Money

In Chapter 16 we learned about the various types of monetary aggregates: M1, the most commonly used definition of the money supply, consists of currency in circulation (cash), plus checkable bank deposits, plus traveler's checks; and M2, a broader definition of the money supply, consists of M1 plus deposits that can easily be transferred into checkable deposits. We also learned why people hold money—to make it easier to purchase goods and services. Now we'll go deeper, examining what determines how much money individuals and firms want to hold at any given time.

The Opportunity Cost of Holding Money

Most economic decisions involve trade-offs at the margin. That is, individuals decide how much of a good to consume by determining whether the benefit they'd gain from consuming a bit more of any given good is worth the cost. The same decision process is used when deciding how much money to hold.

Big Cheese Photo/SuperStock

There is a price to be paid for the convenience of holding money.

Individuals and firms find it useful to hold some of their assets in the form of money because of the convenience money provides: money can be used to make purchases directly, but other assets can't. But there is a price to be paid for that convenience: money normally yields a lower rate of return than nonmonetary assets.

As an example of how convenience makes it worth incurring some opportunity costs, consider the fact that even today—with the prevalence of credit cards, debit cards, and ATMs—people continue to keep cash in their wallets rather than leave the funds in an interest-bearing account. They do this because they don't want to have to go to an ATM to withdraw money every time they want to buy lunch from a place that doesn't accept credit cards or won't accept them for small amounts because of the processing fee. In other words, the convenience of keeping some cash in your wallet is more valuable than the interest you would earn by keeping that money in the bank.

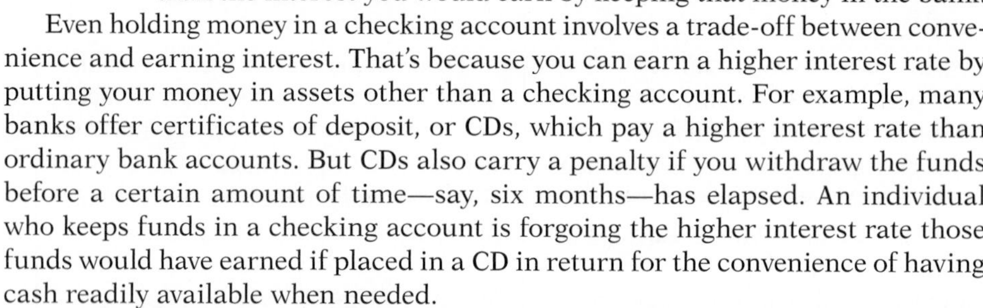

Even holding money in a checking account involves a trade-off between convenience and earning interest. That's because you can earn a higher interest rate by putting your money in assets other than a checking account. For example, many banks offer certificates of deposit, or CDs, which pay a higher interest rate than ordinary bank accounts. But CDs also carry a penalty if you withdraw the funds before a certain amount of time—say, six months—has elapsed. An individual who keeps funds in a checking account is forgoing the higher interest rate those funds would have earned if placed in a CD in return for the convenience of having cash readily available when needed.

So making sense of the demand for money is about understanding how individuals and firms trade off the benefit of holding cash—that provides convenience but no interest—versus the benefit of holding interest-bearing nonmonetary assets—that provide interest but not convenience. And that trade-off is affected by the interest rate. (As before, when we say *the interest rate* it is with the understanding that we mean a nominal interest rate—that is, it's unadjusted for inflation.) Next, we'll examine how that trade-off changed dramatically from June 2007 to June 2008, when there was a big fall in interest rates.

TABLE 17-1 Selected Interest Rates, June 2007

One-month certificates of deposit (CDs)	5.30%
Interest-bearing demand deposits	2.30%
Currency	0

Source: Federal Reserve Bank of St. Louis.

Table 17-1 illustrates the opportunity cost of holding money in a specific month, June 2007. The first row shows the interest rate on one-month certificates of deposit—that is, the interest rate individuals could get if they were willing to tie their funds up for one month. In June 2007, one-month CDs yielded 5.30%. The second row shows the interest rate on interest-bearing demand deposits (specifically, those included in M2, minus small time deposits). Funds in these accounts were more accessible than those in CDs, but the price of that convenience was a much lower interest rate, only 2.30%. Finally, the last row shows the interest rate on currency—cash in your wallet—which was, of course, zero.

Short-term interest rates are the interest rates on financial assets that mature within less than a year.

Long-term interest rates are interest rates on financial assets that mature a number of years in the future.

Table 17-1 shows the opportunity cost of holding money at one point in time, but the opportunity cost of holding money changes when the overall level of interest rates changes. Specifically, when the overall level of interest rates falls, the opportunity cost of holding money falls, too.

Table 17-2 illustrates this point by showing how selected interest rates changed between June 2007 and June 2008, a period when the Federal Reserve was slashing rates in an (unsuccessful) effort to fight off a rapidly worsening recession. A comparison between interest rates in June 2007 and June 2008 illustrates what happens when the opportunity cost of holding money falls sharply. Between June 2007 and June 2008, the federal funds rate, which is the rate the Fed controls most directly, fell by 3.25 percentage points. The interest rate on one-month CDs fell almost as much, 2.8 percentage points. These interest rates are **short-term interest rates**—rates on financial assets that come due, or mature, within less than a year.

TABLE 17-2 Interest Rates and the Opportunity Cost of Holding Money

	June 2007	June 2008
Federal funds rate	5.25%	2.00%
One-month certificates of deposit (CDs)	5.30%	2.50%
Interest-bearing demand deposits	2.30%	1.24%
Currency	0	0
CDs minus interest-bearing demand deposits (percentage points)	**3.00**	**1.26**
CDs minus currency (percentage points)	**5.30**	**2.50**

Source: Federal Reserve Bank of St. Louis.

As short-term interest rates fell between June 2007 and June 2008, the interest rates on money didn't fall by the same amount. The interest rate on currency, of course, remained at zero. The interest rate paid on demand deposits did fall, but by much less than short-term interest rates. As a comparison of the two columns of Table 17-2 shows, the opportunity cost of holding money fell. The last two rows of Table 17-2 summarize this comparison: they give the differences between the interest rates on demand deposits and on currency and the interest rate on CDs. These differences—the opportunity cost of holding money rather than interest-bearing assets—declined sharply between June 2007 and June 2008. This reflects a general result: *The higher the short-term interest rate, the higher the opportunity cost of holding money; the lower the short-term interest rate, the lower the opportunity cost of holding money.*

The fact that the federal funds rate in Table 17-2 and the interest rate on one-month CDs fell by almost the same percentage is not an accident: all short-term interest rates tend to move together, with rare exceptions. The reason short-term interest rates tend to move together is that CDs and other short-term assets (like one-month and three-month U.S. Treasury bills) are in effect competing for the same business. Any short-term asset that offers a lower-than-average interest rate will be sold by investors, who will move their wealth into a higher-yielding short-term asset. The selling of the asset, in turn, forces its interest rate up, because investors must be rewarded with a higher rate in order to induce them to buy it.

Conversely, investors will move their wealth into any short-term financial asset that offers an above-average interest rate. The purchase of the asset drives its interest rate down when sellers find they can lower the rate of return on the asset and still find willing buyers. So interest rates on short-term financial assets tend to be roughly the same because no asset will consistently offer a higher-than-average or a lower-than-average interest rate.

Table 17-2 contains only short-term interest rates. At any given moment, **long-term interest rates**—rates of interest on financial assets that mature, or come due, a number of years into the future—may be different from short-term interest rates. The difference between short-term and long-term interest rates is sometimes important as a practical matter. Moreover, it's short-term rates rather than long-term rates that affect money demand, because the decision to hold money involves trading off the convenience of holding cash versus the payoff from holding assets that mature in the short term—a year or less. For the moment, however, let's ignore the distinction between short-term and long-term rates and assume that there is only one interest rate.

The **money demand curve** shows the relationship between the interest rate and the quantity of money demanded.

The Money Demand Curve

Because the overall level of interest rates affects the opportunity cost of holding money, the quantity of money individuals and firms want to hold is, other things equal, negatively related to the interest rate. In Figure 17-1, the horizontal axis shows the quantity of money demanded and the vertical axis shows the interest rate, *r,* which you can think of as a representative short-term interest rate such as the rate on one-month CDs.

The relationship between the interest rate and the quantity of money demanded by the public is illustrated by the **money demand curve,** *MD,* in Figure 17-1. The money demand curve slopes downward because, other things equal, a higher interest rate increases the opportunity cost of holding money, leading the public to reduce the quantity of money it demands. For example, if the interest rate is very low—say, 1%—the interest forgone by holding money is relatively small. As a result, individuals and firms will tend to hold relatively large amounts of money to avoid the cost and nuisance of converting other assets into money when making purchases.

By contrast, if the interest rate is relatively high—say, 15%, a level it reached in the United States in the early 1980s—the opportunity cost of holding money is high. People will respond by keeping only small amounts in cash and deposits, converting assets into money only when needed.

You might ask why we draw the money demand curve with the interest rate—as opposed to rates of return on other assets, such as stocks or real estate—on the vertical axis. The answer is that for most people the relevant question in deciding how much money to hold is whether to put the funds in the form of other assets that can be turned fairly quickly and easily into money. Stocks don't fit that definition because there are significant transaction fees when you sell stock (which is why stock market investors are advised not to buy and sell too often). Real estate doesn't fit the definition either because selling real estate involves even larger fees and can take a long time as well. So the relevant comparison is with assets that are "close to" money—fairly liquid assets like CDs. And as we've already seen, the interest rates on all these assets normally move closely together.

FIGURE 17-1 The Money Demand Curve

The money demand curve illustrates the relationship between the interest rate and the quantity of money demanded. It slopes downward: a higher interest rate leads to a higher opportunity cost of holding money and reduces the quantity of money demanded. Correspondingly, a lower interest rate reduces the opportunity cost of holding money and increases the quantity of money demanded.

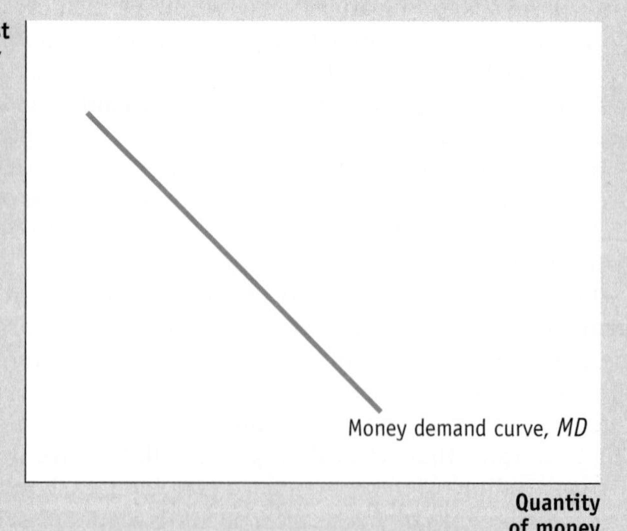

Shifts of the Money Demand Curve

A number of factors other than the interest rate affect the demand for money. When one of these factors changes, the money demand curve shifts. Figure 17-2 shows shifts of the money demand curve: an increase in the demand for money corresponds to a rightward shift of the *MD* curve, raising the quantity of money demanded at any given interest rate; a decrease in the demand for money corresponds to a leftward shift of the *MD* curve, reducing the quantity of money demanded at any given interest rate. The most important factors causing the money demand curve to shift are changes in the aggregate price level, changes in real GDP, changes in credit markets and banking technology, and changes in institutions.

Changes in the Aggregate Price Level Americans keep a lot more cash in their wallets and funds in their checking accounts today than they did in the 1950s. One reason is that they have to if they want to be able to buy anything: almost everything costs more now than it did when you could get a burger, fries, and a drink at McDonald's for 45 cents and a gallon of gasoline for 29 cents. So, other things equal, higher prices increase the demand for money (a rightward shift of the *MD* curve), and lower prices decrease the demand for money (a leftward shift of the *MD* curve).

We can actually be more specific than this: other things equal, the demand for money is *proportional* to the price level. That is, if the aggregate price level rises by 20%, the quantity of money demanded at any given interest rate, such as r_1 in Figure 17-2, also rises by 20%—the movement from M_1 to M_2. Why? Because if the price of everything rises by 20%, it takes 20% more money to buy the same basket of goods and services. And if the aggregate price level falls by 20%, at any given interest rate the quantity of money demanded falls by 20%—shown by the movement from M_1 to M_3 at the interest rate r_1. As we'll see later, the fact that money demand is proportional to the price level has important implications for the long-run effects of monetary policy.

FIGURE 17-2 Increases and Decreases in the Demand for Money

The demand curve for money shifts when non-interest rate factors that affect the demand for money change. An increase in money demand shifts the money demand curve to the right, from MD_1 to MD_2, and the quantity of money demanded rises at any given interest rate. A decrease in money demand shifts the money demand curve to the left, from MD_1 to MD_3, and the quantity of money demanded falls at any given interest rate.

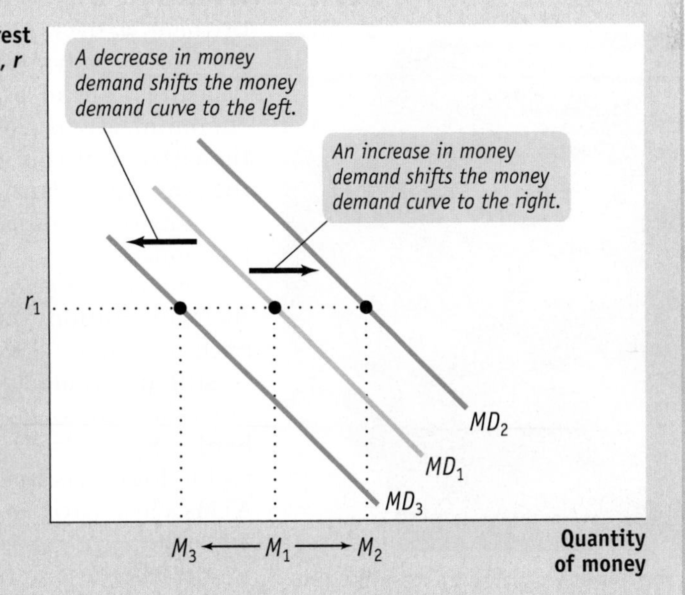

Changes in Real GDP Households and firms hold money as a way to facilitate purchases of goods and services. The larger the quantity of goods and services they buy, the larger the quantity of money they will want to hold at any given interest rate. So an increase in real GDP—the total quantity of goods and services produced and sold in the economy—shifts the money demand curve rightward. A fall in real GDP shifts the money demand curve leftward.

Changes in Credit Markets and Banking Technology Credit cards are everywhere in American life today, but it wasn't always so. The first credit card that allowed customers to carry a balance from month to month (called a "revolving balance") was issued in 1959. Before then, people had to either pay for purchases in cash or pay off their balance every month. The invention of revolving-balance credit cards allowed people to hold less money in order to fund their purchases and decreased the demand for money. In addition, changes in banking technology that made credit cards widely available and widely accepted magnified the effect, making it easier for people to make purchases without having to convert funds from their interest-bearing assets, further reducing the demand for money.

Changes in Institutions Changes in institutions can increase or decrease the demand for money. For example, until Regulation Q was eliminated in 1980, U.S. banks weren't allowed to offer interest on checking accounts. So the interest you would forgo by holding funds in a checking account instead of an interest-bearing asset made the opportunity cost of holding funds in checking accounts very high. When banking regulations changed, allowing banks to pay interest on checking account funds, the demand for money rose and shifted the money demand curve to the right.

ECONOMICS ➤ IN ACTION

A YEN FOR CASH

Japan, say financial experts, is still a "cash society." Visitors from the United States or Europe are surprised at how little use the Japanese make of credit cards and how much cash they carry around in their wallets. Yet Japan is an economically and technologically advanced country and, according to some measures, ahead of the United States in the use of telecommunications and information technology. So why do the citizens of this economic powerhouse still do business the way Americans and Europeans did a generation ago? The answer highlights the factors affecting the demand for money.

Ton Koene/AgeFotostock

No matter what they are shopping for, Japanese consumers tend to pay with cash rather than plastic.

One reason the Japanese use cash so much is that their institutions never made the switch to heavy reliance on plastic. For complex reasons, Japan's retail sector is still dominated by small mom-and-pop stores, which are reluctant to invest in credit card technology. Japan's banks have also been slow about pushing transaction technology; visitors are often surprised to find that ATMs close early in the evening rather than staying open all night.

But there's another reason the Japanese hold so much cash: there's little opportunity cost to doing so. Short-term interest rates in Japan have been below 1% since the mid-1990s. It also helps that the Japanese crime rate is quite low, so you are unlikely to have your wallet full of cash stolen. So why not hold cash?

Quick Review

- Money offers a lower rate of return than other financial assets. We usually compare the rate of return on money with **short-term,** not **long-term, interest rates.**
- Holding money provides liquidity but incurs an opportunity cost that rises with the interest rate, leading to the downward slope of the **money demand curve.**
- Changes in the aggregate price level, real GDP, credit markets and banking technology, and institutions shift the money demand curve. An increase in the demand for money shifts the money demand curve rightward; a decrease in the demand for money shifts the money demand curve leftward.

CHECK YOUR UNDERSTANDING 17-1

1. Explain how each of the following would affect the quantity of money demanded. Does the change cause a movement along the money demand curve or a shift of the money demand curve?
   a. Short-term interest rates rise from 5% to 30%.
   b. All prices fall by 10%.
   c. New wireless technology automatically charges supermarket purchases to credit cards, eliminating the need to stop at the cash register.
   d. In order to avoid paying a sharp increase in taxes, residents of Laguria shift their assets into overseas bank accounts. These accounts are harder for tax authorities to trace but also harder for their owners to tap and convert funds into cash.
2. Which of the following will increase the opportunity cost of holding cash? Reduce it? Have no effect? Explain.
   a. Merchants charge a 1% fee on debit/credit card transactions for purchases of less than $50.
   b. To attract more deposits, banks raise the interest paid on six-month CDs.
   c. It's the holiday shopping season and retailers have temporarily slashed prices to unexpectedly low levels.
   d. The cost of food rises significantly.

Solutions appear at back of book.

Money and Interest Rates

The Federal Open Market Committee decided today to lower its target for the federal funds rate 75 basis points to 2¼ percent.

Recent information indicates that the outlook for economic activity has weakened further. Growth in consumer spending has slowed and labor markets have softened. Financial markets remain under considerable stress, and the tightening of credit conditions and the deepening of the housing contraction are likely to weigh on economic growth over the next few quarters.

So read the beginning of a press release from the Federal Reserve issued on March 18, 2008. (A basis point is equal to 0.01 percentage point. So the statement implies that the Fed lowered the target from 3% to 2.25%.) We learned about the federal funds rate in Chapter 16: it's the rate at which banks lend reserves to each other to meet the required reserve ratio. As the statement implies, at each of its eight-times-a-year meetings, a group called the Federal Open Market Committee sets a target value for the federal funds rate. It's then up to Fed officials to achieve that target. This is done by the Open Market Desk at the Federal Reserve Bank of New York, which buys and sells short-term U.S. government debt, known as Treasury bills, to achieve that target.

As we've already seen, other short-term interest rates, such as the rates on CDs, move with the federal funds rate. So when the Fed reduced its target for the federal funds rate from 3% to 2.25% in March 2008, many other short-term interest rates also fell by about three-quarters of a percentage point.

How does the Fed go about achieving a *target federal funds rate*? And more to the point, how is the Fed able to affect interest rates at all?

According to the **liquidity preference model of the interest rate,** the interest rate is determined by the supply and demand for money.

The **money supply curve** shows how the quantity of money supplied varies with the interest rate.

The Equilibrium Interest Rate

Recall that, for simplicity, we're assuming there is only one interest rate paid on nonmonetary financial assets, both in the short run and in the long run. To understand how the interest rate is determined, consider Figure 17-3, which illustrates the **liquidity preference model of the interest rate;** this model says that the interest rate is determined by the supply and demand for money in the market for money. Figure 17-3 combines the money demand curve, *MD,* with the **money supply curve,** *MS,* which shows how the quantity of money supplied by the Federal Reserve varies with the interest rate.

In Chapter 16 we learned how the Federal Reserve can increase or decrease the money supply: it usually does this through *open-market operations,* buying or selling Treasury bills, but it can also lend via the *discount window* or change *reserve requirements.* Let's assume for simplicity that the Fed, using one or more of these methods, simply chooses the level of the money supply that it believes will achieve its interest rate target. Then the money supply curve is a vertical line, *MS* in Figure 17-3, with a horizontal intercept corresponding to the money supply chosen by the Fed, $\overline{M}$. The money market equilibrium is at *E,* where *MS* and *MD* cross. At this point the quantity of money demanded equals the money supply, $\overline{M}$, leading to an equilibrium interest rate of r_E.

To understand why r_E is the equilibrium interest rate, consider what happens if the money market is at a point like *L,* where the interest rate, r_L, is below r_E. At r_L the public wants to hold the quantity of money M_L, an amount larger than the actual money supply, $\overline{M}$. This means that at point *L,* the public wants to shift some of its wealth out of interest-bearing assets such as CDs into money.

This has two implications. One is that the quantity of money demanded is *more* than the quantity of money supplied. The other is that the quantity of interest-bearing money assets demanded is less than the quantity supplied. So those trying to sell nonmoney assets will find that they have to offer a higher interest rate to attract buyers. As a result, the interest rate will be driven up from r_L until the public wants to hold the quantity of money that is actually available, $\overline{M}$. That is, the interest rate will rise until it is equal to r_E.

FIGURE 17-3 Equilibrium in the Money Market

The money supply curve, *MS,* is vertical at the money supply chosen by the Federal Reserve, $\overline{M}$. The money market is in equilibrium at the interest rate r_E: *the quantity of money demanded by the public is equal to* $\overline{M}$, the quantity of money supplied.

At a point such as *L,* the interest rate, r_L, is below r_E and the corresponding quantity of money demanded, M_L, exceeds the money supply, $\overline{M}$. In an attempt to shift their wealth out of nonmoney interest-bearing financial assets and raise their money holdings, investors drive the interest rate up to r_E. At a point such as *H,* the interest rate r_H exceeds r_E and the corresponding quantity of money demanded, M_H, is less than the money supply, $\overline{M}$. In an attempt to shift out of money holdings into nonmoney interest-bearing financial assets, investors drive the interest rate down to r_E.

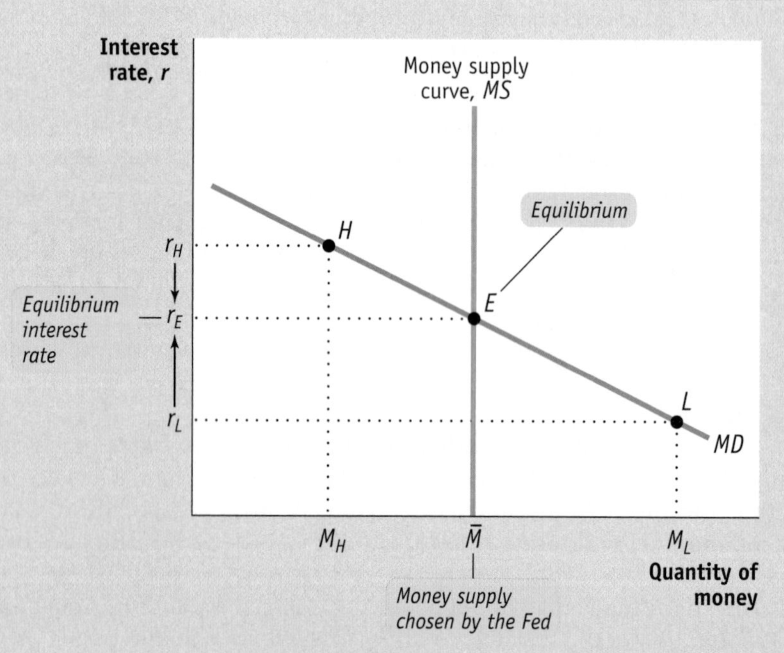

Now consider what happens if the money market is at a point such as H in Figure 17-3, where the interest rate r_H is above r_E. In that case the quantity of money demanded, M_H, is less than the quantity of money supplied, $\overline{M}$. Correspondingly, the quantity of interest-bearing nonmoney assets demanded is greater than the quantity supplied. Those trying to sell interest-bearing nonmoney assets will find that they can offer a lower interest rate and still find willing buyers. This leads to a fall in the interest rate from r_H. It falls until the public wants to hold the quantity of money that is actually available, $\overline{M}$. Again, the interest rate will end up at r_E.

The **target federal funds rate** is the Federal Reserve's desired federal funds rate.

THE TARGET VERSUS THE MARKET

Over the years, the Federal Reserve has changed the way in which monetary policy is implemented. In the late 1970s and early 1980s, it set a target level for the money supply and altered the monetary base to achieve that target. Under this operating procedure, the federal funds rate fluctuated freely. Today the Fed uses the reverse procedure, setting a target for the federal funds rate and allowing the money supply to fluctuate as it pursues that target.

A common mistake is to imagine that these changes in the way the Federal Reserve operates alter the way the money market works. That is, you'll sometimes hear people say that the interest rate no longer reflects the supply and demand for money because the Fed sets the interest rate.

In fact, the money market works the same way as always: the interest rate is determined by the supply and demand for money. The only difference is that now the Fed adjusts the supply of money to achieve its target interest rate. It's important not to confuse a change in the Fed's operating procedure with a change in the way the economy works.

Monetary Policy and the Interest Rate

Let's examine how the Federal Reserve can use changes in the money supply to change the interest rate. Figure 17-4 shows what happens when the Fed increases the money supply from $\overline{M}_1$ to $\overline{M}_2$. The economy is originally in equilibrium at E_1, with an equilibrium interest rate of r_1 and money supply $\overline{M}_1$. An increase in the money supply by the Fed to $\overline{M}_2$ shifts the money supply curve to the right, from MS_1 to MS_2, and leads to a fall in the equilibrium interest rate to r_2. Why? Because r_2 is the only interest rate at which the public is willing to hold the quantity of money actually supplied, $\overline{M}_2$.

So an increase in the money supply drives the interest rate down. Similarly, a reduction in the money supply drives the interest rate up. By adjusting the money supply up or down, the Fed can set the interest rate.

In practice, at each meeting the Federal Open Market Committee decides on the interest rate to prevail for the next six weeks, until its next meeting. The Fed sets a **target federal funds rate,** a desired level for the federal funds rate. This target is then enforced by the Open Market Desk of the Federal Reserve Bank of New York, which adjusts the money supply through the purchase and sale of Treasury bills until the actual federal funds rate equals the target rate. The other tools of monetary policy, lending through the discount window and changes in reserve requirements, aren't used on a regular basis (although the Fed used discount window lending in its efforts to address the 2008 financial crisis).

FIGURE 17-4 The Effect of an Increase in the Money Supply on the Interest Rate

The Federal Reserve can lower the interest rate by increasing the money supply. Here, the equilibrium interest rate falls from r_1 to r_2 in response to an increase in the money supply from $\overline{M}_1$ to $\overline{M}_2$. In order to induce people to hold the larger quantity of money, the interest rate must fall from r_1 to r_2.

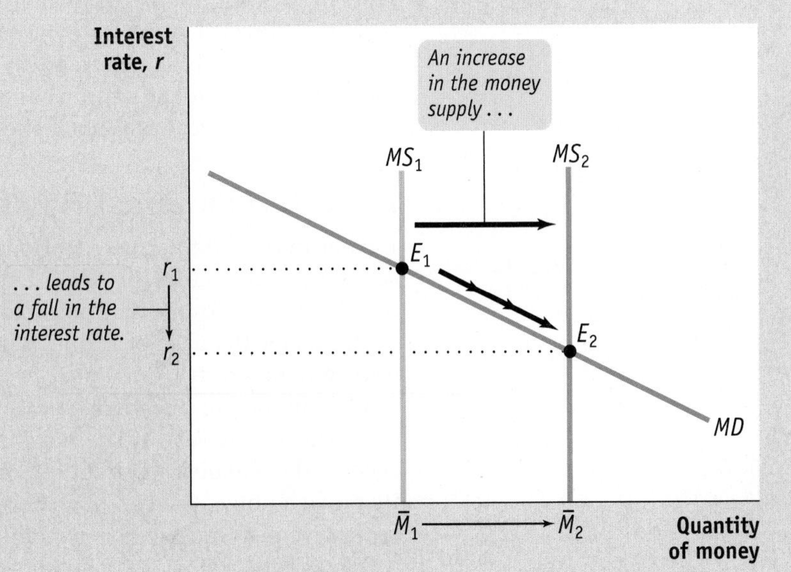

FIGURE 17-5 Setting the Federal Funds Rate

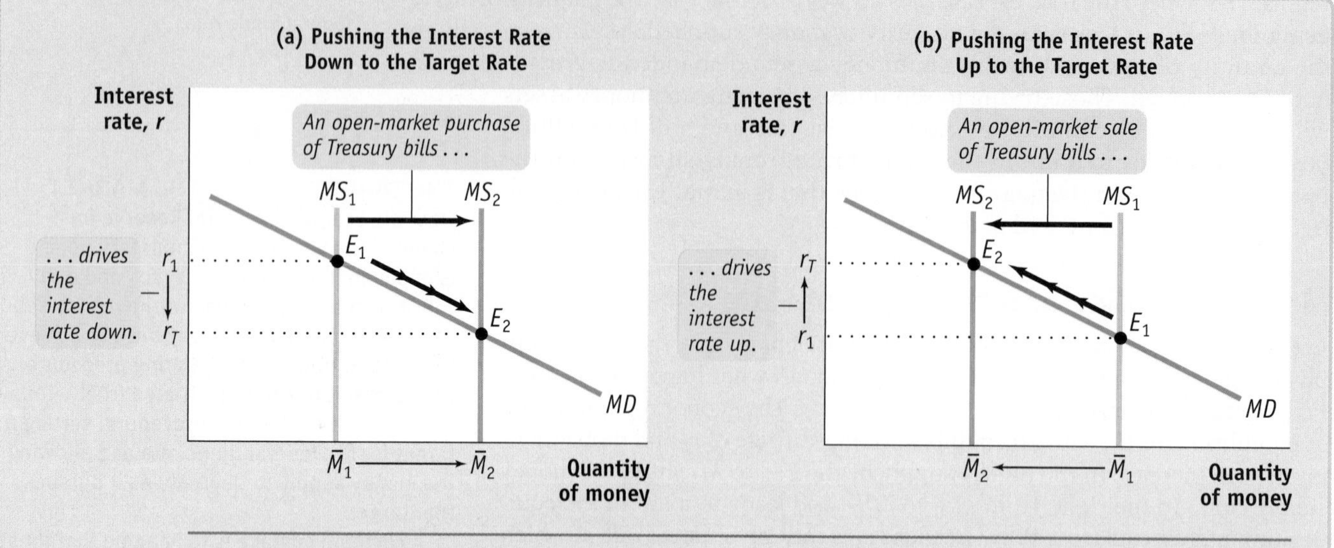

The Federal Reserve sets a target for the federal funds rate and uses open-market operations to achieve that target. In both panels the target rate is r_T. In panel (a) the initial equilibrium interest rate, r_1, is above the target rate. The Fed increases the money supply by making an open-market purchase of Treasury bills, pushing the money supply curve rightward, from MS_1 to MS_2, and driving the interest rate down to r_T. In panel (b) the initial equilibrium interest rate, r_1, is below the target rate. The Fed reduces the money supply by making an open-market sale of Treasury bills, pushing the money supply curve leftward, from MS_1 to MS_2, and driving the interest rate up to r_T.

Figure 17-5 shows how this works. In both panels, r_T is the target federal funds rate. In panel (a), the initial money supply curve is MS_1 with money supply $\overline{M}_1$, and the equilibrium interest rate, r_1, is above the target rate. To lower the interest rate to r_T, the Fed makes an open-market purchase of Treasury bills. As we learned in Chapter 16, an open-market purchase of Treasury bills leads to an increase in the money supply via the money multiplier. This is illustrated in panel (a) by the rightward shift of the money supply curve from MS_1 to MS_2 and an increase in the money supply to $\overline{M}_2$. This drives the equilibrium interest rate down to the target rate, r_T.

Panel (b) shows the opposite case. Again, the initial money supply curve is MS_1 with money supply $\overline{M}_1$. But this time the equilibrium interest rate, r_1, is below the target federal funds rate, r_T. In this case, the Fed will make an open-market sale of Treasury bills, leading to a fall in the money supply to $\overline{M}_2$ via the money multiplier. The money supply curve shifts leftward from MS_1 to MS_2, driving the equilibrium interest rate up to the target federal funds rate, r_T.

Long-Term Interest Rates

Earlier in this chapter we mentioned that *long-term interest rates*—rates on bonds or loans that mature in several years—don't necessarily move with short-term interest rates. How is that possible, and what does it say about monetary policy?

Consider the case of Millie, who has already decided to place $10,000 in U.S. government bonds for the next two years. However, she hasn't decided whether to put the money in one-year bonds, at a 4% rate of interest, or two-year bonds, at a 5% rate of interest. If she buys the one-year bond, then in one year, Millie will receive the $10,000 she paid for the bond (the *principal*) plus interest earned. If instead she buys the two-year bond, Millie will have to wait until the end of the second year to receive her principal and her interest.

You might think that the two-year bonds are a clearly better deal—but they may not be. Suppose that Millie expects the rate of interest on one-year bonds to rise sharply next year. If she puts her funds in one-year bonds this year, she will be able to reinvest the money at a much higher rate next year. And this could give her a two-year rate of return that is higher than if she put her funds into the two-year bonds today. For example, if the rate of interest on one-year bonds rises from 4% this year to 8% next year, putting her funds in a one-year bond today and in another one-year bond a year from now will give her an annual rate of return over the next two years of about 6%, better than the 5% rate on two-year bonds.

The same considerations apply to all investors deciding between short-term and long-term bonds. If they expect short-term interest rates to rise, investors may buy short-term bonds even if long-term bonds bought today offer a higher interest rate today. If they expect short-term interest rates to fall, investors may buy long-term bonds even if short-term bonds bought today offer a higher interest rate today.

As this example suggests, long-term interest rates largely reflect the average expectation in the market about what's going to happen to short-term rates in the future. When long-term rates are higher than short-term rates, as they were in 2010, the market is signaling that it expects short-term rates to rise in the future.

This is not, however, the whole story: risk is also a factor. Return to the example of Millie, deciding whether to buy one-year or two-year bonds. Suppose that there is some chance she will need to cash in her investment after just one year—say, to meet an emergency medical bill. If she buys two-year bonds, she would have to sell those bonds to meet the unexpected expense. But what price will she get for those bonds? It depends on what has happened to interest rates in the rest of the economy. Bond prices and interest rates move in opposite directions: if interest rates rise, bond prices fall, and vice versa.

This means that Millie will face extra risk if she buys two-year rather than one-year bonds, because if a year from now bond prices fall and she must sell her bonds in order to raise cash, she will lose money on the bonds. Owing to this risk factor, long-term interest rates are, on average, higher than short-term rates in order to compensate long-term bond purchasers for the higher risk they face.

Advertising during the two world wars increased the demand for government long-term bonds from savers who might have been otherwise reluctant to tie up their funds for several years.

As we will see later in this chapter, the fact that long-term rates don't necessarily move with short-term rates is sometimes an important consideration for monetary policy.

ECONOMICS ➤ IN ACTION

THE FED REVERSES COURSE

We began this section with the Fed's announcement of March 18, 2008, that it was cutting its target interest rate. This particular action was part of a larger story: a dramatic reversal of Fed policy that began in September 2007.

Figure 17-6 shows two interest rates from the beginning of 2004 to mid-2011: the target federal funds rate, decided by the Federal Open Market Committee, and the effective, or actual, rate in the market. As you can see, the Fed raised its target rate in a series of steps from late 2004 until the middle of 2006; it did this to head off the possibility of an overheating economy and rising inflation (more on that later in this chapter). But the Fed dramatically reversed course beginning in September 2007, as falling housing prices triggered a growing

FIGURE 17-6 The Fed Reverses Course

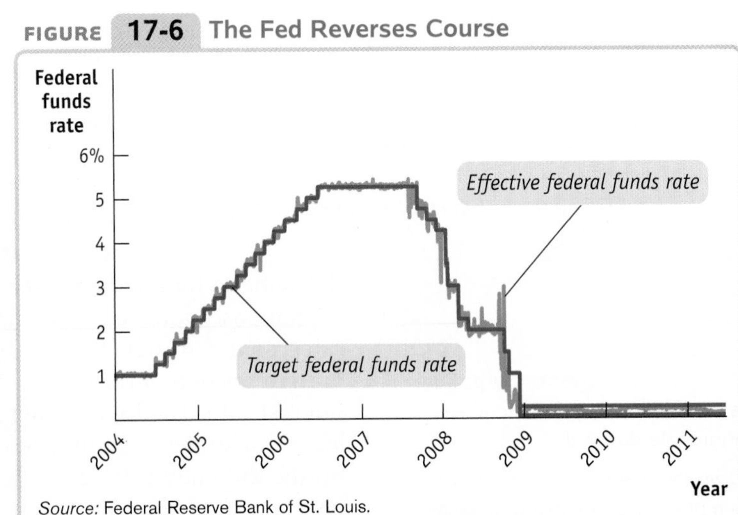

Source: Federal Reserve Bank of St. Louis.

financial crisis and ultimately a severe recession. And in December 2008, the Fed decided to allow the federal funds rate to move inside a target band between 0% and 0.25%. From 2009 to mid-2011, the Fed funds rate was kept close to zero in response to a very weak economy and high unemployment.

Figure 17-6 also shows that the Fed doesn't always hit its target. There were a number of days, especially in 2008, when the effective federal funds rate was significantly above or below the target rate. But these episodes didn't last long, and overall the Fed got what it wanted, at least as far as short-term interest rates were concerned.

Quick Review

- According to the **liquidity preference model of the interest rate,** the equilibrium interest rate is determined by the money demand curve and the **money supply curve.**
- The Federal Reserve can move the interest rate through open-market operations that shift the money supply curve. In practice, the Fed sets a **target federal funds rate** and uses open-market operations to achieve that target.
- Long-term interest rates reflect expectations about what's going to happen to short-term rates in the future. Because of risk, long-term interest rates tend to be higher than short-term rates.

CHECK YOUR UNDERSTANDING 17-2

1. Assume that there is an increase in the demand for money at every interest rate. Using a diagram, show what effect this will have on the equilibrium interest rate for a given money supply.
2. Now assume that the Fed is following a policy of targeting the federal funds rate. What will the Fed do in the situation described in Question 1 to keep the federal funds rate unchanged? Illustrate with a diagram.
3. Frannie must decide whether to buy a one-year bond today and another one a year from now, or buy a two-year bond today. In which of the following scenarios is she better off taking the first action? The second action?
   a. This year, the interest on a one-year bond is 4%; next year, it will be 10%. The interest rate on a two-year bond is 5%.
   b. This year, the interest rate on a one-year bond is 4%; next year, it will be 1%. The interest rate on a two-year bond is 3%.

Solutions appear at back of book.

Monetary Policy and Aggregate Demand

In Chapter 15 we saw how fiscal policy can be used to stabilize the economy. Now we will see how monetary policy—changes in the money supply, and the interest rate—can play the same role.

Robert Mankoff/Cartoonbank.com

"I told you the Fed should have tightened."

Expansionary and Contractionary Monetary Policy

In Chapter 14 we learned that monetary policy shifts the aggregate demand curve. We can now explain how that works: through the effect of monetary policy on the interest rate.

Figure 17-7 illustrates the process. Suppose, first, that the Federal Reserve wants to reduce interest rates, so it expands the money supply. As you can see in the top portion of the figure, a lower interest rate, in turn, will lead, other things equal, to more investment spending. This will in turn lead to higher consumer spending, through the multiplier process, and to an increase in aggregate output demanded. In the end, the total quantity of goods and services demanded at any given aggregate price level rises when the quantity of money increases, and the *AD* curve shifts to the right. Monetary policy that increases the demand for goods and services is known as **expansionary monetary policy.**

Suppose, alternatively, that the Federal Reserve wants to increase interest rates, so it contracts the money supply. You can see this process illustrated in the bottom portion of the diagram. Contraction of the money supply leads to a higher interest rate. The higher interest rate leads to lower investment spending, then to lower consumer spending, and then to a decrease in aggregate output demanded. So the total quantity of goods and services demanded falls when the money supply is reduced, and the *AD* curve shifts to the left. Monetary policy that decreases the demand for goods and services is called **contractionary monetary policy.**

Expansionary monetary policy is monetary policy that increases aggregate demand.

Contractionary monetary policy is monetary policy that decreases aggregate demand.

FIGURE 17-7 Expansionary and Contractionary Monetary Policy

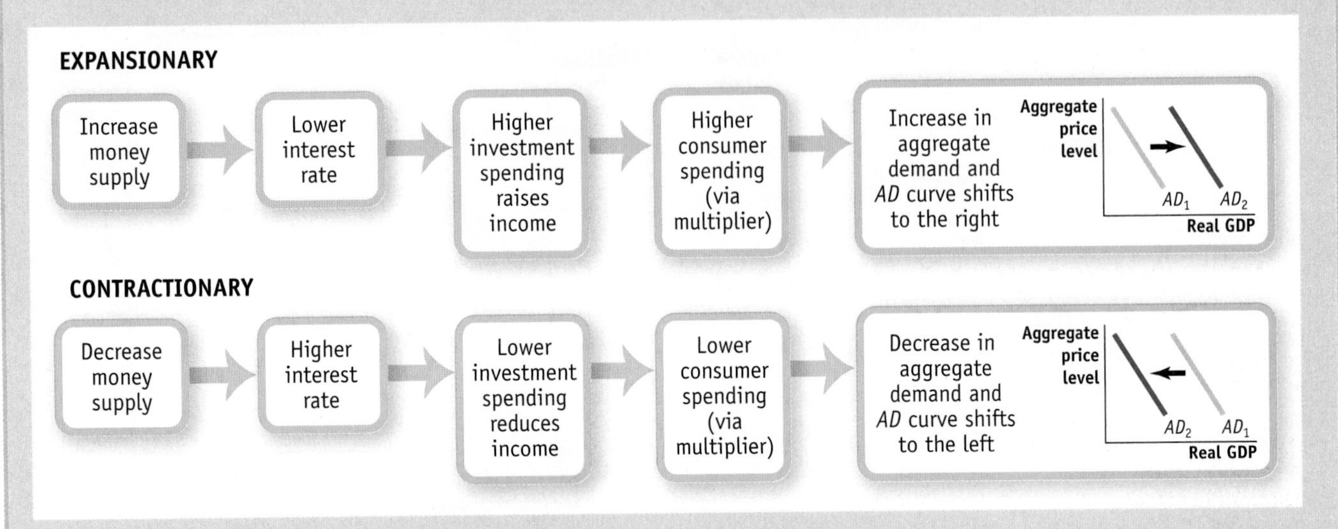

The top portion shows what happens when the Fed adopts an expansionary monetary policy and increases the money supply. Interest rates fall, leading to higher investment spending, which raises income, which, in turn, raises consumer spending and shifts the *AD* curve to the right. The bottom portion shows what happens when the Fed adopts a contractionary monetary policy and reduces the money supply. Interest rates rise, leading to lower investment spending and a reduction in income. This lowers consumer spending and shifts the *AD* curve to the left.

Monetary Policy in Practice

How does the Fed decide whether to use expansionary or contractionary monetary policy? And how does it decide how much is enough? In Chapter 10 we learned that policy makers try to fight recessions, as well as try to ensure *price stability*: low (though usually not zero) inflation. Actual monetary policy reflects a combination of these goals.

In general, the Federal Reserve and other central banks tend to engage in expansionary monetary policy when actual real GDP is below potential output. Panel (a) of Figure 17-8 shows the U.S. output gap, which we defined in Chapter 14 as the percentage difference between actual real GDP and potential output, versus the federal funds rate since 1985. (Recall that the output gap is positive when actual real GDP exceeds potential output.) As you can see, the Fed has tended to raise interest rates when the output gap is rising—that is, when the economy is developing an inflationary gap—and cut rates when the output gap is falling.

The big exception was the late 1990s, when the Fed left rates steady for several years even as the economy developed a positive output gap (which went along with a low unemployment rate). One reason the Fed was willing to keep interest rates low in the late 1990s was that inflation was low. Panel (b) of Figure 17-8 compares the inflation rate, measured as the rate of change in consumer prices excluding food and energy, with the federal funds rate. You can see how low inflation during the mid-1990s, the early 2000s, and the late 2000s helped encourage loose monetary policy in the late 1990s, in 2002–2003, and again beginning in 2008.

The Taylor Rule Method of Setting Monetary Policy

In 1993 Stanford economist John Taylor suggested that monetary policy should follow a simple rule that takes into account concerns about both the business cycle and inflation. He also suggested that actual monetary policy often looks as if the Federal Reserve was, in fact, more or less following the proposed rule. A **Taylor rule for monetary policy** is a rule for setting interest rates that takes

A **Taylor rule for monetary policy** is a rule that sets the federal funds rate according to the level of the inflation rate and either the output gap or the unemployment rate.

FIGURE 17-8 Tracking Monetary Policy Using the Output Gap and Inflation

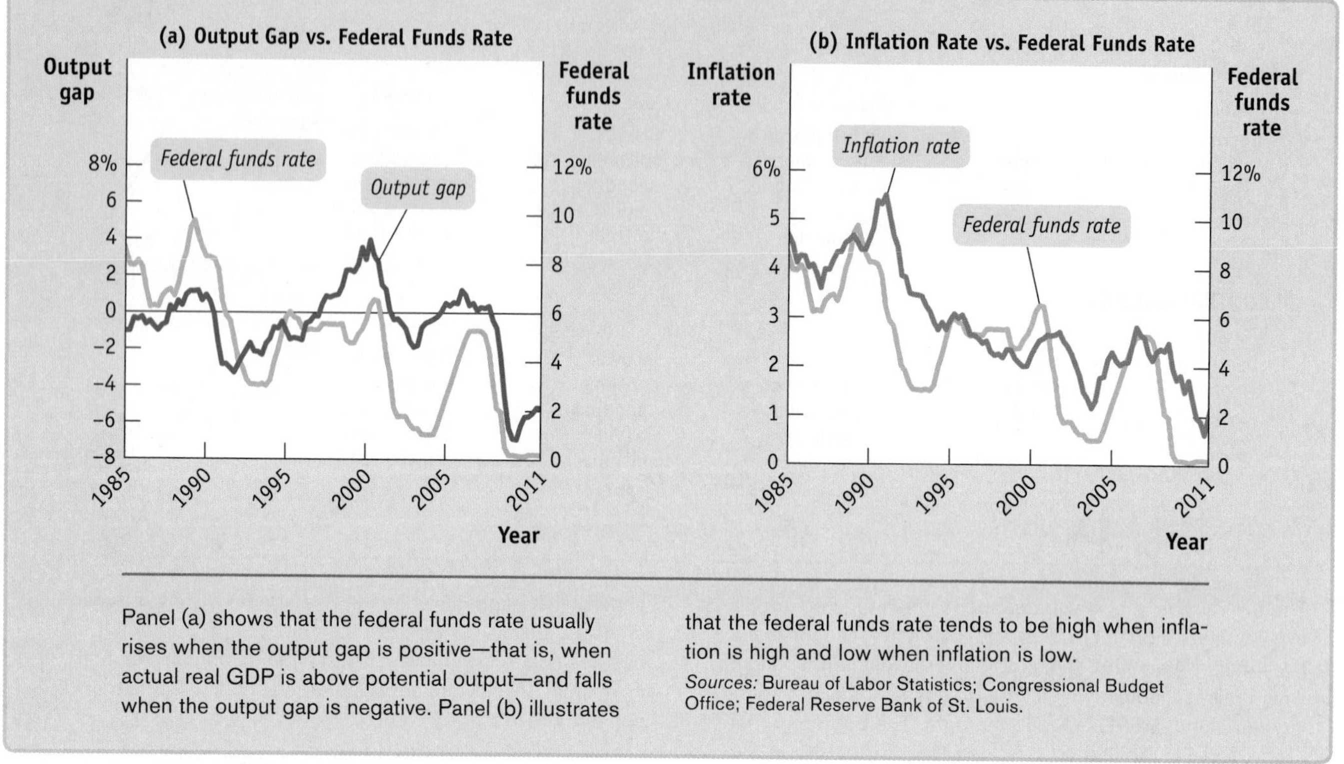

Panel (a) shows that the federal funds rate usually rises when the output gap is positive—that is, when actual real GDP is above potential output—and falls when the output gap is negative. Panel (b) illustrates that the federal funds rate tends to be high when inflation is high and low when inflation is low.

Sources: Bureau of Labor Statistics; Congressional Budget Office; Federal Reserve Bank of St. Louis.

into account the inflation rate and the output gap or, in some cases, the unemployment rate.

A widely cited example of a Taylor rule is a relationship among Fed policy, inflation, and unemployment estimated by economists at the Federal Reserve Bank of San Francisco. These economists found that between 1988 and 2008 the Fed's behavior was well summarized by the following Taylor rule:

$$\text{Federal funds rate} = 2.07 + 1.28 \times \text{inflation rate} - 1.95 \times \text{unemployment gap}$$

where the inflation rate was measured by the change over the previous year in consumer prices excluding food and energy, and the unemployment gap was the difference between the actual unemployment rate and Congressional Budget Office estimates of the natural rate of unemployment.

Figure 17-9 compares the federal funds rate predicted by this rule with the actual federal funds rate from 1985 to early 2011. As you can see, the Fed's decisions were quite close to those predicted by this particular Taylor rule from 1988 through the end of 2008. We'll talk about what happened after 2008 shortly.

Inflation Targeting

Until January 2012, the Fed did not explicitly commit itself to achieving a particular inflation rate. However, in January 2012, Chairman Bernanke announced that the Fed would set its policy to maintain an approximately 2% inflation rate per year. With that statement, the Fed joined a number of other central banks that have explicit inflation targets. So rather than using a Taylor rule to set monetary policy, the central bank instead announces the inflation rate that it wants to achieve—the *inflation target*—and sets policy in an attempt to hit that target. This method of setting monetary policy is called **inflation targeting.** The central

Inflation targeting occurs when the central bank sets an explicit target for the inflation rate and sets monetary policy in order to hit that target.

FIGURE 17-9 The Taylor Rule and the Federal Funds Rate

The red line shows the federal funds rate predicted by the San Francisco Fed's version of the Taylor rule, which relates the interest rate to the inflation rate and the unemployment rate. The green line shows the actual federal funds rate. The actual rate tracked the predicted rate quite closely through the end of 2008. After that, however, the Taylor rule called for negative interest rates, which aren't possible.

Sources: Bureau of Labor Statistics; Congressional Budget Office; Federal Reserve Bank of St. Louis; Glenn D. Rudebusch, "The Fed's Monetary Policy Response to the Current Crisis," *FRBSF Economic Letter* #2009-17 (May 22, 2009).

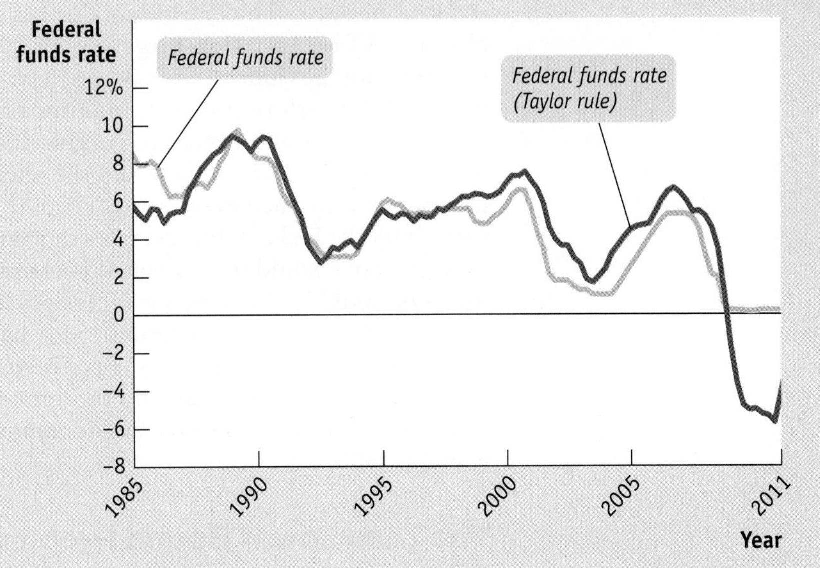

bank of New Zealand, which was the first country to adopt inflation targeting, specified a range for that target of 1% to 3%.

Other central banks commit themselves to achieving a specific number. For example, the Bank of England has committed to keeping inflation at 2%. In practice, there doesn't seem to be much difference between these versions: central banks with a target range for inflation seem to aim for the middle of that range, and central banks with a fixed target tend to give themselves considerable wiggle room.

One major difference between inflation targeting and the Taylor rule method is that inflation targeting is forward-looking rather than backward-looking. That is, the Taylor rule method adjusts monetary policy in response to *past* inflation, but inflation targeting is based on a forecast of future inflation.

GLOBAL COMPARISON INFLATION TARGETS

This figure shows the target inflation rates of six central banks that have adopted inflation targeting. The central bank of New Zealand introduced inflation targeting in 1990. Today it has an inflation target range of from 1% to 3%. The central banks of Canada and Sweden have the same target range but also specify 2% as the precise target. The central banks of Britain and Norway have specific targets for inflation, 2% and 2.5%, respectively. Neither states by how much they're prepared to miss those targets. Since 2012, the U.S. Federal Reserve also targets inflation at 2%.

In practice, these differences in detail don't seem to lead to any significant difference in results. New Zealand aims for the middle of its range, at 2% inflation; Britain, Norway, and the United States allow themselves considerable wiggle room around their target inflation rates.

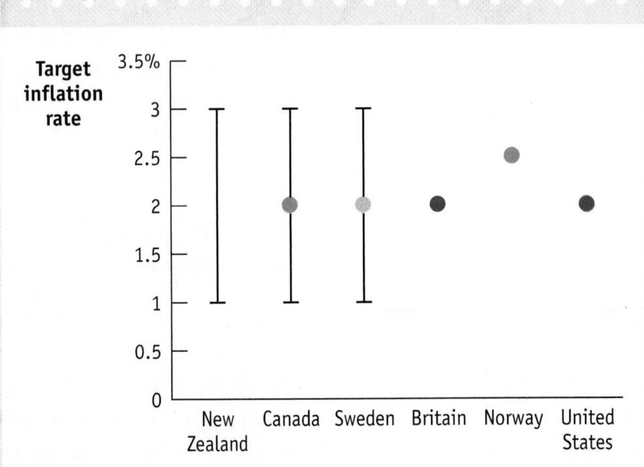

The **zero lower bound for interest rates** means that interest rates cannot fall below zero.

Advocates of inflation targeting argue that it has two key advantages over a Taylor rule: *transparency* and *accountability*. First, economic uncertainty is reduced because the central bank's plan is transparent: the public knows the objective of an inflation-targeting central bank. Second, the central bank's success can be judged by seeing how closely actual inflation rates have matched the inflation target, making central bankers accountable.

Critics of inflation targeting argue that it's too restrictive because there are times when other concerns—like the stability of the financial system—should take priority over achieving any particular inflation rate. Indeed, in late 2007 and early 2008 the Fed cut interest rates much more than either a Taylor rule or inflation targeting would have dictated because it feared that turmoil in the financial markets would lead to a major recession. (In fact, it did.)

Many American macroeconomists have had positive things to say about inflation targeting—including Ben Bernanke. And in January 2012 the Fed declared that what it means by the "price stability" it seeks is 2 percent inflation, although there was no explicit commitment about when this inflation rate would be achieved.

The Zero Lower Bound Problem

As Figure 17-9 shows, a Taylor rule based on inflation and the unemployment rate does a good job of predicting Federal Reserve policy from 1988 through 2008. After that, however, things go awry, and for a simple reason: with very high unemployment and low inflation, the same Taylor rule called for an interest rate less than zero, which isn't possible.

Why aren't negative interest rates possible? Because people always have the alternative of holding cash, which offers a zero interest rate. Nobody would ever buy a bond yielding an interest rate less than zero because holding cash would be a better alternative.

The fact that interest rates can't go below zero—called the **zero lower bound for interest rates**—sets limits to the power of monetary policy. In 2009 and 2010, inflation was low and the economy was operating far below potential, so the Federal Reserve wanted to increase aggregate demand. Yet the normal way it does this—open-market purchases of short-term government debt to expand the money supply—had run out of room to operate because short-term interest rates were already at or near zero.

In November 2010 the Fed began an attempt to circumvent this problem, which went by the somewhat obscure name "quantitative easing." Instead of purchasing only short-term government debt, it began buying longer-term government debt—five-year or six-year bonds, rather than three-month Treasury bills. As we have already pointed out, long-term interest rates don't exactly follow short-term rates. At the time the Fed began this program, short-term rates were near zero, but rates on longer-term bonds were between 2% and 3%. The Fed hoped that direct purchases of these longer-term bonds would drive down interest rates on long-term debt, exerting an expansionary effect on the economy.

This policy may have given the economy some boost in 2011 and 2012, but as of early 2013, recovery remained slow.

ECONOMICS ➤ *IN ACTION*

WHAT THE FED WANTS, THE FED GETS

What's the evidence that the Fed can actually cause an economic contraction or expansion? You might think that finding such evidence is just a matter of looking at what happens to the economy when interest rates go up or down. But it turns out that there's a big problem with that approach: the Fed usually changes interest rates in an attempt to tame the business cycle, raising rates if the economy is expanding and reducing rates if the economy is slumping. So in the actual data, it often looks as if low interest rates go along with a weak economy and high rates go along with a strong economy.

In a famous 1994 paper titled "Monetary Policy Matters," the macroeconomists Christina Romer and David Romer solved this problem by focusing on episodes in which monetary policy wasn't a reaction to the business cycle. Specifically, they used minutes from the Federal Open Market Committee and other sources to identify episodes "in which the Federal Reserve in effect decided to attempt to create a recession to reduce inflation."

FIGURE 17-10 When the Fed Wants a Recession

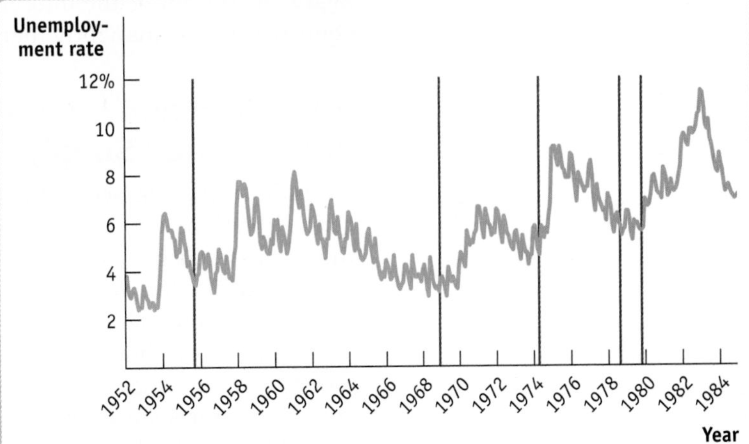

Sources: Bureau of Labor Statistics; Christina D. Romer and David H. Romer, "Monetary Policy Matters," *Journal of Monetary Economics* 34 (August 1994): 75–88.

Figure 17-10 shows the unemployment rate between 1952 and 1984 (orange) and also identifies five dates on which, according to Romer and Romer, the Fed decided that it wanted a recession (vertical red lines). In four out of the five cases, the decision to contract the economy was followed, after a modest lag, by a rise in the unemployment rate. On average, Romer and Romer found, the unemployment rate rises by 2 percentage points after the Fed decides that unemployment needs to go up.

So yes, the Fed gets what it wants.

Quick Review

- The Federal Reserve can use **expansionary monetary policy** to increase aggregate demand and **contractionary monetary policy** to reduce aggregate demand. The Federal Reserve and other central banks generally try to tame the business cycle while keeping the inflation rate low but positive.
- Under a **Taylor rule for monetary policy,** the target federal funds rate rises when there is high inflation and either a positive output gap or very low unemployment; it falls when there is low or negative inflation and either a negative output gap or high unemployment.
- In contrast, some central banks set monetary policy by **inflation targeting,** a forward-looking policy rule, rather than by using the Taylor rule, a backward-looking policy rule. Although inflation targeting has the benefits of transparency and accountability, some think it is too restrictive. Until 2008, the Fed followed a loosely defined Taylor rule. Starting in early 2012, it began inflation targeting with a target of 2% per year.
- There is a **zero lower bound for interest rates**—they cannot fall below zero—that limits the power of monetary policy.
- Because it is subject to fewer lags than fiscal policy, monetary policy is the main tool for macroeconomic stabilization.

CHECK YOUR UNDERSTANDING 17-3

1. Suppose the economy is currently suffering from an output gap and the Federal Reserve uses an expansionary monetary policy to close that gap. Describe the short-run effect of this policy on the following.
   a. The money supply curve
   b. The equilibrium interest rate
   c. Investment spending
   d. Consumer spending
   e. Aggregate output
2. In setting monetary policy, which central bank—one that operates according to a Taylor rule or one that operates by inflation targeting—is likely to respond more directly to a financial crisis? Explain.

Solutions appear at back of book.

Money, Output, and Prices in the Long Run

Through its expansionary and contractionary effects, monetary policy is generally the policy tool of choice to help stabilize the economy. However, not all actions by central banks are productive. In particular, central banks sometimes print money not to fight a recessionary gap but to help the government pay its bills, an action that typically destabilizes the economy.

What happens when a change in the money supply pushes the economy away from, rather than toward, long-run equilibrium? We learned in Chapter 14 that the economy is self-correcting in the long run: a demand shock has only a temporary effect on aggregate output. If the demand shock is the result of a change in the money supply, we can make a stronger statement: in the long run, changes in the quantity of money affect the aggregate price level, but they do not change real aggregate output or the interest rate. To see why, let's look at what happens if the central bank permanently increases the money supply.

Short-Run and Long-Run Effects of an Increase in the Money Supply

To analyze the long-run effects of monetary policy, it's helpful to think of the central bank as choosing a target for the money supply rather than the interest rate. In assessing the effects of an increase in the money supply, we return to the analysis of the long-run effects of an increase in aggregate demand, first introduced in Chapter 14.

Figure 17-11 shows the short-run and long-run effects of an increase in the money supply when the economy begins at potential output, Y_1. The initial short-run aggregate supply curve is $SRAS_1$, the long-run aggregate supply curve is *LRAS*, and the initial aggregate demand curve is AD_1. The economy's initial equilibrium is at E_1, a point of both short-run and long-run macroeconomic equilibrium because it is on both the short-run and the long-run aggregate supply curves. Real GDP is at potential output, Y_1.

Now suppose there is an increase in the money supply. Other things equal, an increase in the money supply reduces the interest rate, which increases investment spending, which leads to a further rise in consumer spending, and so on. So an increase in the money supply increases the quantity of goods and services demanded, shifting the *AD* curve rightward, to AD_2. In the short run, the economy moves to a new short-run macroeconomic equilibrium at E_2. The price level rises from P_1 to P_2, and real GDP rises from Y_1 to Y_2. That is, both the aggregate price level and aggregate output increase in the short run.

FIGURE 17-11 The Short-Run and Long-Run Effects of an Increase in the Money Supply

When the economy is already at potential output, an increase in the money supply generates a positive short-run effect, but no long-run effect, on real GDP.

Here, the economy begins at E_1, a point of short-run and long-run macroeconomic equilibrium. An increase in the money supply shifts the *AD* curve rightward, and the economy moves to a new short-run macroeconomic equilibrium at E_2 and a new real *GDP* of Y_2. But E_2 is not a long-run equilibrium: Y_2 exceeds potential output, Y_1, leading over time to an increase in nominal wages. In the long run, the increase in nominal wages shifts the short-run aggregate supply curve leftward, to a new position at $SRAS_2$.

The economy reaches a new short-run and long-run macroeconomic equilibrium at E_3 on the *LRAS* curve, and output falls back to potential output, Y_1. When the economy is already at potential output, the only long-run effect of an increase in the money supply is an increase in the aggregate price level from P_1 to P_3.

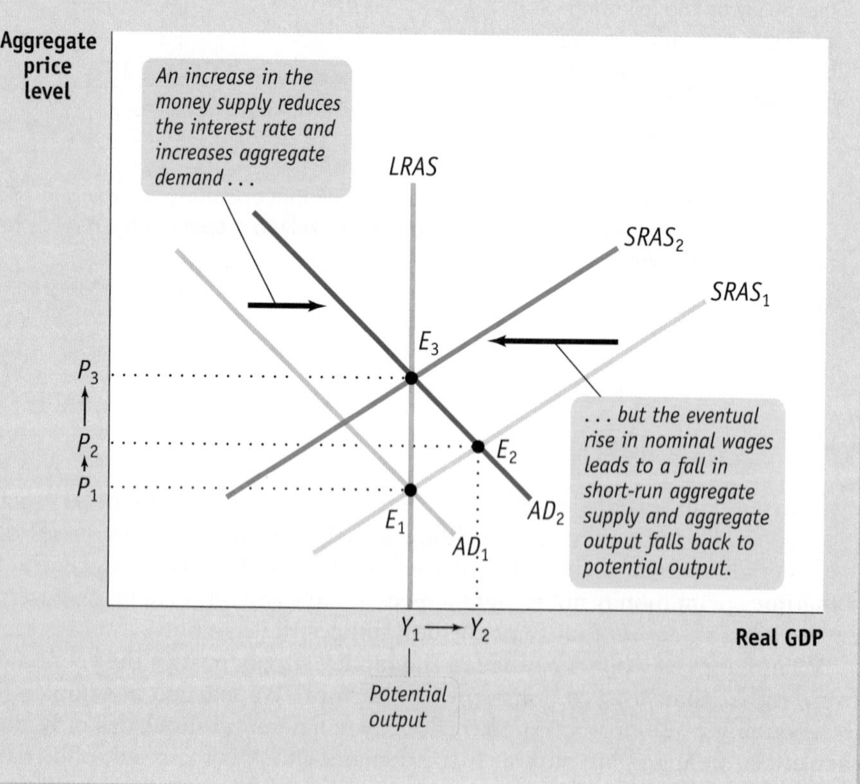

But the aggregate output level, Y_2, is above potential output. As a result, nominal wages will rise over time, causing the short-run aggregate supply curve to shift leftward. This process stops only when the *SRAS* curve ends up at $SRAS_2$ and the economy ends up at point E_3, a point of both short-run and long-run macroeconomic equilibrium. The long-run effect of an increase in the money supply, then, is that the aggregate price level has increased from P_1 to P_3, but aggregate output is back at potential output, Y_1. In the long run, a monetary expansion raises the aggregate price level but has no effect on real GDP.

We won't describe the effects of a monetary contraction in detail, but the same logic applies. In the short run, a fall in the money supply leads to a fall in aggregate output as the economy moves down the short-run aggregate supply curve. In the long run, however, the monetary contraction reduces only the aggregate price level, and real GDP returns to potential output.

According to the concept of **monetary neutrality,** changes in the money supply have no real effects on the economy.

Monetary Neutrality

How much does a change in the money supply change the aggregate price level in the long run? The answer is that a change in the money supply leads to an equal proportional change in the aggregate price level in the long run. For example, if the money supply falls 25%, the aggregate price level falls 25% in the long run; if the money supply rises 50%, the aggregate price level rises 50% in the long run.

How do we know this? Consider the following thought experiment: Suppose all prices in the economy—prices of final goods and services and also factor prices, such as nominal wage rates—double. And suppose the money supply doubles at the same time. What difference does this make to the economy in real terms? The answer is none. All real variables in the economy—such as real GDP and the real value of the money supply (the amount of goods and services it can buy)—are unchanged. So there is no reason for anyone to behave any differently.

We can state this argument in reverse: If the economy starts out in long-run macroeconomic equilibrium and the money supply changes, restoring long-run macroeconomic equilibrium requires restoring all real values to their original values. This includes restoring the real value of the money supply to its original level. So if the money supply falls 25%, the aggregate price level must fall 25%; if the money supply rises 50%, the price level must rise 50%; and so on.

This analysis demonstrates the concept known as **monetary neutrality,** in which changes in the money supply have no real effects on the economy. In the long run, the only effect of an increase in the money supply is to raise the aggregate price level by an equal percentage. Economists argue that *money is neutral in the long run.*

This is, however, a good time to recall the dictum of John Maynard Keynes: "In the long run we are all dead." In the long run, changes in the money supply don't have any effect on real GDP, interest rates, or anything else except the price level. But it would be foolish to conclude from this that the Fed is irrelevant. Monetary policy does have powerful real effects on the economy in the short run, often making the difference between recession and expansion. And that matters a lot for society's welfare.

Changes in the Money Supply and the Interest Rate in the Long Run

In the short run, an increase in the money supply leads to a fall in the interest rate, and a decrease in the money supply leads to a rise in the interest rate. In the long run, however, changes in the money supply don't affect the interest rate.

Figure 17-12 shows why. It shows the money supply curve and the money demand curve before and after the Fed increases the money supply. We assume that the economy is initially at E_1, in long-run macroeconomic equilibrium at potential output, and with money supply $\overline{M}_1$. The initial equilibrium interest rate,

FIGURE 17-12 The Long-Run Determination of the Interest Rate

In the short run, an increase in the money supply from $\overline{M}_1$ to $\overline{M}_2$ pushes the interest rate down from r_1 to r_2 and the economy moves to E_2, a short-run equilibrium. In the long run, however, the aggregate price level rises in proportion to the increase in the money supply, leading to an increase in money demand at any given interest rate in proportion to the increase in the aggregate price level, as shown by the shift from MD_1 to MD_2. The result is that the quantity of money demanded at any given interest rate rises by the same amount as the quantity of money supplied. The economy moves to long-run equilibrium at E_3 and the interest rate returns to r_1.

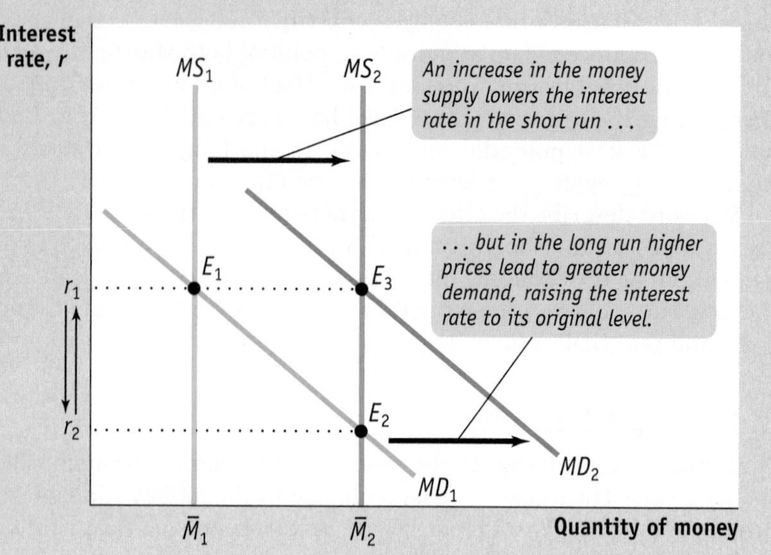
Interest rate, r
MS1
MS2
An increase in the money supply lowers the interest rate in the short run . . .
. . . but in the long run higher prices lead to greater money demand, raising the interest rate to its original level.
E1
E3
E2
r1
r2
MD1
MD2
M̄1
M̄2
Quantity of money

determined by the intersection of the money demand curve MD_1 and the money supply curve MS_1, is r_1.

Now suppose the money supply increases from $\overline{M}_1$ to $\overline{M}_2$. In the short run, the economy moves from E_1 to E_2 and the interest rate falls from r_1 to r_2. Over time, however, the aggregate price level rises, and this raises money demand, shifting the money demand curve rightward from MD_1 to MD_2. The economy moves to a new long-run equilibrium at E_3, and the interest rate rises to its original level at r_1.

And it turns out that the long-run equilibrium interest rate is the original interest rate, r_1. We know this for two reasons. First, due to monetary neutrality, in the long run the aggregate price level rises by the same proportion as the money supply; so if the money supply rises by, say, 50%, the price level will also rise by 50%. Second, the demand for money is, other things equal, proportional to the aggregate price level. So a 50% increase in the money supply raises the aggregate price level by 50%, which increases the quantity of money demanded at any given interest rate by 50%. As a result, the quantity of money demanded at the initial interest rate, r_1, rises exactly as much as the money supply—so that r_1 is still the equilibrium interest rate. In the long run, then, changes in the money supply do not affect the interest rate.

ECONOMICS ➤ IN ACTION

INTERNATIONAL EVIDENCE OF MONETARY NEUTRALITY

These days monetary policy is quite similar among wealthy countries. Each major nation (or, in the case of the euro, the euro area) has a central bank that is insulated from political pressure. All of these central banks try to keep the aggregate price level roughly stable, which usually means inflation of at most 2% to 3% per year.

But if we look at a longer period and a wider group of countries, we see large differences in the growth of the money supply. Between 1970 and the present, the money supply rose only a few percent per year in some countries, such as Switzerland and the United States, but rose much more rapidly in some poorer countries, such as South Africa. These differences allow us to see whether it is really true that increases in the money supply lead, in the long run, to equal percent rises in the aggregate price level.

Figure 17-13 shows the annual percentage increases in the money supply and average annual increases in the aggregate price level—that is, the average rate of inflation—for a sample of countries during the period 1970–2010, with each point representing a country. If the relationship between increases in the money supply and changes in the aggregate price level were exact, the points would lie precisely on a 45-degree line—a line which goes through the origin and has a slope of 1. In fact, the relationship isn't exact, because other factors besides money affect the aggregate price level. But the scatter of points clearly lies close to a 45-degree line, showing a more or less proportional relationship between money and the aggregate price level. That is, the data support the concept of monetary neutrality in the long run.

FIGURE 17-13 The Long-Run Relationship Between Money and Inflation

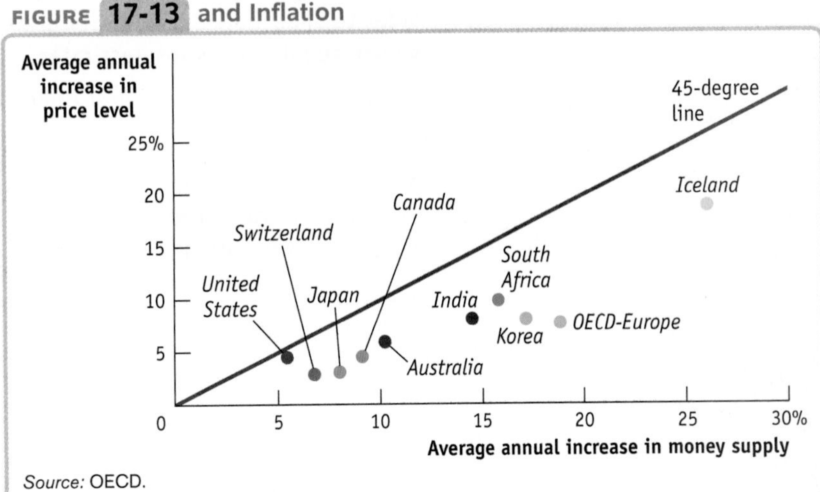

Source: OECD.

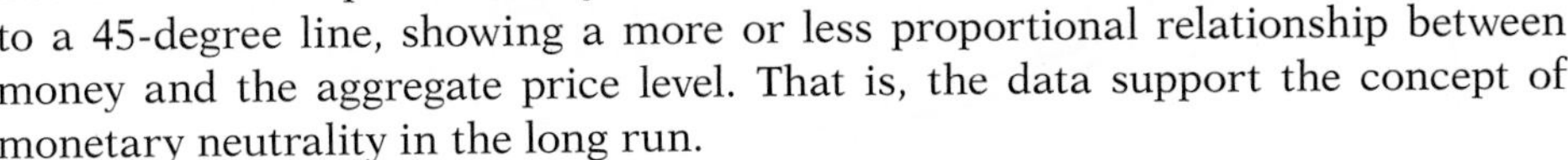

▼ Quick Review

- According to the concept of **monetary neutrality,** changes in the money supply do not affect real GDP, only the aggregate price level. Economists believe that money is neutral in the long run.
- In the long run, the equilibrium interest rate in the economy is unaffected by changes in the money supply.

CHECK YOUR UNDERSTANDING 17-4

1. Assume the central bank increases the quantity of money by 25%, even though the economy is initially in both short-run and long-run macroeconomic equilibrium. Describe the effects, in the short run and in the long run (giving numbers where possible), on the following.
   a. Aggregate output
   b. Aggregate price level
   c. Interest rate
2. Why does monetary policy affect the economy in the short run but not in the long run?

Solutions appear at back of book.

WORKED PROBLEM

The Great Mistake of 1937

In 1937, policy makers at the Fed and in the Roosevelt administration decided that the Great Depression that began in 1929 was over. They believed that the economy no longer needed special support and began phasing out the policies they instituted in the early years of the decade. Spending was cut back, and monetary policy was tightened. The result was a serious relapse in 1938, often referred to at the time as the "second Great Depression."

What caused this relapse? The answer, according to many economists, is that the setback was caused by the policy makers who pulled back too soon, tightening both fiscal and monetary policy, before the economy was on the path to full recovery. Everything else being equal, a tightening of monetary policy causes a drop in GDP. If the economy is starting to heat up and a boom is on its way, this tightening can be important to preventing inflation. But, if the economy is in a fragile state, a tightening of monetary policy can make things worse by decreasing GDP even further.

Using the liquidity preference model and the *AD-AS* model, show how in 1937 monetary policy made things worse for the economy by decreasing GDP in the short run and putting further downward pressure on prices in the short and long run.

STEP 1: Draw the money demand curve, *MD*, and the money supply curve, *MS*, in order to show how the liquidity preference model predicts that a decrease in the money supply raises interest rates.

Read the section "Money and Interest Rates," beginning on page 523. Pay close attention to Figure 17-4 on page 525.

A decrease in the money supply shifts the *MS* curve to the left, from $\overline{M}_1$ to $\overline{M}_2$, as in the following diagram. The interest rate increases from r_1 to r_2 because of the downward sloping money demand curve. ■

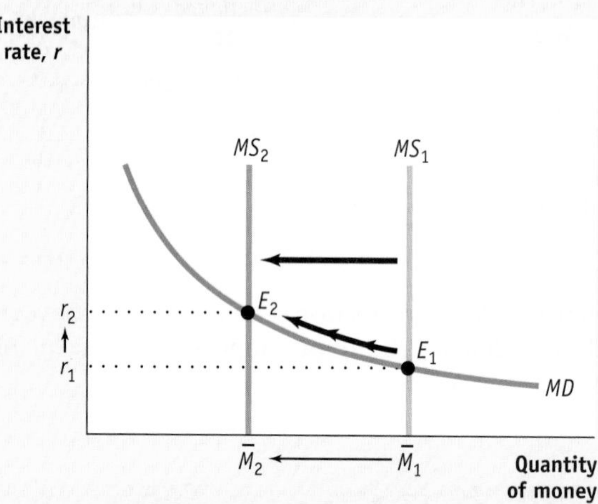

STEP 2: Draw the short-run and long-run effects of a decrease in the money supply on GDP and prices by drawing the *LRAS* curve, the *AD* curves, and the *SRAS* curves before and after a decrease in the money supply.

Read the section "Short-Run and Long-Run Effects of an Increase in the Money Supply," beginning on page 534. Study Figure 17-11 on the same page, but note that a decrease in the money supply shifts the AD curve to the left, not to the right as in the figure.

Other things being equal, a decrease in the money supply increases the interest rate, which reduces investment spending and leads to a further fall in consumer spending. So, as shown in the following diagram, a decrease in the money supply decreases the quantity of goods and services demanded, shifting the *AD* curve leftward to AD_2. The price level falls from P_1 to P_2, and real GDP falls from Y_1 to Y_2.

However, the aggregate output level Y_2 is below potential output. As a result, nominal wages will fall over time, causing the *SRAS* curve to shift rightward. Prices fall further, to P_3, but GDP returns to potential output at Y_1. The economy ends up at point E_3, a point of both short-run and long-run equilibrium.

Thus, in 1937, monetary policy simply made things worse for the economy by decreasing GDP in the short run, and putting further downward pressure on prices in the short and long run. ■

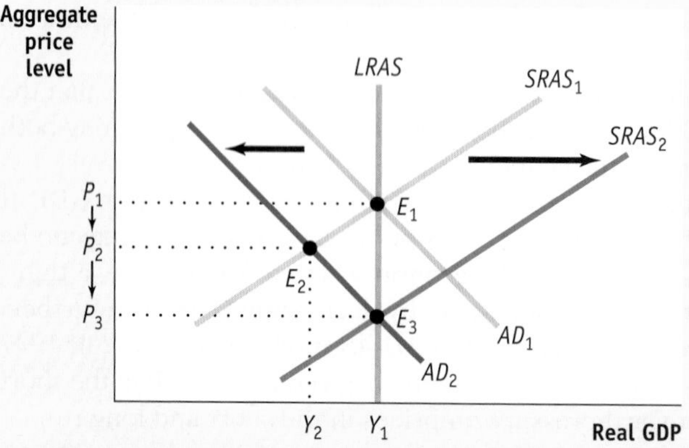

SUMMARY

1. The **money demand curve** arises from a trade-off between the opportunity cost of holding money and the liquidity that money provides. The opportunity cost of holding money depends on **short-term interest rates,** not **long-term interest rates.** Changes in the aggregate price level, real GDP, technology, and institutions shift the money demand curve.
2. According to the **liquidity preference model of the interest rate,** the interest rate is determined in the money market by the money demand curve and the **money supply curve.** The Federal Reserve can change the interest rate in the short run by shifting the money supply curve. In practice, the Fed uses open-market operations to achieve a **target federal funds rate,** which other short-term interest rates generally track. Although long-term interest rates don't necessarily move with short-term interest rates, they reflect expectations about what's going to happen to short-term rates in the future.
3. **Expansionary monetary policy** reduces the interest rate by increasing the money supply. This increases investment spending and consumer spending, which in turn increases aggregate demand and real GDP in the short run. **Contractionary monetary policy** raises the interest rate by reducing the money supply. This reduces investment spending and consumer spending, which in turn reduces aggregate demand and real GDP in the short run.
4. The Federal Reserve and other central banks try to stabilize the economy, limiting fluctuations of actual output around potential output, while also keeping inflation low but positive. Under a **Taylor rule for monetary policy,** the target federal funds rate rises when there is high inflation and either a positive output gap or very low unemployment; it falls when there is low or negative inflation and either a negative output gap or high unemployment. Some central banks (including the Fed as of January 2012) engage in **inflation targeting,** which is a forward-looking policy rule, whereas the Taylor rule method is a backward-looking policy rule. Because monetary policy is subject to fewer implementation lags than fiscal policy, it is the preferred policy tool for stabilizing the economy. Because interest rates cannot fall below zero—the **zero lower bound for interest rates**—the power of monetary policy is limited.
5. In the long run, changes in the money supply affect the aggregate price level but not real GDP or the interest rate. Data show that the concept of **monetary neutrality** holds: changes in the money supply have no real effect on the economy in the long run.

KEY TERMS

Short-term interest rates, p. 519
Long-term interest rates, p. 519
Money demand curve, p. 520
Liquidity preference model of the interest rate, p. 524
Money supply curve, p. 524
Target federal funds rate, p. 525
Expansionary monetary policy, p. 528
Contractionary monetary policy, p. 528
Taylor rule for monetary policy, p. 529
Inflation targeting, p. 530
Zero lower bound for interest rates, p. 532
Monetary neutrality, p. 535

PROBLEMS

1. Go to the FOMC page of the Federal Reserve Board's website (http://www.federalreserve.gov/FOMC/) to find the statement issued after the most recent FOMC meeting. (Click on "Meeting calendars and information" and then click on the most recent statement listed in the calendar.)
   - **a.** What is the target federal funds rate?
   - **b.** Is the target federal funds rate different from the target federal funds rate in the previous FOMC statement? If yes, by how much does it differ?
   - **c.** Does the statement comment on current macroeconomic conditions in the United States? How does it describe the U.S. economy?
2. How will the following events affect the demand for money? In each case, specify whether there is a shift of the demand curve or a movement along the demand curve and its direction.
   - **a.** There is a fall in the interest rate from 12% to 10%.
   - **b.** Thanksgiving arrives and, with it, the beginning of the holiday shopping season.
   - **c.** McDonald's and other fast-food restaurants begin to accept credit cards.
   - **d.** The Fed engages in an open-market purchase of U.S. Treasury bills.
3. **a.** Go to www.treasurydirect.gov. Under "Individuals," go to "Learn about Treasury Bills, Notes, Bonds, and TIPS." Click on "Treasury bills." Under "at a glance," click on "rates in recent auctions." What is the investment rate for the most recently issued 26-week T-bills?

b. Go to the website of your favorite bank. What is the interest rate for six-month CDs?

c. Why are the rates for six-month CDs higher than for 26-week Treasury bills?

4. Go to www.treasurydirect.gov. Under "Individuals," go to "Learn about Treasury Bills, Notes, Bonds, and TIPS." Click on "Treasury notes." Under "at a glance," click on "rates in recent auctions." Use the list of Recent Note, Bond, and TIPS Auction Results to answer the following questions.

a. What are the interest rates on 2-year and 10-year notes?

b. How do the interest rates on the 2-year and 10-year notes relate to each other? Why is the interest rate on the 10-year note higher (or lower) than the interest rate on the 2-year note?

5. An economy is facing the recessionary gap shown in the accompanying diagram. To eliminate the gap, should the central bank use expansionary or contractionary monetary policy? How will the interest rate, investment spending, consumer spending, real GDP, and the aggregate price level change as monetary policy closes the recessionary gap?

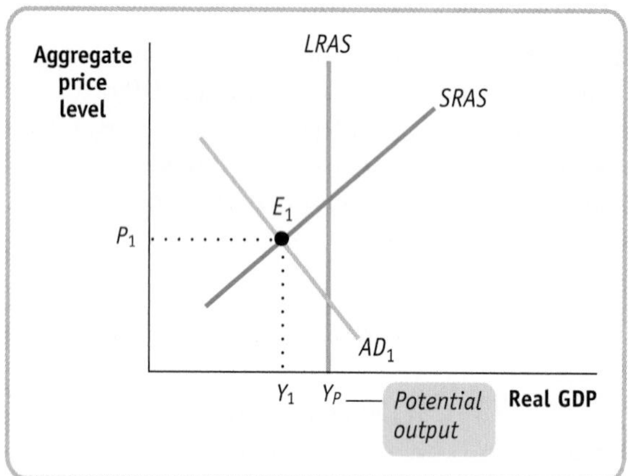

6. An economy is facing the inflationary gap shown in the accompanying diagram. To eliminate the gap, should the central bank use expansionary or contractionary monetary policy? How will the interest rate, investment spending, consumer spending, real GDP, and the aggregate price level change as monetary policy closes the inflationary gap?

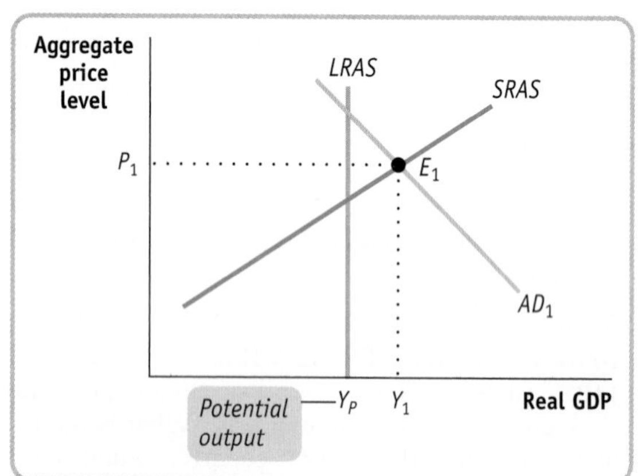

7. In the economy of Eastlandia, the money market is initially in equilibrium when the economy begins to slide into a recession.

a. Using the accompanying diagram, explain what will happen to the interest rate if the central bank of Eastlandia keeps the money supply constant at $\overline{M}_1$.

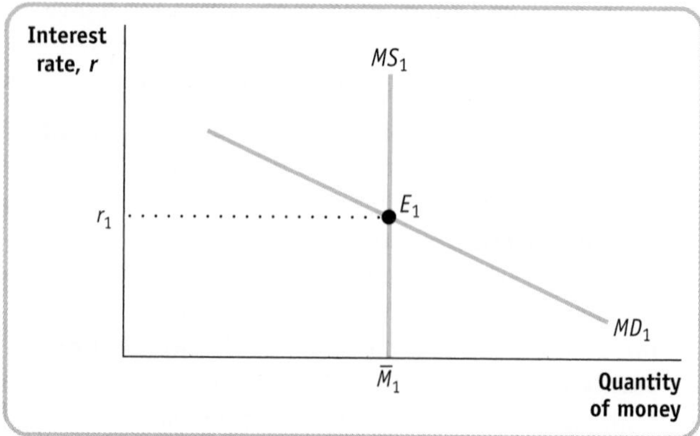

b. If the central bank is instead committed to maintaining an interest rate target of r_1, then as the economy slides into recession, how should the central bank react? Using your diagram from part a, demonstrate the central bank's reaction.

8. Suppose that the money market in Westlandia is initially in equilibrium and the central bank decides to decrease the money supply.

a. Using a diagram like the one in Problem 7, explain what will happen to the interest rate in the short run.

b. What will happen to the interest rate in the long run?

9. An economy is in long-run macroeconomic equilibrium with an unemployment rate of 5% when the government passes a law requiring the central bank to use monetary policy to lower the unemployment rate to 3% and keep it there. How could the central bank achieve this goal in the short run? What would happen in the long run? Illustrate with a diagram.

10. According to the European Central Bank website, the treaty establishing the European Community "makes clear that ensuring price stability is the most important contribution that monetary policy can make to achieve a favourable economic environment and a high level of employment." If price stability is the only goal of monetary policy, explain how monetary policy would be conducted during recessions. Analyze both the case of a recession that is the result of a demand shock and the case of a recession that is the result of a supply shock.

11. The effectiveness of monetary policy depends on how easy it is for changes in the money supply to change interest rates. By changing interest rates, monetary policy affects investment spending and the aggregate demand curve. The economies of Albernia and Brittania have very different money demand curves, as shown in the accompanying diagram. In which economy will changes in the money supply be a more effective policy tool? Why?

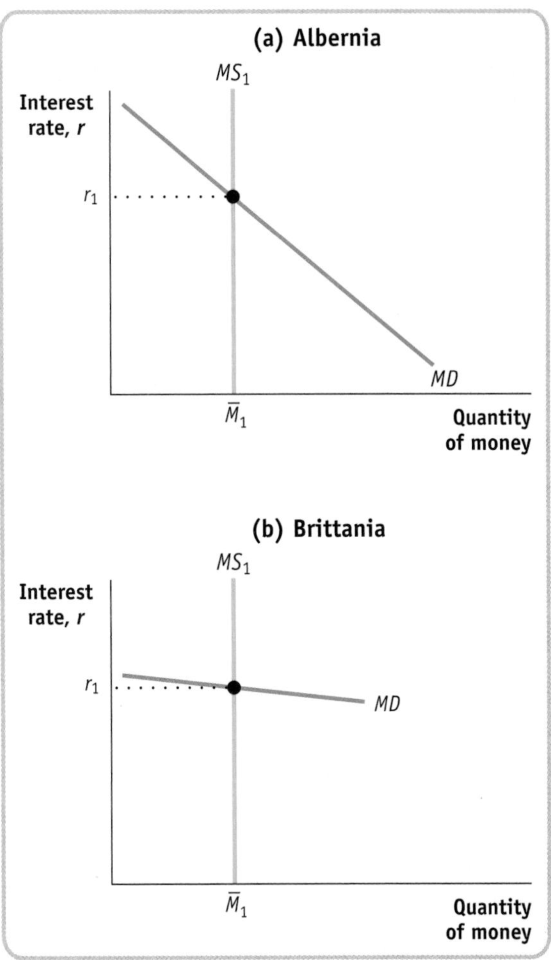

12. During the Great Depression, businesspeople in the United States were very pessimistic about the future of economic growth and reluctant to increase investment spending even when interest rates fell. How did this limit the potential for monetary policy to help alleviate the Depression?

EXTEND YOUR UNDERSTANDING

13. Because of the economic slowdown associated with the 2007–2009 recession, the Federal Open Market Committee of the Federal Reserve, between September 18, 2007 and December 16, 2008, lowered the federal funds rate in a series of steps from a high of 5.25% to a rate between zero and 0.25%. The idea was to provide a boost to the economy by increasing aggregate demand.

a. Use the liquidity preference model to explain how the Federal Open Market Committee lowers the interest rate in the short run. Draw a typical graph that illustrates the mechanism. Label the vertical axis "Interest rate" and the horizontal axis "Quantity of money." Your graph should show two interest rates, r_1 and r_2.

b. Explain why the reduction in the interest rate causes aggregate demand to increase in the short run.

c. Suppose that in 2013 the economy is at potential output but that this is somehow overlooked by the Fed, which continues its monetary expansion. Demonstrate the effect of the policy measure on the *AD* curve. Use the *LRAS* curve to show that the effect of this policy measure on the *AD* curve, other things equal, causes the aggregate price level to rise in the long run. Label the vertical axis "Aggregate price level" and the horizontal axis "Real GDP."

Crises and Consequences

WHAT YOU WILL LEARN IN THIS CHAPTER

- How depository banks and **shadow banks** differ
- Why, despite their differences, both types of banks are subject to bank runs
- What happens during **financial panics** and **banking crises**
- Why the effects of panics and crises on the economy are so severe and long-lasting
- How regulatory loopholes and the rise of **shadow banking** led to the financial crisis of 2008
- How a new regulatory framework seeks to avoid another crisis

FROM PURVEYOR OF DRY GOODS TO DESTROYER OF WORLDS

Press Association via AP Images

The collapse of Lehman Brothers, the once-venerable investment bank, set off a chain of events that led to a worldwide financial panic.

IN 1844 HENRY LEHMAN, A GERMAN immigrant, opened a dry goods store in Montgomery, Alabama. Over time, Lehman and his brothers, who followed him to America, branched out into cotton trading, then into a variety of financial activities. By 1850, Lehman Brothers was established on Wall Street; by 2008, thanks to its skill at trading financial assets, Lehman Brothers was one of the nation's top investment banks. Unlike commercial banks, investment banks trade in financial assets and don't accept deposits from customers.

In September 2008, Lehman's luck ran out. The firm had invested heavily in subprime mortgages—loans to home-buyers with too little income or too few assets to qualify for standard (also called "prime") mortgages. In the summer and fall of 2008, as the U.S. housing market plunge intensified and investments related to subprime mortgages lost much of their value, Lehman was hit hard.

Lehman had been borrowing heavily in the short-term credit market—often using overnight loans that must be repaid the next business day—to finance its ongoing operations and trading. As rumors began to spread about how heavily Lehman was exposed to the tanking housing market, its sources of credit dried up. On September 15, 2008, the firm declared bankruptcy, the largest bankruptcy to date in the United States. What happened would shock the world.

When Lehman fell, it set off a chain of events that came close to taking down the entire world financial system. Because Lehman had hidden the severity of its vulnerability, its failure came as a nasty surprise. Through *securitization* (a concept we defined in Chapter 16) financial institutions throughout the world were exposed to real estate loans that were quickly deteriorating in value as default rates on those loans rose. Credit markets froze because those with funds to lend decided it was better to sit on the funds rather than lend them out and risk losing them to a borrower who might go under like Lehman had. Around the world, borrowers were hit by a global *credit crunch:* they either lost their access to credit or found themselves forced to pay drastically higher interest rates. Stocks plunged, and within weeks the Dow had fallen almost 3,000 points.

Nor were the consequences limited to financial markets. The U.S. economy was already in recession when Lehman fell, but the pace of the downturn accelerated drastically in the months that followed. By the time U.S. employment bottomed out in early 2010, more than 8 million jobs had been lost. Europe and Japan were also suffering their worst recessions since the 1930s, and world trade plunged even faster than it had in the first year of the Great Depression.

All of this came as a great shock because few people imagined that such events were possible in twenty-first-century America. Yet economists who knew their history quickly recognized what they were seeing: it was a modern version of a *financial panic,* a sudden and widespread disruption of financial markets. Financial panics were a regular feature of the U.S. financial system before World War II. The financial panic that hit the United States in 2008 shared many features with the Panic of 1907, whose devastation prompted the creation of the Federal Reserve system. Financial panics almost always include a *banking crisis,* in which a significant portion of the banking sector ceases to function.

On reflection, the panic following Lehman's collapse was not unique, even in the modern world. The failure of Long-Term Capital Management in 1998 also precipitated a financial panic: global financial markets froze until the Federal Reserve rode to the rescue and coordinated a winding-down of the firm's operations. Because the Federal Reserve resolved the LTCM crisis quickly, its fall didn't result in a blow to the economy at large.

Financial panics and banking crises have happened fairly often, sometimes with disastrous effects on output and employment. Chile's 1981 banking crisis was followed by a 19% decline in real GDP per capita and a slump that lasted through most of the following decade. Finland's 1990 banking crisis was followed by a surge in the unemployment rate from 3.2% to 16.3%. Japan's banking crisis of the early 1990s led to more than a decade of economic stagnation.

In this chapter, we'll examine the causes and consequences of banking crises and financial panics, expanding on the discussion of this topic in Chapter 16. We'll begin by examining what makes banking vulnerable to a crisis and how this can mutate into a full-blown financial panic. Then we'll turn to the history of such crises and their aftermath, exploring why they are so destructive to the economy. Finally, we'll look at how governments have tried to limit the risks of financial crises. ■

Banking: Benefits and Dangers

As we learned in earlier chapters, banks perform an essential role in any modern economy. In Chapter 16 we defined commercial banks and savings and loans as financial intermediaries that provide liquid financial assets in the form of deposits to savers and use their funds to finance the illiquid investment spending needs of borrowers. Deposit-taking banks perform the important functions of providing liquidity to savers and directly influencing the level of the money supply.

Lehman Brothers, however, was not a deposit-taking bank. Instead, it was an investment bank in the business of speculative trading for its own profit and the profit of its investors. Yet Lehman got into trouble in much the same way that a deposit-taking bank does: it experienced a loss of confidence and something very much like a bank run—a phenomenon in which many of a bank's depositors try to withdraw their funds due to fears of a bank failure. Lehman was part of a larger category of institutions called shadow banks. *Shadow banking,* a term coined by the economist Paul McCulley of the giant bond fund PIMCO, is composed of a wide variety of types of financial firms: investment banks like Lehman, hedge funds like Long-Term Capital Management (LTCM), and money market funds. (As we will explain in more detail later, "shadow" refers to the fact that before the 2008 crisis these financial institutions were neither closely watched nor effectively regulated.)

Like deposit-taking banks, shadow banks are vulnerable to bank runs because they perform the same economic task: *maturity tranformation,* the transformation of short-term liabilities into long-term assets. From now on, we will use the term *depository banks* for banks that accept deposits (commercial banks and savings and loans) to better distinguish them from shadow banks (investment banks, hedge funds, and money market funds) which do not.

The Trade-off Between Rate of Return and Liquidity

Imagine that you live in a world without any banks. Further imagine that you have saved a substantial sum of money that you don't plan on spending anytime soon. What can you do with those funds?

One answer is that you could simply store the money—say, put it under your bed or in a safe. The money would always be there if you need it, but it would just sit there, not earning any interest.

Alternatively, you could lend the money out, say, to a growing business. This would have the great advantage of putting your money to work, both for you, since the loan would pay interest, and for the economy, since your funds would help pay for investment spending. There would, however, be a potential disadvantage: if you needed the money before the loan was paid off, you might not be able to recover it.

It's true that we asked you to assume that you had no plans for spending the money soon. But it's often impossible to predict when you will want or need to make cash outlays; for example, your car could break down or you could be offered an exciting opportunity to study abroad. Now, a loan is an asset, and there are ways to convert assets into cash. For example, you can try to sell the loan to someone else. But this can be difficult, especially if you need cash on short notice. So, in a world without banks, it's better to have some cash on hand when an unexpected financial need arises.

In other words, without banks, savers face a trade-off when deciding how much of their funds to lend out and how much to keep on hand in cash: a trade-off between liquidity, the ability to turn one's assets into cash on short notice, and the rate of return, in the form of interest or other payments received on one's assets. Without banks, people would make this trade-off by keeping a large fraction of their wealth idle, sitting in safes rather than helping pay for productive investment spending. Banking, however, changes that by allowing people ready access to their funds even while those funds are being used to make loans for productive purposes.

The Purpose of Banking

Banking, as we know it, emerged from a surprising place: it was originally a sideline business for medieval goldsmiths. By the nature of their business, goldsmiths needed vaults in which to store their gold. Over time, they realized that they could offer safekeeping services for their customers, too, because a wealthy person might prefer to leave his stash of gold and silver with a goldsmith rather than keep it at home, where thieves might snatch it.

Someone who deposited gold and silver with a goldsmith received a receipt that could be redeemed for those precious metals at any time. And a funny thing happened: people began paying for their purchases not by cashing in their receipts for gold and then paying with the gold, but simply by handing over their precious metal receipts to the seller. Thus, an early form of paper money was born.

Meanwhile, goldsmiths realized something else: even though they were obligated to return a customer's precious metals on demand, they didn't actually need to keep all of the treasure on their premises. After all, it was unlikely that all of their customers would want to lay hands on their gold and silver on the same day, especially if customers were using receipts as a means of payment. So a goldsmith could safely put some of his customers' wealth to work by lending it out to other businesses, keeping only enough on hand to pay off the few customers likely to demand their precious metals on short notice—plus some additional reserves in case of exceptional demand.

And so banking was born. In a more abstract form, depository banks today do the same thing those enterprising goldsmiths learned to do: they accept the savings of individuals, promising to return them on demand, but put most of those funds to work by taking advantage of the fact that not everyone will want access to those funds at the same time. A typical bank account lets you withdraw as much of your funds as you want, anytime you want—but the bank doesn't actually keep everyone's

Maturity transformation is the conversion of short-term liabilities into long-term assets.

A **shadow bank** is a nondepository financial institution that engages in maturity transformation.

cash in its safe or even in a form that can be turned quickly into cash. Instead, the bank lends out most of the funds placed in its care, keeping limited reserves to meet day-to-day withdrawals. And because deposits can be put to use, banks don't charge you (or charge very little) for the privilege of keeping your savings safe. Depending on the type of account you have, they might even pay you interest on your deposits.

More generally, what depository banks do is borrow on a short-term basis from depositors (who can demand to be repaid at any time) and lend on a long-term basis to others (who cannot be forced to repay until the end date of their loan). This is what economists call **maturity transformation:** converting short-term liabilities (deposits in this case) into long-term assets (bank loans that earn interest). Shadow banks, such as Lehman Brothers, also engage in maturity transformation, but they do it in a way that doesn't involve taking deposits.

Instead of taking deposits, Lehman borrowed funds in the short-term credit markets and then invested those funds in longer-term speculative projects. Indeed, a **shadow bank** is any financial institution that does not accept deposits but does engage in maturity transformation—borrowing over the short term and lending or investing over the longer term. And just as bank depositors benefit from the liquidity and higher return that banking provides compared to sitting on their money, lenders to shadow banks like Lehman benefit from liquidity (their loans must be repaid quickly, often overnight) and higher return compared to other ways of investing their funds.

A generation ago, depository banks accounted for most banking. After about 1980, however, there was a steady rise in shadow banking. Shadow banking has grown so popular because it has not been subject to the regulations, such as capital requirements and reserve requirements, that are imposed on depository banking. So, like the unregulated trusts that set off the Panic of 1907, shadow banks can offer their customers a higher rate of return on their funds. As of July 2007, generally considered the start of the financial crisis that climaxed when Lehman fell in September 2008, the U.S. shadow banking sector was about 1.5 times larger, in terms of dollars, than the formal, deposit-taking banking sector.

As we pointed out in Chapter 16, things are not always simple in banking. There we learned why depository banks can be subject to bank runs. As the cases of Lehman and LTCM so spectacularly illustrate, the same vulnerability afflicts shadow banks. Next we explore why.

Shadow Banks and the Re-emergence of Bank Runs

Because a depository bank keeps on hand just a small fraction of its depositors' funds, a bank run typically results in a bank failure: the bank is unable to meet depositors' demands for their money and closes its doors. Ominously, bank runs can be self-fulfilling prophecies: although a bank may be in fine financial shape, if enough depositors believe it is in trouble and try to withdraw their money, their beliefs end up dooming the bank.

To prevent such occurrences, after the 1930s the United States (and most other countries) adopted wide-ranging banking regulation in the form of regular audits by the Federal Reserve, deposit insurance, capital requirements and reserve requirements, and provisions allowing troubled banks to borrow from the Fed's discount window.

Shadow banks, though, don't take deposits. So how can they be vulnerable to a bank run? The reason is that a shadow bank, like a depository bank, engages in maturity transformation: it borrows short term and lends or invests longer term. If a shadow bank's lenders suddenly decide one day that it's no longer safe to lend it money, the shadow bank can no longer fund its operations. Unless it can sell its assets immediately to raise cash, it will quickly fail. This is exactly what happened to Lehman.

Lehman borrowed funds in the overnight credit market (also known as the *repo* market), funds that it was required to repay the next business day, in order to fund its trading operations. So Lehman was on a very short leash: every day it had to be able to convince its creditors that it was a safe place to park their funds.

And one day, that ability was no longer there. The same phenomenon happened at LTCM: the hedge fund was enormously leveraged (that is, it had borrowed huge amounts of money)—also, like Lehman, to fund its trading operations. One day its credit simply dried up, in its case because creditors perceived that it had lost huge amounts of money during the Asian and Russian financial crises of 1997–1998.

Bank runs are destructive to everyone associated with a bank: its shareholders, its creditors, its depositors and loan customers, and its employees. But a bank run that spreads like a contagion is extraordinarily destructive, causing depositors at other banks to also lose faith, leading to a cascading sequence of bank failures and a banking crisis. This is what happened in the United States during the early 1930s as Americans in general rushed out of bank deposits—the total value of bank deposits fell by 35%—and started holding currency instead. Until 2008, it had never happened again in the United States. Our next topic is to explore how and why bank runs reappeared.

ECONOMICS ➤ IN ACTION

THE DAY THE LIGHTS WENT OUT AT LEHMAN

On Friday night, September 12, 2008, an urgent meeting was held in the New York Federal Reserve Bank's headquarters on Wall Street. Attending was the outgoing Bush Administration's Treasury Secretary, Hank Paulson, and then head of the New York Fed, Tim Geithner (later the Treasury Secretary in the Obama Administration), along with the heads of the country's largest investment banks. Lehman Brothers was rapidly imploding and Paulson called the meeting in the hope of pressing the investment bankers into a deal that would, like the LTCM bailout described in Chapter 16, avert a messy bankruptcy.

Since the forced sale of the nearly bankrupt investment bank Bear Stearns six months earlier to a healthier bank, Lehman had been under increasing pressure. Like Bear Stearns, Lehman had invested heavily in subprime mortgages and other assets tied to real estate. And when Bear Stearns fell as its creditors began calling in its loans and other banks refused to lend to it, many wondered if Lehman would fall next.

In July 2008, Lehman reported a $2.8 billion loss for the second quarter of 2008 (the months April–June), precipitating a 54% fall in its stock price. As its share price fell, Lehman's sources of credit began to dry up and its trading operations withered. CEO of Lehman, Richard Fuld, began a desperate search for a healthier bank to buy shares of Lehman and provide desperately needed funding. By early September 2008, Lehman's loss for the third quarter had risen to $3.9 billion. On September 9, J.P. Morgan Chase, a far healthier investment bank that had been Lehman's major source of financing for its trades, demanded $5 billion in cash as extra collateral or it would freeze Lehman's accounts and cut off its credit. Unable to come up with the cash, Lehman teetered on the edge of bankruptcy.

Alex Wong/Getty Images

Richard Fuld, the head of Lehman, testified before a congressional panel on how the collapse of Lehman precipitated a financial panic.

In the September 12 meeting, Treasury Secretary Paulson urged the investment bankers to put together a package to purchase Lehman's bad assets. But, fearing for their own survival in an extremely turbulent market, they refused unless Paulson would give them a government guarantee on the value of Lehman's assets. The Treasury had made the Bear Stearns sale possible by arranging a huge loan from the New York Fed to its purchaser. This time, facing a backlash from Congress over "bailing out profligate bankers," Paulson refused to provide government help. And in the wee hours of Monday morning, September 15, 2008, Lehman went down, declaring the most expensive bankruptcy in history.

Yet, as Fuld had earlier warned Paulson, the failure of Lehman unleashed the furies. That same day the U.S. stock market fell 504 points, triggering an increase in bank borrowing costs and a run on money-market funds and financial institutions around the world. By Tuesday, Paulson agreed to an $85 billion bailout of another major corporation, the foundering American International Group (AIG), at the time the world's largest insurer. Before the markets stabilized months later, the U.S. government made $250 billion of capital infusions to bolster major U.S. banks. Whether or not Paulson made a catastrophic mistake by not acting to save Lehman is a matter likely to be debated for years to come.

Quick Review

- There is a trade-off between liquidity and yield. Without banks, people would make this trade-off by holding a large fraction of their wealth in idle cash.
- Banks allow savers to make a superior choice in their liquidity–yield trade-off because they engage in **maturity transformation.** Savers can have immediate access to their funds as well as earn interest on those funds.
- Since 1980 there has been a steady rise in shadow banking because **shadow banks**—nondepository financial institutions that engage in maturity transformation—have largely been unregulated, allowing them to pay a higher rate of return to savers. At the time of the Lehman failure, shadow banking was about 1.5 times larger than the depository banking sector.
- Because shadow banks, like depository banks, engage in maturity transformation, they can also be hit by bank runs. Shadow banks depend on short-term borrowing to operate; when short-term lenders won't lend to a shadow bank, their refusal causes the bank to fail.

CHECK YOUR UNDERSTANDING 18-1

1. Which of the following are examples of maturity transformations? Which are subject to a bank-run-like phenomenon in which fear of a failure becomes a self-fulfilling prophecy? Explain.
   a. You sell tickets to a lottery in which each ticket holder has a chance of winning a $10,000 jackpot.
   b. Dana borrows on her credit card to pay her living expenses while she takes a year-long course to upgrade her job skills. Without a better-paying job, she will not be able to pay her accumulated credit card balance.
   c. An investment partnership invests in office buildings. Partners invest their own funds and can redeem them only by selling their partnership share to someone else.
   d. The local student union savings bank offers checking accounts to students and invests those funds in student loans.

Solutions appear at back of book.

Banking Crises and Financial Panics

Bank failures are common: even in a good year, several U.S. banks typically go under for one reason or another. And shadow banks sometimes fail, too. **Banking crises**—episodes in which a large part of the depository banking sector or the shadow banking sector fails or threatens to fail—are relatively rare by comparison. Yet they do happen, often with severe negative effects on the broader economy. What would cause so many of these institutions to get into trouble at the same time? Let's take a look at the logic of banking crises, then review some of the historical experiences.

The Logic of Banking Crises

When many banks—either depository banks or shadow banks—get into trouble at the same time, there are two possible explanations. First, many of them could have made similar mistakes, often due to an *asset bubble.* Second, there may be *financial contagion,* in which one institution's problems spread and create trouble for others.

Shared Mistakes In practice, banking crises usually owe their origins to many banks making the same mistake of investing in an *asset bubble.* In an **asset bubble,** the price of some kind of asset, such as housing, is pushed to an unreasonably high level by investors' expectations of further price gains. For a while, such bubbles can feed on themselves. A good example is the savings and loan crisis of the 1980s, when there was a huge boom in the construction of commercial real estate, especially office buildings. Many banks extended large loans to real estate developers, believing that the boom would continue indefinitely. By the late 1980s, it became clear that developers had gotten carried away, building far more office space than the country needed. Unable to rent out their space or forced to slash rents, a number of developers defaulted on their loans—and the result was a wave of bank failures.

A **banking crisis** occurs when a large part of the depository banking sector or the shadow banking sector fails or threatens to fail.

In an **asset bubble,** the price of an asset is pushed to an unreasonably high level due to expectations of further price gains.

A similar phenomenon occurred between 2002 and 2006, when rapidly rising housing prices led many people to borrow heavily to buy a house in the belief that prices would keep rising. This process accelerated as more buyers rushed into the market and pushed housing prices up even faster. Eventually the market runs out of new buyers and the bubble bursts. At this point asset prices fall; in some parts of the United States, housing prices fell by half between 2006 and 2009. This, in turn, undermines confidence in financial institutions that are exposed to losses due to falling asset prices. This loss of confidence, if it's sufficiently severe, can set in motion the kind of economy-wide vicious downward spiral that marks a financial contagion.

A **financial contagion** is a vicious downward spiral among depository banks or shadow banks: each bank's failure worsens fears and increases the likelihood that another bank will fail.

A **financial panic** is a sudden and widespread disruption of the financial markets that occurs when people suddenly lose faith in the liquidity of financial institutions and markets.

Financial Contagion In especially severe banking crises, a vicious downward spiral of **financial contagion** occurs among depository banks or shadow banks: each institution's failure worsens depositors' or lenders' fears and increases the odds that another bank will fail.

As already noted, one underlying cause of contagion arises from the logic of bank runs. In the case of depository banks, when one bank fails, depositors are likely to become nervous about others. Similarly in the case of shadow banks, when one fails, lenders in the short-term credit market become nervous about lending to others. The shadow banking sector, because it is largely unregulated, is especially prone to fear- and rumor-driven contagion.

There is also a second channel of contagion: asset markets and the vicious cycle of deleveraging. When a financial institution is under pressure to reduce debt and raise cash, it tries to sell assets. To sell assets quickly, though, it often has to sell them at a deep discount. The contagion comes from the fact that other financial institutions own similar assets, whose prices decline as a result of the "fire sale." This decline in asset prices hurts the other financial institutions' financial positions, too, leading their creditors to stop lending to them. This knock-on effect forces more financial institutions to sell assets, reinforcing the downward spiral of asset prices. This kind of downward spiral was clearly evident in the months immediately following Lehman's fall: prices of a wide variety of assets held by financial institutions, from corporate bonds to pools of student loans, plunged as everyone tried to sell assets and raise cash. Later, as the severity of the crisis abated, many of these assets saw at least a partial recovery in prices.

Combine an asset bubble with a huge, unregulated shadow banking system and a vicious cycle of deleveraging and it is easy to see, as the U.S. economy did in 2008, how a full-blown **financial panic**—a sudden and widespread disruption of financial markets that happens when people suddenly lose faith in the liquidity of financial institutions and markets—can arise. A financial panic almost always involves a banking crisis, either in the depository banking sector, or the shadow banking sector, or both.

Because banking provides much of the liquidity needed for trading financial assets like stocks and bonds, severe banking crises almost always lead to disruptions of the stock and bond markets. Disruptions of these markets, along with a headlong rush to sell assets and raise cash, lead to a vicious circle of deleveraging. As the panic unfolds, savers and investors come to believe that the safest place for their money is under their bed, and their hoarding of cash further deepens the distress.

So what can history tell us about banking crises and financial panics?

Historical Banking Crises: The Age of Panics

Between the Civil War and the Great Depression, the United States had a famously crisis-prone banking system. Even then, banks were regulated: most banking was carried out by "national banks" that were regulated by the federal government and subject to rules involving reserves and capital, of the kind described below. However, there was no system of guarantees for depositors. As a result, bank runs were common, and banking crises, also known at the time as panics, were fairly frequent.

Table 18-1 shows the dates of these nationwide banking crises and the number of banks that failed in each episode. Notice that the table is divided into two parts. The first part is devoted to the "national banking era," which preceded the 1913 creation of the Federal Reserve—which was supposed to put an end to such crises. It failed. The second part of the table is devoted to the epic waves of bank failures that took place in the early 1930s.

The events that sparked each of these panics differed. In the nineteenth century, there was a boom-and-bust cycle in railroad construction somewhat similar to the boom-and-bust cycle in office building construction during the 1980s. Like

TABLE 18-1 Number of Bank Failures: National Banking Era and Great Depression

National Banking era (1863–1912)		Great Depression (1929–1941)	
Panic dates	**Number of failures**	**Panic dates**	**Number of failures**
September 1873	101	November–December 1930	806
May 1884	42	April–August 1931	573
November 1890	18	September–October 1931	827
May–August 1893	503	June–July 1932	283
October–December 1907	73*	February–March 1933	Bank holiday

*This understates the scale of the 1907 crisis because it doesn't take into account the role of trusts.

modern real estate companies, nineteenth-century railroad companies relied heavily on borrowed funds to finance their investment projects. And railroads, like office buildings, took a long time to build. This meant that there were repeated episodes of overbuilding: competing railroads would invest in expansion, only to find that collectively they had laid more track than the demand for rail transport warranted. When the overbuilding became apparent, business failures, debt defaults, and an overall banking crisis followed. The Panic of 1873 began when Jay Cooke and Co., a financial firm with a large stake in the railroad business, failed. The Panic of 1893 began with the failure of the overextended Philadelphia and Reading Railroad.

As we'll see later in this chapter, the major financial panics of the nineteenth and early twentieth centuries were followed by severe economic downturns. However, the banking crises of the early 1930s made previous crises seem minor by comparison. In four successive waves of bank runs from 1930 to 1932, about 40% of the banks in America failed. In the end, Franklin Delano Roosevelt declared a temporary closure of all banks—the so-called "bank holiday"—to put an end to the vicious circle. Meanwhile, the economy plunged, with real GDP shrinking by a third and a sharp fall in prices as well.

FPG/Hulton Archive/Getty Images

A typical scene outside a bank during the banking crises of the Great Depression.

There is still considerable controversy about the banking crisis of the early 1930s. In part, this controversy is about cause and effect: did the banking crisis cause the wider economic crisis, or vice versa? (No doubt causation ran in both directions, but the magnitude of these effects remains disputed.) There is also controversy about the extent to which the banking crisis could have been avoided. Milton Friedman and Anna Schwartz, in their famous study *Monetary History of the United States,* argued that the Federal Reserve could and should have prevented the banking crisis—and that if it had, the Great Depression itself could also have been prevented. However, this view has been disputed by other economists.

In the United States, the experience of the 1930s led to banking reforms that prevented a replay for more than 70 years. Outside the United States, however, there were a number of major banking crises.

Modern Banking Crises Around the World

Around the world, banking crises are relatively frequent events. However, the ways in which they occur differ according to the banking sector's particular institutional framework. According to a 2008 analysis by the International Monetary Fund (IMF), no fewer than 127 banking crises occurred around the world between 1970 and 2007. Most of these were in small, poor countries that lack the regulatory safeguards found in advanced countries. In poorer countries, banks generally get in trouble in much the same way: insufficient capital, poor accounting, too many loans and, often, corruption. But banks in advanced countries can also make the same mistakes—for example, there was the Savings and Loans (S&L) crisis in the United States during the 1980s (described in Chapter 16).

In more advanced countries, banking crises almost always occur as a consequence of an asset bubble—typically in real estate. Between 1985 and 1995, three advanced countries—Finland, Sweden, and Japan—experienced banking crises due to the bursting of a real estate bubble. Banks in the three countries lent heavily into a real estate bubble that their lending helped to inflate. Figure 18-1 shows real estate prices, adjusted for inflation, in Finland, Sweden, and Japan from 1985 to 1995. As you can see, in each country a sharp rise was followed by a drastic fall, leading many borrowers to default on their real estate loans, pushing large parts of each country's banking system into insolvency.

FIGURE 18-1 Real Housing Prices in Three Banking Crises

During the period 1985 to 1995, Finland, Sweden, and Japan each experienced a banking crisis due to a real estate bubble. Here you can see how real housing prices (housing prices adjusted for inflation) in each country rose dramatically and then fell sharply. The sharp fall in housing prices pushed a significant part of each country's banking sector into insolvency.

Sources: Bank of Finland; Statistics Sweden; Japan Real Estate Institute; Bank for International Settlements; OECD.

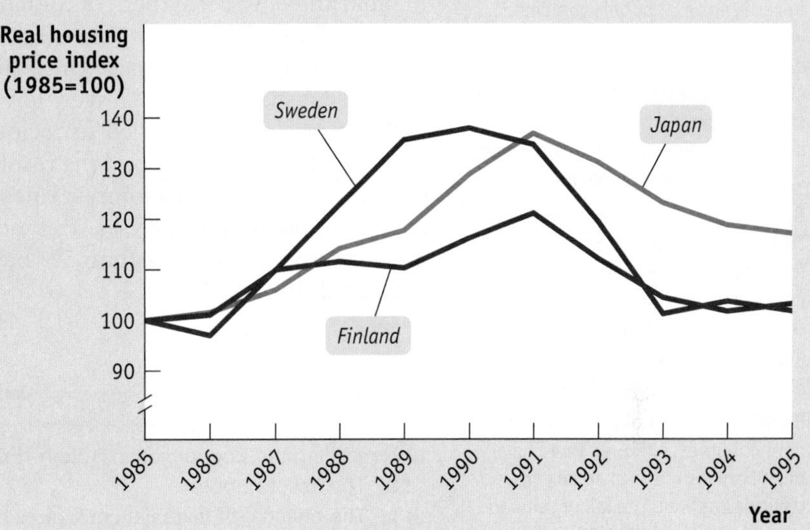

In the United States, the fall of Lehman in September 2008 precipitated a banking crisis in the shadow banking sector that included financial contagion as well as financial panic, but left the depository banking sector largely unaffected. As we discussed in the opening story, the financial crisis of 2008 was devastating because of securitization, which had distributed subprime mortgage loans throughout the entire shadow banking sector both in the United States and abroad.

Immediately after the crisis, the size of the shadow banking sector decreased as investors rediscovered the benefits of regulation and the safety of the depository banking sector. However, the shadow banking sector has since recovered, and it is now significantly larger than it was before the crisis. In the next section, we will learn how troubles in the banking sector soon translate into troubles for the broader economy.

ECONOMICS ➤ *IN ACTION*

ERIN GO BROKE

For much of the 1990s and 2000s, Ireland was celebrated as an economic success story: the "Celtic Tiger" was growing at a pace the rest of Europe could only envy. But the miracle came to an abrupt halt in 2008, as Ireland found itself facing a huge banking crisis.

Like the earlier banking crises in Finland, Sweden, and Japan, Ireland's crisis grew out of excessive optimism about real estate. Irish housing prices began rising in the 1990s, in part a result of the economy's strong growth. However, real estate developers began betting on ever-rising prices, and Irish banks were all too willing to lend these developers large amounts of money to back their speculations. Housing prices tripled between 1997 and 2007, home construction quadrupled over the same period, and total credit offered by banks rose far faster than in any other European nation. To raise the cash for their lending spree, Irish banks supplemented the funds of depositors with large amounts of "wholesale" funding—short-term borrowing from other banks and private investors.

In 2007 the real estate boom collapsed. Home prices started falling, and home sales collapsed. Many of the loans that banks had made during the boom went into default. Now, so-called ghost estates, new housing developments full of unoccupied, crumbling homes, dot the landscape. In 2008, the troubles of the Irish banks threatened to turn into a sort of bank run—not by depositors, but by lenders who had provided the banks with short-term funding through the wholesale interbank lending market. To stabilize the situation, the Irish government stepped in, guaranteeing repayment of all bank debt.

This created a new problem because it put Irish taxpayers on the hook for potentially huge bank losses. Until the crisis struck, Ireland had seemed to be in good fiscal shape, with relatively low government debt and a budget surplus. The banking crisis, however, led to serious questions about the solvency of the Irish government—whether it had the resources to meet its obligations—and forced the government to pay high interest rates on funds it raised in international markets.

Like most banking crises, Ireland's led to a severe recession. The unemployment rate rose from less than 5% before the crisis to more than 14.8%, where it remained throughout 2012.

Quick Review

- Although individual bank failures are common, a **banking crisis** is a rare event that typically will severely harm the broader economy.
- A banking crisis can occur because depository or shadow banks invest in an **asset bubble** or through **financial contagion,** set off by bank runs or by a vicious cycle of deleveraging. Largely unregulated, shadow banking is particularly vulnerable to contagion.
- In 2008, an asset bubble combined with a huge shadow banking sector and a vicious cycle of deleveraging created a **financial panic** and banking crisis, as savers cut their spending and investors hoarded their funds, sending the economy into a steep decline.
- Between the Civil War and the Great Depression, the United States suffered numerous banking crises and financial panics, each followed by a severe economic downturn. The banking reforms of the 1930s prevented another banking crisis until 2008.
- Banking crises usually occur in small, poor countries, although there have been banking crises in advanced countries as well. The fall of Lehman caused a banking crisis and a financial panic in the shadow banking sector, leading investors to shift back into the depository banking sector.

CHECK YOUR UNDERSTANDING 18-2

1. Regarding the Economics in Action "Erin Go Broke," identify the following:
   a. The asset bubble
   b. The channel of financial contagion
2. Again regarding "Erin Go Broke," why do you think the Irish government tried to stabilize the situation by guaranteeing the debts of the banks? Why was this a questionable policy?

Solutions appear at back of book.

The Consequences of Banking Crises

If banking crises affected only banks, they wouldn't be as serious a concern. In fact, however, banking crises are almost always associated with recessions, and severe banking crises are associated with the worst economic slumps. Furthermore, history shows that recessions caused in part by banking crises inflict sustained economic damage, with economies taking years to recover.

Banking Crises, Recessions, and Recovery

A severe banking crisis is one in which a large fraction of the banking system either fails outright (that is, goes bankrupt) or suffers a major loss of confidence and must be bailed out by the government. Such crises almost invariably lead to deep recessions, which are usually followed by slow recoveries. Figure 18-2 illustrates this phenomenon by tracking unemployment in the aftermath of two banking crises widely separated in space and time: the Panic of 1893 in the United States and the Swedish banking crisis of 1991. In the figure, t represents the year of the crisis: 1893 for the United States, 1991 for Sweden. As the figure shows, these crises on different continents, almost a century apart, produced similarly devastating results: unemployment shot up and came down only slowly and erratically so that, even five years after the crisis, the number of jobless remained high by pre-crisis standards.

These historical examples are typical. Figure 18-3, taken from a widely cited study by the economists Carmen Reinhart and Kenneth Rogoff, compares

FIGURE 18-2 Unemployment Rates, Before and After a Banking Crisis

This figure tracks unemployment in the wake of two banking crises: the Panic of 1893 in the United States and the Swedish banking crisis of 1991. *t* represents the year of the crisis—1893 for the United States, 1991 for Sweden. $t-2$ is the date two years before the crisis hit; $t+5$ is the date five years after. In both cases, the economy suffered severe damage from the banking crisis: unemployment shot up and came down only slowly and erratically. In both cases, five years after the crisis the unemployment rate remained high compared to pre-crisis levels.

Sources: Christina D. Romer, "Spurious Volatility in Historical Unemployment Data," *Journal of Political Economy* 94, no. 1 (1986): 1–37; Eurostat.

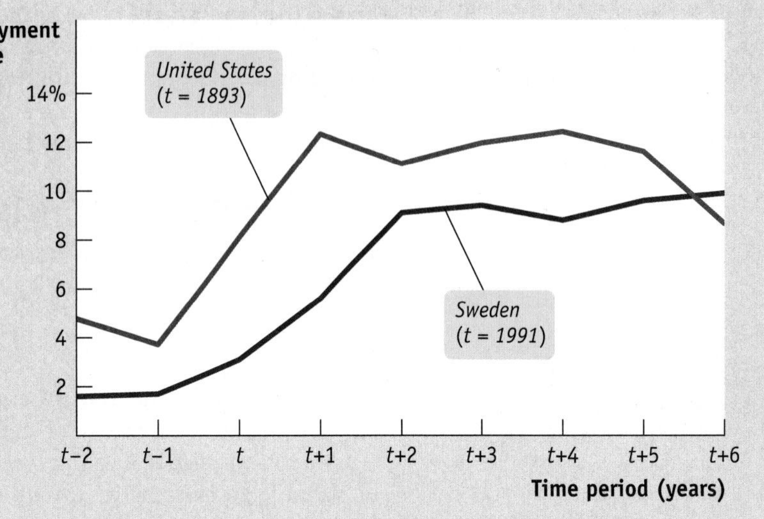

FIGURE 18-3 Episodes of Banking Crises and Unemployment

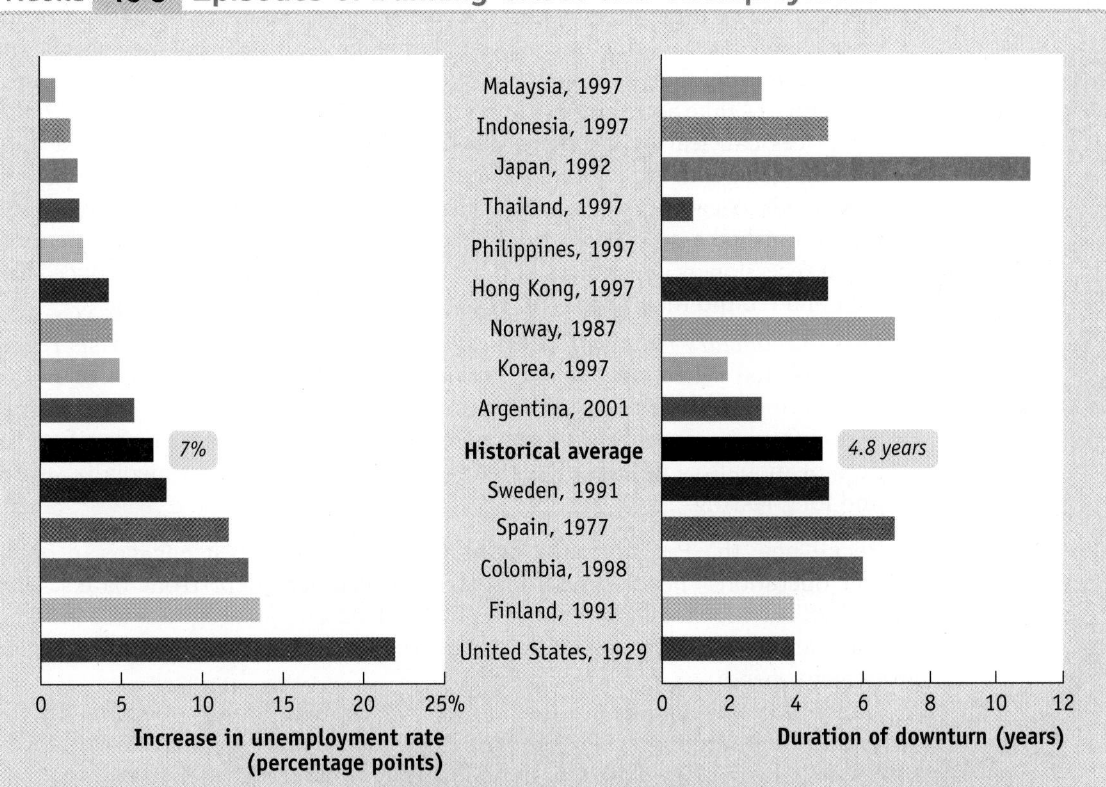

Economists Carmen Reinhart and Kenneth Rogoff have compared employment performance across several countries in the aftermath of a number of severe banking crises. For each country, the bar on the left shows the rise in the unemployment rate during and following the crisis, and the bar on the right shows how long it took for unemployment to begin to fall. On average, severe banking crises have been followed by a 7 percentage point rise in the unemployment rate, and in many cases it has taken four years or more before unemployment even begins to fall, let alone returns to pre-crisis levels.

Source: Carmen M. Reinhart and Kenneth S. Rogoff, "The Aftermath of Financial Crises," *American Economic Review* 99, no. 2 (2009): 466–472.

In a **credit crunch,** potential borrowers either can't get credit at all or must pay very high interest rates.

A **debt overhang** occurs when a vicious circle of deleveraging leaves a borrower with high debt but diminished assets.

employment performance in the wake of a number of severe banking crises. The bars on the left show the rise in the unemployment rate during and following the crisis; the bars on the right show the time it took before unemployment began to fall. The numbers are shocking: on average, severe banking crises have been followed by a 7 percentage point rise in the unemployment rate, and in many cases it has taken four years or more before the unemployment rate even begins to fall, let alone returns to pre-crisis levels.

Why Are Banking-Crisis Recessions So Bad?

It's not difficult to see why banking crises normally lead to recessions. There are three main reasons: a *credit crunch* arising from reduced availability of credit, financial distress caused by a *debt overhang,* and the loss of monetary policy effectiveness.

1. *Credit crunch.* The disruption of the banking system typically leads to a reduction in the availability of credit called a **credit crunch,** in which potential borrowers either can't get credit at all or must pay very high interest rates. Unable to borrow or unwilling to pay higher interest rates, businesses and consumers cut back on spending, pushing the economy into a recession.
2. *Debt overhang.* A banking crisis typically pushes down the prices of many assets through a vicious circle of deleveraging, as distressed borrowers try to sell assets to raise cash, pushing down asset prices and causing further financial distress. As we have already seen, deleveraging is a factor in the spread of the crisis, lowering the value of the assets banks hold on their balance sheets and so undermining their solvency. It also creates problems for other players in the economy. To take an example all too familiar from recent events, falling housing prices can leave consumers substantially poorer, especially because they are still stuck with the debt they incurred to buy their homes. A banking crisis, then, tends to leave consumers and businesses with a **debt overhang:** high debt but diminished assets. Like a credit crunch, this also leads to a fall in spending and a recession as consumers and businesses cut back in order to reduce their debt and rebuild their assets.
3. *Loss of monetary policy effectiveness.* A key feature of banking-crisis recessions is that when they occur, monetary policy—the main tool of policy makers for fighting negative demand shocks caused by a fall in consumer and investment spending—loses much of its effectiveness. The ineffectiveness of monetary policy makes banking-crisis recessions especially severe and long-lasting.

Recall how the Fed normally responds to a recession: it engages in open-market operations, purchasing short-term government debt from banks. This leaves banks with excess reserves, which they lend out, leading to a fall in interest rates and causing an economic expansion through increased consumer and investment spending.

Under normal conditions, this policy response is highly effective. In the aftermath of a banking crisis, though, the whole process tends to break down. Banks, fearing runs by depositors or a loss of confidence by their creditors, tend to hold on to excess reserves rather than lend them out. Meanwhile, businesses and consumers, finding themselves in financial difficulty due to the plunge in asset prices, may be unwilling to borrow even if interest rates fall. As a result, even very low interest rates may not be enough to push the economy back to full employment.

In Chapter 17 we discussed the fact that interest rates can't go below zero—called the *zero bound for interest rates.* A situation in which conventional monetary policy, such as cutting interest rates, can't be used to fight a slump because nominal interest rates are up against the zero bound is known as a

liquidity trap. In fact, all the historical episodes in which the zero bound for interest rates became an important constraint on policy—the 1930s, Japan in the 1990s, and a number of countries after 2008—have occurred after a major banking crisis.

The economy is in a **liquidity trap** when conventional monetary policy is ineffective because nominal interest rates are up against the zero bound.

The inability of the usual tools of monetary policy to offset the macroeconomic devastation caused by banking crises is the major reason such crises produce deep, prolonged slumps. The obvious solution is to look for other policy tools. In fact, governments do typically take a variety of special steps when banks are in crisis.

A **lender of last resort** is an institution, usually a country's central bank, that provides funds to financial institutions when they are unable to borrow from the private credit markets.

Governments Step In

Before the Great Depression, policy makers often adopted a laissez-faire attitude toward banking crises, allowing banks to fail in the belief that market forces should be allowed to work. Since the catastrophe of the 1930s, though, almost all policy makers have believed that it's necessary to take steps to contain the damage from bank failures. In general, central banks and governments take three main kinds of action in an effort to limit the fallout from banking crises:

1. They act as the *lender of last resort.*
2. They offer guarantees to depositors and others with claims on banks.
3. In an extreme crisis, a central bank will step in and provide financing to private credit markets.

1. Lender of Last Resort A **lender of last resort** is an institution, usually a country's central bank, that provides funds to financial institutions when they are unable to borrow from the private credit markets. In particular, the central bank can provide cash to a bank that is facing a run by depositors but is fundamentally solvent, making it unnecessary for the bank to engage in fire sales of its assets to raise cash. This acts as a lifeline, working to prevent a loss of confidence in the bank's solvency from turning into a self-fulfilling prophecy.

Did the Federal Reserve act as a lender of last resort in the 2008 financial crisis? Very much so. Figure 18-4 shows borrowing by banks from the Fed between 2005 and 2010: commercial banks borrowed negligible amounts from the central bank before the crisis, but their borrowing rose to $700 billion in the months

FIGURE 18-4 Total Borrowings of Depository Institutions from the Federal Reserve

Although commercial banks borrowed negligible amounts from the Fed before the crisis hit in 2008, in the months after Lehman's collapse their borrowing surged to $700 billion—an amount 14 times total bank reserves before the crisis.
Source: Federal Reserve Bank of St. Louis.

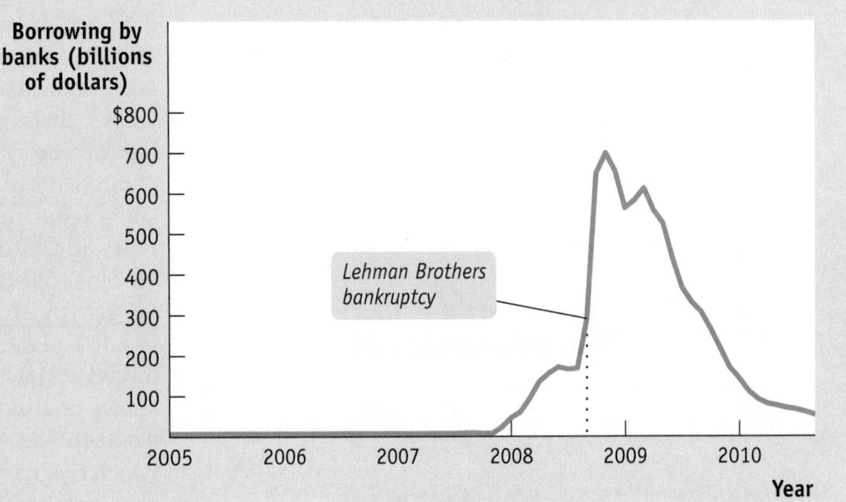

following Lehman's failure. To get a sense of how large this borrowing was, note that total bank reserves before the crisis were less than $50 billion—so these loans were 14 times the banks' initial reserves.

2. Government Guarantees There are limits, though, to how much a lender of last resort can accomplish: it can't restore confidence in a bank if there is good reason to believe the bank is fundamentally insolvent. If the public believes that the bank's assets aren't worth enough to cover its debts even if it doesn't have to sell these assets on short notice, a lender of last resort isn't going to help much. And in major banking crises there are often good reasons to believe that many banks are truly bankrupt.

In such cases, governments often step in to guarantee banks' liabilities. In 2007, a bank run hit the British bank, Northern Rock, ceasing only when the British government stepped in and guaranteed all deposits at the bank, regardless of size. Ireland's government eventually stepped in to guarantee repayment of not just deposits at all of the nation's banks, but all bank debts. Sweden did the same thing after its 1991 banking crisis.

When governments take on banks' risk, they often demand a quid pro quo—namely, they often take ownership of the banks they are rescuing. Northern Rock was nationalized in 2008. Sweden nationalized a significant part of its banking system in 1992. In the United States, the Federal Deposit Insurance Corporation routinely seizes banks that are no longer solvent; it seized 140 banks in 2009. Ireland, however, chose not to seize any of the banks whose debts were guaranteed by taxpayers.

These government takeovers are almost always temporary. In general, modern governments want to save banks, not run them. So they "reprivatize" nationalized banks, selling them to private buyers, as soon as they believe they can.

3. Provider of Direct Financing As we learned in Chapter 16, during the depths of the 2008 financial crisis the Federal Reserve expanded its operations beyond the usual measures of open-market operations and lending to depository banks. It also began lending to shadow banks and buying commercial paper—short-term bonds issued by private companies—as well as buying the debt of Fannie Mae and Freddie Mac, the government-sponsored home mortgage agencies. In this way, the Fed provided credit to keep the economy afloat when private credit markets had dried up.

ECONOMICS ➤ *IN ACTION*

BANKS AND THE GREAT DEPRESSION

According to the official business-cycle chronology, the United States entered a recession in August 1929, two months before that year's famous stock market crash. Although the crash surely made the slump worse, through late 1930 it still seemed to be a more or less ordinary recession. Then the bank failures began. A majority of economists believe that the banking crisis is what turned a fairly severe but not catastrophic recession into the Great Depression.

How did the banking crisis hurt the wider economy? Largely by creating a credit crunch, in which businesses in particular either could not borrow or found themselves forced to pay sharply higher interest rates. Figure 18-5 shows one indicator of this credit crunch: the difference between the interest rates—known as the "spread"—at which businesses with good but not great credit could borrow and the borrowing costs of the federal government.

FIGURE 18-5 The 1930s Banking Crisis and Credit Crunch

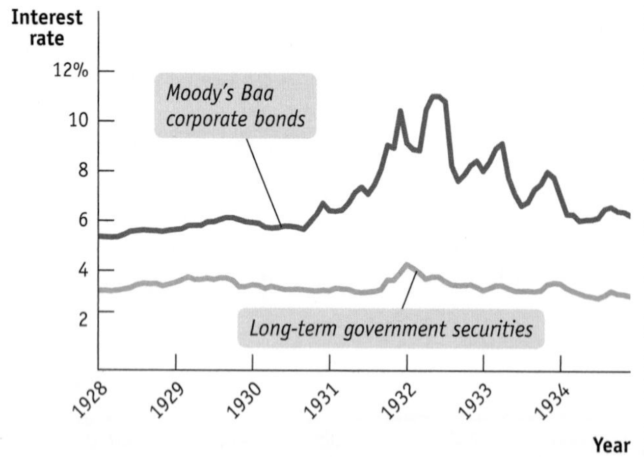

Source: Federal Reserve Bank of St. Louis.

Baa corporate bonds are those that Moody's, the credit rating agency, considers "medium-grade obligations"—debts of companies that should be able to pay but aren't completely reliable. ("Baa" refers to the specific rating assigned to the bonds of such companies.) Until the banking crisis struck, Baa borrowers borrowed at interest rates only about 2 percentage points higher than the interest rates the government borrowed at, and this spread remained low until the summer of 1931. Then it surged, peaking at more than 7 percentage points in 1932. Bear in mind that this is just one indicator of the credit crunch: many would-be borrowers were completely shut out.

One striking fact about the banking crisis of the early 1930s is that the Federal Reserve, although it had the legal ability to act as a lender of last resort, largely failed to do so. Nothing like the surge in bank borrowing from the Fed that took place in 2007–2009 occurred. In fact, bank borrowing from the Fed throughout the 1930s banking crisis was at levels lower than those reached in 1928–1929.

Meanwhile, neither the Fed nor the federal government did anything to rescue failing banks until 1933. So the early 1930s offer a clear example of a banking crisis that policy makers more or less allowed to take its course. It's not an experience anyone wants to repeat.

Quick Review

- Banking crises almost always result in recessions, with severe banking crises associated with the worst economic slumps. Historically, severe banking crises have resulted, on average, in a 7-percentage-point rise in the unemployment rate.
- Recessions caused by banking crises are especially severe because they involve a **credit crunch,** a vicious circle of deleveraging coupled with a **debt overhang,** leading households and businesses to cut spending, further deepening the downturn.
- Slumps induced by bank crises are so severe and prolonged because they make monetary policy ineffective: even though the central bank can lower interest rates, financially distressed households and businesses may still be unwilling to borrow and spend. An economy is in a **liquidity trap** when conventional monetary policy is ineffective because nominal interest rates are up against the zero bound.
- Central banks and governments use two main types of policies to limit the damage from a banking crisis: acting as the **lender of last resort** and offering guarantees that the banks' liabilities will be repaid. In the aftermath of a bank rescue, governments sometimes nationalize the bank and then later reprivatize it. In an extreme crisis, the central bank will provide direct financing to private credit markets.

CHECK YOUR UNDERSTANDING 18-3

1. Explain why, as of late 2010, the Federal Reserve was able to prevent the crisis of 2008 from turning into another Great Depression but was unable to significantly reduce the surge in unemployment that occurred.
2. Explain why, in the aftermath of a severe banking crisis, a very low interest rate—even as low as 0%—may be unable to move the economy back to full employment.

Solutions appear at back of book.

The 2008 Crisis and Its Aftermath

As we've just seen, banking crises have typically been followed by major economic problems. How did the aftermath of the financial crisis of 2008 compare with this historical experience? The answer, unfortunately, is that history has proved a very good guide: once again, the economic damage from the financial crisis was both large and prolonged. And aftershocks from the crisis continue to shake the world economy today, after Lehman's 2008 fall.

Severe Crisis, Slow Recovery

Figure 18-6 shows real GDP in the United States and the European Union, the world's two largest economies, during the crisis and for four years afterward, with the peak pre-crisis quarter—the last quarter of 2007 for the United States, the first quarter of 2008 for the European Union—set equal to 100. What you can see is that both economies suffered severe downturns, shrinking more than 5%, followed by relatively slow recoveries. As of late 2012, Europe had not yet regained its pre-crisis level of output, and the United States was barely above its previous peak.

FIGURE 18-6 Crisis and Recovery in the United States and the European Union

In the aftermath of the 2008 financial crisis, aggregate output in the European Union and in the United States fell dramatically. Real GDP, shown here as an index with each economy's peak pre-crisis quarter set to 100, declined by more than 5%. By late 2011, real GDP in the United States had only barely recovered to pre-crisis levels, and aggregate output in the European Union had still not reached its pre-crisis peak.

Sources: Bureau of Economic Analysis; Eurostat.

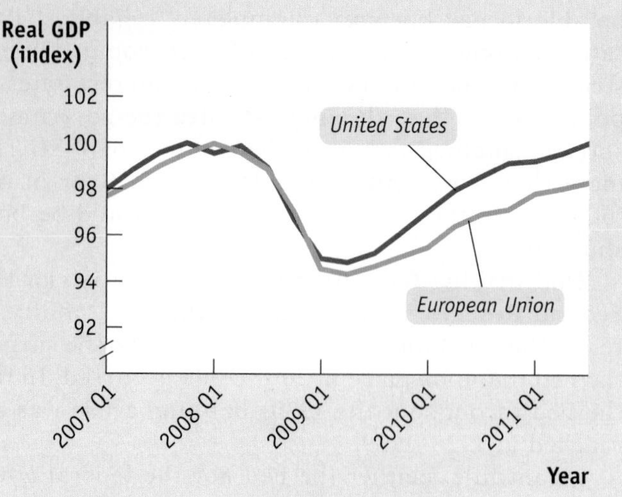

The severe slump and the slow recovery were very bad news for workers, since a healthy job market depends on an economy growing fast enough to accommodate both a growing workforce and rising productivity. Figure 18-7 shows two indicators of unemployment in the United States—the overall unemployment rate and the percentage of the unemployed who had been out of work 27 weeks or more—for the years 2007 through 2011. Both measures shot up during the crisis and remained very high years later, indicating a labor market in which it remained very hard to find a job. As of March 2013, unemployment remained high at 7.6%, with the percentage of long-term unemployed at 39%.

This outcome was, sad to say, about what one should have expected given the severity of the initial financial shock and the historical experience with such shocks. In fact, the U.S. experience with unemployment almost exactly matched the average performance of past economies that had suffered major banking disruptions. America, observed Kenneth Rogoff (whose work we cited earlier), was experiencing a "garden variety severe financial crisis."

FIGURE 18-7 Unemployment in the Aftermath of the 2008 Crisis

After 2008, the unemployment rate increased dramatically and remained high. Long-term unemployment, measured by the percentage of the unemployed who were out of work for 27 weeks or longer, increased at the same time. By 2011, almost half of all unemployed workers were long-term unemployed.

Source: Bureau of Labor Statistics.

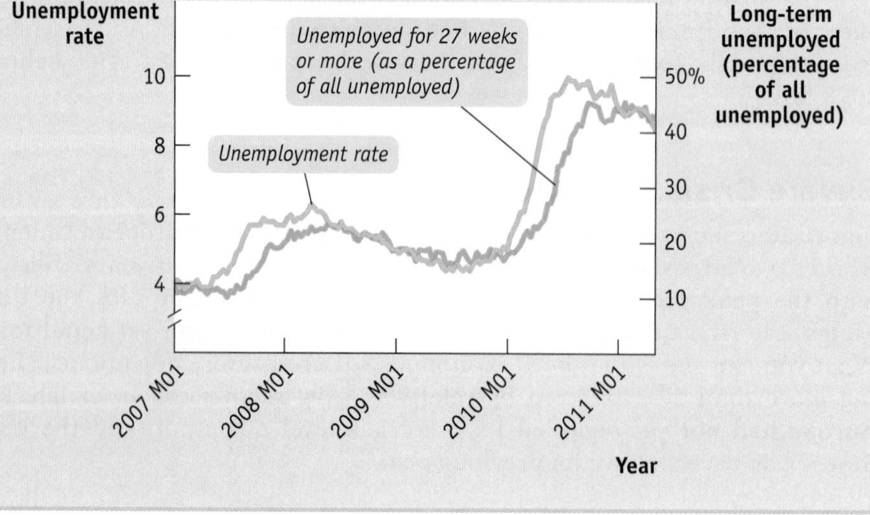

Aftershocks in Europe

One important factor bedeviling hopes for recovery was the emergence of special difficulties in several European nations—difficulties that repeatedly raised the specter of a second financial crisis.

The 2008 crisis was caused by problems with private debt, mainly home loans, which then triggered a crisis of confidence in banks. In 2011 and 2012, fears of a second crisis were focused on public debt, specifically the public debts of Southern European countries plus Ireland.

Europe's troubles first surfaced in Greece, a country with a long history of fiscal irresponsibility. In late 2009, it was revealed that a previous Greek government had understated the size of the budget deficits and the amount of government debt, prompting lenders to refuse further loans to Greece. Other European countries provided emergency loans to the Greek government in return for harsh budget cuts. But these budget cuts depressed the Greek economy, and by late 2011 there was general agreement that Greece could not pay back its debts in full.

By itself, this was probably a manageable shock for the European economy since Greece accounts for less than 3% of European GDP. Unfortunately, foot-dragging by European officials in confronting Greece's problems and the effects of the harsh budget cuts on the Greek economy spooked investors. By the fall of 2011, the crisis had spread beyond the Greek borders, hitting two major European economies: Spain and Italy.

Figure 18-8 shows a measure of pressure on Italy and Spain during the 2008 and 2011 crises: the difference between interest rates on 10-year bonds issued by the two nations' governments and interest rates on German debt, which most people consider a safe investment. Because all three countries use the same currency, the euro, these rates would all be the same if Italian and Spanish government debt were considered as safe as German government debt. The rise in "spreads" therefore indicates a growing perception of risk.

Spain's fiscal problems were mainly fallout from the 2008 crisis. Before that crisis, Spain seemed to be in very good fiscal condition, with low debt and a budget surplus. However, Spain, like Ireland, had a huge housing bubble between 2000 and 2007. When the bubble burst, the Spanish economy fell into a deep slump, depressing tax receipts and causing large budget deficits. At the same time, there were worries that the Spanish government might eventually have to spend large amounts bailing out banks. As a result, investors began worrying about the solvency of the Spanish government and a possible default, driving up interest rates.

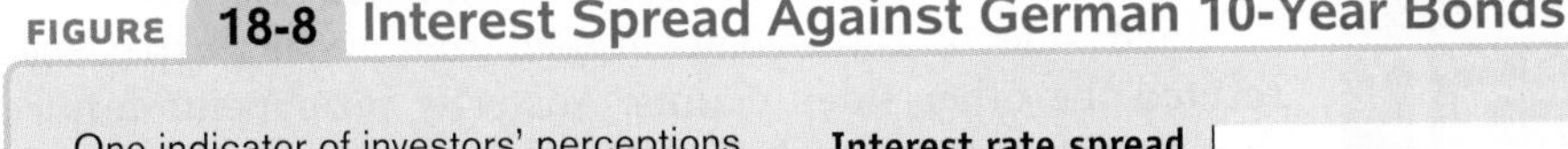

FIGURE 18-8 Interest Spread Against German 10-Year Bonds

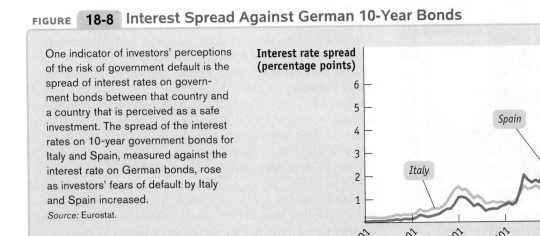

One indicator of investors' perceptions of the risk of government default is the spread of interest rates on government bonds between that country and a country that is perceived as a safe investment. The spread of the interest rates on 10-year government bonds for Italy and Spain, measured against the interest rate on German bonds, rose as investors' fears of default by Italy and Spain increased.

Source: Eurostat.

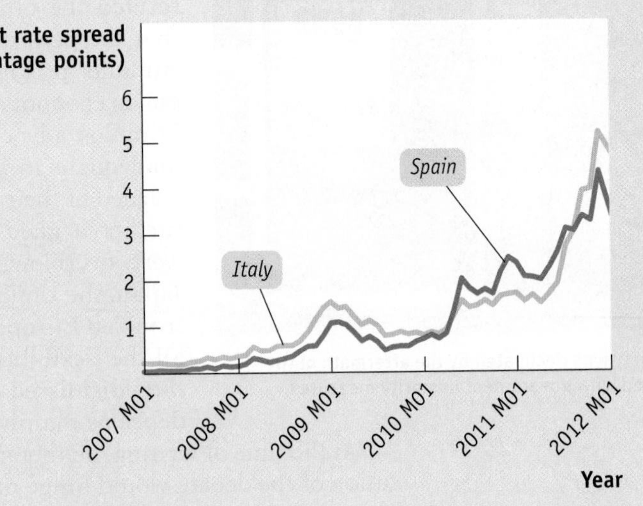

Italy's case was somewhat different. Italy has long had high levels of public debt as a percentage of GDP, but it has not run large deficits in recent years; as late as the spring of 2010 its fiscal position looked fairly stable. At that point, however, investors began to have doubts about the Italian government's solvency, in part because in the aftermath of the 2008 crisis the Italian economy was growing very slowly—too slowly, it was feared, to generate enough tax revenue to repay its public debt. These doubts drove up interest rates on Italian public debt, and this in turn created a vicious circle: higher interest payments, caused by fears about Italian government solvency, worsened Italy's fiscal position even further and pushed it closer to the edge.

At the time of writing, Greece had defaulted on its government bonds, Spanish youth unemployment was over 50%, and it was unclear how much worse the European situation would get. But Europe's difficulties reinforced the sense that the damage from the 2008 financial crisis was by no means over.

The Stimulus–Austerity Debate

The persistence of economic difficulties after the 2008 financial crisis led to fierce debates about appropriate policy responses. Broadly speaking, economists and policy makers were divided as to whether the situation called for more fiscal stimulus—expansionary fiscal measures such as more government spending and possibly tax cuts to promote spending and reduce unemployment—or for fiscal "austerity," contractionary fiscal measures such as spending cuts and possibly tax increases to reduce budget deficits.

The proponents of more stimulus pointed to the continuing poor performance of major economies, arguing that the combination of high unemployment and relatively low inflation clearly pointed to the need for expansionary policies. And since monetary policy was limited by the zero bound for interest rates, stimulus proponents advocated expansionary fiscal policy to fill the gap.

The austerity camp took a very different view. Strongly influenced by the solvency troubles of Greece, Ireland, Spain, and Italy, they argued that the common source of all the problems were high levels of government deficits and debts. In their view, countries like the United States that continued to run large government deficits several years after the 2008 crisis were at risk of suffering a similar loss of investor confidence in their ability to repay their debts. Moreover, austerity advocates claimed that cuts in government spending would not actually be contractionary because they would improve investor confidence and keep interest rates on government debt low.

Oli Scarff/Getty Images

The British economy was decimated by the aftermath of the 2008 crisis coupled with government austerity measures.

Each side of the debate argued that recent experience refuted the other side's claims. Austerity proponents argued that the persistence of high unemployment despite the fiscal stimulus programs adopted by the United States and other major economies in 2009 showed that stimulus doesn't work. Stimulus advocates argued that these programs were simply inadequate in size, pointing out that many economists had warned of their inadequacy from the start. Stimulus advocates further argued that warnings about the dangers of deficits were overblown, that far from rising, borrowing costs for Japan, the United States, and Britain—nations that, unlike the troubled European debtors, still had their own currencies with all the flexibility that implies—had fallen to record lows. And they dismissed claims that spending cuts would raise confidence as mainly fantasy.

At the time of writing, neither side was giving much ground. Clearly, any resolution of the debate would hinge on future economic developments and how they were interpreted.

The Lesson of the Post-Crisis Slump

Almost all major economies had great difficulty dealing with the aftermath of the 2008 financial crisis—high unemployment, low growth and, for some, solvency concerns, and high interest rates on public debt.

Clearly, then, the best way to avoid the terrible problems that arise after a financial crisis is not to have a crisis in the first place. How can you do that? In part, one might hope, through better regulation of financial institutions. We turn next to attempts at regulatory reform.

ECONOMICS ➤ IN ACTION

AUSTERITY BRITAIN

An election in May 2010 led to a shift in power in Britain, with a Labour Party government replaced by a coalition dominated by the Conservative Party under the new prime minister, David Cameron. The new government was firmly committed to the austerity side of the great post-crisis policy debate, and it changed policy accordingly.

Unlike Greece or Ireland, Britain wasn't under any immediate pressure to slash its budget deficit. Like the U.S. government, the British government was still able to borrow cheaply despite its large deficit. And the British economy was, if anything, even more depressed than the U.S. one, with fewer signs of recovery. The Cameron government believed, however, that preemptive cuts in public spending combined with some tax increases were necessary to preserve investor confidence and also that such cuts could boost the economy by improving confidence.

FIGURE 18-9 Business Confidence in Britain

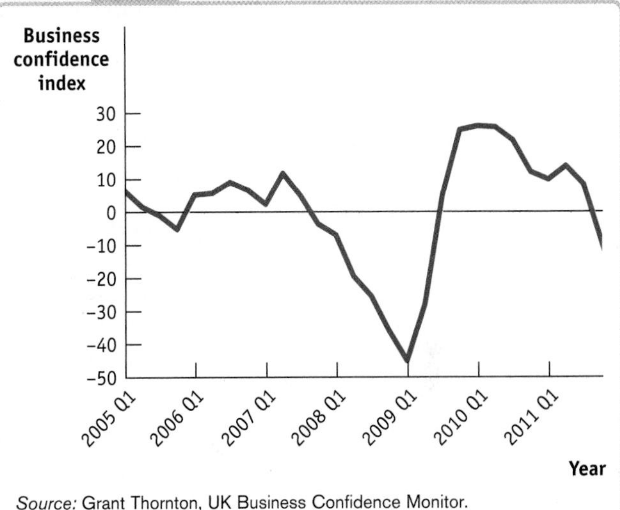

Source: Grant Thornton, UK Business Confidence Monitor.

How have these policies performed? As of mid-2012, the experiment in austerity had yielded disappointing results. British economic growth was weak—in fact, considerably weaker than in the United States, even though U.S. performance was lackluster. And as Figure 18-9 shows, the hoped-for surge in business confidence that austerity measures were supposed to generate had failed to materialize.

Quick Review

- Economic damage from the financial crisis of 2008 was both large and prolonged. Aftershocks from the crisis continue to shake the world economy.
- The world's two largest economies, the United States and the European Union, suffered severe downturns, shrinking more than 5%, followed by relatively slow recoveries. The severe slump and the slow recovery were very bad news for workers.
- The persistence of economic difficulties after the 2008 financial crisis led to severe solvency concerns for several European countries. A fierce debate erupted over whether fiscal stimulus or fiscal austerity was the right policy prescription.

18-4

1. In November 2011, the government of France announced that it was reducing its forecast for economic growth in 2012. It was also reducing its estimates of tax revenue for 2012, since a weaker economy would mean smaller tax receipts. To offset the effect of lower revenue on the budget deficit, the government also announced a new package of tax increases and spending cuts. Which side of the stimulus–austerity debate was France taking?

Regulation in the Wake of the Crisis

By late 2009, interventions by governments and central banks around the world had restored calm to financial markets. However, huge damage had been done to the global economy. In much of the advanced world, countries suffered their deepest slumps since the 1930s. And all indications were that the typical pattern of slow recovery after a financial crisis would be repeated, with unemployment remaining high for years to come.

The banking crisis of 2008 demonstrated, all too clearly, that financial regulation is a continuing process—that regulations will and should change over time to keep up with a changing world. The dependence on very short-term loans (called repos), the lack of regulation, and being outside the lender-of-last-resort system made the shadow banking sector vulnerable to crises and panics. So what changes will the most recent crisis bring? One thing that became all too clear in the 2008 crisis was that the traditional scope of banking regulation was too narrow. Regulating only depository institutions was clearly inadequate in a world in which a large part of banking, properly understood, is undertaken by the shadow banking sector.

In the aftermath of the crisis, then, an overhaul of financial regulation was clearly needed. And in 2010 the U.S. Congress enacted a bill that represented an effort to respond to the events of the preceding years. Like most legislation, the Wall Street Reform and Consumer Protection Act—often referred to as the Dodd-Frank bill—is complex in its details. But it contains four main elements:

1. Consumer protection
2. Derivatives regulation
3. Regulation of shadow banks
4. Resolution authority over nonbank financial institutions that face bankruptcy

1. Consumer Protection One factor in the financial crisis was the fact that many borrowers accepted offers they didn't understand, such as mortgages that were easy to pay in the first two years but required sharply higher payments later on. In an effort to limit future abuses, the new law creates a special office, the Consumer Financial Protection Bureau, dedicated to policing financial industry practices and protecting borrowers.

2. Derivatives Regulation Another factor in the crisis was the proliferation of derivatives, complex financial instruments that were supposed to help spread risk but arguably simply concealed it. Under the new law, most derivatives have to be bought and sold in open, transparent markets, hopefully limiting the extent to which financial players can take on invisible risk.

3. Regulation of Shadow Banks A key element in the financial crisis, as we've seen, was the rise of institutions that didn't fit the conventional definition of a bank but played the role of banks and created the risk of a banking crisis. How can regulation be extended to such institutions? Dodd-Frank does not offer an explicit new definition of what it means to be a bank. Instead, it offers a sort of financial version of "you know it when you see it." Specifically, it gives a special panel the ability to designate financial institutions as "systemically important," meaning that their activities have the potential to create a banking crisis. Such institutions will be subject to bank-like regulation of their capital, their investments, and so on.

4. Resolution Authority The events of 2008 made it clear that governments would often feel the need to guarantee a wide range of financial institution debts in a crisis, not just deposits. Yet how can this be done without creating huge incentive problems, motivating financial institutions to undertake overly risky behavior in the knowledge that they will be bailed out by the government if they get into trouble? Part of the answer is to empower the government to seize control of financial institutions that require a bailout, the way it already does with failing commercial banks and thrifts. This new power, known as resolution authority, should be viewed as solving a problem that seemed acute in early 2009, when several major financial institutions were teetering on the brink. Yet it wasn't clear whether Washington had the legal authority to orchestrate a rescue that was fair to taxpayers.

All this is now law in the United States, but two things remain unclear. (1) How will these regulations be worked into the international financial system? Will other nations adopt similar policies? If they do, how will conflicts among different national policies be resolved? (2) Will these regulations do the trick? Post-1930s bank regulation produced decades of stability, but will that happen again? Or will the new system fail in the face of a serious test?

Nobody knows the answers to these questions. We'll just have to wait and see.

ECONOMICS ➤ IN ACTION

BENT BREAKS THE BUCK

In 1970 a financial innovator named Bruce Bent introduced a new concept to American finance: the money market mutual fund. Most mutual funds offer ways for small investors to buy stocks: when you buy a share in a mutual fund like Fidelity or Vanguard, you are indirectly acquiring a diversified mix of stocks. Bent, however, created a mutual fund that invests only in short-term assets, such as Treasury bills and commercial paper issued by highly rated corporations, which carry a low risk of default. The idea was to give people a safe place to park their money, but one that offered a higher interest rate than a bank deposit. Many people eventually began seeing their investments in money market funds as equivalent to bank accounts, but better.

iStockphoto

In September 2008, the $65 billion Reserve Primary Fund broke the buck after it was caught with bankrupt Lehman Brothers debt, leaving investors in a panic.

But money placed in money market funds was different from money deposited in a bank in one crucial dimension: money market funds weren't federally insured. And on September 16, 2008, the day after Lehman Brothers fell, it became known that one major money market fund had lost heavily on money placed with Lehman, to such an extent that it had "broken the buck"; that is, it no longer had enough assets to pay off all the people who had placed their money at its disposal. As a result, the fund had to suspend withdrawals; in effect, a "bank" had suddenly shut its doors.

And which fund was in this predicament? Reserve Primary Fund, controlled by none other than Bruce Bent. Panicked money market mutual fund customers pulled hundreds of billions of dollars out of money market funds over a two-day period.

The federal government stemmed the panic by instituting a temporary insurance scheme for money market funds, giving them the same protected status as bank deposits. But the money market fund panic was an object lesson in the extent to which financial innovation had undermined the traditional bank safety net.

Quick Review

- When the panic hit after Lehman's fall, governments and central banks around the world stepped in to fight the crisis and calm the markets. Most advanced economies experienced their worst slump since the 1930s.
- In 2010 Congress enacted the Dodd-Frank bill to remedy the regulatory oversights exposed by the crisis of 2007–2009. It created the Consumer Financial Protection Bureau to protect borrowers and consumers, implemented stricter regulation of derivatives, extended the reach of regulation to the shadow banking sector, and empowered the government to seize control of any financial institution requiring a bailout.

CHECK YOUR UNDERSTANDING 18-5

1. Why does the use of short-term borrowing and being outside of the lender-of-last-resort system make shadow banks vulnerable to events similar to bank runs?
2. How do you think the crisis of 2008 would have been mitigated if there had been no shadow banking sector but only the formal depository banking sector?
3. Describe the incentive problem facing the U.S. government in responding to the 2007–2009 crisis with respect to the shadow banking sector. How did the Dodd-Frank bill attempt to address those incentive problems?

Solutions appear at back of book.

SUMMARY

1. Without banks, people would make the trade-off between liquidity and rate of return by holding a large fraction of their wealth in idle cash. Banks engage in **maturity transformation,** transforming short-term liabilities into long-term assets. Banking improves savers' welfare, allowing them immediate access to their funds as well as paying them interest on those funds.

2. **Shadow banks** have grown greatly since 1980. Largely unregulated, they can pay savers a higher rate of return than depository banks. Like depository banks, shadow banks engage in maturity transformation, depending on short-term borrowing to operate and investing in long-term assets. Therefore, shadow banks can also be subject to bank runs.

3. Although **banking crises** are rare, they typically inflict severe damage on the economy. They have two main sources: shared mistakes, such as investing in an **asset bubble,** and **financial contagion.** Contagion is spread through bank runs or via a vicious cycle of deleveraging. When unregulated, shadow banking is particularly vulnerable to contagion. In 2008, a **financial panic** hit the United States, arising from the combination of an asset bubble, a huge shadow banking sector, and a vicious cycle of deleveraging.

4. The United States has suffered numerous banking crises and financial panics, each followed by a severe downturn. The crisis of the 1930s spurred bank reform that prevented another crisis until 2008. Banking crises occur frequently throughout the world, mostly in small, poor countries. In the recent past, though, several advanced countries have had banking crises driven by real estate bubbles.

5. Severe banking crises almost invariably lead to deep and long recessions, with unemployment remaining high for several years after the crisis began. There are three main reasons why banking crises are so damaging to the economy: they result in a **credit crunch,** the vicious circle of deleveraging leads to a **debt overhang,** and monetary policy is rendered ineffective as the economy falls into a **liquidity trap.** As a result, households and businesses are either unable or unwilling to spend, deepening the downturn.

6. Unlike during the Great Depression, governments now step in to try to limit the damage from a banking crisis by acting as the **lender of last resort** and by guaranteeing the banks' liabilities. Sometimes, but not always, governments nationalize the banks and then later reprivatize them. In an extreme crisis, the central bank may directly finance commercial transactions.

7. Economic damage from the financial crisis of 2008 was large and prolonged. The world's two largest economies, the United States and the European Union, suffered severe downturns, shrinking more than 5%, followed by relatively slow recoveries. The persistence of economic difficulties after 2008 led to fierce debates about appropriate policy responses between economists and policy makers calling for more fiscal stimulus—more government spending and possibly tax cuts to promote spending and reduce unemployment—and those favoring fiscal austerity—spending cuts and possibly tax increases to reduce budget deficits.

8. The banking regulatory system put in place during the 1930s has eroded due to the rise of shadow banking. The dependence on short-term financing (repo), the lack of regulation, and being outside the lender-of-last-resort system makes the shadow banking sector vulnerable to a banking panic.

9. The crisis of 2008 began as the shadow banking sector suffered high losses when a real estate bubble burst. Despite the fact that governments and central banks around the world stepped in to fight the crisis and the downturn, most advanced countries experienced their worst slump since the 1930s. Persistently high unemployment is likely to endure for years to come.

10. In the aftermath of the crisis, the U.S. Congress enacted the Dodd-Frank bill in the hope of preventing a replay of the crisis. The main elements of the new reform are stronger consumer protection, greater regulation of derivatives, regulation of shadow banking, and resolution authority for a variety of financial institutions. We have yet to see whether these changes will be adequate or whether they will also be adopted by other countries.

KEY TERMS

PROBLEMS

1. Which of the following are examples of debt overhang? Which examples are likely to lead to a cutback in spending? Explain.
   a. Your uncle starts a restaurant, borrowing to fund his investment. The restaurant fails, and your uncle must shut down but still must pay his debt.
   b. Your parents take out a loan to buy a house. Your father is transferred to a new city, and now your parents must sell the house. The value of the house has gone up during the time your family has lived there.
   c. Your friend's parents take out a loan to buy her a condo to live in while she is at college. Meanwhile, the housing market plummets. By the time your friend leaves college, the condo is worth significantly less than the value of the loan.
   d. You finish college with an honors degree in a field with many good job prospects and with $25,000 in student loans that you must repay.
2. Which of the following are *not* examples of a vicious cycle of deleveraging? Explain.
   a. Your university decides to sell several commercial buildings in the middle of town in order to upgrade buildings on campus.
   b. A company decides to sell its large and valuable art collection because other asset prices on its balance sheet have fallen below a critical level, forcing creditors to call in their loans to the company because of provisions written into the original loan contract.
   c. A company decides to issue more stock in order to voluntarily pay off some of its debt.
   d. A shadow bank must sell its holdings of corporate bonds because falling asset prices have led to a default on the terms of its loans with some creditors.
3. In the following figure showing the Case–Shiller U.S. Home Price Index from 2000 to 2010, did housing prices peak before or after the financial crisis in the United States? Explain your answer.

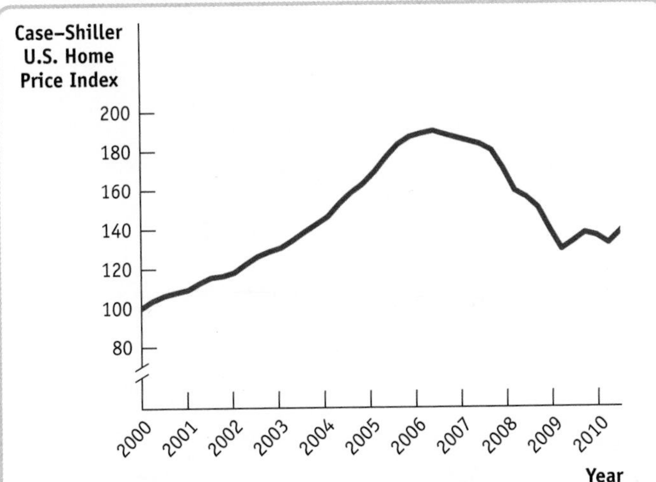

Source: Robert J. Shiller, *Irrational Exuberance*, 2nd ed. (Princeton, NJ: Princeton University Press, 2005); data retrieved from http://www.econ.yale.edu/~shiller/data.htm.

4. Figure 18-2 tracks the unemployment rate in the years before and after the Panic of 1893 in the United States and the banking crisis of 1991 in Sweden.
   a. In Figure 18-2, how many years after the Panic of 1893 did unemployment peak in the United States?
   b. In Figure 18-2, how many years after the banking crisis of 1991 did unemployment peak in Sweden?
5. In 2007–2009, the Federal Reserve, acting as a lender of last resort, stepped in to provide funds when private markets were unable to do so. The Fed also took over many banks. In 2007, it seized 3 banks; in 2008, it seized 25 banks; and in 2009, it seized 140 banks. Go to www.fdic.gov; under "Bank Closing Information," click on "Complete Failed Bank List." Then count the number of banks that the Federal Reserve has seized so far this year. Have bank failures decreased since the crisis in 2008?
6. During the financial crisis in October 2008, the federal government could borrow at a rate of 2.73% (the yield on five-year Treasury securities). During October 2008, though, Baa borrowers (corporate borrowers rated by Moody's as not being completely reliable) had to pay 8.88%.
   a. What was the difference in borrowing costs for these corporate borrowers and the federal government?
   b. Go to www.research.stlouisfed.org/fred2/categories/22. Click on the link for "Treasury constant maturity" and find the most recent interest rate on 10-year U.S. Treasury bonds. Then go back to the original web page and click on the link for "Corporate bonds" and find the rate for Baa corporate bonds. What is the current difference in borrowing costs between corporate borrowers and the U.S. government?
   c. Has this difference in borrowing costs increased or decreased since the height of the financial crisis in October of 2008? Why?
7. Go to www.federalreserve.gov and click on the tab "Banking Information & Regulation." Then select the links "Banking Data" followed by "Large Commercial Banks." Once there, choose the latest release of quarterly data.
   a. Which bank has the largest consolidated assets?
   b. Which bank has the largest domestic assets?
   c. What percent of U.S. GDP are the domestic assets of the bank listed in part b? (*Hint:* You can find U.S. GDP at http://research.stlouisfed.org/fred2/series/GDP?cid=106 using the links "Gross Domestic Product (GDP)" and then "Current-dollar and 'real' GDP.")
8. Go to www.fdic.gov and click on the tab "Industry Analysis" and then on the link "Research & Analysis." Under "Historical Perspectives," select "The First Fifty Years: A History of the FDIC 1933–1983." Open Chapter 3, "Establishment of the FDIC," and scroll

down to the section entitled "The Banking Crisis of 1933" and the section entitled "Federal Deposit Insurance Legislation." Read the section and then answer these questions.

a. President Roosevelt was sworn in on March 4, 1933. What was one of his first official acts in response to the banking crisis?

b. How many banks suspended operations during 1933?

c. Who was the chief proponent of federal deposit insurance in Congress?

d. How much coverage did the temporary fund for federal deposit insurance provide?

9. The U.S. Government Accountability Office (GAO) does research to support congressional decision making. After the Long-Term Capital Management (LTCM) crisis, the GAO produced a summary of the events of the crisis located at http://www.gao.gov/products/GGD-00-3. Read the summary and then answer the following questions.

a. How much of its capital did LTCM lose in 1998?

b. Why did the GAO conclude that LTCM was able to establish leveraged trading positions of a size that posed systemic risk to the banking system?

c. What was the recommendation of the President's Working Group regarding the Securities and Exchange Commission (SEC) and the Commodity Futures Trading Commission (CFTC)?

BUSINESS CASE • Priming the Pumps

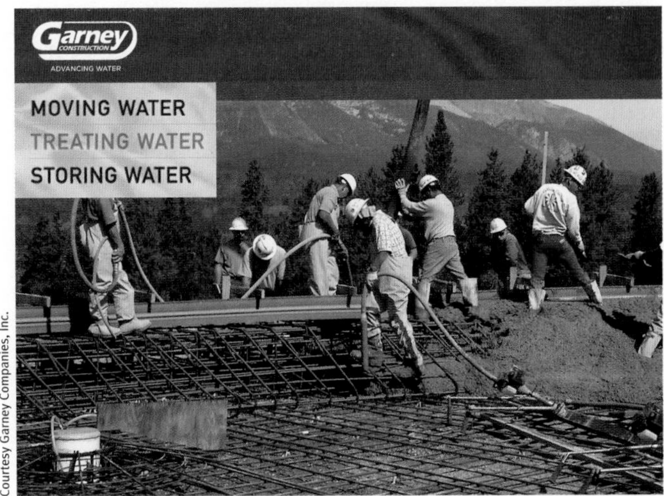

Courtesy Garney Companies, Inc.

In the old days, when fewer Americans had cars but many more people lived in rural areas and drew their water from wells, advocates of fiscal expansion used different metaphors. Instead of talking, as President Obama did, about giving the economy a "jumpstart," they'd talk about "priming the pump." You see, it was often necessary to add water to old-fashioned hand pumps before they would work; similarly, people would argue, you need to add funds to the economy before it will get back to producing jobs and income.

In the case of the Obama stimulus, priming the pump was more than a metaphor: some of the most obvious beneficiaries were companies that made . . . pumps. The Recovery Act allocated $7 billion for drinking-water and wastewater projects, creating a number of new opportunities for companies in the business of moving water around.

A case in point was Garney Construction, a Kansas-City based company specializing in water and sewage projects whose slogan is "Advancing Water." By the summer of 2009, Garney had won contracts to work on nine water- and sewer-related projects that were being financed in whole or in part by the Recovery Act.

None of these infrastructure projects were dreamed up as ways to spend more money; they were all things that state or local governments had been planning to do eventually. "I think most of these projects were sitting on a shelf, waiting for funding," Garney's president told a local business journal.

Although the stimulus was good for Garney, it was not exactly a financial gusher. In 2007, the United States spent about $100 billion on water-supply and wastewater infrastructure; the extra $7 billion coming from the stimulus, not all of it coming in one year, was basically a, well, drop in the bucket by comparison. Indeed, Garney said that only about 10% of its business was coming from stimulus money. And despite the stimulus, the company had less business than it had two years earlier.

Still, Garney and other companies in the water-infrastructure business were clearly getting some benefit from the Recovery Act.

QUESTIONS FOR THOUGHT

1. Some opponents of fiscal expansion have accused it of consisting of make-work projects of little social value. What does the Garney story say about this view?
2. Based on this case, would you say that government spending was competing with the private sector for scarce resources?
3. If a water or sewer project is something we want to do eventually, is the depth of a recession a good or a bad time to undertake that project? Why?

BUSINESS CASE • The Perfect Gift: Cash or a Gift Card?

Richard B. Levine/Alamy

It's always nice when someone shows his or her appreciation by giving you a gift. Over the past few years, more and more people have been showing their appreciation by giving gift cards, prepaid plastic cards issued by a retailer that can be redeemed for merchandise. The best-selling single item for more than 80% of the top 100 American retailers, says GiftCardUSA.com, is their gift cards. What could be more simple and useful, so the thinking goes, than allowing the recipient to choose what he or she wants? And isn't a gift card more personal than cash or a check stuffed in an envelope? (And gift cards have pretty pictures, too.)

Yet several websites are now making a profit from the fact that gift card recipients are often willing to sell their cards at a discount—sometimes at a fairly sizable discount—to turn them into cold, impersonal dollars and cents.

PlasticJungle.com is one such site. At the time of writing, it offers to pay cash to a seller of a Whole Foods gift card equivalent to 95.55% of the card's face value (for example, the seller of a card with a value of $100 would receive $95.55 in cash). But it offers cash equal to only 78.75% of an American Eagle Outfitters card's face value. PlasticJungle.com profits by reselling the card at a premium over what it paid; for example, it buys an American Eagle Outfitters card for 78.75% of its face value and then resells is for 87% of its face value.

Many consumers may be willing to sell at a sizable discount to turn their gift cards into cash, but retailers are eager to promote the use of gift cards over cash. According to GiftCardUSA.com, 5% to 15% of gift cards are never redeemed. Those unredeemed dollars accrue to the retailer, making gift cards a highly profitable line of business. The *Wall Street Journal* placed the value of "breakage," the amount of a gift card that accrues to the retailer rather than to the card holder, at $41 billion between 2005 and 2011.

How does breakage occur? People lose cards. Or they spend only $47 of a $50 gift card, figuring it's not worth the effort to return to the store to spend that last $3. Also, retailers impose fees on the use of the card or make cards subject to expiration dates, which customers forget about. And if a retailer goes out of business, the value of any outstanding gift cards disappears with it.

In addition to breakage, retailers benefit when customers intent on using up the value of their gift card find that it is too difficult to spend exactly the amount of the card; instead, they spend more than the card's face value, sometimes even spending more than they would have in the absence of the gift card.

Gift cards are so beneficial to retailers that those which used to reward customer loyalty with rebate checks have largely switched to dispensing gift cards. As one commentator noted in explaining why retailers prefer gift cards to rebate checks, "Nobody neglects to spend cash."

QUESTIONS FOR THOUGHT

1. Why are gift card owners willing to sell their cards for a cash amount less than their face value?
2. Why do gift cards for retailers like Walmart, Home Depot, and Whole Foods sell for a smaller discount than those for retailers like American Eagle Outfitters and Dick's Sporting Goods?
3. Use your answer from Question 2 to explain why cash never "sells" at a discount.
4. Explain why retailers prefer to reward loyal customers with gift cards instead of rebate checks.
5. Recent legislation restricted retailers' ability to impose fees and expiration dates on their gift cards and mandated greater disclosure of their terms. Why do you think Congress enacted this legislation?

BUSINESS CASE • PIMCO Bets on Cheap Money

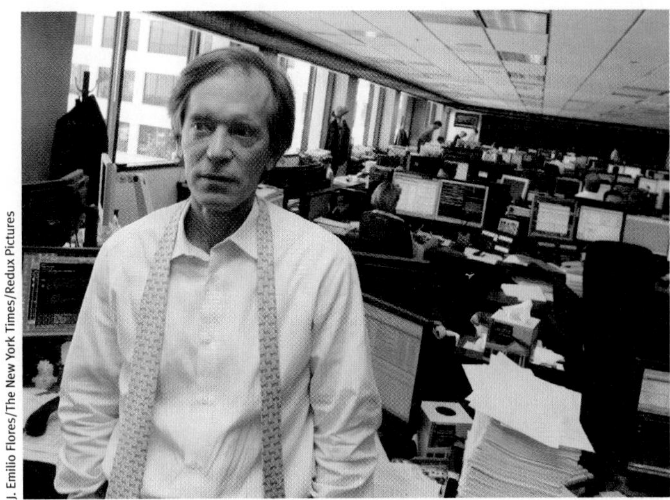
J. Emilio Flores/The New York Times/Redux Pictures

Pacific Investment Management Company, generally known as PIMCO, is one of the world's largest investment companies. Among other things, it runs PIMCO Total Return, the world's largest mutual fund. Bill Gross, shown at left, who heads PIMCO, is legendary for his ability to predict trends in financial markets, especially bond markets, where PIMCO does much of its investing.

In the fall of 2009, Gross decided to put more of PIMCO's assets into long-term U.S. government bonds. This amounted to a bet that long-term interest rates would fall. This bet was especially interesting because it was the opposite of the bet many other investors were making. For example, in November 2009 the investment bank Morgan Stanley told its clients to expect a sharp rise in long-term interest rates.

What lay behind PIMCO's bet? Gross explained the firm's thinking in his September 2009 commentary. He suggested that unemployment was likely to stay high and inflation low. "Global policy rates," he asserted—meaning the federal funds rate and its equivalents in Europe and elsewhere—"will remain low for extended periods of time."

PIMCO's view was in sharp contrast to those of other investors: Morgan Stanley expected long-term rates to rise in part because it expected the Fed to raise the federal funds rate in 2010.

Who was right? PIMCO, mostly. As the accompanying figure shows, the federal funds rate stayed near zero, and long-term interest rates fell through much of 2010, although they rose somewhat very late in the year as investors became somewhat more optimistic about economic recovery. Morgan Stanley, which had bet on rising rates, actually apologized to investors for getting it so wrong.

Bill Gross's foresight, however, was a lot less accurate in 2011. Anticipating a significantly stronger U.S. economy by mid-2011 that would result in inflation, Gross bet heavily against U.S. government bonds early that year. But this time he was wrong, as weak growth continued. By late summer 2011, Gross realized his mistake as U.S. bonds rose in value and the value of his funds sank. He admitted to the *Wall Street Journal* that he had "lost sleep" over his bet, and called it a "mistake."

QUESTIONS FOR THOUGHT

1. Why did PIMCO's view that unemployment would stay high and inflation low lead to a forecast that policy interest rates would remain low for an extended period?
2. Why would low policy rates suggest low long-term interest rates?
3. What might have caused long-term interest rates to rise in late 2010, even though the federal funds rate was still zero?

The Federal Funds Rate and Long-Term Interest Rates, 2009–2011

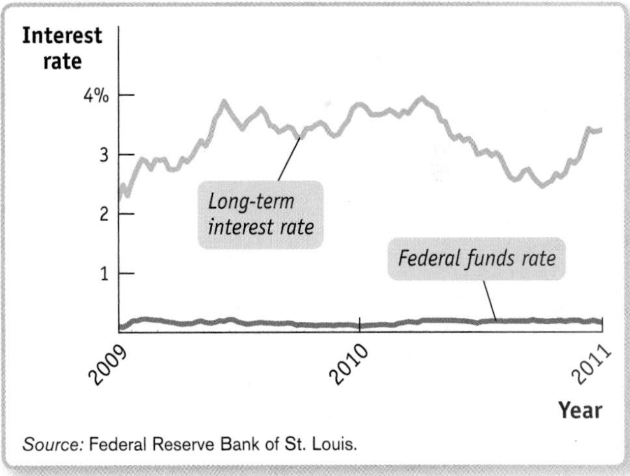

Source: Federal Reserve Bank of St. Louis.

CHAPTER 19

International Trade, Capital Flows, and Exchange Rates

WHAT YOU WILL LEARN IN THIS CHAPTER

- How comparative advantage leads to mutually beneficial international trade
- The sources of international comparative advantage
- Who gains and who loses from international trade, and why the gains exceed the losses
- How **tariffs** and **import quotas** cause inefficiency and reduce total surplus
- The meaning of the **balance of payments accounts** and the determinants of international capital flows
- The role of the **foreign exchange market** and the **exchange rate**

CAR PARTS AND SUCKING SOUNDS

Susana Gonzalez/Bloomberg via Getty Images

Scott Olson/Getty Images

International trade improves the welfare of Mexican producers of auto parts as well as American car buyers and sellers.

STOP IN AN AUTO SHOWROOM, and odds are that the majority of cars on display were produced in the United States. Even if they're Nissans, Hondas, or Volkswagens, most cars sold in this country were made here by the Big Three U.S. auto firms or by subsidiaries of foreign firms. The cars are assembled in "Auto Alley," a north–south corridor roughly defined as the space between Interstate 65, which runs from Chicago to Mobile, and Interstate 75, which runs from Detroit to western Florida.

Although that car you're looking at may have been made in America, a significant part of what's inside was probably made elsewhere, very likely in Mexico. Since the 1980s, U.S. auto production has increasingly relied on factories in Mexico to produce *labor-intensive* auto parts, such as seat parts—products that use a relatively high amount of labor in their production.

Changes in economic policy over the years have contributed greatly to the emergence of large-scale U.S. imports of auto parts from Mexico. Until the 1980s, Mexico had a system of *trade protection*—taxes and regulations limiting imports—that both kept out U.S. manufactured goods and encouraged Mexican industry to focus on selling to Mexican consumers rather than to a wider market. In 1985, however, the Mexican government began dismantling much of its trade protection, boosting trade with the United States. A further boost came in 1993, when the United States, Mexico, and Canada signed the North American Free Trade Agreement (NAFTA), which eliminated most taxes on trade among the three nations and provided guarantees that business investments in Mexico would be protected from arbitrary changes in government policy.

NAFTA was deeply controversial when it went into effect: Mexican workers were paid only about 10% as much as their U.S. counterparts, and many expressed concern that U.S. jobs would be lost to low-wage competition. Most memorably, Ross Perot, a U.S. presidential candidate in 1992, warned that there would be a "giant sucking sound" as U.S. manufacturing moved south of the border. And although apocalyptic predictions about NAFTA's impact haven't come to pass, the agreement remains controversial even now.

Most economists disagreed with those who saw NAFTA as a threat to the U.S. economy. We saw in Chapter 2 how international trade can lead to mutual *gains from trade*. Economists, for the most part, believed that the same logic applied to NAFTA, that the treaty would make both the United States and Mexico richer. But making a nation as a whole richer isn't the same thing as improving the welfare of everyone living in a country, and there were and are reasons to believe that NAFTA hurts some U.S. citizens.

Until now, we have analyzed the economy as if it were self-sufficient, as if the economy produces all the goods and services it consumes, and vice versa. This is, of course, true for the world economy as a whole. But it's not true for any individual country. Assuming self-sufficiency would have been far more accurate 50 years ago, when the United States exported only a small fraction of what it produced and imported only a small fraction of what it consumed.

Since then, however, both U.S. imports and exports have grown much faster than the U.S. economy as a whole. Moreover, compared to the United States, other countries engage in far more foreign trade relative to the size of their economies. To have a full picture of how national economies work, we must understand international trade.

This chapter examines the interaction of national economies. We begin with a discussion of the economics of international trade. With that foundation established, we move on to discuss how trade and capital flows are part of the balance of payments accounts. Finally, we look at the various factors that influence exchange rates.

Goods and services purchased from other countries are **imports;** goods and services sold to other countries are **exports.**

Globalization is the phenomenon of growing economic linkages among countries.

Comparative Advantage and International Trade

The United States buys auto parts—and many other goods and services—from other countries. At the same time, it sells many goods and services to other countries. Goods and services purchased from abroad are **imports;** goods and services sold abroad are **exports.**

As illustrated by the opening story, imports and exports have taken on an increasingly important role in the U.S. economy. Over the last 50 years, both imports into and exports from the United States have grown faster than the U.S. economy. Panel (a) of Figure 19-1 shows how the values of U.S. imports and exports have grown as a percentage of gross domestic product (GDP). Panel (b) shows imports and exports as a percentage of GDP for a number of countries. It shows that foreign trade is significantly more important for many other countries than it is for the United States. (Japan is the exception.)

Foreign trade isn't the only way countries interact economically. In the modern world, investors from one country often invest funds in another nation; many companies are multinational, with subsidiaries operating in several countries; and a growing number of individuals work in a country different from the one in which they were born. The growth of all these forms of economic linkages among countries is often called **globalization.**

FIGURE 19-1 The Growing Importance of International Trade

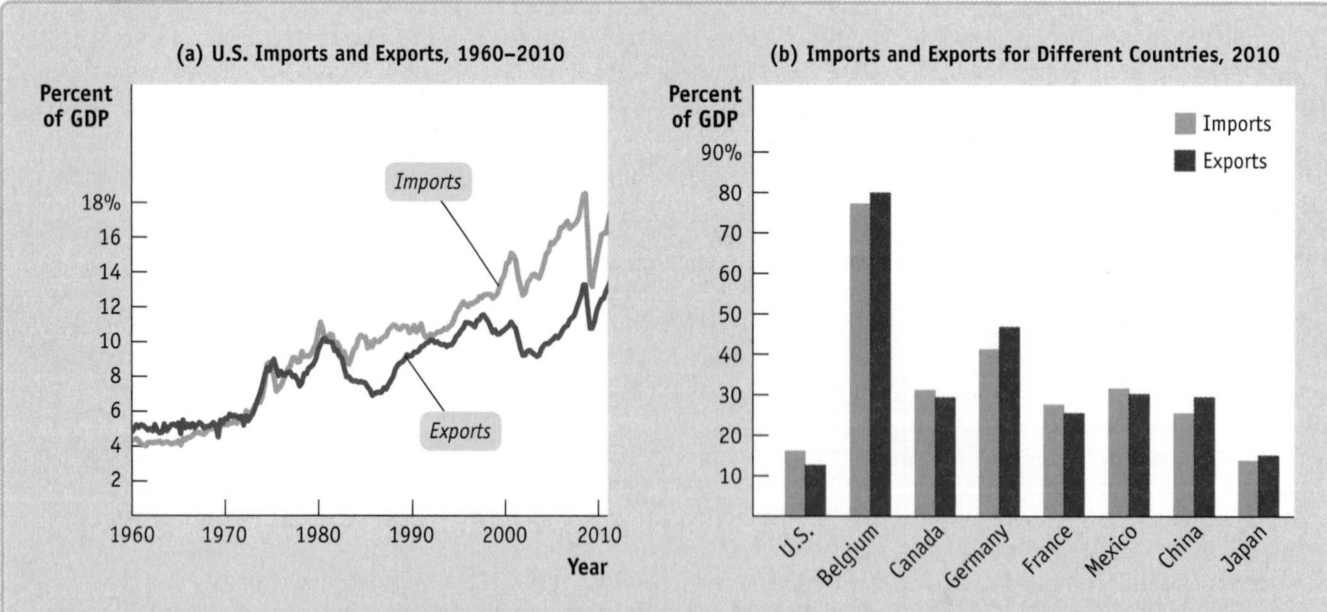

Panel (a) illustrates the fact that over the past 50 years, the United States has exported a steadily growing share of its GDP to other countries and imported a growing share of what it consumes. Panel (b) demonstrates that international trade is significantly more important to many other countries than it is to the United States, with the exception of Japan.

Source: Bureau of Economic Analysis [panel (a)] and World Bank [panel (b)].

We begin by focusing mainly on international trade. To understand why international trade occurs and why economists believe it is beneficial to the economy, we will first review the concept of comparative advantage.

The **Ricardian model of international trade** analyzes international trade under the assumption that opportunity costs are constant.

Production Possibilities and Comparative Advantage, Revisited

To produce auto parts, any country must use resources—land, labor, capital, and so on—that could have been used to produce other things. The potential production of other goods a country must forgo to produce an auto part is the opportunity cost of that part.

In some cases, it's easy to see why the opportunity cost of producing a good is especially low in a given country. Consider, for example, shrimp—much of which now comes from seafood farms in Vietnam and Thailand. It's a lot easier to produce shrimp in Vietnam, where the climate is nearly ideal and there's plenty of coastal land suitable for shellfish farming, than it is in the United States. Conversely, other goods are not produced as easily in Vietnam as in the United States. For example, Vietnam doesn't have the base of skilled workers and technological know-how that makes the United States so good at producing high-technology goods. So the opportunity cost of a ton of shrimp, in terms of other goods such as aircraft, is much less in Vietnam than it is in the United States.

In other cases, matters are a bit less obvious. It's as easy to produce auto parts in the United States as it is in Mexico, and Mexican auto parts workers are, if anything, less efficient than their U.S. counterparts. But Mexican workers are a *lot* less productive than U.S. workers in other areas, such as aircraft and chemical production. This means that diverting a Mexican worker into auto parts production reduces output of other goods less than diverting a U.S. worker into auto parts production. That is, the opportunity cost of producing auto parts in Mexico is less than it is in the United States.

So we say that Mexico has a comparative advantage in producing auto parts. Let's repeat the definition of comparative advantage from Chapter 2: *A country has a comparative advantage in producing a good or service if the opportunity cost of producing the good or service is lower for that country than for other countries.*

Figure 19-2 provides a hypothetical numerical example of comparative advantage in international trade. We assume that only two goods are produced and consumed, auto parts and airplanes, and that there are only two countries in the world, the United States and Mexico. (In real life, auto parts aren't worth much without auto bodies to put them in, but let's set that issue aside.) The figure shows hypothetical production possibility frontiers for the United States and Mexico.

As in Chapter 2, we simplify the model by assuming that the production possibility frontiers are straight lines, as shown in Figure 2-1, rather than the more realistic bowed-out shape shown in Figure 2-2. The straight-line shape implies that the opportunity cost of an auto part in terms of airplanes in each country is constant—it does not depend on how many units of each good the country produces. The analysis of international trade under the assumption that opportunity costs are constant, which makes production possibility frontiers straight lines, is known as the **Ricardian model of international trade,** named after the English economist David Ricardo, who introduced this analysis in the early nineteenth century.

In Figure 19-2 we have grouped auto parts into bundles of 10,000, so, for example, a country that produces 500 bundles of auto parts is producing 5 million individual auto parts. You can see in the figure that the United States can produce 2,000 airplanes if it produces no auto parts, or 1,000 bundles of auto

FIGURE 19-2 Comparative Advantage and the Production Possibility Frontier

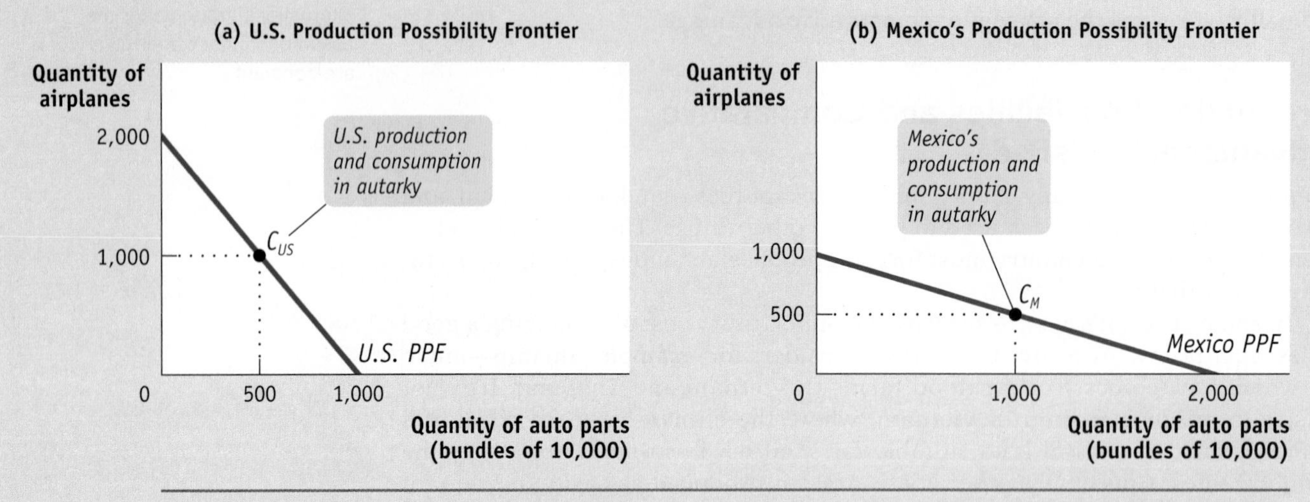

The U.S. opportunity cost of 1 bundle of auto parts in terms of airplanes is 2: for every additional bundle of auto parts, 2 airplanes must be forgone. The Mexican opportunity cost of 1 bundle of auto parts in terms of airplanes is ½: for every additional bundle of auto parts, only ½ of an airplane must be forgone. As a result, the United States has a comparative advantage in airplane production, and Mexico has a comparative advantage in auto parts production. In autarky, each country is forced to consume only what it produces: 1,000 airplanes and 500 bundles of auto parts for the United States; 500 airplanes and 1,000 bundles of auto parts for Mexico.

Autarky is a situation in which a country does not trade with other countries.

parts if it produces no airplanes. Thus, the slope of the U.S. production possibility frontier, or PPF, is –2,000/1,000 = –2. That is, to produce an additional bundle of auto parts, the United States must forgo the production of 2 airplanes.

Similarly, Mexico can produce 1,000 airplanes if it produces no auto parts or 2,000 bundles of auto parts if it produces no airplanes. Thus, the slope of Mexico's PPF is –1,000/2,000 = –1/2. That is, to produce an additional bundle of auto parts, Mexico must forgo the production of 1/2 an airplane.

Economists use the term **autarky** to refer to a situation in which a country does not trade with other countries. We assume that in autarky the United States chooses to produce and consume 500 bundles of auto parts and 1,000 airplanes. We also assume that in autarky Mexico produces 1,000 bundles of auto parts and 500 airplanes.

The trade-offs facing the two countries when they don't trade are summarized in Table 19-1. As you can see, the United States has a comparative advantage in the production of airplanes because it has a lower opportunity cost in terms of auto parts than Mexico has: producing an airplane costs the United States only ½ a bundle of auto parts, while it costs Mexico 2 bundles of auto parts. Correspondingly, Mexico has a comparative advantage in auto parts production: 1 bundle costs it only ½ an airplane, while it costs the United States 2 airplanes.

TABLE 19-1 U.S. and Mexican Opportunity Costs of Auto Parts and Airplanes

	U.S. Opportunity Cost		Mexican Opportunity Cost
1 bundle of auto parts	2 airplanes	>	1/2 airplane
1 airplane	1/2 bundle of auto parts	<	2 bundles of auto parts

As we learned in Chapter 2, each country can do better by engaging in trade than it could by not trading. A country can accomplish this by specializing in the production of the good in which it has a comparative advantage and exporting that good, while importing the good in which it has a comparative *dis*advantage. Let's see how this works.

FIGURE 19-3 The Gains from International Trade

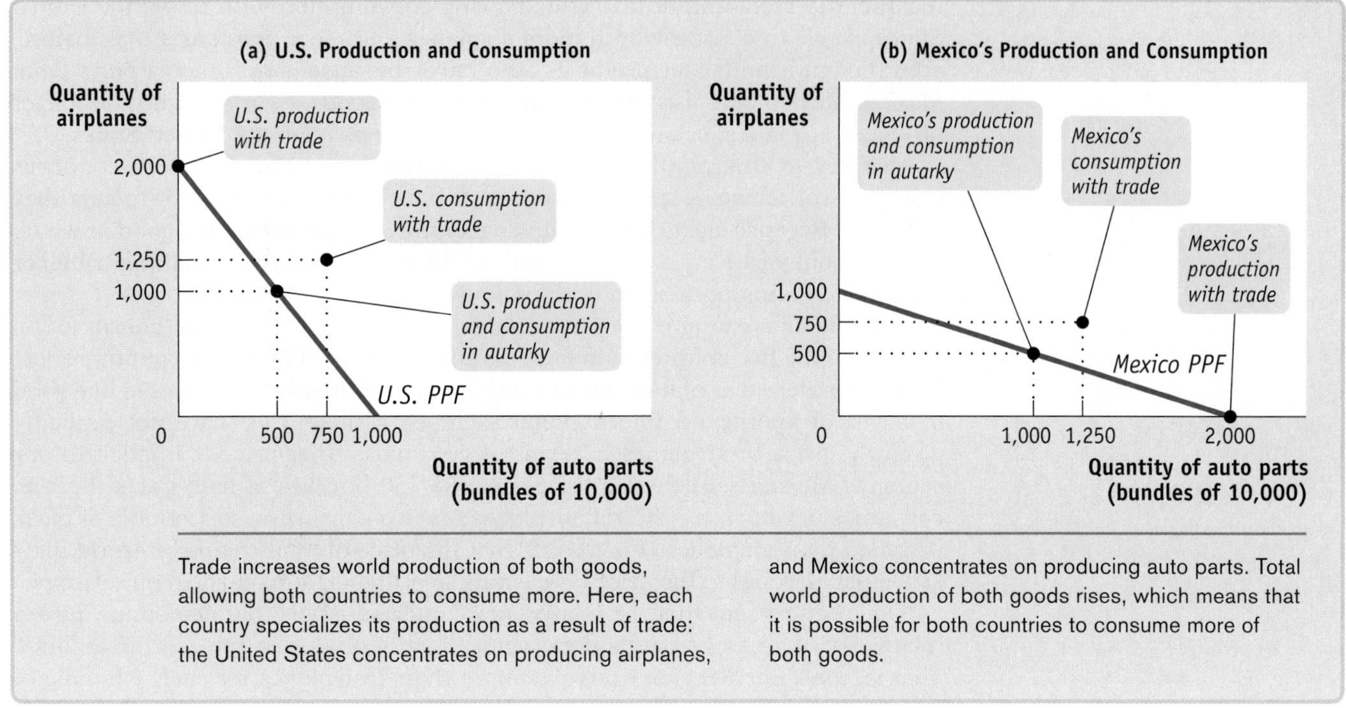

Trade increases world production of both goods, allowing both countries to consume more. Here, each country specializes its production as a result of trade: the United States concentrates on producing airplanes, and Mexico concentrates on producing auto parts. Total world production of both goods rises, which means that it is possible for both countries to consume more of both goods.

The Gains from International Trade

Figure 19-3 illustrates how both countries can gain from specialization and trade, by showing a hypothetical rearrangement of production and consumption that allows *each* country to consume more of *both* goods. Again, panel (a) represents the United States and panel (b) represents Mexico. In each panel we indicate again the autarky production and consumption assumed in Figure 19-2. Once trade becomes possible, however, everything changes. With trade, each country can move to producing only the good in which it has a comparative advantage—airplanes for the United States and auto parts for Mexico. Because the world production of both goods is now higher than in autarky, trade makes it possible for each country to consume more of both goods.

Table 19-2 sums up the changes as a result of trade and shows why both countries can gain. The left part of the table shows the autarky situation, before trade, in which each country must produce the goods it consumes. The right part of the table shows what happens as a result of trade. After trade, the United States specializes in the production of airplanes, producing 2,000 airplanes and no auto parts; Mexico specializes in the production of auto parts, producing 2,000 bundles of auto parts and no airplanes.

TABLE 19-2 How the United States and Mexico Gain from Trade

		In Autarky		With Trade		
		Production	Consumption	Production	Consumption	Gains from trade
United States	Bundles of auto parts	500	500	0	750	+250
	Airplanes	1,000	1,000	2,000	1,250	+250
Mexico	Bundles of auto parts	1,000	1,000	2,000	1,250	+250
	Airplanes	500	500	0	750	+250

The result is a rise in total world production of both goods. As you can see in the Table 19-2 column at far right showing consumption with trade, the United States is able to consume both more airplanes and more auto parts than before, even though it no longer produces auto parts, because it can import parts from Mexico. Mexico can also consume more of both goods, even though it no longer produces airplanes, because it can import airplanes from the United States.

The key to this mutual gain is the fact that trade liberates both countries from self-sufficiency—from the need to produce the same mixes of goods they consume. Because each country can concentrate on producing the good in which it has a comparative advantage, total world production rises, making a higher standard of living possible in both nations.

Now, in this example we have simply assumed the post-trade consumption bundles of the two countries. In fact, the consumption choices of a country reflect both the preferences of its residents and the *relative prices*—the prices of one good in terms of another in international markets. Although we have not explicitly given the price of airplanes in terms of auto parts, that price is implicit in our example: Mexico sells the United States the 750 bundles of auto parts the U.S. consumes in return for the 750 airplanes Mexico consumes, so 1 bundle of parts is traded for 1 airplane. This tells us that the price of an airplane on world markets must be equal to the price of one bundle of 10,000 auto parts in our example.

One requirement that the relative price must satisfy is that no country pays a relative price greater than its opportunity cost of obtaining the good in autarky. That is, the United States won't pay more than 2 airplanes for each 1 bundle of 10,000 auto parts from Mexico, and Mexico won't pay more than 2 bundles of 10,000 auto parts for each 1 airplane from the United States. Once this requirement is satisfied, the actual relative price in international trade is determined by supply and demand—and we'll turn to supply and demand in international trade in the next section. However, first let's look more deeply into the nature of the gains from trade.

Comparative Advantage versus Absolute Advantage

It's easy to accept the idea that Vietnam and Thailand have a comparative advantage in shrimp production: they have a tropical climate that's better suited to shrimp farming than that of the United States (even along the Gulf Coast), and they have a lot of usable coastal area. So the United States imports shrimp from Vietnam and Thailand. In other cases, however, it may be harder to understand why we import certain goods from abroad.

Pornchai Kittiwongsakul/AFP/Getty Images

With their tropical climate, Vietnam and Thailand have a comparative advantage in shrimp production.

U.S. imports of auto parts from Mexico is a case in point. There's nothing about Mexico's climate or resources that makes it especially good at manufacturing auto parts. In fact, it almost surely takes *fewer* hours of labor to produce an auto seat or wiring harness in the United States than in Mexico.

Why, then, do we buy Mexican auto parts? Because the gains from trade depend on *comparative advantage*, not *absolute advantage*. Yes, it takes less labor to produce a wiring harness in the United States than in Mexico. That is, the productivity of Mexican auto parts workers is less than that of their U.S. counterparts. But what determines comparative advantage is not the amount of resources used to produce a good but the opportunity cost of that good—here, the quantity of other goods forgone in order to produce an auto seat. And the opportunity cost of auto parts is lower in Mexico than in the United States.

Here's how it works: Mexican workers have low productivity compared with U.S. workers in the auto parts industry. But Mexican workers have even lower productivity compared with U.S. workers in other industries. Because Mexican labor productivity in industries other than auto parts is relatively very low, producing a wiring harness in Mexico, even though it takes a lot of labor, does not require forgoing the production of large quantities of other goods.

In the United States, the opposite is true: very high productivity in other industries (such as high-technology goods) means that producing an auto seat in the United States, even though it doesn't require much labor, requires sacrificing lots of other goods. So the opportunity cost of producing auto parts is less in Mexico than in the United States. Despite its lower labor productivity, Mexico has a comparative advantage in the production of many auto parts, although the United States has an absolute advantage.

Mexico's comparative advantage in auto parts is reflected in global markets by the wages Mexican workers are paid. That's because a country's wage rates, in general, reflect its labor productivity. In countries where labor is highly productive in many industries, employers are willing to pay high wages to attract workers, so competition among employers leads to an overall high wage rate. In countries where labor is less productive, competition for workers is less intense and wage rates are correspondingly lower.

As the accompanying Global Comparison shows, there is indeed a strong relationship between overall levels of productivity and wage rates around the world. Because Mexico has generally low productivity, it has a relatively low wage rate. Low wages, in turn, give Mexico a cost advantage in producing goods where its productivity is only moderately low, like auto parts. As a result, it's cheaper to produce these parts in Mexico than in the United States.

The kind of trade that takes place between low-wage, low-productivity economies like Mexico and high-wage, high-productivity economies like the United States gives rise to two common misperceptions. One, the *pauper labor fallacy*, is the belief that when a country with high wages imports goods produced by workers who are paid low wages, this must hurt the standard of living of workers in the importing country. The other, the *sweatshop labor fallacy*, is the belief that

PRODUCTIVITY AND WAGES AROUND THE WORLD

Is it true that both the pauper labor argument and the sweatshop labor argument are fallacies? Yes, it is. The real explanation for low wages in poor countries is low overall productivity.

The graph shows estimates of labor productivity, measured by the value of output (GDP) per worker, and wages, measured by the monthly compensation of the average worker, for several countries in 2009. Both productivity and wages are expressed as percentages of U.S. productivity and wages; for example, productivity and wages in Japan were 79% and 91%, respectively, of their U.S. levels. You can see the strong positive relationship between productivity and wages. The relationship isn't perfect. For example, Germany has higher wages than its productivity might lead you to expect. But simple comparisons of wages give a misleading sense of labor costs in poor countries: their low-wage advantage is mostly offset by low productivity.

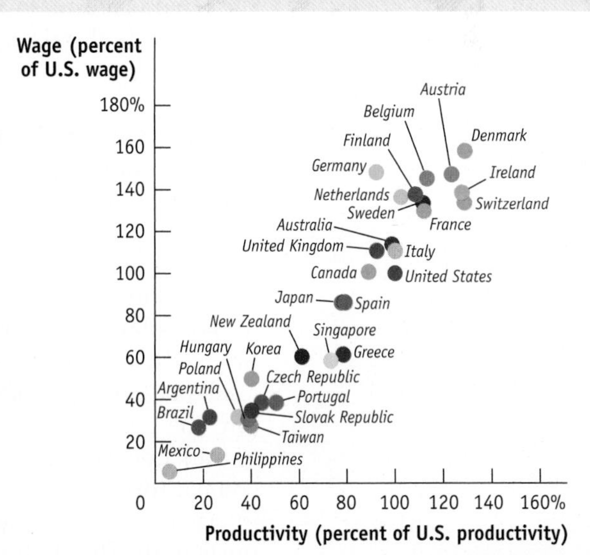

Source: Bureau of Labor Statistics; International Monetary Fund.

trade must be bad for workers in poor exporting countries because those workers are paid very low wages by our standards.

Both fallacies miss the nature of gains from trade: it's to the advantage of *both* countries if the poorer, lower-wage country exports goods in which it has a comparative advantage, even if its cost advantage in these goods depends on low wages. That is, both countries are able to achieve a higher standard of living through trade.

It's particularly important to understand that buying a good made by someone who is paid much lower wages than most U.S. workers doesn't necessarily imply that you're taking advantage of that person. It depends on the alternatives. Because workers in poor countries have low productivity across the board, they are offered low wages whether they produce goods exported to America or goods sold in local markets. A job that looks terrible by rich-country standards can be a step up for someone in a poor country.

International trade that depends on low-wage exports can nonetheless raise a country's standard of living. This is especially true of very-low-wage nations. For example, Bangladesh and similar countries would be much poorer than they are—their citizens might even be starving—if they weren't able to export goods such as clothing based on their low wage rates.

Sources of Comparative Advantage

International trade is driven by comparative advantage, but where does comparative advantage come from? Economists who study international trade have found three main sources of comparative advantage: international differences in *climate,* international differences in *factor endowments,* and international differences in *technology.*

Differences in Climate One key reason the opportunity cost of producing shrimp in Vietnam and Thailand is less than in the United States is that shrimp need warm water—Vietnam has plenty of that, but America doesn't. In general, differences in climate play a significant role in international trade. Tropical countries export tropical products like coffee, sugar, bananas, and shrimp. Countries in the temperate zones export crops like wheat and corn. Some trade is even driven by the difference in seasons between the northern and southern hemispheres: winter deliveries of Chilean grapes and New Zealand apples have become commonplace in U.S. and European supermarkets.

Differences in Factor Endowments Canada is a major exporter of forest products—lumber and products derived from lumber, like pulp and paper—to the United States. These exports don't reflect the special skill of Canadian lumberjacks. Canada has a comparative advantage in forest products because its forested area is much greater compared to the size of its labor force than the ratio of forestland to the labor force in the United States.

Forestland, like labor and capital, is a *factor of production:* an input used to produce goods and services. (Recall from Chapter 2 that the factors of production are land, labor, physical capital, and human capital.) Due to history and geography, the mix of available factors of production differs among countries, providing an important source of comparative advantage. The relationship between comparative advantage and factor availability is found in an influential model of international trade, the *Heckscher–Ohlin model,* developed by two Swedish economists in the first half of the twentieth century.

Two key concepts in the model are *factor abundance* and *factor intensity.* Factor abundance refers to how large a country's supply of a factor is relative to its supply of other factors. Factor intensity refers to the fact that producers use different ratios of factors of production in the production of different goods. For example, oil refineries use much more capital per worker than clothing factories. Economists use the term **factor intensity** to describe this difference among goods: oil refining is capital-intensive, because it tends to use a high ratio of capital to labor, but auto seats production is labor-intensive, because it tends to use a high ratio of labor to capital.

The **factor intensity** of production of a good is a measure of which factor is used in relatively greater quantities than other factors in production.

According to the **Heckscher–Ohlin model,** a country has a comparative advantage in a good whose production is intensive in the factors that are abundantly available in that country.

According to the **Heckscher–Ohlin model,** *a country that has an abundant supply of a factor of production will have a comparative advantage in goods whose production is intensive in that factor.* So a country that has a relative abundance of capital will have a comparative advantage in capital-intensive industries such as oil refining, but a country that has a relative abundance of labor will have a comparative advantage in labor-intensive industries such as auto seats production.

The basic intuition behind this result is simple and based on opportunity cost. The opportunity cost of a given factor—the value that the factor would generate in alternative uses—is low for a country when it is relatively abundant in that factor. Relative to the United States, Mexico has an abundance of low-skilled labor. As a result, the opportunity cost of the production of low-skilled, labor-intensive goods is lower in Mexico than in the United States.

The most dramatic example of the validity of the Heckscher–Ohlin model is world trade in clothing. Clothing production is a labor-intensive activity: it doesn't take much physical capital, nor does it require a lot of human capital in the form of highly educated workers. So you would expect labor-abundant countries such as China and Bangladesh to have a comparative advantage in clothing production. And they do.

That much international trade is the result of differences in factor endowments helps explain another fact: international specialization of production is often *incomplete.* That is, a country often maintains some domestic production of a good that it imports. A good example of this is the United States and oil. Saudi Arabia exports oil to the United States because Saudi Arabia has an abundant supply of oil relative to its other factors of production; the United States exports medical devices to Saudi Arabia because it has an abundant supply of expertise in medical technology relative to its other factors of production. But the United States also produces some oil domestically because the size of its domestic oil reserves in Texas and Alaska makes it economical to do so.

In our supply and demand analysis in the next section, we'll consider incomplete specialization by a country to be the norm. We should emphasize, however, that the fact that countries often incompletely specialize does not in any way change the conclusion that there are gains from trade.

Differences in Technology In the 1970s and 1980s, Japan became by far the world's largest exporter of automobiles, selling large numbers to the United States and the rest of the world. Japan's comparative advantage in automobiles wasn't the result of climate. Nor can it easily be attributed to differences in factor endowments: aside from a scarcity of land, Japan's mix of available factors is quite similar to that in other advanced countries. Instead, Japan's comparative advantage in automobiles was based on the superior production techniques developed by its manufacturers, which allowed them to produce more cars with a given amount of labor and capital than their American or European counterparts.

Japan's comparative advantage in automobiles was a case of comparative advantage caused by differences in technology—the techniques used in production.

The causes of differences in technology are somewhat mysterious. Sometimes they seem to be based on knowledge accumulated through experience—for

FOR INQUIRING MINDS

INCREASING RETURNS TO SCALE AND INTERNATIONAL TRADE

Most analysis of international trade focuses on how differences between countries—differences in climate, factor endowments, and technology—create national comparative advantage. However, economists have also pointed out another reason for international trade: the role of *increasing returns to scale.*

Production of a good is characterized by increasing returns to scale if the productivity of labor and other resources used in production rise with the quantity of output. For example, in an industry characterized by increasing returns to scale, increasing output by 10% might require only 8% more labor and 9% more raw materials. Examples of industries with increasing returns to scale include auto manufacturing, oil refining, and the production of jumbo jets, all of which require large outlays of capital. Increasing returns to scale (sometimes also called economies of scale) can give rise to monopoly, a situation in which an industry is composed of only one producer, because it gives large firms a cost advantage over small ones.

But increasing returns to scale can also give rise to international trade. The logic runs as follows: If production of a good is characterized by increasing returns to scale, it makes sense to concentrate production in only a few locations, so each location has a high level of output. But that also means production occurs in only a few countries that export the good to other countries. A commonly cited example is the North American auto industry: although both the United States and Canada produce automobiles and their components, each particular model or component tends to be produced in only one of the two countries and exported to the other.

Increasing returns to scale probably play a large role in the trade in manufactured goods between advanced countries, which is about 25% of the total value of world trade.

example, Switzerland's comparative advantage in watches reflects a long tradition of watchmaking. Sometimes they are the result of a set of innovations that for some reason occur in one country but not in others. Technological advantage, however, is often transitory. For example, by adopting lean production, American auto manufacturers have now closed much of the gap in productivity with their Japanese competitors. In addition, Europe's aircraft industry has closed a similar gap with the U.S. aircraft industry. At any given point in time, however, differences in technology are a major source of comparative advantage.

ECONOMICS ➤ IN ACTION

SKILL AND COMPARATIVE ADVANTAGE

In 1953 U.S. workers were clearly better equipped with machinery than their counterparts in other countries. Most economists at the time thought that America's comparative advantage lay in capital-intensive goods. But Wassily Leontief made a surprising discovery: America's comparative advantage was in something other than capital-intensive goods. In fact, goods that the United States exported were slightly less capital-intensive than goods the country imported. This discovery came to be known as the Leontief paradox, and it led to a sustained effort to make sense of U.S. trade patterns.

The main resolution of this paradox, it turns out, depends on the definition of *capital.* U.S. exports aren't intensive in *physical* capital—machines and buildings. Instead, they are *skill-intensive*—that is, they are intensive in *human* capital. U.S. exporting industries use a substantially higher ratio of highly educated workers to other workers than is found in U.S. industries that compete against imports. For example, one of America's biggest export sectors is aircraft; the aircraft industry employs large numbers of engineers and other people with graduate degrees relative to the number of manual laborers. Conversely, we import a lot of clothing, which is often produced by workers with little formal education.

In general, countries with highly educated workforces tend to export skill-intensive goods, while countries with less educated workforces tend to export goods whose production requires little skilled labor. Figure 19-4 illustrates this point by comparing the goods the United States imports from Germany, a country with a highly educated labor force, with the goods the United States imports from Bangladesh, where about half of the adult population is still illiterate. In each country industries are ranked, first, according to how skill-intensive they are. Next, for each industry, we calculate its share of exports to the United States. This allows us to plot, for each country, various industries according to their skill intensity and their share of exports to the United States.

In Figure 19-4, the horizontal axis shows a measure of the skill intensity of different industries, and the vertical axes show the share of U.S. imports in each industry coming from Germany (on the left) and Bangladesh (on the right). As you can see, each country's exports to the United States reflect its skill level. The curve representing Germany slopes upward: the more skill-intensive a German industry is, the higher its share of exports to the United States. In contrast, the curve representing Bangladesh slopes downward: the less skill-intensive a Bangladeshi industry is, the higher its share of exports to the United States.

FIGURE 19-4 Education, Skill Intensity, and Trade

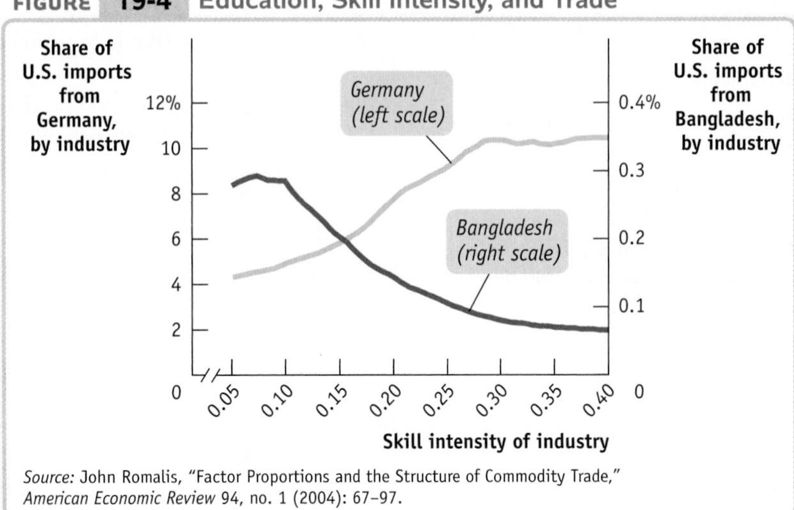

Source: John Romalis, "Factor Proportions and the Structure of Commodity Trade," *American Economic Review* 94, no. 1 (2004): 67–97.

CHECK YOUR UNDERSTANDING 19-1

1. In the United States, the opportunity cost of 1 ton of corn is 50 bicycles. In China, the opportunity cost of 1 bicycle is 0.01 ton of corn.
   a. Determine the pattern of comparative advantage.
   b. In autarky, the United States can produce 200,000 bicycles if no corn is produced, and China can produce 3,000 tons of corn if no bicycles are produced. Draw each country's production possibility frontier assuming constant opportunity cost, with tons of corn on the vertical axis and bicycles on the horizontal axis.
   c. With trade, each country specializes its production. The United States consumes 1,000 tons of corn and 200,000 bicycles; China consumes 3,000 tons of corn and 100,000 bicycles. Indicate the production and consumption points on your diagrams, and use them to explain the gains from trade.
2. Explain the following patterns of trade using the Heckscher–Ohlin model.
   a. France exports wine to the United States, and the United States exports movies to France.
   b. Brazil exports shoes to the United States, and the United States exports shoe-making machinery to Brazil.

Solutions appear at back of book.

Quick Review

- **Imports** and **exports** account for a growing share of the U.S. economy and the economies of many other countries.
- The growth of international trade and other international linkages is known as **globalization.**
- International trade is driven by comparative advantage. The **Ricardian model of international trade** shows that trade between two countries makes both countries better off than they would be in **autarky**—that is, there are gains from international trade.
- The main sources of comparative advantage are international differences in climate, factor endowments, and technology.
- The **Heckscher–Ohlin model** shows how comparative advantage can arise from differences in factor endowments: goods differ in their **factor intensity,** and countries tend to export goods that are intensive in the factors they have in abundance.

Supply, Demand, and International Trade

Simple models of comparative advantage are helpful for understanding the fundamental causes of international trade. However, to analyze the effects of international trade at a more detailed level and to understand trade policy, it helps to return to the supply and demand model. We'll start by looking at the effects of imports on domestic producers and consumers, then turn to the effects of exports.

The **domestic demand curve** shows how the quantity of a good demanded by domestic consumers depends on the price of that good.

The **domestic supply curve** shows how the quantity of a good supplied by domestic producers depends on the price of that good.

The **world price** of a good is the price at which that good can be bought or sold abroad.

The Effects of Imports

Figure 19-5 shows the U.S. market for auto seats, ignoring international trade for a moment. It introduces a few new concepts: the *domestic demand curve,* the *domestic supply curve,* and the domestic or autarky price.

The **domestic demand curve** shows how the quantity of a good demanded by residents of a country depends on the price of that good. Why "domestic"? Because people living in other countries may demand the good, too. Once we introduce international trade, we need to distinguish between purchases of a good by domestic consumers and purchases by foreign consumers. So the domestic demand curve reflects only the demand of residents of our own country. Similarly, the **domestic supply curve** shows how the quantity of a good supplied by producers inside our own country depends on the price of that good. Once we introduce international trade, we need to distinguish between the supply of domestic producers and foreign supply—supply brought in from abroad.

In autarky, with no international trade in auto seats, the equilibrium in this market would be determined by the intersection of the domestic demand and domestic supply curves, point *A*. The equilibrium price of auto seats would be P_A, and the equilibrium quantity of auto seats produced and consumed would be Q_A. As always, both consumers and producers gain from the existence of the domestic market. In autarky, consumer surplus would be equal to the area of the blue-shaded triangle in Figure 19-5. Producer surplus would be equal to the area of the red-shaded triangle. And total surplus would be equal to the sum of these two shaded triangles.

Now let's imagine opening up this market to imports. To do this, we must make an assumption about the supply of imports. The simplest assumption, which we will adopt here, is that unlimited quantities of auto seats can be purchased from abroad at a fixed price, known as the **world price** of auto seats. Figure 19-6 shows a situation in which the world price of an auto seat, P_W, is lower than the price of an auto seat that would prevail in the domestic market in autarky, P_A.

FIGURE 19-5 Consumer and Producer Surplus in Autarky

In the absence of trade, the domestic price is P_A, the autarky price at which the domestic supply curve and the domestic demand curve intersect. The quantity produced and consumed domestically is Q_A. Consumer surplus is represented by the blue-shaded area, and producer surplus is represented by the red-shaded area.

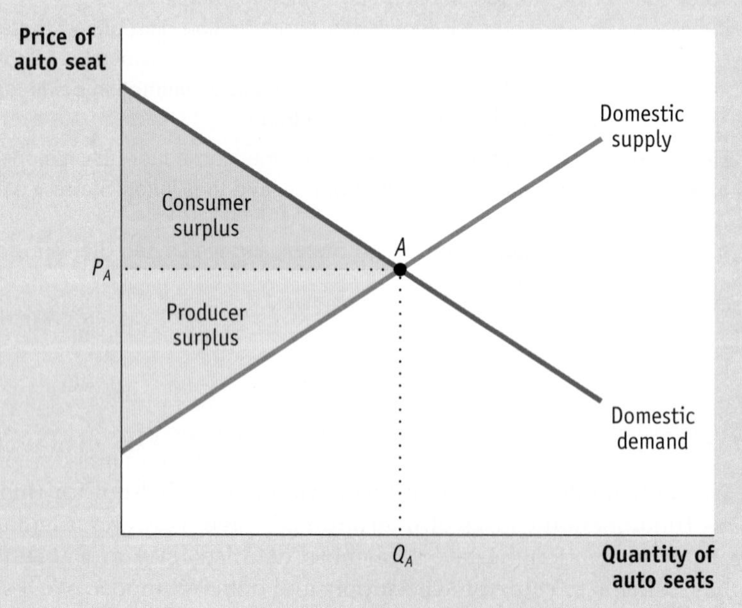

FIGURE 19-6 The Domestic Market with Imports

Here the world price of auto parts, P_W, is below the autarky price, P_A. When the economy is opened to international trade, imports enter the domestic market, and the domestic price falls from the autarky price, P_A, to the world price, P_W. As the price falls, the domestic quantity demanded rises from Q_A to Q_D and the domestic quantity supplied falls from Q_A to Q_S. The difference between domestic quantity demanded and domestic quantity supplied at P_W, the quantity $Q_D - Q_S$, is filled by imports.

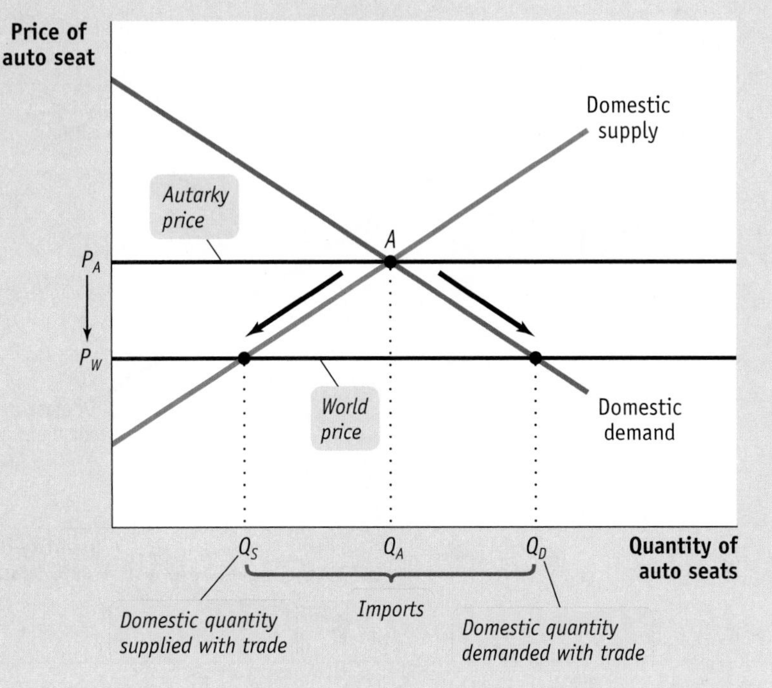

Given that the world price is below the domestic price of an auto seat, it is profitable for importers to buy auto seats abroad and resell them domestically. The imported auto seats increase the supply of auto seats in the domestic market, driving down the domestic market price. Auto seats will continue to be imported until the domestic price falls to a level equal to the world price.

The result is shown in Figure 19-6. Because of imports, the domestic price of an auto seat falls from P_A to P_W. The quantity of auto seats demanded by domestic consumers rises from Q_A to Q_D, and the quantity supplied by domestic producers falls from Q_A to Q_S. The difference between the domestic quantity demanded and the domestic quantity supplied, $Q_D - Q_S$, is filled by imports.

Now let's turn to the effects of imports on consumer surplus and producer surplus. Because imports of auto seats lead to a fall in their domestic price, consumer surplus rises and producer surplus falls. Figure 19-7 shows how this works. We label four areas: *W, X, Y,* and *Z*. The autarky consumer surplus we identified in Figure 19-5 corresponds to *W*, and the autarky producer surplus corresponds to the sum of *X* and *Y*. The fall in the domestic price to the world price leads to an increase in consumer surplus; it increases by *X* and *Z*, so consumer surplus now equals the sum of *W, X,* and *Z*. At the same time, producers lose *X* in surplus, so producer surplus now equals only *Y*.

The table in Figure 19-7 summarizes the changes in consumer and producer surplus when the auto seats market is opened to imports. Consumers gain surplus equal to the areas $X + Z$. Producers lose surplus equal to *X*. So the sum of producer and consumer surplus—the total surplus generated in the auto seats market—increases by *Z*. As a result of trade, consumers gain and producers lose, but the gain to consumers exceeds the loss to producers.

This is an important result. We have just shown that opening up a market to imports leads to a net gain in total surplus, which is what we should have

FIGURE 19-7 The Effects of Imports on Surplus

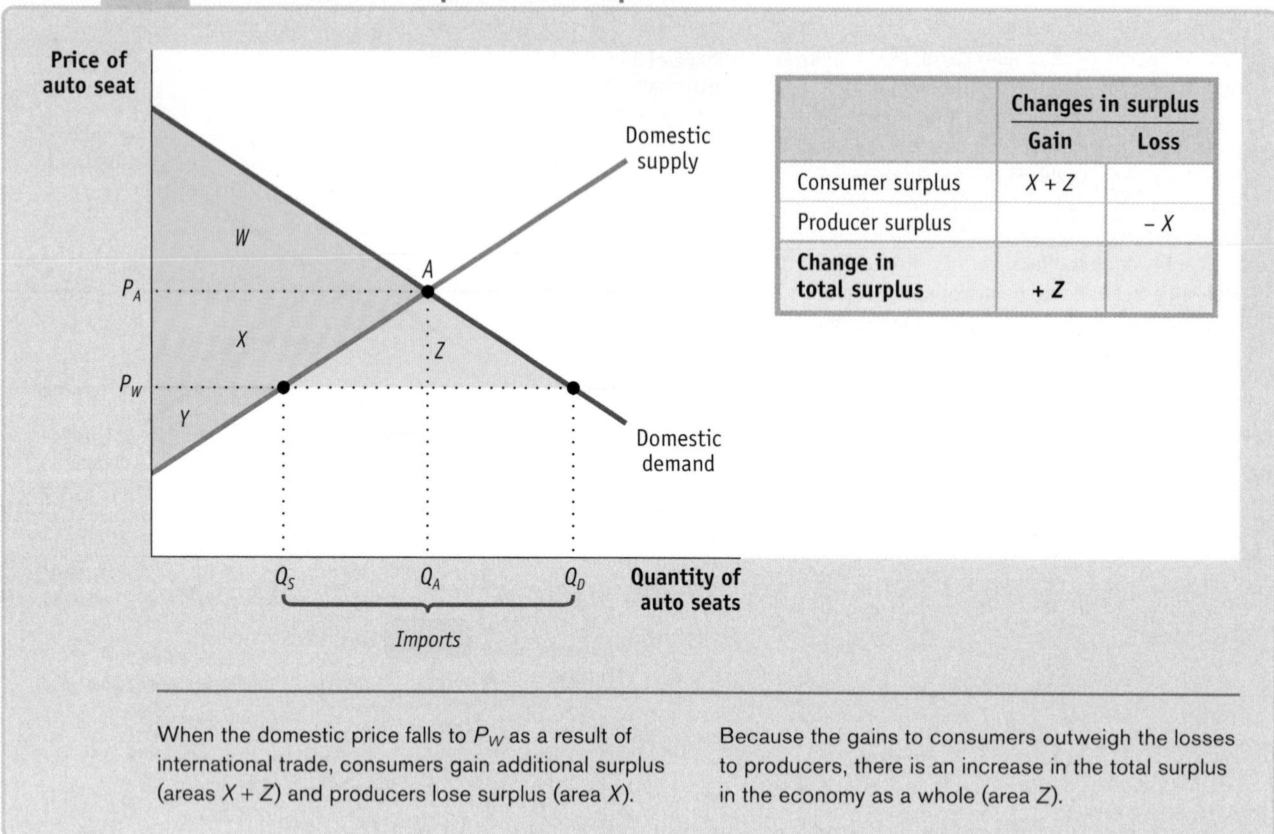

	Changes in surplus: Gain	Changes in surplus: Loss
Consumer surplus	$X + Z$	
Producer surplus		$-X$
Change in total surplus	$+Z$	

When the domestic price falls to P_W as a result of international trade, consumers gain additional surplus (areas $X + Z$) and producers lose surplus (area X). Because the gains to consumers outweigh the losses to producers, there is an increase in the total surplus in the economy as a whole (area Z).

expected given the proposition that there are gains from international trade. However, we have also learned that although the country as a whole gains, some groups—in this case, domestic producers of auto parts—lose as a result of international trade. As we'll see shortly, the fact that international trade typically creates losers as well as winners is crucial for understanding the politics of trade policy.

We turn next to the case in which a country exports a good.

The Effects of Exports

Figure 19-8 shows the effects on a country when it exports a good, in this case airplanes. For this example, we assume that unlimited quantities of airplanes can be sold abroad at a given world price, P_W, which is higher than the price that would prevail in the domestic market in autarky, P_A.

The higher world price makes it profitable for exporters to buy airplanes domestically and sell them overseas. The purchases of domestic airplanes drive the domestic price up until it is equal to the world price. As a result, the quantity demanded by domestic consumers falls from Q_A to Q_D and the quantity supplied by domestic producers rises from Q_A to Q_S. This difference between domestic production and domestic consumption, $Q_S - Q_D$, is exported.

Like imports, exports lead to an overall gain in total surplus for the exporting country but also create losers as well as winners. Figure 19-9 shows the effects of airplane exports on producer and consumer surplus. In the absence of trade, the price of each airplane would be P_A. Consumer surplus in the absence of trade is the sum of areas *W* and *X*, and producer surplus is area *Y*. As a result of trade, price rises from P_A *to* P_W, consumer surplus falls to *W*, and producer surplus rises to $Y + X + Z$. So producers gain $X + Z$, consumers lose *X*, and, as shown in the

FIGURE 19-8 The Domestic Market with Exports

Here the world price, P_W, is greater than the autarky price, P_A. When the economy is opened to international trade, some of the domestic supply is now exported. The domestic price rises from the autarky price, P_A, to the world price, P_W. As the price rises, the domestic quantity demanded falls from Q_A to Q_D and the domestic quantity supplied rises from Q_A to Q_S. The portion of domestic production that is not consumed domestically, $Q_S - Q_D$, is exported.

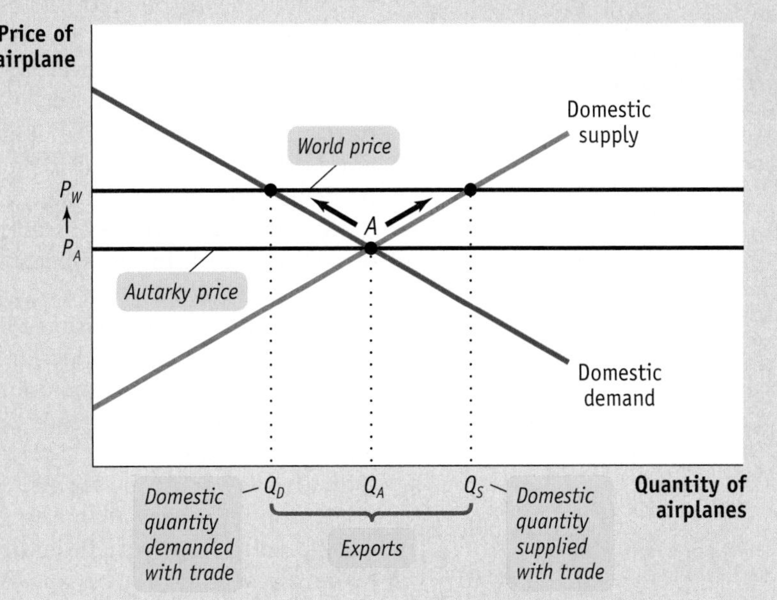

table accompanying the figure, the economy as a whole gains total surplus in the amount of Z.

We have learned, then, that imports of a particular good hurt domestic producers of that good but help domestic consumers, whereas exports of a particular good hurt domestic consumers of that good but help domestic producers. In each case, the gains are larger than the losses.

FIGURE 19-9 The Effects of Exports on Surplus

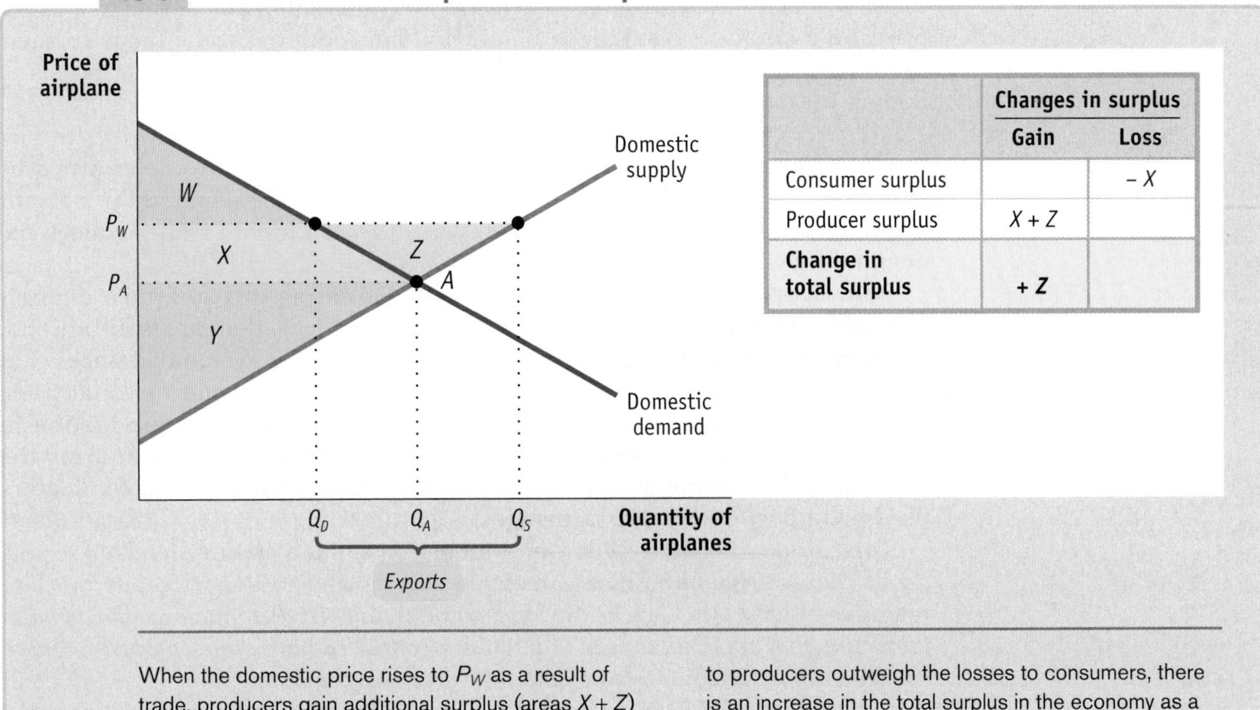

	Changes in surplus	
	Gain	Loss
Consumer surplus		$-X$
Producer surplus	$X + Z$	
Change in total surplus	**$+Z$**	

When the domestic price rises to P_W as a result of trade, producers gain additional surplus (areas $X + Z$) but consumers lose surplus (area X). Because the gains to producers outweigh the losses to consumers, there is an increase in the total surplus in the economy as a whole (area Z).

Exporting industries produce goods and services that are sold abroad.

Import-competing industries produce goods and services that are also imported.

International Trade and Wages

So far we have focused on the effects of international trade on producers and consumers in a particular industry. For many purposes this is a very helpful approach. However, producers and consumers are not the only parts of society affected by trade—so are the owners of factors of production. In particular, the owners of labor, land, and capital employed in producing goods that are exported, or goods that compete with imported goods, can be deeply affected by trade.

Moreover, the effects of trade aren't limited to just those industries that export or compete with imports because *factors of production can often move between industries.* So now we turn our attention to the long-run effects of international trade on income distribution—how a country's total income is allocated among its various factors of production.

To begin our analysis, consider the position of Maria, an accountant at Midwest Auto Parts, Inc. If the economy is opened up to imports of auto parts from Mexico, the domestic auto parts industry will contract, and it will hire fewer accountants. But accounting is a profession with employment opportunities in many industries, and Maria might well find a better job in the aircraft industry, which expands as a result of international trade. So it may not be appropriate to think of her as a producer of auto parts who is hurt by competition from imported parts. Rather, we should think of her as an accountant who is affected by auto part imports only to the extent that these imports change the wages of accountants in the economy as a whole.

The wage rate of accountants is a *factor price*—the price employers have to pay for the services of a factor of production. One key question about international trade is how it affects factor prices—not just narrowly defined factors of production like accountants, but broadly defined factors such as capital, unskilled labor, and college-educated labor.

Earlier in this chapter we described the Heckscher–Ohlin model of trade, which states that comparative advantage is determined by a country's factor endowment. This model also suggests how international trade affects factor prices in a country: compared to autarky, international trade tends to raise the prices of factors that are abundantly available and reduce the prices of factors that are scarce.

We won't work this out in detail, but the idea is simple. The prices of factors of production, like the prices of goods and services, are determined by supply and demand. If international trade increases the demand for a factor of production, that factor's price will rise; if international trade reduces the demand for a factor of production, that factor's price will fall.

Now think of a country's industries as consisting of two kinds: **exporting industries,** which produce goods and services that are sold abroad, and **import-competing industries,** which produce goods and services that are also imported from abroad. Compared with autarky, international trade leads to higher production in exporting industries and lower production in import-competing industries. This indirectly increases the demand for the factors used by exporting industries and decreases the demand for factors used by import-competing industries.

In addition, the Heckscher–Ohlin model says that a country tends to export goods that are intensive in its abundant factors and to import goods that are intensive in its scarce factors. So *international trade tends to increase the demand for factors that are abundant in our country compared with other countries, and to decrease the demand for factors that are scarce in our country compared with other countries.* As a result, *the prices of abundant factors tend to rise, and the prices of scarce factors tend to fall as international trade grows.* In other words, international trade tends to redistribute income toward a country's abundant factors and away from its less abundant factors.

The Economics in Action at the end of the preceding section pointed out that U.S. exports tend to be human-capital-intensive and U.S. imports tend to be unskilled-labor-intensive. This suggests that the effect of international trade on U.S. factor markets is to raise the wage rate of highly educated American workers and reduce the wage rate of unskilled American workers.

This effect has been a source of much concern in recent years. Wage inequality—the gap between the wages of high-paid and low-paid workers—has increased substantially over the last 30 years. Some economists believe that growing international trade is an important factor in that trend. If international trade has the effects predicted by the Heckscher–Ohlin model, its growth raises the wages of highly educated American workers, who already have relatively high wages, and lowers the wages of less educated American workers, who already have relatively low wages. But keep in mind another phenomenon: trade reduces the income inequality *between* countries as poor countries improve their standard of living by exporting to rich countries.

How important are these effects? In some historical episodes, the impacts of international trade on factor prices have been very large. As we explain in the following Economics in Action, the opening of transatlantic trade in the late nineteenth century had a large negative impact on land rents in Europe, hurting landowners but helping workers and owners of capital.

The effects of trade on wages in the United States have generated considerable controversy in recent years. Most economists who have studied the issue agree that growing imports of labor-intensive products from newly industrializing economies, and the export of high-technology goods in return, have helped cause a widening wage gap between highly educated and less educated workers in this country. However, most economists believe that it is only one of several forces explaining the growth in American wage inequality.

ECONOMICS ➤ IN ACTION

TRADE, WAGES, AND LAND PRICES IN THE NINETEENTH CENTURY

Beginning around 1870, there was an explosive growth of world trade in agricultural products, based largely on the steam engine. Steam-powered ships could cross the ocean much more quickly and reliably than sailing ships. Until about 1860, steamships had higher costs than sailing ships, but after that costs dropped sharply. At the same time, steam-powered rail transport made it possible to bring grain and other bulk goods cheaply from the interior to ports. The result was that land-abundant countries—the United States, Canada, Argentina, and Australia—began shipping large quantities of agricultural goods to the densely populated, land-scarce countries of Europe.

This opening up of international trade led to higher prices of agricultural products, such as wheat, in exporting countries and a decline in their prices in importing countries. Notably,

Archive Images/Alamy

International trade redistributes income toward a country's abundant factors and away from its less abundant factors.

the difference between wheat prices in the midwestern United States and England plunged.

The change in agricultural prices created winners and losers on both sides of the Atlantic as factor prices adjusted. In England, land prices fell by half compared with average wages; landowners found their purchasing power sharply reduced, but workers benefited from cheaper food. In the United States, the reverse happened: land prices doubled compared with wages. Landowners did very well, but workers found the purchasing power of their wages dented by rising food prices.

Quick Review

- The intersection of the **domestic demand curve** and the **domestic supply curve** determines the domestic price of a good. When a market is opened to international trade, the domestic price is driven to equal the **world price.**
- If the world price is lower than the autarky price, trade leads to imports and the domestic price falls to the world price. There are overall gains from international trade because the gain in consumer surplus exceeds the loss in producer surplus.
- If the world price is higher than the autarky price, trade leads to exports and the domestic price rises to the world price. There are overall gains from international trade because the gain in producer surplus exceeds the loss in consumer surplus.
- Trade leads to an expansion of **exporting industries,** which increases demand for a country's abundant factors, and a contraction of **import-competing industries,** which decreases demand for its scarce factors.

CHECK YOUR UNDERSTANDING 19-2

1. Due to a strike by truckers, trade in food between the United States and Mexico is halted. In autarky, the price of Mexican grapes is lower than that of U.S. grapes. Using a diagram of the U.S. domestic demand curve and the U.S. domestic supply curve for grapes, explain the effect of these events on the following.
   a. U.S. grape consumers' surplus
   b. U.S. grape producers' surplus
   c. U.S. total surplus
2. What effect do you think this event will have on Mexican grape producers? Mexican grape pickers? Mexican grape consumers? U.S. grape pickers?

Solutions appear at back of book.

The Effects of Trade Protection

Ever since David Ricardo laid out the principle of comparative advantage in the early nineteenth century, most economists have advocated **free trade.** That is, they have argued that government policy should not attempt either to reduce or to increase the levels of exports and imports that occur naturally as a result of supply and demand. Despite the free-trade arguments of economists, however, many governments use taxes and other restrictions to limit imports. Less frequently, governments offer subsidies to encourage exports. Policies that limit imports, usually with the goal of protecting domestic producers in import-competing industries from foreign competition, are known as **trade protection** or simply as **protection.**

Let's look at the two most common protectionist policies, tariffs and import quotas, then turn to the reasons governments follow these policies.

An economy has **free trade** when the government does not attempt either to reduce or to increase the levels of exports and imports that occur naturally as a result of supply and demand.

Policies that limit imports are known as **trade protection** or simply as **protection.**

A **tariff** is a tax levied on imports.

The Effects of a Tariff

A **tariff** is a form of excise tax, one that is levied only on sales of imported goods. For example, the U.S. government could declare that anyone bringing in auto seats must pay a tariff of $100 per unit. In the distant past, tariffs were an important source of government revenue because they were relatively easy to collect. But in the modern world, tariffs are usually intended to discourage imports and protect import-competing domestic producers rather than as a source of government revenue.

The tariff raises both the price received by domestic producers and the price paid by domestic consumers. Suppose, for example, that our country imports auto seats, and an auto seat costs $200 on the world market. As we saw earlier, under free trade the domestic price would also be $200. But if a tariff of $100 per

FIGURE 19-10 The Effect of a Tariff

A tariff raises the domestic price of the good from P_W to P_T. The domestic quantity demanded shrinks from Q_D to Q_{DT}, and the domestic quantity supplied increases from Q_S to Q_{ST}. As a result, imports—which had been $Q_D - Q_S$ before the tariff was imposed—shrink to $Q_{DT} - Q_{ST}$ after the tariff is imposed.

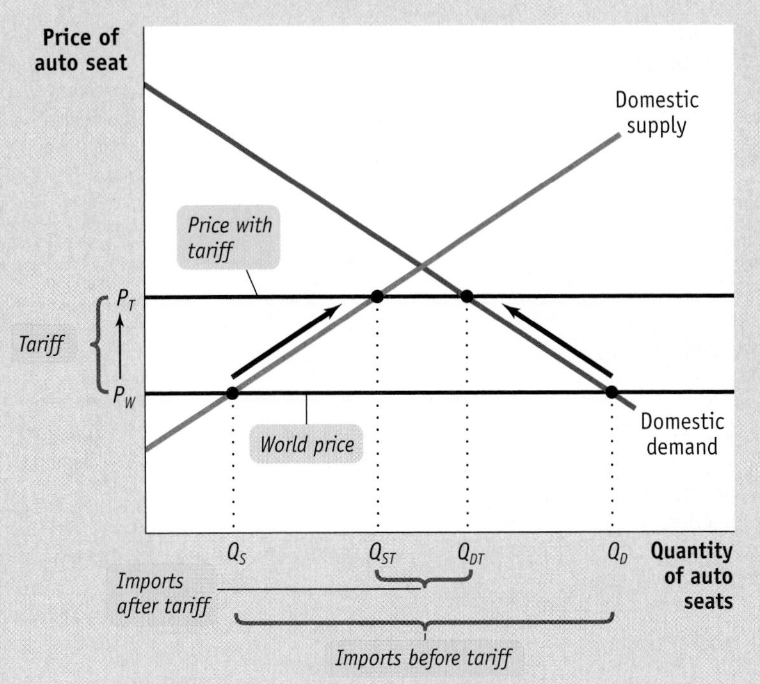

unit is imposed, the domestic price will rise to $300, because it won't be profitable to import auto seats unless the price in the domestic market is high enough to compensate importers for the cost of paying the tariff.

Figure 19-10 illustrates the effects of a tariff on imports of auto seats. As before, we assume that P_W is the world price of an auto seat. Before the tariff is imposed, imports have driven the domestic price down to P_W, so that pre-tariff domestic production is Q_S, pre-tariff domestic consumption is Q_D, and pre-tariff imports are $Q_D - Q_S$.

Now suppose that the government imposes a tariff on each auto seat imported. As a consequence, it is no longer profitable to import auto seats unless the domestic price received by the importer is greater than or equal to the world price *plus* the tariff. So the domestic price rises to P_T, which is equal to the world price, P_W, plus the tariff. Domestic production rises to Q_{ST}, domestic consumption falls to Q_{DT}, and imports fall to $Q_{DT} - Q_{ST}$.

A tariff, then, raises domestic prices, leading to increased domestic production and reduced domestic consumption compared to the situation under free trade. Figure 19-11 shows the effects on surplus. There are three effects:

1. The higher domestic price increases producer surplus, a gain equal to area *A*.
2. The higher domestic price reduces consumer surplus, a reduction equal to the sum of areas *A*, *B*, *C*, and *D*.
3. The tariff yields revenue to the government. How much revenue? The government collects the tariff—which, remember, is equal to the difference between P_T and P_W on each of the $Q_{DT} - Q_{ST}$ units imported. So total revenue is $(P_T - P_W) \times (Q_{DT} - Q_{ST})$. This is equal to area *C*.

The welfare effects of a tariff are summarized in the table in Figure 19-11. Producers gain, consumers lose, and the government gains. But consumer losses are greater than the sum of producer and government gains, leading to a net reduction in total surplus equal to areas $B + D$.

FIGURE 19-11 A Tariff Reduces Total Surplus

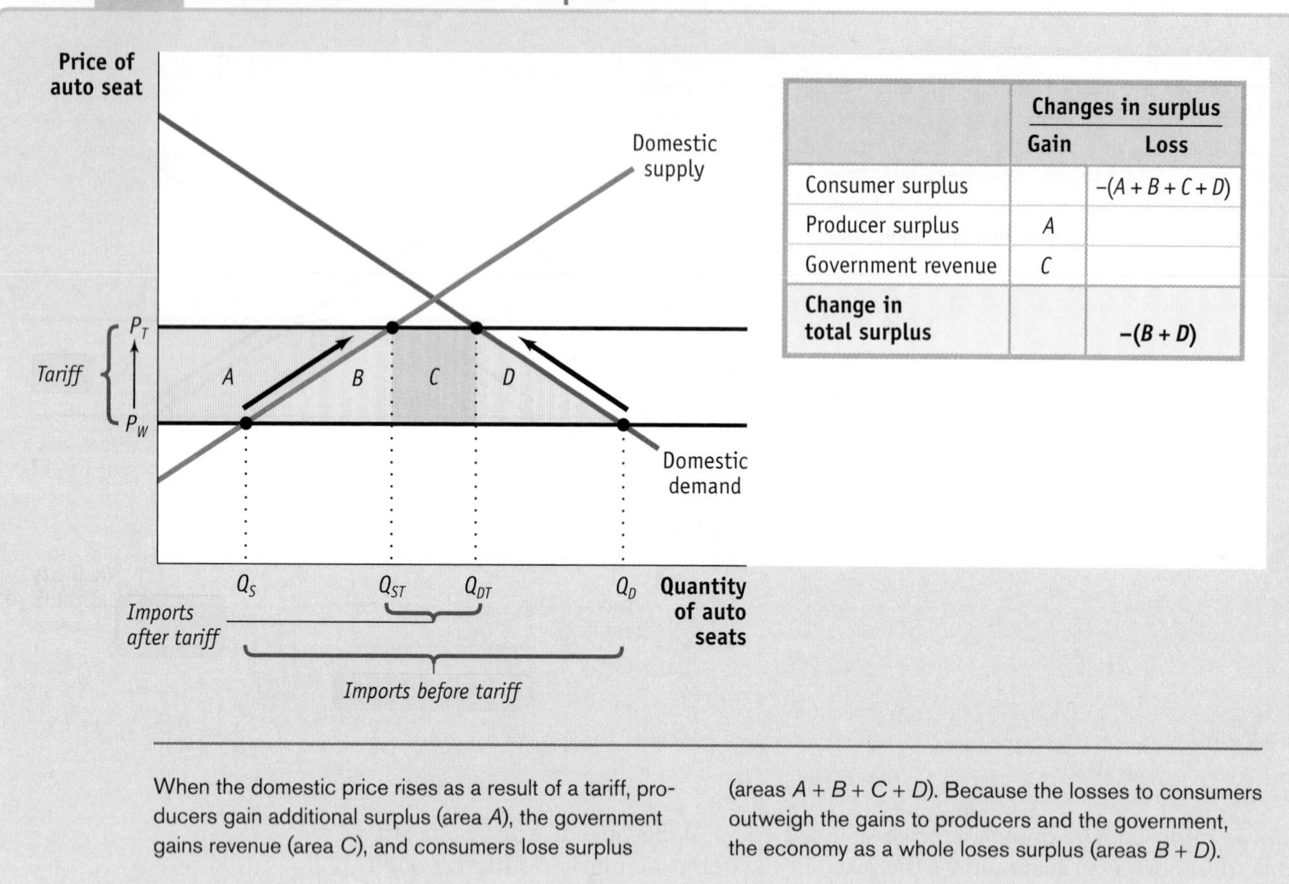

	Changes in surplus	
	Gain	**Loss**
Consumer surplus		$-(A + B + C + D)$
Producer surplus	A	
Government revenue	C	
Change in total surplus		**$-(B + D)$**

When the domestic price rises as a result of a tariff, producers gain additional surplus (area *A*), the government gains revenue (area *C*), and consumers lose surplus (areas *A* + *B* + *C* + *D*). Because the losses to consumers outweigh the gains to producers and the government, the economy as a whole loses surplus (areas *B* + *D*).

An excise tax creates inefficiency, or deadweight loss, because it prevents mutually beneficial trades from occurring. The same is true of a tariff, where the deadweight loss imposed on society is equal to the loss in total surplus represented by areas $B + D$.

Tariffs generate deadweight losses because they create inefficiencies in two ways:

1. Some mutually beneficial trades go unexploited: some consumers who are willing to pay more than the world price, P_W, do not purchase the good, even though P_W is the true cost of a unit of the good to the economy. The cost of this inefficiency is represented in Figure 19-11 by area *D*.
2. The economy's resources are wasted on inefficient production: some producers whose cost exceeds P_W produce the good, even though an additional unit of the good can be purchased abroad for P_W. The cost of this inefficiency is represented in Figure 19-11 by area *B*.

The Effects of an Import Quota

An **import quota** is a legal limit on the quantity of a good that can be imported.

An **import quota,** another form of trade protection, is a legal limit on the quantity of a good that can be imported. For example, a U.S. import quota on Mexican auto seats might limit the quantity imported each year to 500,000 units. Import quotas are usually administered through licenses: a number of licenses are issued, each giving the license-holder the right to import a limited quantity of the good each year.

A quota on sales has the same effect as an excise tax, with one difference: the money that would otherwise have accrued to the government as tax revenue under an excise tax becomes license-holders' revenue under a quota—also known as quota rents. Similarly, an import quota has the same effect as a tariff, with one difference: the money that would otherwise have been government revenue becomes quota rents to license-holders. Look again at Figure 19-11. An import quota that limits imports to $Q_{DT} - Q_{ST}$ will raise the domestic price of auto parts by the same amount as the tariff we considered previously. That is, it will raise the domestic price from P_W to P_T. However, area C will now represent quota rents rather than government revenue.

Who receives import licenses and so collects the quota rents? In the case of U.S. import protection, the answer may surprise you: the most important import licenses—mainly for clothing, to a lesser extent for sugar—are granted to foreign governments.

Because the quota rents for most U.S. import quotas go to foreigners, the cost to the nation of such quotas is larger than that of a comparable tariff (a tariff that leads to the same level of imports). In Figure 19-11 the net loss to the United States from such an import quota would be equal to areas $B + C + D$, the difference between consumer losses and producer gains.

ECONOMICS ➤ IN ACTION

TRADE PROTECTION IN THE UNITED STATES

The United States today generally follows a policy of free trade, both in comparison with other countries and in comparison with its own history. Most imports are subject to either no tariff or to a low tariff. So what are the major exceptions to this rule?

Most of the remaining protection involves agricultural products. Topping the list is ethanol, which in the United States is mainly produced from corn and used as an ingredient in motor fuel. Most imported ethanol is subject to a fairly high tariff, but some countries are allowed to sell a limited amount of ethanol in the United States, at high prices, without paying the tariff. Dairy products also receive substantial import protection, again through a combination of tariffs and quotas.

Until a few years ago, clothing and textiles were also strongly protected from import competition, thanks to an elaborate system of import quotas. However, this system was phased out in 2005 as part of a trade agreement reached a decade earlier. Some clothing imports are still subject to relatively high tariffs, but protection in the clothing industry is a shadow of what it used to be.

The most important thing to know about current U.S. trade protection is how limited it really is, and how little cost it imposes on the economy. Every two years the U.S. International Trade Commission, a government agency, produces estimates of the impact of "significant trade restrictions" on U.S. welfare. As Figure 19-12 shows, over the

FIGURE 19-12 Tariff Rates and Estimated Welfare Gains, 1993–2011

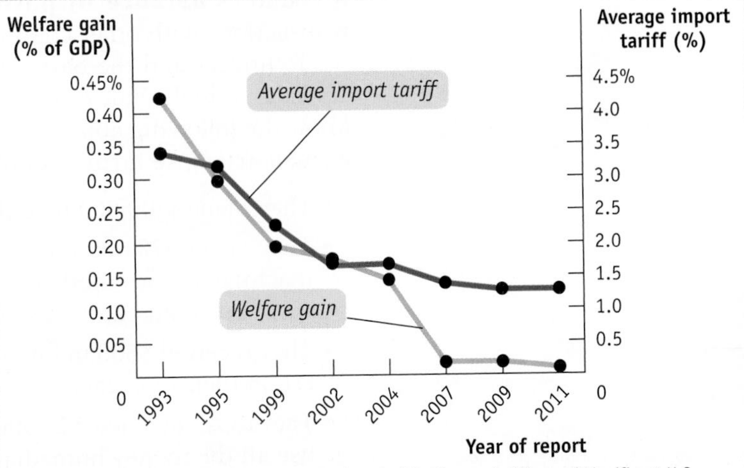

Source: U.S. International Trade Commission (2011), "The Economic Effects of Significant U.S. Import Restraints."

past two decades both average tariff levels and the cost of trade restrictions as a share of national income, which weren't all that big to begin with, have fallen sharply.

Quick Review

- Most economists advocate **free trade,** although many governments engage in **trade protection** of import-competing industries. The two most common protectionist policies are tariffs and import quotas. In rare instances, governments subsidize exporting industries.
- A **tariff** is a tax on imports. It raises the domestic price above the world price, leading to a fall in trade and domestic consumption and a rise in domestic production. Domestic producers and the government gain, but domestic consumer losses more than offset this gain, leading to deadweight loss.
- An **import quota** is a legal quantity limit on imports. Its effect is like that of a tariff, except that revenues—the quota rents—accrue to the license-holder, not to the domestic government.

CHECK YOUR UNDERSTANDING 19-3

1. Suppose the world price of butter is $0.50 per pound and the domestic price in autarky is $1.00 per pound. Use a diagram similar to Figure 19-10 to show the following.
   a. If there is free trade, domestic butter producers want the government to impose a tariff of no less than $0.50 per pound.
   b. What happens if a tariff greater than $0.50 per pound is imposed?
2. Suppose the government imposes an import quota rather than a tariff on butter. What quota limit would generate the same quantity of imports as a tariff of $0.50 per pound?

Solutions appear at back of book.

Capital Flows and the Balance of Payments

In 2010 people living in the United States sold about $3.5 trillion worth of stuff to people living in other countries and bought about $3.5 trillion worth of stuff in return. What kind of stuff? All kinds. Residents of the United States (including firms operating in the United States) sold airplanes, bonds, wheat, and many other items to residents of other countries. Residents of the United States bought cars, stocks, oil, and many other items from residents of other countries.

How can we keep track of these transactions? In Chapter 11 we learned that economists keep track of the domestic economy using the national income and product accounts. Economists keep track of international transactions using a different but related set of numbers, the *balance of payments accounts.*

Balance of Payments Accounts

A country's **balance of payments accounts** are a summary of the country's transactions with other countries.

A country's **balance of payments accounts** are a summary of the country's transactions with other countries.

To understand the basic idea behind the balance of payments accounts, let's consider a small-scale example: not a country, but a family farm. Let's say that we know the following about how last year went financially for the Costas, who own a small artichoke farm in California:

- They made $100,000 by selling artichokes.
- They spent $70,000 on running the farm, including purchases of new farm machinery, and another $40,000 buying food, paying utility bills, replacing their worn-out car, and so on.
- They received $500 in interest on their bank account but paid $10,000 in interest on their mortgage.
- They took out a new $25,000 loan to help pay for farm improvements but didn't use all the money immediately. So they put the extra in the bank.

How could we summarize the Costas' year? One way would be with a table like Table 19-3, which shows sources of cash coming in and money going out, characterized under a few broad headings. The first row of Table 19-3 shows sales and purchases of goods and services: sales of artichokes; purchases of groceries, heating oil, that new car, and so on. The second row shows interest payments: the interest the Costas received from their bank account and the interest they paid on their mortgage. The third row shows cash coming in from new borrowing versus money deposited in the bank.

TABLE 19-3 The Costas' Financial Year

	Sources of cash	Uses of cash	Net
Purchases or sales of goods and services	Artichoke sales: $100,000	Farm operation and living expenses: $110,000	−$10,000
Interest payments	Interest received on bank account: $500	Interest paid on mortgage: $10,000	−$9,500
Loans and deposits	Funds received from new loan: $25,000	Funds deposited in bank: $5,500	+$19,500
Total	**$125,500**	**$125,500**	**$0**

In each row we show the net inflow of cash from that type of transaction. So the net in the first row is −$10,000, because the Costas spent $10,000 more than they earned. The net in the second row is −$9,500, the difference between the interest the Costas received on their bank account and the interest they paid on the mortgage. The net in the third row is $19,500: the Costas brought in $25,000 with their new loan but put only $5,500 of that sum in the bank.

The last row shows the sum of cash coming in from all sources and the sum of all cash used. These sums are equal, by definition: every dollar has a source, and every dollar received gets used somewhere. (What if the Costas hid money under the mattress? Then that would be counted as another "use" of cash.)

A country's balance of payments accounts summarize its transactions with the world with a table basically similar to the way we just summarized the Costas' financial year.

Table 19-4 shows a simplified version of the U.S. balance of payments accounts for 2010. Where the Costa family's accounts show sources and uses of cash, the balance of payments accounts show payments from foreigners—in effect, sources of cash for the United States as a whole—and payments to foreigners.

TABLE 19-4 The U.S. Balance of Payments in 2010 (billions of dollars)

		Payments from foreigners	Payments to foreigners	Net
1	**Sales and purchases of goods and services**	$1,838	$2,338	−$500
2	**Factor income**	663	498	165
3	**Transfers**	—	—	−136
	Current account (1 + 2 + 3)			**−471**
4	**Official asset sales and purchases**	350	−6	356
5	**Private sales and purchases of assets**	910	1,011	−101
	Financial account (4 + 5)			**255**
	Total	—	—	**−216**

Source: Bureau of Economic Analysis.

Row 1 of Table 19-4 shows payments that arise from sales and purchases of goods and services. For example, the value of U.S. wheat exports and the fees foreigners pay to U.S. consulting companies appear in the second column; the value of U.S. oil imports and the fees American companies pay to Indian call centers—the people who often answer your 1-800 calls—appear in the third column.

Row 2 shows *factor income*—the income countries pay for the use of factors of production owned by residents of other countries. Mostly this means investment income: interest paid on loans from overseas, the profits of foreign-owned corporations, and so on. For example, the profits earned by Disneyland Paris, which is owned by the U.S.-based Walt Disney Company, appear in the second column; the profits earned by the U.S. operations of Japanese auto companies appear in the third column. This category also includes some labor income. For example, the wages of an American engineer who works temporarily on a construction site in Dubai are counted in the second column.

Row 3 shows *international transfers*—funds sent by residents of one country to residents of another. The main element here is the remittances that immigrants, such as the millions of Mexican-born workers employed in the United States, send to their families in their country of origin. Notice that Table 19-4 only shows the net value of transfers. That's because the U.S. government only provides an estimate of the net, not a breakdown between payments to foreigners and payments from foreigners.

The next two rows of Table 19-4 show payments resulting from sales and purchases of assets, broken down by who is doing the buying and selling.

A country's **balance of payments on current account,** or **current account,** is its balance of payments on goods and services plus net international transfer payments and factor income.

A country's **balance of payments on goods and services** is the difference between its exports and its imports during a given period.

The **merchandise trade balance,** or **trade balance,** is the difference between a country's exports and imports of goods.

A country's **balance of payments on financial account,** or simply its **financial account,** is the difference between its sales of assets to foreigners and its purchases of assets from foreigners during a given period.

Row 4 shows transactions that involve governments or government agencies, mainly central banks. Row 5 shows private sales and purchases of assets. For example, the 2010 purchase of Ford Motor Company's Volvo brand by the Chinese company Greely Automobile would show up in the second column of row 5; purchases of European stocks by U.S. investors show up in the third column.

In laying out Table 19-4, we have separated rows 1, 2, and 3 into one group and rows 4 and 5 into another. This reflects a fundamental difference in how these two groups of transactions affect the future.

When a U.S. resident sells a good such as wheat to a foreigner, that's the end of the transaction. But a financial asset, such as a bond, is different. Remember, a bond is a promise to pay interest and principal in the future. So when a U.S. resident sells a bond to a foreigner, that sale creates a liability: the U.S. resident will have to pay interest and repay principal in the future. The balance of payments accounts distinguish between transactions that don't create liabilities and those that do.

Transactions that don't create liabilities are considered part of the **balance of payments on current account,** often referred to simply as the **current account:** the balance of payments on goods and services plus net international transfer payments and factor income. The balance of row 1 of Table 19-4, –$500 billion, corresponds to the most important part of the current account: the **balance of payments on goods and services,** the difference between the value of exports and the value of imports during a given period.

By the way, if you read news reports on the economy, you may well see references to another measure, the **merchandise trade balance,** sometimes referred to as the **trade balance** for short. This is the difference between a country's exports and imports of goods alone—not including services. Economists sometimes focus on the merchandise trade balance, even though it's an incomplete measure, because data on international trade in services aren't as accurate as data on trade in physical goods, and they are also slower to arrive.

The current account, as we've just learned, consists of international transactions that don't create liabilities. Transactions that involve the sale or purchase of assets, and therefore do create future liabilities, are considered part of the **balance of payments on financial account,** or the **financial account** for short. (Until a few years ago, economists often referred to the financial account as the *capital account.* We'll use the modern term, but you may run across the older term.)

So how does it all add up? The shaded rows of Table 19-4 show the bottom lines: the overall U.S. current account and financial account for 2010. As you can see, in 2010 the United States ran a current account deficit: the amount it paid to foreigners for goods, services, factors, and transfers was more than the amount it received. Simultaneously, it ran a financial account surplus: the value of the assets it sold to foreigners was more than the value of the assets it bought from foreigners.

In the 2010 official data, the U.S. current account deficit and financial account surplus didn't offset each other: the financial account surplus in 2010 was $216 billion smaller than the current account deficit. But that's just a statistical error, reflecting the imperfection of official data. (That $216 billion discrepancy probably reflected foreign purchases of U.S. assets that official data somehow missed.) In fact, it's a basic rule of balance of payments accounting that the current account and the financial account must sum to zero:

(19-1) Current account (CA) + Financial account (FA) = 0

or

$$CA = -FA$$

Why must Equation 19-1 be true? We already saw the fundamental explanation in Table 19-3, which showed the accounts of the Costa family: in total, the sources of cash must equal the uses of cash. The same applies to balance

FIGURE 19-13 The Balance of Payments

The green arrows represent payments that are counted in the current account. The yellow arrows represent payments that are counted in the financial account. Because the total flow into the United States must equal the total flow out of the United States, the sum of the current account plus the financial account is zero.

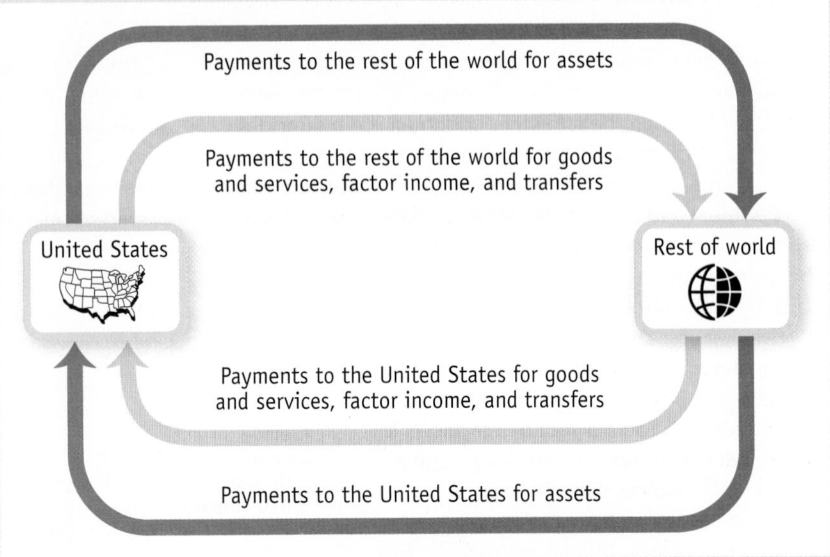

Payments to the rest of the world for assets

Payments to the rest of the world for goods and services, factor income, and transfers

United States

Rest of world

Payments to the United States for goods and services, factor income, and transfers

Payments to the United States for assets

of payments accounts. Figure 19-13, a variant on the circular-flow diagram we have found useful in discussing domestic macroeconomics, may help you visualize how this adding up works. Instead of showing the flow of money *within* a national economy, Figure 19-13 shows the flow of money *between* national economies.

Money flows into the United States from the rest of the world as payment for U.S. exports of goods and services, as payment for the use of U.S.-owned factors of production, and as transfer payments. These flows (indicated by the lower green arrow) are the positive components of the U.S. current account. Money also flows into the United States from foreigners who purchase U.S. assets (as shown by the lower yellow arrow)—the positive component of the U.S. financial account.

At the same time, money flows from the United States to the rest of the world as payment for U.S. imports of goods and services, as payment for the use of foreign-owned factors of production, and as transfer payments. These flows, indicated by the upper green arrow, are the negative components of the U.S. current account. Money also flows from the United States to purchase foreign assets, as shown by the upper yellow arrow—the negative component of the U.S. financial account. As in all circular-flow diagrams, the flow into a box and the flow out of a box are equal. This means that the sum of the yellow and green arrows going into the United States is equal to the sum of the yellow and green arrows going out of the United States. That is,

(19-2) Positive entries on current account (lower green arrow) + Positive entries on financial account (lower yellow arrow) = Negative entries on current account (upper green arrow) + Negative entries on financial account (upper yellow arrow)

Equation 19-2 can be rearranged as follows:

(19-3) Positive entries on current account – Negative entries on current account + Positive entries on financial account – Negative entries on financial account = 0

BIG SURPLUSES

As we've seen, the United States generally runs a large deficit in its current account. In fact, America leads the world in its current account deficit; other countries run bigger deficits as a share of GDP, but they have much smaller economies, so the U.S. deficit is much bigger in absolute terms.

For the world as a whole, however, deficits on the part of some countries must be matched with surpluses on the part of other countries. So who are the surplus nations offsetting U.S. deficits, and what if anything do they have in common?

The accompanying figure shows the average current account surplus of the six countries that ran the largest surpluses over the decade from 2001 to 2010. You may not be surprised to learn that China tops the list. As we explain later in this chapter, China's surplus is largely due to its policy of keeping its currency weak relative to other currencies. But what about the others?

Japan and Germany run current account surpluses for more or less the same reasons: both are rich nations with high savings rates, giving them a lot of money to invest. Since some of that money goes abroad, the result is that they run deficits on the financial account and surpluses on current account.

The other three countries are all major oil exporters. (You may not think of Russia or Norway as "petro-economies," but Russia derives about two-thirds of its export revenue from oil, and Norway owns huge oil fields in the North Sea.) These countries are all deliberately building up assets abroad to help them sustain their spending when the oil runs out.

All in all, the surplus countries are a diverse group. If your picture of the world is simply one of American deficits versus Chinese surpluses, you're missing a large part of the story.

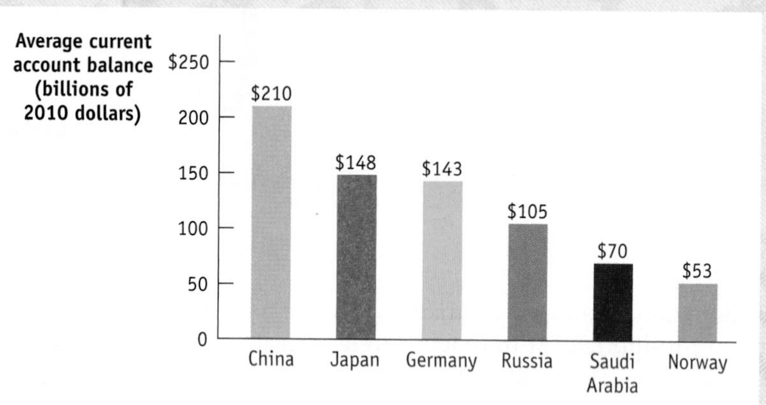

Source: International Monetary Fund.

Equation 19-3 is equivalent to Equation 19-1: the current account plus the financial account—both equal to positive entries minus negative entries—is equal to zero.

But what determines the current account and the financial account?

Underlying Determinants of International Capital Flows

International differences in the demand for funds reflect underlying differences in investment opportunities. In particular, a country with a rapidly growing economy, other things equal, tends to offer more investment opportunities than a country with a slowly growing economy. So a rapidly growing economy typically—though not always—has a higher demand for capital and offers higher returns to investors than a slowly growing economy. As a result, capital tends to flow from slowly growing to rapidly growing economies.

The classic example, described in the upcoming Economics in Action, is the flow of capital from Britain to the United States, among other countries, between 1870 and 1914. During that era, the U.S. economy was growing rapidly as the population increased and spread westward and as the nation industrialized. This created a demand for investment spending on railroads, factories, and so on. Meanwhile, Britain had a much more slowly growing population, was already industrialized, and already had a railroad network covering the country. This left Britain with savings to spare, much of which were lent out to the United States and other New World economies.

International differences in the supply of funds reflect differences in savings across countries. These may be the result of differences in private savings rates, which vary widely among countries. For example, in 2010 gross private savings were 28.5% of Japan's GDP but only 19.2% of U.S. GDP. They may also reflect differences in savings by governments. In particular, government budget deficits, which reduce overall national savings, can lead to capital inflows.

Two-Way Capital Flows

International investment opportunities and differences in savings rates are important determinants of the direction of *net* capital flows—the excess of inflows into a country over outflows, or vice versa. The direction of net flows, other things equal, is determined by differences in interest rates between countries. As we saw in Table 19-4, however, *gross* flows take place in both directions: for example, the United States both sells assets to foreigners and buys assets from foreigners. Why does capital move in both directions?

The answer to this question is that in the real world, as opposed to the simple model we've just learned, there are other motives for international capital flows besides seeking a higher rate of interest.

Individual investors often seek to diversify against risk by buying stocks in a number of countries. Stocks in Europe may do well when stocks in the United States do badly, or vice versa, so investors in Europe try to reduce their risk by buying some U.S. stocks, as investors in the United States try to reduce their risk by buying some European stocks. The result is capital flows in both directions.

Meanwhile, corporations often engage in international investment as part of their business strategy—for example, auto companies may find that they can compete better in a national market if they assemble some of their cars locally. Such business investments can also lead to two-way capital flows, as, say, European car makers build plants in the United States even as U.S. computer companies open facilities in Europe.

Finally, some countries, including the United States, are international banking centers: people from all over the world put money in U.S. financial institutions, which then invest many of those funds overseas.

The result of these two-way flows is that modern economies are typically both debtors (countries that owe money to the rest of the world) and creditors (countries to which the rest of the world owes money). Due to years of both capital inflows and outflows, at the end of 2012, the United States had accumulated foreign assets worth $20.7 trillion, and foreigners had accumulated assets in the United States worth $25.2 trillion.

ECONOMICS ➤ *IN ACTION*

THE GOLDEN AGE OF CAPITAL FLOWS

Technology, it's often said, shrinks the world. Jet planes have put most of the world's cities within a few hours of one another; modern telecommunications transmit information instantly around the globe. So you might think that international capital flows must now be larger than ever.

But if capital flows are measured as a share of world savings and investment, that belief turns out not to be true. The golden age of capital flows actually preceded World War I—from 1870 to 1914.

These capital flows went mainly from European countries, especially Britain, to what were then known as "zones of recent settlement," countries that were attracting large numbers of European immigrants. Among the big recipients of capital inflows were Australia, Argentina, Canada, and the United States.

The large capital flows reflected differences in investment opportunities. Britain, a mature industrial economy with limited natural resources and a slowly growing population, offered relatively limited opportunities for new investment. The zones of recent settlement, with rapidly growing populations and abundant natural resources, offered investors a higher return and attracted capital inflows. Estimates suggest that over this period Britain sent about 40% of its savings abroad, largely to finance railroads and other large projects. No country has matched that record in modern times.

Why can't we match the capital flows of our great-great-grandfathers? Economists aren't completely sure, but they have pointed to two causes: migration restrictions and political risks.

During the golden age of capital flows, capital movements were complementary to population movements: the big recipients of capital from Europe were also places to which large numbers of Europeans were moving. These large-scale population movements were possible before World War I because there were few legal restrictions on immigration. In today's world, by contrast, migration is limited by extensive legal barriers, as anyone considering a move to the United States or Europe can tell you.

The other factor that has changed is political risk. Modern governments often limit foreign investment because they fear it will diminish their national autonomy. And due to political or security concerns, governments sometimes seize foreign property, a risk that deters investors from sending more than a relatively modest share of their wealth abroad. In the nineteenth century such actions were rare, partly because some major destinations of investment were still European colonies, partly because in those days governments had a habit of sending troops and gunboats to enforce the claims of their investors.

Quick Review

- The **balance of payments accounts,** which track a country's international transactions, are composed of the **balance of payments on current account,** or the **current account,** plus the **balance of payments on financial account,** or the **financial account.** The most important component of the current account is the **balance of payments on goods and services,** which itself includes the **merchandise trade balance,** or the **trade balance.**
- Because the sources of payments must equal the uses of payments, the current account plus the financial account sum to zero.
- Capital flows reflect international differences in savings behavior and in investment opportunities.

CHECK YOUR UNDERSTANDING 19-4

1. Which of the balance of payments accounts do the following events affect?
   a. Boeing, a U.S.-based company, sells a newly built airplane to China.
   b. Chinese investors buy stock in Boeing from Americans.
   c. A Chinese company buys a used airplane from American Airlines and ships it to China.
   d. A Chinese investor who owns property in the United States buys a corporate jet, which he will keep in the United States so he can travel around America.

Solutions appear at back of book.

The Role of the Exchange Rate

We've just seen how differences in investment opportunities, savings rates, and interest rates lead to international capital flows. We've also learned that a country's balance of payments on current account plus its balance of payments on financial account add to zero: a country that receives net capital inflows must run a matching current account deficit, and a country that generates net capital outflows must run a matching current account surplus.

The behavior of the financial account—reflecting inflows or outflows of capital—is best described by equilibrium in the international loanable funds market. At the same time, the balance of payments on goods and services, the main component of the current account, is determined by decisions in the international markets for goods and services. So given that the financial account reflects the movement of capital and the current account reflects the movement of goods and services, what ensures that the balance of payments really does balance? That is, what ensures that the two accounts actually offset each other?

Not surprisingly, a price is what makes these two accounts balance. Specifically, that price is the *exchange rate,* which is determined in the *foreign exchange market.*

Currencies are traded in the **foreign exchange market**.

The prices at which currencies trade are known as **exchange rates**.

When a currency becomes more valuable in terms of other currencies, it **appreciates**.

When a currency becomes less valuable in terms of other currencies, it **depreciates**.

Understanding Exchange Rates

In general, goods, services, and assets produced in a country must be paid for in that country's currency. American products must be paid for in dollars; European products must be paid for in euros; Japanese products must be paid for in yen. Occasionally, sellers will accept payment in foreign currency, but they will then exchange that currency for domestic money.

International transactions, then, require a market—the **foreign exchange market**—in which currencies can be exchanged for each other. This market determines **exchange rates,** the prices at which currencies trade. The foreign exchange market is, in fact, not located in any one geographic spot. Rather, it is a global electronic market that traders around the world use to buy and sell currencies.

Table 19-5 shows exchange rates among the world's three most important currencies as of 11:21 A.M., EDT, on November 27, 2012. Each entry shows the price of the "row" currency in terms of the "column" currency. For example, at that time US$1 exchanged for €0.7735, so it took €0.7735 to buy US$1. Similarly, it took US$1.2929 to buy €1. These two numbers reflect the same rate of exchange between the euro and the U.S. dollar: 1/1.2929 = 0.7735.

TABLE 19-5 Exchange Rates, November 27, 2012, 11:21 A.M

	U.S. dollars	Yen	Euros
One U.S. dollar exchanged for	1	82.2304	0.7735
One yen exchanged for	0.0122	1	0.0094
One euro exchanged for	1.2929	106.3112	1

There are two ways to write any given exchange rate. In this case, there were €0.7735 to US$1 and US$1.2929 to €1. Which is the correct way to write it? The answer is that there is no fixed rule. In most countries, people tend to express the exchange rate as the price of a dollar in domestic currency. However, this rule isn't universal, and the U.S. dollar–euro rate is commonly quoted both ways. The important thing is to be sure you know which one you are using! See the accompanying Pitfalls.

When discussing movements in exchange rates, economists use specialized terms to avoid confusion. When a currency becomes more valuable in terms of other currencies, economists say that the currency **appreciates.** When a currency becomes less valuable in terms of other currencies, it **depreciates.** Suppose, for example, that the value of €1 went from $1 to $1.25, which means that the value of US$1 went from €1 to €0.80 (because 1/1.25 = 0.80). In this case, we would say that the euro appreciated and the U.S. dollar depreciated.

Movements in exchange rates, other things equal, affect the relative prices of goods, services, and assets in different countries. Suppose, for example, that the price of an American hotel room is US$100 and the price of a French hotel room is €100. If the exchange rate is €1 = US$1, these hotel rooms have the same price. If the exchange rate is €1.25 = US$1, the French hotel room is 20% cheaper than the American hotel room. If the exchange rate is €0.80 = US$1, the French hotel room is 25% more expensive than the American hotel room.

But what determines exchange rates? Supply and demand in the foreign exchange market.

The Equilibrium Exchange Rate

Imagine, for the sake of simplicity, that there are only two currencies in the world: U.S. dollars and euros. Europeans wanting to purchase American goods, services, and assets come to the foreign exchange market, wanting to exchange euros for U.S. dollars. That is, Europeans demand U.S. dollars from the foreign exchange market and, correspondingly, supply euros to that market. Americans wanting to buy European goods, services, and assets come to the foreign exchange market to exchange U.S. dollars for euros. That is,

WHICH WAY IS UP?

Suppose someone says, "The U.S. exchange rate is up." What does that person mean?

It isn't clear. Sometimes the exchange rate is measured as the price of a dollar in terms of foreign currency, sometimes as the price of foreign currency in terms of dollars. So the statement could mean either that the dollar appreciated or that it depreciated!

You have to be particularly careful when using published statistics. Most countries other than the United States state their exchange rates in terms of the price of a dollar in their domestic currency—for example, Mexican officials will say that the exchange rate is 10, meaning 10 pesos per dollar. But Britain, for historical reasons, usually states its exchange rate the other way. On November 27, 2012, US$1 was worth £0.6240, and £1 was worth US$1.6026. More often than not, this number is reported as an exchange rate of 1.6026. In fact, on occasion, professional economists and consultants embarrass themselves by getting the direction in which the pound is moving wrong!

By the way, Americans generally follow other countries' lead: we usually say that the exchange rate against Mexico is 13 pesos per dollar but that the exchange rate against Britain is 1.60 dollars per pound. But this rule isn't reliable; exchange rates against the euro are often stated both ways.

So it's always important to check before using exchange rate data: which way is the exchange rate being measured?

The **equilibrium exchange rate** is the exchange rate at which the quantity of a currency demanded in the foreign exchange market is equal to the quantity supplied.

Americans supply U.S. dollars to the foreign exchange market and, correspondingly, demand euros from that market. (International transfers and payments of factor income also enter into the foreign exchange market, but to make things simple we'll ignore these.)

Figure 19-14 shows how the foreign exchange market works. The quantity of dollars demanded and supplied at any given euro–U.S. dollar exchange rate is shown on the horizontal axis, and the euro–U.S. dollar exchange rate is shown on the vertical axis. The exchange rate plays the same role as the price of a good or service in an ordinary supply and demand diagram.

The figure shows two curves, the demand curve for U.S. dollars and the supply curve for U.S. dollars. The key to understanding the slopes of these curves is that the level of the exchange rate affects exports and imports. When a country's currency appreciates (becomes more valuable), exports fall and imports rise. When a country's currency depreciates (becomes less valuable), exports rise and imports fall.

To understand why the demand curve for U.S. dollars slopes downward, recall that the exchange rate, other things equal, determines the prices of American goods, services, and assets relative to those of European goods, services, and assets. If the U.S. dollar rises against the euro (the dollar appreciates), American products will become more expensive to Europeans relative to European products. So Europeans will buy less from the United States and will acquire fewer dollars in the foreign exchange market: the quantity of U.S. dollars demanded falls as the number of euros needed to buy a U.S. dollar rises. If the U.S. dollar falls against the euro (the dollar depreciates), American products will become relatively cheaper for Europeans. Europeans will respond by buying more from the United States and acquiring more dollars in the foreign exchange market: the quantity of U.S. dollars demanded rises as the number of euros needed to buy a U.S. dollar falls.

A similar argument explains why the supply curve of U.S. dollars in Figure 19-14 slopes upward: the more euros required to buy a U.S. dollar, the more dollars Americans will supply. Again, the reason is the effect of the exchange rate on relative prices. If the U.S. dollar rises against the euro, European products look cheaper to Americans—who will demand more of them. This will require Americans to convert more dollars into euros.

The **equilibrium exchange rate** is the exchange rate at which the quantity of U.S. dollars demanded in the foreign exchange market is equal to the

FIGURE 19-14 The Foreign Exchange Market

The foreign exchange market matches up the demand for a currency from foreigners who want to buy domestic goods, services, and assets with the supply of a currency from domestic residents who want to buy foreign goods, services, and assets. Here the equilibrium in the market for dollars is at point *E*, corresponding to an equilibrium exchange rate of €0.77 per US$1.

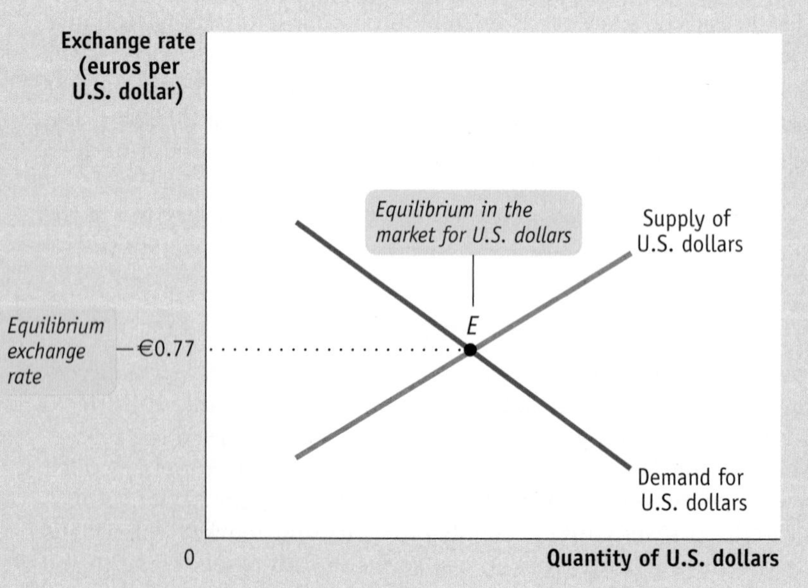

quantity of U.S. dollars supplied. In Figure 19-14, the equilibrium is at point *E*, and the equilibrium exchange rate is 0.77. That is, at an exchange rate of €0.74 per US$1, the quantity of U.S. dollars supplied to the foreign exchange market is equal to the quantity of U.S. dollars demanded.

To understand the significance of the equilibrium exchange rate, it's helpful to consider a numerical example of what equilibrium in the foreign exchange market looks like. A hypothetical example is shown in Table 19-6. The first row shows European purchases of U.S. dollars, either to buy U.S. goods and services or to buy U.S. assets. The second row shows U.S. sales of U.S. dollars, either to buy European goods and services or to buy European assets. At the equilibrium exchange rate, the total quantity of U.S. dollars Europeans want to buy is equal to the total quantity of U.S. dollars Americans want to sell.

TABLE 19-6 A Hypothetical Equilibrium in the Foreign Exchange Market

European purchases of U.S. dollars (trillions of U.S. dollars)	To buy U.S. goods and services: 1.0	To buy U.S. assets: 1.0	**Total purchases of U.S. dollars: 2.0**
U.S. sales of U.S. dollars (trillions of U.S. dollars)	To buy European goods and services: 1.5	To buy European assets: 0.5	**Total sales of U.S. dollars: 2.0**
	U.S. balance of payments on current account: −0.5	**U.S. balance of payments on financial account: +0.5**	

Remember that the balance of payments accounts divide international transactions into two types. Purchases and sales of goods and services are counted in the current account. (Again, we're leaving out transfers and factor income to keep things simple.) Purchases and sales of assets are counted in the financial account. At the equilibrium exchange rate, then, we have the situation shown in Table 19-6: the sum of the balance of payments on current account plus the balance of payments on financial account is zero.

Now let's briefly consider how a shift in the demand for U.S. dollars affects equilibrium in the foreign exchange market. Suppose that for some reason capital flows from Europe to the United States increase—say, due to a change in the preferences of European investors. The effects are shown in Figure 19-15. The demand for U.S. dollars in the foreign exchange market increases as European investors convert euros into dollars to fund their new investments in the United States. This is shown by the shift of the demand curve from D_1 to D_2. As a result, the U.S. dollar appreciates against the euro: the number of euros per U.S. dollar at the equilibrium exchange rate rises from XR_1 to XR_2.

FIGURE 19-15 An Increase in the Demand for U.S. Dollars

An increase in the demand for U.S. dollars might result from a change in the preferences of European investors. The demand curve for U.S. dollars shifts from D_1 to D_2. So the equilibrium number of euros per U.S. dollar rises—the dollar appreciates against the euro. As a result, the balance of payments on current account falls as the balance of payments on financial account rises.

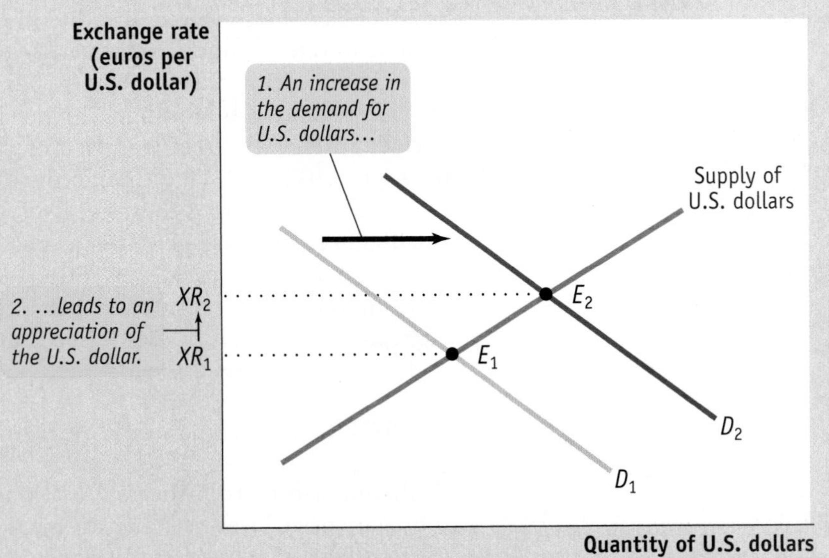

What are the consequences of this increased capital inflow for the balance of payments? The total quantity of U.S. dollars supplied to the foreign exchange market still must equal the total quantity of U.S. dollars demanded. So the increased capital inflow to the United States—an increase in the balance of payments on financial account—must be matched by a decline in the balance of payments on current account. What causes the balance of payments on current account to decline? The appreciation of the U.S. dollar. A rise in the number of euros per U.S. dollar leads Americans to buy more European goods and services and Europeans to buy fewer American goods and services.

Table 19-7 shows a hypothetical example of how this might work. Europeans are buying more U.S. assets, increasing the balance of payments on financial account from 0.5 to 1.0. This is offset by a reduction in European purchases of U.S. goods and services and a rise in U.S. purchases of European goods and services, both the result of the dollar's appreciation. *So any change in the U.S. balance of payments on financial account generates an equal and opposite reaction in the balance of payments on current account.* Movements in the exchange rate ensure that changes in the financial account and in the current account offset each other.

TABLE 19-7 A Hypothetical Example of Effects of Increased Capital Inflows

European purchases of U.S. dollars (trillions of U.S. dollars)	To buy U.S. goods and services: 0.75 (down 0.25)	To buy U.S. assets: 1.5 (up 0.5)	**Total purchases of U.S. dollars: 2.25**
U.S. sales of U.S. dollars (trillions of U.S. dollars)	To buy European goods and services: 1.75 (up 0.25)	To buy European assets: 0.5 (no change)	**Total sales of U.S. dollars: 2.25**
	U.S. balance of payments on current account: −1.0 (down 0.5)	**U.S. balance of payments on financial account: +1.0 (up 0.5)**	

Let's briefly run this process in reverse. Suppose there is a reduction in capital flows from Europe to the United States—again due to a change in the preferences of European investors. The demand for U.S. dollars in the foreign exchange market falls, and the dollar depreciates: the number of euros per U.S. dollar at the equilibrium exchange rate falls. This leads Americans to buy fewer European products and Europeans to buy more American products. Ultimately, this generates an increase in the U.S. balance of payments on current account. So a fall in capital flows into the United States leads to a weaker dollar, which in turn generates an increase in U.S. net exports.

Inflation and Real Exchange Rates

In 1993 one U.S. dollar exchanged, on average, for 3.1 Mexican pesos. By 2011, the peso had fallen against the dollar by almost 75%, with an average exchange rate in 2011 of 12.4 pesos per dollar. Did Mexican products also become much cheaper relative to U.S. products over that 18-year period? Did the price of Mexican products expressed in terms of U.S. dollars also fall by almost 75%? The answer is no, because Mexico had much higher inflation than the United States over that period. In fact, the relative price of U.S. and Mexican products changed little between 1993 and 2011, although the exchange rate changed a lot.

To take account of the effects of differences in inflation rates, economists calculate **real exchange rates,** exchange rates adjusted for international differences in aggregate price levels. Suppose that the exchange rate we are looking at is the number of Mexican pesos per U.S. dollar. Let P_{US} and P_{Mex} be indexes of the aggregate price levels in the United States and Mexico, respectively. Then the real exchange rate between the Mexican peso and the U.S. dollar is defined as:

(19-4) $$\text{Real exchange rate} = \text{Mexican pesos per U.S. dollar} \times \frac{P_{US}}{P_{Mex}}$$

Real exchange rates are exchange rates adjusted for international differences in aggregate price levels.

To distinguish it from the real exchange rate, the exchange rate unadjusted for aggregate price levels is sometimes called the *nominal* exchange rate.

To understand the significance of the difference between the real and nominal exchange rates, let's consider the following example. Suppose that the

Mexican peso depreciates against the U.S. dollar, with the exchange rate going from 10 pesos per U.S. dollar to 15 pesos per U.S. dollar, a 50% change. But suppose that at the same time the price of everything in Mexico, measured in pesos, increases by 50%, so that the Mexican price index rises from 100 to 150. At the same time, suppose that there is no change in U.S. prices, so that the U.S. price index remains at 100. Then the initial real exchange rate is:

$$\text{Pesos per dollar before depreciation} \times \frac{P_{US}}{P_{Mex}} = 10 \times \frac{100}{100} = 10$$

After the peso depreciates and the Mexican price level increases, the real exchange rate is:

$$\text{Pesos per dollar after depreciation} \times \frac{P_{US}}{P_{Mex}} = 15 \times \frac{100}{150} = 10$$

In this example, the peso has depreciated substantially in terms of the U.S. dollar, but the *real* exchange rate between the peso and the U.S. dollar hasn't changed at all. And because the real peso–U.S. dollar exchange rate hasn't changed, the nominal depreciation of the peso against the U.S. dollar will have no effect either on the quantity of goods and services exported by Mexico to the United States or on the quantity of goods and services imported by Mexico from the United States.

To see why, consider again the example of a hotel room. Suppose that this room initially costs 1,000 pesos per night, which is $100 at an exchange rate of 10 pesos per dollar. After both Mexican prices and the number of pesos per dollar rise by 50%, the hotel room costs 1,500 pesos per night—but 1,500 pesos divided by 15 pesos per dollar is $100, so the Mexican hotel room still costs $100. As a result, a U.S. tourist considering a trip to Mexico will have no reason to change plans.

The same is true for all goods and services that enter into trade: *the current account responds only to changes in the real exchange rate, not the nominal exchange rate.* A country's products become cheaper to foreigners only when that country's currency depreciates in real terms, and those products become more expensive to foreigners only when the currency appreciates in real terms. As a consequence, economists who analyze movements in exports and imports of goods and services focus on the real exchange rate, not the nominal exchange rate.

Figure 19-16 illustrates just how important it can be to distinguish between nominal and real exchange rates. The line labeled "Nominal exchange rate" shows the number of pesos it took to buy a U.S. dollar from November 1993 to December

FIGURE 19-16 Real versus Nominal Exchange Rates, 1993–2011

Between November 1993 and December 2011, the price of a dollar in Mexican pesos increased dramatically. But because Mexico had higher inflation than the United States, the real exchange rate, which measures the relative price of Mexican goods and services, ended up roughly where it started.

Source: Federal Reserve Bank of St. Louis.

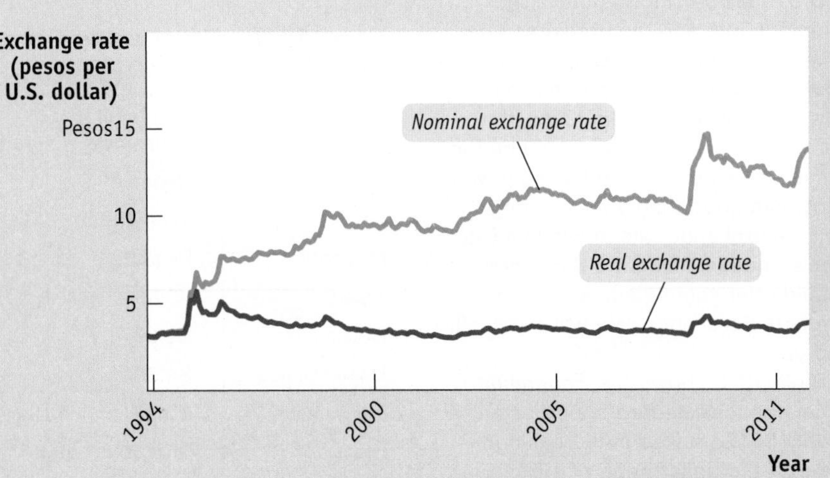

The **purchasing power parity** between two countries' currencies is the nominal exchange rate at which a given basket of goods and services would cost the same amount in each country.

2011. As you can see, the peso depreciated massively over that period. But the line labeled "Real exchange rate" shows the real exchange rate: it was calculated using Equation 19-4, with price indexes for both Mexico and the United States set so that 1993 = 100. In real terms, the peso depreciated between 1994 and 1995, but not by nearly as much as the nominal depreciation. By the end of 2011, the real peso–U.S. dollar exchange rate was just about back where it started.

Purchasing Power Parity

A useful tool for analyzing exchange rates, closely connected to the concept of the real exchange rate, is known as *purchasing power parity*. The **purchasing power parity** between two countries' currencies is the nominal exchange rate at which a given basket of goods and services would cost the same amount in each country. Suppose, for example, that a basket of goods and services that costs \$100 in the United States costs 1,000 pesos in Mexico. Then the purchasing power parity is 10 pesos per U.S. dollar: at that exchange rate, 1,000 pesos = \$100, so the market basket costs the same amount in both countries.

Calculations of purchasing power parities are usually made by estimating the cost of buying broad market baskets containing many goods and services—everything from automobiles and groceries to housing and telephone calls. But as the following For Inquiring Minds explains, once a year the magazine *The Economist* publishes a list of purchasing power parities based on the cost of buying a market basket that contains only one item—a McDonald's Big Mac.

Nominal exchange rates almost always differ from purchasing power parities. Some of these differences are systematic: in general, aggregrate price levels

FOR INQUIRING MINDS

BURGERNOMICS

For a number of years the British magazine *The Economist* has produced an annual comparison of the cost in different countries of one particular consumption item that is found around the world—a McDonald's Big Mac. The magazine finds the price of a Big Mac in local currency, then computes two numbers: the price of a Big Mac in U.S. dollars using the prevailing exchange rate and the exchange rate at which the price of a Big Mac would equal the U.S. price. If purchasing power parity held for Big Macs, the dollar price of a Big Mac would be the same everywhere. If purchasing power parity is a good theory for the long run, the exchange rate at which a Big Mac's price matches the U.S. price should offer some guidance about where the exchange rate will eventually end up.

Table 19-8 shows the *Economist* estimates for selected countries as of July 2012, ranked in increasing order of the dollar price of a Big Mac. The countries with the cheapest Big Macs, and therefore by this measure with the most undervalued currencies, are India and China, both developing countries. But not all developing countries have low-priced Big Macs: the price of a Big Mac in Brazil, converted into dollars, is considerably higher than in the United States. This reflects a sharp appreciation of the *real*, Brazil's currency, in recent years as the country has become a favorite of international investors. And topping the list, with a Big Mac some 50% more expensive than in the United States, is Switzerland—a nation that took extraordinary action in 2011 in an effort to depreciate its currency.

TABLE 19-8 Purchasing Power Parity and the Price of a Big Mac

	Big Mac price		Local currency per dollar	
Country	In local currency	In U.S. dollars	Implied PPP	Actual exchange rate
India	Rupee 89.0	1.58	20.57	56.17
China	Yuan 15.65	2.45	3.62	6.39
Mexico	Peso 32.0	2.70	8.55	13.69
Japan	¥320	4.09	73.95	78.22
Britain	£2.69	4.16	0.62	0.65
United States	\$4.33	4.30		1.00
Euro area	€3.58	4.34	1.21	1.21
Brazil	Real 10.08	4.94	2.33	2.04
Switzerland	SFr 6.5	6.56	1.50	0.99

FIGURE 19-17 Purchasing Power Parity versus the Nominal Exchange Rate, 1990–2011

The purchasing power parity between the United States and Canada—the exchange rate at which a basket of goods and services would have cost the same amount in both countries—changed very little over the period shown, staying near C$1.20 per US$1. But the nominal exchange rate fluctuated widely.

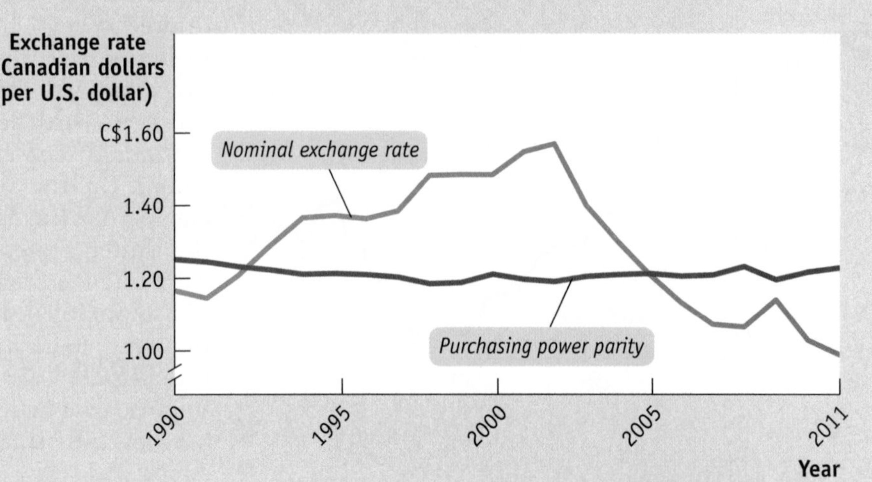

are lower in poor countries than in rich countries because services tend to be cheaper in poor countries. But even among countries at roughly the same level of economic development, nominal exchange rates vary quite a lot from purchasing power parity. Figure 19-17 shows the nominal exchange rate between the Canadian dollar and the U.S. dollar, measured as the number of Canadian dollars per U.S. dollar, from 1990 to 2011, together with an estimate of the purchasing power parity exchange rate between the United States and Canada over the same period. The purchasing power parity didn't change much over the whole period because the United States and Canada had about the same rate of inflation. But at the beginning of the period the nominal exchange rate was below purchasing power parity, so a given market basket was more expensive in Canada than in the United States. By 2002 the nominal exchange rate was far above the purchasing power parity, so a market basket was much cheaper in Canada than in the United States.

Over the long run, however, purchasing power parities are pretty good at predicting actual changes in nominal exchange rates. In particular, nominal exchange rates between countries at similar levels of economic development tend to fluctuate around levels that lead to similar costs for a given market basket. In fact, by July 2005 the nominal exchange rate between the United States and Canada was C$1.22 per US$1—just about the purchasing power parity. By 2011 the cost of living was once again higher in Canada than in the United States and it remained that way throughout 2012.

ECONOMICS ➤ IN ACTION

LOW-COST AMERICA

Does the exchange rate matter for business decisions? And how. Consider what European auto manufacturers were doing in 2008. One report from the University of Iowa summarized the situation as follows:

> While luxury German carmakers BMW and Mercedes have maintained plants in the American South since the 1990s, BMW aims to expand U.S. manufacturing in South Carolina by 50% during the next 5 years. Volvo of Sweden is in negotiations to build a plant in New Mexico. Analysts at Italian carmaker Fiat determined that it needs to build a North American factory to profit from the upcoming re-launch of its Alfa Romeo model. Tennessee recently closed a deal with Volkswagen to build a $1 billion factory by offering $577 million in incentives.

FIGURE 19-18 U.S. Net Exports, 1995–2011

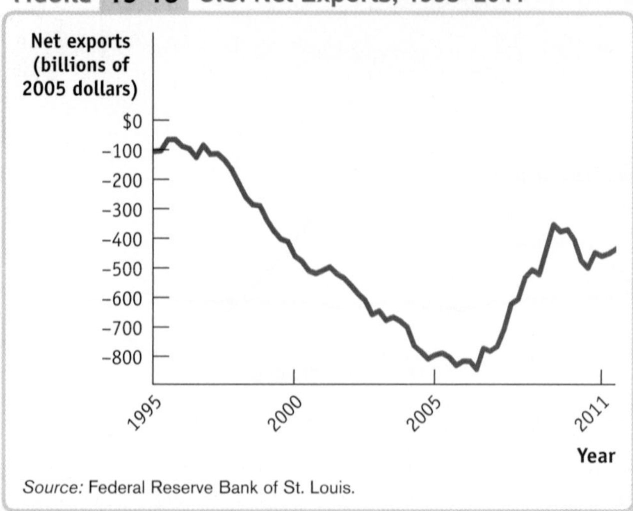

Source: Federal Reserve Bank of St. Louis.

Why were European automakers flocking to America? To some extent because they were being offered special incentives, as the case of Volkswagen in Tennessee illustrates. But the big factor was the exchange rate. In the early 2000s one euro was, on average, worth less than a dollar; by the summer of 2008 the exchange rate was around €1 = $1.50. This change in the exchange rate made it substantially cheaper for European car manufacturers to produce in the United States than at home—especially if the cars were intended for the U.S. market.

Automobile manufacturing wasn't the only U.S. industry benefiting from the weak dollar; across the board, U.S. exports surged after 2006 while import growth fell off. Figure 19-18 shows one measure of U.S. trade performance, real net exports of goods and services: exports minus imports, both measured in 2005 dollars. As you can see, this balance, after a long slide, turned sharply upward in 2006. There was a modest reversal in 2009–2010, as an economy recovering from the 2007–2009 recession pulled in more imports, but a major narrowing of the trade gap remained in place.

Quick Review

- Currencies are traded in the **foreign exchange market,** which determines **exchange rates.**
- Exchange rates can be measured in two ways. To avoid confusion, economists say that a currency **appreciates** or **depreciates.** The **equilibrium exchange rate** matches the supply and demand for currencies on the foreign exchange market.
- To take account of differences in national price levels, economists calculate **real exchange rates.** The current account responds only to changes in the real exchange rate, not the nominal exchange rate.
- **Purchasing power parity** is the nominal exchange rate that equalizes the price of a market basket in the two countries. While the nominal exchange rate almost always differs from purchasing power parity, purchasing power parity is a good predictor of actual changes in the nominal exchange rate.

CHECK YOUR UNDERSTANDING 19-5

1. Mexico discovers huge reserves of oil and starts exporting oil to the United States. Describe how this would affect the following.
   - **a.** The nominal peso–U.S. dollar exchange rate
   - **b.** Mexican exports of other goods and services
   - **c.** Mexican imports of goods and services
2. A basket of goods and services that costs $100 in the United States costs 800 pesos in Mexico, and the current nominal exchange rate is 10 pesos per U.S. dollar. Over the next five years, the cost of that market basket rises to $120 in the United States and to 1,200 pesos in Mexico, although the nominal exchange rate remains at 10 pesos per U.S. dollar. Calculate the following.
   - **a.** The real exchange rate now and five years from now, if today's price index in both countries is 100
   - **b.** Purchasing power parity today and five years from now

Solutions appear at back of book.

WORKED PROBLEM

Trade Is Sweet

The United States has a long-standing policy of trade protection in the sugar industry. As part of the sugar program, the United States Department of Agriculture limits imports to less than 15% of domestic consumption. The policy is controversial, with producers of sodas, candy bars, and other sweetened snacks pitted against sugar growers as well as some public health advocates.

Using the following hypothetical U.S. domestic demand and supply schedule for sugar, determine how many tons of sugar the United States produces in autarky and the equilibrium price per ton.

Price of sugar ($ per metric ton)	Quantity of sugar demanded (millions of tons)	Quantity of sugar supplied (millions of tons)
$650	4	12
600	6	10
550	8	8
500	10	6
450	12	4
400	14	2
350	16	0

If the world price of sugar is $500 per ton, will the United States import or export sugar? How much will they import if there were no import restrictions?

STEP 1: In autarky, how many tons of sugar does the United States produce, and at what price are they bought and sold?

Read the section "Comparative Advantage and International Trade," beginning on page 572 for a definition of autarky. Then, use supply and demand analysis along with the table above to determine the equilibrium price and quantity.

In autarky, the United States produces 8 million tons of sugar, and sugar is sold at $550 per metric ton. This is the quantity and price at which "Quantity of sugar demanded" equals "Quantity of sugar supplied" in the preceding table. At this price and production level, the market is in equilibrium. ■

STEP 2: If the world price of sugar is $500 per ton, will the United States import or export sugar?

Read the section, "Supply, Demand, and International Trade," beginning on page 581. Pay close attention to the section "The Effects of Imports," beginning on page 582 and to Figure 19-6 on page 583.

As shown in Figure 19-6, if the world price is less than the autarky price, then a country will import. In this case, the world price is $500 per ton, and as determined in step 1, the autarky price is $550 per ton, so the United States will import sugar. ■

STEP 3: Determine how much will be imported or exported.

If you need to, re-read the section "Supply, Demand, and International Trade," beginning on page 581, paying close attention to the section "The Effects of Imports," beginning on page 582. Then, working with the preceding table, determine domestic demand at the world price of $500 per ton and domestic supply at the world price of $500 per ton. The difference is the amount that is imported or exported.

Domestic demand at a world price of $500 per ton is 10 million tons, and domestic supply at a world price of $500 per ton is 6 million tons. Since there is a shortage of 4 million tons, the United States will import 4 million tons of sugar if there are no import restrictions.

But in reality, because of the sugar program the United States could not import the required amount of sugar, resulting in higher prices. ■

SUMMARY

1. International trade is of growing importance to the United States and of even greater importance to most other countries. International trade, like trade among individuals, arises from comparative advantage: the opportunity cost of producing an additional unit of a good is lower in some countries than in others. Goods and services purchased abroad are **imports;** those sold abroad are **exports.** Foreign trade, like other economic linkages between countries, has been growing rapidly, a phenomenon called **globalization.**
2. The **Ricardian model of international trade** assumes that opportunity costs are constant. It shows that there are gains from trade: two countries are better off with trade than in **autarky.**
3. In practice, comparative advantage reflects differences between countries in climate, factor endowments, and technology. The **Heckscher–Ohlin** model shows how differences in factor endowments determine comparative advantage: goods differ in **factor intensity,** and countries tend to export goods that are intensive in the factors they have in abundance.
4. The **domestic demand curve** and the **domestic supply curve** determine the price of a good in autarky. When international trade occurs, the domestic price is driven to equality with the **world price,** the price at which the good is bought and sold abroad.
5. If the world price is below the autarky price, a good is imported. This leads to an increase in consumer surplus, a fall in producer surplus, and a gain in total surplus. If the world price is above the autarky price, a good is exported. This leads to an increase in producer surplus, a fall in consumer surplus, and a gain in total surplus.
6. International trade leads to expansion in **exporting industries** and contraction in **import-competing industries.** This raises the domestic demand for abundant factors of production, reduces the demand for scarce factors, and so affects factor prices, such as wages.
7. Most economists advocate **free trade,** but in practice many governments engage in **trade protection.** The two most common forms of **protection** are tariffs and quotas. In rare occasions, export industries are subsidized.
8. A **tariff** is a tax levied on imports. It raises the domestic price above the world price, hurting consumers, benefiting domestic producers, and generating government revenue. As a result, total surplus falls. An **import quota** is a legal limit on the quantity of a good that can be imported. It has the same effects as a tariff, except that the revenue goes not to the government but to those who receive import licenses.
9. A country's **balance of payments accounts** summarize its transactions with the rest of the world. The **balance of payments on current account,** or **current account,** includes the **balance of payments on goods and services** together with balances on factor income and transfers. The **merchandise trade balance,** or **trade balance,** is a frequently cited component of the balance of payments on goods and services. The **balance of payments on financial account,** or **financial account,** measures capital flows. By definition, the balance of payments on current account plus the balance of payments on financial account is zero.
10. Capital flows respond to international differences in interest rates and other rates of return; they can be usefully analyzed using an international version of the loanable funds model, which shows how a country where the interest rate would be low in the absence of capital flows sends funds to a country where the interest rate would be high in the absence of capital flows. The underlying determinants of capital flows are international differences in savings and opportunities for investment spending.
11. Currencies are traded in the **foreign exchange market;** the prices at which they are traded are **exchange rates.** When a currency rises against another currency, it **appreciates;** when it falls, it **depreciates.** The **equilibrium exchange rate** matches the quantity of that currency supplied to the foreign exchange market to the quantity demanded.
12. To correct for international differences in inflation rates, economists calculate **real exchange rates,** which multiply the exchange rate between two countries' currencies by the ratio of the countries' price levels. The current account responds only to changes in the real exchange rate, not the nominal exchange rate. **Purchasing power parity** is the exchange rate that makes the cost of a basket of goods and services equal in two countries. While purchasing power parity and the nominal exchange rate almost always differ, purchasing power parity is a good predictor of actual changes in the nominal exchange rate.

KEY TERMS

Imports, p. 572
Exports, p. 572
Globalization, p. 572
Ricardian model of international trade, p. 573
Autarky, p. 574
Factor intensity, p. 579
Heckscher–Ohlin model, p. 579
Domestic demand curve, p. 582
Domestic supply curve, p. 582
World price, p. 582
Exporting industries, p. 586
Import-competing industries, p. 586
Free trade, p. 588
Trade protection, p. 588
Protection, p. 588
Tariff, p. 588
Import quota, p. 590
Balance of payments accounts, p. 592
Balance of payments on current account (current account), p. 594
Balance of payments on goods and services, p. 594
Merchandise trade balance (trade balance), p. 594
Balance of payments on financial account (financial account), p. 594
Foreign exchange market, p. 599
Exchange rates, p. 599
Appreciation, p. 599
Depreciation, p. 599
Equilibrium exchange rate, p. 600
Real exchange rate, p. 602
Purchasing power parity, p. 604

PROBLEMS

1. Assume Saudi Arabia and the United States face the production possibilities for oil and cars shown in the accompanying table.

Saudi Arabia		United States	
Quantity of oil (millions of barrels)	Quantity of cars (millions)	Quantity of oil (millions of barrels)	Quantity of cars (millions)
0	4	0	10.0
200	3	100	7.5
400	2	200	5.0
600	1	300	2.5
800	0	400	0

a. What is the opportunity cost of producing a car in Saudi Arabia? In the United States? What is the opportunity cost of producing a barrel of oil in Saudi Arabia? In the United States?

b. Which country has the comparative advantage in producing oil? In producing cars?

c. Suppose that in autarky, Saudi Arabia produces 200 million barrels of oil and 3 million cars; similarly, that the United States produces 300 million barrels of oil and 2.5 million cars. Without trade, can Saudi Arabia produce more oil *and* more cars? Without trade, can the United States produce more oil *and* more cars?

2. The production possibilities for the United States and Saudi Arabia are given in Problem 1. Suppose now that each country specializes in the good in which it has the comparative advantage, and the two countries trade. Also assume that for each country the value of imports must equal the value of exports.

a. What is the total quantity of oil produced? What is the total quantity of cars produced?

b. Is it possible for Saudi Arabia to consume 400 million barrels of oil and 5 million cars and for the United States to consume 400 million barrels of oil and 5 million cars?

c. Suppose that, in fact, Saudi Arabia consumes 300 million barrels of oil and 4 million cars and the United States consumes 500 million barrels of oil and 6 million cars. How many barrels of oil does the United States import? How many cars does the United States export? Suppose a car costs $10,000 on the world market. How much, then, does a barrel of oil cost on the world market?

3. Both Canada and the United States produce lumber and music CDs with constant opportunity costs. The United States can produce either 10 tons of lumber and no CDs, or 1,000 CDs and no lumber, or any combination in between. Canada can produce either 8 tons of lumber and no CDs, or 400 CDs and no lumber, or any combination in between.

a. Draw the U.S. and Canadian production possibility frontiers in two separate diagrams, with CDs on the horizontal axis and lumber on the vertical axis.

b. In autarky, if the United States wants to consume 500 CDs, how much lumber can it consume at most? Label this point *A* in your diagram. Similarly, if Canada wants to consume 1 ton of lumber, how many CDs can it consume in autarky? Label this point *C* in your diagram.

c. Which country has the absolute advantage in lumber production?

d. Which country has the comparative advantage in lumber production?

Suppose each country specializes in the good in which it has the comparative advantage, and there is trade.

e. How many CDs does the United States produce? How much lumber does Canada produce?

f. Is it possible for the United States to consume 500 CDs and 7 tons of lumber? Label this point *B* in your diagram. Is it possible for Canada at the same time to consume 500 CDs and 1 ton of lumber? Label this point *D* in your diagram.

4. For each of the following trade relationships, explain the likely source of the comparative advantage of each of the exporting countries.

a. The United States exports software to Venezuela, and Venezuela exports oil to the United States.

b. The United States exports airplanes to China, and China exports clothing to the United States.

c. The United States exports wheat to Colombia, and Colombia exports coffee to the United States.

5. The U.S. Census Bureau keeps statistics on U.S. imports and exports on its website. The following steps will take you to the foreign trade statistics. Use them to answer the questions below.

i. Go to the U.S. Census Bureau's website at www.census.gov

ii. Under the heading "Business & Industry," select "Foreign Trade"

iii. At the top of the page, select "Data"

iv. Then select "Country/Product Trade"

v. Under the heading "North American Industry Classification System (NAICS)-Based," select "NAICS web application"

vi. In the drop-down menu "3-digit and 6-digit NAICS by country," select the product category you are interested in, and hit "Go"

vii. In the drop-down menu "Select 6-digit NAICS," select the good or service you are interested in, and hit "Go"

viii. In the drop-down menus that allow you to select a month and year, select "December" and "2010," and hit "Go"

ix. The right side of the table now shows the import and export statistics for the entire year 2010. For the questions below on U.S. imports, use the column for "Consumption Imports, Customs Value Basis."

a. Look up data for U.S. imports of hats and caps: in step (vi), select "(315) Apparel & Accessories" and in step (vii), select "(315991) Hats and Caps." From which country do we import the most hats and caps? Which of the three sources of comparative advantage (climate, factor endowments, and technology) accounts for that country's comparative advantage in hat and cap production?

b. Look up data for U.S. imports of grapes: in step (vi), select "(111) Agricultural Products" and in step (vii), select "(111332) Grapes." From which country do we import the most grapes? Which of the three sources of comparative advantage (climate, factor endowments, and technology) accounts for that country's comparative advantage in grape production?

c. Look up data for U.S. imports of food product machinery: in step (vi), select "(333) Machinery, Except Electrical" and in step (vii), select "(333294) Food Product Machinery." From which country do we import the most food product machinery? Which of the three sources of comparative advantage (climate, factor endowments, and technology) accounts for that country's comparative advantage in food product machinery?

6. Compare the data for U.S. imports of hats and caps from China in 2010 that you found in Problem 5 with the same data for the year 2000. Repeat the steps outlined in Problem 5, but in step (viii) select "December" and "2000."

a. What happened to the value of U.S. imports of hats and caps from China between 2000 and 2010?

b. What prediction does the Heckscher–Ohlin model make about the wages received by labor in China?

7. Shoes are labor-intensive and satellites are capital-intensive to produce. The United States has abundant capital. China has abundant labor. According to the Heckscher–Ohlin model, which good will China export? Which good will the United States export? In the United States, what will happen to the price of labor (the wage) and to the price of capital?

8. The accompanying table indicates the U.S. domestic demand schedule and domestic supply schedule for commercial jet airplanes. Suppose that the world price of a commercial jet airplane is $100 million.

Price of jet (millions)	Quantity of jets demanded	Quantity of jets supplied
$120	100	1,000
110	150	900
100	200	800
90	250	700
80	300	600
70	350	500
60	400	400
50	450	300
40	500	200

a. In autarky, how many commercial jet airplanes does the United States produce, and at what price are they bought and sold?

b. With trade, what will the price for commercial jet airplanes be? Will the United States import or export airplanes? How many?

9. How would the following transactions be categorized in the U.S. balance of payments accounts? Would they be entered in the current account (as a payment to or from a foreigner) or the financial account (as a sale of assets to or purchase of assets from a foreigner)? How will the balance of payments on the current and financial accounts change?

a. A French importer buys a case of California wine for $500.

b. An American who works for a French company deposits her paycheck, drawn on a Paris bank, into her San Francisco bank.

c. An American buys a bond from a Japanese company for $10,000.

d. An American charity sends $100,000 to Africa to help local residents buy food after a harvest shortfall.

10. The accompanying diagram shows foreign-owned assets in the United States and U.S.-owned assets abroad, both as a percentage of foreign GDP. As you can see from the diagram, both increased around fivefold from 1980 to 2010.

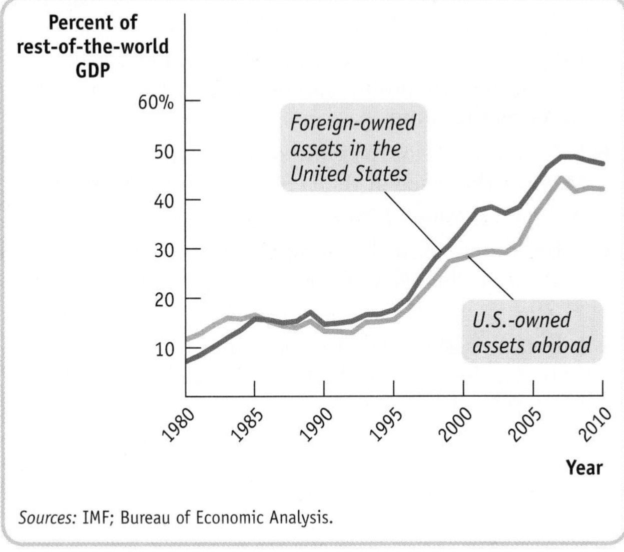

Sources: IMF; Bureau of Economic Analysis.

a. As U.S.-owned assets abroad increased as a percentage of foreign GDP, does this mean that the United States, over the period, experienced net capital outflows?

b. Does this diagram indicate that world economies were more tightly linked in 2010 than they were in 1980?

11. In the economy of Scottopia in 2010, exports equaled $400 billion of goods and $300 billion of services, imports equaled $500 billion of goods and $350 billion of services, and the rest of the world purchased $250 billion of Scottopia's assets. What was the merchandise trade balance for Scottopia? What was the balance of payments on current account in Scottopia? What was the balance of payments on financial account? What was the value of Scottopia's purchases of assets from the rest of the world?

12. In the economy of Popania in 2010, total Popanian purchases of assets in the rest of the world equaled $300 billion, purchases of Popanian assets by the rest of the world equaled $400 billion, and Popania exported goods and services equal to $350 billion. What was Popania's balance of payments on financial account in 2010? What was its balance of payments on current account? What was the value of its imports?

13. Based on the exchange rates for the first trading days of 2011 and 2012 shown in the accompanying table, did the U.S. dollar appreciate or depreciate during 2011? Did the movement in the value of the U.S. dollar make American goods and services more or less attractive to foreigners?

January 3, 2011	January 3, 2012
US$1.55 to buy 1 British pound sterling	US$1.57 to buy 1 British pound sterling
29.08 Taiwan dollars to buy US$1	30.28 Taiwan dollars to buy US$1
US$0.99 to buy 1 Canadian dollar	US$1.01 to buy 1 Canadian dollar
81.56 Japanese yen to buy US$1	76.67 Japanese yen to buy US$1
US$1.34 to buy 1 euro	US$1.31 to buy 1 euro
0.93 Swiss franc to buy US$1	0.93 Swiss franc to buy US$1

14. Go to http://fx.sauder.ubc.ca. Using the table labeled "The Most Recent Cross-Rates of Major Currencies," determine whether the British pound (GBP), the Canadian dollar (CAD), the Japanese yen (JPY), the euro (EUR), and the Swiss franc (CHF) have appreciated or depreciated against the U.S. dollar (USD) since January 3, 2012. The exchange rates on January 3, 2012, are listed in the table in Problem 6 above.

15. Suppose the United States and Japan are the only two trading countries in the world. What will happen to the value of the U.S. dollar if the following occur, other things equal?

a. Japan relaxes some of its import restrictions.

b. The United States imposes some import tariffs on Japanese goods.

c. Interest rates in the United States rise dramatically.

d. A report indicates that Japanese cars last much longer than previously thought, especially compared with American cars.

EXTEND YOUR UNDERSTANDING

16. The accompanying table shows the U.S. domestic demand schedule and domestic supply schedule for oranges. Suppose that the world price of oranges is $0.30 per orange.

Price of orange	Quantity of oranges demanded (thousands)	Quantity of oranges supplied (thousands)
$1.00	2	11
0.90	4	10
0.80	6	9
0.70	8	8
0.60	10	7
0.50	12	6
0.40	14	5
0.30	16	4
0.20	18	3

a. Draw the U.S. domestic supply curve and domestic demand curve.

b. With free trade, how many oranges will the United States import or export?

Suppose that the U.S. government imposes a tariff on oranges of $0.20 per orange.

c. How many oranges will the United States import or export after introduction of the tariff?

d. In your diagram, shade the gain or loss to the economy as a whole from the introduction of this tariff.

17. Before the North American Free Trade Agreement (NAFTA) gradually eliminated import tariffs on goods, the autarky price of tomatoes in Mexico was below the world price and in the United States was above the world price. Similarly, the autarky price of poultry in Mexico was above the world price and in the United States was below the world price. Draw diagrams with domestic supply and demand curves for each country and each of the two goods. As a result of NAFTA, the United States now imports tomatoes from Mexico and the United States now exports poultry to Mexico. How would you expect the following groups to be affected?

a. Mexican and U.S. consumers of tomatoes. Illustrate the effect on consumer surplus in your diagram.

b. Mexican and U.S. producers of tomatoes. Illustrate the effect on producer surplus in your diagram.

c. Mexican and U.S. tomato workers.

d. Mexican and U.S. consumers of poultry. Illustrate the effect on consumer surplus in your diagram.

e. Mexican and U.S. producers of poultry. Illustrate the effect on producer surplus in your diagram.

f. Mexican and U.S. poultry workers.

18. In each of the following scenarios, suppose that the two nations are the only trading nations in the world. Given inflation and the change in the nominal exchange rate, which nation's goods become more attractive?

a. Inflation is 10% in the United States and 5% in Japan; the U.S. dollar–Japanese yen exchange rate remains the same.

b. Inflation is 3% in the United States and 8% in Mexico; the price of the U.S. dollar falls from 12.50 to 10.25 Mexican pesos.

c. Inflation is 5% in the United States and 3% in the euro area; the price of the euro falls from $1.30 to $1.20.

d. Inflation is 8% in the United States and 4% in Canada; the price of the Canadian dollar rises from US$0.60 to US$0.75.

BUSINESS CASE • Li & Fung: From Guangzhou to You

Daniel J. Groshong/Bloomberg via Getty Images

It's a very good bet that as you read this, you're wearing something manufactured in Asia. And if you are, it's also a good bet that the Hong Kong company Li & Fung was involved in getting your garment designed, produced, and shipped to your local store. From Levi's to The Limited to Walmart, Li & Fung is a critical conduit from factories around the world to the shopping mall nearest you.

The company was founded in 1906 in Guangzhou, China. According to Victor Fung, the company's chairman, his grandfather's "value added" was that he spoke English, allowing him to serve as an interpreter in business deals between Chinese and foreigners. When Mao's Communist Party seized control in mainland China, the company moved to Hong Kong. There, as Hong Kong's market economy took off during the 1960s and 1970s, Li & Fung grew as an export broker, bringing together Hong Kong manufacturers and foreign buyers.

The real transformation of the company came, however, as Asian economies grew and changed. Hong Kong's rapid growth led to rising wages, making Li & Fung increasingly uncompetitive in garments, its main business. So the company reinvented itself: rather than being a simple broker, it became a "supply chain manager." Not only would it allocate production of a good to a manufacturer, it would also break production down, allocate production of the inputs, and then allocate final assembly of the good among its 12,000+ suppliers around the globe. Sometimes production would be done in sophisticated economies like those of Hong Kong or even Japan, where wages are high but so is quality and productivity; sometimes it would be done in less advanced locations like mainland China or Thailand, where labor is less productive but cheaper.

For example, suppose you own a U.S. retail chain and want to sell garment-washed blue jeans. Rather than simply arrange for production of the jeans, Li & Fung will work with you on their design, providing you with the latest production and style information, like what materials and colors are hot. After the design has been finalized, Li & Fung will arrange for the creation of a prototype, find the most cost-effective way to manufacture it, and then place an order on your behalf. Through Li & Fung, the yarn might be made in Korea and dyed in Taiwan, and the jeans sewn in Thailand or mainland China. And because production is taking place in so many locations, Li & Fung provides transport logistics as well as quality control.

Li & Fung has been enormously successful. In late 2012 the company had a market value of approximately $13.3 billion, with offices and distribution centers in more than 40 countries. Year after year, it has regularly increased its profits.

QUESTIONS FOR THOUGHT

1. Why do you think it was profitable for Li & Fung to go beyond brokering exports to becoming a supply chain manager, breaking down the production process and sourcing the inputs from various suppliers across many countries?
2. What principle do you think underlies Li & Fung's decisions on how to allocate production of a good's inputs and its final assembly among various countries?
3. Why do you think a retailer prefers to have Li & Fung arrange international production of its jeans rather than purchase them directly from a jeans manufacturer in mainland China?
4. What is the source of Li & Fung's success? Is it based on human capital, on ownership of a natural resource, or on ownership of capital?

Solutions to Check Your Understanding Questions

This section offers suggested answers to the "Check Your Understanding" questions found within chapters.

Chapter One

1-1 CHECK YOUR UNDERSTANDING

1. a. This statement is a feature of a market economy. The invisible hand refers to the way in which the individual pursuit of self-interest can lead to good results for society as a whole.

b. This statement is not a feature of a market economy. In a market economy, production and consumption decisions are the result of decentralized decisions by many firms and individuals. In a command economy, a central authority makes decisions about production and consumption.

c. This statement is a feature of a market economy. Sometimes the pursuit of one's own interests does not promote the interests of society as a whole. This can lead to market failure.

d. This statement is not a feature of a market economy. Although the economy grows over time, fluctuations are regular features of market economies.

1-2 CHECK YOUR UNDERSTANDING

1. a. This illustrates the concept of opportunity cost. Given that a person can only eat so much at one sitting, having a slice of chocolate cake requires that you forgo eating something else, such as a slice of coconut cream pie.

b. This illustrates the concept that resources are scarce. Even if there were more resources in the world, the total amount of those resources would be limited. As a result, scarcity would still arise. For there to be no scarcity, there would have to be unlimited amounts of everything (including unlimited time in a human life), which is clearly impossible.

c. This illustrates the concept that people usually exploit opportunities to make themselves better off. Students will seek to make themselves better off by signing up for the tutorials of teaching assistants with good reputations and avoiding those teaching assistants with poor reputations. It also illustrates the concept that resources are scarce. If there were unlimited spaces in tutorials with good teaching assistants, they would not fill up.

d. This illustrates the concept of marginal analysis. Your decision about allocating your time is a "how much" decision: how much time spent exercising versus how much time spent studying. You make your decision by comparing the benefit of an additional hour of exercising to its cost, the effect on your grades of one less hour spent studying.

2. a. Yes. The increased time spent commuting is a cost you will incur if you accept the new job. That additional time spent commuting—or equivalently, the benefit you would get from spending that time doing something else—is an opportunity cost of the new job.

b. Yes. One of the benefits of the new job is that you will be making $50,000. But if you take the new job, you will have to give up your current job; that is, you have to give up your current salary of $45,000. So $45,000 is one of the opportunity costs of taking the new job.

c. No. A more spacious office is an additional benefit of your new job and does not involve forgoing something else. So it is not an opportunity cost.

1-3 CHECK YOUR UNDERSTANDING

1. a. This illustrates the concept that markets usually lead to efficiency. Any seller who wants to sell a book for at least $30 does indeed sell to someone who is willing to buy a book for $30. As a result, there is no way to change how used textbooks are distributed among buyers and sellers in a way that would make one person better off without making someone else worse off.

b. This illustrates the concept that there are gains from trade. Students trade tutoring services based on their different abilities in academic subjects.

c. This illustrates the concept that when markets don't achieve efficiency, government intervention can improve society's welfare. In this case the market, left alone, will permit bars and nightclubs to impose costs on their neighbors in the form of loud music, costs that the bars and nightclubs have no incentive to take into account. This is an inefficient outcome because society as a whole can be made better off if bars and nightclubs are induced to reduce their noise.

d. This illustrates the concept that resources should be used as efficiently as possible to achieve society's goals. By closing neighborhood clinics and shifting funds to the main hospital, better health care can be provided at a lower cost.

e. This illustrates the concept that markets move toward equilibrium. Here, because books with the same amount of wear and tear sell for about the same price, no buyer or seller can be made better off by engaging in a different trade than he or she undertook. This means that the market for used textbooks has moved to an equilibrium.

2. a. This does not describe an equilibrium situation. Many students should want to change their behavior and switch to eating at the restaurants. Therefore, the situation described is not an equilibrium. An equilibrium will be established when students are equally as well off eating at the restaurants as eating at the dining hall—which would happen if, say, prices at the restaurants were higher than at the dining hall.

b. This does describe an equilibrium situation. By changing your behavior and riding the bus, you would not be made better off. Therefore, you have no incentive to change your behavior.

1-4 CHECK YOUR UNDERSTANDING

1. a. This illustrates the principle that government policies can change spending. The tax cut would increase people's after-tax incomes, leading to higher consumer spending.

b. This illustrates the principle that one person's spending is another person's income. As oil companies increase their spending on labor by hiring more workers, or pay existing workers higher wages, those workers' incomes rise. In turn, these workers increase their consumer spending, which becomes income to restaurants and other consumer businesses.

c. This illustrates the principle that overall spending sometimes gets out of line with the economy's productive capacity. In this case, spending on housing was too high relative to the economy's capacity to create new housing. This first led to a rise in house prices, and then—as a result—to a rise in overall prices, or *inflation*.

Chapter Two

2-1 CHECK YOUR UNDERSTANDING

1. a. False. An increase in the resources available to Boeing for use in producing Dreamliners and small jets changes the production possibility frontier by shifting it outward. This is because Boeing can now produce more small jets and Dreamliners than before. In the accompanying figure, the line labeled "Boeing's original *PPF*" represents Boeing's original production possibility frontier, and the line labeled "Boeing's new *PPF*" represents the new production possibility frontier that results from an increase in resources available to Boeing.

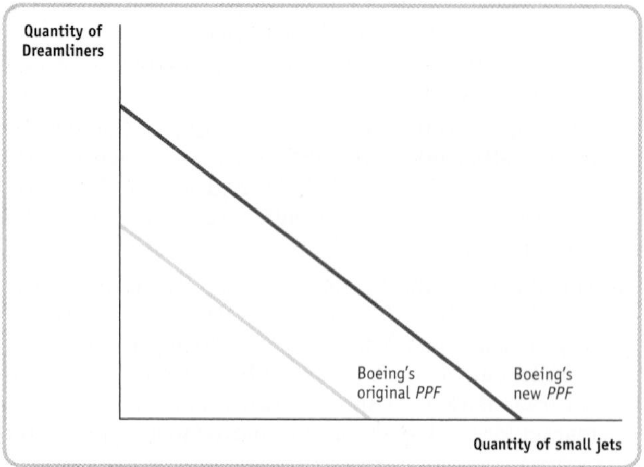

b. True. A technological change that allows Boeing to build more small jets for any amount of Dreamliners built results in a change in its production possibility frontier. This is illustrated in the accompanying figure: the new production possibility frontier is represented by the line labeled "Boeing's new *PPF*," and the original production frontier is represented by the line labeled "Boeing's original *PPF*." Since the maximum quantity of Dreamliners that Boeing can build is the same as before, the new production possibility frontier intersects the vertical axis at the same point as the original frontier. But since the maximum possible quantity of small jets is now greater than before, the new frontier intersects the horizontal axis to the right of the original frontier.

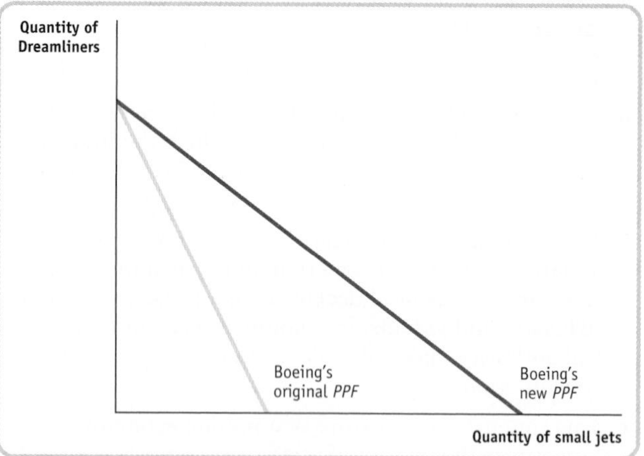

c. False. The production possibility frontier illustrates how much of one good an economy must give up to get more of another good only when resources are used efficiently in production. If an economy is producing inefficiently—that is, inside the frontier—then it does not have to give up a unit of one good in order to get another unit of the other good. Instead, by becoming more efficient in production, this economy can have more of both goods.

2. a. The United States has an absolute advantage in automobile production because it takes fewer Americans (6) to produce a car in one day than Italians (8). The United States also has an absolute advantage in washing machine production because it takes fewer Americans (2) to produce a washing machine in one day than Italians (3).

b. In Italy the opportunity cost of a washing machine in terms of an automobile is $3/8$: $3/8$ of a car can be produced with the same number of workers and in the same time it takes to produce 1 washing machine. In the United States the opportunity cost of a washing machine in terms of an automobile is $2/6 = 1/3$: $1/3$ of a car can be produced with the same number of workers and in the same time it takes to produce 1 washing machine. Since $1/3 < 3/8$, the United States has a comparative advantage in the production of washing machines: to produce a washing machine, only $1/3$ of a car must be given up in the United States but $3/8$ of a car must be given up in Italy. This means that Italy has a comparative advantage in automobiles. This can be checked as follows. The opportunity cost of an automobile in terms of a washing machine in Italy is $8/3$, equal to $2\frac{2}{3}$: $2\frac{2}{3}$ washing machines can be produced with the same number of workers and in the time it takes to produce 1 car in Italy. And the opportunity cost of an automobile in terms of a washing machine in the United States is $6/2$, equal to 3: 3 washing machines can be produced with the same number of workers and in the time it takes to produce 1 car in the United States. Since $2\frac{2}{3} < 3$, Italy has a comparative advantage in producing automobiles.

c. The greatest gains are realized when each country specializes in producing the good for which it has a comparative advantage. Therefore, the United States should specialize in washing machines and Italy should specialize in automobiles.

3. At a trade of 10 U.S. large jets for 15 Brazilian small jets, Brazil gives up less for a large jet than it would if it were building large jets itself. Without trade, Brazil gives up 3 small jets for each large jet it produces. With trade, Brazil gives up only 1.5 small jets for each large jet from the United States. Likewise, the United States gives up less for a small jet than it would if it were producing small jets itself. Without trade, the United States gives up $\frac{3}{4}$ of a large jet for each small jet. With trade, the United States gives up only $\frac{2}{3}$ of a large jet for each small jet from Brazil.

4. An increase in the amount of money spent by households results in an increase in the flow of goods to households. This, in turn, generates an increase in demand for factors of production by firms. So, there is an increase in the number of jobs in the economy.

2-2 CHECK YOUR UNDERSTANDING

1. a. This is a normative statement because it stipulates what should be done. In addition, it may have no "right" answer. That is, should people be prevented from all dangerous personal behavior if they enjoy that behavior—like skydiving? Your answer will depend on your point of view.

b. This is a positive statement because it is a description of fact.

2. a. True. Economists often have different value judgments about the desirability of a particular social goal. But despite those differences in value judgments, they will tend to agree that society, once it has decided to pursue a given social goal, should adopt the most efficient policy to achieve that goal. Therefore economists are likely to agree on adopting policy choice B.

b. False. Disagreements between economists are more likely to arise because they base their conclusions on different models or because they have different value judgments about the desirability of the policy.

c. False. Deciding which goals a society should try to achieve is a matter of value judgments, not a question of economic analysis.

Chapter Three

3-1 CHECK YOUR UNDERSTANDING

1. a. The quantity of umbrellas demanded is higher at any given price on a rainy day than on a dry day. This is a rightward *shift of* the demand curve, since at any given price the quantity demanded rises. This implies that any specific quantity can now be sold at a higher price.

b. The quantity of weekend calls demanded rises in response to a price reduction. This is a *movement along* the demand curve for weekend calls.

c. The demand for roses increases the week of Valentine's Day. This is a rightward *shift of* the demand curve.

d. The quantity of gasoline demanded falls in response to a rise in price. This is a *movement along* the demand curve.

3-2 CHECK YOUR UNDERSTANDING

1. a. The quantity of houses supplied rises as a result of an increase in prices. This is a *movement along* the supply curve.

b. The quantity of strawberries supplied is higher at any given price. This is a rightward *shift of* the supply curve.

c. The quantity of labor supplied is lower at any given wage. This is a leftward *shift of* the supply curve compared to the supply curve during school vacation. So, in order to attract workers, fast-food chains have to offer higher wages.

d. The quantity of labor supplied rises in response to a rise in wages. This is a *movement along* the supply curve.

e. The quantity of cabins supplied is higher at any given price. This is a rightward *shift of* the supply curve.

3-3 CHECK YOUR UNDERSTANDING

1. a. The supply curve shifts rightward. At the original equilibrium price of the year before, the quantity of grapes supplied exceeds the quantity demanded. This is a case of surplus. The price of grapes will fall.

b. The demand curve shifts leftward. At the original equilibrium price, the quantity of hotel rooms supplied exceeds the quantity demanded. This is a case of surplus. The rates for hotel rooms will fall.

c. The demand curve for second-hand snowblowers shifts rightward. At the original equilibrium price, the quantity of second-hand snowblowers demanded exceeds the quantity supplied. This is a case of shortage. The equilibrium price of second-hand snowblowers will rise.

3-4 CHECK YOUR UNDERSTANDING

1. a. The market for large cars: this is a rightward shift in demand caused by a decrease in the price of a complement, gasoline. As a result of the shift, the equilibrium price of large cars will rise and the equilibrium quantity of large cars bought and sold will also rise.

b. The market for fresh paper made from recycled stock: this is a rightward shift in supply due to a technological innovation. As a result of this shift, the equilibrium price of fresh paper made from recycled stock will fall and the equilibrium quantity bought and sold will rise.

c. The market for movies at a local movie theater: this is a leftward shift in demand caused by a fall in the price of a substitute, on-demand films. As a result of this shift, the equilibrium price of movie tickets will fall and the equilibrium number of people who go to the movies will also fall.

2. Upon the announcement of the new chip, the demand curve for computers using the earlier chip shifts leftward, as demand decreases, and the supply curve for these computers shifts rightward, as supply increases.

a. If demand decreases relatively more than supply increases, then the equilibrium quantity falls, as shown here:

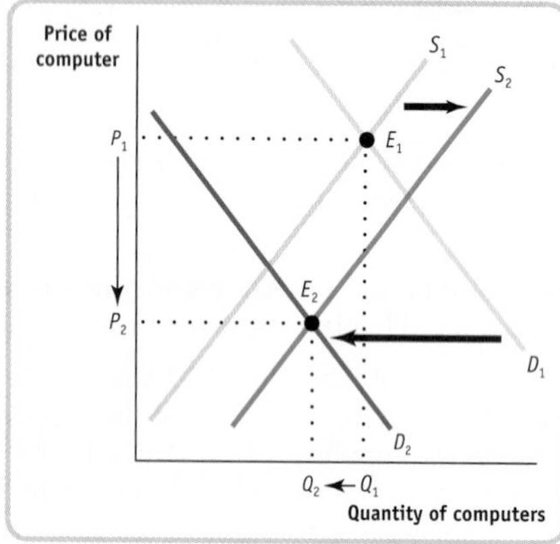

b. If supply increases relatively more than demand decreases, then the equilibrium quantity rises, as shown here:

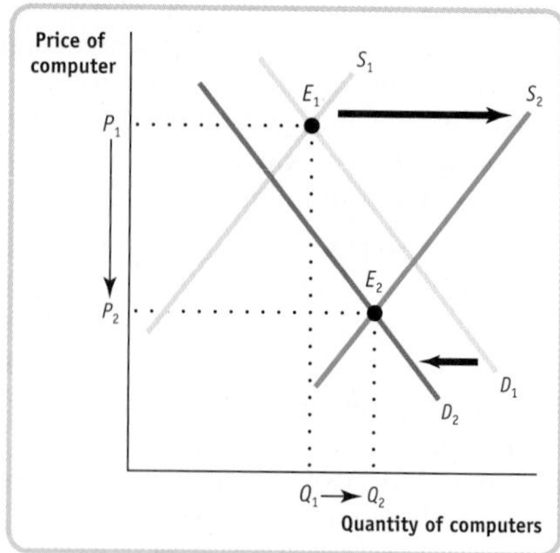

In both cases, the equilibrium price falls.

Chapter Four

4-1 CHECK YOUR UNDERSTANDING

1. a. A consumer buys each pepper if the price is less than (or just equal to) the consumer's willingness to pay for that pepper. The demand schedule is constructed by asking how many peppers will be demanded at any given price. A producer will continue to supply peppers as long as the price is greater than, or just equal to, the producer's cost. The supply schedule is constructed by asking how many peppers will be supplied at any price. The following table illustrates the demand and supply schedules.

b. The quantity demanded equals the quantity supplied at a price of $0.50, the equilibrium price. At that price, a total quantity of five peppers will be bought and sold.

c. Casey will buy three peppers and receive a consumer surplus of $0.40 on his first, $0.20 on his second, and $0.00 on his third pepper. Josey will buy two peppers and receive a consumer surplus of $0.30 on her first and $0.10 on her second pepper. Total consumer surplus is therefore $1.00. Cara will supply three peppers and receive a producer surplus of $0.40 on her first, $0.40 on her second, and $0.10 on her third pepper. Jamie will supply two peppers and receive a producer surplus of $0.20 on his first and $0.00 on his second pepper. Total producer surplus is $1.10. Total surplus in this market is therefore $1.00 + $1.10 = $2.10.

Price of pepper	Quantity of peppers demanded	Quantity of peppers demanded by Casey	Quantity of peppers demanded by Josey	Quantity of peppers supplied	Quantity of peppers supplied by Cara	Quantity of peppers supplied by Jamie
$0.90	1	1	0	8	4	4
0.80	2	1	1	7	4	3
0.70	3	2	1	7	4	3
0.60	4	2	2	6	4	2
0.50	5	3	2	5	3	2
0.40	6	3	3	4	3	1
0.30	8	4	4	3	2	1
0.20	8	4	4	2	2	0
0.10	8	4	4	2	2	0
0.00	8	4	4	0	0	0

2. The new guideline is likely to reduce the total life span of kidney recipients because older recipients (those with young children) are more likely to get a kidney compared to the original guideline. As a result, total surplus is likely to fall. However, this new policy can be justified as an acceptable sacrifice of efficiency for fairness because it's a desirable goal to reduce the chance of a young child losing a parent.

4-2 CHECK YOUR UNDERSTANDING

1. **a.** Fewer homeowners are willing to rent out their driveways because the price ceiling has reduced the payment they receive. This is an example of a fall in price leading to a fall in the quantity supplied. It is shown in the accompanying diagram by the movement from point *E* to point *A* along the supply curve, a reduction in quantity of 400 parking spaces.

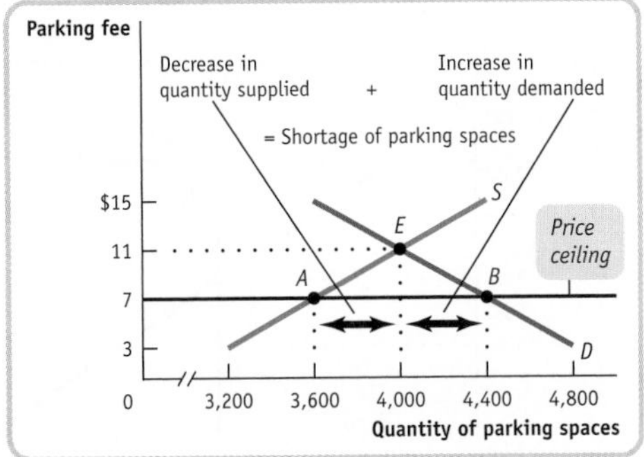

b. The quantity demanded increases by 400 spaces as the price decreases. At a lower price, more fans are willing to drive and rent a parking space. It is shown in the diagram by the movement from point *E* to point *B* along the demand curve.

c. Under a price ceiling, the quantity demanded exceeds the quantity supplied; as a result, shortages arise. In this case, there will be a shortage of 800 parking spaces. It is shown by the horizontal distance between points *A* and *B*.

d. Price ceilings result in wasted resources. The additional time fans spend to guarantee a parking space is wasted time.

e. Price ceilings lead to inefficient allocation of a good—here, the parking spaces—to consumers.

f. Price ceilings lead to black markets.

2. **a.** False. By lowering the price that producers receive, a price ceiling leads to a decrease in the quantity supplied.

b. True. A price ceiling leads to a lower quantity supplied than in an efficient, unregulated market. As a result, some people who would have been willing to pay the market price, and so would have gotten the good in an unregulated market, are unable to obtain it when a price ceiling is imposed.

c. True. Those producers who still sell the product now receive less for it and are therefore worse off. Other producers will no longer find it worthwhile to sell the product at all and so will also be made worse off.

3. **a.** Since the apartment is rented quickly at the same price, there is no change (either gain or loss) in producer surplus. So any change in total surplus comes from changes in consumer surplus. When you are evicted, the amount of consumer surplus you lose is equal to the difference between your willingness to pay for the apartment and the rent-controlled price. When the apartment is rented to someone else at the same price, the amount of consumer surplus the new renter gains is equal to the difference between his or her willingness to pay and the rent-controlled price. So this will be a pure transfer of surplus from one person to another only if both your willingness to pay and the new renter's willingness to pay are the same. Since under rent control apartments are not always allocated to those who have the highest willingness to pay, the new renter's willingness to pay may be either equal to, lower, or higher than your willingness to pay. If the new renter's willingness to pay is lower than yours, this will create additional deadweight loss: there is some additional consumer surplus that is lost. However, if the new renter's willingness to pay is higher than yours, this will create an increase in total surplus, as the new renter gains more consumer surplus than you lost.

b. This creates deadweight loss: if you were able to give the ticket away, someone else would be able to obtain consumer surplus, equal to their willingness to pay for the ticket. You neither gain nor lose any surplus, since you cannot go to the concert whether or not you give the ticket away. If you were able to sell the ticket, the buyer would obtain consumer surplus equal to the difference between their willingness to pay for the ticket and the price at which you sell the ticket. In addition, you would obtain producer surplus equal to the difference between the price at which you sell the ticket and your cost of selling the ticket (which, since you won the ticket, is presumably zero). Since the restriction to neither sell nor give away the ticket means that this surplus cannot be obtained by anybody, it creates deadweight loss. If you could give the ticket away, as described above, there would be consumer surplus that accrues to the recipient of the ticket; and if you give the ticket to the person with the highest willingness to pay, there would be no deadweight loss.

c. This creates deadweight loss. If students buy ice cream on campus, they obtain consumer surplus: their willingness to pay must have been higher than the price of the ice cream. Your college obtains producer surplus: the price is higher than your college's cost of selling the ice cream. Prohibiting the sale of ice cream on campus means that these two sources of total surplus are lost: there is deadweight loss.

d. Given that your dog values ice cream equally as much as you do, this is a pure transfer of surplus. As you lose consumer surplus, your dog gains equally as much consumer surplus.

4-3 CHECK YOUR UNDERSTANDING

1. **a.** Some gas station owners will benefit from getting a higher price. Q_F indicates the sales made by these owners. But some will lose; there are those who make sales at the market equilibrium price of P_E but do not make sales

at the regulated price of P_F. These missed sales are indicated on the graph by the fall in the quantity demanded along the demand curve, from point *E* to point *A*.

b. Those who buy gas at the higher price of P_F will probably receive better service; this is an example of *inefficiently high quality* caused by a price floor as gas station owners compete on quality rather than price. But opponents are correct to claim that consumers are generally worse off—those who buy at P_F would have been happy to buy at P_E, and many who were willing to buy at a price between P_E and P_F are now unwilling to buy. This is indicated on the graph by the fall in the quantity demanded along the demand curve, from point *E* to point *A*.

c. Proponents are wrong because consumers and some gas station owners are hurt by the price floor, which creates "missed opportunities"—desirable transactions between consumers and station owners that never take place. The deadweight loss, the amount of total surplus lost because of missed opportunities, is indicated by the shaded area in the accompanying figure. Moreover, the inefficiency of wasted resources arises as consumers spend time and money driving to other states. The price floor also tempts people to engage in black market activity. With the price floor, only Q_F units are sold. But at prices between P_E and P_F, there are drivers who cumulatively want to buy more than Q_F and owners who are willing to sell to them, a situation likely to lead to illegal activity.

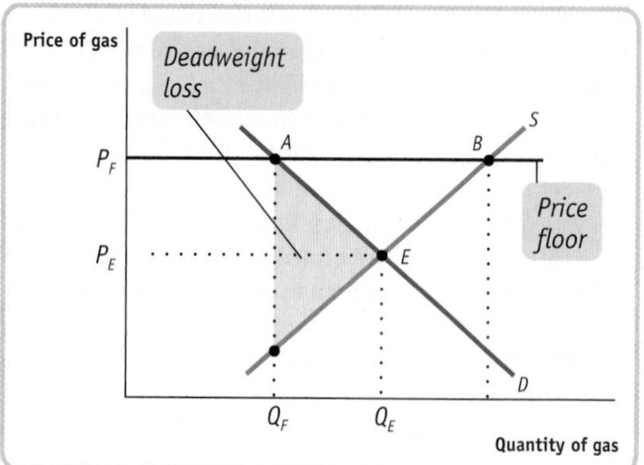

4-4 CHECK YOUR UNDERSTANDING

1. a. The price of a ride is $7 since the quantity demanded at this price is 6 million: $7 is the *demand price* of 6 million rides. This is represented by point *A* in the accompanying figure.

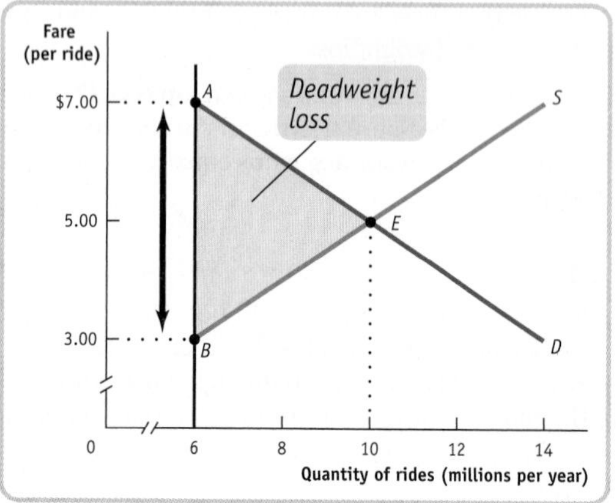

b. At 6 million rides, the supply price is $3 per ride, represented by point *B* in the figure. The wedge between the demand price of $7 per ride and the supply price of $3 per ride is the quota rent per ride, $4. This is represented in the figure above by the vertical distance between points *A* and *B*.

c. The quota discourages 4 million mutually beneficial transactions. The shaded triangle in the figure represents the deadweight loss.

d. At 9 million rides, the demand price is $5.50 per ride, indicated by point *C* in the accompanying figure, and the supply price is $4.50 per ride, indicated by point *D*. The quota rent is the difference between the demand price and the supply price: $1. The deadweight loss is represented by the shaded triangle in the figure. As you can see, the deadweight loss is smaller when the quota is set at 9 million rides than when it is set at 6 million rides.

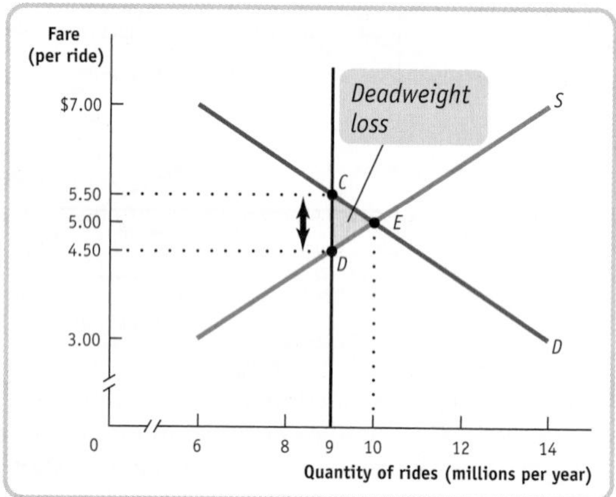

2. The accompanying figure shows a decrease in demand by 4 million rides, represented by a leftward shift of the demand curve from D_1 to D_2: at any given price, the quantity demanded falls by 4 million rides. (For example, at a price of $5, the quantity demanded falls from 10 million to 6 million rides per year.) This eliminates the effect of a quota limit of 8 million rides. At point E_2, the new market equilibrium, the equilibrium quantity is equal to the quota limit; as a result, the quota has no effect on the market.

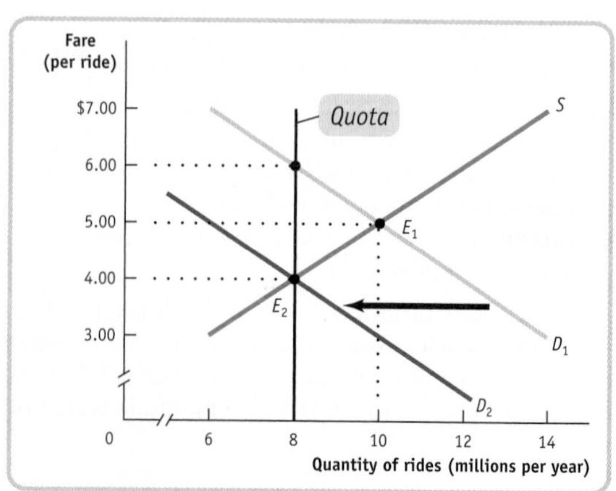

Chapter Five

5-1 CHECK YOUR UNDERSTANDING

1. By the midpoint method, the percent change in the price of strawberries is

$$\frac{\$1.00 - \$1.50}{(\$1.50 + \$1.00)/2} \times 100 = \frac{\$0.50}{\$1.25} \times 100 = -40\%$$

Similarly, the percent change in the quantity of strawberries demanded is

$$\frac{200{,}000 - 100{,}000}{(100{,}000 + 200{,}000)/2} \times 100 = \frac{100{,}000}{150{,}000} \times 100 = 67\%$$

Dropping the minus sign, the price elasticity of demand using the midpoint method is 67%/40% = 1.7.

2. By the midpoint method, the percent change in the quantity of movie tickets demanded in going from 4,000 tickets to 5,000 tickets is

$$\frac{5{,}000 - 4{,}000}{(4{,}000 + 5{,}000)/2} \times 100 = \frac{1{,}000}{4{,}500} \times 100 = 22\%$$

Since the price elasticity of demand is 1 at the current consumption level, it will take a 22% reduction in the price of movie tickets to generate a 22% increase in quantity demanded.

3. Since price rises, we know that quantity demanded must fall. Given the current price of $0.50, a $0.05 increase in price represents a 10% change, using the method in Equation 5-2. So the price elasticity of demand is

$$\frac{\text{change in quantity demanded}}{10\%} = 1.2$$

so that the percent change in quantity demanded is 12%. A 12% decrease in quantity demanded represents 100,000 × 0.12, or 12,000 sandwiches.

5-2 CHECK YOUR UNDERSTANDING

1. **a.** Elastic demand. Consumers are highly responsive to changes in price. For a rise in price, the quantity effect (which tends to reduce total revenue) outweighs the price effect (which tends to increase total revenue). Overall, this leads to a fall in total revenue.

b. Unit-elastic demand. Here the revenue lost to the fall in price is exactly equal to the revenue gained from higher sales. The quantity effect exactly offsets the price effect.

c. Inelastic demand. Consumers are relatively unresponsive to changes in price. For consumers to purchase a given percent increase in output, the price must fall by an even greater percent. The price effect of a fall in price (which tends to reduce total revenue) outweighs the quantity effect (which tends to increase total revenue). As a result, total revenue decreases.

d. Inelastic demand. Consumers are relatively unresponsive to price, so a given percent fall in output is accompanied by an even greater percent rise in price. The price effect of a rise in price (which tends to increase total revenue) outweighs the quantity effect (which tends to reduce total revenue). As a result, total revenue increases.

2. **a.** The demand of an accident victim for a blood transfusion is very likely to be perfectly inelastic because there is no substitute and it is necessary for survival. The demand curve will be vertical, at a quantity equal to the needed transfusion quantity.

b. Students' demand for green erasers is likely to be perfectly elastic because there are easily available substitutes: nongreen erasers. The demand curve will be horizontal, at a price equal to that of nongreen erasers.

5-3 CHECK YOUR UNDERSTANDING

1. By the midpoint method, the percent increase in Chelsea's income is

$$\frac{\$18{,}000 - \$12{,}000}{(\$12{,}000 + \$18{,}000)/2} \times 100 = \frac{\$6{,}000}{\$15{,}000} \times 100 = 40\%$$

Similarly, the percent increase in her consumption of CDs is

$$\frac{40 \quad 10}{(10 \quad 40)/2} \times 100 = \frac{30}{25} \times 100 = 120\%$$

So Chelsea's income elasticity of demand for CDs is 120%/40% = 3.

2. Sanjay's consumption of expensive restaurant meals will fall more than 10% because a given percent change in income (a fall of 10% here) induces a larger percent change in consumption of an income-elastic good.

3. The cross-price elasticity of demand is 5%/20% = 0.25. Since the cross-price elasticity of demand is positive, the two goods are substitutes.

5-4 CHECK YOUR UNDERSTANDING

1. By the midpoint method, the percent change in the number of hours of web-design services contracted is

$$\frac{500{,}000 - 300{,}000}{(300{,}000 + 500{,}000)/2} \times 100 = \frac{200{,}000}{400{,}000} \times 100 = 50\%$$

Similarly, the percent change in the price of web-design services is:

$$\frac{\$150 - \$100}{(\$100 + \$150)/2} \times 100 = \frac{\$50}{\$125} \times 100 = 40\%$$

The price elasticity of supply is 50%/40% = 1.25. So supply is elastic.

2. True. An increase in demand raises price. If the price elasticity of supply of milk is low, then relatively little additional supply will be forthcoming as the price rises. As a result, the price of milk will rise substantially to satisfy the increased demand for milk. If the price elasticity of supply is high, then a relatively large amount of additional supply will be produced as the price rises. As a result, the price of milk will rise only by a little to satisfy the higher demand for milk.

3. False. It is true that long-run price elasticities of supply are generally larger than short-run elasticities of supply. But this means that the short-run supply curves are generally steeper, not flatter, than the long-run supply curves.

4. True. When supply is perfectly elastic, the supply curve is a horizontal line. So a change in demand has no effect on price; it affects only the quantity bought and sold.

5-5 CHECK YOUR UNDERSTANDING

1. a. Without the excise tax, Zhang, Yves, Xavier, and Walter sell, and Ana, Bernice, Chizuko, and Dagmar buy one can of soda each, at \$0.40 per can. So the quantity bought and sold is 4.

b. With the excise tax, Zhang and Yves sell, and Ana and Bernice buy one can of soda each. So the quantity bought and sold is 2.

c. Without the excise tax, Ana's individual consumer surplus is \$0.70 – \$0.40 = \$0.30, Bernice's is \$0.60 – \$0.40 = \$0.20, Chizuko's is \$0.50 – \$0.40 = \$0.10, and Dagmar's is \$0.40 – \$0.40 = \$0.00. Total consumer surplus is \$0.30 + \$0.20 + \$0.10 + \$0.00 = \$0.60. With the tax, Ana's individual consumer surplus is \$0.70 – \$0.60 = \$0.10 and Bernice's is \$0.60 – \$0.60 = \$0.00. Total consumer surplus post-tax is \$0.10 + \$0.00 = \$0.10. So the total consumer surplus lost because of the tax is \$0.60 – \$0.10 = \$0.50.

d. Without the excise tax, Zhang's individual producer surplus is \$0.40 – \$0.10 = \$0.30, Yves's is \$0.40 – \$0.20 = \$0.20, Xavier's is \$0.40 – \$0.30 = \$0.10, and Walter's is \$0.40 – \$0.40 = \$0.00. Total producer surplus is \$0.30 + \$0.20 + \$0.10 + \$0.00 = \$0.60. With the tax, Zhang's individual producer surplus is \$0.20 – \$0.10 = \$0.10 and Yves's is \$0.20 – \$0.20 = \$0.00. Total producer surplus post-tax is \$0.10 + \$0.00 = \$0.10. So the total producer surplus lost because of the tax is \$0.60 – \$0.10 = \$0.50.

e. With the tax, two cans of soda are sold, so the government tax revenue from this excise tax is 2 × \$0.40 = \$0.80.

f. Total surplus without the tax is \$0.60 + \$0.60 = \$1.20. With the tax, total surplus is \$0.10 + \$0.10 = \$0.20, and government tax revenue is \$0.80. So deadweight loss from this excise tax is \$1.20 – (\$0.20 + \$0.80) = \$0.20.

2. a. The demand for gasoline is inelastic because there is no close substitute for gasoline itself and it is difficult for drivers to arrange substitutes for driving, such as taking public transportation. As a result, the deadweight loss from a tax on gasoline would be relatively small, as shown in the accompanying diagram.

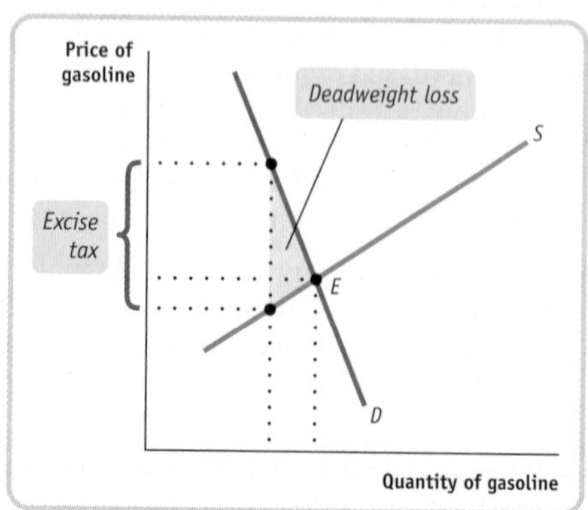

b. The demand for milk chocolate bars is elastic because there are close substitutes: dark chocolate bars, milk chocolate kisses, and so on. As a result, the deadweight loss from a tax on milk chocolate bars would be relatively large, as shown in the accompanying diagram.

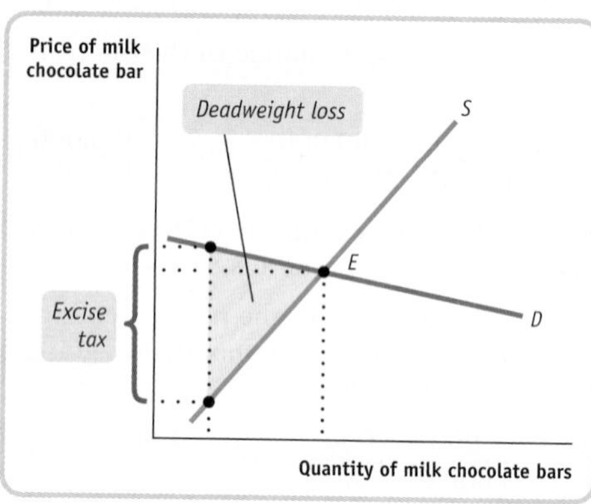

Chapter Six

6-1 CHECK YOUR UNDERSTANDING

1. a. The fixed input is the 10-ton machine, and the variable input is electricity.

b. As you can see from the declining numbers in the third column of the accompanying table, electricity does indeed exhibit diminishing returns: the marginal product of each additional kilowatt of electricity is less than that of the previous kilowatt.

Quantity of electricity (kilowatts)	Quantity of ice (pounds)	Marginal product of electricity (pounds per kilowatt)
0	0	
		1,000
1	1,000	
		800
2	1,800	
		600
3	2,400	
		400
4	2,800	

c. A 50% increase in the size of the fixed input means that Bernie now has a 15-ton machine. So the fixed input is now the 15-ton machine. Since it generates a 100% increase in output for any given amount of electricity, the quantity of output and marginal product are now as shown in the accompanying table.

Quantity of electricity (kilowatts)	Quantity of ice (pounds)	Marginal product of electricity (pounds per kilowatt)
0	0	
		2,000
1	2,000	
		1,600
2	3,600	
		1,200
3	4,800	
		800
4	5,600	

6-2 CHECK YOUR UNDERSTANDING

1. a. As shown in the accompanying table, the marginal cost for each pie is found by multiplying the marginal cost of the previous pie by 1.5. Variable cost for each output level is found by summing the marginal cost for all the pies produced to reach that output level. So, for example, the variable cost of three pies is $1.00 + $1.50 + $2.25 = $4.75. Average fixed cost for *Q* pies is calculated as $9.00/*Q* since fixed cost is $9.00. Average variable cost for *Q* pies is equal to variable cost for the *Q* pies divided by *Q*; for example, the average variable cost of five pies is $13.19/5, or approximately $2.64. Finally, average total cost can be calculated in two equivalent ways: as *TC/Q* or as *AVC* + *AFC*.

Quantity of pies	Marginal cost of pie	Variable cost	Average fixed cost of pie	Average variable cost of pie	Average total cost of pie
0		$0.00	—	—	—
	$1.00				
1		1.00	$9.00	$1.00	$10.00
	1.50				
2		2.50	4.50	1.25	5.75
	2.25				
3		4.75	3.00	1.58	4.58
	3.38				
4		8.13	2.25	2.03	4.28
	5.06				
5		13.19	1.80	2.64	4.44
	7.59				
6		20.78	1.50	3.46	4.96

b. The spreading effect dominates the diminishing returns effect when average total cost is falling: the fall in *AFC* dominates the rise in *AVC* for pies 1 to 4. The diminishing returns effect dominates when average total cost is rising: the rise in *AVC* dominates the fall in *AFC* for pies 5 and 6.

c. Alicia's minimum-cost output is 4 pies; this generates the lowest average total cost, $4.28. When output is less than 4, the marginal cost of a pie is less than the average total cost of the pies already produced. So making an additional pie lowers average total cost. For example, the marginal cost of pie 3 is $2.25, whereas the average total cost of pies 1 and 2 is $5.75. So making pie 3 lowers average total cost to $4.58, equal to (2 × $5.75 + $2.25)/3. When output is more than 4, the marginal cost of a pie is greater than the average total cost of the pies already produced. Consequently, making an additional pie raises average total cost. So, although the marginal cost of pie 6 is $7.59, the average total cost of pies 1 through 5 is $4.44. Making pie 6 raises average total cost to $4.96, equal to (5 × $4.44 + $7.59)/6.

6-3 CHECK YOUR UNDERSTANDING

1. a. The accompanying table shows the average total cost of producing 12,000, 22,000, and 30,000 units for each of the three choices of fixed cost. For example, if the firm makes choice 1, the total cost of producing 12,000 units of output is $8,000 + 12,000 × $1.00 = $20,000. The average total cost of producing 12,000 units of output is therefore $20,000/12,000 = $1.67. The other average total costs are calculated similarly.

	12,000 units	22,000 units	30,000 units
Average total cost from choice 1	$1.67	$1.36	$1.27
Average total cost from choice 2	1.75	1.30	1.15
Average total cost from choice 3	2.25	1.34	1.05

So if the firm wanted to produce 12,000 units, it would make choice 1 because this gives it the lowest average total cost. If it wanted to produce 22,000 units, it would make choice 2. If it wanted to produce 30,000 units, it would make choice 3.

b. Having historically produced 12,000 units, the firm would have adopted choice 1. When producing 12,000 units, the firm would have had an average total cost of $1.67. When output jumps to 22,000 units, the firm cannot alter its choice of fixed cost in the short run, so its average total cost in the short run will be $1.36. In the long run, however, it will adopt choice 2, making its average total cost fall to $1.30.

c. If the firm believes that the increase in demand is temporary, it should not alter its fixed cost from choice 1 because choice 2 generates higher average total cost as soon as output falls back to its original quantity of 12,000 units: $1.75 versus $1.67.

2. a. This firm is likely to experience constant returns to scale. To increase output, the firm must hire more workers, purchase more computers, and pay additional telephone charges. Because these inputs are easily available, their long-run average total cost is unlikely to change as output increases.

b. This firm is likely to experience decreasing returns to scale. As the firm takes on more projects, the costs of communication and coordination required to implement the expertise of the firm's owner are likely to increase.

c. This firm is likely to experience increasing returns to scale. Because diamond mining requires a large initial set-up cost for excavation equipment, long-run average total cost will fall as output increases.

3. The accompanying diagram shows the long-run average total cost curve (*LRATC*) and the short-run average total cost curve corresponding to a long-run output choice of 5 cases of salsa (ATC_5). The curve ATC_5 shows the short-run average total cost for which the level of fixed cost minimizes average total cost at an output of 5 cases of salsa. This is confirmed by the fact that at 5 cases per day, ATC_5 touches *LRATC*, the long-run average total cost curve.

If Selena expects to produce only 4 cases of salsa for a long time, she should change her fixed cost. If she does *not* change her fixed cost and produces 4 cases of salsa, her average total cost in the short run is indicated by point *B* on ATC_5; it is no longer on the *LRATC*. If she changes her fixed cost, though, her average total cost could be lower, at point *A*.

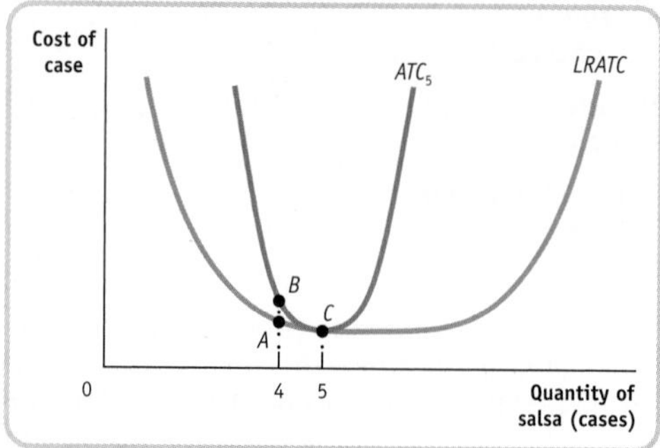

Chapter Seven

7-1 CHECK YOUR UNDERSTANDING

1. a. With only two producers in the world, each producer will represent a sizable share of the market. So the industry will not be perfectly competitive.

b. Because each producer of natural gas from the North Sea has only a small market share of total world supply of natural gas, and since natural gas is a standardized product, the natural gas industry will be perfectly competitive.

c. Because each designer has a distinctive style, high-fashion clothes are not a standardized product. So the industry will not be perfectly competitive.

d. The market described here is the market in each city for tickets to baseball games. Since there are only one or two teams in each major city, each team will represent a sizable share of the market. So the industry will not be perfectly competitive.

7-2 CHECK YOUR UNDERSTANDING

1. a. The firm should shut down immediately when price is less than minimum average variable cost, the shut-down price. In the accompanying diagram, this is optimal for prices in the range 0 to P_1.

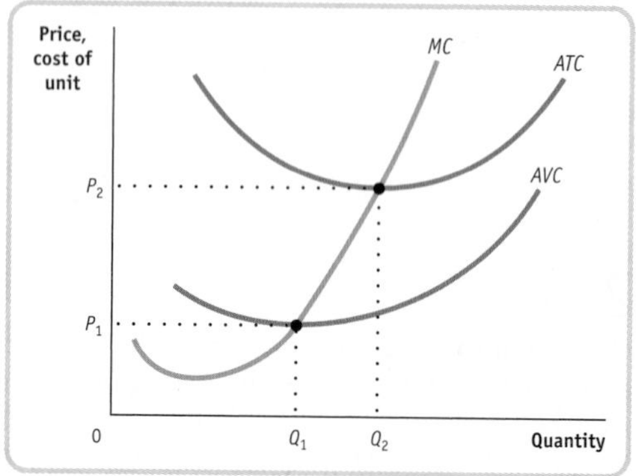

b. When price is greater than minimum average variable cost (the shut-down price) but less than minimum average total cost (the break-even price), the firm should continue to operate in the short run even though it is making a loss. This is optimal for prices in the range P_1 to P_2 and for quantities Q_1 to Q_2.

c. When price exceeds minimum average total cost (the break-even price), the firm makes a profit. This happens for prices in excess of P_2 and results in quantities greater than Q_2.

2. This is an example of a temporary shut-down by a firm when the market price lies below the shut-down price, the minimum average variable cost. In this case, the market price is the price of a lobster meal and variable cost is the variable cost of serving such a meal, such as the cost of the lobster, employee wages, and so on. In this example, however, it is the average variable cost curve rather than the market price that shifts over time, due to seasonal changes in the cost of lobsters. Maine lobster shacks have relatively low average variable cost during the summer, when cheap Maine lobsters are available. During the rest of the year, their average variable cost is relatively high due to the high cost of imported lobsters. So the lobster shacks are open for business during the summer, when their minimum average variable cost lies below price. But they close during the rest of the year, when price lies below their minimum average variable cost.

7-3 CHECK YOUR UNDERSTANDING

1. a. A fall in the fixed cost of production generates a fall in the average total cost of production and, in the short run, an increase in each firm's profit at the current output level. So in the long run new firms will enter

the industry. The increase in supply drives down price and profits. Once profits are driven back to zero, entry will cease.

b. An increase in wages generates an increase in the average variable and the average total cost of production at every output level. In the short run, firms incur losses at the current output level, and so in the long run some firms will exit the industry. (If the average variable cost rises sufficiently, some firms may even shut down in the short run.) As firms exit, supply decreases, price rises, and losses are reduced. Exit will cease once losses return to zero.

c. Price will rise as a result of the increased demand, leading to a short-run increase in profits at the current output level. In the long run, firms will enter the industry, generating an increase in supply, a fall in price, and a fall in profits. Once profits are driven back to zero, entry will cease.

d. The shortage of a key input causes that input's price to increase, resulting in an increase in average variable and average total costs for producers. Firms incur losses in the short run, and some firms will exit the industry in the long run. The fall in supply generates an increase in price and decreased losses. Exit will cease when losses have returned to zero.

2. In the accompanying diagram, point X_{MKT} in panel (b), the intersection of S_1 and D_1, represents the long-run industry equilibrium before the change in consumer tastes. When tastes change, demand falls and the industry moves in the short run to point Y_{MKT} in panel (b), at the intersection of the new demand curve D_2 and S_1, the short-run supply curve representing the same number of egg producers as in the original equilibrium at point X_{MKT}. As the market price falls, an individual firm reacts by producing less—as shown in panel (a)—as long as the market price remains above the minimum average variable cost. If market price falls below minimum average variable cost, the firm would shut down immediately. At point Y_{MKT} the price of eggs is below minimum average total cost, creating losses for producers. This leads some firms to exit, which shifts the short-run industry supply curve leftward to S_2. A new long-run equilibrium is established at point Z_{MKT}. As this occurs, the market price rises again, and, as shown in panel (c), each remaining producer reacts by increasing output (here, from point Y to point Z). All remaining producers again make zero profits. The decrease in the quantity of eggs supplied in the industry comes entirely from the exit of some producers from the industry. The long-run industry supply curve is the curve labeled LRS in panel (b).

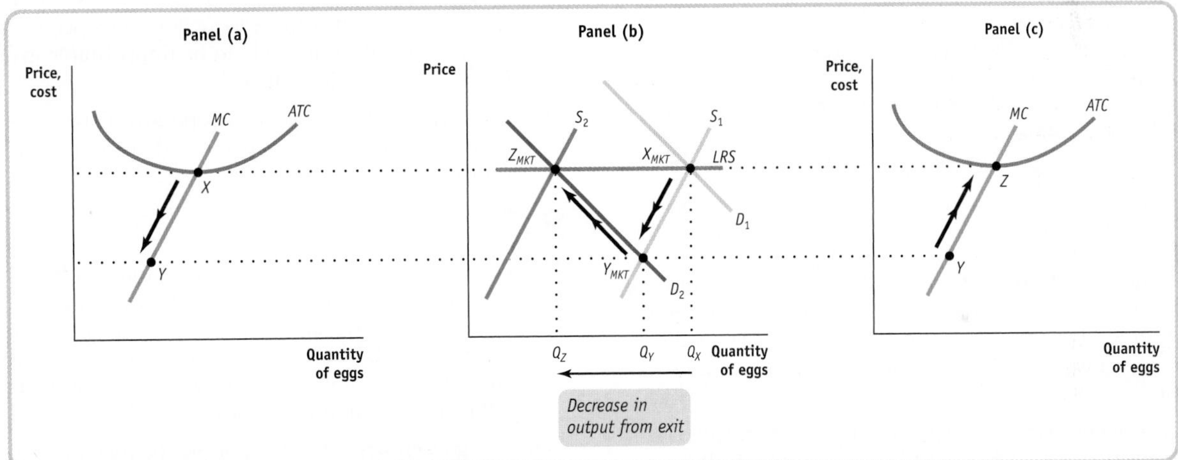

Chapter Eight

8-1 CHECK YOUR UNDERSTANDING

1. a. This does not support the conclusion. Texas Tea has a limited amount of oil, and the price has risen in order to equalize supply and demand.

b. This supports the conclusion because the market for home heating oil has become monopolized, and a monopolist will reduce the quantity supplied and raise price to generate profit.

c. This does not support the conclusion. Texas Tea has raised its price to consumers because the price of its input, home heating oil, has increased.

d. This supports the conclusion. The fact that other firms have begun to supply heating oil at a lower price implies that Texas Tea must have earned sufficient profits to attract the other to Frigid.

e. This supports the conclusion. It indicates that Texas Tea enjoys a barrier to entry because it controls access to the only Alaskan heating oil pipeline.

2. a. The price at each output level is found by dividing the total revenue by the number of emeralds produced; for example, the price when 3 emeralds are produced is $252/3 = $84. The price at the various output levels is then used to construct the demand schedule in the accompanying table.

b. The marginal revenue schedule is found by calculating the change in total revenue as output increases by one unit. For example, the marginal revenue generated by increasing output from 2 to 3 emeralds is ($252 – $186) = $66.

c. The quantity effect component of marginal revenue is the additional revenue generated by selling one more unit of the good at the market price. For example, as shown in the accompanying table, at 3 emeralds, the market price is $84; so when going from 2 to 3 emeralds, the quantity effect is equal to $84.

d. The price effect component of marginal revenue is the decline in total revenue caused by the fall in price when one more unit is sold. For example, as shown in the table, when only 2 emeralds are sold, each emerald sells at a price of $93. However, when Emerald, Inc. sells an additional emerald, the price must fall by $9 to $84. So the price effect component in going from 2 to 3 emeralds is (–$9) × 2 = –$18. That's because 2 emeralds can only be sold at a price of $84 when 3 emeralds in total are sold, although they could have been sold at a price of $93 when only 2 in total were sold.

Quantity of emeralds demanded	Price of emerald	Marginal revenue	Quantity effect component	Price effect component
1	$100			
		$86	$93	–$7
2	93			
		66	84	–18
3	84			
		28	70	–42
4	70			
		–30	50	–80
5	50			

e. In order to determine Emerald, Inc.'s profit-maximizing output level, you must know its marginal cost at each output level. Its profit-maximizing output level is the one at which marginal revenue is equal to marginal cost.

3. As the accompanying diagram shows, the marginal cost curve shifts upward to $400. The profit-maximizing price rises and quantity falls. Profit falls from $3,200 to $300 × 6 = $1,800. Competitive industry profits, though, are unchanged at zero.

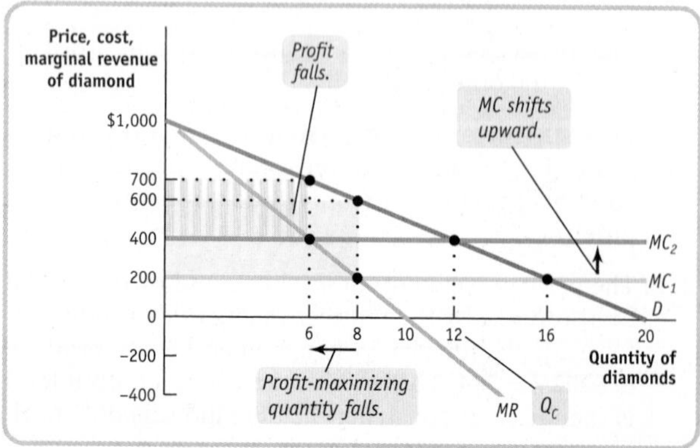

8-2 CHECK YOUR UNDERSTANDING

1. a. The world oil industry is an oligopoly because a few countries control a necessary resource for production, oil reserves.

b. The microprocessor industry is an oligopoly because two firms possess superior technology and so dominate industry production.

c. The wide-body passenger jet industry is an oligopoly because there are increasing returns to scale in production.

2. a. The firm is likely to act noncooperatively and raise output, which will generate a negative price effect. But because the firm's current market share is small, the negative price effect will fall much more heavily on its rivals' revenues than on its own. At the same time, the firm will benefit from a positive quantity effect.

b. The firm is likely to act noncooperatively and raise output, which will generate a fall in price. Because its rivals have higher costs, they will lose money at the lower price while the firm continues to make profits. So the firm may be able to drive its rivals out of business by increasing its output.

c. The firm is likely to collude. Because it is costly for consumers to switch products, the firm would have to lower its price quite substantially (by increasing quantity a lot) to induce consumers to switch to its product. So increasing output is likely to be unprofitable given the large negative price effect.

d. The firm is likely to act uncooperatively because it knows its rivals cannot increase their output in retaliation.

8-3 CHECK YOUR UNDERSTANDING

1. a. Cable Internet service is a natural monopoly. So the government should intervene only if it believes that price exceeds average total cost, where average total cost is based on the cost of laying the cable. In this case it should impose a price ceiling equal to average total cost. Otherwise, it should do nothing.

b. The government should approve the merger only if it fosters competition by transferring some of the company's landing slots to another, competing airline.

2. a. False. As can be seen from Figure 8-8, panel (b), the inefficiency arises from the fact that some of the consumer surplus is transformed into deadweight loss (the yellow area), not that it is transformed into profit (the green area).

b. True. If a monopolist sold to all customers who have a valuation greater than or equal to marginal cost, all mutually beneficial transactions would occur and there would be no deadweight loss.

8-4 CHECK YOUR UNDERSTANDING

1. a. Ladders are not differentiated as a result of monopolistic competition. A ladder producer makes different ladders (tall ladders versus short ladders) to satisfy different consumer needs, not to avoid competition with rivals. So two tall ladders made by two different producers will be indistinguishable by consumers.

b. Soft drinks are an example of product differentiation as a result of monopolistic competition. For example, several producers make colas; each is differentiated in terms of taste, which fast-food chains sell it, and so on.

c. Department stores are an example of product differentiation as a result of monopolistic competition. They serve different clienteles that have different price sensitivities and different tastes. They also offer different levels of customer service and are situated in different locations.

d. Steel is not differentiated as a result of monopolistic competition. Different types of steel (beams versus sheets) are made for different purposes, not to distinguish one steel manufacturer's products from another's.

2. a. Perfectly competitive industries and monopolistically competitive industries both have many sellers. So it may be hard to distinguish between them solely in terms of number of firms. And in both market structures, there is free entry into and exit from the industry in the long run. But in a perfectly competitive industry, one standardized product is sold; in a monopolistically competitive industry, products are differentiated. So you should ask whether products are differentiated in the industry.

b. In a monopoly there is only one firm, but a monopolistically competitive industry contains many firms. So you should ask whether or not there is a single firm in the industry.

Chapter Nine

9-1 CHECK YOUR UNDERSTANDING

1. a. The external cost is the pollution caused by the wastewater runoff, an uncompensated cost imposed by the poultry farms on their neighbors.

b. Since poultry farmers do not take the external cost of their actions into account when making decisions about how much wastewater to generate, they will create more runoff than is socially optimal in the absence of government intervention or a private deal. They will produce runoff up to the point at which the marginal social benefit of an additional unit of runoff is zero; however, their neighbors experience a high, positive level of marginal social cost of runoff from this output level. So the quantity of wastewater runoff is inefficient: reducing runoff by one unit would reduce total social benefit by less than it would reduce total social cost.

c. At the socially optimal quantity of wastewater runoff, the marginal social benefit is equal to the marginal social cost. This quantity is lower than the quantity of wastewater runoff that would be created in the absence of government intervention or a private deal.

2. Yasmin's reasoning is not correct: allowing some late returns of books is likely to be socially optimal. Although you impose a marginal social cost on others every day that you are late in returning a book, there is some positive marginal social benefit to you of returning a book late—for example, you get a longer period to use it in working on a term paper.

The socially optimal number of days that a book is returned late is the number at which the marginal social benefit equals the marginal social cost. A fine so stiff that it prevents any late returns is likely to result in a situation in which people return books although the marginal social benefit of keeping them another day is greater than the marginal social cost—an inefficient outcome. In that case, allowing an overdue patron another day would increase total social benefit more than it would increase total social cost. So charging a moderate fine that reduces the number of days that books are returned late to the socially optimal number of days is appropriate.

9-2 CHECK YOUR UNDERSTANDING

1. This is a misguided argument. Allowing polluters to sell emissions permits makes polluters face a cost of polluting: the opportunity cost of the permit. If a polluter chooses not to reduce its emissions, it cannot sell its emissions permits. As a result, it forgoes the opportunity of making money from the sale of the permits. So despite the fact that the polluter receives a monetary benefit from selling the permits, the scheme has the desired effect: to make polluters internalize the externality of their actions.

2. a. If the emissions tax is smaller than the marginal social cost at Q_{OPT}, a polluter will face a marginal cost of polluting (equal to the amount of the tax) that is less than the marginal social cost at the socially optimal quantity of pollution. Since a polluter will produce emissions up to the point where the marginal social benefit is equal to its marginal cost, the resulting amount of pollution will be larger than the socially optimal quantity. As a result, there is inefficiency: if the amount of pollution is larger than the socially optimal quantity, the marginal social cost exceeds the marginal social benefit, and society could gain from a reduction in emissions levels.

If the emissions tax is greater than the marginal social cost at Q_{OPT}, a polluter will face a marginal cost of polluting (equal to the amount of the tax) that is greater than the marginal social cost at the socially optimal quantity of pollution. This will lead the polluter to reduce emissions below the socially optimal quantity. This also is inefficient: whenever the marginal social benefit is greater than the marginal social cost, society could benefit from an increase in emissions levels.

b. If the total amount of allowable pollution is set too high, the supply of emissions permits will be high and so the equilibrium price at which permits trade will be low. That is, polluters will face a marginal cost of polluting (the price of a permit) that is "too low"—lower than the marginal social cost at the socially optimal quantity of pollution. As a result, pollution will be greater than the socially optimal quantity. This is inefficient.

If the total level of allowable pollution is set too low, the supply of emissions permits will be low and so the equilibrium price at which permits trade will be high. That is, polluters will face a marginal cost of polluting (the price of a permit) that is "too high"—higher than the marginal social cost at the socially optimal quantity of pollution. As a result, pollution will be lower than the socially optimal quantity. This also is inefficient.

9-3 CHECK YOUR UNDERSTANDING

1. College education provides external benefits through the creation of knowledge. And student aid acts like a Pigouvian subsidy on higher education. If the marginal social benefit of higher education is indeed $40 billion, then student aid is an optimal policy.

2. **a.** Planting trees imposes an external benefit: the marginal social benefit of planting trees is higher than the marginal benefit to individual tree planters, since many people (not just those who plant the trees) can benefit from the increased air quality and lower summer temperatures. The difference between the marginal social benefit and the marginal benefit to individual tree planters is the marginal external benefit. A Pigouvian subsidy could be placed on each tree planted in urban areas in order to increase the marginal benefit to individual tree planters to the same level as the marginal social benefit.

   b. Water-saving toilets impose an external benefit: the marginal benefit to individual homeowners from replacing a traditional toilet with a water-saving toilet is zero, since water is virtually costless. But the marginal social benefit is large, since fewer rivers and aquifers need to be pumped. The difference between the marginal social benefit and the marginal benefit to individual home-owners is the marginal external benefit. A Pigouvian subsidy on installing water-saving toilets could bring the marginal benefit to individual homeowners in line with the marginal social benefit.

   c. Disposing of old computer monitors imposes an external cost: the marginal cost to those disposing of old computer monitors is lower than the marginal social cost, since environmental pollution is borne by people other than the person disposing of the monitor. The difference between the marginal social cost and the marginal cost to those disposing of old computer monitors is the marginal external cost. A Pigouvian tax on disposing of computer monitors, or a system of tradable permits for their disposal, could raise the marginal cost to those disposing of old computer monitors sufficiently to make it equal to the marginal social cost.

9-4 CHECK YOUR UNDERSTANDING

1. **a.** Use of a public park is nonexcludable, but it may or may not be rival in consumption, depending on the circumstances. For example, if both you and I use the park for jogging, then your use will not prevent my use—use of the park is nonrival in consumption. In this case the public park is a public good. But use of the park is rival in consumption if there are many people trying to use the jogging path at the same time or when my use of the public tennis court prevents your use of the same court. In this case the public park is a common resource.

   b. A cheese burrito is both excludable and rival in consumption. Hence it is a private good.

   c. Information from a password-protected website is excludable but nonrival in consumption. So it is an artificially scarce good.

   d. Publicly announced information on the path of an incoming hurricane is nonexcludable and nonrival in consumption. So it is a public good.

2. **a.** With 10 Homebodies and 6 Revelers, the marginal social benefit schedule of money spent on the party is as shown in the accompanying table.

Money spent on party	Marginal social benefit
$0	
	(10 × $0.05) + (6 × $0.13) = $1.28
1	
	(10 × $0.04) + (6 × $0.11) = $1.06
2	
	(10 × $0.03) + (6 × $0.09) = $0.84
3	
	(10 × $0.02) + (6 × $0.07) = $0.62
4	

   The efficient spending level is $2, the highest level for which the marginal social benefit is greater than the marginal cost ($1).

   b. With 6 Homebodies and 10 Revelers, the marginal social benefit schedule of money spent on the party is as shown in the accompanying table.

Money spent on party	Marginal social benefit
$0	
	(6 × $0.05) + (10 × $0.13) = $1.60
1	
	(6 × $0.04) + (10 × $0.11) = $1.34
2	
	(6 × $0.03) + (10 × $0.09) = $1.08
3	
	(6 × $0.02) + (10 × $0.07) = $0.82
4	

   The efficient spending level is now $3, the highest level for which the marginal social benefit is greater than the marginal cost ($1). The efficient level of spending has increased from that in part a because with relatively more Revelers than Homebodies, an additional dollar spent on the party generates a higher level of social benefit compared to when there are relatively more Homebodies than Revelers.

   c. When the numbers of Homebodies and Revelers are unknown but residents are asked their preferences, Homebodies will pretend to be Revelers to induce a higher level of spending on the public party. That's because a Homebody still receives a positive individual marginal benefit from an additional $1 spent, despite the fact that his or her individual marginal benefit is lower than that of a Reveler for every additional $1. In this case the "reported" marginal social benefit schedule of money spent on the party will be as shown in the accompanying table.

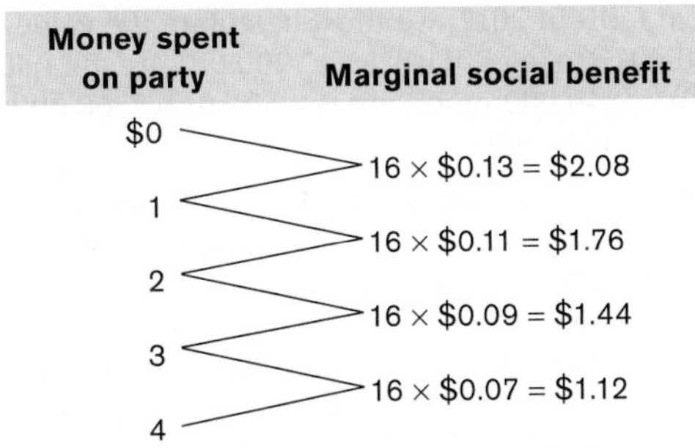

Money spent on party
Marginal social benefit
$0
1
2
3
4
16 × $0.13 = $2.08
16 × $0.11 = $1.76
16 × $0.09 = $1.44
16 × $0.07 = $1.12

As a result, $4 will be spent on the party, the highest level for which the "reported" marginal social benefit is greater than the marginal cost ($1). Regardless of whether there are 10 Homebodies and 6 Revelers (part a) or 6 Homebodies and 10 Revelers (part b), spending $4 in total on the party is clearly inefficient because marginal cost exceeds marginal social benefit at this spending level.

As a further exercise, consider how much Homebodies gain by this misrepresentation. In part a, the efficient level of spending is $2. So by misrepresenting their preferences, the 10 Homebodies gain, in total, 10 × ($0.03 + $0.02) = $0.50—that is, they gain the marginal individual benefit in going from a spending level of $2 to $4. The 6 Revelers also gain from the misrepresentations of the Homebodies; they gain 6 × ($0.09 + $0.07) = $0.96 in total. This outcome is clearly inefficient—when $4 in total is spent, the marginal cost is $1 but the marginal social benefit is only $0.62, indicating that too much money is being spent on the party.

In part b, the efficient level of spending is actually $3. The misrepresentation by the 6 Homebodies gains them, in total, 6 × $0.02 = $0.12, but the 10 Revelers gain 10 × $0.07 = $0.70 in total. This outcome is also clearly inefficient—when $4 is spent, marginal social benefit is only $0.12 + $0.70 = $0.82 but marginal cost is $1.

Chapter Ten

10-1 CHECK YOUR UNDERSTANDING

1. a. This is a microeconomic question because it addresses decisions made by consumers about a particular product.

   b. This is a macroeconomic question because it addresses consumer spending in the overall economy.

   c. This is a macroeconomic question because it addresses changes in the overall economy.

   d. This is a microeconomic question because it addresses changes in a particular market, in this case the market for geologists.

   e. This is a microeconomic question because it addresses choices made by consumers and producers about which mode of transportation to use.

   f. This is a microeconomic question because it addresses changes in a particular market.

   g. This is a macroeconomic question because it addresses changes in a measure of the economy's overall price level.

2. a. When people can't get credit to finance their purchases, they will be unable to spend money. This will weaken the economy, and as others see the economy weaken, they will also cut back on their spending in order to save for future bad times. As a result, the credit shortfall will spark a compounding effect through the economy as people cut back their spending, making the economy worse, leading to more cutbacks in spending, and so on.

   b. If you believe the economy is self-regulating, then you would advocate doing nothing in response to the slump.

   c. If you believe in Keynesian economics, you would advocate that policy makers undertake monetary and fiscal policies to stimulate spending in the economy.

10-2 CHECK YOUR UNDERSTANDING

1. We talk about business cycles for the economy as a whole because recessions and expansions are not confined to a few industries—they reflect downturns and upturns for the economy as a whole. In downturns, almost every sector of the economy reduces output and the number of people employed. Moreover, business cycles are an international phenomenon, sometimes moving in rough synchrony across countries.

2. Recessions cause a great deal of pain across the entire society. They cause large numbers of workers to lose their jobs and make it hard to find new jobs. Recessions hurt the standard of living of many families and are usually associated with a rise in the number of people living below the poverty line, an increase in the number of people who lose their houses because they can't afford their mortgage payments, and a fall in the percentage of Americans with health insurance. Recessions also hurt the profits of firms.

10-3 CHECK YOUR UNDERSTANDING

1. Countries with high rates of population growth will have to maintain higher growth rates of overall output than countries with low rates of population growth in order to achieve an increased standard of living per person because aggregate output will have to be divided among a larger number of people.

2. No, Argentina is not poorer than it was in the past. Both Argentina and Canada have experienced long-run growth. However, after World War II, Argentina did not make as much progress as Canada, perhaps because of political instability and bad macroeconomic policies. Canada's economy grew much faster than Argentina's. Although Canada is now about three times as rich as Argentina, Argentina still had long-run growth of its economy.

10-4 CHECK YOUR UNDERSTANDING

1. a. As some prices have risen but other prices have fallen, there may be overall inflation or deflation. The answer is ambiguous.

   b. As all prices have risen significantly, this sounds like inflation.

   c. As most prices have fallen and others have not changed, this sounds like deflation.

10-5 CHECK YOUR UNDERSTANDING

1. a. This situation reflects comparative advantage. Canada's comparative advantage results from the development of oil—Canada now has an abundance of oil.

   b. This situation reflects comparative advantage. China's comparative advantage results from an abundance of labor; China is good at labor-intensive activities such as assembly.

   c. This situation reflects macroeconomic forces. Germany has been running a huge trade surplus because of underlying decisions regarding savings and investment spending with its savings in excess of its investment spending.

   d. This situation reflects macroeconomic forces. The United States was able to begin running a large trade deficit because the technology boom made the United States an attractive place to invest, with investment spending outstripping U.S. savings.

Chapter Eleven

11-1 CHECK YOUR UNDERSTANDING

1. Let's start by considering the relationship between the total value added of all domestically produced final goods and services and aggregate spending on domestically produced final goods and services. These two quantities are equal because every final good and service produced in the economy is either purchased by someone or added to inventories. And additions to inventories are counted as spending by firms. Next, consider the relationship between aggregate spending on domestically produced final goods and services and total factor income. These two quantities are equal because all spending that is channeled to firms to pay for purchases of domestically produced final goods and services is revenue for firms. Those revenues must be paid out by firms to their factors of production in the form of wages, profit, interest, and rent. Taken together, this means that all three methods of calculating GDP are equivalent.

2. You would be counting the value of the steel twice—once as it was sold by American Steel to American Motors and once as part of the car sold by American Motors.

11-2 CHECK YOUR UNDERSTANDING

1. a. In 2011 nominal GDP was (1,000,000 × \$0.40) + (800,000 × \$0.60) = \$400,000 + \$480,000 = \$880,000. A 25% rise in the price of french fries from 2011 to 2012 means that the 2012 price of french fries was 1.25 × \$0.40 = \$0.50. A 10% fall in servings means that 1,000,000 × 0.9 = 900,000 servings were sold in 2012. As a result, the total value of sales of french fries in 2012 was 900,000 × \$0.50 = \$450,000. A 15% fall in the price of onion rings from 2011 to 2012 means that the 2012 price of onion rings was 0.85 × \$0.60 = \$0.51. A 5% rise in servings sold means that 800,000 × 1.05 = 840,000 servings were sold in 2012. As a result, the total value of sales of onion rings in 2012 was 840,000 × \$0.51 = \$428,400. Nominal GDP in 2012 was \$450,000 + \$428,400 = \$878,400. To find real GDP in 2012, we must calculate the value of sales in 2012 using 2011 prices: (900,000 french fries × \$0.40) + (840,000 onion rings × \$0.60) = \$360,000 + \$504,000 = \$864,000.

   b. A comparison of nominal GDP in 2011 to nominal GDP in 2012 shows a decline of ((\$880,000 – \$878,400) / \$880,000) × 100 = 0.18%. But a comparison using real GDP shows a decline of ((\$880,000 – \$864,000) / \$880,000) × 100 = 1.8%. That is, a calculation based on real GDP shows a drop 10 times larger (1.8%) than a calculation based on nominal GDP (0.18%). In this case, the calculation based on nominal GDP underestimates the true magnitude of the change.

2. A price index based on 2005 prices will contain a relatively high price of electronics and a relatively low price of housing compared to a price index based on 2010 prices. This means that a 2005 price index used to calculate real GDP in 2012 will magnify the value of electronics production in the economy, but a 2010 price index will magnify the value of housing production in the economy.

11-3 CHECK YOUR UNDERSTANDING

1. This market basket costs, pre-frost, (100 × \$0.20) + (50 × \$0.60) + (200 × \$0.25) = \$20 + \$30 + \$50 = \$100. The same market basket, post-frost, costs (100 × \$0.40) + (50 × \$1.00) + (200 × \$0.45) = \$40 + \$50 + \$90 = \$180. So the price index is (\$100/\$100) × 100 = 100 before the frost and (\$180/\$100) × 100 = 180 after the frost, implying a rise in the price index of 80%. This increase in the price index is less than the 84.2% increase calculated in the text. The reason for this difference is that the new market basket of 100 oranges, 50 grapefruit, and 200 lemons contains proportionately more of the items that have experienced relatively lower price increases (the lemons, whose price has increased by 80%) and proportionately fewer of the items that have experienced relatively large price increases (the oranges, whose price has increased by 100%). This shows that the price index can be very sensitive to the composition of the market basket. If the market basket contains a large proportion of goods whose prices have risen faster than the prices of other goods, it will lead to a higher estimate of the increase in the price level. If it contains a large proportion of goods whose prices have risen more slowly than the prices of other goods, it will lead to a lower estimate of the increase in the price level.

2. a. A market basket determined 10 years ago will contain fewer cars than at present. Given that the average price of a car has grown faster than the average prices of other goods, this basket will underestimate the true increase in the cost of living because it contains relatively too few cars.

   b. A market basket determined 10 years ago will not contain broadband Internet access. So it cannot track the fall in prices of Internet access over the past few years. As a result, it will overestimate the true increase in the cost of living.

3. Using Equation 11-2, the inflation rate from 2010 to 2011 is ((224.939 – 218.056)/218.056) × 100 = 3.2%.

Chapter Twelve

12-1 CHECK YOUR UNDERSTANDING

1. The advent of websites that enable job-seekers to find jobs more quickly will reduce the unemployment rate over time. However, websites that induce discouraged workers to begin actively looking for work again will lead to an increase in the unemployment rate over time.

2. a. Rosa is not counted as unemployed because she is not actively looking for work, but she is counted in broader measures of labor underutilization as a discouraged worker.

   b. Anthony is not counted as unemployed; he is considered employed because he has a job.

   c. Grace is unemployed; she is not working and is actively looking for work.

   d. Sergio is not unemployed, but underemployed; he is working part time for economic reasons. He is counted in broader measures of labor underutilization.

   e. Natasha is not unemployed, but marginally attached. She is counted in broader measures of labor underutilization.

3. Both parts a and b are consistent with the relationship, illustrated in Figure 12-5, between above-average or below-average growth in real GDP and changes in the unemployment rate: during years of above-average growth, the unemployment rate falls, and during years of below-average growth, the unemployment rate rises. However, part c is not consistent: it implies that a recession is associated with a fall in the unemployment rate, which is correct.

12-2 CHECK YOUR UNDERSTANDING

1. a. When the pace of technological advance quickens, there will be higher rates of job creation and destruction as old industries disappear and new ones emerge. As a result, frictional unemployment will be higher as workers leave jobs in declining industries in search of jobs in expanding industries.

   b. When the pace of technological advance quickens, there will be greater mismatch between the skills employees have and the skills employers are looking for, leading to higher structural unemployment.

   c. When the unemployment rate is low, frictional unemployment will account for a larger share of total unemployment because other sources of unemployment will be diminished. So the share of total unemployment composed of the frictionally unemployed will rise.

2. A binding minimum wage represents a price floor below which wages cannot fall. As a result, actual wages cannot move toward equilibrium. So a minimum wage causes the quantity of labor supplied to exceed the quantity of labor demanded. Because this surplus of labor reflects unemployed workers, it affects the unemployment rate. Collective bargaining has a similar effect—unions are able to raise the wage above the equilibrium level to a level like W_U in the accompanying diagram. This will act like a minimum wage by causing the number of job-seekers to be larger than the number of workers firms are willing to hire. Collective bargaining causes the unemployment rate to be higher than it otherwise would be, as shown in the accompanying diagram.

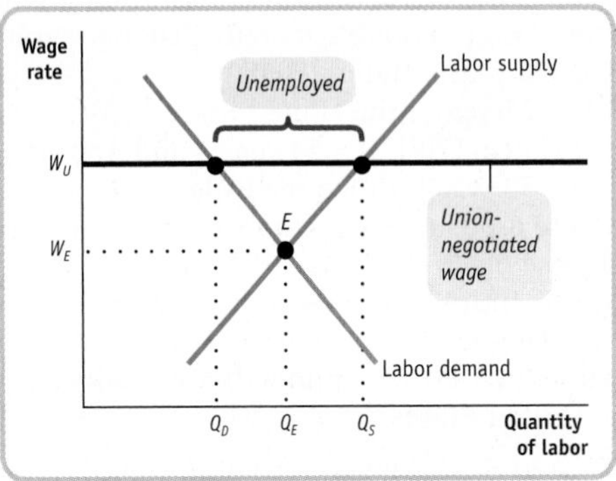

3. An increase in unemployment benefits at the peak of the business cycle reduces the cost to individuals of being unemployed, causing them to spend more time searching for new jobs. So the natural rate of unemployment would increase.

12-3 CHECK YOUR UNDERSTANDING

1. Shoe-leather costs as a result of inflation will be lower because it is now less costly for individuals to manage their assets in order to economize on their money holdings. This reduction in the costs associated with converting other assets into money translates into lower shoe-leather costs.

2. If inflation came to an unexpected and complete stop over the next 15 or 20 years, the inflation rate would be zero, which of course is less than the expected inflation rate of 2% to 3%. Because the real interest rate is the nominal interest rate minus the inflation rate, the real interest rate on a loan would be higher than expected, and lenders would gain at the expense of borrowers. Borrowers would have to repay their loans with funds that have a higher real value than had been expected.

Chapter Thirteen

13-1 CHECK YOUR UNDERSTANDING

1. Economic progress raises the living standards of the average resident of a country. An increase in overall real GDP does not accurately reflect an increase in an average resident's living standard because it does not account for growth in the number of residents. If, for example, real GDP rises by 10% but population grows by 20%, the living standard of the average resident falls: after the change, the average resident has only (110/120) × 100 = 91.6% as much real income as before the change. Similarly, an increase in nominal GDP per capita does not accurately reflect an increase in living standards because it does not account for any change in prices.

For example, a 5% increase in nominal GDP per capita generated by a 5% increase in prices implies that there has been no change in living standards. Real GDP per capita is the only measure that accounts for both changes in the population and changes in prices.

2. Using the Rule of 70, the amount of time it will take for China to double its real GDP per capita is (70/8.9) = 8 years; India, (70/4.2) = 17 years; Ireland, (70/3.1) = 23 years; the United States, (70/1.7) = 41 years; France, (70/1.3) = 54 years; and Argentina (70/1.2) = 58 years. Since the Rule of 70 can only be applied to a positive growth rate, we cannot apply it to the case of Zimbabwe, which experienced negative growth. If India continues to have a higher growth rate of real GDP per capita than the United States, then India's real GDP per capita will eventually surpass that of the United States.

3. The United States began growing rapidly over a century ago, but China and India have begun growing rapidly only recently. As a result, the living standard of the typical Chinese or Indian household has not yet caught up with that of the typical American household.

13-2 CHECK YOUR UNDERSTANDING

1. a. Significant technological progress will result in a positive growth rate of productivity even though physical capital per worker and human capital per worker are unchanged.

   b. The growth rate of productivity will fall but remain positive due to diminishing returns to physical capital.

2. a. If output has grown 3% per year and the labor force has grown 1% per year, then productivity—output per person—has grown at approximately 3% – 1% = 2% per year.

   b. If physical capital has grown 4% per year and the labor force has grown 1% per year, then physical capital per worker has grown at approximately 4% – 1% = 3% per year.

   c. According to estimates, each 1% rise in physical capital, other things equal, increases productivity by 0.3%. So, as physical capital per worker has increased by 3%, productivity growth that can be attributed to an increase in physical capital per worker is 0.3 × 3% = 0.9%. As a percentage of total productivity growth, this is 0.9%/2% × 100% = 45%.

   d. If the rest of productivity growth is due to technological progress, then technological progress has contributed 2% – 0.9% = 1.1% to productivity growth. As a percentage of total productivity growth, this is 1.1%/2% × 100% = 55%.

3. It will take a period time for workers to learn how to use the new computer system and to adjust their routines. And because there are often setbacks in learning a new system, such as accidentally erasing your computer files, productivity at Multinomics may decrease for a period of time.

13-3 CHECK YOUR UNDERSTANDING

1. A country that has high domestic savings is able to achieve a high rate of investment spending as a percent of GDP. This, in turn, allows the country to achieve a high growth rate.

2. It is likely that the United States will experience a greater pace of creation and development of new drugs because closer links between private companies and academic research centers will lead to work more directly focused on producing new drugs rather than on pure research.

3. It is likely that these events resulted in a fall in the country's growth rate because the lack of property rights would have dissuaded people from making investments in productive capacity.

13-4 CHECK YOUR UNDERSTANDING

1. The conditional version of the convergence hypothesis says that countries grow faster, other things equal, when they start from relatively low GDP per capita. From this we can infer that they grow more slowly, other things equal, when their real GDP per capita is relatively higher. This points to lower future Asian growth. However, other things might not be equal: if Asian economies continue investing in human capital, if savings rates continue to be high, if governments invest in infrastructure, and so on, growth might continue at an accelerated pace.

2. The regions of East Asia, Eastern Europe, Western Europe, and the United States support the convergence hypothesis because a comparison among them shows that the growth rate of real GDP per capita falls as real GDP per capita rises. West Asia, Latin America, and Africa do not support the hypothesis because they all have much lower real GDP per capita than the United States but have either approximately the same growth rate (West Asia) or a lower growth rate (Africa and Latin America).

3. The evidence suggests that both sets of factors matter: better infrastructure is important for growth, but so is political and financial stability. Policies should try to address both areas.

13-5 CHECK YOUR UNDERSTANDING

1. Economists are typically more concerned about environmental degradation than resource scarcity. The reason is that in modern economies the price response tends to alleviate the limits imposed by resource scarcity through conservation and the development of alternatives. However, because environmental degradation involves a negative externality—a cost imposed by individuals or firms on others without the requirement to pay compensation—effective government intervention is required to address it. As a result, economists are more concerned about the limits to growth imposed by environmental degradation because a market response would be inadequate.

2. Growth increases a country's greenhouse gas emissions. The current best estimates are that a large reduction

in emissions will result in only a modest reduction in growth. The international burden sharing of greenhouse gas emissions reduction is contentious because rich countries are reluctant to pay the costs of reducing their emissions only to see newly emerging countries like China rapidly increase their emissions. Yet most of the current accumulation of gases is due to the past actions of rich countries. Poorer countries like China are equally reluctant to sacrifice their growth to pay for the past actions of rich countries.

Chapter Fourteen

14-1 CHECK YOUR UNDERSTANDING

1. **a.** This is a shift of the aggregate demand curve. A decrease in the quantity of money raises the interest rate, since people now want to borrow more and lend less. A higher interest rate reduces investment and consumer spending at any given aggregate price level. So the aggregate demand curve shifts to the left.

   b. This is a movement up along the aggregate demand curve. As the aggregate price level rises, the real value of money holdings falls. This is the interest rate effect of a change in the aggregate price level: as the value of money falls, people want to hold more money. They do so by borrowing more and lending less. This leads to a rise in the interest rate and a reduction in consumer and investment spending. So it is a movement along the aggregate demand curve.

   c. This is a shift of the aggregate demand curve. Expectations of a poor job market, and so lower average disposable incomes, will reduce people's consumer spending today at any given aggregate price level. So the aggregate demand curve shifts to the left.

   d. This is a shift of the aggregate demand curve. A fall in tax rates raises people's disposable income. At any given aggregate price level, consumer spending is now higher. So the aggregate demand curve shifts to the right.

   e. This is a movement down along the aggregate demand curve. As the aggregate price level falls, the real value of assets rises. This is the wealth effect of a change in the aggregate price level: as the value of assets rises, people will increase their consumption plans. This leads to higher consumer spending. So it is a movement along the aggregate demand curve.

   f. This is a shift of the aggregate demand curve. A rise in the real value of assets in the economy due to a surge in real estate values raises consumer spending at any given aggregate price level. So the aggregate demand curve shifts to the right.

14-2 CHECK YOUR UNDERSTANDING

1. **a.** This represents a movement along the *SRAS* curve because the CPI—like the GDP deflator—is a measure of the aggregate price level, the overall price level of final goods and services in the economy.

   b. This represents a shift of the *SRAS* curve because oil is a commodity. The *SRAS* curve will shift to the right because production costs are now lower, leading to a higher quantity of aggregate output supplied at any given aggregate price level.

   c. This represents a shift of the *SRAS* curve because it involves a change in nominal wages. An increase in legally mandated benefits to workers is equivalent to an increase in nominal wages. As a result, the *SRAS* curve will shift leftward because production costs are now higher, leading to a lower quantity of aggregate output supplied at any given aggregate price level.

2. You would need to know what happened to the aggregate price level. If the increase in the quantity of aggregate output supplied was due to a movement along the *SRAS* curve, the aggregate price level would have increased at the same time as the quantity of aggregate output supplied increased. If the increase in the quantity of aggregate output supplied was due to a rightward shift of the *LRAS* curve, the aggregate price level might not rise. Alternatively, you could make the determination by observing what happened to aggregate output in the long run. If it fell back to its initial level in the long run, then the temporary increase in aggregate output was due to a movement along the *SRAS* curve. If it stayed at the higher level in the long run, the increase in aggregate output was due to a rightward shift of the *LRAS* curve.

14-3 CHECK YOUR UNDERSTANDING

1. **a.** An increase in the minimum wage raises the nominal wage and, as a result, shifts the short-run aggregate supply curve to the left. As a result of this negative supply shock, the aggregate price level rises and aggregate output falls.

   b. Increased investment spending shifts the aggregate demand curve to the right. As a result of this positive demand shock, both the aggregate price level and aggregate output rise.

   c. An increase in taxes and a reduction in government spending both result in negative demand shocks, shifting the aggregate demand curve to the left. As a result, both the aggregate price level and aggregate output fall.

   d. This is a negative supply shock, shifting the short-run aggregate supply curve to the left. As a result, the aggregate price level rises and aggregate output falls.

2. As the rise in productivity increases potential output, the long-run aggregate supply curve shifts to the right. If, in the short run, there is now a recessionary gap (aggregate output is less than potential output), nominal wages will fall, shifting the short-run aggregate supply curve to the right. This results in a fall in the aggregate price level and a rise in aggregate output. As prices fall, we move along the aggregate demand curve due to the wealth and interest rate effects of a change in the aggregate price level. Eventually, as long-run macroeconomic equilibrium is reestablished, aggregate output will rise to be equal to potential output.

14-4 CHECK YOUR UNDERSTANDING

1. a. An economy is overstimulated when an inflationary gap is present. This will arise if an expansionary monetary or fiscal policy is implemented when the economy is currently in long-run macroeconomic equilibrium. This shifts the aggregate demand curve to the right, in the short run raising the aggregate price level and aggregate output and creating an inflationary gap. Eventually nominal wages will rise and shift the short-run aggregate supply curve to the left, and aggregate output will fall back to potential output. This is the scenario envisaged by the speaker.

   b. No, this is not a valid argument. When the economy is not currently in long-run macroeconomic equilibrium, an expansionary monetary or fiscal policy does not lead to the outcome described above. Suppose a negative demand shock has shifted the aggregate demand curve to the left, resulting in a recessionary gap. An expansionary monetary or fiscal policy can shift the aggregate demand curve back to its original position in long-run macroeconomic equilibrium. In this way, the short-run fall in aggregate output and deflation caused by the original negative demand shock can be avoided. So, if used in response to demand shocks, fiscal or monetary policy is an effective policy tool.

2. Those within the Fed who advocated lowering interest rates were focused on boosting aggregate demand in order to counteract the negative demand shock caused by the collapse of the housing bubble. Lowering interest rates will result in a rightward shift of the aggregate demand curve, increasing aggregate output but raising the aggregate price level. Those within the Fed who advocated holding interest rates steady were focused on the fact that fighting the slump in aggregate demand in the face of a negative supply shock could result in a rise in inflation. Holding interest rates steady relies on the ability of the economy to self-correct in the long run, with the aggregate price level and aggregate output only gradually returning to their levels before the negative supply shock.

Chapter Fifteen

15-1 CHECK YOUR UNDERSTANDING

1. a. This is a contractionary fiscal policy because it is a reduction in government purchases of goods and services.

   b. This is an expansionary fiscal policy because it is an increase in government transfers that will increase disposable income.

   c. This is a contractionary fiscal policy because it is an increase in taxes that will reduce disposable income.

2. Federal disaster relief that is quickly disbursed is more effective than legislated aid because there is very little time lag between the time of the disaster and the time it is received by victims. So it will stabilize the economy after a disaster. In contrast, legislated aid is likely to entail a time lag in its disbursement, potentially destabilizing the economy.

3. This statement implies that expansionary fiscal policy will result in crowding out of the private sector, and that the opposite, contractionary fiscal policy, will lead the private sector to grow. Whether this statement is true or not depends upon whether the economy is at full employment; it is only then that we should expect expansionary fiscal policy to lead to crowding out. If, instead, the economy has a recessionary gap, then we should expect instead that the private sector grows along with the fiscal expansion, and contracts along with a fiscal contraction.

15-2 CHECK YOUR UNDERSTANDING

1. A \$500 million increase in government purchases of goods and services directly increases aggregate spending by \$500 million, which then starts the multiplier in motion. It will increase real GDP by \$500 million × 1/(1 – *MPC*). A \$500 million increase in government transfers increases aggregate spending only to the extent that it leads to an increase in consumer spending. Consumer spending rises by *MPC* × \$1 for every \$1 increase in disposable income, where *MPC* is less than 1. So a \$500 million increase in government transfers will cause a rise in real GDP only *MPC* times as much as a \$500 million increase in government purchases of goods and services. It will increase real GDP by \$500 million × *MPC*/(1 – *MPC*).

2. This is the same issue as in Problem 1, but in reverse. If government purchases of goods and services fall by \$500 million, the initial fall in aggregate spending is \$500 million. If there is a \$500 million reduction in government transfers, the initial fall in aggregate spending is *MPC* × \$500 million, which is less than \$500 million.

3. Boldovia will experience greater variation in its real GDP than Moldovia because Moldovia has automatic stabilizers while Boldovia does not. In Moldovia the effects of slumps will be lessened by unemployment insurance benefits that will support residents' incomes, while the effects of booms will be diminished because tax revenues will go up. In contrast, incomes will not be supported in Boldovia during slumps because there is no unemployment insurance. In addition, because Boldovia has lump-sum taxes, its booms will not be diminished by increases in tax revenue.

15-3 CHECK YOUR UNDERSTANDING

1. The actual budget balance takes into account the effects of the business cycle on the budget deficit. During recessionary gaps, it incorporates the effect of lower tax revenues and higher transfers on the budget balance; during inflationary gaps, it incorporates the effect of higher tax revenues and reduced transfers. In contrast, the cyclically adjusted budget balance factors out the effects of the business cycle and assumes that real GDP is at potential output. Since, in the long run, real GDP tends to potential output, the cyclically adjusted budget balance is a better measure of the long-run sustainability of government policies.

2. In recessions, real GDP falls. This implies that consumers' incomes, consumer spending, and producers' profits

also fall. So in recessions, states' tax revenue (which depends in large part on consumers' incomes, consumer spending, and producers' profits) falls. In order to balance the state budget, states have to cut spending or raise taxes. But that deepens the recession. Without a balanced-budget requirement, states could use expansionary fiscal policy during a recession to lessen the fall in real GDP.

15-4 CHECK YOUR UNDERSTANDING

1. **a.** A higher growth rate of real GDP implies that tax revenue will increase. If government spending remains constant and the government runs a budget surplus, the size of the public debt will be less than it would otherwise have been.

   b. If retirees live longer, the average age of the population increases. As a result, the implicit liabilities of the government increase because spending on programs for older Americans, such as Social Security and Medicare, will rise.

   c. A decrease in tax revenue without offsetting reductions in government spending will cause the public debt to increase.

   d. Public debt will increase as a result of government borrowing to pay interest on its current public debt.

2. In order to stimulate the economy in the short run, the government can use fiscal policy to increase real GDP. This entails borrowing, increasing the size of the public debt further and leading to undesirable consequences: in extreme cases, governments can be forced to default on their debts. Even in less extreme cases, a large public debt is undesirable because government borrowing crowds out borrowing for private investment spending. This reduces the amount of investment spending, reducing the long-run growth of the economy.

3. Fiscal austerity is the same as a contractionary fiscal policy. It reduces government spending, which in turn reduces income and reduces tax revenue. With less tax revenue, the government is less able to pay its debts. Also, a failing economy causes lenders to have less confidence that a government is able to pay its debts and leads them to raise interest rates on the debt. Higher interest rates on the debt make it even less likely the government can repay.

Chapter Sixteen

16-1 CHECK YOUR UNDERSTANDING

1. The defining characteristic of money is its liquidity: how easily it can be used to purchase goods and services. Although a gift certificate can easily be used to purchase a very defined set of goods or services (the goods or services available at the store issuing the gift certificate), it cannot be used to purchase any other goods or services. A gift certificate is therefore not money, since it cannot easily be used to purchase all goods and services.

2. Again, the important characteristic of money is its liquidity: how easily it can be used to purchase goods and services. M1, the narrowest definition of the money supply, contains only currency in circulation, traveler's checks, and checkable bank deposits. CDs aren't checkable—and they can't be made checkable without incurring a cost because there's a penalty for early withdrawal. This makes them less liquid than the assets counted in M1.

3. Commodity-backed money uses resources more efficiently than simple commodity money, like gold and silver coins, because commodity-backed money ties up fewer valuable resources. Although a bank must keep some of the commodity—generally gold and silver—on hand, it only has to keep enough to satisfy demand for redemptions. It can then lend out the remaining gold and silver, which allows society to use these resources for other purposes, with no loss in the ability to achieve gains from trade.

16-2 CHECK YOUR UNDERSTANDING

1. Even though you know that the rumor about the bank is not true, you are concerned about other depositors pulling their money out of the bank. And you know that if enough other depositors pull their money out, the bank will fail. In that case, it is rational for you to pull your money out before the bank fails. All depositors will think like this, so even if they all know that the rumor is false, they may still rationally pull their money out, leading to a bank run. Deposit insurance leads depositors to worry less about the possibility of a bank run. Even if a bank fails, the FDIC will currently pay each depositor up to $250,000 per account. This will make you much less likely to pull your money out in response to a rumor. Since other depositors will think the same, there will be no bank run.

2. The aspects of modern bank regulation that would frustrate this scheme are *capital requirements* and *reserve requirements*. Capital requirements mean that a bank has to have a certain amount of capital—the difference between its assets (loans plus reserves) and its liabilities (deposits). So the con artist could not open a bank without putting any of his own wealth in because the bank needs a certain amount of capital—that is, it needs to hold more assets (loans plus reserves) than deposits. So the con artist would be at risk of losing his own wealth if his loans turn out badly.

16-3 CHECK YOUR UNDERSTANDING

1. Since they only have to hold $100 in reserves, instead of $200, banks now lend out $100 of their reserves. Whoever borrows the $100 will deposit it in a bank, which will lend out $100 × (1 − *rr*) = $100 × 0.9 = $90. Whoever borrows the $90 will put it into a bank, which will lend out $90 × 0.9 = $81, and so on. Overall, deposits will increase by $100/0.1 = $1,000.

2. Silas puts $1,000 in the bank, of which the bank lends out $1,000 × (1 − *rr*) = $1,000 × 0.9 = $900. Whoever borrows the $900 will keep $450 in cash and deposit $450 in a bank. The bank will lend out $450 × 0.9 = $405. Whoever borrows the $405 will keep $202.50 in cash and deposit $202.50 in a bank. The bank will lend out $202.50 × 0.9 = $182.25, and so on. Overall, this leads to

an increase in deposits of \$1,000 + \$450 + \$202.50 + . . . But it decreases the amount of currency in circulation: the amount of cash is reduced by the \$1,000 Silas puts into the bank. This is offset, but not fully, by the amount of cash held by each borrower. The amount of currency in circulation therefore changes by –\$1,000 + \$450 + \$202.50 + . . . The money supply therefore increases by the sum of the increase in deposits and the change in currency in circulation, which is \$1,000 – \$1,000 + \$450 + \$450 + \$202.50 + \$202.50 + . . . and so on.

16-4 CHECK YOUR UNDERSTANDING

1. An open-market purchase of \$100 million by the Fed increases banks' reserves by \$100 million as the Fed credits their accounts with additional reserves. In other words, this open-market purchase increases the monetary base (currency in circulation plus bank reserves) by \$100 million. Banks lend out the additional \$100 million. Whoever borrows the money puts it back into the banking system in the form of deposits. Of these deposits, banks lend out \$100 million × (1 – *rr*) = \$100 million × 0.9 = \$90 million. Whoever borrows the money deposits it back into the banking system. And banks lend out \$90 million × 0.9 = \$81 million, and so on. As a result, bank deposits increase by \$100 million + \$90 million + \$81 million + . . . = \$100 million/*rr* = \$100 million/0.1 = \$1,000 million = \$1 billion. Since in this simplified example all money lent out is deposited back into the banking system, there is no increase of currency in circulation, so the increase in bank deposits is equal to the increase in the money supply. In other words, the money supply increases by \$1 billion. This is greater than the increase in the monetary base by a factor of 10: in this simplified model in which deposits are the only component of the money supply and in which banks hold no excess reserves, the money multiplier is 1/*rr* = 10.

16-5 CHECK YOUR UNDERSTANDING

1. The Panic of 1907, the S&L crisis, and the crisis of 2008 all involved losses by financial institutions that were less regulated than banks. In the crises of 1907 and 2008, there was a widespread loss of confidence in the financial sector and collapse of credit markets. Like the crisis of 1907 and the S&L crisis, the crisis of 2008 exerted a powerful negative effect on the economy.

2. The creation of the Federal Reserve failed to prevent bank runs because it did not eradicate the fears of depositors that a bank collapse would cause them to lose their money. The bank runs eventually stopped after federal deposit insurance was instituted and the public came to understand that their deposits were now protected.

3. The balance sheet effect occurs when asset sales cause declines in asset prices, which then reduce the value of other firms' net worth as the value of the assets on their balance sheets declines. In the vicious cycle of deleveraging, the balance sheet effect on firms forces their creditors to call in their loan contracts, forcing the firms to sell assets to pay back their loans, leading to further asset sales and price declines. Because the vicious cycle of deleveraging occurs across different firms and no single firm can stop it, it is necessary for the government to step in to stop it.

Chapter Seventeen

17-1 CHECK YOUR UNDERSTANDING

1. **a.** By increasing the opportunity cost of holding money, a high interest rate reduces the quantity of money demanded. This is a movement up and to the left along the money demand curve.

   b. A 10% fall in prices reduces the quantity of money demanded at any given interest rate, shifting the money demand curve leftward.

   c. This technological change reduces the quantity of money demanded at any given interest rate. So it shifts the money demand curve leftward.

   d. This will increase the demand for money at any given interest rate. With more of the economy's assets in overseas bank accounts that are difficult to access, people will want to hold more cash to finance purchases.

2. **a.** A 1% processing fee on debit/credit card transactions for purchases less than \$50 reduces the opportunity cost of holding cash because consumers will save money by paying with cash.

   b. An increase in the interest paid on six-month CDs raises the opportunity cost of holding cash because holding cash requires forgoing the higher interest paid.

   c. This reduces the opportunity cost of holding cash because it can now be used to fund purchases at very low prices, compensating its owner for any interest forgone by holding cash.

   d. Because many purchases of food are made in cash, a significant increase in the cost of food reduces the opportunity cost of holding cash.

17-2 CHECK YOUR UNDERSTANDING

1. In the accompanying diagram, the increase in the demand for money is shown as a rightward shift of the money demand curve, from MD_1 to MD_2. This raises the equilibrium interest rate from r_1 to r_2.

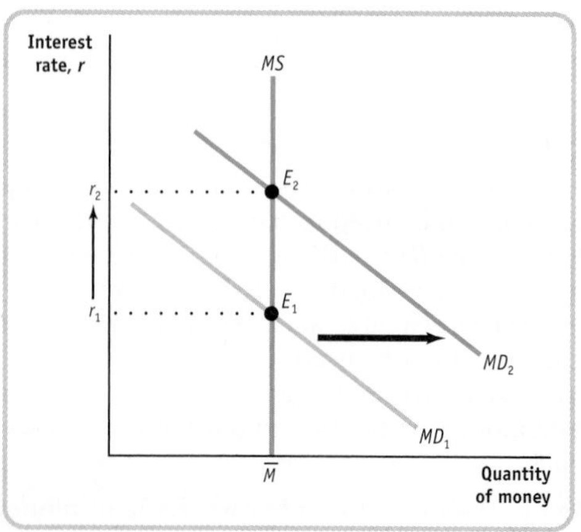

2. In order to prevent the interest rate from rising, the Federal Reserve must make an open-market purchase of Treasury bills, shifting the money supply curve rightward. This is shown in the accompanying diagram as the move from MS_1 to MS_2.

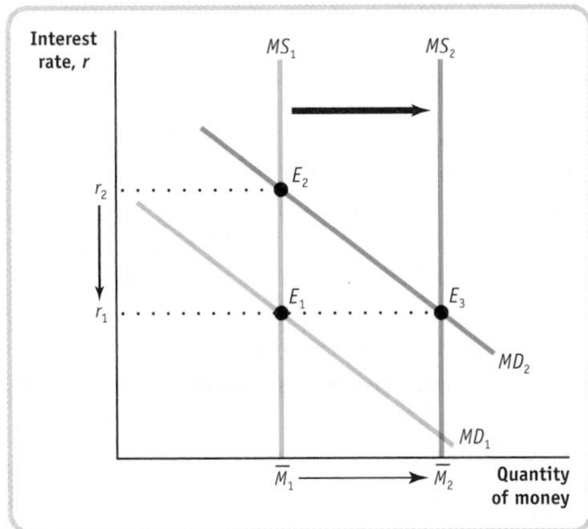

3. a. Frannie is better off buying a one-year bond today and a one-year bond tomorrow because this allows her to get the higher interest rate one year from now.

b. Frannie is better off buying a two-year bond today because it gives her a higher interest rate in the second year than if she bought two one-year bonds.

17-3 CHECK YOUR UNDERSTANDING

1. a. The money supply curve shifts to the right.

b. The equilibrium interest rate falls.

c. Investment spending rises, due to the fall in the interest rate.

d. Consumer spending rises, due to the multiplier process.

e. Aggregate output rises because of the rightward shift of the aggregate demand curve.

2. The central bank that uses a Taylor rule is likely to respond more directly to a financial crisis than one that uses inflation targeting because with a Taylor rule the central bank does not have to set policy to meet a prespecified inflation target.

17-4 CHECK YOUR UNDERSTANDING

1. a. Aggregate output rises in the short run, then falls back to equal potential output in the long run.

b. The aggregate price level rises in the short run, but by less than 25%. It rises further in the long run, for a total increase of 25%.

c. The interest rate falls in the short run, then rises back to its original level in the long run.

2. In the short run, a change in the interest rate alters the economy because it affects investment spending, which in turn affects aggregate demand and real GDP through the multiplier process. However, in the long run, changes in consumer spending and investment spending will eventually result in changes in nominal wages and the nominal prices of other factors of production. For example, an expansionary monetary policy will eventually cause a rise in factor prices; a contractionary policy will eventually cause a fall in factor prices. In response, the short-run aggregate supply curve will shift to move the economy back to long-run equilibrium. So in the long run monetary policy has no effect on the economy.

Chapter Eighteen

18-1 CHECK YOUR UNDERSTANDING

1. a. This is not an example of maturity transformation because no short-term liabilities are being turned into long-term assets. So it is not subject to a bank run.

b. This is an example of maturity transformation: Dana incurs a short-term liability, credit card debt, to fund the acquisition of a long-term asset, better job skills. It can result in a bank-run-like phenomenon if her credit card lender becomes fearful of her ability to repay and stops lending to her. If this happens, she will not be able to finish her course and, as a result, will not be able to get the better job that would allow her to pay off her credit card loans.

c. This is not an example of maturity transformation because there are no short-term liabilities. The partnership itself has no obligation to repay an individual partner's investment and so has no liabilities, short term or long term.

d. This is an example of maturity transformation: the checking accounts are short-term liabilities of the student union savings bank, and the student loans are long-term assets.

18-2 CHECK YOUR UNDERSTANDING

1. a. The asset bubble occurred in Irish real estate.

b. The channel of the financial contagion was the short-term lending that Irish banks depended on from the wholesale interbank lending market. When lenders began to worry about the soundness of the Irish banks, they refused to lend any more money, leading to a type of bank run and putting the Irish banks at great risk of failure.

2. Because the bank run started with fears among lenders to Irish banks, the Irish government sought to eliminate those fears by guaranteeing the lenders that they would be repaid in full. It was a questionable strategy, though, because it put the Irish taxpayers on the hook for potentially very large losses, so large that they threatened the solvency of the Irish government.

18-3 CHECK YOUR UNDERSTANDING

1. The Federal Reserve was able to prevent a replay of the Great Depression because, unlike in the 1930s, it acted as a lender of last resort to stabilize the banking sector and halt the contagion. But it was unable to

significantly reduce the surge in unemployment because the United States experienced a credit crunch and a vicious circle of deleveraging, leaving monetary policy relatively ineffective.

2. In the aftermath of a severe banking crisis, businesses and households have high debt and reduced assets. They cut back on spending to try to reduce their debt. So they are unwilling to borrow regardless of how low the interest rate is.

18-4 CHECK YOUR UNDERSTANDING

1. According to standard macroeconomics, a government should adopt expansionary policies to increase aggregate demand to address an economic slump. France, however, did just the opposite, responding to a weaker economy with a contractionary fiscal policy that would make the economy even weaker. This shows that the French government had adopted the austerity view, believing that it was more important to try to assure markets of its solvency than to support the economy.

18-5 CHECK YOUR UNDERSTANDING

1. Because shadow banks like Lehman relied on short-term borrowing to fund their operations, fears about their soundness could quickly lead lenders to immediately cut off their credit and force them into failure. And without membership in the lender-of-last-resort system, shadow banks like Lehman could not borrow from the Federal Reserve to make up for the short-term loans it had lost.

2. If there had been only a formal depository banking sector, several factors would have mitigated the potential and scope of a banking crisis. First, there would have been no repo financing; the only short-term liabilities would have been customers' deposits, and these would have been largely covered by deposit insurance. Second, capital requirements would have reduced banks' willingness to take on excessive risk, such as holding onto subprime mortgages. Also, direct oversight by the Federal Reserve would have prevented so much concentration of risk within the banking sector. Finally, depository banks are within the lender-of-last-resort system; as a result, depository banks had another layer of protection against the fear of depositors and other creditors that they couldn't meet their obligations. All of these factors would have reduced the potential and scope of a banking crisis.

3. Because the shadow banking sector had become such a critical part of the U.S. economy, the crisis of 2008 made it clear that in the event of another crisis the government would find it necessary to guarantee a wide range of financial institution debts, including those of shadow banks as well as depository banks. This created an incentive problem because it would induce shadow banks to take more risk, knowing that the government would bail them out in the event of a meltdown. To counteract this, the Dodd-Frank bill gave the government the power to regulate "systemically important" shadow banks (those likely to require bailing out) in order to reduce their risk taking. It also gave the government the power to seize control of failing shadow banks in a way that was fair to taxpayers and didn't unfairly enrich the owners of the banks.

Chapter Nineteen

19-1 CHECK YOUR UNDERSTANDING

1. **a.** To determine comparative advantage, we must compare the two countries' opportunity costs for a given good. Take the opportunity cost of 1 ton of corn in terms of bicycles. In China, the opportunity cost of 1 bicycle is 0.01 ton of corn; so the opportunity cost of 1 ton of corn is 1/0.01 bicycles = 100 bicycles. The United States has the comparative advantage in corn since its opportunity cost in terms of bicycles is 50, a smaller number. Similarly, the opportunity cost in the United States of 1 bicycle in terms of corn is 1/50 ton of corn = 0.02 ton of corn. This is greater than 0.01, the Chinese opportunity cost of 1 bicycle in terms of corn, implying that China has a comparative advantage in bicycles.

b. Given that the United States can produce 200,000 bicycles if no corn is produced, it can produce 200,000 bicycles × 0.02 ton of corn/bicycle = 4,000 tons of corn when no bicycles are produced. Likewise, if China can produce 3,000 tons of corn if no bicycles are produced, it can produce 3,000 tons of corn × 100 bicycles/ton of corn = 300,000 bicycles if no corn is produced. These points determine the vertical and horizontal intercepts of the U.S. and Chinese production possibility frontiers, as shown in the accompanying diagram.

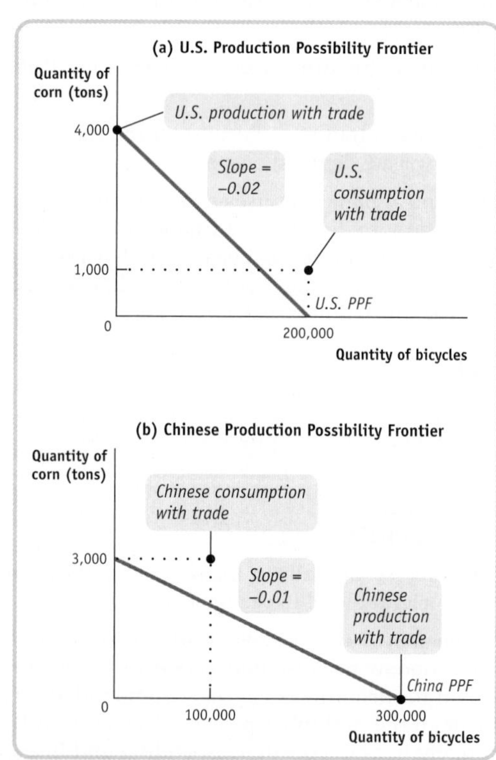

c. The diagram shows the production and consumption points of the two countries. Each country is clearly better off with international trade because each now consumes a bundle of the two goods that lies outside its own production possibility frontier, indicating that these bundles were unattainable in autarky.

2. a. According to the Heckscher–Ohlin model, this pattern of trade occurs because the United States has a relatively larger endowment of factors of production, such as human capital and physical capital, that are suited to the production of movies, but France has a relatively larger endowment of factors of production suited to wine-making, such as vineyards and the human capital of vintners.

b. According to the Heckscher–Ohlin model, this pattern of trade occurs because the United States has a relatively larger endowment of factors of production, such as human and physical capital, that are suited to making machinery, but Brazil has a relatively larger endowment of factors of production suited to shoe-making, such as unskilled labor and leather.

19-2 CHECK YOUR UNDERSTANDING

1. In the accompanying diagram, P_A is the U.S. price of grapes in autarky and P_W is the world price of grapes under international trade. With trade, U.S. consumers pay a price of P_W for grapes and consume quantity Q_D, U.S. grape producers produce quantity Q_S, and the difference, $Q_D - Q_S$, represents imports of Mexican grapes. As a consequence of the strike by truckers, imports are halted, the price paid by American consumers rises to the autarky price, P_A, and U.S. consumption falls to the autarky quantity, Q_A.

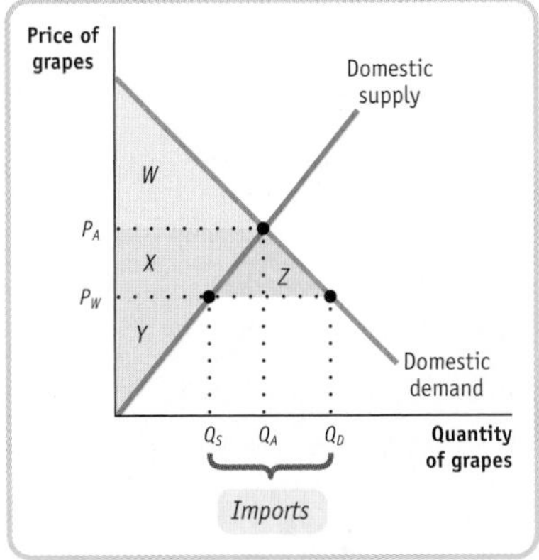

a. Before the strike, U.S. consumers enjoyed consumer surplus equal to areas $W + X + Z$. After the strike, their consumer surplus shrinks to W. So consumers are worse off, losing consumer surplus represented by $X + Z$.

b. Before the strike, U.S. producers had producer surplus equal to the area Y. After the strike, their producer surplus increases to $Y + X$. So U.S. producers are better off, gaining producer surplus represented by X.

c. U.S. total surplus falls as a result of the strike by an amount represented by area Z, the loss in consumer surplus that does not accrue to producers.

2. Mexican grape producers are worse off because they lose sales of exported grapes to the United States, and Mexican grape pickers are worse off because they lose the wages that were associated with the lost sales. The lower demand for Mexican grapes caused by the strike implies that the price Mexican consumers pay for grapes falls, making them better off. U.S. grape pickers are better off because their wages increase as a result of the increase of $Q_A - Q_S$ in U.S. sales.

19-3 CHECK YOUR UNDERSTANDING

1. a. If the tariff is \$0.50, the price paid by domestic consumers for a pound of imported butter is \$0.50 + \$0.50 = \$1.00, the same price as a pound of domestic butter. Imported butter will no longer have a price advantage over domestic butter, imports will cease, and domestic producers will capture all the feasible sales to domestic consumers, selling amount Q_A in the accompanying figure. But if the tariff is less than \$0.50—say, only \$0.25—the price paid by domestic consumers for a pound of imported butter is \$0.50 + \$0.25 = \$0.75, \$0.25 cheaper than a pound of domestic butter. American butter producers will gain sales in the amount of $Q_2 - Q_1$ as a result of the \$0.25 tariff. But this is smaller than the amount they would have gained under the \$0.50 tariff, the amount $Q_A - Q_1$.

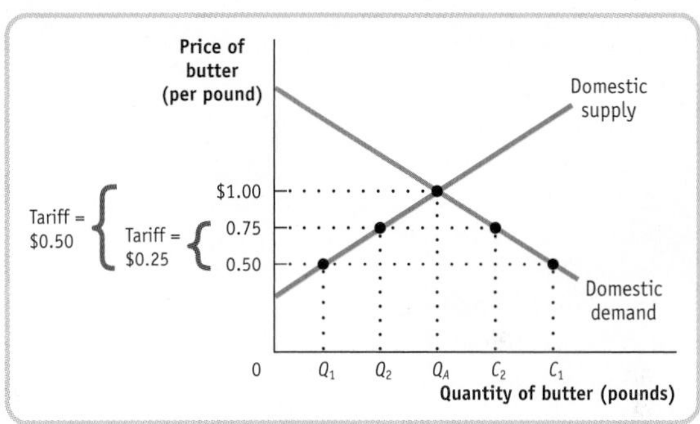

b. As long as the tariff is at least \$0.50, increasing it more has no effect. At a tariff of \$0.50, all imports are effectively blocked.

2. All imports are effectively blocked at a tariff of \$0.50. So such a tariff corresponds to an import quota of 0.

19-4 CHECK YOUR UNDERSTANDING

1. a. The sale of the new airplane to China represents an export of a good to China and so enters the current account.

b. The sale of Boeing stock to Chinese investors is a sale of a U.S. asset and so enters the financial account.

c. Even though the plane already exists, when it is shipped to China it is an export of a good from the United States. So the sale of the plane enters the current account.

d. Because the plane stays in the United States, the Chinese investor is buying a U.S. asset. So this is identical to the answer to part b: the sale of the jet enters the financial account.

19-5 CHECK YOUR UNDERSTANDING

1. a. The increased purchase of Mexican oil will cause U.S. individuals (and firms) to increase their demand for the peso. To purchase pesos, individuals will increase their supply of U.S. dollars to the foreign exchange market, causing a rightward shift in the supply curve of U.S. dollars. This will cause the peso price of the dollar to fall (the amount of pesos per dollar will fall). The peso has appreciated and the U.S. dollar has depreciated as a result.

b. This appreciation of the peso means it will take more U.S. dollars to obtain the same quantity of Mexican pesos. If we assume that the price level (measured in Mexican pesos) of other Mexican goods and services does not change, other Mexican goods and services become more expensive to U.S. households and firms. The dollar cost of other Mexican goods and services will rise as the peso appreciates. So Mexican exports of goods and services other than oil will fall.

c. U.S. goods and services become cheaper in terms of pesos, so Mexican imports of goods and services will rise.

2. a. The real exchange rate equals

$$\text{Pesos per U.S. dollar} \times \frac{\text{Aggregate price level in the U.S.}}{\text{Aggregate price level in Mexico}}$$

Today, the aggregate price levels in both countries are both equal to 100. The real exchange rate today is 10 × (100/100) = 10. The aggregate price level in five years in the U.S. will be 100 × (120/100) = 120, and in Mexico it will be 100 × (1,200/800) = 150. The real exchange rate in five years, assuming the nominal exchange rate does not change, will be 10 × (120/150) = 8.

b. Today, a basket of goods and services that costs $100 costs 800 pesos, so the purchasing power parity is 8 pesos per U.S. dollar. In five years, a basket that costs $120 will cost 1,200 pesos, so the purchasing power parity will be 10 pesos per U.S. dollar.

Italicized terms within definitions are key terms that are defined elsewhere in this glossary.

A

absolute advantage the advantage an individual or country has in an activity if that individual or country can do it better than others.

absolute value the value of a number without regard to a plus or minus sign.

accounting profit a business's revenue minus the *explicit cost* and depreciation; usually larger than economic *profit*.

***AD–AS* model** the basic model used to understand fluctuations in *aggregate output* and the *aggregate price level*. It uses the *aggregate supply curve* and the *aggregate demand curve* together to analyze the behavior of the *economy* in response to shocks or government policy.

administrative costs (of a tax) the *resources* used by government to collect the tax, and by taxpayers to pay it, over and above the amount of the tax, as well as to evade it.

aggregate demand curve a graphical representation that shows the relationship between the *aggregate price level* and the quantity of *aggregate output* demanded by *households*, *firms*, the government, and the rest of the world. The aggregate demand curve has a negative slope due to the *wealth effect of a change in the aggregate price level* and the *interest rate effect of a change in the aggregate price level*.

aggregate output the economy's total quantity of output of *final goods and services*.

aggregate price level a measure of the overall level of prices in the *economy*.

aggregate production function a hypothetical function that shows how productivity (*real GDP* per worker) depends on the quantities of *physical capital* per worker and *human capital* per worker as well as the state of *technology*.

aggregate supply curve a graphical representation that shows the relationship between the *aggregate price level* and the total quantity of *aggregate output* supplied in the *economy*.

antitrust policy efforts undertaken by the government to prevent oligopolistic industries from becoming or behaving like *monopolies*.

appreciation a rise in the value of one currency in terms of other currencies.

asset bubble the price of an asset pushed to an unreasonably high level because of expectations of further price gains.

autarky a situation in which a country does not trade with other countries.

automatic stabilizers government spending and taxation rules that cause *fiscal policy* to be automatically expansionary when the *economy* contracts and automatically contractionary when the economy expands without requiring any deliberate actions by policy makers. Taxes that depend on *disposable income* are the most important example of automatic stabilizers.

autonomous change in aggregate spending an initial rise or fall in *aggregate spending* at a given level of *real GDP*.

average cost an alternative term for *average total cost;* the *total cost* divided by the quantity of output produced.

average fixed cost the *fixed cost* per unit of output.

average total cost *total cost* divided by quantity of output produced. Also referred to as *average cost*.

average variable cost the *variable cost* per unit of output.

B

balance of payments accounts a summary of a country's transactions with other countries, including two main elements: the *balance of payments on current account* and the *balance of payments on financial account*.

balance of payments on current account (current account) transactions that don't create liabilities; a country's *balance of payments on goods and services* plus net international transfer payments and factor income.

balance of payments on financial account (financial account) international transactions that involve the sale or purchase of assets, and therefore create future liabilities.

balance of payments on goods and services the difference between the value of *exports* and the value of *imports* during a given period.

balance sheet effect the reduction in a firm's net worth from falling asset prices.

bank reserves currency held by *banks* in their vaults plus their deposits at the Federal Reserve.

bank run a phenomenon in which many of a *bank's* depositors try to withdraw their funds because of fears of a bank failure.

banking crisis an episode in which a large part of the depository banking sector or the shadow banking sector fails or threatens to fail.

bar graph a graph that uses bars of varying height or length to show the comparative sizes of different observations of a *variable*.

barrier to entry something that prevents other firms from entering an industry. Crucial in protecting the profits of a *monopolist*.

barter a transaction in which people directly exchange goods or services that they have for goods or services that they want.

black market a market in which goods or services are bought and sold illegally, either because it is illegal to sell them at all or because the prices charged are legally prohibited by a *price ceiling*.

break-even price the market price at which a firm earns zero profits.

business cycle the short-run alternation between economic *recessions* and *expansions*.

business-cycle peak the point in time at which the *economy* shifts from *expansion* to *recession*.

business-cycle trough the point in time at which the *economy* shifts from *recession* to *expansion*.

C

cartel an agreement among several producers to obey output restrictions in order to increase their joint profits.

causal relationship the relationship between two *variables* in which the value taken by one variable directly influences or determines the value taken by the other variable.

central bank an institution that oversees and regulates the banking system and controls the *monetary base*.

chained dollars method of calculating *real GDP* that splits the difference between growth rates calculated using early base years and the growth rates calculated using late base years.

checkable bank deposits *bank* accounts on which people can write checks.

circular-flow diagram a diagram that represents the transactions in an *economy* by flows around a circle.

Coase theorem the proposition that even in the presence of *externalities* an *economy* can always reach an *efficient* solution as long as *transaction costs* are sufficiently low.

collusion cooperation among producers to limit production and raise prices so as to raise one another's profits.

commercial bank a *bank* that accepts deposits and is covered by *deposit insurance.*

commodity output of different producers regarded by consumers as the same good; also referred to as a *standardized product.*

commodity-backed money a *medium of exchange* that has no intrinsic value whose ultimate value is guaranteed by a promise that it can be converted into valuable goods on demand.

commodity money a *medium of exchange* that is a good, normally gold or silver, that has intrinsic value in other uses.

comparative advantage the advantage an individual or country has in producing a good or service if the *opportunity cost* of producing the good or service is lower for that individual or country than for others.

competitive market a market in which there are many buyers and sellers of the same good or service, none of whom can influence the price at which the good or service is sold.

complements pairs of goods for which a rise in the price of one good leads to a decrease in the demand for the other good.

constant returns to scale long-run *average total cost* is constant as output increases.

consumer price index (CPI) a measure of the cost of the *market basket* of a typical urban American family.

consumer surplus a term often used to refer both to *individual consumer surplus* and to *total consumer surplus.*

contractionary fiscal policy *fiscal policy* that reduces aggregate demand by decreasing government purchases, increasing taxes, or decreasing transfers.

contractionary monetary policy *monetary policy* that, through the raising of the *interest rate*, reduces aggregate demand and therefore output.

convergence hypothesis a principle of economic growth that holds that international differences in *real GDP* per capita tend to narrow over time because countries that start with lower real GDP per capita tend to have higher growth rates.

copyright gives the creator of a literary or artistic work sole rights to profit from that work.

cost the lowest price at which a seller is willing to sell a good.

cost-benefit analysis the estimation and comparison of the social costs and social benefits of providing a public good.

credit crunch a reduction in the availability of credit in which potential borrowers can't get credit at all or must pay very high interest rates.

cross-price elasticity of demand a measure of the effect of the change in the price of one good on the *quantity demanded* of the other; it is equal to the percent change in the quantity demanded of one good divided by the percent change in the price of another good.

currency in circulation actual cash held by the public.

curve a line on a graph, which may be curved or straight, that depicts a relationship between two *variables*.

cyclical unemployment the difference between the actual rate of *unemployment* and the *natural rate of unemployment* due to downturns in the *business cycle*.

cyclically adjusted budget balance an estimate of what the *budget balance* would be if *real GDP* were exactly equal to *potential output*.

D

deadweight loss the loss in total surplus that occurs whenever an action or a policy reduces the quantity transacted below the efficient market *equilibrium quantity.*

debt overhang high debt but diminished assets, resulting from a vicious circle of deleveraging.

debt–GDP ratio government debt as a percentage of GDP; frequently used as a measure of a government's ability to pay its debts.

decreasing returns to scale long-run *average total cost* increases as output increases.

deflation a fall in the overall level of prices.

demand curve a graphical representation of the *demand schedule,* showing the relationship between *quantity demanded* and price.

demand price the price of a given quantity at which consumers will demand that quantity.

demand schedule shows how much of a good or service consumers will want to buy at different prices.

demand shock an event that shifts the *aggregate demand curve*. A positive demand shock is associated with higher demand for *aggregate output* at any price level and shifts the curve to the right. A negative demand shock is associated with lower demand for aggregate output at any price level and shifts the curve to the left.

dependent variable the determined *variable* in a *causal relationship*.

deposit insurance a guarantee that a *bank*'s depositors will be paid even if the bank can't come up with the funds, up to a maximum amount per account.

depreciation a fall in the value of one currency in terms of other currencies.

diminishing returns to an input the effect observed when an increase in the quantity of an *input,* while holding the levels of all other inputs fixed, leads to a decline in the *marginal product* of that input.

diminishing returns to physical capital the effect on an aggregate *production function* when the amount of *human capital* per worker and the state of technology are held fixed: each successive increase in the amount of *physical capital* per worker leads to a smaller increase in productivity.

discount rate the rate of interest the Federal Reserve charges on loans to *banks* that fall short of *reserve requirements*.

discount window a protection against *bank runs* in which the Federal Reserve stands ready to lend money to *banks* in trouble.

discouraged workers nonworking people who are capable of working but have given up looking for a job given the state of the job market.

discretionary fiscal policy *fiscal policy* that is the direct result of deliberate actions by policy makers rather than rules.

disinflation the process of bringing the *inflation rate* down.

domestic demand curve a *demand curve* that shows how the quantity of a good demanded by domestic consumers depends on the price of that good.

domestic supply curve a *supply curve* that shows how the quantity of a good supplied by domestic producers depends on the price of that good.

duopolist one of the two firms in a *duopoly.*

duopoly an *oligopoly* consisting of only two firms.

E

economic growth the growing ability of the *economy* to produce goods and services.

economic profit a business's revenue minus the *opportunity cost* of *resources;* usually less than the *accounting profit.*

economics the social science that studies the production, distribution, and consumption of goods and services.

economy a system for coordinating society's productive activities.

efficiency wages wages that employers set above the *equilibrium* wage rate as an incentive for workers to deliver better performance.

efficient describes a market or *economy* that takes all opportunities to make some people better off without making other people worse off.

elastic demand when the *price elasticity of demand* is greater than 1.

emissions tax a tax that depends on the amount of pollution a firm produces.

employment the number of people currently employed in the *economy,* either full time or part time.

environmental standards rules established by a government to protect the environment by specifying actions by producers and consumers.

equilibrium an economic situation in which no individual would be better off doing something different.

equilibrium exchange rate the *exchange rate* at which the quantity of a currency demanded in the *foreign exchange market* is equal to the quantity supplied.

equilibrium price the price at which the market is in *equilibrium,* that is, the quantity of a good or service demanded equals the quantity of that good or service supplied; also referred to as the *market-clearing price.*

equilibrium quantity the quantity of a good or service bought and sold at the *equilibrium* (or *market-clearing*) *price.*

equity fairness; everyone gets his or her fair share. Since people can disagree about what's "fair," equity isn't as well defined a concept as efficiency.

excess reserves a *bank's reserves* over and above the reserves required by law or regulation.

exchange rate the price at which currencies trade, determined by the *foreign exchange market.*

excise tax a tax on sales of a good or service.

excludable referring to a good, describes the case in which the supplier can prevent those who do not pay from consuming the good.

expansion period of economic upturn in which output and employment are rising; most economic numbers are following their normal upward trend; also referred to as a recovery.

expansionary fiscal policy *fiscal policy* that increases aggregate demand by increasing government purchases, decreasing taxes, or increasing transfers.

expansionary monetary policy *monetary policy* that, through the lowering of the *interest rate,* increases aggregate demand and therefore output.

explicit cost a cost that involves actually laying out money.

exporting industries industries that produce goods or services that are sold abroad.

exports goods and services sold to other countries.

external benefit a benefit that an individual or firm confers on others without receiving compensation.

external cost an uncompensated cost that an individual or firm imposes on others; also known as *negative externalities.*

externalities *external benefits* and *external costs.*

F

factor intensity the difference in the ratio of factors used to produce a good in various industries. For example, oil refining is capital-intensive compared to clothing manufacture because oil refiners use a higher ratio of capital to labor than do clothing producers.

factor markets markets in which *firms* buy the *resources* they need to produce goods and services.

factors of production the *resources* used to produce goods and services.

federal funds market the *financial market* that allows *banks* that fall short of *reserve requirements* to borrow funds from banks with *excess reserves.*

federal funds rate the *interest rate* at which funds are borrowed and lent in the *federal funds market.*

fiat money a *medium of exchange* whose value derives entirely from its official status as a means of payment.

final goods and services goods and services sold to the final, or end, user.

financial contagion a vicious downward spiral among *depository banks* or *shadow banks:* each bank's failure worsens fears and increases the likelihood that another bank will fail.

financial panic a sudden and widespread disruption of the *financial markets* that occurs when people suddenly lose faith in the liquidity of financial institutions and markets.

firm an organization that produces goods and services for sale.

fiscal policy changes in government spending and taxes designed to affect overall spending.

fiscal year the time period used for much of government accounting, running from October 1 to September 30. Fiscal years are labeled by the calendar year in which they end.

fixed cost a cost that does not depend on the quantity of output produced; the cost of a *fixed input.*

fixed input an *input* whose quantity is fixed for a period of time and cannot be varied.

forecast a simple prediction of the future.

foreign exchange market the market in which currencies can be exchanged for each other.

free entry and exit describes an industry that potential producers can easily enter or current producers can easily leave.

free trade *trade* that is unregulated by government *tariffs* or other artificial barriers; the levels of *exports* and *imports* occur naturally, as a result of supply and demand.

free-rider problem the problem that results when individuals have no *incentive* to pay for their own consumption of a good, they will take a "free ride" on anyone who does pay; a problem with goods that are *nonexcludable.*

frictional unemployment *unemployment* due to time workers spend in *job search.*

G

gains from trade an economic principle that states that by dividing tasks and trading, people can get more of what they want through *trade* than they could if they tried to be self-sufficient.

GDP deflator a price measure for a given year that is equal to 100 times the ratio of *nominal GDP* to *real GDP* in that year.

GDP per capita GDP divided by the size of the population; equivalent to the average GDP per person.

globalization the phenomenon of growing economic linkages among countries.

gross domestic product (GDP) the total value of all *final goods and services* produced in the *economy* during a given period, usually a year.

growth accounting an estimation of the contribution of each of the major factors (physical and human capital, labor, and technology) in the *aggregate production function*.

H

Heckscher–Ohlin model a *model* of international trade in which a country has a *comparative advantage* in a good whose production is intensive in the factors that are abundantly available in that country.

horizontal axis the number line along which values of the *x*-variable are measured; also referred to as the *x-axis*.

horizontal intercept the point at which a *curve* hits the *horizontal axis*; it indicates the value of the *x*-variable when the value of the *y*-variable is zero.

household a person or a group of people who share income.

human capital the improvement in labor created by the education and knowledge embodied in the workforce.

I

imperfect competition a market structure in which no firm is a *monopolist,* but producers nonetheless have *market power* they can use to affect market prices.

implicit cost a cost that does not require the outlay of money; it is measured by the value, in dollar terms, of forgone benefits.

implicit liabilities spending promises made by governments that are effectively a debt despite the fact that they are not included in the usual debt statistics. In the United States, the largest implicit liabilities arise from Social Security and Medicare, which promise transfer payments to current and future retirees (Social Security) and to the elderly (Medicare).

import-competing industries industries that produce goods or services that are also imported.

import quota a legal limit on the quantity of a good that can be imported.

imports goods and services purchased from other countries.

incentive anything that offers rewards to people who change their behavior.

income distribution the way in which total income is divided among the owners of the various *factors of production*.

income-elastic demand when the *income elasticity of demand* for a good is greater than 1.

income elasticity of demand the percent change in the quantity of a good demanded when a consumer's income changes divided by the percent change in the consumer's income.

income-inelastic demand when the *income elasticity of demand* for a good is positive but less than 1.

increasing returns to scale long-run *average total cost* declines as output increases.

independent variable the determining *variable* in a *causal relationship*.

individual choice the decision by an individual of what to do, which necessarily involves a decision of what not to do.

individual consumer surplus the net gain to an individual buyer from the purchase of a good; equal to the difference between the buyer's *willingness to pay* and the price paid.

individual demand curve a graphical representation of the relationship between *quantity demanded* and price for an individual consumer.

individual producer surplus the net gain to an individual seller from selling a good; equal to the difference between the price received and the seller's *cost.*

individual supply curve illustrates the relationship between *quantity supplied* and *price* for an individual consumer.

industrial policy a policy that supports industries believed to yield *positive externalities.*

industry supply curve a graphical representation that shows the relationship between the price of a good and the total output of the industry for that good.

inefficient allocation to consumers a form of inefficiency in which people who want a good badly and are willing to pay a high price don't get it, and those who care relatively little about the good and are only willing to pay a low price do get it; often a result of a *price ceiling.*

inefficient allocation of sales among sellers a form of inefficiency in which those who would be willing to sell a good at the lowest price are not always those who actually manage to sell it; often the result of a *price floor.*

inefficiently high quality a form of inefficiency in which sellers offer high-quality goods at a high price even though buyers would prefer a lower quality at a lower price; often the result of a *price floor.*

inefficiently low quality a form of inefficiency in which sellers offer low-quality goods at a low price even though buyers would prefer a higher quality at a higher price; often a result of a *price ceiling.*

inelastic demand when the *price elasticity of demand* is less than 1.

inferior good a good for which a rise in income decreases the demand for the good.

inflation a rise in the overall level of prices.

inflation rate the percent change per year in a price index—typically the *consumer price index.*

inflation targeting an approach to *monetary policy* that requires that the *central bank* try to keep the *inflation rate* near a predetermined target rate.

inflationary gap exists when *aggregate output* is above *potential output*.

infrastructure *physical capital,* such as roads, power lines, ports, information networks, and other parts of an *economy*, that provides the underpinnings, or foundation, for economic activity.

input a good or service used to produce another good or service.

interaction (of choices) my choices affect your choices, and vice versa; a feature of most economic situations. The results of this interaction are often quite different from what the individuals intend.

interest rate (of a loan) the price, calculated as a percentage of the amount borrowed, that a lender charges a borrower for the use of the borrower's savings for one year.

interest rate effect of a change in the aggregate price level the effect on *consumer spending* and *investment spending* caused by a change in the purchasing power of consumers' money holdings when the *aggregate price level* changes. A rise (fall) in the aggregate price level decreases (increases) the purchasing power of consumers' money holdings. In response, consumers try to increase (decrease) their money holdings, which drives up (down) interest rates, thereby decreasing (increasing) consumption and investment.

intermediate goods and services goods and services, bought from one *firm* by another firm, that are inputs for production of *final goods and services*.

internalize the externality when individuals take into account *external costs* and *external benefits.*

investment bank a *bank* that trades in *financial assets* and is not covered by *deposit insurance.*

invisible hand refers to the way in which the individual pursuit of self-interest can lead to good results for society as a whole.

J

job search the time spent by workers looking for *employment.*

jobless recovery a period in which the *real GDP* growth rate is positive but the *unemployment rate* is still rising.

K

Keynesian economics a theory that states that economic slumps are caused by inadequate spending and they can be mitigated by government intervention.

L

labor force the sum of *employment* and *unemployment.*

labor force participation rate the percentage of the population age 16 or older that is in the *labor force.*

labor productivity output per worker; also referred to as simply *productivity.*

law of demand the principle that a higher price for a good or service, other things equal, leads people to demand a smaller quantity of that good or service.

lender of last resort an institution, usually a country's *central bank,* that provides funds to financial institutions when they are unable to borrow from private credit markets.

leverage the degree to which a financial institution is financing its investments with borrowed funds.

license the right, conferred by the government or an owner, to supply a good.

linear relationship the relationship between two *variables* in which the *slope* is constant and therefore is depicted on a graph by a *curve* that is a straight line.

liquid describes an asset that can be quickly converted into cash without much loss of value.

liquidity preference model of the interest rate a model of the market for money in which the *interest rate* is determined by the supply and demand for money.

liquidity trap the economy is in a liquidity trap when *monetary policy* is ineffective because *nominal interest rates* are up against the *zero bound for interest rates.*

long run the time period in which all *inputs* can be varied.

long-run aggregate supply curve a graphical representation that shows the relationship between the *aggregate price level* and the quantity of *aggregate output* supplied that would exist if all prices, including *nominal wages,* were fully flexible. The long-run aggregate supply curve is vertical because the aggregate price level has no effect on aggregate output in the long run; in the long run, aggregate output is determined by the *economy's potential output.*

long-run average total cost curve a graphical representation showing the relationship between output and *average total cost* when *fixed cost* has been chosen to minimize average total cost for each level of output.

long-run economic growth the sustained upward trend in the *economy's* output over time.

long-run industry supply curve a graphical representation that shows how *quantity supplied* responds to price once producers have had time to enter or exit the industry.

long-run macroeconomic equilibrium the point at which the *short-run macroeconomic equilibrium* is on the *long-run aggregate supply curve;* so *short-run equilibrium aggregate output* is equal to *potential output.*

long-run market equilibrium an economic balance in which, given sufficient time for producers to enter or exit an industry, the *quantity supplied* equals the *quantity demanded.*

long-term interest rate the *interest rate* on *financial assets* that mature a number of years into the future.

lump-sum taxes taxes that don't depend on the taxpayer's income.

M

macroeconomics the branch of *economics* that is concerned with the overall ups and downs in the *economy.*

marginal analysis the study of *marginal decisions.*

marginal benefit the additional benefit derived from producing one more unit of a good or service.

marginal cost the additional cost incurred by producing one more unit of a good or service.

marginal decision a decision made at the "margin" of an activity to do a bit more or a bit less of that activity.

marginal product the additional quantity of output produced by using one more unit of a given *input.*

marginal propensity to consume (MPC) the increase in *consumer spending* when *disposable income* rises by $1. Because consumers normally spend part but not all of an additional dollar of disposable income, *MPC* is between 0 and 1.

marginal revenue the change in *total revenue* generated by an additional unit of output.

marginal revenue curve a graphical representation showing how *marginal revenue* varies as output varies.

marginal social benefit of pollution the additional gain to society as a whole from an additional unit of pollution.

marginal social cost of pollution the additional cost imposed on society as a whole by an additional unit of pollution.

marginally attached workers nonworking individuals who say they would like a job and have looked for work in the recent past but are not currently looking for work.

market basket a hypothetical set of consumer purchases of goods and services.

market-clearing price the price at which the market is in *equilibrium,* that is, the quantity of a good or service demanded equals the quantity of that good or service supplied; also referred to as the *equilibrium price.*

market economy an *economy* in which decisions about production and consumption are made by individual producers and consumers.

market failure refers to the way in which the individual pursuit of self-interest can lead to bad results for society as a whole.

markets for goods and services markets in which *firms* sell goods and services that they produce to *households.*

market power the ability of a firm to raise prices.

market share the fraction of the total industry output accounted for by a given producer's output.

maturity transformation the conversion of short-term liabilities into long-term assets.

maximum the highest point on a *nonlinear curve,* where the *slope* changes from positive to negative.

medium of exchange an asset that individuals acquire for the purpose of trading for goods and services rather than for their own consumption.

menu cost the real cost of changing a listed price.

merchandise trade balance (trade balance) the difference between a country's *exports* and *imports* of goods alone—not including services.

microeconomics the branch of *economics* that studies how people make decisions and how those decisions interact.

midpoint method a technique for calculating the percent change in which changes in a variable are compared with the average, or midpoint, of the starting and final values.

minimum the lowest point on a *nonlinear curve,* where the *slope* changes from negative to positive.

minimum-cost output the quantity of output at which the *average total cost* is lowest—the bottom of the *U-shaped average total cost curve.*

minimum wage a legal floor on the wage rate. The wage rate is the market price of labor.

model a simplified representation of a real situation that is used to better understand real-life situations.

monetary aggregate an overall measure of the *money supply*. The most common monetary aggregates in the United States are M1, which includes *currency in circulation*, traveler's checks, and *checkable bank deposits*, and M2, which includes M1 as well as *near-moneys*.

monetary base the sum of *currency in circulation* and *bank reserves.*

monetary neutrality the concept that changes in the *money supply* have no real effects on the *economy* in the long run and only result in a proportional change in the price level.

monetary policy changes in the quantity of money in circulation designed to alter *interest rates* and affect the level of overall spending.

money any asset that can easily be used to purchase goods and services.

money demand curve a graphical representation of the relationship between the *interest rate* and the quantity of money demanded. The money demand curve slopes downward because, other things equal, a higher interest rate increases the *opportunity cost* of holding money.

money multiplier the ratio of the *money supply* to the *monetary base.*

money supply the total value of *financial assets* in the *economy* that are considered *money*.

money supply curve a graphical representation of the relationship between the quantity of money supplied by the Federal Reserve and the *interest rate*.

monopolist a firm that is the only producer of a good that has no close substitutes.

monopolistic competition a market structure in which there are many competing producers in an industry, each producer sells a differentiated product, and there is *free entry and exit* into and from the industry in the *long run.*

monopoly an industry controlled by a *monopolist.*

movement along the demand curve a change in the *quantity demanded* of a good that results from a change in that good's price.

movement along the supply curve a change in the *quantity supplied* of a good that results from a change in the price of that good.

multiplier the ratio of total change in *real GDP* caused by an *autonomous change in aggregate spending* to the size of that autonomous change.

N

national income and product accounts method of calculating and keeping track of *consumer spending*, sales of producers, business *investment spending*, government purchases, and a variety of other flows of money between different sectors of the *economy*; also referred to as *national accounts*.

natural monopoly exists when *increasing returns to scale* provide a large cost advantage to having all output produced by a single firm.

natural rate of unemployment the normal *unemployment rate* around which the actual unemployment rate fluctuates; the unemployment rate that arises from the effects of *frictional* and *structural unemployment*.

near-money a *financial asset* that can't be directly used as a *medium of exchange* but can be readily converted into cash or *checkable bank deposits*.

negative externalities *external costs.*

negative relationship a relationship between two *variables* in which an increase in the value of one variable is associated with a decrease in the value of the other variable. It is illustrated by a *curve* that slopes downward from left to right.

network externality the increase in the value of a good to an individual is greater when a large number of others own or use the same good.

nominal GDP the value of all *final goods and services* produced in the *economy* during a given year, calculated using the prices current in the year in which the output is produced.

nominal interest rate the *interest rate* in dollar terms.

nominal wage the dollar amount of any given wage paid.

noncooperative behavior actions by firms that ignore the effects of those actions on the profits of other firms.

nonexcludable referring to a good, describes the case in which the supplier cannot prevent those who do not pay from consuming the good.

nonlinear curve a *curve* in which the *slope* is not the same between every pair of points.

nonlinear relationship the relationship between two *variables* in which the *slope* is not constant and therefore is depicted on a graph by a *curve* that is not a straight line.

nonrival in consumption referring to a good, describes the case in which the same unit can be consumed by more than one person at the same time.

normal good a good for which a rise in income increases the demand for that good—the "normal" case.

normative economics the branch of economic analysis that makes prescriptions about the way the *economy* should work.

O

oligopolist a firm in an industry with only a small number of producers.

oligopoly an industry with only a small number of producers.

omitted variable an unobserved *variable* that, through its influence on other variables, creates the erroneous appearance of a direct *causal relationship* among those variables.

open economy an *economy* that trades goods and services with other countries.

open-market operation a purchase or sale of U.S. Treasury bills by the Federal Reserve, normally through a transaction with a *commercial bank*.

opportunity cost the real cost of an item: what you must give up in order to get it.

optimal output rule profit is maximized by producing the quantity of output at which the *marginal revenue* of the last unit produced is equal to its *marginal cost.*

other things equal assumption the assumption that all other relevant factors remain unchanged.

output gap the percentage difference between actual *aggregate output* and *potential output*.

P

patent gives an inventor a temporary monopoly in the use or sale of an invention.

perfectly competitive industry an industry in which all producers are price-takers.

perfectly competitive market a market in which all participants are price-takers.

perfectly elastic demand the case in which any price increase will cause the *quantity demanded* to drop to zero; the *demand curve* is a horizontal line.

perfectly elastic supply the case in which even a tiny increase or reduction in the price will lead to very large changes in the *quantity supplied,* so that the *price elasticity of supply* is infinite; the perfectly elastic *supply curve* is a horizontal line.

perfectly inelastic demand the case in which the *quantity demanded* does not respond at all to changes in the price; the *demand curve* is a vertical line.

perfectly inelastic supply the case in which the *price elasticity of supply* is zero, so that changes in the price of the good have no effect on the *quantity supplied;* the perfectly inelastic *supply curve* is a vertical line.

physical capital manufactured resources, such as buildings and machines.

pie chart a circular graph that shows how some total is divided among its components, usually expressed in percentages.

Pigouvian subsidy a payment designed to encourage activities that yield *external benefits*.

Pigouvian taxes taxes designed to reduce *external costs*.

positive economics the branch of economic analysis that describes the way the *economy* actually works.

positive externalities *external benefits*.

positive relationship a relationship between two *variables* in which an increase in the value of one variable is associated with an increase in the value of the other variable. It is illustrated by a *curve* that slopes upward from left to right.

potential output the level of *real GDP* the *economy* would produce if all prices, including *nominal wages*, were fully flexible.

price ceiling the maximum price sellers are allowed to charge for a good or service; a form of *price control*.

price controls legal restrictions on how high or low a market price may go.

price elasticity of demand the ratio of the percent change in the *quantity demanded* to the percent change in the price as we move along the *demand curve* (dropping the minus sign).

price elasticity of supply a measure of the responsiveness of the quantity of a good supplied to the price of that good; the ratio of the percent change in the *quantity supplied* to the percent change in the price as we move along the *supply curve*.

price floor the minimum price buyers are required to pay for a good or service; a form of *price control*.

price index a measure of the cost of purchasing a given *market basket* in a given year, where that cost is normalized so that it is equal to 100 in the selected base year; a measure of overall price level.

price regulation a limitation on the price a *monopolist* is allowed to charge.

price stability a situation in which the overall level of prices is changing slowly or not at all.

price-taking consumer a consumer whose actions have no effect on the market price of the good or service he or she buys.

price-taking firm's optimal output rule the profit of a price-taking firm is maximized by producing the quantity of output at which the market price is equal to the *marginal cost* of the last unit produced.

price-taking producer a producer whose actions have no effect on the market price of the good or service it sells.

price war a collapse of prices when *tacit collusion* breaks down.

principle of marginal analysis the proposition that the *optimal quantity* is the quantity at which *marginal benefit* is equal to *marginal cost*.

private good a good that is both *excludable* and *rival in consumption*.

producer price index (PPI) a measure of changes in the prices of goods purchased by producers.

producer surplus refers to either *individual producer surplus* or *total producer surplus*.

product differentiation the attempt by a firm to convince buyers that its product is different from the products of other firms in the industry.

production function the relationship between the quantity of *inputs* a firm uses and the quantity of output it produces.

production possibility frontier illustrates the trade-offs facing an *economy* that produces only two goods. It shows the maximum quantity of one good that can be produced for any given quantity produced of the other.

productivity output per worker; a shortened form of the term *labor productivity*.

protection policies that limit *imports;* an alternative term for *trade protection*.

public debt government debt held by individuals and institutions outside the government.

public good a good that is both *nonexcludable* and *nonrival in consumption*.

public ownership when goods are supplied by the government or by a firm owned by the government to protect the interests of the consumer in response to *natural monopoly*.

purchasing power parity (between two countries' currencies) the nominal *exchange rate* at which a given basket of goods and services would cost the same amount in each country.

Q

quantity control an upper limit on the quantity of some good that can be bought or sold; also referred to as a *quota*.

quantity demanded the actual amount of a good or service consumers are willing to buy at some specific price.

quantity supplied the actual amount of a good or service producers are willing to sell at some specific price.

quota an upper limit on the quantity of some good that can be bought or sold; also referred to as a *quantity control*.

quota limit the total amount of a good under a *quota* or *quantity control* that can be legally transacted.

quota rent the difference between the *demand price* and the *supply price* at the *quota limit;* this difference, the earnings that accrue to the license-holder, is equal to the market price of the *license* when the license is traded.

R

real exchange rate the *exchange rate* adjusted for international differences in *aggregate price levels*.

real GDP the total value of all *final goods and services* produced in the *economy* during a given year, calculated using the prices of a selected base year.

real income income divided by the price level.

real interest rate the *nominal interest rate* minus the *inflation rate*.

real wage the wage rate divided by the price level.

recession a period of economic downturn when output and unemployment are falling; also referred to as a contraction.

recessionary gap exists when *aggregate output* is below *potential output*.

research and development (R&D) spending to create new technologies and prepare them for practical use.

reserve ratio the fraction of *bank deposits* that a *bank* holds as reserves. In the United States, the minimum required reserve ratio is set by the Federal Reserve.

reserve requirements rules set by the Federal Reserve that set the minimum *reserve ratio* for banks. For *checkable bank deposits* in the United States, the minimum reserve ratio is set at 10%.

resource anything, such as land, labor, and capital, that can be used to produce something else.

reverse causality the error committed when the true direction of causality between two *variables* is reversed.

Ricardian model of international trade a model that analyzes international *trade* under the assumption that *opportunity costs* are constant.

rival in consumption referring to a good, describes the case in which one unit cannot be consumed by more than one person at the same time.

Rule of 70 a mathematical formula that states that the time it takes *real GDP* per capita, or any other variable that grows gradually over time, to double is approximately 70 divided by that variable's annual growth rate.

S

savings and loans (thrifts) deposit-taking *banks*, usually specialized in issuing home loans.

scarce in short supply; a *resource* is scarce when there is not enough of the resource available to satisfy all the various ways a society wants to use it.

scatter diagram a graph that shows points that correspond to actual observations of the *x*- and *y*-variables; a *curve* is usually fitted to the scatter of points to indicate the trend in the data.

securitization the pooling of loans and mortgages made by a financial institution and the sale of shares in such a pool to other investors.

self-correcting describes an *economy* in which shocks to aggregate demand affect *aggregate output* in the short run but not in the long run.

self-regulating economy an *economy* in which problems such as *unemployment* are resolved without government intervention, through the working of the *invisible hand*.

shadow bank a nondepository financial institution that engages in *maturity transformation*.

shift of the demand curve a change in the *quantity demanded* at any given price, represented by the change of the original *demand curve* to a new position, denoted by a new demand curve.

shift of the supply curve a change in the *quantity supplied* of a good or service at any given price, represented graphically by the change of the original *supply curve* to a new position, denoted by a new supply curve.

shoe-leather costs the increased costs of transactions caused by *inflation*.

short run the time period in which at least one *input* is fixed.

shortage the insufficiency of a good or service that occurs when the *quantity demanded* exceeds the *quantity supplied*; shortages occur when the price is below the *equilibrium price*.

short-run aggregate supply curve a graphical representation that shows the positive relationship between the *aggregate price level* and the quantity of *aggregate output* supplied that exists in the short run, the time period when many production costs, particularly *nominal wages*, can be taken as fixed. The short-run aggregate supply curve has a positive slope because a rise in the aggregate price level leads to a rise in profits, and therefore output, when production costs are fixed.

short-run equilibrium aggregate output the quantity of *aggregate output* produced in *short-run macroeconomic equilibrium*.

short-run equilibrium aggregate price level the *aggregate price level* in *short-run macroeconomic equilibrium*.

short-run individual supply curve a graphical representation that shows how an individual producer's profit-maximizing output quantity depends on the market price, taking *fixed cost* as given.

short-run industry supply curve a graphical representation that shows how the *quantity supplied* by an industry depends on the market price, given a fixed number of producers.

short-run macroeconomic equilibrium the point at which the quantity of *aggregate output* supplied is equal to the *quantity demanded*.

short-run market equilibrium an economic balance that results when the *quantity supplied* equals the *quantity demanded*, taking the number of producers as given.

short-term interest rate the *interest rate* on *financial assets* that mature within less than a year.

shut-down price the price at which a firm ceases production in the short run because the market price has fallen below the minimum *average variable cost*.

slope a measure of the steepness of a line. The slope of a line is measured by "rise over run"—the change in the *y*-variable between two points on the line divided by the change in the *x*-variable between those same two points.

social insurance government programs—like Social Security, Medicare, unemployment insurance, and food stamps—intended to protect families against economic hardship.

socially optimal quantity of pollution the quantity of pollution that society would choose if all the costs and benefits of pollution were fully accounted for.

specialization a situation in which different people each engage in the different task that he or she is good at performing.

stabilization policy the use of government policy to reduce the severity of *recessions* and to rein in excessively strong *expansions*. There are two main tools of stabilization policy: *monetary policy* and *fiscal policy*.

stagflation the combination of *inflation* and falling *aggregate output*.

standardized product output of different producers regarded by consumers as the same good; also referred to as a *commodity*.

sticky wages *nominal wages* that are slow to fall even in the face of high *unemployment* and slow to rise even in the face of labor shortages.

store of value an asset that is a means of holding purchasing power over time.

structural unemployment *unemployment* that results when there are more people seeking jobs in a labor market than there are jobs available at the current wage rate, even when the economy is at the peak of the *business cycle.*

subprime lending lending to home-buyers who don't meet the usual criteria for borrowing.

substitutes pairs of goods for which a rise in the price of one of the goods leads to an increase in the demand for the other good.

sunk cost a cost that has already been incurred and is not recoverable.

supply and demand model a model of how a *competitive market* works.

supply curve a graphical representation showing the relationship between *quantity supplied* and price.

supply price the price of a given quantity at which producers will supply that quantity.

supply schedule a list or table showing how much of a good or service producers will supply at different prices.

supply shock an event that shifts the *short-run aggregate supply curve*. A negative supply shock raises production costs and reduces the *quantity supplied* at any *aggregate price level*, shifting the curve leftward. A positive supply shock decreases production costs and increases the quantity supplied at any aggregate price level, shifting the curve rightward.

surplus the excess of a good or service that occurs when the *quantity supplied* exceeds the *quantity demanded*; surpluses occur when the price is above the *equilibrium price.*

sustainable long-run economic growth long-run growth that can continue in the face of the limited supply of natural resources and the impact of growth on the environment.

T

T-account a simple tool that summarizes a business's financial position by showing, in a single table, the business's assets and liabilities, with assets on the left and liabilities on the right.

tacit collusion cooperation among producers, without a formal agreement, to limit production and raise prices so as to raise one anothers' profits.

tangent line a straight line that just touches a *nonlinear curve* at a particular point; the *slope* of the tangent line is equal to the slope of the nonlinear curve at that point.

target federal funds rate the Federal Reserve's desired level for the *federal funds rate*. The Federal Reserve adjusts the *money supply* through the purchase and sale of Treasury bills until the actual rate equals the desired rate.

tariff a tax levied on *imports.*

tax rate the amount of tax people are required to pay per unit of whatever is being taxed.

Taylor rule for monetary policy a rule for setting the *federal funds rate* that takes into account both the *inflation rate* and the *output gap*.

technological progress an advance in the technical means of the production of goods and services.

technology the technical means for the production of goods and services.

technology spillover an *external benefit* that results when knowledge spreads among individuals and firms.

time-series graph a two-*variable* graph that has dates on the *horizontal axis* and values of a variable that occurred on those dates on the *vertical axis*.

total consumer surplus the sum of the *individual consumer surpluses* of all the buyers of a good in a market.

total cost the sum of the *fixed cost* and the *variable cost* of producing a given quantity of output.

total cost curve a graphical representation of the *total cost,* showing how total cost depends on the quantity of output.

total factor productivity the amount of output that can be produced with a given amount of factor inputs.

total producer surplus the sum of the *individual producer surpluses* of all the sellers of a good in a market.

total product curve a graphical representation that shows how the quantity of output depends on the quantity of the *variable input,* for a given quantity of the *fixed input.*

total revenue the total value of sales of a good or service. It is equal to the price multiplied by the quantity sold.

total surplus the total net gain to consumers and producers from trading in a market; the sum of the *consumer surplus* and the *producer surplus.*

tradable emissions permits *licenses* to emit limited quantities of pollutants that can be bought and sold by polluters.

trade when individuals provide goods and services to others and receive goods and services in return.

trade balance (merchandise trade balance) the difference between a country's *exports* and *imports* of goods alone—not including services.

trade deficit when the value of the goods and services bought from foreigners is more than the value of the goods and services sold to consumers abroad.

trade protection policies that limit *imports;* also known simply as *protection.*

trade surplus when the value of goods and services bought from foreigners is less than the value of the goods and services sold to them.

trade-off a comparison of the costs and benefits of doing something.

transaction costs the expenses of negotiating and executing a deal.

truncated cut; in a truncated axis, some of the range of values are omitted, usually to save space.

U

underemployment the number of people who work part time because they cannot find full-time jobs.

unemployment the total number of people who are actively looking for work but aren't currently employed.

unemployment rate the percentage of the total number of people in the *labor force* who are unemployed.

unit of account a measure used to set prices and make economic calculations.

unit-of-account costs costs arising from the way *inflation* makes money a less reliable unit of measurement.

unit-elastic demand the case in which the *price elasticity of demand* is exactly 1.

U-shaped average total cost curve a distinctive graphical representation of the relationship between output and *average total cost;* the average total cost curve falls at low levels of output, then rises at higher levels.

util a unit of *utility.*

V

value added (of a producer) the value of its sales minus the value of its purchases of intermediate goods and services.

variable a quantity that can take on more than one value.

variable cost a cost that depends on the quantity of output produced; the cost of a *variable input.*

variable input an *input* whose quantity the firm can vary at any time.

vertical axis the number line along which values of the *y*-variable are measured; also referred to as the *y-axis.*

vertical intercept the point at which a *curve* hits the *vertical axis*; it shows the value of the y-variable when the value of the x-variable is zero.

vicious cycle of deleveraging describes the sequence of events that takes place when a *firm's* asset sales to cover losses produce negative *balance sheet effects* on other firms and force creditors to call in their *loans,* forcing sales of more assets and causing further declines in asset prices.

W

wasted resources a form of inefficiency in which people expend money, effort, and time to cope with the shortages caused by a *price ceiling.*

wealth effect of a change in the aggregate price level the effect on *consumer spending* caused by the change in the purchasing power of consumers' assets when the *aggregate price level* changes. A rise in the aggregate price level decreases the purchasing power of consumers' assets, so consumers decrease their consumption; a fall in the aggregate price level increases the purchasing power of consumers' assets, so consumers increase their consumption.

wedge the difference between the *demand price* of the quantity transacted and the *supply price* of the quantity transacted for a good when the supply of the good is legally restricted. Often created by a *quantity control*, or *quota*.

willingness to pay the maximum price a consumer is prepared to pay for a good.

world price the price at which a good can be bought or sold abroad.

X

***x*-axis** the line along which values of the x-variable are measured; also referred to as the *horizontal axis.*

Y

***y*-axis** the line along which values of the y-variable are measured; also referred to as the *vertical axis.*

Z

zero lower bound for interest rates statement of the fact that interest rates cannot fall below zero.

Note: Key terms appear in **boldface** type.

N